Experiencing the Lifespan FOURTH EDITION

JANET BELSKY

Middle Tennessee State University

WORTH PUBLISHERS

A Macmillan Education Imprint
New York

FOR DAVID
A world-class intellectual and the world's best possible husband

Publisher: Rachel Losh

Associate Publisher: Jessica Bayne

Senior Acquisitions Editor: Christine M. Cardone

Developmental Editor: Elaine Epstein

Assistant Editor: Catherine Michaelsen

Marketing Manager: Lindsay Johnson

Marketing Assistant: Allison Greco

Director, Content Management Enhancement: Tracey Kuehn

Media Editor: Lauren Samuelson

Photo Editor: Sheena Goldstein

Art Director: Diana Blume

Cover and Interior Designer: Blake Logan

Managing Editor: Lisa Kinne

Project Editor: Julio Espin

Production Manager: Sarah Segal

Art Manager: Matthew McAdams

Composition: codeMantra

Printing and Binding: RR Donnelley

Cover photo: Stephen St. John/National Geographic Creative

Photo of brain icon: RENGraphic/Getty Images

Photo of flame icon: rilora/Getty Images

Library of Congress Control Number: 2015942394

ISBN-13: 978-1-4641-7594-7
ISBN-10: 1-4641-7594-2

© 2016, 2013, 2010, 2007 by Worth Publishers

Printed in the United States of America

First printing

Worth Publishers
One New York Plaza
Suite 4500
New York, NY
10004-1562

About the Author

Steven James

Born in New York City, Janet Belsky always wanted to be a writer but was also very interested in people. After receiving her undergraduate degree from the University of Pennsylvania, she deferred to her more practical and people-loving side and got her Ph.D. in clinical psychology at the University of Chicago. Janet spent her thirties in New York City teaching at Lehman College, CUNY, and doing clinical work in hospitals and nursing homes. During this time, she wrote one trade book, *Here Tomorrow, Making the Most of Life After 50*, got married, adopted a child and, with the publication of the first undergraduate textbook in the psychology of aging, began what turned into a lifelong developmental science textbook writing career. In 1991, Janet moved to Tennessee with her family to write and teach undergraduate courses in psychology at Middle Tennessee State University. After her husband died in 2012, Janet enrolled in the Master's Program in Liberal Arts at the University of Chicago (a beginning graduate student again at the U of C, after 45-plus years!). Still, she remains committed to her life passion—exciting readers in the marvelous human lifespan through this book.

Brief Contents

Contents

© Nicole Hill/RubberBall/Age Fotostock

Indeed/Getty Images

© IMAGEMORE/Age Fotostock

Fuse/Getty Images

Image Source/Alamy

Preface

I spent my thirties and forties writing textbooks on adult development and aging. I spent more than 15 years writing and revising this book. I've spent almost 40 years (virtually all of my adult life!) joyously teaching this course. My mission in this book is simple: to excite students in our field.

Because I want to showcase the most cutting-edge research, in this edition of *Experiencing the Lifespan*, you will find hundreds of citations dating just from 2013. I've added new sections to every chapter, covering topics as varied as our scientific strides in epigenetics, to the personal experience of providing hospice care. I've constructed dozens of new figures and tables, rewritten almost every sentence, and given this text a new social media–oriented thrust. But, readers who have used *Experiencing the Lifespan* in the past will be comforted to know that this edition has the same familiar structure and plan. It reflects my commitment to convey the beauty of our science in the same compelling way. What *exactly* makes this book compelling? What makes each chapter special? What makes this edition stand out?

What Makes This Book Compelling?

- *Experiencing the Lifespan* **unfolds like a story.** The main feature that makes this book special is the writing style. *Experiencing the Lifespan* reads like a conversation rather than a traditional text. Each chapter begins with a vignette constructed to highlight the material I will be discussing. I've designed my narrative to flow from topic to topic; and I've planned every chapter to interconnect. In this book, the main themes that underlie developmental science flow throughout the *entire* book. I want students to have the sense that they are reading an exciting, ongoing story. Most of all, I want them to feel that they are learning about a coherent, *organized* field.

- *Experiencing the Lifespan* **is uniquely organized to highlight development.** A second mission that has driven my writing is to highlight how our lives evolve. What exactly makes an 8-year-old mentally different from a 4-year-old, or a 60-year-old different from a person of 85. In order to emphasize how children develop, I decided to cover all of childhood in a single three-chapter part. This strategy allowed me to fully explore the magic of Piaget's preoperational and concrete operational stages and to trace the development of aggression, childhood friendships, and gender-stereotyped play. It permitted me to show *concretely* how the ability to think through their actions changes as children travel from preschool through elementary school. I decided to put early and middle adulthood in one unit (Part IV) for similar reasons: It simply made logical sense to discuss important topics that transcend a single life stage, such as marriage, parenting, and work (Chapter 11) and adult personality and cognitive development (Chapter 12) together in the same place. In fact, I've designed this *whole* text to highlight development. I follow the characters in the chapter-opening vignettes throughout each several-chapter book part. I've planned each life-stage segment to flow in a developmental way. In the first infancy chapter, I begin with a discussion of newborn states. The second chapter in this sequence (Infancy: Socioemotional Development) ends with a discussion of toddlerhood. My three-chapter Early and Middle Adulthood book part starts with an exploration of the challenges of emerging adulthood (Chapter 10), then tackles marriage, parenthood, and career (Chapter 11), and culminates with a chapter tracking adult personality and intelligence through midlife, and exploring "older" family roles such as parent care and grandparenthood (Chapter 12). In Part VI, Later Life, I begin with a chapter devoted to topics, such as retirement, that typically take place during the young-old years. Then I focus on physical aging (Chapter 14, The Physical Challenges of Old Age) because sensory-motor impairments, dementing diseases, and interventions for

For this grandmother, mother, and daughter, getting dressed up to visit this Shinto family shrine and pay their respects to their ancestors is an important ritual. It is one way that the lesson "honor your elders" is taught to children living in collectivist societies such as Japan from an early age.

These teens are probably taking great pleasure in serving meals to the homeless as part of their school community-service project. Was a high school experience, like this one, life changing for you?

As she translates an oath of naturalization to her non-English-speaking Iraq mom, this daughter is engaging in a role reversal that can be distressing, but can also offer a lifelong sense of empathy and self-efficacy.

late-life frailty become crucial concerns mainly in the eighties and beyond. Yes, this textbook does—for the most part—move through the lifespan stage by stage. However, it's targeted to highlight the aspects of development—such as constructing an adult life in the twenties or physical disabilities in the eighties—that become salient at particular times of life. I believe that my textbook captures the best features of the chronological and topical approaches.

- *Experiencing the Lifespan* **is both shorter and more in-depth.** Adopting this flexible, development-friendly organization makes for a more manageable, teacher-friendly book. With 15 chapters and at fewer than 475 pages, my textbook *really* can be mastered in a one-semester course! Not being locked into covering each slice of life in defined bits also gives me the freedom to focus on what is most important in special depth. As you will discover while reading my comprehensive discussions of central topics in our field, such as attachment, parenting, puberty, and adult personality consistency and change, omitting superficial coverage of "everything" allows time to explore the core issues in developmental science in a deeper, more thoughtful way.

- *Experiencing the Lifespan* **actively fosters critical thinking.** Guiding students to reflect on what they are reading is actually another of my writing goals. A great advantage of engaging readers in a conversation is that I can naturally embed critical thinking into the actual narrative. For example, as I move from discussing Piaget's ideas on cognition to Vygotsky's theory to the information-processing approach in Chapter 5, I point out the gaps in each perspective and highlight *why* each approach offers a unique contribution to understanding children's intellectual growth. On a policy-oriented level, after discussing day care, teenage storm and stress, or physical aging, I ask readers to think critically about how to improve the way our culture cares for young families, treats teenagers, and can make life more user-friendly for the baby boomers now traveling into their older years.

- *Experiencing the Lifespan* **has a global orientation.** Intrinsic to getting students to evaluate their own cultural practices is the need to highlight alternate perspectives on our developing life. Therefore, *Experiencing the Lifespan* is a firmly international book. I introduce this global orientation in the first chapter when I spell out the differences between collectivist and individualistic cultures and between the developed and developing worlds. In the childhood chapters, when discussing topics from pregnancy to parenting, I pay special attention to cultural variations. In the adulthood sections, standard "Setting the Context" heads, preceding the research, offer snapshots of love and marriage in different nations, discuss retirement around the world, and explore different societal practices and attitudes toward death. (In fact, "How do other groups handle this?" is a question that crops up when I talk about practically every topic in the book!)

- *Experiencing the Lifespan* **highlights the multiple forces that shape development.** Given my emphasis on cultural variations within our universal human experience, it should come as no surprise that the main theoretical framework I've used to organize this book is the developmental systems approach. Throughout the chapters, I explore the many influences that interact to predict life milestones—from puberty to physical aging. Erikson's stages, attachment theory, behavioral genetics, evolutionary theory, self-efficacy, and, especially, the importance of looking at nature and nurture and providing the best person–environment fit—all are concepts that I introduce in the first chapter and continue to stress as the book unfolds. Another theme that runs through this text is the impact of socioeconomic status on shaping everything from breast-feeding practices to the rate at which we age and die.

- *Experiencing the Lifespan* **is applications-oriented, and focused on how to construct a satisfying life.** Because of my background as a clinical psychologist, my other passion is to concretely bring home how we can use the scientific findings to improve the quality of life. So most topics in this text end with "Interventions" sections spelling out practical implications of the research. With its varied Interventions, such as "How Can You Get Babies to Sleep Through the Night?" or "Using Piaget's Theory at Home and at Work," to its adulthood tables, such as "How to Flourish During Adulthood" and sections devoted to "Aging Optimally," *Experiencing the Lifespan* is designed to show how the science of development can make a difference in people's lives.

- *Experiencing the Lifespan* **is a person-centered, hands-on textbook.** This book is also designed to bring the experience of the lifespan home in a personal way. Therefore, in **"Experiencing the Lifespan"** boxes, I report on interviews I've conducted with people ranging from a 16-year-old (a student of mine) who was charged as an adult with second-degree murder to a 70-year-old man with Alzheimer's disease. To entice readers to empathize with the challenges of other life stages, I continually ask students to "imagine you are a toddler" or "a sleep-deprived mother" or "an 80-year-old struggling with the challenges of driving in later life."

This new member of the Efé people of central Africa will be lovingly cared for by the whole community, males as well as females, from his first minutes of life. Because he sleeps with his mother, however, at the "right" age he will develop his primary attachment to her.

Another strategy I use to make the research vivid and personal are questionnaires (often based on the chapter content) that get readers to think more deeply about their own lives: the checklist to identify your parenting priorities in Chapter 7; a scale for "using selective optimization with compensation at home and work" in Chapter 12; surveys for "evaluating your relationships" in Chapters 10 and 11; true/false quizzes at the beginning of my chapters on adolescence (Chapter 9), adult roles (Chapter 11), and later life (Chapter 13) that provide a hands-on preview of the content and entice students into reading the chapter so that they can assess the scientific accuracy of their ideas.

- *Experiencing the Lifespan* **is designed to get students to learn the material while they read.** The chapter-opening vignettes, the applications sections with their summary tables, the hands-on exercises, and the end-of-section questionnaires (such as "Evaluating Your Own Relationship: A Section Summary Checklist" in Chapter 10) are part of an overall pedagogical plan. As I explain in my introductory letter to students on page 2, I want this to be a textbook you don't have to struggle to decode—one that helps you *naturally* cement the concepts in mind. The centerpiece of this effort is the **"Tying It All Together"** quizzes, which follow each major section. These mini-tests, involving multiple-choice, essay, and critical-thinking questions, allow students to test themselves on what they have absorbed. I've also planned the photo program in *Experiencing the Lifespan* to illustrate the major terms and concepts. As you page through the text, you may notice that the pictures and their captions feel organically connected to the writing. They visually bring the main text messages home. When it's important for students to learn a series of terms or related concepts,

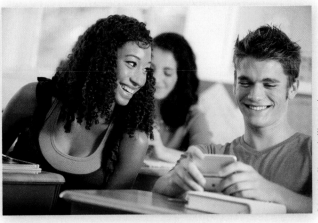

If you can relate to this photo the next time you are tempted to text during that not-so-interesting class, keep this message in mind: *Divided attention tasks* make memory worse!

I provide a summary series of photos. You can see examples in the photographs illustrating the different infant and adult attachment styles on pages 112 and 319, and in Table 3.7 on page 95, highlighting Jean Piaget's infant circular reactions.

As you scan this book, you will see other special features: **"How do we know . . . ?"** boxes in some chapters that delve more deeply into particular research programs; **"Hot in Developmental Science"** sections in each chapter showcasing cutting-edge topics, from prenatal stress to preteen popularity; timelines that pull everything together at the end of complex sections (such as the chart summarizing the landmarks of pregnancy and prenatal development on pages 55–56).

What will make this text a pleasure to teach from? How can I make this book a joy to read? These are questions I have been grappling with as I've been glued to my computer—often seven days a week—during this decade-and-a-half-long labor of love.

What Makes Each Chapter Special?

Now that I've spelled out my general writing missions, here are some highlights of each chapter, and a preview of exactly what's new.

PART I: The Foundation

CHAPTER 1: The People and the Field

- Outlines the basic contexts of development: social class, culture, ethnicity, and cohort.

- Traces the evolution of the lifespan over the centuries and explores the classic developmental science theories that have shaped our understanding of life.

- Spells out the concepts, the perspectives, and the research strategies I will be exploring in each chapter of the book.

What's New?

- Introduces epigenetics and emerging research on environment-sensitive genes (to be discussed in subsequent chapters), and sets readers up for this edition's focus on social media.

- Describes economic trends since the Great Recession.

- Includes psychoanalytic theory as a major perspective in developmental science.

- Revises items in the Tying It All Together quizzes and updates figures to offer data on recent demographic trends. (I've made similar changes to the quiz items and relevant figures throughout the book.)

- Provides a new example to teach students about correlational and experimental research.

CHAPTER 2: Prenatal Development, Pregnancy, and Birth

- Discusses pregnancy rituals and superstitions around the world.

- Highlights the latest research on fetal brain development.

- Fully explores the experience of pregnancy from both the mother's and father's points of view and discusses infertility.

- Looks at the experience of birth historically and discusses policy issues relating to pregnancy and birth in the United States and around the world.

What's New

- Explores the impact of pregnancy stress on the fetus.

- Offers a more thorough look at the emotional effects of infertility.

- Provides international data on smoking and alcohol use during pregnancy.

- Updates material on c-sections and infant mortality worldwide.

Imagine being this terrified woman as she surveys the rubble of her collapsed house. What is the impact of disasters, like this Malaysian landslide, on babies in the womb? Fetal programming research offers fascinating answers.

TEH ENG KOON/AFP/Getty Images

PART II: Infancy

CHAPTER 3: Infancy: Physical and Cognitive Development

- Covers the latest research on brain development.

- Focuses in depth on basic infant states such as eating, crying, and sleep.

- Explores breast-feeding and scans global undernutrition.

- Provides an in-depth, personal, and practice-oriented look at infant motor development, Piaget's sensorimotor stage, and beginning language.

- Explores the cutting-edge findings on infant social cognition.

What's New?

- Discusses physical hurdles to breast-feeding and explores variations in developed-world pressures for new mothers to nurse.

- Showcases research demonstrating that kangaroo care is superior to swaddling, at calming babies.

- Explores how visual pruning during the first year of life may smooth the path to racial prejudice.

- Amplifies my third-edition discussion of infant social cognition by discussing several recent studies suggesting that our basic sense of fairness and morality kicks in at a very young age.

- Includes a new figure illustrating the early neural correlates of emerging language.

CHAPTER 4: Infancy: Socioemotional Development

- Provides unusually in-depth coverage of attachment theory.

- Offers an honest, comprehensive look at day care in the United States and discusses early childhood poverty.

- Highlights exuberant and shy toddler temperaments, explores research on the genetics of temperament, and stresses the need to promote the right temperament–environment fit for each child.

What's New?

- Explores research suggesting plasticity genes may affect how vulnerable infants are to less-than-optimal attachment environments, influence how much attachment can change, and predict how young children adapt to day care. Bottom line: Our "genetics" may set us up to either be more or less reactive to environmental events.

- Updates research exploring the life paths of orphanage-reared babies.

- Introduces the hormones oxytocin and cortisol and discusses the impact of urban and rural poverty on later academic development.

PART III: Childhood

CHAPTER 5: Physical and Cognitive Development

- Begins by exploring why we have childhood, illustrating what makes human beings qualitatively different from other species.

- Covers childhood obesity, including its emotional aspects, in depth.

- Showcases Piaget's, Vygotsky's, and the information-processing models of childhood cognition—with examples that stress the practical implications of these landmark perspectives for parents and people who work with children.

- Discusses ADHD, autobiographical memory, and theory of mind.

What's New?

- Explores new findings suggesting that complex fine-motor skills during early childhood foreshadow later academic performance.

- Offers the latest statistics on child overweight, expands on obesity's epigenetics, and focuses directly on strategies to limit later obesity by changing the environment in utero and during the first months of life.

- Updates the research on ADHD, autobiographical memory, and theory of mind.

- Includes a new section on autism spectrum disorders (accompanied by a figure highlighting autism's increasing prevalence).

CHAPTER 6: Socioemotional Development

- Discusses the development of self-understanding, prosocial behavior, aggression, and fantasy play, and explores friendships and popularity throughout childhood.

- Clearly spells out the developmental pathway to becoming an aggressive child.

- Highlights the challenge of emotion regulation, and focuses on internalizing and externalizing disorders.

- Covers the causes and consequences of bullying in older childhood.

What's New?

- Includes a study showing that praising toddlers for effort enhances later academic self-efficacy.

- Tackles gender differences in prosocial behavior, in depth.

- Showcases findings that toddlers are naturally prosocial, and emphasizes how important it is to allow young children to spontaneously share.

- Explores (in the discussion on play) whether pretend play is crucial to development.

- Revises the popularity discussion (accompanied by a new figure and table) by exploring the impact of relational aggression in promoting high status during elementary school and discussing how children's social goals in fifth grade relate to preteen popularity.

- Provides a new section on cyberbullying.

CHAPTER 7: Settings for Development: Home and School

- This final childhood chapter shifts from the process of development to the major settings for development—home and school—and tackles important controversies in the field, such as the influence of parents versus peers versus genetics in shaping development and the pros and cons of intelligence testing.

- Offers extensive discussions of ethnic variations in parenting styles and describes the latest research on how to stimulate intrinsic motivation.

- Showcases schools that beat the odds and targets the core qualities involved in effective teaching.

Imagine how you would feel if this terrifying, anonymous threat appeared on your screen, and you will immediately understand why cyberbullying is more distressing than bullying of the face-to-face kind.

What's New?

- Expands on the discussion of cultural differences in parenting styles.

- Revises sections on child maltreatment and, especially, divorce; the latter includes an introduction to the concept of parental alienation and more material on custody issues and their
impact on the child (this discussion features a new summary table and figure).

- Describes a newer edition of the WISC and updates the standard IQ diagnostic labels to
reflect the new *DSM-5* terminology.

- Presents the Common Core State Standards for education in a new concluding section.

PART IV: Adolescence

CHAPTER 8: Physical Development

- Offers an in-depth look at puberty, including the multiple forces that program
the timing of this life transition, and looks at historical and cultural variations in
puberty timetables.

- Explores the emotional experience of puberty (an "insider's" view) and the
emotional impact of maturing early for girls.

- Provides up-to-date coverage of teenage body image issues, eating disorders, and
emerging sexuality.

What's New?

- Offers new findings on pubertal progression rates, discusses the impact of being
an early maturer for boys, and showcases a cross-national study (accompanied
by a figure) suggesting that a nation's norms determine the tendency for early-
maturing girls to act out as teens.

- Links dieting problems during puberty to in-utero hormones, discusses
binge-eating disorder, and greatly expands the discussion of eating-disorder
treatments.

What are teens who avidly scan the photos
on a social-network site likely to do? The
surprise is that girls may decide to post more
sexually oriented comments than boys.

- Explores social-media research related to the sexual double standard, and
highlights the global need for relationship education versus just sex education.

CHAPTER 9: Cognitive and Socioemotional Development

- Covers the developmental science research on teenage brain development and various
facets of adolescent "storm and stress."

- Spells out the forces that enable adolescents to thrive and explains what society can do
(and also may not be doing!) to promote optimal development in teens.

- Explores parent–child relationships and discusses teenage peer groups.

What's New?

- Showcases new fMRI research exploring preteens' social sensitivities and impulsiveness.

- Offers a more thorough treatment of nonsuicidal self-injury, explores recent studies tracking
adolescent child–parent separation, and pinpoints the issues that are most problematic for
teens and parents in different world regions.

PART V: Early and Middle Adulthood

CHAPTER 10: Constructing an Adult Life

- Devotes a whole chapter to the concerns of emerging adulthood.

- Offers extensive coverage of diversity issues during this life stage, such as forming an ethnic and biracial identity, interracial dating, and issues related to coming out gay.

- Gives students tips for succeeding in college and spells out career issues for non-college emerging adults.

- Introduces career-relevant topics, such as the concept of "flow," and provides extensive coverage of the research relating to selecting a mate and adult attachment styles.

- Focuses on current social policy issues such as the impact socioeconomic status makes on attending and completing college, and discusses "nest residing," given that so many twenty-somethings now live at home.

What's New?

- Includes an expanded leaving-the-nest discussion, focused more specifically on variations in different European nations.

- Updates the section on identity styles, and introduces a new term, *ruminative moratorium*.

- Discusses self-esteem changes, specifically during college.

- Presents a *completely rewritten* "Finding Love" section that features a variety of new topics such as on-line dating, the tendency for young people to put off having romantic relationships until later in their twenties, and how Facebook is changing contemporary love relationships. This section also features a new table entitled "Everything (or Some Interesting Things) You Wanted to Know About Cyberspace Love Relationships," in addition to updating the research on same-sex relationships and offering a more nuanced look at the qualities we look for in a mate.

CHAPTER 11: Relationships and Roles

- Focuses directly on the core issues of adult life: work and family.

- Provides an extensive discussion of the research relating to how to have happy, enduring relationships, the challenges of parenting, and women's and men's work and family roles.

- Looks at marriage, parenthood, and work in their cultural and historical contexts.

- Offers research-based tips for having a satisfying marriage and career.

- Discusses job insecurity in our more fragile economy.

Having the flexibility to work at home is definitely a double-edged sword. Not only are you tempted to work on assignments when you should be paying attention to your child, but you are probably working far longer hours than if you had gone to the office.

Jamie Grill/Iconica/Getty Images

What's New?

- Includes a rewritten demographics of marriage discussion that explores marriage in India and Iran, current cohabitation trends in the United States, varying attitudes toward cohabitation, and having babies outside of marriage, in different nations (accompanied by two new figures).

- Offers a new section ("Marriage the Second or Third or 'X' Time Around") that discusses remarriage, as well as generally updating the research on what makes for happy marriages.

- Includes a revised parenthood section and features a new summary table entitled "Research Forces that Erode the Quality of the Day-to-Day Motherhood Experience."

- Includes a new section in the Work discussion, entitled "A Final Status Report on Men, Women, and Work" (accompanied by a figure tracking parental leave in Sweden for women and men). This section also introduces the concept of career as a calling.

CHAPTER 12: Midlife

- Describes the complexities of measuring adult personality development.

- Anchors the research on adult intellectual change (the fluid and crystallized distinctions) to lifespan changes in creativity and careers.

- Offers thorough coverage of the research on generativity and adult well-being.

- Provides research-based advice for constructing a fulfilling adult life.

- Covers age-related changes in sexuality, menopause, grandparenthood, and parent care.

What's New?

- Tracks the lifespan impact of conscientiousness in a new Hot in Developmental Science feature.

- Provides (in the section on Personality) additional data suggesting we get happier into later life and that adult stress can sometimes promote emotional growth. (To make these points, I've included several new figures as well as a new research summary table.)

- Introduces the concept of allostatic load (in the discussion on intelligence), and explores how this global index of physical functioning predicts midlife intellectual change.

- Includes a study of on-line relationships between grandparents and grandchildren, and elaborates on the forces that make for closeness or more distance in this core family relationship.

- Features a new section that specifically discusses research demonstrating that sex continues to be highly fulfilling in old age.

PART VI: Later Life

CHAPTER 13: Later Life: Cognitive and Socioemotional Development

- Offers an extensive discussion of Carstensen's socioemotional selectivity theory.

- Helps decode our contradictory stereotypes about later-life emotional states, the core qualities that make for a happy or unsatisfying old age, and offers a section on "aging optimally."

- Describes the research on aging memory, retirement, and widowhood.

- Discusses salient social issues such as age discrimination in hiring and intergenerational equity.

- Looks at later life developmentally by tracing changes from the young-old to the old-old years.

What's New?

- Provides an enhanced discussion of old-age perceptions and includes a new key term, *ageism*.

- Explores new neuroscience research on late-life memory and offers evidence that evoking age stereotypes impairs older people's laboratory performance on memory tests.

- Includes a new term, *age paradox* (in the section on Personality), and showcases research revealing that happiness is high *well into later life*.

- Includes a new Hot in Developmental Science feature exploring current retirement realities in the United States (and other developed nations).

- Offers a rewritten widowhood section showcasing the latest research on spousal mourning, and highlights the importance, specifically, of friends in determining how well older women cope with this life event.

Although his main goal is to greet this woman in a warm, personal way, in order to remember his new friend's name, this elderly man might want to step back and use the mnemonic strategy of forming a mental image, thinking, "I'll remember it's Mrs. Silver because of her hair."

CHAPTER 14: The Physical Challenges of Old Age

- Offers a clear developmental look at how normal aging shades into chronic disease and ADL impairments and looks at the impact of gender and socioeconomic forces on physical aging.

- Focuses on how to change the environment to compensate for sensorimotor declines.

- Provides an in-depth look at neurocognitive disorders, accompanied by compelling first-hand descriptions of their inner experience by people with Alzheimer's disease.

- Explores alternatives to institutionalization and provides a full description of nursing home care.

- Strives to provide a realistic, honest, and yet action-oriented and uplifting portrait of the physical frailties of advanced old age.

What's New?

- Includes a new head (Can we live to 1,000?) that summarizes the biological life-extension research and offers reasons why extending our human maximum lifespan, in the near future, is an unrealistic dream.

The huge domed ceilings are awe-inspiring, but combined with bare floors and the clatter of commuters they make New York City's Grand Central Station an acoustic nightmare. However, thanks to the miracle of the hearing loop, people can now bypass that background noise via loudspeaker train announcements beamed directly to their hearing aids.

- Ties the socioeconomic health gap directly to biology, by looking at telomeres and allostatic load; explores the impact specifically of education on longevity; and introduces a new key term, *healthy-life years*.

- Expands the gender discussion by offering an E.U. nation-by-nation chart, graphically showing that women spend more time than men living frailer.

- Updates sections on vision and hearing, and also provides new data on late-life falling and driving (the latter in a new Hot in Developmental Science feature).

- Revises the diagnostic labels for serious aging pathologies such as Alzheimer's disease and neurocognitive disorder (dementia) to conform with DSM-5, as well as exploring the latest findings relating to these conditions.

- Discussion in the section on options for the frail elderly section includes research on "social issues" related to moving to continuing care.

- Includes updates in the nursing home discussion.

PART VII: Epilogue

CHAPTER 15: Death and Dying

- Explores cross-cultural variations in dying and offers an historical look at death practices from the Middle Ages to today.

- Discusses the pros and cons of the hospice movement, with its focus on dying at home.

- Offers a look at the pros and cons of different types of advance directives and explores controversial topics such as physician-assisted suicide.

What's New?

- Includes a new Hot in Developmental Science feature devoted to mourning, accompanied by a table summarizing the research on children's bereavement, and introduces new key terms, *complex bereavement-related disorder* and *prolonged grief*.

- Includes a new section devoted to the concerns caregivers face in providing home hospice care. (In this edition, I also discuss my experience caring for my husband in hospice—in a new Experiencing the Lifespan interview.)

- Offers data on how euthanasia attitudes vary in different European nations, how older people feel about physician-assisted suicide, and generally updates the findings on advance directives.

Final Thoughts

This wrap-up section summarizes my new four top-pick research trends since the previous edition of *Experiencing the Lifespan*.

What Media and Supplements Come with This Book?

When you decide to use this book, you're adopting far more than just this text. You have access to an incredible learning system—everything from tests to video clips that bring the material to life. The Worth team and several dozen dedicated instructors have worked to provide an array of supplements to my text to foster student learning and make this course memorable: Video clips convey the magic of prenatal development, clarify Piaget's tasks, highlight child under-nutrition, and showcase the life stories of active and healthy people in their ninth and tenth decades of life. Lecture slides and clicker questions make class sessions more visual and inter-active. My publisher has amassed a rich archive of developmental science materials. For additional information, please contact your Worth Publishers sales consultant or look at the Worth Web site at http://www.macmillanhighered.com/Catalog/product/experiencingthelifespan-fourthedition-belsky. Here are descriptions of the supplements:

A comprehensive Web resource for teaching and learning, Worth Publishers' online course space offers:

- Prebuilt units for each chapter, curated by experienced educators, with relevant media organized and ready to be assigned or customized to suit your course

- One location for all online resources, including an interactive e-Book, LearningCurve's adaptive quizzing (see below), videos, activities, and more

- Intuitive and useful analytics, with a gradebook that lets you track how students in the class are performing individually and as a whole

- A streamlined and intuitive interface that lets you build an entire course in minutes

The LaunchPad can be previewed at www.macmillanhighered.com/launchpad/

LearningCurve

The **LearningCurve** quizzing system reflects the latest findings from learning and memory research. LearningCurve's adaptive and formative quizzing provides an effective way to get students involved in the coursework. It combines:

- A unique learning path for each student, with quizzes shaped by each individual's correct and incorrect answers

- A personalized study plan to guide students' preparation for class and for exams

- Feedback for each question with live links to relevant e-Book pages, guiding students to the resources they need to improve their areas of weakness

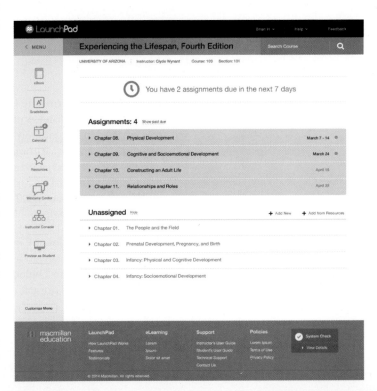

The LearningCurve system combines adaptive question selection, immediate feedback, and an interactive interface to engage students in a learning experience that is unique to them. Each LearningCurve quiz is fully integrated with other resources in LaunchPad, so students will be able to review using Worth's extensive library of videos and activities. And state-of-the-art question-analysis reports allow instructors to track the progress of individual students as well as their class as a whole.

You'll find the following in our LaunchPad:

Human Development Videos

In collaboration with dozens of instructors and researchers, Worth has developed an extensive archive of video clips. This collection covers the full range of the course, from classic experiments (like the Strange Situation and Piaget's conservation tasks) to investigations of children's play, to adolescent risk taking. Instructors can assign these videos to students through LaunchPad or choose one of 50 popular video activities that combine videos with short-answer and multiple-choice questions. For presentation purposes, our videos are available in a variety of formats to suit your needs, and highlights of the series appear periodically in the text's margin.

Interactive Presentation Slides

A new extraordinary series of "next generation" interactive presentation lectures give instructors a dynamic, yet easy-to-use, new way to engage students during classroom presentations of core developmental psychology topics. Each lecture provides opportunities for discussion and interaction and enlivens the psychology classroom with an unprecedented number of embedded video clips and animations.

Lecture Slides

There are two slide sets for each chapter of *Experiencing the Lifespan* (one featuring a full chapter lecture, the other featuring all chapter art and illustrations).

Instructor's Resources in Launchpad

Now fully integrated with LaunchPad, this collection of resources has been hailed as a rich collection of instructor's resources in developmental psychology. The resources include learning objectives, springboard topics for discussion and debate, handouts for student projects, course-planning suggestions, ideas for term projects, and a guide to audiovisual and online materials.

Assessment

- **LearningCurve: Formative Quizzing Engine.** Developed by a team of psychology instructors with extensive backgrounds in course design and online education, LearningCurve combines adaptive question selection, personalized study plans, and state-of-the-art question analysis reports. LearningCurve is based on the simple yet powerful concept of testing-to-learn, with gamelike quizzing activities that keep students engaged in the material while helping them learn key concepts. A team of dedicated instructors have worked closely to develop more than 3,000 quizzing questions developed specifically for this edition of *Experiencing the Lifespan*.

- Downloadable **Diploma Computerized Test Bank (for Windows and Macintosh).** This Test Bank offers an easy-to-use test-generation system that guides you through the process of creating tests. The Diploma software allows you to add an unlimited number of questions, edit questions, format a test, scramble questions, and include pictures, equations, or multimedia links. The Diploma software will also allow you to export into a variety of formats that are compatible with many Internet-based testing products. For more information on Diploma, visit: www.brownstone.net/publishers/products/dip6.asp.

Course Management

Worth Publishers supports multiple Course Management Systems with enhanced cartridges for upload into Blackboard, Desire2Learn, Sakai, Canvas, and Moodle. Cartridges are provided free upon adoption of *Experiencing the Lifespan* and can be downloaded from Worth's online catalog at www.macmillanhighered.com. Deep integration is also available between LaunchPad products and Blackboard, Brightspace by D2L, and Canvas. These deep integrations offer educators single sign-on and gradebook sync now with autorefresh.

Who Made This Book Possible?

This book was a completely collaborative endeavor engineered by the finest publishing company in the world: Worth (and not many authors can make that statement)! Firstly, again heartfelt thanks go to Elaine Epstein. Elaine, who I have been fortunate to have as my "developmental editor" for several editions of this book, has been working more than full time on this edition for over a year. She meticulously pored over every sentence of this manuscript multiple times, helped prepare all the figures and tables, skillfully guided everything into production, and is guiding this book into print as we speak. Elaine, as usual, is my real, unseen, full partner on this book.

The other genuine collaborator on this book is my masterful hands-on acquisitions editor Chris Cardone. After decades spent working with publishers, I can honestly say that in terms of attentiveness to authors, sensitivity to their needs, reliability, and genuine good smarts, Chris ranks in the top 1 percent. (Kudos also go to my editors for previous editions of this book, Catherine Woods and Jessica Bayne.)

Then there are the talented people who transformed this manuscript into print. Thanks go to Julio Espin, my hardworking Project Editor, for coordinating this intricate process, to Catherine Michaelsen, Assistant Editor, and to Sarah Segal, my Production Manager, for helping ensure everything fit together and pushing everyone to get things out on time. It's been my great fortune to rely on the advice of Worth's accomplished Director of Content Management Enhancement Tracey Kuehn, and to have Deb Heimann, my eagle-eyed copy editor check the manuscript for accuracy. Sheena Goldstein had the heroic task of helping select photos that embodied my thoughts. At the final stage of this process, Christine Hastings meticulously picked through the manuscript to place my commas correctly and make sure each sentence made grammatical sense.

Then there are the talented people who make *Experiencing the Lifespan* look like a breathtaking work of art. As you delight in looking at these fabulous pictures, you can thank Sheena Goldstein for coordinating the photo program. The Art Director, Diana Blume, along with Designer Blake Logan are responsible for planning this book's gorgeous design.

Thanks to Laura Burden my Media Editor, and to the supplements and media authors.

Without good marketing, no one would read this book. And, as usual, this arm of the Worth team gets my A+ rating. Kate Nurre, our Executive Marketing Manager, and Lindsay Johnson, Senior Marketing Manager, do an outstanding job. They go to many conferences and spend countless hours in the field advocating for my work. Although I may not meet many of you personally, I want take this chance to thank all the sales reps for working so hard to get "Belsky" out in the real world.

I am grateful for those student readers who took the time to personally e-mail and tell me, "You did a good job," or, "Dr. Belsky, I like it; but here's where you went wrong." These kinds of comments really make an author's day! This book has benefited from the insights of an incredible number of reviewers over the years. Here are the lifespan instructors who helped improve each edition of *Experiencing the Lifespan*:

Heather Adams, *Ball State University*

Daisuke Akiba, *Queens College*

Cecilia Alvarez, *San Antonio College*

Andrea S. Anastasiou, *Mary Baldwin College*

Emilie Aubert, *Marquette University*

Pamela Auburn, *University of Houston Downtown*

Tracy Babcock, *Montana State University*

Harriet Bachner, *Northeastern State University*

Carol Bailey, *Rochester Community and Technical College*

Thomas Bailey, *University of Baltimore*

Shelly Ball, *Western Kentucky University*

Mary Ballard, *Appalachian State University*

Lacy Barnes-Mileham, *Reedley College*

Kay Bartosz, *Eastern Kentucky University*

Laura Barwegen, *Wheaton College*

Jonathan Bates, *Hunter College, CUNY*

Don Beach, *Tarleton State University*

Lori Beasley, *University of Central Oklahoma*

Martha-Ann Bell, *Virginia Tech*

Daniel Bellack, *Trident Technical College*

Jennifer Bellingtier, *University of Northern Iowa*

Karen Bendersky, *Georgia College and State University*

Keisha Bentley, *University of La Verne*

Robert Billingham, *Indiana University*

Kathi J. Bivens, *Asheville-Buncombe Technical Community College*

Jim Blonsky, *University of Tulsa*

Cheryl Bluestone, *Queensborough Community College, CUNY*

Greg Bonanno, *Teachers College, Columbia University*

Aviva Bower, *College of St. Rose*

Marlys Bratteli, *North Dakota State University*

Bonnie Breitmayer, *University of Illinois, Chicago*

Jennifer Brennom, *Kirkwood Community College*

Tom Brian, *University of Tulsa*

Sabrina Brinson, *Missouri State University*

Adam Brown, *St. Bonaventure University*

Kimberly D. Brown, *Ball State University*

Donna Browning, *Mississippi State University*

Janine Buckner, *Seton Hall University*

Ted Bulling, *Nebraska Wesleyan University*

Holly Bunje, *University of Minnesota, Twin Cities*

Melinda Burgess, *Southwestern Oklahoma State University*

Barbara Burns, *University of Louisville*

Marilyn Burns, *Modesto Junior College*

Joni Caldwell, *Spalding University*

Norma Caltagirone, *Hillsborough Community College, Ybor City*

Lanthan Camblin, *University of Cincinnati*

Debb Campbell, *College of Sequoias*

Lee H. Campbell, *Edison Community College*

Robin Campbell, *Brevard Community College*

Kathryn A. Canter, *Penn State Fayette*

Peter Carson, *South Florida Community College*

Michael Casey, *College of Wooster*

Kimberly Chapman, *Blue River Community College*

Tom Chiaromonte, *Fullerton College*

Yiling Chow, *North Island College, Port Albernia*

Toni Christopherson, *California State University, Dominguez Hills*

Wanda Clark, *South Plains College*

Judy Collmer, *Cedar Valley College*

David Conner, *Truman State University*

Deborah Conway, *University of Virginia*

Diana Cooper, *Purdue University*

Ellen Cotter, *Georgia Southwestern State University*

Deborah M. Cox, *Madisonville Community College*

Kim B. Cragin, *Snow College*

Charles P. Cummings, *Asheville-Buncombe Technical Community College*

Karen Curran, *Mt. San Antonio College*

Antonio Cutolo-Ring, *Kansas City (KS) Community College*

Ken Damstrom, *Valley Forge Christian College*

Leslie Daniels, *Florida State College at Jacksonville*

Nancy Darling, *Bard College*

Paul Dawson, *Weber State University*

Janet B. Dean, *Asbury University*

Lynda DeDee, *University of Wisconsin, Oshkosh*

David C. Devonis, *Graceland University*

Charles Dickel, *Creighton University*

Darryl Dietrich, *College of St. Scholastica*

Stephanie Ding, *Del Mar College*

Lugenia Dixon, *Bainbridge College*

Benjamin Dobrin, *Virginia Wesleyan College*

Delores Doench, *Southwestern Community College*

Melanie Domenech Rodriguez, *Utah State University*

Sundi Donovan, *Liberty University*

Lana Dryden, *Sir Sanford Fleming College*

Gwenden Dueker, *Grand Valley State University*

Bryan Duke, *University of Central Oklahoma*

Trisha M. Dunkel, *Loyola University, Chicago*

Robin Eliason, *Piedmont Virginia Community College*

Traci Elliot, *Alvin Community College*

Frank Ellis, *University of Maine, Augusta*

Kelley Eltzroth, *Mid Michigan Community College*

Marya Endriga, *California State University, Stanislaus*

Lena Ericksen, *Western Washington University*

Kathryn Fagan, *California Baptist University*

Daniel Fasko, *Bowling Green State University*

Nancy Feehan, *University of San Francisco*

Meredyth C. Fellows, *West Chester University of Pennsylvania*

Gary Felt, *City University of New York*

Martha Fewell, *Barat College*

Mark A. Fine, *University of Missouri*

Roseanne L. Flores, *Hunter College, CUNY*

John Foley, *Hagerstown Community College*

James Foster, *George Fox University*

Geri Fox, *University of Illinois, Chicago*

Thomas Francigetto, *Northampton Community College*

James Francis, *San Jacinto College*

Doug Friedrich, *University of West Florida*

Lynn Garrioch, *Colby-Sawyer College*

Bill Garris, *Cumberland College*

Caroline Gee, *Palomar College*

C. Ray Gentry, *Lenoir-Rhyne College*

Carol George, *Mills College*

Elizabeth Gersten, *Victor Valley College*

Linde Getahun, *Bethel University*

Afshin Gharib, *California State University, East Bay*

Nada Glick, *Yeshiva University*

Andrea Goldstein, *Kaplan University*

Arthur Gonchar, *University of La Verne*

Helen Gore-Laird, *University of Houston, University Park*

Tyhesha N. Goss, *University of Pennsylvania*

Dan Grangaard, *Austin Community College, Rio Grande*

Julie Graul, *St. Louis Community College, Florissant Valley*

Elizabeth Gray, *North Park University*

Stefanie Gray Greiner, *Mississippi University for Women*

Erinn L. Green, *Wilmington College*

Dale D. Grubb, *Baldwin-Wallace College*

Laura Gruntmeir, *Redlands Community College*

Lisa Hager, *Spring Hill College*

Michael Hall, *Iowa Western Community College*

Andre Halliburton, *Prairie State College*

Laura Hanish, *Arizona State University*

Robert Hansson, *University of Tulsa*

Richard Harland, *West Texas A&M University*

Gregory Harris, *Polk Community College*

Virginia Harvey, *University of Massachusetts, Boston*

Margaret Hellie Huyck, *Illinois Institute of Technology*

Janice L. Hendrix, *Missouri State University*

Gertrude Henry, *Hampton University*

Rod Hetzel, *Baylor University*

Heather Hill, *University of Texas, San Antonio*

Elaine Hogan, *University of North Carolina, Wilmington*

Judith Holland, *Hawaii Pacific University*

Debra Hollister, *Valencia Community College*

Heather Holmes-Lonergan, *Metropolitan State College of Denver*

Rosemary Hornak, *Meredith College*

Suzy Horton, *Mesa Community College*

Rebecca Hoss, *College of Saint Mary*

Cynthia Hudley, *University of California, Santa Barbara*

Alycia Hund, *Illinois State University*

David P. Hurford, *Pittsburgh State University*

Elaine Ironsmith, *East Carolina University*

Jessica Jablonski, *Richard Stockton College*

Sabra Jacobs, *Big Sandy Community and Technical College*

David Johnson, *John Brown University*

Emilie Johnson, *Lindenwood University*

Mary Johnson, *Loras College*

Mike Johnson, *Hawaii Pacific University*

Peggy Jordan, *Oklahoma City Community College*

Lisa Judd, *Western Wisconsin Technical College*

Tracy R. Juliao, *University of Michigan Flint*

Elaine Justice, *Old Dominion University*

Steve Kaatz, *Bethel University*

Jyotsna M. Kalavar, *Penn State New Kensington*

Chi-Ming Kam, *City College of New York, CUNY*

Richard Kandus, *Mt. San Jacinto College*

Skip Keith, *Delaware Technical and Community College*

Michelle L. Kelley, *Old Dominion University*

Richie Kelley, *Baptist Bible College and Seminary*

Robert Kelley, *Mira Costa College*

Jeff Kellogg, *Marian College*

Colleen Kennedy, *Roosevelt University*

Sarah Kern, *The College of New Jersey*

Marcia Killien, *University of Washington*

Kenyon Knapp, *Troy State University*

Cynthia Koenig, *Mt. St. Mary's College of Maryland*

Steve Kohn, *Valdosta State University*

Holly Krogh, *Mississippi University for Women*

Martha Kuehn, *Central Lakes College*

Alvin Kuest, *Great Lakes Christian College*

Rich Lanthier, *George Washington University*

Peggy Lauria, *Central Connecticut State University*

Melisa Layne, *Danville Community College*

John LeChapitaine, *University of Wisconsin, River Falls*

Barbara Lehmann, *Augsburg College*

Rhinehart Lintonen, *Gateway Technical College*

Nancy Lobb, *Alvin Community College*

Martha V. Low, *Winston-Salem State University*

Carol Ludders, *University of St. Francis*

Dunja Lund Trunk, *Bloomfield College*

Vickie Luttrell, *Drury University*

Nina Lyon Jenkins, *University of Maryland, Eastern Shore*

Christine Malecki, *Northern Illinois University*

Marlowe Manger, *Stanly Community College*

Pamela Manners, *Troy State University*

Kathy Manuel, *Bossier Parish Community College*

Howard Markowitz, *Hawaii Pacific University*

Jayne D. B. Marsh, *University of Southern Maine, Lewiston-Auburn College*

Esther Martin, *California State University, Dominguez Hills*

Jan Mast, *Miami Dade College, North Campus*

Pan Maxson, *Duke University*

Nancy Mazurek, *Long Beach City College*

Christine McCormick, *Eastern Illinois University*

Jim McDonald, *California State University, Fresno*

Clark McKinney, *Southwest Tennessee Community College*

George Meyer, *Suffolk County Community College*

Barbara J. Miller, *Pasadena City College*

Christy Miller, *Coker College*

Mary Beth Miller, *Fresno City College*

Al Montgomery, *Our Lady of Holy Cross College*

Robin Montvilo, *Rhode Island College*

Peggy Moody, *St. Louis Community College*

Michelle Moriarty, *Johnson County Community College*

Wendy Bianchini Morrison, *Montana State University-Bozeman*

Ken Mumm, *University of Nebraska, Kearney*

Joyce Munsch, *Texas Tech University*

Jeannette Murphey, *Meridian Community College*

Lori Myers, *Louisiana Tech University*

Lana Nenide, *University of Wisconsin, Madison*

Margaret Nettles, *Alliant University*

Gregory Newton, *Diablo Valley College*

Barbara Nicoll, *University of La Verne*

Nancy Nolan, *Nashville State Community College*

Harriett Nordstrom, *University of Michigan, Flint*

Wendy North-Ollendorf, *Northwestern Connecticut Community College*

Elizabeth O'Connor, *St. Mary's College*

Susan O'Donnell, *George Fox University*

Jane Ogden, *East Texas Baptist University*

Shirley Ogletree, *Texas State University*

Claudius Oni, *South Piedmont Community College*

Randall E. Osborne, *Texas State University, San Marcos*

John Otey, *Southern Arkansas University*

Carol Ott, *University of Wisconsin, Milwaukee*

Patti Owen-Smith, *Oxford College*

Heidi Pasek, *Montana State University*

Margaret Patton, *University of North Carolina, Charlotte*

Julie Hicks Patrick, *West Virginia University*

Evelyn Payne, *Albany State University*

Ian E. Payton, *Bethune-Cookman University*

Carole Penner-Faje, *Molloy College*

Michelle L. Pilati, *Rio Hondo College*

Meril Posy, *Touro College, Brooklyn*

Shannon M. Pruden, *Temple University*

Ellery Pullman, *Briarcrest Bible College*

Samuel Putnam, *Bowdoin College*

Jeanne Quarles, *Oregon Coast Community College*

Mark Rafter, *College of the Canyons*

Cynthia Rand-Johnson, *Albany State University*

Janet Rangel, *Palo Alto College*

Jean Raniseski, *Alvin Community College*

Frances Raphael-Howell, *Montgomery College*

Celinda Reese, *Oklahoma State University*

Ethan Remmel, *Western Washington University*

Paul Rhoads, *Williams Baptist College*

Kerri A. Riggs, *Lourdes College*

Mark Rittman, *Cuyahoga Community College*

Jeanne Rivers, *Finger Lakes Community College*

Wendy Robertson, *Western Michigan University*

Richard Robins, *University of California, Davis*

Millie Roqueta, *Miami Dade College*

June Rosenberg, *Lyndon State College*

Christopher Rosnick, *University of South Florida*

Trisha Rossi, *Adelphi University*

Rodger Rossman, *College of the Albemarle*

Lisa Routh, *Pikes Peak Community College*

Stephanie Rowley, *University of Michigan, Ann Arbor*

Randall Russac, *University of North Florida*

Dawn Ella Rust, *Stephen F. Austin State University*

Tara Saathoff-Wells, *Central Michigan University*

Traci Sachteleben, *Southwestern Illinois College*

Douglas Sauber, *Arcadia University*

Chris Saxild, *Wisconsin Indianhead Technical College*

Barbara Schaudt, *California State University, Bakersfield*

Daniela E. Schreier, *Chicago School of Professional Psychology*

Pamela Schuetze, *SUNY College at Buffalo*

Donna Seagle, *Chattanooga State Technical Community College*

Bonnie Seegmiller, *Hunter College, CUNY*

Chris Seifert, *Montana State University*

Marianne Shablousky, *Community College of Allegheny County*

Susan Shapiro, *Indiana University, East*

Elliot Sharpe, *Maryville University*

Lawrence Shelton, *University of Vermont*

Shamani Shikwambi, *University of Northern Iowa*

Denise Simonsen, *Fort Lewis College*

Penny Skemp, *Mira Costa College*

Peggy Skinner, *South Plains College*

Barbara Smith, *Westminster College*

Valerie Smith, *Collin County Community College*

Edward Sofranko, *University of Rio Grande*

Joan Spiegel, *West Los Angeles College*

Jason S. Spiegelman, *Community College of Baltimore County*

Carolyn I. Spies, *Bloomfield College*

Scott Stein, *Southern Vermont College*

Stephanie Stein, *Central Washington University*

Sheila Steiner, *Jamestown College*

Jacqueline Stewart, *Seminole State College*

Robert Stewart, Jr., *Oakland University*

Cynthia Suarez, *Wofford College*

Joshua Susskind, *University of Northern Iowa*

Josephine Swalloway, *Curry College*

Emily Sweitzer, *California University of Pennsylvania*

Chuck Talor, *Valdosta State University*

Jamie Tanner, *South Georgia College*

Norma Tedder, *Edison Community College*

George Thatcher, *Texas Tech University*

Shannon Thomas, *Wallace Community College*

Donna Thompson, *Midland College*

Vicki Tinsley, *Brescia University*

Eugene Tootle, *Barry University*

David Tracer, *University of Colorado, Denver*

Stephen Truhon, *Austin Peay Centre, Fort Campbell*

Dana Van Abbema, *St. Mary's College of Maryland*

Mary Vandendorpe, *Lewis University*

Janice Vidic, *University of Rio Grande*

Steven Voss, *Moberly Area Community College*

William Walkup, *Southwest Baptist University*

Anne Weiher, *Metropolitan State College of Denver*

Robert Weis, *University of Wisconsin, Stevens Point*

Lori Werdenschlag, *Lyndon State College*

Noel Wescombe, *Whitworth College*

Andrea White, *Ithaca College*

Meade Whorton, *Louisiana Delta Community College*

Wanda A. Willard, *Monroe Community College*

Joylynne Wills, *Howard University*

Nancy A. Wilson, *Haywood Community College*

Steffen Wilson, *Eastern Kentucky University*

Bernadette Wise, *Iowa Lakes Community College*

Steve Wisecarver, *Lord Fairfax Community College*

Alex Wiseman, *University of Tulsa*

Rebecca Witt Stoffel, *West Liberty State College*

Nanci Woods, *Austin Peay State University*

Chrysalis L. Wright, *University of Central Florida*

Stephanie Wright, *Georgetown University*

David Yarbrough, *Texas State University*

Nikki Yonts, *Lyon College*

Ling-Yi Zhou, *University of St. Francis*

On the home front, I am indebted to my colleagues at Middle Tennessee State University and to my students over the years. As any teacher will tell you, I learn as much—or more—from you each semester as you do from me. I want to thank my incredibly competent reference checker, Jac Mitchell, for performing the difficult task of ferreting out the full source of every new citation in this book. I'm grateful to my baby, Thomas, for being born, and giving my life such meaning, and to Shelly for brightening my life since I moved to Chicago this past year. But the real credit for this book still belongs to my late husband David, for putting this book and my happiness center stage and for giving me the best possible life.

Janet Belsky
August 25, 2015

The Foundation

This two-chapter part offers you the foundations for understanding the lifespan journey.

Chapter 1–**The People and the Field** introduces *all* the major concepts and themes in this course. In this chapter, I'll describe our discipline's basic terminology, provide a bird's-eye view of the evolving lifespan, offer a framework for how to think about world cultures, and highlight some new twenty-first-century life stages. Most important, in this chapter you will learn about the themes, theories, and research strategies that have shaped our field. Bottom line: Chapter 1 gives you the tools you will need for understanding this book.

Chapter 2–**Prenatal Development, Pregnancy, and Birth** lays the foundation for our developing lives. Here, you will learn about how a baby develops from a tiny clump of cells, and get insights into the experience of pregnancy from the point of view of mothers and fathers. This chapter describes pregnancy rituals in different cultures, discusses the impact of prenatal issues such as stress and infertility, and offers an in-depth look at the miracle of birth.

PART I

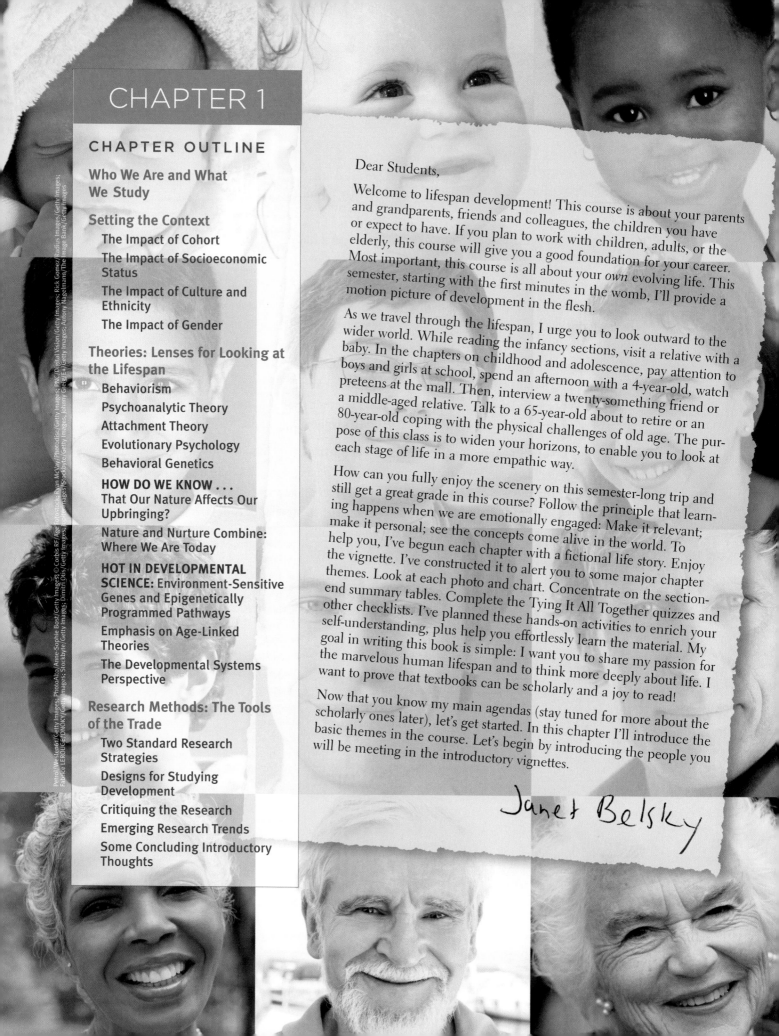

CHAPTER 1

CHAPTER OUTLINE

Dear Students,

Welcome to lifespan development! This course is about your parents and grandparents, friends and colleagues, the children you have or expect to have. If you plan to work with children, adults, or the elderly, this course will give you a good foundation for your career. Most important, this course is all about your *own* evolving life. This semester, starting with the first minutes in the womb, I'll provide a motion picture of development in the flesh.

As we travel through the lifespan, I urge you to look outward to the wider world. While reading the infancy sections, visit a relative with a baby. In the chapters on childhood and adolescence, pay attention to boys and girls at school, spend an afternoon with a 4-year-old, watch preteens at the mall. Then, interview a twenty-something friend or a middle-aged relative. Talk to a 65-year-old about to retire or an 80-year-old coping with the physical challenges of old age. The purpose of this class is to widen your horizons, to enable you to look at each stage of life in a more empathic way.

How can you fully enjoy the scenery on this semester-long trip and still get a great grade in this course? Follow the principle that learning happens when we are emotionally engaged: Make it relevant; make it personal; see the concepts come alive in the world. To help you, I've begun each chapter with a fictional life story. Enjoy the vignette. I've constructed it to alert you to some major chapter themes. Look at each photo and chart. Concentrate on the section-end summary tables. Complete the Tying It All Together quizzes and other checklists. I've planned these hands-on activities to enrich your self-understanding, plus help you effortlessly learn the material. My goal in writing this book is simple: I want you to share my passion for the marvelous human lifespan and to think more deeply about life. I want to prove that textbooks can be scholarly and a joy to read!

Now that you know my main agendas (stay tuned for more about the scholarly ones later), let's get started. In this chapter I'll introduce the basic themes in the course. Let's begin by introducing the people you will be meeting in the introductory vignettes.

Janet Belsky

The People and the Field

Susan is having a party to celebrate Carl's wonderful life. Losing her husband was tough, but Susan takes comfort in the fact that during their 50-plus-year-long marriage, she and her husband amassed so many friends—people of every age, ethnicity, and social group. After Carl's death, everyone flooded Susan's Facebook page with expressions of love. But, being from a different era, Susan craves having her friends physically close, to hug and reminisce about Carl.

First to arrive on Saturday were Maria and baby Josiah, whom Susan and Carl met on a cross-country trip to Las Vegas five years ago. Then, Mathew and Jamila, the lovely couple who were on last year's Alaskan cruise, knocked on the door. For Susan, bonding with her new 40-something friends on that 10-day trip through the Glaciers offered a lesson in how the world has changed. Susan and Carl married at age 21—at a time when middle-class women often stopped working after getting married, and gender roles were clearly defined. Jamila waited until she got her career in order at age 35 to get married, met Matt on-line, and even selected a husband of a different race. How, despite juggling step-kids and full-time jobs, have Matt and Jamila mastered the secret of staying in love for more than 10 years?

Finally, Kim, her husband Jeff, and baby Elissa drove up. Although Susan was devastated when this close neighborhood couple moved across the country 9 months ago, she has been thrilled to witness Elissa's transformations through the miracles of Skype. Now, it's time to (finally) envelope that precious 1-year-old in her arms and hear, in person, about everyone else's lives!

As they sit down to dinner, Kim reports that since Elissa began walking, she doesn't slow down for a minute. Actually, it's kind of depressing. Elissa used to go to Susan with a smile. Now, all she wants is Mom. The transformation in Josiah is even more astonishing. Now that he is 8, that precious child can talk to you like an adult!

Over the next hour, the talk turns to deeper issues: Kim shares her anxieties about putting Elissa in day care. Matt talks about the trials and joys of step-fatherhood. Maria opens up about the challenges of being a single parent, an immigrant, and ethnic minority in the United States. Jamila informs the group that she wants to make a difference. She is returning to school for a Ph.D. But can she make it academically at age 53?

Susan tells the group not to worry. The sixties and early seventies (until Carl's massive stroke) were the happiest time of their lives. Now, with her slowness, her progressing vision problems, and especially that frightening fall she took at Kroger's last week, the future looks bleaker. Susan knows that life is precious. She treasures every moment she has left. But the eighties won't be like the seventies. What will happen when she really gets old?

Is Susan right that the sixties and early seventies are life's happiest stage? If you met Susan at age 30 or 50, would she be the same upbeat person as today? Are Jamila's worries about her mental abilities realistic, and what *are* some secrets for staying passionately in love with your spouse? Why do 1-year-olds such as Elissa get clingy just as they begin walking, and what mental leaps make children at age 8, such as Josiah, seem so grown up? How has the social media revolution affected how we relate?

Developmentalists, also called **developmental scientists**—researchers who study the lifespan—are about to answer these questions and hundreds of others about our unfolding life.

developmentalists
Researchers and practitioners whose professional interest lies in the study of the human lifespan.

lifespan development
The scientific study of development through life.

child development The scientific study of development from birth through adolescence.

gerontology The scientific study of the aging process and older adults.

adult development The scientific study of the adult part of life.

normative transitions
Predictable life changes that occur during development.

non-normative transitions
Unpredictable or atypical life changes that occur during development.

Who We Are and What We Study

Lifespan development, the scientific study of human growth throughout life, is a latecomer to psychology. Its roots lie in **child development,** the study of childhood and the teenage years. Child development traces its origins back more than a century. In 1877, Charles Darwin published an article based on notes he had made about his baby during the first years of life. In the 1890s, a pioneering psychologist named G. Stanley Hall established the first institute in the United States devoted to research on the child. Child development began to take off between World Wars I and II (Lerner, 1998). It remains the passion of thousands of developmental scientists working in every corner of the globe.

Gerontology, the scientific study of aging—the other core discipline in lifespan development—had a slower start. Researchers began to really study the aging process only after World War II (Birren & Birren, 1990). Gerontology and its related field, **adult development,** underwent their phenomenal growth spurt during the final third of the twentieth century.

Lifespan development puts it all together. It synthesizes what researchers know about our unfolding life. Who works in this huge mega-discipline, and what passions drive developmentalists?

- **Lifespan development is multidisciplinary.** It draws on fields as different as neuroscience, nursing, psychology, and social policy to understand human development. A biologically oriented developmentalist might examine toddlers' output of salivary cortisol (a stress hormone) when they arrive at day care. An anthropologist might look at cultural values shaping the day-care choice. A social policy expert might explore the impact of offering universal government-funded day care in Finland and France. A biochemist who studies Alzheimer's disease might decode what produces the plaques and tangles that ravage the brain. A nurse might head an innovative Alzheimer's unit. A research-oriented psychologist might construct a scale to measure the impairments produced by this devastating disease.

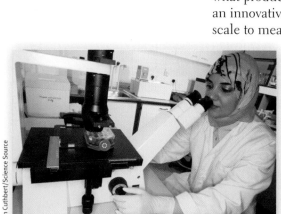

This researcher is among the thousands of developmental scientists whose mission is to decode the causes of that later life scourge, Alzheimer's disease.

- **Lifespan development explores the predictable milestones on our human journey,** from walking to working, to Elissa's sudden shyness and attachment to her mother. Are people right to worry about their learning abilities in their fifties? What is physical aging, or puberty, or menopause all about? Are there specific emotions we feel as we approach that final universal milestone, death?

- **Lifespan development focuses on the individual differences that give spice to human life.** Can we really see the person we will be at age 73, by age 50, or 30? How much does personality or intelligence change as we travel through life? Developmentalists want to understand what *causes* the striking differences between people in temperament, talents, and traits. They are interested in exploring individual differences in the timing of developmental milestones, too; examining, for instance, why people reach puberty earlier or later or age more quickly or slowly than their peers.

- **Lifespan development explores the impact of life transitions and practices.** It deals with **normative,** or predictable, **transitions,** such as retirement, becoming parents, or beginning middle school. It focuses on **non-normative,** or atypical, **transitions,** such as divorce, the death of a child, or how declines in the economy affect how we approach the world. It explores life practices, such as smoking, spanking, or sleeping in the same bed with your child.

Developmentalists realize that life transitions that we consider normative, such as retiring or starting middle school, are products of living in a particular time in

Colin Cuthbert/Science Source

history. They understand that practices such as smoking or sleeping in bed with a child vary, depending on our social class and cultural background. They know that several basic markers, or overall conditions of life, affect our development.

Now it's time to introduce some **contexts of development**, or broad general influences, which I will be continually discussing throughout this book.

Setting the Context

How does being born in a particular historical time affect our lifespan journey? What about our social class, cultural background, or that basic biological difference, being female or male?

The Impact of Cohort

Cohort refers to our birth group, the age group with whom we travel through life. In the vignette, you can immediately see the heavy role our cohort plays in influencing adult life. Susan reached adult life in 1960, when women married in their early twenties and typically stayed married for life. Jamila came of age during the final decade of the twentieth century, when women began to feel they needed to get their careers together before finding a mate. As an interracial couple, Matt and Jamila are taking a life path unusual even for today! Because they are in their late forties, this couple is at an interesting cutting point. They are traveling through life after that huge bulge in the population called the baby boom.

The **baby boom cohort,** defined as people born from 1946 to 1964, has made a huge impact on the Western world as it moves through society. The reason lies in size. When soldiers returned from World War II and got married, the average family size ballooned to almost four children. When this huge group was growing up during the 1950s, families were traditional, with the two-parent, stay-at-home-mother family being our national ideal. Then, as rebellious adolescents during the 1960s and 1970s, the baby boomers helped usher in a radical transformation in these attitudes and roles (more about this lifestyle revolution soon). Society, as we know, is now experiencing an old-age explosion as the baby boom cohort floods into later life.

The cohorts living in the early twenty-first century are part of an endless march of cohorts stretching back thousands of years. Let's now take a brief historical tour to get a sense of the dramatic changes in childhood, old age, and adulthood during just the past few centuries, and pinpoint what our lifespan looks like today.

Changing Conceptions of Childhood

At age ten he began his work life helping . . . manufacture candles and soap. He . . . wanted to go to sea, but his father refused and apprenticed him to a master printer. At age 17 he ran away from Boston to Philadelphia to search for work.

His father died when he was 11, and he left school. At 17 he was appointed official surveyor for Culpepper County in Virginia. By age 20 he was in charge of managing his family's plantation.

(Mintz, 2004)

Who were these boys? Their names were Benjamin Franklin and George Washington.

Imagine being born in Colonial times. In addition to reaching adulthood at a much younger age, your chance of having *any* lifespan would have been far from secure. In seventeenth-century Paris, roughly 1 in every 3 babies died in early infancy (Ariès, 1962; Hrdy, 1999). As late as 1900, almost 3 of every 10 U.S. children did not live beyond age 5 (Konner, 2010; Mintz, 2004).

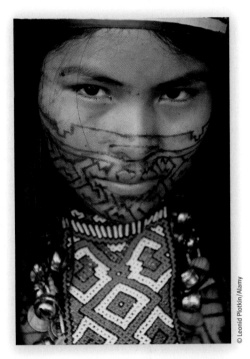

© Leonid Plotkin/Alamy

Our cultural background affects every aspect of development. So, culturally oriented developmentalists might study how this coming-of-age ritual expresses this society's messages about adult life.

contexts of development Fundamental markers, including cohort, socioeconomic status, culture, and gender, that shape how we develop throughout the lifespan.

cohort The age group with whom we travel through life.

baby boom cohort The huge age group born between 1946 and 1964.

The incredible childhood mortality rates, plus poverty, may have partly explained why child-rearing practices that we would label as abusive used to be routine. Children were often beaten and, at their parents' whim, might be abandoned at birth (Konner, 2010; Pinker, 2011). In the early 1800s in Paris, about one in five newborns was "exposed"—placed in the doorways of churches, or simply left outside to die. In cities such as St. Petersburg, Russia, the statistic might have been as high as one in two (Ariès, 1962; Hrdy, 1999).

In addition, for most of history, people did not have our feeling that childhood is a special life stage (Ariès, 1962; Mintz, 2004). Children, as you saw above, began to work at a young age. During the early industrial revolution, poor boys and girls made up more than a third of the labor force in British mills (Mintz, 2004).

Library of Congress, Prints & Photographs Division, National Child Labor Committee Collection

In the nineteenth century, if you visited factories such as this cannery, you would see many young children at work—showing how far we have come in just a bit more than a century in our attitudes about childhood.

In the seventeenth and eighteenth centuries, enlightenment philosophers such as John Locke and Jean Jacques Rousseau spelled out a strikingly different vision of childhood and human life (Pinker, 2011). Locke believed that human beings are born a *tabula rasa*, a blank slate on which anything could be written, and that the way we treat children shapes their adult lives. Rousseau argued that babies enter life totally innocent; he felt we should shower these dependent creatures with love. However, this message could fully penetrate society only when the advances of the early twentieth century dramatically improved living standards, and we entered our modern age.

One force producing this kinder, gentler view of childhood was universal education. During the late nineteenth century in Western Europe and much of the United States, attendance at primary school became mandatory (Ariès, 1962). School kept children from working and insulated these years as a protected, dependent life phase. Still, as late as 1915, only 1 in 10 U.S. children attended high school; most people entered their work lives after seventh or eighth grade (Mintz, 2004).

At the beginning of the twentieth century, the developmentalist G. Stanley Hall (1904/1969) identified a stage of "storm and stress," located between childhood and adulthood, which he named *adolescence*. However, it was during the Great Depression of the 1930s, when President Franklin Roosevelt signed a bill making high school attendance mandatory, that adolescence became a standard U.S. life stage (Mintz, 2004). Our famous teenage culture has existed for only 70 or 80 years!

In recent decades, with many of us going to college and graduate school, we have delayed the beginning of adulthood to an older age. Developmentalists (see Tanner & Arnett, 2010) have identified a new in-between stage of life in affluent countries. **Emerging adulthood,** lasting from age 18 to roughly the late twenties, is devoted to exploring our place in the world. One reason that we feel comfortable postponing marriage or settling down to a career is that we can expect to live an amazingly long time.

Changing Conceptions of Later Life

In every culture, a few people always lived to "old age." However, for most of history, largely due to the high rates of infant and childhood mortality, **average life expectancy,** our fifty-fifty chance at birth of living to a given age, was shockingly low. In Maryland during Colonial times, average life expectancy was only age 20, for both masters and their slaves (Fischer, 1977).

Toward the end of the nineteenth century, life expectancy in the United States rapidly improved. By 1900, it was 46. Then, in the next century, it shot up to 76.7. During the twentieth century, life expectancy in North America and Western Europe increased by almost 30 years! (Centers for Disease Control and Prevention [CDC], Health United States, 2007.)

emerging adulthood The phase of life that begins after high school, tapers off toward the late twenties, and is devoted to constructing an adult life.

average life expectancy A person's fifty-fifty chance at birth of living to a given age.

The **twentieth-century life expectancy revolution** may be the most important milestone in human history. The most dramatic increases in longevity occurred about 100 years ago, when public health improvements and medical advances, such as antibiotics, wiped out deaths from many *infectious diseases*. Since these illnesses, such as diphtheria, killed both the young and old, their conquest allowed us to live past midlife. In the last 50 years, our progress has been slower because the illnesses we now die from, called *chronic diseases*—such as heart disease, cancer, and stroke—are tied to the aging process itself.

As you can see in Figure 1.1, the outcome is that today, life expectancies have zoomed into the upper seventies in North America, Western Europe, New Zealand, Israel, and Japan. A baby born in affluent parts of the world, especially if that child is female, now has a good chance of making it close to our **maximum lifespan,** the biological limit of human life (about age 105).

This extension of the lifespan has changed how we think about *every* life stage. It has moved grandparenthood, once a sign of being "old," down into middle age. If you become a grandparent in your forties, expect to be called grandma or grandpa for half of your life! Women can start new careers in their early fifties, given that U.S. females at that age can expect to live on average for roughly 32 more years (U.S. Census Bureau, 2012). Most important, we have moved the beginning of old age beyond age 65.

Today, people in their sixties and even early seventies are often active and relatively healthy. But in our eighties, our chance of being disabled by disease increases dramatically. Because of this, developmentalists make a distinction between two groups of older adults. The **young-old,** defined as people in their sixties and early seventies, often look and feel middle-aged. They reject the idea that they are old (Lachman, 2004). The **old-old,** people in their late seventies and beyond, seem in a different class. Since they are more likely to have physical and mental disabilities, they are more prone to fit the stereotype of the frail, dependent older adult. In sum, Susan in the vignette was right: Today the eighties are a different stage of life!

Changing Conceptions of Adult Life

If health-care strides during the early twentieth century allowed us to survive to old age, during the last third of the twentieth century, a revolution in lifestyles changed the way we live our adult lives. This transformation, in the West, which has now spread around the globe, began when the baby boomers entered their teenage years.

The 1960s "Decade of Protest" included the civil rights and women's movements, the sexual revolution, and the "counterculture" movement that emphasized liberation in every area of life (Bengtson, 1989). People could have sex without being married. Women could fulfill themselves in a career. We encouraged husbands to share the housework and child care equally with their wives. Divorce became an acceptable alternative to living in an unfulfilling marriage. To have a baby, women no longer needed to be married at all.

Today, with women making up more than half the U.S. labor force, only a minority of couples fit the traditional 1950s roles of breadwinner husband and homemaker wife (U.S. Bureau of Labor Statistics, 2014). With roughly one out of two U.S. marriages ending in divorce, we can no longer be confident of staying together for life. While divorce rates are now declining, the Western trend toward having children without being married continues to rise. As of 2013, almost 48 percent of U.S. babies were born to single moms (Hymowitz and others, 2013).

twentieth-century life expectancy revolution The dramatic increase in average life expectancy that occurred during the first half of the twentieth century in the developed world.

maximum lifespan The biological limit of human life (about 105 years).

young-old People in their sixties and seventies.

old-old People in their late seventies and older.

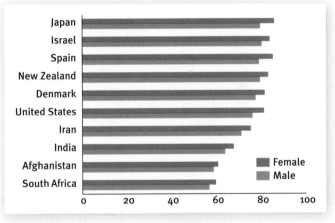

FIGURE 1.1: **Average life expectancy of men and women in some selected nations, 2013:** Notice the gap in life expectancy between the developed and developing worlds. Notice also the astonishingly high life expectancy for women in Spain, New Zealand, Israel, and Japan. Women today can expect to live close to the maximum lifespan in these developed countries. (As of 2007, the United States ranked forty-ninth globally in average life expectancy.)

Data from: http://www.worldlifeexpectancy.com/ retrieved September 3, 2014.

The healthy, active couple in their sixties *(left)* have little in common with the disabled 90-year-old man living in a nursing home *(right)*—showing why developmentalists divide the elderly into the *young-old* and the *old-old.*

The timeline at the bottom of this page illustrates the twentieth-century shifts in life expectancy and family life, as well as charting the passage of the mammoth baby boom as it moves through life. In later chapters, I'll pay special attention to the late-twentieth-century lifestyle revolution—highlighting single parenthood, the trend toward having stepchildren, exploring gay and bisexual relationships, and shedding light on the changing family roles of women and men. While this text does divide development into its standard categories (infancy, childhood, adolescence, adulthood, and later life), I'll also devote a chapter to emerging adulthood—that life stage many of you are in right now. In the later-life section, I'll continually emphasize the distinction between the young-old and old-old (being 60 is miles different physically and mentally from being 80 or 95) and focus on the issues we face as the baby boomers flood into their older years.

But, as history is always advancing, let's end this section by touching on two twenty-first-century transformations: The first is a permanent change in how we relate; the second temporarily affects the economic path we take as adults.

From Relating in the Real World to Residing in Cyberspace: On-line Relationships

> Meet the Alvin family. . . . Sandra, a former journalist . . . has over 800 followers on twitter and keeps an elaborate . . . blog; their 16-year-old daughter Zara is a fanatic Facebook user—464 friends right now—and she also uses Pinterest for "pinning and sharing photos". . . .
>
> (quoted in Van Dijck, 2013, p 3)

> Julia, . . . a Sophomore at a . . . public high school turns texting into a kind of polling. After Julia sends out a text, she is uncomfortable until she gets one back: "I'm always looking for a text that says, "Oh I'm sorry" or "Oh that's great." Without this feedback, she says, "It's hard to calm down." Julia describes how painful it is to text about her feelings and get no response: "If . . . they don't answer me . . . I'll text them again "are you mad? . . . Is everything Ok?"
>
> (adapted from Turkle, 2011, p. 175)

How many of you feel the urge to check Facebook or your cell phone as you are reading these lines? Perhaps, like Sandra, you have followers on Twitter or keep a

TIMELINE	Selected Twentieth-Century Milestones and the Progress of the Huge Baby Boom													
	1900	1910	1920	1930	1940	1950	1960	1970	1980	1990	2000	2010	2020	2030
MAJOR SOCIETAL CHANGE	Life Expectancy Takes Off Deaths shift from infectious to chronic diseases								Lifestyle Revolution Women's movement/rise in divorce and single parenthood/more lifestyle freedom					
BABY BOOM COHORT						Born		Teenagers			Young-old	→		Old-old

personal blog, or can relate to Julia's anxiety when you text and don't get an immediate response.

Cell phones and texting instituted what one expert (Van Dijck, 2013) has labeled our twenty-first century "culture of connectivity," by tethering us to our significant others every moment of the day. Then that early-twentieth-century advance in technology, called Web 2.0, accelerated this revolution, by allowing us to interact 24/7 with strangers around the globe (Van Dijck, 2013). In particular, Web 2.0 fostered the development of **social networking sites**, such as Facebook, that permit us to broadcast every feeling to an expanding array of "friends."

How has Facebook transformed romantic relationships? Does bullying online differ from real-life bullying, and can texting (or sexting) reveal our inner lives? Stay tuned for subsequent chapters when I showcase studies delving into the impact of the on-line revolution on how we relate.

From Living in an Expanding Economy, to Facing Financial Hardship: The Great Recession

© Doug Steley C/Alamy

> I was laid off from my job on April 1st. I've used up all my retirement funds and savings. I have never seen anything this bad in this country.
>
> (Sandra K, Cleveland Heights, Ohio)

Welcome to the **Great Recession of 2008,** which began with the bursting of an 8-trillion-dollar-housing bubble, producing sharp cutbacks in U.S. consumer spending, followed by a loss of 8.4 million jobs within the following two years (Economic Policy Institute [EPI], 2011). The Great Recession has caused us to rethink standard adult markers, from retirement to leaving home for college (see Chapters 10 and 13). It has weakened our historic American faith in constructing a secure middle-class life. As this storm rolled in, it uncovered a festering problem called **income inequality**—the widening gap between the superrich and everyone else (EPI, 2011; Wilkinson & Pickett, 2009).

As I'm writing this chapter (in early 2015), the economy has improved in the United States and many European nations. Will the economic landscape turn truly sunny as you are reading these pages? Whatever the answer, our economic situation has an important impact on our journey through life. How *exactly* does being affluent or poor affect how we develop and behave?

The Impact of Socioeconomic Status

This question brings up the role of **socioeconomic status (SES)**—a term referring to our education and income—on our unfolding lives. As you will see throughout this book, living in poverty makes people vulnerable to a cascade of problems—from being born less healthy, to attending lower-quality schools; from living in more dangerous neighborhoods, to dying at a younger age. Not only do developmentalists rank individuals by socioeconomic status, but they rank nations, too.

Developed-world nations are defined by their wealth, or high median per-person incomes. In these countries, life expectancy is high (Central Intelligence Agency [CIA], 2007). Technology is advanced. People have widespread access to education and medical care. Traditionally, the United States, Canada, Australia, New Zealand, and Japan, as well as every Western European nation, have been classified in this "most affluent" category, although its ranks *may* be expanding as the economies of nations such as China and India explode.

Developing-world countries stand in sharp contrast to these most affluent world regions. Here people may not have indoor plumbing, clean running water, or access to education. They even may die at a young age from "curable" infectious disease. Babies born in the poorest regions of the globe face a twenty-first-century lifespan that has striking similarities to the one developed-world children faced more than a century ago.

This consequence of the social-media revolution is all too familiar. In Chapter 6, you will learn what forces might make cyberbullying more distressing than bullying of the face-to-face kind.

social networking sites Internet sites whose goal is to forge personal connections between users.

Great Recession of 2008 Dramatic loss of jobs (and consumer spending) that began with the bursting of the U.S. housing bubble in late 2007.

income inequality The gap between the rich and poor within a nation. Specifically, when income inequality is wide, a nation has a few very affluent residents and a mass of disadvantaged citizens.

socioeconomic status (SES) A basic marker referring to status on the educational and—especially—income rungs.

developed world The most affluent countries in the world.

developing world The more impoverished countries of the world.

collectivist cultures Societies that prize social harmony, obedience, and close family connectedness over individual achievement.

individualistic cultures Societies that prize independence, competition, and personal success.

For this grandmother, mother, and daughter, getting dressed up to visit this Shinto family shrine and pay their respects to their ancestors is an important ritual. It is one way that the lesson "honor your elders" is taught to children living in collectivist societies such as Japan from an early age.

The Impact of Culture and Ethnicity

Residents of developing nations often have shorter, more difficult lives. Still, if you visited these places, you might be struck by a sense of community you might not find in the West. Can we categorize societies according to their basic values, apart from their wealth? Developmentalists who study culture answer yes.

Collectivist cultures place a premium on social harmony. The family generations expect to live together, even as adults. Children are taught to obey their elders, to suppress their feelings, to value being respectful, and to subordinate their needs to the good of the wider group.

Individualistic cultures emphasize independence, competition, and personal success. Children are encouraged to openly express their emotions, to believe in their own personal power, to leave their parents, to stand on their own as self-sufficient and independent adults. Traditionally, Western nations score high on indices of individualism. Nations in Asia, Africa, and South America rank higher on collectivism scales (Hofstede, 1981, 2001; Triandis, 1995).

Imagine how your perspective on life might differ if becoming independent from your parents or honestly sharing your feelings was viewed as an inappropriate way to behave. How would you treat your children, choose a career, or select a spouse? What concerns would you have as you were facing death?

As we scan development around the world, I will regularly distinguish between collectivist and more individualistic societies. I'll highlight the issues families face when they move from these traditional cultures to the West, and explore research relating to the major U.S. ethnic groups listed in Figure 1.2.

As you read this information, keep in mind that what unites us as people outweighs any distinctions based on culture, ethnicity, or race. Moreover, making diversity generalizations is hazardous because of the diversity that exists *within* each nation and ethnic group. In the most individualistic country (no surprise, that's the United States), people have a mix of collectivist and individualistic worldviews. Due to globalization, traditionally collectivistic cultures, such as China and Japan, now have developed more individualistic, Western worldviews.

If the census labels you as "Hispanic American," you also are probably aware that this label masks more than it reveals. As a third-generation Cuban American, do you really have much in common with a recent immigrant from Mexico or Belize? Given that people arrive in Western nations from hundreds of culturally different countries, does it make sense to lump people into a small number of ethnic groups? There is, however, one distinction that we can agree on—being female or male.

FIGURE 1.2: The major ethnic groups in the United States, their percentages in 2013, and a few mid-twenty-first-century projections: By 2042, more than half of the U.S. population is projected to be ethnic minorities. Notice, in particular, the huge increase in the fraction of Hispanic Americans.

Data from: http://quickfacts.census.gov/qfd/states/00000.html, Retrieved September 3, 2014.

The Impact of Gender

Obviously, our culture's values shape our development as males and females. Are you living in a society or at a time in history when men are encouraged to be househusbands and women to be corporate CEOs? Biology is crucial in driving at least one fundamental difference in the pathways of women and men: Throughout the world, females outlive males by at least two years (World Life Expectancy, 2011). Because they must survive childbearing and carry an extra X chromosome, women are the physiologically hardier sex.

Table 1.1: Is It Males or Females?

1. Who are more likely to survive the hazards of prenatal development, male or female fetuses? (You will find the answer in Chapter 2.)

2. Who are more likely to be diagnosed with ADHD, girls or boys? (You will find the answer in Chapter 5.)

3. Who are more aggressive, boys or girls? (You will find the answer in Chapter 6.)

4. Who are more likely to be diagnosed with learning disabilities in school, boys or girls? (You will find the answer in Chapter 7.)

5. Who, when they reach puberty at an earlier-than-typical age, are more at risk of developing problems, boys or girls? (You will find the answer in Chapter 8.)

6. Who are likely to stay in the "nest" (at home) longer during the emerging-adult years, men or women? (You will find the answer in Chapter 10.)

7. Who tend to earn more today, women or men? (You will find the answer in Chapter 11.)

8. Who are more at risk of having emotional problems after being widowed, men or women? (You will find the answer in Chapter 13.)

9. Who are apt to live longer, sicker men or women? (You will find the answer in Chapter 14.)

10. Who care more about being closely attached, males or females—or both sexes? (You will find the answer throughout this book.)

Are boys more aggressive than girls? When we see male/female differences in caregiving, career interests, and childhood play styles, are these differences mainly due to the environment (societal pressures or the way we are brought up) or to inborn, biological forces? Throughout this book, I'll examine these questions as we explore the scientific truth of our gender stereotypes and spell out other fascinating facts about sex differences. To introduce this conversation, you might want to take the "Is It Males or Females?" quiz in Table 1.1. Keep a copy. As we travel through the lifespan, you can check the accuracy of your ideas.

Now that you understand that our lifespan is a continuing work in progress that varies across cultures and historical times, let's get to the science. After you complete this section's Tying It All Together review quiz below, I will introduce the main theories, research methods, concepts, and scientific terms in this book.

 Tying It All Together

1. Imagine you were born in the eighteenth century. Which statement would be *least true* of your life?

   a. You would have a good chance of dying during childhood.
   b. You might be severely beaten by your parents.
   c. You would start working right after high school.
   d. You would not have an adolescence.

2. Rosa is 80. Ramona is 65. In a sentence, describe the major statistical difference between these two women, and then label each person's life stage.

3. Carlos was in his twenties during the 1980s; his grandfather reached adulthood in 1945. In comparing their lives, plug in the statistically correct items: Carlos was *more/less likely* to have divorced; Carlos entered the workforce at an *older/younger* age and got married *later/earlier* than his grandfather. Carlos had *more/fewer* years of education than his grandfather.

4. Pablo says, "I would never think of leaving my parents or living far from my brothers and sisters. A person must take care of his extended family before satisfying his own needs." Peter says, "My primary commitment is to my wife and children. A person needs, above all, to make an independent life." Pablo has a(n) _____ worldview, while Peter's worldview is more _____.

5. List and (possibly discuss with the class) the merits and downsides of Facebook.

Answers to the Tying It All Together questions can be found at the end of this chapter.

theory Any perspective explaining why people act the way they do. Theories allow us to predict behavior and also suggest how to intervene to improve behavior.

nature Biological or genetic causes of development.

nurture Environmental causes of development.

traditional behaviorism The original behavioral worldview that focused on charting and modifying only "objective," visible behaviors.

operant conditioning According to the traditional behavioral perspective, the law of learning that determines any voluntary response. Specifically, we act the way we do because we are reinforced for acting in that way.

Theories: Lenses for Looking at the Lifespan

During her twenties, Jamila was probably searching for her identity. Susan's sunny, people-oriented personality is genetic. If Elissa's mother gives her a lot of love during her first years of life, she will grow up to be a loving, secure adult. If any of these thoughts entered your mind while reading about the people in the opening chapter vignette, you were using a major theory that developmentalists use to understand human life.

Theories attempt to explain what causes us to act as we do. They may allow us to predict the future. Ideally, they give us information about how to improve the quality of life. Theories in developmental science may offer broad explanations of behavior that apply to people at every age, or describe changes that occur at particular ages. This section provides a preview of both kinds of theories.

Let's begin by outlining some theories (one is actually a research discipline) that offer general explanations of behavior. I've organized these theories somewhat chronologically—based on *when* they appeared during the twentieth century—but mainly according to their position on that core issue: Is it the environment, or the wider world, that determines how we develop? Are our personalities, talents, and traits shaped mainly by biological or genetic forces? This is the famous **nature** (biology) versus **nurture** (environment) question.

This photo shows B. F. Skinner with his favorite research subject for exploring operant conditioning—the pigeon. By charting how often pigeons pecked to get reinforced by food and varying the patterns of reinforcement, this famous behaviorist was able to tell us a good deal about how humans act.

Behaviorism: The Original Blockbuster "Nurture" Theory

Give me a dozen healthy infants . . . and I'll guarantee to take any one at random and train him to be any specialist I might select—doctor, lawyer, artist, merchant-chief, and yes, even beggar man and thief.
(Watson, 1930, p. 104)

So proclaimed the early-twentieth-century psychologist John Watson as he spelled out the nurture-is-all-important position of traditional behaviorism. Intoxicated by the scientific advances that were transforming society, Watson and his fellow behaviorist B. F. Skinner (1960, 1974) dreamed of a science of human behavior that would be as rigorous as physics. These theorists believed that we could not study feelings and thoughts because inner experiences could not be observed. It was vital to chart only measurable, observable responses. Moreover, according to these **traditional behaviorists,** a few general laws of learning explain behavior in every situation at every time of life.

Exploring Reinforcement

According to Skinner, the general law of learning that causes each voluntary action, from forming our first words to mastering higher math, is **operant conditioning.** Responses that we reward, or reinforce, are learned. Responses that are not reinforced go away or are *extinguished*. So what accounts for Watson's beggar men and thieves, the out-of-control kids, all of the marriages that start out so loving and then fall apart? According to Skinner, the reinforcements are operating as they should. The problem is that instead of reinforcing positive behavior, we often reinforce the wrong things.

One excellent place to see Skinner's point is to take a trip to your local Walmart or restaurant. Notice how when children act up at the store parents often buy them a toy to quiet them down. At dinner, as long as a toddler is playing quietly, adults ignore her. When she starts to hurl objects off the table, they pick her up, kiss her, and take her outside. Then, they complain about their child's difficult personality, not realizing that their *own* reinforcements have produced these responses!

One of Skinner's most interesting concepts, derived from his work with pigeons, relates to *variable reinforcement schedules.* This is the type of reinforcement that typically occurs in daily life: We get reinforced unpredictably, so we keep responding, realizing that if we continue, *at some point* we will be reinforced. Readers with children will understand how difficult it is to follow the basic behavioral principle to be consistent or not let a negative variable schedule emerge. At Walmart, even though you vow, "I won't give in to bad behavior!" as your toddler's tantrums escalate, you cave in, simply to avoid other shoppers' disapproving stares ("What an out-of-control mother and bratty kid!"). Unfortunately, your child has learned, "If I keep whining, *eventually* I'll get what I want."

Imagine wheeling this whining toddler through your Walmart grocery aisle. Wouldn't you be tempted to reinforce this unpleasant behavior by silencing the child with an enticing object on the shelf?

Reinforcement (and its opposite process, *extinction*) is a powerful force for both good and bad. It explains why, if a child starts out succeeding early in elementary school (being reinforced by receiving A's), he is apt to study more. If a kindergartner begins failing socially (does not get positive reinforcement from her peers), she is at risk for becoming incredibly shy or highly aggressive in third or fourth grade (see Chapter 6). If you were not being reinforced by people, wouldn't you withdraw or act in socially inappropriate ways?

Behaviorism makes sense of why, after starting out loving, marriages can end in divorce. As newlyweds, couples are continually reinforcing each other with expressions of love. Then, over time, husbands and wives tend to ignore the good parts of their partner and pay attention when there is something wrong.

The theory even offers an optimistic environmental explanation for the physical and mental impairments of old age. If you were in a nursing home and weren't being reinforced for remembering or walking, wouldn't your memory or physical abilities decline? The key to producing well-behaved children, enduring, loving marriages, and fewer old-age disabilities is simple. According to traditional behaviorists, we need to reinforce the right things.

However, things are not that simple. Human beings *do* think and reason. People do not need to be personally reinforced to learn.

Taking a Different Perspective: Exploring Cognitions

Enter **cognitive behaviorism (social learning theory),** launched by Albert Bandura (1977; 1986) and his colleagues in the 1970s, in studies demonstrating the power of **modeling,** or learning by watching and imitating what other people do.

Because we are a social species, modeling (both imitating other people, and others reciprocally imitating us) is endemic in daily life. Given that we are always modeling everything from the latest hairstyle on, who are we most likely to *generally* model as children and adults?

Bandura (1986) finds that that we tend to model people who are nurturing, or relate to us in a caring way. (The good news here is that being a loving, hands-on parent is the best way to naturally embed your values and ideas.) We model people whom we categorize as being like us. At age 2, you probably modeled anything from the vacuum cleaner to the behavior of the family dog. As we grow older, we tailor our modeling selectively, based on our understanding of who we are.

Modeling similar people partly explains why, after children understand their gender label (girl or boy) at about age 2 1/2, they separate into sex-segregated play groups and prefer to play with their "own group" (see Chapter 6). It makes sense of why at-risk teenagers gravitate to the druggies group at school, and then model the leader who most embodies the group norms (see Chapter 9). While I will use modeling to explain behavior at several points in this book, another concept— also devised by Bandura—will be a *genuine* foundation in the chapters to come: self-efficacy.

reinforcement Behavioral term for reward.

cognitive behaviorism (social learning theory) A behavioral worldview that emphasizes that people learn by watching others and that our thoughts about the reinforcers determine our behavior. Cognitive behaviorists focus on charting and modifying people's thoughts.

modeling Learning by watching and imitating others.

self-efficacy According to cognitive behaviorism, an internal belief in our competence that predicts whether we initiate activities or persist in the face of failures, and predicts the goals we set.

This man is clearly upbeat and ebullient. In Chapter 13, you will learn what health benefits result from having his efficacious sense of purpose in life.

Freud, pictured here in his robust middle age, alerted us to the power of childhood experiences and unconscious motivations in shaping human life.

Self-efficacy refers to our belief in our competence, our sense that we can be successful at a given task. According to Bandura (1989, 1992, 1997), efficacy feelings determine the goals we set. They predict which activities we engage in as we travel through life. When self-efficacy is low, we decide not to tackle that difficult math problem. We choose not to ask a beautiful stranger for a date. When self-efficacy is high, we not only take action, but also continue to act long after the traditional behavioral approach suggests that extinction should occur.

Let's imagine that your goal is to be a nurse, but you get an F on your first test in this course. If your academic self-efficacy is low, you might conclude: "I'm basically not smart." You might not put forth any effort on the next exam. You might even drop out of school. But if you have high self-efficacy, you will think: "I just need to work harder. I can do it. I'm *going* to get a good grade in this class!"

How do children develop low or high self-efficacy? Can efficacy feelings predict success decades later in life? What role does self-efficacy play in happiness at any age? These are the kinds of questions we will explore in examining efficacy feelings throughout life.

By now, you may be impressed with behaviorism's simple, action-oriented concepts. Be consistent. Don't reinforce negative behavior. Reinforce positive things (from traditional behaviorism). Draw on the principles of modeling and stimulate efficacy feelings to help children and adults succeed (from cognitive behaviorism).

Still, many developmentalists, even people who believe that nurture (or the environment) is important, find behaviorism unsatisfying. Aren't we more than just efficacy feelings or reinforced responses? Isn't there a basic core to personality, and aren't the lessons we learn in childhood vital in shaping adult life? Notice that behaviorism doesn't address that core question: What *really* motivates us as people? To address these gaps, developmental scientists, particularly in the past, turned to the insights of that world-class genius, Sigmund Freud.

Psychoanalytic Theory: Focus on Early Childhood and Unconscious Motivations

Freud's ideas are currently not in vogue in developmental science. However, no one can dispute the fact that Sigmund Freud (1856–1939) transformed the way we think about human beings. Anytime you say, "I must have done that unconsciously" or "My problems are due to my childhood," you are quoting Freudian thought.

Freud, a Viennese Jewish physician, wrote more than 40 books and monographs in a burst of brilliance during the early twentieth century. His ideas revolutionized everything from anthropology to the arts, in addition to jump-starting the modern field of mental health. Freud's mission, however, was simple: to decode why his patients were in emotional pain.

Freud's theory is called *psychoanalytic* because it analyzes the psyche or our inner life. By listening to his patients, Freud became convinced that our actions are dominated by feelings of which we are not aware. The roots of emotional problems lay in repressed (made unconscious) feelings from early childhood. Moreover, "mothering," during the first five years of life, determines adult mental health.

Specifically, Freud posited three hypothetical structures. The *id*, present at birth, is the mass of instincts, needs, and feelings we have when we arrive in the world. During early childhood, the conscious, rational part of our personality—called *the ego*—emerges. Ego functions involve thinking, reasoning, planning, and fulfilling our id desires in realistic ways. Finally, a structure called the *superego*—the moral arm of our personality—exists in opposition to the id's desires.

According to Freud and his followers, if our parents are excellent caregivers, we will develop a strong ego, which sets us up to master the challenges of life. If they are insensitive or their caregiving is impaired, our behavior will be id driven, and our lives will be out of control. The purpose of his therapy, called *psychoanalysis,* was to enable his patients to become aware of the repressed early childhood experiences causing their symptoms and liberate them from the tyranny of the unconscious to live rational, productive lives. (As Freud famously put it, where *id* there was, *ego* there will be.)

In sum, according to Freud: (1) Human beings are basically irrational; (2) life-long mental health depends on our parents' caregiving during early life; and (3) self-understanding is the key to living a fulfilling adult life.

By now many of you might be on a similar page as Freud. Where you are apt to part serious company with the theory relates to Freud's stages of sexuality. Freud argued that sexual feelings (which he called *libido*) are the motivation driving human life, and he put forth the shocking idea—especially in that time—that babies are sexual human beings. As the infant develops, he argued, sexual feelings are centered on specific areas of the body called *erogenous zones.* During the first year of life, the erogenous zone is the mouth (the famous *oral stage*). Around age 2, with toilet training, sexual feelings center on elimination (the *anal stage*). Finally, around ages 3 and 4, sexual feelings shift to the genitals (the *phallic stage*). During this time, the child develops sexual fantasies relating to the parent of the opposite sex (the *Oedipus complex*), and the same-sex parent becomes a rival. Then, sexuality is repressed, the child identifies with that parent, the superego is formed, and we enter *latency*—an asexual stage that lasts through elementary school.

Partly because his sexual stages seem so foreign to our thinking, we tend to reject psychoanalytic theory as outdated—an artifact of a distant era. A deeper look suggests we might be wrong. Like Freud, contemporary developmentalists believe that self-understanding—being able to reflect on and regulate our emotions—is the defining quality of being mature. Like Freud, developmental scientists are passionate to trace the roots of lifelong development to what happens in our earliest months and years of life. As you read through this book, perhaps you will agree with me, that—despite its different terminology and approaches—our field owes a great philosophical debt to Freud. Moreover, psychoanalytic theory gave birth to that important modern perspective called attachment theory.

Attachment Theory: Focus on Nurture, Nature, and Love

British psychiatrist John Bowlby formulated **attachment theory** during the mid-twentieth century. Bowlby, like Freud, believed that our early experiences with caregivers shape our adult ability to love, but he focused on what he called the *attachment response.*

In observing young children separated from their mothers, Bowlby noticed that babies need to be physically close to a caregiver during the time when they are beginning to walk (Bowlby, 1969, 1973; Karen, 1998). Disruptions in this biologically programmed attachment response, he argued, if prolonged, might cause serious problems later in life. Moreover, our impulse to be close to a "significant other" is a basic human need during every stage of life.

How does the attachment response develop? Are Bowlby and Freud right that our early attachments determine adult mental health? How can we draw on attachment

attachment theory Theory formulated by John Bowlby centering on the crucial importance to our species' survival of being closely connected with a caregiver during early childhood and being attached to a significant other during all of life.

Bowlby believes that the intense, loving bond between this father and infant son will set the baby up for a fulfilling life. In Chapter 4, I will describe exactly how the attachment bond unfolds, and whether this core principle of Bowlby's theory is correct.

evolutionary psychology
Theory or worldview highlighting the role that inborn, species-specific behaviors play in human development and life.

behavioral genetics Field devoted to scientifically determining the role that hereditary forces play in determining individual differences in behavior.

twin study Behavioral genetic research strategy, designed to determine the genetic contribution of a given trait, that involves comparing identical twins with fraternal twins (or with other people).

theory to understand everything from adult love relationships to our concerns as we approach death? Stay tuned for answers as we explore this influential theory throughout this book.

Why did Bowlby's ideas eclipse psychoanalytic theory? A main reason was that Bowlby agreed with a late-twentieth-century shift in the way developmentalists understood human motivations. Yes, Bowlby did believe in the power of caregiving (nurture), but he firmly anchored his theory in nature (genetics). Bowlby (1969, 1973, 1980) argued that the attachment response is genetically programmed into our species to promote survival. Bowlby was an early evolutionary psychologist.

Evolutionary Psychology: Theorizing About the "Nature" of Human Similarities

Evolutionary psychologists are the mirror image of behaviorists. They look to nature, or inborn biological forces that have evolved to promote survival, to explain how we behave. Why do pregnant women develop morning sickness just as the fetal organs are being formed, and why do newborns prefer to look at attractive faces rather than ugly ones? (That's actually true!) According to evolutionary psychologists, these reactions cannot be changed by modifying the reinforcers. They are based in the human genetic code that we all share.

Evolutionary psychology lacks the practical, action-oriented approach of behaviorism, although it does alert us to the fact that we need to pay close attention to basic human needs. Still, as we look at how far flung topics—from the timing of puberty (Chapter 8), to the purpose of grandparents (Chapter 12)—are being viewed through an evolutionary psychology lens, you will realize just how influential this "look to the human genome" perspective has become in our field. What *first* convinced developmentalists that genetics is important in determining the person we become? A simple set of research techniques.

Behavioral Genetics: Scientifically Exploring the "Nature" of Human Differences

Behavioral genetics is the name for research strategies devoted to examining the genetic contribution to the *differences* we see between human beings. How genetic is the tendency to bite our nails, develop bipolar disorders, have specific attitudes about life? To answer these kinds of questions, scientists typically use twin and adoption studies.

How "genetic" are these children's friendly personalities? To answer this question, researchers compare identical twins, such as these two girls *(left)*, with fraternal twins, like this girl and boy *(right)*. If the identicals (who share exactly the same DNA) are much more similar to each other than the fraternals in their scores on friendliness tests, friendliness is defined as a highly heritable trait.

In **twin studies,** researchers typically compare identical (monozygotic) twins and fraternal (dizygotic) twins on the trait they are interested in (playing the oboe, obesity, and so on). Identical twins develop from the same fertilized egg (it splits soon after the one-cell stage) and are genetic clones. Fraternal twins, like any brother or sister, develop from separate conceptions and so, on average, share 50 percent of their genes. The idea is that if a given trait is highly influenced by genetics, identical twins should be much more alike in that quality than fraternal twins. Specifically, behavioral geneticists use a statistic called *heritability* (which ranges from 1 = totally genetic, to 0 = no genetic contribution) to summarize the extent to which a given behavior is shaped by genetic forces.

For instance, to conduct a twin study to determine the heritability of friendliness, you would select a large group of identical and fraternal twins. You would give both sets of twins tests measuring outgoing attitudes, and then compare the strength of the relationships you found for each twin group. Let's say the identical twins' scores were incredibly similar—almost like the same person taking the tests twice—and the fraternal twins' test scores varied a great deal from one another. Your heritability statistic would be high, and you could conclude: "Friendliness is a mainly genetically determined trait."

In **adoption studies,** researchers compare adopted children with their biological and adoptive parents. Here, too, they evaluate the impact of heredity on a trait by looking at how closely these children resemble their birth parents (with whom they share only genes) and their adoptive parents (with whom they share only environments).

Twin studies of children growing up in the same family and adoption studies are fairly easy to carry out. The most powerful evidence for genetics comes from the rare **twin/adoption studies,** in which identical twins are separated in childhood and reunited in adult life. If Joe and James, who have exactly the same DNA, have similar abilities, traits, and personalities, even though they grow up in *different families,* this would be strong evidence that genetics plays a crucial role in who we are.

Consider, for instance, the Swedish Twin/Adoption Study of Aging. Researchers combed national registries to find identical and fraternal twins adopted into different families in that country—where birth records of every adoptee are kept. Then they reunited these children in late middle age and gave the twins a battery of tests (Finkel & Pedersen, 2004; Kato & Pedersen, 2005).

While specific qualities varied in their heritabilities, you might be surprised to know that the most genetically determined quality was IQ (Pedersen, 1996). In fact, if one twin took the standard intelligence test, statistically speaking we could predict that the other twin would have an almost identical IQ despite living apart for almost an entire lifetime!

Behavioral genetic studies such as these have opened our eyes to the role of nature in shaping who we are (Turkheimer, 2004). Our tendencies to be religious, vote for conservative Republicans (Bouchard and others, 2004), drink to excess (Agrawal & Lynsky, 2008), or get divorced—qualities we thought *must* be due to how our parents raised us—are all somewhat shaped by genetic forces (Plomin and others, 2003).

These studies have given us tantalizing insights into nurture too. It's tempting to assume that children growing up in the same family share the same nurture, or environment. But as you can see in the How Do We Know research box on page 18, that assumption is wrong. We inhabit different life spaces than our brothers and sisters, even when we eat at the same dinner table and share the same room—environments that are influenced by our genes (Rowe, 2003).

adoption study Behavioral genetic research strategy, designed to determine the genetic contribution to a given trait, that involves comparing adopted children with their biological and adoptive parents.

twin/adoption study Behavioral genetic research strategy that involves comparing the similarities of identical twin pairs adopted into different families, to determine the genetic contribution to a given trait.

evocative forces The nature-interacts-with-nurture principle that our genetic temperamental tendencies and predispositions evoke, or produce, certain responses from other people.

bidirectionality The crucial principle that people affect one another, or that interpersonal influences flow in both directions.

active forces The nature-interacts-with-nurture principle that our genetic temperamental tendencies and predispositions cause us to actively choose to put ourselves into specific environments.

HOW DO WE KNOW. . .
that our nature affects our upbringing?

For much of the twentieth century, developmentalists assumed that parents treated all of their children the same way. We could classify mothers as either nurturing or rejecting, caring or cold. The Swedish Twin/Adoption Study turned these basic parenting assumptions upside down (Plomin & Bergeman, 1991).

Researchers asked middle-aged identical twins who had been adopted into different families as babies to rate their parents along dimensions such as caring, acceptance, and discipline styles. They were astonished to find similarities in the ratings, even though the twins were evaluating different families!

What was happening? The answer, the researchers concluded, was that the genetic similarities in the twins' personalities *created* similar family environments. If Joe and Jim were both easy, kind, and caring, they evoked more loving parenting. If they were temperamentally difficult, they caused their adoptive parents to react in more rejecting, less nurturant ways.

I vividly saw this *evocative,* child-shapes-parenting relationship in my own life. Because my adopted son has dyslexia and is very physically active, in our house we ended up doing active things like sports. As Thomas didn't like to sit still for story time, I probably would have been described as a "less than optimally stimulating" parent had some psychologist come into my home to rate how much I read to my child.

And now, the plot thickens. When I met Thomas's biological mother, I found out that she also has dyslexia. She's energetic and peppy. It's one thing to see the impact of nature in my son, as his mother revealed. But I can't help wondering. . . . Maureen is a very different person than I am (although we have a terrific time together—traveling and doing active things). Would Thomas have had the *same* kind of upbringing (at least partly) that I gave my son if he had grown up with his biological mom?

The bottom line is that there is no such thing as nature *or* nurture. To understand human development, scientists need to explore how nature *and* nurture combine.

Nature and Nurture Combine: Where We Are Today

Let's now lay out two basic nature-plus-nurture principles, and then introduce cutting-edge developmental science research relating to how nature and nurture interact.

Principle One: Our Nature (Genetic Tendencies) Shapes Our Nurture (Life Experiences)

Developmentalists understand that nature and nurture are not independent entities. Our genetic tendencies shape our wider-world experiences in two ways.

Evocative forces refer to the fact that our inborn talents and temperamental tendencies evoke, or produce, certain responses from the world. A joyous child elicits smiles from everyone. A child who is temperamentally irritable, hard to handle, or has trouble sitting still is unfortunately set up to get the kind of harsh parenting she least needs to succeed. Human relationships are **bidirectional.** Just as you get grumpy when with a grumpy person, fight with your difficult neighbor, or shy away from your colleague who is paralyzingly shy, who we are as people causes other people to react to us in specific ways, driving our development for the good and the bad.

Active forces refer to the fact that we *actively select* our environments based on our genetic tendencies. A child who is talented at reading gravitates toward

Because this musically talented girl is choosing to spend hours playing the piano, she is likely to become even more talented as she gets older, illustrating the fact that we actively shape our environment to fit our genetic tendencies and talents.

Jesse Kunerth/Hemera/Getty Images

devouring books and so becomes a better reader over time. His brother, who is well coordinated, may play baseball three hours a day and become a star athlete in his teenage years. Because we choose activities to fit our biologically based interests and skills, what start out as minor differences between people in early childhood snowball—ultimately producing huge gaps in talents and traits. The high heritabilities for IQ in the Swedish Twin/Adoption Study are lower in similar behavioral genetic studies conducted during childhood (Plomin & Spinath, 2004). The reason is that, like heat-seeking missiles, our nature causes us to gravitate toward specific life experiences, so we literally become *more like ourselves* genetically as we travel into adult life (Scarr, 1997).

person–environment fit
The extent to which the environment is tailored to our biological tendencies and talents. In developmental science, fostering this fit between our talents and the wider world is an important goal.

Principle 2: We Need the Right Nurture (Life Experiences) to Fully Express Our Nature (Genetic Talents)

Developmentalists understand that even if a quality is mainly genetic, its expression can be 100 percent dependent on the outside world. Let's illustrate by returning to the high heritabilities for intelligence. If you lived in an impoverished developing country, were malnourished, and worked as a laborer in a field, having a genius-level IQ would be irrelevant, as there would be no chance to demonstrate your hereditary gifts.

The most fascinating example that a high-quality environment can bring our human genetic potential relates specifically to IQ. As you will see in Chapter 7, over the past century, scores on the standard intelligence test have been rising. The same correct items a twenty-first-century teenager needed to be ranked as "average" in intelligence would have boosted that same child into the top third of the population in 1950. A century ago, having the identical number of items correct would get that child labeled as gifted, in the top 2 percent of his peers (Pinker, 2011)!

What is causing this upward shift? Obviously, our "genetic," intellectual capacities can't have changed. It's just that as human beings have become better nourished, more educated, and more technologically adept, they perform better, especially on the kinds of abstract-reasoning items on the IQ test (see Flynn, 2007; Pinker, 2011). So even when individual differences in IQ are "genetic," the environment makes a dramatic difference in how people perform.

My discussion brings home the fact that to promote our human potential, we need to provide the best possible environment. This is why a core goal of developmental science is to foster the correct **person–environment fit**—making the wider world bring out our human "best."

 ### Hot in Developmental Science: Environment-Sensitive Genes and Epigenetically Programmed Pathways

It's a no brainer that we need to provide a superior environment for every child (and adult). But why does one child sail through traumas, such as poor parenting, while another breaks down under the smallest stress? What causes that same "genetically fragile" boy or girl to excel in a nurturing setting, such as high-quality day care, while his hardier peer seems immune to the gifts this exceptional environment provides? These questions are driving the hunt for genes that make people either more or less reactive to life events (see Belsky and others, 2014). In the childhood chapters, I'll be outlining findings suggesting some of us are like cactuses, set up biologically to survive in less than nourishing environments; others seem similar to fragile orchids, capable of providing gorgeous flowers but only with special care. I'll also showcase exciting findings suggesting our genetics may be altered by early life events.

epigenetics Research field exploring how early life events alter the outer cover of our DNA, producing lifelong changes in health and behavior.

Erikson's psychosocial tasks In Erik Erikson's theory, each challenge that we face as we travel through the eight stages of the lifespan.

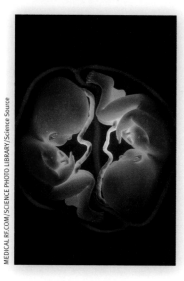

As you will learn in Chapter 8, due to an *epigenetic process,* this female fraternal twin fetus may be more insulated from developing an eating disorder by being exposed to the circulating testosterone her brother's body is giving off.

With his powerful writings on identity and, especially, his concept of age-related psychosocial tasks, Erik Erikson (shown here with his wife, Joan) has become a father of our field.

Epigenetics refers to the study of how our environment—often, but not exclusively, intrauterine and early childhood experiences—alters the outer cover of our DNA, causing effects that last throughout life. Can obesity, our tendency to develop gender atypical behavior, or even our predisposition to die at a younger age be partly programmed by events in the womb? Stay tuned for fascinating epigenetic hints in the chapters to come. 🌀

Emphasis on Age-Linked Theories

Now that I've highlighted this book's basic nature combines with nurture message, it's time to explore the ideas of two psychologists who view human development as occurring in defined stages. Let's start with Erik Erikson.

Erik Erikson's Psychosocial Tasks

Erikson, born in Germany in 1904, was an analyst who, like Bowlby, adhered to most tenets of psychoanalytic theory; but rather than emphasizing sexuality, Erikson (1963) saw becoming an independent self and relating to others as our basic motivations (which explains why Erikson's theory is called *psychosocial* to distinguish it from Freud's psychosexual stages). Erikson, however, is often labeled the father of lifespan development because, unlike Freud, he believed development occurs throughout life. He spelled out unique challenges we face at each life stage.

You can see these **psychosocial tasks,** or challenges, listed in Table 1.2. Each task, Erikson argued, builds on another because we cannot master the issue of a later stage unless we have accomplished the developmental milestones of the previous ones.

Notice how parents take incredible joy in satisfying their baby's needs and you will understand why Erikson believed that *basic trust* (the belief that the human world is caring) is our fundamental life task in the first year of life. Erikson's second psychosocial task, *autonomy,* makes sense of the infamous "*no* stage" and "terrible twos." It tells us that we need to *celebrate* this not-so-pleasant toddler behavior as the blossoming of a separate self! Think back to elementary school, and you may realize why Erikson used the term *industry,* or learning to work—at friendships, sports, academics—as our challenge from age 6 to 12. Erikson's adolescent task, the search for *identity,* has now become a household word.

How have developmentalists expanded on Erikson's ideas about identity? Is Erikson right that nurturing the next generation, or *generativity,* is the key to a fulfilling adult life? These are just two questions I'll be addressing as we draw on Erikson's theory to help us think more deeply about the challenges we face at each life stage.

Erikson offered a general emotional roadmap for our developing lives. But—in brilliance and transformational thinking—there is only one human development rival to Freud: Jean Piaget.

Table 1.2: Erikson's Psychosocial Stages

Life Stage	Primary Task
Infancy (birth to 1 year)	Basic trust versus mistrust
Toddlerhood (1 to 2 years)	Autonomy versus shame and doubt
Early childhood (3 to 6 years)	Initiative versus guilt
Middle childhood (6 years to puberty)	Industry versus inferiority
Adolescence (teens into twenties)	Identity versus role confusion
Young adulthood (twenties to early forties)	Intimacy versus isolation
Middle adulthood (forties to sixties)	Generativity versus stagnation
Late adulthood (late sixties and beyond)	Integrity versus despair

Piaget's Cognitive Developmental Theory

A 3-year-old tells you "Mr. Sun goes to bed because it's time for me to go to sleep." A toddler is obsessed with flushing different-sized wads of paper down the toilet and can't resist touching everything she sees. Do you ever wish you could get into the heads of young children and understand how they view the world? If so, you share the passion of our foremost genius in child development: Piaget.

Piaget, born in 1894 in Switzerland, was a child prodigy himself. As the teenaged author of several dozen articles on mollusks, he was already becoming well known in that field (Flavell, 1963; Wadsworth, 1996). Piaget's interests shifted to studying children when he worked in the laboratory of a psychologist named Binet, who was devising the original intelligence test. Rather than ranking children according to how much they knew, Piaget became fascinated by children's *incorrect* responses. He spent the next 60 years meticulously devising tasks to map the minds of these mysterious creatures in our midst.

Piaget believed—in his **cognitive developmental theory**—that from birth through adolescence, children progress through *qualitatively different* stages of cognitive growth (see Table 1.3). The term *qualitative* means that rather than simply knowing less or more (on the kind of scale we can rank from 1 to 10), infants, preschoolers, elementary-school-age children, and teenagers think about the world in *completely* different ways. However, Piaget also believed that at every life stage human beings share a hunger to learn and mentally grow. Mental growth occurs through **assimilation:** We fit the world to our capacities or existing cognitive structures (which Piaget calls *schemas*). And then **accommodation** occurs. We change our thinking to fit the world (Piaget, 1971).

Let's illustrate by reflecting on your own thinking while you were reading the previous section. Before reading this chapter, you probably had certain ideas about heredity and environment. In Piaget's terminology, let's call them your "heredity/environment schemas." Perhaps you felt that if a trait is highly genetic, changing the environment doesn't matter; or you may have believed that genetics and environment were totally separate. While fitting (assimilating) your reading into these existing ideas, you entered a state of disequilibrium—"Hey, this contradicts what I've always believed"—and were forced to accommodate. The result was that your nature/nurture schemas became more complex and you developed a more advanced

Jean Piaget, in his masterful studies spanning much of the twentieth century, transformed the way we think about children's thinking.

Bill Anderson/Science Source

Table 1.3: Piaget's Stages of Development

Age	Name of Stage	Description
0–2	Sensorimotor	The baby manipulates objects to pin down the basics of physical reality. This stage, ending with the development of language, will be described in Chapter 3.
2–7	Preoperations	Children's perceptions are captured by their immediate appearances. "What they see is what is real." They believe, among other things, that inanimate objects are really alive and that if the appearance of a quantity of liquid changes (for instance, if it is poured from a short, wide glass into a tall, thin one), the amount actually becomes different. You will learn about all of these perceptions in Chapter 5.
8–12	Concrete operations	Children have a realistic understanding of the world. Their thinking is really on the same wavelength as adults'. While they can reason conceptually about concrete objects, however, they cannot think abstractly in a scientific way.
12+	Formal operations	Reasoning is at its pinnacle: hypothetical, scientific, flexible, fully adult. The person's full cognitive human potential has been reached. We will explore this stage in Chapter 9.

Piaget's cognitive developmental theory Jean Piaget's principle that from infancy to adolescence, children progress through four qualitatively different stages of intellectual growth.

assimilation In Jean Piaget's theory, the first step promoting mental growth, involving fitting environmental input to our existing mental capacities.

accommodation In Piaget's theory, enlarging our mental capacities to fit input from the wider world.

Table 1.4: Summary of the Major Current Theories in Lifespan Development

	Nature vs. Nurture Emphasis and Ages of Interest	Representative Questions
Behaviorism	Nurture (all ages)	What reinforcers are shaping this behavior? Who is this person modeling? How can I stimulate self-efficacy?
Psychoanalytic theory	Nurture	What unconscious motives, stemming from early childhood, are motivating this person?
Attachment theory	Nature and nurture (infancy but also all ages)	How does the attachment response unfold in infancy? What conditions evoke this biologically programmed response at every life stage?
Evolutionary theory	Nature (all ages)	How might this behavior be built into the human genetic code?
Behavioral genetics	Nature (all ages)	To what degree are the differences I see in people due to genetics?
Erikson's theory	(all ages)	Is this baby experiencing basic trust? Where is this teenager in terms of identity? Has this middle-aged person reached generativity?
Piaget's theory	Children	How does this child understand the world? What is his thinking like?

(intelligent) way of perceiving the world! Like a newborn who assimilates every new object to her small sucking schema, or a neuroscientist who incorporates each new finding into her huge knowledge-base, while assimilating each object or fact to what we already know, we must accommodate, and so—inch by inch—cognitively advance.

Piaget was a great advocate of hands-on experiences. He felt that we learn by acting in the world. Rather than using an adult-centered framework, he had the revolutionary idea that we need to understand how children experience life *from their point of view.* As we explore the science of lifespan development, I hope you will adopt this hands-on, person-centered perspective to understand the human experience from the perspective of 1-year-olds to people aged 101.

By now, you may be overwhelmed by theories and terms. But take heart. You have the basic concepts you need for understanding this semester well in hand! Now, let's conclude by exploring a worldview that says, "Let's embrace *all* of these influences on development and explore how they interact." (For a summary of the theories, see Table 1.4.)

The Developmental Systems Perspective

An influential child psychologist named Urie Bronfenbrenner (1977) was among the earliest lifespan theorists to highlight the principle that real-world behavior has *many* different causes. Bronfenbrenner, as you can see in Figure 1.3, viewed each of us at the center of an expanding circle of environmental influences. At the inner circle, development is shaped by the relationships between the child and people he relates to in his immediate setting, such as family, church, peers, and school. The next wider circles, that indirectly feed back to affect the child, lie in overarching influences such as his community, the media environment, the health-care community, and the school system itself. At the broadest levels, as you saw earlier in the chapter, our culture, economic trends, and cohort crucially shape behavior, too. Bronfenbrenner's plea to examine the total *ecology*, or life situation, of the child

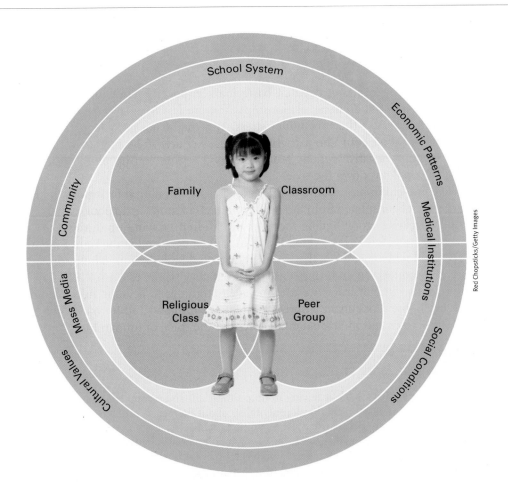

Red Chopsticks/Getty Images

FIGURE 1.3: **Bronfenbrenner's ecological model:** This set of imbedded circles spells out the multiple forces that Bronfenbrenner believed shape development. First and foremost, there are the places that form the core of the child's daily life: family, church, peers, classroom (orange). What is the child's family, school, and religious life like? Who are his friends? How does the child interact with his siblings, his parents, his teacher, and his peers? Although its influence is more indirect, development also depends on the broader milieu—the media, the school system, the community where the boy or girl lives (see blue circle). At the most macro—or broadest—level, we also need to consider that child's culture, the prevailing economic and social conditions of his society (green circle), and, his cohort or the time in history in which he lives. Bottom line: Human behavior depends on multiple complex forces!

forms the heart of a contemporary perspective called the **developmental systems approach** (Ford & Lerner, 1992; Lerner, 1998; Lerner, Dowling, & Roth, 2003). Specifically:

• **Developmental systems theorists stress the need to use many different approaches.** There are *many* valid ways of looking at behavior. Our actions *do* have many causes. To fully understand development, we need to draw on the principles of behaviorism, attachment theory, evolutionary psychology, and Piaget. At the widest societal level, to explain our actions, we need to look outward to our culture and cohort. At the molecular level, we need to look inward to our genes. We have to embrace the input of everyone, from nurses to neuroscientists from anthropologists to molecular biologists, to make sense of each individual life.

• **Developmental systems theorists emphasize the need to look at how processes interact.** Bronfenbrenner pointed out that our genetic tendencies influence the cultures we construct; the cultures we live in affect the expression of our genes.

developmental systems perspective An all-encompassing outlook on development that stresses the need to embrace a variety of theories, and the idea that all systems and processes interrelate.

In the same way that our body systems and processes are in constant communication, continual back-and-forth influences are what human development is all about (see Diamond, 2009).

For example, let's consider that basic marker: poverty. Growing up in poverty might affect your attachment relationships. You are less likely to get attention from your parents because they are under stress. You might not get adequate nutrition. Your neighborhood could be a frightening place. Each stress might overload your body, activating negative genetic tendencies and setting you up physiologically for emotional problems down the road.

But some children, because of their genetics, their cultural background, or their cohort, might be insulated from the negative effects of growing up poor. Others might thrive. In a classic study tracing the lives of children growing up during the Great Depression, researchers discovered that if this event occurred at the right time in the life cycle (adolescence, when the young person could take action to help support the family), it produced an enduring sense of self-efficacy (Elder & Caspi, 1988). During adulthood, as you will learn, we even need life traumas to become fully mature! In sum, development occurs in surprising directions for good and for bad. Diversity of change processes and individual differences are the spice of human life.

 Tying It All Together

1. Ricardo, a third grader, is having trouble sitting still and paying attention in class, so Ricardo's parents consult developmentalists about their son's problem. Pick which comments might be made by: (1) a traditional behaviorist; (2) a cognitive behaviorist; (3) a Freudian theorist; (4) an evolutionary psychologist; (5) a behavioral geneticist; (6) an Eriksonian; (7) an advocate of developmental systems theory.

   a. Ricardo has low academic self-efficacy. Let's improve his sense of competence at school.

   b. Ricardo, like other boys, is biologically programmed to run around. If the class had regular gym time, Ricardo's ability to focus in class would improve.

   c. Ricardo is being reinforced for this behavior by getting attention from the teacher and his classmates. Let's reward appropriate classroom behavior.

   d. Did you or your husband have trouble focusing in school? Perhaps your son's difficulties are hereditary.

   e. Ricardo's behavior may have many causes, from genetics, to the reinforcers at school, to growing up in our twenty-first-century Internet age. Let's use a variety of different approaches to help him.

   f. Ricardo is having trouble mastering the developmental task of industry. How can we promote the ability to work that is so important at this age?

   g. By refusing to pay attention in class, Ricardo may be unconsciously acting out his anger at the birth of his baby sister Heloise.

2. In the above question, which suggestion involves providing the right person–environment fit?

3. Dr. Kaplan, a scientist, wants to determine how being born premature might alter our genetic propensity to develop chronic disease. The field Dr. Kaplan is working in is called (pick one): *outergenetics/epigenetics*.

4. Billy, a 1-year-old, mouths everything—pencils, his favorite toy, DVDs—changing his mouthing to fit the object that he is "sampling." According to Piaget, the act of mouthing everything refers to _____, while changing the mouthing behavior to fit the different objects refers to _____.

5. Samantha, a behaviorist, is arguing for her worldview, while Sally is pointing up behaviorism's flaws. First, take Samantha's position, arguing for the virtues of behaviorism, and then discuss some limitations of the theory.

Answers to the **Tying It All Together** questions can be found at the end of this chapter.

Research Methods: The Tools of the Trade

Theories give us lenses for interpreting behavior. *Research* allows us to find the scientific truth. I already touched on the research technique designed to determine the genetic contributions to behavior. Now let's sketch out the general research strategies that developmental scientists use.

Two Standard Research Strategies: Correlations and Experiments

What impact does poverty have on relationships, personality, or physical health? What forces cause children to model certain people? Does a particular intervention to help improve self-efficacy really work? To answer any question about the impact one condition or entity (called a *variable*) has on another, developmentalists use two basic research designs: correlational studies and true experiments.

In a **correlational study**, researchers chart the relationships between the dimensions they are interested in exploring as they naturally occur. Let's say you want to test the hypothesis that parents who behave more lovingly have first graders with superior social skills. Your game plan is simple: Select a group of children by going to a class. Relate their interpersonal skills to the nurturing that parents provide.

Immediately, you will be faced with decisions related to choosing your participants. Are you going to explore the practices of mothers and fathers or mothers alone, confine yourself to a middle-class group, consider two- versus one-parent families, look at a mix of ethnicities or not? You would need to get permission from the school system. You would need to get the parents to volunteer. Are you choosing a **representative sample**—a group that reflects the characteristics of the population about whom you want to generalize?

Then you would face your most important challenge—accurately measuring your variables. Just as a broken thermometer can't tell us if we have a fever, if we don't have adequate indices of the concepts we are measuring, we can't conclude anything at all.

With regard to the parent dimension, one possibility might be to visit parents and children and observe how they relate. This technique, called **naturalistic observation,** is appealing because you are seeing the behavior as it occurs in "nature," or real life. However, this approach presents a huge practical challenge: the need to travel to each home to observe each family on many occasions. Plus, when we watch parent–child interactions, or any socially desirable activity, people try to act their best. Wouldn't you make an effort to act especially loving if a psychologist arrived at your house?

The most cost-effective strategy would be to give the parents a questionnaire with items such as: "Do you make an effort to kiss, hug, and praise your daughter? Is it important to avoid yelling at your child?" This **self-report strategy,** in which people evaluate their behavior anonymously, is the main approach researchers use with adults. Still, it has its own biases. Do you think that people can report accurately on their activities? Is there a natural human tendency to magnify our positive behaviors and minimize our negative ones?

Now, turning to the child side of your question, one reasonable way to assess social skills would be to have teachers evaluate each student via a questionnaire: "Does this child make friends easily?"; "Does he relate to his peers in a mature way?" Or, we could ask children to rank their classmates by showing photos: "Does Calista or Cory get a smiley face?"; "Pick your three best friends." Evaluations from expert observers, such as teachers, and even peers, are often used to assess concepts such as popularity and personality during the childhood years.

correlational study A research strategy that involves relating two or more variables.

representative sample A group that reflects the characteristics of the overall population.

naturalistic observation A measurement strategy that involves directly watching and coding behaviors.

self-report strategy A measurement having people report on their feelings and activities through questionnaires.

Table 1.5: Common Strategies Developmentalists Use to Measure Specific Variables
(Behaviors or Concepts of Interest)

Type	Strategy	Commonly Used Ages	Pluses and Problems
Naturalistic observation	Observes behavior directly; codes actions, often by rating the behavior as either present or absent (either in real life or the lab)	Typically during childhood, but also used with impaired adults	**Pluses:** Offers a direct, unfiltered record of behavior **Problems:** Very time intensive; people behave differently when watched
Self-reports	Questionnaires in which people report on their feelings, interests, attitudes, and thoughts	Adults and older children	**Pluses:** Easy to administer; quickly provides data **Problems:** Subject to bias if the person is reporting on undesirable activities and behaviors
Observer reports	Knowledgeable person such as a parent, teacher, or trained observer completes scales evaluating the person. Sometimes peers rank the children in their class	Typically during childhood; also used during adulthood if the person is mentally or physically impaired	**Pluses:** Offers a structured look at the person's behavior **Problems:** Observers—in particular teachers and parents—have their own biases

Table 1.5 spells out the uses, and the pluses and minuses, of these frequently used ways of measuring concepts: naturalistic observation, self-reports, and observer evaluations. Now, returning to our study, suppose you found a relationship, that is, a correlation, between having nurturing parents and children's interpersonal skills. Could you infer that a loving home environment *causes* children to socially flower? The answer is no!

- **With correlations, we may be mixing up the result with the cause.** Given that parent–child relationships are bidirectional, does loving parenting really *cause* superior social skills, or do socially skilled children provoke parents to act in loving ways? ("My son is such an endearing person. You want to just love him up.") This evocative chicken-or-egg argument applies to far more than child–parent interactions. Does exercising promote health in later life, or are some older adults likely to become physically active because they are *already* in good health?

- **With correlations, there may be another variable that explains the results.** In view of our discussion of heritability, with regard to the social skills study, the immediate third force that comes to mind is genetics. Wouldn't parents who are genetically blessed with superior social skills provide a more caring home environment and genetically pass down these same positive personality traits to their sons and daughters? Wouldn't older adults who go to the gym or ski regularly also be likely to watch their diet and generally take better care of their health? Given that these other activities should naturally be associated with keeping physically fit, can we conclude that exercise *alone* accounts for the association we find?

To rule out these confounding forces, the solution is to conduct a **true experiment** (see Figure 1.4). Researchers isolate their variable of interest by manipulating that condition (called the *independent variable*), and then randomly assign people to either receive that treatment or another, *control* intervention. If we *randomly assign* people to different groups (say, like tossing a coin), there can't be any preexisting differences between our participants that would bias our results. If the group does differ in the way we predict, we have to say that our intervention *caused* the particular result.

The problem is that we could never assign children to different kinds of parents! If, as Figure 1.4 suggests, developmentalists trained one group of mothers to relate in more caring ways and withheld this "intervention" from another group, the

true experiment The only research strategy that can determine that something causes something else; involves randomly assigning people to different treatments and then looking at the outcome.

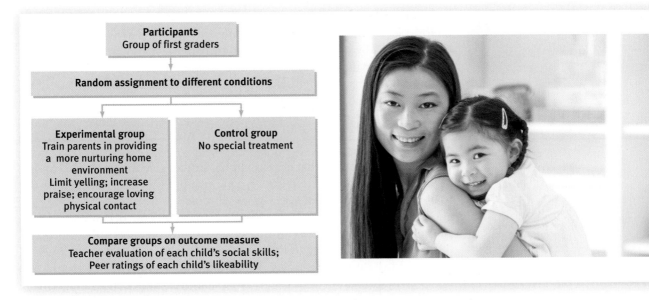

FIGURE 1.4: **How an experiment looks:** By randomly assigning children to different groups and then giving an intervention (this is called *the independent variable*), we know that our treatment (nurturing parents) *caused* better social skills (this outcome is called *the dependent variable*).

researchers would run into ethical problems. Would it be fair to deprive the control group of that treatment? In the name of science, can we take the risk of doing people harm? Experiments are ideal for determining what causes behavior. But to tackle the most compelling questions about human development, we *have* to conduct correlational research—and control as best we can for competing explanations that might bias our results.

Designs for Studying Development: Cross-Sectional and Longitudinal Studies

Experiments and correlational studies are standard, all-purpose research strategies. In studying development, however, we have a special interest: How do people change with age? To answer this question, scientists also use two research designs—cross-sectional and longitudinal studies.

Cross-Sectional Studies: Getting a One-Shot Snapshot of Groups

Because cross-sectional research is relatively easy to carry out, developmentalists typically use this strategy to explore changes over long periods of life (Hertzog, 1996). In a **cross-sectional study**, researchers compare *different age groups at the same time* on the trait or characteristic they are interested in, be it political attitudes, personality, or physical health. Consider a study that (among other questions) explored this interesting issue: "How do our feelings about human nature change with age?"

Researchers gave 2,138 U.S. adults a questionnaire measuring their beliefs in a benevolent world (Poulin & Silver, 2008). Presented with items such as "Human nature is basically good," people ranging in age from 18 to 101 ranked each statement on a scale from "agree strongly" to "disagree." As you scan the findings in Figure 1.5, notice that the youngest age group has the most negative perceptions about humanity. The elderly feel most optimistic about people and the world. If you are in your early twenties, does this mean you can expect to grow less cynical as you age?

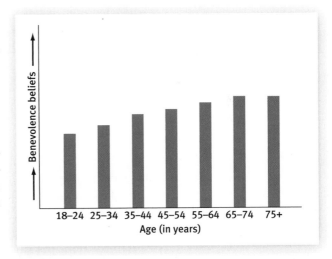

FIGURE 1.5: **"Benevolence beliefs," or faith in humanity across different age groups in a study of U.S. adults:** Notice that, while young people feel worst about human nature, the elderly have the most positive feelings about their fellow human beings.
Data from: Poulin & Silver, 2008.

cross-sectional study A developmental research strategy that involves testing different age groups at the same time.

Don't you think that these innocent 1950s-era twenty-somethings would have a more optimistic view of human nature than young people today? So could we really conclude from a cross-sectional study comparing these now elderly people with the young that "faith in humanity" grows with age?

Not necessarily. Perhaps your cohort has special reasons to feel suspicious about human motivations. After all, today the media delights in exposing the cheating and lying of authority figures, from senators to school principals. Previous cohorts of young people were never exposed to this drumbeat of messages highlighting human nature at its worst. In fact, if we conducted this same poll during the 1950s (in the Eisenhower era of *Leave It to Beaver* and *Father Knows Best*) we might find the opposite pattern: Positive feelings about human nature were highest among the young and declined with age!

The bottom line is that cross-sectional studies give us a current snapshot of differences among cohorts (or age groups); but they don't necessarily tell us about real *changes that occur as we grow old.*

Cross-sectional studies have a more basic problem. Because they measure only *group differences*, they can't reveal anything about the individual differences that give spice to life. If you are a real pessimist, will your worldview stay the same as you age? What influences might make people feel better about humanity during adulthood, and what experiences might make people feel worse? To answer these questions about how *individuals* develop, as well as to look at what makes for specific changes, it's best to be on the scene to measure what is going on. This means doing longitudinal research.

Longitudinal Studies: The Gold-Standard Developmental Science Research Design

In **longitudinal studies**, researchers typically select a group of a particular age and periodically test those people over years (the relevant word here is *long*). Consider the Dunedin Multidisciplinary Health and Development Study: An international team of researchers descended on Dunedin, a city in New Zealand, to follow more than 1,000 children born between April 1972 and March 1973, examining them at two-year intervals during childhood and roughly every three years after that. At each evaluation, they examined participants' personalities and looked at parenting practices and life events. The scientists are now tracking these babies as they move into middle age (Dunedin Multidisciplinary Health and Development Research Unit, 2014).

The outcome has been an incredible array of findings related to personality and psychological problems. Can we predict adult emotional difficulties as early as age 3? Do chronic anxiety and depression produce cellular damage as we travel through adolescence and early adult life (Shalev and others, 2014)? As you will learn in Chapter 12, scientists have discovered that a personality trait called *conscientiousness*, measured during emerging adulthood, powerfully predicts following good health habits—from not smoking, to exercising, and to watching one's diet as participants travel into middle age (Israel and others, 2014).

Moreover, because they are using cutting-edge DNA technology, this landmark research was the first to identify candidate genes that may make us more or less responsive to wider world stress. Plus, like other longitudinal research, the Dunedin Study offers a crystal ball into those questions at the heart of our field: How will I change as I get older? When should we worry about children, and when should we *not* be concerned?

Longitudinal studies are exciting, but they have their own problems. They involve a tremendous amount of time, effort, and expense. Imagine the resources involved in planning this particular study. Think of the hassles involved in searching out the participants and getting them to return again and again to take the tests. The researchers must fly the overseas Dunedin volunteers back for each evaluation. They need to reimburse people for their time and lost wages. These logistical and financial

longitudinal study A developmental research strategy that involves testing an age group repeatedly over many years.

problems become more serious the longer a study continues. For this reason, we have hundreds of studies covering infancy, childhood, or defined segments of adult life, such as the old-old years. Only a precious handful trace development from childhood to later life.

The difficulty with getting people to return for testing leads to an important bias in itself. People who stay in longitudinal studies, particularly during adulthood, tend to be highly motivated. Think of which classmates are going to attend your high school reunion. Aren't they apt to be the people who are successful, versus those who have made a mess of their lives? Participants in longitudinal research are typically elite, better than average groups. While they offer us unparalleled information, these gold-standard studies have their biases, too.

Critiquing the Research

So to summarize, when you are scanning the findings in our field, keep these concerns in mind:

- Consider the study's participants. How were they selected? Ask yourself, "Can I generalize from this particular group to the wider world?"

- Examine the study's measures. Are they accurate? What biases might they have?

- In looking at the *many* correlational studies in this book, be attuned to the fact that their findings might be due to other forces. What competing interpretations can you come up with to explain this researcher's results?

- With cross-sectional findings, beware of making assumptions that this is the way people *really* change with age.

- Look for longitudinal studies and welcome their insights. However, understand that—especially during adult life—these investigations are probably tracing the lives of the best and brightest people rather than the average adult.

Emerging Research Trends

Developmental scientists are attuned to these issues. In conducting correlational studies, they typically try to control for other influences that might explain their findings. They are apt to use several measures, such as teacher ratings, formal questionnaires, and peer input, as well as direct observations, to make sure they are measuring their concepts accurately. As you will see throughout this book, current developmental research has an international flavor, with researchers from nations as different as Iran and Ireland or China and Cameroon offering country-by-country insights on core topics in our field. Still, in addition to becoming more global, our research is getting up close and personal, too.

Quantitative research techniques—the strategies I have been describing, using groups of people and statistical tests—are the main approaches that researchers use to study human behavior. In order to make general predictions about people, we need to examine the behavior of different individuals. We need to pin down our concepts by using scales or ratings with numerical values that can be tallied and compared. Developmentalists who conduct **qualitative research** are not interested in making numerical comparisons. They want to understand the unique lives of people by conducting in-depth interviews. In this book, I will be focusing mainly on quantitative research because that is how we find out the scientific "truth." But I also will highlight the increasing number of qualitative interview studies to put a human face on our developing life.

quantitative research
Standard developmental science data-collection strategy that involves testing groups of people and using numerical scales and statistics.

qualitative research
Occasional developmental science data-collection strategy that involves interviewing people to obtain information that cannot be quantified on a numerical scale.

Some Concluding Introductory Thoughts

This discussion brings me back to the letter on page 2 and my promise to let you in on my other agendas in writing this text. Because I want to teach you to critically evaluate research, in the following pages I'll be analyzing individual studies and—in the How Do We Know features that appear in some chapters—focusing on research-related issues in more depth. To bring home the personal experience of the lifespan, I've filled the chapters with quotations, and—in the Experiencing the Lifespan boxes—occasionally interviewed people myself. To bring home the principle that our lifespan is a work in progress, I'll be starting many chapters by setting the historical and cultural context. To emphasize the power of research to improve lives, I'll conclude most sections by spelling out interventions that improve the quality of life.

This book is designed to be read like a story with each chapter building on concepts and terms mentioned in the previous ones. It's planned to emphasize how our insights about earlier life stages relate to older ages. I will be discussing three major aspects of development—physical development, cognitive development, and personality and social relationships (*socioemotional development*)—separately. However, I'll be continually stressing how these aspects of development connect. After all, we are not just bodies, minds, and personalities, but whole human beings!

While I want you to share my excitement in the research, please don't read this book as "the final word." Science—like the lifespan—is always evolving. Moreover, with any research finding, take the phrase "it's all statistical" to heart. Yes, developmentalists are passionate to make general predictions about life; but, because human beings are incredibly complex, at bottom, each person's lifespan journey is a beautiful surprise.

Now, beginning with prenatal development and infancy (Chapters 2, 3, and 4); then moving on to childhood (Chapters 5, 6, and 7); adolescence (Chapters 8 and 9); early and middle adulthood (Chapters 10, 11, and 12); later life (Chapters 13 and 14); and, finally, that last milestone, death (Chapter 15), welcome to the lifespan and to the rest of this book!

 Tying It All Together

1. Four developmentalists are studying whether eating excessive sugar has detrimental effects on the body and mind: Alicia relates the amount of sugar elementary schoolers eat at breakfast to aggression, by going to a playground and counting the frequency of hitting on selected days. Betty randomly assigns students in a high school class into two groups, tells one group to eat a healthy diet and another to eat candy bars, and compares their grades on tests. Calista measures the sugar consumption of teens and then retests them periodically into their fifties. David constructs a questionnaire exploring sugar consumption and gives it to adults of different ages. For each question below, link the appropriate person's name to the correct study.

   a. Who is conducting a cross-sectional study?
   b. Who is using naturalistic observation?
   c. Who is conducting a correlational study?
   d. Who can prove that eating a lot of sugar *causes* problems—but is doing an unethical study?
   e. Who is going to have a huge problem with dropouts?
   f. Who can tell you that if you are a sugar junkie in your twenties, you might still be eating an incredible amount of sugar (compared to everyone else) as you age?

2. Plan a longitudinal study to test a developmental science question. Describe how you would select your participants, how your study would proceed, what measures you would use, and what problems and biases your study would have.

Answers to the Tying It All Together questions can be found at the end of this chapter.

Who We Are and What We Study

Lifespan development is a mega-discipline encompassing **child development, gerontology,** and **adult development. Developmental scientists,** or **developmentalists,** chart universal changes from birth to old age, explore individual differences in development, study the impact of **normative** and **non-normative** life transitions, and explore every other topic relevant to our unfolding lives.

Several major **contexts of development** shape our lives. The first is our **cohort,** or the time in history in which we live. The huge **baby boom cohort,** born in the years following World War II, has changed society as it passes through the lifespan. Cohorts of babies born before the twentieth century faced a shorter, harsher childhood, and many did not survive. As life got easier and education got longer, we first extended the growing-up phase of life to include adolescence and, in recent years, with a new life stage called **emerging adulthood,** have put off the starting date of full adulthood to our late twenties.

The **early-twentieth-century life expectancy revolution,** with its dramatic advances in curing *infectious disease* and shift to deaths from *chronic illnesses,* allowed us to survive to later life. **Average life expectancy** is now within striking distance of the **maximum lifespan** in affluent nations, and we distinguish between the healthy **young-old** (people in their sixties and seventies) and the frail **old-old** (people in and over their eighties). The second major twentieth-century change occurred in the 1960s with the lifestyle revolution, which has given us freedom to engineer our own adult path. Today, the Internet and **social networking sites** have transformed relationships, while the lingering effects of the **Great Recession of 2008** and widening **income inequalities** are still clouding the economic landscape of twenty-first century life.

Socioeconomic status (SES) greatly affects our lifespan—with poor people in each nation facing a harsher, more stressful, and shorter life. The gaps between **developed world** countries and **developing world** countries are even more dramatic, with the least-developed countries lagging well behind in terms of health, wealth, and technology.

Our cultural and ethnic background also determines how we develop. Scientists distinguish between **collectivist cultures** (typically non-Western), which stress social harmony and extended-family relationships, and **individualistic cultures** (often Western), which value independence and personal achievement. We need to be aware, however, that residents living in all nations have a mix of individualistic and collectivist worldviews; the practice of lumping people into broad ethnic labels masks diversity within each group. Finally, our gender influences our travels through life. Women outlive men by at least two years in the developed world.

Theories: Lenses for Looking at the Lifespan

Theories offer explanations about what causes people to act the way they do. The main theories in developmental science offering general explanations of behavior vary in their position on the **nature** versus **nurture** question. Behaviorists believe nurture is all-important. **Traditional behaviorists,** in particular B. F. Skinner, believe **operant conditioning** and **reinforcement** determine all voluntary behaviors. According to **cognitive behaviorism/social learning theory, modeling** and **self-efficacy**—our internal sense that we can competently perform given tasks—predict how we act.

Sigmund Freud, in his psychoanalytic theory, believed our adult personality is shaped by the way our parents treated us during the first five years of life. Freud also felt human beings are dominated by unconscious drives, mental health depends on self-awareness, and sexuality (different erogenous zones) motivates behavior during the early childhood years. John Bowlby's **attachment theory** draws on the psychoanalytic principle that parenting during early life (or our attachment relationships) determines later mental health, but he believes that the attachment response is genetically built in to our species to promote survival. **Evolutionary psychologists** adopt this nature perspective, seeing actions and traits as programmed into our DNA. **Behavioral genetic** research—in particular, **twin studies, adoption studies,** and occasionally **twin/adoption studies**—convinced developmental scientists of the power of nature, revealing genetic contributions to almost any way we differ from each other as human beings.

Developmental scientists today, are exploring how nature *and* nurture combine. Due to **evocative** and **active forces,** we shape our environments to go along with our genetic tendencies, and human relationships are **bidirectional**—our temperamental qualities and actions influence the others, just as their actions influence us. A basic developmental science challenge is to foster an appropriate **person–environment fit.** We need to match our genetically based talents and abilities to the right environment. New research suggests that people differ genetically in how responsive they are to environmental events, and that early life environments may alter our genome, producing long-lasting **epigenetic** effects.

Erik Erikson spelled out eight **psychosocial tasks** that we must master as we travel from birth to old age. According to Jean Piaget's **cognitive developmental theory,** children progress through four qualitatively different stages of intellectual development, and all learning occurs through **assimilation** and **accommodation.**

Most developmental scientists today adopt the **developmental systems perspective.** They welcome input from every theory and realize that many interacting influences shape who we are. They understand that diversity among people and change processes is the essence of development.

Research Methods: The Tools of the Trade

The two main research strategies scientists use are **correlational studies,** which relate naturally occurring variations among people, and **true experiments,** in which researchers manipulate a variable (or give a specific treatment) and randomly assign people to receive that intervention or not. With correlational studies, there are always competing possibilities for the relationships we find. While experiments do allow us to prove causes, they are often unethical and impractical. In conducting research, it's best to strive for a **representative sample,** and it's essential to have accurate measures. **Naturalistic observation, self-reports,** and observer evaluations are three common measurement strategies developmental scientists use.

The two major designs for studying development are longitudinal and cross-sectional research. **Cross-sectional studies,** which involve testing people of different age groups at the same time, are very easy to carry out. However, they may confuse differences between age groups with true changes that occur as people age, and they can't tell us about individual differences in development.

Longitudinal studies can answer vital questions about how people develop. However, they involve following people over years and may sample atypical, elite groups.

Quantitative research—studies involving groups of participants, and using statistical tests—is still the standard way we learn the scientific truth. But developmentalists are now occasionally conducting **qualitative research**—interviewing people in depth. Our research is generally getting more global and sophisticated, too.

KEY TERMS

developmentalists (developmental scientists), p. 3
lifespan development, p. 4
child development, p. 4
gerontology, p. 4
adult development, p. 4
normative transitions, p. 4
non-normative transitions, p. 4
contexts of development, p. 5
cohort, p. 5
baby boom cohort, p. 5
emerging adulthood, p. 6
average life expectancy, p. 6
twentieth-century life expectancy revolution, p. 7
maximum lifespan, p. 7
young-old, p. 7

old-old, p. 7
social networking sites, p. 9
Great Recession of 2008, p. 9
income inequality, p. 9
socioeconomic status (SES), p. 9
developed world, p. 9
developing world, p. 9
collectivist cultures, p. 10
individualistic cultures, p. 10
theory, p. 12
nature, p. 12
nurture, p. 12
traditional behaviorism, p. 12
operant conditioning, p. 12
reinforcement, p. 13
cognitive behaviorism (social learning theory), p. 13

modeling, p. 13
self-efficacy, p. 14
attachment theory, p. 15
evolutionary psychology, p. 16
behavioral genetics, p. 16
twin study, p. 16
adoption study, p. 17
twin/adoption study, p. 17
evocative forces, p. 18
bidirectionality, p. 18
active forces, p. 18
person–environment fit, p. 19
epigenetics, p. 20
Erikson's psychosocial tasks, p. 20

Piaget's cognitive developmental theory, p. 21
assimilation, p. 21
accommodation, p. 21
developmental systems approach, p. 21
correlational study, p. 25
representative sample, p. 25
naturalistic observation, p. 25
self-report strategy, p. 25
true experiment, p. 26
cross-sectional study, p. 27
longitudinal study, p. 28
quantitative research, p. 29
qualitative research, p. 29

ANSWERS TO Tying It All Together QUIZZES

Setting the Context

1. C. There was no real high school in the eighteenth century.

2. Rosa is more likely to be physically disabled than Ramona. Rosa is old-old; Ramona is young-old.

3. Carlos was *more likely* to have divorced, probably entered the workforce at an *older age,* and got married later than his grandfather. Carlos probably had *more years* of education than his grandpa.

4. Pablo has a collectivist worldview, while Peter's worldview is individualistic.

5. Your answers here will all vary.

Theories: Lenses for Looking at the Lifespan

1. (1) c; (2) a; (3) g; (4) b; (5) d; (6) f ; (7) e

2. b. As Ricardo and other children need to run around, regular gym time would help to foster the best person–environment fit.

3. Dr. Kaplan is working in a field called epigenetics.

4. assimilation; accommodation

5. Samantha might argue that behaviorism is an ideal approach to human development because it is simple, effective, and easy to carry out. Behaviorism's easily mastered, action-oriented concepts—be consistent, reinforce positive behavior, draw on principles of modeling, and stimulate efficacy feelings—can make dramatic improvements in the quality of life. Also, because behaviorism doesn't blame the person but locates problems in the learning environment, it has special appeal. Sally might argue that behaviorism's premise that nurture is all-important neglects the powerful impact genetic forces have in determining who we are. So the theory is far too limited—offering a wrongheaded view about development. We need the insights of attachment theory, evolutionary psychology, behavioral genetics, plus Piaget's and Erikson's theories to fully understand what motivates human beings.

Research Methods: The Tools of the Trade

1. a. David; b. Alicia; c. Alicia; d. Betty; e. Calista; f. David

2. After coming up with your hypothesis, you would need to adequately measure your concepts—choosing the appropriate tests. Your next step would be to solicit a large representative sample of a particular age group, give them these measures, and retest these people at regular intervals over an extended period of time. In addition to the investment of time and money, it would be hard to keep track of your sample and entice participants to undergo subsequent evaluations. Because the most motivated fraction of your original group will probably continue, your results will tend to reflect how the "best people" behave and change over time (not the typical person).

CHAPTER 2

Petrol/Westend61/Getty Images

Prenatal Development, Pregnancy, and Birth

It's hard to explain, Kim told me. You are two people now. When you wake up, shop, or plan meals, this other person is always with you. You are always thinking, "What will be good for the baby? What will be best for the two of us?"

Feeling the first kick—like little feathers brushing inside me—was amazing. At first I felt like I could never explain this to my husband. But Jeff is wonderful. I think he gets it. So I feel lucky. I can't imagine what this experience would be like if I was going through nine months completely alone.

Now that it's the thirtieth week and my little girl can survive, there is another shift. I'm focused on the moment she will arrive: What will it be like to hold my baby? Will she be born healthy?

The downside is the fear that she will be born with some problem. Being an older mom, it took me two years to get pregnant. Now that I've gone through those exhausting procedures and they worked (hooray!), I'd never risk having an invasive genetic test. So, you eat right and never take a drink; but there are concerns. I worry about the stress I've been undergoing, since my mom died right before I conceived. And, of course, I worry about labor and delivery. Suppose I have some problem during birth, or my baby has a serious genetic disease?

Another downside is that, until recently, I still felt tired. Some days, I could barely make it to work. (Everything they told you about morning sickness only lasting through the first trimester is wrong—at least for me!)

But nothing equals the thrill of having my little girl inside—fantasizing about her future, watching her grow into a marvelous adult. I also adore what happens when I'm at the mall. People light up and grin, wish me good luck, or give me advice. It's like the world is watching out for me, rooting for me, cherishing me.

AP Photo/Matt York

In this traditional southern Indian ceremony performed at the sixth or eighth month of pregnancy, family members and friends gather around to protect the woman and fetus from "the evil eyes." Rituals such as this one are common around the world and embody our fears about this special time of life.

uterus The pear-shaped muscular organ in a woman's abdomen that houses the developing baby.

cervix The neck, or narrow lower portion, of the uterus.

fallopian tube One of a pair of slim, pipelike structures that connect the ovaries with the uterus.

ovary One of a pair of almond-shaped organs that contain a woman's ova, or eggs.

ovum An egg cell containing the genetic material contributed by the mother to the baby.

fertilization The union of sperm and egg.

ovulation The moment during a woman's monthly cycle when an ovum is expelled from the ovary.

hormones Chemical substances released in the bloodstream that target and change organs and tissues.

Setting the Context

The joy and fear Kim is experiencing seem built into our humanity. Throughout history, societies have seen pregnancy as an exciting and frightening time of life. Cultures used to make heroic efforts to keep pregnant women calm and happy. They might use good luck charms to keep evil spirits away—a pregnancy girdle in medieval England, a garlic-filled sack in Guatemala (Aldred, 1997; Von Raffler-Engel, 1994), a cotton pregnancy sash in Japan (Ito & Sharts-Hopko, 2002).

In the past, societies celebrated pregnancy milestones, too. In Bulgaria, the first kick was the signal for a woman to bake bread and take it to the church. In Bali, at the seventh month, a prayer ceremony took place to recognize that there was now, finally, a person inside whom the spirits should protect from harm (Kitzinger, 2000; Von Raffler-Engel, 1994). This chapter draws on the miracle of twenty-first century science to explore each pregnancy concern as I chart the marvelous milestones of prenatal development, pregnancy, and birth.

The First Step: Fertilization

Before embarking on this journey let's focus on the starting point. What structures are involved in reproduction? What physiological process is involved in conceiving a child? What happens at the genetic level when a sperm and an egg unite to form a human being?

The Reproductive Systems

The female and male reproductive systems are shown in Figure 2.1. Notice that the female system has several basic parts:

- Center stage is the **uterus,** the pear-shaped muscular organ that carries the baby to term. The uterus is lined with a velvety tissue, the *endometrium,* which thickens in preparation for pregnancy and, if that event does not occur, sheds during menstruation.

- The lower section of the uterus is the **cervix.** During pregnancy, this thick uterine neck must perform an amazing feat: Be strong enough to resist the pressure of the expanding uterus; be flexible enough to open fully at birth.

- Branching from the upper ends of the uterus are the **fallopian tubes.** These slim, pipelike structures serve as conduits to the uterus.

- The feathery ends of the fallopian tubes surround the **ovaries,** the almond-shaped organs where the **ova,** the mother's egg cells, reside.

The Process of Fertilization

The pathway that results in **fertilization**—the union of sperm and egg—begins at **ovulation.** This is the moment, typically around day 14 of a woman's cycle, when a mature ovum erupts from the ovary wall. **Hormones**—chemical substances that target certain tissues and body processes and cause them to change—orchestrate ovulation as well as the other events that program pregnancy.

At ovulation, a fallopian tube suctions the ovum in, and the tube begins vigorous contractions that propel the ovum on its three-day journey toward the uterus.

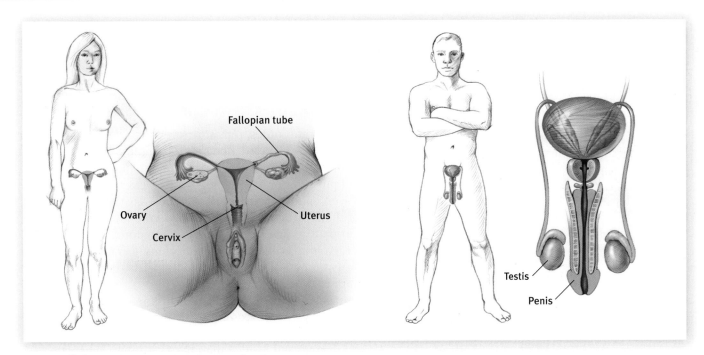

FIGURE 2.1: **The female and male reproductive systems**

Now the male's contribution to forming a new life arrives. In contrast to females, whose ova are all mainly formed at birth, the **testes**—male structures comparable to the ovaries—are continually manufacturing sperm. An adult male typically produces several hundred million sperm a day. During sexual intercourse these cells are expelled into the vagina, where a small proportion enter the uterus and wend their way up the fallopian tubes.

testes Male organs that manufacture sperm.

To promote pregnancy, it's best to have intercourse around ovulation. The ovum is receptive for about 24 hours while in the tube's outer part. Sperm take a few hours to journey from the cervix to the tube. However, sperm can live almost a week in the uterus, which means that intercourse several days prior to ovulation may also result in fertilization (Marieb, 2004).

Although the ovum emits chemical signals as to its location, the tiny tadpole-shaped travelers cannot easily make the perilous journey upward into the tubes. So, of the estimated several hundred million sperm expelled at ejaculation, only 200 to 300 reach their destination, find their target, and burrow in.

What happens now is a team assault. The sperm drill into the ovum, penetrating toward the center. Suddenly, one reaches the innermost part. Then the chemical composition of the ovum wall changes, shutting out the other sperm.

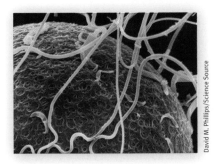

The sperm surround the ovum.

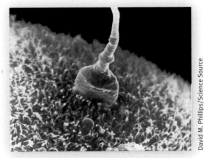

One sperm burrows in (notice the large head).

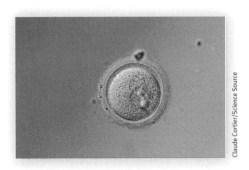

The nuclei of the two cells fuse. The watershed event called fertilization has occurred.

chromosome A threadlike strand of DNA located in the nucleus of every cell that carries the genes, which transmit hereditary information.

DNA (deoxyribonucleic acid) The material that makes up genes, which bear our hereditary characteristics.

gene A segment of DNA that contains a chemical blueprint for manufacturing a particular protein.

The nuclei of the male and female cells move slowly together. When they meld into one cell, the landmark event called fertilization has occurred. What is happening genetically when the sperm and egg combine?

The Genetics of Fertilization

The answer lies in looking at **chromosomes**, ropy structures composed of ladder-like strands of the genetic material **DNA.** Arrayed along each chromosome are segments of DNA called **genes**, which serve as templates for creating the proteins responsible for carrying out the physical processes of life (see Figure 2.2). Every cell in our body contains 46 chromosomes—except the sperm and ova, which have half this number, or 23. When the nuclei of these two cells, called *gametes*, combine at fertilization, their chromosomes align in pairs to again comprise 46. So nature has a marvelous mechanism to ensure that each human life has an identical number of chromosomes and every human being gets half of its genetic heritage from the parent of each sex.

You can see the 46 paired male chromosomes in Figure 2.3. Notice that each chromosome pair (one from our mother and one from our father) is a match, except for the sex chromosomes. The X is longer and heavier than the Y. Because each ovum carries an X chromosome, our father's contribution determines our sex. If a lighter, faster-swimming, Y-carrying sperm fertilizes the ovum, we get a boy (XY). If the victor is a more resilient, slower-moving X, we get a girl (XX).

In the race to fertilization, the Y's are statistically more successful; scientists estimate that 20 percent more male than female babies are conceived. But the prenatal period is particularly hard on males. If a family member learns that she is pregnant, the odds still favor her having a boy; but because more males die in the uterus, only 5 percent more boys than girls make it to birth (Werth & Tsiaras, 2002). And throughout life, males continue to be the less hardy sex, dying off at higher rates at every age. Recall from Chapter 1 that, throughout the developed world, women outlive men by at least two years.

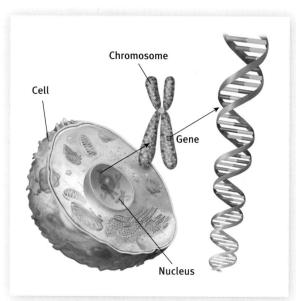

FIGURE 2.2: **The human building blocks:** The nucleus of every human cell contains chromosomes, each of which is made up of two strands of DNA connected in a double helix.

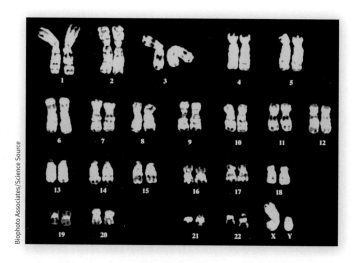

FIGURE 2.3: **A map of human chromosomes:** This magnified grid, called a karyotype, shows the 46 chromosomes in their matched pairs. The final pair, with its X and Y, shows that this person is a male. Also, notice the huge size of the X chromosome compared to the Y.

Tying It All Together

1. In order, list the structures involved in "getting pregnant." Choose from the following: *uterus, fallopian tubes, ovaries*. Then, name the structure in which fertilization occurs.

2. The _____ house the female's genetic material, while the _____ contain the sperm. (Identify the correct names)

3. Tiffany feels certain that if she has intercourse at the right time, she will get pregnant—but asks you, "What is the right time?" Give Tiffany your answer, referring to the text discussion.

4. If a fetus has the XX chromosomal configuration *he/she* is *more/less* apt to survive the prenatal journey (and live longer) and is *more/less* apt to be conceived.

Answers to the Tying It All Together questions can be found at the end of this chapter.

Prenatal Development

Now that we understand the starting point, let's chart prenatal development, tracing how the microscopic, fertilized ovum divides millions of times and differentiates into a living child. This miraculous transformation takes place in three stages.

First Two Weeks: The Germinal Stage

The first approximately two weeks after fertilization—when the cell mass has not fully attached to the uterine wall—is called the **germinal stage** (see Figure 2.4). Within 36 hours, the fertilized ovum, now a single cell called the **zygote,** makes its first cell division. Then the tiny cluster of cells divides every 12 to 15 hours as it wends its way down the fallopian tube. When the cells enter the uterine cavity, they differentiate into layers—some destined to form the pregnancy support structures, others the child-to-be. Now called a **blastocyst,** this ball of roughly 100 cells faces the challenge called **implantation**—embedding into the uterine wall.

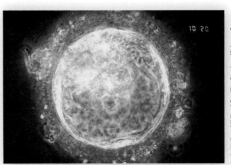

This is a photo of the blastocyst, the roughly 100-cell ball, soon to attach itself to the uterine wall. When implantation occurs, this event will signal the end of the germinal phase.

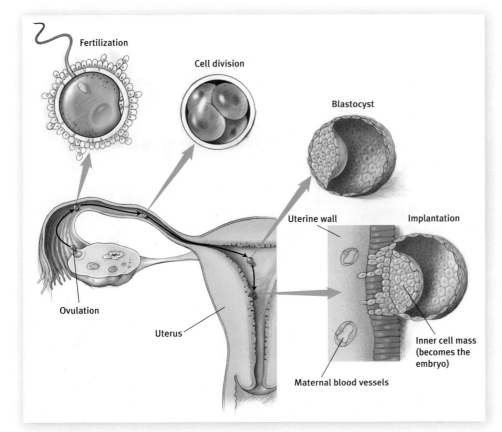

germinal stage The first 14 days of prenatal development, from fertilization to full implantation.

zygote A fertilized ovum.

blastocyst The hollow sphere of cells formed during the germinal stage in preparation for implantation.

implantation The process in which a blastocyst becomes embedded in the uterine wall.

FIGURE 2.4: **The events of the germinal stage:** The fertilized ovum divides on its trip to the uterus, then becomes a hollow ball called a blastocyst, and finally fully implants in the wall of the uterus at about 14 days after fertilization.

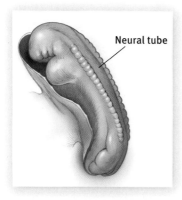

FIGURE 2.5: The neural tube: This structure is one of the first to form after implantation. The brain and spinal cord will develop from it.

placenta The structure projecting from the wall of the uterus during pregnancy through which the developing baby absorbs nutrients.

embryonic stage The second stage of prenatal development, lasting from week 3 through week 8.

neural tube A cylindrical structure that forms along the back of the embryo and develops into the brain and spinal cord.

neuron A nerve cell.

proximodistal sequence The developmental principle that growth occurs from the most interior parts of the body outward.

The blastocyst seeks a landing site on the upper uterus. Its outer layer develops projections and burrows in. From this landing zone, blood vessels proliferate to form the **placenta,** the lifeline that passes nutrients from the mother to the developing baby. Then, the next stage of prenatal development begins: the all-important embryonic phase.

Week 3 to Week 8: The Embryonic Stage

Although the **embryonic stage** lasts roughly only six weeks, it is the most fast-paced period of development. During this time, all the major organs are constructed. By the end of this stage, what began as a clump of cells looks like a recognizable human being!

One early task is to construct the conduit responsible for all development. After the baby hooks up to the maternal bloodstream—which will nourish its growth—nutrients must reach each rapidly differentiating cell. So by the third week after fertilization, the circulatory system (our body's transport system) forms, and its pump, the heart, starts to beat.

At the same time, the rudiments of the nervous system appear. Between 20 and 24 days after fertilization, an indentation forms along the back of the embryo and closes up to form the **neural tube** (see Figure 2.5). The upper part of this cylinder becomes the brain. Its lower part forms the spinal cord. Although it is possible to "grow" new brain cells throughout life, almost all of those remarkable branching structures, called **neurons,** which cause us to think, respond, and process information, originated in neural tube cells formed during our first months in the womb.

Meanwhile, the body is developing at an astounding rate. At day 26, arm buds form; by day 28, leg swellings erupt. At day 37, rudimentary feet start to develop. By day 41, elbows, wrist curves, and the precursors of fingers can be seen. Several days later, raylike structures that will become toes emerge. By about week 8, the internal organs are in place. What started out looking like a curved stalk, then an outer-space alien, now appears like a *human* being.

Principles of Prenatal Development

In scanning the photographs of the developing embryo below, can you spell out three guiding principles related to the sequence of development I just described?

• Notice that from a cylindrical shape, the arms and legs grow outward and then (not unexpectedly) the fingers and toes protrude. So growth follows the **proximodistal sequence,** from the most interior (proximal) part of the body to the outer (distal) sides.

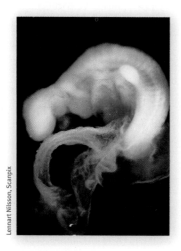

At about week 3, the embryo (the upside-down U across the top) looks like a curved stalk.

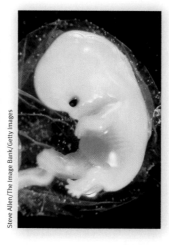

At week 4, you can see the indentations for eyes and the arms and legs beginning to sprout.

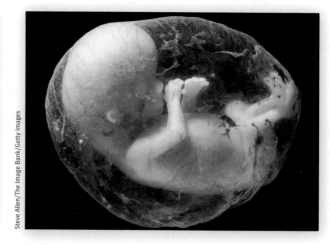

At week 9, the baby-to-be has fingers, toes, and ears. All the major organs have developed, and the fetal stage has begun!

- Notice that from a huge swelling that makes the embryo look like a mammoth head, the arms emerge and the legs sprout. So, development takes place according to the **cephalocaudal sequence,** meaning from top (*cephalo* = head) to bottom (*caudal* = tail).

- Finally, just as in constructing a sculpture, nature starts with the basic building blocks and then fills in details. A head forms before eyes and ears; legs are constructed before feet and toes. So the **mass-to-specific sequence,** or gross (large, simple) structures before smaller (complex) refinements, is the third principle of body growth.

Keep these principles in mind. As you will see in the next chapters, the same patterns apply to growth and motor skills *after* the baby leaves the womb.

Week 9 to Birth: The Fetal Stage

During the embryonic stage, body structures literally sprout. In the **fetal stage,** development occurs at a more leisurely pace. From the eyebrows, fingernails, and hair follicles that develop from weeks 9 to 12, to the cushion of fat that accumulates during the final weeks, it takes seven months to transform the embryo into a resilient baby ready to embrace life.

Why does our species need this long refining period? One reason is to allow ample time for that masterpiece organ—the human brain—to form. Let's now look at this process of making a brain.

During the late embryonic stage, a mass of cells accumulates within the neural tube that will eventually produce the more than 100 billion neurons composing our brain (Stiles & Jernigan, 2010). From this zone, the neurons migrate to a region just under the top of the differentiating tube (see Figure 2.6). When the cells assemble in their "staging area," by the middle of the fetal period, they lengthen, develop branches, and interlink. This interconnecting process—responsible for every human thought and action—continues until almost our final day of life.

Figure 2.7 shows the mushrooming brain. Notice that the brain almost doubles in size from month 4 to month 7. By now, the brain has the wrinkled structure of an adult.

This massive growth has a profound effect. At around month 6, the fetus can hear (Crade & Lovett, 1988). By month 7, the fetus is probably able to see (Del Giudice, 2011). And by this time, with high-quality medical care, a few babies can survive.

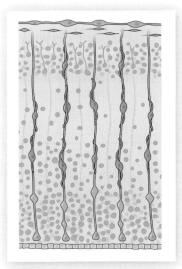

FIGURE 2.6: **Forming a brain: climbing neurons:** During the earlier part of the fetal period, the neurons destined to make up the brain ascend these ladder-like filaments to reach the uppermost part of what had been the neural tube.
Data from: Huttenlocher, 2002.

cephalocaudal sequence The developmental principle that growth occurs in a sequence from head to toe.

mass-to-specific sequence The developmental principle that large structures (and movements) precede increasingly detailed refinements.

fetal stage The final period of prenatal development, lasting seven months, characterized by physical refinements, massive growth, and the development of the brain.

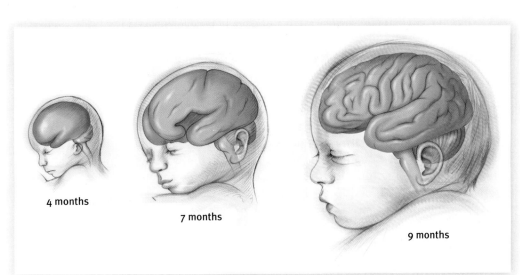

4 months

7 months

9 months

FIGURE 2.7: **The expanding brain:** The brain grows dramatically month by month during the fetal period. During the final months, it develops its characteristic folds.

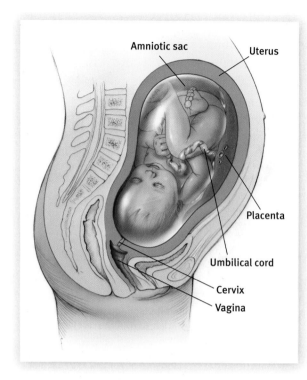

Amniotic sac

Uterus

Placenta

Umbilical cord

Cervix

Vagina

FIGURE 2.8: **Poised to be born:** This diagram shows the fetus inside the woman's uterus late in pregnancy. Notice the placenta, amniotic sac, and umbilical cord.

Today, the **age of viability,** or earliest date at which we can be born and *possibly* live, has dropped to 22 to 23 weeks—almost halving the 38 weeks the fetus normally spends in the womb. By week 25, in affluent nations, the odds of survival are more than fifty-fifty (Lawn and others, 2011).

However, it is *vitally* important that the fetus stay in the uterus as long as possible. As I will describe later, being born too early (and too small) can make a lifelong impact in health.

Figure 2.8 shows the fetus during the final month of pregnancy, when its prenatal nest is cramped and birth looms on the horizon. Notice the baby's support structures: the placenta, projecting from the uterine wall, which supplies nutrients from the mother to the fetus; the **umbilical cord,** protruding from what will be the baby's bellybutton, the conduit through which nutrients flow; the **amniotic sac,** the fluid-filled chamber within which the baby floats. This encasing membrane provides insulation from infection and harm.

At this stage, parents may be running around, buying the crib or shopping for baby clothes. Middle-class women may be marveling at the items their precious son or daughter "must have": a pacifier, a receiving blanket, a bassinet . . . and what else! What is happening during *all* nine months from the mother's—and father's—point of view?

Tying It All Together

1. In order, name the three stages of prenatal development. Then, identify the stage in which the organs are formed.

2. A pregnant friend asks you, "How does my baby's brain develop?" Describe the process of neural migration—when it occurs, and when it is complete.

3. Match the following in utero descriptions to the correct names. (Choose from *cephalocaudal/proximodistal/mass-to-specific.*)

   (a) The fingers form before the fingernails; (b) The head forms first and the feet last; (c) the neural tube develops and then the arms.

4. You are horrified to learn that your friend went into premature labor yesterday. Pick the minimum pregnancy age that she might be able to have a live birth: *around 12 weeks; around 22–23 weeks; around 30 weeks.*

Answers to the Tying It All Together questions can be found at the end of this chapter.

age of viability The earliest point at which a baby can survive outside the womb.

umbilical cord The structure that attaches the placenta to the fetus, through which nutrients are passed and fetal wastes are removed.

amniotic sac A bag-shaped, fluid-filled membrane that contains and insulates the fetus.

gestation The period of pregnancy.

trimester One of the 3-month-long segments into which pregnancy is divided.

Pregnancy

The 266- to 277-day **gestation** period (or pregnancy) is divided into three segments called **trimesters,** each comprising roughly three months. (Because it is difficult to know exactly when fertilization occurs, health-care professionals date the pregnancy from the woman's last menstrual period.)

Pregnancy differs, however, from the universally patterned process of prenatal development. Despite having classic symptoms, here individual differences are the *norm.*

Scanning the Trimesters

With the strong caution that the following symptoms vary—from person to person (and pregnancy to pregnancy)— let's now offer an in-the-flesh sense of how each trimester feels.

First Trimester: Often Feeling Tired and Ill

After the blastocyst implants in the uterus—a few days before the woman first misses her period—pregnancy often signals its presence through unpleasant symptoms. Many women feel faint. (Yes, fainting can be a sign of pregnancy!) They may get headaches or have to urinate frequently. Like Kim in the introductory chapter vignette, they may feel incredibly tired. Their breasts become tender, painful to the touch. So, many women do not need that tip-off—a missed menstrual period—to realize they are carrying a child.

Hormones trigger these symptoms. After implantation, the production of *progesterone* (literally *pro*, or "for," *gestation*)—the hormone responsible for maintaining the pregnancy—surges. The placenta produces its own unique hormone, *human chorionic gonadotropin (HCG)*, thought to prevent the woman's body from rejecting the "foreign" embryo.

Given this hormonal onslaught, the body changes, and the fact that the blood supply is being diverted to the uterus, the tiredness, dizziness, and headaches make sense. What about that other early pregnancy sign—morning sickness?

Morning sickness—nausea and sometimes vomiting—affects at least two out of every three women during the first trimester (Beckmann and others, 2002). This well-known symptom is not confined to the morning. Many women feel queasy all day. A few cannot keep any food down. And men sometimes develop morning sickness along with their wives! This phenomenon has its own special name: *couvade* (Munroe, 2010).

But morning sickness seems senseless: Doesn't the embryo need all the nourishment it can get? Why, during the first months of pregnancy, might it be "good" to stop eating particular foods?

Consider these clues: The queasiness is at its height when the organs are forming, and, like magic, toward the end of the first trimester, usually (but not always) disappears. Munching on bread products helps. Strong odors make many women gag. Evolutionary psychologists theorize that, before refrigeration, morning sickness prevented the mother from eating spoiled meat or toxic plants, which could be especially dangerous during the embryo phase (Bjorklund & Pellegrini, 2002). If you have a friend struggling with morning sickness, you can give her this heartening information: Some research suggests that women with morning sickness are more likely to carry their babies to term.

This brings up that upsetting event: **miscarriage**. Roughly 1 in 10 pregnancies end in a first trimester fetal loss. For women in their late thirties, the chance of miscarrying during these weeks escalates to 1 in 5. Many miscarriages are inevitable—caused by genetic problems in the embryo that are incompatible with life.

Second Trimester: Feeling Much Better and Connecting Emotionally

Morning sickness, the other unpleasant symptoms, and the relatively high chance of miscarrying make the first trimester less than an unmitigated joy. During the second trimester, the magic kicks in.

By week 14, the uterus dramatically grows, often creating a need to shop for maternity clothes. The wider world may notice the woman's expanding body: "Are you pregnant?" "How wonderful!" "Take my seat." Around week 18, an event called **quickening**—a sensation like bubbles that signals the baby kicking in the womb—appears. The woman feels viscerally connected to a growing human being.

Another landmark event that alters the emotional experience of pregnancy occurs at the beginning of the third trimester, when the woman can give birth to a living child. This important late-pregnancy marker explains why some societies build in celebrations at month 6 or 7 to welcome the baby to the human community.

miscarriage The naturally occurring loss of a pregnancy and death of the fetus.

quickening A pregnant woman's first feeling of the fetus moving inside her body.

© Robin Sachs/Photo Edit

Imagine what this woman is feeling while watching her husband paint the newborn's nursery during her final months of pregnancy. "Not only is my spouse a full partner in building our family nest, he is physically showing me his love."

Third Trimester: Getting Very Large and Waiting for Birth

Look at a pregnant woman struggling up the stairs and you'll get a sense of her feelings during this final trimester: backaches (think of carrying a bowling ball); leg cramps; numbness and tingling as the uterus presses against the nerves of the lower limbs; heartburn, insomnia, and anxious anticipation as focus shifts to the birth ("When will this baby arrive?!"); uterine contractions occurring irregularly as the baby sinks into the birth canal and delivery draws very near.

Although women often do work up to the day of delivery, health-care workers advise taking time off to rest and relying on caring loved ones to help cook and clean during the final months. Actually, having caring loved ones is vital during all nine months!

Pregnancy Is Not a Solo Act

I don't know what it's like for you and your partner to hear the baby's heartbeat, or see the ultrasound together, or feel the first kick. I lived through nine months of pregnancy alone. I thought this was supposed to be the happiest time of your life. I found myself losing weight instead of gaining and being depressed most of the time.

When I told my husband I was pregnant, he got furious, said he couldn't afford the baby and moved out. So now what do I do—I've been laid off from my job. I'm frightened about how I can cope.

As these quotations reveal, pregnancy has a different emotional flavor depending on the wider world. What forces turn this joyous time of life into nine months of distress?

One influence, as suggested above, lies in economic concerns. Studies routinely show that low socioeconomic status puts pregnant women at risk of feeling demoralized and depressed (see, for instance, Guardino & Schetter, 2014). Imagine coping with the stresses associated with being poor—worrying about making ends meet, perhaps not getting adequate prenatal care—and you will understand why pregnancy is more likely to be one of life's great joys when an expectant mother is comfortably middle class.

The main force, however, that predicts having a joyous pregnancy applies to both affluent and economically deprived women alike—feeling loved by one's mate (Rahman, Iqbal, & Harrington, 2003; Savage and others, 2007). From dealing with problems on the pregnancy pathway, to handling birth and the new baby, having a caring partner is critically important in how women cope (Guardino & Schetter, 2014).

Because she is being cherished and pampered by loving friends, this single mom is likely to find the pregnancy journey very fulfilling.

Does this mean going through pregnancy without a mate is a terrible thing? The answer is no. What matters is whether a woman feels *generally* cared about and loved (Abdou and others, 2010). Listen to this comment of an impoverished single woman whom researchers ranked as "thriving" during this time of life: "We've always been a close-knit family, and they were there to get me through. . . . They called me every night to make sure I was eating right" (Savage and others, 2007, p. 219).

Suppose, like the woman quoted at beginning of this section, you were married, but your spouse was hostile to your pregnancy. Wouldn't you rather be going through this journey with a loving family or good friends?

bikeriderlondon/Shutterstock

What About Dads?

This brings up the emotions of the standard pregnancy partner: dads. Given the attention we lavish on pregnant women, it should come as no surprise that fathers have been relatively ignored in the research exploring this transition of life. But fathers are also bonded to their babies-to-be (Vreeswijk and others, 2014). They can feel just as devastated when a pregnancy doesn't work out. Here are some comments about miscarriage from the male point of view:

Richard anguished,

I keep thinking that my wife is still pregnant. Where is my little girl? I was so ready to spoil her and treat her like a princess . . . but now she is gone. I don't think I'll ever be the same again.

(quoted in Jaffe & Diamond, 2011, p. 218)

And another grieving dad reported,

I had to be strong for Kate. I had to let her cry on me and then I would . . . drive up into the hills and cry to myself. I was trying to support her even though I felt my whole life had just caved in. . . .

(quoted in McCreight, 2004, p. 337)

As you saw in the quotation above, in coping with this trauma, men have a double burden. They may feel compelled to put aside their feelings to focus on their wives (Jaffe & Diamond, 2011; Rinehart & Kiselica, 2010). Plus, because the loss of a baby is typically seen as a "woman's issue," the wider world tends to marginalize their pain. These examples remind us that husbands are "pregnant" in spirit along with their wives. We should *never* thrust their feelings aside.

So, by returning to the beginning of the chapter, we now know that the cultural practice of pampering pregnant women makes excellent psychological sense—for both the mother *and* her child. But we also need to realize that expectant fathers need cherishing, too!

Table 2.1 summarizes these points in a brief "stress during pregnancy" questionnaire. Now, let's return to the baby and tackle that common fear: "Will my child be healthy?"

Table 2.1: Measuring Stress in Mothers-to-Be: A Short Section Summary Questionnaire

1. Does this woman have serious financial troubles, or is she living in poverty?
2. Is this woman having marital problems, and does her husband want this baby?
3. Is the woman a single mother? If so, does she have a supportive network of friends and family?
4. If the woman is living in poverty, does she feel connected to others in loving, positive ways?

 Tying It All Together

1. Samantha just entered her second trimester. Explain how she is likely to feel for the next few months. What symptoms was Samantha apt to describe during the first trimester, after learning she was pregnant?

2. You just learned your cousin is pregnant. What two forces might best predict her emotional state?

3. As a clinic director, you are concerned that men are often left out of the pregnancy experience. Design a few innovative interventions to make your clinic responsive to the needs of fathers-to-be.

Answers to the Tying It All Together questions can be found at the end of this chapter.

birth defect A physical or neurological problem that occurs prenatally or at birth.

teratogen A substance that crosses the placenta and harms the fetus.

sensitive period The time when a body structure is most vulnerable to damage by a teratogen, typically when that organ or process is rapidly developing or coming "on line."

Threats to the Developing Baby

In this section, we'll explore the prenatal reasons for **birth defects,** or health problems at birth. I'll also discuss new research exploring how wider-world events while "in the womb" can potentially affect a fetus's lifelong health. In reading this catalogue of "things that can go wrong," keep these thoughts in mind: The vast majority of babies are born healthy. Many birth defects don't seriously impair a baby's ability to have a fulfilling life. Often birth defects result from a complex nature-plus-nurture interaction. Fetal genetic vulnerabilities combine with environmental hazards in the womb. However, this section separates these conditions into two categories: toxins that flow through the placenta to impair development and genetic diseases.

Threats from Outside: Teratogens

The universal fears about the growing baby are expressed in cultural prohibitions: "Don't use scissors or your baby will have cut lips" (a cleft palate) Afghanistan; "Avoid looking at monkeys [Indonesia] or gossiping [China] or your baby will be deformed."

If you think these practices are strange, consider the standard mid-twentieth-century medical advice. Physicians put women in the United States on a strict diet if they gained over 15 pounds. They encouraged mothers-to-be to smoke and drink to relax (Von Raffler-Engel, 1994; Wertz & Wertz, 1989). Today, these pronouncements might qualify as fetal abuse! What *can* hurt the developing baby? When is damage most apt to occur?

A **teratogen** (from the Greek word *teras,* "monster," and *gen,* "creating") is the name for any substance that crosses the placenta to harm the fetus. A teratogen may be an infectious disease; a medication; a recreational drug; environmental hazards, such as radiation or pollution; or as you will see later, the hormones produced by a pregnant woman who is under extreme stress. Table 2.2 describes potential teratogens in various categories.

This Honduran baby is a testament to the horrible damage teratogens can potentially cause during the embryonic period, as his condition was believed to be due to his mother's exposure to pesticides during early pregnancy.

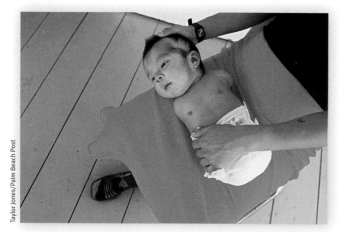

Taylor Jones/Palm Beach Post

Basic Teratogenic Principles

Teratogens typically exert their damage during the **sensitive period**—the timeframe when a particular organ or system is coming "on line." For example, the infectious disease called rubella (German measles) often damaged a baby's heart or ears, depending on the week during the first trimester when a mother contracted the disease. The sedative Thalidomide, prescribed in Europe during the late 1950s to prevent morning sickness, impaired limb formation, depending on which day after fertilization the drug was imbibed. In general, with regard to teratogens, the following principles apply:

1. **Teratogens are most likely to cause major structural damage during the embryonic stage.** Before implantation, teratogens have an all-or-nothing impact. They either inhibit implantation and cause death, or they leave the not-yet-attached blastocyst unscathed. It is during organ formation (after implantation through week 8) that major body structures are most likely to be affected. This is why—unless expectant mothers have a chronic disease that demands continuing—physicians advise forgoing any medications during the first trimester (American Academy of Pediatrics [AAP], Committee on Drugs, 2000).

2. **Teratogens can affect the developing brain throughout pregnancy.** As you saw earlier, because the brain is forming during the second and third trimesters, the potential for neurological damage extends for all nine months. Typically, during

Table 2.2: Examples of Known Teratogens and the Damage They Can Do

Teratogen	Consequences of Exposure
INFECTIOUS DISEASES	
Rubella (German measles)	If a pregnant woman contracts rubella during the embryonic stage, the consequence is, not infrequently, intellectual disability, blindness, or eye, ear, and heart abnormalities in the baby—depending on the week the virus enters the bloodstream. Luckily, women of childbearing age are now routinely immunized for this otherwise minor adult disease.
Cytomegalovirus	About 25% of babies infected with this virus develop vision or hearing loss; 10% develop neurological problems.
AIDS	HIV-infected women can transmit the virus to their babies prenatally through the placenta, during delivery (when blood is exchanged between the mother and child), or after birth (through breast milk). Rates of transmission are much lower if infected mothers take the anti-AIDS drug AZT or if newborns are given a new drug that blocks the transmission of HIV at birth. If a mother takes these precautions, does not breastfeed, and delivers her baby by c-section, the infection rate falls to less than 1%. While mother-to-child transmission of HIV has declined dramatically in the developed world, it remains a devastating problem in sub-Saharan Africa and other impoverished regions of the globe (AVERT, 2005).
Herpes	This familiar sexually transmitted disease can cause miscarriage, growth retardation, and eye abnormalities in affected fetuses. Doctors recommend that pregnant women with active genital herpes undergo c-sections to avoid infecting their babies during delivery.
Toxoplasmosis	This disease, caused by a parasite found in raw meat and cat feces, can lead to blindness, deafness, and intellectual disability in infants. Pregnant women should avoid handling raw meat and cat litter.
MEDICATIONS	
Antibiotics	Streptomycin has been linked to hearing loss; tetracycline to stained infant tooth enamel.
Thalidomide	This drug, prescribed in the late 1950s in Europe to prevent nausea during the first trimester, prevented the baby's arms and legs from developing if taken during the embryonic period.
Anti-seizure drugs	These medications have been linked to developmental delays during infancy.
Anti-psychotic drugs	These drugs may slightly raise the risk of giving birth to a baby with heart problems.
Antidepressants	Although typically safe, third-trimester exposure to selective serotonin reuptake inhibitors and tricyclic antidepressants has been linked to temporary jitteriness and excessive crying and to eating and sleeping difficulties in newborns. Rarely, these drugs can produce a serious syndrome involving seizures and dehydration, as well as higher rates of miscarriage.
RECREATIONAL DRUGS	
Cocaine	This drug is linked to miscarriage, growth retardation, and learning and behavior problems.
Methamphetamine	This drug may cause miscarriage and growth retardation.
ENVIRONMENTAL TOXINS	
Radiation	Japanese children exposed to radiation from the atomic bomb during the second trimester had extremely high rates of severe intellectual disability. Miscarriages were virtually universal among pregnant women living within 5 miles of the blast. Pregnant women are also advised to avoid clinical doses of radiation such as those used in X-rays (and especially cancer treatment radiation).
Lead	Babies with high levels of lead in the umbilical cord may show impairments in cognitive functioning (Bellinger and others, 1987). Maternal exposure to lead is associated with miscarriage.
Mercury and PCBs	These pollutants are linked to learning and behavior problems.
VITAMIN DEFICIENCIES	In addition to eating a balanced diet, every woman of childbearing age should take folic acid supplements. This vitamin, part of the B complex, protects against the incomplete closure of the neural tube during the first month of development—an event that may produce *spina bifida* (paralysis in the body below the region of the spine that has not completely closed) or *anencephaly* (failure of the brain to develop—and certain death) if the gap occurs toward the top of the developing tube.

Data from: Huttenlocher, 2002, and the references in this chapter.

the second and third trimesters, exposure to teratogens increases the risk of **developmental disorders.** This term refers to any condition that compromises normal development—from delays in reaching basic milestones, such as walking or talking, to learning problems and hyperactivity.

3. **Teratogens have a threshold level above which damage occurs.** For instance, women who drink more than four cups of coffee a day throughout pregnancy have a slightly higher risk of miscarriage; but having an occasional Diet Coke is fine (Gilbert-Barness, 2000).

4. **Teratogens exert their damage unpredictably, depending on fetal and maternal vulnerabilities.** Still, mothers-to-be metabolize toxins differently, and babies differ genetically in susceptibility. So the damaging effects of a particular teratogen can vary. On the plus side, you may know a child in your local school's gifted program whose mother drank heavily during pregnancy. On the negative side, we do not know where the teratogenic threshold lies in any particular case. Therefore, during pregnancy, it's best to err on the side of caution.

Although the damaging impact of a teratogen may show up during infancy, it can also manifest itself years later. An unfortunate example of this teratogenic time bomb took place in my own life. My mother was given a drug called diethylstilbestrol (DES) while she was pregnant with me. (DES was prescribed routinely in the 1950s and 1960s to prevent miscarriage.) During my early twenties, I developed cancerous cells in my cervix—and, after surgery, had three miscarriages before being blessed by adopting my son.

The Teratogenic Impact of Medicines and Recreational Drugs

The fact that some medications are teratogenic presents dilemmas for women. Do you stop taking your anti-epilepsy drugs and risk having a seizure? In one survey, many women with this condition didn't understand their medicines could effect the babies' developing brain (McGrath and others, 2014). Or, suppose you are among the millions of people taking antidepressant drugs. You may be aware of the research suggesting your medicine slightly raises the risk of premature birth (Huang and others, 2014; Deligiannidis, Byatt, & Freeman, 2014; Jensen and others, 2013). But you worry that stopping will cause excessive anxiety which—as we will see soon—also may compromise your baby's health.

As these comments illustrate, with medications and pregnancy, it can be a balancing act. Sometimes there are no perfect choices.

With recreational drugs, the choice is clear. Each substance is potentially teratogenic. So it's best to just say *no!*

Because tobacco and alcohol are woven into the fabric of daily life, let's now focus on these widely used teratogens. What *can* happen to the baby when pregnant women smoke and drink?

SMOKING Each time she reads the information on a cigarette pack, a pregnant woman gets a reminder that she may be doing her baby harm. Still, with polls showing that anywhere from 1 in 12 people (in the Netherlands) and 1 in 3 pregnant women (in Spain) smoke, tobacco use during this time is far from rare (De Wilde and others, 2013). Because this practice is such a "no, no," these surveys almost certainly underestimate the fraction of smoking mothers-to-be. When scientists in a national U.S. study measured blood levels of cotinine (a biological indicator of tobacco use), they discovered that roughly 1 in 4 pregnant smokers had earlier falsely reported: "Oh yes, I definitely quit!" (See Dietz and others, 2011.)

The main danger with smoking is giving birth to a smaller-than-normal baby (Krstev and others, 2013). Nicotine constricts the mother's blood vessels, reducing blood flow to the fetus and so not allowing a full complement of nutrients to reach the child. In particular, smoking—and giving birth to a small child—raises the risk of developmental problems like hyperactivity (Keyes, Smith, & Susser, 2014), and makes newborns less able to regulate their sleep (Hernandez-Martinez and others, 2012).

The good news is that the many U.S. pregnant smokers who take the difficult step of quitting for the health of their babies (see Chisolm, Cheng, & Terplan, 2014) feel more efficacious and less depressed (De Wilde and others, 2013). The bad news is that women still get ammunition—even from health-care professionals—for continuing to smoke: "My doctor told me stopping would put stress on the baby" . . . "I've seen . . . many people do it and had healthy babies" (quoted in Naughton, Eborall, & Sutton, 2013, pp. 27 and 28). Plus, unfortunately, many former smokers resume using tobacco after giving birth (Xu and others, 2013; De Wilde and others, 2013).

ALCOHOL As you saw earlier, it used to be standard to encourage pregnant women to have a nightcap to relieve stress. In Italy, drinking red wine during pregnancy was supposed to produce a healthy, rosy-cheeked child! (See Von Raffler-Engel, 1994.) During the 1970s, as evidence mounted for a disorder called **fetal alcohol syndrome (FAS),** these prescriptions were quickly revised. Whenever you hear the word *syndrome*, it is a signal that the condition has a constellation of features that are present to varying degrees. The defining qualities of fetal alcohol syndrome include a smaller-than-normal birth weight and brain; facial abnormalities (such as a flattened face); and developmental disorders ranging from serious intellectual disability to seizures and hyperactivity (Dean & Davis, 2007; Roussotte, Soderberg, & Sowell, 2010).

fetal alcohol syndrome (FAS) A cluster of birth defects caused by the mother's alcohol consumption during pregnancy.

Women who binge-drink (have more than four drinks at a sitting), or pregnant women who regularly consume several drinks nightly, are at highest risk of giving birth to a baby with fetal alcohol syndrome. Their children, at a minimum, may be born with a less severe syndrome called *fetal alcohol spectrum disorders*, characterized by deficits in learning and impaired mental health (Wedding and others, 2007). As alcohol crosses the placenta, it causes genetic changes that impair neural growth (Hashimoto-Torii and others, 2011).

Faced with these warnings, New Zealand researchers found about half of women in a national poll reported stopping drinking after learning they were pregnant (Parackal Parackal, & Harraway, 2013). Ironically, however, *trying* to conceive has no influence on alcohol use (Terplan, Cheng, & Chisolm, 2014). Pregnant women who drink regularly tend to be anxious or depressed (Beijers and others, 2014). Surprisingly, however, one study in the Netherlands showed *well-educated*, expectant moms were more likely to report still using alcohol or restarting at some point (Pfinder and others, 2014)!

This unexpected finding may reflect cultural norms. Every U.S. public health organization recommends no alcohol during pregnancy. In Europe, having a cocktail or glass of wine is an expected practice during meals. This may explain why European physicians disagree with their U.S. counterparts: "One drink per day can't *possibly* do the fetus harm" (Paul, 2010; Royal College of Obstetricians and Gynaecologists [RCOG], 1999).

As this woman downed her many drinks, she put her baby at risk of fetal alcohol syndrome— explaining why patrons at a bar who saw this scenario would get very upset!

Measurement Issues

Why is there *any* debate about a safe amount of alcohol to drink? For answers, imagine the challenges you would face as a researcher exploring the impact of tobacco or alcohol on the developing child: The need to ask thousands of pregnant women to estimate how often they indulged in these "unacceptable" behaviors and then track the children for decades, looking for problems that might appear as late as adult life. Plus, because your study is *correlational*, the difficulties you find might be due to other confounding causes. Pregnant women who drink are more likely to smoke (Mallard, Connor, & Houghton, 2013). As I've implied, these people may be generally stressed out. Could you isolate the child's symptoms to just tobacco or alcohol? Wouldn't simply feeling overly anxious damage the developing child?

Hot in Developmental Science: What Is the Impact of Prenatal Stress?

I introduced this chapter by emphasizing that anxiety is *normal* during pregnancy. Will my baby be all right? I discussed how throughout history people intuitively believed that stress could harm the fetus, so societies went to heroic lengths to keep mothers calm. What does the research suggest about the impact of pregnancy stress?

One concern is that excessive anxiety may cause premature labor, causing women to miscarry or have an unhealthy infant (Guardino & Schetter, 2014). High levels of the stress hormone cortisol, as it turns out, are transmitted to the fetus via the amniotic fluid, making babies irritable during the first months of life (Baibazarova and others, 2013). Now—as with teratogens in general—let's list two forces that increase these risks:

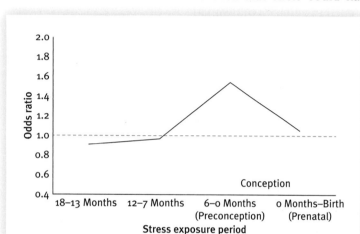

FIGURE 2.9: Odds of infant mortality following maternal stress (defined as the woman's having experienced the death of a first degree relative) at varying times before conception and during pregnancy: In this remarkable study tracking the more than 3 million Swedish babies born between 1973 and 2008, notice that the risk of a baby's dying soon after birth rose only when the mom experienced this life stressor within 6 months of conception—suggesting that, strangely, distress immediately prior to getting pregnant may weigh most heavily in determining the baby's health. After reading the information on fetal programming below this section, can you think of some possible reasons why this might be so?
Data from: Class and others, 2013.

- **The intensity, quality, and timing of the stress may matter.** Does the person have an overload of problems, few social supports, or is she experiencing a difficult (perhaps unwanted) pregnancy? Anxieties about fetal health, not unexpectedly, are more common in older moms (Bayrampour and others, 2013). One study showed excessive stress in the latter part of pregnancy increased the chance of premature labor (Cole-Lewis and others, 2014). Then, ironically—as if women didn't have enough to worry about—notice from Figure 2.9, that other researchers discovered traumatic events *prior* to getting pregnant compromised the baby's health (Class and others, 2013)!

- **The person's personality and coping style matters most.** In thoughtfully reviewing these confusing findings, developmentalists concluded that the critical variable relates to the way women *handle* stress (Guardino & Schetter, 2014). Does the person behave proactively, taking constructive steps to confront problems, or bury her difficulties by using avoidant strategies? Denying distress, or passively breaking down, and, of course, resorting to binge drinking or smoking to cope, raises the risk of giving birth early and having a frail child.

But suppose the trauma is so overwhelming that it's impossible to constructively cope. Imagine that while a woman is pregnant a disaster occurs—a war or an earthquake—or a person is so poor she doesn't have enough to eat. Can these experiences have a lifelong impact on her child?

Is Pregnancy a Programmer of Old Age?

The answer may be yes. For instance, during World War II, in 1944, the Germans cut off the food supply to Holland, putting that nation in a semi-starvation condition for a few months. As you might imagine, miscarriages and stillbirths were far more frequent during this "Hunger Winter." But even the surviving babies had enduring scars. Midlife heart disease rates were higher if a baby had been in the womb *specifically* during the Hunger Winter (Paul, 2010). Another landmark study had a similar result: Babies born in the most impoverished sections of England and Wales were more susceptible to dying from cardiovascular disease at a young age (Paul, 2010).

Why might deprivation in the womb be linked to premature, age-related disease? Speculations again center on being born too small. When fetuses are deprived of nutrients and/or exposed to intense maternal stress, researchers hypothesize, the resulting impaired growth primes the baby to enter the world expecting "a state of deprivation" and to eat excessively or store fat. But while this strategy promotes survival when nutrition is scarce, it boomerangs—promoting obesity and a potentially shorter life—when a child arrives in the world in today's era of overabundant food.

Is obesity (and adult chronic disease) caused just by personal lifestyle choices or partly promoted by a poor body-environment fit at birth? These tantalizing questions are driving **fetal programming research**—studies exploring how intrauterine events may *epigenetically* change our genetic code (Belsky & Pluess, 2011).

Imagine being this terrified woman as she surveys the rubble of her collapsed house. What is the impact of disasters, like this Malaysian landslide, on babies in the womb? Fetal programming research offers fascinating answers.

Freud revolutionized the twentieth century by arguing that childhood experiences shape personality. Will twenty-first-century scientists trace the roots of human development to experiences in the womb?

Fetal programming research is action oriented. Ideally, we can take steps before birth to influence a child's fate. With these next conditions, the problems are often more serious. They are frequently diagnosed at birth. This is because the child's condition is "genetic." It was sealed at conception with the union of an egg and sperm.

Threats from Within: Chromosomal and Genetic Disorders

When a birth defect is classified as "genetic," there are two main causes. The child might have an unusual number of chromosomes, or a faulty gene (or set of genes) might be the problem.

Chromosomal Problems

As we know, the normal human chromosomal complement is 46. However, sometimes a baby with a missing or extra chromosome is conceived. The vast majority of these fertilizations end in first-trimester miscarriages, as the cells cannot differentiate much past the blastocyst stage.

Still, babies can be born with an abnormal number of sex chromosomes (such as an extra X or two, an extra Y, or a single X) and survive. In this case, although the symptoms vary, the result is often learning impairments and sometimes infertility.

Survival is also possible when a child is born with an extra chromosome on a specific other pair. The most common example—happening in roughly 1 in every 700 births (National Down Syndrome Society [NDSS], n.d.)—produces a baby with Down syndrome.

Down syndrome typically occurs because a cell-division error, called *nondisjunction*, in the egg or sperm causes an extra chromosome or piece of that copy to adhere to chromosome pair 21. (Figure 2.3, on page 38, shows this is the smallest matching set, so the reason extra material adhering to chromosome 21 is not uniformly lethal is that this pair generally contains the fewest genes.) The child is born with 47 chromosomes instead of the normal 46.

This extra chromosome produces familiar physical features: a flat facial profile, an upward slant to the eyes, a stocky appearance, and an enlarged tongue. Babies born with Down syndrome are at high risk for having heart defects and childhood leukemia. Here, too, there is a lifespan time-bomb impact. During midlife, many adults with Down syndrome develop Alzheimer's disease. The most well-known problem with this familiar condition, however, is mild to moderate intellectual disability.

A century ago, Down syndrome children rarely lived to adulthood. They were shunted to institutions to live severely shortened lives. In the United States today,

fetal programming research
New research discipline exploring the impact of traumatic pregnancy events and intense stress on producing low birth weight, obesity, and long-term physical problems.

Down syndrome The most common chromosomal abnormality, causing intellectual disability, susceptibility to heart disease, and other health problems; and distinctive physical characteristics, such as slanted eyes and stocky build.

Lauren Shear/Science Source

Knowing a Down syndrome child has a powerful effect on every person. Will this older girl become a more caring, sensitive adult through having played with this much loved younger friend?

due to medical advances, these babies have an average life expectancy of 60 years (NDSS, retrieved 2014). Ironically, this longevity gain can be a double-edged sword. Elderly parent caregivers may worry what will happen to their middle-aged child when they die or become physically impaired (Gath, 1993).

This is not to say that every Down syndrome baby is dependent on a caregiver's help. These children can sometimes learn to read and write. They can live independently, hold down jobs, marry and have children, construct fulfilling lives. Do you know a child with Down syndrome like the toddler in this photo who is the light of her loving family and friends' lives?

Although women of any age can give birth to Down syndrome babies, the risk rises exponentially among older mothers. Over age 40, the chance of having a Down syndrome birth is 1 in 100; over age 45, it is 1 in 30 (NDSS, n.d.). The reason is that, with more time "in storage," older ova are more apt to develop chromosomal faults.

Down syndrome is typically caused by a spontaneous genetic mistake. Now let's look at a different category of genetic disorders—those passed down in the parents' DNA to potentially affect *every* child.

Genetic Disorders

Most illnesses—from cancer to heart disease to schizophrenia—are caused by complex nature-plus-nurture interactions. Several, often unknown, genes act in conjunction with murky environmental forces. A *single*, known gene causes these next disorders that often appear at birth.

Single-gene disorders are passed down according to three modes of inheritance: They may be *dominant, recessive,* or *sex-linked.* To understand these patterns, you might want to look back again at the paired arrangement of the chromosomes in Figure 2.3 (page 38) and remember that we get one copy of each gene from our mother and one from our father. Also, in understanding these illnesses, it is important to know that one member of each gene pair can be dominant. This means that the quality will always show up in real life. If both members of the gene pair are not dominant (that is, if they are recessive), the illness will manifest itself only if the child inherits two of the faulty genes.

Dominant disorders are in the first category. In this case, if one parent harbors the problem gene (and so has the illness), each child the couple gives birth to has a fifty-fifty chance of also getting ill.

Recessive disorders are in the second category. Unless a person gets two copies of the gene, one from the father and one from the mother, that child is disease free. In this case, the odds of a baby born to two carriers—that is, parents who each have one copy of that gene—having the illness are 1 in 4.

The mode of transmission for **sex-linked single-gene disorders** is more complicated. Most often, the woman is carrying a recessive (non-expressed in real life) gene for the illness on *one* of her two X chromosomes. Since her daughters have another X from their father (who doesn't carry the illness), the female side of the family is typically disease free. Her sons, however—with just one X chromosome that might code for the disorder—have a fifty-fifty chance of getting ill, depending on whether they get the normal or abnormal version of their mother's X.

single-gene disorder An illness caused by a single gene.

dominant disorder An illness that a child gets by inheriting one copy of the abnormal gene that causes the disorder.

recessive disorder An illness that a child gets by inheriting two copies of the abnormal gene that causes the disorder.

sex-linked single-gene disorder An illness, carried on the mother's X chromosome, that typically leaves the female offspring unaffected but has a fifty-fifty chance of striking each male child.

Because their single X leaves them vulnerable, sex-linked disorders typically affect males. But as an intellectual exercise, you might want to figure out when females can get this condition. If you guessed that it's when the mother is a carrier (having one faulty X) and the dad has the disorder (having the gene on his single X), you are right!

Table 2.3 visually decodes these modes of inheritance and describes a few of the best-known single-gene diseases. In scanning the first illness on the chart, Huntington's

Table 2.3: Some Examples of Dominant, Recessive, and Sex-Linked Single-Gene Disorders

Dominant Disorders

- **Huntington's disease (HD)** This fatal nervous system disorder is characterized by uncontrollable jerky movements and irreversible intellectual impairment (dementia). Symptoms usually appear around age 35, although the illness can occasionally erupt in childhood and in old age. There is no treatment for this disease.

Recessive Disorders

- **Cystic fibrosis (CF)** This most common single-gene disorder in the United States is typically identified at birth by the salty character of the sweat. The child's body produces mucus that clogs the lungs and pancreas, interfering with breathing and digestion and causing repeated medical crises. As the hairlike cells in the lungs are destroyed, these vital organs degenerate and eventually cause premature death. Advances in treatment have extended the average life expectancy for people with CF to the late twenties. One in 28 U.S. Caucasians is a carrier for this disease.*

- **Sickle cell anemia** This blood disorder takes its name from the characteristic sickle shape of the red blood cells. The blood cells collapse and clump together, causing oxygen deprivation and organ damage. The symptoms of sickle cell anemia are fatigue, pain, growth retardation, ulcers, stroke, and, ultimately, a shortened life. Treatments include transfusions and medications for infection and pain. One in 10 African Americans is a carrier of this disease.*

- **Tay-Sachs disease** In this universally fatal infant nervous system disorder, the child appears healthy at birth, but then fatty material accumulates in the neurons and, at 6 months, symptoms such as blindness, intellectual disability, and paralysis occur and the baby dies. Tay-Sachs is found most often among Jewish people of Eastern European ancestry. An estimated 1 in 25 U.S. Jews is a carrier.†

Sex-Linked Disorders

- **Hemophilia** These blood-clotting disorders typically affect males. The most serious forms of hemophilia (A and B) produce severe episodes of uncontrolled joint bleeding and pain. In the past, these episodes often resulted in death during childhood. Today, with transfusions of the missing clotting factors, affected children can have a fairly normal life expectancy.

*Sickle cell anemia may have remained in the population because having the trait (one copy of the gene) conferred an evolutionary advantage: It protected against malaria in Africa. Scientists also speculate that the cystic fibrosis trait may have conferred immunity to typhoid fever.

†Due to a vigorous public awareness program in the Jewish community, potential carriers are routinely screened and the rate of Tay-Sachs disease has declined dramatically.

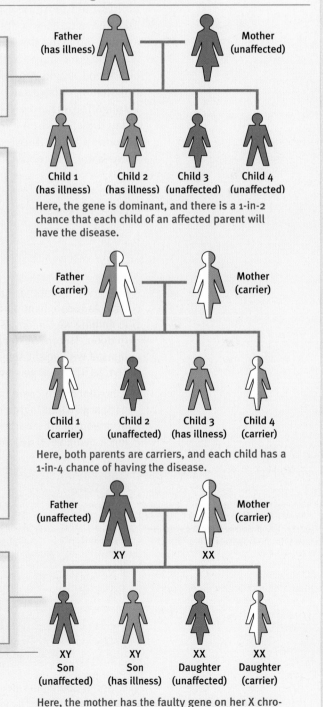

Here, the gene is dominant, and there is a 1-in-2 chance that each child of an affected parent will have the disease.

Here, both parents are carriers, and each child has a 1-in-4 chance of having the disease.

Here, the mother has the faulty gene on her X chromosome, so the daughters are typically disease-free, but each son has a 1-in-2 chance of getting ill.

disease, imagine your emotional burden as a genetically at-risk child. People with Huntington's develop an incurable dementia in the prime of life. As a child you would probably have watched a beloved parent lose his memory and bodily functions, and then die. You would know that your odds of suffering the same fate are 1 in 2. (Although babies born with lethal dominant genetic disorders typically die before they can have children, Huntington's disease remained in the population because it, too, operates as an internal time bomb, showing up during the prime reproductive years.)

With the other illnesses in the table—programmed by recessive genes—the fears relate to bearing a child. If both you and your partner have the Tay-Sachs carrier gene, you may have seen a beloved baby die in infancy. With cystic fibrosis, your affected child would be subject to recurrent medical crises as his lungs filled up with fluid, and he would face a dramatically shortened life. Would you want to take the 1-in-4 chance of having this experience again?

The good news, as the table shows, is that the prognoses for some routinely fatal childhood single-gene disorders are no longer as dire. With hemophilia, the life-threatening episodes of bleeding can be avoided by supplying the missing blood factor through transfusions. While surviving to the teens with cystic fibrosis used to be rare, today these children can expect on average to live to their twenties and sometimes beyond (CysticFibrosis.com, n.d.). Still, with Tay-Sachs or Huntington's disease, there is *nothing* medically that can be done.

HOW DO WE KNOW . . .
about the gene for Huntington's disease?

Nancy Wexler and her sister got the devastating news from their physician father, Milton: "Your mother has Huntington's disease. She will die of dementia in a horrible way. As a dominant single gene disorder, your chance of getting ill is fifty-fifty. There is nothing we can do. (See Table 2.3.) But that doesn't mean we are going to give up." In 1969, Milton Wexler established the Hereditary Disease Foundation, surrounded himself with scientists, and put his young daughter, Nancy, a clinical psychologist, in charge. The hunt was on for the Huntington's gene.

A breakthrough came in 1979, when Nancy learned that the world's largest group of people with Huntington's lived in a small, inbred community in Venezuela—descendants of a woman who harbored the gene mutation that caused the disease. After building a pedigree of 18,000 family members, collecting blood samples from thousands

more, and carefully analyzing the DNA for differences, the researchers hit pay dirt. They isolated the Huntington's gene.

Having this diagnostic marker is the first step to eventually finding a cure. So far the cure is elusive, but the hunt continues. Nancy still serves as the head of the foundation, vigorously agitating for research on the illness that killed her mother. She works as a professor in Columbia University's Neurology and Psychiatry Department. But every year, she comes back to the village in Venezuela to counsel and just visit with her families—her relatives in blood.

Acey Harper/The LIFE Images Collection/Getty Images

In sum, the answer to the question "Can single-gene disorders be treated and cured?" is "It depends." Although people still have the faulty gene—and so are not "cured" in the traditional sense—through advances in nurture (or changing the environment), we have made remarkable progress in treating what used to be uniformly fatal diseases.

Our most dramatic progress, however, lies in **genetic testing.** Through a simple blood test, people can find out whether they carry the gene for these (and other) illnesses.

These diagnostic breakthroughs bring up difficult issues. Would you really want to know whether you have the gene for Huntington's disease? The inspiring story of Nancy Wexler, the psychologist who helped discover the Huntington's gene and whose mother died of the disease, is instructive here (see the How Do We Know box). While Nancy will not say whether she has been tested, her sister Alice refused to be screened because she felt not knowing was better emotionally than the anguish of living with a positive result.

Interventions

The advantages of genetic testing are clearer when the issue relates to having a child. Let's imagine for instance that you and your spouse know you are carriers of the cystic fibrosis gene. If you are contemplating having children, what should you do?

Sorting Out the Options: Genetic Counseling

Your first step would be to consult a **genetic counselor,** a professional skilled in both genetics and counseling, to help you think through your choices. In addition to laying out the odds of having an affected child, genetic counselors describe advances in treatment. For example, they inform couples who are carriers for cystic fibrosis about biological strategies on the horizon, such as gene therapy. They also highlight the interpersonal and economic costs of having a child with this disease. But they are trained never to offer advice. Their goal is to permit couples to make a *mutual decision* on their own.

Now, suppose that armed with this information, you and your partner go ahead and conceive. Let's scan the major tests that are available to every woman carrying a child.

Tools of Discovery: Prenatal Tests

Blood tests performed during the first trimester can detect (with reasonable accuracy) various chromosomal conditions, such as Down syndrome. Brain scans (MRIs) offer a vivid prenatal window on the developing brain (Jokhi & Whitby, 2011). The standard fetal diagnostic test has been a staple for over 40 years: the **ultrasound.**

Ultrasounds, which now provide a clear image of fetus (see the accompanying photo), are used to date the pregnancy and assess in utero growth, in addition to revealing physical abnormalities. By making the baby visually real, ultrasound visits have become emotional landmarks on the pregnancy journey itself (Paul, 2010). Imagine the thrill of getting this vivid photo of your baby months before she is born!

Pregnant women embrace ultrasound technology and noninvasive genetic tests (Verweij and others, 2013). They tend to be more wary of the next procedures, because those require entering the womb.

During the first trimester, **chorionic villus sampling (CVS)** can diagnose a variety of chromosomal and genetic conditions. A physician inserts a catheter into the woman's abdomen or vagina and withdraws a piece of the developing placenta for analysis. The advantage of CVS, is knowing early on about problems; however, this test can be slightly dangerous, as it carries a risk of miscarriage and limb impairments (Karni, Leshno, & Rapaport, 2014).

genetic testing A blood test to determine whether a person carries the gene for a given genetic disorder.

genetic counselor A professional who counsels parents-to-be about their own or their children's risk of developing genetic disorders, as well as about available treatments.

ultrasound In pregnancy, an image of the fetus in the womb that helps to date the pregnancy, assess the fetus's growth, and identify abnormalities.

chorionic villus sampling (CVS) A relatively risky first-trimester pregnancy test for fetal genetic disorders.

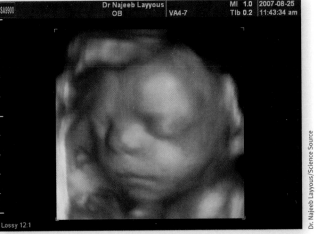

Dr. Najeeb Layyous/Science Source

Due to the miracles of 3D ultrasound technology, when women visit their health-care provider, they can have the thrill of clearly seeing their baby's face. As they peer through this "window on the womb," doctors can get vital information about the health of this 26-week-old fetus, too.

TIMELINE	Prenatal Development, Pregnancy, Prenatal Threats, Tools of Discovery		
	Germinal stage (weeks 1 and 2)	**Embryonic stage (weeks 3–8)**	**Fetal stage (weeks 9–38)**
PRENATAL DEVELOPMENT	Zygote → blastocyst, which implants in uterus.	All major organs and structures form.	Massive growth and refinements; brain develops; live birth is possible at 22–24 weeks.
THREATS	At fertilization: chromosomal and single-gene diseases.	Teratogens can cause basic structural abnormalities.	Teratogens can impair growth, affect the brain, and so cause developmental disorders. They can also produce miscarriage or premature labor.

amniocentesis A second-trimester procedure that involves inserting a syringe into a woman's uterus to extract a sample of amniotic fluid, which is tested for a variety of genetic and chromosomal conditions.

During the second trimester, a safer test, called **amniocentesis,** can determine the fetus's fate. The doctor inserts a syringe into the woman's uterus and extracts a sample of amniotic fluid. The cells can reveal a host of genetic and chromosomal conditions, as well as the fetus's sex.

Amniocentesis is planned for a gestational age (typically week 14) when there is enough fluid to safely siphon out and time to decide whether or not to carry the baby to term. However, it, too, carries a small chance of infection and miscarriage, depending on the skill of the doctor performing the test (Karni, Lescho & Rapaport, 2014). Moreover by the time the results of the "amnio" arrive, quickening may have occurred. The woman must endure the trauma of labor should she decide to terminate the pregnancy at this late stage.

Because their risk of having a child with chromosomal disorders is higher, many doctors suggest that patients over age 35 have these procedures. But, not unexpectedly, more women in their forties agree to tested; and, because it is safer, more people undergo amniocentesis than CVS (Godino and others, 2013).

When these couples receive a diagnosis of serious chromosomal problems, most do terminate the pregnancy—roughly 8 in 10 in one study at a U.S. hospital (Hawkins and others, 2013). Still, some people who would never consider abortion undergo testing to ease their anxieties or to prepare in advance if their baby does have a genetic disease. While a diagnosis of serious fetal problems is devastating to both moms and dads, for women specifically—perhaps because they are carrying the child inside—it may be more traumatic to get this news during pregnancy than at birth (Fonseca, Nazare, & Canavarro, 2014).

The summary timeline spanning these pages shows these procedures and charts the landmark events of prenatal development and pregnancy. I cannot emphasize strongly enough that giving birth to a baby with serious birth defects is rare. That is not true of the topic I turn to now—problems in conceiving a child.

Infertility and New Reproductive Technologies

I'll never forget the comment my sister made . . . when I was about 13. I said, "I'm a woman because I have my period" . . . . And she said, "You are not a woman until you have a baby" (from a woman who after years of infertility adopted a child).

(quoted in Loftus & Androit, 2012, p. 23)

According to Psalm 127:3, "Children are a heritage unto the Lord and the fruit of his womb is His Reward." So why didn't I get this gift? I asked myself over and over if I was being punished.

(quoted in Ferland and Caron, 2013, p. 183)

These quotations have an ageless quality. Since biblical times, humanity has equated womanhood with bearing a child. The message that "being barren" is a terrible,

	First trimester (month 1–month 3)	Second trimester (month 4–month 6)	Third trimester (month 7–month 9)
PREGNANCY	Morning sickness, tiredness, and other unpleasant symptoms may occur; miscarriage is a worry.	Woman looks pregnant. Quickening occurs (around week 18). Mother can feel intensely bonded to baby.	Woman gets very large and anxiously waits for birth.
TOOLS OF DISCOVERY	Ultrasound Blood tests Chorionic villus sampling (CVS) around week 10	Ultrasound Amniocentesis (around week 15)	Ultrasound

female fate is an underlying message beginning in *Genesis*. When his beloved wife Sarah couldn't get pregnant, the Biblical patriarch Abraham felt compelled to "procreate" with a substitute wife.

Infertility—the inability to conceive a child after a year of unprotected intercourse—is far from rare. In affluent nations, it affects an estimated 1 in 6 couples. In poor countries, the statistics may be as high as 1 in 4. Moreover, infertility rates have been rising over the past half-century, due to sexually transmitted diseases in the developing world and the fact that so many developed world women today are delaying childbearing to their thirties and beyond (Petraglia, Serour, & Chapron, 2013).

While infertility can affect women (and men) of every age, just as with miscarriage and Down syndrome—as we know from the standard phrase, "the ticking of the biological clock"—getting pregnant is far more difficult at older ages. Within the first six months of trying, roughly 3 out of 4 women in their twenties conceives. At age 40, only 1 out of 5 achieves that goal (Turkington & Alper, 2001). Because of their more complicated anatomy, many of us assume infertility is usually a "female" problem. Not so! Male issues—which can vary from low sperm motility to varicose veins in the testicles—are *equally* likely to be involved (Turkington & Alper, 2001).

Infertility puts stress on both partners. Still, as the quotes at the beginning of this section suggest, this life trauma is apt to hit women hardest (Teskereci & Oncel, 2013). Although they are more immune from feelings of having personally failed (Herrera, 2013), males have pressures to prove their manhood by fathering a child. In one Danish questionnaire study, almost 1 in 3 patients at a male fertility clinic confessed that their condition affected their sense of masculinity and self-esteem (Mikkelsen, Madsen, & Humaidan, 2013).

The impact varies in intensity, depending on one's culture. In places like Iran, where not being able to bear a child is sometimes an accepted reason for divorce (more about this in Chapter 11), infertility can leave a woman shunned by family and friends (Behboodi-Moghamdam and others, 2013). There may be a feeling of being socially isolated, even in the liberal West. Imagine going to dinner parties and needing to listen quietly as everyone at the table bonds around the joys and trials of having kids.

And, when you are in these situations, do you discuss your situation, or clam up? Revealing your problem to parents—especially those who are anxious for a grandchild—demands planning: As one woman reported: "They (my husband's parents) live over 3 hours away and we didn't want to start the conversation over the phone. And so we went to visit" (quoted in Bute, 2013 p. 172).

Does telling people help? If, and *only if*, you have a caring, social-support system, you may feel relieved by being upfront: "Yes, I'm trying to get pregnant but it's not working, Mom" (Martins and others, 2013). But, the bottom-line message is that, in coping with infertility, having a supportive partner matters most (Darwiche and

infertility The inability to conceive after a year of unprotected sex. (Includes the inability to carry a child to term.)

others, 2013). Read this lovely comment taken from another interview study conducted with long-time infertile women:

> When I told him (my second husband) when we were dating that I could not have children, he said, "If god wanted me to have kids, he would have made me fall in love with a woman who could have them."
>
> (quoted in Ferland & Caron, 2013, p. 186)

Just as with the Biblical patriarch Abraham, whose decision to stay with Sarah is an ageless model for marital love, infertility can offer a chance to demonstrate a person's loving commitment to a mate.

Today, communicating collaboratively around fertility issues is essential, as science offers couples so many options to help fulfill the quest to have a (partly) biological child.

INTERVENTIONS: Exploring ART

For females, there are treatments to attack every problem on the reproductive chain (see the illustration in Figure 2.10)—from fertility drugs to stimulate ovulation, to hormonal supplements to foster implantation; from surgery to help clean out the uterus and the fallopian tubes, to artificial insemination (inserting the sperm into the woman's uterus through a syringe). Males may take medications or undergo surgery to increase the quality and motility of the sperm. Then there is that ultimate approach: **assisted reproductive technology (ART).**

Assisted reproductive technology refers to any strategy in which the egg is fertilized outside the womb. The most widely used ART procedure is **in vitro fertilization (IVF).** After the woman is given fertility drugs (which stimulate multiple ovulations), her eggs are harvested and put in a laboratory dish, along with the partner's sperm, to be fertilized. A few days later, the fertilized eggs are inserted into the uterus. Then, the couple anxiously waits to find out if the cells have implanted in the uterine wall.

In vitro fertilization, initially developed to bypass blocked fallopian tubes, has spawned amazing variations. A sperm may be injected directly into the ovum if it cannot penetrate the surface on its own. The woman may use a donor egg—one from another woman— in order to conceive. Or, she may go to a sperm bank to utilize a donor sperm. The fertilized eggs may be inserted into a "carrier womb"—a surrogate mother, who carries the couple's genetic offspring to term.

Imagine the emotions that can arise when another person is carrying your baby, or if the child you are carrying has another woman's (or man's) genes. And,

assisted reproductive technology (ART) Any infertility treatment in which the egg is fertilized outside the womb.

in vitro fertilization An infertility treatment in which conception occurs outside the womb; the developing cell mass is then inserted into the woman's uterus so that pregnancy can occur.

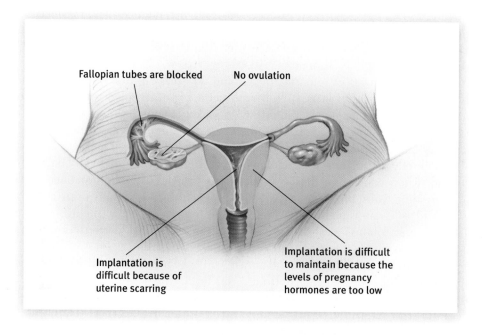

FIGURE 2.10: Some possible missteps on the path to reproduction: In this diagram, you can see some problems that may cause infertility in women. You can also use it to review the ovulation-to-implantation sequence.

Fallopian tubes are blocked

No ovulation

Implantation is difficult because of uterine scarring

Implantation is difficult to maintain because the levels of pregnancy hormones are too low consider the expense of these added "pregnancy players." As the cost of soliciting a donor egg can be as high as $30,000, and fees to the donor vary from $5,000 to $15,000, an ART investment can top $40,000—and that's *before* each roughly $12,000 round of treatments even begins (See Jaffe & Diamond, 2011.)!

Now, imagine enduring the invasive techniques used to harvest and insert the eggs, and managing your monthly anguish if a pregnancy doesn't occur. According to 2012 U.S. data, the odds of a woman under age 35 getting pregnant after a round of in vitro treatments was less than fifty/fifty. Over age 42, success rates per cycle slid down to less than 1 in 10 (Society for Assisted Reproductive Technologies, retrieved 2014).

Critics emphasize the headaches (and heartaches) involved in ART; the pain, expense, and the chance of miscarrying if many eggs take (often to counter this risk, doctors engage in a procedure gently named "fetal reduction"); the virtual certainty of having fragile, small babies when several conceptions come to term (Gentile, 2014; Centers for Disease Control and Prevention (CDC), retrieved 2014); or the issues attached to third-party arrangements: ("Should I meet my egg or sperm donor?" "Do I tell my child this person exists?") (Johnson, 2013). In nations such as Israel—which has the highest ART rates in the world—people argue about whether the government should fund this procedure for women "simply" for wanting a second or third child (Gooldin, 2013).

These complaints ignore the gift ART provides. This landmark technology has given thousands of infertile couples their only chance to have a biological child: "I could never have accomplished all of this myself," gushed one grateful Taiwanese woman. Another said: "I no longer felt pitiful. . . . My child represents the continuation of my life" (quoted in Lin, Tsai, and Lai, 2013, p. 194).

Tying It All Together

1. Teratogen A caused limb malformations. Teratogen B caused developmental disorders. Teratogen A wreaked its damage during the_____ stage of prenatal development and was taken during the_____ trimester of pregnancy, while teratogen B probably did its damage during the _____stage and was taken during the _____ trimester.

2. Seto and Brandon's mothers contracted rubella (German measles) during different weeks in their first trimester of pregnancy. Seto has heart problems; Brandon has hearing problems. Which teratogenic principle is illustrated here?

3. Monique is planning to become pregnant and asks her physician if it will be okay for her to have a glass of wine with dinner each night. What would her doctor answer if Monique lived in the United States? What might the doctor say if Monique lived in France?

4. Imagine that in 2016, a tornado hits Nashville, Tennessee. Based on the fetal programming research, which *two* predictions might you make about babies who were in-utero during that time?

   a. They might be at higher risk of being born small.
   b. They might be at higher risk of developing premature heart disease.
   c. They might be at higher risk of being very thin throughout life.

5. Latasha gives birth to a child with Down syndrome, while Jennifer gives birth to a child with cystic fibrosis. Which woman should be more worried about having another child with that condition, and why?

6. To a friend who is thinking of choosing between chorionic villus sampling (CVS) and amniocentesis, mention the advantages and disadvantages of each procedure.

7. Jennifer and Brad are considering ART, after years of unsuccessful fertility treatments. First describe some pros and cons of this procedure. According to the text, what force is most critical in determining how well Jennifer has been coping with her troubles getting pregnant?

Answers to the Tying It All Together questions can be found at the end of this chapter.

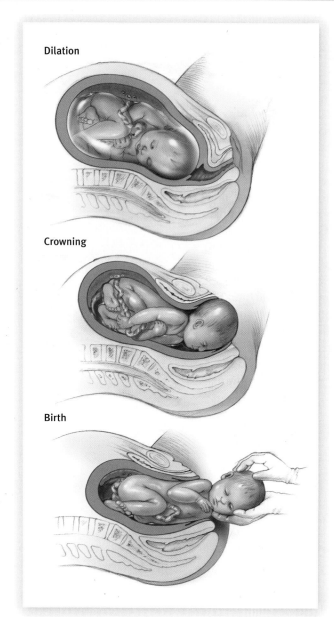

Dilation

Crowning

Birth

FIGURE 2.11: **Labor and childbirth:** In the first stage of labor, the cervix dilates; then, in the second stage, the baby's head emerges and the baby is born.

Now let's look at what happens when these wished-for pregnancies—or any pregnancies—reach the final step: exploring the miracle of birth.

Birth

During the last weeks of pregnancy, the fetus's head drops lower into the uterus. On their weekly visits to the health-care provider, women, such as Kim in the opening chapter vignette, may be told, "It should be any minute now." The uterus begins to contract as it prepares for birth. The cervix thins out and softens under the weight of the child. Anticipation builds . . . and then—she waits!

> I am 39 weeks and desperate for some sign that labor is near, but so far NOTHING—no softening of the cervix, no contractions, and the baby has not dropped—the idea of two more weeks makes me want to SCREAM!!!

What sets off labor? One hypothesis is that the trigger is a hormonal signal that the fetus sends to the mother's brain. Once it's officially under way, labor proceeds through three stages.

Stage 1: Dilation and Effacement

This first stage of labor is the most arduous. The thick cervix, which has held in the expanding fetus for so long, has finished its job. Now it must *efface*, or thin out, and *dilate*, or widen from a tiny gap about the size of a dime to the width of a coffee mug or a medium-sized bowl of soup. This transformation is accomplished by *contractions*—muscular, wavelike batterings against the uterine floor. The uterus is far stronger than a boxer's biceps. Even at the beginning of labor, the contractions put about 30 pounds of pressure on the cervix to expand to its cuplike shape.

The contractions start out slowly, perhaps 20 to 30 minutes apart. They become more frequent and painful as the cervix more rapidly opens up. Sweating, nausea, and intense pain can accompany the final phase—as the closely spaced contractions reach a crescendo, and the baby is poised for the miracle of birth (see Figure 2.11).

Stage 2: Birth

The fetus descends through the uterus and enters the vagina, or birth canal. Then, as the baby's scalp appears (an event called *crowning*), parents get their first exciting glimpse of this new life. The shoulders rotate; the baby slowly slithers out, to be captured and cradled as it enters the world. The prenatal journey has ended; the journey of life is about to begin.

Stage 3: The Expulsion of the Placenta

In the ecstasy of the birth, the final event is almost unnoticed. The placenta and other supporting structures must be pushed out. Fully expelling these materials is essential to avoid infection and to help the uterus return to its pre-pregnant state.

Threats at Birth

Just as with pregnancy, a variety of missteps may happen during this landmark passage into life: problems with the contraction mechanism; the inability of the cervix to fully dilate; deviations from the normal head-down position as the fetus descends and positions itself for birth (this atypical positioning, with feet, buttocks, or knees first, is called a *breech birth*); difficulties stemming from the position of the placenta or the umbilical cord as the baby makes its way into the world. Today, these in-transit troubles are easily surmounted through obstetrical techniques. This was not true in the past.

Birth Options, Past and Present

For most of human history, pregnancy was a grim nine-month march to an uncertain end (Kitzinger, 2000; Wertz & Wertz, 1989). The eighteenth-century New England preacher Cotton Mather captured the emotions of his era when, on learning that a parish woman was pregnant, he thundered, "Your death has entered into you!" Not only were there the hazards involved in getting the baby to emerge, but a raging infection called childbed fever could also set in and kill a new mother (and her child) within days.

Women had only one another or lay midwives to rely on during this frightening time. So birth was a social event. Friends and relatives flocked around, perhaps traveling miles to offer comfort when the woman's due date drew near. Doctors were of little help, because they could not view the female anatomy directly. In fact, due to their clumsiness (using primitive forceps to yank the baby out) and their tendency to spread childbed fever by failing to wash their hands, eighteenth- and nineteenth-century doctors often made the situation worse (Wertz & Wertz, 1989).

Techniques gradually improved toward the end of the nineteenth century, but few wealthy women dared enter hospitals to deliver, as these institutions were hotbeds of contagious disease. Then, with the early-twentieth-century conquest of many infectious diseases, it became fashionable for affluent middle-class women to have a "modern" hospital birth. By the late 1930s, the science of obstetrics gained the upper hand, fetal mortality plummeted, and birth became genuinely safe (Leavitt, 1986). By the turn of this century, in the developed world, this conquest was virtually complete. In 1997, there were only 329 pregnancy-related maternal deaths in the United States (Miniño and others, 2002).

This watershed medical victory was accompanied by discontent. The natural process of birth had become an impersonal event. Women protested the assembly-line hospital procedures; the fact that they were strapped down and sedated in order to give birth. They eagerly devoured books describing the new Lamaze technique, which taught controlled breathing, allowed partner involvement, and promised undrugged births. During the women's movement of the 1960s and early 1970s, the natural-childbirth movement arrived.

Natural Childbirth

Natural childbirth, a vague label for returning the birth experience to its "true" natural state, is now embedded in the labor and birth choices available to women today. To avoid the hospital experience, some women choose to deliver in homelike birthing centers. They may use certified midwives rather than doctors, and draw on the help of a *doula,* a nonmedical pregnancy and labor coach. Women who are committed to the most natural experience may give birth in their own homes. (Table 2.4 on page 62 describes some natural birth options, as well as some commonly used medical procedures.)

At the medical end of the spectrum, as Table 2.4 shows, lies the arsenal of physician interventions designed to promote a less painful and safer birth. Let's now pause for a minute to look at the last procedure in the table: the cesarean section.

This classic nineteenth-century illustration shows just why early doctors were clueless about how to help pregnant women. They could not view the relevant body parts!

natural childbirth A general term for labor and birth without medical interventions.

Table 2.4: The Major Players and Interventions in Labor and Birth

Natural-Birth Providers and Options

Certified midwife: Certified by the American College of Nurse Midwives, this health-care professional is trained to handle *low-risk* deliveries, with obstetrical backup should complications arise.

- *Plus:* Offers a birth experience with fewer medical interventions and more humanistic care.
- *Minus:* If the delivery suddenly becomes high risk, an obstetrician may be needed on the scene.

Doula: Mirroring the "old-style" female experience, this person provides loving emotional and physical support during labor, offering massage and help in breathing and relaxation, but not performing actual health-care tasks, such as vaginal exams. (Doulas have no medical training.)

- *Plus:* Provides caring support from an advocate.
- *Minus:* Drives up the birth expense.

Lamaze method: Developed by the French physician Ferdinand Lamaze, this popular method prepares women for childbirth by teaching pain management through relaxation and breathing exercises.

- *Plus:* Offers a shared experience with a partner (who acts as the coach) and the sense of approaching the birth experience with greater control.
- *Minus:* Doesn't necessarily work for pain control "as advertised"!

Bradley method: Developed by Robert Bradley in the 1940s, this technique is designed for women interested in having a completely natural, nonmedicated birth. It stresses good diet and exercise, partner coaching, and deep relaxation.

- *Plus:* Tailored for women firmly committed to forgoing any medical interventions.
- *Minus:* May set women up for disappointment if things don't go as planned and they need those interventions.

Medical Interventions

Episiotomy: The cutting of the perineum or vagina to widen that opening and allow the fetus to emerge (not recommended unless there is a problem delivery).*

- *Plus:* May prevent a fistula, a vaginal tear into the rectal opening, which produces chronic incontinence and pain.
- *Minus:* May increase the risk of infection after delivery and hinder healing.

Epidural: This most popular type of anesthesia used during labor involves injecting a painkilling medication into a small space outside the spinal cord to numb the woman's body below the waist. Epidurals are now used during the active stage of labor—effectively dulling much of the pain—and during c-sections, so that the woman is awake to see her child during the first moments after birth.

- *Plus:* Combines optimum pain control with awareness; because the dose can be varied, the woman can see everything, and she has enough feeling to push during vaginal deliveries.
- *Minus:* Can slow the progress of labor in vaginal deliveries, can result in headaches, and is subject to errors if the needle is improperly inserted. Concerns also center on the fact that the newborn may emerge "groggy."

Electronic fetal monitor: This device is used to monitor the fetus's heart rate and alert the doctor to distress. With an external monitor, the woman wears two belts around her abdomen. With an internal monitor, an electrode is inserted through the cervix to record the heart rate through the fetal scalp.

- *Plus:* Shown to be useful in high-risk pregnancies.
- *Minus:* Can give false readings, leading to a premature c-section. Also, its superiority over the lower-tech method of listening to the baby's heartbeat with a stethoscope has not been demonstrated.

C-section: The doctor makes an incision in the abdominal wall and the uterus and removes the fetus manually.

- *Plus:* Is life-saving to the mother and baby when a vaginal delivery cannot occur (as when the baby is too big to emerge or the placenta is obstructing the cervix). Also is needed when the mother has certain health problems or when the fetus is in serious distress.
- *Minus:* As a surgical procedure, it is more expensive than vaginal delivery and can lead to more discomfort after birth.

*Late-twentieth-century research has suggested that the once-common U.S. practice of routinely performing episiotomies had no advantages and actually hindered recovery from birth. Therefore, in recent decades, the episiotomy rate in the United States has declined.

The Cesarean Section

cesarean section (c-section) A method of delivering a baby surgically by extracting the baby through incisions in the woman's abdominal wall and in the uterus.

A **cesarean section** (or **c-section**), in which a surgeon makes incisions in the woman's abdominal wall and enters the uterus to remove the baby, is the lifesaving final solution for labor and delivery problems. This operation exploded in popularity during the 1970s. By the turn of this century, c-sections accounted for an astonishing 1 in 3 U.S. deliveries (Martin and others, 2005).

Some c-sections are planned to occur before labor because the physician knows in advance that there are dangers in a vaginal birth. If the woman is affluent, she can sometimes choose to have a c-section rather than go through labor on her own. As one South African woman graphically explained, "I don't want to push and sweat and moan and tear . . . I don't want to lie and pooh in front of everyone" (Chadwick & Foster, 2013).

Most c-sections, however, occur when there are difficulties once labor has begun. To what degree are these procedures unnecessary, due to health care workers fears of legal liability ("I might get sued unless I get this baby out")? We don't know. What we do know is that the best-laid birth plans may not work out, and some women can feel upset if they had been counting on having a child "the natural way":

> "I sort of feel like I failed in the birthing arena," said one Australian woman . . . "Logically I knew that the c-section was necessary, but somehow I think if I was slim . . . and had not eaten as much ice cream that would not have happened."
>
> (quoted in Malacrida & Boulton, 2014, p. 18)

Finally, while affluent women may bemoan their c-sections, the real tragedy is the horrifying lack of access to high-quality medical interventions in the least-developed regions of the world. In 2010, an estimated 287,000 people died of pregnancy-related causes, typically postpartum hemorrhage, infections, or pregnancy blood-pressure complications that would prompt an immediate c-section in the developed world (Souza and others, 2013; Buttenheim & Asch, 2013). While some relatively poor nations—for instance Iran, Honduras, Thailand, and most central European countries—have made great progress in reducing maternal mortality, others have lost ground. Perhaps due to its chronic wars, child marriage, and the prevalence of HIV (Raj & Boehmer, 2013), sub-Saharan Africa had *worse* maternal death statistics in 2010 than in 1990 (Lawson & Keirse, 2013)! So let's keep in mind that billions of developing world mothers-to-be still approach birth with a more basic concern than their Western counterparts. Their worries are not, "Should I *choose* a c-section?" It's not, "What birth method should I use?" Unfortunately, all too often, it's still: "Will I survive my baby's birth?" (Lester, Benfield, & Fathalla, 2010; Potts, Prata, & Sahin-Hodoglugil, 2010).

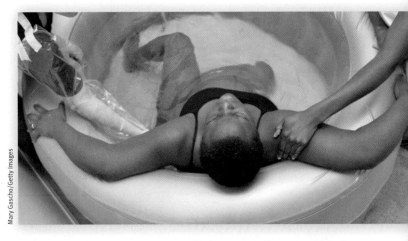

Today, women have a variety of birth choices in the developed world. The woman in this photo is having a water birth.

Mary Gascho/Getty Images

 Tying It All Together

1. Melissa says that her contractions are coming every 10 minutes now. Sonia has just seen her baby's scalp emerge. In which stages of labor are Melissa and Sonia?

2. To a friend interested in having the most natural birth possible, spell out some of these options.

3. C-sections may sometimes *be over-/under* used in the developed world; but life-saving medical interventions are *underutilized/overutilized* in poor areas of the globe.

Answers to the Tying It All Together questions can be found at the end of this chapter.

The Newborn

Now that we have examined how the baby arrives in the world, let's focus on that tiny arrival. What happens after the baby is born? What dangers do babies face after birth?

Tools of Discovery: Testing Newborns

The first step after the newborn enters the world is to evaluate its health in the delivery room with a checklist called the **Apgar scale.** The child's heart rate, muscle tone, respiration, reflex response, and color are rated on a scale of 0 to 2 at one minute and then again at five minutes after birth. Newborns with five-minute Apgar scores over 7 are usually in excellent shape. However, if the score stays below 7, the child must be monitored or resuscitated and kept in the hospital for a while.

Apgar scale A quick test used to assess a just-delivered baby's condition by measuring heart rate, muscle tone, respiration, reflex response, and color.

Threats to Development Just After Birth

After their babies have been checked out medically, most mothers and fathers eagerly take their robust, full-term baby home. But other parents hover at the hospital and anxiously wait. The reason, most often, is that their child has arrived in the world too small and/or too soon.

Born Too Small and Too Soon

low birth weight (LBW) A body weight at birth of less than 5 1/2 pounds.

very low birth weight (VLBW) A body weight at birth of less than 3 1/4 pounds.

neonatal intensive care unit (NICU) A special hospital unit that treats at-risk newborns, such as low-birth-weight and very-low-birth-weight babies.

In 2010, about 15 million babies were born *preterm*, or premature—they entered the world more than three weeks early (Chang and others, 2013). In the United States, about 1 in every 11 babies are categorized as **low birth weight.** They arrive in the world weighing less than 5 1/2 pounds. Babies can be designated low birth weight because they either arrived before their due date or did not grow sufficiently in the womb.

Earlier in this chapter, I highlighted smoking and maternal stress as risk factors for going into labor early and/or having a low birth weight baby. But, uncontrollable influences—such as an infection that prematurely ruptures the amniotic sac, or a cervix that cannot withstand the pressure of the growing fetus's weight—also can cause this too-early or excessively small arrival into life.

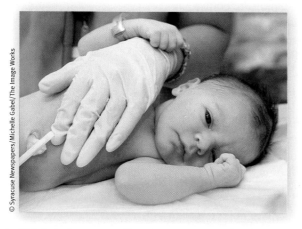

This baby has an excellent Apgar score. Notice his healthy, robust appearance.

You might assume that prematurity has declined in tandem with our pregnancy medical advances. Not so! Ironically, the same cutting-edge procedures discussed earlier, such as c-sections on demand and ART, boost the probability of a baby leaving the womb early and being more frail (Chang and others, 2013).

Many early arrivals are fine. The vulnerable newborns are the 1.4 percent classified as **very low birth weight,** babies weighing less than 3 1/4 pounds. When these infants are delivered, often *very* prematurely, they are immediately rushed to a major medical center to enter a special hospital unit for frail newborns—the **neonatal intensive care unit.**

> At 24 weeks my water broke, and I was put in the hospital and given drugs. I hung on, and then, at week 26, gave birth. Peter was sent by ambulance to Children's Hospital. When I first saw my son, he had needles in every point of his body and was wrapped in plastic to keep his skin from drying out. Peter's intestines had a hole in them, and the doctor had to perform an emergency operation. But Peter made it! . . . Now it's four months later, and my husband and I are about to bring our miracle baby home.

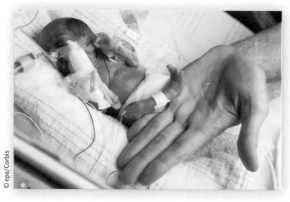

This baby weighing less than one pound was incredibly lucky to make it out of the womb alive—but she is at high risk for having enduring problems as she travels through life.

Peter was lucky. He escaped the fate of the more than 1 million babies who die each year as a consequence of being very premature (Chang and others, 2013). Is this survival story purchased at the price of a life of pain? Enduring health problems are a serious risk with newborns such as Peter, born too soon and excessively small. Study after study suggests low birth weight can compromise brain development (Rose and others, 2014; Yang and others, 2014). It may impair preschoolers' growth and motor abilities (Raz and others, 2014). It can limit intellectual and social skills throughout childhood (Murray and others, 2014) and the adolescent years (Healy and others, 2013; Yang and others, 2014)—in addition, as you know, to possibly promoting overweight and early age-related disease. And what about the costs? Astronomical sums are required to keep frail babies such as Peter alive—expenses that can bankrupt families and are often borne by society as a whole (Caplan, Blank, & Merrick, 1992).

When a child is born at the cusp of viability—at around 22 weeks—doctors, not infrequently, refuse to vigorously intervene (Duffy & Reynolds, 2011; Ramsay & Santella, 2011). But survival rates vary, depending on the individual baby—and very important—that child's access to high-quality care (Sjörs, 2010). Plus, due to dramatic neonatal advances occurring during the 1980s, many more small babies are now living to adulthood unimpaired (Baron & Rey-Casserly, 2010). I have vividly seen these statistics in operation when, in recent years, a student proudly informed our class: "I weighed less than 2 pounds at birth" or "I was born at the twenty-sixth week of life."

Even when they do have disabilities, these tiny babies can have a full life. Listen to my former student Marcia, whose 15-ounce body at birth would have easily fit in the palm of your hand—and whom no doctor believed was capable of surviving. Marcia, as the Experiencing the Lifespan box describes, is partially deaf, blind in one eye, and suffers from the disorder cerebral palsy. But rarely have I met someone so upbeat, joyous, and fully engaged in the world.

The Unthinkable: Infant Mortality

In the developed world, prematurity is the primary cause of **infant mortality**—the term for deaths occurring within the first year of life. The good news is that in affluent nations, infant mortality is at an historic low (see Figure 2.12). The bad news is the dismal standing of the United States compared to many other industrialized countries. Why does the United States rank a humiliating forty-sixth in this basic marker of a society's health?

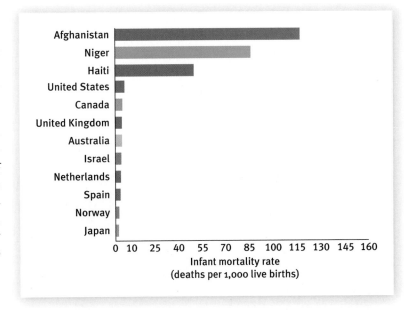

FIGURE 2.12: Deaths of infants under one year of age per 1,000 live births in selected countries (estimated data for 2014): Infant mortality rates vary tremendously around the globe. Notice the huge disparities between affluent and least-developed countries. Also notice that the United States has more than twice the infant mortality rate of Norway and Japan.

Data from: World Factbook, Central Intelligence Agency, Retrieved August 7, 2014.

infant mortality Death during the first year of life.

Experiencing the Lifespan: Marcia's Story

The service elevator at Peck Hall takes forever to get there, then moves in extra-slow motion up to the third floor. If, as sometimes happens, it's out of service, you are out of luck. It's about a 30-minute drive from my dorm in the motorized wheelchair, including the ramps. When it rains, there's the muck—slowing you up—keeping you wet. So I try to leave at least an hour to get to class.

My goal is to be at least five minutes early so I don't disrupt everything as I move the chair, back and forth, back and forth, to be positioned right in front. Because my bad eye wanders to the side, you may not think I can read the board. That's no problem, although it takes me weeks to get through a chapter in your book! The CP [cerebral palsy], as you know, affects my vocal cords, making it hard to get a sentence out. But I won't be ashamed. I am determined to participate in class. I have my note-taker. I have my hearing amplifier turned up to catch every sound. My mind is on full alert. I'm set to go.

I usually can take about two courses each semester—sometimes one. I'm careful to screen my teachers to make sure they will work with me. I'm almost 30 and still only a junior, but I'm determined to get my degree. I'd like to be a counselor and work with CP kids. I know all about it—the troubles, the physical pain, what people are like.

I'm not sure exactly what week I was born, but it wasn't really all that early; maybe two months at the most. My problem was being incredibly small. They think my mom might have gotten an infection that made me born less than one pound. The doctors were sure I'd never make it. But I proved everyone wrong. Once I got out of the ICU and, at about eight months, went into convulsions, and then had a stroke, everyone thought that would be the end again. They were wrong. I want to keep proving them wrong as long as I live.

I've had tons of physical therapy, and a few surgeries; so I can get up from a chair and walk around a room. But it took me until about age five to begin to speak or take my first step. The worst time of my life was elementary school—the kids who make fun of you; call you a freak. In high school, and especially here at MTSU, things are much better. I've made close friends, both in the disability community and outside. Actually, I'm a well-known figure, especially since I've been here so long! Everyone on campus greets me with a smile as I scoot around.

In my future? I'd love to get married and adopt a kid. OK, I know that's going to be hard. Because of my speech problem, I know you're thinking it's going to be hard to be a counselor, too. But I'm determined to keep trying, and take every day as a blessing. Life is very special. I've always been living on borrowed time.

(Central Intelligence Agency [CIA], 2014.) The main cause lies in income inequalities, stress, poor health practices, and limited access to high-quality prenatal care.

The socioeconomic link to pregnancy and birth problems is particularly troubling. In every affluent nation—but especially the United States—poverty puts women at higher risk of delivering prematurely or having their baby die before age 1. So, sadly, I must end this chapter on a downbeat note. At this moment in history, our wealthiest nations are falling short of "cherishing" each woman during this landmark journey of life.

Families come in many forms, and the love you have for *all* your adopted children is no different than if you personally gave birth. Take it from me as an adoptive mom!

A Few Final Thoughts on Biological Determinism and Biological Parents

But I also can't leave you with the downbeat impression that what happens during pregnancy is destiny. Yes, researchers now believe events "in-utero" play a role in how we develop. But a basic message of this book is that human beings are resilient. A quality environment matters greatly in shaping our life path (and even can change our biology) well into old age.

Now that we are on the topic of biology, I feel compelled to highlight a personal point, as an adoptive mom. In this chapter, you learned about the feelings of attachment (or mother-child bond) that often begin before birth. But I can assure you that to bond with a baby, you don't need to personally carry that child inside or share the same set of genes. So, just a reminder for later chapters when we scan the beautiful mosaic of families on our landscape today: The bottom-line blessing is being a parent, not being pregnant. Parenting is far different from personally giving birth!

The next two chapters turn directly to the joys of babyhood, as we catch up with Kim and her daughter Elissa, and track development during the first two years of life.

Tying It All Together

1. Baby David gets a two-minute Apgar score of 8; at five minutes, his score is 9. What does this mean?

2. Rates of premature births have *risen/declined* due to ART and low birth weight *always causes serious problems/can produce problems/has no effects* on later development.

3. Bill says, "Pregnancy and birth are very safe today." George says, "Hey, you are very wrong!" Who is right?
   a. Bill, because worldwide maternal mortality is now very low.
   b. George, because birth is still unsafe around the world.
   c. Both are partly correct: Birth is typically very safe in the developed world, but maternal and infant mortality remains unacceptably high in the poorest regions of the globe.

4. Sally brags about the U.S. infant mortality rate, while Samantha is horrified by it. First make Sally's case and then Samantha's, referring to the chapter points.

5. You want to set up a program to reduce prematurity and neonatal mortality among low-income women. List some steps that you might take.

Answers to the Tying It All Together questions can be found at the end of this chapter.

SUMMARY

The First Step: Fertilization

Every culture cherishes pregnant women. Some build in rituals to announce the baby after a certain point during pregnancy, and many use charms to ward off fetal harm. Pregnancy is a time of intense mixed emotions—joyous expectations coupled with uneasy fears.

The female reproductive system includes the **uterus** and its neck, the **cervix;** the **fallopian tubes;** and the **ovaries,** housing the **ova.** To promote **fertilization,** the optimum time for intercourse is when the egg is released. **Hormones** program **ovulation** and all of the events of pregnancy. At intercourse, hundreds of millions of sperm, produced in the **testes,** are ejaculated, but only a small fraction make their way to the fallopian tubes to reach the ovum. When the single victorious sperm penetrates the ovum, the two 23 **chromosome** pairs (composed of **DNA,** segmented into **genes)** unite to regain the normal complement of 46 that form our body's cells.

Prenatal Development

During the first stage of pregnancy, the two-week-long **germinal phase,** the rapidly dividing **zygote** travels to the uterus, becomes a **blastocyst,** and faces the next challenge—**implantation.** The second stage of pregnancy, the **embryonic stage,** begins after implantation and ends around week 8. During this intense six-week period, the **neural tube** forms and all the major body structures are constructed—according to the **proximodistal, cephalocaudal,** and **mass-to-specific** principles of development.

During the third stage of pregnancy, the **fetal stage,** development is slower paced. The hallmarks of this stage are enormous body growth and construction of the brain as the neurons migrate to the top of the tube and differentiate. Another defining landmark of this seven-month phase occurs around week 22, when the fetus can possibly be **viable,** that is, survive outside the womb if born.

Pregnancy

The nine months of **gestation,** or pregnancy, are divided into **trimesters.** The first trimester is often characterized by unpleasant symptoms, such as morning sickness, and a relatively high risk of **miscarriage.** The landmarks of the second trimester are looking clearly pregnant, experiencing **quickening,** and often feeling intensely emotionally connected to the child. During the third trimester, the woman's uterus gets very large, and she anxiously awaits the birth.

The emotional experience of being pregnant varies, depending on socioeconomic status and, most importantly, social support. To really enjoy her pregnancy, a woman needs to feel cared about and loved. Fathers, the neglected pregnancy partners, also feel bonded to their babies too.

Threats to the Developing Baby

Rarely babies are born with a **birth defect.** One cause is **teratogens,** toxins from the outside that exert their damage during the **sensitive period** for the development of a particular body part.

In general, the embryonic stage is the time of greatest vulnerability, although toxins can affect the developing brain during the second and third trimesters also, producing **developmental disorders.** While there is typically a threshold level beyond which damage can occur, teratogens have unpredictable effects. Damage may not show up until decades later.

Any recreational drug is potentially teratogenic. Smoking during pregnancy is a risk factor for having a smaller-than-optimal-size baby. Drinking excessively during pregnancy can produce **fetal alcohol syndrome,** or *fetal alcohol spectrum disorder.* If the woman has poor coping abilities, stress during pregnancy can produce premature labor. **Fetal programming research** suggests that societal upheavals experienced during pregnancy can have enduring effects, by producing small babies and promoting weight gain and premature, age-related chronic diseases.

The second major cause of prenatal problems is genuinely "genetic"—chromosomal problems and single-gene diseases. **Down syndrome** is one of the few disorders in which babies born with an abnormal number of chromosomes survive. Although Down syndrome, caused by having an extra chromosome on pair 21, produces intellectual disability and other health problems, people with this condition do live fulfilling lives.

With **single-gene disorders,** a specific gene passed down from one's parents, causes the disease. In **dominant disorders,** a person who harbors a single copy of the gene gets ill, and each child born to this couple (one of whom has the disease) has a fifty-fifty chance of developing the condition. If the disorder is **recessive,** both parents carry a single copy of the "problem gene" that is not expressed in real life, but they have a 1-in-4 chance of giving birth to a child with that disease (that is, a son or daughter with two copies of the gene). With **sex-linked disorders,** the problem gene is recessive and lies on the X chromosome. If a mother carries a single copy of the gene, her daughters are spared (because they have two Xs), but each male baby has a fifty-fifty risk of getting the disease. Through advances in genetic testing, couples (and individuals) can find out if they harbor the genes for many diseases. **Genetic testing** poses difficult issues with regard to whether people want to find out if they have incurable adult-onset diseases.

Couples at high risk for having a baby with a single-gene disorder (or any couple) may undergo genetic counseling to decide whether they should try to have a child. During pregnancy, tests, including the **ultrasound,** and more invasive procedures such as **chorionic villus sampling** (during the first trimester) and **amniocentesis** (during the second trimester) allow us to determine the baby's genetic fate.

Infertility can be emotionally traumatic and socially isolating, especially for women because of their historic imperative to bear children. Problems getting pregnant are far from rare today, especially at older ages. The most radical intervention, **assisted reproductive technologies (ART),** such as **in vitro fertilization (IVF),** in which the egg is fertilized outside of the womb, is emotionally and physically demanding, costly, and offers no guarantee of having a baby. However, this landmark procedure has given couples who could never have conceived the chance to have a biological child.

Birth

Labor and birth consist of three stages. During the first stage of labor, contractions cause the cervix to efface and fully dilate. During the second stage, birth, the baby emerges. During the third stage, the placenta and supporting structures are expelled.

For most of history, childbirth was life-threatening to both the mother and the child. During the first third of the twentieth century, birth became much safer. This victory set the stage for the later-twentieth-century **natural childbirth** movement. Today women in the developed world can choose from a variety of birth options, including **cesarean sections**. Impoverished, developing-world women do not have this kind of access or luxury of choices. Their main concern is surviving the baby's birth.

The Newborn

After birth, the **Apgar scale** and other tests are used to assess the baby's health. While most babies are healthy, **low birth weight** can compromise development. **Very-low-birth-weight** infants are most apt to have enduring problems and need careful monitoring in the **neonatal intensive care unit** during their early weeks or months of life.

Infant mortality is a serious concern in the developing world. While rates of infant mortality are generally very low in developed world countries, the United States has a comparatively dismal standing compared to other affluent countries on this basic health parameter. Even though the environment in the womb (stress during pregnancy) can affect the baby, providing a high-quality environment shapes development at every life stage.

KEY TERMS

uterus, p. 36

cervix, p. 36

fallopian tube, p. 36

ovary, p. 36

ovum, p. 36

fertilization, p. 36

ovulation, p. 36

hormones, p. 36

testes, p. 37

chromosome, p. 38

DNA (deoxyribonucleic acid), p. 38

gene, p. 38

germinal stage, p. 39

zygote, p. 39

blastocyst, p. 39

implantation, p. 39

placenta, p. 40

embryonic stage, p. 40

neural tube, p. 40

neuron, p. 40

proximodistal sequence, p. 40

cephalocaudal sequence, p. 41

mass-to-specific sequence, p. 41

fetal stage, p. 41

age of viability, p. 42

umbilical cord, p. 42

amniotic sac, p. 42

gestation, p. 42

trimester, p. 42

miscarriage, p. 43

quickening, p. 43

birth defect, p. 46

teratogen, p. 46

sensitive period, p. 46

developmental disorders, p. 48

fetal alcohol syndrome (FAS), p. 49

fetal programming research, p. 51

Down syndrome, p. 51

single-gene disorder, p. 52

dominant disorder, p. 52

recessive disorder, p. 52

sex-linked single-gene disorder, p. 52

genetic testing, p. 55

genetic counselor, p. 55

ultrasound, p. 55

chorionic villus sampling (CVS), p. 55

amniocentesis, p. 56

infertility, p. 57

assisted reproductive technology (ART), p. 58

in vitro fertilization (IVF), p. 58

natural childbirth, p. 61

cesarean section (c-section), p. 62

Apgar scale, p. 63

low birth weight (LBW), p. 64

very low birth weight (VLBW), p. 64

neonatal intensive care unit (NICU), p. 64

infant mortality, p. 65

ANSWERS TO **Tying It All Together** QUIZES

The First Step: Fertilization

1. ovaries, fallopian tubes, uterus; fertilization occurs in the fallopian tubes

2. ovaries for female; testes for male

3. Tell Tiffany that the best time to have intercourse is around the time of ovulation, as fertilization typically occurs when the ovum is in the upper part of the fallopian tube.

4. *she* is *more* apt to survive and *less* apt to be conceived.

Prenatal Development

1. germinal; embryonic; fetal. Organs are formed during the embryonic stage.

2. From the neural tube, a mass of cells differentiates during the late embryonic phase. During the next few months, the cells ascend to the top of the neural tube, completing their migration by week 25. In the final months of pregnancy, the neurons elongate and begin to assume their mature structure.

3. (a) mass to specific (b) cephalocaudal (c) proximodistal

4. Around 22–23 weeks

Pregnancy

1. In this second trimester, she will feel better physically and perhaps experience an intense sense of emotional connectedness when she feels the baby move. During the first trimester she may have been very tired, perhaps felt faint, and had morning sickness.

2. Does she feel as though she is supported and loved? Does she have economic problems?

3. You may come up with a host of interesting possibilities. Here are a few of mine: Include fathers in all pregnancy and birth educational materials the clinic provides; strongly encourage men to be present during prenatal exams; alert female patients about the need to be sensitive to their partners; set up a clinic-sponsored support group for fathers-to-be.

Threats to the Developing Baby

1. Teratogen A most likely caused damage during the *embryonic stage* of development and was taken during the *first trimester* of pregnancy. Teratogen B probably did its damage during the *fetal stage* and was taken during the *second or third trimesters*.

2. Teratogens exert damage during the sensitive period for the development of a particular organ.

3. A doctor in the United States would advocate no alcohol, while a physician in France might say a glass of wine is fine.

4. a & b. They might be at higher risk of being born small and of developing premature heart disease.

5. Jennifer. Down syndrome is typically caused by an unlikely, random event. With cystic fibrosis, that single-gene recessive disorder, the mom (in this case, Jennifer) has a 1-in-4 chance of giving birth to another child with that disease.

6. Tell your friend that the plus of chorionic villus sampling is finding out a child's genetic fate in the first trimester. However, this procedure is more dangerous, carrying a slight risk of limb malformations and, possibly, miscarriage.

Amniocentesis is much safer and can show a fuller complement of genetic disorders but must be performed in the second trimester—meaning she will have to undergo the trauma of a full labor should she decide to end the pregnancy.

7. Cons: ART can be expensive, demands effort and time, has unpleasant physical symptoms, and the chance of actually getting pregnant per cycle is small—especially for older women. Pros: ART gives women (and men) who could never otherwise have a biological child a chance to have a baby who is genetically theirs! The best predictor of Jennifer's coping well is having a supportive spouse.

Birth

1. Melissa is in stage 1, effacement and dilation of the cervix. Sonia is in stage 2, birth.

2. "You might want to forgo any labor medications, and/or give birth in a birthing center under a midwife's (and doula's) care. Look into new options such as water births, and, if you are especially daring, consider giving birth at home."

3. C-sections may sometimes be *overused* in the developed world. But they are seriously *underutilized* in poor areas of the globe.

The Newborn

1. Baby David is in excellent health.

2. Rates of premature births *have risen* due to ART; and low birth weight *can produce problems* in later development.

3. c. While birth is very safe in the developed world, maternal and infant mortality remain serious problems in the least-developed countries.

4. Sally: The United States—like other developed countries—has made tremendous strides in conquering infant mortality. Samantha: The fact that the United States has higher infant mortality rates than many other developed countries is incredibly distressing.

5. You can come up with your own suggestions. Here are a few of mine: Increase the number of nurse-practitioners and obstetrician-gynecologists in poor urban and rural areas. Provide special monetary incentives to health-care providers to treat low-income women. Offer special "healthy baby" educational programs at schools, community centers, and local churches in low-income neighborhoods targeted for female teens. Make it easier for low-wage workers to actually see a health-care provider by providing incentives to employers. Set up volunteer programs to visit isolated pregnant single moms and provide social support. Target nutrition programs to low-income mothers-to-be (actually, this is the goal of the WIC program, described in the next chapter).

Infancy

This two-chapter part is devoted to infancy and toddlerhood (the period from birth through age 2). How does a helpless newborn become a walking, talking, loving child?

Chapter 3—**Infancy: Physical and Cognitive Development** starts by offering an overview of brain development, then explores those basic newborn states: feeding, crying, and sleeping. Next, I chart sensory and motor development: What do babies see? How do newborns develop from lying helplessly to being able to walk? What can caregivers do to keep babies safe as they travel into the world? Finally, I'll offer an overview of infants' evolving cognition and their first steps toward language, the capacity that allows us to really enter the human community.

Chapter 4—**Infancy: Socioemotional Development** looks at what makes us human: our relationships. First, I'll explore the attachment relationship between caregiver and child, then examine poverty and day care. The final part of this chapter focuses on toddlerhood—roughly from age 1 to 2 1/2. Toddlers are intensely attached to their caregivers and passionate to be independent. During this watershed age, when we are walking and beginning to talk, we first learn the rules of the human world.

PART II

CHAPTER 3

Infancy: Physical and Cognitive Development

In Chapter 2 I talked to Kim at the beginning of the third trimester, anxiously waiting for her child's birth. Now, let's pay her a visit and meet Elissa, her baby girl.

She's been here for 5 months and 10 days, and I feel like she's been here forever. For me, it was love at first sight and, of course, the same for Jeff. But the real thrill is watching a wonderful person emerge day by day. Take what's happening now. At first, she couldn't care less, but about a month ago, it was like, "Wow, there's a world out there!" See that baby seat? Elissa can make the colored buttons flash by moving her legs. When I put her in it, she bats her legs like crazy. She can't get enough of those lights and sounds. Now that she is finally able to reach, notice her hunger to grab for everything and the way she looks at your face—like she can get into your soul. Sometimes, I think she understands what I'm feeling . . . but I know she must be way too young for this.

Elissa doesn't cry much—nothing like other babies during the first three months. Actually, I was worried. I asked the doctor whether there was something wrong. Crying is vital to communicating what you need! The same is true of sleeping. I'm almost embarrassed to tell you that I have the only baby in history who has been regularly giving her mom a good night's sleep since she was 2 months old.

Breast-feeding is indescribable. It feels like I am literally making her grow. But, here I also was concerned. Could I do this? What helped me persevere through the painful first weeks was my supportive husband—and most important, the fact that Jeff makes enough money to let me take off work for five months. I feel so sad for my friend, Nora, who had to abandon this incredible experience when she needed to go back to her job right after her son's birth.

Pick her up. Feel what it's like to hold her—how she melts into you. But notice how she squirms to get away. It's as if she is saying, "Mom, my agenda is to get moving into the world." I plan to YouTube every step now that she's traveling into life.

At five months of age, Elissa has reached a milestone. She is poised to physically encounter life. This chapter charts the transformation from lying helplessly to moving into the world and the other amazing physical and cognitive changes that occur during infancy—that magic first two years of life.

To set the context, I'll first spell out some brain changes (and principles) that program development. Then, returning to infancy, I'll chart those basic newborn states—eating, crying, and sleeping—and track babies' emerging vision and motor skills. The final sections of this chapter tour cognition and emerging language, the capacity that makes our species unique.

What does this young baby see and understand about the tremendous loving object he is facing? That is the mystery we will be exploring in this chapter.

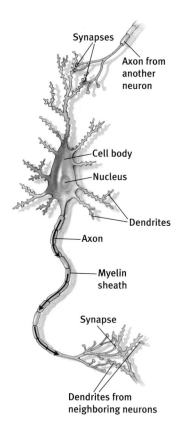

FIGURE 3.1: The neuron and synapses: Here is an illustration of the remarkable structure that programs every developing skill, perception, and thought. Notice the dendrites receiving information at the synapses and how impulses flow down the long axon to connect up with the dendrites of the adjoining cells.

Setting the Context

What causes the remarkable changes—from seeing to walking to speaking—that unfold during infancy? Answers come from scanning development in that master-piece structure—the human brain.

The Expanding Brain

The **cerebral cortex,** the outer, furrowed mantle of the brain, is the site of every conscious perception, action, and thought. With a surface area 10 times larger than the monkey's and 1,000 times larger than the rat's, our cortex is what makes human beings different from any other species on earth.

Because of our immense cortex, humans are also unique in the amount of brain growth that occurs outside of our womb. During the first four years of life, brain volume quadruples (Stiles & Jernigan, 2010). It takes more than two decades for the brain to fully mature. Actually, the cortex only starts taking over our behavior a few months *after* birth.

Recall from Chapter 2 that by the middle of the fetal period the cells that compose the brain have migrated to the top of the neural tube. During the final months of pregnancy, and the first year of life, they differentiate into their mature form. The cells form long **axons**—fibers that conduct impulses away from the cell body. They sprout **dendrites**—treelike, branching ends. As the dendrites proliferate at junctions, or **synapses,** the axons and dendrites interconnect (see Figure 3.1).

Synaptogenesis, the process of making myriad connections, programs every skill—from Elissa's vigorous push-ups to composing symphonies or solving problems in math. Another critical transformation is called **myelination:** The axons form a fatty layer around their core. Just as a stream of water prevents us from painfully bumping down a water park slide, the myelin sheath is the lubricant that permits the neural impulses to speedily flow. This insulating layer may also determine which cells thrive (Stiles & Jernigan, 2010).

Synaptogenesis and myelination occur at different rates in specific brain regions (Dean and others, 2014). In the visual cortex, the part of the brain responsible for interpreting visual stimuli, the axons are myelinated by about age 1. In the frontal lobes, the brain region involved in reasoning, the myelin sheath is still forming into our twenties.

This makes sense. Seeing is a skill we need soon after birth. Visual abilities, as you will learn in this chapter, develop rapidly during our first year of life. But we won't need the skills to compose symphonies, do higher math, or competently make our way in the world until we become adults. So there are parallels between our unfolding abilities and the way our brain matures.

Neural Pruning and Brain Plasticity

So far, you might imagine that more neural connections equal superior skills. Not so! Neural loss is critical to development, too. Following a phase of lavishly producing synapses, each cortical region undergoes synaptic pruning and neural death. This shedding timetable also reflects our expanding abilities. It begins around age 1 in the visual cortex. It starts during late childhood in the frontal lobes. Just as weeding is critical to sculpting a beautiful garden, we need to get rid of the unnecessary neurons to permit the essential cells to flower.

Why does the brain undergo this frantic overproduction, followed by cutting back? Clues come from research suggesting that during infancy, synaptic connections progressively strengthen in more distant areas of the brain (Damaraju and others, 2014). Perhaps, having an oversupply of connections allows us to "recruit" from this wider pool and redirect these extra neurons to perform other functions, should we have a major sensory deficit or brain insult early in life (Fox, Levitt, & Nelson,

2010; Stiles & Jernigan, 2010). Actually, our cortex is malleable or **plastic** (able to be changed), particularly during infancy and the childhood years.

Using the fMRI, which measures the brain's energy consumption, researchers find that among people blind from birth, activity in the visual cortex is intense while reading Braille and localizing sounds in space. This suggests that, without environmental stimulation from the eye, the neurons programmed for vision are captured, or taken over, to strengthen hearing and touch (Collignon and others, 2011; Fox, Levitt, & Nelson, 2010).

A similar process occurs with language, normally represented in the left hemisphere of the brain. If an infant has a left-hemisphere stroke, with intense verbal stimulation, the right hemisphere takes over, and language develops normally (Rowe and others, 2009). Compare this to what happens when an older person has a left-hemisphere stroke after language is located firmly in its appropriate places. The result can be devastating—a permanent loss in understanding speech or forming words.

So, brain plasticity highlights the basic nature-combines-with-nurture principle that governs human life. Yes, the blueprint for our cortex is laid out at conception. But, environmental stimulation is vital in strengthening specific neural networks and determining which connections will be pruned (Fox, Levitt, & Nelson, 2010). Before the pruning phase, our brain is particularly malleable—permitting us to grow a somewhat different garden should disaster strike. Still, as synaptogenesis is a lifelong process, we continue to grow, to learn, to develop intellectually, from age 1 to age 101.

Table 3.1 on page 76 offers additional fascinating facts about neurons, synaptogenesis, and the pruning phase. Notice from the last item that, in the same way as the houses in your subdivision look different—although they may have had the same original plan (as each owner took charge of decorating his personal space)—scientists find remarkable variability in the brains of *normally* developing girls and boys (Giedd and others, 2010). Actually, why should these variations be a surprise, given the diversity of interests and talents we develop in life!

cerebral cortex The outer, folded mantle of the brain, responsible for thinking, reasoning, perceiving, and all conscious responses.

axon A long nerve fiber that usually conducts impulses away from the cell body of a neuron.

dendrite A branching fiber that receives information and conducts impulses toward the cell body of a neuron.

synapse The gap between the dendrites of one neuron and the axon of another, over which impulses flow.

synaptogenesis Forming of connections between neurons at the synapses. This process, responsible for all perceptions, actions, and thoughts, is most intense during infancy and childhood but continues throughout life.

myelination Formation of a fatty layer encasing the axons of neurons. This process, which speeds the transmission of neural impulses, continues from birth to early adulthood.

plastic Malleable, or capable of being changed (used to refer to neural or cognitive development).

Susan Watts/NY Daily News Archive via Getty Images

This resilient baby has survived major surgeries in which large sections of his brain had to be removed. Remarkably—because the cortex is so *plastic* at this age—he is expected to be left with few, if any, impairments.

Table 3.1: Brain-Busting Facts to Wrap Your Head Around

- Our adult brain is composed of more than 1 billion neurons and, via synaptogenesis, makes roughly 60 trillion neural connections.

- As preschoolers, we have roughly double the number of synapses we have as adults—because, as our brain develops, roughly 40 percent of our synapses are ultimately pruned (see the text). So, ironically, the overall cortical thinning during elementary school and adolescence is a symptom of brain maturation.

- Specific abilities such as language, that scientists had believed were localized in one part of the cortex, are dependent on many brain regions. Moreover, the cortical indicators of "being advanced" in an ability shift in puzzling ways as a child gets older. For instance, while rapid myelination in the left frontal lobe predicts language abilities at age 1, by age 4 this relationship reverses, with linguistically advanced preschoolers showing more myelin in the right frontal lobe. Although when a given child shows rapid IQ declines there is a steeper-than-normal loss in cortical thickness, boys and girls whose intelligence scores rise show no special cortical changes.

- Boys' brains, on average, are 10 percent larger than girls' brains, even during childhood, when both sexes are roughly the same size, body-wise.

- The most amazing finding relates to the surprising, dramatic variability in brain size from child to child. Two normal 10-year-old boys might have a twofold difference in brain volume, without showing any difference in intellectual abilities!

Information from: Giedd and others, 2010; Stiles & Jernigan, 2010; Muircheartaigh and others, 2013; Burgaleta and others, 2014.

Now keeping in mind the basic brain principles—(1) development unfolds "in its own neurological time" (you can't teach a baby to do something before the relevant part of the brain comes on-line); (2) stimulation sculpts neurons (our wider-world experiences physically change our brain); and (3) the brain is still "under construction" (and shaped by those same experiences) for as long as we live—let's explore how the expanding cortex works magic during the first two years of life.

 Tying It All Together

1. Cortez and Ashley are arguing about what makes our brain unique. Cortez says it's the immense size of our cortex. Ashley says it's the fact that we "grow" most of our brain after birth and that the cortex continues to mature for at least two decades. Who is right—Cortez, Ashley, or both students?

2. Latisha tells you that the myelin sheath speeds neural impulses and the more synaptic connections, the higher the level of development. Is Latisha totally correct? If not, describe how she is wrong?

3. When babies have a stroke, they may end up (choose one) *more/less* impaired than they would be as adults, due to a phenomenon called brain (choose one) *myelination/plasticity.*

4. Which neural process is occurring right now in your mom and your elderly grandma? (Choose one) *myelination/synaptogenesis*

Answers to the Tying It All Together questions can be found at the end of this chapter.

Basic Newborn States

Visit a newborn and you will see simple activities: She eats, she cries, she sleeps. In this section, I'll spotlight each state.

Eating: The Basis of Living

Eating undergoes amazing changes during infancy. Let's scan these transformations and then discuss nutritional topics that loom large in the first years of life.

Developmental Changes: From Newborn Reflexes to Two-Year-Olds' Food Cautions

Newborns seem to be eating even when they are sleeping—a fact vividly brought home to me by the loud smacking that rhythmically erupted from my son's bassinet. The reason is that babies are born with a powerful **sucking reflex**—they suck virtually all the time. Newborns also are born with a **rooting reflex.** If *anything* touches their cheek, they turn their head in that direction and suck.

Reflexes are automatic activities. Because they do not depend on the cortex, they are not under conscious control. It is easy to see why the sucking and rooting reflexes are vital to surviving after we exit the womb. If newborns had to learn to suck, they might starve before mastering that skill. Without the rooting reflex, babies would have trouble finding the breast.

Sucking and rooting have clear functions. What about the other infant reflexes shown in Figure 3.2? Do you think the grasping reflex may have helped newborns survive during hunter-gatherer times? Can you think of why newborns, when stood on a table, take little steps (the stepping reflex)? Whatever their value, these reflexes, and a few others, must be present at birth. They must disappear as the cortex grows.

As the cortex matures, voluntary processes replace these special newborn reflexes. By month four or five, babies no longer suck continually. Their sucking is governed by *operant conditioning*. When the breast draws near, they suck in anticipation of that delicious reinforcer: "Mealtime has arrived!" Still, Sigmund Freud named infancy the oral stage for good reason: During the first years of life, the theme is "Everything in the mouth."

This impulse to taste everything leads to scary moments as children crawl and walk. There is nothing like the sickening sensation of seeing a baby put a forgotten pin in his mouth or taste your possibly poisonous plant. My personal heart-stopping experience occurred when my son was almost 2. I'll never forget the frantic race to the emergency room after Thomas toddled in to joyously share a treasure, an open vial of pills!

Luckily, a mechanism may protect toddlers from sampling every potentially lethal substance during their first travels into the world. Between ages 1 1/2 and 2, children can revert to eating a few familiar foods, such as peanut butter sandwiches and apple juice. Evolutionary psychologists believe that, like morning sickness, this behavior is adaptive. Sticking to foods they know reduces the risk of children poisoning themselves when they begin to walk (Bjorklund & Pellegrini, 2002). Because this *2-year-old food caution* gives caregivers headaches, we need to reassure frantic parents: Picky eating can be *normal* during the second year of life (as long as your child eats a reasonable amount of food).

sucking reflex The automatic, spontaneous sucking movements newborns produce, especially when anything touches their lips.

rooting reflex Newborns' automatic response to a touch on the cheek, involving turning toward that location and beginning to suck.

reflex A response or action that is automatic and programmed by noncortical brain centers.

Rooting: Whenever something touches their cheek, newborns turn their head in that direction and make sucking movements.

Sucking: Newborns are programmed to suck, especially when something enters their mouth.

Grasping: Newborns automatically vigorously grasp anything that touches the palm of their hand.

FIGURE 3.2: **Some newborn reflexes:** If the baby's brain is developing normally, each of these reflexes is present at birth and gradually disappears after the first few months of life. In addition to the reflexes illustrated here, other newborn reflexes include the Babinski reflex (stroke a baby's foot and her toes turn outward), the stepping reflex (place a baby's feet on a hard surface and she takes small steps), and the swimming reflex (if placed under water, newborns can hold their breath and make swimming motions).

What is the best diet during a baby's first months? When is not having enough food a widespread problem? These questions bring up breast-feeding and global malnutrition.

Breast Milk: Nature's First Food

During the late nineteenth century, U.S. babies faced perils after birth. A major threat was diarrhea, which caused a spike in infant mortality in the teeming city tenements. The newborns of immigrant Eastern European Jews, however, were less likely to develop diarrhea and other infectious diseases, because Jewish tradition dictated that mothers breast-feed their daughters and sons (Preston, 1991).

In the past, because it protected babies against impure milk, breast-feeding was a life-saving act. That choice has an impact today. Breast milk provides immunities to middle ear infections and gastrointestinal problems. It makes toddlers more resistant to colds and the flu (McNiel, Labbok, & Abrahams, 2010). Breast-fed babies show accelerated myelin formation (Deoni and others, 2013). They get higher scores on intelligence tests (Karns, 2001; Mortensen and others, 2002; Bernard, 2013). At age 1, they seem less physiologically reactive to stress (Beijers, Riksen-Walraven, & De Weerth, 2013).

Still, these findings involve correlations. And, as we know, just because there is a relationship between two variables does not mean one *causes* the other. The research exploring breast milk's benefits rarely controls for that important "third variable"—social class. Caucasian women, who breast-feed for months, tend to be older, well educated, and affluent (Dennis and others, 2013). They spend more time in hands-on infant care (Smith & Ellwood, 2011). Women who nurse for months, one study showed, are less prone to becoming depressed as their baby travels into the stressful toddler years (Hahn-Holbrook and others, 2013). Is it really breast *milk* that promotes health, or the extra nurturing that goes along with providing this natural food?

As with pregnancy advice (recall Chapter 2), breast-feeding pronouncements have undergone fascinating historical shifts. During the 1950s, doctors pushed formula as the "scientific" best food. Since research revealed nursing's benefits, health care organizations such as the American Academy of Pediatrics (2005) and UNICEF (2009) campaigned for *exclusive* breast-feeding during the first six months of life.

Contemporary women listened. Today, three out of four new U.S. mothers start out determined to breast-feed. But only a small percentage persists to the five- or six-month mark (Foss, 2010). Why?

Breast-feeding challenges

One cause has to do with the need to work (Flower and others, 2008; Vaughn, 2010). Although U.S. employers must permit new mothers to pump their milk, imagine your problems following the six-month recommendation as a server or supermarket clerk who had to return to work soon after delivery (Guendelman and others, 2009). Women complain that breast-feeding is not practical. They are embarrassed to nurse their babies in public, especially if men are around (Vaaler and others, 2010; Vaughn, 2010).

Interesting nation-to-nation nursing-rate differences in the West reveal the impact that "other people" (in this case, society) make on breast-feeding. In Ireland, where people view formula as fine, most women bottle-feed soon after birth (Tarrant and others, 2013). In Canada and especially Norway, where breast-feeding is the *only* socially acceptable option, mothers try valiantly to nurse for the full six months (Andrews and Knaak, 2013).

This pressure to live up to the image of the ideal breast-feeding mom presents problems. Not only can nursing be inconvenient, but it can also be physically hard. As one U.S. mother reported: "I never realized . . . that I would be reduced to tears every time I fed" (Sheehan Schmied, & Barclay, 2013, p. 23). A Canadian woman, forced to abandon the breast, reported: "I felt so horrible . . . that I couldn't do this for my child . . . You feel like less of a mother, less of a person (quoted in Andrews and Knaak, 2013, p. 95).

Therefore, it comes as no surprise that some Western moms are rebelling against breast-feeding "police" (Williams and others, 2013; Leeming and others, 2013; Regan and Ball, 2013). As Chloe, a U.S mother forced to give up the breast, rationalized: "I remember reading that . . . even just getting the first two weeks . . . is apparently really worthwhile . . . ." (quoted in Williams, Donaghue, & Kurz, 2013, p. 37). One British woman even took the step of viewing breast-feeding as narcissistic, when she argued, "I like . . . bottles because it gives her a chance to bond with my partner . . . and her grandma . . . ." (Leeming and others, 2013).

These quotes suggest we need to rethink the health-care message that automatically equates nursing with ideal motherhood. Many women (such as your author) cannot breast-feed. Millions of children (including your author) born during the mid-twentieth century, when bottle-feeding was standard, grew up to live successful lives. Rather than your milk delivery method, what's really important is the way you love and bond with your child!

Malnutrition: A Serious Developing-World Concern

Breast-feeding allows *every* newborn a chance to thrive. However, there comes a time—at around 6 months of age—when babies need solid food. Then, the horrifying inequalities in global nutrition hit (Caulfield and others, 2006).

How many young children suffer from **undernutrition,** having a serious lack of adequate food? For answers, epidemiologists measure **stunting,** the percentage of children under age 5 who in a given region rank below the fifth percentile in height, according to the norms for their age. This very short stature is a symptom of *chronic* inadequate nutrition, which compromises every aspect of development and activity of life (Abubakar and others, 2010; UNICEF, 2009).

The good news is that in recent decades, stunting rates declined in poor regions of the world (UNICEF, 2002a). The tragedy, as Figure 3.3 shows, is that this sign of serious malnutrition still affects an alarming 209 million children, roughly two in five developing-world girls and boys (UNICEF, 2000). In Africa and South Asia, **micronutrient deficiencies**—inadequate levels of nutrients such as iron or zinc or Vitamin A—are rampant. Disorders, such as Kwashiorkor (described in the Experiencing the Lifespan box on page 80), can even strike when there is ample food.

This breast-feeding mom is probably thrilled to provide her baby with the best first start; but, unfortunately, her choice might be more difficult than experts have led her to believe.

undernutrition A chronic lack of adequate food.

stunting Excessively short stature in a child, caused by chronic lack of adequate nutrition.

micronutrient deficiency Chronically inadequate level of a specific nutrient important to development and disease prevention, such as Vitamin A, zinc, and/or iron.

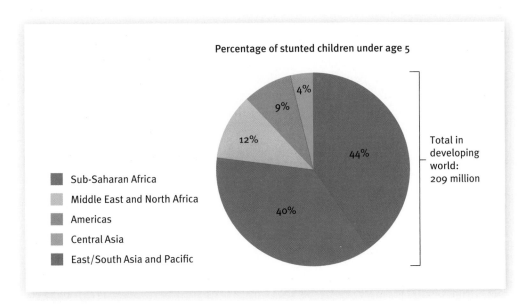

Percentage of stunted children under age 5

- Sub-Saharan Africa
- Middle East and North Africa
- Americas
- Central Asia
- East/South Asia and Pacific

4%
9%
12%
44%
40%

Total in developing world: 209 million

FIGURE 3.3: **Percentage of stunted children under age 5 in the developing world:** This upsetting chart shows that stunting is common in much of the developed world—affecting many millions of young children, especially in East and South Asia and the Pacific regions and Sub-Saharan Africa.
Adapted from: UNICEF, 2000.

Experiencing the Lifespan: A Passion to Eradicate Malnutrition: A Career in Public Health

What is it like to battle malnutrition in the developing world? Listen to Richard Douglass describe his career:

I grew up on the South Side of Chicago—my radius was maybe 4 or 5 blocks in either direction. Then, I spent my junior year in college in Ethiopia, and it changed my life. I lived across the street from the hospital, and every morning I saw a flood of people standing in line. They would wait all day . . . , and eventually a cart would come and take away the dead. When I saw the lack of doctors, I realized I needed to get my Master's and Ph.D. in public health.

In public health we focus on primary prevention, how to prevent diseases and save thousands of people from getting ill. My interest was in helping to eradicate Kwashiorkor in Ghana. What the name literally means is "the disease that happens when the second child is born." The first child is taken off the breast too soon and given a porridge that doesn't have amino acids, and so the musculature and the diaphragm break down. You get a bloated look (swollen stomach), and then you die. If a child does survive, he ends up stunted, and so looks maybe 5 years younger.

Once someone gets the disease, you can save their life. But it's a 36-month rehabilitation that requires taking that child to the clinic for treatment every week. In Ghana it can mean traveling a dozen miles by foot. So a single mom with two or three kids is going to drop out of the program as soon as the child starts to look healthy. Because of male urban migration, the African family is in peril. If a family has a grandmother or great-auntie, the child can make it because this woman can take care of the children. So the presence of a grandma saves kids' lives.

Most malnutrition shows up after wars. In Ghana there is tons of food. So it's a problem of ignorance, not poverty. The issue is partly cultural. First, among some groups, the men eat, then women, then older children, then the babies get what is left. So the meat is gone, the fish is gone, and then you just have that porridge. We have been trying to impose a cultural norm that everyone sits around the dining table for meals, thereby ensuring that all the children get to eat. The other issue is just pure public health education—teaching families "just because your child looks fat doesn't mean that he is healthy."

I feel better on African soil than anywhere else. With poor people in the developing world who are used to being exploited, they are willing to write you off in a heartbeat if you give them a reason; but if you make a promise and follow through, then you are part of their lives. I keep going back to my college experience in Ethiopia . . . watching those people standing at the hospital, waiting to die. Making a difference for them is the reason why I was born.

How many young children are stunted or chronically hungry in the United States? According to the U.S. Department of Agriculture, in 2012 roughly one in six U.S. households with children was designated as **food insecure**. This means that people reported sometimes not affording to provide a balanced diet, or being worried that their money for food might run out. About one in 20 families reported *severe food insecurity*. They sometimes went hungry due to lack of funds (Coleman-Jensen and others, 2013). However, because the United States provides nutrition-related entitlement programs described in Table 3.2, in our nation and other developed countries, poor children are spared the *ongoing* hunger that limits the life chances of so many boys and girls around the globe.

Crying: The First Communication Signal

At 2 months, when Jason cried, I was clueless. I picked him up, rocked him, and kept a pacifier glued to his mouth; I called my mother, the doctor, even my local pharmacist, for advice. Since it put Jason to sleep, my husband and I took car rides at three in the morning—the only people on the road were teenagers and other new parents like us. Now that my little love is 10 months old, I know why he is crying, and those lonely countryside tours are long gone.

Crying, that vital way we communicate our feelings, reaches its lifetime peak at around one month after birth (St. James-Roberts, 2007). However, a distinctive change in crying occurs at about month 4. As the cortex blossoms, crying rates decline, and babies use this communication to express their needs.

It's tempting to think of crying as a negative state. However, because crying is as vital to survival as sucking, when babies cry too little, this can signal a neurological

food insecurity According to U.S. Department of Agriculture surveys, the number of households that report needing to serve unbalanced meals, worrying about not having enough food at the end of the month, or having to go hungry due to lack of money (latter is *severe food insecurity*).

> **Table 3.2:** Major U.S. Federal Nutrition Programs Serving Young Children
>
> **Food Stamp Program (Now called SNAP, Supplemental Nutrition Assistance Program):** This mainstay federal nutrition program provides electronic cards that participants can use like a debit card to buy food. To qualify, a family must have no more than $2,000 in resources, such as a bank account, or $3,250 in resources if one person is disabled or age 60 and over. Families with young children make up the majority of food stamp recipients.*
>
> **Special Supplemental Nutrition Program for Women, Infants, and Children (WIC):** This federally funded grant program is specifically for low-income pregnant women and mothers with children under age 5. To be eligible, a family must be judged nutritionally at risk by a health-care professional and earn below 185 percent of the poverty line. WIC offers a monthly package of supplements tailored to the family's unique nutritional needs (such as infant formula and baby cereals) plus nutrition education and breast-feeding support.*
>
> **Child and Adult Care Food Program (CACFP):** This program reimburses child-care facilities, day-care providers, after-school programs, and providers of various adult services for the cost of serving high-quality meals. Surveys show that children in participating programs have higher intakes of key nutrients and eat fewer servings of fats and sweets than do children who attend child-care facilities that do not participate.
>
> Information from: U.S. Department of Agriculture, Food and Nutrition Service, accessed September 10, 2014, http://www.fns.usda.gov/snap/supplemental-nutrition-assistance-program
>
> *As of 2012, about 42 million households received Food Stamps (over 50 million were eligible). Participation rates in WIC are lower, with slightly more than half eligible U.S. families getting this aid.

problem (Zeskind & Lester, 2001). When babies cry, we pick them up, rock them, and give them loving care. So, up to a certain point, crying helps cement the infant–parent bond.

Still, there is a limit. When a baby cries continually, she may have that bane of early infancy—**colic.** Despite what some "friends" (unhelpfully) tell new mothers, it's a myth that inept parents produce colicky babies. Colic is caused by an immature nervous system. After they exit the cozy womb, some babies get unusually distressed when bombarded by stimuli, such as being handled or fed (St. James-Roberts, 2007). So, we need to back off from blaming stressed-out moms and dads for this biological problem of early infant life.

The good news is that colic is short-lived. Most parents find that around month 4, their baby suddenly becomes a new, pleasant person overnight. For this reason, there is only cause for concern when a baby cries excessively after this age (Schmid and others, 2010).

Imagine having a baby with colic. You feel helpless. You cannot do anything to quiet the baby down. There are few things more damaging to parental self-efficacy than an infant's out-of-control crying (Keefe and others, 2006).

INTERVENTIONS: What Quiets a Young Baby?

WHAT SOOTHES A CRYING BABY? One strategy is to hold and rock the baby and provide a pacifier, a breast, a bottle, or anything that satisfies the need to suck. Another traditional approach is **swaddling** (wrapping) a newborn tight.

Interestingly, because it distances the baby from the mom's body, swaddling has the downside of limiting skin-to-skin contact between caregiver and child (Kelmanson, 2013; Dumas and others, 2013). Continuous *human* touch is most effective at calming crying during the first days of life (Cecchini and others, 2013). The best example comes from the !Kung San hunter-gatherers of Botswana. In this collectivist culture, where mothers strap infants to their bodies and feed them on demand, the frequency of colic is dramatically reduced.

Kangaroo care, or using a baby sling, can even help premature infants grow (World Health Organization [WHO], 2003b). In one experiment, developmentalists

colic A baby's frantic, continual crying during the first three months of life; caused by an immature nervous system.

swaddling The standard Western infant calming technique of wrapping a baby tightly in a blanket or other garment.

kangaroo care Carrying a young baby in a sling close to the caregiver's body. This technique is most useful for soothing an infant.

Kangaroo care, because it promotes this intense skin-to-skin bonding, is superior to swaddling—the standard Western baby-calming technique.

had mothers with babies in an intensive care unit carry their infants in baby slings for one hour each day. Then, they compared these children's development with that of a comparable group given standard care. At 6 months of age, the kangaroo-care babies scored higher on developmental tests. Their parents were rated as providing a more nurturing home environment, too (Feldman & Eidelman, 2003).

Imagine having your baby whisked away at birth to spend weeks with strangers. Now, think of being able to caress his tiny body, the sense of self-efficacy that would flow from helping him thrive. So it makes sense that any cuddling intervention can have an impact on the baby and the parent–child bond.

Another baby-calming strategy is infant massage. From helping premature infants gain weight, to treating toddler (and adult) sleep problems, to reducing old-age pain, massage enhances well-being from the beginning to the end of life (Field, Diego, & Hernandez-Reif, 2007, 2011).

We all know the power of a cuddle or a relaxing massage to soothe our troubles. Can holding and stroking in early infancy *generally* insulate us against stress? Consider this study with rats.

Because rodent mothers (like humans) differ in the "hands-on" contact they give their babies, researchers classified rats who had just given birth into high licking and grooming, average licking and grooming, and low licking and grooming groups. As adults, the lavishly licked and groomed rats reacted in a more placid way when exposed to stress (Menard & Hakvoort, 2007). We need to be cautious about generalizing this finding to humans. Advocating for the !Kung San approach to caregiving might be asking too much of modern moms. Still, the implication is clear: During the first months of life (or, for as long as you can), keep touching and loving 'em up!

Cuddles calm us from day 1 to age 101. However, crying also undergoes fascinating developmental changes. The long car ride that magically quieted a 2-month-old evokes agony in a toddler who cannot stand to be confined. First, it's swaddling, then watching a mobile, then seeing Mom enter the room that has the power to soothe. In preschool, it's monsters that cause wailing; during elementary school and teenager-hood, it's failing or being rejected by our social group. As emerging adults, we weep for lost love. Finally, among mature adults and old folks (as we reach Erikson's stage of generativity), we stop crying for ourselves and cry when our loved ones are in pain. Our crying shows where we are developmentally throughout our lives!

Sleeping: The Main Newborn State

If crying is a crucial baby (and adult) communication signal, sleep is the quintessential newborn state. Visit a relative who has recently given birth. Will her baby be crying or eating? No, she is almost certain to be asleep. Full-term newborns typically sleep for 18 hours out of a 24-hour day. As Figure 3.4 shows, although they cycle through different stages, newborns are in the sleeping/drowsy phase about 90 percent of the time (Thoman & Whitney, 1990). And there is a reason for the saying, "She sleeps like a baby." Perhaps because it mirrors the whooshing sound in the womb, noise helps newborns zone out. The problem for parents is that babies wake up and start wailing, like clockwork, every 3 to 4 hours.

Developmental Changes: From Signaling, to Self-Soothing, to Shifts in REM Sleep

During the first year of life, infant sleep patterns adapt to the human world. Nighttime awakenings become less frequent. Then, by about 6 months of age, there is a

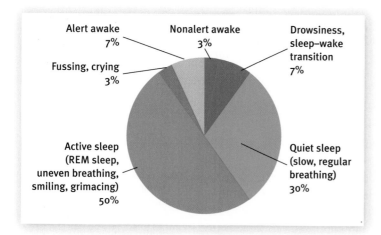

FIGURE 3.4: **Newborns sleep most of the time:** During each 24-hour period, newborns cycle through various states of arousal. Notice, however, that babies spend the vast majority of their time either sleeping or in the getting-to-sleep phase.
Adapted from: Thoman & Whitney, 1990.

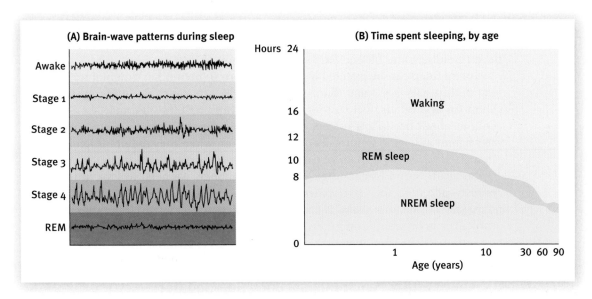

FIGURE 3.5: **Sleep brain waves and lifespan changes in sleep and wakefulness:** In chart A, you can see the EEG patterns associated with the four stages of sleep that first appear during adolescence. After we fall asleep, our brain waves get progressively slower (these are the four stages of non-REM sleep) and then we enter the REM phase during which dreaming is intense. Now, notice in chart B the time young babies spend in REM. As REM sleep helps consolidate memory, is the incredible time babies spend in this phase crucial to absorbing the overwhelming amount of information that must be mastered during the first years of life?
Adapted from: Roffwarg, Muzio, & Dement, 1966.

milestone. The typical baby sleeps for 6 hours a night. At age 1, the typical pattern is roughly 12 hours of sleep a night, with an additional morning and afternoon nap. During year 2, the caretaker's morning respite to do housework or rest is regretfully lost, as children give up the morning nap. Finally, by late preschool, sleep often (although not always) occurs only at night (Anders, Goodlin-Jones, & Zelenko, 1998).

In addition to its length and on-again-off-again pattern, infant sleep differs physiologically from our adult pattern. When we fall asleep, we descend through four stages, involving progressively slower brain-wave frequencies, and then cycle back to **REM sleep**—a phase of rapid eye movement, when dreaming is intense and our brain-wave frequencies look virtually identical to when we are in the lightest sleep stage (see Figure 3.5). When infants fall asleep, they immediately enter REM and spend most of their time in this state. It is not until adolescence that we have the adult sleep cycle, with four distinct stages (Anders, Goodlin-Jones, & Zelenko, 1998).

Although parents are thrilled to say, "My child is sleeping though the night," this statement is false. Babies *never* sleep continuously through the night. However, by about 6 months of age, many have the skill to become **self-soothing.** They put themselves back to sleep when they wake up (Goodlin-Jones and others, 2001).

Imagine being a new parent. Your first challenge is to get your baby to develop the skill of nighttime self-soothing. Around age 1, because your child is now put into the crib while still awake, there may be issues getting your baby to *go* to sleep. During preschool and elementary school, the sleep problem shifts again. Now, it's concerns about getting the child *into* bed: "Mommy, can't I stay up later? Do I *have* to turn off the lights?"

Although it may make them cranky, parents expect to be sleep-deprived with a young baby; but once a child has passed the 5- or 6-month milestone, they get agitated if the infant has never permitted them a full night's sleep. Parents expect sleep problems when their child is ill or under stress, but not the zombielike irritability that comes from being chronically sleep-deprived for years. There is a poisonous

REM sleep The phase of sleep involving rapid eye movements, when the EEG looks almost like it does during waking. REM sleep decreases as infants mature.

self-soothing Children's ability, usually beginning at about 6 months of age, to put themselves back to sleep when they wake up during the night.

bidirectional effect here: Children with chronic sleep problems produce irritable, stressed-out parents. Irritable, stressed-out parents produce childhood problems with sleep (Goldberg and others, 2013).

Infant sleep can be affected by everything from the mother's mental state, to her relationship with her mate (Kim and Teti, 2014), to the stress of living in poverty (Sheridan and others, 2013). Moreover, a mother's mental state may skew her perceptions about her infant's sleep. In one survey, depressed moms were apt to label their babies as having serious sleep problems even when they did not (Goldberg and others, 2013).

So again, in understanding sleep during infancy, we need to look at the wider context—adopting the *developmental systems approach*. Moreover, we sometimes might take complaints about "a baby's serious sleep issues" with a grain of salt. Child problems can be seen through the eye of the beholder—and that's another theme I'll be returning to in later chapters.

INTERVENTIONS: What Helps a Baby Self-Soothe?

What should parents do when their baby signals (cries out) from the crib? At one end of the continuum stand the behaviorists: "Don't reinforce crying by responding—and be consistent. Never go in and comfort the baby lest you let a variable reinforcement schedule unfold, and the child will cry longer." At the other, we have John Bowlby with his emphasis on the attachment bond, or Erik Erikson with his concept of *basic trust* (see Table 3.3). During the first year of life, both Bowlby and Erikson imply that caregivers should sensitively respond when an infant cries. These contrasting points of view evoke passions among parents, too:

> I feel the basic lesson parents need to teach children is how to be independent, not to let your child rule your life, give him time to figure things out on his own, and not be attended to with every whimper.

> I am going with my instincts and trying to be a good, caring mommy. Putting a baby in his crib to "cry it out" seems cruel. There is no such thing as spoiling an infant!

Where do you stand on this "Teach 'em" versus "Give unconditional love" controversy? Given that in a young baby the cortex has not fully come on-line, the behavioral "teach 'em not to cry" doesn't work during early infancy (Douglas and Hill, 2013; Stremler and others, 2013). But, by about month 7 or 8, it may be better to hang back,

---

Table 3.3: Erikson's Psychosocial Stages

Life Stage	Primary Task
INFANCY (BIRTH TO 1 YEAR)	**BASIC TRUST VERSUS MISTRUST**
Toddlerhood (1 to 2 years)	Autonomy versus shame and doubt
Early childhood (3 to 6 years)	Initiative versus guilt
Late childhood (6 years to puberty)	Industry versus inferiority
Adolescence (teens into twenties)	Identity versus role confusion
Young adulthood (twenties to early forties)	Intimacy versus isolation
Middle adulthood (forties to sixties)	Generativity versus stagnation
Late adulthood (late sixties and beyond)	Integrity versus despair

According to Erikson, in the first year of life, our mission is to feel confident that the human world will lovingly satisfy our needs. Basic trust is the foundation for the challenges we face at every other life stage.

as babies who are quickly picked up may have more trouble learning to self-soothe (St. James-Roberts, 2007). So, if parents care vitally about getting a good night's sleep, it's best not to react to every nighttime whimper—but only when an infant approaches age 1 and can "learn" to get to sleep on her own.

Vigorous "settling activities"—carrying a child around at bedtime, making a big deal of an infant's getting to sleep—are correlated with sleep difficulties at age 5 (Sheridan and others, 2013). Therefore, new parents might metaphorically err on the side of letting sleeping dogs lie, meaning not make excessive efforts to quiet the child. Still, this doesn't mean don't get involved!

When researchers videoed the bedtime behavior of mothers with infants, they found that women who responded sensitively to their babies around bedtime (those who used gentle, loving, pre-bed soothing routines) had children with fewer sleep problems (Teti and others, 2010). So, apart from any specific strategy, the real key to promoting infant sleep is to put a baby to bed with love.

This makes sense. Notice that when you feel disconnected from loved ones and anxious, you have trouble sleeping. To sleep soundly at *any age*, we need to feel cushioned by love.

The same principles—listen to the research, but act with love—apply to having a baby sleep in your bed.

By lovingly preparing his baby for bed, this man is helping ensure a better night's sleep for *both* father and child. He also may be fostering basic trust—according to Erikson, the core foundation for having a good life.

To Co-sleep or Not to Co-sleep: A Cultural and Personal Choice

> It was a standard nighttime routine in our house—one by one we'd wander in and say, "Mommy I'm afraid of witches and ghosts," and soon all four of us would be happily nestled in our parents' huge king-sized bed. I never realized that—in the 1950s, in our uptight, middle-class New York suburb—this family bed-sharing qualified as a radical act.

How do you feel about **co-sleeping** or sharing a bed with a child? If you live in the United States and feel queasy about my parents' decision, you are not alone. Until recently, experts in our individualistic society cautioned parents against co-sleeping (see Ferber, 1985). Behaviorists warned that sharing a bed with a child could produce "excessive dependency." Freudian theorists implied that bed-sharing might place a child at risk for sexual abuse.

In collectivist cultures, people would laugh at these ideas (Latz, Wolf, & Lozoff, 1999; Yang & Hahn, 2002). Japanese parents, for instance, often separate to give each child a sleeping partner, because they believe co-sleeping is crucial to babies developing into caring, loving adults (Kitahara, 1989).

Today, in the West, co-sleeping has come out of the closet. Surveys show that, yes, like my parents, many people do it (Ball, 2007; Germo and others, 2007). But, because some mothers and fathers are still reluctant to admit that fact, Table 3.4 on page 86 provides three typical anti-bed-sharing stereotypes and some relevant research so you can decide which choice works best for you.

In this next section, we'll explore the topic raised by the third stereotype in the table: What causes a baby to die while sleeping, or succumb to *sudden infant death syndrome (SIDS)?*

co-sleeping The standard custom, in collectivist cultures, of having a child and parent share a bed.

Table 3.4: Classic Co-sleeping Stereotypes and Some Relevant Research

1. Stereotype: Co-sleeping makes a child less independent and mature.

Relevant research: Among parents of preschoolers, researchers looked at three groups: (1) people who decided to co-sleep; (2) "reactive co-sleepers," who reluctantly brought a child into their bed because of sleep troubles; and (3) solitary sleepers—those who slept apart from their babies (Keller & Goldberg, 2004). The preschoolers whose parents had decided to co-sleep were more self-reliant (for example, able to dress themselves) and socially independent (for example, more able to make friends by themselves) compared to the other two groups. In a more recent study, co-sleeping early in life had calming effects. The more time a child spent bed-sharing from birth to 6 months of age, the lower a baby's cortisol production (a stress hormone) after being exposed to a stressor at age 1 (Beijars, Riksen-Walraven, & De Weerth, 2013). Therefore, if we look simply at parents who *choose* to co-sleep, bed-sharing may promote greater resilience and maturity, not less!

2. Stereotype: Co-sleeping disrupts parents' and children's sleep.

Relevant research: Co-sleeping infants do awaken more often at night than solitary sleepers. However, co-sleeping babies get back to sleep in a shorter time (Latz, Wolf, & Lozoff, 1999; Mao and others, 2004). With regard to adults, one EEG sleep study found that parents who shared a bed with their infant spent a bit less time in the deepest sleep stages. However, because they did not have to go into the child's room, these parents did not spend fewer hours sleeping than the non-bed-sharing moms and dads (Mosko, Richard, & McKenna, 1997). Bottom line: Co-sleeping is not detrimental to sleep.

3. Stereotype: Co-sleeping is dangerous because it can cause a baby to be smothered.

Relevant research: Here, there may be a few concerns. While some authors argue that co-sleeping helps regulate babies' breathing and so *may* help prevent suffocating at night (see St. James-Roberts, 2007), bed-sharing infants spend a good fraction of their sleep time face down (Mao and others, 2004). This sleep position, as you can see in the Hot in Developmental Science feature does not offer the best protection against the ultimate smothering tragedy, SIDS.

 Hot in Developmental Science: SIDS

sudden infant death syndrome (SIDS) The unexplained death of an apparently healthy infant, often while sleeping, during the first year of life.

Sudden infant death syndrome (SIDS) refers to the unexplained death of an apparently healthy infant, often while sleeping, during the first months of life. Although it strikes only about 1 in 1,000 U.S. babies, SIDS is a top-ranking cause of infant mortality in the developed world (Karns, 2001).

What causes SIDS? In autopsying infants who died during the peak risk zone for SIDS (about 1 to 10 months), researchers targeted abnormalities in a particular region of the brain. Specifically, SIDS infants had either too many or too few neurons in a section of the brain stem involved in coordinating tongue movements and maintaining the airway when we inhale (Lavezzi and others, 2010). SIDS has been linked to pathologies in the part of the brain stem producing cerebrospinal fluid, too (Lavezzi and others, 2013).

But even if SIDS is caused by biological pre-birth problems, this tragedy can have post-birth environmental causes. In particular, SIDS is linked to infants being inadvertently smothered, by being placed face down in a "fluffy" crib. During the early 1990s, this evidence prompted the American Academy of Pediatrics to urge parents to put infants to sleep on their backs. The "Back to Sleep" campaign worked, because from 1992 to 1997, there was a 43 percent reduction in SIDS deaths in the United States (Gore & DuBois, 1998).

Still, because placing babies on their backs can demand infants' sleep separately in a crib, the "Back to Sleep" public health message contradicts the strong pro co-sleeping culture among non-Western groups. To circumvent this barrier, New Zealand scientists devised a strategy to permit Maori mothers to follow their traditional sleeping style and minimize the SIDS risk. They encouraged these women to return to another old-style practice—weaving a baby sleeping-basket. By placing this basket on parents' beds, co-sleeping has now become scientifically "correct" (Ball & Volpe, 2013)!

studiomoment/iStock/Getty Images

This portable sleeping basket is user friendly around the world, but in the Maori culture, it qualifies as culture friendly, too.

Table 3.5 offers a section summary in the form of practical tips for caregivers dealing with infants' eating, crying, and sleeping. Now it's time to move on to sensory development and moving into the world.

Table 3.5: Infants' Basic States: Summary Tips for Caregivers (and Others)

Eating

- Don't worry about continual newborn sucking and rooting. These are normal reflexes, and they disappear after the first months of life.
- As the baby becomes mobile, be alert to the child's tendency to put everything into the mouth and baby-proof the home (see the next section's discussion).
- Try to breast-feed, but if nursing becomes too difficult, don't berate yourself. The benefits breast-fed babies show may mainly result from having more loving "bonding time."
- Employers should make efforts to support breast-feeding in the workplace. Society should celebrate women who nurse in public. However, people should not criticize women for "failing" at this task.
- After the child is weaned, provide a balanced diet. But don't get frantic if a toddler limits her intake to a few "favorite foods" at around age 1 1/2—this pickiness is normal and temporary.

Crying

- Appreciate that crying is crucial—it's the way babies communicate their needs—and realize that this behavior is at its peak during the first months of life. The frequency of crying declines and the reasons why the child is crying become far clearer after early infancy.
- If a baby has colic, hang in there. This condition typically ends at month 4. Moreover, understand that colic has nothing to do with insensitive mothering.
- During the day, carry a young infant around in a "baby sling" as much as possible. In addition, employ infant massage to soothe the baby.

Sleeping

- Expect to be sleep-deprived for the first few months, until the typical infant learns to self-soothe; meanwhile, try to take regular naps. After that, expect periodic sleep problems and understand that children will give up their daytime nap at around age 2.
- After about 6 to 8 months of age, to promote self-soothing, don't go to the infant at the first whimper. But the choice is really up to you—as the best way to promote sleep is to put your baby to bed with love.
- Co-sleeping—having a child sleep in your bed—is a personal decision. Although most of the stereotypes about co-sleeping are wrong, this practice may not be completely safe with young infants, as bed-sharing may slightly increase the risk of SIDS.

Tying It All Together

1. You're a nurse in the obstetrics ward, and new parents often ask you why their babies turn their heads toward anything that touches their cheek and then suck. You say (pick two): *This is called the rooting reflex; This behavior is programmed by the lower brain centers to automatically occur at birth and disappear as the brain matures; This is a sign of early intelligence.*

2. Elaine tells you that breast-feeding is more difficult than medical authorities suggest. Make her argument, drawing on the points in this section.

3. Your sister and her husband are under enormous stress because of their 1-month-old's crying. Based on this section, give your relatives advice for soothing their child. What standard child-soothing strategy mentioned in the text would you *not* recommend?

4. Jorge tells you that he's thrilled because last night his 6-month-old finally slept through the night. Is Jorge's child ahead of schedule, behind, or on time for this milestone? Is Jorge right in saying, "My child is sleeping *through* the night"?

5. Take a poll of your classmates, asking them if they believe in co-sleeping and whether they would immediately go in to quiet a crying infant. Do you find any differences in their answers by ethnicity, by gender, or by age?

Answers to the Tying It All Together questions can be found at the end of this chapter.

Sensory and Motor Development

Sleeping, eating, and crying are easy to observe; but suppose you could time-travel back to your first days of life. What would you experience through your senses?

One sense is definitely operational before we leave the womb. Using ultrasound, researchers can see startle reactions in fetuses in response to noise, showing that rudimentary hearing capacities exist before birth. Recall from the previous chapter that the basics of vision may also be in place by about the seventh month of fetal life.

Table 3.6 lists other interesting facts about newborn senses. Now, let's focus on vision because the research in this area is so extensive, the findings are so astonishing, and the studies devised to get into babies' heads are so brilliantly planned.

What Do Newborns See?

Imagine you are a researcher who wants to figure out what a newborn can see. What do you do? As might be logical, you put the baby into an apparatus, present images, and watch her eyes move. Specifically, researchers use the **preferential-looking paradigm**—the principle that human beings are attracted to novelty and look selectively at new things. They also draw on a process called **habituation**—the fact that we naturally lose interest in a new object after some time.

You can notice preferential looking and habituation in operation right now in your life. If you see or hear something new, you look up with interest. After a minute, you habituate and return to reading this book.

By showing newborns small- and large-striped patterns and measuring preferential looking, researchers have found that at birth our ability to see clearly at distances is very poor. With a visual acuity score of roughly 20/400 (versus our ideal adult 20/20), a newborn would qualify as legally blind in many states (Kellman & Banks, 1998). Because the visual cortex matures quickly, vision improves rapidly, and by about age 1, infants see just like adults.

What visual capacities *do* we have at birth? A century ago, the first American psychologist, William James, described the inner life of the newborn as "one buzzing, blooming confusion." Studies exploring **face perception** (making sense of human faces) offer scientific data about the truth of James' ideas.

preferential-looking paradigm A research technique to explore early infant sensory capacities and cognition, drawing on the principle that we are attracted to novelty and prefer to look at new things.

habituation The predictable loss of interest that develops once a stimulus becomes familiar; used to explore infant sensory capacities and thinking.

face-perception studies Research using preferential looking and habituation to explore what very young babies know about faces.

Table 3.6: Some Interesting Facts About Other Newborn Senses

Hearing: Fetuses can discriminate different tones in the womb (Lecanuet and others, 2000). Newborns prefer women's voices, as they are selectively sensitive to higher-pitched tones. At less than 1 week of age, babies recognize their mother's voice (DeCasper & Fifer, 1980). By 1 month of age, they tune in to infant-directed speech (described on page 101) communications tailored to them.

Smell: Newborns prefer the odor of breast milk to that of amniotic fluid (Marlier, Schaal, & Soussignan, 1998). The smell of breast milk, unlike formula, increases blood flow in newborn's frontal lobes—which may be another benefit of nursing for 6 months (Aoyama and others, 2010). Plus, smelling breast milk has a soothing effect; newborns cry more vigorously when facing a scentless breast (one covered with a transparent film) (Doucet and others, 2007).

Taste: Newborns are sensitive to basic tastes. When they taste a bitter, sour, or salty substance, they stop sucking and wrinkle their faces. They will suck more avidly on a sweet solution, although they will stop if the substance grows too sweet. Having babies suck a sweet solution before a painful experience, such as a heel stick, reduces agitation and so can be used as a pain-management technique (Fernandez and others, 2003; Gibbins & Stevens, 2001).

Focusing on Faces

Actually, when we emerge from the womb, we are primed to selectively attend to the social world. When presented with the paired stimuli in Figure 3.6, newborns spend more time looking at the face pattern than at the scrambled pattern. They follow that facelike stimulus longer when it is moved from side to side (Farroni, Massaccesi, & Simion, 2002; Slater and others, 2010).

The story gets more interesting. Newborns can make amazing distinctions. During their first week of life, they prefer to look at a photo of their mother compared to one of a stranger (Bushnell, 1998). Newborns prefer attractive-looking people too!

Researchers selected photos of attractive and unattractive women, then took infants from the maternity ward and measured preferential looking. The attractive faces got looked at significantly longer—61 percent of the time (Slater and others, 2010). By 3 to 6 months of age, babies preferentially look at good-looking infants and children. They even prefer handsome men and pretty women of different racial groups (Slater, 2001). Unhappily, our tendency to gravitate toward people for their looks seems somewhat biologically built in. (In case you are interested, more symmetrical faces tend to be rated as better-looking.)

We also seem prewired to gravitate to *relationships*. Newborns look longer at faces when the "eyes" are gazing directly at them (Frischen, Bayliss, & Tipper, 2007). They can mimic facial expressions that an adult makes, such as sticking out the tongue (Meltzoff & Moore, 1977). So if you have wondered why you get uncomfortable when someone stares at you, or have agonized at your humiliating tendency to mimic everyone else's gestures and facial tics, this research offers answers. It's not a personal problem. It's built into our human biology, beginning from day one!

With experience, our sensitivity to faces—and the emotions they reveal—markedly improves. But fascinating research suggests that early experience also shapes what we learn *not* to see (Slater and others, 2010).

Developmentalists tested European American babies at different points during their first year of life for their ability to discriminate between different faces within their own racial group and those belonging to other ethnicities (African American, Middle Eastern, and Chinese). While the 3-month-olds preferentially looked at "new faces" of every ethnicity, showing they could see the differences between individuals in each group, by 9 months of age, the babies could only discriminate between faces of their own ethnicity.

Why did this skill disappear? The cause, as you may have guessed, is cortical pruning—the fact that unneeded synapses in our visual system atrophy or are lost (Slater and others, 2010). So if you have wondered why other races look more alike (compared to your own ethnic group, of course!), it's a misperception. You learned not to see these differences during your first year of life!

Is Prejudice Partly Prewired?

This tantalizing research suggests that spending our first years of life in a racially homogenous environment might promote prejudice because the resulting neural atrophy could blunt our ability to decode the emotions of other ethnic groups. Amazingly, in testing U.S. teens adopted from Eastern European or Asian orphanages (places where infants are only exposed to caregivers of their ethnicity), scientists discovered that this was true. The longer a child lived in an orphanage, the less sensitive that adolescent was at picking up facial expressions of people from other races. Moreover, fMRI recordings showed an unusual spike in the amygdala (our brain's fear center) when these young people viewed "foreign" faces. Therefore, simply being born in a multicultural city, such as New York or Chicago, might make us more toler-

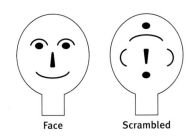

Face   Scrambled

FIGURE 3.6: **Babies prefer faces:** When shown these illustrations, newborns looked most at the facelike drawing. Might the fact that infants are biologically programmed to selectively look at faces be built into evolution to help ensure that adults give babies loving care?

ant because that experience prewires us *visually* to be more sensitive to the feelings of other races (Telzer and others, 2013)!

The main conclusion, however, is that William James was wrong. Newborns don't experience the world as a "blooming, buzzing confusion." We arrive in life with a built-in antenna to tune into the human world. But also, visual skills change as we mature, in sometimes surprising ways.

Now let's trace another visual capacity as it comes on-line—the ability to see and become frightened of heights.

Seeing Depth and Fearing Heights

depth perception The ability to see (and fear) heights.

visual cliff A table that appears to "end" in a drop-off at its midpoint; used to test for infant depth perception.

Imagine you are a researcher facing a conundrum: How can I find out when babies develop **depth perception**—the ability to "see" variations in heights—without causing them harm? Elinor Gibson's ingenious solution: Develop a procedure called the **visual cliff**. As Figure 3.7 shows, Gibson and her colleague placed infants on one end of a table with a checkerboard pattern while their mothers stood at the opposite end (Gibson & Walk, 1960). At the table's midpoint, the checkerboard design moved from table to floor level, so it appeared to the babies that if they crawled beyond that point, they would fall. Even when parents encouraged their children to crawl to them, by 8 months of age, babies refused to venture beyond what looked like the drop-off—showing that depth perception fully comes on-line, but only about this age.

In sum, the sick feeling you have when leaning over a balcony—"Wow, I'd better avoid falling into that space below"—emerged when you started moving into the world and needed that fear to protect you from getting hurt. How does mobility unfold?

FIGURE 3.7: The visual cliff: Even though his mother is on the other side, this 8-month-old child gets anxious about venturing beyond what looks like the drop-off point in the table—demonstrating that by this age babies have depth perception.

Expanding Body Size

Our brain may expand dramatically after birth. Still, it's out-paced by the blossoming of the envelope in which we live. Our bodies grow to 21 times their newborn size by the time we reach adulthood (Slater, 2001). This growth is most dramatic during infancy, slows down during childhood, and increases in velocity again during the preadolescent years. Still, looking at overall height and weight statistics is not that revealing. This body sculpting occurs in a definite way.

Imagine taking time-lapse photographs of a baby's head from birth to adulthood and comparing your photos to snapshots of the body. While you would not see much change in the overall size and shape of the head, the body would elongate and thin out. Newborns start out with tiny "frog" legs timed to slowly straighten out by about month 6. Then comes the stocky, bowlegged toddler, followed by the slimmer child of kindergarten and elementary school. So during childhood, growth follows the same principle as inside the womb: Development proceeds according to the *cephalocaudal sequence*—from the head to the feet.

Now think of Mickey Mouse, Big Bird, and Elmo. They, too, have relatively large heads and small bodies. Might our favorite cartoon characters be enticing because they mimic the proportions of a baby? Did the deliciously rounded infant shape evolve to seduce adults into giving babies special care?

Mastering Motor Milestones

Actually, all three growth principles spelled out in the previous chapter—*cephalocaudal*, *proximodistal*, and *mass-to-specific*—apply to infant *motor milestones*, the exciting progression of physical abilities during the first year of life. First, babies lift their head, then pivot their upper body, then sit up without support, and finally stand (the cephalocaudal sequence). Infants have control of their shoulders before they can make their arms and fingers obey their commands (proximodistal sequence, from interior to outer parts).

But the most important principle programming motor abilities throughout childhood is the *mass-to-specific* sequence (large before small and detailed). From the wobbly first step at age 1 to the home run out of the ballpark during the teenage years—as the neurons myelinate—big, uncoordinated movements are honed and perfected as we move from infancy to adult life.

The tiny frog legs of very early infancy straighten out by month 6 and then become longer and fully functional for carrying us around (as toddlers)—demonstrating the cephalocaudal principle of development.

Variations (and Joys) Related to Infant Mobility

Charting these milestones does not speak to the joy of witnessing them unfold—that landmark moment when your daughter masters turning over, after those practice "push-ups," or first connects with the bottle, grasps it, and awkwardly moves it to her mouth. I'll never forget when my own son, after what seemed like years of cruising around holding onto the furniture, finally ventured (so gingerly) out into the air, flung up his hands, and, yes, yes, took his ecstatic first step!

The charts don't mention the hilarious glitches that happen when a skill is emerging—the first days of creeping, when a baby can only move backward and you find him huddled in the corner in pursuit of objects that get farther way. Or when a child first pulls herself to a standing position in the crib, and her triumphant expression changes to bewilderment: "Whoops, now tell me, Mom, *how do I get down?*"

Actually, rather than viewing motor development in static stages, researchers now stress the variability and ingenuity of babies' passion to get moving into life (Adolph, 2008). Consider the "creeping" or belly-crawling stage. Some babies scoot; others hunch over or launch themselves forward from their knees, roll from side to side, or scrape along with a cheek on the floor (Adolph & Berger, 2006). And can I *really* say that there was a day when my son mastered walking? When walking, or any other major motor skill first occurs, children do not make steady progress (Adolph & Berger, 2006). They may take their first solo step on Monday and then revert to crawling for a week or so before trying, oh so tentatively, to tackle toddling again.

At 8 or 10 months of age, getting around is a challenge that babies approach in a variety of creative, unique ways.

But suppose a child is behind schedule. Let's say your son is almost 15 months old and has yet to take his first solo step? And what about the fantasies that set in when an infant is ahead? "Only 8 months old, and he's walking. Perhaps my baby is special, a genius!"

What typically happens is that, within weeks, the worries become a memory and the fantasies about the future are shown to be completely wrong. Except in the case of children who have developmental disorders, the rate at which babies master motor milestones has no relation to their later intelligence. Since different regions of the cortex develop at different times, why should our walking or grasping-an-object timetable predict development in a complex function such as grasping the point of this book?

But even if a baby's early locomotion (physically getting around) does not mean he will end up an Einstein, each motor achievement provokes other advances.

Motor Milestones Have Widespread Effects

Consider, for instance, that landmark event: reaching. Because it allows babies to physically make contact with the world, the urge to grasp objects propels sitting, as a child will tolerate plopping over in her hunger to touch everything she can (Harbourne and others, 2013).

Now consider how crawling changes the parent–child bond (Campos and others, 2000). When infants crawl, parents see their children as more independent—people with a mind of their own. Many say this is the first time they discipline their child. So as babies get mobile, our basic child-rearing agenda emerges: Children's mission is to explore the world. A parent's job, for the next two decades, lies in setting limits to that exploration, as well as giving love.

baby-proofing Making the home safe for a newly mobile infant.

INTERVENTIONS: **Baby-Proofing, the First Person–Environment Fit**

Motor development presents perils. Now safety issues become a concern. How can caretakers encourage these emerging skills and still protect children from getting hurt? The answer is to strive for the right person–environment fit—that is, to **baby-proof** the house.

Get on the floor and look at life from the perspective of the child. Cover electrical outlets and put dangerous cleaning substances on the top shelf. Unplug countertop appliances. Take small objects off tables. Perhaps pad the furniture corners, too. The challenge is to anticipate possible dangers and to stay one step ahead. There will come a day when that child can pry out those outlet covers or ascend to the top of the cleanser-laden cabinet. Unfortunately, those exciting milestones have a downside, too!

Tying It All Together

1. Your 3-month-old perks up when you start the vacuum cleaner, and then after a moment, loses interest. You are using a kind of _____ paradigm; and the scientific term for when your baby loses interest is _____.

2. Tania says, "Visual capacities improve dramatically during the first year of life." Thomas replies, "No, in some ways our vision gets worse." Who is correct: Tania, Thomas, or both students? Why?

3. One implication of the face perception studies is that the roots of adult prejudice begin (choose one) *at birth/during the second 6 months of life/after age 2.*

4. If Alicia's 8-month-old daughter is participating in a visual cliff study, when she approaches the drop-off, she should (choose one): *crawl over it/be frightened.*

5. What steps would you take to baby-proof the room you are sitting in right now?

Answers to the Tying It All Together questions can be found at the end of this chapter.

Cognition

Why *do* infants have an incredible hunger to explore, to reach, to touch, to get into every cleanser-laden cabinet and remove outlet plugs? For the same reason that, if you landed on a different planet, you would need to get the basics of reality down.

Imagine stepping out onto Mars. You would roam the new environment, exploring the rocks and the sand. While exercising your *walking schema*, or habitual way of physically navigating, you would need to make drastic changes. On Mars, with its minimal gravity, when you took your normal earthling stride, you would probably bounce up 20 feet. Just like a newly crawling infant, you would have to accommodate, and in the process reach a higher mental equilibrium, or a better understanding of life. Moreover, as a scientist, you would not be satisfied to perform each movement only once. The way to pin down the physics of this planet would be to repeat each action over and over again. Now you have the basic principles of Jean Piaget's **sensorimotor stage** (see Table 3.7).

Piaget's Sensorimotor Stage

Specifically, Piaget believed that during our first two years on this planet, our mission is to make sense of physical reality by exploring the world through our senses. Just as in the above Mars example, as they *assimilate*, or fit the outer world to what they are capable of doing, infants *accommodate* and so gradually mentally advance. (Remember my example in Chapter 1 of how, in the process of assimilating this information to your current knowledge schemas or mental slots, you are accommodating and so expanding what you know.)

Let's take the "everything into the mouth" schema that figures so prominently during the first year of life. As babies mouth each new object—or, in Piaget's words, assimilate everything to their mouthing schema—they realize that objects have different characteristics. Some are soft or prickly. Others taste terrible or great. Through continual assimilation and accommodation, by age 2, babies make a dramatic mental leap—from relying on a set of reflexes, to reasoning and using symbolic thought.

Circular Reactions: Habits That Pin Down Reality

By observing his own three children, Piaget discovered that driving all these advances were what he called **circular reactions**—habits, or action-oriented schemas, the child repeats again and again.

sensorimotor stage Piaget's first stage of cognitive development, lasting from birth to age 2, when babies' agenda is to pin down the basics of physical reality.

circular reactions In Piaget's framework, repetitive action-oriented schemas (or habits) characteristic of babies during the sensorimotor stage.

Table 3.7: Piaget's Stages: Focus on Infancy

Age	Name of Stage	Description
0–2	Sensorimotor	The baby manipulates objects to pin down the basics of physical reality. This stage ends with the development of language.
2–7	Preoperations	Children's perceptions are captured by their immediate appearances. "What they see is what is real." They believe, among other things, that inanimate objects are really alive and that if the appearance of a quantity of liquid changes (for example, if it is poured from a short, wide glass into a tall, thin one), the amount actually becomes different.
8–12	Concrete operations	Children have a realistic understanding of the world. Their thinking is really on the same wavelength as adults. While they can reason conceptually about concrete objects, however, they cannot think abstractly in a scientific way.
12+	Formal operations	Reasoning is at its pinnacle: hypothetical, scientific, flexible, fully adult. Our full cognitive human potential has been reached.

primary circular reactions In Piaget's framework, the first infant habits during the sensorimotor stage, centered on the body.

secondary circular reactions In Piaget's framework, habits of the sensorimotor stage lasting from about 4 months of age to the baby's first birthday, centered on exploring the external world.

tertiary circular reactions In Piaget's framework, "little-scientist" activities of the sensorimotor stage, beginning around age 1, involving flexibly exploring the properties of objects.

little-scientist phase The time around age 1 when babies use tertiary circular reactions to actively explore the properties of objects, experimenting with them like "scientists."

means–end behavior In Piaget's framework, performing a different action to get to a goal—an ability that emerges in the sensorimotor stage as babies approach age 1.

From the newborn reflexes, during months 1 to 4, **primary circular reactions** develop. These are repetitive actions centered on the child's body. A thumb randomly makes contact with his mouth, and a 2-month-old removes that interesting object, observes it, and moves it in and out. Waving her legs captivates a 3-month-old for hours.

At around 4 months of age, **secondary circular reactions** appear. As the cortex blossoms and the child begins to reach, action-oriented schemas become centered on the *outside* world. Here is how Piaget described his daughter Lucienne's first secondary circular reactions:

> Lucienne at 0:4 [4 months] is lying in her bassinet. I hang a doll over her feet which . . . sets in motion the schema of shakes. Her feet reach the doll . . . and give it a violent movement which Lucienne surveys with delight . . . . After the first shakes, Lucienne makes slow foot movements as though to grasp and explore . . . . When she tries to kick the doll, and misses . . . she begins again very slowly until she succeeds [without looking at her feet].
>
> (Piaget, 1950, p. 159 [as cited in Flavell, 1963, p. 103])

During the next few months, secondary circular reactions become better coordinated. By about 8 months of age, babies can simultaneously employ two circular reactions, using both grasping and kicking together to explore the world.

Then, around a baby's first birthday, **tertiary circular reactions** appear. Now, the child is no longer constrained by stereotyped schemas. He can operate just like a real scientist, flexibly changing his behavior to make sense of the world. A toddler becomes captivated by the toilet, throwing toys and different types of paper into the bowl. At dinner, he gleefully spits his food out at varying velocities and hurls his bottle off the high chair in different directions to see where it lands.

How important are circular reactions in infancy? Spend time with a young baby, as she bats at her mobile or joyously pinwheels her legs. Try to prevent a 1-year-old from hurling plates from a high chair, flushing money down the toilet, or inserting bits of cookie into a USB slot. Then you will understand: Infancy is all about the insatiable drive to repeat interesting acts. (See Table 3.8 for a recap of the circular reactions, as well as a look at the sensorimotor substages.)

Piaget's concept of circular reactions offers a new perspective on those obsessions that drive adults crazy during what researchers call the **little-scientist phase** (and parents call the "getting into everything" phase). This is the time, around age 1, when the child begins experimenting with objects in a way that mimics how a scientist behaves: "Let me try this, then that, and see what happens." The reason you can't derail a 1-year-old from putting oatmeal into the computer, or clogging the toilet with your hard-earned wages (making a plumber a parent's new best friend) is that circular reactions allow infants to pin down the basic properties of the world.

Why do *specific* circular reactions, such as flushing dollar bills down the toilet, become irresistible during the little-scientist phase? This question brings me to Piaget's ideas about how babies progress from reflexes to the ability to think.

Tracking Early Thinking

How do we know when infants begin to think? According to Piaget, one hallmark of thinking is deferred imitation—repeating an action that was witnessed at an earlier time. When Piaget saw Lucienne, at 16 months of age, mimic a tantrum she had seen another child have days earlier, he realized she had the mental skills to keep that image in her mind, mull it over, and translate it into action on her own. Another sign of reasoning is make-believe play. To pretend you are cleaning the house or talking on the phone like Mommy, you must realize that something *signifies*, or stands for, something else.

But the most important sign of emerging reasoning is **means–end behavior**—when the child is able to perform a separate, or different, action to get to a goal. Pushing the toilet lever to make the water swirl down, manipulating a switch to turn

Table 3.8: The Circular Reactions: A Summary Table (with a Look at Piaget's Sensorimotor Substages)

Primary Circular Reactions: 1–4 months

Description: Repetitive habits center around the child's own body.

Examples: Sucking toes; sucking thumb.

Rommel/Masterfile

Secondary Circular Reactions: 4 months–1 year

Description: Child "wakes up to wider world." Habits center on environmental objects.

Examples: Grabbing for toys; batting mobiles; pushing one's body to activate the lights and sounds on a swing.

Substages: From 4 to 8 months, children use single secondary circular reactions such as those above; from 8 to 12 months, they employ two circular reactions in concert to attain a goal (i.e., they may grab a toy in each hand, bat a mobile back and forth, coordinate the motions of toys).

© Christina Kennedy/PhotoEdit

Tertiary Circular Reactions: 1–2 years

Description: Child flexibly explores the properties of objects, like a "little scientist."

Examples: Exploring the various dimensions of a toy; throwing a bottle off the high chair in different directions; putting different kinds of food in the computer; flushing dollars down the toilet.

Substages: From 12 to 18 months, the child experiments with concrete objects; from 18 to 24 months, his little-scientist behavior transcends what is observable and involves using symbols to stand for something else. (I'll be describing the many advances ushered in by this ability to reason symbolically in later chapters.)

American Images Inc/Getty Images

on the light, screwing open a bottle to extract the juice—all are examples of "doing something different" to reach a particular end.

If you have access to a 1-year-old, you might try to construct your own means–end task. First, show the child something she wants, such as a cookie or a toy. Then, put the object in a place where the baby must perform a different type of action to get the treat. For instance, you might put the cookie in a clear container and cover the top with Saran Wrap. Will the baby ineffectively bang the side of the container, or will she figure out the *different* step (removing the cover) essential to retrieving what she wants? If you conduct your test by putting the cookie in an opaque container, the baby must have another basic understanding: She must realize that—although she doesn't see it—the cookie still exists.

Object Permanence: Believing in a Stable World

Object permanence refers to knowing that objects exist even when we no longer see them—a perception that is, obviously, fundamental to our sense of living in a stable world. Suppose you felt that this book disappeared when you averted your eyes or

object permanence In Piaget's framework, the understanding that objects continue to exist even when we can no longer see them, which gradually emerges during the sensorimotor stage.

A minute ago, this 4-month-old girl was delightedly grabbing this little dog but, when this barrier blocked her image, it was "out of sight, out of mind." If you have access to a young baby, can you perform this test to track the beginning of *object permanence?*

A-not-B error In Piaget's framework, a classic mistake made by infants in the sensorimotor stage, whereby babies approaching age 1 go back to the original hiding place to look for an object even though they have seen it get hidden in a second place.

that your house rematerialized out of nothing when you entered your driveway. Piaget believed that object permanence is not inborn. This perception develops gradually throughout the sensorimotor stage.

Piaget's observations suggested that during babies' first few months, life is a series of disappearing pictures. If an enticing image, such as her mother, passed her line of sight, Lucienne would stare at the place from which the image had vanished as if it would reappear out of thin air. (The relevant phrase here is "out of sight, out of mind.") Then, around month 5, when the *secondary circular reactions* are first flowering, there was a milestone. An object dropped out of sight and Lucienne leaned over to look for it, suggesting that she knew it existed independently of her gaze. Still, this sense of a stable object was fragile. The baby quickly abandoned her search after Piaget covered that object with his hand.

Hunting for hidden objects under covers becomes an absorbing game as children approach age one. Still, around 9 or 10 months of age, children make a surprising mistake called the **A-not-B error.** If you put an object in full view of a baby into one out-of-sight location, have the baby get it, and then move it to another place while the child is watching, she will look for it in the initial place!

See if you can perform this classic test if you have access to a 10-month-old: Place an object, such as a toy, under a piece of paper (A). Then have the baby find it in that place a few times. Next, remove the toy as the infant watches and put it under a different piece of paper (B). What happens? Even though the child saw you put the toy in the new location, he will probably look under the A paper again, as if it had migrated unseen to its original place!

After their first birthday, children seem to master the basic principle. Move an object to a new hiding place and they look for it in the correct location. However, as Piaget found when he used this strategy but *covered* the object with his hand, object permanence does not fully emerge until children are almost 2 years old.

Emerging object permanence explains many puzzles about development. Why does peek-a-boo become a favorite activity at around 8 months? The reason is that a child now thinks there is *probably* still someone behind those hands, but doesn't know for sure.

Emerging object permanence offers a wonderful perspective on why younger babies are so laid back when you remove an interesting object, and then become possessive by their second year of life. Those toddler tantrums do not signal a new, awful personality trait called "the terrible twos." They simply show that children are smarter. They have the cognitive skills to know that objects still exist when you take them away.

Finally, the concept of object permanence, or fascination with disappearing objects, plus means–end behavior, makes sense of that passion to flush dollar bills down the toilet or the compulsion to stick bits of cookie in a USB port. What could be more tantalizing during the little-scientist phase than taking a new action to get to a goal plus causing things to disappear and possibly reappear? It also explains why you can't go wrong if you buy your toddler nephew a pop-up toy.

But during the first year of life there is no need to arrive with any toy. Buy a toy for an infant and he will push it aside to play with the box. Your nephew probably prefers fiddling with the TV remote to any object from Toys R Us. Toys only become interesting once we realize that they are different from real life. So, a desire for dolls or action figures—or for anything that requires make-believe play—shows that a child is making the transition from the sensorimotor period to symbolic thought. With the concepts of circular reactions, emerging object permanence, and means–end behavior, Piaget masterfully made sense of the puzzling passions of infant life!

Critiquing Piaget

Piaget's insights have transformed the way we think about childhood. Research confirms the fact that children are, at heart, little scientists. The passion to decode the world is built into being human from our first months of life (Gopnik, 2010). However, Piaget's timing was seriously off. Piaget's trouble was that he had to rely on babies' actions (for instance, taking covers off hidden objects) to figure out what they knew. He did not have creative strategies, like preferential looking and habituation, to decode what babies' understand before they can physically respond. Using these techniques, researchers realized that young infants know far more about life than this master theorist ever believed. Specifically, scientists now know that:

For this 1-year-old, pushing the buttons on the TV remote is utterly captivating. Information processing researchers want to understand what specific skills made this boy capable of achieving this miraculous means–end feat.

- **Infants grasp the basics of physical reality well before age 1.** To demonstrate this point, developmentalist Renée Baillargeon (1993) presented young babies with physically impossible events such as showing a traveling rabbit that never appeared in a gap it had to pass through to reach its place on the other side (illustrated in Figure 3.8A). Even 5-month-olds looked astonished when they saw these impossible events. You could almost hear them thinking, "I know that's not the way objects should behave."

- **Infants' understanding of physical reality develops gradually.** For instance, while Baillargeon discovered that the impossible event of the traveling rabbit in the figure provoked astonishment around month 5, other research shows it takes until age 1 for babies to master other basics about the world, such as the fact that you cannot take a large rabbit out of a little container (shown in Figure 3.8B). (As an aside, that explains why "magic" suddenly becomes interesting only around age 2 or 3.) Therefore, rather than viewing development in huge qualitative stages, many contemporary researchers adopt a more specific approach: focusing on particular mental processes such as memory; decoding step by step how cognition *gradually* emerges.

Information-processing researchers use the metaphor of a computer with separate processing steps to decode children's (and adults') intellectual skills. For instance, instead of seeing means–end behavior as a capacity that suddenly emerges at age 1, a psychologist using this approach would isolate the talents involved in this milestone—memory, attention, the ability to inhibit your immediate perception—and chart how each skill develops over time.

information-processing approach A perspective on understanding cognition that divides thinking into specific steps and component processes, much like a computer.

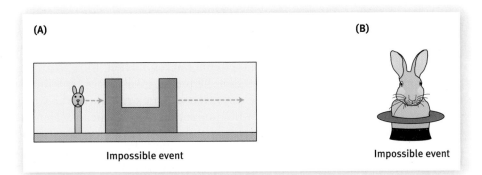

(A)

Impossible event

(B)

Impossible event

FIGURE 3.8: **Two impossible events:** At about 5 months of age babies were surprised by the physically impossible sequence in A—but they did not look surprised by the event in B till about age one. The bottom line: Infants understand the physical world far earlier than Piaget believed, but this knowledge occurs gradually.

Adapted from: Baillargeon, 1993; Baillargeon & DeVos, 1991; Baillargeon & Graber, 1987.

Table 3.9: Infant Memory and Conceptual Abilities: Some Interesting Findings

Memory: By using deferred imitation (see the text discussion), researchers find that babies as young as 9 months of age can "remember" events from the previous day. Infants will push a button if they saw an adult performing that act 24 hours earlier. In another study, most 10-month-olds imitated an action they saw one month earlier. There even have been cases where babies this age saw an action and then remembered it a year later.*

Forming categories: By 7 to 9 months of age, babies are able to distinguish between animals and vehicles. They will feed an animal or put it to bed, but even if they watch an adult put a car to bed, they will not model her action. So the first classification babies make is between something that moves by itself or cannot move on its own. (Is it alive, like an animal, or inanimate?) Then, categorization abilities get more refined depending on familiarity. Eleven-month-old infants, for example, can often distinguish between dogs and cats but not among dogs, rabbits, and fish.

Understanding numbers: By about 5 months of age, infants can make differentiations between different numbers—for instance, after seeing three dots on a screen, they will look preferentially at a subsequent screen showing four dots. They also have an implicit understanding of addition and subtraction. If they see someone add one doll to another, or take away a doll from a set, they look surprised when they see an image on a screen showing the incorrect number of dolls.

Information from: Mandler, 2007.

*Because deferred imitation reflects the child's memory capacities, a preverbal baby's skill in this area predicts the rapidity of language development and later IQ scores.

---

social cognition Any skill related to understanding feelings and negotiating interpersonal interactions.

Table 3.9 showcases insights about babies' memories and mathematical capacities, derived from using this gradual, specific approach. Stay tuned for Chapters 5 and 13, to see how information processing sheds light on memory and thinking during elementary school and old age. Now, it's time to tackle another question: What do babies understand about human minds?

Tackling the Core of What Makes Us Human: Infant Social Cognition

Social cognition refers to any skill related to managing and decoding people's emotions, and getting along with other human beings. One hallmark of being human is that we are always making inferences about people's feelings and goals, based on their actions. ("He's running, so he must be late." "She slammed the door in my face, so she must be angry.") When do these judgments first occur? Piaget would say not before age 2 (or much later) because infants in the sensorimotor period can't think conceptually. Here, too, Piaget was incorrect. Babies make sophisticated judgments about intentions at an incredibly young age!

After seeing this video sequence of events, even infants under 6 months of age preferentially reached for the "nice" tiger rather than the "mean dog"—showing that the fundamental human *social-cognitive* awareness, "he's acting mean or nice" emerges at a remarkably young age.

The strategy here is to first show infants a video of a puppet or stuffed animal helping another puppet complete a challenging task (the nice puppet). In the next scene, another puppet hinders the stuffed animal from reaching his goal (the mean puppet). (See the photos at left.) Then, the experimenter offers the baby both puppets and sees if she preferentially grabs for either one. And guess what? By the time they can reach (at about month 5), most infants grasp the nice puppet rather than the puppet that acted "mean" (Hamlin & Wynn, 2011; Hamlin, 2013).

This remarkable finding suggests we clue into motivations such as "She's not nice!" months before we begin to speak (Hamlin, 2013). More astonishing, 8-month-old babies can make adultlike judgments about intentions. They preferentially reach for a stuffed animal that tried to help a puppet, but failed. Here the reasoning may be: "He is a good guy. Even though he didn't succeed, he tried" (Hamlin, 2013a). Notice that these infants have intuitively mastered modern legal concepts we use in assessing criminal intent. Our system must determine: Was this an accident or did he mean it? He should only be punished if he meant to do harm.

PBS Courtesy of Karen Wynn

But I cannot leave you with the sense that our species is primed to be mini-biblical King Solomons, behaving in a wise, ethical way. Some not-so-appealing human tendencies also erupt before age 1.

Using a similar procedure, the same research group found that 8-month-olds reach for a puppet they previously viewed hindering (acting mean) to another puppet if they view that puppet as different from themselves (Hamlin, 2013b; Hamlin and others, 2013). The principle here seems to be: "The enemy of my enemy is my friend." Or put more graphically: "I *like* people who are mean to people who are different than me." (In the next chapter, you will learn that a fear of anyone different—meaning, not a baby's primary caregiver—kicks in at exactly 8 months of age!)

In sum, during our second six months on this planet, we can decode intentions—inferring underlying motivations from the way people behave. This mind-reading talent (probably unique to our species) paves the way for that other human milestone: language, communicating our thoughts through words.

 Tying It All Together

1. You are working at a child-care center, and you notice Darien repeatedly opening and closing a cabinet door. Then Jai comes over and pulls open the door. You decide to latch it. Jai—undeterred—pulls on the door and, when it doesn't open, begins jiggling the latch. And then he looks up, very pleased, as he manages to figure out how to open the latch. Finally, you give up and decide to play a game with Sam. You hide a stuffed bear in a toy box while Sam watches. Then Sam throws open the lid of the box and scoops out the bear. Link the appropriate Piagetian term to each child's behavior: *circular reaction; object permanence; means–end behavior.*

2. Jose, while an avid Piaget fan, has to admit that in important ways, this master theorist was wrong. Jose can legitimately make which two criticisms? (1) Cognition develops gradually, not in stages; (2) Infants understand human motivations; (3) Babies understand the basic properties of objects at birth.

3. Baby Sara watches her big brother hit the dog. Based on the research in this section, Sara might first understand her brother is being "mean" (choose one) *months before/at/months after* age 1.

Answers to the Tying It All Together questions can be found at the end of this chapter.

Language: The Endpoint of Infancy

Piaget believed that language signals the end of the sensorimotor period because this ability requires understanding a symbol stands for something else. True, in order to master language, you must grasp the idea that the abstract word-symbol *textbook* refers to what you are reading now. But the miracle of language is that we string together words in novel, understandable ways. What causes us to master this feat, and how does language evolve?

Nature, Nurture, and the Passion to Learn Language

The essential property of language is elasticity. How can I come up with this new sentence, and why can you understand its meaning, although you have never seen it before? Why does every language have a **grammar**, with nouns, verbs, and rules for organizing words into sentences? According to linguist Noam Chomsky, the reason is that humans are biologically programmed to make "language," via what he labeled the **language acquisition device (LAD).**

Chomsky developed his nature-oriented concept of a uniquely human LAD in reaction to the behaviorist B. F. Skinner's nurture-oriented proposition that we learn to speak through being reinforced for producing specific words (for instance, Skinner

grammar The rules and word-arranging systems that every human language employs to communicate meaning.

language acquisition device (LAD) Chomsky's term for a hypothetical brain structure that enables our species to learn and produce language.

social-interactionist perspective An approach to language development that emphasizes its social function, specifically that babies and adults have a mutual passion to communicate.

babbling The alternating vowel and consonant sounds that babies repeat with variations of intonation and pitch and that precede the first words.

holophrase First clear evidence of language, when babies use a single word to communicate a sentence or complete thought.

telegraphic speech First stage of combining words in infancy, in which a baby pares down a sentence to its essential words.

argued that we learn to say "I want cookie" by being rewarded for producing those sounds by getting that treat). This pronouncement was another example of the traditional behaviorist principle that "all actions are driven by reinforcement" run amok (see Chapter 1). It defies common sense to suggest that we can generate billions of new sentences by having people reinforce us for every word!

Still, Skinner is correct in one respect. I speak English instead of Mandarin Chinese because I grew up in New York City, not Beijing. So the way our genetic program for making language gets expressed depends on our environment. Once again, nature plus nurture work together to explain every activity of life!

Currently, developmentalists adopt a **social-interactionist** perspective on this core skill. They focus on the motivations that propel language (Hoff-Ginsberg, 1997). Babies are passionate to communicate. Adults are passionate to help babies learn to talk. How does the infant passion to communicate evolve?

Tracking Emerging Language

The pathway to producing language occurs in stages. Out of the reflexive crying of the newborn period comes *cooing* (*oooh* sounds) at about month 4. At around month 6, delightful vocal circular reactions called **babbling** emerge. Babbles are alternating consonant and vowel sounds, such as "da da da," that infants playfully repeat with variations of intonation and pitch.

The first word emerges out of the babble at around 11 months, although that exact landmark is difficult to define. There is little more reinforcing to paternal pride than when your 8-month-old genius repeats your name. But when does "da da da" really refer to Dad? In the first, **holophrase** stage of true speech, one word, accompanied by gestures says it all. When your son says "ja" and points to the kitchen, you know he wants juice . . . or was it a jelly sandwich, or was he referring to his sister Jane?

Children accumulate their first 50 or so words, centering on the important items in their world (people, toys, and food), slowly (Nelson, 1974). Then, typically between ages 1 1/2 and 2, there is a vocabulary explosion as the child begins to combine words. Because children pare communication down to its essentials, just like an old-style telegram ("Me juice"; "Mommy, no"), this first word-combining stage is called **telegraphic speech.** Table 3.10 summarizes these language landmarks, along with offering examples and the approximate time each milestone occurs.

Just as with the other infant achievements described in this chapter, developmentalists are passionate to trace language to its roots. It turns out, for instance, that newborns are prewired to gravitate to the sounds of living things—as they suck longer when reinforced by hearing monkey and/or human vocalizations (versus pure tones). By 3 months of age, preferences get more selective. Now babies perk up *only* when they hear human speech (Vouloumanos and others, 2010). By 8 months of age (notice the similarity to the visual-system atrophy research described early in this chapter), infants—like adults—lose their ability to hear sound tones in languages not their own, such as Hindi (Gervain & Mehler, 2010). Simultaneously, a remarkable sharpening occurs. When language starts

Table 3.10: Language Milestones from Birth to Age 2*

Age	Language Characteristic
2–4 months	Cooing: First sounds growing out of reflexes. Example: "oooo"
5–11 months	Babbling: Alternate vowel–consonant sounds. Examples: "ba-ba-ba," "da-da-da"
12 months	Holophrases: First one-word sentences. Example: "ja" ("I want juice.")
18 months–2 years	Telegraphic speech: Two-word combinations, often accompanied by an explosion in vocabulary. Example: "Me juice"

*Babies vary a good deal in the ages at which they begin to combine words.

to explode, toddlers can hear the difference between similar sounds like "bih" and "dih" and link them to objects after *just hearing this connection once!*

Caregivers promote these achievements by continually talking to babies. Around the world, they train infants in language by using *infant-directed speech.*

Infant-directed speech (IDS) (what you and I call *baby talk*) uses simple words, exaggerated tones, elongated vowels, and has a higher pitch than we use in speaking to adults (Hoff-Ginsberg, 1997). Although IDS sounds ridiculous ("Mooommy taaaaking baaaaby ooooout!" "Moommy looooves baaaaby!"), infants perk up when they hear this conversational style (Santesso, Schmidt, & Trainor, 2007). So we naturally use infant-directed speech with babies, just as we are compelled to pick up and rock a child when she cries. Does IDS really help promote emerging language? The answer is yes.

Babies identify individual words better when they are uttered in exaggerated IDS tones (Thiessen, Hill, & Saffran, 2005). When adults are learning a new language, they also benefit from the slow, repetitive IDS style. Therefore, rather than being just for babies, IDS is a strategy that teaches language across the board (Ratner, 2013). In fact, notice that when you are teaching a person *any* new skill (or, as you will see in Chapter 14, when talking to an older person you perceive as impaired,) you, too, are apt to automatically use IDS!

The close link between brain development at 7 months of age and children's speech understanding at age 1, shown in Figure 3.9, suggests that we can physically "see" the roots of language before that talent appears (Deniz Can, Richards, and Kuhl, 2013; see also Dean and others, 2014). But even if this growth rate is mainly genetically programmed (meaning due to biological differences), parents who use more IDS communications have babies who speak at a younger age (Ratner, 2013).

IDS is different than other talk. You don't hear this speech style on TV, at the dinner table, or on videos designed to produce Einstein's at 8 months of age. IDS kicks in *only* when we communicate with babies one on one. So, if parents are passionate to accelerate language, investing millions in learning tools seems a distant second best to spending time *talking* to a child (Ratner, 2013)!

infant-directed speech (IDS) The simplified, exaggerated, high-pitched tones that adults and children use to speak to infants that function to help teach language.

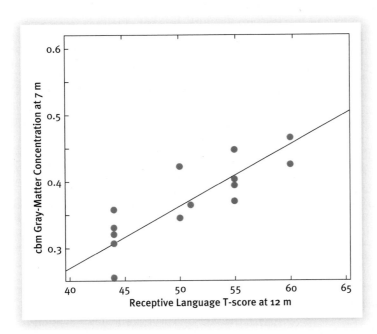

FIGURE 3.9: **The relationship between grey matter (synaptogenesis) concentration in the cerebellum at 7 months of age and language comprehension at a child's first birthday:** This chart shows a close correlation between the quantity, or amount, of synaptogenesis that has taken place in this particular brain region and a child's ability to understand language at age 1. The surprise is that this part of the brain—the cerebellum—does not qualify as a "higher brain center," as it programs balance and coordination.
Data from: Deniz Can Dilara, Richards. Todd Kuhl, Patricia K., (2013).

A basic message of this chapter is that—from language, to face perception, to social cognition—our main agenda is to connect with the human world. The next chapter focuses on this number-one infant (and adult) agenda by exploring attachment relationships during our first two years of life.

 Tying It All Together

1. "We learn to speak by getting reinforced for saying what we want." "We are biologically programmed to learn language." "Babies are passionate to communicate." Identify the theoretical perspective reflected in each of these statements: *Skinner's operant conditioning perspective; Chomsky's language acquisition device; a social-interactionist perspective on language.*

2. Baby Ginny is 4 months old; baby Jamal is about 7 months old; baby Sam is 1 year old; baby David is 2 years old. Identify each child's probable language stage by choosing from the following items: *babbling; cooing; telegraphic speech; holophrases.*

3. A friend makes fun of adults who use baby talk. Given the information in this section, is her teasing justified?

Answers to the Tying It All Together questions can be found at the end of this chapter.

SUMMARY

Setting the Context: Brain Blossoming and Sculpting

Because our large **cerebral cortex** develops mainly after birth, during the first two years of life, the brain mushrooms. **Axons** elongate and develop a fatty cover called myelin. **Dendrites** sprout branches and at **synapses** link up with other cells. **Synaptogenesis** and **myelination** program every ability and human skill. Although the brain matures for decades, we do not simply "develop more synapses." Each region undergoes rapid synaptogenesis, followed by pruning (or cutting back). Before pruning, the brain is particularly **plastic**, allowing us to compensate for early brain insults—but synaptogenesis and learning occur throughout life.

Basic Newborn States

Eating undergoes dramatic changes during infancy. We emerge from the womb with **sucking** and **rooting reflexes,** which jump-start eating, as well as other **reflexes,** which disappear after the early months of life. Although the "everything into the mouth" phase of infancy can make life scary for caregivers, a 2-year-old's food caution can protect toddlers from poisoning themselves.

Even though its specific health benefits are not always clear-cut, every public health organization advocates exclusive breast-feeding for the first 6 months of life. However, only a minority of women follows this recommendation. Mothers may find breast-feeding difficult and rebel against the social pressure to nurse for 6 months. We need to realize that breast-feeding is not for everyone and avoid equating nursing with being a good mom.

Undernutrition, both **stunting** (very short stature) and **micro-nutrient deficiencies,** are common in young children living in the developing world. Although families with children in the United States may suffer from **food insecurity,** due to government entitlement programs, severe, chronic hunger is very rare.

Crying is at its height during early infancy and declines around month 4 as the cortex develops. **Colic,** excessive crying that disappears after early infancy, is basically a biological problem. Strategies for quieting crying babies include rocking, holding, and providing an outlet for the urge to suck. The skin-to-skin contact involved in infant massage, and **kangaroo care,** is preferable to **swaddling,** another classic technique. These practices may help infants—especially at-risk premature babies—grow.

Sleep is the basic newborn state, and from the 18-hour, waking-every-few hours newborn pattern, babies gradually adjust to falling asleep at night. **REM sleep** lessens and shifts to the end of the cycle. Babies, however, really do not ever sleep through the night. At about 6 months, many learn **self-soothing,** putting themselves back to sleep when they wake up. The decision about whether to "let a baby cry it out" or respond immediately at night is personal, because the best way to foster sleep is to provide a caring bedtime routine. **Co-sleeping** (or bed-sharing)—the norm in collectivist cultures—although still controversial in the West, is also a personal choice.

Sudden infant death syndrome (SIDS)—when a young baby stops breathing, often at night, and dies—is a main cause of developed-world infant mortality. Although SIDS may be caused by impairments in the developing fetal brain—it tends to occur most often when babies sleep face down. Therefore, a late-twentieth-century SIDS campaign urging parents to put babies to sleep on their backs (not stomachs) has been effective, although delivering this message is difficult in cultures that prize co-sleeping.

Sensory and Motor Development

The **preferential-looking paradigm** (exploring what objects babies look at) and **habituation** (the fact that we get less interested in looking at objects that are no longer "new") are used to determine what very young babies can see. Although at birth visual acuity is poor, it improves very rapidly. **Face-perception studies** show that newborns look at facelike stimuli, recognize their mothers, and even prefer good-looking people from the first weeks of life. At the same time that our visual capacities improve, due to neural pruning, we lose the ability to "see" facial differences we really don't need. Sadly, this neural atrophy may bias us against other races. **Depth perception** studies using the **visual cliff** show that babies get frightened of heights around the time they begin to crawl.

Infants' bodies lengthen and thin out as they grow. The cephalocaudal, proximodistal, and mass-to-specific principles apply to how the body changes and emerging infant motor milestones. Although they do progress through stages when getting to walking, babies show incredible creativity and variability when they first attain skills. Reaching, in particular, literally opens babies up to encountering life. Earlier-than-normal motor development does not predict advanced cognition; but as babies get more mobile, parents need to discipline their children and **baby-proof** their home.

Cognition

During Piaget's **sensorimotor stage**, babies master the basics of physical reality through their senses and begin to symbolize and think. **Circular reactions** (habits the baby repeats) help babies pin down the basics of the physical world. **Primary circular reactions**—body-centered habits, such as sucking one's toes—emerge first. **Secondary circular reactions**, habits centered on making interesting external stimuli last (for example, batting mobiles), begin around month 4. **Tertiary circular reactions**, also called **"little-scientist"** activities—like spitting food at different velocities just to see where the oatmeal lands—are the hallmark of the toddler years. A major advance in reasoning that occurs around age 1 is **means–end behavior**—understanding you need to do something different to get to a goal.

Piaget's most compelling concept is **object permanence**—knowing that objects exist when you no longer see them. According to Piaget, this understanding develops gradually during the first years of life. When this knowledge is developing, infants make the **A-not-B error**, looking for an object in the place where they first found it, even if it has been hidden in another location before their eyes.

Using preferential looking, and watching babies' expressions of surprise at impossible events, researchers now know that babies understand physical reality far earlier than Piaget believed. Because Piaget's stage model also does not fit the gradual way cognition unfolds, contemporary developmentalists may adopt an **information-processing approach,** breaking thinking into separate components and steps. Scientists studying **social cognition** find that babies understand people's motivations (and prefer people, based on judging their inner intentions) remarkably early in life.

Language: The Endpoint of Infancy

Language, specifically our use of **grammar** and our ability to form infinitely different sentences, sets us apart from any other animal. Although B. F. Skinner believed that we learn to speak through being reinforced, the more logical explanation is Chomsky's idea that we have a biologically built-in **language acquisition device (LAD)**. **Social-interactionists** focus on the mutual passion of babies and adults to communicate.

First, babies coo, then **babble**, then use one-word **holophrases**, and finally, at 1 1/2 or 2, progress to two-word combinations called **telegraphic speech**. Caregivers naturally use **infant-directed speech** (exaggerated intonations and simpler phrases) when they talk to babies. Talking to babies in **IDS** is better than any baby-genius tape in promoting this vital human skill.

KEY TERMS

cerebral cortex, p. 74
axon, p. 74
dendrite, p. 74
synapse, p. 74
synaptogenesis, p. 74
myelination, p. 74
plastic, p. 75
sucking reflex, p. 77
rooting reflex, p. 77
reflex, p. 77
undernutrition, p. 79
stunting, p. 79

micronutrient deficiency, p. 79
food insecurity, p. 80
colic, p. 81
swaddling, p. 81
kangaroo care, p. 81
REM sleep, p. 83
self-soothing, p. 83
co-sleeping, p. 85
sudden infant death syndrome (SIDS), p. 86
preferential-looking paradigm, p. 88
habituation, p. 88

face-perception studies, p. 88
depth perception, p. 90
visual cliff, p. 90
baby-proofing, p. 92
sensorimotor stage, p. 93
circular reactions, p. 93
primary circular reactions, p. 94
secondary circular reactions, p. 94
tertiary circular reactions, p. 94
little-scientist phase, p. 94
means–end behavior, p. 94

object permanence, p. 95
A-not-B error, p. 96
information processing approach, p. 97
social cognition, p. 98
grammar, p. 99
language acquisition device (LAD), p. 99
social-interactionist view, p. 100
babbling, p. 100
holophrase, p. 100
telegraphic speech, p. 100
infant-directed speech (IDS), p. 101

ANSWERS TO Tying It All Together QUIZZES

Setting the Context: Brain Blossoming and Sculpting

1. Both Cortez and Ashley are right. We are unique in our massive cerebral cortex, in growing most of our brain outside of the womb, and in the fact that the human cortex does not reach its adult form for more than two decades.

2. Latisha is only partly right. Synaptic loss and neural pruning are essential to fostering our emerging abilities.

3. When babies have a stroke, they may end up *less* impaired than during adulthood, due to *brain plasticity.*

4. *Synaptogenesis* is occurring in your mom and grandma. *Myelination* (or formation of the myelin sheath) ends by our mid-twenties.

Basic Newborn States

1. You need to pick the first two statements: The rooting reflex is programmed by the low brain centers to appear at birth and then go away as the cortex matures. Its appearance is definitely *not* a sign of early intelligence.

2. Elaine should say breast-feeding is inconvenient for new moms who need to work full-time at working-class jobs. It can be embarrassing to nurse in public. Plus, breast-feeding can be painful.

3. Tell your relatives to carry the child around in a baby sling (kangaroo care). Also, perhaps make heavy use of a pacifier and employ baby massage. Don't recommend swaddling, though—as it limits skin-to-skin contact.

4. Jorge's child is right on schedule, but he's wrong to say his child is sleeping through the night. The baby has simply learned to self-soothe.

5. The answers here will depend on the class.

Sensory and Motor Development

1. You are using a kind of *preferential-looking* paradigm; the scientific term for when your baby loses interest is *habituation.*

2. Both Tania and Thomas are right. In support of Tania's "dramatic improvement" position, while newborns are legally blind, vision improves to 20/20 by age 1. (Another example is the visual cliff research.) Thomas is also correct that in some ways vision gets worse during infancy. He should mention the fact that by 9 months of age we have "unlearned" the ability to become as sensitive to facial distinctions in people of other ethnic groups.

3. The roots of adult prejudice may begin *during the second 6 months of life.*

4. At 8 months of age, the child should *be frightened* of the cliff.

5. Your answers might include installing electrical outlet covers; putting sharp, poisonous, and breakable objects out of a baby's reach; carpeting hard floor surfaces; padding furniture corners; installing latches on cabinet doors; and so on.

Cognition

1. Circular reaction = Darien; means–end behavior = Jai; object permanence = Sam.

2. Cognition develops gradually rather than in distinct stages; infants understand human motivations.

3. Baby Sara should pick up this idea *months before* age 1.

Language: The Endpoint of Infancy

1. The idea that we learn language by getting reinforced reflects Skinner's operant conditioning perspective; Chomsky hypothesized that we are biologically programmed to acquire language; the social-interactionist perspective emphasizes the fact that babies and adults have a passion to communicate.

2. Baby Ginny is cooing; baby Jamal is babbling; baby Sam is speaking in holophrases (one-word stage); and baby David is using telegraphic speech.

3. No, your friend is wrong!!! Baby talk—or in developmental science terms, infant-directed speech (IDS)—helps promote early language.

CHAPTER 4

CHAPTER OUTLINE

Infancy: Socioemotional Development

Now that we've talked to Kim during pregnancy and visited when Elissa was a young baby, let's catch up with mother and daughter now that Elissa is 15 months old.

Elissa had her first birthday in December. She's such a happy baby, but now if you take something away, it's like, "Why did you do that?" Pick her up. For a second everything is fine, and then her face changes and she squirms and her arms go out toward me. She's really busy walking, busy exploring, but she's always got an eye on me. The minute I make a motion to leave, she stops and races near. I think Elissa has a stronger connection to her dad, because now that I'm working, Jeff has arranged his schedule to watch the baby late in the afternoon . . . but when she's tired or sick, it's still Mom.

It was difficult to go back to work. You hear terrible things about day care, stories of babies being neglected. I looked at the center in town, but there were just so many kids. Finally I settled on a neighbor who watches a few toddlers in her home. I saw how much this woman loves children, and felt secure knowing who would be caring for my child. But you still worry, feel guilty. The worst was Elissa's reaction—the way she screamed the first week when I left her off. But it's obvious that she's happy now. Every morning she runs smiling to Ms. Marie's arms.

It's bittersweet to see my baby separating from me, running into the world, becoming her own little person—with some very strong likes and dislikes. The clashes are becoming more frequent now that I'm turning up the discipline, expecting more in terms of behavior from my "big girl." But mainly it's so hard to be apart. I think about Elissa 50 million times a day. I speed home to see her. I can't wait to glimpse her glowing face in the window, how she jumps up and down, and we run to kiss and cuddle again.

Imagine being Kim, with your child the center of your life. Imagine being Elissa, wanting to be independent but needing your mother close. In this chapter, I'll focus on **attachment**, the powerful bond of love between caregiver and child.

My discussion of attachment—which takes up much of this chapter—starts a conversation that continues throughout this book. Attachment is not only at the core of infancy, but human life. After exploring this vital one-to-one relationship, I'll turn to the wider world, first examining how that basic marker, socioeconomic status (SES), affects young children's development, then spotlighting day care, the setting where so many developed-world babies spend their days. The last section of this chapter focuses on **toddlerhood,** the famous time lasting roughly from age 1 to 2 1/2 years. (Your tip-off that a child is a toddler is that classic endearing "toddling" gait that characterizes the second year of life.)

attachment The powerful bond of love between a caregiver and child (or between any two individuals).

toddlerhood The important transitional stage after baby-hood, from roughly 1 year to 2 1/2 years of age; defined by an intense attachment to caregivers and by an urgent need to become independent.

Attachment: The Basic Life Bond

Perhaps you remember being intensely in love. You may be in that wonderful state right now. You cannot stop fantasizing about your significant other. Your moves blend with your partner's. You connect in a unique way. Knowing that this person is there gives you confidence. You can conquer the world. You feel uncomfortable when you are separated. Your world depends on having your lover close. Now you know how Elissa feels about her mother and the powerful emotions that flow from Kim to her child.

Mark Hall/Getty Images

The adoring expressions on the faces of parents and babies as they gaze at each other make it obvious why the attachment relationship in infancy is our basic model for romantic love in adulthood.

Nina Leen/The LIFE Picture Collection/Getty Images

Ethologist Konrad Lorenz arranged to become the first living thing that newly hatched geese saw at their species-specific critical time for attachment. He then became the goslings' "mother," the object whom they felt compelled never to let out of their sight.

Setting the Context: How Developmentalists (Slowly) Got Attached to Attachment

During much of the twentieth century, U.S. psychologists seemed indifferent to these feelings. At a time when psychology was dominated by behaviorism, studying love seemed unscientific. Behaviorists minimized our need for attachment, suggesting that babies wanted to be close to their mothers because this "maternal reinforcing stimulus" provided food. Worse yet, one famous early behaviorist named John Watson seemed *hostile* to attachment when he crusaded against the dangers of "too much" mother love:

When I hear a mother say "bless its little heart" when it falls down, I . . . have to walk a block or two to let off steam. . . . Can't she train herself to substitute a kindly word . . . for . . . the coddling? . . . Can't she learn to keep away from the child a large part of the day? [And then he made this memorable statement:] . . . I sometimes wish that we could live in a community of homes [where] . . . we could have the babies fed and bathed each week by a different nurse. (!)

(Watson, 1928/1972, pp. 82–83)

European psychoanalysts felt differently. They discovered that attachment was far from dangerous. It was crucial to infant life.

Consider a heart-rending mid-twentieth-century film that showed the fate of babies living in orphanages (Blum, 2002; Karen, 1998). In these sterile, impeccably maintained institutions, behaviorists would have predicted that infants should thrive. So why did babies lie listless on cots—unable to eat, withering away?

Now consider that ethologists—the forerunners of today's evolutionary psychologists—noticed that *every* species had a biologically programmed attachment response (or drive to be physically close to their mothers) that appeared at a specific point soon after birth. When the famous ethologist Konrad Lorenz (1935) arranged to become this attachment-eliciting stimulus for goslings, as this compelling photograph shows, Lorenz became the adored Pied Piper the baby geese tried to follow to the ends of the earth.

However, it took a rebellious psychologist named Harry Harlow, who studied monkeys, to convince U.S. psychologists that the behaviorist meal-dispenser model of mother love was wrong. In a classic study, Harlow (1958) separated baby monkeys from their mothers at birth and raised them in a cage with a wire-mesh "mother" (which offered food from a milk bottle attached to its chest) and a cloth "mother" (which was soft and provided contact comfort). The babies stayed glued to the cloth mother, making occasional trips to eat from the wire mom. In stressful situations, they scurried to the cloth mother for comfort. Love won, hands down, over getting fed!

Moreover, there were serious psychological consequences for the monkeys raised without their moms. The animals couldn't have sex. They were frightened of their peers. After being artificially inseminated and giving birth, the "motherless mothers" were uncaring, abusive parents. One mauled her baby so badly that it later died (Harlow and others, 1966; Harlow, C. M., 1986).

Then, in the late 1960s, John Bowlby put the evidence together—the orphanage findings, Lorenz's ethological studies, Harlow's research, his own clinical work with children who had been hospitalized or separated from their mothers (Hinde, 2005). In a landmark series of books, Bowlby (1969, 1973, 1980) argued that there is no such thing as "excessive mother love." Having a loving **primary attachment figure** is crucial to our development. It is essential to living fully at any age. By the final decades of the twentieth century, attachment moved to the front burner in developmental science. It remains front and center today.

Exploring the Attachment Response

Bowlby (1969, 1973) made his case for the crucial importance of attachment based on evolutionary theory. He believed that, as with other species, human beings have a critical period when the attachment response "comes out." As with Lorenz's ducks, attachment is built into our genetic code to allow us to survive. Although the attachment response is programmed to emerge during our first years of life, **proximity-seeking behavior**—our need to make contact with an attachment figure—is activated when our survival is threatened at *any* age.

Bowlby believed that threats to survival come in two categories. They may be activated by our internal state. When a child clings only to her mom, you know she must be tired. When you go to the hospital, you make sure that your family is close. You immediately text your "significant other" when you have a fever or the flu.

They may be evoked by dangers in the external world. During childhood, it's a huge dog that causes us to run anxiously into our parent's arms. As adults, it's a professor's nasty comment or a humiliating experience at work that provokes a frantic call to our primary attachment figure, be it our spouse, our father, or our best friend.

Although we all need to touch base with our significant others when we feel threatened, adults and older children can be separated from their attachment figures for some time. During infancy and early childhood, simply being physically apart causes distress. Now, let's trace step-by-step how human attachment unfolds.

Attachment Milestones

According to Bowlby, during their first three months of life, babies are in the **preattachment phase.** Remember that during this reflex-dominated time infants have yet to wake up to the world. However, at around 2 months there is a milestone called the **social smile.** Bowlby believed that this first real smile does not show attachment to *a* person. Because it pops up in response to any human face, it is just one example of an automatic reflex such as sucking or grasping that evokes care from adults.

Still, a baby's eagerly awaited first smile can be an incredible experience if you are a parent. Suddenly, your relationship with your child shifts to a different plane. Now, I have a confession to make: During my first 2 months as a new mother, I was worried, as I did not feel anything for this beautiful child I had waited so long to adopt. I date Thomas's first endearing smile as the defining event in my lifelong attachment romance.

In Harlow's landmark study, baby monkeys clung to the cloth-covered "mother" (which provided contact comfort) as they leaned over to feed from the wire-mesh "mother"—vividly refuting the behaviorist idea that infants become "attached" to the reinforcing stimulus that feeds them.

primary attachment figure The closest person in a child's or adult's life.

proximity-seeking behavior Acting to maintain physical contact or to be close to an attachment figure.

preattachment phase The first phase of John Bowlby's developmental attachment sequence, during the first three months of life, when infants show no visible signs of attachment.

social smile The first real smile, occurring at about 2 months of age.

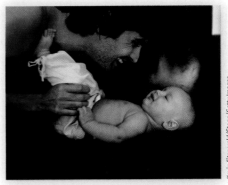

A baby's first social smile, which appears at the sight of any face at about 2 to 3 months of age, is biologically programmed to delight adults and charm them into providing love and care.

attachment in the making
Second phase of Bowlby's attachment sequence, when, from 4 to 7 months of age, babies slightly prefer the primary caregiver.

clear-cut attachment Critical human attachment phase, from 7 months through toddlerhood, defined by separation anxiety, stranger anxiety, and needing a primary caregiver close.

separation anxiety Signal of clear-cut attachment when a baby gets upset as a primary caregiver departs.

stranger anxiety Beginning at about 7 months of age, when a baby grows wary of people other than a primary caregiver.

social referencing A baby's checking back and monitoring a caregiver for cues as to how to behave while exploring; linked to clear-cut attachment.

A few weeks ago this 7-month-old boy would have happily gone to his neighbor. But everything changes during the phase of clear-cut attachment when stranger anxiety emerges.

As she socially references her mom this baby wants to know: Is that giant with the strange object really safe?

At roughly 4 months of age, infants enter a transitional period, called **attachment in the making.** At this time, Piaget's environment-focused secondary circular reactions are unfolding (recall Chapter 3). The cortex is coming on-line. Babies may show a slight preference for their primary caregiver. But still, a 4- or 5-month-old can be the ultimate party person, thrilled to be cuddled by anyone—from Grandma, to a neighbor, to a stranger at the mall.

By around 7 or 8 months of age, this changes. At this age, as you saw in Chapter 3, babies are hunting for hidden objects—showing that they have the cognitive skills to miss their caregivers. Now that they can crawl, or walk holding onto furniture, children can really get hurt. The stage is set for **clear-cut** (or *focused*) **attachment**—the beginning of the full-blown attachment response. This phase of intense attachment will last throughout the toddler years.

Separation anxiety signals this milestone. When your baby is about 7 or 8 months old, she suddenly gets uncomfortable when you leave the room. Then, **stranger anxiety** appears. Your child gets agitated when any unfamiliar person picks her up. So, as children travel toward their first birthday, the universal friendliness of early infancy is gone. While they may still joyously gurgle at the world from their caregiver's arms, it's normal for babies to forbid any "stranger"—a nice day-care worker or even a loving Grandma who flies in for a visit—to invade their space.

Between ages 1 and 2, the distress reaches a peak. A toddler clings and cries when mom or dad makes a motion to leave. It's as if an invisible string connects the caregiver and the child. In one classic study at a park, 1-year-olds played within a certain distance from their mothers. Interestingly, this zone of optimum comfort (about 200 feet) was identical for both the parent and the child (Anderson, 1972).

To see these changes, pick up a young baby (such as a 4-month-old) and an older infant (perhaps a 10-month-old) and compare their reactions. Then, observe 1-year-olds at a local park. Can you measure this attachment zone of comfort? Do you notice the busy, exploring toddlers periodically checking back to make sure a caregiver is still there?

Social referencing is the term developmentalists use to describe this checking-back behavior. Social referencing helps alert the baby to which situations are dangerous and which ones are safe. ("Should I climb up this slide, Mommy?" "Does Daddy think this object is OK to explore?")

Social referencing is not only the glue that permits babies to safely venture into the world; we depend on this core *social cognitive* skill ("She is looking upset. I'd better not do that!") to pace our behavior from age 1 to 101. When does the infant attachment response—or need to be physically close to a caregiver—go away? Although the marker is hazy, babies typically leave this stage at about age 3. Children still care just as much about their primary attachment figure. But now, according to Bowlby, they have the cognitive skills to carry a **working model,** or internal representation, of this number-one person in their minds (Bretherton, 2005).

The bottom-line message is that our human critical period for attachment is timed to unfold during our most vulnerable time of life—when we first become mobile and are most in danger of getting hurt. Moreover, what compensates parents for the frustrations of having a Piagetian "little scientist" is enormous gratification. Just when a toddler is continually messing up the house and saying "No!" parents know that their child's world revolves totally around them.

Do children differ in the way they express this priceless sense of connection? And if so, what might these differences mean about the quality of the infant–parent bond?

Attachment Styles

Mary Ainsworth answered these questions by devising a classic test of attachment—the **Strange Situation** (Ainsworth, 1967; Ainsworth and others, 1978).

The Strange Situation procedure begins when a mother and a 1-year-old enter a room full of toys. After the child has time to explore, an unfamiliar adult enters the room. Then, the mother leaves the baby alone with the stranger and, a few minutes later, returns to comfort the child. Next, the mom leaves the baby totally alone for a minute; the stranger enters; and finally, the mother returns (see Figure 4.1). By observing the child's reactions to these separations and reunions through a one-way mirror, developmentalists categorize infants as either *securely* or *insecurely attached*.

Securely attached children use their mother as a secure base, or anchor, to explore the toys. When she leaves, they may or may not become highly distressed. Most important, when she returns, their eyes light up with joy. Their close relationship is apparent in the way they run and melt into their mothers' arms. **Insecurely attached** children react in one of three ways:

In kindergarten, this child can say goodbye with minimal separation anxiety because she is in the working-model phase of attachment.

- Infants classified as **avoidant** seem excessively detached. They rarely show separation anxiety or much emotion—positive or negative—when their primary attachment figure returns. They seem wooden, disengaged, without much feeling at all.

- Babies with an **anxious-ambivalent attachment** are at the opposite end of the spectrum—clingy, nervous, too frightened to explore the toys. Terribly distressed by their mother's departure, these infants may show contradictory emotions when she returns—clinging and then striking out in anger. Often, they are inconsolable, unable to be comforted when their attachment figure comes back.

- Children showing a **disorganized attachment** behave in a genuinely bizarre manner. They freeze, run around erratically, or even look frightened when the caregiver returns.

Developmentalists point out that the insecure attachments illustrated in my summary in Figure 4.2 on page 112 do not show a weakness in the *underlying* connection. Avoidant infants are just as bonded to their caregivers as babies ranked secure. Anxious-ambivalent infants are not more closely attached even though they show intense separation distress. To take an analogy from adult life, when a person who cares deeply about you pretends to be indifferent, is this individual less in love? Is a lover who can't let his partner out of sight more attached than a person who allows his significant other to have an independent life? Unless they experience the grossly abnormal rearing conditions described later in this section, *every infant* is closely attached (Zeanah, Berlin, & Boris, 2011).

working model In Bowlby's theory, the mental representation of a caregiver allowing children over age 3 to be physically apart from that primary attachment figure.

Strange Situation Mary Ainsworth's procedure to measure attachment at age 1, involving planned separations and reunions with a caregiver.

secure attachment Ideal attachment response when a child responds with joy at being united with a primary caregiver; or, in adulthood, the genuine intimacy that is ideal in love relationships.

insecure attachment Deviation from the normally joyful response of being united with a primary caregiver, signaling problems in the caregiver–child relationship.

avoidant attachment An insecure attachment style characterized by a child's indifference to a primary caregiver at being reunited after separation.

FIGURE 4.1: **The Strange Situation:** The classic Strange Situation, involving separations and reunions from a caregiver, can tell us whether this one year old girl is securely or insecurely attached.

Secure Attachment: The child is thrilled to see the caregiver.

Avoidant Attachment: The child is unresponsive to the caregiver.

Anxious-Ambivalent Attachment: The child cannot be calmed by the caregiver.

Disorganized Attachment: The child seems frightened and behaves bizarrely when the caregiver arrives.

FIGURE 4.2: **Secure and insecure attachments: A summary photo series**

anxious-ambivalent attachment An insecure attachment style characterized by a child's intense distress when reunited with a primary caregiver after separation.

disorganized attachment An insecure attachment style characterized by responses such as freezing or fear when a child is reunited with the primary caregiver in the Strange Situation.

synchrony The reciprocal aspect of the attachment relationship, with a caregiver and infant responding emotionally to each other in a sensitive, exquisitely attuned way.

temperament A person's characteristic, inborn style of dealing with the world.

The blissful rapture, the sense of being totally engrossed and in tune with each other, is the reason why developmentalists use the word *synchrony* to describe parent–infant attachment.

The Attachment Dance

Look at a baby and a caregiver and it is almost as if you are seeing a dance. The partners are alert to each other's signals. They know when to come on stronger and when to back off. They are absorbed and captivated, oblivious to the world. This blissful **synchrony,** or sense of being totally emotionally in tune, is what makes the infant–mother relationship our model for romantic love. Ainsworth and Bowlby believed that the parent's "dancing potential," or sensitivity to a baby's signals, produces secure attachments (Ainsworth and others, 1978). Were they correct?

The Caregiver

Decades of studies suggest that the answer is yes. Sensitive caregivers tend to have babies who are securely attached. Parents who misread their baby's signals or are rejecting, disengaged, or depressed are more apt to have infants ranked insecure (see Behrens, Parker, & Haltigan, 2011 and Zeanah, Berlin, & Boris, 2011 for a review).

Still, because these are *correlations*, if we find that securely attached parents have open, loving children or that distant moms and dads have avoidant babies, couldn't these people be passing these styles of responding down in their genes? Furthermore, by blaming children's attachment issues on parents, aren't we neglecting the fact that there are *two* partners in the dance?

The Child

Listen to any mother comparing her babies ("Sara was fussy; Matthew is easier to soothe") and you will realize that not all infants are born with the same dancing talent. Babies differ in **temperament**—characteristic, inborn behavioral styles of approaching the world.

In a pioneering study, developmentalists classified a group of middle-class babies into three temperamental styles: *Easy* babies—the majority of the children—had rhythmic eating and sleeping patterns; they were happy and easily soothed. More wary babies were labeled *slow to warm up.* One in 10 babies were ranked as *difficult*—hypersensitive, unusually agitated, reactive to every sight and sound (Thomas & Chess, 1977; Thomas, Chess, & Birch, 1968). Here is an example:

> Everything bothers my 5-month-old little girl—a bright light, a rough blanket, a sudden noise—even, I'm ashamed to admit, sometimes my touch. I thought colic went away by month 3. I'm getting discouraged and depressed.

Now, consider the stressful experiences a baby must go through during the Strange Situation. Do you see why some developmentalists have argued that biologically based differences in temperamental "reactivity"—not the quality of a mother's caregiving— determine attachment status at age 1? (See, for example, Kagan, 1984.)

Does a baby's biology (nature) or poor caregiving (nurture) produce insecure attachments? As you might imagine—given the nature-plus-nurture message of this book—the answer is, a little of both. Biologically hardy babies—children who have a gene associated with resilience to stress (more about this later)—tend to be securely attached in the face of less sensitive parenting. However, when a child is fragile emotionally, he needs exceptionally nurturing caregiving to be classified as secure (Barry, Kochanska, & Philibert, 2008; Pace & Zavattini, 2011; Pluess and Belsky, 2010). So, a skillful dancer can sometimes shift a temperamentally "difficult" baby from insecure to secure.

But with biologically vulnerable infants, there is a limit to what the most sensitive parent can achieve. Suppose a child was extremely premature or autistic, or had some serious disease. Would it be fair to label the baby's attachment issues as the caregiver's fault?

Moreover, because "it takes two to tango" (that is, the dance is bidirectional), a child's temperament affects the parent's sensitivity, too. To use an analogy from real-life dancing, imagine waltzing with a partner who couldn't keep time with the music; or think of a time you tried to soothe a person who was too agitated to connect. Even a prize-winning dancer or someone with world-class relationship skills would feel inept.

The Caregiver's Other Attachments

And, to continue the analogy, it takes more than two to tango. Just as a woman's attitudes about being pregnant depend on feeling supported by the wider world (recall Chapter 2), it is difficult to be a sensitive caregiver if your other attachment relationships are not working out. When mothers (and fathers) are unhappily married, or don't dance well with each other, their babies are more likely to be rated as insecurely attached (Cowan, Cowan, & Mehta, 2009; Moss and others, 2005).

Figure 4.3 on the next page—illustrating how the caregiver, the baby, and the parent's other relationships interact to shape attachment—brings home the need to adopt a *developmental systems approach.* Many forces shape the attachment dance. By assuming that problems were due simply to the parent's personality, Bowlby and Ainsworth were taking an excessively limited view. What about the general theory? Is attachment to a primary caregiver universal? Do infants in different countries fall into the same categories of secure and insecure?

Is Infant Attachment Universal?

From Chicago to Capetown, from Naples to New York, Bowlby's and Ainsworth's ideas about attachment get high marks (van IJzendoorn & Sagi, 1999). Babies around the world get attached to a primary caregiver at roughly the same age. As Figure 4.4 on page 114 shows, the percentages of infants ranked secure in different countries are remarkably similar— roughly 60 to 70 percent (Sroufe, 2000; Tomlinson, Cooper, & Murray, 2005).

FIGURE 4.3: Three pathways to insecure attachment: Above left: The mother is too depressed to connect. Above center: The child has temperamental vulnerabilities. Above right: The caregiver's other attachment relationships make it difficult to "dance" with her baby.

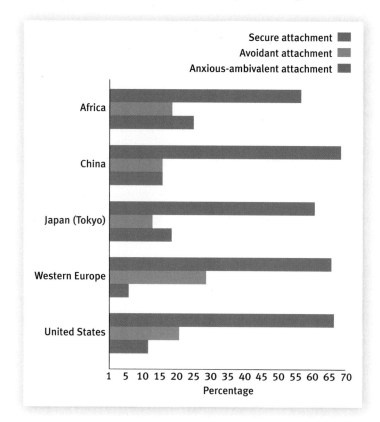

FIGURE 4.4: Snapshots of attachment security (and insecurity) around the world: Around the world, roughly 60 to 70 percent of 1-year-olds are classified as securely attached—although there are interesting differences in the percentages of babies falling into the different insecure categories.

Data from: van IJzendoorn & Sagi, 1999, p. 729.

The most amazing validation of attachment's universal quality comes from the Efé, a communal hunter-gatherer people living in Africa. Efé newborns nurse from any lactating woman, even when their own parent is around. They are dressed and cared for by the whole community. But Efé babies still develop a primary attachment to their mothers at the typical age! (See van IJzendoorn & Sagi, 1999.)

So far you might be thinking that during the phase of clear-cut attachment, babies are connected to only one person. Wrong! A toddler may be attached to her father and day-care provider, as well as her mom. And, just as you and I connect differently with each "significant other," a baby can be securely attached to his father and insecurely attached to his mom.

Interestingly, when babies are upset, they run to their primary caregiver—the parent who spends the most time with them—even if they are insecurely attached to this adult. So, the *amount* of hands-on caregiving (not necessarily its quality) evokes the biologically programmed, security-seeking response (Umemura and others, 2013). The good news is that if a child is securely attached *to one parent* that may be all that matters for his future life.

In a heartening longitudinal study, 15-month-olds labeled "double insecure" (insecurely attached to both caregivers) were prone to have behavior problems in third grade. But children with a secure attachment to either parent were as insulated from poor mental health as those who were securely attached to both mom and dad (Kochanska & Kim, 2013). This suggests that having *one* nurturing figure during infancy—a father, a grandma, or aunt—may be all we need to protect us from problems down the road. How *does* infant attachment relate to problems down the road?

Does Infant Attachment Predict Later Relationships and Mental Health?

Bowlby's core argument, in his working-model concept, is that our attachment relationships in infancy determine how we relate to other people and feel about ourselves (Bretherton, 2005). A baby who acts avoidant with his parents will be aloof and uncaring with friends; he may be unresponsive to a teacher's demands. An anxious-ambivalent infant will behave in a needy way in her other love relationships. A secure baby is set up to succeed socially.

Again, decades of research support Bowlby's prediction. Securely attached babies tend to be more socially competent and popular (McElwain and others, 2011; Rispoli and others, 2013). Insecure attachment foreshadows anxiety (Madigan and others, 2013), trouble managing one's emotions, and interpersonal problems, later on (Pasco Fearon and others, 2010; Kochanska and others, 2010; von der Lippe and others, 2010).

Interestingly, the most potent predictor of problems is the disorganized attachment style. This erratic, confused infant response is a risk factor for "acting-out issues" (aggression, disobedience, difficulty controlling one's behavior) as children travel through elementary school (Bohlin and others, 2012; Pasco Fearon & Belsky, 2011).

However, the operative word here is "risk factor." Landmark longitudinal studies measuring attachment at age 1 and tracking babies into their adult years suggest that, while there is "moderate continuity," attachments do change (Grossmann and others, 2005; Simpson and others, 2007; Sroufe and others, 2005; Pinquart and others, 2013).

One obvious cause relates to the environment. Sensitive, loving relationships—at every stage of life—can transform our "attachment status" from insecure to secure (Zayas and others, 2011). Unfortunately, the most blissful early life does not inoculate us against traumas later on.

Consider a boy named Tony, in one major infant-to-adult attachment study, ranked securely attached at age 1. While in preschool and early elementary school, Tony was popular, self-assured, and still securely attached; as a teenager, he suffered devastating attachment blows. First his parents went through a difficult divorce. Then, his mother was killed in a car accident and his father moved to another state, leaving Tony with his aunt. It should come as no surprise that as an angry, depressed adolescent, Tony was classified as insecurely attached. But at age 26, Tony recovered. He met a wonderful woman and became a father. His status slowly returned to secure (Sroufe and others, 2005).

It seems logical that life experiences might change our attachment relationships for the better or the worse. But research—involving the "love hormone" oxytocin—suggests genetics is also involved.

This new member of the Efé people of central Africa will be lovingly cared for by the whole community, males as well as females, from his first minutes of life. Because he sleeps with his mother, however, at the "right" age he will develop his primary attachment to her.

Exploring the Genetics of Attachment Stability and Change

Oxytocin qualifies as the attachment hormone, as this substance elicits bonding, caregiving, and nurturing in mammals and in our own species (Rilling, 2013). When researchers in the infant-to-adult attachment study explored variations in a gene involved in producing oxytocin, they found that young people, like Tony, who changed in attachment status, showed one variant of this particular gene. Others, with a different, less environment-responsive genetic profile, were apt to stay stable in attachment from age 1. Therefore, our infant attachment style may be more or less important in shaping our adult fate, depending on our genes. (Stay tuned throughout this chapter for research with a similar theme.)

oxytocin The hormone whose production is centrally involved in bonding, nurturing, and caregiving behaviors in our species and other mammals.

The bottom-line theme, however, of *all* these studies is that Bowlby was wrong. We are not destined for lifelong problems if we suffered from inadequate caregiving early in life. But what if a baby has experienced not just poor caregiving, but *no* caregiving at all?

Hot in Developmental Science: Experiencing Early Life's Worst Deprivation

"When I . . . walked into the . . . building (in 1990)," said a British school teacher . . . "what I saw was beyond belief . . . babies lay three and four to a bed, given no attention. . . . There were no medicines or washing facilities, . . . physical and sexual abuse were rife . . . I particularly remember . . . the basement. There were kids there who hadn't seen natural light in years."

(McGeown, 2005, para. 4)

This scene was not from some horror movie. It was real. This woman had entered a Romanian orphanage, the bitter legacy of the dictator Ceausescu's decision to forbid contraception, which caused a flood of unwanted babies that destitute parents dumped on the state.

When the "Iron Curtain" fell and revealed these grisly Eastern European scenes, British and American families rushed in to adopt these children. But then parents began to report distressing symptoms—sons and daughters who displayed a strange, indiscriminate friendliness and never showed interest in any specific adult (see Kreppner and others, 2011). These responses did not qualify as insecure attachment. They showed a *lack* of any attachment response.

Which institution-reared babies are apt to show these deficits? Can children recover from this deprivation, and is there an age at which help might come too late? Studies tracking the Romanian babies, as well as children adopted from orphanages in China and Russia, offer these tantalizing conclusions (Julian, 2013):

First, babies adopted from the most intensely depriving institutions—such as in Romania—are most at risk for problems. In these places, damage can appear if adoption occurs after 6 months of age. In orphanages, like those in Russia that are classified as "socially depriving" but satisfy infants' basic health needs, the cut-off point for beginning to show deficits is close to 18 months. Therefore, just as Bowlby would predict, the zone of attachment (7–18 months) is a sensitive period for receiving caregiving. But, there also is a **dose–response effect**—meaning that the intensity (dose) of deprivation predicts the impact (response) on a given child. The probability of having enduring problems depends on *when* a child is adopted and the kind of place from *where* the adoption occurs.

What are these children's symptoms? A classic sign of this "institutionalization syndrome" is the indiscriminate friendliness I just described (this is called *reactive attachment disorder*). Another is deficits in attention (McLaughlin and others, 2010; Wiik and others, 2011). EEG studies suggest the reason for this impaired focusing ability is that lack of stimulation delays the maturation of the brain (McLaughlin and others, 2010).

As they tracked babies subjected to these unfortunate "natural experiments," scientists discovered that institutionalized boys are more vulnerable than girls to having enduring attachment problems (McLaughlin and others, 2012). While a massive catch-up growth often occurs after moving to a new, loving home (Sheridan and others, 2010), symptoms can persist, or erupt again, in the adolescent years (Julian, 2013). By exploring these grossly abnormal, worst-case early-life scenarios, developmentalists are learning vital information about human resilience, brain plasticity, and its limits in human beings. ❖

dose–response effect Term referring to the fact that the amount (dose) of a substance, in this case the depth and length of deprivation, determines its probable effect or impact on the person. (In the orphanage studies, the "response" is subsequent emotional and/or cognitive problems.)

Wrapping Up Attachment

To summarize, infancy is a special zone of sensitivity for forming relationships. The attachment response that unfolds during our first years of life lays down the foundation for healthy development in a variety of life realms. Still, attachment capacities (and human brains) are malleable, and negative paths can be altered provided the deprivation is not too profound and the wider world provides special help. How does the wider world affect development during infancy and beyond? To explore this question, let's look at two crucial infant wider-world contexts: poverty and day care.

 Tying It All Together

1. List an example of "proximity-seeking in distress" in your own life within the past few months.

2. Muriel is 1 month old, Janine is 5 months old, Ted is 1 year old, and Tania is age 3. List each child's phase of attachment.

3. Match term to the correct definition: (1) social referencing; (2) working model; (3) synchrony; (4) Strange Situation.

   a. A researcher measures a child's attachment at age 1 in a series of separations and reunions with the mother.

   b. A toddler keeps looking back at the parent while exploring at a playground.

   c. An elementary school child keeps an image of her parent in mind to calm herself when she gets on the school bus in the morning.

   d. A mother and baby relate to each other as if they are totally in tune.

4. Your cousin is the primary caregiver of her 1-year-old son. On a recent visit to her house, you notice that the baby shows no emotion when his mother leaves the room, and—more important—seems indifferent when she returns. How might you classify this child's attachment?

5. Manuel is arguing for the validity of attachment theory as spelled out by Bowlby and Ainsworth. Manuel should say (pick one, neither, or both): *Infants around the world get attached to a primary caregiver at roughly the same age/a child's attachment status as of age 1 never changes.*

6. Jasmine is adopting a 2-year-old from an orphanage in Haiti. List a few child issues Jasmine might have to deal with, and then give Jasmine a piece of good attachment news.

You can find Answers to the Tying It All Together questions at the end of this chapter.

Settings for Development

What happens to children in the United States who spend their first years of life in poverty? And what about that crucial setting of early childhood—day care?

The Impact of Poverty in the United States

In Chapter 3, I examined the physical effects of extreme poverty—the high rates of stunting in the developing world. While the United States doesn't have the kind of poverty that causes undernutrition, early-childhood poverty in the United States can compromise a developing life. How common is child poverty in the United States? How does growing up poor affect children's later well-being?

FIGURE 4.5: Poverty rates by age, 1959–2010: Notice that since the 1970s, children under 6 years of age have been more likely to live under the poverty line than other age groups in the United States. (FYI—Although the "poverty line" designation theoretically describes the minimum income needed to survive, experts feel that families need twice that amount of money to really make ends meet.)

Data from: Economic Policy Institute (2012). The State of Working America: Poor children. Retrieved January 12, 2014, http://stateofworkingamerica.org/

FIGURE 4.6: Resting cortisol levels among low- and middle-income children from age 7 months through age 4 years: Notice that low-income babies, toddlers, and preschoolers show elevated levels of the stress hormone cortisol, which may impair their ability to regulate their behavior and wear down the body, causing premature illness and death.

Data from: Evans and Kim, 2013, p. 45.

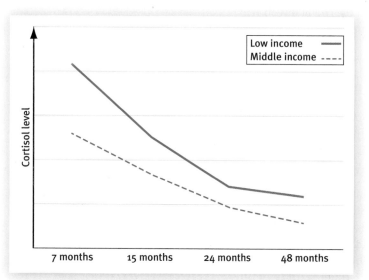

How Common Is Early-Childhood Poverty?

As Figure 4.5, shows, unfortunately, child poverty is prevalent in the United States. In 2013, almost one in four children (22 percent) lived under the poverty line. If we consider children in "low income" families (those earning within two times the official poverty cut-off), the statistic rises to 45 percent (National Center for Children in Poverty [NCCP], 2014)! Moreover, notice that, since the 1970s, young children have been more likely to live in poverty than other age groups in the United States.

One cause is single motherhood. Imagine how difficult it would be as a woman raising a baby alone to work, pay for child care, and still have money to make ends meet. Now imagine how difficult it would be for *any* person to support a family with a full-time job that pays under $12 an hour. In 2013, more than 1 in 4 U.S. *working men*, age 25–34, earned less than this amount (Gould, 2014). So, it's no wonder that economic disadvantage can be the price of starting families during the very time young people are supposed to marry and give birth.

How Does Early-Childhood Poverty Affect Later Development?

Unfortunately, spending one's first years of life in poverty can have long-term effects. As Figure 4.6 shows, poor children show chronically elevated levels of the stress hormone cortisol (Evans & Kim, 2013), which may wear down the body and promote premature illnesses and death (Miller, Chen, & Parker, 2011; recall also my discussion of deprivation in the womb, in Chapter 2).

The educational impact is pronounced. You might be surprised to know that being poor during the first four years of life makes it statistically less likely for a child to graduate from high school (Duncan & Brooks-Gunn, 2000; Duncan, Ziol-Guest, & Kalil, 2010).

Why can early-childhood poverty limit later academic success? One possibility is that it is difficult to make up for what you have lost if you enter school "left behind," not knowing your letters or numbers, without the basic building blocks to succeed. (Kozol, 2005, p. 53.)

Poverty also can impair the attachment dance, especially among at-risk children who need unusually sensitive care. Imagine arriving home exhausted from a low-wage job or being unemployed, *food insecure*, and worried about getting evicted because you can't pay the rent. How would you deal with the kind of temperamentally irritable infant I described in the previous section, a baby who was difficult to soothe (Paulussen-Hoogeboom and others, 2007). So although money cannot buy loving parents, it can buy any parent breathing space to try to do her best.

Moreover, poor children may not have the *concrete* breathing space to learn (Leventhal & Newman, 2010). If a boy or girl lives in crowded, substandard housing or is among the roughly 1 in 3 low-income children in the United States whose family must repeatedly move (Miller, Sadegh-Nobari, & Lillie-Blanton, 2011), it's hard to focus on academics or get connected to school. And if a child lives in a dangerous area, she cannot escape the household chaos by venturing outside. Her neighborhood is likely to be a scary place (Anakwenze & Zuberi, 2013).

Unfortunately, the impact of a chaotic environment may appear before a child ventures outside. When researchers explored how well 6-month-olds were able to focus their attention, the low-SES babies performed worse than the average child that age (Clearfield & Jedd, 2013).

If you are thinking this research has eerie similarities to the orphanage-caused attention abnormalities, you may be right. However, with poverty, the same earlier (attachment) principles apply. Individual children are more or less genetically reactive to this stress. There is dose–response effect. Deficits in the ability to focus and modulate one's behavior are more probable if a child has been chronically poor (Raver and others, 2013).

There also is a rural–urban U.S. distinction. While one study suggested the risk of experiencing preschool problems was *three times greater* if a poor child lived in a large city (versus the country), over a certain economic threshold ($32,000), city preschoolers benefited most (Miller and others, 2013). Blighted, impoverished urban neighborhoods seem especially toxic to young children's well-being. But having

Growing up in a bucolic rural setting offers a lovely tranquil childhood, but it can't top the intellectual stimulation this city provides—explaining why, beyond "a threshold income level," urban preschoolers do better on early-childhood cognitive tests.

"a bit more money" allows city parents to expose their preschoolers to museums, parks, and the many enriching experiences this kind of world-class environment provides.

Luckily, low-income parents have access to one enriching experience *no matter* where they live—Head Start.

INTERVENTIONS: Giving Disadvantaged Children an Intellectual and Social Boost

Head Start A federal program offering high-quality day care at a center and other services to help preschoolers aged 3 to 5 from low-income families prepare for school.

Early Head Start A federal program that provides counseling and other services to low-income parents and children under age 3.

preschool A teaching-oriented group setting for children aged 3 to 5.

The famous government program called **Head Start,** established in 1965, aims to provide the kind of high-quality preschool experience to make poverty-level children as ready for kindergarten as their middle-class peers. By the beginning of the twenty-first century most states also offered free pre-K (prekindergarten) programs targeted to children in economic need (U.S. Department of Health and Human Services, 2003).

Early Head Start extends this help to infants and toddlers. This federal program focuses on training parents to be more effective caregivers, as well as supports low-income pregnant women with home visits and other services (Phillips & Lowenstein, 2011).

Do these interventions work? The answer is yes. Provided the programs are high quality, study after study shows Head Start and pre-K programs make a difference in low-income children's lives (Bassok, 2010; Votruba-Drzal, 2013; Magnuson & Shager, 2010; Miller, Sadegh-Nobari, & Lillie-Blanton, 2011; Phillips & Lowenstein, 2011; Li and others, 2013). In a genuine experiment, in which researchers randomly assigned disadvantaged children to a high-quality pre-K, this one-shot intervention had an impact, decades later, in improved college graduation rates! (See Pungello and others, 2010.)

Unfortunately, however, excellent **preschools** (teaching-oriented group programs beginning at age 3) are most available to affluent young children (Magnuson & Shager, 2010). Moreover, no one-shot magic intervention at age 3 or 4 compensates for the academic barriers poor children face during their *entire* school careers. As you will learn in Chapter 7, low-income children typically attend the poorest-quality kindergartens. Their educational experiences—without adequate books, mold-encrusted classrooms, and teachers who often quit just a few months into the school year—qualify as a national shame (Kozol, 1988, 2005).

Finally, I must emphasize that preschool doesn't work in isolation. Yes, early-childhood programs can be a nurturing lifeline for a child whose home environment is poor (Phillips & Lowenstein, 2011; Berry and others, 2014). But what matters most is the quality of care at school and home (Crosnoe and others, 2010; Stein and others, 2013).

This brings up that vital influence: parents! Mothers and fathers at *every* income level differ in the enriching experiences they provide. Every study agrees: What happens at home matters most (Lugo-Gil & Tamis-LeMonda, 2008). Some affluent parents are neglectful. Some poverty-level moms and dads work overtime to nurture their daughters and sons.

Can we identify the core qualities of these special low-income parents? In one study, researchers found that if people felt good about their own childhoods and were optimistic, they could put aside their problems and offer their children the ultimate in tender-loving care (Kochanska and others, 2007). As a student of mine commented, "I don't see my family in your description of poverty. My mom is my hero. We grew up poor, but in terms of parenting, we were very rich."

The Impact of Child Care

As a well-off parent, poverty issues can seem distant from your life. Child care affects every family, from millionaires, to middle-class urban mothers and fathers, to the rural poor. One in every two mothers in the United States returns to work during a baby's

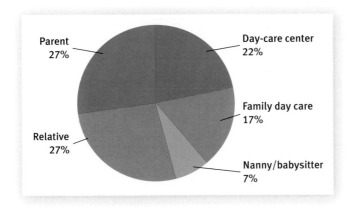

FIGURE 4.7: **Day-care arrangements for infants and toddlers with employed mothers, late 1990s:** Notice that, while most infants and toddlers with working mothers are cared for by other family members, 1 in 5 attend licensed day-care centers.
Data from: Shonkoff & Phillips 2000, p. 304.

first year of life. With child-care costs currently ranging from $5,000 to 15,000 per year, the expense of putting even *one* baby in day care is daunting, even to couples who are middle class (Palley & Shdaimah, 2011). When we combine these economic concerns ("This is taking up a huge chunk of my paycheck!") with anxieties about "leaving my baby with strangers," it makes sense that many new parents struggle to keep child care in the family. They may rely on grandma or juggle work schedules so that one spouse is always home (Phillips & Lowenstein, 2011).

People who use paid caregivers have several options. Well-off families often hire a nanny or babysitter. Less-affluent parents, or those who want a more inexpensive option, often turn to **family day care,** where a neighbor or local parent cares for a small group of children in her home.

The big change on the child-care landscape has been the dramatic increase in licensed **day-care centers**—larger settings catering to children of different ages. By the late twentieth century, roughly 1 in 2 U.S. preschoolers attended these facilities. The comparable figure for infants and toddlers was more than 1 in 5 (see Figure 4.7).

family day care A day-care arrangement in which a neighbor or relative cares for a small number of children in her home for a fee.

day-care center A day-care arrangement in which a large number of children are cared for at a licensed facility by paid providers.

Child Care and Development

Imagine you are the mother of an infant and must return to work. You probably have heard the media messages that link full-time day care with less-than-adequate mothering. So you are feeling guilty, and perhaps feel compelled to explain your decision to disapproving family and friends (Fothergill, 2013). You may wonder, "Will my child be securely attached if I see her only a few hours a day?" You certainly worry about the quality of care your child would receive: "Will my baby get enough attention at the local day-care center?" "Am I *really* harming my child?"

To answer these kinds of questions, in 1989, developmentalists began the National Institute of Child Health and Human Development (NICHD) Study of Early Child Care. They selected more than 1,000 newborns in 10 regions of the United States and tracked the progress of these children, measuring everything from attachment to academic abilities, from mental health, to mothers' caregiving skills. They looked at the hours each child spent in day care, and assessed the quality of each setting. The NICHD newborns are being followed as they travel into adult life (Vandell and others, 2010).

The good news is that putting a baby in day care does not weaken the attachment bond. Most infants attending day care are securely attached to their parents. The important force that promotes attachment is the *quality* of the dance—whether a parent is a sensitive caregiver—not whether she works (Phillips & Lowenstein, 2011; Nomaguchi and DeMaris, 2013). Moreover, as I emphasized earlier, what happens at home is the crucial influence affecting how young children develop, outweighing long hours spent in day care during the first years of life (Belsky and others, 2007b; Stein and others, 2013).

However, when we look *just* at the impact of spending those long hours, the findings are less upbeat. As you saw in the previous section, attending an excellent preschool has intellectual benefits (Vandell and others, 2010). But when we look at the impact of attending day care *throughout the first five years of life*, there is troubling news.

Earlier NICHD research raised alarm bells by reporting that children who spent long hours in "nonrelative care" were slightly more likely to be rated as "difficult to control" by caregivers and kindergarten teachers (NICHD, Early Child Care Research Network, 2003, 2004, 2006; see also Coley and others, 2013). Now we know that long hours spent in day care, beginning early in life, still predict an elevated risk of "acting-out issues" as teens (Vandell and others, 2010).

These results do not offer comfort to the millions of parents with babies who rely heavily on day care. Luckily, the correlations are weak (Vandell and others, 2010). Because these settings can be a refuge from the chaotic home environments described earlier, for infants living in poverty, attending full-time day care may promote well-being (Berry and others, 2014). Moreover, day care's negative effects apply mainly to children attending large centers, not smaller, family day care (Groeneveld and others, 2010; Coley and others, 2013).

What is the trouble with day-care centers? For hints, let's scan the state of child care in the United States.

Exploring Child-Care Quality in the United States

Visit several facilities and you will immediately see that U.S. day care varies in quality. In some places, babies are warehoused and ignored. In others, every child is nurtured and loved.

The essence of quality day care again boils down to the dance—that is, the attachment relationship between caretakers and the children. Children develop intense attachments to their day-care providers. If a particular caregiver is sensitive, a child in her care tends to be securely attached (Ahnert, Pinquart, & Lamb, 2006; De Schipper and others, 2008).

Child-care providers and parents agree: To be effective in this job, you need to be patient, caring, empathic, and child-centered (Berthelsen & Brownlee, 2007; Virmani & Ontai, 2010). It's not so much formal education that matters, but being able to reflect on your interactions (Virmani & Ontai, 2010) and being committed to this field (Martin and others, 2010).

You also need to work in a setting where you can relate to children in a one-to-one way. To demonstrate this point, researchers videotaped teachers at 64 Dutch preschools, either playing with three children or with five. Teachers acted more empathic in the three-child group. They were more likely to criticize and get angry with the group of five (de Schipper, Riksen-Walraven, & Geurts, 2006). These differences in teachers' tone and style were especially pronounced with younger children (the 3-year-olds). So, group size matters; and the lower the child–teacher ratio, the better, especially earlier in life.

Another important dimension is consistency of care (Harrist, Thompson, & Norris, 2007). Forming an attachment takes time. Therefore, children are more apt to be securely attached to a caregiver when that person has been there a longer time (Ahnert, Pinquart, & Lamb, 2006).

However, partly because of the abysmal pay (in the United States, it's often close to the minimum wage), day-care workers are apt to quit. They may feel rejected even when they have valuable input to provide. As one woman in an interview study complained, "When . . . you try to tell them (some parents) anything, it's like 'yeah right.' They never want to hear what you have to say" (quoted in Fothergill, 2013, p. 440).

Now, combine this feeling of being unappreciated, with burnout from being overwhelmed. While the recommended ratio is one caregiver to four toddlers, only

Can these day-care workers give enough attention to the babies, toddlers, and preschoolers in their care? Unfortunately, with a child–caregiver ratio at over 3 to 1 at this center, the answer may be no.

eight states follow this guideline (Stebbins & Knitzner, NCCP, 2007). Some allow as many as one teacher per 12 children, even during the first year of life.

In sum, now we know why day-care centers are at risk of providing inadequate care. Their culprit is size. In family day care, there is a smaller number of children and often more stability (since the person is watching the children in her home) than in a large facility, where caregivers keep leaving and babies can be warehoused in larger groups (Gerber, Whitebrook, & Weinstein, 2007; Ahnert, Pinquart, & Lamb, 2006; Groeneveld and others, 2010).

INTERVENTIONS: Choosing Child Care

Given these findings, what should parents do? The take-home message is not "avoid a day-care center," but rather "choose the best possible place." Look for a low staff turnover; see if the caregivers are empathic and warm; if you have an infant or toddler, make sure your baby will spend the day in a small group. You might find these conditions at your next-door neighbor's house. Perhaps you'll find these attributes at the largest child-care facility in town.

Finally, here, too, we can look to the child's biology. While attending a low-quality day care is harmful for infants and toddlers with an environment-responsive genetic profile, these same children may flourish if a program is top notch (Belsky and Pluess, 2013). So, as we learn more about environment-sensitive genes, making blanket generalizations—such as "day care is bad (or good)"—may not be appropriate. It depends on the quality of the program, a person's home life, and, now, the biology of a given child.

Table 4.1 draws on these messages in a checklist. And if you are a parent who relies heavily on day care, keep those guilty thoughts at bay. Your child may blossom at a high-quality day care. Moreover, *your* responsiveness matters most. You are your child's major teacher and the major force in making your child secure.

Now that we have examined attachment, poverty, and day care, it's time to turn directly to the topic I have been implicitly talking about all along—being a toddler.

Table 4.1: Choosing a Day-Care Center: A Checklist

Overall Considerations

- Consider the caregiver(s). Are they nurturing? Do they love babies? Are they interested in providing a good deal of verbal stimulation to children?

- Ask about stability, or staff turnover. Have caregivers left in the last few months? Can my infant have the same caregivers when she moves to the toddler room?

- Look for a low caregiver-to-baby ratio (and a small group). The ideal is one caregiver to every two or three babies.

- Look at the physical setting. Is it safe and clean, set up with children's needs in mind? (With toddlers, look for a variety of age-appropriate play materials, clearly defined social spaces and more private nooks, child-sized furniture, clear pathways for children to circulate, and sensitive placement of play areas, such as areas for painting situated near sinks.)

Additional Suggestions

- For infants and toddlers in full-time care, limit exposure by having a child take occasional vacations or building in special time with the child every day.

- Consider the home environment. If your home life is chaotic or you live in a dangerous neighborhood, your child may be better off spending the day at a structured, stable place.

- Consider a child's temperament. While biologically reactive (highly environment-sensitive) babies have special trouble coping with less-than-optimal care, these same toddlers may flourish in a high-quality setting.

- And finally, for society, pay day-care workers decently and make the qualities you are looking for in this checklist the norm!

Background information from: The authors cited in this section.

Tying It All Together

1. Hugo is explaining which low SES children are at higher risk of having cognitive deficits. Pick the statement he should **NOT** make: *These children's families are chronically poor/These children live in rural areas/These children are genetically reactive to stress.*

2. Nancy has just put her 6-month-old in day care, and she is anxious about her decision. Give a "good news" statement to ease Nancy's mind, and then be honest and give a "not such good news" statement about day care.

3. You are making a presentation to a Senate committee investigating early child care. What should you tell the senators about the impact of preschool on development? What improvements can you suggest with regard to day care itself?

Answers to the Tying It All Together questions can be found at the end of this chapter.

Toddlerhood: Age of Autonomy *and* Shame and Doubt

Imagine time-traveling back to when you were a toddler. Everything is entrancing—a bubble bath, the dishwasher soap box, the dirt and bugs in your backyard. You are just cracking the language barrier and finally (yes!) traveling on your own two feet. Passionate to sail into life, you are also intensely connected to that number-one adult in your life. So, during our second year on this planet, the two agendas that make us human first emerge: We need to be closely connected, and we want to be free, autonomous selves. This is why Erik Erikson (1950) used the descriptive word **autonomy** to describe children's challenge as they emerge from the cocoon of babyhood (see Table 4.2).

Autonomy involves everything from the thrill a 2-year-old feels when forming his first sentences, to the delight children have in dressing themselves. But it also involves those not-so-pleasant traits we associate with the "terrible twos." Overwhelmed by these classic 2-year-old meltdowns, in one study, 1 in 3 parents labeled their child as having behavior problems that were "off the charts" (Schellinger & Talmi, 2013). This may be a misperception, as Figure 4.8 on the opposite page shows. Difficulties "listening" and angry outbursts (Barry & Kochanska, 2010) are *normal* during that magic age when children's life passion is to explore the world (recall Piaget's little scientist behaviors).

autonomy Erikson's second psychosocial task, when toddlers confront the challenge of understanding that they are separate individuals.

Table 4.2: Erikson's Psychosocial Stages

Life Stage	Primary Task
Infancy (birth to 1 year)	Basic trust versus mistrust
Toddlerhood (1 to 2 years)	**Autonomy versus Shame and Doubt**
Early childhood (3 to 6 years)	Initiative versus guilt
Late childhood (6 years to puberty)	Industry versus inferiority
Adolescence (teens into twenties)	Identity versus role confusion
Young adulthood (twenties to early forties)	Intimacy versus isolation
Middle adulthood (forties to sixties)	Generativity versus stagnation
Late adulthood (late sixties and beyond)	Integrity versus despair

Erikson used the words *shame* and *doubt* to refer to the situation when a toddler's drive for autonomy is not fulfilled. But feeling shameful and doubtful is also vital to shedding babyhood and entering the human world. During their first year of life, infants show joy, fear, and anger. At age 2, more complicated, uniquely human emotions emerge—pride and shame. The appearance of these **self-conscious emotions** is a milestone—showing that a child is becoming aware of having a self. The gift (and sometimes curse) of being human is that we are capable of self-reflection, able to get outside of our heads and observe our actions from an outsider's point of view. Children show signs of this uniquely human quality between age 2 and 3, when they feel ashamed and clearly are proud of their actions for the first time (Kagan, 1984).

Socialization: The Challenge for 2-Year-Olds

Shame and pride are vital in another respect. They are essential to **socialization**—being taught to live in the human community.

Parents begin socializing their children by making requests such as "eat that cookie," as early as 6 months of age. There are cultural differences, with Indian mothers giving their babies more instructions and getting higher rates of compliance than do U.S. moms (Reddy and others, 2013).

When does the U.S. socialization pressure *heat up*? For answers, developmentalists surveyed middle-class parents about their rules for their 14-month-olds and when the children just turned 2 (Smetana, Kochanska, & Chuang, 2000). While rules for younger toddlers centered on safety issues ("Stay away from the stove!"), by age 2, parents were telling their children to "share," "sit at the table," and "don't disobey, bite, or hit." Therefore, we expect children to begin to act "like adults" around their second birthdays. No wonder 2-year-olds are infamous for those tantrums called "the terrible twos"!

Figure 4.8 shows just how difficult it is for 1-year-olds to follow socialization rules when their parents are around. When do children have the capacity to follow unwanted directions when a parent *isn't* in the room? To answer this question related to early *conscience*—the ability to adopt internal standards for our behavior, or have that little voice inside us that says, "even though I want to do this, it's wrong"—researchers devised an interesting procedure. Accompanied by their mothers, children enter a laboratory full of toys. Next, the parent gives an unwelcome instruction—telling the child either to clean up the toys or not to touch another easily reachable set of enticing toys. Then, the mother leaves the room, and researchers watch the child through a one-way mirror.

Not unexpectedly, children's ability to "listen to a parent in their head" and stop doing what they want improves dramatically from age 2 to 4 (Kochanska, Coy, & Murray, 2001). Still, the really interesting question is: Who is better or worse at this feat of self-control?

Again, the marked differences in self-control that emerge during toddlerhood (or even earlier) have genetic roots (Wang & Saudino, 2013; Gartstein and others, 2013).

This toddler has reached a human milestone: She can feel shame, which means that she is beginning to be aware that she has a separate self.

self-conscious emotions Feelings of pride, shame, or guilt, which first emerge around age 2 and show the capacity to reflect on the self.

socialization The process by which children are taught to obey the norms of society and to behave in socially appropriate ways.

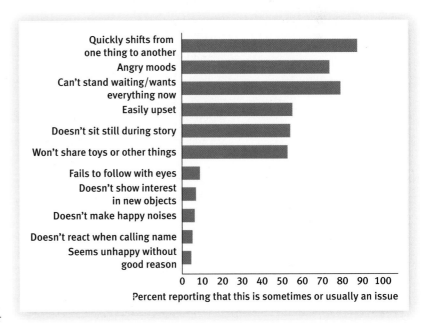

Percent reporting that this is sometimes or usually an issue

FIGURE 4.8: **Typical and unusual difficult toddler behaviors, based on a survey of Dutch parents of 6,491 infants aged 14 to 19 months:** Notice that it's normal for toddlers not to listen, have temper tantrums, and refuse to sit still or share—but the other difficult behaviors in red should be warning signs of a real problem.
Data from: Beernick and others, 2007.

Some of us are biologically better able to resist temptation at any age! Parenting matters, too. While having a responsive mother seems most important at promoting compliance during toddlerhood, a father's warmth weighs heavily at older ages (Lickenbrock and others, 2013; Schueler & Prinz, 2013). So dad's socializing influence—at least in traditional two-parent families—is important, but mainly when children move beyond the clear-cut attachment zone.

What temperamental traits provoke early compliance? Here the answer comes as no surprise. Fearful toddlers are more obedient (Aksan & Kochanska, 2004; see also the How Do We Know box). Exuberant, joyful, fearless, intrepid toddler-explorers are especially hard to socialize! (See Kochanska & Knaack, 2003.)

HOW DO WE KNOW ...
that shy and exuberant children differ dramatically in self-control?

How do researchers measure the toddler temperaments discussed below? How do they test later self-control? Their first step is to design situations tailored to elicit fear, anger, and joy and then observe how toddlers act.

In the fear eliciting "treatment," a child enters a room filled with frightening toy objects, such as a dinosaur with huge teeth or a black box covered with spider webs. The experimenter asks that boy or girl to perform a mildly risky act, such as putting a hand into the box. To measure anger, the researchers restrain a child in a car seat and then rate how frustrated the toddler gets. To tap into exuberance, the researchers entertain a child with a set of funny puppets. Will the toddler respond with gales of laughter or be more reserved?

Several years later, the researchers set up a situation provoking noncompliance by asking the child, now age 4, to perform an impossible task (throw Velcro balls at a target from a long distance without looking) to get a prize. Then, they leave the room and watch through a one-way mirror to see if the boy or girl will cheat.

Toddlers at the high end of the fearless, joyous, and angry continuum, show less "morality" at age 4. Without the strong inhibition of fear, their exuberant "get closer" impulses are difficult to dampen down. So they succumb to temptation, sneak closer, and look directly at the target as they hurl the balls (Kochanska & Knaack, 2003).

Being Exuberant and Being Shy

Adam [was a vigorous, happy baby who] began walking at 9 months. From then on, it seemed as though he could never stop.

(10 months) Adam . . . refuses to be carried anywhere. . . . He trips over objects, falls down, bumps himself.

(12 months) The word *osside* appears. . . . Adam stands by the door, banging at it and repeating this magic word again and again.

(19 months) Adam begins attending a toddler group. . . . The first day, Adam climbs to the highest rung of the climbing structure and falls down. . . . The second day, Adam upturns a heavy wooden bench. . . . The fourth day, the teacher [devastates Adam's mother] when she says, "I think Adam is not ready for this."

. . .

(13 months) (Erin begins to talk in sentences the same week as she takes her first steps.) . . . Rather suddenly, Erin becomes quite shy. . . . She cries when her mother leaves the room, and insists on following her everywhere.

(15 months) Erin and her parents go to the birthday party of a little friend. . . . For the first half-hour, Erin stays very close to her mother, intermittently hiding her face on her mother's skirt.

(18 months) Erin's mother takes her to a toddlers' gym. Erin watches the children . . . with a "tight little face." . . . Her mother berates herself for raising such a timid child.
(Lieberman, 1993, pp. 83–87, 104–105)

Observe any group of 1-year-olds and you will immediately pick out the Erins and the Adams. Some children are wary and shy. Others are whirlwinds of activity, constantly in motion, bouncing off the walls. I remember my own first toddler group at the local Y, when—just like Adam's mother—I first realized how different my exuberant son was from the other children his age. After enduring the horrified expressions of the other mothers as Thomas whirled gleefully around the room while everyone else sat obediently for a snack, I came home and cried. How was I to know that the very qualities that made my outgoing, joyous, vital baby so charismatic during his first year of life might go along with his being so difficult to tame?

My exuberant son—shown enjoying a sink bath at 9 months of age—began to have problems at 18 months, when his strong, joyous temperament collided with the need to "please sit still and listen, Thomas!"

The classic longitudinal studies tracing children with shy temperaments have been carried out by Jerome Kagan. Kagan (1994; see also Degnan, Almas, & Fox, 2010) classifies about 1 in 5 middle-class European American toddlers as inhibited. Although they are comfortable in familiar situations, these 1-year-olds, like Erin, get nervous when confronted with anything new. Inhibited 13-month-olds shy away from approaching a toy robot, a clown, or an unfamiliar person. They take time to venture out in the Strange Situation, get agitated when the stranger enters, and cry bitterly when their parent leaves the room.

This tendency to be inhibited is also moderately "genetic" (Smith and others, 2012), and we can get clues to its appearance very early in life. At 4 months of age, toddlers destined to be inhibited excessively fret and cry (Moehler and others, 2008; Marysko and others, 2010). At 9 months of age, they are less able to ignore distracting stimuli such as flashing lights or background noise. Their attention wanders to any off-topic, irrelevant unpleasant event (Pérez-Edgar and others, 2010a).

Inhibited toddlers are more prone to be fearful throughout childhood (Degnan, Almas, & Fox, 2010). They overfocus on threatening stimuli in their teens (Pérez-Edgar and others, 2010a). This temperamental sensitivity to threat shows up in adult life. Using brain scans, Kagan's research team found that his inhibited toddlers, now as young adults, showed more activity in the part of the brain coding negative emotions when shown a stranger's face on a screen (Schwartz and others, 2003). So for all of you formerly very shy people (your author included) who think you have shed that childhood wariness, you still carry your physiology inside.

Still, if you think you have come a long way in conquering your *incredible* childhood shyness, you are probably correct. Many anxious toddlers (and exuberant explorers) get less inhibited as they move into elementary school and the teenage years (Degnan, Almas, & Fox, 2010; Pérez-Edgar and others, 2010b).

INTERVENTIONS: Providing the Right Temperament–Socialization Fit

Faced with a temperamentally timid toddler such as Erin or an exuberant explorer like Adam or Thomas, what can parents do?

Socializing a Shy Baby

In dealing with fearful children, parents' impulse is to back off ("Erin is emotionally fragile, so I won't pressure her to go to day care or clean up her toys"). This "treat 'em like glass" approach is apt to backfire, provoking more wariness down the road (Natsuaki and others, 2013). With shy children, be caring and responsive (Barnett and others, 2010; Degnan, Almas, & Fox, 2010), but provide a gentle push. Exposing a shy toddler to *supportive* new social situations—such as family day care—helps teach that child to cope.

Raising a Rambunctious Toddler

When faced with fearless explorers, like Adam and Thomas, it's tempting to adopt a discipline style called **power assertion**—yelling, screaming, and hitting a child who is bouncing off the walls (Verhoeven and others, 2010). Once they have defined their toddler as "impossible to control," parents are prone to come down more harshly, misreading defiance even into benign acts. Another reaction is to give up—abandoning any attempt to discipline a child (Mence and others, 2014).

Both strategies are counterproductive. Power assertion strongly predicts behavior problems down the road (Brotman and others, 2009; Kochanska & Knaack, 2003; Leve and others, 2010). Disengaging from discipline robs the child of the tools to modify his behavior. Plus, it conveys the message, "You are out of control and there is nothing I can do."

The key to reducing "noncompliance" in *any toddler* is to offer positive guidance; meaning to set limits in a calm, clear way (Christopher and others, 2013). With fearless explorers, it's especially crucial to foster a secure attachment, getting a child to *want* to be good for mom and dad (Kochanska and Kim, 2013). As my husband insightfully commented, "Punishment doesn't matter much to Thomas. What he does, he does for your love."

Table 4.3 offers a summary of this discussion, showing these different toddler temperaments, their infant precursors, their pluses and potential later dangers, and lessons for socializing each kind of child. Now let's look at some general temperament-sensitive lessons for raising every child.

An Overall Strategy for Temperamentally Friendly Childrearing

Clearly, one key to socializing children is to provide a secure, loving attachment. However, another is to understand each child's temperament and work with that unique behavioral style. This principle was demonstrated in the classic study I mentioned earlier, in which developmentalists classified babies as "easy," "slow-to-warm-up," and "difficult."

Table 4.3: Exuberant and Inhibited Toddler Temperaments: A Summary

Inhibited, Shy Toddler

- **Developmental precursor:** Responds with intense motor arousal to external stimulation in infancy.

- **Plus:** Easily socialized; shows early signs of conscience; not a discipline problem.

- **Minus:** Shy, fearful temperament can persist into adulthood, making social encounters painful.

- **Child-rearing advice:** Don't overprotect the child. Expose the baby to unfamiliar people and supportive new situations.

Sakdawut Tangtongsap/Shutterstock

Exuberant Toddler

- **Developmental precursor:** Emotionally intense but unafraid of new stimuli.

- **Plus:** Joyous; fearless; outgoing; adventurous.

- **Minus:** Less easily socialized; potential problems with conscience development; at higher risk for later "acting-out" behavior problems.

- **Child-rearing advice:** Avoid power assertion and harsh punishment. Offer clear rules, but provide lots of love.

© Picture Partners/Alamy

In following the difficult babies into elementary school, the researchers found that intense infants were more likely to have problems with their teachers and peers (Thomas & Chess, 1977; Thomas, Chess, & Birch, 1968). However, some children learned to compensate for their biology and to shine. The key, the researchers discovered, lay in a parenting strategy labeled **goodness of fit.** Parents who carefully arranged their children's lives to minimize their vulnerabilities and accentuate their strengths had infants who later did well.

Understanding that their child was overwhelmed by stimuli, these parents kept the environment calm. They did not get hysterical when faced with their child's distress. They may have offered a quiet environment for studying and encouraged their child to do activities that took advantage of his or her talents. They went overboard to provide their child with a placid, nurturing, low-stress milieu.

Here, too, emerging genetic studies suggest these parents were right. Again, researchers find that children may be genetically predisposed to be reactive or relatively immune to environmental events (Ellis and others, 2011a). In typical settings, sensitive babies can be labeled "difficult" because they are wired to react negatively to changes. These same infants however, may flourish when the environment is exceptionally calm (for review, see Belsky & Pleuss, 2009). In fact, in one study, when "environment reactive" children were put in a nurturing, placid environment, they performed *better* than their laid-back peers (Obradović, Burt & Masten, 2010)!

I must emphasize that this genetically oriented research is in its infancy. Each study I've highlighted in this chapter has targeted a *different* environment-reactive marker gene! But the lesson here is that making assumptions about the enduring importance of infant attachment, categorizing poverty and full-time day care as universal stressors, or, in this case, labeling a baby (or person) as "difficult" or "easy" may not be appropriate. With the right person–environment fit, what looks like a liability might be a gift!

How can we promote goodness of fit, or person–environment fit, at every stage of life? What happens to babies who are shy or exuberant, difficult or easy, as they journey into elementary school and adolescence? How do Ainsworth's attachment styles play out in adult romance? Stay tuned for answers to these questions in the rest of this book.

goodness of fit An ideal parenting strategy that involves arranging children's environments to suit their temperaments, minimizing their vulnerabilities and accentuating their strengths.

 Tying It All Together

1. If Amanda has recently turned 2, what predictions are you *not* justified in making about her?

   a. Amanda wants to be independent, yet closely attached.

   b. Amanda is beginning to show signs of self-awareness and can possibly feel shame.

   c. Amanda's parents haven't begun to discipline her yet.

2. To a colleague at work who confides that he's worried about his timid toddler, what words of comfort can you offer?

3. Think back to your own childhood: Did you fit into either the shy or exuberant temperament type? How did your parents cope with your personality style?

Answers to the Tying It All Together questions can be found at the end of this chapter.

SUMMARY

Attachment: The Basic Life Bond

For much of the twentieth century, many psychologists in the United States—because they were behaviorists—minimized the mother–child bond. European psychoanalysts such as John Bowlby were finding, however, that attachment was a basic human need. Harlow's studies with monkeys convinced U.S. developmentalists of the importance of **attachment,** and Bowlby transformed developmental science by arguing that having a loving **primary attachment figure** is biologically built in, and crucial to our development. Although threats to survival at any age evoke **proximity-seeking behavior**—especially during **toddlerhood**—being physically apart from an attachment figure elicits distress.

According to Bowlby, life begins with a three-month-long **preat-tachment phase**, which is characterized by the first **social smile**. After an intermediate phase called **attachment in the making**, at about 7 months of age, the landmark phase of **clear-cut attach-ment** begins, signaled by **separation anxiety** and **stranger anxi-ety**. During this period spanning toddlerhood, children need their caregiver to be physically close, and they rely on **social referenc-ing** to monitor their behavior. After age 3, children can tolerate separations, as they develop an internal **working model** of their caregiver—which they carry into life.

To explore individual differences in attachment, Mary Ainsworth devised the **Strange Situation**. Using this test, involving planned separations, and especially reunions, developmentalists label 1-year-olds as **securely** or **insecurely attached**. Securely attached 1-year-olds use their primary attachment figure as a secure base for exploration and are delighted when she returns. **Avoidant** infants seem indifferent. **Anxious-ambivalent** children are incon-solable and sometimes angry when their caregiver arrives. Chil-dren with a **disorganized attachment** react in an erratic way and often show fear when their parent reenters the room.

Caregiver–child interactions are characterized by a beautiful **syn-chrony,** or attachment dance. Although the caregiver's respon-siveness to the baby is a major determinant of attachment security at age 1, infant attachment is also affected by the **tem-perament** of the child and depends on the quality of a caregiver's other relationships, too.

Cross-cultural studies support the idea that attachment to a pri-mary caregiver is universal, with similar percentages of babies in various countries classified as securely attached. When they are distressed, babies run to the caregiver who spends the most time with them, but infants can be attached to several people, and having a secure attachment to only one caregiver may be all that children need for optimal mental health.

As Bowlby predicted in his working-model concept, securely attached babies have superior mental health. Infants with inse-cure attachments (especially disorganized attachments) are at risk for later problems. However, the good-news/bad-news find-ing is that, when the caregiving environment changes, attach-ment security can change for the better or worse. A gene related to **oxytocin** production may make us more or less responsive to the attachment environment. Babies exposed to the worst-case attachment situation, living in an orphanage with virtually no caregiving, experience a **dose–response effect.** Although the risk of having enduring problems sets in during the "attachment zone," damage depends on the depth of the deprivation and the age when a child leaves that institution.

Settings for Development

Early-childhood poverty—widespread in the United States—can have long-lasting effects on health, emotional development, and,

particularly, school success. Again, this impact varies depend-ing on the duration of the deprivation, the child's genetics, and, interestingly, whether a poor preschooler lives in a rural or urban area. Although **Head Start** and **Early Head Start,** as well as other high-quality preschool experiences, make a difference for disad-vantaged children, they can't totally erase the impact of attend-ing inadequate schools. Poverty-level parents can be excellent parents, and the quality of children's home life matters most.

Going back to work in a baby's first year of life is common, but due to day care's expense and anxieties about leaving their baby with strangers, parents in the United States ideally prefer to keep infant care in the family. Paid child-care options include nannies (for affluent parents), **family day care** (where a person takes a small number of children in her home), and larger **day-care centers.**

The NICHD Study of Early Child Care showed that the best pre-dictor of being securely attached at age 1 is having a sensitive parent, not the number of hours a child spends in day care. While high quality day care can compensate for a chaotic family life, unfortunately, children who spend many hours in day-care centers (versus family care) are at a slightly higher risk of having acting-out behaviors.

In choosing day care, search out loving teachers and a setting where caregivers can relate in a one-to-one way. Because day-care workers are so poorly paid in the United States and may not get respect, staff turnover is a serious problem. This issue, plus their large size, may explain why day-care centers can be prob-lematic. Babies who are genetically environment-reactive may also be more vulnerable to low-quality day care.

Toddlerhood: Age of Autonomy *and* Shame and Doubt

Erikson's **autonomy** captures the essence of toddlerhood, the landmark age when we shed babyhood, become able to observe the self, and enter the human world. **Self-conscious emotions** such as pride and shame emerge and are crucial to socialization, which begins in earnest at around age 2. Difficulties with focusing and obeying are normal during toddlerhood, but at this age, dramatic individual differences appear in children's ability to control them-selves. Temperamentally fearful children show earlier signs of "con-science," following adult prohibitions when not being watched. Exuberant, active toddlers are especially hard to socialize.

As young babies, shy toddlers react with intense motor activity to stimuli. They are more inhibited in elementary school and adoles-cence and show neurological signs of social wariness as young adults. Still (with sensitive parenting), many shy toddlers and fear-less explorers lose these extreme tendencies as they grow older.

To help an inhibited baby don't overprotect the child. Socialize a fearless explorer by avoiding **power assertion,** offering con-sistent rules, and providing lots of love. While fostering secure

attachments is essential in raising *all* children, another key is to promote goodness of fit—tailoring one's parenting to a child's temperamental needs. Genetically environment-sensitive children, although prone to break down in stressful situations, may blossom when the wider world is caring and calm.

KEY TERMS

attachment, p. 107

toddlerhood, p. 107

primary attachment figure, p. 109

proximity-seeking behavior, p. 109

preattachment phase, p. 109

social smile, p. 109

attachment in the making, p. 110

clear-cut attachment, p. 110

separation anxiety, p. 110

stranger anxiety, p. 110

social referencing, p. 110

working model, p. 110

Strange Situation, p. 111

secure attachment, p. 111

insecure attachment, p. 111

avoidant attachment, p. 111

anxious-ambivalent attachment, p. 111

disorganized attachment, p. 111

synchrony, p. 112

temperament, p. 112

oxytocin, p. 115

dose–response effect, p. 116

Head Start, p. 120

Early Head Start, p. 120

preschool, p. 120

family day care, p. 121

day-care center, p. 121

autonomy, p. 124

self-conscious emotions, p. 125

socialization, p. 125

power assertion, p. 128

goodness of fit, p. 129

ANSWERS TO Tying It All Together QUIZZES

Attachment: The Basic Life Bond

1. Your responses will differ, but any example you give, such as "I called Mom when that terrible thing happened at work," should show that in a stressful situation your immediate impulse was to contact your attachment figure.

2. Muriel = preattachment; Janine = attachment in the making; Ted = clear-cut attachment: Tania = working model.

3. (1) b; (2) c; (3) d; (4) a

4. The child has an avoidant attachment.

5. Manuel should say: Infants around the world get attached to a primary caregiver at roughly the same age.

6. Caution Jasmine that her child may show problems with attention and indiscriminant friendliness and, if Jasmine is adopting a boy, have special difficulties developing a secure attachment. However, you can also say these problems *should* improve with loving care.

Settings for Development

1. These children live in rural areas. Children are at highest risk of having deficits when their families are chronically poor and they are temperamentally reactive to stress. (Urban poverty, at least under a certain economic threshold, seems more detrimental to young children's development.)

2. The good news is that the quality of Nancy's parenting is the main force in determining her child's attachment (and emotional health). The bad news is that many day-care centers leave a good deal to be desired, and long hours spent in these centers are associated with a higher risk of having "acting-out issues" in school.

3. Tell the Senate committee that 1) high-quality preschools can have a lasting effect on cognitive development. But 2) we have an imperative need to raise day-care conditions in the United States. Pass laws mandating (not simply recommending) small child-to-caregiver ratios; pay day-care workers decently; give this job the status it deserves! Also, consider providing government-funded toddler and infant child care and mandating paid family leave, so working parents can afford to stay home after a child's birth.

Toddlerhood: Age of Autonomy *and* Shame and Doubt

1. c. Parents typically start serious discipline around age 2.

2. You might tell him that most children grow out of their shyness, even if they do not completely shed this temperamental tendency. But be sure to stress the advantages of being shy: His baby will be easier to socialize, not likely to be a behavior problem, and may have a stronger conscience, too.

3. These answers will be totally your own.

Childhood

In this three-chapter book part covering childhood, the first two chapters trace children's unfolding abilities. In the final chapter, I'll explore the two settings within which children develop: home and school.

The first part of Chapter 5—**Physical and Cognitive Development** examines children's expanding motor skills and focuses on health issues such as obesity. Then comes the heart of this chapter: an exploration of children's minds. If you have ever wondered about the strange ways preschoolers think, want a basic framework for teaching, or would like to understand how memory and reasoning develop, this section is for you. This chapter also charts developing language and two types of social knowledge that evolve during childhood.

In Chapter 6—**Socioemotional Development** my focus shifts to personality and relationships. Here, I will trace growing self-awareness, aggression, caring acts, play, friendships, and popularity from preschool through elementary school. A special focus of this chapter is on boys and girls who are having trouble relating to their peers and adults.

The first half of Chapter 7—**Settings for Development: Home and School** tackles children's family lives. Is there an ideal way of parenting? Why do some children thrive in spite of devastatingly dysfunctional early lives? What is the impact of spanking, child abuse, and divorce on the child? In the second section on school, you will learn all about intelligence tests, what makes schools successful, and how teachers can make every child eager to learn. This chapter concludes with a section outlining the Common Core Standards, that educational transformation in U.S. public schools.

CHAPTER 5

© Corbis RF/Age Fotostock

Physical and Cognitive Development

As the 3-year-olds drift in to Learning Preschool, Ms. Angela fills me in:

"We do free play, then structured games. Then we go outside. At 11 we have snack. We focus on the skills the kids need for school and life: sit still; follow directions; listen; share. During free play, they need to remember three rules: four kids to an activity center; clean up before you leave; don't take the toys from one center when you go to another place."

In the kitchen corner, Kanesha is pretending to scrub pots. "What is your name?" "You know!" says Kanesha, looking at me as if I'm totally dumb. "This is a picnic," Kanesha continues, giving me a plate: "Let's have psghetti and Nadia makeacake." We are having a wonderful time talking as she loads me up with plastic food. The problem is that we aren't communicating. Who is Nadia, that great cook? Then some girls run in with Barbies from the dress-up corner: "Our babies need food!" We're happily feeding our toys when Ms. Angela pipes up: "No moving stuff from the play centers! Don't you remember our four kids to a center rule?" . . .

I move to the crafts table, where Moriah, a dreamy frail girl, and Josiah are surrounded by paper: "Hey!" Moriah yells, after Josiah cuts his paper into pieces, "Josiah has more than me!" Josiah tenderly gives Moriah his bunny, and gives me a heart-melting, welcoming smile: "I'm [holds up three fingers]." (Moriah and Josiah are obviously interested in what I'm doing.) "I'm taking notes for a book." "Taking nose," both children giggle and hold their noses. Moriah is making beautiful circles with paste. Josiah tries to copy her but can only make random lines. These children are so different in their physical abilities, even though they are the same age. But, oh, no, here come the kids from the kitchen corner with plastic vegetables, forgetting the "don't move the toys" and "four children to a center" rules! Luckily, it's time for structured games.

Ms. Angela shows the class cards picturing a sun, an umbrella with raindrops, and clouds, and asks: "What is the weather today?" Josiah proudly picks the umbrella. "How many people think Josiah is right?" Everyone raises a hand. "Who feels it's sunny?" Everyone yells: "Me!" "Who thinks it's cloudy?" Everyone agrees. Then Ms. Angela puts on a tape: "Dance fast, fast . . . slower slower . . . Now speed up!" The kids frantically dance around, and it's time to go outside. Soon the wind starts gusting (it really is about to rain), and everyone gets excited: "Let's catch the wind. . . . Oh, he ran away again!" And now (whew!) it's 11:00 and time for snack.

These 3-year-olds have amazing skills. They can cut, climb, follow directions, tell me about their lives, and (occasionally) remember the teacher's rules. But it will take another decade before they can reason like adults. What were the children thinking during the pretend feedings, and why was Kanesha sure I *had* to know her name? Why did Moriah assume Josiah had more paper when he cut his sheet into pieces, and why did *everyone* have so much trouble remembering the center's rules? In this chapter you'll find answers as we track physical and cognitive development during **early childhood** (age 3 through kindergarten) and **middle childhood** (elementary school).

Before tackling these topics, let's explore *why* our species needs so much time to mentally grow up.

early childhood The first phase of childhood, lasting from age 3 through kindergarten, or about age 5.

middle childhood The second phase of childhood, covering the elementary school years, from about age 6 to 11.

frontal lobes The area at the uppermost front of the brain, responsible for reasoning and planning our actions.

Setting the Context

The monkeys in this photo reached adulthood at roughly age 7 or 8 (Poirier & Smith, 1974). Why do human preschoolers take twice as long to grow up?

Special Mindreading Skills

The reason is that our species has a unique capacity—the ability to build on each generation's intellectual advances. Three-year-olds born in biblical times had the same biology as today's preschoolers, but these twenty-first-century children will grow up using iPads and surfing online. They might even take vacations on the moon or Mars.

What talent allowed humanity to mentally take off? Evolutionary theorists believe at the core of our achievements lies our *social cognitive* capacity to put ourselves in other people's heads and decode intentions (recall Chapter 3). Monkeys show glimmers of this mindreading ability (see Buttelmann, Call, & Tomasello, 2009); but because they don't have our language capacities (also described in Chapter 3), our close mammal cousins can't draw on *each other's* insights to transform the world. ("Oh, now I understand what you were trying to do. Let's work together to improve on that.") Capitalizing on these insights, in turn, demands a large, slow-growing brain.

© Markus Botzek/zefa/Corbis

Imagine that these chimps could *really* share what insights were going on in each other's minds. Wouldn't they be inventing the Internet and traveling into outer space?

Slow-Growing Frontal Lobes

Actually, our huge *cerebral cortex* takes more than two full decades to mature. The *myelin sheath*—the fatty neural cover—grows into our twenties. *Synaptogenesis* (the process of making billions of connections between neurons) is on an extended blossoming and pruning timetable, too, especially in the brain region responsible for thinking through our actions—the **frontal lobes.**

Figure 5.1, which compares the size of our cortex to that of other species, shows the huge frontal lobes positioned at the top of the brain. During early childhood, the neurons in the visual and motor cortices are in their pruning phase, which explains why vision develops rapidly and why we master basic physical milestones, such as

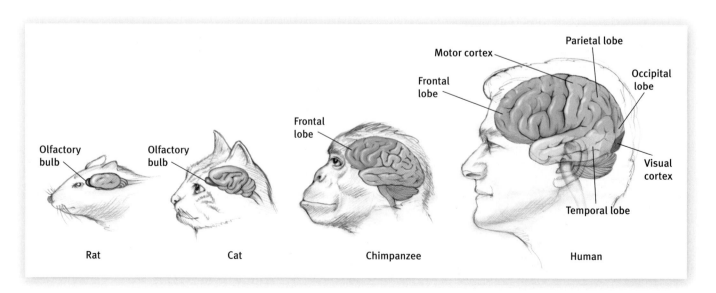

FIGURE 5.1: **The human cortex and that of some other species:** Notice the size of our cortex in comparison to other species. Also notice the dramatic increase in the size of our frontal lobes. It is our mammoth cortex and especially our huge frontal lobes that are responsible for everything that makes our species unique.

walking, at a relatively young age. However, the frontal lobes are only beginning their synaptic blossoming when we start toddling around. Pruning in this part of the brain will not start until about age 9.

Their slow frontal-lobe timetable explains why preschoolers have so much trouble controlling their behavior, and why our ability to plan, think through, and inhibit our actions improves over years. It even accounts for the high expectations we have of elementary schoolers when the frontal lobes enter their pruning phase. We expect fourth and fifth graders to understand long division and take responsibility for completing their homework. After all, they can sometimes beat us at baseball and outscore us at the bowling alley, too.

In addition to allowing us to have the inner control to study (rather than watching TV) and the cognitive abilities to grasp long division, the frontal lobes are vital to mastering physical abilities, from tennis, to tightrope walking, to getting to the toilet at about age 3.

So, understanding that *many* regions of the brain work together to program every action and thought, let's use our slow frontal-lobe timetable as a model to track how children's physical and cognitive abilities unfold.

Tying It All Together

1. In a sentence, explain why language is the core ability that makes human beings special.

2. When Steven played hide-and-seek with his 4-year-old nephew, he realized that while Ethan could run very well, the child was having trouble not betraying his hiding place and understanding the rules of the game. The reason is that Ethan's _____ cortex is on an earlier developmental timetable than his _____ lobes.

3. If you learn that a colleague was in an accident and has frontal-lobe damage, what impairments might you expect?

Answers to the Tying It All Together questions can be found at the end of this chapter.

Physical Development

Look at children of different ages and you will immediately see the *cephalocaudal principle* of physical growth discussed in Chapters 2 and 3. Three-year-olds have large heads and squat, rounded bodies. As children get older, their limbs lengthen and their bodies thin out. Although from age 2 to 12 children double their height and weight, after infancy growth slows down considerably (National Health and Nutrition Examination Survey, 2004). Because they grow at similar rates, boys and girls are roughly the same size until they reach the preadolescent years.

What tips us off about the ages of the children in these two photographs relates to the *cephalocaudal principle* of development. We know that the children in the left photo are preschoolers because they have squat shapes and relatively large heads, while the longer bodies in the right photo are typical of the middle childhood years.

Table 5.1: Selected Motor Skill Milestones: Progression from Age 2 to Age 6

At age 2	At age 4
Picks up small objects with thumb and forefinger, feeds self with spoon	Cuts paper, approximates circle
Walks unassisted, usually by 12 months	Walks down stairs, alternating feet
Rolls a ball or flings it awkwardly	Catches and controls a large bounced ball across the body
At age 5	**At age 6**
Prints name	Copies two short words
Walks without holding on to railing	Hops on each foot for 1 meter but still holds railing
Tosses ball overhand with bent elbows	Catches and controls a 10-inch ball in both hands with arms in front of body

gross motor skills Physical abilities that involve large muscle movements, such as running and jumping.

fine motor skills Physical abilities that involve small, coordinated movements, such as drawing and writing one's name.

These boys—being generally advanced in the gross motor skills—may be the victors when they compete with girls in this potato sack race. But this girl's exceptional fine motor talents have set her up to do well at school.

Now visit a playground or take out your childhood artwork to see the *mass-to-specific* principle—the progression from clumsy to sure, swift movements year by year. Three-year-olds have trouble making circles; third graders draw bodies and faces. At age 4, children catch a ball with both hands; by fourth grade, they may be able to hit home runs. You can see the changes from mass to specific in a few skills in Table 5.1.

Two Types of Motor Talents

Developmentalists divide physical skills into two categories. **Gross motor skills** refer to large muscle movements, such as running, climbing, and hopping. **Fine motor skills** involve small, coordinated movements, such as drawing faces and writing one's name.

The stereotype that boys are better at gross motor abilities and girls at fine motor tasks is true—although often the differences are small. The largest sex difference in sports-related abilities occurs in throwing speed. During preschool and middle childhood, boys can typically hurl a ball much faster and farther than can girls (Geary, 1998; Thomas & French, 1985). Does this mean that girls can't compete with boys on a Little League team? Not necessarily. The boys probably will be faster pitchers and more powerful hitters. But the female talent at connecting with the ball, which involves fine motor coordination, may even things out.

If a preschooler has precocious physical abilities, will that child be advanced at school? The answer is yes, if we look at complex fine motor skills. Researchers asked 5-year-olds to copy images and then reproduce designs displayed on another page. Performance on this more difficult test (involving fine motor coordination and the ability to judge spatial dimensions) strongly predicted elementary school math and writing skills (Carlson, Rowe, & Curby 2013).

This study suggests that to improve academic abilities we might train young children to reproduce images, in addition to teaching them numbers or how to sound out words. The problem is that pressuring (forcing) preschoolers to unwillingly perform physical tasks can be counterproductive. During early childhood, we should provide activities—such as cutting paper or scaling the monkey bars—that kids' naturally enjoy (Zaichkowsky & Larson, 1995). Allow young children to exercise their unfolding talents, but don't push, and provide the right person–environment fit.

Now that we've scanned what normally happens physically, let's look at what can go wrong.

Threats to Growth and Motor Skills

I discussed the main threat to growth and motor skills in Chapter 3: lack of food. In addition to causing stunting, undernutrition impairs gross and fine motor skills because it compromises the development of the bones, muscles, and brain. Most important, when children are hungry, they are too tired to move and so don't get the experience crucial to developing their physical skills.

During the 1980s, researchers observed how undernourished children in rural Nepal maximized their growth by cutting down on play (Anderson & Mitchell, 1984). Play does more than exercise our bodies. It can help prime neural development and is crucial in promoting *social cognition*, helping children learn how to get along with their peers. So, the lethargy that malnutrition produces is as detrimental to children's relationships as it is to their bodies and brains. Notice how, after skipping just one meal, you become listless, unwilling to talk, less interested in reaching out to people in a loving way.

Keeping in mind that undernutrition *remains* the top-ranking twenty-first-century global physical threat, let's now explore the condition that is ringing alarm bells in the developed world: childhood obesity.

Childhood Obesity

Have you ever wondered about the source of the numbers in the charts showing the ideal weights for people of different heights? These statistics come from a regular U.S. national poll called the National Health and Nutrition Examination Study (NHANES). Since the 1960s, the federal government has literally been measuring the size of Americans by charting caloric intakes, heights, and weights. The familiar statistic researchers use to monitor overweight is **body mass index (BMI)**—the ratio of a person's weight to height. If the BMI is at or over the 85 percentile for the norms in the first poll, a child is defined as "overweight." At the 95th percentile or above, the label is "obese."

body mass index (BMI) The ratio of weight to height; the main indicator of overweight or underweight.

childhood obesity A body mass index at or above the 95th percentile compared to the U.S. norms established for children in the 1970s.

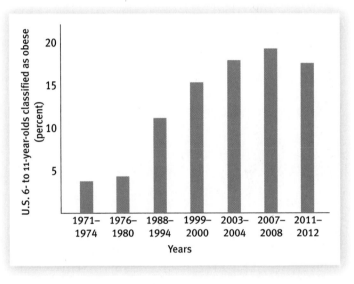

Exploring the Epidemic's Size

Childhood obesity ballooned about 35 years ago. During the late 1980s, the NHANES researchers were astonished to find that the fraction of obese elementary school children had doubled over a decade (see Figure 5.2). By 2012, roughly 1 out of every 6 North American children and teens was obese—four times the number in the original poll (Gordon-Larson, The, & Adair, 2010; Centers for Disease Control and Prevention [CDC], Childhood obesity facts, 2011). To bring this increase home, if you entered a second-grade classroom in the early 1970s, two children might stand out as very overweight. *Eight or nine* would fit that category today.

This late twentieth-century scourge has spread throughout the developed world. From Finland to France and Great Britain to Greece, governments have targeted child obesity as a public health threat (Stamatakis and others, 2010; Swinburn & de Silva-Sanigorski, 2010; Tambalis and others, 2010).

The shape of the threat, however, differs by nation. Obesity rates are lower in Scandinavia than in Mediterranean countries and the United States (Faeh & Bopp, 2010). In the developing world, childhood obesity is most common in cities and among affluent boys and girls (Berkowitz & Stunkard, 2002). In the United States, obesity rates are higher in rural areas (Davis and others, 2011), and *far* more common among the poor. There is also an ethnic dimension to the epidemic. Obesity is most prevalent among Latino and African American boys and girls (Boonpleng and others, 2013).

FIGURE 5.2: **Percentage of U.S. children aged 6–11 classified as obese, selected years:** This chart shows that the prevalence of child obesity almost tripled during the 1980s, continued to rise slowly, and then declined slightly in 2011. The wonderful news is that, as I note in the text, the prevalence of preschool obesity has recently decreased significantly. Adapted from: National Center for Health Statistics, CDC, 2007–2008, CDC, Prevalence of childhood obesity in the United States 2011–2012.

The great news is that in recent years, the prevalence of preschool obesity declined significantly, from roughly 14 percent in 2003–2004 to 8.4 percent in 2011–2012. The bad news is that this condition is still so common throughout the childhood years (CDC, Childhood obesity facts, 2012). Why, despite vigorous attention, is obesity resistant to change?

Exploring the Epidemic's Wider-World Roots

The reason lies in a perfect storm of societal "obesogenic" forces (Finegood, Merth, & Rutter, 2010; Swinburn & deSilva-Sanigorski, 2010): stressed out working parents who don't have time to prepare nutritious, sit-down meals (Morrissey, Dunifon, & Kalil, 2011); expanding restaurant portion sizes; and easy access to low-cost calorie-dense foods—such as chips and sugar-laced sodas tailored to tempt the palates of children (and adults) (Cornwell & McAlister, 2011).

Lack of exercise plays an important role. With the Internet and TV, playing outside—that typical childhood vehicle for burning up calories—has sharply declined. Obese children, being less physically active than their normal-weight peers, lag behind in gross motor abilities (Soric & Misigoj-Durakovic, 2010). There may be a poisonous *bidirectional* effect here. When children feel bad about their "big clumsy bodies," they withdraw from physical activity, watch more TV, and snack more.

When we see overweight women and their children eating together, some not- so- nice reactions cross our minds. What do you think when you see families like this?

To tackle the weight of obesity-promoting forces, governments have developed a host of policies, from requiring school cafeterias to limit fattening foods, to mandating calorie counts for sodas and Big Macs. Still, societal efforts have been less than effective, partly because individuals vary greatly in the tendency to pack on pounds. When researchers tracked thousands of preschoolers, they found that, yes, the school and neighborhood fast-food milieu played some role; but the primary predictor of a child's kindergarten "weight status" was his mother's weight (Boonpleng and others, 2013).

It's tempting to see this striking correlation (overweight parents have overweight children) and conclude that obesity is genetic, so there is nothing we can do. Or perhaps you (like many of us) have mentally accused overweight parents for loading themselves and their kids up with fattening foods.

Exploring the Epidemic's Epigenetics

Tantalizing research suggests obesity has a partly epigenetic, pre-birth root. Women who gain excessive weight during pregnancy, and so give birth to large babies, are at higher risk of having an obese child (Boonpleng and others, 2013). Recall from Chapter 2 that being born premature and excessively small may also "turn on" the biological tendency to overeat and store fat. Therefore, events in the womb and at birth might set us up to pack on pounds by literally changing our DNA.

Interestingly, scientists can predict this predisposition soon after we emerge from the womb. Rapid weight gain during infancy and early childhood is a strong predictor of later obesity—outweighing even a child's genetic propensity to gain weight (Belsky, 2013; Belsky, Moffitt, & Caspi, 2013). So what happens during our earliest years can biologically set us up to battle obesity for life (see Belsky, 2014, for review).

Exploring the Epidemic's Consequences

This lifelong battle takes a social toll. From being less likely to get hired (Puhl & Heuer, 2010) or finish college (Fowler-Brown and others, 2010) to having problems getting elected to public office (Miller & Lundgren, 2010), obesity can present serious barriers to living a successful life.

These barriers begin soon after babyhood (Puhl & Latner, 2007). In a classic study, elementary schoolers were shown pictures of an overweight child, a child in a wheelchair, another with facial disfigurements, and several others with disabilities. When asked, "Whom would you choose as a friend?" the children ranked the obese boy or girl last. By age 3, children describe chubby boys and girls as "mean" and "sloppy." So it's no wonder that, in the West, overweight children are at risk of suffering from depression in their teens (Pitrou and others, 2010; Sánchez-Villegas and others, 2010).

Attitudes are less harsh in other cultures. In Bangladesh, obesity actually promotes high self-worth (Asghar and others, 2010). There are differences by ethnicity, with African Americans more weight tolerant than their Caucasian counterparts (more about this in Chapter 8). And of course, there are variations from family to family. Parents who care vitally about physical beauty hold especially negative stereotypes about overweight people, and are prone to monitor a child's every bite (Puhl & Latner, 2007).

This pressure can backfire (no surprise), producing binge eating (Matton and others, 2013), compounding an elementary schooler's already fragile self-esteem. Therefore, many parents go in the opposite direction. They minimize weight issues in their child (Luttikhuis, Stolk, & Sauer, 2010). "My daughter may be chubby, but she's perfectly fine." Ironically, then, in one study, the very people who could most benefit from an obesity prevention program—mothers with overweight preschoolers—were *least* likely to enroll (Taveras and others, 2011).

Let's understand where these adults are coming from. Faced with the prejudices their children are *already* enduring, parents want to protect their sons and daughters from further pain. As one woman reported, "He's a highly sensitive child, and he's got very low self-esteem generally . . . I think, (if he participated in the program) . . . he would . . . think, 'what's wrong with me?'" (quoted in Barratt and others, 2013, p. 61).

Moreover—perhaps because by age 4 or 5, obesity is more resistant to change—family-focused weight-control programs, even when they show initial success (Sung-Chan and others, 2013) often don't work in the long term. Plus, once a boy or girl moves out of the family orbit, friends' eating practices make a huge difference in that child's food choices (Hemar-Nicolas and others, 2013).

INTERVENTIONS: Limiting Overweight

My discussion shows that the best strategy to control overweight is to start early on. Rather than intervening during preschool or elementary school, when self-esteem has taken a nosedive and the child's epigenetic path has formed, focus on pregnancy and the earliest year of life. Specifically,

- Never put a pregnant woman on a diet. Instead, point out that excessive weight gain during pregnancy may have obesity-promoting effects—not just for the mom, but also for her child. (Taking steps to reduce prematurity rates would also help.)

- Limit excessive feeding during the first year of life. Overweight women are more apt to soothe their infants by immediately offering the bottle or breast (Anzman-Frasca and others, 2013). Depressed women also may promote infant weight gain, by overlabeling their babies as fussy and prematurely providing solid food (Gaffney and others, 2013). Mothers, one study showed, can be taught to minimize nursing for non-hunger related distress (Paul and others, 2011). Encourage *every* new parent to feed until her baby is satisfied, and not beyond.

- Understand that limiting intake is especially difficult for overweight children (Skoranski and others, 2013) and that obesity control programs are apt to be rejected if they seem insulting to parents or attack children's self-esteem. Make interventions palatable by having families serve as the experts in what they should do (Jurkowski and others, 2013).

Although we might think there couldn't be any danger in pushing food on this adorable 8-month-old girl, we would be wrong, as rapid weight gain at this age strongly predicts lifelong struggles with weight. (NOTE: You NEVER, EVER want to put a baby on a diet, though.)

Without denying that we are making strides in combatting preschool obesity, I think you might agree that self-help programs cannot fully counter the temptations of living in a calorie-rich milieu. Therefore, the next step is for scientists to wage war on an internal, biological front: Can researchers decode the biochemical mechanisms producing the rapid infant weight gain that sets some of us up to battle weight issues for life? (See Belsky, Moffitt, & Caspi, 2013; Belsky, 2014.)

Tying It All Together

1. Jessica has terrific gross motor skills but trouble with fine motor skills. Select the two sports from this list that Jessica would be most likely to excel at: long-distance running, tennis, water ballet, the high jump, bowling.

2. The prevalence of obesity is _____ during preschool. *(rising/leveling off/declining)*

3. Melanie is a toddler. In predicting her chance of later weight struggles, you might look to *(pick right alternative)*: *Melanie's mom's weight; whether Melanie was born premature; Melanie's weight again during the past year; all of these forces.*

4. The best age to intervene to prevent obesity is: *(a) birth–age 1; (b) age 3–4; (c) the teenage years (choose a, b, or c).*

5. Your friend wants to develop a child obesity intervention at your local church. Explain in a sentence why some people might be unwilling to participate, and what your friend might do to ensure more families enroll.

Answers to the Tying It All Together questions can be found at the end of this chapter.

Cognitive Development

In this section, we turn to the heart of this chapter: cognition. How do children develop intellectually as they travel from age 3 into elementary school? In our search for answers, we explore three perspectives on mental growth, starting with that master theorist Jean Piaget.

Piaget's Preoperational and Concrete Operational Stages

Recall from Chapter 1 that Piaget believed that through assimilation (fitting new information into their existing cognitive structures) and accommodation (changing those cognitive slots to fit input from the world), children undergo qualitatively different stages of cognitive growth. In Chapter 3, I discussed Piaget's sensorimotor stage. Now, it's time to tackle the next two stages, in Table 5.2: the preoperational and concrete operational stages.

As their names imply, we need to discuss these two stages together. **Preoperational thinking** is defined by what children are missing—the ability to step back from their immediate perceptions. **Concrete operational thinking** is defined by what children possess: the ability to reason about the world in a more logical, adult-like way.

When children leave infancy and enter the stage of preoperational thought, they have made tremendous mental strides. Still, their thinking seems on a different planet from that of adults. The problem is that preoperational children are unable to look beyond the way objects immediately appear. By about age 7 or 8, children can mentally transcend what first hits their eye. They have entered the concrete operational stage.

The Preoperational Stage: Taking the World at Face Value

You saw vivid examples of this "from another planet" preschool thinking in my chapter-opening vignette. Now, let's enter the minds of young children and explore how they reason about physical substances and the social world.

preoperational thinking In Piaget's theory, the type of cognition characteristic of children aged 2 to 7, marked by an inability to step back from one's immediate perceptions and think conceptually.

concrete operational thinking In Piaget's framework, the type of cognition characteristic of children aged 8 to 11, marked by the ability to reason about the world in a more logical, adult way.

Table 5.2: Piaget's Stages: Focus on Childhood

Age	Name of Stage	Description
0–2	Sensorimotor	The baby manipulates objects to pin down the basics of physical reality. This stage ends with the development of language.
2–7	Preoperations	Children's perceptions are captured by their immediate appearances. "What they see is what is real." They believe, among other things, that inanimate objects are really alive and that if the appearance of a quantity of liquid changes (for example, if it is poured from a short, wide glass into a tall, thin one), the amount becomes different.
8–12	Concrete operations	Children have a realistic understanding of the world. Their thinking is really on the same wavelength as adults'. While they can reason conceptually about concrete objects, however, they cannot think abstractly in a scientific way.
12+	Formal operations	Reasoning is at its pinnacle: hypothetical, scientific, flexible, fully adult. Our full cognitive human potential has been reached.

Strange Ideas About Substances

The fact that preoperational children are locked into immediate appearances is illustrated by Piaget's (1965) famous **conservation tasks.** In Piaget's terminology, *conservation* refers to knowing that the amount of a given substance remains identical despite changes in its shape or form.

In the conservation of mass task, for instance, an adult gives a child a round ball of clay and asks that boy or girl to make another ball "just as big and heavy." Then she reshapes the ball so it looks like a pancake and asks, "Is there still the same amount now?" In the conservation of liquid task, the procedure is similar: present a child with two identical glasses with equal amounts of liquid. Make sure he tells you, "Yes, they have the same amount of water or juice." Then, pour the liquid into a tall, thin glass while the child watches and ask, "Is there more or less juice now, or is there the same amount?"

Typically, when children under age 7 are asked this final question, they give a peculiar answer: "Now there is more clay" or "The tall glass has more juice." "Why?" "Because now the pancake is bigger" or "The juice is taller." Then, when the clay is remolded into a ball or the liquid poured into the original glass, they report: "Now it's the same again." The logical conflict in their statements doesn't bother them at all. In Figure 5.3 on the next page, I have illustrated these procedures as well as additional Piagetian conservation tasks to perform with children you know.

Why can't young children conserve? For two reasons, Piaget believes. First, children don't grasp a concept called **reversibility.** This is the idea that an operation (or procedure) can be repeated in the opposite direction. Adults accept the fact that we can change various substances, such as our hairstyle, or the color of our room, and reverse them to their original state. Young children lack this fundamental *schema*, or cognitive structure, for interpreting the world.

A second issue lies in a perceptual style that Piaget calls **centering.** Young children interpret things according to what first hits their eye, rather than taking in the entire visual array. In the conservation of liquid task, they become captivated by the height of the liquid. They don't notice that the width of the original container makes up for the height of the current one. When children reach concrete operations, they **decenter.** They can step back from a substance's immediate appearance and understand that an increase in one dimension makes up for a loss in the other one.

Centering—the tendency to fix on what is visually most striking—impairs **class inclusion.** This is the knowledge that a category can encompass subordinate elements. Spread 20 Skittles and a few Gummi Bears on a plate and ask a 3-year-old,

conservation tasks Piagetian tasks that involve changing the shape of a substance to see whether children can go beyond the way that substance visually appears to understand that the amount is still the same.

reversibility In Piaget's conservation tasks, the concrete operational child's knowledge that a specific change in the way a given substance looks can be reversed.

centering In Piaget's conservation tasks, the preoperational child's tendency to fix on the most visually striking feature of a substance and not take other dimensions into account.

decentering In Piaget's conservation tasks, the concrete operational child's ability to look at several dimensions of an object or substance.

class inclusion The understanding that a general category can encompass several subordinate elements.

Type of conservation	Initial step and question	Transformation and next question	Preoperational child's answer
Number	Two equal rows of pennies.  "Are these two rows the same?" (Yes.)	Increase spacing of pennies in one line.  "Now is the amount of money the same?"	 "No, the longer row has more."
Mass	Two equal balls of clay. 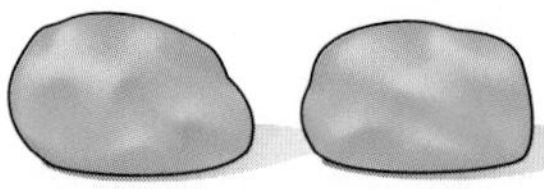 "Do these two balls have the same amount of clay?" (Yes.)	Squeeze one ball into a long pancake shape. 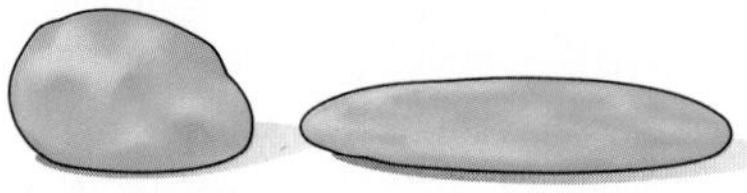 "Now is the amount of clay the same?"	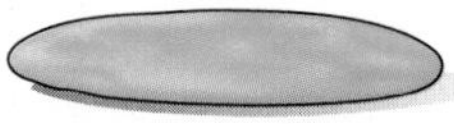 "No, the long, thin one has more clay."
Volume or liquid	Two glasses of the same size with liquid.  "Do these glasses have the same amount of juice?" (Yes.)	Pour one into a taller, narrower glass.  "Now do these glasses have the same amount of juice?"	 "No, the taller glass has more juice."
Matter*	Two identical cubes of sugar.  "Do these cubes have the same amount of sugar?" (Yes.)	Dissolve one cube in a glass of water. 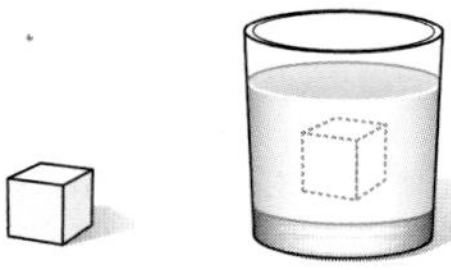 "Now is there the same amount of sugar?"	 "No, because you made one piece of sugar disappear."

*That is, the idea that a substance such as sugar is "still there" even though it seems to have disappeared (by dissolving).

FIGURE 5.3: **Four Piagetian conservation tasks:** Can you perform these tasks with a child you know?

"Would you rather have the Skittles or the candy?" and she is almost certain to say, "The Skittles," even when you have determined beforehand that both types of candy have equal appeal. She gets mesmerized by the number of Skittles and does not notice that "candy" is the label for both.

This tendency to focus on immediate appearances explains why, in the opening chapter vignette, Moriah believed that Josiah had more paper when he cut his sheet into sections. Her attention was captured by the spread-out pieces, and she believed that now there must be more paper than before.

The idea that "bigger" automatically equals "more" extends to every aspect of preoperational thought. Ask a 3-year-old if he wants a nickel or a dime, and he will choose the first option. (This is a great source of pleasure to older siblings asked to equally share their funds.) Perhaps because greater height means "older" in their own lives, children even believe that a taller person has been on earth for a longer time:

I was substitute teaching with a group of kindergarten children—at the time I was about 22—and when I met a student's mother, she was shocked. "When I asked Ben about you," she said, "he told me you were much older than his regular teacher." This teacher was in her mid- to late fifties and looked it. However, then we figured out the difference. This woman was barely 5 feet tall, and I am 6 feet two!

Peculiar Perceptions About People

Young children's tendency to believe that "what hits my eye right now is real" explains why a 3-year-old thinks her mommy is transformed into a princess when she dresses up for Halloween, or cries bitterly after her first visit to the beauty salon, believing that her short haircut has transformed her into a boy. It makes sense of why a favorite strategy of older sisters and brothers (to torture younger siblings) is to put on a mask and see the child run in horror from the room. As these examples show, young children lack **identity constancy.** They don't realize that people are still their essential selves despite changes in the way they visually appear.

I got insights into this identity constancy deficit at my son's fifth birthday party, when I hired a "gorilla" to entertain the guests (some developmental psychologist!). As the hairy 6-foot figure rang the doorbell, mass hysteria ensued—requiring the gorilla to take off his head. After the children calmed down, and the gorilla put on his head again to enact his skit, guess what? Pure hysteria again! Why did that huge animal cause pandemonium? The reason is that the children believed that the gorilla, even though a costumed figure, was really alive.

Animism refers to the difficulty young children have in sorting out what is really alive. Specifically, preschoolers see inanimate objects—such as dolls or costumed figures—as having consciousness, too. Look back at the beginning chapter vignette and you will notice several examples of animistic thinking—for example, the Barbies that were hungry or the wind that ran away. Now think back to when you were age 5 or 6. Do you remember being afraid the escalator might suck you in? Or perhaps you recall believing, as in the Stephen King Experiencing the Lifespan box on page 146, that your dolls came alive at night.

Listen to young children talking about nature, and you will hear delightful examples of animism: "The sun gets sleepy when I sleep." "The moon likes to follow me in the car." The practice of assigning human motivations to natural phenomena is not something we grow out of as adults. Think of the Greek thunder god Zeus, or the ancient Druids who worshiped the spirits that lived within trees. Throughout history, humans have regularly used animism to make sense of a frightening world.

A related concept is called **artificialism.** Young children believe that human beings have made everything in nature. Here is an example of this "daddy power" from Piaget's 3-year-old daughter, Laurent:

> L was in bed in the evening and it was still light: "Put the light out please" . . . (I switched the electric light off.) "It isn't dark"—"But I can't put the light out outside" . . . "Yes you can, you can make it dark." . . . "How?" . . . "You must turn it out very hard. It'll be dark and there will be little lights everywhere (stars)."

(Piaget, 1951/1962, p. 248)

When her dad puts on a mask, he suddenly becomes a scary monster to this 4-year-old girl because she has not yet grasped the principle of identity constancy.

His animistic thinking causes this 4-year-old to believe that the bear is really going to enjoy the ride he is about to provide.

identity constancy In Piaget's theory, the preoperational child's inability to grasp that a person's core "self" stays the same despite changes in external appearance.

animism In Piaget's theory, the preoperational child's belief that inanimate objects are alive.

artificialism In Piaget's theory, the preoperational child's belief that human beings make everything in nature.

Experiencing the Lifespan: Childhood Fears, Animism, and the Power of Stephen King

There was one shadow that would constantly cast itself on my bedroom wall. It looked just like a giant creeping towards me with a big knife in his hand.

I used to believe that Satan lived in my basement. The light switch was at the bottom of the steps, and whenever I switched off the light it was a mad dash to the top. I was so scared that Satan was going to stab my feet with knives.

Boy, do I remember the doll that sat on the top of my dresser. I called it "Chatty Kathy." This doll came to life every night. She would stare at me, no matter where I went.

My mother used to take me when she went to clean house for Mrs. Handler, a rich lady. Mrs. Handler had this huge, shiny black grand piano, and I thought it came alive when I was not looking at it. It was so enormous, dark, and quiet. I remember pressing one of the bass keys, which sounded really deep and loud and it terrified me.

I remember being scared that there was something alive under my bed. I must tell you I sometimes still get scared that someone is under my bed and that they are going to grab me by my ankles. I don't think I will ever grow out of this, as I am 26.

Can you relate to any of these childhood memories collected from my students? Perhaps your enemy was that evil creature lurking in your basement; the frightening stuffed animal on your wall; a huge object (with teeth) such as that piano; or your local garbage truck.

Now you know where that master storyteller Stephen King gets his ideas. King's genius is that he taps into the preoperational thoughts that we have papered over, though not very well, as adults. When we read King's story about a toy animal that clapped cymbals to signal someone's imminent death, or about Christine, the car with a mind of its own, or about the laundry-pressing machine that loved human blood—these stories fall on familiar childhood ground. Don't you still get a bit anxious when you enter a dark basement? Even today, on a dark night, do you have an uneasy feeling that some strange monster might be lurking beneath your bed?

Animism and artificialism perfectly illustrate Piaget's concept of assimilation. The child knows that she is alive and so applies her "alive" schema to every object. Having seen adults perform heroic physical feats, such as turning off lights and building houses, a 3-year-old generalizes the same "big people control things" schema to the universe. Imagine that you are a young child taking a family vacation. After you visited that gleaming construction called Las Vegas, wouldn't it make sense that people carved out the Grand Canyon and the Rocky Mountains, too?

The sun and moon examples illustrate another aspect of preoperational thought. According to Piaget, young children believe that they are the literal center of the universe, the pivot around which everything else revolves. Their worldview is characterized by **egocentrism**—the inability to understand that other people have different points of view.

By *egocentrism*, Piaget does not mean that young children are vain or uncaring, although they will tell you they are the smartest people on earth and the activities of the heavenly bodies are at their beck and call. Many of their most loving acts show egocentrism. There is nothing more touching than a 3-year-old's offer of a favorite "blankee" if he sees you upset. The child is egocentric, however, because he assumes that what comforts *him* will automatically comfort you.

You can see delightful examples of egocentrism when having a conversation with a young child. Have you ever had a 3-year-old discuss an event at school without providing any background information, as if you *automatically* knew her teacher and the rest of the class?

Piaget views egocentrism as a perfect example of centering in the human world. Young children are unable to decenter from their own mental processes. They don't realize that what is in their mind is not in everyone else's awareness, too.

egocentrism In Piaget's theory, the preoperational child's inability to understand that other people have different points of view from their own.

The Concrete Operational Stage: Getting on the Adult Wavelength

Piaget discovered that the transition from preoperations to concrete operations happens gradually. First, children are preoperational in every area. Then, between ages 5 and 7, their thinking gets less static, or "thaws out" (Flavell, 1963). A 6-year-old, when given the conservation of liquid task, might first say the taller glass had more liquid, but then, after it is poured back into a wide glass, becomes unsure: "Is it bigger or not?" She has reached the tipping point where she is poised to reason on a higher cognitive plane.

By age 8, the child has reached this higher-level, concrete operational state: "Even though the second glass is taller, the first is wider" (showing decentering); "You can pour the liquid right back into the short glass and it would look the same" (illustrating reversibility). Now, she doesn't realize that she ever thought differently: "Are you silly? Of course it's the same!"

Piaget also found that specific conservations come in at different ages. First, children master conservation of number and then mass and liquid. They may not figure out the most difficult conservations until age 11 or 12. Imagine the challenge of understanding the last task in Figure 5.3 (see p. 144)—realizing that when sugar is dissolved in water, it exists, but in a molecular form.

Still, according to Piaget, age 8 is a landmark for looking beyond immediate appearances, for understanding seriation and categories, for decentering in the physical and social worlds, for abandoning the tooth fairy and the idea that our stuffed animals are alive, and for entering the planet of adults.

Table 5.3 shows examples of different kinds of preoperational ideas. Now, test yourself by seeing if you can classify each statement in Piagetian terms.

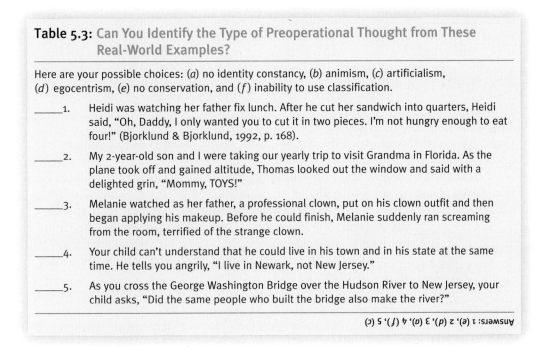

Table 5.3: Can You Identify the Type of Preoperational Thought from These Real-World Examples?

Here are your possible choices: (a) no identity constancy, (b) animism, (c) artificialism, (d) egocentrism, (e) no conservation, and (f) inability to use classification.

_____1. Heidi was watching her father fix lunch. After he cut her sandwich into quarters, Heidi said, "Oh, Daddy, I only wanted you to cut it in two pieces. I'm not hungry enough to eat four!" (Bjorklund & Bjorklund, 1992, p. 168).

_____2. My 2-year-old son and I were taking our yearly trip to visit Grandma in Florida. As the plane took off and gained altitude, Thomas looked out the window and said with a delighted grin, "Mommy, TOYS!"

_____3. Melanie watched as her father, a professional clown, put on his clown outfit and then began applying his makeup. Before he could finish, Melanie suddenly ran screaming from the room, terrified of the strange clown.

_____4. Your child can't understand that he could live in his town and in his state at the same time. He tells you angrily, "I live in Newark, not New Jersey."

_____5. As you cross the George Washington Bridge over the Hudson River to New Jersey, your child asks, "Did the same people who built the bridge also make the river?"

Answers: 1 (e), 2 (d), 3 (a), 4 (f), 5 (c)

INTERVENTIONS: Using Piaget's Ideas at Home and at Work

Piaget's concepts provide marvelous insights into young children's minds. For teachers, the theory explains why you need the same-sized cups at a kindergarten lunch table or an argument will erupt, even if you poured each drink from identical cans. Nurses understand that rationally explaining the purpose of a painful medical procedure to a 4-year-old may not be as effective as providing a magic doll to help the child cope.

The theory makes sense of why forming a baseball team with a group of 4- or 5-year-olds is an impossible idea. Grasping the rules of a game requires abstract conceptualization—a skill that preoperational children do not possess. It tells us

In late elementary school, children take great pride in collecting, classifying, and trading items like Yu-Gi-Oh cards because they are practicing their new concrete operational skills.

why young children are terrified of the dark and scary clowns at the amusement park. So for parents who feel uneasy about playing into their child's fantasies when they provide "anti-monster spray" to calm those bedtime fears, one justification is that, according to Piaget, when your child is ready, she will naturally grow out of her ideas.

Piaget's concepts also give us insights into children's passions at different ages. They explain the power of pretending in early childhood (more about this in Chapter 6) and the lure of that favorite holiday, Halloween. When a 4-year-old child dresses up as Batman, he may be grappling with the challenge of understanding that you can look different yet still remain your essential self. The theory accounts for why third or fourth graders become captivated with games such as soccer, and can be avid collectors of baseball cards. Now that they can understand rules and categories, concrete operational children are determined to exercise their new conceptual and classification skills.

The theory explains why "real school," the academic part, fully begins at about age 7. Children younger than this age often don't have the intellectual tools to understand reversibility, a concept critical to understanding mathematics (if 2 plus 4 is 6, then 6 minus 4 must equal 2). Even empathizing with the teacher's agenda is a concrete operational skill.

The fact that age 8 is a coming-of-age marker is represented by the classic movie *Home Alone*. The plot of this film would have been unthinkable if its hero were 5, or even 6. If the star were 11, the movie would be not be interesting because, by this age, a child could competently take care of himself. Eight is when we begin to make the transition to being able to make it "home alone." It is the age when we shift from worrying about monsters—things that are not real—to grappling with the dangers that we really face as adults.

Evaluating Piaget

Piaget has clearly transformed the way we think about young children. Still, as you saw with infancy, in important areas, Piaget was incorrect.

I described a major problem with Piaget's ideas in Chapter 3: just as he minimized what babies know, Piaget underestimated preoperational children's capacities. In particular, Piaget overstated young children's egocentrism. If babies

Because this girl growing up in Mexico gets so much practice at weaving, we might expect her to grasp concrete operational conservation tasks related to spatial concepts at a relatively early age.

can decode intentions, the first awareness that we live in "different heads" must dawn on children at a far younger age than 8! (At the end of this chapter, you'll learn when this mindreading ability fully comes on.)

We might also take issue with Piaget's idea that we grow out of animism by age 8 or 9. Maybe he was giving us too *much* credit here. Do you have a good luck charm that keeps the plane from crashing, or a place you go for comfort where you can hear the trees whispering to you?

Children around the world do learn to conserve (Dasen, 1977, 1984). But because nature interacts with nurture, the ages at which they master specific conservation tasks vary from place to place. An example comes from a village in Mexico, where weaving is the main occupation. Young children in this collectivist culture grasp conservation tasks involving spatial concepts when they are younger than age 7 or 8 because they have so much hands-on training in this kind of skill (Maynard & Greenfield, 2003). This brings up a crucial dimension that Piaget's theory leaves out: the impact of teaching in promoting cognitive growth.

Vygotsky's Zone of Proximal Development

Piaget implies that children naturally construct an adult view of the world. We can't convince preschoolers that their dolls are not alive or that the width of the glass makes up for the height. They must grow out of those ideas on their own. The Russian psychologist Lev Vygotsky (1962, 1978) had a different perspective: people propel mental growth.

Vygotsky was born in the same year as Piaget. He showed as much brilliance at a young age, but—unlike Piaget, who lived to a ripe old age—he died of tuberculosis in his late thirties. Still, Vygotsky's writings have given him towering status in developmental science today. One reason is that Vygotsky was, at heart, an educator. He believed that what *we* do helps children mentally advance.

Vygotsky theorized that learning takes place within the **zone of proximal development,** which he defined as the difference between what the child can do by himself and his level of "potential development as determined through problem solving under adult guidance or in collaboration with more capable peers" (Vygotsky, 1978, p. 86; also, see the diagram in Figure 5.4). Teachers must tailor their instruction to a child's proximal zone. Then, as that child becomes more competent, they should slowly back off and allow the student more responsibility for directing that learning activity on his own. This sensitive pacing has a special name: **scaffolding** (Wood, Bruner, & Ross, 1976).

You saw scaffolding in operation in Chapter 3 in my discussion of infant-directed speech, the simplified language that adults use when talking to babies. Recall that baby talk has an adult function. It permits caregivers to penetrate a young child's proximal zone for language and so helps scaffold emerging speech. Now, let's explore scaffolding as we read about a mother teaching her 5-year-old daughter how to play her first board game, Chutes and Ladders:

> Tiffany threw the dice, then looked up at her mother. Her mother said, "How many is that?" Tiffany shrugged her shoulders. Her mother said, "Count them," but Tiffany just sat and stared. Her mother counted the dots aloud, and then said to her daughter, "Now you count them," which Tiffany did. This was repeated for the next five turns. Tiffany waited for her mother to count the dots. On her sixth move, however, Tiffany counted the dots on the dice on her own after her mother's request. . . . Eventually, Tiffany threw the dice and counted the dots herself and continued to do so, practicing counting and moving the pieces on both her own and her mother's turns.
>
> (Bjorklund & Rosenblum, 2001)

Notice that this mother was a superb scaffolder. By pacing her interventions to Tiffany's capacities, she paved the way for her child to master the game. But this process did not just flow from parent to child. Tiffany was also teaching her mother how to respond. Just as your professor is getting new insights into lifespan development while teaching every class—or at this minute, as I struggle to write this page, I'm learning to better connect with Vygotsky's ideas—education is a *bidirectional,* mind-expanding duet (Scrimsher & Tudge, 2003).

In our culture, we have definite ideas about what makes a good scaffolder. Enter a child's proximal zone. Actively instruct, but be sensitive to a child's responses. However, in collectivist societies, such as among the Mayans living in Mexico's Yucatán Peninsula, children learn by observation. They listen. They watch. They are not explicitly taught the skills they need for adult life (Rogoff and others, 2003). So the qualities our culture sees as vital to socializing children are not necessarily part of the ideology of good parenting around the globe.

zone of proximal development (ZPD) In Vygotsky's theory, the gap between a child's ability to solve a problem totally on his own and his potential knowledge if taught by a more accomplished person.

scaffolding The process of teaching new skills by entering a child's zone of proximal development and tailoring one's efforts to that person's competence level.

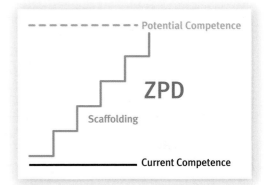

FIGURE 5.4: Vygotsky's zone of proximal development: These lines illustrate the ZPD—the gap between where a child is currently "at" intellectually and where he can potentially be. If a teacher sensitively teaches within this zone and employs scaffolding (see step-wise lines)—providing support, then backing off when help is no longer needed—students will reach their full intellectual potential.

This girl in Thailand is learning to weave just by observing her mother—a strategy that we might find unusual in our teaching-oriented culture.

INTERVENTIONS: **Becoming an Effective Scaffolder**

In our teaching-oriented society, what do superior scaffolders do? Let's list a few techniques:

- They foster a secure attachment, as nurturing, responsive interactions are a basic foundation for learning (Laible, 2004).

- They break a larger cognitive challenge, such as learning Chutes and Ladders, into manageable steps (Berk & Winsler, 1999).

- They continue helping until the child has fully mastered the concept before moving on, as Tiffany's mother did earlier.

As you will learn in Chapter 7, these same scaffolding principles—identify each core skill, cement-in learning within the child's proximal zone, move to the next level up in the academic "ladder" when the child is ready— underlie the Common Core State Standards now being used in elementary schools across the United States.

Table 5.4 compares Vygotsky's and Piaget's perspectives and offers capsule summaries of the backgrounds that shaped these world-class geniuses' ideas (Vianna & Stetsenko, 2006). Although often described in opposing terms, these two theories form an ideal pair. Piaget gave us insights into the developing structure of childhood cognition. Vygotsky offered us an engine to transform children's lives.

Table 5.4: Piagetian and Vygotskian Perspectives on Life and Learning

	Lev Vygotsky (1896–1934)	Jean Piaget (1896–1980)

Biography	Russian, Jewish, communist (reached teenage years during the Russian Revolution), believed in Marx	Swiss, middle-class family
Basic interests	Education, literature, literary criticism	Biology, mollusks
	Wanted to know how to stimulate thinking	Wanted to trace the evolution of thought in stages
Overall orientation	Look at interpersonal processes and the role of society in cognition	Look for universal developmental processes
Basic ideas	1. We develop intellectually through social interactions.	1. We develop intellectually through physically acting on the world.
	2. Development is a collaborative endeavor.	2. Development takes place on our own inner timetable.
	3. People cause cognitive growth.	3. When we are internally ready, we reach a higher level of cognitive development.
Implications for education	Instruction is critical to development. Teachers should sensitively intervene within each child's zone of proximal development.	Provide ample materials to let children explore and learn on their own.

The Information-Processing Perspective

Vygotsky filled in the missing social pieces of Piaget's theory and gave us a framework for stimulating mental growth. But he did not address the gaps in the theory itself. Why are children able to decenter? What *specific* skills allow children to understand that the width of the glass makes up for the height?

Piaget never mentions how crucial abilities such as memory, concentration, and planning develop. Was Ms. Angela, the teacher in the opening chapter vignette, asking too much of her 3-year-olds to remember those free-play rules? How can teachers best teach spelling to a third-grade class? Parents might want guidelines as to what to expect from a child at a particular age: "Can my 6-year-old daughter take responsibility for caring for a puppy?" "When will my son be able to get ready for school on his own?" Clinical psychologists and caregivers would want to understand why a particular child has so much trouble focusing and obeying at school and at home. To get this information, everyone would gravitate toward the *information-processing approach.*

Information-processing theorists, as you learned in Chapter 3, break cognitive processes into components and divide thinking into steps. Let's illustrate this approach by examining memory, the basis of all thought.

Making Sense of Memory

Information-processing theorists believe that on the way to becoming "a memory," information passes through different stores, or stages. First, we hold stimuli arriving from the outside world briefly in a sensory store. Then, features that we notice enter the most important store, called working memory.

Working memory is where the "cognitive action" takes place. Here, we keep information in awareness and act to either process it or discard it. Working memory is made up of limited-capacity holding bins. It also consists of an "executive processor," which allows us to focus on what we need to remember as well as to manipulate the material in working memory to prepare it for permanent storage (Baddeley, 1992; Best & Miller, 2010). Once we have moved information through working memory, it enters a more long-lasting store, and we can recall it at a later time.

You can get a real-life example of the fleeting quality of working memory when you get a phone number from information and call from a landline phone. You know that you can dial the number without having to write it down, and your memory will not fail *if you get to finish.* If you are interrupted by a beep from another caller and lose focus, the number evaporates. In fact, for adults, the typical bin size of working memory is about the size of a local phone number: seven chunks (in this case, digits) of information.

Just as they vary in motor talents, young children differ in working memory abilities, and these differences predict school readiness skills (Fizpatrick & Pagani, 2012; Preßler, Krajewski, & Hasselhorn, 2013). Moreover, while the basic structure of working memory, described above, swings into operation by about age 6 (Michalczyk and others, 2013), this capacity enlarges dramatically during elementary school (Alloway & Alloway, 2013; Thaler and others, 2013). Actually, the fact that memory-bin capacity expands from about two to five bits of information by age 7 (Dempster, 1981) explains why we reach concrete operations at roughly that age (Case, 1999). Now, children have the memory capacities to step back from their first impressions and remember that what they saw previously (for instance, a wider glass) compensates for what they are seeing right now.

Exploring Executive Functions

Executive functions refer to any skill related to managing our memory, controlling our cognitions, planning our behavior, and inhibiting our responses. Executive functions depend on the brain's master planner—the frontal lobes. Now, let's look at three examples of executive functions that make children in concrete operations very different thinkers than at age 4 or even 5.

working memory In information-processing theory, the limited-capacity gateway system, containing all the material that we can keep in awareness at a single time. The material in this system is either processed for more permanent storage or lost.

executive functions Any frontal-lobe ability that allows us to inhibit our responses and to plan and direct our thinking.

rehearsal A learning strategy in which people repeat information to embed it in memory.

selective attention A learning strategy in which people manage their awareness so as to attend only to what is relevant and to filter out unneeded information.

Older Children Rehearse Information

A major way we learn information is through **rehearsal.** We repeat material to embed it in memory. In a classic study, developmentalists had kindergarteners, second graders, and fifth graders memorize objects (such as a cat or a desk) pictured on cards (Flavell, Beach, & Chinsky, 1966). Prior to the testing, the research team watched the children's lips to see if they were repeating the names of the objects to themselves. Eighty-five percent of the fifth graders used rehearsal; only 10 percent of the kindergarteners did. So one reason why older children are superior learners is that they understand that they need to rehearse.

Older Children Understand How to Selectively Attend

The ability to manage our awareness so we focus on what we need to know and filter out extraneous information is called **selective attention.** In a classic study illustrating young children's problems in this area, researchers presented boys and girls of different ages with cards. On one half of each card was an animal photo; on the other half was a picture of some household item (see Figure 5.5). The children were instructed to remember only the animals.

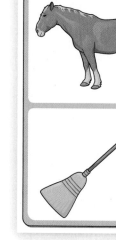

FIGURE 5.5: **A selective attention study:** In this study measuring selective attention, children were asked only to memorize the animals on the top half of the cards. Then researchers looked for age differences in their memory for the irrelevant household items.

As you might expect, older children were better at recalling the animal names. But now comes the interesting part: when the children were asked how many irrelevant items they could recall, the performance differences evaporated—suggesting that the young children wasted effort looking at the objects they did not need to know (Bjorklund, 2005). This suggests that, in addition to having smaller memory bins, young children clog their bin space with irrelevant information. They can't focus their attention on what is relevant and filter out extraneous stimuli as well.

Older Children Are Superior at Inhibition

Turn back to the vignette at the beginning of this chapter to see the problems young children have inhibiting their impulses. Notice how the 3-year-olds ran into the different activity centers without thinking, "That's not what I'm supposed to do." The most fascinating example occurred during the weather report. Because the temptation to say yes was so strong, the children could not restrain themselves from agreeing when the teacher asked *any* question about the weather that day.

To measure differences in inhibition directly, researchers may ask children to perform some action that contradicts their immediate tendencies, such as instructing them to say the word *black* when they see the word *white* (Diamond, Kirkham, & Amso, 2002). Or the child may be instructed, "Press a button as fast as you can each time you see an animal on the screen, but don't respond when you see a dog" (Pnevmatikos & Trikkaliotis, 2013). This "go, don't go" challenge is exemplified by the classic childhood game Simon Says.

The childhood game of Simon Says is far from all fun and games—it's tailored to train executive functions by giving children practice in the skill of inhibiting their immediate responses.

Performance on these tasks improves markedly during preschool, and gradually gets better with age (Best & Miller, 2010). Actually, fostering inhibition—not doing what you feel like doing—is a primary *socialization* goal. From following the preschool rules to resisting checking Facebook while you are reading this page, inhibiting our responses is essential to succeeding at school and life.

Moreover, if you think these self-control feats are difficult, imagine being a young child. And never, ever tell a 4- or 5-year-old to keep a "big secret." Her automatic response will be to immediately blurt it out!

Given that the exciting news is on this child's mind and the frontal lobes are still under construction, there is no such thing as a secret!

INTERVENTIONS: Using Information-Processing Theory at Home and at Work

So, to return to the beginning of this section, teachers *cannot* assume that third graders will automatically understand how to memorize spelling words. Scaffolding study skills, such as the need to rehearse, or teaching strategies to promote selective attention, such as putting large stars next to the relevant words for a test, should be an integral part of education, beginning in elementary school.

Parents will probably need to regularly remind a child, even at age 6 or 7, to feed the dog. Expect activities requiring different information-processing tasks, such as getting dressed and remembering to take homework and pencils to class, to be difficult *throughout* elementary school (and beyond). Scaffold organizational strategies, such as helping a second grader get everything ready for school before bedtime and teaching that child to put important items in specific places. For everyone else, the information-processing research suggests that executive functions—from inhibiting yourself, to selectively attending—improve gradually over *many years* (Best & Miller, 2010; Zhan and others, 2011). (See Table 5.5 for some general information-processing tips.)

Now that we know how thinking normally develops, let's look at the insights information-processing research offers caregivers who want to understand children with executive-function issues—boys and girls with attention-deficit/hyperactivity disorder, or ADHD.

Table 5.5: Information-Processing Guidelines for Teachers and Parents

Early childhood

1. Don't expect a child to remember, without considerable prompting, regular chores such as feeding a pet, the details of a show, or the name of the person who telephoned.

2. Expect the child to have a good deal of trouble with any situation that involves inhibiting a strong "prepotent impulse"—such as not touching toys, following unpleasant rules, or keeping a secret.

Middle childhood

1. Actively teach the child studying skills (such as rehearsing information) and selective attention strategies (such as underlining important points).

2. Scaffold organizational strategies for school and life. For example, get the child to use a notebook for each class assignment and keep important objects, such as eyeglasses, in a specific place.

3. Expect situations that involve multiple tasks, such as getting ready for school, to present problems. Also expect trouble with activities that involve *ongoing* inhibition, such as refraining from watching TV before finishing homework. Build in a clear structure for mastering these difficult executive-functioning tasks: "At 8 or 9 p.m., it's time to get everything ready for school." "Homework must be completed by dinnertime, or the first thing after you get home from school."

4. To promote selective attention (and inhibition), have a child do homework, or any task that involves concentration, in a room away from tempting distractions such as the TV or Internet.

Hot in Developmental Science: Attention-Deficit/Hyperactivity Disorder

Attention-deficit/hyperactivity disorder (ADHD), defined by inattentiveness, and hyperactivity/distractibility is the most widely diagnosed childhood disorder in the United States, affecting roughly 1 in 9 or 10 girls and boys (CDC Attention deficit hyperactivity disorder, n.d.). This condition is currently diagnosed in preschoolers and during the adult years. But since sitting still and focusing becomes mandatory in elementary school, boys and girls typically receive this label during those years. Actually, boys are several times more likely to receive this label than are girls (CDC Attention deficit hyperactivity disorder, n.d.).

ADHD follows a bewildering array of paths: from first appearing in preschool, to erupting during adulthood; from persisting for decades, to fading after months (Sonuga-Barke & Halperin, 2010). While twin and adoption studies confirm this condition has primarily genetic causes (Thapar and others, 2013), a bewildering set of biological triggers may produce this familiar contemporary condition of childhood (and now adult) life (Sánchez-Mora and others, 2013).

ADHD has been linked to everything from prenatal maternal smoking, to breathing problems at birth (Owens & Hinshaw, 2013). One widely accepted idea is that this condition results from a lower-than-normal output of dopamine, the neurotransmitter that modulates sensitivity to rewards (Hoogman and others, 2013; Silvetti and others, 2014). Some scientists feel ADHD is caused by the delayed maturation of the frontal lobes. Others speculate that impairments in lower brain centers are to blame. Neuropsychologists have linked symptoms to everything from smaller brain volume (de Mello and others, 2013), to structural abnormalities in specific cortical regions (Ghassabian and others, 2013), and documented a range of abnormal neural activation patterns when these children perform learning tasks (Berger and others, 2013; Wang and others, 2013; Hoogman and others, 2013; Wilson and others, 2013; Clerkin and others, 2013).

The hallmark of ADHD, however, is deficits in executive functions (Halperin & Healey, 2011). These children have problems with working memory (Alderson and others, 2013; Dovis and others, 2013) and especially inhibition (Barkley, 1998, 2003; Berger and others, 2013). When told, "Don't touch the toys," boys and girls diagnosed with ADHD have special trouble resisting this impulse.

These children also have difficulties with selective attention. Researchers asked elementary schoolers to memorize a series of words. Some words were more valuable to remember (that is, worth more points), and others less. Boys and girls with ADHD memorized an equal number of words as a comparison group; but, like the preschoolers in the previous section, they got lower scores because they clogged their memory bins with less valuable words (Castel and others, 2010).

As you might imagine, performing a sequence of tasks under time pressure, such as getting ready for school by 7:00 a.m., presents immense problems for boys and girls with ADHD. These children have more trouble estimating time (Gooch, Snowling, & Hulme, 2011; Hurks & Hendriksen, 2011; Hwang and others, 2010). Moreover, perhaps because of their dopamine deficit, they seem less affected by punishments and rewards (Stark and others, 2011). So, yelling, or threatening, simply may not work.

These issues explain why school is so problematic for boys and girls with ADHD. Working memory is critical to performing any academic task. Focusing on a teacher demands inhibitory and selective attention skills. Taking tests can involve exceptional time-management talents, too.

Because the same difficulties lead to problems at home, frustrated parents are apt to resort to *power-assertion* disciplinary techniques (Wymbs & Pelham, 2010). They lash out at a 9-year-old who seems incapable of getting his things in order. They scream at, hit, and punish a daughter who can't "just sit still." Therefore, due to an *evocative* process, boys and girls with ADHD are *least* likely to get the sensitive parenting that they need. Their difficult behavior can provoke marital conflict (Wymbs & Pelham, 2010) and routinely cause these children to fail with their peers (Normand and others, 2013; Staikova and others, 2013).

Frequent social failures seem to be most upsetting for girls (Becker and others, 2013). Anxiety—for females especially—is an unfortunate side consequence of having ADHD (Skogli and others, 2013). Given these dangers, what should a caring adult do? 🔊

INTERVENTIONS: Helping Children with ADHD

The well-known treatment for ADHD is psycho-stimulant medications (Barkley & Murphy, 2006; Wender and others, 2011; Pearson and others, 2013), often supplemented by parent (and sometimes teacher) training. Parent training may be especially vital because adults with ADHD, being at a higher genetic risk of having children with this condition, tend to inflate their positive parenting skills (Lui and others, 2013) ("I'm doing everything fine! What can I learn from you?").

Parent training often takes a behavioral approach by teaching adults to target upsetting behaviors (rather than ineffectually yelling), pay attention to positive acts, consistently use time out, and offer children concrete rewards for behaving (Ryan-Krause, 2011; Young & Amarasinghe, 2010). It's important not to pressure sons and daughters to complete demanding time-based tasks.

Another strategy focuses on helping children enhance working memory, attention, and inhibition. And then there are interventions focused on diet—limiting the child's intake of additives or sugar-laced foods.

One summary of the incredible 2,000-plus intervention studies in this area suggested that dietary changes—for some children—are effective (Sonuga-Barke and others, 2013). Unfortunately, because adults are invested in seeing progress after enrolling a child in a program ("Yes, my kid is better because we did this"), we cannot *prove* that parent or child training has long-lasting effects (Rapport and others, 2013; Melby-Lervåg & Hulme, 2013; Sonuga-Barke and others, 2013).

What does work? Children with ADHD learn better in noisy environments. So, to enhance a 9- or 10-year-old's ability to focus on homework, it may help to provide "white" background noise (Soderlund, Sikstrom, & Smart, 2007). Because they have so much trouble delaying gratification, it's preferable to give frequent small reinforcers for good behavior, rather than waiting for a big prize (10 minutes on the computer later today works better than promising a family trip to Disney World next month) (Scheres, Tontsch, & Thoeny, 2013). As providing regular recess also helps (Ridgway and others, 2003), schools should build more physical activity into the day (which, by the way, helps *every* child perform better!). Presenting learning tasks in a gaming format, or making any task more high energy and less distracting, is especially beneficial for children and adults with ADHD (Forster and others, 2014).

Students have told me that getting absorbed in high-energy activities, such as games or sports, was the treatment that "cured" a sibling's ADHD. Traditional, medication-oriented experts are listening

Parent training will ideally help mothers and fathers feel more in control (and be far less angry and impatient) when dealing with this child who has ADHD.

Although he may regularly tune out in class, this boy clearly has no problem being riveted to this game. Therefore, it makes sense that providing high-intensity academics-related video games may help cure wandering school minds.

(see Halperin & Healey, 2011). Medicines, scientists point out, even when they work, can have upsetting side effects. Once a person stops the treatment, symptoms return (Graham and others, 2011; Sonuga-Barke & Halperin, 2010). Exercise, as you will see later in this book, helps stimulate neurogenesis and *may* reduce the risk of getting later-life Alzheimer's disease. Might intense exercise or even providing time for playing games help mend a child's brain?

But perhaps some brains don't need mending. ADHD symptoms appear on a continuum (Bell, 2011; Larsson and others, 2012). Where should we *really* put the cutting point between normal childhood inattentiveness and a diagnosed "disease"? The dramatic early-twenty-first-century U.S. rise in the prevalence of ADHD (CDC, 2010b) is troubling. So is the male tilt to this diagnosis, as boys are more physically active than girls. Without denying that ADHD can cause considerable heartache, what role might a poor elementary school child–environment fit play in this "disorder" at this moment in history?

Wrapping Up Cognition

Now that I have reached the end of our survey of cognition, it should be clear why our species needs a decade (or two) beyond infancy to master the intellectual challenges of the adult world. Now, imagine the insights we would be missing if we left out any theory. What if you wanted to make sense of the strange ideas preschoolers have, or needed a general strategy for stimulating intellectual growth, or were looking for guidance about what to expect from children in terms of listening, following directions, and sitting still? You would have to turn to Piaget, Vygotsky, and the information-processing perspective. Has a particular theory been especially valuable in helping you understand the children you know?

 Tying It All Together

1. While with your 3-year-old nephew Mark, you observe many examples of preoperational thought. Give the Piagetian label—egocentrism, animism, no conservation, artificialism, identity constancy—for each of the following:

   a. Mark tells you that the big tree in the garden is watching him.

   b. When you stub your toe, Mark gives you his favorite stuffed animal.

   c. Mark tells you that his daddy made the sun.

   d. Mark says, "There's more now," when you pour juice from a wide carton into a skinny glass.

   e. Mark tells you that his sister turned into a princess yesterday when she put on a costume.

2. In a sentence, explain the basic mental difference between an 8-year-old in the concrete operational stage and a preoperational 4-year-old.

3. Four-year-old Christopher can recognize the alphabet, and is beginning to sound out words in books. Drawing on Vygotsky's theory, Chris' parents should (choose one): *buy alphabet books, because their son will succeed at recognizing the words; buy "easy-to-read" books just above their son's skill level; challenge Chris by getting him books with complicated stories.*

4. Turn back to the opening chapter vignette on page 135. List three activities specifically tailored to help train these preschoolers in the skills of regulating and inhibiting their responses.

5. Laura's son has been diagnosed with ADHD. Based on this chapter, suggest some environmental strategies she might use to help her child.

Answers to the Tying It All Together questions can be found at the end of this chapter.

Language

So far, I have been discussing the cognitive and physical milestones in this chapter as if they occurred in a vacuum. But, as I highlighted at the beginning of this chapter, that uniquely human skill, language, is vital to every childhood advance. Vygotsky (1978) actually put language—or speaking—front and center in everything we learn.

Inner Speech

According to Vygotsky, learning takes place when the words a child hears from parents and other scaffolders migrate inward to become talk directed at the self. For instance, using the earlier example of Chutes and Ladders, after listening to her mother say "Count them" a number of times, Tiffany learned the game by repeating "Count them" to herself. Thinking, according to Vygotsky, is **inner speech.**

Support for this idea comes from listening to young children monitor their actions. A 3-year-old might say, "Don't touch!" as she moves near the stove; or she could remind herself to be "a good girl" at preschool that day (Manfra & Winsler, 2006). We may feel the same way as adults. If something is *really important*—and if no one is listening—have you ever given yourself instructions "Be sure to do X, Y, and Z" out loud?

Developing Speech

How does language *itself* unfold? Actually, during early childhood language does more than unfold. It explodes.

By our second birthday, we are just beginning to put together words (see Chapter 3). By kindergarten, we basically have adult language nailed down. When we look at the challenges involved in mastering language, this achievement becomes more remarkable. To speak like adults, children must articulate word sounds. They must string units of meaning together in sentences. They must produce sentences that are grammatically correct. They must understand the meanings of words.

The word sounds of language are called **phonemes.** When children begin to speak in late infancy, they can only form single phonemes—for instance, they call their bottle *ba*. They repeat sounds that seem similar, such as calling their bottle *baba*, when they cannot form the next syllable of the word. By age 3, while children have made tremendous strides in producing phonemes, they still—as you saw in the introductory chapter vignette—have trouble pronouncing multisyllabic words (like *psghetti*). Then, early in elementary school, these articulation problems disappear— but not completely. Have you ever had a problem pronouncing a difficult word that you were able to read on a page?

The meaning units of language are called **morphemes** (for example, the word *boys* has two units of meaning: *boy* and the plural suffix *s*). As children get older, their average number of morphemes per sentence—called their **mean length of utterance (MLU)**—expands. A 2-year-old's sentence, "Me juice" (2 MLUs), becomes, "Me want juice" (3 MLUs), and then, at age 4, "Please give me the juice" (5 MLUS). Also around age 3 or 4, children are fascinated by producing long, jumbled-together sentences strung together by *and* ("Give me juice and crackers and milk and cookies and . . .").

This brings up the steps to mastering grammar, or **syntax.** What's interesting here are the classic mistakes that young children make. As parents are aware, one of the first words that children utter is *no*. First, children typically add this word to the beginning of a sentence ("No eat cheese" or "No go inside"). Next, they move the negative term inside the sentence, next to the main verb ("I no sing" or "He no do it"). A question starts out as a declarative sentence with a rising intonation: "I have a drink, Daddy?" Then it, too, is replaced by the correct word order: "Can I have a

---

inner speech In Vygotsky's theory, the way in by which human beings learn to regulate their behavior and master cognitive challenges, through silently repeating information or talking to themselves.

According to Vygotsky, by talking to her image in the mirror "out loud," this girl is learning to monitor her behavior. Have you ever done the same thing when no one was watching?

phoneme The sound units that convey meaning in a given language—for example, in English, the *c* sound of *cat* and the *b* sound of *bat*.

morpheme The smallest unit of meaning in a particular language—for example, *boys* contains two morphemes: *boy* and the plural suffix *s*.

mean length of utterance (MLU) The average number of morphemes per sentence.

syntax The system of grammatical rules in a particular language.

semantics The meaning system of a language—that is, what the words stand for.

overregularization An error in early language development, in which young children apply the rules for plurals and past tenses even to exceptions, so irregular forms sound like regular forms.

overextension An error in early language development in which young children apply verbal labels too broadly.

underextension An error in early language development in which young children apply verbal labels too narrowly.

drink, Daddy?" Children typically produce grammatically correct sentences by the time they enter school.

The most amazing changes occur in **semantics**—understanding word meanings. Here, children go from three- or four-word vocabularies at age 1 to knowing about 10,000 words by age 6! (See Slobin, 1972; Smith, 1926.) While we have the other core abilities under our belts by the end of early childhood, our vocabularies continue to grow from age 2 to 102.

One mistake young children make while learning language is called **overregularization**. Around age 3 or 4, they often misapply general rules for plurals or past tense forms even when exceptions occur. A preschooler will say *runned, goed, teached, sawed, mouses, feets,* and *cup of sugars* rather than using the correct irregular form (Berko, 1958).

Another error lies in children's semantic mistakes. Also around age 3, children often use **overextensions**—meaning they extend a verbal label too broadly. In Piaget's terminology, they assimilate the word *horsey* to all four-legged creatures, such as dogs, cats, and lions in the zoo. Or they use **underextensions**—making name categories too narrow. A 3-year-old may tell you that only her own pet is a dog and insist that all the other neighborhood dogs must be called something else. As children get older, through continual assimilation and accommodation, they sort these glitches out.

Table 5.6 summarizes these challenges. Now you might want to have a conversation with a 3- or 4-year-old child. Can you pick out examples of overregularization, overextensions or underextensions, problems with syntax (grammar), or difficulties pronouncing phonemes (word sounds)? Can you figure out the child's MLU?

Table 5.6: Challenges on the Language Pathway: A Summary Table

Type of challenge	Description	Example
Phonemes	Has trouble forming sounds	*Baba, psghetti*
Morphemes	Uses few meaning units per sentence	*Me go home*
Syntax (grammar)	Makes mistakes in applying rules for forming sentences	*Me go home*
Semantics	Has problems understanding word meanings	*Calls the family dog a horsey*
Overregularization	Puts irregular pasts and plurals into regular forms	*Foots; runned*
Over/underextension	Applies verbal labels too broadly/narrowly	*Calls every old man grandpa; tells another child he can't have a grandpa because grandpa is the name for his grandfather alone*

Tying It All Together

1. A 5-year-old is talking out loud and making comments such as "Put the big piece here," while constructing a puzzle. What would Vygotsky say about this behavior?

2. You are listening to a 3-year-old named Joshua. Pick out the example of overregularization and the overextension from the following comments.

   a. When offered a piece of cheese, Joshua said, "I no eat cheese."

   b. Seeing a dog run away, Joshua said, "The doggie runned away."

   c. Taken to a petting zoo, Joshua pointed excitedly at a goat and said, "Horsey!"

Answers to the Tying It All Together questions can be found at the end of this chapter.

Specific Social Cognitive Skills

Language makes us capable of uniquely human *social cognitive* understandings. We are the only species that reflects on our past and future (Fivush, 2011). The essence of being human, as I highlighted at the beginning of this chapter, is that we effortlessly transport ourselves into each other's heads, decoding what people are thinking from their own point of view. How do children learn they have an ongoing life history? When do we *fully* grasp that "other minds" are different from our own?

Constructing Our Personal Past

Autobiographical memories refer to reflecting on our life histories: from our earliest memories at age 3 or 4, to that incredible experience we had at work last week. Children's understanding that they have a unique autobiography is scaffolded through a specific kind of talk. Caregivers reminisce with young children: "Remember going on a train to visit Grandma?" "What did we do at the beach last week?" These *past-talk conversations* are teaching a lesson: "You have a past and future. You are an enduring self."

Past-talk conversations typically begin with parents doing the "remembering" when children first begin to speak (Harley & Reese, 1999). Then, children become partners in these mutual stories, and finally, at age 4 or 5, initiate past-talk conversations on their own (Nelson & Fivush, 2004). Listen to this vivid autobiographical memory produced by a 6-year-old:

INTERVIEWER TO 6-YEAR-OLD: Can you tell me about the ballet recital?

CHILD: It was driving me crazy.

INTERVIEWER: Really?

CHILD: Yes, I was so scared because I didn't know any of the people and I couldn't see mom and dad. They were way on top of the audience. . . . Ummm, we were on a slippery surface and we all did "Where the Wild Things Are" and we . . . Mine had horns sticking out of it . . . And I had baggy pants.

(adapted from Nelson & Fivush, 2004)

As this girl reaches adolescence, she will link these kinds of memories to each other, and construct a timeline of her life (Habermas, Negele, & Mayer, 2010; Chen, McAnally, & Reese, 2013). By about age 16, she will use these events to reflect on her enduring personality ("This is the kind of person I am, as shown by how I felt at age 4 or 5 or 9"). Then she will have achieved that Eriksonian milestone—an *identity* to carry through life (more about this in Chapter 10).

Caregivers can help stimulate autobiographical memory by sensitively asking questions about exciting experiences they shared with their child (Valentino and others, 2014). ("Wasn't the Circus amazing! What did you like best?") Moreover, the quality of our teenage autobiographical memories vary depending on the loving past talk experiences we receive. In one study, young teens who produced rich personal autobiographies were apt to report close, trusting relationships with their mothers (Bosmans and others, 2013). Conversely, overly general autobiographical memories ("I used to go shopping") rather than recalling specific events ("I remember how I went to Green Hills Mall on that Tuesday with my friends") can be a symptom of an unhappy life (Valentino and others, 2014). In another study, having been abused, plus an inability to recall details about one's past, was linked to a young teen's experiencing depression down the road (Stange and others, 2013).

The most chilling example of this autobiographical memory failure (Freud might label it *repression*) occurred when researchers tested children who were removed from an abusive home. If a parent was insecurely attached, a child either was apt to make false statements about what took place that day or to deny remembering anything about the traumatic event (Melinder and others, 2013).

autobiographical memories Recollections of events and experiences that make up one's life history.

When they get home, this mother can help her daughter construct her "personal autobiography" by starting a dialogue about their wonderful day at the beach.

Paul Avis/Getty Images

The take-home message is that having a personal autobiography (or full sense of self) is taught through responsive parent–child encounters. As the sociologist George Herbert Mead suggested a century ago by using different terminology, or as Vygotsky implied in a different context in this chapter, relationships are the medium that teach us to be a self.

Moreover, when researchers train parents in the rich reminiscence styles described above, they find that past-talk conversations enhance the child's ability to relate to other minds (Taumoepeau & Reese, 2013). When does this vital mindreading ability really lock in?

Making Sense of Other Minds

Listen to 3-year-olds having a conversation, and it's as if you are hearing monologues, or mental ships passing in the night. Around age 4 or 5, children start relating in a *give-and-take* way. They have reached that landmark called **theory of mind**. Developmentalists have a creative procedure to demonstrate this milestone—*the false-belief task*.

With a friend and a young child, see if you can perform this classic theory of mind task in Figure 5.6 (Wimmer & Perner, 1983). Hide a toy in a place (location A) while the child and your friend watch. Then, have your friend leave the room. Once she is gone, move the toy to another hiding place (location B). Next, ask the child where *your friend* will look for the toy when she returns. If the child is under age 4, he will typically answer the second hiding place (location B), even though your friend could not possibly know the toy has been moved. It's as if the child doesn't grasp the fact that what *he* observed can't be in your friend's head, too.

What Are the Consequences and Roots of Theory of Mind?

Having a theory of mind is not only vital to having a real conversation; it is crucial to convincing someone to do what you say. Researchers asked children to persuade a puppet to do something aversive, either eat broccoli or brush its teeth. Even controlling for verbal abilities, the number of arguments a given boy or girl made was linked to advanced theory of mind (Slaughter, Peterson, & Moore, 2013).

Theory of mind is essential to understanding people may not have your best interests at heart. One developmentalist had children play a game with "Mean Monkey," a puppet the experimenter controlled (Peskin, 1992). Beforehand, the researcher had asked the children which sticker they wanted. Then, she had Mean Monkey pick each child's favorite choice. Most 4-year-olds figured out how to play the game and told Mean Monkey the opposite of what they wanted. Three-year-olds never caught on. They always pointed to their favorite sticker and got the "yucky" one instead.

A remark from one of my students brings home the real-world message of this research. She commented that her 4-year-old nephew had reached the stage where he was beginning to tell lies. Under age 4, children don't fully have the mental abilities to understand that their parents don't know the thoughts in their head. So lying is an important cognitive advance! (See Evans, Xu, & Lee, 2011.)

The false-belief studies, conducted during the last decades of the twentieth century, convinced developmentalists that Piaget's ideas about preoperational egocentrism were wrong. Although theory-of-mind abilities mature well into later childhood (Devine & Hughes, 2013) and our teens (Dumontheil, Apperly, & Blakemore, 2010; Lagattuta, Sayfan, & Blattman, 2010; Samson & Apperly, 2010), remember that children first grasp the principle that there are other minds out there, during the first 6 months of life!

Do Individual Children (and Adults) Differ in Theory of Mind?

While most preschoolers pass theory-of-mind tasks at around 4 or 5, perhaps because parent–child disagreements are less acceptable in collectivist societies, children in these cultures take a bit longer to grasp the idea that people have conflicting opinions

theory of mind Children's first cognitive understanding, which appears at about age 4, that other people have different beliefs and perspectives from their own.

(1) Another adult and a young child watch while you hide a toy in a place like a desk drawer.

(2) The other adult [Ms. X] leaves the room.

(3) You hide the toy under the bed and then ask the child, "Where will Ms. X look for the toy?"

FIGURE 5.6: **The false-belief task:** In this classic test for *theory of mind,* when children under age 4 are asked, "Where will Ms. X look for the toy?" they are likely to say, "Under the bed," even though Ms. X could not possibly know the toy was moved to this new location.
Based on Wimmer & Perner, 1983.

than do Western 4-year-olds (Shahaeian and others, 2011; see also Table 5.7 on page 162 for some fascinating neural findings related to theory of mind and the collectivist/individualistic distinction).

Conversely, because they have so much hands-on experience in colliding (meaning arguing) with other minds—"Hey, I want that toy!" "No, I do!"—Western preschoolers with brothers and sisters tend to pass theory-of-mind tasks at somewhat younger ages than only children do (McAlister & Peterson, 2013).

Table 5.7: Brain-Imaging Theory-of-Mind and Autobiographical-Memory Findings to Wrap Your Head Around

Reflecting on the self and others' mental states is a frontal-lobe activity involving slightly different brain regions: When Westerners are asked to recall autobiographical memories, a brain region called the *medial frontal cortex* lights up. When given theory-of-mind–type tasks, a slightly different area of the medial frontal cortex is activated. So thinking about ourselves and motivations of other people involves distinctive (but closely aligned) brain areas.

Interesting cultural variation: This classic neural separation does not exist when Chinese adults think about themselves and their mothers. More astonishing, thinking about yourself and family members activates either the same or more separate brain regions, depending on whether you have a collectivist (interdependent) or individualistic (self-oriented) worldview.

Interesting variation from person to person: When you judge the mental state of someone you view as similar, such as a good friend, a closely aligned brain region lights up as when you are asked to reflect on yourself (as if you are drawing on your feelings about how you would respond in interpreting this person). But, inferring the mental states of dissimilar others— people you view as very different—activates truly separate brain areas. Imagining the feelings of disliked out-group members (e.g., as a Palestinian being asked to empathize with the perspective of a Jewish-Israeli West Bank settler) may elicit reduced activity in the "social" brain!

Conclusion: Our attitudes about the self in relationship to other human beings are mirrored in the physical architecture of our brain.

Data from: Abu-Akel & Shamay-Tsoory, 2011; Heatherton, 2011; Oddo and others, 2010; Rabin and others, 2010.

For this Latino girl, the challenge of switching to English to recite this poem to the class may provide a lifelong cognitive boost.

autism spectrum disorders (ASDs) Conditions characterized by persistent, severe, widespread social and conversational deficits; lack of interest in people and their feelings; and repetitive, restricted behavior patterns, such as rocking, ritualized behavior, hypersensitivity to sensory input, and a fixation on inanimate objects. A core characteristic of these disorders is impairments in theory of mind.

Bilingual preschoolers—because they must sensitively switch between languages, depending on their conversational partner—also reach this social milestone earlier than the typical child (Adi-Japha, Berberich-Artzi, & Libnawi, 2010; Chertkow and others, 2010; Cushen & Wiley, 2011). So do preschoolers who are emotionally reactive and, possibly, more attuned to social cues (Lane and others, 2013), and boys and girls with parents who talk about other people's mental states from a very young age (Lundy, 2013; Pavarini, de Hollanda Souza, & Hawk, 2013).

My discussion implies that interpersonal or social skills are intimately involved in grasping theory-of-mind tasks. So it comes as no surprise that the core condition associated with "mind-blindness"—difficulties with theory of mind—is autism, that well-known impairment in the ability to socially relate (Baron-Cohen, 1999; Steele, Joseph, & Tager-Flusberg, 2003). As autism spectrum disorders—the current umbrella name encompassing Asperger's syndrome and autism—are such compelling contemporary concerns, let's end this chapter by outlining what these devastating conditions are like.

Hot in Developmental Science: Autism Spectrum Disorders

Autism spectrum disorders (ASDs) actually are defined by deficits in theory of mind—the inability to have normal back-and-forth conversations, share feelings (or be self-aware), and a lack of interest in relationships or friends. To qualify for this diagnosis, according to the recent *Diagnostic and Statistical Manual (DSM-5)*, these severe social impairments must be combined with restricted, stereotyped, repetitive-behavior patterns: rocking, flipping objects, a hypersensitivity to sensory input, an abnormal fixation on the nonhuman world (American Psychiatric Association, 2013).

Unlike ADHD, the symptoms of autism spectrum disorders routinely appear in early childhood and persist, wreaking lifelong havoc. Deteriorating executive functions (Rosenthal and others, 2013), poor social understanding (Bal and others, 2013), and worsening vocational adjustment (Taylor & Mailick, 2014) can be an unfortunate path this disorder takes during the adult years.

© Bill Aron/PhotoEdit

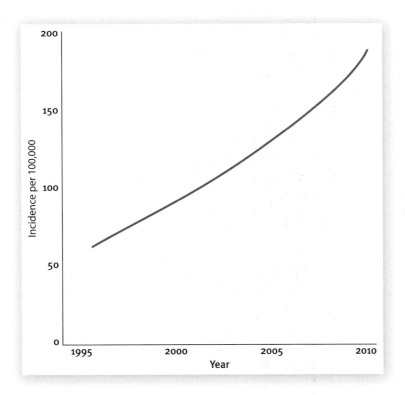

FIGURE 5.7: Time trends of autism spectrum diagnoses among children aged 4-6 in Denmark, 1995–2010: This chart vividly shows the rise in autism spectrum diagnoses among young children over the past decades in one representative Western nation (Denmark). Is this alarming increase partly due to the massive media attention focused on this condition? We do not know. Interestingly, however, as the new criteria for labeling autism spectrum disorders are more stringent, the number of children diagnosed with this condition may decline a bit in subsequent years.
Data from: Jensen, C, Steinhausen, H., & Lauritson, M. B. (1914).

The good news is that in contrast to ADHD, this fuzzy, multi-symptom syndrome (Williams & Bowler, 2014) is rare, affecting roughly 1 in every 88 children in the United States (Yudell and others, 2013). The problem is the alarming increase in autism spectrum diagnoses over the past two decades (Yudell and others, 2013). (See Figure 5.7 for an example from Denmark.) As with ADHD, autism spectrum disorders are several times more common in boys than girls (Volkmar and others, 2014).

What causes these devastating brain conditions? The fact that autism spectrum disorders run in families suggests these diseases may partly have genetic causes (Rosti and others, 2014). A puzzling array of environmental risk factors have been linked to autism, from air pollution (Volk and others, 2013), to maternal abusive relationships (Roberts and others, 2013); from prenatal medication use (Christensen and others, 2013), to having a premature birth. Given that pregnancy and birth problems seem involved, it's no surprise that older parents are at higher risk of having a child with this condition. But astonishingly, one study traced the risk back a generation—to the advanced age of the granddad (See Frans and others, 2013)!

What are the treatments? The most well-known intervention, developed about 40 years ago, is applied behavioral analysis. This is an intensive, hands-on approach in which a clinician reinforces each appropriate behavior. Children with autism spectrum disorders may receive services from a variety of professionals, while their parents get educational training and their peers are taught strategies to help these boys and girls at school. Unlike with ADHD, medications are not effective with the basic autistic symptoms, although they can ameliorate the challenging behaviors and emotional distress the disease produces (Volkmar and others, 2014).

Unfortunately, however, despite decades of nonstop media attention, little progress has been made at finding a magic-bullet intervention or decoding what *really* causes these devastating diseases (Yudell and others, 2013).

Autism spectrum disorders are poster-child diseases for the devastation that occurs when our human capacity to relate to other minds is impaired. In the next chapter, I'll focus directly on charting children's relationships (and self-awareness), as I explore socioemotional development during the childhood years.

Tying It All Together

1. Andrew said to Madison, his 3-year-old son: "Remember when we went to Grandma and Grandpa's last year? . . . . It was your birthday, and what did Grandma make for you?" This _____ conversation will help scaffold Madison's _____ .

2. Pick the statement that would *not* signify that a child has developed a full-fledged theory of mind:

   a. He's having a real give-and-take conversation with you.

   b. He realizes that if you weren't there, you can't know what's gone on—and tries to explain to you what happened while you were absent.

   c. When he has done something he shouldn't do, he is likely to lie.

   d. He's learning to read.

3. Autism spectrum disorders are becoming *more/less* prevalent, and we are *making great progress/not making much progress* in determining their causes.

Answers to the Tying It All Together questions can be found at the end of this chapter.

SUMMARY

Setting the Context

Childhood comprises two phases—**early** and **middle childhood**—and this period of life lasts longer in our species than in any other animal. We need this time to absorb the lessons passed down by previous generations, and to take advantage of our finely tuned ability to decode intentions—the talent that has allowed us to advance. The **frontal lobes,** in particular, take two decades to become "adult." As this region of the brain—involved in reasoning and planning— develops, every childhood ability improves.

Physical Development

Physical growth slows down after infancy. Girls and boys are roughly the same height during preschool and much of elementary school. Boys are a bit more competent at **gross motor skills.** Girls are slightly superior in **fine motor skills.** Although preschool fine motor skills predict elementary school success, we need to be careful not to push young children too hard. Undernutrition severely impairs motor skill development by making children too tired to exercise and play.

Rates of **childhood obesity**—defined by a **high body mass index (BMI)**—dramatically increased starting about 40 years ago, although the prevalence of this epidemic differs across nations and in specific demographic groups. While the main general cause for this modern scourge lies in toxic environmental forces (too little exercise, an abundance of tasty, calorie-dense foods, and so on), children differ genetically in their tendencies to be overweight, and the best predictor of later obesity is rapid weight gain early in life. Because prejudices against overweight children are intense, parents tend to minimize their children's weight issues and can be reluctant to participate in family interventions. Rather than just changing society, it's important to discourage overfeeding babies and decode the biochemical conditions causing vulnerable infants to gain excessive weight.

Cognitive Development

Piaget's preoperational stage lasts from about age 3 to 7. The concrete operational stage lasts from about age 8 to 11.

Preoperational thinkers focus on the way objects and substances (and people) immediately appear. **Concrete operational thinkers** can step back from their visual perceptions and reason on a more conceptual plane. In Piaget's **conservation tasks,** children in preoperations believe that when the shape of a substance has changed, the amount of it has changed. One reason is that young children lack the concept of **reversibility,** the understanding that an operation can be repeated in the opposite way. Another is that children **center** on what first captures their eye and cannot **decenter,** or focus on several dimensions at one time. Centering also affects **class inclusion** (understanding overarching categories). Preoperational children believe that if something *looks* bigger visually, it always equals "more."

Preoperational children lack **identity constancy**—they don't understand that people are "the same" in spite of changes in external appearance. Their thinking is characterized by **animism** (the idea that inanimate objects are alive) and by **artificialism** (the belief that everything in nature was made by humans). They are **egocentric,** unable to understand that other people have different perspectives from their own. Although Piaget's ideas offer a wealth of insights into children's thinking, he underestimated what young children know. Children in every culture do progress from preoperational to concrete operational thinking—but the learning demands of the particular society make a difference in the age at which specific conservations are attained.

Lev Vygotsky, with his concept of the **zone of proximal development,** suggested that learning occurs when adults tailor instruction to a child's capacities and then use **scaffolding** to gradually promote independent performance. Education, according to Vygotsky, is a collaborative, bidirectional learning experience.

Information-processing theory provides another perspective on cognitive growth. In this framework on memory, material must be processed through a limited-capacity system, called **working memory,** in order to be recalled at a subsequent time. As children get older, their working memory-bin capacity dramatically expands, which may explain why children reach concrete operations at age 7 or 8.

Executive functions—the ability to think through our actions and manage our cognitions—dramatically improve over time. Children adopt learning strategies such as **rehearsal.** They get better at **selective attention** and inhibiting their immediate responses. The research on rehearsal, selective attention, and inhibition provides a wealth of insights that can be applied in real life.

Attention-deficit/hyperactivity disorder (ADHD), the most common childhood disorder in the United States, involves impairments in executive functions such as working memory, inhibition, and selective attention, and presents widespread problems at home and school. This condition, usually diagnosed in elementary school (more often among boys), can have a bewildering array of pathways and possible brain causes. Treatments involve medication, training for parents and children, dietary interventions, providing white noise, exercise, and high-intensity games. The dramatic rise in contemporary Western ADHD diagnoses could be partly a product of a poor child-environment fit.

Language

Language makes every other childhood skill possible. Vygotsky believed that we learn everything through using **inner speech.** During early childhood, language abilities expand dramatically. **Phonemic** (sound articulation) abilities improve. As the number of **morphemes** in children's sentences increases, their **mean length of utterance (MLU)** expands. **Syntax,** or knowledge of grammatical rules, improves. **Semantic** understanding (vocabulary) shoots up. Common language mistakes young children make include **overregularization** (using regular forms for irregular verbs and nouns), **overextension** (applying word categories too broadly), and **underextension** (applying word categories too narrowly).

Specific Social Cognitive Skills

Autobiographical memories, the child's understanding of having a personal past, is socialized by caregivers through past-talk conversations, questioning young children about shared life events. Specific autobiographical memories consolidate into a coherent identity during the teens. Overly general autobiographical memories (or not recalling salient events from the past) may indicate a child's having an abusive early life.

Theory of mind, our knowledge that other people have different perspectives from our own, is measured by the false-belief task. Children around the world typically pass this milestone at about age 4 or 5, although the roots of this uniquely human ability appear before age 1. Cultural forces, being bilingual, having older siblings, and having parents' continually talk about people's mental states predict the emergence of this vital skill.

Autism spectrum disorders (ASDs), characterized by severely impaired social skills and abnormal repetitive behaviors, are emblematic of impaired theory of mind. These devastating disorders, which typically are diagnosed in early childhood, are rising in prevalence, and have unknown causes.

KEY TERMS

early childhood, p. 135

middle childhood, p. 135

frontal lobes, p. 136

gross motor skills, p. 138

fine motor skills, p. 138

body mass index (BMI), p. 139

childhood obesity, p. 139

preoperational thinking, p. 142

concrete operational
    thinking, p. 142

conservation tasks, p. 143

reversibility, p. 143

centering, p. 143

decentering, p. 143

class inclusion, p. 143

identity constancy, p. 145

animism, p. 145

artificialism, p. 145

egocentrism, p. 146

zone of proximal
    development, p. 149

scaffolding, p. 149

working memory, p. 151

executive functions, p. 151

rehearsal, p. 152

selective attention, p. 152

attention-deficit/hyperactivity
    disorder (ADHD), p. 154

inner speech, p. 157

phoneme, p. 157

morpheme, p. 157

mean length of utterance
    (MLU), p. 157

syntax, p. 157

semantics, p. 158

overregularization,
    p. 158

overextension, p. 158

underextension, p. 158

autobiographical memories,
    p. 159

theory of mind, p. 160

autism spectrum disorders
    (ASDs), p. 162

ANSWERS TO **Tying It All Together** QUIZZES

Setting the Context

1. Language is what really allows us to penetrate other minds—and our superior mindreading ability is what makes us different from other animals.

2. Ethan's *motor* cortex is on an earlier developmental timetable than his *frontal lobes*.

3. This is a disaster! Your colleague might have trouble with everything from regulating his physical responses, to analyzing problems, to inhibiting his actions.

Physical Development

1. Long-distance running and the high jump would be ideal for Jessica, as these sports heavily tap into gross motor skills.

2. The prevalence of obesity is declining during preschool.

3. All of these forces predict later overweight.

4. The best age to intervene to prevent obesity is birth age 1.

5. Because parents—especially those with an overweight child—might be unwilling to participate to protect their own and their child's self-esteem, empower families by having them plan the intervention strategies.

Amos Morgan/Photodisc/Getty Images

Cognitive Development

1. (a) animism; (b) egocentrism; (c) artificialism; (d) can't conserve; (e) (no) identity constancy

2. Children in concrete operations can step back from their current perceptions and think conceptually, while preoperational children can't go beyond how things immediately appear.

3. Buy Chris easy-to-read books that are just above his skill level.

4. (1) Following the play center rules to clean up, not take toys outside, and keep oneself from entering if there are four children; (2) having the class sit still and raise their hands to speak; (3) the dance slower and faster activity.

5. Don't put your son in demanding situations involving time management. When he studies, provide "white" background noise. Use small immediate reinforcers, such as prizes for good behavior that day. Get your son involved in sports or playing exciting games. Avoid power assertion (yelling and screaming), and go out of your way to provide lots of love.

Language

1. Vygotsky would say it's normal—the way children learn to think through their actions and control their behavior.

2. (b) = overregularization; (c) = overextension

Specific Cognitive Skills

1. This *past-talk* conversation will help stimulate Madison's *autobiographical memory.*

2. d

3. Autism spectrum disorders are becoming *more* prevalent, and we are *not making great progress* in determining their causes.

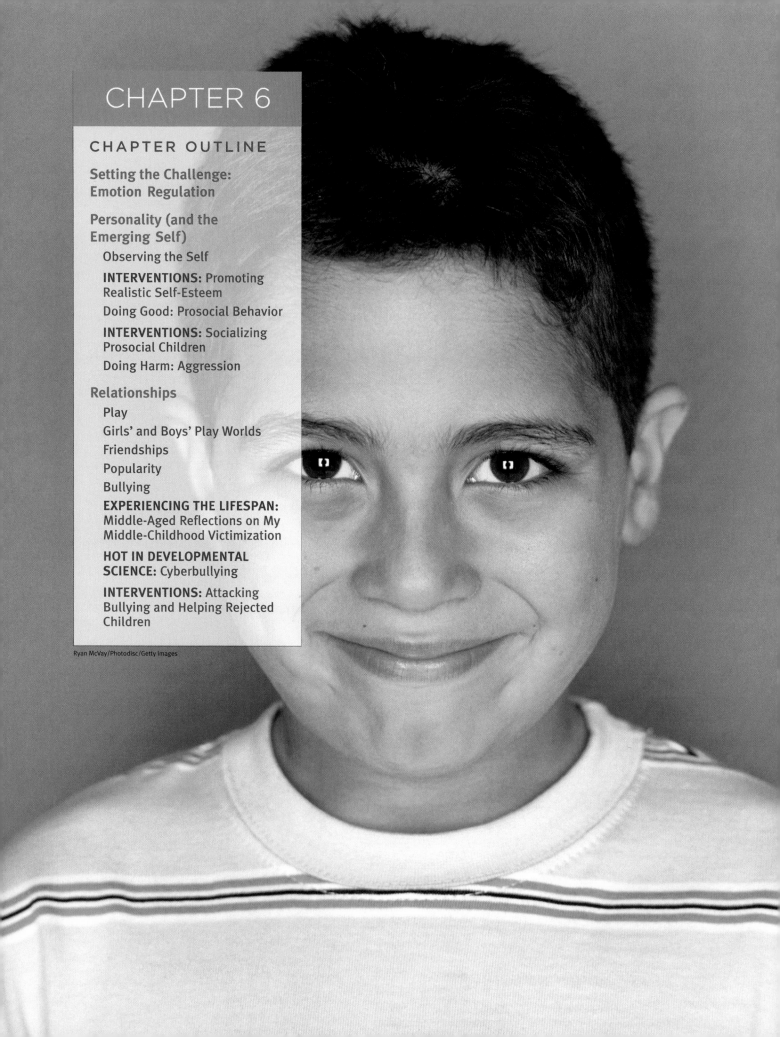

CHAPTER 6

Ryan McVay/Photodisc/Getty Images

Socioemotional Development

Nine-year-old Josiah has a new best friend, Matt. The boys bonded over their love of soccer and their "so-called" hatred of girls. Although they aren't in the popular kids group, these best buddies are the kind of caring, take-charge kids you want to have around. A perfect example of what these kids add to the class happened last week when the boys decided to physically (!) play tag using a video game.

As she saw the kids jostling, filling up the recess area with joyous noise, Moriah—who had earlier made the memorable statement, "Girls' stuff is stupid" (comments that quickly earned her the label "dork" from the female members of the class)—ran over and asked, "Can I play?"

Everyone closed ranks, yelling, "No girls allowed!"

Then Mark pushed in, as usual, disrupting the game, hogging the device the kids had renamed "the ball." A few minutes later, Jimmy, an anxious child, worked up the guts to timidly enter the group.

"Get out!" erupted Mark, "You wuss. You girl!"

Mark bopped Jimmy over the head, and—as usual—a few boys laughed. Jimmy started to cry and began to slink away. But suddenly, Josiah slowed down.

"Cool it, guys," he said. "Man, are you all right? Come join us."

Josiah comforted Jimmy and managed to tell the other boys to lay off Moriah ("Hey, guys, she's really cool!"), while Matt did his best to keep Mark from messing up the game. All of this earned these two good-guy heroes exuberant fist pumps from the teacher and the rest of the class!

Have you ever wondered why children, such as Josiah and Matt, are competent and caring, while others, like Mark, seem insensitive, aggressive, and rude? Perhaps you are curious about what makes children bond together as best friends, or why people, like Jimmy and Moriah, seem isolated from their peers. Have you puzzled over why boys love to run around or wondered why elementary schoolchildren (say) they love to hate the other sex? Maybe you simply want to understand your own and other people's behavior in a deeper way. If so, this chapter, covering children's emotional and social development, is for you.

In the following pages, you'll be getting insights into the challenges in *social cognition* that children face as they travel from preschool through elementary school. But this chapter has another purpose: to help children such as Moriah, Mark, and Jimmy, who are having troubles relating in the world. With this goal in mind, let's begin by highlighting that fundamental human challenge—managing our emotions.

Setting the Challenge: Emotion Regulation

In Chapter 5, you saw how the ability to control our behavior underpins every childhood cognitive advance. We need the same *executive function* skills to succeed socially and emotionally, too. When we get angry, we must cool down our feelings, rather than lash out. We have to overcome our anxieties and talk to that scary professor, or conquer our shyness and go to a party because we might meet that special person who will be the love of our life. **Emotion regulation** is the term developmentalists use for the skills involved in managing our feelings so that they don't get in the way of a productive life.

Children with **externalizing tendencies** have special trouble with this challenge. Like Mark in the introductory chapter vignette, they act on their immediate emotions and often behave disruptively and aggressively. Perhaps you know a child who bursts into every scene, fighting, bossing people around, wreaking havoc with his classmates and adults.

Children with **internalizing tendencies** have the opposite problem. Like Jimmy, they hang back in social situations. They are timid and self-conscious, frightened and depressed.

The beauty of being human is that we vary in our temperamental tendencies—to be shy or active, boisterous or reserved. In collectivist cultures such as India, ones that traditionally put a premium on being self-effacing, shyness is not necessarily a social liability (Bowker & Raja, 2011). In our individualistic society, being aggressive can be a social plus (as you will see later). But having serious trouble *controlling* one's aggression or anxiety puts children around the world at a disadvantage (Chen & French, 2008; Prakash & Coplan, 2007). Externalizing and internalizing tendencies—at their extremes—present universal barriers to succeeding with people and in life.

In Chapter 4, you learned about the temperaments that put toddlers at risk for having these emotion regulation issues—being highly exuberant or inhibited. Now, let's look at what happens if these tendencies evolve to the point where they cause suffering during the childhood years.

emotion regulation The capacity to manage one's emotional state.

externalizing tendencies A personality style that involves acting on one's immediate impulses and behaving disruptively and aggressively.

internalizing tendencies A personality style that involves intense fear, social inhibition, and often depression.

 Tying It All Together

1. Krista, a school psychologist, is concerned about two students: Paul, who bursts out in rage and is continually misbehaving; and Jeremy, who is timid, anxious, and sad. Krista describes Paul as having *internalizing/externalizing* tendencies and Jeremy as having *internalizing/externalizing tendencies*, and she says that issues with emotion regulation are a problem for *Paul/Jeremy/both boys*.

Answers to the Tying It All Together questions can be found at the end of this chapter.

Personality (and the Emerging Self)

As they get older, how do children's perceptions about themselves change and how do these changes affect self-esteem? What makes children (and adults) act in caring or hurtful ways?

Observing the Self

Developmentalist Susan Harter (1999) has explored the first questions in her research program examining how children view themselves. To make sense of her findings, Harter draws on Piaget's distinction between preoperational and concrete operational thinking—a difference I will be highlighting throughout this chapter. So let's take another look at the mental leap that Piaget believes takes place when children reach age 7 or 8.

Children in the concrete operational stage:

- Look beyond immediate appearances and think abstractly about inner states.

- Give up their egocentrism and realize they are but one person among many others in this vast world.

To examine how these changes affect **self-awareness**—the way children reflect on who they are as people—Harter asks boys and girls of different ages to describe themselves. Here are examples illustrating the responses she finds:

> I am 3 years old and I live in a big house. . . . I have blue eyes and a kitty that is orange. . . . I love my dog Skipper. . . . I'm always happy. I have brown hair. . . . I'm really strong.

> I'm in fourth grade, and I'm pretty popular. . . . That's because I'm nice to people . . . , although if I get into a bad mood I sometimes say something that can be a little mean. At school I'm feeling pretty smart in . . . Language Arts and Social Studies. . . . But I'm feeling pretty dumb in Math and Science. . . .

> (adapted from Harter, 1999, pp. 37, 48)

Notice that the 3-year-old talks about herself in terms of external facts. The fourth grader's descriptions are internal and psychological, anchored in her feelings, abilities, and inner traits. The 3-year-old describes herself in unrealistic, positive ways as "always happy." The fourth grader lists her deficiencies and strengths in many areas of life. Moreover, while the younger child talks about herself as if she were living in a bubble, the older child focuses on how she measures up compared to her classmates. So Harter believes that when they reach concrete operations, children realistically evaluate their abilities and decide whether they like or dislike the person they see. **Self-esteem**—the tendency to feel good or bad about ourselves—first becomes a *major issue* during elementary school.

Actually, studies around the world show that self-esteem tends to decline during early elementary school (Frey & Ruble, 1985, 1990; Harter & Pike, 1984; Super & Harkness, 2003). A mother may sadly notice this change when her 8-year-old daughter starts to make comments such as, "I am not pretty" or "I can't do math." ("What happened to that self-confident child who used to feel she was the most beautiful, intelligent kid in the world?") Caring teachers struggle with the same comparisons, the fact that their fourth graders are exquisitely sensitive to who is popular, which classmates are getting A's, and who needs special academic help.

Harter's research beautifully dovetails with Erik Erikson's early and middle childhood developmental tasks. Erikson, as you can see in Table 6.1, labeled the preschool psychosocial challenge as **initiative versus guilt**. Children's mission at this age, he believed, is to courageously test their abilities in the wider world. From risking racing

self-awareness The ability to observe our abilities and actions from an outside frame of reference and to reflect on our inner state.

self-esteem Evaluating oneself as either "good" or "bad" as a result of comparing the self to other people.

initiative versus guilt Erik Erikson's term for the preschool psychosocial task involving actively taking on life tasks.

Table 6.1: Erikson's Psychosocial Stages

Life Stage	Primary Task
Infancy (birth to 1 year)	Basic trust versus mistrust
Toddlerhood (1 to 2 years)	Autonomy versus shame and doubt
Early childhood (3 to 6 years)	**Initiative versus guilt**
Middle childhood (6 years to puberty)	**Industry versus inferiority**
Adolescence (teens into twenties)	Identity versus role confusion
Young adulthood (twenties to early forties)	Intimacy versus isolation
Middle adulthood (forties to sixties)	Generativity versus stagnation
Late adulthood (late sixties and beyond)	Integrity versus despair

In Erikson's framework, during preschool our agenda is to take the initiative to try out our skills in the wider world. During elementary school, our task is to learn to work for what we want.

Exuberantly taking off on your tricycle versus listening to the teacher and making sure you have finished your homework before raising your hand in class captures the essential difference between Erikson's *initiative* and *industry* tasks. It also shows why early childhood is a magical Garden of Eden interlude, before we enter the real world (aka concrete operations) and face the need to "work."

industry versus inferiority Erik Erikson's term for the psychosocial task of middle childhood involving managing our emotions and realizing that real-world success involves hard work.

learned helplessness A state that develops when a person feels incapable of affecting the outcome of events, and so gives up without trying.

your tricycle in the street to scaling the school monkey bars, our challenge in early childhood is taking the initiative to confront life.

In middle childhood (from age 6 to 12) our task shifts to **industry versus inferiority**—the need to manage our emotions and work for what we want to achieve (industry). Now we know that we are not just wonderful, and are vulnerable to low self-esteem—or inferiority—having the painful sense that we don't measure up. In other words, the price of leaving the preoperational bubble, or early-childhood Garden of Eden, is becoming realistically aware of our abilities and the demands of living in the "real world."

Still, all is not lost because this new, realistic understanding produces another change. Notice how the fourth grader on page 171 compares her abilities in different areas such as personality and school. As they get older, this means children's self-esteem doesn't hinge on one quality. Even if they are not doing well in one area, they can take comfort in the places where they really shine.

According to Harter, children draw on five areas to determine their self-esteem: *scholastic competence* (academic talents); *behavioral conduct* (obedience or being "good"); *athletic skills* (performance at sports); *peer likeability* (popularity); and *physical appearance* (looks). To diagnose how a child feels in each domain, Harter devised the kinds of questions in Figure 6.1.

As you might expect, children who view themselves as "not so good" in several domains often report low self-esteem. However, to really understand a given child's self-esteem, it is important to know that person's priorities—the value that a boy or girl attaches to doing well in a particular area of life.

To understand this point, take a minute to rate yourself in your people skills, politeness or good manners, your intellectual abilities, looks, and your physical abilities. If you label yourself "not so good" in an area you don't care about (for me, it would be physical skills), it won't make a dent in your self-esteem. If you care deeply about some area where you feel deficient, you would get pretty depressed.

This discounting process ("It doesn't matter if I'm not a scholar; I have great relationship skills") is vital. It lets us gain self-esteem from the areas in which we shine. The problem is that some children take this discounting to an extreme—minimizing their problems in *essential* areas of life.

Two Kinds of Self-Esteem Distortions

Normally, we base our self-esteem on the signals from the outside world: "Am I succeeding or not doing so well?" However, when children with externalizing problems *are* failing—for instance, being rejected or performing poorly at school—they may deny reality (Chung-Hall & Chen, 2010) and blame others to preserve their unrealistically high self-worth (Miller & Daniel, 2007). Perhaps you know an adult whose anger gets him into regular trouble at home and at work, but who copes by taking the position, "I'm wonderful. It's their fault." Because this person seems impervious to his flaws and has such difficulty regulating his emotions, he cannot change his behavior and so ensures that he continues to fail.

Children with internalizing tendencies have the opposite problem. Their hypersensitivity to environmental cues (recall Chapter 4) may cause them to read failure into benign events. ("My teacher hates me because she looked at me the wrong way.") They are at risk of developing **learned helplessness** (Abramson, Seligman, & Teasdale, 1978), the feeling that they are powerless to affect their fate. They give up at the starting gate, assuming, "I know I'm going to fail, so why should I try?"

So, children and adults with externalizing and internalizing tendencies face a similar danger—but for different reasons. When people minimize their real-world

FIGURE 6.1: **How do children view themselves?:** Harter has devised this questionnaire format to measure children's feelings of competence in her five different areas of life. The item in the top panel is derived from Harter's scale designed for young children; the questions in the bottom panel are from a similar scale for elementary school children.
Data from: Harter, 1999, pp. 121–122.

An examiner points to a girl to a preschooler's right and says, "This girl isn't good at doing puzzles." She then points to a girl to the child's left and says, "This girl is good at doing puzzles." Then she asks the child to point to the appropriate circle under each girl. If "this really fits me," the child points to the large circle. If "this fits me a little bit," the child points to the small circle.

Really True for Me	Sort of True for Me				Sort of True for Me	Really True for Me
☐	☐	Some kids are often *unhappy* with themselves.	BUT	Other kids are pretty *pleased* with themselves.	☐	☐
☐	☐	Some kids feel like they are *just as smart* as other kids their age.	BUT	Other kids aren't so sure and *wonder* if they are as smart.	☐	☐

Here the elementary schoolchild reads the items and checks the box that applies to her.

difficulties or assume they are incompetent, they cut off the chance of working to change their behavior and so ensure that they *will* fail.

Table 6.2 summarizes these self-esteem problems and their real-world consequences. Then, Table 6.3 offers a checklist, based on Harter's five dimensions, for

Table 6.2: Externalizing and Internalizing Problems, Self-Esteem Distortions, and Consequences—A Summary Table

Description	Self-Esteem Distortion	Consequence
CHILDREN WITH EXTERNALIZING PROBLEMS		
Act out "emotions," are impulsive and often aggressive.	May ignore real problems and have unrealistically high self-esteem.	Continue to fail because they don't see the need to improve.
CHILDREN WITH INTERNALIZING PROBLEMS		
Are intensely fearful.	Can read failure into everything and have overly low self-esteem.	Continue to fail because they decide that they cannot succeed and stop working.

Table 6.3: Identifying Your Self-Esteem Distortions: A Checklist Using Harter's Five Domains

You have externalizing issues if you regularly have thoughts like these:

1. **Academics:** "When I get poor grades, it's because my teachers don't give good tests or teach well." "I have very little to learn from other people." "I'm much smarter than practically everyone else I know."

2. **Physical skills:** "When I play baseball, soccer, etc., and my team doesn't win, it's my teammates' fault, not mine." "I believe it's OK to take physical risks, such as not wearing a seatbelt or running miles in the hot sun, because I know I won't get hurt." "It's all statistics, so I shouldn't be concerned about smoking four packs a day or about drinking a six-pack of beer every night."

3. **Relationships:** "When I have trouble at work or with my family, it's typically my co-workers' or family's fault." "My son (or mate, friend, mother) is the one causing all the conflict between us."

4. **Physical appearance:** "I don't think I have to work to improve my appearance because I'm basically gorgeous."

5. **Conduct:** "I should be able to come to work late (or turn in papers after the end of the semester, talk in class, etc.)." "Other people are too uptight. I have a right to behave any way I want to."

Diagnosis: You are purchasing high self-esteem at the price of denying reality. Try to look at the impact of your actions more realistically and take steps to change.

You have internalizing issues if you regularly have thoughts like these:

1. **Academics:** "I'm basically stupid." "I can't do well on tests." "My memory is poor." "I'm bound to fail at science." "I'm too dumb to get through college." "I'll never be smart enough to get ahead in my career."

2. **Physical skills:** "I can't play basketball (or some other sport) because I'm uncoordinated or too slow." "I'll never have the willpower to exercise regularly (or stick to a diet, stop smoking, stop drinking, or stop taking drugs)."

3. **Relationships:** "I don't have any people skills." "I'm doomed to fail in my love life." "I can't be a good mother (or spouse or friend)."

4. **Physical appearance:** "I'm basically unattractive." "People are born either good-looking or not, and I fall into the not category." "There is nothing I can do to improve my looks."

5. **Conduct:** "I'm incapable of being on time (or getting jobs done or stopping talking in class)." "I can't change my tendency to rub people the wrong way."

Diagnosis: Your excessively low self-esteem is inhibiting your ability to succeed. Work on reducing your helpless and hopeless attitudes and try for change.

evaluating yourself. Are there areas where you gloss over your deficiencies? Do you have pockets of learned helplessness that prevent you from living a full life?

INTERVENTIONS: Promoting Realistic Self-Esteem

This discussion shows why school programs focused *just* on raising self-esteem—those devoted to instilling the message, "You are a terrific kid"—are missing the boat (Baumeister and others, 2003; Swann, Chang-Schneider, & McClarty, 2007). Drawing on Erikson's theory, true self-esteem is derived from "industry"—working for our goals. Therefore, when children are having difficulties in a vital life domain, it's important to (1) enhance *self-efficacy*, or the feeling, "I can succeed if I work" (Miller & Daniel, 2007) and (2) promote *realistic* perceptions about the self. As a caring adult, how might you carry out this two-pronged approach?

ENHANCING SELF-EFFICACY. As developmentalist Carol Dweck has demonstrated, one key to enhancing academic self-efficacy is to praise children for effort ("You are trying so hard!"), rather than to make comments about basic ability ("You are incredibly smart!"). In her studies, elementary schoolers who were praised for being "very intelligent," after successfully completing problems, later had *lower* self-efficacy. They were afraid to tackle other challenging tasks ("I'd better not try this or everyone might learn I'm really dumb!") (Molden & Dweck, 2006; Mueller & Dweck, 1998).

You might think that praising kids for effort would only be effective when children have reached concrete operations and developed fixed ideas about the self ("I am basically dumb"). But when researchers videotaped mothers' interactions with their 2-year-olds, and tracked these toddlers into elementary school, guess what? Parents who years earlier made more statements that praised effort ("You worked so hard on that drawing," versus, "You are a great artist!") had 8-year-olds who (1) preferred tackling challenging tasks, (2) attributed academic success to hard work, and (3) believed that a person's intelligence and personality can be changed (Gunderson and others, 2013). Therefore, instilling the efficacious message, "working is what matters," should be a parental socialization goal starting from age one!

By praising her 3-year-old for being such a hard worker, this mom is socializing her child to tackle challenging tasks in third grade.

ENCOURAGING ACCURATE PERCEPTIONS. Still, if a child—for instance, Jimmy in the beginning chapter vignette—has internalizing tendencies, efficacy-enhancing interventions may not be enough. These children often see themselves as failing when they are not. Therefore, adults must continually provide accurate feedback: "The class doesn't hate you. Notice that Matt and Josiah wanted you in the game last week." And, if an elementary schooler with externalizing tendencies discounts his failures at the price of preserving an inflated sense of self-esteem, gently point out reality, too: Using the example of Mark, you might say, "The kids don't like you when you barge in and take over those games" (Thomaes, Stegge, & Olthof, 2007).

There is a way of softening this painful "You are not doing so well" message that is the price of realistically seeing the self. Harter (1999, 2006) finds that feeling loved by their attachment figures provides a cushion when children understand they are having trouble in an important area of life. So, returning to the beginning of this section, school programs (and adults) that stress the message "I care about you," plus foster self-efficacy ("You can succeed if you work hard"), are the key to promoting *true* self-esteem (Miller & Daniel, 2007).

Doing Good: Prosocial Behavior

On the morning of September 11, 2001, the nation was riveted by the heroism of the firefighters who ran into the World Trade Center buildings, risking almost certain death. We marveled at the "ordinary people" working in the Twin Towers, whose response to this emergency was to help others get out first.

Prosocial behavior is the term developmentalists use to describe such amazing acts of self-sacrifice, as well as the minor acts of helping, comforting, and sharing that we perform during daily life. Do we need to be taught to open a door when we see someone struggling with a package, to hug a distressed friend, or to reach out to include a shy kid who wants to play in our elementary school group?

What qualities made hundreds of New York City firefighters run into the burning Twin Towers on September 11, knowing that they might be facing death? This is the kind of question that developmentalists who study prosocial behavior want to answer.

The answer is no. Each prosocial activity naturally appears early in life (Hepach, Vaish, & Tomasello, 2013; Thompson & Newton, 2013). Toddlers will help a researcher retrieve an out-of-reach object; or comfort that person when she bangs her finger and says "Ouch!" (Dunfield & Kuhlmeir, 2013.) Eighteen-month-olds even perform sharing acts that go beyond the adult norm, giving some of their own stickers to an experimenter when that person has acted selfishly in a previous trial (Sebastián-Enesco, Hernández-Lloreda, & Colmenares, 2013).

This impetus to help, comfort, and share, which blossoms during toddlerhood, appears in cultures around the world (House and others, 2013). Moreover, doing

prosocial behavior Sharing, helping, and caring actions.

The fact that toddlers naturally take joy in giving suggests that giving is built into being human.

good makes young children feel good. Toddlers look happier after giving a treat to another person than when they get that treat for themselves. They seem especially joyous when engaging in costly giving—giving up something they *wanted to get* (Aknin, Hamlin, & Dunn, 2012). So, the principle that it feels better to give than receive doesn't need to be vigorously instilled in us at our mosque, temple, or church. It seems baked into the human genome from birth (Hepach and others, 2013)!

Individual and Gender Variations

However, as you saw in the vignette at the beginning of the chapter, children differ in the strength of this impulse to help, comfort, and spontaneously share. Developmentalists visited preschool classrooms and looked specifically at spontaneous sharing, the coming-from-the-heart giving that is different from being ordered: "Share!" When they tested these children in elementary school, during adolescence, and in emerging adulthood, the 3-year-olds who shared most readily were more prosocial at every age (Eisenberg and others, 1999; Eisenberg and others, 2014). So, if your 4-year-old niece seems unusually generous (especially at cost to herself), she may grow up to be an unusually prosocial adult.

What about your 4-year-old nephew? Are females generally more prosocial than males? As one Dutch study confirmed, women report more prosocial attitudes on questionnaires. However, when researchers used the EEG to tap into one facet of caring, being sensitive to other people's feelings, they found fewer variations by sex. Scenes depicting strong human emotions equally activated both male and female brains. But the women showed comparatively more arousal when viewing images of anguished people—which suggests that females may indeed be more attuned to others distress (Groen and others, 2013). The problem is that being sensitive to people's emotional pain may not result in *acting* in a prosocial way.

Decoding Prosocial Behavior in a Deeper Way

empathy Feeling the exact emotion that another person is experiencing.

sympathy A state necessary for acting prosocially, involving feeling upset *for* a person who needs help.

Empathy is the term developmentalists use for directly feeling another person's emotion. You get anxious when you hear your boss berating a co-worker. You were overcome by horror as you saw a video of the Twin Towers go down.

Sympathy is the more muted feeling that we experience *for* another human being. You feel terrible *for* your co-worker, but don't feel her intense distress. Your heart went out to the people who were trapped in the Twin Towers that day. Rather than empathy, developmentalists argue, sympathy is related to behaving in a prosocial way (Eisenberg, 1992, 2003; Trommsdorff, Friedlmeier, & Mayer, 2007).

The reason is that experiencing another person's distress can provoke a variety of reactions, from becoming immobilized with fear to behaving in a far-from-caring way. We can vividly see this when, out of empathic embarrassment, we burst out laughing after a waiter spills a restaurant tray, or become paralyzed by terror as we see a highway crash. So to be prosocial, children need to mute their empathic feelings into a sympathetic response (Eisenberg, 1992; Liew, Friedlmeier, & Mayer, 2011).

Acting prosocial, especially after preschool, also requires superior information processing skills. You need to decide *when* to be generous, which explains why 2-year-olds share with everyone, but, around age 4 or 5, children become selective, sharing mainly with people who are kind to them (Paulus & Moore, 2014). You must draw on your blossoming, concrete operational talents to assess the situation and decide if you *can* offer aid. Preoperational children will automatically give you their blankee when you are upset, because they are egocentric and assume that everything that comforts them will comfort you. However, just as I would not run into a flaming building because I'm not a firefighter, the reasons elementary school children report for not acting prosocial are that they don't have the skills to help (Denham, 1998; Eisenberg & Fabes, 1998).

Returning to gender differences, this suggests we take a more nuanced approach to the idea that females are more (or less) prosocial than males. Yes, women qualify as more prosocial if we measure comforting someone in emotional pain. Men, however, may be more prosocial in their own competence realm—changing a motorist's tire; helping a stranger lift a heavy object; opening doors for people; paying for dinner; or taking prosocial charge of a group during the fast-paced physical elementary school situation in the opening chapter vignette. After all, that's what being a gentleman—or gentleman-in-training—is traditionally all about!

Finally, people are more apt to reach out prosocially when they are happy—explaining why, when we are immersed in our own problems, we are less likely to help a friend, and why children who are fearful (those prone to internalizing disorders), as well as those who are relatively nonempathic (children with externalizing problems), tend to be less prosocial than their peers (Liew and others, 2011; Saarni, 1999).

To summarize, the impulse to share, to help, and to comfort is built into our species. But to predict who acts on that impulse, we need to ask specific questions: "Does this child have good executive functions?" "Does he have the concrete skills to help?" "Is she a confident, upbeat human being?"

Now that we've targeted the qualities involved in being prosocial, what can adults do to encourage these behaviors in a child?

Who tends to help a stranded stranger on the highway, carry your heavy load of packages, or be there to offer aid when you move? With that in mind, can we conclude that males are generally less prosocial than the other sex?

INTERVENTIONS: Socializing Prosocial Children

As some of you might imagine, offering concrete reinforcements, such as giving prizes for sharing, is counterproductive. External reinforcers undercut the happiness that flows from spontaneously performing costly prosocial acts. In one fascinating study, children who had earlier been given the chance to make a difficult prosocial decision—sharing desirable stickers with an experimenter—were more likely to be generous later on. So, the first step in promoting generosity is to give children space to spontaneously give (Chernyak & Kushnir, 2013).

Providing a caring socialization climate is important. Model prosocial behavior, making sure your toddler sees you regularly help people in need (Williamson, Donohue, & Tully, 2013). Behave in a caring, cooperative way with your spouse (Scrimgeour and others, 2013). Encourage a young child to talk about her emotions, and respond to her distress in a sympathetic way (Taylor and others, 2013). Be attuned to the caring things that your child does and attribute them to her personality—for instance, saying, "You really are a caring person for doing that," instead of "That was a nice thing you did" (Eisenberg, 2003). So, by complimenting your niece for being a kind person, you may be getting her to define herself as caring and helping to socialize her to be a prosocial adult (see Kochanska and others, 2010).

Most studies of prosocial behavior focus on a socialization technique called **induction** (Hoffman, 1994, 2001). Caregivers who use induction point out the ethical issues when a child has performed a hurtful act. Now, imagine that classic situation when your 8-year-old daughter has invited everyone in class but Sara to her birthday party. Instead of punishing your child—or giving that other classic response, "Kids will be kids"—here's what you should say: "It's hurtful to leave Sara out. Think of how terrible she must feel!"

Induction has several virtues: It offers children concrete feedback about exactly what they did wrong and moves them off of focusing on their own punishment ("Now, I'm really going to get it!") to the *other* child's distress ("Oh, gosh, she must feel hurt"). Induction also allows for reparations, the chance to make amends. Induction works because it stimulates the emotion called guilt.

induction The ideal discipline style for socializing prosocial behavior, involving getting a child who has behaved hurtfully to empathize with the pain he has caused the other person.

shame A feeling of being personally humiliated.

guilt Feeling upset about having caused harm to a person or about having violated one's internal standard of behavior.

When parents use shame to discipline, a child's impulse is to get furious. But by pointing out how disappointed a parent is in a "good girl," a parent can produce guilt—and so ultimately have a more prosocial child.

Shame Versus Guilt and Prosocial Acts

Think back to an event during childhood when you felt terrible about yourself. Perhaps it was the day you were caught cheating and sent to the principal. What you may remember was feeling so ashamed. Developmentalists, however, distinguish between feeling ashamed and experiencing guilt. **Shame** is the primitive feeling we have when we are *personally* humiliated. **Guilt** is the more sophisticated emotion we experience when we have violated a personal moral standard or hurt another human being.

I believe that Erikson may have been alluding to this maturity difference when he labeled "shame" as the emotion we experience as toddlers, and reserved "guilt" for the feeling that arises during preschool, when our drive to master the world causes other people distress (see Table 6.1 on page 171). While shame and guilt are both "self-conscious" relationship-oriented emotions, they have opposing effects. Shame causes us to withdraw from people, to slink away, and crawl into a hole (Thomaes and others, 2007). We feel furious at being humiliated and want to strike back. Guilt connects us to people. We feel terrible about what we have done and try to make amends. So, shame diminishes us. Guilt—*in moderation* (see Soenens & Vansteenkiste, 2010)—can cause us to act prosocially and emotionally enlarge (Olthof, 2012).

This suggests that socialization techniques involving shame are especially poisonous. If, when you arrived at the principal's office, he shamed you ("In the next school assembly, I'll announce what a terrible person you are!"), you might change your behavior, but at an emotional price. You would feel humiliated. You might decide you hated school. But if the principal induced guilt ("I feel disappointed because you're such a good kid"), you could act to enhance self-efficacy ("Dr. Jones, what can I do to make it up?"). You might end up feeling better about yourself and more connected to school. Has feeling guilty and apologizing ever made you feel closer to someone you love?

Table 6.4 summarizes these section messages and offers an additional tip. And, for readers who are thinking, "I'm prosocial, even though I didn't grow up in that kind of home," there is the reality that people can draw on shaming childhood experiences to construct prosocial lives. Perhaps you have a friend who grew up in an abusive family whose mission it is to work with abused children or (like me) have been privileged to meet childhood survivors of Hitler's holocaust who have devoted their lives to teaching people "never again!" Then you will realize that, while love is the best prosocial socializer, life's adversities can promote exceptional altruism, too (more about this compelling topic in Chapter 12).

Now that we have analyzed what makes us do good (the angel side of personality), let's enter the darker side of human nature: aggression.

Table 6.4: How to Produce Prosocial Children: A Summary Table

- Hold off and give the child opportunities to experience the joy of spontaneously sharing.

- Avoid giving treats or special privileges to reward prosocial acts. Instead, praise the child effusively when she is being prosocial, and label her as a caring child.

- When the child has hurt another person, use induction: Clearly point out the moral issue, and alert him to how the other person must feel.

- Avoid teasing and shaming. When the child has done something wrong, tell her you are disappointed and give her a chance to make amends.

- Don't think that you have fulfilled your responsibility to teach prosocial behavior by having a child participate in school or church drives to help the unfortunate. Morality isn't magically learned on Sunday. Model caring by having a loving, cooperative marriage, being sensitive to your child's feelings, and performing random acts of kindness in your daily life.

Doing Harm: Aggression

Aggression refers to acts designed to cause harm, from shaming to shoving, from gossiping to starting unprovoked wars. It should come as no surprise that physical aggression reaches its life peak at around age 2 1/2 (Dodge, Coie, & Lynam, 2006; van Aken and others, 2008). During this critical age for socialization, children are vigorously being disciplined but don't have the capacity to inhibit their responses. Imagine being a toddler continually ordered by giants to do impossible things, such as sharing and sitting still. Because being frustrated provokes aggression, it makes perfect sense that hitting and throwing tantrums are normal during "the terrible twos."

As preschoolers become more skilled at regulating their emotions and can make better sense of adults' rules, rates of open aggression (yelling or hitting) dramatically decline (Dishion & Tipsord, 2011). As children get older, the reasons for aggression change. Preschool fights center on objects, such as toys. During elementary school, when children have developed a full-fledged sense of self-esteem, aggression becomes personal. We strike out when we are wounded as human beings (Coie & Dodge, 1998). How do researchers categorize aggressive acts?

Types of Aggression

One way developmentalists classify aggression is by its motive. **Proactive aggression** refers to hurtful behavior that is initiated to achieve a goal. Johnny kicks Manuel to gain possession of the block pile. Sally spreads a rumor about Moriah to replace her as Sara's best friend. **Reactive aggression** occurs in response to being hurt, threatened, or deprived. Manuel, infuriated at Johnny, kicks him back.

Its self-determined nature gives proactive aggression a calculated, "cooler" emotional tone. When we behave aggressively to get something, we plan our behavior. We may feel a sense of self-efficacy as we carry out the act. Reactive aggression involves white-hot, disorganized rage. When you hear that your best friend has betrayed you, or even have a minor frustrating experience such as being caught in traffic, you get furious and blindly lash out (Deater-Deckard and others, 2010).

This feeling is normal. According to a classic theory called the *frustration-aggression hypothesis,* when human beings are thwarted, we are biologically primed to retaliate or strike back.

In addition to its motive—proactive or reactive—developmentalists distinguish between different forms of aggression. Hitting and yelling are direct forms of aggression. A more devious type of aggression is **relational aggression,** acts designed to hurt our relationships. Not inviting Sara to a birthday party, spreading rumors, or tattling on a disliked classmate all qualify as relationally aggressive acts.

Because it targets self-esteem and involves more sophisticated social skills, relational aggression follows a different developmental path than openly aggressive acts. Just as rates of open aggression are declining, during middle childhood, relational aggression rises. In fact, the overabundance of relational aggression during late elementary school and early adolescence (another intensely frustrating time) may explain why we label these ages as the "meanest" times of life.

Most of us assume relational aggression is more common in girls, but, in research, this "obvious" gender difference does not appear. Yes, overt aggression is severely sanctioned in females, so girls make relational aggression their major mode (Ostrov & Godleski, 2010; Smith, Rose, & Schwartz-Mette, 2010). But as spreading rumors and talking trash about your competitors can be vital to dethroning adversaries and climbing the social ranks, one study showed teenage boys were just as relationally aggressive as teenage girls (Mayeux & Cillessen, 2008)!

aggression Any hostile or destructive act.

proactive aggression A hostile or destructive act initiated to achieve a goal.

reactive aggression A hostile or destructive act carried out in response to being frustrated or hurt.

relational aggression A hostile or destructive act designed to cause harm to a person's relationships.

As he lunges for his friend's book, the boy on the right may feel powerful (*proactive aggression*). But his furious buddy is apt to react by bopping him on the head (*reactive aggression*).

Excluding someone from your group is a classic sign of *relational aggression*—which really gets going in middle childhood. Can you remember being the target of the behavior shown here when you were in fourth or fifth grade?

Table 6.5: Aggression: A Summary of the Types

What Motivated the Behavior?

Proactive aggression: Acts that are actively instigated to achieve a goal.

Examples: "I'll hit Tommy so I can get his toys." "I'll cut off that car so I can get ahead of him." "I want my boss's job, so I'll spread a rumor that he is having an affair."

Characteristics: Emotionally cool and more carefully planned.

Reactive aggression: Acts that occur in response to being frustrated or hurt.

Examples: "Jimmy took my toy, so I'm going to hit him." "That guy shoved me to take my place in line, so I'm going to punch him out." "Joe took my girlfriend, so I'm gonna get a gun and shoot him."

Characteristics: Furious, disorganized, impulsive response.

What Was Its Form?

Direct aggression: Everyone can see it.

Examples: Telling your boyfriend you hate his guts. Beating up someone. Screaming at your mother. Having a tantrum. Bopping a playmate over the head with a toy.

Characteristics: At its peak at about age 2 or 3; declines as children get older. More common in boys than in girls, especially physical aggression.

Relational aggression: Carried out indirectly, through damaging or destroying the victim's relationships.

Examples: "Sara got a better grade than me, so I'm going to tell the teacher that she cheated." "Let's tell everyone not to let Sara play in our group." "I want Sara's job, so I'll spread a rumor that she is stealing money from the company." "I'm going to tell my best friend that her husband is cheating on her because I want to break up their marriage."

Characteristics: Occurs mainly during elementary school and may be at its peak during adolescence, although—as we all know—it's common *throughout* adult life.

Table 6.5 summarizes the different types of aggression and gives examples from childhood and adult life. While scanning the table, notice that we all behave in *every* aggressive way. Also, being aggressive is not "bad." As I just implied, it is vital to making our way in the world. Children who are popular don't abandon being aggressive (Guerra, Williams, & Sadek, 2011; Roseth and others, 2011). Proactive aggression, as you will see later, particularly the relational kind, helps children climb the social ranks (White, Jarrett, & Ollendick, 2013; Rodkin and others, 2013; Waasdorp and others, 2013). Without reactive aggression (fighting back when attacked), our species would never survive. Still, this disorganized, rage-filled aggression definitely doesn't work. Excessive reactive aggression *ensures* having troubles in the social world (White and others, 2013).

Understanding Highly Aggressive Children

You just saw that, as they get older, boys and girls typically get less openly aggressive. However, a percentage of children remain unusually aggressive into elementary school. These children are labeled with externalizing disorders defined by high rates of aggression. They are classified as defiant, antisocial kids.

THE PATHWAY TO PRODUCING PROBLEMATIC AGGRESSION. Longitudinal studies suggest that there may be a poisonous two-step, nature-plus-nurture pathway to being labeled as a highly aggressive child:

STEP 1: The toddler's exuberant (or difficult) temperament evokes harsh discipline. When toddlers are exuberant (Degnan, Almas, & Fox, 2010), temperamentally fearless (Gao and others, 2010), and have problems regulating their attention (Kim & Deater-Deckard, 2011)—recall that caregivers often react by using *power-assertion*

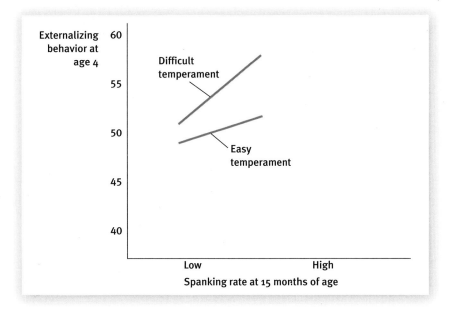

FIGURE 6.2: **The relationship between mothers' reports of spanking at 15 months and externalizing behavior at age 4, for temperamentally difficult and easy children, from a longitudinal study:** In this research, notice that if a child was temperamentally easy, being regularly spanked during toddlerhood slightly increased the risk of having later externalizing problems. However, this discipline style had a huge negative impact on development for toddlers with difficult temperaments. Bottom line: Power assertion is poisonous for a temperamentally at-risk child. Data from: Mulvaney & Mebert, 2007.

discipline—they shame, scream, and hit: "Shut up! You are impossible. You'll get a beating from mom." Physically punishing a "difficult" toddler is apt to back-fire (Boden, Fergusson, & Horwood, 2010; Edwards and others, 2010). Notice, for instance, from scanning the study findings in Figure 6.2, that regularly spanking a difficult 15-month-old magnified that child's risk of developing externalizing problems at age 4. Therefore, unfortunately, the very toddlers who most need sensitive, loving parenting are primed to get the harshest, most punitive care.

STEP 2: The child is rejected by teachers and peers in school. Typically, the transition to being defined as an "antisocial child" occurs during early elementary school. As impulsive, by now clearly aggressive, children travel outside the family, they get rejected by their classmates. Being socially excluded is a powerful stress that provokes paranoia and reactive aggression at any age (DeWall and others, 2009; Lansford and others, 2010). Moreover, because aggressive children *generally* have trouble inhibiting their behavior (Runions & Keating, 2010), during elementary school they may start failing in their academic work (Romano and others, 2010). This amplifies the frustration ("I'm not making it in any area of life!") and compounds the tendency to lash out ("It's their fault, not mine!").

A HOSTILE WORLDVIEW. As I just implied, reactive-aggressive children also think differently in social situations. They may have a **hostile attributional bias** (Crick & Dodge, 1996). They see threat in benign social cues. A boy gets accidentally bumped at the lunch table, and he sees a deliberate provocation. A girl decides that you are her enemy when you look at her the wrong way. So the child's behavior provokes a more hostile world.

To summarize, let's enter the mind of a reactive aggressive child, such as Mark in the opening chapter vignette. As a toddler, your fearless temperament continually got you into trouble with your parents. You have been harshly disciplined for years. In school, you are failing academically and shunned by your classmates. So you never have a chance to interact with other children and improve your social skills. In fact, your hostile attributional bias makes perfect sense. You are living in a "sea of negativity" (Jenson and others, 2004). And yes, the world *is* out to do you in!

hostile attributional bias The tendency of highly aggressive children to see motives and actions as threatening when they are actually benign.

This boy who has been shunned by other children for his disruptive behavior in elementary school may respond by developing a hostile attributional bias, unrealistically feeling that his classmates are out to do him in.

Finally, as you saw in the Chapter 5 discussion of ADHD, there is a gender difference in the risk of being defined as "an acting-out, antisocial child." Because they are more "exuberant" and physical when they play, boys are more likely than girls to show the physically aggressive behavior that gets them labeled with an externalizing problem in elementary school (Vazsonyi & Chen, 2010).

How *do* boys and girls relate when they play? Now, I'll turn to this question and others as we move to part two of this chapter: relationships.

Tying It All Together

1. You interviewed a 4-year-old and a fourth grader for your class project in lifespan development, but mixed up your interview notes. Which statement was made by the 4-year-old?
   a. "My friend Megan is better at math than me."
   b. "Sometimes I get mad at my friends, but maybe it's because I'm too stubborn."
   c. "I have a cat named Kit, and I'm the smartest girl in the world."

2. Identify which of the following boys has internalizing or externalizing tendencies and then, for one of these children, design an intervention using principles spelled out in this section: Ramon sees himself as wonderful, but he is having serious trouble getting along with his teachers and the other kids; Jared is a great student, but when he gets a B instead of an A, he decides that he's "dumb" and gets too depressed to work.

3. Cotonia tells you that children need to be taught to be caring and helpful. Calista disagrees, saying that the impulse to be prosocial is built into human nature. In a sentence or two explain why both statements are correct.

4. A teacher wants to intervene with a student who has been teasing a classmate. Identify which statement is guilt-producing, which is shame-producing, and which involves the use of induction. Then, name which response(s) would promote prosocial behavior.
   a. "Think of how bad Johnny must feel."
   b. "If that's how you act, you can sit by yourself. You're not nice enough to be with the other kids."
   c. "I'm disappointed in you. You are usually such a good kid."

5. Alyssa wants to replace Brianna as Chloe's best friend, so she spreads horrible rumors about Brianna. Brianna overhears Alyssa dissing her and starts slapping Alyssa. Of the four types of aggression discussed in this section—*direct, proactive, reactive, relational*—which two describe Alyssa's behavior, and which two fit Brianna's actions?

6. Mario, a fourth grader, feels that everyone is out to get him. Give the name for Mario's negative worldview.

Answers to the Tying It All Together questions can be found at the end of this chapter.

Relationships

Think back to your days pretending to be a superhero or supermodel, getting together with the girls or boys to play, your best friends, and whether you were popular at school. Now, beginning with play, moving on to the play worlds of girls and boys, then friendships and popularity, and finally tackling bullying—that important contemporary concern—let's explore each relationship-related topic one by one.

Play

rough-and-tumble play
Play that involves shoving, wrestling, and hitting, but in which no actual harm is intended; especially characteristic of boys.

Developmentalists classify children's "free play" (the non-sports-oriented kind) into different categories. **Rough-and-tumble play** refers to the excited shoving, wrestling, and running around that is most apparent with boys. Actually, rough-and-tumble play is classically boy behavior. It seems biologically built into being male (Bjorklund & Pellegrini, 2002; Pellegrini, 2006).

Pretending: The Heart of Early Childhood

Fantasy play, or *pretending,* is different. Here, the child takes a stance apart from reality and makes up a scene, often with a toy or other prop. While fantasy play also can be immensely physical, this "as if" quality makes it unique. Children must pretend to be pirates or superheroes as they wrestle and run. Because fantasy play is so emblematic of early childhood, let's delve into pretending in depth.

THE DEVELOPMENT AND DECLINE OF PRETENDING. Fantasy play first emerges in toddlerhood, as children realize that a symbol can stand for something else. In a classic study, developmentalists watched 1-year-olds with their mothers at home. Although toddlers often initiated a fantasy episode, they needed a parent to expand on the scene (Dunn, Wooding, & Hermann, 1977). So a child would pretend to make a phone call, and his mother would pick up the real phone and say, "Hello, this is Mommy. Should I come home now?"

At about age 3, children transfer the skill of pretending with mothers to peers. **Collaborative pretend play,** or fantasizing *together* with another child, really gets going at about age 4 (Smolucha & Smolucha, 1998). Because they must work together to develop the scene, collaboratively pretending shows that preschoolers have a *theory of mind*—the knowledge that the other person has a different perspective. (You need to understand that your fellow playwright has a different script in his head.) Collaboratively pretending, in turn, helps teach young children the skill of making sense of different minds (Nicolopoulou and others, 2010).

Anyone involved with a young child can see these changes firsthand. When a 2-year-old has his "best friend" over, they play in parallel orbits—if things go well. More likely, a titanic battle erupts, full of proactive and reactive aggression, as each child attempts to gain possession of the toys. By age 4, children can play *together.* At age 5 or 6, they can pretend together for hours—with only a few major fights that are usually resolved.

Although fantasy play can continue into early adolescence, when children reach concrete operations, their interest shifts to structured games (Bjorklund & Pellegrini, 2002). At age 3, a child pretends to bake in the kitchen corner; at 9, he wants to bake a cake. At age 5, you ran around playing pirates; at 9, you tried to hit the ball like the Pittsburgh Pirates do.

THE PURPOSES OF PRETENDING. Interestingly, around the world, when children pretend, their play has similar plots. Let's eavesdrop at a U.S. preschool:

Boy 2: I don't want to be a kitty anymore.

Girl: You are a husband?

Boy 2: Yeah.

Boys 1 and 2: Husbands, husbands! (Yell and run around the play house)

Girl: Hold it, Bill, I can't have two husbands.

Boys 1 and 2: Two husbands! Two husbands!

Girl: We gonna marry ourselves, right?

(adapted from Corsaro, 1985, pp. 102–104)

Why do young children play "family," and assume the "correct" roles when they play mommy and daddy? For answers, let's turn to Lev Vygotsky's insights.

Rough-and-tumble play is not only tremendously exciting, but it seems to be genetically built into being "male."

For these 4-year-old girls (aka women who have dressed up to go to a party), their *collaborative pretend play* is teaching them vital lessons about how to compromise and get along.

fantasy play Play that involves making up and acting out a scenario; also called *pretend play.*

collaborative pretend play Fantasy play in which children work together to develop and act out the scenes.

Play allows children to practice adult roles. Vygotsky (1978) believed that pretending allows children to rehearse being adults. The reason girls pretend to be mommy and baby is that women are the main child-care providers around the world. Boys play soldiers because this activity offers built-in training for the wars they face as adults (Pellegrini & Smith, 2005).

Play allows children a sense of control. As the following preschool conversation suggests, pretending has a deeper psychological function, too:

GIRL 1: Yeah, and let's pretend when Mommy's out until later.

GIRL 2: Ooooh. Well, I'm not the boss around here, though. 'Cause mommies are the bosses.

GIRL 1: (Doubtfully) But maybe we won't know how to punish.

GIRL 2: I will. I'll put my hand up and spank. That's what my mom does.

GIRL 1: My mom does too.

(adapted from Corsaro, 1985, p. 96)

Courtesy of Dr. William Corsaro

Imagine that, like the supersized preschooler shown here (Professor William Corsaro), you could spend years going down slides, playing family, and bonding with 3- and 4-year-olds—and then get professional recognition for your academic work. What an incredible career!

While reading the previous two chapters, you may have been thinking that the so-called carefree early childhood years are hardly free of stress. We expect children to regulate their emotions when their frontal lobes aren't fully functional. We discipline toddlers and preschoolers when they cannot make sense of the mysteries of adult rules. Vygotsky (1978) believed that, in response to this sense of powerlessness, young children enter "an illusory role" in which their desires are realized. In play, *you* can be the spanking mommy or the queen of the castle, even when you are small, and sometimes feel like a slave.

To penetrate the inner world of preschool fantasy play, sociologist William Corsaro (1985, 1997) went undercover, entering a nursery school as a member of the class. (No problem. The children welcomed their new playmate, whom they called Big Bill, as a clumsy, enlarged version of themselves.) As Vygotsky would predict, Corsaro found that preschool play plots often centered on mastering upsetting events. There were separation/reunion scenarios ("Help! I'm lost in the forest." "I'll find you.") and danger/rescue plots ("Get in the house. It's gonna be a rainstorm!"). Sometimes, play scenarios centered on that ultimate frightening event, death:

CHILD 1: We are dead, we are dead! Help, we are dead! (Puts animals on their sides)

CHILD 2: You can't talk if you are dead.

CHILD 1: Oh, well, Leah's talked when she was dead, so mine have to talk when they are dead. Help, help, we are dead!

(adapted from Corsaro, 1985 p. 204)

Notice that these themes are basic to Disney movies and fairy tales. From *Finding Nemo*, *Bambi*, and *The Lion King* to—my personal favorite—*Dumbo*, there is nothing more heart-wrenching than being separated from your parent. From the greedy old witch in *Hansel and Gretel* to the jealous queen in *Sleeping Beauty*, no scenario is as sweet as triumphing over evil and possible death.

Play furthers our understanding of social norms. Corsaro (1985) found that death was a touchy play topic. When children proposed these plots, their partners might try to change the script. This relates to Vygotsky's third insight about play: Although children's play looks unstructured, it has boundaries and rules. Plots involving dead animals waking up make children uncomfortable because they violate the conditions of life. Children get especially uneasy when a play partner proposes scenarios with gory themes, such as cutting off people's heads (Dunn & Hughes, 2001). Therefore, play teaches children how to act and how not to behave. Wouldn't you want to retreat if someone showed an intense interest in decapitation while having a conversation with you?

Evaluating the Impact of Play

Many educators believe fantasy play is vital to developing our social and intellectual skills (see, for instance, Lindsey & Colwell, 2013). They agonize about the Internet revolution, worrying that hours glued to computers are robbing today's preschoolers of the vital lessons that play provides (as reported in Lillard and others, 2013). Is pretend play important to developing a full human being?

In reviewing the data, scientists concluded the jury is out (Lillard and others, 2013). Many studies showing play's value are correlational. So they may be confusing outcomes with causes. If preschoolers who pretend more are advanced socially and cognitively, does pretending cause these benefits, or do these qualities *cause* children to pretend more? Perhaps it is the myriad of adult activities that go along with fantasy play—talking about emotions, reading to a child—that help preschoolers cope with stress and make sense of the puzzling adult world. But even if it's not essential to development, pretending is definitely a main feature of childhood. Moreover, during elementary school, boys and girls play in different ways.

gender-segregated play
Play in which boys and girls associate only with members of their own sex—typical of childhood.

Girls' and Boys' Play Worlds

[Some] girls, all about five and a half years old, are looking through department store catalogues, . . . concentrating on what they call "girls' stuff" and referring to some of the other items as "yucky boys' stuff." . . . Shirley points to a picture of a couch . . . "All we want is the pretty stuff," says Ruth. Peggy now announces, "If you come to my birthday, every girl in the school is invited. I'm going to put a sign up that says, 'No boys allowed!'" "Oh good, good, good," says Vickie. "I hate boys."

(adapted from Corsaro, 1997, p. 155)

Does this conversation bring back childhood memories of being 5 or 6? How does **gender-segregated play** develop? What are the differences in boy versus girl play, and what causes the sexes to separate into these different camps?

Exploring the Separate Societies

Visit a playground and observe children of different ages. Notice that toddlers show no sign of gender-segregated play. In preschool, children start to play mainly in sex-segregated groups (Martin & Ruble, 2010). By elementary school, gender-segregated play is entrenched. On the playground, boys and girls do play in mixed groups (Fabes, Martin, & Hanish, 2003). Still, with friendships, there is a split: boys are typically best friends with boys and girls with girls (Maccoby, 1998).

A visit to this elementary school vividly brings home the fact that middle childhood is traditionally defined by *gender-segregated play.*

Now, go back to the playground and look at the *way* boys and girls relate. Do you notice that boy and girl play differs in the following ways?

BOYS EXCITEDLY RUN AROUND; GIRLS CALMLY TALK. Boys' play is more rambunctious. Even during physical games such as tag, girls play together in calmer, more subdued ways (Maccoby, 1998; Pellegrini, 2006). The difference in activity levels is striking if you have the pleasure of witnessing one gender playing with the opposite sex's toys. In one memorable episode, after my son and a friend invaded a girl's stash of dolls, they gleefully ran around the house bashing Barbie into Barbie and using their booty as swords.

BOYS COMPETE IN GROUPS; GIRLS PLAY COLLABORATIVELY, ONE-TO-ONE. Their exuberant, rough-and-tumble play explains why boys burst on the scene, running and yelling, dominating every room. Another difference lies in playgroup *size.* Boys get together in packs. Girls play in smaller, more intimate groups (Maccoby, 1990, 1998; Ruble, Martin, & Berenbaum, 2006).

Boys and girls also differ in the *way* they relate. Boys try to establish dominance and compete to be the best. This competitive versus cooperative style spills over into children's talk. Girl-to-girl collaborative play really sounds collaborative ("I'll be the doctor, OK?"). Boys give each other bossy commands ("I'm doing the operation. Lie down, now!") (Maccoby, 1998). Girl-to-girl fantasy play involves nurturing themes. Boys prefer the warrior, superhero mode.

The stereotypic quality of girls' fantasy play came as a shock when I spent three days playing with my visiting 7-year-old niece. We devoted day one to setting up a beauty shop, complete with nail polishes and shampoos. We had a table for massages and a makeover section featuring all the cosmetics I owned. Then, we opened for business for the visiting relatives and, (of course!)—by charging for our services—made money for toys. We spent the last day playing with a "pool party" Barbie combo my niece had selected at Walmart that afternoon.

Boys' and girls' different play interests show why the kindergartners in the vignette at the beginning of this section came to hate those "yucky" boys. Another reason why girls turn off to the opposite sex is the unpleasant reception they get from the other camp. In observing at a preschool, researchers found that while active girls played with the boys' groups early in the year, they eventually were rejected and forced to play with their own sex (Pellegrini and others, 2007). Therefore, boys are the first to erect the barriers: "No girls allowed!" Moreover, the gender barriers are *generally* more rigid for males.

BOYS LIVE IN A MORE EXCLUSIONARY, SEPARATE WORLD. My niece did choose to buy Barbies, but she also plays with trucks. She loves soccer and baseball, not just doing her nails. So, even though they may dislike the opposite sex, girls do cross the divide. Boys are more likely to avoid that chasm—refusing to venture down the Barbie aisle or consider buying a toy labeled "girl." So boys live in a more roped-off gender world (Boyle and others, 2003).

Now, you might be interested in what happened during my final day pretending with the pool party toys. After my niece said, "Aunt Janet, let's pretend we are the popular girls," our Barbies tried on fancy dresses ("What shall I wear, Jane?") in preparation for a "popular girls" pool party, where the dolls met up to discuss—*guess what*—where they shopped and who did their hair!

What Causes Gender-Stereotyped Play?

Why do children, such as my niece, play in gender-stereotyped ways? Answers come from exploring three forces: biology (nature), socialization (nurture), and cognitions (or thoughts).

A BIOLOGICAL UNDERPINNING. Ample evidence suggests that gender-segregated play is biologically built in. Children around the world form separate play societies (Maccoby, 1998). Troops of juvenile rhesus monkeys behave *exactly* like human children. The males segregate into their own groups and engage in rough-and-tumble play (Pellegrini, 2006). Grooming activities similar to my niece's beauty-shop behaviors are prominent among young female monkeys, too (Bjorklund & Pellegrini, 2002; Suomi, 2004).

Actually, we can predict male gender-typed play from measuring hormone levels during the first months of life. Researchers looked at the naturally occurring amount of salivary testosterone in 3-month-old boys and girls (females also produce this classic male sex hormone). Remarkably, both sexes with high concentrations of testosterone displayed more male play behaviors at age two (Saenz & Alexander, 2013).

Moreover girls exposed to high levels of testosterone *before birth* show more masculine interests as teens and emerging adults (Udry, 2000)! After taking maternal blood samples during the second trimester—the time, you may recall from Chapter 2, when the neurons are being formed—one researcher tracked the female fetuses of these women for the next two decades.

Females with high levels of prenatal testosterone, he discovered, were more interested in traditionally male occupations, such as engineering, than their lower-hormone-level counterparts. They were less likely to wear makeup. In their twenties, they showed more stereotypically male interests (such as race-car driving). So, in utero testosterone epigenetically affects our DNA—programming a more "feminized" or "masculinized" brain.

THE AMPLIFYING EFFECT OF SOCIALIZATION. The wider world helps biology along. From the images displayed in preschool coloring books (Fitzpatrick & McPherson, 2010) to parents' different toy selections for daughters and sons; from the messages beamed out in television sitcoms (Collins, 2011; Paek, Nelson, & Vilela, 2011) to teachers' differential treatment of boys and girls in school (Chen & Rao, 2011)—everything brings home the message: Males and females act in different ways.

Peers play a powerful role in this programming. When they play in mixed-gender groups, children act in less gender-stereotyped ways (Fabes and others, 2003); with girls, boys tone down their rough-and-tumble activities; girls are less apt to play quietly with dolls when they are pretending with boys. Therefore, the act of splitting into separate play societies trains children to behave in ways typical of their own sex (Martin & Fabes, 2001).

Same-sex playmates reinforce one another for selecting gender-stereotyped activities ("Let's play with dolls." "Great!"). They model one another as they play together in "gentle" or "rough" ways. The pressure to toe the gender line is promoted by social sanctions. Children who behave in "gender atypical ways" (girls who hit a lot or boys who play with dolls) are rejected by their peers (Lee & Troop-Gordon, 2011; Smith and others, 2010).

THE IMPACT OF COGNITIONS. A cognitive process reinforces these external messages. According to **gender schema theory** (Bem, 1981; Martin & Dinella, 2002), once children understand their category (girl or boy), they selectively attend to the activities of their own sex.

When do we first grasp our gender label and start this lifelong practice of modeling our group? The answer is at about age 2 1/2, right after we begin to talk (Martin & Ruble, 2010)! Although they may not learn the real difference until much later (here it helps to have an opposite-sex sibling to see naked), 3-year-olds can tell you that girls have long hair, and cry a lot, while boys fight and play with trucks. At about age 5 or 6, when they are mastering the similar concept of identity constancy (the knowledge that your essential self doesn't change when you dress up in a gorilla costume), children grasp the idea that once you start out as a boy or girl, you stay that way for life (Kohlberg, 1966). However, mistakes are common. I once heard my 5-year-old nephew ask my husband, "Was that jewelry from when you were a girl?"

In sum, my niece's beauty-shop activities had a biological basis, although a steady stream of nurture influences from adults and playmates helped this process along. Identifying herself as "a girl," and then spending hours modeling the women in her life, promoted classically "feminine" sex role behavior, too.

But are the gender norms loosening? U.S. children now feel it's "unfair" to exclude boys from ballet class (Martin & Ruble, 2010). My students today often describe having had good friends of the other sex in elementary school, something that would *never* have occurred when I was a child. Do you think our less gender-defined adult world is reducing the childhood pressures to "act like a girl or boy"? Who were your best friends when you were age 7 or 9?

gender schema theory
Explanation for gender-stereotyped behavior that emphasizes the role of cognitions; specifically, the idea that once children know their own gender label (girl or boy), they selectively watch and model their own sex.

Just imagine the powerful message about traditional female behavior this 5 year old girl is getting from being dressed in pink alongside her mom as they both pore over this pink hued book.

Children spend hours modeling their own sex, demonstrating why *gender schema theory* (the idea "I am a boy" or "I am a girl") also encourages behaving in gender-stereotyped ways.

Friendships

This last question brings me friends. *Why* do children choose specific friends, and what benefits do childhood friendships provide?

The Core Qualities: Similarity, Trust, and Emotional Support

The essence of friendship is feeling similarity (Poulin & Chan, 2010). Children gravitate toward people who are "like them" in interests and activities (Dishion & Tipsord, 2011). In preschool, an active child will tend to make friends with a classmate who likes to run around. A 4-year-old who loves the slide will most likely become best buddies with a child who shares this passion (Rubin, Bukowski, & Parker, 2006).

In elementary school, children choose friends based on deeper similarities , such as shared morals (McDonald and others, 2014; Spencer and others, 2013). ("I like Josiah, because we think the same way about what's right.") As they reach concrete operations, children also develop the concept of loyalty ("I can trust Josiah to stand up for me") and the sense that friends share their inner lives (Hartup & Stevens, 1997; Newcomb & Bagwell, 1995). Listen to these fourth and fifth graders describing their best friend:

> He is my very best friend because he tells me things and I tell him things.

> Me and Tiff share our deepest, darkest secrets and we talk about boys, when we grow up, and shopping.

> Jessica has problems at home and with her religion and when something happens she always comes to me and talks about it. We've been through a lot together.
>
> (quoted in Rose & Asher, 2000, p. 49)

These quotations would resonate with the ideas of personality theorist Harry Stack Sullivan. Sullivan (1953) believed that a chum (or best friend) fulfills the developmental need for self-validation and intimacy that emerges at around age 9. Sullivan also believed that this special relationship serves as a stepping-stone to adult romance.

The Protecting and Teaching Functions of Friends

In addition to offering emotional support and validating us as people, friends stimulate children's personal development in two other ways:

FRIENDS PROTECT AND ENHANCE THE DEVELOPING SELF. Perhaps you noticed this protective function in the quotation above in which the fourth grader spoke about how she helped her best friend when she had problems at home. Friends help insulate children from being bullied at school (Scholte, Sentse, & Granic, 2010). Close friends can even mute children's genetic tendency toward developing depression (Brendgen and others, 2013) or reduce symptoms of ADHD (Becker and others, 2013).

Left: Preschool best friends connect through their shared passion for physical activities such as going down slides. *Right:* In late elementary school, best friends bond by sharing values, secrets and plans.

Mel Yates/Getty Images

Windsor & Wiehahn/Getty Images

FRIENDS TEACH US TO MANAGE OUR EMOTIONS AND HANDLE CONFLICTS. One reason is that friends offer on-the-job training in being our "best"(meaning prosocial) self. Your parents will love you no matter what you do, but the love of a friend is contingent. To keep a friendship, children must dampen down their immediate impulses and attune themselves to the other person's needs (Bukowski, 2001; Denham and others, 2003).

This is not to say that friends are always positive influences. They can bring out a child's worst self by encouraging relational aggression ("We are best friends, so you can't play with us") and daring one another to engage in dangerous behavior ("Let's sneak out of the house at 2 a.m.") Best friends can promote an "us-against-them mentality" and promote a shared, hostile attributional worldview ("It's their fault you are getting into trouble. Only *I* can protect you from the outside world") (Spencer and others, 2013; more about this dark side of friendship in Chapter 9). However, in general, Sullivan may be right: Friends do teach us how to relate as adults.

Popularity

Friendship involves relating with a single person in a close one-to-one way. Popularity is a group concern. It requires rising to the top of the social totem pole.

Although children differ in social status in preschool, you may remember from childhood that "Who is popular?" becomes an absorbing question during later elementary school. Entering concrete operations makes children sensitive to making social comparisons. The urge to rank classmates according to social status is heightened by the confining conditions of childhood itself. In adulthood, popularity fades more into the background because we select our own social circles. Children must make it on a daily basis in a classroom full of random peers.

Who Is Popular and Who Is Unpopular?

How do children vary in popularity during the socially stressful later elementary school years? Here are the main categories researchers find when they ask third, fourth, or fifth graders to list the two or three classmates they like most and really dislike:

- *Popular children* are frequently named in the most-liked category and never appear in the disliked group. They stand out as being really liked by everyone.

- *Average children* receive a few most-liked and perhaps one or two disliked nominations. They rank around the middle range of status in the class.

- *Rejected children* land in the disliked category often and never appear in the preferred list. They stand out among their classmates in a negative way.

What qualities make children popular? What gets elementary schoolers rejected by their peers?

Decoding Popularity

Especially in elementary school, popular children are often friendly and outgoing, prosocial, and kind (Mayberry & Espelage, 2007). However, starting as early as third grade, popularity can be linked to being relationally aggressive (Rodkin & Roisman, 2010; Ostrov and others, 2013).

Figure 6.3, on the next page, based on a study conducted in an inner city school, illustrates this unfortunate truth. Notice that relationally aggressive third to fifth graders were more apt to be rated as popular class leaders. But notice that the association between this poisonous interpersonal form of aggression and popularity was much stronger for girls—which offers insights into why we see relational aggression as mainly a girl activity. Yes, relational aggression gains status for both girls and boys. But this behavior earns females more social mileage than males.

FIGURE 6.3: **How relational aggression related to popularity among 227 elementary schoolers attending a low income, urban school:** In this city school, being relationally aggressive "worked" to make children—both males and females—more popular; but this type of aggression was far, far more often effective at promoting popularity among girls.

Data from: Waasdorp and others, 2013, p. 269.

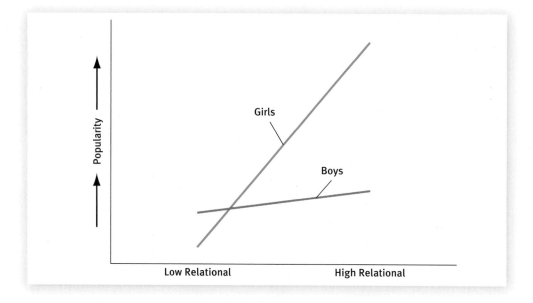

Relational aggression, as you will see in Chapter 9, is especially effective at propelling social mileage during preadolescence, when rebellion is in full flower and the pressure to form status cliques is intense (Werner & Hill, 2010; Witvliet and others, 2010). The good news is that the study described in Table 6.6 shows being in the popular crowd is different from being personally liked.

Table 6.6: Social Goals in Fifth Grade and How They Relate to Peer Preferences a Year Later

1) I like it when I learn new ways to make a friend.

2) I try to figure out what makes for a good friend.

3) I try to get to know other kids better.

4) It's important to me that the other kids think I'm popular.

5) I want to be friendly with the popular kids.

6) It's important to me to have cool friends.

7) It's important to me that I don't embarrass myself around my friends.

8) When I am around other kids, I mostly just try not to goof up.

9) I try to avoid doing things that make me look foolish around other kids.

Researchers had 980 fifth graders fill out these questionnaire items and then charted children's social rankings in the fall and spring of the following year. Boys and girls who checked the yellow items were more likely to ascend the classroom social hierarchy (that was their goal); but children checking the blue items were increasingly preferred as friends. Unfortunately, however, agreeing with the red items predicted being increasingly disliked during the next year.

Data from: Rodkin and others, 2013, p. 1142.

When researchers asked fifth graders questions such as those in the table, and then tracked their social status over time, boys and girls whose agenda was being popular (those agreeing with the yellow items) did rise in the social ranks. But as they reached sixth grade, the class increasingly preferred people with the blue agendas—children with caring, prosocial goals. So, behaving in a caring way is important at every age if we look at what *really* matters: being liked as a human being.

Now let's focus on the third group of kids, fifth graders who checked the red items—children terrified about being embarrassed or socially goofing up. This socially anxious group became more unpopular over time (Rodkin and others, 2013). Who, exactly, do peers reject?

REJECTED CHILDREN HAVE EXTERNALIZING (AND OFTEN INTERNALIZING) PROBLEMS. Actually, the traits that universally land a child into the unpopular, rejected category are externalizing issues. Classmates shun boys and girls (like Mark in the introductory chapter vignette) who make reactive aggression a major life mode as early as age 5 (Hawley and others, 2007; Sturaro and others, 2011). Children with internalizing disorders may or may not be rejected. However, if a child—such as Jimmy in the introductory vignette or the fifth graders who agreed with the red items on the table—is *socially anxious*, that person is apt to be avoided as early as first grade (Degnan and others, 2010).

Moreover, a poisonous nature-evokes-nurture interaction can set in when a child enters school extremely socially shy. As children pick up on the fact that people are avoiding them, their shyness gets more intense. So they become less socially competent—and increasingly likely to be rejected (and, as you will see, victimized)—as they advance from grade to grade (Booth-LaForce & Oxford, 2008).

A bidirectional process is also occurring. The child's anxiety makes other children nervous. They get uncomfortable and want to retreat when they see this person approach. In response to your own awkward encounters, have you ever been tempted to walk in the opposite direction when you saw a very shy person approaching in the hall?

REJECTED CHILDREN DON'T FIT IN WITH THE DOMINANT GROUP. Children who stand out as different are also at risk of being rejected: boys and girls (like Moriah in the opening vignette) who don't fit the gender stereotypes (Lee & Troop-Gordon, 2011); low-income children in middle-class schools (Zettergren, 2007); immigrant children in ethnically homogenous societies (Strohmeier, Kärnä, & Salmivalli, 2010)—any child whom classmates label as "different," "weird," or "not like us."

Exploring the Fate of the Rejected

Is childhood rejection a prelude to poor adult mental health? The answer is "sometimes." Highly physically aggressive children are at risk for getting into trouble—at home, in school, and with the law—during adolescence and in their adult years (Alatupa and others, 2013; more about this pathway in Chapter 9). Unfortunately, one longitudinal study suggested that women who were unpopular as preteens had high rates of anxiety disorders and depression during midlife (Modin, Östberg, & Almquist, 2011).

But there is variability, especially if a child has been rejected due to being "different" from the group. Consider an awkward little girl named Eleanor Roosevelt, who was socially rejected at age 8, or a boy named Thomas Edison, whose preference for playing alone got him defined as a "problem" child. Because they were so different, these famous adults were dismal failures during elementary school. To get insights into the fleeting quality of childhood peer status, you might organize a reunion of your fifth- or sixth-grade class. You might be surprised at how many unpopular classmates flowered during their high school or college years.

His shyness may set this boy up for social rejection because his anxiety will make the other children uneasy and he may not have the courage to reach out to his classmates.

Photography by Mijang Ka/Getty Images

Because he prefers to hang back and observe the group scene from afar, this cerebral boy is not winning popularity contests in fourth grade. But, the same introspective qualities that are giving him problems in elementary school might produce a world-class author or brilliant psychologist during adult life.

© Daniel Atkin/Alamy

Bullying: A Core Contemporary Childhood Concern

> You can get bullied because you are weak or annoying or because you are different. Kids with big ears get bullied. Dorks get bullied. . . . Teacher's pet gets bullied. If you say the right answer in class too many times, you can get bullied.
>
> (quoted in Guerra and others, 2011, p. 306)

bullying A situation in which one or more children (or adults) harass or target a specific child for systematic abuse.

bully-victims Exceptionally aggressive children (with externalizing disorders) who repeatedly bully and get victimized.

Children who are different can excel in the proving ground of life. This is not the case on the proving ground of the playground. As you just read, being different, weak, socially awkward, or even "too good" is a recipe for **bullying**—being teased, made fun of, and verbally or physically abused by one's peers.

As I implied earlier, bullying is "normal" as children jockey for power and status in the group. But the roughly 10 to 20 percent of children subject to chronic harassment fall into two categories. The first—the less common type—are **bully-victims.** These children are highly aggressive boys and girls who bully, get harassed, then bully again in an escalating cycle of pain (Deater-Deckard and others, 2010; Waasdorp and others, 2011). The classic victim, however, has internalizing issues (Crawford & Manassis, 2011). These children are anxious, shy, low on the social hierarchy, and unlikely to fight back (Cook and others, 2010; Degnan and others, 2010; Scholte and others, 2010; also, see my personal confession in the Experiencing the Lifespan box).

Home used to be a refuge for children harassed at school. No more! Facebook, cell phones, and the Internet have made bullying a 24/7 concern.

Experiencing the Lifespan: Middle-Aged Reflections on My Middle-Childhood Victimization

It was a hot August afternoon when the birthday present arrived. As usual, I was playing alone that day, maybe reading or engaging in a favorite pastime, fantasizing that I was a princess while sitting in a backyard tree. The gift, addressed to Janet Kaplan, was beautifully wrapped—huge but surprisingly light. This is amazing! I must be special! Someone had gone to such trouble for me! When I opened the first box, I saw another carefully wrapped box, and then another, smaller box, and yet another, smaller one inside. Finally, surrounded by ribbons and wrapping paper, I eagerly got to the last box and saw a tiny matchbox—which contained a small burnt match.

Around that time, the doorbell rang, and Cathy, then Ruth, then Carol, bounded up. "Your mother called to tell us she was giving you a surprise birthday party. We had to come over right away and be sure to wear our best dresses!" But their excitement turned to disgust when they learned that no party had been arranged. My ninth birthday was really in mid-September—more than a month away. It turned out that Nancy and Marion—the two most popular girls in class—had masterminded this relational aggression plot directed at me.

Why was I selected as the victim among the other third-grade girls? I had never hurt Nancy or Marion. In fact, in confessing their role, they admitted to some puzzlement: "We really don't dislike Janet at all." Researching this chapter has offered me insights into the reasons for this 60-year-old wound.

Although I did have friends, I was fairly low in the classroom hierarchy. Not only was I shy, but I was that unusual girl—a child who genuinely preferred to play alone. But most important, I was the perfect victim. I dislike competitive status situations. When taunted or teased, I don't fight back.

As an older woman, I still dislike status hierarchies and social snobberies. I'm not a group (or party) person. I far prefer talking one-to-one. I am happy to spend hours alone. Today, I consider these attributes a plus (after all, having no problem sitting by myself for many thousands of hours was a prime skill that allowed me to write this text!), but they caused me anguish in middle childhood. In fact, when I'm in status-oriented peer situations even today—as a widowed older woman—I still find myself occasionally getting teased by the group!

(P.S. I can honestly tell you that what happened to me in third grade is irrelevant to my life. I can't help wondering, though. Suppose, as would be likely today, my classmates had been invited to my so-called birthday via Facebook: "Janet is having a party, and she is inviting X, Y, and Z." Could being targeted through this humiliating, public venue have caused more enduring emotional scars?)

Hot in Developmental Science: **Cyberbullying**

Cyberbullying, aggressive behavior repeatedly carried out via electronic media is potentially more toxic than traditional bullying in several ways: Broadcasting demeaning comments on Facebook ensures a large, amorphous audience that multiplies the victim's distress. Sending a text anonymously can be scarier than confronting the person face to face. ("Who hates me this much?" "Perhaps it's someone I trusted as a friend?") (See Sticca & Perren, 2013.)

    Moreover, the temptation to bully on-line is easier emotionally, as it removes all inner controls. You can lash out and be free from immediate consequences (Runions, 2013). You don't have to worry about the sympathy (and guilt) linked to seeing your victim's pained face.

    Cyberbullying's ease, nonstop quality, and scary public nature explain why teens see this behavior as worse than traditional bullying (Sticca & Perren, 2013). In one study of Canadian adolescents, involvement in cyberbullying—either as a perpetrator or victim—predicted having internalizing difficulties over and above participating in traditional harassing acts (Bonanno & Hymel, 2013).

    Still, the same motives propel both cyberbullying and harassment of the face-to-face kind: Kids bully for revenge (as reactive aggression, or to get back at someone). Kids bully for recreation (for fun). Kids bully because this activity offers social rewards, or reinforcement from one's peers (Runions, 2013).

    Actually, bullying—of any kind—often demands an appreciative audience. One person (or a few people) does the harassing, while everyone else eggs the perpetrator on by laughing, posting similar comments on-line, or passively standing by. Therefore, children are less apt to bully when their classmates don't condone this behavior (Christian Elledge and others, 2013; Elsaesser, Gorman-Smith, & Henry, 2013; Hinduja & Patchin, 2013). Conversely, when bullying is frequent in a given classroom, or the class norm supports relational aggression, *everyone* is prone to bullying *regardless of whether or not people personally believe this behavior is wrong* (Scholte and others, 2010; Werner & Hill, 2010).

    The fact that the nicest children bully if the atmospheric conditions are right explains why school programs to attack bullying focus on changing the peer-group norms.

cyberbullying Systematic harassment conducted through electronic media.

Imagine how you would feel if this terrifying, anonymous threat appeared on your screen, and you will immediately understand why cyberbullying is more distressing than bullying of the face-to-face kind.

INTERVENTIONS: **Attacking Bullying and Helping Rejected Children**

In the Olweus Bully Prevention Program, for example, administrators plan a school assembly to discuss bullying early in the year. Then, they form a bullying-prevention committee composed of children from each grade. Teachers and students are kept on high alert for bullying in their classes. The goal is to develop a school-wide norm to not tolerate peer abuse (Olweus, Limber, & Mihalic, 1999).

    Do the many bullying-prevention programs now in operation work? The answer is: "Yes, to some extent" (Espelage & De La Rue, 2013). But, as bullying or relational aggression is such an effective way of gaining status (Witvliet and others, 2010), this phenomenon, present at *every age*, is a bit like bad weather—not in our power to totally control (Guerra and others, 2011).

    That's why I'd like to end this chapter by returning to the classic recipients of this unfortunate, universal human activity—children who are socially shy. How can we help these boys and girls succeed?

    In following a group of shy 5-year-olds, researchers found that if a child developed friends in kindergarten or first grade, that boy or girl became less socially anxious over time (Gazelle & Ladd, 2003). So, to help a temperamentally anxious child, parents

U.S. Department of Defense

What was this incredibly brave prosocial soldier really like at age 1 or 2? Probably a fearless handful!

need to immediately connect their son or daughter—preferably in preschool—with a playmate who might become a close friend.

With toddlers at risk for externalizing disorders, as I've stressed earlier, providing loving, sensitive parenting is just as important (see Kochanska and others, 2010b). Adults also need to understand that, with active explorers, the same traits that *can* spell trouble can also be potential life assets. In an amazing decades-long study, when researchers measured temperament during infancy and then looked at personality during adulthood, the *one* quality that predicted being highly competent at age 40 was having been rated fearless during the first year of life (Blatney, Jelinek, & Osecka, 2007). So with the right person–environment fit, a "difficult to tame" toddler may turn into a caring soldier or a true prosocial hero, like the firefighters on 9/11!

How important are peer groups versus parents in shaping our behavior? What can schools do to generally help children thrive? Stay tuned as I delve into these questions—and related topics—in the next chapter, which is devoted to home and school.

Tying It All Together

1. When Melanie and Miranda play, they love to make up pretend scenes together. Are these two girls likely to be about age 2, age 5, or age 9?

2. In watching boys and girls at recess in an elementary school, which two observations are you likely to make?

   a. The boys are playing in larger groups.
   b. Both girls and boys love rough-and-tumble play.
   c. The girls are quieter and they are doing more negotiating.

3. Erik and Maria are arguing about the cause of gender-stereotyped behavior. Erik says the reason why boys like to run around and play with trucks is biological. Sophia argues that gender-stereotyped play is socialized by adults and other children. First, argue Erik's position and then, make Sophia's case by referring to specific data in this section.

4. Best friends in elementary school (pick false statement): *support each other/have similar moral values/encourage good behavior.*

5. Describe in a sentence or two the core difference between being popular and well liked.

6. Which of the following children is NOT at risk of being rejected in later elementary school?

   a. Miguel, a shy, socially anxious child
   b. Lauren, a tomboy who hates "girls' stuff"
   c. Nicholas, who lashes out in anger randomly at other kids
   d. Elaine, who is relationally aggressive

7. (a) If a child (or adult) is being regularly bullied, name the core qualities that may be making this person an easy target. (b) Then, based on what you just read, describe in a sentence what you personally might do to change this situation.

Answers to the Tying It All Together questions can be found at the end of this chapter.

SUMMARY

Setting the Challenge: Emotion Regulation

Emotion regulation, the ability to manage and control our feelings, is crucial to having a successful life. Children with **externalizing tendencies** often "act out their emotions" and behave aggressively. Children with **internalizing tendencies** have problems managing intense fear. Both temperamental tendencies, at their extreme, cause problems during childhood.

Personality (and the Emerging Self)

Self-awareness changes dramatically as children move into middle childhood. Concrete operational children think about themselves in psychological terms, realistically scan their abilities, and evaluate themselves in comparison with peers. These realistic self-perceptions explain why **self-esteem** normally declines during elementary school. Comparing Erikson's early childhood task (**initiative versus guilt**) with **industry versus inferiority** highlights the message that, in middle childhood, we fully wake up to the realities of life. Relationships, academics, behavior, sports, and looks are the five areas from which elementary schoolchildren derive their self-esteem.

Children with externalizing tendencies minimize their difficulties with other people and may have unrealistically high self-esteem. Children with internalizing tendencies may develop **learned helplessness,** the feeling that they are incapable of doing well. Because both attitudes keep children from improving their behavior, the key to helping *every* child is to focus on enhancing self-efficacy, promote realistic views of the self, and offer love.

Prosocial behaviors—helping, comforting, and sharing acts—seem built into our biology and appear spontaneously during toddlerhood. There also is consistency, with prosocial preschoolers tending to be prosocial later on. While girls may be more attuned than boys to upsetting feelings, females are not necessarily more prosocial than males.

Acting prosocially—at older ages—involves transforming one's **empathy** (directly experiencing another's feelings) into **sympathy** (feeling for another person), having the information processing skills to decide when to be prosocial, feeling you can effectively offer help, and being happy. Promote prosocial behavior by allowing the child to naturally experience the joy of performing prosocial acts, model caring in your relationships, define the child as "a good person," and use **induction** (get a child who has behaved hurtfully to understand the other person's feelings). Induction helps because it induces **guilt.** Child-rearing techniques involving **shame** (personal humiliation) backfire, making children angry and less likely to act in prosocial ways.

Aggression, or hurtful behavior, is also basic to being human. Rates of open aggression (hitting, yelling) dramatically decline as children get older. **Proactive aggression** is hurtful behavior we initiate. **Reactive aggression** occurs in response to being frustrated or hurt. **Relational aggression** refers to acts of aggression designed to damage social relationships. Relational aggression increases during late elementary school and middle school, and is present in girls and boys. High levels of reactive aggression present problems getting along in the world.

A two-step pathway may produce a highly aggressive child. When toddlers are very active (exuberant) or difficult, caregivers may respond harshly and punitively—causing anger and aggression. Then, during school, the child's "bad" behavior causes social rejection which leads to more reactive aggression. Highly aggressive children may have a **hostile attributional bias.** This "the world is out to get me" outlook is understandable since aggressive children may have been living in a rejecting environment since their earliest years. Because boys tend to act out their feelings, they are more likely to be diagnosed as having "problematic aggression" than are girls.

Relationships

Play is at the heart of childhood. **Rough-and-tumble play** (play fighting and wrestling), is typical of boys. **Fantasy play** or pretending—typical of all children—begins in later infancy and becomes mutual at about age 4, with the beginning of **collaborative pretend play.** Fantasy play declines during concrete operations, as children become interested in organized activities.

Fantasy play may help children practice adult roles; offer a sense of control; and teach the need to adhere to norms and rules. Although educators view fantasy play as vitally important, the idea that pretending is critical to children's development has yet to be proved.

Gender-segregated play unfolds during preschool, and in elementary school girls and boys typically play mainly with their own sex. Boy-to-boy play is rambunctious, while girls play together in quiet, collaborative ways. Boys tend to compete in groups; girls play one-to-one. Boys' play is more excluding of girls. Gender-stereotyped play seems to have a biological basis, as shown by the fact that high testosterone levels during our early months and in utero promote stereotypically male behaviors. It is also socialized by adults and by peers as children play together in same-sex groups. According to **gender schema theory,** once children understand that they are a boy or a girl, they attend to and model behaviors of their own sex.

In childhood (and adulthood) we select friends who are similar to ourselves, and when children get older, deeper qualities, such as sharing feelings, having similar moral worldviews, and loyalty, become important. Friends provide children with emotional support and teach us to modulate our emotions.

While popular children are often prosocial, relational aggression helps children gain status. Still, being kind—not relationally aggressive—gets children well liked by their peers. Rejected children are disliked—either because of serious externalizing or internalizing problems, or because they are different from the group. Although unpopular children are at risk for later problems, children who are rejected for being different may flower as adults.

Children who are unpopular—either aggressive **bully-victims** or, more typically, shy, anxious kids—are vulnerable to chronic **bullying.** Its anonymous, 24/7 public nature makes **cyberbullying** more toxic than face-to-face harassment. Because bullying of any kind depends on peer reinforcement, school bully prevention programs work to change the class norms favoring relational aggression. To help socially anxious children, connect timid preschoolers with a friend. Give at-risk exuberant toddlers lots of love, and understand that these "difficult" girls and boys can flourish in the right environment.

KEY TERMS

ANSWERS TO Tying It All Together QUIZZES

Setting the Challenge: Emotion Regulation

1. Paul has *externalizing tendencies;* Jeremy has *internalizing tendencies;* and issues with emotion regulation are problems for *both* boys.

Personality (and the Emerging Self)

1. c

2. Ramon = externalizing tendencies. Jared = internalizing tendencies. *Suggested intervention for Ramon:* Point out his realistic problems ("You are having trouble in X, Y, Z areas."), but cushion criticisms with plenty of love. *Suggested intervention for Jared:* Continually point out reality ("No one can always get A's. In fact, you are a fabulous student."). Get

Jared to identify his "hopeless and helpless" ways of thinking, and train him to substitute more accurate perceptions.

3. Calista is right that the impulse to be prosocial seems biologically built in, as toddlers get joy from spontaneously performing helpful acts. Cotonia is correct, however, that adults need to nurture this behavior by modeling caring acts, being sensitive to a child's emotions, defining the child as good, and using induction.

4. a = induction; good for promoting prosocial behavior; b = shame; bad strategy; and c = guilt; good for promoting prosocial behavior

5. Alyssa = proactive, relational. Brianna = direct, reactive

6. Mario has a hostile attributional bias.

Relationships

1. About age 5

2. a and c

3. Erik can argue that gender-stereotyped play must be biologically built in, as this behavior occurs in primates and appears in societies around the world. He can mention that masculine-type play and interests are programmed by high levels of testosterone. Sophia can say differing gender roles are strongly socialized by parents, teachers, and media messages from a young age. Most important, peers powerfully reinforce traditional "girl" or "boy" behavior as they segregate into same-sex play groups. Children are highly motivated to conform to these "correct" ways of acting or risk being socially excluded.

4. Friends can promote negative behavior (third alternative is wrong).

5. Being popular refers to being in the in-group. But being in the high-status crowd does not necessarily mean a child is personally well liked by the other kids.

6. d. (Unfortunately, relationally aggressive children can be popular.)

7. (a) She may be highly aggressive, and is bullied, then victimized. Or, more typically, she is anxious, has few friends, and has trouble standing up for herself. (b) Speak up against the perpetrators while the group is around, or—if the situation involves cyberbullying—post a comment on-line, telling the writer to "lay off X. He is a real prince."

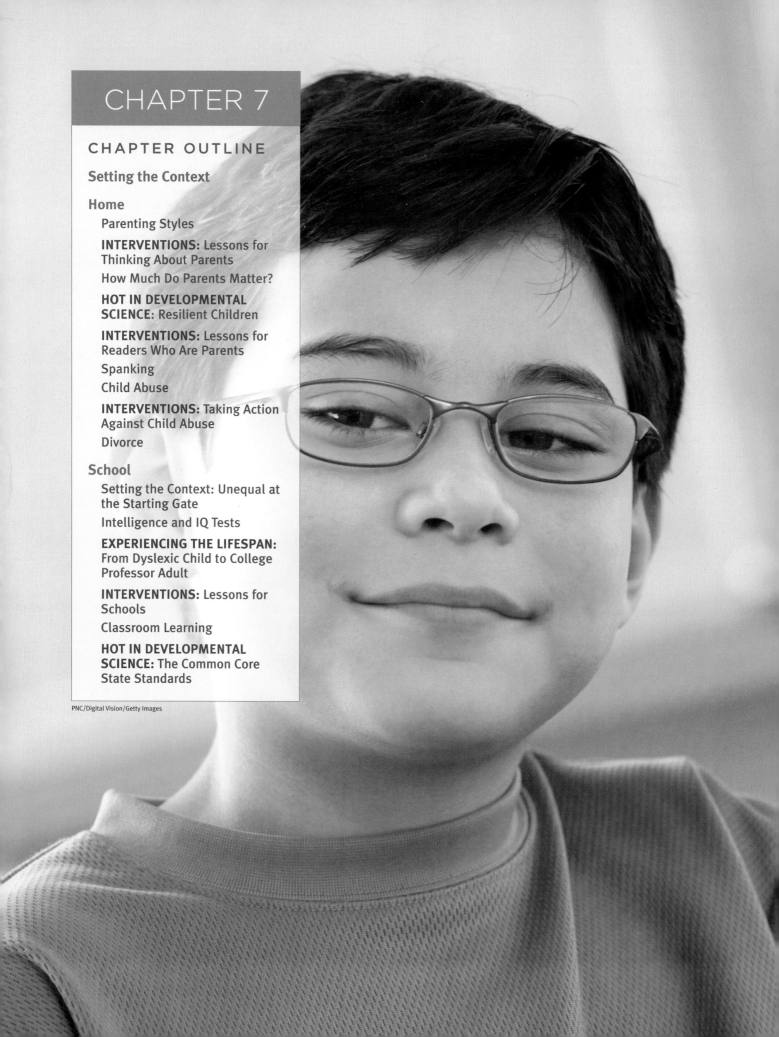

CHAPTER 7

CHAPTER OUTLINE

Settings for Development: Home and School

Josiah's parents migrated from Honduras to Las Vegas when he was a baby. Leaving their close, extended family was painful, but they knew their son would not have a future in their dangerous town.

At first, life was going well. Manuel joined the Culinary Workers' Union. Maria got a housekeeping job at Caesar's Palace. They sent money to relatives and made a down payment on a condo in the best school district in the city. Liberated from the horrifying conditions in her country, where parents had to confine their children to the house to keep them safe, Maria was thrilled to relax and lavish love on her child. Lavishing love was easy, because Maria was blessed to have such a sunny, talented boy. At age 5, Josiah could repair household appliances. He put together puzzles that would stump children twice his age. He was picking up English beautifully, even though his parents, who only spoke Spanish, could not help him with school.

Then, when Josiah was 7, Manuel was laid off. He started to drink. He came home late to regularly yell at his wife. Maria fell into a depression, agonizing over whether to break her family apart. When she finally had that difficult conversation: "Dad and I will be living separately," Josiah cried for months. This painful talk couldn't have been more poorly planned. The next day, Josiah was tested for the gifted program at school.

Josiah's block design performance was off the charts. But growing up in a Spanish-speaking family was a handicap. Josiah's full-scale score didn't make the cut off, because his vocabulary skills were still below the mean.

It's three years later and Maria's becoming the loving mother she used to be. Josiah is returning to his old, delightful self. Maria sings the praises of the fourth-grade teacher—for understanding her son's gifts and having the know-how to implement the Common Core State Standards. She appreciates the fact that due to the new state custody laws, Josiah can spend as much time as he wants at his father's house. (Actually, she hates to admit it, but Manuel is a good dad!) The thorn in Maria's side is Grandma—or, to be exact, Josiah's attitude toward Grandma. Having her mother in the house is a godsend. Josiah doesn't have to stay home alone when Maria works double shifts to keep the family above the poverty line. But Josiah now feels ashamed to bring friends home to see that "Old World" lady. He wants to be a regular American boy. The downside of seeing your baby blossom beautifully in this country is watching your heritage fade.

How do children such as Josiah react after their parents get divorced? Given that we must succeed in the world, how important are the lessons we learn from our parents as opposed to our peers? What was that test Josiah took, and what strategies can teachers use to make every child eager to learn. What *are* the U.S. Common Core State Standards all about? Now, we tackle these questions, and others, as I focus on the settings within which children develop: home and school.

While my discussion applies to all children, in every home and school, in this chapter, I'll pay special attention to children such as Josiah, whose families differ from the traditional two-parent, middle-class, European American norm. So let's begin our exploration of home and school by scanning the tapestry of families in the twenty-first-century United States.

Setting the Context

As of 2012, the *traditional nuclear family*—heterosexual married couples with biological children—had dwindled to less than half of U.S. households. Of these, a significant percent were *blended families*—spouses divorced and remarried—so children had stepparents and, often, stepsiblings. Five percent of U.S. children were raised by unmarried couples; two million had gay or bisexual parents; a smaller but growing number of boys and girls (1.3 million) were being brought up by their grandparents alone (Healthychildren.org, n.d.).

The most important distinction relates to the 1 in 4 U.S. children being raised by single parents (see Figure 7.1). In particular, in motherheaded families, poverty is not an infrequent fate—2 out of 5 of these children live under the poverty line (see Vespa, Lewis, & Kreider, 2013).

On a brighter note, due to a global influx of immigrants, the developed world is blessed with a beautiful mosaic of ethnicities. What is your country of origin? What generation American, or Australian, or Scandinavian are you?

Comstock/Stockbyte/Getty Images

Parenting grandmothers, such as this woman helping her grandson with his homework, show that strong, loving families come in many forms. What exactly is this grandma doing right? This is the question we will explore in this next section.

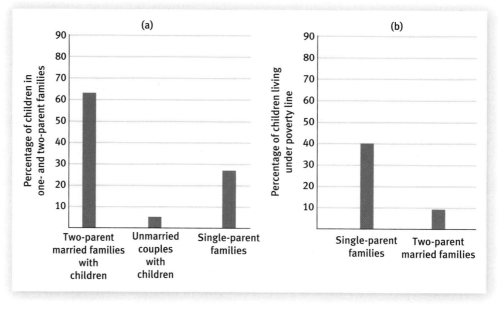

FIGURE 7.1: **Living arrangements of children in U.S. families:** Chart (a) shows that the two-parent married couple family is still the most common one—a family form that includes the traditional nuclear family and nontraditional forms. Chart (b) shows that children who live in single-mother families have roughly four times the odds of living under the poverty line as boys and girls whose parents are married.
Source: Vespa and others, 2013.

Home

Can children thrive in every family? The answer is yes. The key lies in what parents do. We know that parents need to promote a secure attachment and be sensitive to a child's temperamental needs. Is there an overall discipline style that works best? In landmark studies conducted 40 years ago, developmentalist Diana Baumrind (1971) decided yes.

Parenting Styles

Think of a parent you admire. What is that mother or father doing right? Now think of parents who you feel are not fulfilling this job. Where are they falling short? Most likely, your list will center on two functions. Are these people nurturing? Do they provide discipline or rules? By classifying parents on these two dimensions—being child-centered, and giving "structure"—Baumrind (1971) and other researchers spelled out the following **parenting styles:**

- **Authoritative parents** rank high on nurturing and setting limits. They set clear standards for their children but also provide some freedom and lots of love. In this house, there are specific bed and homework times. However, if a daughter wants to watch a favorite TV program, these parents might relax the rule that homework must be finished before dinner. They could let a son extend his regular 9:00 p.m. bedtime for a special event. Although authoritative parents believe in structure, they understand that rules don't take precedence over human needs.

- **Authoritarian parents** are more inflexible. Their child-rearing motto is, "Do just what I say." In these families, rules are not negotiable. While authoritarian parents may love their children deeply, their child-rearing style can seem inflexible, rigid, and cold.

- **Permissive parents** are at the opposite end of the spectrum from authoritarian parents. Their parenting mantra is, "Provide total freedom and unconditional love." In these households, there may be no set bedtimes and no homework demands. The child-rearing principle here is that children's wishes rule.

- **Rejecting-neglecting parents** are the worst of both worlds—low on structure and on love. In these families, children are neglected, ignored, and emotionally abandoned. They are left to raise themselves (see Figure 7.2 for a recap).

In relating the first three discipline studies to children's behavior (the fourth was added later), Baumrind found that children with authoritative parents were more successful and socially skilled. Hundreds of twentieth-century studies confirmed this finding: Authoritative parenting works best (Maccoby & Martin, 1983).

Decoding Parenting in a Deeper Way

At first glance, Baumrind's authoritative category offers a beautiful blueprint for the right way to raise children: Provide structure and lots of love. However, if you classify your parents along these dimensions, you may find problems. Perhaps one parent was permissive and another authoritarian. Or, your families' rules might randomly vary from authoritative to permissive over time.

According to one global study, the worst situation—in terms of a teenager's mental health—occurs when families have inconsistent rules (Dwairy, 2010). If one parent is more authoritarian and the other permissive, you do have predictability ("I can get away with things with Mom, but not with Dad"), although you might feel a bit upset. But imagine how disoriented you would be if your parents sometimes came down very hard on you and, in *similar situations*, seemed not to care. Rather than adhering to a single parenting style, parents should provide a *consistent* roadmap for their child.

But aren't there times when parenting styles should vary, or situations when every child *needs* a more authoritarian or permissive approach? These questions bring me to two other classic parenting styles critiques:

CRITIQUE 1: PARENTING STYLES VARY FROM CHILD TO CHILD AND MAY SHIFT AT DIFFERENT LIFE STAGES. Perhaps your parents came down harder on a brother or sister because that sibling needed more discipline, while your personality flourished with a permissive style. As you learned earlier in this book, good parents *should* vary their child-rearing, depending on the unique personality of a specific child.

parenting style In Diana Baumrind's framework, how parents align on two dimensions of child-rearing: nurturance (or child-centeredness) and discipline (or structure and rules).

authoritative parents In the parenting-styles framework, the best possible child-rearing style, in which parents rank high on both nurturance and discipline, providing both love and clear family rules.

authoritarian parents In the parenting-styles framework, a type of child-rearing in which parents provide plenty of rules but rank low on child-centeredness, stressing unquestioning obedience.

permissive parents In the parenting-styles framework, a type of child-rearing in which parents provide few rules but rank high on child-centeredness, being extremely loving but providing little discipline.

rejecting-neglecting parents In the parenting-styles framework, the worst child-rearing approach, in which parents provide little discipline and little nurturing or love.

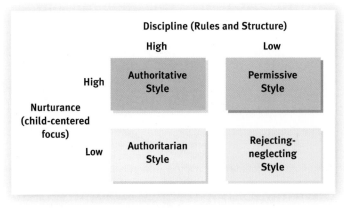

FIGURE 7.2: **Parenting styles:** A summary diagram.
Source: Adapted from Baumrind, 1971.

Unfortunately, however, as you also learned in previous chapters, when children are "high maintenance" (difficult to raise), due to an *evocative process*, parenting styles are apt to change for the worse. A mom may become excessively controlling (authoritarian) when her child has a chronic illness (Pinquart, 2013). She might yell, scream, and wall herself off emotionally from a son or daughter with ADHD (Gau & Chang, 2013).

A study conducted in Finland suggested mothers were most likely to retreat into walled-off, distant caregiving when raising a temperamentally grumpy child (Laukkanen and others, 2014). Therefore, it makes sense that U.S. researchers find that parents are most likely to abandon being authoritative when their sons and daughters reach adolescence—that grumpier, less compliant life stage. Interestingly, this U.S. study showed, when caregivers did withdraw emotionally during puberty, preteens were most at risk for delinquency later on (Schroeder & Mowen, 2014).

So again, parenting is far more "bidirectional" (and child evoked) than Baumrind assumes. Moreover, parents are apt to become less loving in the very situations when children need extra loving the most. Does adopting a rule-focused, authoritarian parenting style *ever* work best?

CRITIQUE 2: PARENTING STYLES CAN VARY DEPENDING ON ONE'S SOCIETY.

Baumrind's styles perspective, developmentalists point out, reflects a Western middle-class perspective on child-rearing. Yes, we think structure (rules) is vital, but we put a premium on loving and listening to our sons and daughters. If you know families from Korea or China, or Latinos or African Americans, you may be struck by the more authoritarian agendas of these moms and dads: "Be obedient," "Don't talk back," "I make the rules" (Fuller & García Coll, 2010; Mistry, Chaudhuri, & Diez, 2003).

This cultural difference, specifically in Asian parenting, was spelled out in a controversial book called *The Battle Hymn of The Tiger Mother* (2011). Amy Chua, a second-generation Chinese American parent, made the case that, in contrast to our laid-back democratic style, "traditional Chinese" parenting was superior at producing a high-achieving child (see Chua, 2011; Lui & Rollock, 2013).

Do Asian-heritage U.S. parents *typically* adopt Chua's authoritarian parenting style? If we consider first-generation immigrants (Nomaguchi & House, 2013) or people living in ethnically homogenous enclaves such as urban Chinatowns (Lee and others, 2014), the answer is yes. But, in contrast to our stereotypes, Asian American parents are normally not more authoritarian than anyone else (Choi and others, 2013; Kim and others, 2013). In fact, if you grew up in India, you would probably have been raised more "permissively" than a European-heritage child born in the United States! (See Barnhart and others, 2013; Ferguson and others, 2013.)

Should Western parents adopt Chua's rule-oriented child-rearing advice? The answer is definitely no. Among contemporary Asian families—both in the United States (Lee and others, 2014; Kim and others, 2013) and Japan (Uji and others, 2014)—authoritative parenting is correlated with superior child mental health.

In the past, parents needed to act authoritarian to socialize their children for life in harsh, dictatorial societies or protect their offspring from the horrors of war or disease. In dangerous places today, such as El Salvador, people still report reluctantly using these rigid child-rearing techniques. As one mother in this violence-wracked nation bemoaned: ". . . I do not let my son go outside . . . . I think we have become overprotective against our will" (Rojas-Flores and others, 2013, p. 278). But in the contemporary West, having "authoritarian values" is a symptom of feeling unhappier and more stressed out in the parenting role (Nomaguchi & House, 2013).

Hero Images/Getty Images

The stereotype is that this mother should be raising her child using an authoritarian style. The reality is that this Indian mom's childrearing approach is apt to be more permissive than ours!

INTERVENTIONS: **Lessons for Thinking About Parents**

How can you use these insights to think about parents in a more empathic way?

- Understand that parenting styles don't operate in a vacuum. They vary depending on a family's unique life situation and a unique child.

- Understand that retreating emotionally is normal when dealing with a child who has problems, but realize that in our culture, adopting this distant, authoritarian style signals parenting distress.

- Rather than accusing parents of being "soft" or permissive, celebrate the fact that today we *can* be child-centered, in the sense of listening empathically to our daughters and sons. Without minimizing the need for consistent rules, ideal twenty-first-century parenting boils down to three joyous principles: "Listen, nurture, offer lots of love!"

Table 7.1 gives you a chance to step back and list your specific parenting priorities in a deeper way. Let's now consider that deeper philosophical question: Is parenting critically important to how children turn out?

Table 7.1: Checklist for Identifying Your Parenting Priorities

Rank the following goals in order of their importance to you, from 1 (for highest priority) to 8 (for lowest priority). It's OK to use the same number twice if two goals are equally important to you.

_____ Producing an obedient, well-behaved child

_____ Producing a caring, prosocial child

_____ Producing an independent, self-sufficient child

_____ Producing a child who is extremely close to you

_____ Producing an intelligent, creative thinker

_____ Producing a well-rounded child

_____ Producing a happy, emotionally secure child

_____ Producing a spiritual (religious) child

What do your rankings reveal about the qualities you most admire in human beings?

How Much Do Parents Matter?

The most inspiring place to start is with those world-class role models who had terrible childhoods, but succeeded brilliantly as adults.

 Hot in Developmental Science: Resilient Children

His aristocratic parents spent their time gallivanting around Europe; they never appeared at the nursery doors. At age 7, he was wrenched from the only person who loved him—his nanny—and shipped off to boarding school. Insolent, angry, refusing to obey orders or sit still, he was regularly beaten by the headmaster and teased by the other boys. Although gifted at writing, he was incapable of rote memorization; he couldn't pass a test. When he graduated at the bottom of his boarding school class, his father informed him that he would never amount to anything. His name was Winston Churchill. He was the man who stood up to Hitler and carried England to victory in World War II.

Churchill's upbringing was a recipe for disaster. He had neglectful parents, behavior problems, and was a failure at school. But this dismal childhood produced the leader who saved the modern world.

Resilient children, like Churchill, confront terrible conditions such as parental abuse, poverty, and war and go on to construct successful, loving lives. What qualities allow these unusual children to thrive?

resilient children Children who rebound from serious early life traumas to construct successful adult lives.

The Library of Congress

Abandoned by his father at about age 9 to be cared for by a teenaged sister for several years after his mother's premature death, raised in a dirt-floor Kentucky shack without any chance to attend school—Abraham Lincoln grew up to become our most beloved president and perhaps the greatest man of the nineteenth century. What qualities made this incredibly resilient child thrive? The answer: towering intellectual gifts, a remarkable drive to learn, optimism, self-efficacy, and—most of all—a world-class talent for understanding human motivations and connecting with people in a caring, prosocial way. By the way, while he guided a battered nation, "father Abraham"—shown here with his son—also made time to be a totally permissive, hands-on dad.

Developmentalists find that resilient children often have a special talent, such as Churchill's gift for writing, or superior cognitive skills. They are skilled at regulating their emotions. They have a high sense of self-efficacy and an optimistic worldview (Brodhagan & Wise, 2008; Pitzer & Fingerman, 2010). They possess a strong faith or sense of meaning in life (Wright & Masten, 2005).

Being resilient depends on inner resources—having good executive functions and intellectual and social skills (Deater-Deckard, Ivy, & Smith, 2005). But the quantity of environmental setbacks also matters (Greenfield, 2010). If you are exposed to a series of tragedies—for instance, having your parents get divorced after recently becoming homeless due to experiencing a disaster such as a hurricane—it's more difficult to preserve your efficacy feelings or rebound to construct a happy life (Becker-Blease, Turner, & Finkelhor, 2010; Kronenberg and others, 2010).

Not only is the quantity of life stress important, so are "social supports." Children who succeed against incredible odds typically have at least one close, caring relationship with a parent or another adult (such as Churchill's nanny). Like a plant that thrives in the desert, resilient children have the internal resources to extract love from their parched environment. But they cannot survive without any water at all.

Might these children have resilience-promoting genes? Remember that scientists feel a genetic profile may set some people up to be relatively immune to stressful life events, but that this same "immunity" gene-form is a liability when the wider world is nurturing and calm. So, yes, some lucky people may arrive in this world biologically blessed to weather the hurricanes of human life. ◐

Making the Case That Parents Don't Matter

What matters more in how we develop, our life experiences or our genes? Twin and adoption studies, as I mentioned in Chapter 1, come down firmly on the "it's mainly genetic" side. Faced with this nature-oriented behavioral-genetic research message, one developmentalist famously concluded that it doesn't matter if you were raised in your particular family or the one down the street. Given reasonably adequate parenting, children grow up to express their genetic fate (see Scarr, 1997; Scarr & Deater-Deckard, 1997).

The most interesting twist on this "parents don't matter" argument was put forth by psychologist Judith Harris. Harris (1995, 1998, 2002, 2006) believes that the environment has a dramatic impact on our development; but—rather than parents—our peer group socializes us to become adults.

Harris begins by taking aim at the principle underlying attachment theory—that the lessons we learn from our parents transfer to our other relationships. Learning, Harris believes, is context-specific. We cannot use the same *working model* with our mother and with the classroom bully, or we would never survive. Furthermore, because we live our lives in the wider world, she argues, the messages we absorb from the culture of our contemporaries must take precedence over the lessons we are taught at home.

Any parent can relate to Harris's peer-power principle when she is horrified to witness her 3-year-old picking up every bad habit from her classmates after entering preschool. You saw a chilling example of a similar group infection in the last chapter when I described how aggressive middle-school norms evoke bullying in the "nicest kids."

The most compelling evidence for Harris's theory, however, comes from looking at immigrants. As I implied in the introductory chapter vignette, **acculturation**—children's rapid shift to embrace new cultures—offers a vivid testament that Harris has an important point.

These arguments that genetics and our culture shape development alert us to the fact that, when you see children "acting out," you cannot leap to the assumption that "it's the parents' fault." As developmental systems theory predicts, a variety of influences—from genetics, to peer groups, to everything else—affect how children behave. But you may be thinking that the idea that parents are *not* important goes too far.

Many experts agree. For children to realize their genetic potential, parents should provide the best possible environment (Ceci and others, 1997; Kagan, 1998; Maccoby, 2002). In fact, when children are vulnerable or fragile as I've been pointing out, superior parenting is required.

Making the Case for Superior Parenting

Imagine, for instance, that your daughter is temperamentally "difficult." You know from reading this book that you may be tempted to disengage emotionally from your child. You also know that adopting this less-responsive parenting style can make the situation much worse. So, you inhibit your use of *power assertion*. You provide lots of love. You arrange the environment to minimize your child's vulnerabilities and highlight her strengths.

Actually, when a child is biologically fragile, or genetically reactive, sensitive caregiving can make a critical difference. From studies showing that loving touch helps premature infants grow (recall Chapter 3), to my suggestions for raising fearful or exuberant kids (see Chapters 4 and 6), the message is the same: When children are "at risk," superior parenting matters most.

So let's celebrate the fact that resilient children can flower in the face of difficult life conditions and less-than-ideal parenting styles. But when a baby needs special nurturing, the importance of high-quality nurture shines out.

INTERVENTIONS: **Lessons for Readers Who Are Parents**

Now let's summarize our discussion by talking directly to the parent readers of this book:

There are no firm guidelines about how to be an effective parent—except to show lots of love and provide consistent rules. But it also is critical to adapt your discipline to your unique child. You will face special challenges if you live in a dangerous environment or have a son or daughter who is "harder to raise" (where you may have to work harder to stay loving and attached). Your power is limited at best.

Try to see this message as liberating. Children cannot be massaged into having an idealized adult life. Your child's future does not totally depend on you. Focus on the quality of your relationship, and enjoy these wonderful years. And if your son or daughter is having difficulties, draw inspiration from Winston Churchill's history. Predictions from childhood to adult life can be hazy. Your unsuccessful child may grow up to save the world!

Now that I've covered the general territory, let's turn to specifics. First, we'll examine that controversial practice, spanking; then, focus on the worst type of parenting, child abuse; and finally, we'll explore that common transition, divorce.

acculturation Among immigrants, the tendency to become similar in attitudes and practices to the mainstream culture after time spent living in a new society.

Look at these exuberant boys, passionate to fit in with their friends. Then, ask yourself whether these children are acting the same way they were taught to behave at home. Suddenly, doesn't Judith Harris's theory that "peer groups shape our development" make a good deal of sense?

Spanking

corporal punishment The use of physical force to discipline a child.

Poll friends and family about **corporal punishment**—any discipline technique using physical measures such as spanking—and you are likely to get strong reactions. Some people adhere to the biblical principle, "Spare the rod and spoil the child." They may blame the decline in spanking for every social problem. Others blame corporal punishment for *creating* those social problems. They believe that parents who rely on "hitting" are implicitly teaching children the message that it is OK to respond in a violent way. To put these positions into perspective, let's take a brief tour of a total turnaround in corporal punishment attitudes in recent times.

Until the twentieth century, corporal punishment used to be standard practice. Flogging was routine in prisons (Gould & Pate, 2010), the military, and other places (Pinker, 2011). In the United States, it was legal for men to "physically chastise" their wives (Knox, 2010). Today, while these practices still occur in less developed nations, in Western democracies they are widely condemned (Knox, 2010).

Moreover in recent years—from Spain to Sweden or Croatia to Costa Rica—a remarkable 24 nations have passed laws banning child corporal punishment. Organizations from the American Academy of Pediatrics, to the United Nations, to the Methodist Church have also passed resolutions calling spanking children "inhumane" (Knox, 2010).

In the United States, we've been listening—a bit. Spanking is illegal at schools and day-care centers in most states. But any person proposing a bill to ban this behavior would be laughed off the congressional floor. Not only is our individualistic society wary about government intrusions in family life, but *most* U.S. parents spank their daughters and sons.

Still, with surveys showing only one in ten parents saying they "often spank," corporal punishment is not the preferred U.S. discipline mode. Today, the most frequent punishments parents report are "time-outs" and removal of privileges and, to a lesser extent, getting sent to one's room (Barkin and others, 2007).

Who in Western nations is most likely to spank? Corporal punishment is widely accepted in the African American community (Burchinal, Skinner, & Reznick, 2010; Lorber, O'Leary, & Smith Slep, 2011). As one Black woman reported: "I would rather me discipline them than (the police)" (Taylor, Hamvas, & Paris, 2011, p. 65). As you might imagine from the "spare the rod, spoil the child" injunction, people who believe the Bible is literally true are most apt to strongly advocate this disciplinary technique (Rodriguez & Henderson, 2010).

Adults who were spanked as children see more value in this child-rearing approach (Simons & Wurtele, 2010). (In my classes, I often hear students report: "I was spanked and it helped; so I plan to do the same with my kids.") But if you feel that physical punishment got out of hand during your childhood, you are probably passionate about never hitting your own daughter or son (Gagne and others, 2007).

What do experts advise? Here, there is debate. Many psychologists argue that physical punishment is *never* appropriate (Gershoff, 2002; Knox, 2010). They believe that hitting a child conveys the message that it is acceptable for big people to give small people pain. Yes, spanking, these psychologists point out, does produce compliance. But, it impairs prosocial behavior because it gets children to only focus on themselves (Andero & Stewart, 2002; Benjet & Kazdin, 2003; Knox, 2010).

Other experts believe that mild spanking is not detrimental (Baumrind, Larzelere, & Cowan, 2002; Larzelere & Kuhn, 2005; Oas, 2010). They suggest that, if we rule out corporal punishment, caregivers may resort to more damaging, shaming responses such as saying, "I hate you. You will never amount to anything." But these psychologists have clear limits as to how and when this type of discipline might be used:

- Never hit an infant. *Babies can't control their behavior. They don't know what they are doing wrong.* For a preschooler, a few light swats on the bottom can be a last resort disciplinary technique if a child is engaging in dangerous activities—such as running into the street—that need to be immediately stopped (Larzelere & Kuhn, 2005).

- This action, however, must be accompanied by a verbal explanation ("What you did was wrong because . . .") Spanking should rarely be considered only as a last ditch backup when other strategies, such as time-outs, fail.

The problem is that spanking is often not a final backup—particularly among the very children whom physical punishment *does* most harm—boys and girls at risk for externalizing problems (recall Chapter 6). Therefore, parent training is crucial. We need to emphasize the behavioral principle that positive reinforcement (giving rewards for good behavior) is more effective than any punishment, be it spanking or being sent to a room. We must *vigorously* dispel the misconception that it's possible to spoil a baby, and that spanking produces a well-behaved child (Burchinal, Skinner, & Reznick, 2010).

Frequent spanking promotes the very behavior it is supposed to cure. To take one example, researchers found that parents who believed strongly in spanking had kids who said it was fine, during disagreements with a playmate, to "hit" that other child (Simons & Wurtele, 2010). Worse yet, what might start out as a spanking can escalate as a parent "gets into it," the child cries more, and soon you have that worst-case scenario: child abuse.

Child Abuse

Child maltreatment—the term for acts that endanger children's physical or emotional well-being—comprises four categories. *Physical abuse* refers to bodily injury that leaves bruises. It encompasses everything from overzealous spanking to battering that may lead to a child's death. *Neglect* refers to caregivers' failure to provide adequate supervision and care. It might mean abandoning the child, not providing sufficient food, or failing to enroll a son or daughter in school. *Emotional abuse* refers to continual shaming or terrorizing or exploiting a child. *Sexual abuse* covers the spectrum from rape and incest to fondling and exhibitionistic acts.

Everyone can identify serious forms of maltreatment; but there is a gray zone as to what activities cross the line (Greenfield, 2010). Does every spanking that leaves bruises qualify as physical abuse? If a single mother leaves her toddler in an 8-year-old sibling's care, is she neglectful? Are parents who walk around naked in the house guilty of sexual abuse? Emotional abuse is inherently murky to define, although this form of maltreatment may be the most common of all (Foster and others, 2010).

This labeling issue partly explains why maltreatment statistics vary, depending on who we ask. In one global summary (involving an amazing 150 studies and 10 million participants), scientists estimated that roughly 3 of 1,000 children worldwide were physically maltreated, using informant's (meaning, other people's) reports. In polling adults themselves, the rates were 10 times higher than that (Stoltenborgh and others, 2013). Considering all forms of abuse, the figures are alarming: 15 percent of teenage boys were labeled as abused in a city in Iran (Mikaeili, Barahmand, & Abdi, 2013). In Canada, 1 in 4 adults reported being maltreated as a child (MacMillan and others, 2013).

Obviously, far more individuals will report ("I was abused"), than the "objective" abuse-rate statistics in any particular community indicate. But another force that accounts for these variations are cultural norms. Do you live in a patriarchal society where corporal punishment is traditionally routine (as in Iran)? Do your society's values stress family loyalty (as in China or Japan)? (See Foynes and others, 2014.) In both cases, we would expect fewer maltreatment reports than in the West.

What we can say is that, while a few adults are prone to err in the over-reporting direction (saying "I was abused" when they are chronically angry with a mom or dad), outsider-reported rates qualify as the iceberg's tiny tip (Greenfield, 2010). Why is maltreatment swept under the rug in our day and age? Before answering this question, let's look at what provokes this parenting pathology and probe its effects.

child maltreatment Any act that seriously endangers a child's physical or emotional well-being.

Exploring the Risk Factors

As developmental systems theory would predict, several categories of influence cause child abuse to flare up (Wolfe, 2011):

PARENTS' PERSONALITY PROBLEMS ARE IMPORTANT. People who abuse their children tend to suffer from psychological disorders such as depression and externalizing problems (Annerbäck, Svedin, & Gustafsson, 2010). They often have hostile attributional biases (Berlin, Appleyard, & Dodge, 2011; Crouch and others, 2010), assuming "bad" behavior from benign activities, like a toddler's running around. Their determination not to "spoil" their babies is accompanied by other unrealistic expectations. They may believe that 3-month-olds can be taught not to cry or that 8-month-olds can be totally toilet trained (Bissada & Briere, 2001).

LIFE STRESS ACCOMPANIED BY SOCIAL ISOLATION CAN BE CRUCIAL. Abusive parents are often young and poorly educated (Bartlett & Easterbrooks, 2012; Sieswerda-Hoogendoorn and others, 2013). They tend to be coping with an overload of upsetting life events, from domestic violence to severe poverty (Annerbäck, Svedin, & Gustafsson, 2010). Most important, they feel cut off from other people. Social isolation, plus severe economic distress, is the match that is most apt to ignite child abuse (Berlin, Appleyard, & Dodge, 2011; Li, Godinet, & Arnsberger, 2011).

CHILDREN'S VULNERABILITIES PLAY A ROLE. A child who is emotionally fragile can fan this fire—a baby who cries excessively (Reijneveld and others, 2004), has a medical problem (Svensson, Bornehag, & Janson, 2011), or is premature (Sieswerda-Hoogendoorn and others, 2013). Therefore, in a terrible irony, the very children that require special loving care are most apt to provoke an out-of-control caregiver's wrath." The fact that abusive parents may target just one child was brought home to me when I was working as a clinical psychologist at a city hospital in New York. A mother was referred for treatment for abusing her "spiteful" 10-year-old, although she never harmed his "sweet" 3-year-old brother. So disturbances in the attachment relationship are a core ingredient in the poisonous recipe for producing a battered child.

Exploring the Consequences

As you learned in Chapter 4, maltreated children often have insecure attachments (Stronach and others, 2011). They tend to suffer from internalizing and externalizing problems (Mills and others, 2013), and get rejected by their peers (Kim & Cicchetti, 2010). Just as with the orphanage-reared babies discussed in Chapter 4, brain-imaging studies suggest child maltreatment may compromise the developing frontal lobes (van Harmelen and others, 2010). In one study, children exposed to sexual abuse even showed epigenetic changes in their DNA (Beach and others, 2013).

Because terrible childhood experiences prime us *epigenetically* to biologically break down (Shapero and others, 2014), it comes as no surprise that the long-term effects of child maltreatment span the spectrum: from adolescent antisocial tendencies (Beach and others, 2013; Brody and others, 2014), to adult executive-function deficits (Nikulina & Widom, 2013); from depression and substance abuse (Herrenkohl and others, 2013; Mills and others, 2013), to higher rates of midlife heart disease (Midei and others, 2013). These children are primed to get embroiled in abusive, adult love relationships (McCloskey, 2013) and have more trouble lovingly bonding with their babies (Muzik and others, 2013). So yes, abused children are at higher risk of maltreating their own children when they become moms and dads.

Still most abused children become decent, caring parents (Woodruff and Lee, 2011). Some are passionate to never, ever hit their daughters and sons (Berlin, Appleyard, & Dodge, 2011). As one woman described: "I made a vow to protect my children no matter what. . . . It was almost like a mantra, that I'm never going to strike (my child)" (quoted in Hall, 2011, p. 38).

People who break the cycle of abuse tend to have good intellectual and coping skills (Hengartner and others, 2013). They are blessed to have a DNA profile that I alluded to earlier, that makes them genetically more resistant to stress (Banducci and others, 2014). Being blessed to have a stable, loving marriage also offers potent insulation from repeating the trauma of abuse (Jaffe and others, 2013).

INTERVENTIONS: Taking Action Against Child Abuse

What should you do if you suspect child abuse? The law requires teachers, social workers, health-care professionals, and, sometimes, any concerned citizen, to report the situation to child protective services. Children in imminent danger are removed from the home, and the cases are referred to juvenile court. Judges do not have the power to punish abusive parents, but they can place their children in foster care and limit or terminate their parental rights.

Unfortunately, there are powerful temptations not to speak up. If you make a false report, you risk ruining a family's life. You may feel that you don't have the training to make a difficult judgment call, or fear your life would be in danger from a vengeful parent if you made a report (see Chen and others, 2010; Osofsky and Lieberman, 2010): "Are those injuries normal accidents, or are the patterned bruises characteristic of being hit by a cord or belt?" (Harris, 2010.) "If I do report the situation, will authorities take any action?"

This last fear seems justified. In one Swedish study, even in the face of accusations of severe abuse, only about 10 percent of children were physically examined. Roughly 1 percent of the cases actually went to trial (Otterman, Lainpelto, & Lindblad, 2013). This is unfortunate, because with abuse, the family situation can get worse. In one study tracking U.S. families with documented histories of maltreatment, the home environment deteriorated from preschool to kindergarten, with mothers doing more yelling and having fewer caring interactions, especially with sons (Haskett, Neupert, & Okado, 2014).

Having a loving family life—and particularly a caring relationship with one's spouse—can break the intergenerational cycle of abuse.

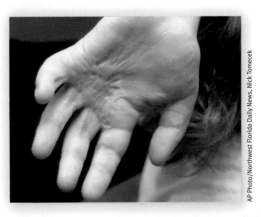

Imagine you are a teacher who sees these kinds of suspicious burns on a student's hands. You know that unusual injuries like this can signal child abuse, but you aren't absolutely sure. Would you immediately report the situation to the authorities? Would you talk to the parents first? What exactly would you do?

Divorce

Although developed-world child abuse rates have declined (see Pinker, 2011), this parenting pathology still is unacceptably frequent today. However, since the late-twentieth-century lifestyle revolution, even more children undergo another unwelcome family change: divorce. How does divorce affect children, and what issues do families undergoing this life transition face?

Let's start with the bad news. Studies comparing children of divorce with their counterparts in intact married families show that these boys and girls are at a disadvantage—academically, socially, and in terms of mental health (Amato, 2010; Potter, 2010). Worse yet, Swedish researchers found that—while this statistical disparity has shrunk, as divorce has become "normal"—it still exists (Gähler & Garriga, 2013). In large part, the problem may be economic. Divorce can propel a newly mother-headed household into poverty, even though that family had previously been middle class (Schramm and others, 2013; see also Figure 7.1a on p. 200 of this chapter).

The good news is that most children cope with divorce very well, especially if this family event is fairly drama free. Still, I don't want to minimize the guilt parents feel when making this choice. One woman in a Finnish study revealed these predictable feelings when she anguished: "What am I to change two close people's lives . . . Was a thought that did not leave me for a long time" (as reported in Kiiski & Määttä Uusiautti, 2013).

Imagine coping with feeling you have failed your family and then needing to have a conversation that upends your children's world. And it's not just that you explain, "Mommy and Daddy need to live apart, but we still love you," and children get over the news. One Israeli woman described a fairly common scenario when she reported that for months her daughter's conversations started with the phrase, "Soon, when Dad will come back home" (quoted in Cohen, Leichtentritt, & Volpin, 2014).

In this interview study exploring the feelings of newly divorced Israeli mothers, women said their main agenda was to minimize their children's pain. So, they struggled to put aside their vengeful feelings and not bad-mouth their former spouses. One mother helped her child cope with his father's hurtful absence by making it into a shared game: "I laugh. I tell him, 'OK you miss daddy. But where is he?' And he says 'far, far away'". Others vowed to avoid mentioning the gritty details: "I don't want to hurt him," said a woman named Trina. "I won't tell them that his father pointed a gun at his mother."

parental alienation The practice among divorced parents of badmouthing a former spouse, with the goal of turning a child against that person.

This is not to say that **parental alienation**—poisoning children against ex-partners—is rare. Even many years after separating, some people can't resist denigrating the other parent, especially after an acrimonious divorce (see Lowenstein, 2013).

The compelling lure to succumb to *relational aggression* (that is, enlisting children against a former spouse) brings up the subject of custody and visitation. When the divorce is bitter (or high conflict) should a child be allowed to frequently see both the dad and mom?

For almost the entire twentieth century, the mother was given custody unless there was a serious problem with her parenting (based on the psychoanalytic principle that women are inherently superior nurturers)—a practice that unfairly limited dads from being involved in their children's lives. Today, Western nations—from Canada, to Italy, to Sweden—have rectified this wrong by passing laws encouraging joint custody (see Lavadera, Caravelli, & Togliatti, 2013). Spouses don't have to split living arrangements 50/50. But when the parents share custody, even when the child lives with the mother, the father can see his sons and daughters any time.

Does this permeable visiting schedule help children cope? Actually, "it depends." Researchers found that after a divorce, moving an infant child from house to house predicted greater attachment insecurity. In contrast, adolescent research suggested that teens who split their living arrangements between ex-spouses had better mental health than their single-parent counterparts (Carlsund and others, 2013).

The most informative finding comes from scanning Figure 7.3. While more overnights with a dad who provides positive parenting promotes adjustment, if a father had

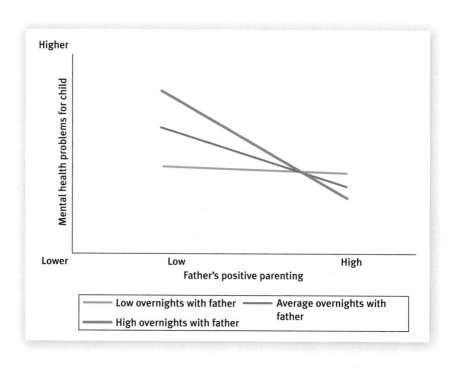

FIGURE 7.3: Child mental-health problems as a function of father's positive parenting and whether the child spent many or few overnights at that parent's house: Notice from the red line that staying over often at a divorced dad's house is good for children, *if* that man is a good parent. But frequent overnights with a father who has poor parenting skills are clearly detrimental to children's mental health.
Source: Sandler, Wheeler, & Braver, 2013.

poor parenting skills, children's emotional problems escalated (Sandler, Wheeler, & Braver, 2013).

So with custody and visitation, we need to take an individual-centered, developmental systems approach. Go for shared arrangements in the abstract, but if a father is antisocial or the spouses continually bad mouth each other, limit access to one or both parents, to protect the child (see DeGarmo, 2010; Lessard and others, 2010). Moreover, with divorce, the ongoing parenting matters most. A child should spend the most time with the parent who parents the best!

Should children be able to decide which custody and visitation arrangement they prefer? One experiment, comparing standard divorce mediation with approaches centered more on child wishes, suggested yes (Ballard and others, 2013).

Do you think this girl should be testifying in court about whether to live with mom or dad? Clearly there are some serious minuses here.

Still, in a poll of divorced families, everyone recoiled at the idea of putting *total* decision-making burden on a child (Cashmore & Parkinson, 2008). Imagine forcing a son or daughter to publically admit, "I prefer to live with Mom or (Dad)." And imagine the coercion that might ensue from the parent side. During this semester's divorce discussion, a student poignantly described this scenario, when she told the class: "My daughter told the judge she wanted to live with her father, and then, years later said, 'Mom, I wanted you, but I was afraid to say so because I was frightened of Dad.'"

At this point some of you might be thinking unhappy couples should try to bite the bullet and stay together for the sake of their children. If the marriage is labeled "high conflict," think again. For children subjected to continual marital fighting, ending the marriage improves well-being (Amato, 2010). As another student explained during the class divorce discussion, "Because the atmosphere at home was terrible, I felt much happier after my parents divorced."

Table 7.2 summarizes these points in a parenting-related divorce questionnaire. In Chapter 11, I'll fully explore divorce from the adult point of view. Now it's time to turn to that other setting within which children develop—school.

Table 7.2: Parenting Questions to Ask to Predict How Well a Given Child Is Apt to Cope with Divorce

1. Do the parents continually fight and badmouth each other? (Engaging in parental alienation is poisonous for the child.)

2. Can the child see the dad frequently? (Frequent overnights are a positive thing if the father is a good parent, but can be detrimental when the man's parenting skills are poor.)

3. Does the child have input into custody decisions? (This can be a net positive, provided the child does not have full decision-making capacity and a parent doesn't force the child to make unwanted choices.)

4. What is the quality of the custodial parenting? (This is the main force determining how well the child copes!)

Tying It All Together

1. Montana's parents make firm rules but value their children's input about family decisions. Pablo's parents have rules for everything and tolerate no *ifs, ands,* or *buts.* Sara's parents don't really have rules. At their house it's always playtime and time to indulge the children. Which parenting style is being used by Montana's parents? By Pablo's parents? By Sara's parents?

2. Chloe grew up in a happy middle-class family, but Amber and Sierra both had difficult childhoods. Sierra is struggling in college and often feels very unhappy, but both Amber and Chloe are doing well at school. To which student does the term resilient best apply?

3. Melissa's son Jared, now in elementary school, was premature and has a difficult temperament. What might Judith Harris advise about fostering this child's development, and what might this chapter recommend?

4. Your sister is concerned about a friend who uses corporal punishment with her baby and her 4-year-old. She asks you what the experts say. Pick the following two positions developmentalists might take.

    a. Never spank children of any age.

    b. Mild spanking is OK for the infant.

    c. Mild spanking is OK for the 4-year-old, as a backup.

    d. If the child has a difficult temperament, regular corporal punishment might help.

5. Ms. Johnson, an elementary school teacher, is worried about a student who has been coming to school unwashed and with torn clothes. Yesterday, she saw what looked like burn marks on the child's arms. Describe how Ms. Johnson might feel about reporting this situation, and what might happen if she formally accuses the parent of abuse or neglect.

6. Imagine you are a family court judge deciding to award joint custody. In a phrase, explain your main criterion for awarding unlimited overnights with a particular divorced dad.

Answers to the Tying It All Together questions can be found at the end of this chapter.

FIGURE 7.4: Socioeconomic status and kindergartners' scores on tests of readiness for reading and math: As children's socioeconomic status rises, so do average scores on tests of math and reading readiness. Notice the dramatic differences between low-income and affluent children.
Source: Lee & Burkam, 2002, p. 18.

School

What was that test Josiah (in the introductory chapter vignette) took, and what does intelligence really mean? What makes for good teaching and superior schools? Before looking at these school-related topics, let's step back and, once again, explore the impact of that basic marker, poverty, on young children's cognitive skills.

Setting the Context: Unequal at the Starting Gate

In Chapter 4, you learned that living in poverty for the first years of life has damaging effects on cognition. Figure 7.4 reveals that devastation directly by offering sobering statistics with regard to a turn of the century entering U.S. kindergarten class (Lee & Burkam, 2002). Notice that children from low-income families, on average, do markedly worse than their upper-middle-class counterparts on tests of reading readiness and math. When we compare poverty-level Latino and African American children to the wealthiest European Americans, the test-score gap becomes a chasm. The most disadvantaged U.S. children enter school academically several years behind their most affluent counterparts.

You would think that when children start a race miles behind, they should be given every chance to catch up. The

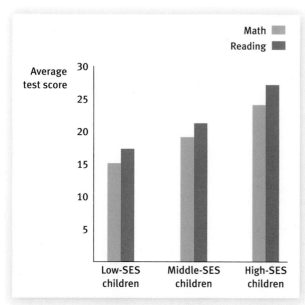

reality is the reverse. From class size, to the quality of teacher training, to the attractiveness of the physical building—U.S. kindergartens serving poor children rank at the bottom of the educational heap. As one group of researchers put it:

> The consistency of these findings . . . is . . . troubling. The least advantaged of America's children, who also begin their formal schooling at a substantial cognitive disadvantage, are systematically mapped into our nation's worst schools.
>
> (Lee & Burkam, 2002, p. 77)

Now, let's keep these inequalities in mind as we explore the controversial topic of intelligence tests.

Intelligence and IQ Tests

What does it mean to be intelligent? Ask classmates the question, and they will probably mention both academic and "real life" skills (Sternberg, Grigorenko, & Kidd, 2005). Conceptions of what it means to "be intelligent" differ from society to society, and among different ethnic groups. Latino parents, for instance, focus more on social competence (getting along with people), while our mainstream culture views intelligence in terms of cognitive traits (Sternberg, 2007).

Traditional intelligence tests reflect the mainstream view. They measure only cognitive abilities. Intelligence tests, however, differ from **achievement tests**—the yearly evaluations children take to measure knowledge in various subjects. The intelligence test is designed to predict a person's general academic potential, or ability to master any school-related task. Do the tests measure mainly genetic capacities? Do they have any relevance beyond school? To approach these hot-button issues, let's examine the intelligence test that children typically take today: the WISC.

achievement tests Measures that evaluate a child's knowledge in specific school-related areas.

WISC (Wechsler Intelligence Scale for Children) The standard intelligence test used in childhood, consisting of different scales composing a variety of subtests.

Examining the WISC

The **WISC (Wechsler Intelligence Scale for Children)**, now in repeated revisions, was devised by David Wechsler and is the current standard intelligence test. As you can see in Table 7.3, the WISC samples a child's performance in a variety of areas. However, as it is divided into main sections—each testing a basic ability—testers can give a child a separate IQ score for each part.

Achievement tests are administered to groups. The WISC is given individually to a child by a trained psychologist, a process that often includes several hours of testing and concludes with a written report. If the child scores at the 50th percentile for his

---

Table 7.3: A WISC-IV Subtest Sampler

Verbal Comprehension

Subtest	Sample (simulated) Item
Similarities (analogies)	Cat is to kitten as dog is to _____.
Vocabulary (defining words)	What is a table?

Perceptual Reasoning

Picture completion	Pick out what is missing in this picture.
Block design	Arrange these blocks to look like the photograph on the card.

Processing Speed

Coding	Using the key above, put each symbol in the correct space below.

Working Memory Index

Digit span	Repeat these numbers forward. Now repeat these numbers backward.

intellectual disability The label for significantly impaired cognitive functioning, measured by deficits in behavior accompanied by having an IQ of 70 or below.

specific learning disorder The label for any impairment in language or any deficit related to listening, thinking, speaking, reading, writing, spelling, or understanding mathematics.

dyslexia A learning disorder that is characterized by reading difficulties, lack of fluency, and poor word recognition that is often genetic in origin.

gifted The label for superior intellectual functioning characterized by an IQ score of 130 or above, showing that a child ranks in the top 2 percent of his age group.

age group, his IQ is defined as 100. If that child's IQ is 130, he ranks at roughly the 98th percentile, or in the top 2 percent of children his age. If a child's score is 70, he is at the opposite end of the distribution, performing in the lowest 2 percent of children that age. Put on a graph, this score distribution, as you can see in Figure 7.5, looks like a bell-shaped curve.

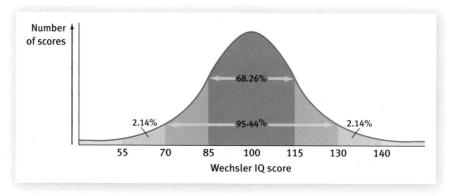

FIGURE 7.5: **The bell-shaped curve:** The WISC scores are arranged to align in a normal distribution. Notice from the chart that about 68 percent of the population has scores between 85 and 115 and about 95 percent of the scores are between 70 and 130.

When do children take this test? The answer, most often, is during elementary school when there is a question about a given child's classroom performance. School personnel then use the IQ score as one component of a multifaceted assessment, which includes achievement test scores, teachers' ratings, and parents' input, to determine whether a boy or girl needs special help (Sattler, 2001). If a child's low score (under 70) and other behaviors warrant this designation, she may be classified as **intellectually disabled.** If a child's IQ is far higher than would be expected, compared to her performance on achievement tests, she is classified as having a **specific learning disorder,** an umbrella term for any impairment in language or difficulties related to listening (such as ADHD), thinking, speaking, reading, spelling, or math.

Although children with learning disabilities often score in the average range on IQ tests, they have trouble with schoolwork. Many times, they have a debilitating impairment called **dyslexia** that undercuts every academic skill. Dyslexia, a catchall term referring to any reading disorder, may have multiple causes (Nicolson & Fawcett, 2011; Zoccolotti and Friedmann, 2010). What's important is that, despite having good instruction and doing well on tests of intelligence, a dyslexic child is still struggling to read (Shaywitz, Morris, & Shaywitz, 2008).

My son, for instance, has dyslexia, and our experience shows just how important having a measure of general intelligence can be. Because Thomas was falling behind in the third grade, my husband and I arranged to have our son tested. Thomas was defined as having a learning disability because his IQ score was above average but his achievement scores were well below the norm for his grade. Although we were aware of our son's reading problems, the testing was vital in easing our anxieties. Thomas—just as we thought—was capable intellectually. Now we just had to get our son through school with his sense of self-efficacy intact!

Often, teachers and parents urge testing for a happier reason: They want to confirm that a child is intellectually advanced. If the child's IQ exceeds a certain number, typically 130, or in the top 2 percent (see Figure 7.4), she is labeled **gifted** and is eligible for special programs. In U.S. public schools, the law mandates intelligence testing before children can be assigned to a gifted program or remedial class (Canter, 1997; Sattler, 2001).

Table 7.4 offers a fact sheet about dyslexia. The Experiencing the Lifespan box provides a firsthand view of what it is like to triumph over this debilitating condition. Now that we have explored the measure and when it is used, let's turn to what the scores mean.

© Ray Stott/The Image Works

This second grader, taking a subtest of the WISC, will be tested for at least an hour and a half. Then, the examiner will write a report and compare her scores with those of other children that age. If this girl's IQ is at least 130—ranking her at roughly the top 2 percent of his age group—she will be eligible for the school's gifted program.

Table 7.4: Some Interesting Facts About Dyslexia

- Reading difficulties are shockingly prevalent among U.S. children. According to one 2005 survey, more than 1 in 4 high school seniors were reading below the most basic levels. The figures were higher for fourth graders—over 1 in 3 had trouble grasping the basic points of a passage designed for their grade.

- Specific learning disabilities (including dyslexia) are a mainly male diagnosis—affecting roughly three times as many boys as girls around the world. However, because a referral bias favors boys, there may be more undiagnosed females with dyslexia than had previously been thought.

- Dyslexia is inherited and "genetic" in origin. However, multiple genes are involved in this condition, and, as I mentioned in the text, problems learning to read have a variety of different causes.

- Late-appearing language (entering the word-combining phase of speech at an older-than-typical age, such as close to age 2 1/2 [see Chapter 3]) and especially phonemic deficits (the inability to differentiate sounds [see Chapter 5]) are early predictors of dyslexia.

- Children prone to dyslexia may even be identified during their first weeks after birth—by looking at the pattern of their brain waves evoked by different sounds. These newborns have a slightly slower shift from positivity to negativity on "event-related potentials" when exposed to noises of different frequencies.

- Although many children with dyslexia eventually learn to read, this condition persists to some extent into adulthood. Early interventions—involving intensive instruction in teaching "at-risk" kindergartners and first graders to identify phonemes—can be effective, but to really work this special help should be continued into elementary school.

- Boys and girls with dyslexia unfortunately perform more poorly on general tests of executive functions. They are also at higher risk for developing other mental health problems—such as depressive and anxiety disorders. About 15 to 50 percent also have ADHD.

Sources: Beneventi and others, 2010; Gooch, Snowling, & Hulme, 2011; Henry, Messer, & Nash, 2012; Hensler and others, 2010; Landerl & Moll, 2010; Leppänen and others, 2010; Shaywitz and others, 2008.

Experiencing the Lifespan: From Dyslexic Child to College Professor Adult

Aimee Holt, a colleague of mine who teaches our school psychology students, is beautiful and intelligent, the kind of golden girl you might imagine would have been a great childhood success. When I sat down to chat with Aimee about her struggles with dyslexia and other learning disabilities, I found first impressions can be very misleading:

In first grade, the teachers at school said I was mentally retarded. I didn't notice the sounds that went along with letters. I walked into walls and fell down a lot. My parents refused to put me in a special school and finally got me accepted at a private school, contingent on getting a good deal of help. I spent my elementary school years being tutored for an hour before school, an hour afterwards, and all summer.

Socially, elementary school was a nightmare . . . I remember kids laughing at me, calling me stupid. There was a small group of people that I was friendly with, but we were all misfits. One of my closest friends had an inoperable brain tumor. Because of my problems coordinating my vision with my motor skills, I couldn't participate in normal activities, such as sports or dance. By seventh grade, after years of working every day with my wonderful reading teacher, I was reading at almost grade level.

Then when we moved to Tennessee in my freshman year of high school, I felt like a new person. Nobody knew that I had learning difficulties. We moved to a rural community, so I got to be a top student, because I'd had the same classes in my Dallas private school the year before. In the tenth and eleventh grades, I was making A's and B's. I got a scholarship to college, where I was a straight-A student (with a GPA of 3.9).

My mom is the reason I've done well. She always believed in me, always felt I could make it; she never gave up. Plus, as I mentioned, I had an exceptional reading teacher. My goal was always to be an elementary school teacher, but, after teaching for years and realizing that a lot of the kids in my classes were not being accurately diagnosed, I decided to go to graduate school to get my Ph.D.

Today, in addition to teaching, I do private tutoring with children like me. First, I get kids to identify word sounds (phonemes) because children with dyslexia have a problem decoding the specific sounds of words. I'll have the children identify how many sounds they hear in a word. . . . "Which sounds rhyme, which don't?" . . . "If I change the word from cat to hat, what sound changes?" Most children naturally pick up on these reading cues. Kids with dyslexia need to have these skills directly taught.

Many children I tutor are in fourth or even sixth grade and have had years of feeling like a failure. They develop an attitude of "Why try? I'm going to fail anyway." I can tell them that I've been there and that they can succeed. So I work on academic self-efficacy—teaching them to put forth effort. Most of these kids are intelligent, but as they progress through school, their IQ drops because they are not being exposed to written material at their grade level. I try to get them to stay in the regular class-room, with modifications such as books on tape and oral testing, to prevent that false drop in their knowledge base. I was so fortunate—with a wonderful mother, an exceptional reading teacher, getting the help I needed at exactly the right time—that I feel my mission is to give something back.

Decoding the Meaning of the IQ Test

reliability In measurement terminology, a basic criterion of a test's accuracy that scores must be fairly similar when a person takes the test more than once.

validity In measurement terminology, a basic criterion for a test's accuracy involving whether that measure reflects the real-world quality it is supposed to measure.

Flynn effect Remarkable and steady rise in overall performance on IQ tests that has been occurring around the world over the past century.

"g" Charles Spearman's term for a general intelligence factor that he claimed underlies all cognitive activities.

The first question we need to grapple with in looking at the meaning of the test relates to a measurement criterion called **reliability.** When people take a test thought to measure a basic trait, such as IQ, more than one time, their results should not vary. Imagine that your IQ score randomly shifted from gifted to average, year by year. Clearly, this test score would not tell us anything about a stable attribute called intelligence.

The good news is that, in elementary school, IQ test performance does typically remain stable (Ryan, Glass, & Bartels, 2010). In one amazing study, people's scores remained fairly similar when they first took the test in childhood and then were retested more than a half-century later (see Deary and others, 2000). Still, among individual children, the IQ can change. Scores are most likely to shift when children have undergone life stresses.

This research tells us that we should never evaluate a child's IQ during a family crisis such as divorce. But being reliable is only the first requirement. The test must be **valid.** This means it must predict what it is supposed to be measuring. Is the WISC a valid test?

If our predictor is academic performance, the answer is yes. A child who gets an IQ score of 130 will tend to perform well in the gifted class. A child whose IQ is 80 will probably need remedial help. But now we turn to the controversial question: Does the test measure genetic learning potential or biological smarts?

ARE THE TESTS A GOOD MEASURE OF GENETIC GIFTS? When we are evaluating children living in poverty (or boys and girls growing up in non-English-speaking families), logic tells us that the answer should be no. Look back at the items on the WISC verbal comprehension scale (Table 7.3 on p. 213), and you will immediately see that if parents stimulate a child's vocabulary, she will be at a test-taking advantage. If a family cannot buy books and learning toys, their children will be handicapped on this part of the test.

An excellent argument that the environment weighs heavily in IQ comes from that remarkable century-long increase in intelligence test scores described in Chapter 1. This worldwide rise in IQ scores, called the **Flynn effect** (named for its discoverer James Flynn) is dramatic. More years of education, plus the modern media, have made twenty-first-century children and adults far better "thinkers" than their parents and grandparents were at the same age. Incredibly, Flynn (2007) calculates that the average-scoring child taking the WISC in 1900 would rank as "mentally retarded" using today's IQ norms!

We also have newer research confirming that a poor life situation artificially limits IQ. For low-income children, the IQ score mainly reflects environmental forces. For upper-middle-class children, the test score is more reflective of genetic gifts (Turkheimer and others, 2003). So if an elementary schooler comes from a poverty-level family and attends a low-quality school, yes, his IQ may predict his current school performance. But we should not assume that score reflects true intellectual potential unless a child has been exposed to the incredible learning advantages upper-middle-class life provides.

Now, imagine that you are an upper-middle-class child. You were regularly read to, taken to museums, and attended the best schools. Your IQ score is only 95 or 100. Is your intellectual potential limited for life?

DO IQ SCORES PREDICT REAL-WORLD PERFORMANCE? When a student comes up after this class lecture and proudly admits that his IQ is 130 or 140, he is not thinking of school learning. He assumes that his score measures a basic "smartness" that carries over to every life activity. In measurement terminology, this student would agree with Charles Spearman. Spearman believed that IQ test scores reflect a general underlying, all-encompassing intelligence factor called "**g.**"

Psychologists debate the existence of "g." Many strongly believe that the IQ test *generally* predicts intellectual capacities. They argue that we can use the IQ as a summary measure of a person's cognitive potential for all life tasks (Herrnstein & Murray, 1994; Rushton & Jensen, 2005). Others believe that people have unique intellectual talents. There is no one-dimensional quality called "g" (Eisner, 2004; Schlinger, 2003; Sternberg, 2007). These critics believe it inappropriate to rank people on a continuum from highly intelligent to not very smart (Gould, 1981; Sternberg, Grigorenko & Kidd, 2005).

Tantalizing evidence for "g" lies in the fact that people differ in the speed with which they process information (Brody, 2006; Rushton & Jensen, 2005). Intelligence test scores also correlate with various indicators of life success, such as occupational status. However, the problem is that the gateway to high-status professions, such as law and medicine, is school performance, which is what the tests predict (Sternberg, 1997; Sternberg, Grigorenko, & Bundy, 2001).

One problem with believing that IQ tests offer a *total* X-ray into intellectual capacities is that people may carry around their test-score ranking as an inner wound. A psychologist supervisor once confessed to me that he was really not that intelligent because his IQ was only 105. He devalued the criterion the scores were supposed to predict—his years of real-life success—by accepting what, in his case, was an invalid score!

A high test score can produce its own problems. Suppose the student who told me his IQ was 140 decided he was so intelligent he didn't have to open a book in my class. He might be in for a nasty surprise when he found out that what *really* matters is your ability to work. Or that person might worry: "I'd better not try in Dr. Belsky's class because, if I do put forth effort and *don't* get an A, I will discover that my astronomical IQ score was wrong." (Recall the research in Chapter 6 that showed how telling elementary schoolers "you are smart" made them afraid to tackle challenging academic tasks.)

Even the firmest advocate of "g" would admit that some of us are marvelous mechanically and miserable at math, wonderful at writing but hopeless at reading maps.

Toward a Broader View of Intelligence

But if intelligence involves different abilities, such as Josiah's mechanical talents (recall the introductory vignette), perhaps we should go beyond the IQ test to measure those skills in a broader way. Psychologists Robert Sternberg and Howard Gardner have devoted their careers to providing this broader view of what it means to be smart.

STERNBERG'S SUCCESSFUL INTELLIGENCE. Robert Sternberg (1984, 1996, 1997) has been a man on a mission. In hundreds of publications, this psychologist transformed the way we think about intelligence. Sternberg's passion comes from the heart. He began school with a problem:

> As an elementary school student, I failed miserably on the IQ tests. . . . Just the sight of the school psychologist coming into the classroom to give . . . an IQ test sent me into a wild panic attack. . . . You don't need to be a genius to figure out what happens next. My teachers in the elementary school grades certainly didn't expect much from me. . . . So I gave them what they expected. . . . Were the teachers disappointed? Not on your life. They were happy that I was giving them what they expected.
>
> (Sternberg, 1997, pp. 17–18)

Sternberg actually believes that traditional intelligence tests do damage in the school environment. As I implied earlier, the relationship between IQ scores and schooling is somewhat bidirectional. Children who attend inferior schools, or who miss months of classroom work due to illness, perform more poorly on intelligence tests (Sternberg, 1997). Worse yet, Sternberg argues, when schools assign children to lower-track, less demanding classes on the basis of their low test scores, their IQs gradually decline year by year.

Most importantly, Sternberg (1984) believes that conventional intelligence tests are too limited. Although they do measure one type of intelligence, they do not cover the total terrain.

IQ tests, according to Sternberg, measure **analytic intelligence.** They test how well people can solve academic-type problems. They do not measure **creative intelligence,** the ability to "think outside the box," or to formulate problems in new ways. Nor do they measure a third type of intelligence called **practical intelligence,** common sense, or "street smarts."

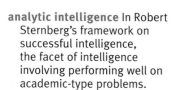

Being a math wiz (*analytic intelligence*) demands different skills from deftly snagging this fish (*practical intelligence*). That's why Robert Sternberg believes that IQ tests, which mainly measure school type analytic skills, do not tap into many of the abilities that make people successful in the real world.

Brazilian street children who make their living selling flowers show impressive levels of practical intelligence. They understand how to handle money in the real world. However, they do poorly on measures of traditional IQ (Sternberg, 1984, 1997). Others, such as Winston Churchill, can be terrible scholars but flower after they leave their academic careers. Then, there are people who excel at IQ test taking and traditional schooling but fail abysmally once in the real world. Sternberg argues that to be **successfully intelligent** in life requires a balance of all three "intelligences." (As a postscript, Sternberg recently added a fourth type of intellectual gift—that rare attribute called wisdom. See Sternberg, 2010.)

GARDNER'S MULTIPLE INTELLIGENCES. Howard Gardner (1998) did not have Sternberg's problem with intelligence tests:

> As a child I was a good student and a good test taker . . . but . . . music . . . and the arts were important parts of my life. Therefore when I asked myself what optimal human development is, I became more convinced that [we] had to . . . broaden the definition of intelligence to include these activities, too.
>
> (Gardner, 1998, p. 3)

Gardner is not passionately opposed to standard intelligence tests. Still, he believes that using the single IQ score is less informative than measuring children's unique talents and gifts. (Gardner's motto is: "Ask not *how* intelligent you are, but *how* are you intelligent?") According to Gardner's (2004, 2006) **multiple intelligences theory,** human abilities come in eight, and possibly nine, distinctive forms.

In addition to the verbal and mathematical skills measured by traditional IQ tests, people may be gifted in *interpersonal intelligence,* or understanding other people. Their talents may lie in *intrapersonal intelligence,* the skill of understanding oneself. They may be gifted in *spatial intelligence,* grasping where objects are arranged in space. (You might rely on a friend who is gifted in spatial intelligence to beautifully arrange the furniture in your house.) Some people have high levels of *musical intelligence, or kinesthetic intelligence* (the ability to use the body well), or *naturalist intelligence* (the gift for dealing with animals or plants and trees). There may even be an *existential (spiritual) intelligence,* too.

analytic intelligence In Robert Sternberg's framework on successful intelligence, the facet of intelligence involving performing well on academic-type problems.

creative intelligence In Robert Sternberg's framework on successful intelligence, the facet of intelligence involved in producing novel ideas or innovative work.

practical intelligence In Robert Sternberg's framework on successful intelligence, the facet of intelligence involved in knowing how to act competently in real-world situations.

successful intelligence In Robert Sternberg's framework, the optimal form of cognition, involving having a good balance of analytic, creative, and practical intelligence.

multiple intelligences theory In Howard Gardner's perspective on intelligence, the principle that there are eight separate kinds of intelligence—verbal, mathematical, interpersonal, intrapersonal, spatial, musical, kinesthetic, naturalist—plus a possible ninth form, called spiritual intelligence.

EVALUATING THE THEORIES. These perspectives on intelligence are exciting. Some of you may be thinking, "I'm gifted in practical or musical intelligence. I always knew there was more to being smart than school success!" But let's use our practical intelligence to critique these approaches. Why did Gardner select these particular eight abilities and not others (Barnett, Ceci, & Williams, 2006; White, 2006)? Yes, parents may marvel at a 6-year-old's creative or kinesthetic intelligence; but, it is analytic intelligence that will get this child into the school gifted program, not his artistic productions or how well his body moves (Eisner, 2004).

We can also criticize Sternberg's ideas. Is there such a thing as creative or practical intelligence apart from a particular field? Adopting the idea that there is a single "creative" intelligence might lead to the conclusion that Michelangelo would be a talented musician or that Mozart could beautifully paint the Sistine Chapel.

The bottom line is that neither Gardner nor Sternberg has developed replacements for our current IQ test. But this does not matter. Their mission is to transform the way schools teach (Gardner & Moran, 2006; Sternberg, 2010).

Being a world-class gymnast (*kinesthetic intelligence*) doesn't necessarily mean that you will also shine in reading or math. That's why Howard Gardner believes that schools need to broaden their focus to teach to the different kinds of intelligences that we all possess.

INTERVENTIONS: Lessons for Schools

Gardner's theory has been embraced by teachers who understand that intelligence involves more than having traditional academic skills. However, to implement his ideas requires revolutionizing the way we structure education. Therefore, the main use of multiple intelligences theory has been in helping "nontraditional learners" succeed (Schirduan & Case, 2004). Here is how Mark, a dyslexic teenager, describes how he uses his spatial intelligence to cope with the maze of facts in history:

> I'll picture things; for example, if we are studying the French revolution . . . Louis the 16th. . . . I'll have a picture of him in my mind [and I'll visualize] the castle and peasants to help me learn.
>
> (quoted in Schirduan & Case, 2004, p. 93)

Sternberg, being an experimentalist, has put his theory to rigorous test. Does instruction tailored to each different type of intelligence produce better achievement than teaching in the traditional way? Initial encouraging findings suggested yes (Sternberg, Torff, & Grigorenko, 1998). But when Sternberg's research team carried out a massive intervention trial, assigning 7,702 fourth graders in 223 classrooms to either be taught according to his theory or several typical approaches, the outcome was inconsistent at best (Sternberg and others, 2014). So, while the concept of successful intelligence is intuitively appealing, it's not clear that Sternberg's ideas merit changing the way classrooms operate. How *do* classrooms operate?

Classroom Learning

The diversity of intelligences, cultures, and educational experiences at home is matched by the diversity of American schools. There are small rural schools and large urban schools, public schools and private schools, highly traditional schools where students wear uniforms and schools that teach to Gardner's intelligences. There are single-sex schools, charter schools, religious schools, magnet schools that cater to gifted students, and alternative schools for children with behavior problems or learning disabilities.

Can students thrive in every school? The answer is yes, provided schools have an intense commitment to student learning and teachers can excite students to learn. The rest of this chapter focuses on these challenges.

Examining Successful Schools

What qualities make a school successful? Insights come from surveying elementary schools that are beating the odds. These schools, while serving high fractions of economically disadvantaged children, have students who are thriving.

A school's physical appearance can also make a real difference in whether children "beat the odds." This boy attends a model public school, designed and built by a well-known architect and located in an impoverished section of New York City.

In the Vista School, located on a Native American reservation, for instance, virtually all the children are eligible for a free lunch. However, Vista consistently boasts dramatic improvements on statewide reading and math tests. According to Ms. Thompson, the principal, "Our job is not to make excuses for students, but just to give them every possible opportunity. At Vista, teachers refuse to dumb down the curriculum. We offer tons of high-level conceptual work" (quoted in Borko and others, 2003, p. 177).

At Beacon Elementary School, two out of every three students exceed state-mandated writing standards despite coming from impoverished backgrounds. Here, Susie Murphy, the principal, comments: "You can . . . say, these kids are poor. You just need to love them. Or you can come to a school like this where the philosophy is that the best way to love them is to give them an education so they can make choices in their life" (quoted in Borko and others, 2003, p. 186). Beacon teachers, she continues, "are here . . . by choice. They are committed to proving that kids who live in poverty can learn every bit as well as other kids" (p. 192). At Beacon, the teachers' goal is to challenge all their students. The school builds in opportunities for teachers to share ideas: "We have mini-workshops in geometry, or problem solving. Our whole staff talks about the general focus and where math is going" (p. 194).

Committed teachers, professional collaboration, and a mission to "deliver for *all* our kids" explains why a rural Florida elementary school, serving mainly low-income children, dramatically boosted the test scores of its most struggling students in a single year. Rather than isolating boys and girls with "learning differences," this school took the unusual step of embedding every child into its academic life. Before instituting their focus on inclusiveness, only one in three at-risk child ranked proficient in math and language arts. At the year's end, these rates shot upward—to roughly two in three.

As Ms. Richards, the principal, explained: "We've got to improve to meet all kids needs. . . . That's how we started and it didn't turn into. . . a fix for one group, but how to make . . . everyone successful." A special education teacher named Ms. Wood probably summed up this school's teaching strategy best when she said, "We have ongoing conversations about challenging students . . . at our school . . . the meat of the curriculum is presented to everyone" (adapted from McLeskey, Waldron, & Redd, 2014, p. 63).

To summarize, successful schools set high standards. Teachers believe that every child can benefit from challenging, conceptual work. These schools offer an excess of nurture—both to students, and to one another. In Baumrind's parenting-styles framework, these schools are authoritative in their approach.

Now that we have the outlines for what is effective, let's tackle the challenge every teacher faces: getting students eager to learn.

Producing Eager Learners

But to go to school in a summer morn,

O! it drives all joy away;

Under a cruel eye outworn,

The little ones spend the day

In sighing and dismay.

—William Blake, from "The Schoolboy" (1794)

Jean Piaget believed that the hunger to learn is more important than food or drink. Why then do children over the centuries lament, "I hate school"? The reason is that learning loses its joy when it becomes a requirement instead of an activity we choose to engage in for ourselves.

THE PROBLEM: AN EROSION OF INTRINSIC MOTIVATION. Developmentalists divide motivation into two categories. **Intrinsic motivation** refers to self-generated actions, those we take from our inner desires. When Piaget described our hunger to learn, he was referring to intrinsic motivations. **Extrinsic motivation** refers to activities that we undertake in order to get external reinforcers, such as praise or pay, or a good grade.

Unfortunately, the learning activity you are currently engaged in falls into the extrinsic category. You know you will be tested on what you are reading. Worse yet, if you decided to pick up this book for an intrinsic reason—because you wanted to learn about human development—the very fact that you might be graded would make your basic interest fall off.

Numerous studies show that when adults give external reinforcers for activities that are intrinsically motivating, children are less likely to want to perform those activities for themselves (Patall, Cooper, & Robinson, 2008; Stipek, 1996). In one classic example, researchers selected preschoolers who were intrinsically interested in art. When they gave a "good player" award (an outside reinforcer) for the art projects, the children later showed a dramatic decline in their interest in doing art for fun (Lepper, Greene, & Nisbett, 1973). This research makes sense of the question you may have wondered about: "Why, after taking that literature class, am I less interested in reading on my own?"

Young children enter kindergarten brimming with intrinsic motivation. When does this love affair with school turn sour? Think back to your childhood, and you will realize that enchantment wanes during early elementary school, when teachers provide those external reinforcers—grades (Stipek, 1997). Moreover, during first or second grade, classroom learning often becomes abstract and removed from life. Rote activities, like filling in worksheets and memorizing multiplication tables, have replaced the creative hands-on projects of kindergarten. So ironically school may be the very setting where Piaget's little-scientist activities are *least* likely to occur.

Then, as children enter concrete operations—at around age 8— they begin comparing their performance to that of their peers. This competitive orientation erodes intrinsic motivation (Dweck, 1986; Self-Brown & Mathews, 2003). The focus shifts from "I want to improve for myself" to "I want to do *better* than my friends."

In sum, several forces explain why many children dislike school: School involves extrinsic reinforcers (grades). School learning, because it often involves rote memorization, is not intrinsically interesting. In school, children are not free to set their own learning goals. Their performance is judged by how they measure up to the rest of the class.

It is no wonder, therefore, that studies in Western nations document an alarming decline in intrinsic motivation as children travel through school (Katz, Kaplan, & Gueta, 2010; Spinath & Steinmayr, 2008). Susan Harter (1981) asked children to choose

intrinsic motivation The drive to act based on the pleasure of taking that action in itself, not for an external reinforcer or reward.

extrinsic motivation The drive to take an action because that activity offers external reinforcers such as praise, money, or a good grade.

Compare the activities of this kindergarten class of "little scientists" with older children in your local elementary school and you will immediately understand why by about age 8 many children begin to say, "I hate school."

between two statements: "Some kids work really hard to get good grades" (referring to extrinsic motivation) or "Some kids work really hard because they like to learn new things" (measuring intrinsic motives). When she gave her measure to hundreds of California public school children, intrinsic motivation scores fell off from third to ninth grade.

Still, external reinforcers can be vital hooks that get us intrinsically involved. Have you ever reluctantly read a book for a class and found yourself captivated by the subject? Perhaps you enrolled in this course because it was required for graduation but are now so interested in the material that you want to make some aspect of developmental science your career. Given that extrinsically motivating activities are basic to school and life, how can we make them work best?

THE SOLUTION: MAKING EXTRINSIC LEARNING PART OF US. To answer this question, Edward Deci and Richard Ryan (1985, 2000) make the point that we engage in some types of extrinsic learning unwillingly: "I have to take that terrible anatomy course because it is a requirement for graduation." We enthusiastically embrace other extrinsic tasks, which may not be inherently interesting, because we identify with their larger goal: "I want to memorize every bone of the body because that information is vital to my nursing career." In the first situation, the learning activity is irrelevant. In the second, the task has become intrinsic because it is connected to our inner self. Therefore, the key to transforming school learning from a chore into a pleasure is to make extrinsic learning relate to children's goals and desires.

The most boring tasks take on an intrinsic aura when they speak to children's passions. Imagine, for instance, how a first grader's motivation to sound out words might change if a teacher, knowing that student was captivated by dinosaurs, gave that boy the job of sounding out dinosaur names. Deci and Ryan believe that learning becomes intrinsic when it satisfies our basic need for relatedness (attachment). Think back to the discussion of schools that beat the odds. Imagine how motivated those children might be to learn to read when they understood that their success would make their beloved school proud. Finally, extrinsic tasks take on an intrinsic feeling when they foster autonomy, or offer choices of how to do our work (Patall, Cooper, & Robinson, 2008; Ryan and others, 2006).

Studies around the globe suggest that when teachers and parents take away children's autonomy—by controlling, criticizing, or micromanaging learning tasks—they erode intrinsic motivation (see Jang, Reeve, & Deci, 2010; Soenens & Vansteenkiste, 2010). We can see this principle in our own lives. By continually denigrating our work, or hovering over every move, a controlling supervisor has the uncanny ability to turn us off to the most intrinsically interesting job.

Our need for autonomy explains why, as I suggested in the section on successful schools, assigning high-level conceptual learning tasks can be effective with every child. Conversely, the poisonous effects of taking away autonomy suggests why the U.S. practice of grading teachers (an extrinsic motivator) based on students' performance on standardized exams erodes satisfaction in this field ("I can't teach the way I want. I have to teach to the test or I'll get fired"). Plus, because curriculum changes are typically dictated from on "high" (and so take away autonomy), it makes sense that teachers can be unmotivated to implement new reading and math directives even when those changes might work.

But, in a national experiment, when certain school districts gave staff the chance to *choose* between several new programs and provided *clear data* about their effectiveness, teachers modified their behavior—and, after 4 years, students made impressive gains on standard reading tests (Slavin and others, 2013). Therefore, providing autonomy (giving choices) and fostering relevance (pointing out the importance of an activity to that person's goals) benefits *both* students and teachers!

Table 7.5 summarizes these messages for teachers: Focus on relevance, enhance relatedness, and provide autonomy. The table also pulls together other teaching tips based on Gardner's and Sternberg's perspectives on intelligence and our look at what makes schools successful. Now, let's conclude by touching briefly on that sea change in the U.S. public school landscape—the Common Core State Standards.

Table 7.5: Lessons for Teachers: A Recap of This Chapter's Insights

1. **Foster relevance.** For instance, in teaching reading, tailor the books you are assigning so that they fit children's passions. And entice students to learn to read in other ways, such as getting first and second graders energized by telling them that they will now be able to break a code that the world uses, just like a detective!

2. **Foster relatedness.** Develop a secure, loving attachment with every student. Continually tell each child how proud you are when that person tries hard or succeeds.

3. **Foster autonomy.** As much as possible, allow your students to select among several equivalent assignments (such as choosing which specific books to read). Don't give time limits, such as "It's 9:30 and this has to be done by 10:00," or hover, take over tasks, or make negative comments. Stand by to provide informational comments and careful scaffolding (see Chapter 5) when students ask. Build in assignments that allow high-level thinking, such as using essays in preference to rote work such as copying sentences or filling out worksheets.

Teaching Tips Based on Gardner's and Sternberg's Theories

1. Offer balanced assignments that capitalize on students' different kinds of intelligence—creative work such as essays; practical-intelligence activities such as calculating numbers to make change at a store; single-answer analytic tasks (using Sternberg's framework); and classroom time devoted to music, dance, the arts, and caring for plants (capitalizing on Gardner's ideas).

2. Explicitly teach students to use their different intelligences in mastering classroom work.

Additional Teaching Tips

1. Don't rely on IQ test scores, especially in assessing the abilities of low-income and ethnic-minority students.

2. Avoid praising children for being "brilliant." Compliment them for hard work.

3. Go beyond academics to teach children interpersonal skills.

4. Strive for excellence. Expect all students to succeed.

5. Foster collaborative working relationships with your colleagues and students' parents.

6. Minimize grade-oriented comparisons (such as who got A's, B's, C's, etc.). Emphasize the importance of personal improvement to students. Experiment with giving grades for individual progress.

Hot in Developmental Science: The Common Core State Standards

At this point in the chapter, you are fully aware of the dispiriting problems plaguing U.S. schools. Affluent middle-class students get the best teachers and go to superior schools. Simply by residing in the "wrong" zip codes, low-income children are left behind from kindergarten onward. Because classwork involves rote memorization, a steady erosion of intrinsic motivation sets in as children travel through school.

How can we change this scenario so that boys and girls—no matter where they live—are literally on the same learning page? Now that we understand each child can benefit from challenging work, can't we inject more conceptual thinking into every class?

Enter the **Common Core State Standards.** Rather than learning benchmarks differing in a crazy-quilt pattern from state to state, the Common Core spells out consistent, *demanding* requirements for students attending every U.S. public school (Kornhaber, Griffith, & Tyler, 2014). Rather than passively accepting the spit-back information strategy that has caused children throughout the ages to love to hate school, the Common Core encourages teachers to stress innovative thinking, problem solving, and communication skills. Instead of presenting learning tasks haphazardly, the Common Core also specifically utilizes the Vygotskian principle of scaffolding (see Chapter 5). Teachers are taught to tailor each assignment to flow in a stepwise manner from what students have previously absorbed.

As of this writing, this landmark in education has been adopted in 45 states and the District of Columbia (Kornhaber, Griffith, and Tyler, 2014). But the revolution has miles to go (Rothman, 2014). Teachers need to learn how to teach using scaffolding and

Common Core State Standards Transformative U.S. public school changes, spelling out universal learning benchmarks and emphasizing teaching through scaffolding, problem solving, and communication skills.

Masterfile

This teacher is using the Common Core principles of scaffolding, and stressing creative thinking in teaching this computer class–getting these boys to think through their answers on their own.

more Socratic (questioning, discussion-based) classroom techniques. Teacher evaluations and student end-of-year tests need to be aligned with the learning goals in the Common Core. In addition to using fill-in-the-bubble multiple-choice tests, for instance, student-generated portfolios may be required to test the deeper thinking this approach to learning demands.

Will school systems give teachers the space to creatively collaborate in how best to implement the Common Core, or will these guidelines be viewed as another airy set of autonomy-eroding dictums from on high? Will having clear benchmarks and putting a premium on thinking really make a difference for students in less desirable zip codes (aka poor children) and for every U.S. public school child? Stay tuned for data, as most states implement these changes after this book goes to press.

The Common Core State Standards embody the equity and inclusiveness that we hope for when children arrive on the planet in this enlightened day and age. I hope this chapter has alerted you to *generally* think about development in a more enlightened, inclusive way. Child-rearing priorities are shaped by our particular society. Poverty-level children need a more level academic playing field. We need to provide an environment that allows parents to effectively parent and schools to teach in a way that permits every child to succeed.

Tying It All Together

1. If Devin, from an upper-middle-class family, and Adam, from a low-income family, are starting kindergarten, you can predict that (pick one):

   a. Both children will perform equally well on school readiness tests, but Adam will fall behind because he is likely to go to a poor-quality kindergarten.

   b. Devin will outperform Adam on school readiness tests, and the gap will probably widen because Adam will go to a poor-quality kindergarten.

2. Malik hasn't been doing well in school, and his achievement test scores have consistently been well below average for his grade. On the WISC, Malik gets an IQ score of 115. What is your conclusion?

3. You are telling a friend about the deficiencies of relying on a child's IQ score. Pick out the two arguments you might make.

   a. The tests are not reliable; children's scores typically change a lot during the elementary school years.

   b. The tests are not valid predictors of school performance.

   c. As people have different abilities, a single IQ score may not tell us much about a child's unique gifts.

   d. As poor children are at a disadvantage in taking the test, you should not use the IQ scores as an index of "genetic school-related talents" for low-income children.

4. Josh doesn't do well in reading or math, but he excels in music and dance, and he gets along with all kinds of children. In terms of Sternberg's theory of successful intelligence, Josh is not good in _____, but he is skilled in _____ and _____. In terms of Gardner's theory of _____, Josh is strong in which intelligences?

5. A principal of a school asks for tips to help her students with learning difficulties. Based on this section, you should advise (*pick one*): *making the material simple/ putting these children together in a special class/providing high-level creative work and embedding these children in the life of the school.*

6. (a) Define intrinsic and extrinsic motivation. (b) Give an example of a task in your life right now that is driven by each kind of motivation. (c) From reading the chapter, can you come up with some ways to make the unpleasant extrinsic tasks you do feel more intrinsic?

Answers to the Tying It All Together questions can be found at the end of this chapter.

SUMMARY

Home

Families vary, from never-divorced two-parent couples to blended families, from gay-parent families to unmarried couples or grand-parents raising a child. The main distinction is that mother-headed families are far more likely to live in poverty than their two-parent counterparts. Today, in the West, families vary dramatically by ethnicity and immigrant status. Children, however, can thrive in any kind of family, depending on the care parents provide.

According to Diana Baumrind's **parenting styles** approach, based on providing rules and nurturing, parents are classified as **authoritative, authoritarian, permissive,** and **rejecting-neglecting.** Although, generally speaking, parents who provide clear rules and are highly child-centered tend to raise the most well-adjusted children, above all, parents should provide consistent discipline. Child-rearing approaches actually vary from child to child, with at-risk children evoking poorer parenting. Even though Asian-heritage families have been portrayed as authoritarian, they, too, adopt a child-centered authoritative style. Having rigid rules, while appropriate in the past, are symptoms of contemporary parenting distress.

Resilient children, boys and girls who do well in the face of traumatic experiences, tend to have good executive functions; other talents; one close, secure attachment and not be faced with an overload of life blows. A specific genetic profile may offer some children biological resilience in the face of stress.

Behavioral-genetic researchers argue that children grow up to fulfill their genetic destiny, and adequate parenting is all that is necessary. Judith Harris believes that peer groups (and the wider society)—not parents—are the main socializers in children's lives. While the findings relating to **acculturation** (immigrant children taking on the norms of the new society) support Harris's theory, high-quality parenting matters greatly when children are biologically and socially "at risk." Parents need to be flexible, tailoring their child-rearing to their environment and to their children's needs. They should also relax and enjoy these fleeting years.

Attitudes about **corporal punishment** have changed dramatically, with many developed nations now outlawing spanking. Passing similar bans however is unlikely in the United States. Although physical punishment is not the preferred discipline, it is still used by many U.S. parents and strongly endorsed by certain groups. Experts disagree as to whether corporal punishment can ever be used, but we do know that spanking is particularly detrimental with "at-risk" children, people should never hit a baby, and positive reinforcement is far preferable to any punishment.

Child maltreatment—physical abuse, neglect, emotional abuse, and sexual abuse—can sometimes be hard to classify. The prevalence of this parenting disaster varies from nation to nation, and maltreatment statistics differ, depending on whether we ask adults to reflect on their childhoods or consider observers' reports. However, in general, parents' personality problems, environmental stress, plus low social support and having an at-risk child are the main factors that can provoke abuse. Abused children often have problems that can persist into adult life, in part because this trauma can produce epigenetic changes in our DNA. Although teachers and health-care professionals are required to report suspected abuse, it is difficult to speak up, and authorities often do not follow through on reports. So, unfortunately, child-abuse statistics underestimate the magnitude of this problem today.

Children of divorce are at risk for negative life outcomes, but most boys and girls adapt well to this common childhood event. Parents find it difficult to tell their children they are divorcing, and struggle not to badmouth an ex-spouse. The key to making divorce less traumatic lies in minimizing **parental alienation,** giving children some say in custody arrangements, and promoting high-quality custodial parenting. Joint custody is a common arrangement today, but it only works if the dad is a reasonably good parent.

School

Many children from low-income families enter kindergarten well behind their affluent counterparts in basic academic skills. These inequalities at the starting gate are magnified by the fact that poor children are likely to attend the poorest-quality kindergartens.

Achievement tests measure a child's body of knowledge. IQ tests measure a child's basic potential for classroom work. The **Wechsler Intelligence Scale for Children (WISC),** is the main childhood IQ test. This time-intensive test, involving a variety of subtests, is given individually to a child. If the child's IQ score is below 70—and if other indicators warrant this designation—that boy or girl may be labeled **intellectually disabled.** If the child's score is much higher than his performance on achievement tests, he is classified as having a **specific learning disorder** such as **dyslexia.** If a child's IQ score is at or above 130, she is considered **gifted** and is eligible to be placed in an accelerated class.

IQ scores satisfy the measurement criterion called **reliability,** meaning that people tend to get roughly the same score if the test is taken more than once. However, stressful life experiences can artificially lower a child's score. The test is also **valid,** meaning that it predicts performance in school. Some psychologists claim that the test score reflects a single quality called **"g"** that relates to cognitive performance in every area of life; others feel that intelligence involves multiple abilities and argue that it is inappropriate to rank people as intelligent or not based on a single IQ score. The remarkable **Flynn effect** (century-long test performance increase due to improved environments), suggests that, for disadvantaged children, the IQ score cannot be viewed as an index of genetic gifts.

Robert Sternberg and Howard Gardner argue that we need to expand our measures of intelligence beyond traditional tests. Sternberg believes that there are three types of intelligence: **analytic intelligence** (academic abilities), **creative intelligence,** and **practical intelligence** (real-world abilities, or "street smarts"). **Successful intelligence** requires having a balance among these three skills. Gardner, in his **multiple intelligences theory,** describes eight (or possibly nine) types of intelligences. Although neither of these psychologists has developed alternatives to conventional IQ tests, their ideas have been used to rethink the way we teach.

Schools serving disadvantaged students who flower academically share a mission to have every child succeed. They provide a challenging academic environment and assume that each student can do well at high-level work. Teachers support and mentor one another at these authoritative schools.

Why do many children dislike school? The reason is that classroom learning is based on **extrinsic motivation** (external reinforcers such as grades), which impairs **intrinsic motivation** (the desire to learn for the sake of learning). School learning is inherently less interesting because it often involves rote memorization. Being evaluated in comparison to the class also erodes a child's interest in learning for its own sake. Studies show a disturbing decline in intrinsic motivation as children progress through elementary school.

Teachers (and parents) can make extrinsic learning tasks more intrinsic by offering material relevant to children's interests, fostering relatedness (or a close attachment), and giving students choices about how to do their work. Stimulating intrinsic motivation by offering more autonomy (providing choices) helps motivate teachers to adopt new effective teaching strategies. The **Common Core State Standards,** by providing universal learning benchmarks and teaching with an emphasis on scaffolding, creativity, and problem solving, provide a potential sea change in U.S. education. Schools need to provide a better planned, more interesting, consistent learning experience for every child.

KEY TERMS

parenting style, p. 201

authoritative parents, p. 201

authoritarian parents, p. 201

permissive parents, p. 201

rejecting-neglecting parents, p. 201

resilient children, p. 203

acculturation, p. 205

corporal punishment, p. 206

child maltreatment, p. 207

parental alienation, p. 210

achievement tests, p. 213

WISC (Wechsler Intelligence Scale for Children), p. 213

intellectual disability, p. 214

specific learning disorder, p. 214

dyslexia, p. 214

gifted, p. 214

reliability, p. 216

validity, p. 216

Flynn effect, p. 216

"g," p. 216

analytic intelligence, p. 218

creative intelligence, p. 218

practical intelligence, p. 218

Sternberg's successful intelligence, p. 218

Gardner's multiple intelligences theory, p. 218

intrinsic motivation, p. 221

extrinsic motivation, p. 221

Common Core State Standards, p. 223

Amos Morgan/Photodisc/Getty Images

ANSWERS TO Tying It All Together QUIZZES

Home

1. Montana's parents = authoritative. Pablo's parents = authoritarian. Sara's parents = permissive.

2. Amber

3. Judith Harris's advice = Get your son in the best possible peer group. This chapter's recommendation = Provide exceptionally sensitive parenting.

4. a and c

5. Ms. Johnson might feel torn about reporting her observations, because she is afraid of parents retaliating or worried about making false accusations. Even if she does make a report, there is a good chance authorities will not investigate the situation.

6. The main criterion for awarding joint custody—or unlimited visits—should be whether the father is a good parent.

School

1. b

2. Malik has a learning disability.

3. c and d

4. Analytic intelligence . . . creative intelligence and practical intelligence . . . multiple intelligences . . . Josh's strengths are in musical, kinesthetic, and interpersonal intelligence.

5. You should advise giving these children high-level creative work and embed them in the life of the school.

6. (a) Intrinsic motivation is self-generated—we work at something simply because it gives us joy. Extrinsic motivation refers to activities propelled by external reinforcers like grades. (b) Ask yourself: Am I doing this because I love it or only because this activity results in an external reward? (c) 1. Make disliked, extrinsic tasks relevant to a larger personal goal. ("Cleaning the house will help me become a more organized person. Plus, it's great exercise, so I'll become healthier.") 2. Increase your sense of autonomy or feeling of having choices around this activity. ("I'll do my housecleaning at the time of day that feels least burdensome while I listen to my favorite CD.") 3. Enhance attachments ("If my significant other comes home to a clean house, she'll feel wonderful!")

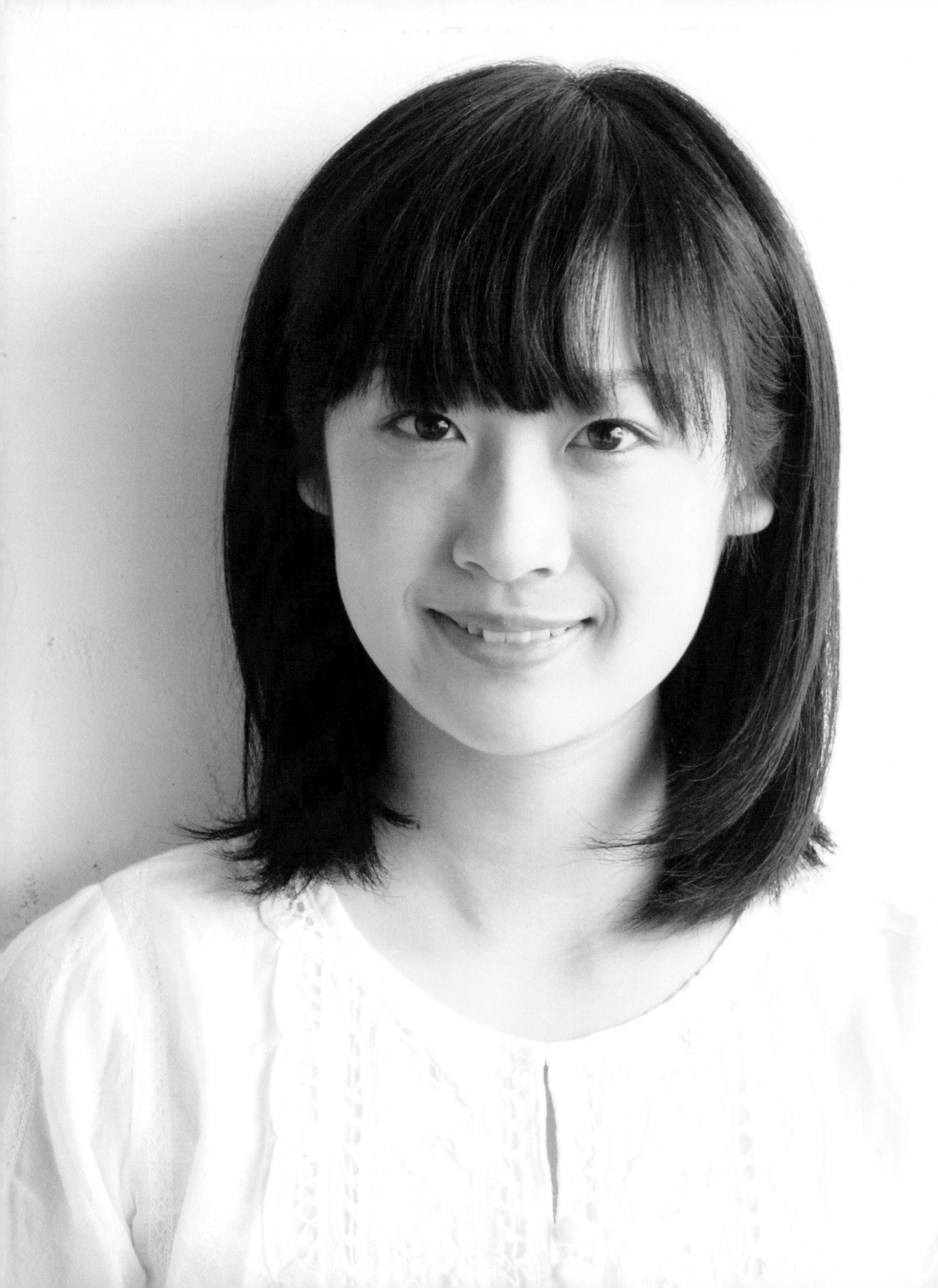

Adolescence

This two-chapter part dealing with the teenage years actually progresses a bit chronologically. That's because my first topic, puberty, can begin to take place as early as age 9 or 10.

In Chapter 8—**Physical Development**—I'll spend a good deal of time exploring puberty, that early adolescent total body change. However, I'll also be focusing on two other teenage body-oriented topics: body image (and eating disorders) and adolescent sexuality.

Chapter 9—**Cognitive and Socioemotional Development**—begins by examining the dramatic advances in reasoning and morality that occur during adolescence. Next, I'll be looking at teenagers' emotional states and offering insights into which children are prone to have problems or flourish during this special decade of life. The last part of this chapter concerns relationships—how teenagers behave with their parents; how they act with their peers.

PART IV

CHAPTER 8

Rick Gomez/Radius Images/Getty Images

Physical Development

Samantha and her twin brother, Sam, were so much alike—in their physical features, their personalities, their academic talents. Except for the sex difference, they seemed like identical twins. Then, when Samantha was 10, she started to tower over Sam and the rest of the fifth-grade class.

Yes, there were downsides to being first to develop—needing to hide behind a locker when you dressed for gym; not having anyone to talk to when you got your period at age 10; being teased by the other kids about your big, strange body. But, oh, what fun! From being a neglected, pudgy elementary school child, by sixth grade, Samantha leaped into the ranks of most popular. At age 12, Samantha was smoking and drinking. By 14, she regularly defied her helpless parents and often left the house at 2 a.m.

Samantha's parents were frantic, but their daughter couldn't care less. Everything else was irrelevant compared to exploring being an adult. It took a life-changing tenth-grade trip to Costa Rica with Sara, and a pregnancy scare, to get Samantha on track. Samantha had abandoned Sara, her best friend from first grade on, for her new "mature" friends. But when the girls got close again that memorable summer, Sara's calming influence woke Samantha up. Samantha credits comments like, "Why are you putting yourself in danger by having unprotected sex?" with saving her life. Plus, her lifelong competition with her brother didn't hurt. Although Sam was also an early developer, when he shot up to 6 feet in the spring of seventh grade, he was great at sports and also a social star.

Now that Samantha is 30, married, and expecting her first child, it's interesting for the three of them to get together and talk (for the first time) about the teenage years. Sam remembers the thrill of getting so much stronger and his first incredible feelings of being in love. Samantha recalls being excited about her changing body, but she also remembers obsessively worrying about being too fat. Then, there is Sara, who says middle school was no problem because she didn't menstruate until age 14. Everyone goes through puberty, but why does everyone react in different ways?

Why did Samantha have trouble as an early-maturing girl, while Sam and Sara sailed through these landmark years? This chapter focuses on that question and others as I explore **puberty,** the name for the internal and external changes related to physically becoming adult. I'll begin by exploring this landmark life transition—examining what sets off puberty, tracking the unfolding changes, focusing on how teens react to their bodies. Next, I'll discuss body image issues and, finally, explore sexuality during this watershed time of life. As you read this chapter, think back to when you were 10 or 12 or 14. How did you feel about your body during puberty? When did you begin dating and fantasizing about having sex?

puberty The hormonal and physical changes by which children become sexually mature human beings and reach their adult height.

puberty rite A "coming of age" ritual, usually beginning at some event such as first menstruation, held in traditional cultures to celebrate children's transition to adulthood.

secular trend in puberty A century-long decline in the average age at which children reach puberty in the developed world.

menarche A girl's first menstruation.

spermarche A boy's first ejaculation of live sperm.

Puberty

Compare photos of yourself from late elementary school and high school to get a vivid sense of the changes that occur during puberty. From the size of our thighs to the shape of our nose, we become a different-looking person during the early teenage years. Although children's timetables vary, today puberty—which lasts about five years from start to finish—typically is a pre-teen and early adolescent change (Archibald, Graber, & Brooks-Gunn, 2003). Moreover, today, as you saw with Samantha, who started menstruating at age 10 and has just gotten pregnant at age 30, the gap between being physically able to have children and actually having children can be twice as long as infancy and childhood combined.

These photographs of fourth graders and high school juniors at the prom offer a vivid visual reminder of the total body transformation that takes place as children travel through puberty during early adolescence.

This lack of person–environment fit, when our body is passionately saying "have sex" and society is telling us to "just say no" to intercourse, explains why issues relating to teenage sexuality provoke such anxiety among Western adults. Our concerns are recent. They are a product of living in the contemporary developed world.

Setting the Context: Culture, History, and Puberty

For this rural Vietnamese boy, reaching puberty means it's time to assume his adult responsibilities as a fisherman. This is the reason why having puberty rites to mark the end of childhood makes excellent sense in less-industrialized cultures, but not in our own.

As my sisters and I went about doing our daily chores, we choked on the dust stirred up by the herd of cattle and goats that had just arrived in our compound. . . . These animals were my bride wealth, negotiated by my parents and the family of the man who had been chosen as my husband. . . . I am considered to be a woman, so I am ready to marry, have children, and assume adult privileges and responsibilities. My name is Telelia ole Mariani. I am 14 years old.

(quoted in Wilson, Ngige, & Trollinger, 2003, p. 95)

As you can see in this quotation from a girl in rural Nigeria, throughout most of history and even today in agrarian cultures, having sex as a teenager was "normal." The reason is that puberty was often society's signal to find a spouse (Schlegel, 1995; Schlegel & Barry, 1991). The fact that a young person's changing body meant entering a new adult stage of life produced a different attitude toward the physical changes. In our culture, we downplay puberty because we don't want teenagers to act on their sexual feelings for years. In traditional societies, people might celebrate the changes in a coming-of-age ceremony called the **puberty rite.**

Celebrating Puberty

Puberty rites were emotional events, carefully scripted to highlight a young person's entrance into adulthood. Often, children were removed from their families and asked to perform challenging tasks. There was anxiety ("Can I really do this thing?") and feelings of awe and self-efficacy, as the young person returned to joyfully enter the community as an adult (Feixa, 2011; Weisfeld, 1997).

So as this photo shows in one South African tribe, after a private group initiation, boys returned to their tribe and were labeled as "warriors" in a community celebration. In the Amazon, males were required to prove their manhood by killing a large animal and then, metaphorically, "die"—by drinking a hallucinogen and spending time in isolation to "be born again" as adults. Among the Masai of Africa, male children first faced the challenge of undergoing a painful circumcision without showing distress. After passing this test, they entered a segregated compound to learn military maneuvers before proudly returning home and taking wives (Feixa, 2011).

For girls, menstruation was the standard marker to celebrate one's arrival into womanhood. In the traditional Navajo Kinaalda ceremony, for instance, girls in their first or second menstrual cycle, guided by a female mentor, performed the long-distance running ritual, sprinting for miles. (Imagine your motivation to train for this event, when you understood that the length of your run symbolized how long you would live!) The female role model massaged the girl's body, painted her face, and supervised her as she prepared a huge corn cake (a symbol of fertility) to be served to the community during a joyous, all-night sing. The Navajo believe that when females begin menstruating, they possess special spiritual powers, so everyone would gather around for the girl's blessings as they gave her a new adult name.

Today, however, girls may menstruate at age 10 or even 9. At that age—in *any* society—could people be ready for adult life? The answer is no. In the past, we reached puberty at an older age.

The Declining Age of Puberty

You can see this fascinating decline, called the **secular trend in puberty,** in Figure 8.1. In the 1860s, the average age of **menarche,** or first menstruation, in northern Europe was over 17 (Tanner, 1978). In the 1960s, in the developed world, it dropped to under 13 (Parent and others, 2003). Then, after a pause, about 20 years ago, the menarche marker began to slide downward again (Lee & Styne, 2013).

This means, a century ago, many girls could not get pregnant until their late teens. Today, many girls can have babies *before* their teenage years.

Researchers typically use menarche as their benchmark for charting the secular trend because it is an obvious sign of being able to have a child. The male signal of fertility, **spermarche,** or first ejaculation of live sperm, is a hidden event.

This photo shows South African boys returning from an "initiation school" to welcome their entry into adulthood. As is classic, in this culture the puberty ritual involves separation from one's family, symbolically being "reborn" or changed (in this case, being circumcised), and intensive instruction in the conduct befitting their new status as men.

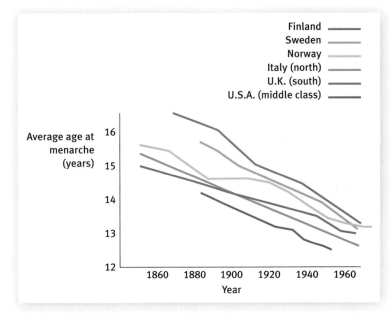

Finland _____
Sweden _____
Norway _____
Italy (north) _____
U.K. (south) _____
U.S.A. (middle class) _____

Average age at menarche (years)

FIGURE 8.1: **The secular trend in puberty:** Notice that the average age of menarche dramatically declined in developed countries during the first half of the twentieth century. Why exactly is this decline continuing? Stay tuned for surprising answers later in this chapter.

Data from: Tanner 1978, p. 103.

If they had grown up a century ago, these seventh graders at a summer computer camp would really have looked like girls. Due to the secular trend in puberty, females today mature physically at a younger age than they did one hundred years ago.

In addition, because it reflects better nutrition, in the same way as with stunting in early childhood (remember Chapter 3), we can use the secular trend in puberty as an index of a nation's economic development. In the United States, African American girls begin to menstruate at close to age 12. In impoverished African nations, such as Senegal, the average age of menarche is over 16 (Parent and others, 2003)!

Given that nutrition is intimately involved, what *exactly* sets puberty off? For answers, let's focus on the hormonal systems that program the physical changes.

The Hormonal Programmers

Puberty is programmed by two command centers. One system, located in the adrenal glands at the top of the kidneys, begins to release its hormones at about age 6 to 8, several years before children show observable signs of puberty. The **adrenal androgens**, whose output increases to reach a peak in the early twenties, eventually produce (among other events) pubic hair development, skin changes, body odor, and, as you will read later in this chapter, our first feelings of sexual desire (McClintock & Herdt, 1996).

About two years later, the most important command center kicks in. Called the **HPG axis**—because it involves the hypothalamus (in the brain), the pituitary (a gland at the base of the brain), and the **gonads** (the *ovaries* and the *testes*)—this system produces the major body changes.

As you can see in Figure 8.2, puberty is set off by a three-phase chain reaction. At about age 9 or 10, pulsating bursts of the hypothalamic hormone stimulate the pituitary gland to step up production of its hormones. This causes the ovaries and testes to secrete several closely related compounds called estrogens and the hormone called **testosterone.**

As the blood concentrations of estrogens and testosterone float upward, these hormones unleash a physical transformation. Estrogens produce females' changing shape by causing the hips to widen and the uterus and breasts to enlarge. They set in motion the cycle of reproduction, stimulating the ovaries to produce eggs. Testosterone causes the penis to lengthen, promotes the growth of facial and body hair, and is responsible for a dramatic increase in muscle mass and other internal masculine changes.

Boys and girls *both* produce estrogens and testosterone. Testosterone and the adrenal androgens are the desire hormones. They are responsible for sexual arousal in females and males. However, women produce mainly estrogens. The concentration of testosterone is roughly eight times higher in boys after puberty than it is in girls; in fact, this classic "male" hormone is responsible for *all* the physical changes in boys.

Now, to return to our earlier question: What primes the triggering hypothalamic hormone? As Figure 8.2 illustrates, many forces help unleash the pulsating hypothalamic bursts—from genetics, to exposure to light; from possible chemicals in our water and food, to environmental stress (more about this fascinating force later). Central to this process is a threshold amount of a hormone called leptin, which is tied to the level of body fat (McCarthy, 2013; Lee & Styne, 2013). This explains why boys and girls whose bodies are stunted due to lack of food reach puberty at older ages. It accounts for the role that the obesity epidemic may play in the declining age of puberty in recent years (Lee & Styne, 2013; more about this later). These puberty primers unleash a cascade of physical changes.

adrenal androgens Hormones produced by the adrenal glands that program various aspects of puberty, such as growth of body hair, skin changes, and sexual desire.

HPG axis The main hormonal system programming puberty; it involves a triggering hypothalamic hormone that causes the pituitary to secrete its hormones, which in turn cause the ovaries and testes to develop and secrete the hormones that produce the major body changes.

gonads The sex organs—the ovaries in girls and the testes in boys.

testosterone The hormone responsible for the maturation of the organs of reproduction and other signs of puberty in men, and for hair and skin changes during puberty and for sexual desire in both sexes.

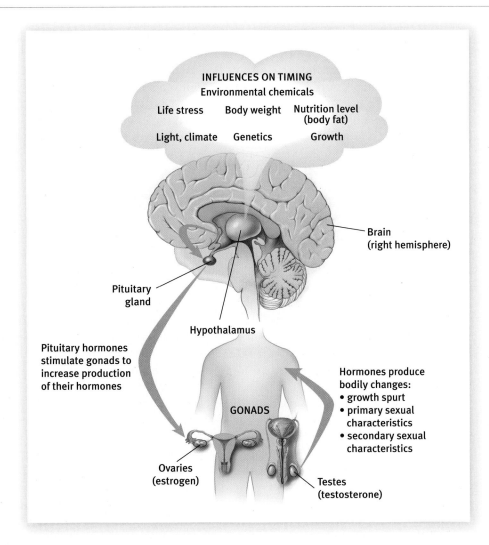

INFLUENCES ON TIMING
Environmental chemicals

Life stress   Body weight   Nutrition level (body fat)

Light, climate   Genetics   Growth

Brain (right hemisphere)

Pituitary gland

Hypothalamus

Pituitary hormones stimulate gonads to increase production of their hormones

GONADS

Hormones produce bodily changes:
• growth spurt
• primary sexual characteristics
• secondary sexual characteristics

Ovaries (estrogen)

Testes (testosterone)

FIGURE 8.2: **The HPG axis: The three-phase hormonal sequence that triggers puberty:** As you can see here, in response to various genetic and environmental influences, the hypothalamus releases a hormone that stimulates the pituitary gland to produce its own hormones, which cause the ovaries in girls and the testes in boys to grow and secrete estrogens and testosterone, producing the physical changes of puberty.
Adapted from Tanner, 1978, p. 103.

The Physical Changes

Puberty causes a total *psychological* as well as physical transformation. As the hormones flood the body, they affect specific brain regions, making teenagers more emotional, sensitive to social cues, and interested in taking risks (as you will read in Chapter 9). Scientists divide the physical changes into three categories:

- **Primary sexual characteristics** refer to the body changes directly involved in reproduction. The growth of the penis and menstruation are examples of primary sexual characteristics.

- **Secondary sexual characteristics** is the label for the hundreds of other changes that accompany puberty, such as breast development, the growth of pubic hair, voice changes, and alterations in the texture of the skin.

- The **growth spurt** merits its own special category. At puberty—as should come as no surprise—there is a dramatic increase in height and weight.

    Now, let's offer a motion picture of these changes, first in girls and then in boys.

For Girls

The first sign of puberty in girls is the growth spurt. During late childhood, girls' growth picks up speed, accelerates, and then begins to decrease (Abbassi, 1998). On a visit to my 11-year-old niece, I got a vivid sense of this "peak velocity" phase of growth.

primary sexual characteristics Physical changes of puberty that directly involve the organs of reproduction, such as the growth of the penis and the onset of menstruation.

secondary sexual characteristics Physical changes of puberty that are not directly involved in reproduction.

growth spurt A dramatic increase in height and weight that occurs during puberty.

Six months earlier, I had towered over her. Now, she insisted on standing back-to-back to demonstrate: "Look, Aunt Janet, I'm taller than you!"

About six months after the growth spurt begins, girls start to develop breasts and pubic hair. On average, girls' breasts take about four years to grow to their adult form (Tanner, 1955, 1978).

Menarche typically occurs in the middle to final stages of breast and pubic hair development when growth is winding down (Christensen and others, 2010; Peper & Dahl, 2013; Lee & Styne, 2013). So you can tell your 12-year-old niece, who has just begun to menstruate, that, while her breasts are still "works in progress," she is probably about as tall today as she will be as an adult.

When they reach menarche, can girls get pregnant? Yes, but there is often a window of infertility until the system fully gears up. Does puberty unfold in the same way for every girl? The answer is no. Because the hormonal signals are complex, in some girls, pubic hair development (programmed by the adrenal androgens) is underway before the breasts begin to enlarge. Occasionally, a girl does grow much taller after she begins to menstruate.

The most fascinating variability relates to the *rate* of change. Some children are developmental "tortoises." Their progression through puberty is slow-paced. Others are "hares." They speed through the body changes. For instance, while breast development *on average* takes four years, the process—from start to finish—can range from less than two to an incredible nine years! (See Mendle and others, 2010.)

New research suggests the pace at which children progress through puberty is affected by when the process starts. Girls who begin to develop earlier often proceed at a slower rate. Late starters pass through puberty for a shorter time. So if your 13-year-old niece is worried because she has just begun developing breasts, you can tell her that she may catch up a bit with the rest of the class now that her puberty system has locked into gear.

In tracking puberty in females, researchers focus on charting pubic hair and breast development because they can measure these external secondary sexual changes in stages. But the internal changes are equally dramatic. During puberty the uterus grows, the vagina lengthens, and the hips develop a cushion of fat. The vocal cords get longer, the heart gets bigger, and the red blood cells carry more oxygen. So, in addition to looking very different, after puberty, girls become much stronger (Archibald, Graber, & Brooks-Gunn, 2003). The increases in strength, stamina, height, and weight are astonishing in boys.

For Boys

In boys, researchers also chart how the penis, testicles, and pubic hair develop in stages. However, because these organs of reproduction begin developing first, boys still look like children to the outside world for a year or two after their bodies start changing. Voice changes, the growth of body hair, and that other visible sign of being a man—needing to shave—all take place after the growth of the testes and penis are underway (Tanner, 1978). Now, let's pause to look at the most obvious signals that a boy is becoming a man—the mammoth alterations in body size, shape, and strength.

Recall from Chapter 5 that elementary school boys and girls are roughly the same size. Then, during the puberty growth spurt, males shoot up an incredible average of 8 inches, compared to 4 inches for girls (Tanner, 1978). Boys also become far stronger than the other sex.

Photography by Alan Antiporda/Moment/Getty Images

Because the landmark change, shaving, occurs fairly late in the sequence of puberty, we can be sure that this 14-year-old-boy has been looking like a man, for some time, in ways we can't see in this photo.

One reason lies in the tremendous increase in muscle mass. Another lies in the dramatic cardiovascular changes. At puberty, boys' hearts increase in weight by more than one-third. In particular, notice in Figure 8.3 that, compared to females, after puberty, males have many more red blood cells and a much greater capacity for carrying oxygen in their blood. The visible signs of these changes are a big chest, wide shoulders, and a muscular frame. The real-world consequence is that after puberty, males get a boost in gross motor skills that give them an edge in everything from soccer to sprinting; from cycling to carrying heavy loads.

Do you know seventh- or eighth-grade boys? If so, you might notice that growth during puberty takes place in the opposite pattern to the one that occurs earlier in life. Rather than following the *cephalocaudal* and *proximodistal* sequences (from the head downward and from the middle of the body outward), at puberty, the hands, feet, and legs grow first. While this happens for both sexes, because their growth is so dramatic, these changes are especially obvious in boys.

Their long legs and large feet explain why, in their early teens, boys look so gawky (and unattractive!). Adding to the problem is the crackly voice produced by the growing larynx, the wispy look of beginning facial hair, and the fact that during puberty a boy's nose and ears grow before the rest of his face catches up. Plus, the increased activity of the sweat glands and enlarged pores leads to the condition that results in so much emotional agony: acne. Although girls also suffer from acne, boys are more vulnerable to this condition because testosterone, which males produce in abundance, produces changes in the hair and skin.

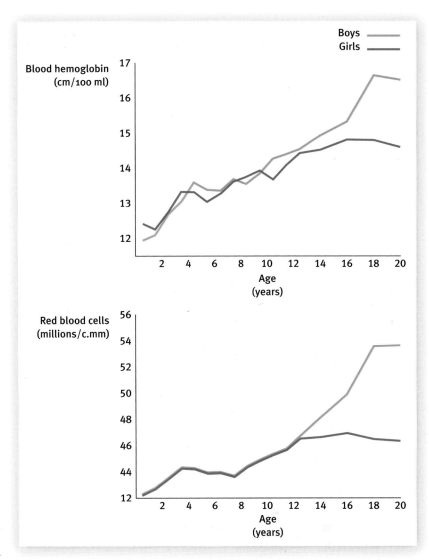

FIGURE 8.3: **Changes in blood hemoglobin and red blood cells during puberty in males and females:** At puberty, increases in the amount of hemoglobin in the blood and in the number of red blood cells cause children of both sexes to get far stronger. But notice that these changes are more pronounced in boys than in girls. Data from: Tanner, 1955, p. 103.

Are Boys on a Later Timetable? A Bit

Now, visit a middle school and you will be struck by the fact that boys, on average, appear to reach puberty two years later than girls. But appearances can be deceiving. In girls, as I mentioned earlier, the externally visible signs of puberty, such as the growth spurt and breast development, take place toward the beginning of the sequence. For boys, the hidden development—growth of the testes—occurs first (Huddleston & Ge, 2003; Lee & Styne, 2013).

If we look at the *real* sign of fertility, the timetables for girls and boys are not very far apart. In one study, boys reported that spermarche occurred at roughly age 13, only about six months later than the average age of menarche (Stein & Reiser, 1994).

Figure 8.4, on the next page, graphically summarizes some changes I have been discussing. Now, let's explore the numbers inside the chart. Why do children undergo puberty at such different ages?

FIGURE 8.4: **The sequence of some major events of puberty:** This chart shows the ages at which some important changes of puberty occur in the average boy and girl. The numbers below each change show the range of ages at which that event begins. Notice that girls are on a slightly earlier timetable than boys, that boys' height spurt occurs at a later point in their development, and that there are dramatic differences from child to child in the timing of puberty.

Data from: Tanner, 1978, pp. 23, 29.

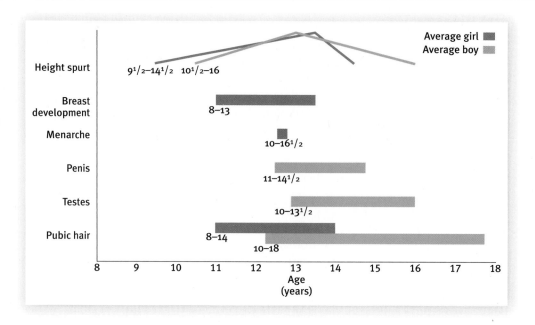

Individual Differences in Puberty Timetables

> I'm seventeen already. But I still look like a kid. I get teased a lot, especially by the other guys. . . . Girls aren't interested in me, either, because most of them are taller than I am. When will I grow up?
>
> (adapted from an on-line chat room)

The gender difference in puberty timetables can cause anxiety. As an early-maturing girl, I vividly remember slumping to avoid the humiliation of having my partner's head encounter my chest in sixth-grade dancing class! But nature's cruelest blow may relate to the individual differences in timing. What accounts for the five-year difference in puberty timetables between children who live in the same environment? (See Parent and others, 2003.)

Not expectedly, genetics is important. Identical twins go through puberty at roughly the same ages (Silventoinen and others, 2008; Lee & Styne, 2013). Asian Americans tend to be slightly behind other U.S. children in puberty timetables (Sun and others, 2002). African American and Hispanic boys and girls are ahead of other North American groups (Rosenfield, Lipton, & Drum, 2009; Lee & Styne, 2013).

But remember that in impoverished African countries—where children are poorly nourished—girls begin to menstruate, on average, as late as age 16. Recall from Chapter 5 that, in the United States, obesity rates are skyrocketing among African American elementary school girls and boys. Given that body fat is intimately involved, and the secular trend picked up steam during the past 20 years, does childhood weight predict when a boy or girl physically matures?

Look at female middle school friends—such as these girls getting ready for a dance—and you will be struck with the differences in puberty timetables. As you can see, a variety of interesting forces predict why children mature earlier or later than their peers.

Overweight and Early Puberty (It's All About Girls)

The answer is yes— if we consider female children *only*. Controlling for other forces, having a high BMI (body mass index) during elementary school does predict entering puberty earlier for girls (Rosenfield, Lipton, & Drum, 2009; Lee & Styne, 2013). Most tantalizing, rapid weight gain in the *first nine months of life* is strongly linked to menstruating at a younger age! (See Walvoord, 2010.)

Recall that this finding dovetails with the research in Chapter 5, suggesting that our overweight path is set in motion early in life. Now—in addition to foreshadowing later obesity—weight gain during infancy may even predict when we sexually mature. What I find strangest, however, is that the data for boys is inconsistent. Some studies show obese boys mature early; others suggest these children develop later than their peers! (See Lee & Styne, 2013.)

Now let's turn to a more astonishing environmental influence predicting puberty, specifically in girls—the quality of family life.

In Chapter 5 you learned that pushing food on this adorable 8-month-old girl might program her body to put on excessive weight. Now we know overfeeding can have another negative epigenetic effect—priming this baby to reach puberty at an early age.

Family Stress and Early Puberty (Again, It's About Girls)

Drawing on an *evolutionary psychology perspective*, some developmentalists argue that when family stress is intense, nature might build in a mechanism to accelerate sexual maturity and free a child from an inhospitable nest (Belsky, Steinberg, & Draper, 1991). Just as stress in the womb "instructs" the baby to store fat (recall the fetal programming hypothesis in Chapter 2), researchers believe that an unhappy childhood signals the body to expect a short life and pushes adult fertility to a younger age (Belsky, Houts, & Pasco Fearon, 2010).

I must emphasize that "genetics" is the most important force predicting your puberty timetable (when your mother or father developed). But, if a girl is temperamentally vulnerable, *controlling for every other influence* (genetics, body weight, and so on), her family life makes its small, tantalizing contribution, too (Ellis and others, 2011b). Early-maturing girls are more apt to grow up in mother-headed households (Graber, Nichols, & Brooks-Gunn, 2010; Neberich and others, 2010) and report intense childhood stress (Ellis, 2004; Allison & Hyde, 2013). In one longitudinal study, mothers' use of *power-assertive* discipline during preschool—yelling, shaming, rejecting—was associated with earlier menstruation (Belsky and others, 2007a, 2010). Even being insecurely attached at age 1 predicts reaching menarche at a younger age (Belsky, Houts, & Pasco Fearon, 2010).

Why—specifically in girls—is the hypothalamic timer sensitive to body weight and family stress? We do not know. But, these surprising studies emphasize the developmental-systems theory message that underlies this book: To understand *every aspect* of who we are, look to a variety of influences—from genetics to gender, from physiology to parenting, to everything else.

Table 8.1 summarizes these points by spelling out questions that predict a female child's chance of reaching puberty at a younger-than-average age. If you were an early maturer, how many—if any—of these forces applied to you?

Now that I've described the physical process, let's shift to an insider's perspective, exploring how children feel about three classic signs of puberty—breast development, menstruation, and first ejaculation—then, looking at the consequences of reaching puberty relatively early or late.

Table 8.1: Predicting a Girl's Chances of Early Puberty: Some Questions

1. Did this girl's parents reach puberty early?

2. Is this girl African American?

3. Is this girl overweight? Did she gain weight rapidly during her first year of life?

4. Has this girl's family life been stressful and unhappy? Did she have an insecure attachment?

An Insider's View of Puberty

If you think back to how you felt about your changing body during puberty, you probably remember a mixture of emotions: fear, pride, embarrassment, excitement. Now, imagine how you would react if a researcher asked you to describe your inner state. Would you want to talk about how you *really* felt? The reluctance of pre-teens to discuss what is happening ("Yuck! Just don't go there!") explains why, to study reactions to puberty, researchers often ask adults to remember this time of life, or use indirect measures, such as having children tell stories about pictures, to reveal their inner concerns.

The Breasts

In a classic study, researchers used this indirect strategy to explore how girls feel in relation to their parents while undergoing that most visible sign of becoming a woman—breast development (Brooks-Gunn and others, 1994). They asked a group of girls to tell a story about the characters in a drawing that showed an adult female (the mother) taking a bra out of a shopping bag while an adolescent girl and an adult male (the father) watched. While girls often talked about the mother in the picture as being excited and happy, they typically described the teenager as humiliated by her father's presence in the room. Moreover, girls in the middle of puberty told the most negative stories about the fathers, suggesting that body embarrassment is at its height when children are undergoing the physical changes.

Because society strongly values this symbol of being a woman (and our contemporary culture sees bigger as better!), other research suggests that U.S. girls feel proud of their developing breasts (Brooks-Gunn & Warren, 1988). However, among girls in ballet schools, where there are strong pressures to look prepubescent, breast development evokes distress (Brooks-Gunn & Warren, 1985). The principle that children's reactions to puberty depend on messages from the wider world holds true for menstruation, too.

Imagine how these girls auditioning at a premier ballet academy in New York City will feel when they develop breasts and perhaps find that their womanly body shape interrupts their career dreams, and you will understand why children's reactions to puberty depend totally on their unique environment.

David Sacks/The Image Bank/Getty Images

Menstruation

Think of being a Navajo girl and knowing that when you begin to menstruate, you enter a special spiritual state. Compare this with the less-than-glowing portrait Western societies paint about "that time of the month" (Brooks-Gunn & Ruble, 1982; Costos, Ackerman, & Paradis, 2002). From the advertisements for pills strong enough to handle even menstrual pain to its classic description as "the curse," there's no wonder that in the past, girls approached this milestone with dread (Brooks-Gunn & Ruble, 1982).

Luckily, upper-middle-class, baby boom mothers have changed these cultural scripts. When 18- to 20-year-old students at Oregon State University were asked in 2006 to write about their "first period experiences," 3 out of 4 women recalled their moms as being thrilled ("She treated me like a princess"). One person wrote that, the day after she told her mother, "I saw an expensive box of chocolates and a card addressed to me. It said 'Congrats on becoming a woman'" (quoted in Lee, 2008, p. 1332).

Positive responses make a difference. In contrast to earlier research, about half of these young women described menarche as positive or "no big deal." But negative emotions linger. Even when they described their mothers as supportive, 1 in 3 students remembered feeling "disgusted" or, more likely, ambivalent—both ashamed and happy—when menarche arrived.

First Ejaculation

Daughters must confide in their mothers about menarche because this change demands specific coping techniques. Spermarche, as I mentioned earlier, is hidden, because this event doesn't require instructions from the outside world. Who talks to male adolescents about first ejaculation, and how do teenagers feel about their signal of becoming a man? Read these memories from some 18-year-olds (Stein & Reiser, 1994):

> I woke up the next morning and my sheets were pasty. . . . After you wake up your mind is kind of happy and then you realize: "Oh my God, this is my wet dream!"
>
> (quoted in Stein & Reiser, 1994, p. 380)

> My mom, she knew I had them. It was all over my sheets and bedspread and stuff, but she didn't say anything, didn't tease me and stuff. She never asked if I wanted to talk about it—I'm glad. I never could have said anything to my mom.
>
> (quoted in Stein & Reiser, 1994, p. 377)

Most of these boys reported that they needed to be secretive. They didn't want to let *anyone* know. And notice from the second quotation—as you saw earlier with fathers and pre-teen girls—that boys also view their changing bodies as especially embarrassing around the parent of the opposite sex.

Is this tendency for children to hide the symptoms of puberty around the parent of the other gender programmed into evolution to help teenagers emotionally separate from their families? We do not know. Where we do have massive scientific information is on the emotional impact of being early or late.

Being Early: It Can Be a Problem for Girls

Imagine being an early-maturing girl. How would you feel if you looked like an adult while everyone else in your class still looked like a child? Now imagine being a late maturer and thinking, "What's wrong with my body? Will I *ever* grow up?"

Actually, the timing of development matters, but again the results differ for boys and girls. Early-maturing boys are more prone to abuse substances, particularly if these teens are low in impulse control (Castellanos-Ryan and others, 2013). They also may be at risk for depression if they have prior personality problems and an unhappy family life (Benoit, Lacourse, & Claes, 2013). But, because of being physically stronger (and so better at sports) and on time for the average girl, maturing early provides boys a popularity and self-esteem boost (Li and others, 2013).

Unfortunately, the research is consistently downbeat for the other sex: *Hundreds of studies suggest early-maturing girls can have widespread difficulties during their adolescent years.*

EARLY-MATURING GIRLS ARE AT RISK OF DEVELOPING EXTERNALIZING PROBLEMS. Because we choose friends who are "like us," early-maturing girls may gravitate toward becoming friends with older girls and boys. So they tend to get involved in "adult activities" such as smoking, drinking, and taking drugs at a younger age. Maturing early heightens the tendency—described in the next chapter—for teens to make dangerous, impulsive decisions with their peers (Kretsch & Harden, 2014.)

Because they are so busy testing the limits, in one classic study, early-maturing girls tended to get worse grades than their classmates in the sixth and seventh grades (Simmons & Blyth, 1987). By their twenties, Swedish researchers found, early-maturing girls were several times less likely to have graduated from high school than their later-developing peers (Stattin & Magnusson, 1990).

Then, there is the main concern with having a mature body early on: having unprotected sex. Because they may not have the cognitive abilities to resist this social pressure and often have older boyfriends, early-maturing girls are more likely to have

While early-maturing girls may be prone to get into trouble, for these manlike seventh-grade boys, developing earlier can be a social plus, as they are right on time for the average girl in this class.

Laurence Mouton/PhotoAlto Agency RF Collections/Getty Images

intercourse at a younger age (Graber, Nichols, & Brooks-Gunn, 2010). They are less apt to use contraception, making them more vulnerable to becoming pregnant as teens (Allison & Hyde, 2013). Imagine being a sixth- or seventh-grade girl thrilled to be pursued by the high school boys. Would you have the presence of mind to "just say no"?

EARLY-MATURING GIRLS ARE AT RISK OF GETTING ANXIOUS AND DEPRESSED. As if this were not enough, early-maturing girls are also more prone to feel bad about themselves (Carter, Silverman, & Jaccard, 2013; Joinson & others, 2013). As I implied in the introductory chapter vignette, in fourth or fifth grade, these girls can be bullied by their peers, because they look so different from the other children in class (Allison & Hyde, 2013). Then, there is the shame (and peer harassment) attached to *generally* having a larger body size. Not only are early-maturing girls apt to be heavier during elementary school, but they also end up shorter and stockier because their height spurt occurs at an earlier point in their development (Adair, 2008; Must and others, 2005). Late-maturing girls are more prone to fit the tall ultra-slim model shape. Reaching puberty early sets girls up for a poor body image and low self-esteem.

So far, I've been painting a dismal portrait of early-maturing girls. But, as with any aspect of development, it's important to look at the *whole* context of a person's life. Early maturation may not pose body image problems in ethnic groups that have a healthier, more inclusive idea about the ideal female body size (more about this later).

Most important, these negative effects happen mainly when there are other risk factors in a child's life. If a girl is exposed to harsh parenting (Deardorff and others, 2013) or if she is living in poverty, then, yes, early maturation can be the straw that breaks the camel's back (Lynne-Landsman, Graber, & Andrews, 2010). But, when a child has close relationships with her parents, strong religious values, and doesn't get involved with older "at-risk" friends, her puberty timetable will not matter at all (Stattin & Magnusson, 1990).

The risks linked with maturing early also seem dependent on the society in which a girl grows up. In one interesting international comparison, while early-maturing Swedish girls were more prone to get into trouble than late maturers, this was not true in Slovakia (see Figure 8.5). The reason, these researchers argue, is that Scandinavia is a permissive society that accepts adolescent sex, while Slovakia severely restricts these activities (Skoog and others, 2013). So, again, a protective milieu can cushion a girl (or any child) from acting on the behavioral messages her blossoming body gives off.

This brings up that important teenage milieu: school. In a classic study, researchers (Simmons & Blyth, 1987) found that early-maturing girls were set up to have problems when they transferred to a large middle school versus staying in a smaller K–8 school. In fact, in this landmark research, moving to middle school predicted getting poor grades and being more stressed out for every child.

Based on these findings, developmentalists have argued that it's best not to "warehouse" boys and girls in middle schools during the stressful pubertal years (see Eccles & Roeser, 2003). But, the following study suggests we might rethink this classic scientific advice.

In tracking students in 36 rural school systems that did and did not offer middle school, the researchers were surprised to find that bullying was less frequent among

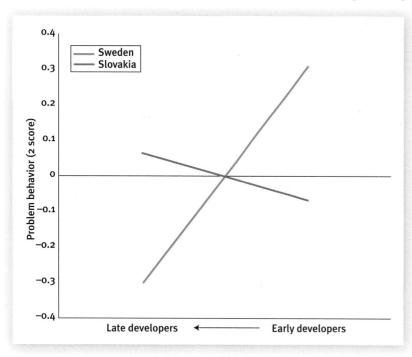

FIGURE 8.5: The interaction between culture and pubertal timing in predicting girls' problem behavior in Sweden (red line) and Slovakia (blue line): Notice that in sexually-permissive Sweden, being early has a huge impact on a girl's risk of getting into trouble (with drugs, ignoring curfews, being truant at school, and so on); but a girl's puberty timetable makes far less difference if that child lives in Slovakia.

Data from: Skoog and others, 2013.

the sixth graders who moved to middle schools. Moreover, the middle schoolers reported having more supportive class environments than children who remained in K–8 or K–12 schools (Farmer and others, 2011).

This study highlights the fact that with pre-teens (and every child), we need to go beyond a school's structure to consider more basic questions: Is this a nurturing, *authoritative* environment (see Chapter 7)? Does this school have caring peer norms (see Chapter 6)? Moreover, imagine being locked into the calcified status-hierarchies that can solidify, based on spending your whole childhood with the same group of peers. The advantage of middle school is that it offers you (and everyone else) a liberating new start!

Wrapping Up Puberty

Now, let's summarize these messages:

- **Children's reactions to puberty depend on the environment in which they physically mature.** Negative feelings are more likely to occur when society looks down on a given sign of development (as with menstruation) or when the physical changes are not valued in a person's particular group (as with breast development in ballerinas). Living in a sexually permissive society or changing to a non-nurturing school during puberty magnifies the stress of body changes.

- **With early-maturing girls, we should take special steps to arrange the right body–environment fit.** Having an adult body at a young age is dangerous for girls, but only when the changes happen in a high-risk milieu. Therefore, when a girl reaches puberty early, it's important to arrange her life with special care.

- **Communication about puberty should be improved—especially for boys.** While some contemporary mothers may be doing a fine job discussing menstruation with their daughters, boys, in particular, seem to enter puberty without any guidance about what to expect (Omar, McElderry, & Zakharia, 2003).

INTERVENTIONS: Minimizing Puberty Distress

Given these findings, what are the lessons for parents? What changes should society make?

LESSONS FOR PARENTS. It's tempting for parents to avoid discussing puberty because children are so sensitive about their changing bodies (see Elliot, 2012; Hyde and others, 2013). This reluctance is a mistake. Developmentalists urge parents to discuss what is happening with a same-sex child. They advise beginning these discussions when the child is at an age when talking is emotionally easier, before the changes take place (Graber, Nichols, & Brooks-Gunn, 2010). Fathers, in particular, need to make special efforts to talk about puberty with their sons (Paikoff & Brooks-Gunn, 1991).

Finally, parents of early-maturing daughters should try to get their child involved in positive activities, especially with friends her own age and, if possible, carefully pick the best school environment.

LESSONS FOR SOCIETY. No matter what a child's puberty timetable, the implicit message of this section is that the school environment matters *tremendously* at this gateway-to-adulthood age. Rather than viewing sixth or seventh grade as relatively unimportant (compared, let's say, to high school), understand that nurturing schools are vital to setting young teens on the right path.

It also seems critical to provide more adequate puberty education. Think back to what you wanted to know about your changing body ("My breasts don't look right"; "My penis has a strange shape"), and you will realize that offering a few fifth-grade health lectures at school is not enough. Formal sex education in the United States typically begins in high school, after puberty has occurred (Guttmacher Institute, 2011a). (That's like locking the barn door after the horses have been stolen!)

UNESCO has developed global guidelines aimed at teaching young children (aged 5 to 8) to respect their bodies. But, with the exception of a few European nations, schools routinely ignore this document—offering "too little too late" alarmist-oriented instruction focused on pubertal damage control: "Don't get pregnant," "Avoid STDs" (Goldman & Coleman, 2013). Suppose our culture really *celebrated* children's blossoming bodies, as the Navajo do? Perhaps this might cause a revolution where we celebrated every body size.

Tying It All Together

1. In contrast to earlier times, give the main reason why our culture can't celebrate puberty today?

2. You notice that your 11-year-old cousin is going from looking like a child to looking like a young woman. (a) Outline the three-phase hormonal sequence that is setting off the physical changes; and then (b) name the three classes of hormones involved in puberty.

3. Kendra has recently begun to menstruate. Calista has just shot up in height. Carl is developing facial hair. Statistically speaking, which child is at the beginning of puberty?

4. Brianna, an overweight second grader, has a harsh, rejecting family life. Based on this chapter, you might predict that Briana should enter puberty *earlier/later* than her peers.

5. Based simply on knowing a child's puberty timetable, spell out who is most at risk of getting into trouble (e.g., with drugs or having unprotected sex) as a teen.

6. You are on an international advisory committee charged with developing programs to help children cope emotionally with puberty. What recommendations might you make?

Answers to the Tying It All Together questions can be found at the end of this chapter.

Body Image Issues

What do you daydream about?

Being skinny.

—Amanda (quoted in Martin, 1996, p. 36)

Puberty is a time of intense physical preoccupations, and there is hardly a teenager who isn't concerned about some body part. How important is it for young people to be *generally* satisfied with how they look?

Consider this finding: Susan Harter (1999) explored how feeling competent in each of her five "self-worth" dimensions—scholastic abilities, conduct, athletic skills, peer likeability, and appearance (recall Chapter 6)—related to teenagers' overall self-esteem. She found that being happy about one's looks outweighed *anything else* in determining whether adolescents generally felt good about themselves.

This finding is not just true of teenagers in the United States. It appears in surveys conducted in Western countries among people at various stages of life. If we are happy with the way we look, we are likely to be happy with who we are as human beings.

Feeling physically appealing is important to everyone—for boys, surprisingly, one study suggested, more than for girls (Mellor and others, 2010). But, girls (no surprise) are prone to be especially unhappy with their looks (Lawler and Nixon, 2011; Warren, Schoen, & Schafer, 2010). One reason for pervasive body dissatisfaction comes as no surprise—the intense cultural pressure to be thin.

The Differing Body Concerns of Girls and Boys

The distorting impact of the **thin ideal**, or pressure to be abnormally thin, was graphically suggested in an Irish survey. The researchers found that 3 out of 4 female teens with average BMIs felt they were too fat. An alarming percentage—2 out of 5—of

thin ideal Media-driven cultural idea that females need to be abnormally thin.

When did our culture develop the idea that women should be unrealistically thin? Historians trace this change to the 1970s, when extremely slim actresses like Audrey Hepburn became our cultural ideal. More recently, as you can see in the second photo, similar body pressures have infected the other sex, causing this vulnerable eighth-grade boy to struggle to attain the muscled male shape that is our contemporary cultural ideal.

underweight girls also wanted to shed pounds (Lawler & Nixon, 2011). While some boys (those who were genuinely heavy in this study, for instance) also worried about their weight, especially in our twenty-first century culture, males have another concern: They want to build up their muscles—spending hours at the gym, sometimes using dangerous anabolic steroids to increase their body mass (Parent & Moradi, 2011; Smolak & Stein, 2010).

These preoccupations may be set in motion by biological forces. As you will see in the next chapter, the hormonal changes of puberty prime pre-teens to be unusually sensitive to social cues. New research suggests that the female obsession to be thin may have roots even before we emerge from the womb. In one incredible study, scientists found female twin pairs were more apt to develop unhealthy dieting practices at puberty than females in fraternal twin pairs where the other twin was male—suggesting that testosterone (given off by the male twin's body) may dampen down the female tendency to become weight obsessed during the pubertal years (Culbert and others, 2013).

Still, even if the signal "be supersensitive to your body" is hormonal, outer-world pressures prime the pump: Pre-teens love to tease one another about weight ("Ha, ha, you are getting fat!") (Compian, Gowen, & Hayward, 2004; Jackson & Chen, 2008; Lawler & Nixon, 2011). When children are already unhappy, this teasing can provoke an obsession with dieting—for either sex (Benas, Uhrlass, & Gibb, 2010; Hutchinson, Rapee, & Taylor, 2010).

A primary culprit is the media, for its regular drumbeat advocating the thin ideal. As early as preschool, one study showed, girls have internalized the message, "You need to be thin" (Harriger and others, 2010). Digitally altered images beamed from TV, the Internet, and magazines set body-size standards that are often impossible to attain (López-Guimerà and others, 2010). So it's no wonder that being shown snapshots of ultra-thin women activates body dissatisfaction in temperamentally vulnerable teens and adults (Anschutz and others, 2011; Roberts & Good, 2010).

Still, some children are less susceptible to the media messages. In Albert Bandura's social learning framework, for instance, African American and Latino girls should be more insulated from the thin ideal because their media role models, such as Queen Latifah and Beyonce, demonstrate that beauty comes in ample sizes. As one young

Interestingly, due to an epigenetic process, this fraternal twin girl may be more insulated from developing an eating disorder as a teen by simply being exposed to the circulating testosterone her brother's body is giving off.

© Sayre Berman/Corbis

Queen Latifah embodies the fact that bodies are beautiful at every size. Not only is she a role model for women of color, but for every woman in our culture.

eating disorder A pathological obsession with getting and staying thin. The two best-known eating disorders are *anorexia nervosa* and *bulimia nervosa*.

anorexia nervosa A potentially life-threatening eating disorder characterized by pathological dieting (resulting in severe weight loss and, in females, loss of menstruation) and by a distorted body image.

bulimia nervosa An eating disorder characterized by at least biweekly cycles of binging and purging (by inducing vomiting or taking laxatives) in an obsessive attempt to lose weight.

binge eating disorder A newly labeled eating disorder defined by recurrent, out-of-control binging accompanied by feelings of disgust.

African American woman in an interview study explained: "I feel like . . . for the woman of color . . . the look is like thick thighs, you know fat butt . . . (men) like, like want you to have meat on your body" (quoted in Hesse-Biber and others, 2010, p. 704).

Does this mean that, unless they are obese, Latino and African American teens don't worry about their weight? No! If an ethnic minority girl identifies with the mainstream, Western thin ideal, she is just as vulnerable to developing eating disorders as any other teen (Sabik, Cole, & Ward, 2010). What *exactly* are eating disorders like?

Eating Disorders

> In the morning I'll have a black coffee. At noon I have a mix of shredded lettuce, carrots and cabbage. At around dinnertime I have 9 mini whole-wheat crackers. On a bad day I may have. . . . with my (morning) black coffee an egg white, . . .
> (adapted from Juarascio, Shoaib, & Timko, 2010, p. 402)

> Scales are evil! But I'm obsessed with them! I'm on the damn thing like 3 times a day!
> (adapted from Gavin, Rodham, & Poyer, 2008, pp. 327–328)

As these quotations from "pro-anorexia" social network sites show, **eating disorders** differ from "normal" dieting. Here, eating is the sole focus of life. Imagine waking up and planning each day around eating (or not eating). You monitor every morsel. You are obsessed with checking and rechecking your weight. Or you have the impulse to gorge every time you approach the refrigerator or buy a box of candy at the store. Let's now explore three major forms these total food fixations take: anorexia, bulimia, and binge eating disorder.

Anorexia nervosa, the most serious eating disorder, is defined by self-starvation—specifically to the point of being 85 percent of one's ideal body weight or less. (This means that if 110 pounds is the ideal weight for your height, you would now weigh less than 95 pounds.) Another common feature of this primarily female disorder is that leptin levels have become too low to support adult fertility and the girl has stopped menstruating. A hallmark of eating disorders—among both girls and boys—is a distorted body image (Espeset and others, 2011). Even when people look skeletal, they feel fat. They often compulsively exercise, running miles for hours, abandoning their other commitments to spend every day at the gym (Holland, Brown, & Keel, 2014). They may be disconnected from reality, denying that their symptoms apply to them ("Oh no, I don't binge and purge") (Gratwick-Sarll, Mond, & Hay, 2013). Sometimes they literally don't see their true body size: As one girl named Sarah commented: "I remember . . . passing an open door and saw myself in the mirror . . . and thought "Oh gosh, she is thin!" but then when I understood that it was actually me, I didn't see me as thin anymore" (quoted in Espeset and others, 2011, p. 183).

Anorexia is a life-threatening disease. When people reach two-thirds of their ideal weight or less, they need to be hospitalized and fed—intravenously, if necessary—to stave off death (Diamanti and others, 2008). A student of mine who runs a self-help group for people with eating disorders provided a vivid reminder of the enduring physical toll anorexia can cause. Alicia informed the class that she had permanently damaged her heart muscle during her bout with this devastating disease.

Bulimia nervosa is typically not life threatening because the person's weight often stays within a normal range. However, because this disorder involves frequent binging (at least once weekly eating sprees in which thousands of calories may be consumed in a matter of hours) and either purging (getting rid of the food by vomiting or misusing laxatives and diuretics) or fasting, bulimia can seriously compromise health. In addition to producing deficiencies of basic nutrients, the purging episodes can cause mouth sores, ulcers in the esophagus, and the loss of tooth enamel due to being exposed to stomach acid.

Binge eating disorder, which first appeared in the new *Diagnostic and Statistical Manual (DSM-5)* in 2013, involves recurrent out-of-control eating. The person wolfs down huge quantities of food and then is wracked by disgust, guilt, and shame. This mental disorder was added to the *DSM-5* because (no surprise) it is intimately tied to obesity and so presents a serious threat to health (Myers & Wiman, 2014). Binge eating disorder, like anorexia and bulimia, can wreak enduring havoc on the person's life (Goldschmidt and others, 2014).

How common are these mainly female disorders, which most frequently erupt in the early twenties or late teens? In one eight-year-long community survey, binge eating disorder was most prevalent, affecting roughly 3 in 100 young women over that time; bulimia ranked second (at 2.6 in 100). Thankfully, the most serious condition, anorexia, struck only 8 out of a thousand girls. The bad news is that subclinical (less severe) forms of eating disorders may affect an astonishing 18 million people in the United States at some point in life (Forbush & Hunt, 2014).

What causes these conditions? Twin studies suggest anorexia and bulimia have a hereditary component (Striegel-Moore & Bulik, 2007). One nonspecific risk factor is prior internalizing symptoms—a tendency during middle childhood to be anxious and depressed (Touchette and others, 2011). At puberty, if these "I hate myself" attitudes translate into a commitment to the *thin ideal*, an obsession with dieting or binge eating and purging can result (Espinoza, Penelo, & Raich, 2010; Stice, Ng, & Shaw, 2010).

Researchers find teens and young adults with eating disorders have other psychological symptoms: insecure attachments, an extreme need for approval (Abbate-Dega and others, 2010), or rigidity (Masuda, Boone, & Timko, 2011). They often have trouble expressing their needs (Norwood and others, 2011). One hallmark of eating disorders is incredibly poor self-worth, that is, feeling like a terrible human being (Fairchild & Cooper, 2010). At bottom, these teens have low *self-efficacy*—feeling out of control of their lives.

If a young person develops anorexia or bulimia, how do these feelings get channeled into an obsession with being too fat? Hints come from an experiment in which researchers told girls with an eating disorder and others a comparison group to think about an event in which they felt useless or incapable. After the "feeling incompetent" instructions, the girls with an eating disorder automatically focused on their body flaws (McFarlane, Urbszat, & Olmsted, 2011). So when girls are temperamentally prone to low self-esteem and believe that the key to happiness is being ultrathin, negative emotions may be displaced into feeling "I'm too fat," and warded off by extreme measures to control one's weight.

Table 8.2 offers a summary checklist for determining if a teenager you love is at risk for serious body dissatisfaction. Still, if you know a young person who is struggling with an eating disorder, there is brighter news. Most adolescents grow out of eating problems as they get older and construct a satisfying adult life (Keel and others, 2007). Moreover, contrary to popular opinion, therapy for eating disorders works!

A temperamental tendency to be anxious, low self-efficacy, a great need for approval, and the inability to express your legitimate needs. These poisonous forces, plus a commitment to the *thin ideal*, may have produced this child's eating disorder. Moreover, because whenever she feels bad about herself, she automatically thinks, "I'm too fat"—self-starvation has become her main mode of dealing with stress.

Table 8.2: Is a Teenager at Risk for Serious Body Dissatisfaction? A Checklist

(Background influences: Has this child reached puberty? Is this child female?)

1. Is this child temperamentally prone to anxiety and depression?
2. Does this child vigorously subscribe to the thin ideal?
3. Is this child becoming obsessed with dieting (or, if male, becoming obsessed with building up his muscles)?
4. Does this child have insecure attachments, trouble expressing her feelings, and excessively low self-efficacy and self-esteem?
5. When this child gets rejected or experiences a negative event, does she automatically think, "I feel fat"?

INTERVENTIONS: **Improving Teenagers' Body Image**

Perhaps the first place to begin to treat young people with eating disorders is to examine how girls who embrace their bodies reason and think. As one interview study suggested, these teens do not deny their "imperfections," but they discount negative comments and focus on their physical pluses. Yes, they do care deeply about their looks, but they view being beautiful as taking care of their physical health—eating nutritious foods, exercising, appreciating what their bodies can do (Frisén & Holmqvist, 2010). These adolescents are often spiritually oriented (Boisvert & Harrell, 2013). They understand what *really* makes people beautiful in life. As one woman named Heather put it: "You have to remind yourself that even though (the thin ideal) is what (the media are) . . . promoting, self-esteem really looks the best" (Wood-Barcalow, Tylka, & Augustus-Horvath, 2010, p. 115).

Heather's remarks explain why a popular eating-disorder treatment (called dialectic behavior therapy) teaches meditation, as well as strategies to promote self-efficacy (feeling in control of one's life) (Lenz and others, 2014). Therapists have devised other creative approaches, such as repeatedly exposing women to video images of themselves, to train them to see their real body size (Trentowska, Svaldi, & Tuschen-Caffier, 2014).

One innovative therapy ignores *any* underlying psychological causes. Arguing that eating disorders are totally biologically based, therapists have had success by keeping the girl's body temperature warm and training her in the appropriate amount to eat via a scale under a plate that measures her intake (Bergh and others, 2013).

While, as I just mentioned, eating disorders have the reputation of being hard to cure, the reverse seems true. This may explain why therapists who treat these young people have lower burnout rates than do their colleagues (Thompson-Brenner, 2013; Warren and others, 2013) and find such personal meaning in this work (Zerbe, 2013).

The same upbeat message is typical of much (but not all) of the research relating to our final topic: teenage sex.

 Tying It All Together

1. Kimberly, an eleventh grader, tells you, "I am ugly," but knows she is terrific in sports and academics. According to Harter's studies, is Kimberly likely to have high or low self-esteem?

2. Amy is regularly on a diet, trying for that Barbie-doll figure. Jasmine, who is far below her ideal body weight, is always exercising and has cut her food intake down to virtually nothing. Sophia, whose weight is normal, goes on eating sprees followed by purges every few days. Clara also has regular, out-of-control eating sprees, after which she says she feels like a bloated "blimp." Identify which girls have an eating disorder, and name each person's specific problem.

3. Pick which three female teens seem protected from developing an eating disorder: *Cotonya whose role model is Beyonce; Caroline who has high self-efficacy; Cora who has a twin brother; Connie who exercises for an hour every day.*

4. Eating disorders are very hard to treat. True or False?

Answers to the Tying It All Together questions can be found at the end of this chapter.

Sexuality

548: Immculate ros: Sex sex sex that all you think about?

559: Snowbunny: people who have sex at 16 r sick:

560: Twonky: I agree

564: 00o0CaFfEinNe; no sex until ur happily married—Thtz muh rule

566: Twonky: I agree with that too.

567: Snowbunny: me too caffine!

(quoted in Subrahmanyam, Greenfield, & Tynes, 2004, p. 658)

Sex is the elephant in the room of teenage life. Everyone knows it's a top-ranking issue, but the adult world often shies from mentioning it. Celebrated in the media, minimized or ignored by anxious parents ("If I talk about it, I'll encourage my child to do it") (see Elliot, 2012; Hyde and others, 2013), the issue of when and whether to have sex is left for teenagers to decide on their own as they filter through the conflicting messages and—as you can see above—vigorously stake out their positions in on-line chats.

It is a minefield issue that contemporary young people negotiate in different ways. Take a poll of your classmates. Some people, as with the teenagers quoted above, may advocate abstinence, believing that everyone should remain a virgin until marriage. Others probably believe that having sex within a loving relationship is fine. Some students, if they are being honest, will admit, "I want to try out the sexual possibilities, but I promise to use contraception!"

This increasing acceptability (within limits) of carving out our own sexual path was highlighted in sexual surveys polling U.S. high school seniors in 1950, 1972, and 2000 (Caron & Moskey, 2002). Over the years, the number of seniors who decided, "It's okay for teenagers to have sex," shot up from a minority to more than 70 percent. But in the final turn-of-the-century poll, more teens agreed that a person could decide to not have sex and still be popular. Most felt confident they would use birth control when they were sexually active, and could wait to have intercourse until they got married. How are these efficacious attitudes translated into action? Let's begin our exploration at the sexual starting gate—with desire.

Exploring Sexual Desire

David, age 14: Since a year or so ago, I just think about sex and masturbation ALL THE TIME! I mean I just think about having sex no matter where I am and I'm aroused all the time. Is that normal?

Expert's reply: Welcome to the raging hormones of adolescence!

(adapted from a teenage sexuality on-line advice forum)

At what age does sexual desire begin? Although scientists had long assumed that the answer was during puberty, when testosterone is pumping through the body, research with homosexual adults caused them to rethink this idea. When gay women and men were asked to recall a watershed event in their lives—the age when they first realized that they were physically attracted to a person of the same sex—their responses centered around age 10. At that age the output of the adrenal androgens is rising but testosterone production has not yet fully geared up (McClintock & Herdt, 1996). So, our first sexual feelings seem programmed by the adrenal androgens and appear before we undergo the visible changes of puberty, by about fourth grade!

How do sex hormone levels relate to teenagers' sexual desires? According to researchers, we need a threshold androgen level to prime our initial feelings of desire (Udry, 1990; Udry & Campbell, 1994). Then, signals from the environment feedback to heighten our interest in sex. As children see their bodies changing, they think of themselves in a new, sexual way. Reaching puberty evokes a different set of signals from the outside world. A ninth-grade boy finds love notes in his locker. A seventh-grade girl notices men looking at her differently as she walks down the street. It is the physical changes of puberty and how outsiders react to those changes that usher us into our lives as sexual human beings. Which young people act on those desires by having intercourse as teens?

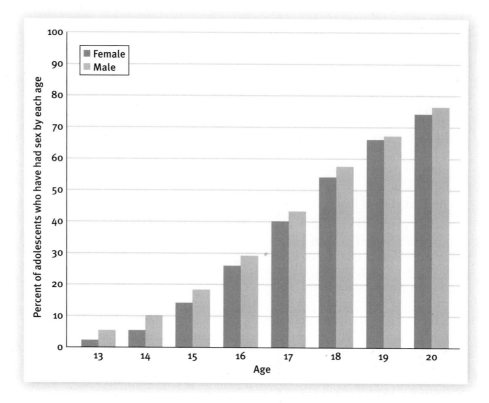

FIGURE 8.6: **Percent of U.S. teens who have had intercourse, at different ages:** This chart pinpoints late adolescence as the tipping point when most American teens have had sex; but, it also shows (not unexpectedly) that intercourse rates begin to rise dramatically after age 15.

Data from: Guttmacher Institute, 2014.

Who Is Having Intercourse?

Today, the average age of first intercourse in the United States is age 17.8 for women and 18 for men (Finer & Philbin, 2014). But about 1 in 8 children make a "sexual debut" by age 15 (Guttmacher Institute, 2014; see also Figure 8.6).

As developmental systems theory suggests, a variety of forces predict making what researchers call an earlier *transition to intercourse.* One influence, for both boys and girls, is biological—being on an earlier puberty timetable. Ethnicity and socioeconomic status (SES) also matter. African Americans and lower-income males are more apt to be sexually active at younger ages (Moilanen and others, 2010; Zimmer-Gembeck & Helfand, 2008; Finer & Philbin, 2014).

Personality makes a difference. Teens who are more impulsive, that is, those with externalizing tendencies, are apt to make the transition earlier (Moilanen and others, 2010). For European American girls, one study has suggested, having a risk-taking personality plus low social self-worth (but not depression) correlates with being more advanced sexually—that is, engaging in pre-intercourse activities such as fondling at age 12 (Hipwell and others, 2010). Conversely, also for girls, having religious parents predicts staying a virgin because it makes it more likely that a teen will be religious and so have friends who agree that abstinence is the way to go (Landor and others, 2011).

This brings up the crucial role of peers. As I suggested earlier in the discussion of early-maturing girls, we can predict a teenager's chance of having intercourse by looking at the company she (or he) chooses. Having an older boyfriend, or girlfriend (no surprise), raises the chance of a child's becoming sexually active (Martin, 1996). In fact, scientists can make precise statistical calculations of a teen's intercourse odds based on the number of people in that child's social circle who have gone "all the

Is my teenage daughter having intercourse? Researchers can now offer parents precise odds by determining how many people in this crowd of best buddies have gone "all the way."

way" (Ali & Dwyer, 2011). So, just as with other aspects of teenage behavior, to understand whether a teen you know is sexually active, look at the values and behaviors of his (or her) group.

You also might want to look at what a child watches on TV. In one fascinating study, researchers were able to predict which virgin boys and girls were likely to become sexually active from looking at their prior TV watching practices. Teens who reported watching a heavy diet of programs with sexually oriented talk were twice as likely to have intercourse in the next year as the children who did not (Collins and others, 2004).

Since sexual experiences (affairs, and so on) are a common media theme, we might predict that simply watching a good deal of television would promote an earlier transition to intercourse. We would be wrong. Teens are at special risk when they watch sexually suggestive programs in mixed gender groups (Parkes and others, 2013). With any media, it's the content that matters—whether a child prefers sex-laced cable channels (Bersamin and others, 2008), gravitates to Internet porn, or avidly consumes magazines like *Cosmo* rather than sticking to *Seventeen* (Walsh, 2008).

Should we blame *Cosmo* reports such as "101 Ways to Drive Him Wild in Bed" for *causing* teenagers to start having sex? A bidirectional influence is probably in operation here. If a teenager is *already* interested in sex, that boy or girl will gravitate toward media that fit this passion. For me, the tip-off was raiding my parents' library to read the steamy scenes in that forbidden book, D. H. Lawrence's *Lady Chatterley's Lover*. Today, parents know that their child has entered a different mental space when she abandons the Discovery Channel in favor of MTV. Swimming in this sea of media sex then, naturally, further inflames a teenager's desires.

The image of this girl absorbed in reading the sex-laden articles in *Cosmo* may be a tip-off that she is poised to make the transition to intercourse.

Who Are Teens Having Intercourse With?

Internet pornography celebrates anonymous sex. Many intercourse episodes on TV involve one-night stands (Grube and others, 2008). Are children imitating these models when they start having intercourse? With most U.S. teens (70 percent of girls and 56 percent of boys) reporting they first had sex with a steady partner, the answer is no. But as roughly 1 in 5 teens report making the transition to intercourse outside of a committed relationship (Guttmacher Institute, 2014), let's pause to look briefly at what these nonromantic encounters are like.

Do adolescents who have sex with a person they are not dating hook up with a stranger or a good friend? For answers, we have an interview study in which researchers asked high schoolers in Ohio about their experiences with "noncommitted" sex (Manning, Giordano, & Longmore, 2006).

Of the teens who admitted to a nonromantic sexual encounter, 3 out of 4 reported that their partner was a person they knew very well. As one boy, who lost his virginity with his best friend described: ". . . I wouldn't really consider dating her . . . but I've known her so long . . . anytime I feel down or she feels down, we just talk to each other" (quoted in Manning, Giordano, & Longmore, 2006, p. 469). Sometimes, the goal of having sex was to change a friendship to a romance: "After we started sleeping together . . . having a relationship came up." Or, a teenager might fall into having sex with an ex-boyfriend or girlfriend: "Well, it (sex) kind of happened like towards the end when we were both friends" (quoted in Manning, Giordano, & Longmore, 2006, p. 470).

So far, I have painted a benign portrait of these more casual, "friends with benefits" experiences. Wrong! Especially for girls, as you will read in Chapter 10, having one-night stands is a serious risk factor for getting depressed. This brings me to the supposedly clashing sexual agendas of women and men.

Hot in Developmental Science: Is There Still a Sexual Double Standard?

It's different for boys, it's like . . . if they have sex with somebody and then they are rewarded . . . and all the guys are just like "That's great!" You have sex, and you're a girl and it's like "Slut." That's how it is . . .

(quoted in Martin, 1996, p. 86)

sexual double standard A cultural code that gives men greater sexual freedom than women. Specifically, society expects males to want to have intercourse and expects females to remain virgins until they marry and to be more interested in relationships than in having sex.

These complaints from a 16-year-old girl named Erin refer to the well-known **sexual double standard.** Boys are supposed to want sex; girls are supposed to resist. Teenage boys get reinforcement for "getting to home base." Intercourse is fraught with ambivalence and danger for girls: "Should I do it? Will he love me if I do it? Will he love me if I don't? Will I get pregnant? What will my friends and my parents think?"

Basic to the stereotype of the double standard is the idea that girls are looking for committed relationships and that boys mainly want sex. The Ohio study, discussed in the previous section, offered a different view (Manning, Giordano, & Longmore, 2006). These interviews confirmed the statistics showing that teenage sex often happens within a committed relationship. In fact, feeling emotionally intimate, most teens reported, was the reason why *both* boys and girls decided to have sex. And, when a couple did take that step, the decision was often as difficult for guys as girls.

Read what a boy named Tim had to say:

That was something that I had been saving. I really wanted to save it for marriage, but I was curious and um she was special enough to me that I could give her this part of my life that I had been saving and um . . . She felt the same way because she wanted to wait till marriage, but we had decided and we was [were] both curious I guess and so it just happened"

(quoted in Giordano, Manning, & Longmore, 2010, p. 1007)

Moreover, when sex happened too quickly, as this next quotation shows, boys—as much as girls—were turned off:

She was like . . . moving too fast . . . like she wanted to have sex with me in the car and I'm like "No" and then she starts touching me and I'm like "I'm cool, I'm cool; I got to go". . . . And I did that and I left. . . . I was just, I don't know; she wasn't the girl I wanted to have sex with. . . . She wasn't the right girl.

(quoted in Giordano, Manning, & Longmore, 2010, p. 1002)

In this study, *both* male and female teens reported that the decision to have sex was mutual; no one was pressuring anyone else. Or, as another boy named Tim delightfully put it:

So if a girl says yes and a boy says no; it's a maybe. If a guy doesn't know and a girl says yes, it's yes . . . . If a girl says yes and a guy says yes, it's yes . . . . So I think the women have more control because their opinion matters more in that situation.

(quoted in Giordano, Manning, & Longmore, 2010, p. 1007)

Is it really true, as Tim implies, that females are the main initiators (aggressors) when it comes to sex? Consider this revealing evidence from the virtual world: When researchers analyzed the profile photo comments on a popular Belgian social network site, they found that girls' sexually-oriented responses to boys' posted photos far outnumbered boys' comments to the photos posted by girls.

Here are a few enthusiastic female posts that a boy named Kendeman's photo evoked: "You are ****.. ... beautiful!" "I just wanted to say this because I think you are wonderfuuuuuul. Nobody can compete with you!" (Quoted from De Ridder & Van Bauwell, 2013, p. 576.)

So, even though the double standard seems firmly in operation, when we hear male teens brag about their exploits or listen to people make snide comments about

What are teens who avidly scan the photos on a social-network site likely to do? The surprise is that girls may decide to post more sexually oriented comments than boys.

"sluts and studs," the reality is complex. Boys want sex in a loving relationship—just like girls (Ott and others, 2006). In terms of making the first sexually oriented moves, either on-line or, sometimes, in the flesh—if anything, an *anti*-double standard can apply! 🌀

Wrapping Up Sexuality: Contemporary Trends

In summary, the news about teenage sexuality is good. Teenagers today feel more confident about charting their sexual path. Most sexual encounters occur in committed love relationships. The decision to have teenage sex is not typically taken lightly, but in a climate of caring and mutual decision making for both girls and boys. Girls have far more control in the sexual arena than we think!

These changes are mirrored in the encouraging statistics in Figure 8.7: fewer U.S. teenagers are having intercourse, and most teens report they use condoms when they do have sex. In fact, over a decade spanning the late 1990s to the early twenty-first century, teen pregnancy rates in the United States dipped from more than 5 to 4 per thousand girls.

Still, with regard to teenage pregnancy, the United States ranks near the pinnacle of the developed world. While European teens have comparable levels of sexual activity as U.S. adolescents, E.U. pregnancy rates put the United States to shame (Guttmacher Institute, 2014; McKay & Barrett, 2010). Compared to Western Europe, the prevalence of gonorrhea and chlamydia among U.S. adolescents is very high (Guttmacher Institute, 2011b).

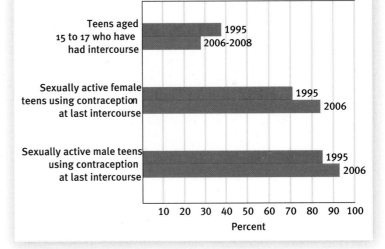

FIGURE 8.7: **Encouraging snapshots of twenty-first-century teenage sexuality in the United States:** This news about teenage sex is good! Fewer young people are having intercourse and more sexually active adolescents report using contraception.
Data from: Guttmacher Institute, 2011a, 2011b; 2014; Mckay & Barrett, 2010.

INTERVENTIONS: **Toward Teenager-Friendly Sex Education**

These less-than-flattering statistics bring us back to the issue I alluded to in the discussion of puberty: sex education. Clearly, in its mission to prevent teenage pregnancy, the United States is falling short. Could *one* reason be that teens are not getting the "correct" information in school sex education classes?

Actually, around the world, school sex education offers a patchwork of slipshod strategies. Some school systems and countries teach only abstinence. Others discuss contraception and sexually transmitted diseases (STDs). Some teach teens about alternative lifestyles, such as being gay. Other nations teach nothing about sex in school at all. The reason comes as no surprise: From Canada, to Australia

Because teens really want to know how to have loving relationships, this high school couple might love romance education classes!

(Goldman & Coleman, 2013), to South Africa (Francis & DePalma, 2014), parents are deeply divided about what to say to teens about sex (Elliot, 2012).

One classic fear is that teaching contraception might encourage teens to have intercourse. This *we know* is not true. When Irish researchers compared young people in that nation who had high school sex education and a group with no instruction, girls and boys exposed to sex education classes became sexually active at an *older age* than their peers (Bourke and others, 2014).

Some of you reading the above information might say, "Ok, Dr. Belsky, perhaps that's true, but having my child's school discuss contraception is ethically distasteful, because I believe abstinence is the only way to go." Perhaps everyone might agree with the following alternate approach.

For decades, teens have complained that high school sex-education is irrelevant to their lives. Adolescents say they are hungering for different information: "How can I develop a relationship?" "What does it mean to fall in love?" (see Martin 1996).

Therefore, stale controversies about whether to teach contraception may be missing the boat. In contrast to the alarmist messages, we now understand that most teens are not passionate to have random sex. Young people are lusting—if anything—to find love. We also know that parents have difficulty discussing these new, embarrassing "adult" yearnings with their daughters and sons. Therefore, to really speak to teenagers' passions, sex education can't focus mainly on sex. Schools need romance education classes!

Designing an optimal romance (or relationship) class depends on knowing how adolescents think and reason about life. The next chapter focuses on this topic in depth.

 Tying It All Together

1. When a mother asks you when her son may experience his first sexual feelings, you should answer: *around age 10, before the physical signs of puberty occur/around age 13 or 14/in the middle of puberty/toward the end of puberty.*

2. Your friend thinks her teenage daughter may be having sex. So she asks for your opinion. All the following questions are relevant for you to ask *except*:

   a. Are your daughter's friends having sex?

   b. Is your daughter's school teaching abstinence?

   c. Is your daughter watching sexually explicit cable channels with her male friends and reading *Cosmo?*

   d. Does your daughter have an older boyfriend?

3. Tom is discussing trends in teenage sex and pregnancy. Which two statements should he make?

   a. Today, sex often happens in a committed relationship.

   b. Today, the United States has lower teenage pregnancy rates than other Western nations.

   c. In recent decades, rates of teenage births in the United States have declined.

   d. Today, boys are still the sexual initiators.

4. Imagine you are designing a "model" sex-education program. According to this section, you should focus on:

   a. encouraging abstinence

   b. providing information about birth control and STDs

   c. discussing how to have loving relationships

Answers to the Tying It All Together questions can be found at the end of this chapter.

SUMMARY

Puberty

Today, the physical changes of **puberty** occur during early adolescence, and there can be decades between the time children physically mature and the time they enter adult life. Because in traditional agrarian societies a person's changing body used to be the signal to get married, many cultures devised **puberty rites** to welcome the physical changes. The **secular trend in puberty** has magnified the separation between puberty and full adulthood, the fact that **menarche** (and **spermarche**) have been occurring at much younger ages.

Two hormonal command centers program puberty. The adrenal glands produce **adrenal androgens** starting in middle childhood. The **HPG axis,** the main system that sets the bodily changes in motion, involves the hypothalamus, the pituitary, and the **gonads** (ovaries and testes), which produce estrogens and **testosterone** (found in both males and females). Leptin levels and a variety of environmental influences trigger the initial hypothalamic hormone.

The physical changes of puberty are divided into **primary sexual characteristics, secondary sexual characteristics,** and the **growth spurt.** Although in females puberty begins with the growth spurt and menarche occurs late in the process, the rate and sequence of this total-body transformation varies from child to child. Because for males the externally visible changes of puberty occur later and the organs of reproduction are the first to start developing, the puberty timetables of the sexes are not as far apart as they appear.

The striking individual differences in the timing of puberty are mainly genetically programmed. African American children tend to reach puberty at a younger age. For girls, being overweight and having stressful family relationships are tied to reaching puberty earlier. These "environmental events" push up the hypothalamic timer, but strangely, only for females.

How children feel about their changing bodies varies, depending on the social environment. Breast development often evokes positive emotions. Feelings about menstruation seem more positive than in the past because today's mothers are more apt to celebrate this change. First ejaculation is rarely talked about. Children tend to be embarrassed about their changing bodies when they are around the parent of the opposite sex.

Girls who mature early are at risk of getting into trouble as teens (for example, taking drugs, getting pregnant, or doing poorly in school), but only if they reach puberty in a stressful environment or live in a permissive culture, and get involved with older friends. Because they often end up heavier and shorter, these girls tend to have a poor body image and are more prone to be anxious and depressed.

Although, based on older research, developmentalists have argued it's better not to move children undergoing puberty to a new school, there may be interesting pluses to moving to middle school. In general, our mission should be to provide nurturing schools to children at this vulnerable age. Parents need to talk about puberty with their children, especially their sons. We need to be alert to the potential for problems with early-maturing girls. We need to implement global guidelines for elementary school education that generally focus on respecting your body.

Body Image Issues

How children feel about their looks is closely tied to their overall self-esteem. Girls tend to feel worse about their looks than boys do, partly because society expects women to adhere to the **thin ideal.** Boys feel pressured to build up their muscles. The impulse to be thin may be rooted in biological forces for girls, but peer pressures and media images play an important role in this passion.

The two classic **eating disorders** are **anorexia nervosa** (severe underweight resulting from obsessive dieting) and **bulimia nervosa** (chronic binging and, often, purging) accompanied by body image distortions. **Binge eating disorder** (involving binging alone) was recently added to the list. Genetic vulnerabilities, prior internalizing tendencies, and low self-esteem put teenage and young adult girls at special risk for these problems. Children with eating disorders have low self-efficacy, and may cope with distressing feelings by "projecting" these emotions onto their body shape. Eating disorder interventions take varied forms, and treatments for these so-called intractable problems often do work.

Sexuality

Teenagers today feel freer to make their own sexual decisions, including whether or not to begin to have intercourse. While sexual desire is triggered by the adrenal androgens, and first switches on at around age 10, sexual signals from the outside world feed back to cause children to really become interested in sex.

Factors that predict making the transition to intercourse include, among others, race, SES, family and peer influences, and gravitating to sex-laden media. Most teens have their first intercourse experience in a romantic relationship. Noncommitted sex most often takes place with someone a teen knows well. Although the **sexual double standard** suggests that boys just want sex and girls are interested in relationships, both males and females are mainly interested in love. Ironically, our image of men as the sexual aggressors may operate in the opposite way in the "real world."

The good news about teenage sexuality in the United States is that children feel freer to make their own sexual choices, and teens typically report having sex in a committed relationship. Rates of teen pregnancies have dramatically declined, although they are still markedly higher in the United States than in other Western nations. Rather than arguing about whether to teach contraception, educators should provide sex-education classes relevant to young people's real concerns: relationships and romance.

KEY TERMS

puberty, p. 231

puberty rite, p. 232

secular trend in puberty, p. 233

menarche, p. 233

spermarche, p. 233

adrenal androgens, p. 234

HPG axis, p. 234

gonads, p. 234

testosterone, p. 234

primary sexual characteristics, p. 235

secondary sexual characteristics, p. 235

growth spurt, p. 235

thin ideal, p. 244

eating disorder, p. 246

anorexia nervosa, p. 246

bulimia nervosa, p. 246

binge eating disorder, p. 246

sexual double standard, p. 252

ANSWERS TO **Tying It All Together** QUIZZES

Puberty

1. Today, puberty occurs a decade or more before we can fully reach adult life.

2. (a) The initial hypothalamic hormone triggers the pituitary to produce its hormones, which cause the ovaries and testes to mature and produce their hormones, which, in turn, produce the body changes. (b) Estrogens, testosterone, and the adrenal androgens.

3. Calista

4. *earlier*

5. An early maturing girl

6. *Possible recommendations:* Pay special attention to providing nurturing schools in sixth and seventh grade.

Push for more adequate, "honest" puberty education at a younger age, possibly in a format—such as on-line— where children can talk anonymously about their concerns. Institute a public awareness program encouraging parents to talk about puberty with a same-sex child. Encourage mothers to speak positively about menstruation and have dads discuss events such as spermarche with sons. Make everyone alert to the dangers associated with being an early-maturing girl and develop formal interventions targeted to this "at-risk" group. Institute sensitive, school-based "respect your body" discussions—based on the UNESCO guidelines— for children beginning in the early elementary school years.

Amos Morgan/Photodisc/Getty Images

Body Image Issues

1. Unfortunately, low self-esteem
2. Jasmine, Sophia, and Clara have eating disorders. Jasmine has the symptoms of anorexia nervosa; Sophia has the symptoms of bulimia nervosa. Clara has binge eating disorder.
3. Cotonya, Caroline, and Cora (We don't know about Connie— but, if she obsessively exercises just to stay thin, she might be at higher risk)
4. False (new research suggests eating disorders are treatable)

Sexuality

1. around age 10, before the physical signs of puberty occur
2. b
3. a and c
4. c, discuss how to have loving relationships

CHAPTER 9

Fabrice LEROUGE/ONOKY/Getty Images

Cognitive and Socioemotional Development

Samantha's father began to worry when his daughter was in sixth grade. Suddenly, his sweet little princess was becoming so selfish, so moody, and so rude. She began to question everything, from her 10 o'clock curfew to why poverty exists. At the same time, she had to buy clothes with the right designer label and immediately download the latest music. She wanted to be an individual, but her clique shaped every decision. She got hysterical if anyone looked at her the wrong way. Worse yet, Samantha was hanging out with the middle school "popular" crowd—smoking, drinking, not doing her homework, cutting class.

Her twin brother, Sam, couldn't have been more different. Sam was obedient, an honor student, captain of the basketball team. He mellowly sailed into his teenage years. Actually, Sam defied the categories. He was smart and a jock; he really had heart. Sam volunteered with disabled children. He effortlessly moved among the nerdy brains, the popular kids, and the artsy groups at school. Still, this model child was also caught smoking and sampling the occasional joint. The most heart-stopping example happened when the police picked up Sam and a carload of buddies for drag racing on the freeway. Sam's puzzled explanation: "Something just took over and I stopped thinking, Dad."

If you looked beneath the surface, however, both of his children were great. They were thoughtful, caring, and capable of having the deepest discussions about life. They simply seemed to get caught up in the moment and lose their minds—especially when they were with their friends. What really is going on in the teenage mind?

Think of our contradictory stereotypes about the teenage mind. Teenagers are supposed to be idealistic, thoughtful, and introspective; concerned with larger issues; pondering life in deeper ways; but also impulsive, moody, and out of control. We expect them to be the ultimate radicals, rejecting everything adults say, and the consummate conformists, dominated by the crowd, driven by the latest craze, totally influenced by their peers.

These contradictory ideas are mirrored in a confusing welter of laws relating to when teens are considered "adult." In the United States, adolescents can sometimes be tried in adult court at 14, at an age when they are barred from seeing R-rated movies. Deemed mature enough to vote at age 18, U.S. teens are unable to buy liquor until age 21. How is science shedding light on the elusive teenage mind? That is the subject of the chapter you are about to read.

Setting the Context

Youth are heated by nature as drunken men by wine.

Aristotle (n.d.)

I would that there were no age between ten and twenty-three . . ., for there's nothing in between but getting wenches with child, wronging the ancientry, stealing, fighting. . . .

William Shakespeare, *The Winter's Tale*, Act III

As the quotations above illustrate, throughout history, wise observers of human nature have described young people as being emotional, hot-headed, and out of control. When, in 1904, G. Stanley Hall first identified a new life stage characterized by **"storm and stress,"** which he called "adolescence," he was only echoing these timeless ideas. Moreover, as the mission of the young is to look at society in fresh, new ways, it makes sense that most cultures would view each new generation in ambivalent terms—praising young people for their energy and passion; fearing them as a menace and threat.

"storm and stress" G. Stanley Hall's phrase for the intense moodiness, emotional sensitivity, and risk-taking tendencies that characterize the life stage he labeled adolescence.

However, until fairly recently, young people never had years to explore life or rebel against society because they took on adult responsibilities at an early age. As you may remember from Chapter 1, adolescence only became a distinct stage of life in the United States during the twentieth century, when—for most children—going to high school became routine (Mintz, 2004; Modell, 1989; Palladino, 1996).

As this famous 1930s photograph of a migrant family traveling across the arid Southwest to search for California jobs illustrates, early in the Great Depression, there was no chance to go to high school and no real adolescence because children had, at a very young age, to work to help support their families.

Look into your family history and you may find a great-grandparent who finished high school or college. But a century ago, these events were fairly rare, as the typical U.S. child left school after sixth or seventh grade to find work (Mintz, 2004). Unfortunately, however, during the Great Depression of the 1930s, there was little work to find. Idle and at loose ends, young people took to roaming the countryside, angry, demoralized, and depressed. Alarmed by the situation, the federal government took action. At the same time that it instituted the Social Security system to provide for the elderly (to be discussed in Chapter 13), the Roosevelt administration implemented a national youth program to lure young people to school. The program worked. By 1939, 75 percent of all U.S. teenagers were attending high school.

High school boosted the intellectual skills of a whole cohort of Americans. But it produced a generation gap between these young people and their less educated, often immigrant parents and encouraged teens to spend their days together as an isolated, age-segregated group. Then, during the 1950s, when entrepreneurs began to target products to this new, lucrative "teen" market, we developed our familiar adolescent culture with its distinctive music and dress (Mintz, 2004; Modell, 1989). The sense of an adolescent society bonded together (against their elders) reached its height during the late 1960s and early 1970s. With "Never trust anyone over 30" as its slogan, the huge teenage baby boom cohort rejected the conventional rules related to marriage and gender roles and transformed the way we live our adult lives.

In this chapter, we will explore the experience of being adolescent in the contemporary developed world—a time in history when we expect teenagers to go to high school (and now college) and society insulates young people from adult responsibilities for a decade or more. First, I'll be examining the cognitive abilities and emotional

Table 9.1: Stereotypes About Adolescence: True or False?

T/F	1.	Adolescents think about life in deeper, more thoughtful ways than children do.
T/F	2.	Adolescence is when we develop our personal moral code for living.
T/F	3.	Adolescents are highly sensitive to what other people think.
T/F	4.	Adolescents are unusually susceptible to peer influences.
T/F	5.	Adolescents are highly emotional compared to other age groups.
T/F	6.	Adolescents are prone to taking risks.
T/F	7.	Most adolescents are emotionally disturbed.
T/F	8.	Rates of suicide are at their peak during adolescence.
T/F	9.	Adolescents feel more stressed out with their parents than with their peers.
T/F	10.	Getting in with a bad crowd makes it more likely for teenagers to "go down the wrong path."

(Answers: 1. T, 2. T, 3. T, 4. T, 5. T, 6. T, 7. F, 8. F, 9. T, 10. T)

lives of teens. Then, I'll chart how teenagers separate from their parents and relate to one another in groups. This chapter ends by touching on some issues that affect the millions of young people living in impoverished regions of the world, who can't count on having a life stage called adolescence at all.

Before beginning your reading, you might want to take the "Stereotypes About Adolescence: True or False?" quiz in Table 9.1. In the following pages, I'll be discussing why each stereotype is right or wrong.

The Mysterious Teenage Mind

Thoughtful and introspective, but impulsive, moody, and out of control; peer-centered conformists and rebellious risk takers; being able to make adult decisions, but needing to be sheltered from the real world: Can teenagers *really* be all these things? In our search to explain these contradictions, let's first look at three classic theories of teenage thinking, then explore the research related to teenage storm and stress.

Three Classic Theories of Teenage Thinking

Have a thoughtful conversation with a 16-year-old and a 10-year-old and you will be struck by the remarkable mental growth that occurs during adolescence. It's not so much that teenagers know much more than they did in fourth or fifth grade, but that adolescents *think* in a different way. With an elementary school child in the concrete operational stage, you can have a rational talk about daily life. With a teenager, you can have a rational talk about *ideas*. This ability to reason abstractly about concepts is the defining quality of Jean Piaget's formal operational stage (see Table 9.2 on p. 262).

Formal Operational Thinking: Abstract Reasoning at Its Peak

Children in concrete operations can look beyond the way objects immediately appear. They realize that when Mommy puts on a mask, she's still Mommy "inside." They understand that when you pour a glass of juice or milk into a different-shaped glass, the amount of liquid remains the same. Piaget believed that when children reach the **formal operational stage**, at around age 12, this ability to think abstractly takes

formal operational stage Jean Piaget's fourth and final stage of cognitive development, reached at around age 12 and characterized by teenagers' ability to reason at an abstract, scientific level.

Table 9.2: Piaget's Stages: Focus on Adolescence

Age	Name of Stage	Description
0–2	Sensorimotor	The baby manipulates objects to pin down the basics of physical reality.
2–7	Preoperations	Children's perceptions are captured by their immediate appearances. "What they see is what is real." They believe, among other things, that inanimate objects are really alive and that if the appearance of a quantity of liquid changes (for example, if it is poured from a short, wide glass into a tall, thin one), the amount actually becomes different.
8–12	Concrete operations	Children have a realistic understanding of the world. Their thinking is really on the same wavelength as adults'. While they can reason conceptually about concrete objects, however, they cannot think abstractly in a scientific way.
12+	Formal operations	Reasoning is at its pinnacle: hypothetical, scientific, flexible, fully adult. Our full cognitive human potential has been reached.

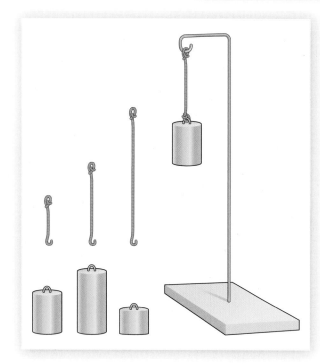

FIGURE 9.1: **Piaget's pendulum apparatus: A task to assess whether children can reason scientifically:** Piaget presents the child with the different weights and string lengths illustrated here and shows the boy or girl how to attach them to the pendulum (and to one another). Then he says, "Your task is to discover what makes the pendulum swing more or less rapidly from side to side—is it the length of the string, the heaviness of the weight, or the height (and force) from which you release the pendulum?" and watches to see what happens.

a qualitative leap. Teenagers are able to reason logically in the realm of pure thought. Specifically, according to Piaget:

ADOLESCENTS CAN THINK LOGICALLY ABOUT CONCEPTS AND HYPOTHETICAL POSSIBILITIES. Ask fourth- or fifth-graders to put objects such as sticks in order from small to large, and they will have no problem performing this *seriation* task. But present a similar task verbally: "Bob is taller than Sam, and Sam is taller than Bill. Who is the tallest?" and the same children will be lost. The reason is that, during adolescence, we first become capable of logically manipulating concepts in our minds (Elkind, 1968; Flavell, 1963).

Moreover, if you give a child in concrete operations a reasoning task that begins, "Suppose snow is blue," she will refuse to go further, saying, "That's not true!" Adolescents in formal operations have no problem tackling that challenge because once our thinking is liberated from concrete objects, we are comfortable reasoning about concepts that may *not* be real.

ADOLESCENTS CAN THINK LIKE REAL SCIENTISTS. When our thinking occurs on an abstract plane, we can approach problems in a systematic way, devising a strategy to scientifically prove that something is true.

Piaget designed an exercise to reveal this new scientific thought: He presented children with a pendulum apparatus and unattached strings and weights (see Figure 9.1). Notice that the strings differ in their length and the weights vary in size or heaviness. Children's task was to connect the weights to the strings, then attach them to the pendulum, to decide which influence determined how quickly the pendulum swung from side to side. Was it the length of the string, the heaviness of the weight, or the height from which the string was released?

Think about how to approach this problem, and you may realize that it's crucial to be systematic—keeping everything constant but the factor whose influence you want to assess (remember my explanation of an experiment in Chapter 1). To test whether it's the heaviness of the weight, you must keep the string length and the height from which you drop it constant, varying only the weight. Then, you need to isolate another variable, keeping everything else the same. And when you vary the length of the string, keeping everything else the same, you will realize that the string length alone affects how quickly the pendulum swings.

Elementary school children, Piaget discovered, approach these problems haphazardly. Only adolescents adopt a scientific strategy to solve reasoning tasks (Flavell, 1963; Ginsburg & Opper, 1969).

HOW DOES THIS CHANGE IN THINKING APPLY TO REAL LIFE? This new ability to think hypothetically and scientifically explains why it's not until in high school that we can thrill to a poetic metaphor or comprehend chemistry experiments (Kroger, 2000). It's only during high school that we can join the debate team and argue the case for and against capital punishment, no matter what we *personally* believe. In fact, reaching the formal operational stage explains why teenagers are famous for debating *everything* in their lives. A 10-year-old who wants to stay up till 2 a.m. to watch a new movie will just keep saying, "I don't want to go to bed." A teenager will lay out his case point by point: "Mom, I got enough sleep last night. Besides, I only need six hours. I can sleep after school tomorrow."

But, do *all* adolescents reach formal operations? The answer is no. For one thing—rather than being universal—formal operational reasoning only occurs in scientifically oriented Western cultures. Worse yet, even in our society, most people don't make it to Piaget's final stage. In a classic study, one researcher discovered only a fraction of U.S. adults approached the pendulum problem scientifically. More disheartening, when asked to debate a controversial issue, such as capital punishment, most people did not even realize that they needed to use logic to construct their case (Kuhn, 1989).

Still, even if many of us never reason like real scientists or master debaters, we can see the qualities involved in formal operational thinking if we look at how adolescents—especially older teenagers—reason about their *own lives*.

If you are a traditional emerging-adult student, think back to the organizational skills it took to get into college. You may have learned about your options from an adviser, researched each possibility on the Internet, visited campuses, and constructed different applications to showcase your talents. Then, when you got accepted, you needed to reflect on your future self again: "This school works financially, but is it too large? How will I feel about moving far from home?" Would you have been able to mentally weigh these possibilities, and project yourself into the future in this way, at age 10, 12, or even 14?

The bottom line is that reaching concrete operations allows us to be on the same wavelength as the adult world. Reaching formal operations allows us to *act* in the world like adults.

Kohlberg's Stages of Moral Judgment: Developing Internalized Moral Values

This new ability to reflect on ourselves as people allows us to reflect on our personal values. Therefore, drawing on Piaget's theory, developmentalist Lawrence Kohlberg (1981, 1984) argued that during adolescence we become capable of developing a moral code that guides our lives. To measure this moral code, Kohlberg constructed ethical dilemmas, had people reason about these scenarios, and asked raters to chart the responses according to the three levels of moral thought outlined in Table 9.3 on p. 264. Before looking at the table, take a minute to respond to the "Heinz dilemma," the most famous problem on Kohlberg's moral judgment test:

> A woman was near death from cancer. One drug might save her. The druggist was charging . . . ten times what the drug cost him to make. The . . . husband, Heinz, went to everyone he knew to borrow the money but he could only get together about half of what it cost. [He] asked the . . . druggist to sell it cheaper or let him pay later. But the druggist said NO! Heinz broke into the man's store to steal the drug. . . . Should he have done that? Why?

The advances in scientific thinking that allow teenagers to solve the pendulum problem are the core qualities that made it possible for this undergraduate to be a real research collaborator in his professor's chemistry lab.

Discussing your plans with an adviser, filling out college applications, and realistically assessing your interests and talents involve the kind of future-oriented adult thinking that only becomes possible in late adolescence. So, even if they don't reason at the formal operational level on Piaget's laboratory tasks, these Portland, Maine, high school seniors are probably firmly formal operational in terms of thinking about their own lives.

Table 9.3: Kohlberg's Three Levels of Moral Reasoning, with Sample Responses to the Heinz Dilemma*

Preconventional level:

Description: Person operates according to a "Will I be punished or rewarded?" mentality.

Reasons given for acting in a certain way: (1) to avoid getting into trouble or to get concrete benefits. (2) person discusses what will best serve his own needs ("Will it be good for me?"), although he may also recognize that others may have different needs.

Examples: (1) Heinz shouldn't steal the drug because then the police will catch him and he will go to jail. (2) Heinz should steal the drug because his wife will love him more.

Conventional level:

Description: Person's morality centers on the need to obey society's rules.

Reasons given for acting in a certain way: (1) to be thought of as a "good person"; (2) the idea that it's vital to follow the rules to prevent a breakdown in society.

Examples: (1) Heinz should steal the drug because that's what "a good husband" does; or Heinz should not steal the drug because good citizens don't steal. (2) Heinz can't steal the drug—even though it might be best—because, if one person decides to steal, so will another and then another, and then the laws would all break down.

Postconventional level:

Description: Person has a personal moral code that transcends society's rules.

Reasons given for acting in a certain way: (1) talks about abstract concepts, such as taking care of the welfare of all people; (2) discusses the fact that there are universally valid moral principles that transcend anything society says.

Examples: (1) Although it's wrong for Heinz to steal the drug, there are times when rules must be disobeyed to provide for people's welfare. (2) Heinz must steal the drug because the obligation to save a human life is more important than every other consideration.

*Within each general moral level, the reasons and examples numbered (1) reflect a slightly lower substage of moral reasoning than those numbered (2).

Source: Adapted from Reimer, Paolitto, & Hersh, 1983.

preconventional level of morality In Lawrence Kohlberg's theory, the lowest level of moral reasoning, in which people approach ethical issues by considering the personal punishments or rewards of taking a particular action.

conventional level of morality In Lawrence Kohlberg's theory, the intermediate level of moral reasoning, in which people respond to ethical issues by considering the need to uphold social norms.

postconventional level of morality In Lawrence Kohlberg's theory, the highest level of moral reasoning, in which people respond to ethical issues by applying their own moral guidelines apart from society's rules.

If you thought in terms of whether Heinz would be personally punished or rewarded for his actions, you would be classified at the lowest level of morality, the **preconventional level.** Responses such as "Heinz should not take the drug because he will go to jail," or "Heinz should take the drug because then his wife will treat him well," suggest that—because your focus is solely on external consequences, whether Heinz will get in trouble or be praised—you are not demonstrating *any* moral sense.

If you made comments such as "Heinz should [or shouldn't] steal the drug because it's a person's duty to obey the law [or to stick up for his wife]" or "Yes, human life is sacred, but the rules must be obeyed," your response would be classified at the **conventional level**—right where adults typically are. This shows your morality revolves around the need to uphold society's norms.

People who reason about this dilemma using their own moral guidelines *apart* from society's rules are operating at Kohlberg's highest **postconventional level.** A response showing postconventional reasoning might be, "No matter what society says, Heinz had to steal the drug because nothing outweighs the universal principle of saving a life."

When he conducted studies with different age groups, Kohlberg discovered that at age 13, preconventional answers were universal. By 15 or 16, most children around the world were reasoning at the conventional level. Still, many of us stop right there. Although some of Kohlberg's adults did think postconventionally, using his *incredibly* demanding criteria, almost no person consistently made it to the highest moral stage (Reimer, Paolitto, & Hersh, 1983; Snarey, 1985).

HOW DOES KOHLBERG'S THEORY APPLY TO REAL LIFE? Kohlberg's categories get us to think deeply about our values. Do you have a moral code that guides your actions? Would you intervene, no matter what the costs, to save a person's life? These categories give us insights into other people's moral priorities, too. While reading about Kohlberg's preconventional level, you might have thought: "I know someone just like this. This person has no ethics. He only cares about whether or not he gets caught!"

However, Kohlberg's research has been severely criticized. For one thing, Kohlberg was wrong when he said that children can't go beyond a punishment and reward mentality. Remember from Chapters 3 and 6, developmentalists now know that our basic sense of morality naturally kicks in at an incredibly young age.

In a classic late-twentieth-century critique, feminist psychologist Carol Gilligan argued that Kohlberg's stages offer a specifically male-centered approach to moral thought. Recall that being classified at the postconventional stage requires abstractly weighing ideals of justice. People must verbalize the tension between societies' rules and universal ideals. Women's morality, Gilligan believes, revolves around concrete, caring-oriented criteria: "Hurting others is wrong"; "Moral people take responsibility to reach out in a nurturing way" (Gilligan & Attanucci, 1988).

Gilligan's criticisms bring up an interesting question: Is Kohlberg's scale *valid*? Does the way people reason about his scenarios relate to the attitudes and behaviors, which, as you learned in Chapter 6, predict acting prosocially in life? Unfortunately, the answer is "not necessarily." When outstandingly prosocial teenagers—community leaders who set up programs for the homeless—took Kohlberg's test, researchers rated their answers at the same conventional level as non-prosocial teens! (See Reimer, 2003.)

Concerns about whether responses to artificial vignettes predict real-world morality are heightened when we look around. We all know people who can spout the highest ethical principles but behave pretty despicably: the minister who lectures his congregation about the sanctity of marriage while cheating on his wife; the chairman of the ethics committee in the state legislature who has been taking bribes for years.

Still, when he describes the changes in moral reasoning that take place during adolescence, Kohlberg has an important point. Teenagers are famous for questioning society's rules, for seeing the injustice of the world, and for getting involved in idealistic causes. Unfortunately, this ability to step back and see the world as it should be, but rarely is, may produce the emotional storm and stress of teenage life.

Elkind's Adolescent Egocentrism: Explaining Teenage Storms

This was David Elkind's (1978) conclusion when he drew on Piaget's concept of formal operations to make sense of teenagers' emotional states. Elkind argues that, when children make the transition to formal operational thought at about age 12, they can see beneath the surface of adult rules. A sixth-grader realizes that his 10 o'clock bedtime, rather than being carved in stone, is an arbitrary number capable of being contested and changed. A socially conscious 14-year-old becomes acutely aware of the difference between what adults say they do and how they really act. The same parents and teachers who punish you for missing your curfew or being late to class can't get to the dinner table or a meeting on time.

The realization that the emperor has no clothes ("Those godlike adults are no better than me"), according to Elkind, leads to anger, anxiety, and the impulse to rebel. From arguing with a ninth-grade English teacher over a grade to testing the limits by driving fast, teenagers are well known for protesting anything just because it's "a rule."

Taking to the streets to protest environmental destruction (fracking) is apt to be a life-changing experience for this teen. It also is a developmental landmark, as advances in moral reasoning make adolescents highly sensitive to social injustices.

Look at the worried expressions on the faces of these freshmen cheerleaders and you can almost hear them thinking, "If I make a mistake during the game, everyone will laugh at me for my whole life!" According to David Elkind, the imaginary audience can make daily life intensely humiliating for young teens.

More tantalizing, Elkind draws on formal operational thinking to make sense of the classic behavior we often observe in young teens—their incredible sensitivity to what other people think. According to Elkind, when children first become attuned to other people's flaws, this feeling turns inward to become an obsession with what others think about their *own* personal flaws. This leads to **adolescent egocentrism**—the distorted feeling that one's own actions are at the center of everyone else's consciousness.

So 13-year-old Melody drives her parents crazy. She objects to everything from the way they dress to how they chew their food. When her mother picks her up from school, she will not let this humiliating person emerge from the car: "Mom, I don't know you!" She does not spare herself: A minuscule pimple is a monumental misery; stumbling and spilling her food on the school lunch line is a source of shame ("Everyone is laughing at me! My life is over!"). According to Elkind, this intense self-consciousness is caused by one facet of adolescent egocentrism called the **imaginary audience.** By that term, he meant that young teens, such as Melody, literally feel that they are on stage, with everyone watching everything they do.

A second component of adolescent egocentrism is the **personal fable.** Teenagers feel that they are invincible and that their own life experiences are unique. So Melody believes that no one has ever had so disgusting a blemish. She has the *most* embarrassing mother in the world.

These mental distortions explain the exaggerated emotional storms we laugh about during the early adolescent years. Unfortunately, the "It can't happen to me" component of the personal fable may lead to tragic acts. Boys put their lives at risk by drag racing on the freeway because they imagine that they can never die. A girl does not use contraception when she has sex because, she reasons, "Yes, *other* girls can get pregnant, but not me. Plus, if I do get pregnant, I will be the center of attention, a real heroine."

Studying Three Aspects of Storm and Stress

Are teenagers unusually sensitive to people's reactions? Is Elkind (like other observers, from Aristotle to Shakespeare to G. Stanley Hall) correct in saying that risk taking is intrinsic to being a "hot-headed youth"? Are adolescents really intensely emotional and/or likely to be emotionally disturbed? Now, let's turn to research related to these three core aspects of teenage storm and stress.

Are Adolescents Exceptionally Socially Sensitive?

In the last chapter, you learned that, when they reach puberty, children—especially girls—become attuned to their bodies' flaws. In Chapter 6, you saw how the passion to fit in socially (and target people who don't!) causes bullying to flare up during the early teens. In one revealing study, when researchers asked middle schoolers to list their priorities, pre-teens ranked socially succeeding as their top concern. Being in the "in crowd" was more important than being a scholar, being nice, or even having friends! (See LaFontana & Cillessen, 2010.)

Moreover, as Elkind would predict, when they reach puberty, children are especially sensitive to social disapproval. If presented with unfamiliar faces on a screen, and told they were unexpectedly rejected by those virtual peers, pre-teen girls' heart rates dramatically slow (Gunther Moor and others, 2014). When scientists constructed a cyber ball game and then arranged for study participants to get ostracized (no one threw these people the ball)—as the researchers predicted, adolescents reacted to this social slight more intensely than did adults (Sebastian and others, 2010).

adolescent egocentrism David Elkind's term for the tendency of young teenagers to feel that their actions are at the center of everyone else's consciousness.

imaginary audience David Elkind's term for the tendency of young teenagers to feel that everyone is watching their every action; a component of adolescent egocentrism.

personal fable David Elkind's term for the tendency of young teenagers to believe that their lives are special and heroic; a component of adolescent egocentrism.

More telling, young teens are prone to act impulsively, *specifically* in situations involving arousing social cues (Blakemore & Mills, 2014). As Figure 9.2 reveals, they selectively fail Simon Says–like tasks, but only when an enticing, smiling person says "Simon Says, 'don't go'" (Casey & Caudle, 2013). As the landmark study in the How Do We Know box spells out, boys tend to make risky driving decisions, but *only* with their friends (Steinberg, 2005; 2008). After being socially excluded (via the cyber ball game) especially teens who are highly rejection-sensitive overreact by impulsively taking these scary driving risks (Peake and others, 2013).

Moreover, fMRI studies show that this predisposition to act precipitously in emotional situations is mirrored in specific brain changes (Blakemore & Mills, 2014; Peake and others, 2013). So, the answer to the question, "Are adolescents more socially sensitive?" is "absolutely yes," especially around the pubertal years!

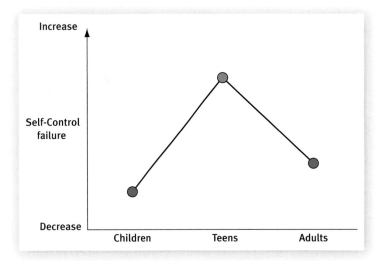

FIGURE 9.2: **Developmental differences in a go, no go, Simon Says–like task:** This chart shows teens made more impulsive "I'll go ahead" errors than either children or adults when a welcoming, smiling face said, "Don't go," suggesting that adolescents, in particular, are apt to lose control in enticing peer situations.

Data from: Casey & Caudle, 2013, p. 84.

HOW DO WE KNOW . . .
that adolescents make riskier decisions when they are with their peers?

Their heightened social sensitivity gives us strong evidence that teenagers do more dangerous things in arousing situations with their friends. About a decade ago, an ingenious video study drove this point scientifically home. Researchers (Gardner & Steinberg, 2005) asked younger teenagers (aged 13 to 16), emerging adults (aged 18 to 22), and adults (aged 24-plus) to play a computer game in which they could earn extra points by taking risks, such as continuing to drive a car after a traffic light had turned yellow. They assigned the members of each age group to two conditions: Either play the game alone or in the presence of two friends.

The chart below shows the intriguingly different findings for young teenagers and for people over age 24. Notice that, while being with other people had no impact on risky decision making in the adults, it had an enormous effect on young teens, who were much more likely to risk crashing the car by driving farther after the yellow light appeared when with friends. The bottom line: Watch for risky behavior when groups of teenagers are together—a fact to consider the next time you see a car full of adolescents barreling down the road with music playing full blast!

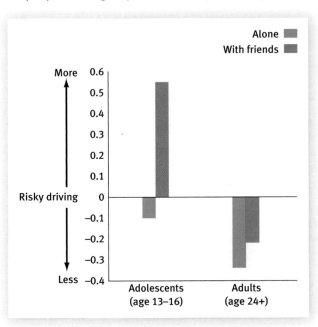

Are Adolescents Risk Takers?

> Doing something and getting away with it. . . . You are driving at 80 miles an hour and stop at a stop sign and a cop will turn around the corner and you start giggling. Or you are out drinking or maybe you smoked a joint, and you say "hi" to a police officer and he walks by. . . .
>
> (quoted in Lightfoot, 1997, p. 100)

This quotation from a teen in an interview study, plus the research in the previous section, suggests that (no surprise) the second storm-and-stress stereotype is *definitely true*. From the thrill of taking that first drink to the lure of driving fast, pushing the envelope is a basic feature of teenage life (Dahl, 2004; Steinberg, 2010).

Consider, for instance, the findings of yearly nationwide University of Michigan–sponsored polls tracking U.S. young people's lives. In examining data spanning 1997 to 2008, researchers found that 1 in 6 teens had been arrested by age 18. By age 23, the arrest rate slid up to an astonishing almost 1 in 3! (See Brame and others, 2012.) In the 2010 survey, roughly 2 in 10 high school seniors admitted to binge drinking (defined as having five or more drinks at a time for males and four or more drinks in a row for females) (Johnston and others, 2011). (Table 9.4 showcases some interesting research facts related specifically to alcohol and adolescents.)

The good news is that, as you can see in Figure 9.3, in contrast to our images of rampant teenage substance abuse, most high school seniors do not report using *any* drugs. The most recent 2013 University of Michigan poll found the *lowest* rates of teenage alcohol use since the survey was instituted four decades ago! (See Johnston and others, 2014.) The bad news is that—for an alarming fraction of young people in the United States—encounters with the criminal justice system are a depressing feature of modern life.

Younger children also rebel, disobey, and test the limits. But, if you have seen a group of teenage boys hanging from the top of a speeding car, you know that the

---

Table 9.4: Stereotypes and Surprising Research Facts About Alcohol and Teens

Stereotype #1: Teenagers who drink are prone to abuse alcohol later in life.

Research answer: "It depends on *when* you begin." Drinking during puberty is a risk factor for later alcohol problems, with animal research suggesting that alcohol use specifically at this time of life primes the brain physiologically to want alcohol later on (Blomeyer and others, 2013). However, during the late teens and twenties, drinking—at least in Western societies—is normative. So we can't predict well from a person's consumption at these peak-use ages to the rest of adulthood.

Stereotype #2: Involvement in academics and/or athletics protects a teen from abusing alcohol.

Research answer: "It's complicated." While excelling at academics protects children at high genetic risk from drinking to excess as a teen (Benner and others, 2014), heavy athletic involvement is correlated with binge drinking (Barnes and others, 2007; Peck, Vida, & Eccles, 2008) for boys. In both cases, this research points (again) to the pivotal role of the peer environment. Drinking (no surprise) is apt to be a prominent feature of the high school jock culture, and more of a "no, no" in the society of scholars, *specifically* during the high school years (see below).

Stereotype #3: Middle childhood problems are risk factors for later excessive drinking.

Research answer: "Both true and surprisingly false." As you might expect, impulse control problems predict teenage and adult problem-drinking (Englund and others, 2008; Pitkanen and others, 2008; Lopez-Caneda and others, 2014). However, two longitudinal investigations—conducted in the United States and Great Britain—revealed that, for girls, high academic achievement was a risk factor for heavy drinking in the early twenties! (Englund and others, 2008; Maggs, Patrick, & Feinstein, 2008.) To explain this uncomfortable finding, researchers suggest that girls who do well academically may be more likely to go to college, where, as many of you know, again the peer culture encourages drinking to excess.

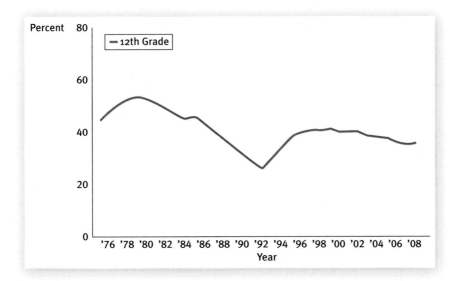

FIGURE 9.3: **Trends in prevalence of illicit drug use, reported by U.S. high school seniors from the mid-1970s to 2010:** Contrary to our stereotypes, only 2 in 5 U.S. high school seniors reports using any illicit drugs (including alcohol) over the past year. Notice also that drug use was actually somewhat more common during the late 1970s and early 1980s—among the parents of today's teens, during their own adolescence.

Data from: Johnston and others, 2011.

risks adolescents take can be threatening to life. At the very age when they are most physically robust, teenagers—especially males—are most likely to die of preventable causes such as accidents (Dahl, 2004; Spear, 2008). So, yes, parents can worry about their children—particularly their sons—when they haven't made it home from a party and it's already 2 a.m.!

Are Adolescents More Emotional, More Emotionally Disturbed, or Both?

Given this information, it should come as no surprise that the third major storm-and-stress stereotype is also correct: Adolescents are more emotionally intense than adults. Developmentalists could not arrive at this conclusion by using surveys in which they asked young people to reflect on how they *generally* felt. They needed a method to chart the minute-to-minute ups and downs of teenagers' emotional lives.

Imagine that you could get inside the head of a 16-year-old as that person went about daily life. About 40 years ago, Mihaly Csikszentmihalyi and Reed Larson (1984) accomplished this feat through developing a procedure called the **experience-sampling technique.** The researchers asked students at a suburban Chicago high school to carry pagers programmed to emit a signal at random intervals during each day for a week. When the beeper went off, each teenager filled out a chart like the one you can see in Figure 9.4 on page 270. Notice, if you turn to Greg's record, that the experience-sampling procedure gives us insights into what experiences make teenagers (and people of other ages) feel joyous or distressed. Let's now look at what the charts revealed about the intensity of adolescents' moods.

The records showed that adolescents do live life on an intense emotional plane. Teenagers reported experiencing euphoria and deep unhappiness far more often than a comparison sample of adults. Teenagers also had more roller-coaster shifts in moods. While a 16-year-old was more likely to be back to normal 45 minutes after feeling terrific, an adult was likely to still feel happier than average hours after reporting an emotional high.

experience-sampling technique A research procedure designed to capture moment-to-moment experiences by having people carry pagers and take notes describing their activities and emotions whenever the signal sounds.

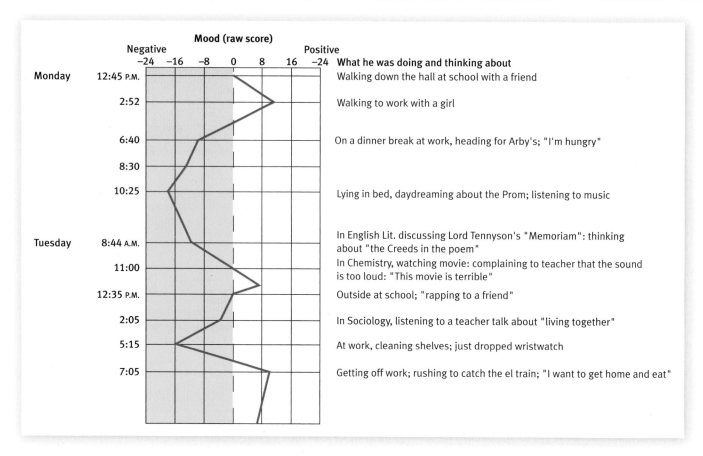

FIGURE 9.4: **Two days in the life of Gregory Stone: An experience-sampling record:** This chart is based on two days of self-reports by a teenager named Greg Stone, as he was randomly beeped and asked to rate his moods and what he was doing at that moment. By looking at the ups and downs of Greg's mood, can you identify the kinds of activities that he really enjoys or dislikes? Now, as an exercise, you might want to monitor your own moods for a few days and see how they change in response to your own life experiences. What insights does your internal mental checklist reveal about which activities are most enjoyable for you?
Adapted from Csikszentmihalyi & Larson, 1984, p. 111.

Does this mean that adolescents' moods are irrational? The researchers concluded that the answer was no. As Greg's experience-sampling chart shows, teenagers don't get excited or down in the dumps for no reason. It's hanging out with their friends that makes them feel elated. It's a boring class that bores them very, very much.

Does this mean that *most* adolescents are emotionally disturbed? Now, the answer is *definitely* no. Although the distinction can escape parents when their child wails, "I got a D on my chemistry test; I'll kill myself!" there is a difference between being highly *emotional* and being emotionally disturbed.

Actually, when developmentalists ask teenagers to evaluate their lives, they get an upbeat picture of how young people generally feel. Most adolescents around the world are confident and hopeful about the future (Gilman and others, 2008; Lewin-Bizan and others, 2010). In one U.S. poll, researchers classified 4 out of 10 adolescents as "flourishing"—efficacious, zestful, connected to family and friends. Only 6 percent were "languishing," totally demoralized about life (Keys, 2007).

So the stereotypic impression that most teenagers are unhappy or suffer from serious psychological problems is false. Still, as you just read, the picture is far from totally rosy. Their risk-taking propensities make the late teens the peak crime years (Warr, 2007; see Figure 9.5). Teenagers' emotional storms can produce other distressing symptoms, too. Again, contrary to our stereotypes, adolescent suicide is rare (Males, 2009). As I'll describe in Chapter 13, the peak life stage for suicide is old age! But, in several international polls, researchers found an alarming fraction of teens—between 1 in 4, to 1 in 6 young people—have engaged in **nonsuicidal self-injury**

nonsuicidal self-injury
Cutting, burning, or purposely injuring one's body to cope with stress.

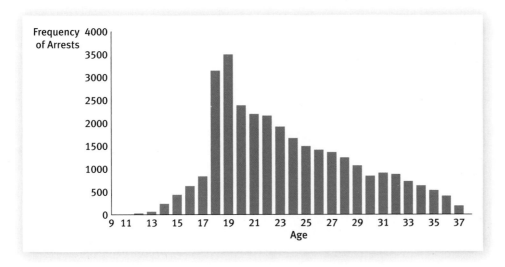

FIGURE 9.5: Frequency of arrests by age in a California study of offenders: This chart shows the standard age pattern around the world. The peak years for law breaking are the late teens, after which criminal activity falls off.
Data from: Natsuaki, Ge, & Wenk, 2008.

(Muehlenkamp and others, 2012; Giletta and others, 2012). These adolescents cut themselves, or perform other self-mutilation acts, to deal with stress.

Scientists are passionate to make sense of this global epidemic. The impulse to self-injure, they find, unlike addictions such as drinking or taking drugs, is used specifically to cope with distress. Cutting episodes erupt when emotionally fragile teens experience bouts of incredibly low self-esteem (Victor, Glenn, & Klonsky, 2012; Anestis and others, 2013). As one adolescent in an interview study explained: [It's due to] "pure black hatred of the self that has failed at everything else" (Breen, Lewis, & Sutherland, 2013, p. 59). Still, another child who regularly self-injured admitted a poisonous positive feeling is involved: "I love looking at my scars. They are an important part of me that I know will always be with me even if nothing else is." (p. 60) Therefore, in some distorted way, cutting may be a strategy for defining one's identity and ironically *preserving* the sense of an enduring self. Which brings up an interesting question. Given that cutting can flare up—and externalizing behaviors such as risk-taking become common—do depression rates rise during the adolescent years?

Unfortunately, the answer is yes. Moreover, while the prevalence of this mental disorder is about equal for each sex during childhood, by the mid-teens, the adult gender pattern kicks in. Throughout life, women are roughly twice as susceptible to depression as are men. So, while they are worrying about their teenage sons, mothers might be a bit concerned about their daughters, too (see Oldehinkel & Bouma, 2011, for review).

Depression rates may escalate during adolescence because the hormonal changes of puberty make the teenage brain more sensitive to stress (Romeo, 2013). But why is depression a mainly female disorder during adult life? Are women biologically primed to internalize their problems when under stress, and could this gender difference have roots in the womb? We do not know. What we do know is that if a child's fate is to battle *any* serious mental health disorder, from depression to schizophrenia, that condition often has its onset in late adolescence or the early emerging-adult years.

Moreover, I believe that the push to be socially successful (or popular) may explain *many* classic distressing symptoms during the early teens.

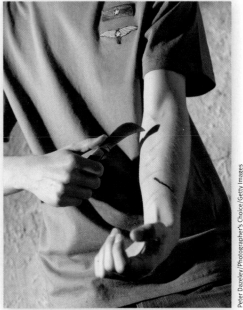

Most teens are upbeat and happy, and suicide is very, very rare during the adolescent years. But, engaging in cutting, or nonsuicidal self-injury, is upsettingly prevalent at this age around the world.

Hot in Developmental Science: A Potential Pubertal Problem, Popularity

Young teens' drive for social status, for instance, seems partly to blame for the fact that academic motivation often takes a nosedive in middle school (LaFontana & Cillessen, 2010; Li & Lerner, 2011). Worse yet—because at this age it can be "cool" to rebel (recall Chapter 6)—for aggressive children, being in the "popular group" is a risk factor for failing in school (Troop-Gordon, Visconti, & Kuntz, 2011). Therefore, chasing popularity can have academic costs. Plus, young teens may be faced with a difficult choice: "Either be in the 'in crowd' or do well in school" (Wilson, Karimpour, & Rodkin, 2011).

Being in the elite "in crowd" at school is probably a thrilling experience for these girls. But, now that their quest to be popular has succeeded, they may develop some not-so-nice qualities as a result of having climbed the status rungs.

Making it into the in crowd can also have personal costs. Pre-teens often base their friendships on similarities in social status—not on shared interests or anything else (Logis and others, 2013). Higher-status adolescents tend to reject their lower-status peers (Berger & Dijkstra, 2013). Plus, when a child is passionate about being popular and ascends to the high status group, this achievement leads to more aggression over time (Dawes & Xie, 2014).

Finally, because social standing is so important at this age (Molloy, Gest, & Rulison, 2011), getting isolated from the "in crowd" can lead to becoming depressed (Buck & Dix, 2012; Witvliet and others, 2010). Popularity pressures seem implicated in *both* the upsurge in unhappiness and acting out during the early teens!

Different Teenage Pathways

So far, I seem to be sliding into stereotyping "adolescents" as a monolithic group. This is absolutely not true! Teenagers, as we know, differ—in their passion to be popular, in their school connectedness, in their tendencies to take risks or get depressed. As diversity at this life stage—and any other age—is the norm, the critical question is, "Who gets derailed and who thrives during this landmark decade of life?"

Which Teens Get into Serious Trouble?

Without denying that serious adolescent difficulties can unpredictably erupt, here are three thunderclouds that foreshadow stormy weather ahead:

AT-RISK TEENS TEND TO HAVE PRIOR EMOTION REGULATION PROBLEMS. It should come as no surprise that one thundercloud relates to elementary school externalizing tendencies and academic difficulties. Not only is the lure of getting into trouble overwhelming, when a child's problems regulating his behavior are already causing him to fail (Hirschfield & Gasper, 2011; Li & Lerner, 2011; Sibley and others, 2011), as I will describe later, children who are not succeeding with the mainstream kids gravitate toward antisocial groups of friends, who then give each other reinforcement for doing dangerous things.

Therefore, tests of *executive functions*—measures charting whether girls and boys are having difficulties generally thinking through their behavior—strongly predict adolescent storms (Pharo and others, 2011; May & Beaver, 2014). Moreover, the same self-regulation issues that lead to teenage turmoil are apt to appear earlier in life.

AT-RISK TEENS TEND TO HAVE POOR FAMILY RELATIONSHIPS. Feeling alienated from one's parents can also be a warning sign of developing storms. When researchers explored the emotions of teens who self-injured, these children often anguished: "My parents are way too critical"; "I can't depend on my mom or dad" (Bureau and others, 2010; You, Lin, & Leung, 2013).

In essence, these young people were describing an insecure attachment. Teenagers want to be listened to and respected. They need to know they are unconditionally loved (Allen and others, 2007). So, to use the attachment metaphor spelled out in Chapter 4, with adolescents, parents must be skillful dancers. They should understand when to back off and when to stay close. In Chapter 7's terms, adolescents require an *authoritative* discipline style.

Given what you learned in previous chapters, it comes as no surprise that parent–child problems appearing years earlier foreshadow teenage distress. From disorganized infant attachment (Spangler & Zimmermann, 2014) to lack of maternal warmth (Morgan, Shaw, & Forbes, 2014)—what happens relationship-wise during infancy and early childhood may epigenetically alter how the adolescent brain reacts to stress. Moreover, it comes as no shock that, just as conflict-ridden parent–child interactions evoke pre-teen depression, being depressed impairs a young person's ability to communicate with her mom or dad (Brière, Archambault, & Janosz, 2013).

This brings up the fact that the attachment dance at *any age* is bidirectional. When we see correlations between teenagers' reporting distant family relationships and having troubles, it's not *simply* parents who are at fault. Imagine that you are a 15-year-old who is having unprotected sex, taking drugs, or withdrawing from the world. Would you tell your parents about your life? And when you withdrew to your room or lied about your activities, wouldn't you feel even more alienated: "My family knows zero about who I am" (Bradley & Corwyn, 2013).

Yes, it's easy to say that being authoritative is vital in parenting teens. But take it from me (I've been there!), when your teenager is on the road to trouble, confronting him about his activities is apt to backfire. So, it can be difficult for frantic parents to understand how to *really* act authoritatively in a much-loved son or daughter's life.

AT-RISK TEENS LIVE IN A RISK-TAKING ENVIRONMENT. Focusing on parent–child relationships neglects the role the social milieu plays in seeding teenage storms. If your much-loved older brother is into drugs (Solmeyer, McHale, & Crouter, 2014), your boyfriend is robbing stores (Monahan, Dimitrieva, & Cauffman, 2014), or the values at your school encourage risk-taking (Rambaran, Dijkstra, & Stark, 2013), your chance of getting into trouble as an adolescent accelerates. To rephrase the old saying: "It may take a village to raise a child, but it *really* takes a nurturing village to help a teenager thrive." Now, let's look at who thrives during their teens.

Which Teens Flourish?

In high school I really got it together. I connected with my lifelong love of music. I'll never forget that feeling when I got that special prize in band my senior year.

At about age 15, I decided the best way to keep myself off the streets was to get involved in my church youth group. It was my best time of life.

As the quotations show, these attributes offer a mirror image of the qualities I just described: Teenagers thrive when they have superior executive functions and can thoughtfully direct their lives (Gestsdottir and others, 2010; Urban, Lewin-Bizan, & Lerner, 2010). They flourish when they are connected to school (Lewis and others, 2011). Having a mentor or VIP (very important non-parental adult) boosts young people's self-esteem (Haddad, Chen, & Greenberger, 2011)—and so does having a

Suppose this 16-year-old chess wiz had no adult mentors to encourage and nurture his passion. He would probably never have a chance to express his talent and flourish during his teenage years.

life interest, like music, provided caring adults nurture your passion (Scales, Benson, & Roehlkepartain, 2011). In two-parent families in particular, attending religious services in later childhood with your parents and siblings promotes thriving later on (Petts, 2014).

Thriving does not mean staying out of trouble. Adolescents who are flourishing may also engage in considerable risk taking during the early and middle teens (Lerner and others, 2010). So again, we need to approach adolescent behavior by adopting the developmental systems approach. Those human beings called teens, like human beings of any age, are not all angel or devil, but complex mixtures of frailties and strengths (Larson & Tran, 2014). Testing the limits is a *normal* adolescent experience even among the happiest, healthiest teens.

And let's not give up on children who *do* get seriously derailed. Developmentalists make a distinction between **adolescence-limited turmoil** (antisocial behavior during the teenage years) and **life-course difficulties** (antisocial behaviors that continue into adult life) (Moffitt, 1993). Perhaps you have a friend who used to stay out all night partying, drinking, or taking drugs, but later became a responsible parent. Or you may know an extremely "troubled teen" who is succeeding incredibly well after finding the right person–environment fit at college or work. (For a compelling example, stay tuned for page 276.) If so, you understand a main message of the next chapter: We change the most during our emerging-adult years. (Table 9.5 offers a checklist so you can evaluate whether a child you love might have a stormy or sunny adolescence.)

Table 9.5: Predicting Whether a Child Is Prone to Teenage Storms or to Flourish: A Section Summary Checklist

Threatening Thunderclouds

1. Does this child have emotion regulation difficulties and academic problems?

2. Does this child have distant or conflict-ridden family relationships?*

3. Does this child live in an environment where risk taking is prized?

Sunny Signs

4. Does this child have good executive functions and/or is she connected to school?

5. Does this child have a mentor or close family relationships?

6. Does this child have a passion or talent that is being nurtured by caring adults?

7. Does this child live in a two-parent family and did she regularly attend church with her parents and siblings during elementary school?

Source: Adapted from Masten (2004), p. 315, and the sources in this section.

*As I will describe later in this chapter, some conflict (and distancing) from parents predictably occurs during early adolescence.

adolescence-limited turmoil Antisocial behavior that, for most teens, is specific to adolescence and does not persist into adult life.

life-course difficulties Antisocial behavior that, for a fraction of adolescents, persists into adult life.

Wrapping Things Up: The Blossoming Teenage Brain

Now, let's put it all together: the mental growth; the morality; the emotionality; and the sensitivity to what others think. Give teenagers an intellectual problem and they reason in mature ways. But younger teens tend to be captivated by popularity, and get overwhelmed in arousing situations when with their friends.

According to adolescence specialists, these qualities make sense when we look at the developing brain. During the teens, a dramatic pruning occurs in the frontal lobes (see Table 9.6). The insulating *myelin sheath* has years to go before reaching its

Table 9.6: Teenage Brain-Imaging Questions and Findings

Question #1: How does the brain change during adolescence?

Answer: *Dramatically, in different ways:* Frontal lobe grey matter (the neurons and synapses) peaks during the pre-teen years, and then declines due to pruning—meaning the cortex "gets thinner" over the teenage years. In the meantime, white matter (the myelin sheath) steadily grows into the twenties.

Question #2: Are there gender differences in this brain development?

Answer: *Yes.* Girls are on an earlier brain-development timetable than boys, with grey matter peaking at a younger age (10 for girls and 12 for boys), and white matter increasing at a faster rate in the female brain. Might these differences relate to emerging gender differences in depression, or the male tendency to take dangerous risks? We do not know.

Question #3: Do the brain-imaging findings mirror the behavioral research in this section?

Answer: *Not really.* For instance, although as suggested above, the teen brain matures in definite ways from adolescence to adulthood, studies exploring specific activation pattern differences between teens and adults—as they relate to social sensitivities, risky decisions, and so on—have sometimes confusing results.

Conclusion: While we do have good general data on teenage brain development, we still have far to go in neuroscientifically mapping the teenage (and adult!) mind.

Sources: Blakemore, Burnett, & Dahl, 2010; Bramen and others, 2011; Burnett and others, 2011; Lenroot & Giedd, 2010; Luciana, 2010; Negriff and others, 2011; Bava and others, 2010; Koolschijn & Crone, 2013; Moreno & Trainor, 2013.

Note: The final statement here is based on my own impressions from reviewing the research cited above.

mature form. At the same time, puberty heightens the output of certain neurotransmitters, which provokes the passion to take risks (Guerri & Pascual, 2010; Steinberg, 2010). As Laurence Steinberg (2008; Smith, Chein, & Steinberg, 2013) explains, it's like starting the engine of adulthood with an unskilled driver. This heightened activation of the "socioemotional brain," with a cognitive control center still "under construction," makes adolescence a potentially dangerous time.

But from an evolutionary standpoint, it is logical to start with an emotional engine in high gear. Teenagers' risk-taking tendencies propel them to venture into the world. Their passion to make it with their peers is vital to leaving their parents and forming new, close attachments as adults. The unique qualities of the adolescent mind are beautifully tailored to help young people make the leap from childhood to the adult world (Dahl, 2004; Steinberg, 2008).

INTERVENTIONS: **Making the World Fit the Teenage Mind**

Table 9.7 summarizes these section messages in a chart for parents. Now, let's explore our discussion's ramifications for society.

Table 9.7: Tips for Parents of Teens

1. Understand that strong emotions may not have the same meaning for your teen as for you. So try not to take comments like "I hate myself" or "I'm the dumbest person in the world" very seriously. Also, during the early teen years, new research—discussed later in this chapter—suggests it's normal for your child to become more secretive and rebellious. But just because your daughter gets furious at you, don't think she doesn't love you.

2. Understand that, while sampling forbidden activities is normal, if your teen is getting involved in clearly illegal activities or seems seriously depressed, you do need to be concerned.

3. Understand that your child's peer choices (and peer-group status) offer good hints about her behavior, and that striving to be in the "popular crowd"—while normal—can have unpleasant consequences.

4. Roll with the punches, encourage your child's passions, and enjoy your teenager!

Don't punish adolescents as if they were mentally just like adults. If the adolescent brain is a work in progress, it doesn't make sense to have the same legal sanctions for teenagers who commit crimes that we have for adults. Rather than locking adolescents up, it seems logical that at this young age we focus on rehabilitation. As Laurence Steinberg (2008) and virtually every other adolescence expert suggest, with regard to the legal system, "less guilty by reason of adolescence" is the way to go.

Is the U.S. legal system listening to the adolescence specialists? The answer is "a bit, but only recently." In 2005, the Supreme Court outlawed the death penalty for adolescents and, in 2012, eliminated mandatory life sentences without the possibility of parole for teens (Shulman & Cauffman, 2013). Still, today, as the Experiencing the Lifespan Box suggests, officers and prosecutors can transfer selected adolescents accused of violent crimes out of the juvenile justice system and have those teens tried as adults. Yes, as my amazing interview with Jason suggests, with luck and a resilient temperament, a shockingly punitive approach can help turn a person around. However, statistically speaking, there is no evidence that condemning adolescents to the gulag of dysfunctional adult prisons deters later criminal acts (Fabian, 2011). Do you believe that it's *ever* acceptable to try teenagers as adults?

Pass laws user-friendly to the teenage mind. Putting adolescents in adult prisons is counterproductive, simply because it exposes this socially-sensitive age group to the kind of social milieu that encourages criminal acts. Therefore, we need to craft legislation taking teenagers mental processes into account. One good example is graduated driving rules, which limit young people just getting their license from operating cars

Experiencing the Lifespan: Innocently Imprisoned at 16

If you think the U.S. legal system protects 16-year-olds from adult jail and that citizens can't be falsely incarcerated without a trial, think again. Then, after reading Jason's story, you might link his horrific teenage years to the qualities involved in resilience I discussed in Chapter 7.

I grew up with crazy stuff. My mom was a drug dealer and my dad passed away so I was adopted by my grandparents. I was kicked out of four schools before ninth grade. By age 15, I was involved with a street gang and heavy gun trading in Birmingham, Alabama. I was in a car with some older guys during a drive-by shooting, got pulled over, and that was the last time I saw daylight for over 3 years.

The original charge was carrying a concealed weapon, and I was sent to a juvenile boot camp. Then, two days after being discharged, detectives were knocking on my door with the full charges: three counts of attempted murder. The arresting officers decided to transfer me to county jail, where I ended up for 19 months. If you go to trial and lose, you get the maximum sentence, 20 years to life, so—even though I was innocent—avoiding trial is the thing you want to do. What happens is that your lawyers keep negotiating plea bargains. First, I was offered 20 to life, with the idea I'd be out in 10 years; then 15 years, then 10. Not very appealing for a 16-year-old kid! Finally, by incredible good luck, I got a lawyer who takes kids from prisons and puts them into rehab

facilities, and he convinced the judge that was best for me. I quickly had to take what they offered—being sent to the Nashville Rescue Mission and then a halfway house for 2 years—because my trial date was coming up very soon.

Jail was unbelievable. The ninth floor of the Jefferson County Jail is well known because that's where they send criminals from the penitentiary who have committed the most violent crimes to await trial. My first cellmate had cut a guy's head off. Every time you get to know a group, the next week another group arrives in jail and you have to fight again. The guards were no better. If they didn't like a prisoner, they would persuade inmates to beat the living daylights out of that person.

What helped me cope were my dreams, because you are not in jail in your dreams. I wrote constantly, read all the time. What ultimately helped was being sent out of state (so I couldn't get involved with my old friends) and, especially, my counselors at the mission. I never met guys so humble; such amazing people. Also, if I got into trouble again, I knew where I could be heading. Scared the heck out of me. Now, everything I do is dependent on being normal. I'm 22. I have good friends but I haven't told anyone anything about my past. I have a 3.5 average. I'm working two jobs. I'll be the first person in my family to graduate college. I want to go to grad school to get my psychology Ph.D.

while in groups of peers. Better yet, let's draw on adolescents' social sensitivities and passion to connect with the wider world in a positive way.

Provide group activities that capitalize on adolescents' strengths. How can we help teenagers forge growth-enhancing peer relationships and promote their inner development?

Youth development programs fulfill this mission. They give adolescents safe places to explore their passions during the late afternoon hours, when teens are most prone to get into trouble while hanging out with their friends (Goldner and others, 2011). From 4-H clubs, to church groups, to high school plays, youth development programs ideally foster qualities that developmentalist Richard Lerner has named the five C's: *competence, confidence, character, caring,* and *connections*. They provide an environment that allows young people to thrive (Bowers and others, 2010; Lerner, Dowling, & Anderson, 2003).

I wish I could say that every youth program fostered flourishing. But as anyone who has spent time at a girls' club or the local Y knows, these settings can encourage group bullying and antisocial acts (Rorie and others, 2011). Therefore, youth programs must be structured and well supervised. They have to promote the five C's. At the same time, they should be places where young people can exercise their autonomy and relax, let loose, or joke around (Adachi & Willoughby, 2014). So, rather than just saying, "Afterschool activities are great," we need to consider what each specific program actually provides.

It also helps to embed less academic offerings into the school day. In one heartening study, having strong high school arts programs boosted children's academic performance, making students feel more engaged in *all* of their classes (Martin and others, 2013). Intense involvement, specifically in high school clubs, predicts work success years down the road (Gardner, Roth, & Brooks-Gunn, 2008; Linver, Roth, & Brooks-Gunn, 2009)—which brings me to that important issue: For the sake of *both* their present and future, how can we get more teens connected to school?

Change high schools to provide a better adolescent–environment fit. Adolescents who feel imbedded in nurturing schools tend to feel good about themselves (Hirschfield & Gasper, 2011; Lewis and others, 2011) and the world (Flanagan & Stout, 2010). School can offer at-risk teens a haven when they are having problems at home (Loukas, Roalson, & Herrera, 2010).

Unfortunately, however, many Western high schools are not nurturing places. In one disheartening international poll, although teenagers were generally upbeat about other aspects of their lives, they rated their high school experience as only "so-so" (Gilman and others, 2008). How can we turn this situation around?

In surveys, teenagers say that they are yearning for the experiences that characterize high-quality elementary schools (described in Chapter 7)—autonomy-supporting work that encourages them to think and teachers who respect their point of view (LaRusso, Romer, & Selman, 2008); courses that are relevant to their lives (Wagner, 2000).

In addition to injecting more creativity into the day through the arts, service-learning classes can make a lasting difference in later development (McIntosh, Metz, & Youniss, 2005). Here is what one African American young man had to say about his junior-year course in which he volunteered at a soup kitchen: "I was on the brink of becoming one of those hoodlums the world so fears. This class was one of the major factors in my choosing the right path" (quoted in Yates & Youniss, 1998, p. 509).

youth development program
Any after-school program or structured activity outside of the school day that is devoted to promoting flourishing in teenagers.

These teens are probably taking great pleasure in serving meals to the homeless as part of their school community-service project. Was a high school experience, like this one, life changing for you?

Jose Luis Pelaez Inc./Getty Images

Could this have been you in high school, particularly toward the end of the week? Did you decide not to take early-morning classes this semester because you realized the same thing would happen to you today? Do you think that we are making a mistake by resisting teenagers' biological clocks and insisting that their school day start at 8 a.m.?

Finally, we might rethink the school day to take into account teenagers' unique sleep requirements. During early adolescence, the sleep cycle is biologically pushed back (Colrain & Baker, 2011; Feinberg & Campbell, 2010). Although adolescents often need at least nine hours of sleep to function at their best, because they tend to go to bed after 11 and must wake up for school at 6 or 7 a.m., the typical U.S. teen sleeps fewer than 7 hours each day (Colrain & Baker, 2011). Worse yet, children who strongly show this evening circadian shift are *generally* at risk for a stormy teenage life. They tend to have poorer family relationships (Díaz-Morales and others, 2014), are often lonely, and are less mentally tough (Brand and others, 2014; Doane & Thurston, 2014). Because sleep deprivation throws the cognitive and socioemotional control systems more out of whack, these adolescents are apt to be impulsive (Peach & Gaultney, 2013) and engage in deviant acts (Telzer and others, 2013), in addition to (no surprise) doing poorly in class.

For this reason, researchers are exploring how strategies such as reducing ambient light at night might better promote teenage sleep (Shochat, Cohen-Zion, & Tzischinsky, 2014; Short and others, 2013). But perhaps these scientists should consider a simpler route: Start school at 10 or even 11 a.m.!

Think back to your high school—what you found problematic; what helped you cope; what may have allowed you to thrive. Do you have other ideas about how we might change schools, or any other aspect of the environment, to help teenagers make the most of these special years?

Another Perspective on the Teenage Mind

Until now, I've been highlighting the mainstream developmental science message: "Because of their brain immaturity, teens need protection from the world." Let's consider some different views: Do we know enough about how the brain functions to make these kinds of neural attributions? Given the somewhat confusing findings in Table 9.6, some experts legitimately answer no (Epstein, 2010; Sercombe, 2010). Might scientists be over-invoking biology, to inappropriately label teenagers as out-of-control?

Consider, for instance, that the brain evidence targeting the early teens as a time for trouble is out of sync with many *real-world* risk-taking facts. From the frequency of arrests, to bingeing on alcohol, the peak age-zone for deviant behavior is late adolescence and early emerging adulthood—when the frontal lobes are almost fully mature. Furthermore, is teenage risk taking that dangerous compared to the impulsive activities we engage in *throughout* adult life—from marrying multiple times, to making investments we can't afford, to starting unprovoked wars (see Willoughby and others, 2013)?

The most innovative critique of the immature adolescent brain was put forth by psychologist Robert Epstein. Epstein (2010) reminds us that the life stage called adolescence is an artificial construction. Nature intended us to enter adulthood at puberty. Now young people may be forced into depression and dangerous risk taking by languishing for a decade under the ill-fitting label "child." How many "predictable" teenage symptoms of storm and stress, Epstein argues, have little to do with faulty frontal lobes and everything to do with a poor contemporary body–environment fit? Do teenagers *really* have immature brains, or are adults to blame for shackling teenagers' minds? Let's keep these thoughts in mind, as we turn now to explore parent–teenager relationships in depth.

Keren Su/The Image Bank/Getty Images

Assuming adult responsibilities right after puberty, like fishing for a living, is what nature intended for our species (see Chapter 8). Therefore, Robert Epstein believes so-called teenage "dysfunction" is produced by a dysfunctional contemporary society.

Tying It All Together

1. Robin, a teacher, is about to transfer from fourth grade to the local high school, and she is excited by all the things that her older students will be able to do. Based on what you have learned about Piaget's formal operational stage and Kohlberg's theory of moral reasoning, pick out which two new capacities Robin may find among her students.

   a. The high schoolers will be able to memorize poems.

   b. The high schoolers will be able to summarize the plots of stories.

   c. The high schoolers will be able to debate different ideas even if they don't personally agree with them.

   d. The high schoolers will be able to develop their own moral principles.

2. Eric is the coach of a basketball team. The year-end tournament is tomorrow, and the star forward has the flu and won't be able to play. Terry, last year's number one player, offers to fill in—even though this is a violation of the conference rules. Eric agonizes about the ethical issue. Should he deprive his guys of their shot at the championship, or go against the regulations and put Terry in? How would you reason about this issue? Now, fit your responses into Kohlberg's categories of moral thought.

3. A 14-year-old worries that everyone is watching every mistake she makes; at the same time, she is fearless when her friends dare her to take life-threatening risks like bungee jumping off a cliff. According to Elkind, this feeling that everyone is watching her illustrates _____; the risk taking is a sign of _____; and both are evidence of the overall process called _____.

4. In your 15-year-old nephew, pick which symptom(s) is unusual and so might indicate a real psychological problem: *intense mood swings and social sensitivities/depression/a tendency to engage in risky behavior with friends.*

5. Your child has finally made it into the popular kids crowd at school. You should feel (*Pick one*): *proud because that means he is able to get along with the kids/worried because he may be at risk for acting out behaviors such as aggression.*

6. There has been a rise in teenage crimes in your town, and you are at a community meeting to explore solutions. Given what you know about the teenage mind, which two interventions should you definitely support?

   a. Push the state legislature to punish teenage offenders as adults. Let them pay for their crimes!

   b. Encourage the local high school to expand its menu of arts classes.

   c. Think about postponing the beginning of the school day to 10 a.m.

7. Imagine you are a college debater. Use your formal operational skills to argue first for and then against the proposition that society should try teens as adults.

Answers to the Tying It All Together questions can be found at the end of this chapter.

Teenage Relationships

What exactly are teenager–parent interactions like? Now, it's time to tackle this question, as I focus on those two adolescent agendas—separating from parents and connecting with peers.

Separating from Parents

> When I'm with my dad fishing, or when my family is just joking around at dinner—it's times like these when I feel completely content, loved, the best about life and myself.

In their original experience-sampling study, Csikszentmihalyi and Larson (1984) discovered that teenagers' most uplifting experiences occurred when they were with their families—sharing a joke around the dinner table or having a close moment with

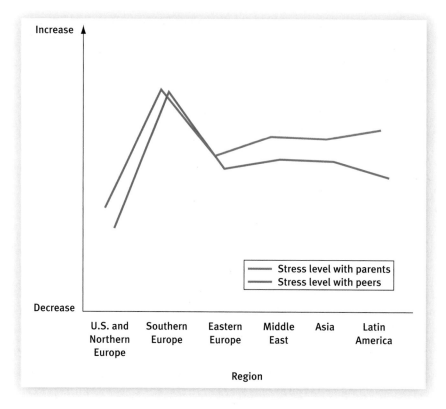

Increase

Decrease

Stress level with parents
Stress level with peers

U.S. and Northern Europe   Southern Europe   Eastern Europe   Middle East   Asia   Latin America

Region

FIGURE 9.6: **Mean of parent–child stress versus stress with peers, as reported by teens in various regions of the globe:** Notice that with the exception of southern Europe, worldwide, adolescent stress with parents is more intense than stress with peers.

Data from: Persike & Seiffge-Krenke, 2014, p. 499.

mom or dad. Unfortunately, however, those moments were few. In fact, while peer encounters were more apt to evoke passionate highs, when adolescents were with their families, unhappy emotions outweighed positive ones 10 to 1.

This tendency to lock horns with our parents seems built into the adolescent experience, as the global poll illustrated in Figure 9.6 shows. Notice that, while the magnitude of the gap differs from nation to nation, teens worldwide typically rank stress in the parent–child relationship as more upsetting than stress with peers (Persike & Seiffge-Krenke, 2014).

The Issue: Pushing for Autonomy

Why does family life produce such teenage pain? As developmentalists point out, if our home life is good, our family provides our cocoon. Home is the place where we can relax, be ourselves, and feel completely loved. However, in addition to being our safe haven, parents must be a source of pain. The reason is that parents' job is both to love us and to limit us. When this parental limiting function gets into high gear, teenage distress becomes acute.

What do teenagers and their parents argue about? This global poll offers insights into unique cultural parenting priorities in different regions of the world (Persike & Seffge-Krenke, 2014). In northern Europe and the United States, arguments around academic issues loom large ("I hate that pressure to get good grades!"). For Japanese and Chinese teens, as you might imagine, these kinds of school-related conflicts outweigh everything else.

Perhaps, because it's especially crucial in these collectivist societies to marry within "one's own group," in the Middle East, micromanaging peer relationships is a major stress ("My parents won't let me see the friends I want!"). In southern Europe, where children still live with their parents well into their late twenties and early thirties, dependency and general parent–child acrimony is a serious concern ("We fight all the time!" "They won't let me grow up!"). (More about these cultural priorities in Chapters 10 and 11.)

But it should come as no surprise that the underlying issue in *every nation* centers around independence ("Why can't I do what I want? You have too many rules!").

Moreover, the most intense clashes occur just when peer group popularity pressures reach their height—around the early to middle teens (De Goede, Branje, & Meeus, 2009; Daddis, 2011.)

The Process: Exploring the Dance of Autonomy

Actually, parent–adolescent conflict flares up while children are in the midst of puberty (Steinberg, 2005; Steinberg & Hill, 1978). From an evolutionary perspective, the hormonal surges of puberty may propel this struggle for autonomy ("You can't tell me what to do!") that sets in motion the dance of separation intrinsic to becoming an independent adult.

How does the dance of autonomy unfold? Based on periodically asking teens questions—such as, "Do your parents know what you do in your free time?" or "Do you tell your parents who you hang out with?"—and exploring parental rules, Canadian researchers offered a motion picture of changing parent–child relationships over the teenage years (Keijsers & Poulin, 2013).

As it turns out, children first initiate the push for independence by becoming secretive and distant in their early teens. But, parents only respond by steadily granting their children much more freedom beginning after age 15.

Why is mid- to later adolescence a crucial autonomy-granting cutting point? The reason may be that by about their Junior year of high school, parents feel their children are more responsible and mature (Wray-Lake, Crouter, & McHale, 2010). As we get closer to high school graduation, our priorities start to shift from rebelling to constructing an adult life. Now, we must get it together and think concretely about college and a career (Malin and others, 2014).

Even the major social markers of independence at around age 16 or 17 eliminate sources of family strain. Think about how getting your first job, or your license, removed an important area of family conflict. You no longer had to ask your parents for every dime or rely on mom or dad to get around.

Passing a driving test and finally getting the keys to the car is a joyous late-teenage transition into adult liberation. It's almost the developed-world equivalent of a puberty rite!

These adult landmarks put distance between parents and teenagers in the most basic, physical way. The experience-sampling charts showed that ninth-graders spent 25 percent of their time with family members. Among high school seniors, the figure dropped to 14 percent (Csikszentmihalyi & Larson, 1984).

So the process of separating from our families makes it possible to have a more harmonious family life. The delicate task for parents, as I suggested earlier, is to give teens space to explore their new, adult selves and still remain closely involved (Steinberg, 2001). One mother of a teenager explained what ideally should happen, when she said: "I don't treat her like a young child anymore, but we're still very, very close. Sort of like a friendship, but not really, because I'm still in charge. She's my buddy" (quoted in Shearer, Crouter, & McHale, 2005, p. 674).

This quotation brings up a fascinating gender difference in the parent–child intimacy dance. Boys, the earlier Canadian study showed, maintained their new, distant pubertal communication pattern as they traveled into the late teens—not telling mothers much about their activities, avoiding sharing their lives. But, after becoming more secretive and distant as young teens, during mid- and later adolescence, girls reached out to their moms to reconnect again as confidants and "best friends."

Sharing a real woman-to-woman talk is one joy of being an older female teen, as, during later adolescence, girls often reconnect emotionally with their mothers again.

Cultural Variations on a Theme

My parents won't let me date anyone who isn't Hindi—or go to parties. They never tell me they love me. I have to be at home right after school to do the grocery shopping and other family chores. Why can't they just let me be a normal American kid?

In individualistic societies, we strive for parent–child adult relationships that are less hierarchical, more like friends. What about teens—such as the young person quoted above—whose parents have collectivist values centered on obedience and putting family obligations first? How do these immigrant teens cope with separation issues?

AP Photo/Lincoln Journal Star, Krista Niles

As she translates an oath of naturalization to her non-English-speaking Iraqi mom, this daughter is engaging in a role reversal that can be distressing, but can also offer a lifelong sense of empathy and self-efficacy.

As researchers point out, with immigrant adolescents, the normal impulse to separate can be exacerbated by issues relating to *acculturation* (Kim & Park, 2011; Park and others, 2010; Wu & Chao, 2011; Kim and others, 2013). Teens want to become "real" Americans. They may think: "My parents have old-fashioned attitudes. Their values have nothing to do with my life." As Judith Harris's *peer group socialization* theory might predict (recall Chapter 7), with immigrant adolescents, parent–child disagreements may go beyond bickering about family rules to involve a fundamental difference in worldviews (Arnett, 1999).

Family pressures, as you saw in the example above, present special hurdles for immigrant teens. Straddling two cultures can upend the normal parent–child relationship—catapulting some second-generation children into becoming the family adults. As one teacher who works with Chinese immigrants commented, "The kids may be doing the interpreting and translating…, they may be the de facto parents" (quoted in Lim and others, 2009).

Given these strains, are immigrant teens at risk for poor parent–child relations? The answer is, "it depends." Rules that seem rigid to Western eyes have a different meaning when young people understand that their parents have sacrificed everything for their well-being (Wu & Chao, 2011). As one touching, international poll showed, the core quality that makes adolescents feel loved *worldwide* is feeling their parents have gone out of their way to do things that are rare and emotionally hard (McNeely & Barber, 2010).

So, knowing that one's parents made a rare sacrifice ("giving up their happiness and moving for my future") can create unusually close parent–child bonds. Helping a non-English-speaking mom or dad negotiate this unfamiliar culture can promote self-efficacy and empathy, too. As one 19-year-old revealingly commented: "My entire childhood, I was translating simple things day to day . . . (it made me feel) . . . empowered, proud, frustrated at times, (but) understanding of my parents' struggle" (Guan, Greenfield, & Orellana, 2014, p. 332).

immigrant paradox The fact that despite living in poverty, going to substandard schools, and not having parents who speak the language, many immigrant children do far better than we might expect at school.

This quotation may explain a phenomenon called the **immigrant paradox.** Despite coping with an overload of stresses (Cho & Haslam, 2010), many immigrant children living in poverty do better than their peers (van Geel & Vedder, 2011). But like all children, immigrant teens take different paths—some flourish and others flounder (Suárez-Orozco and others, 2010). One force can be critical in predicting failure or success—no surprise, it's a person's group of peers.

Connecting in Groups

Go to your local mall and watch sixth and seventh graders hanging out to get a first-hand glimpse of the group passion that takes over during the early teens. Now that we understand peer group's potentially destructive effects, let's turn to the vital positive functions pre-teen peer groups serve.

Defining Groups by Size: Cliques and Crowds

Developmentalists classify teenage peer groups into categories. **Cliques** are intimate groups having a membership size of about six. Your group of closest friends would constitute a clique. **Crowds** are larger groupings. Your crowd comprises both your best buddies and a more loose-knit set of people you get together with less regularly.

In a 1960s observational study in Sydney, Australia, one researcher found that these groups serve a crucial purpose: They are the vehicles that convey teenagers to relationships with the opposite sex (Dunphy, 1963).

As you can see in the photos in Figure 9.7, children enter their pre-teen years belonging to unisex cliques, the close associations of same-gender best friends that I talked about in Chapter 6. Relationships start to change when cliques of boys and girls enter a public space and "accidentally" meet. At the mall, notice the bands of sixth- or seventh-grade girls who have supposedly arrived to check out the stores, but who really have another agenda: They know that Sam or José and his buddies will be there. A major mode of interaction when these groups meet is loud teasing. When several cliques get together to walk around the stores, they have melded into that larger, first genuinely mixed-sex group called a crowd (Cotterell, 1996).

The crowd is an ideal medium to bridge the gap between the sexes because there is safety in numbers. Children can still be with their own gender while they are crossing into that "foreign" land. Gradually, out of these large-group experiences, small heterosexual cliques form. You may recall this stage during high school, when your dating activities occurred in a small group of girls *and* boys. Finally, at the end of adolescence, the structure collapses. It seems babyish to get together as a group. You want to be with your romantic partner alone.

You might be surprised to know that the progression outlined in this 50-year-old research still rings true (Child Trends Data Bank, 2008): First, teenagers get together in large mixed-sex crowds; next, they align into smaller heterosexual groups; then, they form one-to-one relationships, or date.

What Is the Purpose of Crowds?

Crowds have other functions. They allow teenagers to connect with people who share their values. Just as we select friends who fit our personalities, we gravitate to the crowd that fits our interests. We disengage from a crowd when its values diverge from ours. As one academically focused teenager lamented: "I see some of my friends changing. . . . They are getting into parties and alcohol. . . . We used to be good friends . . . and now, I can't really relate to them . . . . That's kind of sad" (quoted in Phelan, Davidson, & Yu, 1998, p. 60).

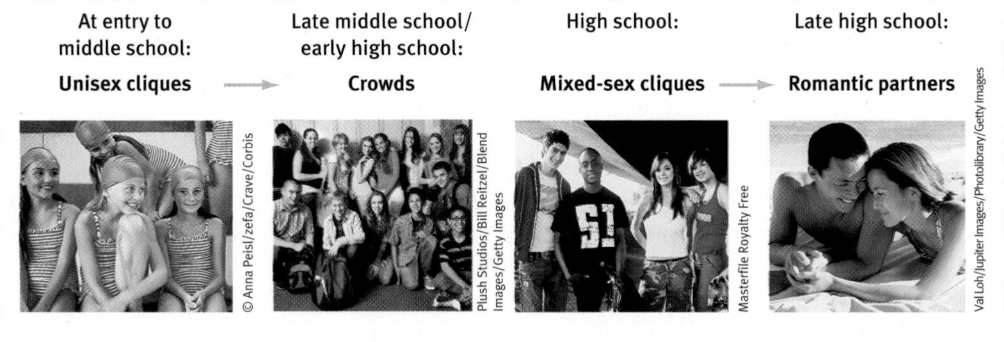

clique A small peer group composed of roughly six teenagers who have similar attitudes and who share activities.

crowd A relatively large teenage peer group.

At entry to middle school:	Late middle school/ early high school:	High school:	Late high school:
Unisex cliques →	**Crowds** →	**Mixed-sex cliques** →	**Romantic partners**

FIGURE 9.7: **The steps from unisex elementary cliques to adult romantic relationships: A visual summary:** Unisex cliques meld into large heterosexual crowds, then re-form as heterosexual cliques, and then break up into one-to-one dating relationships. Does this sequence match your own teen experience?

Allen Russell/Photolibrary/Getty Images

As you pass this group of "punks" on the street, you may think, "Why do they dress in this crazy way?" But for this group, their outlandish hair and clothes are a message that "I'm very different, and I don't agree with what society says," and most important, they are a signal to attract other fellow minds: "I'm like you. I'm safe. I have the same ideas about the world."

Crowds, actually, serve as a roadmap, allowing teens to connect with "our kind of people" in an overwhelming social world (Smetana, Campione-Barr, & Metzger, 2006). Interestingly, it's mainly in large high schools that teens align into defined crowds such as "the Goths" or "the brains," who share activities, attitudes, and a special type of dress. Therefore, one developmentalist suggested that a school's size plays a vital role in promoting the teenage crowd (Cotterell, 1996). When your classes are filled with unfamiliar faces, it is helpful to develop a mechanism for finding a smaller set of people just like you. Teenagers adopt a specific look—like having blue hair and wearing grungy jeans—to signal: "I'm your type of person. It's okay to be friends with me."

What Are the Kinds of Crowds?

In affluent societies, there is consistency in the major crowd categories. The intellectuals (also called brains, nerds, grinds, or geeks), the popular kids (also known as hotshots, preppies, elites, princesses), the deviants (burnouts, dirts, freaks, druggies, potheads), and a residual type (Goths, alternatives, grubs, loners, independents) appear in high schools throughout the West (Sussman and others, 2007).

How much mixing occurs between different crowds? Although teens do straddle different groups (Lonardo and others, 2009), adolescents tend to have friends in similar status crowds. So a popular boy, as suggested earlier in the chapter, associates with the popular kids. He shuns the socially more marginal groups, such as the deviants (bad kids) or nerdy brains. Moreover, as being brainy and especially advertising that you work for high grades can go against the group norms, intellectuality does not gain teenagers kudos in the peer world, at least in the standard public school (Sussman and others, 2007).

A study tracking children's self-esteem, as they moved from elementary school into high school, documents exactly how being brainy can be transformed from a plus to a greater teenage liability, and also charts the wider peer group scene (Prinstein & La Greca, 2002). Notice in Figure 9.8 that children who end up in the popular kids and jocks crowds became more self-confident during adolescence. (These are the people who would tell you, "I wasn't very happy in elementary school, but high school was my best time of life.") The brains group followed the opposite path—happiest during elementary school, less self-confident as teens.

Finally, notice that the teenagers in the deviant burnout group tend to be most depressed before adolescence and stay at the low end of the happiness continuum in high school (see also Heaven, Ciarrochi, & Vialle, 2008). We already know that failing in middle childhood predicts gravitating toward groups of "bad" peers. Now, let's explore why joining that bad crowd makes a teenager even more likely to fail.

"Bad Crowds"

The classic defense that parents give for a teenager's delinquent behavior is, "My child got involved with a bad crowd." Without ignoring the principle of selection (birds of a feather flock together), there are powerful reasons why bad crowds do cause kids to do bad things.

For one thing, as we know, teenagers are incredibly swayed by their peers. Moreover, each group has a leader, the person who most embodies the group's goals. So, if a child joins the brains group, his school performance is apt to improve because everyone is jockeying for status by competing for grades (Cook, Deng, & Morgano, 2007; Molloy, Gest, & Rulison, 2011). However, in delinquent groups, the pressure is to model the most antisocial member. Therefore, the activities of this most acting-out leader set the standard for how the others want to behave.

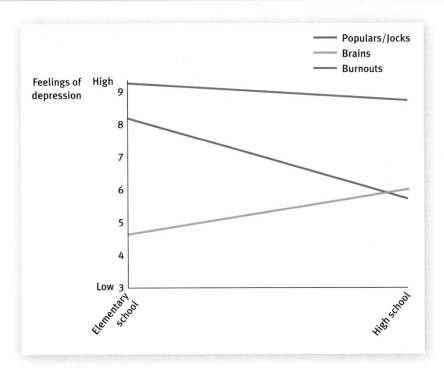

FIGURE 9.8: **Feelings of depression in late elementary school and high school, for children who ended up in three different high school crowds:** In this "follow-back" study, researchers tested children in grades four and six and then looked at their depression levels in high school and explored their particular high school crowds. Notice that the boys and girls in the high-status "popular" and "jocks" crowds became happier during high school. The children destined to be in the "brains" crowd felt happiest during elementary school. The teens who became "burnouts" were more depressed than any other group both in late elementary school and in high school. If you remember being in one of these high school crowds, how do these findings relate to your feelings in elementary school versus high school?
Data from: Prinstein & La Greca, 2002, p. 340.

So, in the same way you felt compelled to jump into the icy water at camp when the bravest of your bunkmates took the plunge, if one group member begins selling guns or drugs, the rest must follow the leader or be called "chicken." Moreover, when children compete for status by getting into trouble, this creates ever-wilder antisocial modeling and propels the group toward taking increasingly risky actions.

Combine this principle with the impact of just being in a group. When young people get together, a group high occurs. Talk gets louder and more outrageous. People act in ways that would be unthinkable if they were alone. From rioting at rock concerts to being in a car with your buddies during a drive-by shooting (recall the earlier Experiencing the Lifespan box), groups do cause people to act in dangerous ways (Cotterell, 1996).

By videotaping groups of boys, developmentalists have documented the **deviancy training,** or socialization into delinquency, that occurs as a function of simply talking with friends in a group (Dishion, McCord, & Poulin, 1999; Rorie and others, 2011). The researchers find that at-risk pre-teens forge friendships through specific kinds of conversations: They laugh, egg one another on, and reinforce one another as they discuss committing antisocial acts. So peer interactions in early adolescence are a medium by which problem behavior gets established, solidified, and entrenched.

As a group euphoria sets in and people start surging for the stage, these teenagers at a rock festival in England might trample one another—and then later be horrified that they could ever have acted this way.

deviancy training
Socialization of a young teenager into delinquency through conversations centered on performing antisocial acts.

The lure of entering an antisocial peer group is especially strong for at-risk kids because they are already feeling "it's me against the world" (Veenstra and others, 2010). Put yourself in the place of a child whose impulsive behavior is causing him to get rejected by the "regular" kids. You need to connect with other children like yourself because you have failed at gaining entry anywhere else. Once in the group, your buddies reinforce your *hostile attributional bias.* Your friends tell you that it's fine to go against the system. You are finally finding acceptance in an unfriendly world.

In middle-class settings, popular kids sometimes get into trouble. "Self-identifying" as a jock is actually a risk factor for abusing alcohol or having unprotected sex (Cook, Deng, & Morgano, 2007). (At this point, any reader who has lived through adolescence is probably saying, "Duh!") But in affluent communities, children with prior problems tend to gravitate toward the druggy or delinquent groups. In economically deprived neighborhoods, however, there may be few achievers to hang out with. Flourishing is difficult because the community is a toxic place. The only major crowd may be the antisocial group called a gang.

Society's Nightmare Crowd: Teenage Gangs

gang A close-knit, delinquent peer group. Gangs form mainly under conditions of economic deprivation; they offer their members protection from harm and engage in a variety of criminal activities.

The **gang**, a close-knit, delinquent peer group, embodies society's worst nightmares. Gang members share a collective identity, which they often express by adopting specific symbols and claiming control over a certain territory or turf (Shelden, Tracy, & Brown, 1997). This mainly male group appears in different cultures and historical eras. However, with gangs, the socioeconomic context looms large: Adverse economic conditions promote gangs (again for a vivid example, turn back to the Experiencing the Lifespan box on page 276).

Gangs provide teenagers with status. They offer physical protection in dangerous neighborhoods (Shelden, Tracy, & Brown, 1997). When young people have few options for making it in the conventional way, gangs offer a pathway to making a living (for example, by selling drugs or stealing). So, in dangerous neighborhoods, what starts as time-limited adolescent turmoil is more likely to turn into a life-course criminal career.

This suggests that moving inner city children to middle-class communities might turn them around. Not so fast! When impoverished ghetto families were randomly assigned by lottery to move to subsidized housing in an affluent suburban town, the "mover" teenagers actually did worse than the children who were left behind! (See Fauth, Leventhal, & Brooks-Gunn, 2007.) When we think more deeply, it makes sense that relocating disadvantaged children to a potentially unfriendly place might backfire. If a specific group is defined as "not like us"—in this case, rejected as "those scary kids who live in subsidized housing"—these young people will feel more isolated from a caring community than before. Again, it takes a *nurturing* village for adolescents to thrive.

A Note on Adolescence Worldwide

It also takes a kinder, gentler society for adolescence to exist. So, children growing up in impoverished areas of the world are less apt to have this extra decade insulated from adult life. Unfortunately, adolescence has been eliminated for the approximately 1 million children who enter the sex trade every year (United Nations Children's Fund [UNICEF], 2002). Some of these boys and girls are street children, living in gangs in cities in Latin America and Southeast Asia. Or destitute parents may sell their daughters into the sex industry in order for the family to survive (Gajic-Veljanowki & Stewart, 2007). In poor regions of the globe, parents may force their female children into unwanted marriages as early as age 13 (Erulkar, 2013).

This 14-year-old soldier and devastated child bride in Africa offer a stark testament that, in some regions of the world, young people still are deprived of an adolescence.

Adolescence has been eliminated for the hundreds of thousands of child soldiers. Many combatants in the poorest regions of the globe are teenage boys. Some are coerced into fighting as young as age 10 or 8 (Child Soldiers Global Report, 2008; UNICEF, 2002a).

Yes, many teenagers in the world's affluent areas are flourishing. But children in the least-developed regions of the globe may not have the chance to be teenagers or construct a decent adult life. Although critics, such as Robert Epstein, bemoan the shackles of Western teens, having an extra decade liberated from grown-up responsibilities can be critical to flourishing during the adult years.

How can you personally flourish during your adult years? Stay tuned for research relating to this question in the next part of the book.

Tying It All Together

1. Chris and her parents are arguing again. Based on this chapter, at what age might arguments between Chris and her parents be most intense? Around what age would Chris's parents have begun to seriously loosen their rules? Choose between ages 12, 16, and 19.

2. Your niece Heather hangs around with a small group of girlfriends. You see them at the mall giggling at a group of boys. According to the standard pattern, what is the next step?

    a. Heather and her friends will begin going on dates with the boys.

    b. Heather and her clique will meld into a large heterosexual crowd.

    c. Heather and her clique will form another small clique composed of both girls and boys.

3. Mom #1 says, "Getting involved with the 'bad kids' makes teens get into trouble." Mom #2 disagrees: "It's the kid's personality that causes him to get into trouble." Mom #3 says, "You both are correct—but also partly wrong. The kid's personality causes him to gravitate toward the 'bad kids,' and then that peer group encourages antisocial acts." Which mother is right?

4. You want to intervene to help prevent at-risk pre-teens from becoming delinquents. First, devise a checklist to assess who might be appropriate for your program. Then, applying the principles in this chapter, offer suggestions for how you would turn potentially "troublemaking teens" around.

Answers to the Tying It All Together questions can be found at the end of this chapter.

SUMMARY

The Mysterious Teenage Mind

Wise observers have described the "hot-headed" qualities of youth for millennia. However, adolescence, first identified by G. Stanley Hall in the early 1900s and characterized by **"storm and stress,"** became a life stage in the United States during the twentieth century, when high school became universal and "isolated" teens together as a group.

Jean Piaget believes that when teenagers reach the **formal operational stage,** they can think abstractly about hypothetical possibilities and reason scientifically. Although even most adults don't typically reason like scientists, older teenagers use the skills involved in formal operations to plan their adult futures.

According to Lawrence Kohlberg, reaching formal operations makes it possible for teenagers to develop moral values that guide their lives. By examining how they reason about ethical dilemmas, Kohlberg has classified people at the **preconventional level** (a level of moral judgment in which only punishment and reward are important); the **conventional level** (moral judgment that is based on obeying social norms); and the highest, **postconventional level** (moral reasoning that is based on one's own moral ideals, apart from society's rules). Despite the fact that Kohlberg's criteria for measuring morality have serious problems, adolescence is when we become attuned to society's flaws.

According to David Elkind, this ability to evaluate the flaws of the adult world produces **adolescent egocentrism.** The **imaginary audience** (the feeling that everyone is watching everything one does) and the **personal fable** (feeling invincible and utterly unique) are two components of this intense early-teenage sensitivity to what others think.

Studies suggest that many, but not all, storm-and-stress stereotypes about teenagerhood are true. Adolescents are highly socially sensitive. In arousing peer situations, they are apt to take dangerous risks. This risk-taking (and sometimes law-breaking) propensity, especially with friends, makes adolescence a potentially dangerous time. Research, using the **experience-sampling technique,** shows teens are more emotionally intense than adults. Contrary to our stereotypes, however, most adolescents are upbeat and happy. Still, teenage **nonsuicidal self-injury** is prevalent around the world and depression rates rise during adolescence—especially among females. The push to be popular may explain many unfortunate behaviors during the pubertal years.

The minority of teenagers who get into *serious* trouble tend to have prior emotional and school problems, feel distant from their families (and create more family distance), and live in a risk-taking social milieu. Being connected to academics and having personal and wider-world resources helps teens thrive. However, even adolescents who are succeeding experiment with forbidden activities, and even serious **adolescence-limited turmoil** may not lead to **life-course difficulties.** Many problem teens construct fulfilling adult lives.

The unique characteristics of the developing teenage brain may make early adolescence a relatively dangerous life stage. The frontal lobes are still maturing. Puberty heightens teenagers' social sensitivities and emotional states. The lessons for society are: Don't punish teenagers who break the law in the same ways that adult offenders are punished; pass legislation that takes teenage sensitivities into account; and, most of all, channel teenage passions in a positive way through *high-quality* **youth development programs.** We also need to make high school more appealing and adjust the school day to fit adolescent sleep needs. While the "immature brain" conception of adolescence is currently in vogue, critics suggest that it minimizes teenagers' strengths.

Teenage Relationships

Teenagers' struggles with parents are most intense during puberty, and issues relating to independence loom large in these conflicts around the world (with interesting cultural variations). After young teens initiate the push for autonomy by distancing themselves from their families, by mid- and later adolescence, parents respond by relaxing their rules. Eventually, the goal is to develop a more friendlike relationship with one's parents as adults. Immigrant adolescents from families with collectivist values face unique family separation stresses, although the **immigrant paradox** suggests that caring for a non-English-speaking mother or father can make teens self-confident, empathic, and mature.

Teenage peer groups comprise **cliques** and **crowds.** These different sized groups convey adolescents, in stages, toward romantic involvement. Crowds, such as the jocks or the brains, give teenagers an easy way of finding people like themselves in large high schools. The popular kids and the jocks (in contrast to the lower-status brains) feel better about themselves in high school than during elementary school. Children who enter delinquent groups tend to be unhappy before high school and remain distressed during their teenage years.

Entering a "bad crowd" may smooth the way to antisocial behavior because group members model the most antisocial leader and compete for leadership by performing delinquent acts. **Deviancy training,** in which pre-teens egg one another on by talking about doing dangerous things, leads directly to delinquency as at-risk children travel into high school. **Gangs,** mainly male teenage peer groups that engage in criminal acts, are most common in impoverished communities. In poor regions of the world, young people may not have any adolescence at all.

KEY TERMS

"storm and stress," p. 260

formal operational stage, p. 261

preconventional level of morality, p. 264

conventional level of morality, p. 264

postconventional level of morality, p. 264

adolescent egocentrism, p. 266

imaginary audience, p. 266

personal fable, p. 266

experience-sampling technique, p. 269

nonsuicidal self-injury, p. 270

adolescence-limited turmoil, p. 274

life-course difficulties, p. 274

youth development program, p. 277

immigrant paradox, p. 282

clique, p. 283

crowd, p. 283

deviancy training, p. 285

gang, p. 286

ANSWERS TO **Tying It All Together** QUIZZES

The Mysterious Teenage Mind

1. c and d

2. If your arguments centered on getting punished or rewarded (the coach needs to put Terry in because that's his best shot at winning; or, the coach can't put Terry in because, if someone finds out, he will be in trouble), you are reasoning at the preconventional level. Comments such as "going against the rules is wrong" might be classified as conventional. If you argued, "Putting Terry in goes against my values, no matter what the team or the rules say," your response might qualify as postconventional.

3. the imaginary audience; the personal fable; adolescent egocentrism

4. depression

5. worried, because he is at risk for acting out behaviors such as aggression

6. b and c

7. Trying teens as adults. Pro arguments: Kohlberg's theory clearly implies teens know right from wrong, so if teens knowingly do the crime, they should "do the time." Actually, the critical dimension in deciding on adult punishment should be a person's culpability— premeditation, seriousness of the infraction, and so on, not age.

Con arguments: The research in this chapter shows that teens are indeed biologically and behaviorally different, so it is cruel to judge their behavior by adult standards. Moreover, if the U.S. bars young people from voting or serving in the military until age 18, and won't let people buy alcohol until age 21, it's unfair to put teens in adult prisons.

Teenage Relationships

1. At age 12, the arguments would be most intense; by age 16, Chris's parents would be giving her much more freedom

2. b

3. Mom #3 is correct.

4. Checklist: (1) Is this child unusually aggressive? (2) Is he failing at school and being rejected by the mainstream kids? (3) Does this child have poor relationships with his parents? (4) Does he live in a dangerous community, or a risk-taking environment? (Or, because he is poor, is he being defined as "dangerous" by the community?) Your possible program: Provide positive extracurricular activities that nurture each child's interests. Offer service-learning opportunities. Possibly, institute group sessions with parents to solve problems around certain issues. Definitely try to get these teens connected with caring mentors and a different set of (prosocial) friends.

Early and Middle Adulthood

This three-chapter book part spans the time from high school graduation (at roughly age 18) until society labels us as senior citizens (in our mid-sixties)—a lifespan chunk that covers almost 50 years!

Chapter 10—**Constructing an Adult Life** tackles the challenges of making it to full adulthood—a process that often takes a decade after we reach age 18. In this chapter, among other topics, I'll tackle the challenges of college, choosing a career, and finding a mate—including paying special attention to the on-line revolution in romance. If you are a traditional college student or a twenty-something young adult, this chapter is about your life.

Chapter 11—**Relationships and Roles** continues this focus on work and love by exploring marriage, parenthood, and careers. In the marriage section, you will get insights into how different societies view this core relationship, how marriages change over time and, especially, learn the latest research relating to having enduring, satisfying love. In the parenthood section, you'll find out how becoming parents changes a marriage and learn what twenty-first-century motherhood and fatherhood is really like. The last section of the chapter addresses work: How have our career lives been changing? What makes for happiness in this vital role? Do men's and women's career attitudes and pathways differ today?

Chapter 12—**Midlife.** In much of this chapter, my focus is, "How do people change over the adult years?" Once again, as I survey the research on personality and intellectual change, you'll be getting a wealth of insights into what makes for a fulfilling adult life. The last sections of this chapter cover topics specific to middle age: grandparenthood, caring for elderly parents, and age-related changes in sexuality.

PART V

CHAPTER 10

Stockbyte/Getty Images

Constructing an Adult Life

After graduating from high school in the top third of his class, Matt looked forward to pursuing his dream of becoming a lawyer. But his freshman year at State U was a nightmare. His courses felt irrelevant. He zoned out during lectures. Compared to high school, the work seemed impossibly hard. Most important, with his full-time job at the supermarket, and five classes a semester, he lost his scholarship after the first year. The only rational solution seemed to be to drop out for a while and move back with his parents, so he could work his way up to management and then consider going back.

Six years later, Matt is doing well. In June he was promoted to store supervisor and (finally) moved out of the house. One reason is that he met a terrific girl on Facebook named Clara—his first real relationship in five years. Clara and Matt share many values even though, he must admit, she is more mature. He respects Clara's strong woman ethic and the fact that she has been caring for her disabled sister, while working and going to nursing school full time. Clara—being the take-charge person in their relationship—is pushing Matt to return to college. But it's going to be such a stretch, financially. And—frankly—Matt is worried that he won't get into the work.

Should he give up his job or cut down his hours? And what will he major in if he returns to State U? Adulthood can be thrilling—but the choices you face during the twenties are much harder than you'd expect!

Can you identify with Matt's financial troubles or his decision-making problems centered on school? Perhaps, like Clara, you are struggling to balance work and family responsibilities while getting your degree. No matter what your situation, if you are in your twenties, you might feel a bit "in between." You are clearly not a child, but you still haven't reached those classic goals of adulthood—marriage, parenthood, embarking on your "real" career. You fit into that new life category Jeffrey Arnett labels (2004, 2007) *emerging adulthood.*

This chapter is devoted to this new life phase. It explores that time lasting roughly from age 18 through the late twenties, when we are constructing an adult life. First, I'll explore the features of emerging adulthood and describe the challenges we face during this watershed, transitional life stage. The last half of this chapter focuses on three crucial emerging-adult concerns: career, college, finding love.

Emerging into Adulthood

emerging adulthood The phase of life that begins after high school, tapers off toward the late twenties, and is devoted to constructing an adult life.

role The characteristic behavior that is expected of a person in a particular social position, such as student, parent, married person, worker, or retiree.

As you learned in Chapter 1, **emerging adulthood** is not a universal life stage. It exists for a minority of young people—those living at this point in history in the Western world. Its function is exploration—trying out options before committing to adult **roles.** Emerging adults often are "not quite ready" to settle down. They don't feel financially or emotionally secure. They may be exploring trial pathways—moving from job to job, entering and then exiting college or a parent's home, testing out relationships before they commit (Arnett, 2007; Arnett & Tanner, 2010).

Emerging adulthood is defined by testing out different possibilities and developing the self. Its other core quality, according to Arnett, is often exuberant optimism about what lies ahead (Tanner & Arnett, 2010). Emerging adults, as Table 10.1 shows, are at their physical peak. Their abilities to think and to reason are in top form. Still, the challenges of this age are perhaps more daunting than those we face at any time of life.

We need to re-center our lives. Our parents protect us during adolescence. Now, our task is to take control of ourselves and act like "real adults" (Tanner, 2006; Tanner & Arnett, 2010). We used to count on the standard roles of marriage or supporting a family to make us feel adult. No more! Parents in collectivist countries such as China disagree with their developed world counterparts, viewing the core characteristics of adulthood in relational terms—such as keeping the family safe (see Nelson and others, 2013). But, Westerners view the benchmarks of adulthood in internal ways: Being adult means accepting responsibility. Adults financially support themselves. Adults make their own independent decisions about life (Arnett, 2007).

We have entered an unstructured, unpredictable path. During adolescence, high school organizes our days. We wake up, go to class; we are on an identical track. Then, at age 18, our lives diverge. Many of us go to college; others enter the world of work. Some people get married; others never enter that state. Emerging adults live alone or with friends, stay with their parents or move far away. For some emerging adults, constructing an adult life takes decades. For others—people who have children, get married, and enter the work world at age 18 or 19—there may be no life stage called emerging adulthood at all. So emerging adulthood is defined by variability—as we each set sail on our own. Why did this structure-free life stage emerge?

Table 10.1: A Twenty-Something Body at Its Physical Peak, and Snapshots of How a Few Capacities Decline Over Time*†

The skeleton: Our height peaks at age 20 and then, due to the compression of the joint cartilage and bones, declines, especially after midlife. So by age 70, we are roughly 2–5 percent shorter. (Erosion in the joint cartilage and fragile bones also produces classic age-related illnesses called osteoarthritis and osteoporosis, explained in Chapter 14.)

The muscles: The contracting skeletal muscle fibers allow us to perform physical tasks. As we age, these fibers atrophy and are replaced by fat, causing an average 30–40 percent decline in strength by the seventies.

The heart: During exercise, cardiac output, or our heart's pumping capacity, dramatically increases—delivering more oxygen to the muscles. With age the cardiac muscle weakens and thickens, so this maximum pumping ability declines, and we easily get winded. Fatty deposits and a loss of elasticity of the artery walls also compromise our strength and stamina over time.

The lungs: The lungs are the bellows that deliver oxygen to the blood. Our ability to breathe in deeply and exhale forcefully peaks in the twenties, and declines year by year, even for nonsmokers. This loss in vital capacity (and related measures) also explains why physical performance declines with age.

Data from: Spense, 1989; Masoro, 1999.

* In general, losses accelerate after midlife.
† People differ greatly in the extent of these losses.

Setting the Context: Culture and History

Emerging adulthood was made possible because of our dramatic twentieth-century longevity gains. Imagine reaching adulthood a half-century ago. With a life expectancy in the mid-sixties, you could not have the luxury of spending almost a decade constructing an adult life. Now, with life expectancy floating up to the late seventies in industrialized nations, putting off adult commitments until an older age makes excellent sense.

Emerging adulthood was solidified by the need for more education. A half-century ago, high school graduates could climb to the top rungs in their careers. Today, in the United States, college is often crucial to adult success (Danziger & Ratner, 2010; Furstenberg, 2010). But, although most emerging adults enter college, it typically takes six years to get an undergraduate degree, especially because so many people need to work to finance school. If we add in graduate school, constructing a career can normally take until the mid-twenties and beyond (Johnson, Crosnoe, & Elder, 2011).

Emerging adulthood was promoted by uniquely individualistic attitudes about what makes for a satisfying adult life (Côté & Levine, 2002; Yeung & Hu, 2013). This life-stage took hold in a late-twentieth-century Western culture that stresses self-expression and "doing your own thing," in which people make dramatic changes *throughout* their adult years.

Longevity, the need for education, and a Western ethic that stresses personal freedom made emerging adulthood possible. Still, the forces that drive this life stage vary from place to place. For snapshots of this variability, let's travel to southern Europe, Scandinavia, and then enter the United States.

The Mediterranean Model: Living with Parents and Having Trouble Making the Leap to Adult Life

In southern Europe, sagging economies make it difficult for young people to find jobs. The Italian and Spanish cultures, in particular, have norms against **cohabitation,** or living together (Seiffge-Krenke, 2013). People only push to leave home when they find a serious romantic partner and can support a spouse. This means young people in Portugal, Italy, Spain, and Greece often spend their emerging-adult years in their parents' house (Mendonça & Fontaine, 2013; Seiffge-Krenke, 2013). Unfortunately, in Mediterranean nations, at the time of this writing (early 2015), family traditions, plus financial constraints, have seriously impeded young people's travels into an independent life.

Many Greek men in their late twenties and thirties are still living with their families, in some cases because they cannot afford to the leave the nest and construct an adult life. If you were in this situation, how would you react?

cohabitation Sharing a household in an unmarried romantic relationship.

nest-leaving Moving out of a childhood home and living independently.

The Northern European Plan: Expect to Live Independently, Hopefully with Government Help

These impediments do not exist in northern European nations, where the economy is better (again, as of this writing) and where young people often live together and can have babies outside of marriage. In Norway, Sweden, and Denmark the government subsidizes university attendance. A strong social safety net provides free health care and other benefits to citizens of every age. So (although the reality can be different) in northern Europe, **nest-leaving**—moving out of a parent's home to live independently—traditionally begins at the brink of the emerging-adult years (Furstenberg, 2010; Hendry & Kloep, 2010; Seiffge-Krenke, 2013). In the Nordic countries, in particular, the twenties are a stress-free interlude—a time for exploring, for testing out different relationships and careers before settling down to adult life (Buhl & Lanz, 2007).

The United States: Alternating Between Independence and Dependence

Emerging adulthood in the United States has features of both the northern European and Mediterranean scenes. As in northern Europe, in the United States, young people often live together and increasingly have children before they get married. Our individualistic culture has traditionally encouraged moving out of a parent's home at 18. However, as in southern Europe, the United States does not help young people find work and has its own sluggish economy, so it can be difficult to exit the nest (more about this issue in the next section).

The reality is that our dramatic *income inequalities*, plus diversity of cultures, make U.S. young people emerging into adulthood very different at the starting gate (Furstenberg, 2010). We also have a more erratic passage to constructing an adult life (Settersten & Ray, 2010).

This bumpy path became evident several decades ago when researchers tracked several hundred New York State young people from ages 17 to 27, looking at their progress toward reaching classic adulthood markers such as financial independence, marriage, and living on their own (Cohen and others, 2003). Yes, there was an overall shift to more mature adult status as people moved deeper into their twenties. But notice from Figure 10.1 that, when we look at individuals, we see variability and movement backward and forward toward the benchmarks of being adult.

FIGURE 10.1: **The ups and downs of the emerging-adult years:** In a 10-year study tracing how young people develop from age 17 to 27, researchers discovered that many emerging adults move backward and forward on their way to constructing an adult life. These graphs illustrate the adult pathways of five different people in the areas of financial independence and romantic relationships.

Data from: Cohen and others, 2003.

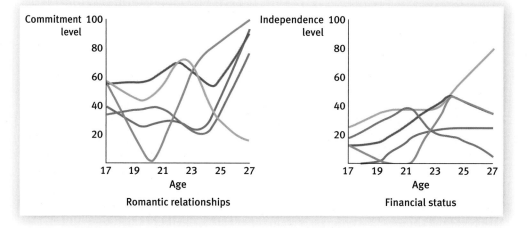

So, at age 22, a man might be cohabiting with the idea of getting married. At 25, he might break up with his fiancée and begin dating again. A woman could be financially independent at 21, then slide backward, depending on her parents' help after losing her job and returning to school.

If you are in your mid- or upper-twenties, think about your progress to adulthood in terms of relationships, career, and becoming financially independent. Does your pathway also show these ups and downs? When do you expect to *fully* arrive at adulthood?

Beginning and End Points

This last question brings up an interesting issue: When *does* emerging adulthood begin and end?

Exploring the "So-Called" Entry Point: Nest-Leaving

If you are like many middle-class Westerners, you might mark the event that launches emerging adulthood as moving out of a parent's home. Leaving home after high school for college, a job, or—if your parents are affluent—a gap year traveling the world is often viewed as a rite of passage. It forces people to take that first step toward independent adulthood—taking care of their needs on their own. It also causes a re-centering in family relationships, as parents see their children in a different, adult way. Listen to this British mother gushing about her 20-year-old daughter: "To be honest I'm real proud of her. . . . She keeps her flat tidy which was a total shocker to me; I'd expected to be a laundry and maid service to her but fair play, she's done all her washing and cleaning" (quoted in Kloep & Hendry, 2010, p. 824).

This quotation hints at two potential benefits of leaving home: It should produce more harmonious family relationships; it should force young people to "grow up."

For this mother, being invited to her daughter's first apartment may be a thrilling experience: "My baby did grow up to become a responsible woman!"

DOES LEAVING HOME PRODUCE BETTER PARENT–CHILD RELATIONSHIPS? U.S. research suggests the answer to this common perception is yes. In several longitudinal studies, both young people and their parents reported less conflict and more adult-to-adult relationships when college-bound children left the nest (Whiteman, McHale, & Crouter, 2007; Morgan, Thorne, & Zubriggen, 2010). However, this is not the case in Portugal, where family dependence is prized and staying at home is "normal" during the emerging-adult years. In this nation, where more than one-half of all people between the ages of 18 and 35 live with their parents, one study showed that staying in the nest had no impact on parent–child relationships. Ironically, Portuguese parents got more agitated when their children moved out! (See Mendonça & Fontaine, 2013.)

I must emphasize that, even in the United States, physically leaving home does not mean having distant family relationships. Judging by the 24/7 texts that fly back and forth between my students and their mothers, the impulse to stay closely connected to parents is more intense among this cohort of twenty-somethings than when I was a college student decades ago (see Levine & Dean, 2012). Having close mother–child relationships and even calling each other frequently is correlated with adjusting well to college and homing in on a satisfying career (Gentzler and others, 2011; Melendez & Melendez, 2010; Stringer & Kerpelman, 2010). Although they may not be making the meals or doing the laundry, mothers in particular remain a vital support as young people exit the nest and travel into the wider world.

DOES LEAVING HOME MAKE PEOPLE MORE ADULT? Here, European studies imply the answer is yes. In the Portuguese research I just described, young people who lived on their own managed their lives more competently than did their peers who stayed in the nest (Mendonça & Fontaine, 2013). When Belgian researchers compared young people in their early twenties who never left home with a same-aged group who moved out, the "nest residers" were less likely to be in a long-term relationship, felt more emotionally dependent on their parents, and were less satisfied with life (Kins & Beyers, 2010; see also Seiffge-Krenke, 2010). One Belgian emerging-adult named Adam spelled his feelings out: "(It) is comparable to living in a hotel actually. I have no charges . . . my meals are prepared, my laundry is done" (quoted in Kins, de Mol, & Beyers, 2014, p. 104). Another British mom put it more graphically: "He is my little boy, a mummy's boy if you like. . . . And 'cos he lives at home still . . . I do his clothes, his washing, tidy his room . . . and even still do packed lunch for him to take to work" (quoted in Kloep & Hendry, 2010, p. 826).

These quotations reinforce our negative images about emerging adults who stay in the nest (yes, in the developed world, they tend more often to be males): They are lazy, babyish, and unwilling to grow up. The problem is that we are confusing consequences with causes. In southern Europe, the push to move out is often propelled by finding a serious romantic relationship ("Now that I found my life love, I must leave home!").

This college student is living at home to save money. How can she and her mother negotiate the difficult task of getting along as adults? Stay tuned for suggestions right now.

social clock The concept that we regulate our passage through adulthood by an inner timetable that tells us which life activities are appropriate at certain ages.

age norms Cultural ideas about the appropriate ages for engaging in particular activities or life tasks.

on time Being on target in a culture's timetable for achieving adult life tasks.

off time Being too late or too early in a culture's timetable for achieving adult life tasks.

In every nation, as I implied earlier, nest-leaving has a clear economic cause (Seiffge-Krenke, 2013). Young people stay at home, or return to live with their families, because they cannot afford to live on their own (Berzin & De Marco, 2010; Britton, 2013).

In addition to economic issues, there is another barrier to moving out for some immigrant and ethnic minority youth—values (Furstenberg, 2010; Kiang & Fuligni, 2009). If a young person's collectivist worldview says, "put family first," or if a family really needs help, children may stay in the nest for very adult-centered reasons—to help with the finances and the chores. As one Latino 20-year-old explained: "I can't leave my mom by herself, she is a single mother. The only person she's got is me. . . ." (quoted in Sánchez and others, 2010, p. 872).

So, does nest-leaving qualify as the entry point of emerging adulthood? The answer is "not really anymore." Do young people *need* to live independently to act mature? The answer is definitely no. The real challenge for families is to construct adult-to-adult relationships with their children no matter where the younger generation lives (see Table 10.2 for some suggestions). And the challenge for young people is to assemble the building blocks to construct a satisfying adult life. When should this constructing phase end and full adulthood arrive? The answer brings up a classic concept in adult development.

Table 10.2: Tips for Getting Along as Co-residing Adults

1. **For parents:** Don't baby your child or micromanage or hover—texting or calling when your child comes home "late." Support and scaffold your child's passage into adulthood.

2. **For children:** Resist the lure of being babied, but lean on your parents for emotional support. Understand, if you are making progress to adulthood, that's the important issue—not that you are living "at home."

3. **For parents and children:** Talk openly about your living together concerns and set up shared rules if you think they will help: How will you divide household tasks? Is it important that your son or daughter stays in school or is looking for a job? Then, vow to treat each other like loving adults.

Exploring the Fuzzy End Point: The Ticking of the Social Clock

Our feelings about when we should get our adult lives in order reflect our culture's **social clock** (Neugarten, 1972, 1979). This phrase refers to shared **age norms** that act as guideposts to what behaviors are appropriate at particular ages. If our passage matches up with the normal timetable in our culture, we are defined as **on time**; if not, we are **off time**—either too early or too late in terms of where we should be at a given age.

So in the twenty-first-century West, exploring different options is considered "on time" during our twenties, but these activities become off time if they extend well into the next decade of life. A parent whose 39-year-old son is "just dating" and shows no signs of deciding on a career or moves back home for the third or fourth time may become impatient: "Will my child ever grow up?" A woman traveling through her thirties may get uneasy: "I'd better hurry up if I want a family," or "Do I still have time to go to medical school?"

Society sets the general social-clock guidelines. Today, with the average age of marriage in most E.U. countries floating up to the late twenties for women and the early thirties for men (Shulman & Connolly, 2013), it's fine to date for more than a decade if you live in the West. But in China, everyone is expected to get married, and the

When this not-so-young man in his forties finally proposed to his long-time, 38-year-old girlfriend, she and her family were probably thrilled. Feeling "off time" in the late direction in your social-clock timetable can cause considerable distress.

marriage age is lower now than in the past (Yeung & Hu, 2013). So, in Beijing, it's shameful, as a female, to be over age 30 without a mate: "The older generation cannot understand why I keep being single . . . ," said one woman. "Many people will think . . . I must have some mental or physical deficiencies" (quoted in Wang & Abbott, 2013, p. 226).

Personal preferences make a difference, too. In one survey, developmentalists found that they could predict a given student's social-clock timetable by asking a simple question: "Is having a family your main passion?" People who said that "marriage is my top-ranking agenda," or "I can't wait to be a mom or dad," often had an earlier timetable for entering adult life (Carroll and others, 2007). So, the limits of emerging adulthood are set both by the culture and shaped by our own priorities and goals.

The problem, however, is that our personal social-clock agendas are not totally under our control. You cannot simply "decide" to marry the love of your life at a defined age. This sense of being "out of control," combined with the pressures to get our adult life in order, may explain why emerging adulthood is both an exhilarating *and* emotionally challenging time. On the positive side, most emerging adults are optimistic about their futures (Frye & Liem, 2011; Pryor and others, 2011). On the minus side, especially in the first year after entering college emotional distress can be intense (Pryor and others, 2011).

For many young people, the issue lies in failing at the task of taking adult responsibility. As one emerging adult anguished: "My life looks like a . . . gutter and effort to fight that gutter . . . then back in the gutter . . . I just don't have any control over myself" (quoted in Macek, Bejcek, & Vanickova, 2007, p. 466). For others, concerns center around balancing multiple commitments, such as the need to work full time and go to school. Or, some emerging adults may have the feeling of not knowing where they are going in life: "We do have more possibilities . . . but that's why it's harder" . . . "You study and you wonder what it is good for" (quoted in Macek, Bejcek, & Vanickova, 2007, p. 468). The reason for this inner turmoil is that, during emerging adulthood, we undergo a mental makeover. We decide who to be as adults.

For a surprising number of people, coping with the demands of college can seem like an insurmountable challenge. You need to struggle with the anxious feeling of "can I make it academically?" plus take responsibility for handling all those fast-paced deadlines, all on your own. This shock of first bumping up against adult realities helps explain why—as you will see later—many college freshmen report high levels of emotional distress.

© Myrleen Pearson/PhotoEdit

Tying It All Together

1. You are giving a toast at your friend Sarah's twenty-first birthday party, and you want to offer some predictions on what the next years might hold for her. Given your understanding of emerging adulthood, which of the following would NOT be a safe prediction?

   a. Sarah may not reach all the standard markers of adulthood until her late twenties.

   b. Sarah's pathway to adulthood will flow smoothly, with steady, predictable steps forward.

   c. Sarah might need to move back into the nest or might still be living at home.

2. Which twenty-something person is LEAST likely to be in the nest?

   a. Manuel who lives in Madrid

   b. Jose who just lost his job

   c. Paula whose parents are living under the poverty line

   d. Silvia who lives in Stockholm

3. Staying in the nest during the twenties today is typically a "symptom" of a child's refusing to grow up. (True or False)

4. Which person is most apt to worry about a social-clock issue: Martha, age 50, who wants to apply to nursing school, or Lee, age 28, who has just become a father?

Answers to the Tying It All Together questions can be found at the end of this chapter.

Constructing an Identity

Erik Erikson was the theorist who highlighted the challenge of transforming our childhood self into the person we will be as adults. Recall he called this process the search for **identity** (see Table 10.3).

identity In Erikson's theory, the life task of deciding who to be as a person in making the transition to adulthood.

Table 10.3: Erikson's Psychosocial Stages

Life Stage	Primary Task
Infancy (birth to 1 year)	Basic trust versus mistrust
Toddlerhood (1 to 2 years)	Autonomy versus shame and doubt
Early childhood (3 to 6 years)	Initiative versus guilt
Late childhood (6 years to puberty)	Industry versus inferiority
Adolescence (teens into twenties)	**Identity versus role confusion**
Young adulthood (twenties to early forties)	Intimacy versus isolation
Middle adulthood (forties to sixties)	Generativity versus stagnation
Late adulthood (late sixties and beyond)	Integrity versus despair

---

role confusion Erikson's term for a failure in identity formation, marked by the lack of any sense of a future adult path.

Time spent wandering through Europe to find himself sensitized Erikson to the difficulties young people face in constructing an adult self. Erikson's fascination with identity as a developmental task, however, crystallized when he worked as a psychotherapist in a psychiatric hospital for troubled teens. Erikson discovered that young patients suffered from a problem he labeled **role confusion.** They had no sense of any adult path:

> [The person feels as] if he were moving in molasses. It is hard for him to go to bed and face the transition into . . . sleep; and it is equally hard for him to get up . . . Such complaints as . . . "I don't know" . . . "I give up" . . . "I quit" . . . are often expressions of . . . despair.
>
> (Erikson, 1968, p. 169)

Some young people felt a frightening sense of falseness about themselves: "If I tell a girl I like her, if I make a gesture . . . this third voice is at me all the time—'You're doing this for effect; you're a phony'" (quoted in Erikson, 1968, p. 173). Others could not cope with having any future and planned to end their lives on their eighteenth birthday or some other symbolic date.

This derailment, which Erikson called confusion—an aimless drifting, or shutting down—differs from the active search process he labeled *moratorium* (1980). Taking time to explore various paths, Erikson argued, is crucial to forming a solid adult identity. Having witnessed Hitler's Holocaust, Erikson believed that young people must discover their own identities. He had seen a destructive process of identity formation firsthand. To cope with that nation's economic problems after World War I, German teenagers leaped into pathological identities by entering totalitarian organizations such as the Hitler Youth.

Can we categorize the different ways people tackle the challenge of constructing an adult identity? Decades ago, James Marcia answered yes.

Marcia's Identity Statuses

Marcia (1966, 1987) devised four **identity statuses** to expand on Erikson's powerful ideas:

identity statuses Marcia's four categories of identity formation: identity diffusion, identity foreclosure, moratorium, and identity achievement.

identity diffusion An identity status in which the person is aimless or feels totally blocked, without any adult life path.

- **Identity diffusion** best fits Erikson's description of the most troubled teens—young people drifting aimlessly toward adulthood without any goals: "I don't know where I am going." "Nothing has any appeal."

This young woman may fit Marcia's category of *identity diffusion*. She seems listless and depressed.

This student, forced by his dad to get a degree in computer science in order to get a well-paying job, feels incredibly bored. People who follow their parents' career choices without exploring other possibilities are in *identity foreclosure*. (While Erikson and Marcia linked this status to poor mental health—as you will see on page 302—young people "in foreclosure" can also feel happy about this state.)

This young woman who has accepted a company internship is in *identity moratorium*, because she wants to figure out if she likes working in this career. We need to know, however, if she is happily exploring her options, or unproductively obsessing about her choices.

This delighted man is in *identity achievement*, because he has discovered his life passion lies in computer design.

- **Identity foreclosure** describes a person who adopts an identity without any self-exploration or thought. At its violent extreme, foreclosure might apply to a Hitler Youth member or a person who becomes a terrorist in his teens. In general, however, researchers define young people as being in foreclosure when they adopt a life path handed down by some authority: "My parents want me to take over the family business, so that's what I will do."

- The person in **moratorium** is engaged in the exciting, healthy search for an adult self. While this internal process may provoke anxiety, because it involves wrestling with different philosophies and ideas, Marcia (and Erikson) felt it is critical to arriving at the final stage.

- **Identity achievement** is the end point: "I've thought through my life. I want to be a computer artist, no matter what my family says."

Marcia's categories offer a marvelous framework for pinpointing what is going wrong (or right) in a young person's life. Perhaps while reading these descriptions you were thinking, "I have a friend in diffusion. Now, I understand exactly what this person's problem is!" How do these statuses really play out in life?

identity foreclosure An identity status in which the person decides on an adult life path (often one spelled out by an authority figure) without any thought or active search.

moratorium An identity status in which the person actively searches out various possibilities to find a truly solid adult life path. A mature style of constructing an identity.

identity achievement An identity status in which the person decides on a definite adult life path after searching out various options.

The Identity Statuses in Action

Marcia originally believed that, as we move through adolescence, we pass from diffusion to moratorium to achievement. Who thinks much about adulthood in ninth or tenth grade? At that age, your agenda is to cope with puberty. You test the limits. You sometimes act in ways that seem tailor-made to undermine your adult life (see Chapter 9). Then, as older adolescents and emerging adults, we undertake a moratorium search as adulthood looms in full view. At some point during our twenties, we have reached achievement, finalizing our search for an adult identity.

However, in real life, identity pathways are erratic. People move backward and forward in statuses *throughout* their adult years (Côté & Bynner, 2008; Waterman, 1999). A woman might enter college exploring different faiths, then become a committed Catholic, start questioning her choice again at 30, and finally settle on her spiritual identity in Bahai at age 45. As many older students are aware, you may have gone through moratorium and firmly believed you were in identity achievement in your career, and now have shifted back to moratorium when you realized, "I need a more secure, fulfilling job."

This lifelong shifting is appropriate. It's unrealistic to think we reach a final identity as emerging adults. The push to rethink our lives, to change directions, to have plans and goals, is what makes us human. It is essential at any age. Moreover, revising our identity is vital to living fully since our lives are always being disrupted—as we change careers, become parents, are widowed, or adapt to our children leaving the nest (McAdams, 2001b, 2013).

The bad news is that people can be stuck in unproductive places in their identity search. In some studies, an alarming 1 in 4 undergraduates is locked in diffusion (Côté & Bynner, 2008). They don't have *any* career goals. Or, as I see in my classes, students are sampling different paths, but without much Eriksonian moratorium joy. Is your friend who keeps changing his major and putting off graduation excitedly exploring his options, or is he afraid of entering the real world? Are the emerging adults who spend their twenties moving from low-wage job to low-wage job really in moratorium or randomly drifting into adult life?

Actually, Erikson and Marcia's assumption that we need to sample *many* fields in order to construct a solid career identity, is not accurate. Having a career goal in mind from childhood, such as knowing you want to be a nurse from age nine (the status Marcia dismisses as "foreclosure") is fine (Ryeng, Kroger, & Martinussen, 2013). Anxiously obsessing about possibilities, or being locked in a state called **ruminative moratorium,** causes more distress (Ritchie and others, 2013; Luyckx and others, 2014). ("I don't know if I want to be an anesthesiologist or an actor and that's driving me crazy.")

There can even be problems with being identity achieved. Suppose after considerable searching you adopt a devalued identity. ("Yes, I'll give up and go to medical school, but I'm not convinced being a doctor is really me.") It doesn't matter *how* you got there. What's crucial is to make a commitment *and* feel confident that this decision expresses your true self (see Meeus, 2011; Schwartz and others, 2013 for reviews).

ruminative moratorium When a young person is unable to decide between different identities, becoming emotionally paralyzed and highly anxious.

Ethnic Identity, a Minority Theme

The emotional pluses of committing to our identity and feeling positive about that choice are underlined by examining **ethnic identity**—our sense of belonging to an ethnic category, such as "Asian American." If, like me, you are part of the mainstream culture, you rarely think of your ethnicity. For minority young people, labeling yourself as part of a group, with defined characteristics, tends to happen during concrete operations (recall Chapter 6), although the need to explore one's relationship to that label waxes and wanes at older ages. For instance, although ethnic identity issues often become intense during the teens, one study showed that in college, people grapple with that consciousness again (Syed & Azmitia, 2009).

ethnic identity How people come to terms with who they are as people relating to their unique ethnic or racial heritage.

People cope with this consciousness in various ways. They may develop dual minority and mainstream identities (acting African American in one setting and not another), or reject one identity in favor of another ("I never think of myself as Black, just as American," or "I never think of myself as American, just as Black") (Phinney, 2006).

Studies routinely show that identifying with one's ethnicity is correlated with a host of positive attributes and traits (Acevedo-Polakovich and others, 2014; Kiang, Witkow, & Champagne, 2013). Being proud of one's heritage as an African American or Asian American buffers young people from becoming depressed or resorting to risk taking when faced with discrimination in the wider world (Polanco-Roman & Miranda, 2013; Toomey and others, 2013). But, it's important to reach out to the wider culture, too. Actually, firmly connecting with the mainstream culture ("I'm also proud of being American") is one sign that an ethnic minority young person has the skills to reach out fully in love.

The challenges for **biracial or multiracial** emerging adults, people from mixed racial or ethnic backgrounds (like President Obama), are particularly poignant. These young people may feel adrift without any ethnic home (Literte, 2010). But, here, too, reaching identity achievement can have widespread benefits. Fascinating research suggests having a biracial or bicultural background pushes people to think in more creative, complex ways about life (Tadmor, Tetlock, & Peng, 2009). It can promote resilience, too. As one biracial woman in her early thirties put it: "When I was younger I felt I didn't belong anywhere. But now I've just come to the conclusion that my home is inside myself" (Phinney, 2006, p. 128).

Making sense of one's "place in the world" as an ethnic minority is literally a minority identity theme. But every young person has to grapple with those two universal identity issues: choosing a career and finding love. The rest of this chapter tackles those agendas.

© Winter Media/Corbis

Coming to terms with a biracial background ("Should I identify with my African or European heritage?" "Where do I *really* fit in?") can help develop a crucial life strength—the capacity to think more deeply and thoughtfully about the world.

biracial or multiracial identity How people of mixed racial backgrounds come to terms with who they are as people in relation to their heritage.

Tying It All Together

1. You overheard your psychology professor saying that his daughter Emma shows symptoms of Erikson's identity confusion. Emma must be _____ (drifting, actively searching for an identity), which in Marcia's identity status framework is a sign of _____ (diffusion, foreclosure, moratorium).

2. Joe said, "I've wanted to be a lawyer since I was a little boy." Kayla replied, "I don't know what my career will be, and I've been obsessing about the possibilities day and night." Joe's identity status is _____ (moratorium, foreclosure, diffusion, or achievement), while Kayla's status is _____ (moratorium, foreclosure, diffusion, or achievement). According to the latest research, who is apt to be most anxious and disturbed?

3. Your cousin Clara has enrolled in nursing school. To predict her feelings about this decision, pick the correct question to ask: *Have you explored different possibilities?/Do you feel nursing expresses your inner self?*

4. Confronting the challenge of a biracial or multiracial identity tends to make people think in more rigid ways about the world. (True or False)

Answers to the Tying It All Together questions can be found at the end of this chapter.

Finding a Career

In a famous statement, Sigmund Freud, when asked to sum up the definition of ideal mental health, answered with the simple words, "the ability to love and work." Let's now look at finding ourselves in the world of work.

When did you begin thinking about your career? What influences are drawing you to psychology, nursing, or business—a compelling class, a caring mentor, or the conviction that this field would fit your talents best? How do young people feel about their careers, their futures, and working?

To answer these kinds of questions, Mihaly Csikszentmihalyi and Barbara Schneider (2000) conducted a pioneering study of teenagers' career dreams. They selected 33 U.S. schools and interviewed students from sixth to twelfth grade. To chart how young people felt—when at home, with friends, when at school—they used the *experience-sampling method* (discussed in Chapter 9). Now, let's touch on their insights and other studies as we track young people entering and moving through the emerging adult years.

Entering with High (but Often Unrealistic) Career Goals

Almost every teenager, the researchers found, expects to go to college. Almost everyone wants to have a professional career. The tendency to aim high appears regardless of gender or social class. Whether male or female, rich or poor, adolescents have lofty career goals. Moreover, I believe that the experts who view today's young people as over coddled (Levine & Dean, 2012), narcissistic (Twenge, 2006), and "basically" unmotivated are unfair. Due to the lingering effects of the Great Recession, young people face a far harsher economic climate than we baby boomers encountered when we emerged into adult life (Economic Policy Institute, n.d.). In one survey of U.S. college freshmen, young people reported being more driven to work hard than their counterparts in previous years (Pryor and others, 2011).

The real problem, however, is that teens are (naturally) clueless about what it takes to implement their dream careers. Can someone who "hates reading" really spend a decade getting a psychology Ph.D.? What happens when my students learn they have to have a GPA close to 3.7 to enter our university's nursing program, or they can't go to law school because of the astronomical costs? Career disappointment can lurk right around the corner for young people as they emerge from the cocoon of high school and confront the real world. How do people react as they enter their college years?

Self-Esteem and Emotional Growth During College and Beyond

Interestingly, one U.S. survey showed that self-esteem dips dramatically during the first semester of college (Chung and others, 2014) and then gradually rises over the next few years (see also Wagner and others, 2013; Higher Education Research Institute [HERI], 2013). Because students tend to inflate their academic abilities (Chung and others, 2014), it can be a shock when those disappointing first-semester grades arrive. The other bad news is that, due to the well-known social reinforcement in college for activities such as binge drinking (recall the previous chapter), emerging adulthood offers ample room for addictions to flower (Sussman & Arnett, 2014). Still, as the research described in Figure 10.2 shows, there is diversity, with some people getting unhappier and others improving in mental health from age 18 to 22 (Frye & Liem, 2011).

Who thrives? The figure implies that personality matters. Young people who enter emerging adulthood upbeat and competent are set up to flourish when confronting the demands of college life. In their study, Csikszentmihalyi and Schneider

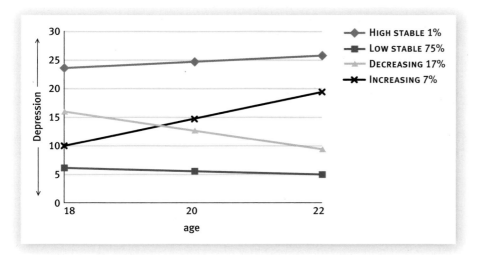

FIGURE 10.2: **The diverse ways depression changed in an economically diverse sample of over 1,000 young people traveling from age 18 to age 22:** Notice from this chart that the vast majority of young people are happy both during their teens and as they emerge into their early twenties (red). Those teens with major depressive disorders are still battling their condition three years later (blue). But a reasonable percentage of moderately depressed teens become happier as they make the transition to adult life (yellow line)—although, granted, some do become more depressed.
Data from: Frye & Liem, 2011.

(2000) called these efficacious teens "workers"—the 16-year-olds who amaze you with their ability to balance band, a part-time job, and honors classes. It's also a no-brainer that succeeding at academics boosts self-esteem (Chung and others, 2014). But, the most interesting discovery of the studies tracking people as they traveled through their early twenties was the impact of having a stable love relationship on young people's self-worth.

You might think finding love would be especially important for females. You would be wrong. Interestingly, men, in particular, felt especially good about themselves if they were in a caring relationship by age 23 (Wagner and others, 2013).

In what ways do people change for the better during this landmark decade? Growth is most apt to occur in a temperamental dimension that researchers call *conscientiousness*—becoming more reliable; developing self-control (see Cramer, 2008; Donnellan, Conger, & Burzette, 2007; Walton and others, 2013); being better able to manage your emotions (Zimmermann & Iwanski, 2014); reasoning in more thoughtful ways (Labouvie-Vief, 2006; more about these qualities in Chapter 12).

To explain this rise in *executive functions*—what you and I would call "maturity"—adolescent specialists might look to the fully developed frontal lobes. But an equally plausible cause lies in the wider world. Shedding an unproductive adolescent risk-taking identity in college (recall Jason's story in the previous chapter) or finding a satisfying job can transform troubled teens into "workers," in Mihaly Csikszentmihalyi's terms (Dennissen, Asendorpf, & van Aken, 2008). A powerful inner state—also spelled out by Csikszentmihalyi—can help transform us into "workers" and lock people into the right career.

Finding Flow

Think back over the past week to the times you felt energized and alive. You might be surprised to discover that events you looked forward to—such as relaxing at home or watching a favorite TV program—do not come to mind. Many of life's most uplifting experiences occur when we connect deeply with people. Others take place when we are immersed in some compelling task. Csikszentmihalyi names this intense task absorption **flow**.

flow Csikszentmihalyi's term for feeling total absorption in a challenging, goal-oriented activity.

For this graduate student who is puzzling over the meaning of a difficult paper in his field, the hours may fly by. Challenging activities that fully draw on our talents and skills produce that marvelous inner state called "flow."

Flow is different from "feeling happy." We enter this state when we are immersed in an activity that stretches our capacities, such as the challenge of decoding a difficult academic problem, or (hopefully) getting absorbed in mastering the material in this class. People also differ in the kinds of activities that cause flow. For some of us, it's hiking in the Himalayas that produces this feeling. For me, it has been writing this book. When we are in flow, we enter an altered state of consciousness in which we forget the outside world. Problems disappear. We lose a sense of time. The activity feels infinitely worth doing for its own sake. Flow makes us feel completely alive.

Csikszentmihalyi (1990), who has spent his career studying flow, finds that some people rarely experience this feeling. Others feel flow several times a day. If you feel flow only during a rare mountain-climbing experience or, worse, when robbing a bank, Csikszentmihalyi argues that it will be difficult to construct a satisfying life. The challenge is to find flow in ways related to your career.

Flow depends on being *intrinsically motivated*. We must be mesmerized by what we are doing right now for its own sake, not for an extrinsic reward. But there also is a future-oriented dimension to feeling flow. Flow, according to Csikszentmihalyi, happens when we are working toward a goal.

For example, the idea that this book will be published two years from now is the goal that is pushing me to write this very page. But what riveted me to my chair this morning is the actual process of writing. Getting into a flow state is often elusive. On the days when I can't construct a paragraph, I get anxious. But if I could not regularly find flow in my writing, I would never be writing this book.

Figure 10.3 shows exactly why finding flow can be difficult. That state depends on a delicate person–environment fit. When a task seems beyond our capacities, we become anxious. When an activity is too simple, we grow bored. Ideally, the activities in which we feel flow can alert us to our ideal careers. Think about some situation in which you recently felt flow. If you are in ruminative moratorium or worry you may be in career diffusion, can you use this feeling to clue you in to a particular field?

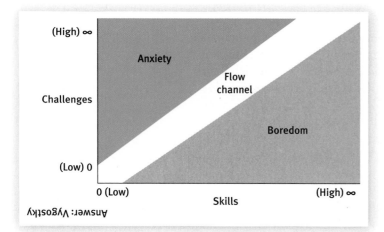

Answer: Vygostky

FIGURE 10.3: The zone of flow: Notice that the flow zone (white area) depends on a delicate matching of our abilities and the challenge involved in a particular real-world task. If the task is too difficult or beyond our capacities, we land in the upper red area of the chart and become anxious. If the task is too easy, we land in the lower, gray area of the chart and become bored. Moreover, as our skills increase, the difficulty of the task must also increase to provide us with the sense of being in flow. Which theorist's ideas about teaching and what stimulates mental growth does this model remind you of? (Turn page upside down for answer.)

Data from: Csikszentmihalyi, 1990.

Drawing on the concept of flow, my discussion of identity, as well as recent economic concerns, let's now look at two career paths emerging adults in the United States follow.

Emerging into Adulthood Without a College Degree (in the United States)

"I never want this kind of job for my kids." This comment, from a 35-year-old high school graduate working at a construction job, sums up the contemporary feeling in the United States that college is vital for having a good life (Furstenberg, 2010). Actually, more than 2 of every 3 U.S. high school graduates enroll in college right after high school. However, as time passes, the ranks thin. For students beginning at four-year institutions, the odds of graduating within the next six years are about 3 in 5 (National Center on Education Statistics, n.d.). The graduation rates for their community-college counterparts are far lower than this.

People in the United States who don't go to college or who never get their degree can have fulfilling careers. Some may excel at Robert Sternberg's practical or creative intelligence (described in Chapter 7) but do not do well at academics.

When they find their flow in the work world, they blossom. Consider the career of that college failure, the famous filmmaker named Woody Allen, or even that of Bill Gates, who found his undergraduate courses too confining and left Harvard to pioneer a new field.

Unfortunately, these famous college dropouts are a statistical blip. The bleak reality is that non-college graduates have a far harder time constructing a middle-class life. As you can see in Figure 10.4A, the well-known difference in earnings, based on education, has stayed relatively stable in the past 15 years. In 2012, the median income of people aged 25 to 35 with master's degrees, who worked full time, was roughly $70,000 per year. Their counterparts, with only high school diplomas, earned less than one-half of that amount—$30,000 (National Center on Health Statistics, n.d.). And, of course, college graduates are more likely to find jobs. In 2013, in the age group of 25 to 34, roughly 1 out of 10 non-college graduates were unemployed. The comparable statistic for young people with a B.A. degree or higher was 6 percent (National Center for Health Statistics, n.d.).

Given these realities, why do many emerging adults drop out of school? Our first assumption is that most of these people are not "college material"—uninterested in academics, poorly prepared in high school, and/or can't do the work.

True, to succeed in college, prior academic aptitude is important. As a C student in your public school class, your odds of getting a bachelor's degree are less than 1 in 5 (Engle, n.d.). But, as Figure 10.4B shows, economic considerations matter greatly. The unfortunate reality is that talented, low-SES young people are far less likely to graduate from college than their affluent peers (Carnevale & Strohl, 2010).

When the Gates Foundation commissioned a survey of more than 600 young adults ages 22 to 30 who had dropped out of college, they discovered the same message—money matters. Only 1 in 10 students said they left school because the courses were too difficult or they weren't interested in the work. The main reason was that they had to work full time to finance school, and the strain became too much (Johnson & Rochkind, 2011).

This twenty-something high school graduate probably felt lucky to find this low-wage job. For emerging adults who do not go to college, the current U.S. economic realities are bleak.

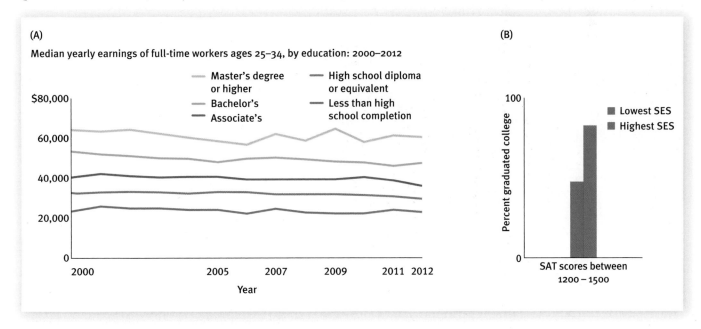

FIGURE 10.4: **Snapshots of economic inequality, with regard to higher education, earnings, and getting a college degree:** Chart (A) shows that the high school versus higher-education earnings gap has been pronounced for the past decade, underlining the fact that people without a college degree are "left behind" economically. Chart (B) shows that for intellectually talented young people, family income makes a huge difference in getting that degree. Bottom line: In the United States, finishing college is vital and low-income high-ability students are at a severe disadvantage.

Data from: Chart (A) ICS National Center on Education Statistics, n.d. Chart (B) adapted from data in Carnevale & Strohl, 2010.

The silver lining is that most of these people did plan to return. And, as many nontraditional student readers are aware, there can be emotional advantages to leaving and then coming back. In Sweden, the social clock for college is programmed to start ticking a few years after high school (Arnett, 2007). The reasoning is that time spent in the wider world helps people home in on what to study in school.

Moreover, as you saw in the beginning chapter vignette, emerging adults can sometimes advance in their careers without a college degree. Employers look for reliability and a good work ethic, virtues that can be demonstrated once someone gets his foot in the door. When British researchers explored the qualities that distinguished people who left school at 16 and had gone on to do well economically during midlife (granted, during better economies), the main predictor that stood out was prior academic skills (Schoon & Duckworth, 2010). So, if a non-college graduate is a "worker" and intellectually competent, that person can *sometimes* succeed against the odds.

INTERVENTIONS: Smoothing the School Path and School-to-Work Transition

Still, we can't let society off of the hook. The fact that financing college is difficult for U.S. young people is a national shame. The standard practice of taking out loans means that young people face frightening economic futures after getting their degrees. In 2012, more than half of U.S. emerging adults left college owing the government and private lenders $20,000 or more. Moreover, in the same poll, more than 1 out of 2 graduating seniors searching for a full-time job were still looking for work (HERI, 2013).

What can colleges do? Rather than having students languish, unproductively shifting from major to major, offer centralized advising to get students on the right track during the freshman year (Kot, 2014). As of this writing, states are experimenting with low-cost alternatives—such as MOOCS and credit for work experience—to streamline college costs and cut down on the time it takes to earn a degree.

Most important, we need to rethink our contemporary emphasis on college as the *only* ticket to a decent life. As some people are skilled at working with their hands, or excel in practical intelligence, why force non-academically oriented emerging adults to suffer, enduring a poor talent–environment fit? Can't we develop the kinds of apprentice programs that have been successful in Germany? (See Cook & Furstenberg, 2002; Seiffge-Krenke, Persike, & Luyckx, 2013.) In that nation, employers partner with schools that offer on-the-job training. Graduates emerge with a *definite* position in that specific firm.

Germany, like other Western countries, has a youth unemployment problem. But because its apprenticeship programs offer young people careers outside of college, this nation helps undercut the unproductive ruminative-identity moratorium that can cause so much angst in the Western world. In one German national survey, having a job or being enrolled in an apprentice program predicted both identity achievement and occupational self-efficacy down the road (Seiffge-Krenke, Persike, & Luyckx, 2013).

After joyously getting their degree, these new CUNY graduates now must face the dispiriting experience of feeling like a number as they wend their way through this impersonal job-fair line. At least in the United States, negotiating the school-to-work transition can be difficult.

How many young people are locked in diffusion or moratorium because the United States lacks a defined **school-to-work transition** (school-to-career path)? Rather than leaving the anxiety-ridden, post-education job hunt to luck, random contacts, and putting the burden on the so-called "inner" talents of kids, let's devise creative strategies to help young people confront this crucial social-clock challenge of adult life.

school-to-work transition The change from the schooling phase of life to the work world.

Table 10.4 summarizes the main messages of this section, by offering suggestions for emerging adults and society at large. Now, it's time to immerse ourselves in the undergraduate experience.

Table 10.4: Succeeding in College/Finding a Career Identity Tips for Young People and Society

For Young People

1. Understand that it's common to have high expectations about your abilities and to expect a let down when you enter college. It takes time to get adjusted to the demands of this new life stage!

2. Focus on finding your flow in selecting a career. Try to avoid obsessing about different possibilities, but understand that it can take time to formulate a career plan.

3. If you need to drop out for some time, understand it's not the end of the world. Having a year or two off may help you home in on a career identity and be a better student.

For Society

1. Assign counselors for incoming freshmen to map out classroom and financial options, and link students to community employers.

2. Reach out to low-income undergraduates, and offer special services for students who are parents or working adults.

3. Set up apprenticeship programs linked to jobs—ones that offer a conduit to the work world without college.

4. Make negotiating young people's school-to-work transition a national priority!

Being in College

So far, I've been implying that the only purpose of going to college is to find a career. Thankfully, in surveys, most U.S. college graduates disagree. They report the main value of their undergraduate years was to help them "grow intellectually and personally" (Hoover, 2011).

How does this inner growth progress during college? According to William Perry (1999), freshmen come in blindly accepting the facts that authorities hand down, and then they move to relativism (understanding that there are multiple truths); by senior year, they make their own ethical commitments in the face of appreciating diverse points of view.

Perry's findings are based on studies conducted with Harvard undergraduates 40 years ago. But another longitudinal study (granted, also at a selective university) confirms that this inner development occurs—and most important—it takes place *specifically* during the undergraduate years (Bauer & MacAdams, 2010).

If you are a traditional college student, here are tips to make your college experience an inner-growth flow zone.

INTERVENTIONS: Making College an Inner-Growth Flow Zone

GET THE BEST PROFESSORS (AND TALK TO THEM OUTSIDE OF CLASS!). It's a no-brainer that exciting teachers loom large in student success (Komarraju, Musulkin, & Bhattacharya, 2010; Schreiner and others, 2011). Outstanding professors adore their subject and can vividly communicate their passion to students (Bane, 2004). Just like their elementary school counterparts (see Chapter 7), they respect their students' talents and are committed to nurturing undergraduates' growth. So reach out and talk to your professors. Students from every end of the academic spectrum agree that feeling listened to can be a peak experience in one's academic life:

From a Harvard senior:

> He began by asking me which single book had the biggest impact on me. He was the first professor who was interested in what matters to me. . . . You can't imagine how excited I was.

(quoted in Light, 2001, pp. 82–83)

From a community college student:

> You know, what he does more than anything else is that . . . he really listens. I was in his office last semester and I was telling him how I was struggling. . . . He really let me talk myself into doing what I needed to pass. It's like, you know he gives a damn.

(quoted in Schreiner and others, 2011, p. 324)

CONNECT YOUR CLASSES TO POTENTIAL CAREERS. Professors' mission is to excite you in their field. But classes can't provide the hands-on experience you need to actually find your personal zone of flow. So, institute your personal school-to-work transition. Set up independent studies involving volunteer work. If you are interested in science, work in a professor's lab. If your passion is politics, do an internship with a local legislator. In one study, college seniors mentioned that the highlight of their undergraduate experience occurred during a mentored project in the real world (Light, 2001).

IMMERSE YOURSELF IN THE COLLEGE MILIEU. Following this advice is easier if you are attending a small residential school. The college experience is at your doorstep, ready to be embraced. At a large university, especially a commuter school, you'll need to make efforts to get involved in campus life. If possible, spend your first year living in a college dormitory. Join a college organization, or two, or three. Working for the college newspaper or becoming active in the drama club not only will provide you with a rich source of friends, but can help promote your career identity, too.

CAPITALIZE ON THE DIVERSE HUMAN CONNECTIONS COLLEGE PROVIDES. As you saw in previous chapters, the peer groups we select help shape who we become. At college, it is tempting to find a single clique and then not reach out to other crowds. Resist this impulse. A major growth experience college provides is the chance to connect with people of different points of view (Hu & Kuh, 2003; see also Leung & Chiu, 2011). Here's what another Harvard undergraduate had to say:

> I have re-evaluated my beliefs. . . . At college, there are people of all different religions around me. . . . Living . . . with these people marks an important difference. . . . [It] has made me reconsider and ultimately reaffirm my faith.

(quoted in Light, 2001, p. 163)

But this community college student summed it up best:

> When I come home and have all these great stories; they think college is the most amazing thing . . . and that's because of all the people I'm surrounded with.

(quoted in Schreiner and others, 2011, p. 337)

Being surrounded by interesting people has another benefit: It smoothes the way to Erikson's other emerging adult task: finding love.

College is an ideal time to connect with people from different backgrounds. So go for it!

Photodisc

Tying It All Together

1. Your 17-year-old cousin is graduating from high school. Given what you learned in this section, you might predict that she has *overly high/overly low* expectations about her abilities to do college work.

2. Juan has just turned 19; all of these forces predict he may have high self-esteem as he travels through his early twenties EXCEPT:

   a. Juan is a "worker," a person who thrives on mastering challenging tasks.

   b. Juan gets good college grades.

   c. Juan puts off having a close love relationship during these years.

3. Hannah confesses that she loves her server job—but only during busy times. When the restaurant is hectic, she gets energized. Time flies by. She feels exhilarated, at the top of her form, like a multitasking whiz! Hannah is describing a _____ experience.

4. Josiah says the reason why his classmates drop out of college is that they can't do the work. Jocasta says, "Sorry, it's the need to work incredible hours to pay for school." Make each person's case, using the information from this chapter.

5. Your cousin Juan, who is about to enter his freshman year, asks you for tips about how to succeed in college. Based on the information in this section, pick the advice you should not give:

   a. Get involved in campus activities.

   b. Search out friends who have exactly the same ideas as you do.

   c. Select the best professors and reach out to make connections with them.

Answers to the Tying It All Together questions can be found at the end of this chapter.

Finding Love

How do emerging adults negotiate Erikson's first task of adult life (see Table 10.5)— **intimacy**, the search for love? Let's first explore two major cultural shifts in the ways we choose mates before turning to our main topic: finding fulfilling love.

intimacy Erikson's first adult task, involving connecting with a partner in a mutual loving relationship.

Table 10.5: Erikson's Life Stages and Their Psychological Tasks

Life Stage	Primary Task
Infancy (birth to 1 year)	Basic trust versus mistrust
Toddlerhood (1 to 2 years)	Autonomy versus shame and doubt
Early childhood (3 to 6 years)	Initiative versus guilt
Late childhood (6 years to puberty)	Industry versus inferiority
Adolescence (teens into twenties)	Identity versus role confusion
Young adulthood (twenties to early forties)	**Intimacy versus isolation***
Middle adulthood (forties to sixties)	Generativity versus stagnation
Late adulthood (late sixties and beyond)	Integrity versus despair

*Although this next section is devoted to the early adult search for intimacy, I'll spend more time on this topic in the Chapter 11 discussion of marriage.

Setting the Context: Seismic Shifts in Searching for Love

The following quotations perfectly introduce our first total transformation in how we search for enduring love:

Daolin Yang lives in Hebie Province, China. . . . At age 15, he married his wife Yufen, then 13. . . . A matchmaker proposed the marriage on behalf of the Yang family. They have been married for 62 years. . . . He says that they married first and dated later. It is "cold at the start and hot in the end." The relationship gets better and better over the years.

(Xia & Zhou, 2003, p. 231)

I got married a month ago to the woman . . . I met on Match a year ago. I met my wife just a week after setting up my profile, and we have been together ever since . . . Thanks to the profiles, local singles matching, and easy chats, I found the girl of my dreams.

(Adapted from, Top 10 Best Dating Sites, 2014)

Many More Potential Partners

Throughout history, as I just illustrated in the first example, in many regions of the world, parents chose a child's marital partner (often during puberty), and newlyweds hoped (if they were lucky) to later fall in love. Today, even in places like India, where, until recently, arranged marriages had been standard, many people accept freely choosing a mate (Gala & Kapadia, 2014, more about this topic in the next chapter).

Moreover, until very recently, romantic choices were confined to our own social network. People searched for their soul mates at parties, at school, or at synagogue. Often, they relied on family and friends to fix them up.

Today, with the explosion of on line dating, as we all know, the Internet has globalized the search for love. By the second decade of the twentieth century, an incredible 1 in 3 married couples in the United States had met on-line. Plus, new research suggests on-line marriages are more likely to be happy than those in which spouses meet in the old-style traditional way! (See Cacioppo and others, 2013.)

At the same time, since the 1960s lifestyle revolution, Western young people are far more willing to date outside of their own ethnic group. By the turn of the twenty-first century, 1 in 3 European Americans reported getting romantically involved with someone of a different ethnicity or race. More than one-half of all African Americans, Hispanic Americans, and Asian Americans had also made that claim (Yancey & Yancey, 2002).

Interest in dating and/or marrying outside one's own ethnicity varies from person to person. In one survey of on-line daters, females—especially White women—were less open to contacting someone of another ethnic group than were men. As implied by the statistic above, minorities are more open to interethnic dating than are Whites. Interestingly, in this poll, there was special reluctance to getting romantically involved with African Americans, again if someone was female and White (Hwang, 2013).

Religious attitudes also make a difference. Contrary to popular opinion, one national U.S. poll found that having a strong religious faith might not matter. But if someone is White and accepts the bible as literal truth (and doesn't attend a multi-racial congregation), this person is apt to be more opposed to this widening of love choices (Perry, 2013).

Christians who believe biblical injunctions must be obeyed word for word are particularly aghast (no surprise!) at that other contemporary expansion in the landscape of love: same-sex romance.

Hot in Developmental Science: Same-Sex Romance

In the 1990s, when I began teaching at my southern university, I remember being disturbed by the snickering that would erupt when I mentioned issues related to being gay. No more! Although the gay rights movement exploded on the scene in the late 1960s in New York City, its most revolutionary strides took place during the early twenty-first century. As one expert put it, within a few years, the announcement "I'm gay" went from evoking shock to producing yawns—"So, what else is new?" (See Savin-Williams, 2001, 2008.) In an era in which emerging adults define themselves as "mostly straight," "sometimes gay," "occasionally bisexual," or "heterosexual but attracted to the other gender," even limiting one's sexual identity to a defined category is becoming passé (see Morgan, 2013).

This is not to say that **homophobia,** fear and dislike of gays and lesbians, is rare. Despite our landmark U.S. strides in legalizing same sex marriage in all 50 states—as we know from the use of derogatory terms for gays and lesbian—many people—even in enlightened Western nations—have serious qualms about embracing this new form of love (see Jowett, 2014; Peltz, 2014).

Given this continuing (although more covert) social scorn, it makes sense that sexual-minority young people can undergo considerable emotional turmoil during their teens (see Table 10.6). Interestingly, however, while self-loathing may still be prevalent in traditional world regions, such as in Asia (Li, Johnson, & Jenkins-Guarnieri, 2013), these feelings are *not the norm* in the United States today. In a recent survey of 165 bisexual, gay, and lesbian young people, the largest group (about 4 in 5 adolescents and emerging adults) was classified as identity achieved. These people said they felt comfortable about their sexual identity. They reported few qualms about being rejected by their close attachment figures when they came out. The concern was the 1 in 5 respondents the researchers labeled as "struggling." While these young people "knew" their sexual identity, they worried about disclosing this fact to disapproving parents and friends (Bregman and others, 2013).

Another at-risk group may be people who are "identity confused." When researchers explored the mental health of women who defined themselves as

homophobia Intense fear and dislike of gays and lesbians.

This cake decoration, created in the early twenty-first century for the first gay marriage show in Seattle, was a perfect harbinger of the quickly evolving times, as in just a brief decade, same-sex marriage became far more widely accepted throughout the Western world.

Table 10.6: Homosexual Stereotypes and Scientific Facts

Stereotype: Overinvolved mothers and distant fathers "cause" boys to be homosexual.

Scientific fact: There is no evidence that this or any other parenting problem causes homosexuality. The causes of homosexuality are unknown—however, recent research suggests that levels of prenatal testosterone may help program a fetus' later gender orientation (see Chapter 6).

Stereotype: Homosexual couples have lower-quality relationships—their interactions are "psychologically immature."

Scientific fact: Researchers have compared the relationships of committed gay couples with their heterosexual counterparts via a variety of strategies. The typical finding: There are usually NO differences in the quality of heterosexual and homosexual relationships. When same-sex partners have personality issues, they fight a good deal, just like any couple does (Markey and others, 2014). But, in a recent Swiss study, lesbian couples reported less conflict than a comparable heterosexual group. These women also showed a trend to being more satisfied with their mates (Meuwly and others, 2013).

Stereotype: Homosexual parents have pathological family interactions and disturbed children.

Scientific fact: When British researchers (Golombok and others, 2003) compared lesbian-mother, two-parent-heterosexual, and single-mother families, they found that children raised in lesbian families had no problems with their gender identity and had no signs of impaired mental health. In fact, the lesbian mothers showed signs of superior parenting—hitting their children less frequently and engaging in more fantasy play.

Stereotype: Homosexuals are emotionally disturbed.

Scientific fact: Unfortunately, in the past, elevated rates of psychological problems, such as suicidal thoughts, depression, and drug abuse, were common when gay young people formulated their sexual identities and dealt with anxieties relating to coming out (Saewyc, 2011). However, as you can see above, intense distress is not the norm today in the West.

heterosexual but reported having mainly same-sex attractions, this group was as prone to be distressed as a comparison sample who openly labeled themselves as gay (Johns, Zimmerman, & Bauermeister, 2013). ◓

Again, I think this research underlines the importance of being identity achieved in a positive way. Once you *embrace* your identity (or self), whether as a gay person or ethnic minority, there is a feeling of self-efficacy and relief. Problems arise if your other attachment figures cause you to dislike the person you "really" are, or when you languish untethered in moratorium for an extended time.

A More Erratic, Extended Dating Phase

Unfortunately, however, as I implied earlier in this chapter, romantic moratorium is built into Western society because the untethered dating phase of mate selection lasts so long (Shulman & Connolly, 2013). As the average age of marriage has shifted upward, people not only are delaying making serious love commitments, but younger emerging adults are even putting off getting romantically involved.

In tracking over 500 economically diverse young people from age 18 to 25, U.S. researchers found a fraction—about 1 in 4 respondents—did find an enduring, stable relationship soon after leaving their teens. Interestingly, the largest group—almost 1 in 3 people—fit into the low-involvement categories, having only sporadic relationships or no romantic involvement throughout those years (Rauer and others, 2013).

Brocreative/Shutterstock

This once standard campus scene is less typical today, as more undergraduates are putting off romance until they have their careers in place. But I believe that this new lengthening of the unattached phase of love can have emotional downsides.

When emerging adults do find romance, they may have off-again on-again relationships. In another U.S. survey, nearly one-half of couples in their twenties who broke up, got back together again at some point. And, after ending the relationship, one-half continued to have sex with their ex (Halpern-Meekin and others, 2013).

This extended finding-love phase is related to the time it takes to construct a career (Shulman & Connolly, 2013). In Argentina, where young people have few enticing work identities, young people are passionate to find love in their early twenties (Facio & Resett, 2014). In Holland (Branje and others, 2014), the United States, and especially in Finland where there are many career options, people put relationships on the back burner until their mid-twenties when they are finished with school (Mayseless & Keren, 2014; Ranta, Dietrich, & Salmela-Aro, 2014). ("My first priority is to become a doctor or lawyer. I need to get my career in order before finding romance.")

What happens when young people delay making love commitments? We might think that having casual sexual encounters is a risk-free way of spending these years. Unfortunately, data suggests otherwise. In tracking a national sample of U.S. emerging adults, people who reported one-night stands or friends-with-benefits encounters were at risk of having poorer mental health (Sandberg-Thoma & Kamp Dush, 2014). Friends-with-benefits relationships are less problematic for women than one-night stands. One-night stands have fewer mental health downsides for men than for the other sex (Claxton & van Dulmen, 2013). On the other hand, recall from page 305 that having a stable love relationship during the early twenties seems most critical to self-esteem for males!

At the risk of going out on a limb (your class can debate this point), I'm going to agree with Erikson that finding intimacy—meaning a significant other—is immensely helpful *throughout* the turbulent twenties. A high-quality love relationship helps buffer people from the ups and downs of this life stage and the ups and downs we face at *every* age. How can people achieve this goal?

Similarity and Structured Relationship Stages: A Classic Model of Love, and a Critique

Bernard Murstein's now-classic **stimulus-value-role theory** (1999) views finding a satisfying love as a three-phase process. During the **stimulus phase,** we see a potential partner and make our first decision: "Could this be a good choice for me?" "Would this person want me?" Since we know nothing about the person, our judgment is based on superficial signs, such as looks or the way the individual dresses. In this assessment, we compare our own reinforcement value to the other person's along a number of dimensions (Murstein, 1999): "True, I am not as good-looking, but she may find me desirable because I am better educated." If the person seems of equal value, we decide to go on a date.

When we start actually dating, we enter the **value-comparison phase.** Here, our goal is to select the right person by matching up in terms of inner qualities and traits: "Does this person share my interests? Do we have the same values?" If this person seems "right," we enter the **role phase,** in which we work out our shared lives.

So, at a party, Aaron scans the room and decides that Samantha with the tattoos and frumpy-looking Abigail are out of the question. If he is searching on Facebook or Cupid's Arrow, he might be put off by Georgette, who looks too gorgeous or has posted photos of her glorious vacation at San Tropez. Aaron gravitates to Ashley, whose appearance and self-presentation suggests that she is more low maintenance, and maybe—like him—a bit shy. As Aaron and Ashley begin dating, he discovers that they are on the same wavelength. They enjoy the same movies; they both love the mountains; they have the same worldview. The romance could still end. On their third or tenth date, there may be a revelation that "this person is too different." But, if things go smoothly, Aaron and Ashley begin planning their future. Should they move to California when they graduate? Will their wedding be small and intimate or big and expensive?

The "equal-reinforcement-value partner" part of Murstein's theory explains why we expect couples to be similar in social status. We're not surprised if the best-looking girl in high school dates the captain of the football team. When we find serious partner status mismatches, we search for reasons to explain these discrepancies (Murstein, Reif, & Syracuse-Siewert, 2002): "That handsome young lawyer must have low self-esteem to have settled for that unattractive older woman." "Perhaps he chose that woman because she has millions in the bank."

Most important, Murstein's theory suggests that opposites do not attract. In love relationships, as in childhood and adolescent friendships, the driving force is **homogamy** (similarity). We want to find a soul mate, a person who matches us, not just in external status, but also in interests and attitudes about life.

The principle that homogamy promotes happiness (the eHarmony, Match, and Christian Mingle approaches to love) has scientific truth. Late-twentieth-century research consistently showed that sharing basic values promotes a happy married life (see Belsky, 1999 for review). Moreover, when people connect through their mutual passions ("I met my love on a theater blog"), they find an interesting side benefit. As you will see in the next chapter, sharing flow activities such as acting helps keep marital passion alive.

The Limits to Looking for a Similar Mate

But should couples be similar in *every* respect? When psychologists asked undergraduates to describe their ideal mate, in accordance with the homogamy principle, people selected someone with a similar personality. But, in actually examining happiness among long-married couples, these researchers discovered relationships worked best when one partner was more dominant and the other more submissive (Markey & Markey, 2007).

stimulus-value-role theory Murstein's mate-selection theory that suggests similar people pair up and that our path to commitment progresses through three phases (called the stimulus, value-comparison, and role phases).

stimulus phase In Murstein's theory, the initial mate-selection stage, in which we make judgments about a potential partner based on external characteristics such as appearance.

value-comparison phase In Murstein's theory, the second mate-selection stage, in which we make judgments about a partner on the basis of similar values and interests.

role phase In Murstein's theory, the final mate-selection stage, in which committed partners work out their future life together.

homogamy The principle that we select a mate who is similar to us.

Logically, matching up two strong personalities should be unlikely to promote romantic bliss (people would probably fight). Two passive partners might frustrate each other. ("Why doesn't my lover take the lead?") Yes, in general, similarity is important. (Birds of a feather should flock together!) But, as in the other familiar saying, "opposites attract," couples can mesh best when they have a *few* carefully selected opposing personality preferences and styles.

Moreover, suppose a given couple is very similar but in unpleasant traits, such as their tendency to fly off the handle or be pathologically shy. What really matters in happiness is not so much objective similarity (the eHarmony approach of matching people whose personality test scores agree), but believing that one's significant other has terrific personality traits. People who see their partner as outgoing and emotionally stable ("He is a real people person, and open to new things") have better relationships over time (Furler, Gomez, & Grob, 2013; Furler, Gomez, & Grob, 2014).

Admiring each other's talents in their shared life passion ("I love how brilliant my significant other is at acting") predicts future happiness for this young couple. It also may make these emerging adults feel as if they are becoming better performers just from being together—and it certainly helps if they inflate each other's talents, too. (My partner is going to be the next Denzel Washington!)

The bottom-line message is that finding a soul mate means something different than selecting a clone. We don't want a reflection of our current real self. We want someone who embodies our "ideal self"—the person we would like to be. One study showed that when people believe their significant other embodies their best self ("I fell in love with him because he's a wonderful actor, and that's always been my goal"), they tend to grow emotionally as people, becoming more like their ideal. Idealizing a partner's good qualities promotes more happiness over time (Rusbult and others, 2009).

Actually rather than "objectively" matching up, happy couples see their mates through rose-colored glasses (Murray & Holmes, 1997). They inflate their partner's virtues (Murray and others, 2000). They overestimate the extent to which they and that person are alike in values and goals (Murray and others, 2002). So, science confirms George Bernard Shaw's classic observation: "Love is a gross exaggeration of the difference between one person and everyone else."

The Limits to Charting Love in Stages

As soon as I met R, . . . he was just so kind and thoughtful and he was considerate. So we started talking on email and the phone and when I got back from the trip, and he came over a month after the cruise . . . I knew like right away . . . It was just like kind of a confirmation that, I don't know, we were meant to be together.

(quoted in Mackinnon and others, 2011, p. 607)

This quotation implies that, by viewing mate selection in defined steps, Murstein is also missing the magical essence of real-world love. Couples may suddenly fall in love when they meet after months of emails. Or there may be an epiphany, at some point in your relationship, when you decide, "This person is the one." As I mentioned earlier, couples often break up and then reconsider that decision and get back together again.

While turbulent relationships can spark passion, especially for men (that's the thrill of the chase), one study found that married couples who recalled their courtship as accelerating in a positive direction were more likely to report being happy with their mates (Wilson & Huston, 2013). Happily married spouses, it turned out, recalled having similar levels of love as their relationship developed. They were on the same page about how their feelings progressed. Still, even though we should become surer of our love over time, *any romance* has some doubts and ups and downs.

To get insights into this ebb and flow, researchers asked couples who were seriously dating to graph their chances (from 0 to 100 percent) of marrying their partner (Surra & Hughes, 1997; Surra, Hughes, & Jacquet, 1999). They then had the young people return each month to chart changes in their commitment and asked them to describe the reasons for any dramatic relationship turning points, for better or worse.

Hill Street Studios/Blend Images/Getty Images

You can see examples of these turning points in Table 10.7. Notice that relationships do often hinge on homogamy issues ("This person is really right for me"). Other causes may be turning points, too—from the input of family and friends ("I really like that person") to social comparisons ("Our relationship seems better than theirs") to the insight, "I'm too young to get involved." Today, one milestone in the commitment journey is becoming "Facebook official" with your mate.

Table 10.7: Some Major Positive (+) and Negative (–) Turning Points in a Relationship

Personal Compatibility/Homogamy*

We spent a lot of time together. +

We had a big fight. –

We had similar interests. +

Compatibility with Family and Friends

My friends kept saying that Sue was bad for me. –

I fit right in with his family. +

Her dad just hated me. –

Other Random Forces

I just turned 21, so I don't want to be tied down to anyone. –

The guy I used to date started calling me. –

Information from: Surra, Hughes, & Jacquet, 1999.

*Notice that homogamy issues can be critically involved in relationship turning points; but also that other forces provoke turning points, too—from the input of family and friends, to having other romantic possibilities, to simply deciding, "I'm too young to get involved."

Hot in Developmental Science: Facebook Romance

Facebook is a double-edged relationship sword. On one hand, this medium widens the field of romantic possibilities. On the other hand, Facebook is tailor-made to evoke jealousy when your partner's friend list is laden with competing attractive possibilities, or your lover uses Facebook as a tool to make you jealous and spy on your life. Imagine your shock to wake up, check Facebook, and find your lover has changed his status from "in a relationship" to " it's complicated." And how do you feel about needing to change your own status to "it's complicated," and thereby broadcast to the world the humiliating fact that your relationship is not working out?

In one focus-group study exploring these issues, young people agreed it's not kosher to defriend a former lover. Still, it can be impossible to get over a breakup when you witness your ex cavorting with new females (or males) in cyberspace. Even when you delete that person, you are vulnerable to seeing hurtful images, because you share so many friends. Posting multiple mushy statements ("I love my sweet baby so much") on a partner's wall, respondents agreed, is a "no, no." But some people felt it's important to log in at least one caring comment every day.

The universal perception of the young people in this study, however, was that, in their words: "Facebook is a trap"; "It's a total . . . train wreck"; "It's not going to make a relationship better but it could make it worse"(quoted in Fox, Osborn, & Warber, 2014, p. 531). Unfortunately, however, everyone still felt wedded to this technology. In spite of reporting numerous negative experiences, 46 of these 47 young adults still maintained a Facebook page. The one emerging adult who had deleted his profile

Table 10.8: Everything (or Some Interesting Things) You Wanted to Know About Cyberspace Love Relationships

Question 1: *Should I worry if there is a huge assortment of potentially competing romantic possibilities on my partner's Facebook friends list?*

Research answer: Actually no, but you should be concerned if your lover seems interested in adding *new friends*. In one study exploring commitment in 145 college students, researchers found that people in a relationship who reported lower feelings of love for their partners were apt to solicit new Facebook friends. But the sheer number of romantic possibilities on a friend list had nothing to do with the odds that a person was less committed or would stray. Bottom line: Ignore your lover's existing Facebook friends, but beware of the ones she adds! (See Drouin, Miller, & Dibble, 2014.)

Question 2: *My lover texts me constantly every day. Does that mean he is anxious about my love?*

Research answer: Not really, but you might be alert to whether he prefers texting to contacting you in other ways. In measuring relationship satisfaction among 364 daters, and controlling for background variables such as physical distance, one psychologist (Luo, 2014) found that the absolute number of texts per day didn't matter. However, overusing this communication mode, when compared to calling or meeting face to face, predicted relationship distress. So, it may be OK to receive love texts every hour. But when your lover's cyberspace messages are replacing "real life" interactions, that person may be feeling uneasy about your love.

Question 3: *I must admit that I've been guilty of sexting my partner. Does that mean I'm a loose woman or have personality issues?*

Research answer: Contrary to the media alarm bells, sexting is not a symptom of having mental health problems (Gordon-Messer and others, 2013). Actually, the main correlate of engaging in this activity is having a close romantic relationship (Delevi & Weisskirch, 2013; Samimi & Alderson, 2014). Still, among females, unwanted sexting is fairly common—with more than one-half of girls in one study reporting they engaged in this behavior to please their mates (Drouin & Tobin, 2014). There also is an interesting difference between European nations. While living in a country with traditional values (such as Italy) does not affect sexting prevalence, it does predict gender differences in this activity. In permissive societies such as Scandinavia, females are more apt to sext than males. In conservative countries, by far the main sexters are men (Baumgartner and others, 2014).

was reconsidering getting a new one, ironically, "just to keep tabs on his girlfriend" (p. 533). (Check out Table 10.8 for other interesting research facts related to romance in the on-line age.) 🌀

Although it makes romance (in Facebook terms) "complicated," the on-line revolution is not apt to make or break a relationship. Studies tracking the real-world couples that I've been describing offer that crystal ball. To summarize: It helps to be similar in values to your partner and on the same page about your feelings of love; it's a good sign if your relationship progresses without too much turmoil. It's important to idealize your partner ("My mate is the greatest!") and to find someone whose personal attributes you respect. This brings me to the importance of that final, critical personal attribute—Find someone who can reach out in love!

Love Through the Lens of Attachment Theory

Think back to Chapter 4's discussion of the different infant attachment styles. Remember that Mary Ainsworth (1973) found that *securely attached* babies run to Mom with hugs and kisses when she appears in the room. *Avoidant* infants act cold, aloof, and indifferent in the Strange Situation when the caregiver returns. *Anxious-ambivalent* babies are overly clingy, afraid to explore the toys, and angry and inconsolable when their caregiver arrives. Now, think of your own romantic relationships, or the love relationships of family members or friends. Wouldn't these same attachment categories apply to adult romantic love? Cindy Hazan and Phillip Shaver (1987) had the same insight: Let's draw on Ainsworth's dimensions to classify people into different **adult attachment styles**.

People with a **preoccupied/ambivalent** type of insecure attachment fall quickly and deeply in love (see the How Do We Know box). But, because they are engulfing and needy, they often end up being rejected or feeling chronically unfulfilled. Adults with an **avoidant/dismissive** form of insecure attachment are at the opposite end of the spectrum—withholding, aloof, reluctant to engage. You may have dated this kind of person, someone whose main mottos seem to be "stay independent," "don't share," "avoid getting close" (Feeney, 1999).

adult attachment styles The different ways in which adults relate to romantic partners, based on Mary Ainsworth's infant attachment styles. (Adult attachment styles are classified as secure, or preoccupied/ambivalent insecure, or avoidant/dismissive insecure.)

preoccupied/ambivalent insecure attachment An excessively clingy, needy style of relating to loved ones.

avoidant/dismissive insecure attachment A standoffish, excessively disengaged style of relating to loved ones.

HOW DO WE KNOW . . .

that a person is securely or insecurely attached?

How do developmentalists classify adults as either securely or insecurely attached? In the *current relationship interview,* they ask people questions about their goals and feelings about their romantic relationships; for example, "What happens when either of you is in trouble? Can you rely on each other to be there emotionally?" Trained evaluators then code the responses.

People are labeled securely attached if they coherently describe the pluses and minuses of their own behavior and of the relationship, if they talk freely about their desire for intimacy, and if they adopt an other-centered perspective, seeing nurturing the other person's development as a primary goal. Those who describe their relationship in formal, stilted ways, emphasize "autonomy issues," or talk about the advantages of being together in non-intimate terms ("We are buying a house"; "We go places"), are classified as avoidant/dismissive. Those who express total dependence ("I can't function unless she is nearby"), anger about not being treated correctly, or fears of being left are classified as preoccupied/ambivalent.

This in-depth interview technique is time intensive. But many attachment researchers argue that it reveals a person's attachment style better than questionnaires in which people simply check "yes" or "no" to indicate whether items on a scale apply to them.

Secure attachment

- **Definition:** Capable of genuine intimacy in relationships.
- **Signs:** Empathic, sensitive, able to reach out emotionally. Balances own needs with those of partner. Has affectionate, caring interactions. Probably in a loving, long-term relationship.

Avoidant/dismissive insecure attachment

- **Definition:** Unable to get close in relationships.
- **Signs:** Uncaring, aloof, emotionally distant. Unresponsive to loving feelings. Abruptly disengages at signs of involvement. Unlikely to be in a long-term relationship.

Preoccupied/ambivalent insecure attachment

- **Definition:** Needy and engulfing in relationships.
- **Signs:** Excessively jealous, suffocating. Needs continual reassurance of being totally loved. Unlikely to be in a loving, long-term relationship.

Securely attached people are fully open to love. They give their partners space to differentiate, yet are firmly committed. Like Ainsworth's secure infants, their faces light up when they talk about their partner. Their joy in their love shines through. Decades of studies exploring these different attachment styles show that insecurely attached adults have trouble with relationships. Securely attached people are more successful in the world of love.

secure attachment The genuine intimacy that is ideal in love relationships.

Securely attached adults have happier marriages. They report more satisfying romances (Feeney, 1999; Mikulincer and others, 2002; Morgan & Shaver, 1999). Avoidant husbands are disengaged when their wives get upset (Barry & Lawrence, 2013). Perhaps because they are so frightened about being left, anxiously attached spouses are more apt to have affairs (Russell, Baker, & McNulty, 2013). Insecurely attached people get far more dissatisfied with their lovers over time (Hadden, Smith, & Webster, 2014). But, securely attached adults hang in during difficulties. They freely support their partner in times of need. Using the metaphor of mother–infant attachment, described in Chapter 4, people with secure attachments are wonderful dancers. They excel at being emotionally responsive and in tune.

Recall that Bowlby and Ainsworth believe that the dance of attachment between the caregiver and baby is the basis for feeling securely attached in infancy and for dancing well in other relationships in life. If you listen to friends anguishing about their relationship problems, you will hear similar ideas: "The reason I act clingy and jealous is that, during my childhood, I felt unloved." "It's hard for me to warm up and respond to kisses because my mom was rejecting and cold." We already know that attachment styles can change throughout childhood and adolescence (see Chapter 4). In fact, a better predictor of being securely attached in your twenties is not your attachment status during infancy, but maintaining close friendships as a teen (Fraley and others, 2013; Pascuzzo, Cyr, & Moss, 2013). Once entering adulthood, how much can attachment styles change from year to year?

To answer this question, researchers measured the attachment styles of several hundred women at intervals over two years (Cozzarelli and others, 2003). They found that almost one-half of the women had changed categories over that time. So the good news is that we can change our attachment status from insecure to secure. And—as will come as no surprise to many readers—we can also move in the opposite direction, temporarily feeling insecurely attached after a terrible experience with love. The best way to understand attachment styles, then, is as somewhat enduring and consistent, arising, in part, from our recent experiences in love.

One reason attachment styles stay stable is that they may operate as a self-fulfilling prophecy. A preoccupied, clingy person does tend to be rejected repeatedly. An avoidant individual remains isolated because piercing that armored shell takes such a heroic effort. A secure, loving person gets more secure over time because his caring behavior evokes warm, loving responses (Davila & Kashy, 2009).

By now, you are probably impressed with the power of the attachment-styles perspective to predict real-world love. But alert readers might notice that these *correlational* findings have conceptual flaws: Let's say, for instance, that a person labels his childhood as unhappy, is classified as having an insecure attachment style, and experiences relationship distress. It's tempting to say that "poor parenting" caused this insecure worldview, which then produced the current problems; but couldn't the causal chain go in the opposite way? "I'm not getting along with my partner, so I believe love can't work out, and it must be my parents fault." Or, couldn't these *self-reports* be caused by a third force having nothing to do with attachment: being depressed. If you have a gloomy worldview, wouldn't you see both your childhood and current relationship as dissatisfying, and also have an "avoidant" or "preoccupied" attachment style?

Still, as a framework for understanding people (and ourselves), the attachment styles perspective has great appeal. Who can't relate to having had a lover (or friend or parent) with a "dismissing" or "preoccupied" attachment? Don't the defining qualities of secure attachment give us a beautiful roadmap for how we personally should relate to the significant others in our lives? Attachment theory allows us to look at *every* love relationship through a fascinating new lens.

INTERVENTIONS: **Evaluating Your Own Relationship**

How can you use *all* of the insights in this section to ensure smoother-sailing romance? Select someone who is similar in values and interests, but don't necessarily search for a partner with your personality traits. Find someone who you respect as an individual, a person whose qualities embody the "self" you want to be—but it's best if you each differ on the need to take charge. Focus on the outstanding "special qualities" of your significant other. Look for someone who is securely attached and secure as a human being. It's a good sign if your relationship progresses fairly smoothly, but expect bumps along the way. Still, however, notice the other implicit message of the research on relationship turning points (see Table 10.7 on page 317): If things don't work out, it easily may have *nothing* to do with you, the other person, or any problem basic to how well you get along! If you want to evaluate your own relationship, you might take the questionnaire based on these chapter points in Table 10.9.

Table 10.9: Evaluating Your Own Relationship: A Section Summary Checklist

	Yes	No
1. Are you and your partner similar in interests and values?	☐	☐
You don't have to be clones of each other, but the research shows that the more similar you are in many worldviews, the greater your chances of a happy relationship.*		
2. Do you believe that your partner has a great personality and, in important ways, embodies your ideal self?	☐	☐
Seeing your partner as having wonderful qualities and as someone you want to be like predicts staying together happily as well as growing emotionally toward your ideal.		
3. Do you see your partner as utterly terrific and unique?	☐	☐
Deciding that this person has no human flaws is not necessary—but seeing your partner as "unique and special" also predicts being happy together.		
4. Is your relationship getting better and better, with you two becoming more committed over time?	☐	☐
If you experience minor ups and downs in your feelings of love, that's fine, but it's best if your relationship generally continues on an upward trajectory.		
5. Is your partner able to fully reach out in love, neither intensely jealous nor aloof?	☐	☐
Some jealousy or hesitation about commitment can be normal, but in general, your partner should be securely attached and able to love.		

If you checked "yes" for all six of these questions, your relationship is in excellent shape. If you checked "no" for every question, your "relationship" does not exist! One or two no's mixed in with yes's suggest areas that need additional work.

*Recall that it may be best if one of you has a stronger, or more dominant, personality.

So far, I have just begun my exploration into those adult agendas: love and work. In the next chapter, we'll focus directly on that core adult love relationship—marriage—and talk in more depth about careers. Then stay tuned, in Chapter 12, for exciting findings exploring how we change as people during adulthood, and tips for constructing a fulfilling adult life.

Tying It All Together

1. If Latoya is discussing with James how relationships have changed in recent decades, which *two* statements should she make?

   a. There is now more interracial and interethnic dating.

   b. Same-sex relationships are now much more acceptable.

   c. Homophobia is now rare.

2. Today, relatively *few/many* single people are open to Internet dating, and on-line relationships are *less/more* apt to be successful than traditional relationships.

3. Natasha and Akbar met at a friend's New Year's Eve party and just started dating. They are about to find out whether they share similar interests, backgrounds, and worldviews. This couple is in Murstein's (choose one) *stimulus/value-comparison/role* phase of romantic relationships.

4. Catherine tells Kelly, "To have a happy relationship, find someone as similar to you as possible." Go back and review this section. Then list the ways in which Catherine is somewhat wrong.

5. Kita is clingy and always feels rejected. Rena runs away from intimate relationships. Sam is affectionate and loving. Match the attachment status of each person to one of the following alternatives: *secure, avoidant-dismissive, or preoccupied*.

Answers to the Tying It All Together questions can be found at the end of this chapter.

Emerging into Adulthood

Psychologists have identified a new life phase called **emerging adulthood**. This in-between, not-quite-fully-adult time of life, beginning after high school and tapering off by the late twenties, involves testing out adult **roles**. The main challenge of this least-structured life stage is taking adult responsibility for our lives. This new, developed-world life stage differs from person to person and country to country. In southern Europe, young people typically live at home until they marry, and they often have great trouble becoming financially independent. In northern Europe, **cohabitation** and having babies before marriage are widespread. In these nations, better economies, plus an emphasis on independence, make early **nest-leaving** the norm. In the United States, there is tremendous variability, with people moving backward and forward on the way to constructing an adult life.

We often think of the entry point of emerging adulthood as leaving the nest. But, although, in many nations, parent–child relationships improve after emerging adults move out, this is not true in places such as Portugal where most young people stay in the nest through their twenties. The idea that we must leave home to "act adult" is also incorrect. Young people typically live with their parents because they cannot afford to live alone. Ethnic-minority young people, in particular, may stay in the nest to help their families as "full adults."

Social-clock pressures, or **age norms**, set the boundaries of emerging adulthood. Exploring is **on time**, or appropriate, in the twenties, but **off time** if it extends well into the thirties. Although society sets the overall social-clock guidelines, people also have their own personal timetables for when to get married and reach other adult markers. Social-clock pressures, plus other forces, make emerging adulthood both an exhilarating life stage and a time of special stress.

Constructing an Identity

Deciding on one's **identity**, Erikson's first task in becoming an adult, is the major challenge facing emerging adults. Erikson believed that exploring various possibilities and taking time to ponder this question is critical to developing a solid adult self. At the opposite pole lies **role confusion**—drifting and seeing no adult future.

James Marcia identified four **identity statuses: identity diffusion** (drifting aimlessly), **identity foreclosure** (leaping into an identity without any thought), **moratorium** (exploring different pathways), and **identity achievement** (settling on an identity). In contrast to Marcia's idea that we progress through these stages and reach achievement in the twenties, people shift from status to status throughout life. Emerging adults may not need to sample different fields to develop a secure career identity. Being paralyzed by different possibilities, or locked in **ruminative moratorium**, produces special distress. In terms of identity—including one's **ethnic (biracial or multiracial identity)**—it's important to make a choice, feel positive about your identity, and believe that your decision expresses your inner self.

Finding a Career

Teenagers have high career goals. The downside is that, because many teens overinflate their abilities, self-esteem often drops when young people enter college. Emerging adults follow diverse emotional paths as they leave high school and move through their early twenties. Getting good grades, being someone who enjoys mastering challenges (a "worker"), and finding a stable love relationship (if you are a male) seem important in boosting self-worth. Emerging adulthood, in general, is a time of emotional growth, with young people getting more conscientious, gaining self-control, and thinking about life in more complex ways. "Troubled teens," in particular, tend to grow emotionally if they lock into a satisfying job.

Flow is a feeling of total absorption in a challenging task. The hours seem to pass like minutes, intrinsic motivation is high, and our skills are in balance with the demands of a given task. Flow states can alert us to our ideal careers.

Although higher education is more necessary than ever, and most young people in the United States enroll in college, many drop out before finishing. Economics looms large in who leaves college, as high-performing young people from low-income backgrounds are less apt to finish school than their affluent counterparts. While there may be advantages to leaving college and coming back, we need to make it easier for financially strapped young people to get a B.A. and offer non-college alternatives that lead directly to jobs. The absence of a real **school-to-work transition** in the United States is a national crisis.

Ideally, the college experience should be a time of inner growth. Get the best professors (and reach out to them); explore career-relevant work; become involved in campus activities; and reach out to students of different backgrounds to make the most of these special years.

Finding Love

Erikson's second emerging-adult task, **intimacy**—finding committed love—has changed dramatically in recent decades. People now find romance on-line, and are far more likely to date outside their ethnicity and race, although White women and Christians who accept biblical pronouncements as literal truth are less open to interethnic romance. Same-sex relationships are "out in the open," in the West, although **homophobia** still exists. Western gay teens are more comfortable about coming out than in the past. The dating phase of life lasts longer, too, with more young people putting off serious romantic involvements until they establish a career. Unfortunately, putting relationships on the back burner can have negative effects, as casual sex has emotional downsides, and having a caring partner seems important during the early twenties, especially for men.

Stimulus-value-role theory spells out a three-stage process leading to marriage. First, we select a potential partner who looks appropriate (the **stimulus phase**); then, during the **value-comparison phase,** we find out whether that person shares our interests and worldview. Finally, during the **role phase,** we plan our lives together. **Homogamy,** people's tendency to choose similar partners and partners of equivalent status to themselves, is the main principle underlying this theory.

Although it does help to be similar in values, there are qualifications to the idea that we should search for a similar mate. Relationships flourish when people respect their partner's personality, and two very dominant (or submissive) personalities might not mesh. It helps to view a lover as embodying your "ideal self" and idealize that person's virtues. While the experience of love doesn't fall into patterned stages, it helps to gradually get closer, too—although every relationship has ups and downs. Facebook, that new medium for selecting and announcing one's love, can make things more complicated by evoking jealousy and distress. Relationship success, however, depends on the above qualities, and one final attribute: finding someone who is securely attached.

Researchers have spelled out three **adult attachment styles.** Adults ranked as insecurely attached—either **preoccupied/ambivalent** (overly clingy and engulfing) or **avoidant/dismissive** (overly aloof and detached)—have poorer-quality relationships. **Securely attached** adults tend to be successful in love and marriage. Although we can question the validity of this research, the attachment-styles framework offers fascinating insights into the qualities we should search for in selecting a mate.

KEY TERMS

ANSWERS TO **Tying It All Together** QUIZZES

Emerging into Adulthood

1. b. Sara's pathway to adulthood will flow smoothly
2. d. Silvia who lives in Stockholm
3. False (there are many rational "adult reasons" people stay in the nest)
4. Martha, who is starting a new career at age 50; she will be most worried about the ticking of the social clock.

Constructing an Identity

1. drifting; diffusion

2. foreclosure; moratorium. Kayla is most likely to be distressed (in moratorium).
3. Do you feel nursing expresses your inner self?
4. False

Finding a Career

1. Overly high
2. c. Juan might do best if he finds a close caring relationship during these years
3. flow

4. Josiah might argue that prior academic performance predicts college completion, with low odds of finishing for high school graduates with a C-average or below. Jocasta should reply that money is crucial because academically talented low-income kids are far less likely to finish college than their affluent peers, and drop-outs cite "financial issues" as the main reason for leaving.

5. b

Finding Love

1. a and b

2. Today *many* people are open to internet dating and on-line relationships are *more* apt to be successful than traditional relationships.

3. value-comparison phase

4. Actually, people who have dominant personalities might be better off with more submissive mates (and vice versa). Respecting a partner's personality is more important than being alike in every attribute and trait. Rather than searching for a clone, it's best to find a mate who is similar to one's ideal self. Overinflating that person's virtues helps tremendously, too!

5. Kita's status is preoccupied. Rena is avoidant/dismissing. Sam is securely attached.

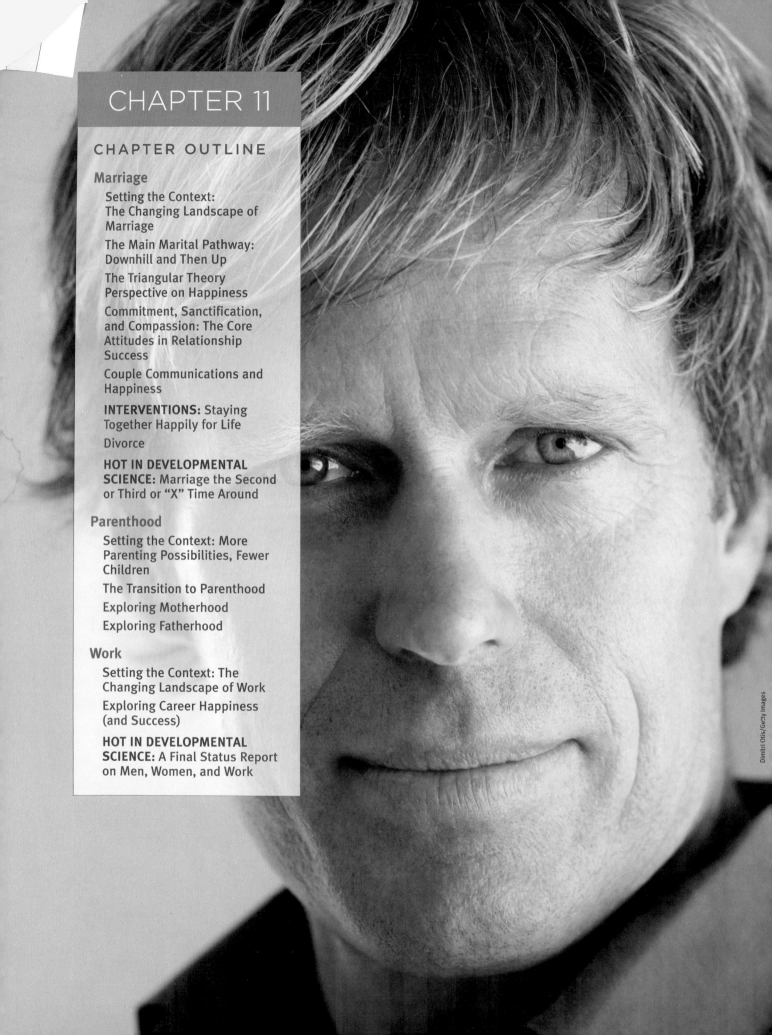

CHAPTER 11

Dimitri Otis/Getty Images

Relationships and Roles

Home at 3 a.m. from closing the restaurant and hopefully to bed by 4. Then, Jamila wakes up and gets the kids ready for school to arrive at her job at 9.

Matt's first marriage to Clara ended in a disastrous divorce. He feels blessed to have this second chance for happiness at age 35. Matt and Jamila met at a community-wide faith celebration. They share the same values. They understand that marriage involves commitment and sacrifice. They believe that god has sanctified their marriage.

After a difficult year struggling to connect with the twins, Matt finally knows that his stepchildren see him as their real dad—he knows he would die for these precious children and more. But supporting his family means being apart more than he would like. Matt wants to make enough money to give the kids a top-notch education and allow his wife to quit her high-stress job to spend more time at home.

That's why Matt just "supplemented" his store manager position with a weekend shift running the local health food store. Yes, the 70-plus-hour workweeks will be exhausting, but Matt is thrilled. What a blessing to find not just one, but two decently paying jobs. It's a 24/7 struggle, but this marriage must work for life!

Do you know someone like Matt who is trying to be a caring husband, a sensitive father, and support his family? Perhaps like Jamila, you have a friend who feels overwhelmed by a high-pressure job and wants to spend more time at home with her kids. If so, you know a twenty-first-century adult.

This chapter is devoted to the main role challenges involved in being adult. Here, I'll build on the Chapter 10 discussion of love and career by focusing directly on marriage, parenthood, and work. Before beginning your reading, you might want to take the family and work quiz in Table 11.1 on the next page.

Soon you will learn *why* each stereotype is right or wrong.

Although I will discuss them separately, I must emphasize that we cannot look at marriage, parenthood, and career as separate. Our work situation determines *if* we decide to get married (recall the last chapter). Having children changes a marriage and, as with Matt, affects our feelings about our career. As *developmental systems theory* suggests, marriage, parenthood, and career are tri-directional, interlocking roles. Moreover, how we approach these core adult roles depends on the time in history and the society in which we live.

Table 11.1: Stereotypes About Family and Work: A Quiz

Write "True" or "False" next to each of the following statements. To see how accurate your beliefs about family and work are, look at the correct answers, printed upside down below the table. As you read through the chapter, you'll find out exactly why each statement is true or false.

_____ 1. Americans today are not as interested in getting married as they were in the past.

_____ 2. Poor people often don't get married because they are basically less interested in having a permanent commitment.

_____ 3. People are happiest in the honeymoon phase of a marriage.

_____ 4. Having children brings married couples closer.

_____ 5. People who don't have children are self-absorbed and narcissistic.

_____ 6. Mothers used to spend more time with their children in the past than they do today.

_____ 7. Most dads today share the childcare 50/50 with their wives.

_____ 8. Technology has reduced the hours we spend at work.

_____ 9. People work fewer hours than they used to, at least in the United States.

_____ 10. Traditional gender roles have mainly disappeared in the world of work.

Answers: 1. F, 2. F, 3. T, 4. F, 5. F, 6. F, 7. F, 8. F, 9. F, 10. F

Marriage

Ask people to describe their ideal marriage (or relationship) and you may hear phrases such as "soul mates," "equal sharing," and "someone who fulfills my innermost self" (Amato, 2007; Dew & Wilcox, 2011). This vision of "lovers for life," who work and share the housework equally, is a product of living in the contemporary, developed world.

Setting the Context: The Changing Landscape of Marriage

Throughout history, as I implied in Chapter 10, people often got married based on practical concerns. With marriages often being arranged by the couple's parents, and daily life being so difficult, we did not have the luxury of marrying for love. In addition, in the not-so-distant past, life expectancy was so low that the typical marriage only lasted a decade or two before one partner died.

Then, in the early twentieth century, as life got easier and health care advances allowed us to routinely live into later life, in Western nations, we developed the idea that people should get married in their twenties and be lovers for a half-century or more. The traditional 1950s *Leave It to Beaver* marriage, with defined gender roles, reflected this vision of enduring love (Amato, 2007; Cherlin, 2004; Coontz, 1992).

In the last third of the twentieth century, Western ideas about marriage took another turn. The women's movement told us that women should have careers and spouses should share the child care. As a result of the 1960s lifestyle revolution, which stressed personal fulfillment, we rejected the idea that people should stay in an unhappy marriage. We could get divorced, have babies without being married, and choose not to get married at all.

The outcome was the dramatic change that social scientists call the **deinstitutionalization of marriage** (Cherlin, 2004, 2010). This phrase means that marriage has been transformed from the standard adult "institution" into an optional choice.

deinstitutionalization of marriage The decline in marriage and the emergence of alternate family forms that occurred during the last third of the twentieth century.

From the 1950s stay-at-home mom to the two-career marriage with fully engaged dads—over the last third of the twentieth century, a revolution occurred in our ideas about married life. How do you feel about these lifestyle changes?

Figure 11.1 shows one symptom of this transformation in the United States: A steady cohort-by-cohort rise in cohabitation rates during the emerging adult years. When people born in the late 1950s and early 1960s (shown in the first bar of the figure) were in their twenties, only 1 in 3 women dared move in with a romantic partner without a wedding ring. (This was called "living in sin.") With the cohabitation odds now reversing to 2 in 3, living together before getting married is a normal event (Vespa, 2014).

The most revealing change relates to **serial cohabitation**—living with different partners sequentially during adult life. When emerging adults cohabit with only one person, they are more apt to see this arrangement as a step to a wedding ring ("We want to see if we can make it as husband and wife"). Serial cohabiters are unlikely to have any marriage goals (Vespa, 2014). They may join the millions of contemporary women who give birth without a spouse.

This brings up the most controversial U.S. change: unmarried parenthood. During the 1950s, if a U.S. woman dared to have a baby without being married, her family

serial cohabitation Living sequentially with different partners outside of marriage.

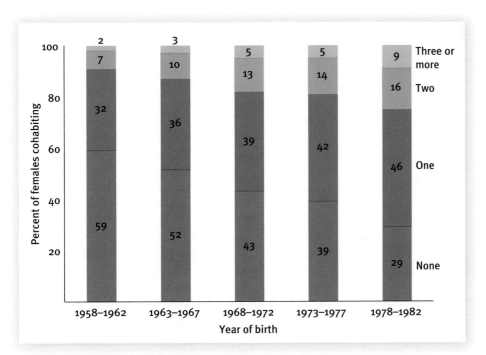

FIGURE 11.1: Percent of women who cohabited during emerging adulthood: Notice how, over time, cohabitation has become a normal event during the twenties (red, green and orange bars). Also notice the increase in serial cohabitation— living together with different partners on the way to becoming an adult (green and orange bars).

Data from: Vespa, 2014, p. 211.

might ship her off to a home for unwed mothers or insist that she marry the dad (the infamously named "shotgun marriage"). A half-century later, with only 11 percent of U.S. women without a college degree being married before giving birth (Gibson-Davis & Rackin, 2014), the disconnect between marriage and a baby carriage, for less well-educated Americans, is a predictable path (see also Manning, Brown, & Payne, 2014).

Acceptance of divorce, cohabitation, and unmarried motherhood clearly varies around the globe. How are these lifestyles playing out in countries famous for rigid marriage rules? For answers, let's travel to Iran and India.

Iran: Eroding Male Dominated Marriage

When we imagine cultures most horrified by our "decadent" Western practices, countries such as Iran might come to mind. In Iran, in accordance with fundamentalist Islamic Law, marriage is the *only* acceptable life path. Moreover, Iran's Civil Code includes provisions suggesting that women are subservient to men. A daughter should be pure—meaning a virgin—until she marries, on pain of shaming the family name. After she marries, a wife is expected to obey a spouse. Husbands traditionally can forbid their wives to go to school and to work, as a female's proper role is to care for children and the house.

Just as shocking to Western eyes were Iranian regulations surrounding divorce: Husbands have decision-making power to dissolve a marriage. Ex-wives are barred from receiving alimony. The man automatically gets custody of the children once they are over a certain age. So, it's no wonder that Iranian mothers classically warned their daughters: "A woman will go to her husband's house with her veil and come out with her . . . (shroud)" (quoted in Aghajanian & Thompson, 2013, p. 113).

Within the past 15 years, these pronouncements lost force. Iranian women can now initiate divorce proceedings and draw up prenuptial agreements, spelling out their right to work; they can insist on getting half of the man's property if the couple splits up.

Moreover, in recent decades, women in Iran made massive strides in moving into the wider world. In Iran today—as in the West—more women enroll in universities than men (Abbas-Shavazi, Mohammad, & McDonald, 2008). Although—in contrast to the West—only about 1 in 5 married Iranian women are in the labor force, women are postponing marriage until older ages. In fact, in the last 15 years, divorce rates in this nation accelerated, to outpace those in Catholic countries such as Ireland, Italy, and Spain. Bottom line: Iran is becoming a more gender equal nation, where the first stages of the deinstitutionalization of marriage have arrived (see Aghajanian & Thompson, 2013).

India: From Arranged Marriages to Eloping for Love

India is an even stronger "anti-Western" marriage model because of its *arranged marriages*, unions in which parents choose their child's spouse. As late as 2005, most wives in India reported that their families had made the primary decision about whom they would wed, and many barely knew their husbands before their wedding day. However, with the younger generation now having veto power over parental choices, here, too, arranged marriage is in steep decline.

The most radical change relates to what people in India call *elopements*: Young people run away and get engaged without their parents' consent. What typically happens here is that the girl leaves home without telling her parents (or the boy and girl both leave home). Then, the boy's family goes to the girl's family, informs them of her whereabouts and gets consent for the marriage. A few months later, unless the girl's parents forbid the union, the couple formally weds (Allendorf, 2013).

If you visited this family, the mother would almost certainly have had an arranged marriage. There would be a good chance that the daughter would choose a mate on her own.

What do people think about this change? For answers researchers traveled to a rural area of India to conduct interviews. While believing that each type of marriage had its pluses and minuses, most residents were in favor of elopements. Well-educated people in particular used the phrases, "modern," "advanced," and "forward" to describe this trend.

India is miles from Western in its marriage views. However, in this nation, it seems appropriate to cite the lyrics, "The times they are a changing."

Western Variations

The deinstitutionalization of marriage is the melody now being played throughout the developed world. Still, as Figure 11.2 shows, attitudes toward alternate family forms differ from nation to nation in the West. Because the United States is ambivalent about unmarried motherhood, women who give birth without a wedding ring, particularly those who move from cohabiting relationship to relationship, are far more likely to be poor (Farber & Miller-Cribbs, 2014; Nepomnyaschy & Teitler, 2013). Scandinavia has no stigma attached to these lifestyle choices. So in this nation, unmarried couples with children cohabit at every educational and economic rung (Vanassche, Swicegood, & Matthijs, 2013).

The reality is that the United States is still in love with marriage. Roughly 8 out of 10 U.S. young people want to *eventually* get married—the same fraction as in the past (Manning, Longmore, & Giordano, 2007). But before taking this step, we want to be sure we have the foundations in place.

Think about your requirements for getting married if you are single—or, if you are married, think of your personal goals before you were wed. In addition to finding the right person, if you are like most people, you probably believe that making this commitment demands reaching a certain place in your development. It's important to have a solid sense of identity and to be financially secure (Gibson-Davis, 2009; Umberson, Pudrovska, & Reczek, 2010; also, recall Chapter 10). Therefore, because we select partners according to *homogamy*, the marriage market for less-well-educated

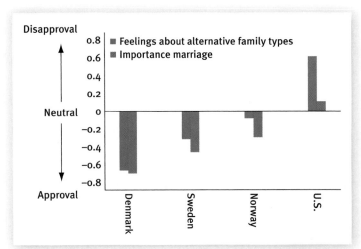

FIGURE 11.2: **Importance of marriage and feelings about alternate family types in samples of adults aged 22–55 in Scandinavian nations and the United States (based on data from the International Social Survey program):** Notice that Scandinavians—especially residents of Denmark—are fine with non-marriage alternatives (red bars) and don't place great emphasis on getting married (blue bars), while in the United States, people still strongly disapprove of family forms such as unmarried motherhood. Data from: Vanassche, Swicegood, & Matthijs, 2013.

If you visited this Scandinavian family, these parents might be happily cohabiting without feeling they needed a wedding ring. In the United States we believe that making it to a marriage ceremony is ideal.

young people is poor (Gibson-Davis, 2009; Gibson-Davis & Rackin, 2014). Even when couples are committed to each other, it can be difficult to move from living together to getting engaged.

Read what Candace, a 25-year-old, had to say about her marriage plans:

> Um, we have certain things that we want to do before we get married. We both want very good jobs. . . . He's been looking out for jobs everywhere and we— . . . we're trying. We just want to have—we gotta have everything before we say, "Let's get married."

(quoted in Smock, Manning, & Porter, 2005, p. 690)

As this comment implies, rather than blaming a "culture of irresponsibility" (see Murray, 2012), the lack of well-paying jobs is a major reason why many U.S. young people at the lower end of the economic spectrum never wed (Bianchi & Milkie, 2010). Today, for increasing numbers of young women, having babies is the main marker of adulthood. Getting married can seem like a hazy, far-in-the-future goal (Edin & Kefalas, 2005; Parham-Payne, Dickerson, & Everette, 2013).

Another goal that seems hard to reach—for everyone, rich or poor—is staying married for life. I got insights into the awe young people feel about this achievement when a college-student server came up to my husband and me at a local restaurant and shyly asked for our secret when we said we had been married for over 30 years.

Is our dream of finding a life soul mate too idealistic, given that we never expected people to stay madly in love for 50 or more years? How can couples stay together for decades when there are so many alternatives to marriage today? In the next section, I'll focus on this question as I explore the insights that research offers for having enduring, happy relationships. Let's begin, however, by tracing how marital happiness *normally* changes through the years.

U-shaped curve of marital satisfaction The most common pathway of marital happiness in the West, in which satisfaction is highest at the honeymoon, declines during the child-rearing years, then rises after the children grow up.

The Main Marital Pathway: Downhill and Then Up

Many of us enter marriage (or any romantic relationship) with blissful expectations. Then, disenchantment sets in. Hundreds of studies conducted in Western countries show that marital satisfaction is at its peak during the honeymoon and then decreases (Blood & Wolfe, 1960; Glenn, 1990; Lavner & Bradbury, 2010). As the decline—statistically speaking—is steepest during the first few years, some researchers believe that if people make it beyond four years of marriage, they have passed the main divorce danger zone (Bradbury & Karney, 2004).

Notice the interesting similarity to John Bowlby's ideas about the different attachment phases. In the first year or two of marriage, couples are in the phase of clear-cut attachment, when they are madly in love and see their significant other as the center of life. As they move into their relationship's working model phase—developing more separate lives, getting involved in the wider world—they risk disconnecting from their spouse.

The good news is that there is a positive change to look forward to later on. According to the **U-shaped curve of marital satisfaction,** after it dips to a low point, couples can get happier at the empty nest, when the children leave the house and husbands and wives have the luxury of focusing on each other again (Glenn, 1990; White & Edwards, 1990). And, at retirement, the curve can swing up even more. Compared to middle-aged couples, elderly spouses fight less. They relate in kinder, less combative ways (Carstensen, Graff, Levenson & Gottman, 1996; Windsor & Butterworth, 2010).

Andrew Olney/Masterfile

The so-called "difficulties" of the empty nest are highly overrated. In fact, many couples find that, when the children leave, they can joyously rekindle marital love!

Happy elderly couples actually embody many of the good love-relationship principles spelled out in Chapter 10. They idealize their partners ("Your grandma is the best woman in the world!"); and, you might be interested to know, men who rank themselves as disagreeable are especially likely to display this trait ("How did I deserve this woman? I married a saint!") (O'Rourke and others, 2010). And, not only is there a well-known correlation between being married and living longer (Robles and others, 2014), being old-old and *happily married* mutes feelings of distress when old age disabilities strike (Waldinger & Schultz, 2010). So, we are right to yearn to stay married "till death do us part"—if (and this is a very important "if") our marriage is a happy one.

This brings up individual differences. Many of you may know miserable, long-married 80-year-olds who may be *making* each other ill, or be fortunate to have friends who buck the U-shaped curve and grow happier as the years pass. For some newlyweds, marital happiness declines sharply during the first four years; for others, it wanes slightly. Interestingly, we can predict the steepness of this early downslide by examining marriage attitudes on the wedding day.

Almost everyone gets married convinced the statistics don't apply to them: "We are going to live happily ever after. Our relationship will improve over time, and it certainly won't get worse." Ironically, in tracking newly married couples, researchers found women who held these optimistic ideas to an extreme were at special risk of being disenchanted, or totally turned off, in the next few years (Lavner, Karney, & Bradbury, 2013).

Why might seeing one's *marriage*—in particular—as flawless promote distress? For answers, researchers made the interesting distinction between being a generally optimistic person and being optimistic about a marriage. People who were generally upbeat, they found, were prone to constructively solve marital conflicts. But spouses who magically believed, "We can't have problems," developed a shocked, learned-helplessness attitude when reality hit. Unprepared for disagreements, expecting romance to conquer all, they were blindsided when things didn't go as planned, and so poorly equipped to deal with the normal ups and downs of married life (Neff & Geers, 2013).

What does it mean to constructively handle conflicts, and what other attitudes help us stay together happily for life? To offer some perspective on these issues let's first spell out a familiar psychologist's (that is, from his theory of intelligence, described in Chapter 7) conceptualizations about love—Robert Sternberg's *triangular theory*.

The Triangular Theory Perspective on Happiness

According to Sternberg's (1986, 1988, 2004) **triangular theory of love**, we can break adult love relationships into three components: passion (sexual arousal), intimacy (feelings of closeness), and commitment (typically marriage, but also exclusive, lifelong cohabiting relationships). When we arrange them on a triangle such as Figure 11.3, as I'll describe next, we get a portrait of the different kinds of relationships in life.

With passion alone, we have a crush, the fantasy obsession for the girl down the street or a handsome professor we don't really know. With intimacy alone, we have the caring that we feel for

triangular theory of love Robert Sternberg's categorization of love relationships into three facets: passion, intimacy, and commitment. When arranged at the points of a triangle, their combinations describe all the different kinds of adult love relationships.

FIGURE 11.3: Sternberg's triangle: The different types of love: The three facets of love form the points of this triangle. The relationships along the triangle's sides reflect combinations of the facets. At the center is the ideal relationship: consummate love.
Data from: Sternberg, 1988.

a best friend. *Romantic love* combines these two qualities. Walk around your campus and you can see this relationship. Couples are passionate and clearly know each other well but have probably not made a commitment to form a lifelong bond.

On the marriage side of the triangle, commitment alone results in "empty marriages." In these emotionally barren, loveless marriages (luckily, fairly infrequent today), people stay together physically but live separate lives. Intimacy plus commitment produces *companionate marriages*, the best-friend relationships that long-married couples may have after passion is gone. Finally, recall from the bottom of the diagram that a few married couples stay together because they share sexual passion and nothing else. The ideal in our culture is **consummate love**—a relationship that combines passion, intimacy, and commitment.

Why is consummate love fragile? One reason is that, with familiarity, passion often falls off. It's hard to keep lusting after your mate when you wake up together day after day for years (Klusmann, 2002). This sexual decline has an unfortunate hormonal basis. Married couples—both men and women—show lower testosterone levels than their single or divorced counterparts (Barrett and others, 2013; Gettler and others, 2013).

As couples enter into the working-model phase of their marriage, and move out into the world, intimacy can also wane. You and your partner don't talk the way you used to. Work or the children are more absorbing. You may become "ships passing in the night."

Sternberg's theory beautifully alerts us to why marriages normally get less happy. But it does not offer clues as to how we can beat the odds and stay romantically connected for life. Actually, a fraction of couples (roughly 1 in 10 people) do stay passionate for decades (Acevedo & Aron, 2009). What are these marital role models doing right? For answers, researchers decided to decode the experience of falling in love.

When we fall in love, they discovered, efficacy feelings are intense. We feel powerful, competent, capable of doing wonderful things (Aron and others, 2002). Given that romantic love causes a joyous feeling of self-expansion (and boosts testosterone!), couldn't we teach people to preserve passion and intimacy by encouraging couples to share exciting activities that expand the self?

To test this idea, the psychologists asked married volunteers to list their most exciting activities—the passions that gave them a sense of flow (see Chapter 10). Then, they instructed one group of husbands and wives to engage in the stimulating activities *both* partners had picked out (for example, going to concerts or skiing) frequently over 10 weeks. As they predicted, marital happiness rose among these couples compared to control groups who were told to engage in pleasant but not especially interesting activities (such as going out to dinner) or just to follow their normal routine (Reissman, Aron, & Bergen, 1993).

So, to stay passionate for decades, people may not need to take trips to Tahiti, or even have candlelit dinners with a mate. The secret is to *continue* to engage in the flow-inducing activities that may have brought couples together in the first place. If you connected through your commitment to church, take mission trips with your mate. If you met through your passion for skate boarding, sharpen those skills with your spouse. The problem is that during the working-model phase of a relationship, arousing activities that expand ourselves tend to migrate outside of married life. When work does become more compelling (or flow-inducing), people may find their partner dull. Worse yet, they may fall in love with someone who is on the scene to promote their most efficacious, attractive self: "I feel so competent, powerful, and energized at my job. Hey, wait a second! It's my co-worker, not my wife, who is bringing out my best self!" Keeping "growth experiences" within a marriage helps keep marital (and sexual) passion alive.

consummate love In Robert Sternberg's triangular theory of love, the ideal form of love, in which a couple's relationship involves all three of the major facets of love: passion, intimacy, and commitment.

Peathegee Inc/Blend Images/Getty Images

This couple is doing more than sharing a wonderful experience. They are actually "working" on their relationship. Engaging in mutually exciting activities helps preserve marital passion.

Commitment, Sanctification, and Compassion: The Core Attitudes in Relationship Success

But sharing exciting activities may not be sufficient to keep couples glued to one another during the stresses and storms of daily life. People must be committed to a spouse.

Researchers are passionate to identify the glue called "commitment," the inner attitudes that keep couples hanging in happily together over years (Epstein, Pandit, & Thakar, 2013). One force that fosters commitment, they find, is believing one's union is sanctified by god ("My marriage is an expression of god's will") (Stafford, David, & McPherson, 2014; Kusner and others, 2014). This conviction of being destined for a particular person—Jewish people use the evocative word *bashert,* or meant to be—explains why arranged marriages, because they eliminate any choice, can sometimes be happier than those that happen the romantic way (Epstein, Pandit, & Thakar, 2013). When you marry with the idea of "this must work," love can unexpectedly flower. As one African American man married for decades, explained to researchers:

Imagine how this father-to-be feels when he pampers his wife and you will understand why the thrill of "sacrificing" for a loved one helps relationships lovingly survive.

> I was committed to proving them [others' predictions] wrong . . . somewhere along in trying to stay in there to prove everyone wrong, I fell in love. I probably should have fallen in love before I said "I do" . . . but I wasn't you know . . . —it's amazing!
>
> (quoted in Hurt, 2013, p. 870)

But if you assume commitment means making the best of a relationship because there is no alternative (as in the lyrics, "If you can't be with the one you love, love the one you're with"), you are wrong. Commitment involves immensely positive emotions, too.

Committed spouses are dedicated to a partner's "inner growth" (Fincham, Stanley, & Beach, 2007; Overall, Fletcher, & Simpson, 2010). Specifically, commitment involves sacrifice, giving up one's desires to further the other person's joy. When people sacrifice for their partner, they are benefiting themselves. Drawing on our natural high from performing costly prosocial acts (recall Chapters 4 and 6), there is no greater joy than performing personally difficult acts for the people we love (Kogan and others, 2010).

Intrinsic to sacrifice is compassion, being devoted to the other person's well-being. In one study, older couples who checked items such as "I spend a lot of time concerned about my partner," were particularly likely to have happy married lives (Sabey, Rauer, & Jensen, 2014). Here, too, compassion benefited givers more than receivers. Feeling compassion *for* a spouse—not believing one's partner had that feeling—cemented one's attachment to a mate. These commitment attitudes, in turn, translate into specific communication styles.

Couple Communications and Happiness

Watch happy couples, whether they are age 80 or 18, and you will be struck with the way they relate. Like mothers and babies enjoying the dance of attachment, loving couples share joyous experiences. They are playful, affectionate. They use humor to signal, "I love you," even when they disagree (Driver & Gottman, 2004). During disagreements, women in happy relationships regulate their emotions. They dampen down angry feelings rather than letting the situation get out of hand (Bloch, Haase, & Levenson, 2014).

© moodboard/Corbis

Their delighted facial expressions tip us off that this young married man and woman are blissfully in love. But, specifically, how do happy couples communicate when they talk? The answers are listed right here.

But have you ever spent an evening with friends and had the uneasy feeling, "This relationship isn't working out"? By listening to couples talk, psychologist John Gottman (1994, 1999) can tell, with uncanny accuracy, whether a marriage is becoming unglued. Here are three communication styles that distinguish thriving relationships from those with serious problems:

- **Happy couples engage in a high ratio of positive to negative comments.** People can fight a good deal and still have a happy marriage. The key is to be sure that your caring comments *strongly* outweigh critical ones. In videotaping couples discussing problems in his "love lab," Gottman has discovered that when the ratio of positive to negative interactions dips well below 5 to 1, the risk of getting divorced escalates.

- **Happy couples don't get personal when they disagree.** When happy couples fight, they confine themselves to the problem: "I don't like it when I come home and the house is messy. What can we do?" Unhappy couples personalize their conflicts: They use put-downs and sarcasm. They look disgusted. They roll their eyes. Expressions of contempt for a partner are poisonous to married life.

- **Happy couples are sensitive to their partner's need for "space."** Another classic way of interacting that signals a relationship is in trouble occurs when one person provides too much "support" (Brock & Lawrence, 2014). A husband gives his wife excessive advice about her clothes or raising the children; a wife intrusively micromanages her partner's life. You would not be surprised to learn that these actions don't qualify as compassion, even when a person says, "I'm doing this for your well-being." People who sensitively perform the dance of attachment—whether moms with infants or married couples—know when to be close *and* when to back off (Feeney & Noller, 2002; Murray and others, 2003; Brock & Lawrence, 2014).

INTERVENTIONS: Staying Together Happily for Life

How can you draw on *all* of these insights to have an enduring, happy relationship? Understand the natural time course of love. Be fully committed to your partner. Act on that feeling by being devoted to the person's development and taking joy in sacrificing for your mate. Preserve intimacy and passion by sharing arousing, exciting activities. Be very, very positive after you get negative. Avoid getting personal when you fight. Be sensitive to your partner's need for space. Table 11.2 offers a checklist based on these points to evaluate your current relationship or to keep on hand for the love relationships you will have as you travel through life.

As a final caution, however, I must emphasize that commitment is sometimes misplaced. One key to sacrificing is reciprocity. If a relationship is totally one-sided—for instance, one man complained that "he worked all day and then had to cook the evening meals" (Paechter, 2013)—or someone is being treated with a lack of compassion—"He criticized everything about me," said a wife. "He made fun of my C section. He told me my teeth weren't white enough" (quoted in Watson & Ancis, 2013, p. 173)—it's time to reconsider one's commitment and contemplate divorce.

Table 11.2: Evaluating Your Close Relationship: A Checklist

Answer these questions as honestly as you can. The more "yes" boxes you check, the stronger your relationship is likely to be.

	Yes	No
1. Do you have realistic expectations about your relationship—realizing that passion and intimacy don't magically last forever?	☐	☐
2. Do you engage in activities that your partner feels as passionate about as you do?	☐	☐
3. Do you feel your relationship was blessed by god or "meant to be"?	☐	☐
4. Does sacrificing your own needs to make your partner happy give you pleasure, and are you devoted to your mate's well-being?	☐	☐
5. Are you affectionate and positive with your partner?	☐	☐
6. Do you solve differences of opinion in a constructive way—and do not get personal when you fight?	☐	☐
7. Are you able to give your partner space to make his or her own decisions and choices?	☐	☐

Divorce

Researchers stress that we need to think of divorce as having specific phases. When people consider this major life change, they weigh the costs of leaving against the benefits (Hopper, 1993; Kelly, 2000). You and your spouse are not getting along, but perhaps you should just hang on. One deterrent is financial: "Can I afford the loss in income after a divorce?" But if the couple has children, money issues are trumped by a more critical concern: "How will divorce affect my parenting?" "Will this damage my daughter or son?" (See Poortman & Seltzer, 2007; recall also Chapter 7.)

Couples typically cite communication problems like those I've been discussing, and lack of "attachment," as the reasons for their divorce (Bodenmann and others, 2007). In extreme cases, women report being denigrated and completely controlled: "If I had a . . . contrary opinion," (one woman complained) "then the reaction would be, 'Well what do you know?'" (Adapted from Watson & Ancis, 2013, p.173.)

Once a couple separates, they experience an overload of changes: the need to move or perhaps find a better-paying job (Amato, 2010). Housework burdens rise, particularly for men (Hewitt, Haynes, & Baxter, 2013). There are the legal hassles, anxieties about the children, and telling loved ones ("How will my friends and family feel?").

Still, divorce can produce emotional growth and enhanced efficacy feelings as people learn they can make it on their own (Fahs, 2007; Hetherington & Kelly, 2002). And, of course, ending a marriage can come as a welcome relief (Montemurro, 2014). Perhaps aided by that burst of testosterone, some women rediscover their sexuality, too. Listen to a 58-year-old woman whose husband divorced her after

William Thomas Cain/Getty Images

Compare the body language of this man and woman with the joyous couples in the previous three photos and you can graphically see why the marital disconnect labeled in the text as "lack of attachment" can provoke a divorce.

The fact that their marriage is so conflict ridden suggests that this couple may feel much better after they divorce—but simply splitting up because you find your relationship "somewhat unfulfilling" predicts feeling more depressed after a marriage breaks up.

years of an unfulfilling sexual relationship: "I've been like reborn almost . . . in the sexual realm. . . . It's like a renewal" (Montemurro, 2014, p. 83).

Who feels relieved or sexually energized after divorce? Insights come from considering why people separate. In one U.S. study tracking married couples, researchers put divorced couples into two categories: spouses who had reported being miserable in their marriage, and couples who divorced, even though they had previously judged their marital happiness as "fairly good" (Amato, 2010; Amato & Hohmann-Marriott, 2007).

People in very unhappy marriages did feel liberated after divorcing. But relatively satisfied couples who later divorced, perhaps thinking, "I just don't find our relationship fulfilling," reported subsequent declines in well-being! Given this finding, family expert Paul Amato (2007, 2010) suggests that perhaps our cultural fantasy of finding a life soul mate (or the sense that something is missing if we don't *automatically* have intimacy and passion for life) lures people to leave a marriage who might be better off remaining with their spouse. And what happens to children when couples make this choice? If your house is a battleground, as I described in Chapter 7, it's better for the children if you divorce. But imagine being shocked to learn that your parents are separating when you always believed their marriage was perfectly fine. Then, think of having to adjust to a new family when your mom or dad remarries again.

Hot in Developmental Science: Marriage the Second or Third or "X" Time Around

This brings up that common sequel to divorce: remarriage. Today, about 1 in 4 U.S. marriages occur between previously divorced partners, and almost 1 in 2 involve a spouse who has been married at least once before (see Shafer & James, 2013). Are people correct that they might do better the second or third time around?

Before considering the issue, let's spell out some realities. If you are a woman, and especially if you have children (and are older), it's harder to find a mate. One U.S. study showed that after they divorce, women have 60 percent lower odds of remarrying than men (Shafer & James, 2013).

Are remarried couples happier? The fact that one Swedish study showed women select second husbands similar in education and earnings suggests yes (Åström and others, 2013). Remarried people *say* they communicate better with their current spouse. Still, these reports go along with a gingerly approach to disagreements—more withholding and avoidance when couples talk (Mirecki, Brimhall, & Bramesfeld, 2013). Have these spouses decided, "not to sweat the small stuff," or will this gun-shy approach to conflict cause them to harbor resentments down the road?

Whatever the answer, remarriages face unique barriers. These couples seem less committed, in the sense that they express more positive attitudes toward divorcing if they don't get along (Whitton and others, 2013). Bringing children into the marriage involves complications that go well beyond just relating to a husband or wife (Mirecki and others, 2013).

Stepchildren are a loose cannon in remarriage, because they naturally feel angry and resentful of a stepparent for "replacing" my real mom or dad. Therefore, stepparents must tread carefully: "Be there" to give support, but do not step far into that landmine area for trouble—the disciplinarian role (Kinniburgh-White, Cartwright, & Seymour, 2010).

When children live with a stepfather, do they become more attached to this person than their biological dad? One study showed length of residence trumps biology. The preference for biological fathers is attenuated the longer a child lives with a stepdad (Kalmijn, 2013). If there is open communication between children and their mothers, a happy family climate, and parents agree on child-rearing, stepchildren are more apt to lovingly connect (Jensen, Shafer, & Larson, 2014).

Yes, attachment-wise, this new family form presents hurdles (van der Pas, van Tilburg, & Silverstein, 2013). But stepchildren can enlarge our circle of attachments, too. One encouraging Dutch study showed that the percentage of remarried adults who enveloped a stepchild in their attachment network rose from 69 percent in 1992 to 85 percent in 2009 (Suanet, van der Pas, & van Tilberg, 2013).

Most important, these new sons and daughters can provide incredible joy: As one woman reported: "I don't look at her as a stepdaughter because that implies they are not . . . your child . . . she's my only child and I just accept the fact that she has another mother as well" (quoted in Whiting and others, 2007, p. 102). And a stepfather put it more bluntly: "I don't introduce her as my stepdaughter because I didn't step on her. I introduce her, 'This is my daughter.' . . . I'd go crazy if something happened to her" (quoted in Marsiglio, 2004, p. 32). 🚱

Will this girl see this stepfather as her real dad? A good deal depends on the quality of her home life, and how long this man has been raising his child.

Now, let's explore the feelings these men and women are experiencing by turning to parenthood, that second important adult role.

Tying It All Together

1. Jared is describing marriage around the world. Which *two* statements can he make?

   a. In Sweden, unmarried couples with children are far more likely to be poor.

   b. In the United States, we no longer believe in marriage.

   c. In Iran today, married women have far more rights than in the past.

   d. In India, arranged marriages are in decline.

2. Three couples are celebrating their silver anniversaries. Which relationship has followed the "classic" marital pathway?

   a. After being extremely happy with each other during the first three years, Ted and Elaine now find that their marriage has gone steadily downhill.

   b. Steve and Betty's marriage has had many unpredictable ups and downs over the years.

   c. Dave and Erika's marital satisfaction declined, especially during the first four years, but has dramatically improved now that their children have left home.

3. Describe the triangular theory to a friend and give an example of (a) romantic love, (b) consummate love, and (c) a companionate marriage. Can you think of couples who fit each category? At what stage of life are couples most likely to have companionate marriages?

4. Jennifer says, "I am trying to do exciting things with my spouse." Mark says, "I'm passionate about focusing on my wife's well-being." Explain in a sentence why each strategy promotes marital happiness.

5. You are a marriage counselor. Drawing on the research with regard to (1) keeping passion alive, (2) commitment, and (3) couple communications, formulate a suggestion for "homework" to give couples who come to your office for help.

6. Your best friend (who has children) is getting remarried. Without being excessively negative, explain frankly why her new relationship can be at risk.

Answers to the Tying It All Together questions can be found at the end of this chapter.

Parenthood

I have never felt the joy that my daughter brings me when I wake up and see her . . . when you are laying there and . . . and feel this little hand tapping on your hand . . . that has been the most joyful thing I ever have experienced. . . . I've never been able to get that type of joy anywhere else.

(quoted in Palkovitz, 2002, p. 96)

Setting the Context: More Parenting Possibilities, Fewer Children

Poll parents and you will hear similar comments: "The love and joy you have with children is impossible to describe." The great benefit of the 1960s lifestyle revolution is that more people than ever can participate in this life-changing experience, from stepparents, to gay couples, to never-married adults.

At the same time, people have freedom not to be parents—and more adults are making that choice. One sign of the times is the decline in **fertility rates,** or the average number of births per woman, in many developed countries. And whatever happened to those huge Spanish, Italian, or Greek families? As Figure 11.4 shows, adults in these southernmost European nations have some of the lowest fertility rates in the world.

Why has fertility dropped well below the level to keep the population constant (2.1 births) in every European nation, as well as in Russia and Asia? (See Li and others, 2011.) A major cause, in Europe, lies in the stalled progress people are making toward adulthood. Remember from Chapter 10 that, in Italy, Spain, and Greece, most twenty-somethings don't have the financial resources to get married and have children.

Are people who decide not to have children more materialistic and narcissistic than their peers? The answer is no! (See Gerson, Posner, & Morris, 1991.) Childless adults—especially if they have freely chosen this path—are just as happy as parents (Nelson, Kushlev, & Lyubomirsky, 2014). Moreover, the stereotype that having children makes a relationship stronger (or that having a child saves an unhappy relationship) is equally false. How does having a baby change people's lives?

The Transition to Parenthood

To see how becoming parents affects a marriage, researchers conduct longitudinal studies, selecting couples when the wife is pregnant, then tracking those families for a few years after the baby's birth. Understanding that parenthood arrives via many routes, social scientists have explored how having a child affects the bond between gay partners (Goldberg, Smith, & Kashy, 2010) and cohabiting couples, too (Kamp Dush and others, 2014). Here are the conclusions of these studies exploring the *transition to parenthood:*

- *Parenthood makes couples less intimate and happy.* Look back to the infancy chapters—especially the discussion of infant sleep in Chapter 3—and you will immediately see why a baby's birth is apt to change passion and intimacy for the worse. In fact, look at any couple struggling with an infant at your local restaurant and you will understand why researchers find that feelings about one's partner shift from lover to "fellow worker" after the baby arrives (Belsky, Lang, & Rovine, 1985).

Rachel Epstein/Photo Edit, Inc.

In the past, gay couples such as these women could never have hoped to be parents. They would have had to hide their relationship from the outside world. Today, they proudly can fulfill their life dream.

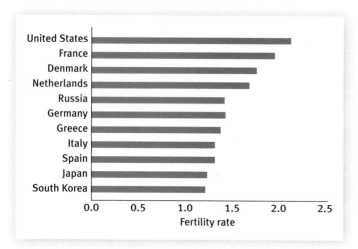

FIGURE 11.4: Fertility rates in selected developed countries, 2008: This chart reveals just why declining fertility is a crucial concern in Western Europe, where fertility rates are now below the replacement level (2.1 children) in every country. Notice, also, that childbearing rates are especially low in the southernmost European nations, Russia, and several Asian countries.

Data from: Central Intelligence Agency, 2008.

This tendency to get less satisfied (and certainly less romantic) applies equally to heterosexual couples and gay couples who are adopting a child (Goldberg, Smith, & Kashy, 2014; Tornello & Patterson, 2012). Still, in one tantalizing U.S. study, heterosexual men in cohabiting relationships felt especially hemmed in and unhappy after a child's arrived (Kamp Dush and others, 2014). We need to be cautious about interpreting these results, because recall that unmarried U.S. cohabiting couples are apt to be less economically secure. However, these findings clearly imply that—in the United States—a wedding ring can heighten our commitment to family life.

- *If the couple is heterosexual, parenthood produces more traditional (and potentially conflict-ridden) marital roles.* Among heterosexual partners, having children accentuates traditional gender roles (Katz-Wise, Priess, & Hyde, 2010). Even when the man and woman have been sharing the household tasks fairly equally, women often take over most of the housework and child care after the baby arrives. Often this occurs because, as you will see later in this chapter, after having children, a woman may leave her job or reduce her hours at work. However, even when both spouses work full time, mothers tend to do more of the diaper changing and household chores than dads (Bryan, 2013). This change can provoke conflicts centered on **marital equity**, or feelings of unfairness: Women get angry with men for not doing their share around the house (Dew & Wilcox, 2011; Feeney and others, 2001).

What compounds the sense of over-sacrificing are clashes centered on differing parenting styles (recall Chapter 7). One unhappy wife described this kind of disagreement when she informed her husband: "What's really getting to me . . . is that we hardly ever agree on how to handle [the baby]. I think you are too rough, and you think I'm spoiling her, and none of us wants to change" (quoted in Cowan & Cowan, 1992, p. 112).

These examples show exactly why we can't expect having a child to draw people closer together, whether the partners are gay or heterosexual, married or not. (Here the most relevant saying may be, "Three is a crowd.") However, after becoming parents, one classic study revealed that about 1 in 3 spouses did report more love for a husband or wife (Belsky & Rovine, 1990).

To predict which relationships are prone to develop serious problems, survive, or flourish, we need to adopt a developmental systems approach—looking at everything from the family's financial situation, to the baby's temperament (recall Chapter 4), to whether the couple really wanted this child (Chapter 2).

The pre-baby attachment dance matters most (see Feeney and others, 2001). How did the couple cope with disagreements before the child arrived? In the words of pioneering researchers, "The transition to parenthood seems to act as an amplifier, tuning couples into their strengths and turning up the volume on existing difficulties in managing their . . . [love]" (Cowan & Cowan, 1992, p. 206).

Now that we've looked at its impact on the couple, let's turn to parenthood from mothers' and fathers' points of view.

Exploring Motherhood

I've already talked about the love that mothers feel for their children, especially in the infancy section of this book. Drawing on the previous section, children are our prime vehicles for expressing compassion. They embody the joy we get from sacrificing for a beloved person's well-being.

fertility rate The average number of children a woman in a given country has during her lifetime.

marital equity Fairness in the "work" of a couple's life together. If a relationship lacks equity, with one partner doing significantly more than the other, the outcome is typically marital dissatisfaction.

Will this young couple's relationship seriously deteriorate after the baby? Will it improve? To answer these questions, we need to look at what their marriage was like before having a child.

Still, the downside of this 24/7 sacrifice—lack of sleep, financial strains, spending hours in less than fun (aka boring) activities, a messy house, dealing with tantrums, time taken away from being with our partner, and so on—can tip the balance from pleasure to pain. In surveys, mothers rank child care on an emotional par with house-keeping, and it's far less enjoyable than shopping and watching TV. Studies routinely show mothers are no happier (and sometimes far less happy) on a daily basis than their counterparts without children or people in the empty nest (Nelson, Kushlev, & Lyubomirsky, 2014).

Table 11.3 offers a research-based checklist for parent readers, listing forces that make the motherhood experience "better or worse." Now, let's turn to a decades-old interview study, to get insights into that experience in the flesh.

Table 11.3: Research Forces that Erode the Quality of the Day-to-Day Motherhood Experience: A Questionnaire for Moms

1. Do you have serious money worries, a rocky relationship with your partner, and/or are you a single parent? (These stresses make daily life difficult and also can impair the quality of your attachments to your children.)

2. Do you have several children and/or infants and toddlers? (Both forces make mothering a more overwhelming job.)

3. Do you have a temperamentally difficult son or daughter, and/or a child with chronic medical problems? (Again, these conditions increase the hands-on burden, plus may affect the attachment response.)

4. Are you a young mom? (Yes, older parents—women over 25—seem to cope better with the normal stresses of motherhood!)

These questions are based on Nelson, Kushlev, & Lyubomirsky, 2014.

The Inner Motherhood Experience

One downside of motherhood, women in this U.S. national poll reported, is that it destroys cherished fantasies people have about how they expected to behave (Genevie & Margolies, 1987). One in two mothers admitted that they had trouble controlling their temper. Disobedience, disrespect, and even typical behaviors such as a child's whining might provoke reactions bordering on rage. When confronted with real-life children, these mothers found that their dream of being the ideal calm, empathetic, and always in control mother came tumbling down (Genevie & Margolies, 1987).

Given the bidirectional quality of the parent–child bond, it should come as no surprise that a main force that affected how closely a woman fit her motherhood ideal lay in her attachment with a given child. Children who were temperamentally difficult provoked more irritation and lowered a mother's self-esteem. An easy child evoked loving feelings and made that mother feel competent in her role. As one woman wrote:

> Lee Ann has been my godsend. My other two have given me so many problems and are rude and disrespectful. Not Lee Ann. . . . I disciplined her in the same way . . . except that she seemed to require less of it. Usually she just seemed to do the right thing. She is . . . my chance for supreme success after two devastating failures.
>
> (quoted in Genevie & Margolies, 1987, pp. 220–221.)

These emotions destroy another motherhood ideal: Mothers love all their children equally. Many women in this study did admit they had favorites. Typically, a favorite child was "easy" and successful in the wider world. However, most important, again, was the attachment relationship, the feeling of being totally loved by a particular child. As one woman reported:

> There will always be a special closeness with Darrell. He likes to test my word. . . . There are times he makes me feel like pulling my hair out. . . . But when he comes to "talk" to mom that's an important feeling to me.
>
> (quoted in Genevie & Margolies, 1987, p. 248)

Not only does the experience of motherhood vary dramatically from child to child, it shifts from minute to minute and day to day:

> Good days are getting hugs and kisses and hearing "I love you." The bad days are hearing "you are not my friend." Good days are not knowing the color of the refrigerator because of the paintings and drawings all over it. Bad days are seeing a new drawing on a just painted wall.
>
> (quoted in Genevie & Margolies, 1987, p. 412)

In sum, motherhood is wonderful and terrible. It evokes the most uplifting emotions *and* offers painful insights into the self. Now that we understand the individual situations that make motherhood more challenging, let's explore how the wider world can amplify mothers' distress.

Expectations and Motherhood Stress

Society provides women with an airbrushed view of motherhood—from the movie stars who wax enthusiastic about the joys of having babies ("much better than that terrible old career") to the family members who gush at bleary-eyed, sleep-deprived new mothers: "How wonderful you must feel!" By portraying motherhood as total bliss, are we doing women a disservice when they realize that their own experience does not live up to this glorified image? (See Douglas & Michaels, 2004.)

The blissful image of a mother and baby is nothing like contending with the reality of continual sleep deprivation and a screaming newborn—explaining why the idealized media images can make the first months of motherhood come as a total shock.

What compounds the problem are unrealistic performance pressures. Good children, as you saw in the above quotation, make a mother feel competent. "Difficult" children can make a woman feel like a failure. Despite all we know about the crucial role of genetics, peers, and the wider society in affecting development, mothers still bear the responsibility for the way their children turn out (Coontz, 1992; Crittenden, 2001; Douglas & Michaels, 2004; Garey & Arendell, 2001).

Single mothers face the most intense pressures as they struggle with financial hurdles, working full time, plus trying to fulfill the "blissful" mom ideal. But *every* woman is subject to the intense pressures of contemporary motherhood: be patient; cram in reading; provide enriching lessons; produce a perfect child. To what degree is the so-called epidemic of "helicopter" mothers a by-product of these intense demands, which compel women to go overboard in their hovering to prove that they are not slacking off in the motherhood role?

This photograph shows the reality of motherhood today. Working mothers are spending much more time teaching their children than their own stay-at-home mothers did in the past!

I'm sure you've heard that today's moms are not giving children the same attention as in "the good old days." Figure 11.5, on the next page, proves this "obvious" assumption is wrong. Notice that twenty-first-century mothers spend more time with their children than their counterparts did a generation ago (Bianchi, Robinson, & Milkie, 2006). In particular, notice the dramatic increase in hours spent teaching and playing. This cohort of young mothers—including those remarkable single moms—is spending almost *twice as much time* engaging in child cognition-stimulating activities as their own mothers spent with them!

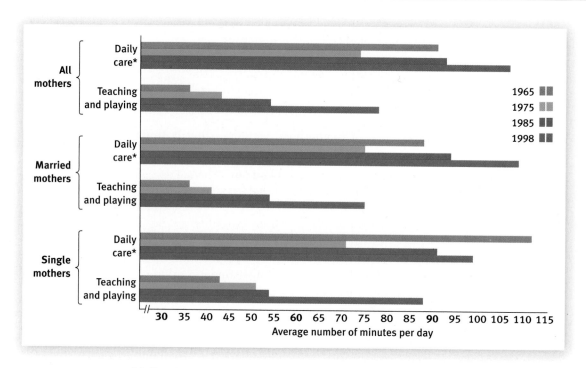

FIGURE 11.5: **Minutes per day devoted to hands-on child care by U.S. mothers from diary studies during the last third of the 20th century:** Notice in particular that, in contrast to our myths, in more recent years, mothers are spending much more time teaching and playing with their children than in previous decades.

Data from: Sayer, Bianchi, & Robinson, 2004.

*Refers to routine kinds of care, such as helping the child get dressed.

Where are fathers in his picture? Earlier, when I talked about equity issues during the transition to parenthood, I might have given the impression that contemporary dads are slacking off. Not so! Today's fathers are often making valiant efforts to be involved parents, too.

Exploring Fatherhood

When women first entered the workforce in large numbers in the 1970s, it became a badge of honor for fathers, in addition to fulfilling the traditional **breadwinner role,** to change the diapers and to be deeply involved in caring for their children. From Slovakia (Švab & Humer, 2013) to Sweden (Björk, 2013) and from Australia (Thompson, Lee, & Adams, 2013) to Japan and the United States (Ito & Izumi-Taylor, 2013), the **nurturer father** has become one masculine ideal. Furthermore, according to psychologists, we expect fathers to be good sex-role models, giving children a road map for how men should ideally behave. Sometimes, we want them to be ultimate authority figures, people responsible for laying down the family rules (as in the old saying: "Wait until your father gets home!").

The lack of guidelines leaves fathers with contradictory demands. "Should I be strict, or nurturing, sensitive, or strong? Should I work full time to feed my family or reduce my hours at work and stay home to feed my child?" (Björk, 2013; McGill, 2014; Mooney and others, 2013). Given that there may be no "right" way to be a father, how do men carry out their role?

How Fathers Act

As you would expect from the principle that they should be good sex-role models, fathers, on average, spend more time with their sons than their daughters

breadwinner role Traditional concept that a man's job is to support a wife and children.

nurturer father Husband who actively participates in hands-on child care.

(Bronstein, 1988). They play with their children in classically "male," rough-and-tumble ways (see Chapter 6). Fathers run, wrestle, and chase. They dangle infants upside down (Belsky & Volling, 1987). Although children adore this whirl-the-baby-around-by-the-feet play (in our house we called it "going to Six Flags"), it can give mothers palpitations as they wonder: "Help! Is my baby going to be hurt?"

How much hands-on nurturing do today's fathers perform? Diary studies show that, although in Western countries a genuine father-as-caregiver revolution occurred about 20 years ago, statistically speaking, contemporary child care remains mainly a female job (Bianchi, Robinson, & Milkie, 2006). On average, Western women do roughly twice as much hands-on child care as do men (Craig & Mullan, 2010).

Furthermore, these studies don't tell us which parent is taking bottom-line responsibility for the children—making that dentist appointment, arranging for a babysitter, planning the meals, and being on call when a child is sick. Having bottom-line responsibility may not translate into many hours spent physically with a daughter or son, but the weight and worry make this aspect of parenting a 24/7 job.

Based on the earlier discussion of society's expectations, it seems likely that mothers typically continue to take bottom-line responsibility. When we look at where the parenting buck stops, the gender dimension of being a parent is fully revealed (Lamb, 1997).

In sum, although today's fathers are doing far more hands-on child care than in the past, their involvement still is skewed toward play activities, particularly of the rough-and-tumble, "Six Flags" kind. Dads are often more involved with their sons than their daughters. Mothers remain the caregivers of final resort.

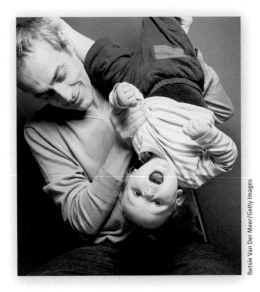

Think back to the thrilled expressions on the faces of the boys engaged in rough-and-tumble play in Chapter 6 and you can understand why this male "hang 'em upside down" play style is a compelling bonding experience for both fathers and their sons. It's also clear why "daddy play" is apt to give moms fits.

Variations in Fathers' Involvement

If you look at the fathers you know, however, you will be struck by the variations in this profile. There are divorced men who never see their children, and traditional "I never touch a diaper" dads; there are househusbands who assume primary caregiving responsibilities, and men who take sole care of the kids. What statistical forces predict how involved a given father is likely to be?

In two-parent couples, a good deal depends on a man's attitudes. In one U.S. study, researchers found men who cared deeply about being hands-on dads heroically blended 50-hour workweeks with devoting their leisure time to playing with their child (McGill, 2014). Still, physical hours at work make a difference, especially when a man has more traditional fatherhood ideas. Jobless fathers—even those living in male-dominated cultures such as Palestine—ramp up their time spent on child care (Strier, 2014).

Dads in gay relationships are apt to be full caregiving partners (Golombok and others, 2014), as are married heterosexual men who have good relationships with their mates (Perry & Langley, 2013)—giving us another reason why male/female cohabiting parents, at least in the United States, seem most at risk. Liberal family-leave policies, such as those in Sweden, that permit men and women more than a year off with pay after a child's birth, can seduce dads into giving up the breadwinner role and opting for part-time work (Björk, 2013).

This last consideration brings up the greatest barrier that keeps fathers from being completely involved: the need to be the primary breadwinner. For all our talk about equal family roles, supporting a family is at the core of many men's identities as adults. Men—like women—complain that working long hours interferes with family time (Bryan, 2013; more about this soon). Still, fathers around the world who cannot fulfill the provider role are apt to feel distressed (Bryan, 2013; Strier, 2014; Thompson, Lee, & Adams, 2013).

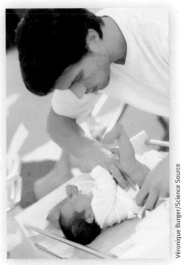

Contemporary fathers differ in how willing they are to change diapers. To explain this young man's behavior, we would predict that he has "father as hands-on caregiver" gender-role ideas, and—if he has traditional conceptions of a man's role—that he may have been laid off or is working many fewer hours than his wife.

How are things *really* changing with regard to work for women and men? First, let's sum up these section messages in Table 11.4, then explore this question as we turn to the third vital adult role: work.

Table 11.4: Advice for Parents: A Checklist

Coping with the Transition to Parenthood

• Don't expect your romantic feelings about each other to stay the same—they won't.

• Try to agree on who is going to do what around the house, but understand that you may fall into more traditional roles.

• Work on your communication skills before the baby arrives.

For Mothers

• Understand that you won't and can't be the perfect mother—in fact, sometimes you will be utterly terrible—and accept yourself for being human!

• Don't buy into the fantasy of producing a perfect child. Children cannot be micromanaged into being perfect. Focus on enjoying and loving your child as he or she is (see also Chapter 7).

• Don't listen to people who say that working outside the home automatically means that you can't be an involved mother. Remember the findings discussed in this section.

For Fathers

• Understand that your role is full of contradictions—and that there is no "perfect" way to be a dad.

• Be aware of your attitudes toward doing the diapers and other hands-on nurturing, and clearly communicate these feelings to your partner.

• Know your work priorities, too. If—as may be typical—fulfilling the breadwinner role is vital to you, don't beat yourself up for those feelings, but also take care to communicate your priorities to your partner.

• If you are not married to the mother of your child, take special care to bond together as a family.

Tying It All Together

1. Jenna and Charlie, a married couple, are expecting their first child. According to the research, how might their marital satisfaction change after having the baby? How might their happiness change if they were a same-sex couple or they were not married?

2. Akisha, a new mother, is feeling unexpectedly stressed and unhappy. She and other mothers might cope better if they experienced which two of the following?

   a. Got a less rosy, more accurate picture about motherhood from the media

   b. Had more experts giving them parenting advice

   c. Had less pressure placed on them from the outside world to "be perfect"

3. Your grandmother is complaining that children today don't get the attention from their parents that they got in the "good old days." How should you respond, based on this chapter? Be specific with regard to both mothers and fathers.

4. Construct a questionnaire to predict how heavily involved in child care a particular man is likely to be, and give it to some fathers you know.

Answers to the Tying It All Together questions can be found at the end of this chapter.

Work

What is work like in the Western world, and how can you construct a fulfilling career life?

Setting the Context: The Changing Landscape of Work

Let's begin our discussion by spelling out three changes in the developed-world career landscape over the past half-century (I'll be discussing that other sea change, women in the work force, at the end of the chapter):

- *More career (and job) changes.* Work used to have a structured path. Right after high school or college, men found a job and often stayed in that same organization until they retired (Super, 1957). This **traditional stable career** is now atypical. People move from job to job, or change direction, starting new careers as they travel through life. Today adults experience a shifting work pattern called **boundaryless careers** (DeFillippi & Arthur, 1994). Our less-defined career path is mirrored by less definition to work itself.

- *The disappearing barrier between work and family.* Work life used to be separate from home life (Davies & Frink, 2014). You went to your job from 9 to 5 on Monday through Friday and spent weekends and evenings with your children and spouse. Today, with people working flexible hours, nonstandard work hours have become common (Cappelli & Keller, 2013). More important, technology has moved work out of the office to permeate family life (Perrone-McGovern and others, 2014).

The benefit of the on-line revolution is work flexibility. People can telecommute from an office that is halfway around the world; or, even if their office is around the corner, work on their own schedule at home. This melding of work and home time, however, is a double-edged sword. Yes, not having to go into the office allows you to take the kids to the dentist or pick them up from school, but you are potentially on the job 24 hours a day. In fact, in several U.S. polls, people who reported working 50-plus hours per week had the most flexible schedules of all! (See Golden, 2008; see also Bianchi & Milkie, 2010; DiRenzo, Greenhaus, & Weer, 2011.)

- *Longer working hours (and more job insecurity).* Actually it's a myth that the U.S. work ethic has diminished and that Americans worked longer hours in the "good old days." Educated men (and, of course, women) in the United States are putting in more hours per week at their full-time jobs than their parents or grandparents did.

Consider findings from the National Survey of the Changing Workforce (NSCW), a U.S. poll that regularly monitors the hours that workers work (Families and Work Institute, 2009). The survey showed that by the beginning of the twenty-first century, the 40-hour workweek was a relic of the past. In 2002, the typical male worker spent an average of 49 hours a week on his so-called 40-hour-a-week job (Galinsky and others, 2005).

In the European Union, governments limit overwork by requiring member states to keep work time to less than 48 hours per week. Japan, with its routine 50-plus workweek, clocks in with the longest working hours in the developing world. But because the United States doesn't regulate work hours, employers are free to "encourage" their employees to stay on their jobs as much as they can (Fuwa, 2014).

One force propelling the drive to work longer hours is job insecurity. Especially since the Great Recession of 2008, people know that unless they perform well, they are at risk of getting fired. So one co-worker at your law firm works 100 hours per week. In order to keep your job, you feel compelled to work 75. Soon, not working weekends and evenings is defined as slacking off.

Clearly these kinds of treadmill pressures limit our joy in a job. What specifically makes for career happiness and success?

traditional stable career A career path in which people settle into their permanent life's work in their twenties and often stay with the same organization until they retire.

boundaryless career Today's most common career path for Western workers, in which people change jobs or professions periodically during their working lives.

Having the flexibility to work at home is definitely a double-edged sword. Not only are you tempted to work on assignments when you should be paying attention to your child, but you are probably working far longer hours than if you had gone to the office.

Exploring Career Happiness (and Success)

Suppose you wanted to predict which high school classmates would be successful at their careers. It's a no-brainer that you might bet on the class valedictorian or your friend from an affluent family. But some of you may know Harvard Ph.D.s or people with billionaire parents who are failing miserably to live up to their career potential. What are these people missing in life?

Clues come from that regular University of Michigan poll exploring health behaviors and attitudes in different cohorts of teens (discussed in Chapter 9). At their first evaluation, sampling high schoolers in 1979, the researchers measured what they called "core self-evaluations": whether a person had high self-esteem, was optimistic or depressed, and felt in control of his life. Among people who graduated college, this single evaluation from decades earlier predicted work success by early midlife! (See Judge & Hurst, 2007.)

Why do attitudes such as optimism and self-efficacy matter so much when we are on the college or graduate track? One reason is that people who generally feel good about themselves gravitate to more rewarding fields (Drago, 2011). So, given equal GPAs, your college classmates with high self-esteem will tend to "go for" a more fulfilling career.

Once at work, people who have high self-efficacy proactively shape their jobs. They seek realistic feedback from their supervisors and ask for the kind of support that will make them effective employees (W. Li and others, 2014; L. Li and others, 2014). Interestingly, one study, sampling Israeli workers, showed having this efficacious "workerlike" attitude made a special difference when people saw their jobs as less than meaningful (Steger and others, 2013). Anyone can become engaged in a job if they are lucky to have compelling work. The challenge is to find meaning in less-than-optimal jobs.

Because they view making a difference for young children as their life calling and this job fits their nurturing personalities, these male childcare workers have had the courage to choose a "gender atypical" career.

Other personality traits that go along with work success are having the emotion-regulation talents to disengage from job stress (Hülsheger and others, 2014) and gravitating to challenging tasks (Fossen & Vredenburgh, 2014). The goal is to view our job as a calling—perfectly expressing our identity, embodying our mission in life.

Are you blessed to see your work as a life calling? As I can tell you, there is no greater gratification than finding a career that you feel called to do. We might think that living a calling causes us to be committed to our work. One longitudinal study suggested the reverse. In a way similar to marriage, researchers found developing this feeling grew out of time spent committed to a career (Duffy and others, 2014). So, the reason I see writing textbooks as my life calling (it's beshert!) came from years spent making writing the center of my life.

But seeing writing textbooks as my calling involved more than being committed to working hard. I lucked into a career that matched my personality!

Strategy 1: Match Career to Your Personality

According to John Holland's (1997) classic theory, the key to work happiness is to find my kind of personality–career match. People who are sociable, those who crave continual human interaction, should not be textbook writers. If I needed to spend a lot of time outside, I would not be happy devoting days to scanning this computer screen. The closer we get to our ideal personality–career fit, Holland argues, the more satisfied and successful we can be at our jobs.

To promote this fit, Holland classifies six personality types, described in Table 11.5, and fits them to occupations. Based on their answers to items on a career inventory,

> **Table 11.5:** Holland's Six Personality Work Types
>
> **Realistic type:** These people enjoy manipulating machinery or working with tools. They like physical activity and being outdoors. If you fit this profile, your ideal career might be in construction, appliance repair, or car repair.
>
> **Investigative type:** These people like to find things out through doing research, analyzing information, and collecting data. If you fit this pattern, you might get special satisfaction in some scientific career.
>
> **Artistic type:** These people are creative and nonconforming, and they love to freely express themselves in the arts. If this is your type, a career as a decorator, dancer, musician, or writer might be ideal.
>
> **Social type:** These people enjoy helping others and come alive when they are interacting with other human beings. If this description fits you, a career as a bartender, practicing physician, or social worker might be right.
>
> **Entrepreneurial type:** These people like to lead others, and they enjoy working on organizational goals. As this kind of person, you might find special joy as a company manager or in sales.
>
> **Conventional type:** These people have a passion for manipulating data and getting things organized. If you fit this type, you would probably be very happy as an accountant, administrative assistant, or clerk.
>
> Take a minute to think about your three-letter code. Can you use this framework to come up with your ideal career?

people get a three-letter code, showing the three main categories into which they fit, in descending order of importance. If a person's ranking is SAE (social, artistic, and entrepreneurial), that individual might find fulfillment directing an art gallery or managing a beautiful restaurant. If your code is SIE (social, investigative, and entrepreneurial), you might be better off marketing a new medicine for heart disease, or spending your work life as a practicing veterinarian.

Still, even when people have found work that fits their personality, there is no guarantee that they will be happy at a job. What if your gallery director job involves mountains of paperwork and little time exercising your creative or social skills? Suppose your gallery is in financial trouble, and you have a micromanaging owner in charge? To find work happiness, it's vital to consider the actual workplace too.

Strategy 2: Find an Optimal Workplace

What constitutes an ideal job situation? Workers agree that jobs should give us autonomy to exercise our creativity. We want caring colleagues, and organizations that are sensitive to our needs (Fossen & Vredenburgh, 2014). Remember from Chapter 7 that these same qualities—autonomy, nurturing, and relatedness—define ideal school environments. Ideally, we are looking for **intrinsic career rewards**—work that is fulfilling in itself.

Extrinsic career rewards, or external reinforcers, such as salary, can also be crucial, depending on a person's situation. For instance, one longitudinal study showed intrinsic career rewards become less vital to work satisfaction as people (particularly men) moved through their twenties and had families—again suggesting that the breadwinner role remains a priority for twenty-first-century married men (Porfeli & Mortimer, 2010). As people age, they feel freer to focus more on enjoying working in itself (Kooij, Bal, & Kanfer, 2014; Allen & Finkelstein, 2014). Moreover, while money does not make for happiness, below a certain salary, family income has a dramatic impact on well-being. So, for the many workers who are struggling to make it from paycheck to paycheck, salary is a prime job concern. Unfortunately, having the luxury of viewing a job as an intrinsically gratifying, flow-inducing experience depends on having our "security needs" satisfied or knowing we can economically survive.

intrinsic career rewards
Work that provides inner fulfillment and allows people to satisfy their needs for creativity, autonomy, and relatedness.

extrinsic career rewards
Work that is performed for external reinforcers, such as pay.

Remember from Chapter 10 that flow states require that our skills match the demands of a given task. Therefore, it should come as no surprise that one poisonous job-related stress is "role ambiguity," or a lack of clear work demands (Gilboa and others, 2008). If you are unsure of what people expect at your job, or have no guidelines as to how you can be effective, there is no chance of feeling "in flow." If you are a nurse (and by extension, any worker), one Dutch study showed, feeling powerless to shape your work conditions is tailor-made to produce alienation ("I have to follow these ridiculous regulations. Plus I'm overwhelmed by paperwork, not patient care") (Tummers & Den Dulk, 2013). A related problem is **role overload**—having way too much to do, to do an effective job—or **role conflict**—being torn between competing life demands.

This brings up the topic of **family–work conflict.** As hundreds of studies document, being pulled between the demands of a job and family is a major stress for women and men, especially during their parenting years (see, for example, Wattis, Standing, & Yerkes, 2013). But, without minimizing the fact that work-to-family conflict ("I feel guilty about not spending enough time with my son or daughter") and family-to-work interference ("If I stay home with my sick child, I might get fired") can cause anguish, a fulfilling job also energizes people to relate better as a parent or spouse (van Steenbergen, Kluwer, & Karney, 2014; Dunn & O'Brien, 2013; Gatrell and others, 2013).

How do women and men behave when faced with the competing pulls of family and career? For answers, let's end this chapter with a status report on gender and work.

role overload A job situation that places so many requirements or demands on workers that it becomes impossible to do a good job.

role conflict A situation in which a person is torn between two or more major responsibilities— for instance, parent and worker—and cannot do either job adequately.

family–work conflict A situation in which people— typically parents—are torn between the demands of family and work.

Hot in Developmental Science: A Final Status Report on Men, Women, and Work

Today, men *say* they are searching for well-educated, successful working-wives (Perrone-McGovern and others, 2014). How much have things changed with regard to twenty-first-century gender work roles?

With women now more likely than men to graduate from college in many nations, we might expect females to overtake males in their careers. Still, for the reasons below, traditional gender attitudes are alive and well in the world of work.

- *Women (especially when they are married) have more erratic, less continuous "careers" than men.* For one thing, husbands are more apt to work continuously, while wives move in and out of the workforce to provide family care (Bianchi & Milkie, 2010). The first exit may occur early in adulthood. As one U.S. longitudinal survey showed, a pregnant woman has three times higher odds of leaving work than her counterpart who is not planning to have a child (Shafer, 2011). Another may happen in midlife, when she takes off time to care for her elderly parents as they become physically frail (see the next chapter for more information).

In places like Japan, which provide minimal government support for family care, an astonishing 3 out of 4 married working women exits the labor force after having a child (Fuwa, 2014). But in Sweden, a nation that encourages gender equality and offers both sexes equally lavish family leave, after becoming parents, women also become less committed to their jobs (Evertsson, 2014). Swedish leave-time statistics actually offer our best evidence that traditional work attitudes are alive and well (Duvander, 2014). Notice from Figure 11.6 that while women take ample leave time after giving birth, men in that nation more quickly leap to go back to their jobs!

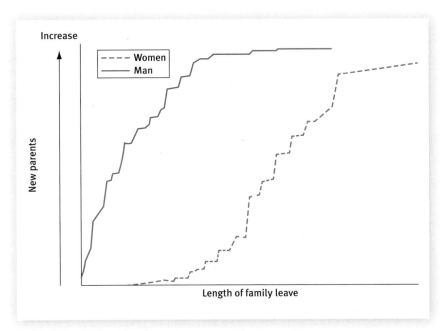

FIGURE 11.6: **Parental leave time taken in Sweden for women (broken red line) and men (blue line):** This chart shows that, in Sweden, women are apt to use far more family leave after a couple's child is born than men—suggesting that in this most gender equal nation, traditional family and work roles still exist.

Data from: Duvander, 2014.

- *Women earn less than men, and jobs are gender defined.* This difference may be partly due to economics. Men who work full time earn more than their female counterparts. In the United States in 2011, for instance, women's wages on average stood at 82.4 percent of men's salaries when both genders worked full time (U.S. Department of Labor, 2011).

We might think the cause is **occupational segregation,** meaning that work is divided into classically "male" (higher paying) and "female" (lower paying) jobs (Charles, 1992; Cohen, 2004; Reskin, 1993). Female-type jobs such as secretary or home health aide typically pay at the lower ends of the wage scale. However, the same wide salary gap occurs *within* comparable careers. So, as a U.S. female engineer, you can expect to earn considerably more than someone who majored in the arts; but you still will make, on average, a whopping $17,000 a year less than the typical male in that same field!

occupational segregation
The separation of men and women into different kinds of jobs.

- *Society prioritizes salaries for fathers and expects married men to out-earn their wives.* Although this wage disparity is partly due to women's less continuous careers, societal attitudes also are involved. In the United States, fatherhood is associated with a wage rise of 4 percent (Killewald, 2013). The interesting fact that stepfathers and cohabiting men don't show this statistical income jump suggests that employers implicitly believe that men deserve to bring home more bacon when they are married and father a child.

Actually, the fact that (at least in the United States) people don't feel it's quite kosher for married women to bring home most of the bacon is supported by other evidence: Researchers gave undergraduates fictitious scenarios in which they were asked to rate the qualifications of a person for promotion. When they arranged to have everything be equal, but made the main wage earner a wife (saying her salary was $100,000 in a household reporting an income of $150,000), *both* males and females rated this person as basically less qualified to advance (Triana, 2011).

There is even a sexual counterpart to this connection to traditional gender roles. When researchers studied prescription-use patterns (in Denmark, no less), married men in that nation whose wives out-earned them were more apt to take erectile

If we learn that this female executive is greatly out-earning her spouse, some not-so-nice images may pop into our minds.

dysfunction medication than their peers (Pierce, Dahl, & Nielson, 2013). And, just as depressing, U.S. researchers found that spouses who adopted the traditional housework arrangement, with the wives doing the cooking and cleaning, reported having more marital sex! (See Kornrich, Brines, & Leupp, 2013.)

The bottom line is that the women's movement seems to have changed society (and our inner sex-role feelings) less than we thought. But if you think I'm advocating reverting back to the 1950s *Leave It to Beaver* era, you are wrong. The great benefit of the lifestyle revolution is that today *both* women and men can express their human potential in work and love. The next chapter is all about expressing your human potential during adult life.

Tying It All Together

1. Michael, age 30, has just begun his career. Compared to his grandfather, who entered his career 50 years ago, what two predictions can you make for Michael?
    a. Michael will change jobs more often than his grandpa.
    b. Michael will work fewer hours per week than his grandpa.
    c. Michael will have less traditional work hours than his grandpa.

2. Vanessa, a bubbly, outgoing 30-year-old, has what her friends see as a perfect job: She's a researcher in a one-person office, with flexible hours; she has a large, quiet work-space; a boss who is often away; job security; and great pay. Yet Vanessa is unhappy with the job. According to Holland's theory, what is the problem?

3. Malia and her husband work full time. Statistically speaking, you can make two of the following predictions:
    a. Malia will probably take more time off from work for family caregiving.
    b. Malia will probably earn less than her spouse.
    c. Malia will probably be less well-educated than her spouse.

4. According to this chapter, with regard to family and work, traditional gender roles *still exist/no longer exist*.

Answers to the Tying It All Together questions can be found at the end of this chapter.

SUMMARY

Marriage

Marriages used to be practical unions often arranged by families. In the early twentieth century, as life expectancy increased dramatically, we developed the idea that couples should be best friends and lovers for life. During the late twentieth century, with the women's movement, divorce, rising **serial cohabitation** rates, and the dramatic increase in unwed motherhood, marriage became **deinstitutionalized**—less of a standard path in the Western world.

While male-dominated marriage used to be standard in Iran, today divorce is becoming more common, and married women in this nation have more rights than before. Arranged marriages, once the only option in India, are being replaced by the Western practice of marrying for love. Marriage attitudes differ in the West, with Scandinavians seeing unmarried motherhood as fully acceptable, but people in the U.S. caring far more about being married before having children. U.S. marriage has a socioeconomic dimension, with parents often not getting married if they are at the lower ends of the income rungs.

Especially during the first four years after being married, couples can expect a decline in happiness; but, for people who stay together, there may be a **U-shaped curve of marital satisfaction,** with happiness rising at the empty-nest stage. Ironically, expecting one's relationship to be perfect may predict becoming especially disenchanted after the honeymoon phase.

According to Robert Sternberg's **triangular theory of love**, married couples start out with **consummate love**, but passion and intimacy can decline as partners construct separate lives. To preserve passion and intimacy, share exciting experiences with your mate, be totally committed to the marriage, feel devoted to a partner's well-being, and take joy in sacrificing for your mate. When they communicate, happy couples make a high ratio of positive to negative comments and don't get personally hurtful or offer their partners excessive advice.

Divorce, that common adult event, has negative causes and consequences. Still this life event can result in greater well-being, and even a sexual rebirth (for females), especially if couples were very distressed (versus simply feeling "a bit" unfulfilled) with their mates. Although many people do remarry after divorcing, the odds of finding a new mate don't favor females, and second marriages can be difficult, because it's hard for stepchildren to get attached to a "new" mom or dad. Attachments are more likely when stepfamilies provide a loving atmosphere, and a stepdad lives with the children for an extended time. Stepchildren give both men and women tremendous joy.

Parenthood

Although many more people can become parents in our twenty-first-century society, a major concern in Europe and Asia is declining **fertility rates**. Despite our negative stereotypes, childless adults are not more self-centered or unhappy than parents.

The transition to parenthood tends to lessen romance and happiness, for both gay and heterosexual couples, and especially for men who have not married the mother. Gender roles become more traditional. Conflicts centered on **marital equity** can arise. Still, some couples grow closer after the baby is born. Coping constructively with conflicts before becoming parents predicts how a relationship will fare after the child arrives.

The emotional quality of motherhood is affected by a variety of forces, and this experience, although meaningful, is tailor-made to destroy women's images of how they thought they would behave. Society conveys a sanitized view of motherhood. We tend to blame mothers for their children's "deficiencies," and we sometimes berate women who work for not spending enough time with their children. In contrast to our images of an epidemic of uninvolved mothers, twenty-first-century women spend much more time (especially teaching time) with their children than in the past. Contemporary mothers (and fathers) are giving their children unparalleled attention and love—even while they hold down jobs.

Today, we expect men to be **breadwinners** and **nurturer fathers** as well as good sex-role models and, sometimes, disciplinarians. In recent decades, dads do far more hands on caregiving, although, statistically speaking, women typically still do more. Fathers play with their children in traditionally male, active ways, and vary in their involvement, depending on their fatherhood attitudes and work schedules. Despite our new nurturer fatherhood ideals, men still vitally care about fulfilling the traditional breadwinner role.

Work

We used to have **traditional stable careers**. Today, we often have **boundaryless careers**. Technology, while it offers more flexibility with regard to physically being at an office, has led to a blurring of family and work time. We also work longer hours than in the past, partly because Western adults have less job security than in previous decades.

Among college graduates, high core self-evaluations, measured in high school, predict mid-life career happiness and career success. People who have high self-efficacy and optimistic attitudes seek out challenging work, proactively shape their jobs, and manage to enjoy their jobs even when engaged in less meaningful work. The ideal is to see our career as a calling, fully expressing our life mission.

Career happiness (and seeing our job as a calling) involves working hard at a job and, especially, finding an ideal personality–work fit. People want jobs that offer **intrinsic career rewards** although **extrinsic career rewards**, such as pay, become salient when people need to support a family or need a paycheck to economically survive. **Role overload** (too much work to do) and **role conflict** (being pulled between family and work) impair career satisfaction. While **family–work conflict** is endemic, especially during the parenting years, work can also enrich family life.

Traditional gender roles still operate in the world of work. Because they are more apt to periodically leave the workforce to provide family care, women have more erratic careers than men. **Occupational segregation** also explains (a bit) why females who work full time continue to earn less than males. Society gives priority to married fathers in salaries and expects men to out-earn their wives. Unfortunately, when a wife is the primary breadwinner and the husband engages in most of the housework, a couple's sexual life may be affected.

KEY TERMS

deinstitutionalization of marriage, p. 328
serial cohabitation, p. 329
U-shaped curve of marital satisfaction, p. 332
triangular theory of love, p. 333

consummate love, p. 334
fertility rate, p. 340
marital equity, p. 341
breadwinner role, p. 344
nurturer father, p. 344

traditional stable career, p. 347
boundaryless career, p. 347
intrinsic career rewards, p. 349
extrinsic career rewards, p. 349

role overload, p. 350
role conflict, p. 350
family–work conflict, p. 350
occupational segregation, p. 351

ANSWERS TO **Tying It All Together** QUIZZES

Marriage

1. c and d

2. c

3. According to Sternberg, by looking at three dimensions—passion, intimacy, and commitment—and exploring their combinations we can get a portrait of all the partner love relationships that exist in life. By exploring how these facets change over time, we can also understand why marital happiness might naturally decline over the years. (a) This couple is extremely emotionally involved (has intimacy and passion) but has not decided to get married or enter a fully committed relationship. (b) This couple has it all: intimacy, passion, and commitment. Most likely, they are newlyweds. (c) This couple is best friends (intimate) and married (committed) but no longer passionate. Couples who have been married for decades are most likely to have companionate marriages.

4. Sharing mutually exciting activities cements passion. Commitment grows out of (and is embodied by) feeling devoted to a partner's well-being.

5. (1) Spend time together doing exciting activities you both enjoy. (2) Practice sacrificing for your mate (giving up activities you might enjoy to further your partner's happiness). (3) Keep disagreements to the topic; never get personal when fighting; hold off from giving too much advice.

6. Be careful! You may more quickly contemplate leaving your new spouse when you disagree. Your children are apt to feel threatened by your new relationship, and may place barriers to your getting along.

Amos Morgan/Photodisc/Getty Images

Parenthood

1. Statistically speaking, you would expect this couple's marital satisfaction to decline (same would be true if this couple were gay). If Jenna and Charlie were not married, Charlie might be especially dissatisfied after Jenna gave birth.

2. a and c

3. Tell grandma that's not true! Parents are spending more time with their children than in the past. Moms do far more hands-on teaching—even when they have full-time jobs. And of course, fathers are also much more involved. Not only are dads spending more time playing, particularly, with their sons; but depending on their attitudes, they are even doing more routine care.

4. My questions (but you can think of others!): (1) Do you think child care is basically a woman's job, or should couples share this responsibility? (2) Are females basically superior at child-rearing than men? (3) How important is it to you to be the primary breadwinner? (4) How much does your wife earn compared to you? (5) Have you been laid off at work? (6) Do you live in a patriarchal society?

Work

1. a and c

2. Vanessa's isolated work environment doesn't fit her sociable personality. She needs ample chances to interact with people during the day.

3. a and b

4. still exist

CHAPTER 12

CHAPTER OUTLINE

Jupiterimages/Stockbyte/Getty Images

Midlife

At 20, I was so anxious about life. But there is nothing like 30-plus years of living to teach you who you really are. I mainly credit the life-changing experience of having twins for making me mature. Children lock you into the fact that you have a mission larger than the self. The down-times strengthened me, too: raising my own babies as a single mom, helping to take care of Dad during his final years. At age 53, I have zero fears about physical aging. Getting through menopause was no problem; my sex life is actually better than it was at 25! My anxiety relates to my mind. Now that the kids are grown, I'm passionate to make a difference in the world. I want to return to school to get a Ph.D. in public policy. But can I succeed in the classroom at my age? Am I too old to get a job?

Then, there are anxieties about time. I'm watching my new grandbaby during the week, while my daughter is at work. Not only is day care expensive, I can't let Joshua spend his first year of life with strangers. Child care is a grandma's job!

Still, I'm up for these challenges, especially since I can rely on my life love, Matt, to cheer me on. In most ways, I'm the same person I was at 20—just as outgoing, caring—but much more responsible, of course. And, it's now or never. I feel the clock ticking when I look around. My friend Charron recently died of cancer. My baby brother retired after having a stroke last year. I get my inspiration from Mom—at age 75, still the youth group director at Church. Mom—well, she's supposed to be old, but she's really middle-aged.

When you think of middle age, what images come to mind? As is true of Jamila in the vignette, you might imagine adults at the peak of their powers: confident, mature, taking on empty nest challenges, focused on making a difference in the world. But you might also think of people fearful about mental loss, and grappling with sexual decline. You could imagine vigorous, happy grandparents, or midlife daughters overburdened by caring for their parents in old age. In this chapter, devoted to the long life stage that psychologist Carl Jung (1933) poetically labeled "the afternoon of life," we'll explore these joys and heartaches, challenges, and changes.

Let's start by setting boundaries. When are people middle-aged?

Setting the Context

If you are like most people reading this chapter, you believe we enter middle age at about age 40 and exit this life stage at age 60 or 65 (Etaugh & Bridges, 2006; Lachman, 2004). Your parents or grandparents might not agree. In U.S. surveys, roughly *half* of all people in their late sixties and seventies call themselves middle-aged (Lachman, 2004). They may be right. When a woman, such as Jamila's mother, is healthy and working in her seventies, should we call her middle-aged or old? When someone is starting a family at age 45 or 50, is that individual middle-aged or a young adult?

At the other extreme, you may know a middle-aged person who does feel "old": a relative in his fifties coping with heart disease or a colleague who acts like 80 even though she is 45.

What causes one midlife adult to embrace aging and another to feel frightened about the years ahead? One poll showed an important influence fostering a downbeat view of the future, as I just suggested, is health concerns—having an *off-time* chronic disease.

Gender and socioeconomic status make a difference, with females and affluent adults having more upbeat aging attitudes than their peers (more about these forces in Chapter 14). But personality matters most. A basic temperamental trait called neuroticism is almost certain to cloud people's view about the older years (Miche and others, 2014).

What exactly is neuroticism, and how do personality and cognition change as we travel into life's afternoon? What role concerns become salient during the middle years? This chapter tackles these topics one by one.

Although the calendar would categorize these seventy-something dance instructors as "senior citizens," they would almost certainly say, "No, we are middle-aged." When people are healthy and active, middle age extends well into later life!

Exploring Personality (and Well-Being)

Actually, we have *contradictory* views about how our personality changes during adulthood. One is that we don't change: "If Calista is irascible in college, she will be bitter in the nursing home." Another is that entering new life stages, or having life-changing experiences, propels emotional growth: "Since getting married, I'm a more stable person." "Coming close to death in my car accident transformed how I think about the world."

Do people stay the same or grow as the years pass? As we see now, by looking at the research, both ideas are true!

Tracking the Big Five

Today, the main way psychologists measure personality is by ranking people according to five basic temperamental qualities. As you read this list, take a minute to think of where you stand on these largely genetically determined dimensions, which Paul Costa and Robert McCrae have named the **Big Five** traits:

Big Five: Five core psychological predispositions—neuroticism, extraversion, openness to experience, conscientiousness, and agreeableness—that underlie personality.

- *Neuroticism* refers to our general tendency toward mental health versus psychological disturbance. Are you resilient, stable, and well-adjusted, someone who bounces back after setbacks; or hostile, high-strung, hysterical, and impulsive, a person who others might label as psychologically disturbed? (Children with serious externalizing and internalizing tendencies, for instance, would rank high on neuroticism.)

- *Extraversion* describes outgoing attitudes, such as warmth, gregariousness, activity, and assertion. Are you sociable, friendly, a real "people person," someone who thrives on meeting new friends and going to parties, or are you most comfortable curling up alone with a good book? Do you get antsy when you are by yourself, thinking "I've got to get out and be with people," or do you prefer living a reflective, solitary life?

- *Openness to experience* refers to our passion to seek out new experiences. Do you adore traveling the world, adopting different perspectives, having people shake up your preconceived ideas? Do you believe life should be a continual adventure and relish getting out of your comfort zone? Or are you cautious, rigid, risk averse, and comfortable mainly with what you already know?

- *Conscientiousness* describes having the kind of efficacious, worker personality described in Chapters 10 and 11. Are you hardworking, self-disciplined, and reliable, someone others count on to take on demanding jobs and get things done? Or are you erratic and irresponsible, prone to renege on obligations and forget appointments, a person your friends and co-workers really can't trust?

- *Agreeableness* has to do with kindness, empathy, and the ability to compromise. Are you pleasant, loving, and easy to get along with; or stubborn, hot-tempered, someone who continually seems offended and gets into fights? (Agreeable people, for instance, have secure attachment styles.)

Look at these exuberant women enjoying themselves at a party and you will understand why extroverts are generally happy (and also why simply being around a "people person" makes us feel more upbeat). How would you rank yourself on extraversion, and each of the other Big Five traits I just described?

Hundreds of studies show that our Big Five rankings have consequences for our lives. Because they are upbeat and happy, extraverts have more fulfilling relationships (Butkovic, Brkovic, & Bratko, 2011; Cox and others, 2010). People high on neuroticism, being impulsive and depressed, are more apt to suffer from chronic diseases (Sutin and others, 2013). Passionate to expand their horizons, adults high on openness are set up to grow emotionally (Lilgendahl, Helson, & John, 2013) and stay cognitively sharp (von Stumm, 2013) as the years pass. One longitudinal study even suggested that openness to experience and conscientiousness might help protect us against developing Alzheimer's disease (Duberstein and others, 2011).

Without neglecting the role of each Big Five trait in constructing a successful life, researchers are particularly interested in the impact of conscientiousness as we travel from childhood to old age. So let's pause to look at the lifespan path of this personality dimension in more depth. (Unless otherwise noted, these findings come from Shanahan and others, 2014; Reiss, Eccles, & Nielson, 2014.)

Hot in Developmental Science: Tracking the Fate of C (Conscientiousness)

The childhood quality that defines conscientiousness is good *executive functions*—meaning being able to think through your actions and modulate your emotions. Therefore, it makes sense that this Big Five quality is closely correlated with educational success. In fact C (conscientiousness) may be as important as IQ in predicting our GPA! Because, as teens, they are less apt to succumb to risky behaviors, conscientious boys and girls arrive at the brink of adulthood blessed with superior academic credentials and good health. During adulthood, their conscientious, "workerlike" personalities smooth the path to further success.

Conscientious adults have more stable marriages. They tend to be affluent or middle class. Study after study suggests they live longer than their peers because they take such good care of their health (see, for instance, Hampson and others, 2013; Sutin and others, 2013).

For example, let's take Sara, who ranked high on conscientiousness at age 10. Her hard-working personality ensured that she got into a good college, graduated at the top of her class, and got an excellent first job. As she traveled through her career, Sara was praised for her industriousness, got promotions, and eventually landed an executive position at a firm. Sara was committed to her marriage, had the emotion regulation talents to communicate well with her mate and—because we match up by *homogamy*—selected a conscientious spouse. At age 55, Sara's life is a testament to the power of hard work in building a fulfilling life. Because Sara and her husband take care to exercise and eat right, this couple is on track to live healthy, wealthy, and happy, into old age.

Now, imagine Joe, an emerging-adult friend, who ranks low on this Big Five dimension. In his teens, Joe became ensnared in alcohol and drugs, so he never made it through school. Because Joe was so unreliable, he continually lost jobs and—over the decades—had several bitter divorces. At age 60, when you bump into Joe, he has serious health concerns and appears years older than his age. His decades of failure have left your friend penniless, demoralized, and depressed.

These descriptions suggest that because our nature (or basic temperamental traits) shape specific life experiences, we should become more like ourselves as we age. Due to an *evocative and active* process, Sara's conscientious personality paved the way for her to outshine her contemporaries dramatically at each adult stage. Joe and Calista (mentioned earlier in this chapter), are set up to fail socially and work-wise, and become bitter over time. In addition to genetic and environmental forces both converging to promote consistency, we expect similar behaviors from people such as Sara, Joe, and Calista ("She's a nasty you-know-what!") because we yearn for a stable world (Allemand, Steiger, & Hill, 2013). If you have ever been shocked when a family member acted totally "out of character," you know what I mean.

Therefore, what's astonishing is that twin studies show personality gets *less* heritable as we age and encounter the random ups and downs of life (Bleidorn, Kandler, & Caspi, 2014; Briley & Tucker-Drob, 2014; Specht and others, 2014). Moreover, although the main theme is consistency (who you are as a person probably won't basically change), the good news is that during adulthood many of us get more mature.

Making the Maturity Case

One early influence fostering maturity is confronting the challenges of adult life (see Hutteman and others, 2014). As I suggested in Chapters 9 and 10, after leaving the cocoon of our families, we need to emotionally grow up. In a mammoth study exploring the Big Five in 62 nations, researchers found that in every society, agreeableness and extraversion increased from youth into middle age (Bleidorn and others, 2013). Not unexpectedly, however, worldwide conscientiousness rose the most (Walton and others, 2013).

This study also offered compelling evidence that assuming adult roles makes us more mature. In cultures with an earlier onset of marriage or parenthood, people became more conscientious and agreeable at younger ages (Bleidorn and others, 2013).

A delightful example of the power of adult relationships to mold our character (meaning the Big Five trait of conscientiousness) comes from a German study exploring personality changes in relation to the living arrangements of emerging adults. While young people who cohabited with roommates did not increase much in conscientiousness over a four-year period, moving in with a romantic partner was apt to be accompanied by a real boost in that core trait (Jonkmann and others, 2014). Bottom line: close, adult encounters—especially of the romantic kind—force us to toe the maturity line.

But emotional growth doesn't just stop after we assume adult roles. Many people feel more in control of their lives and grow self-assured well into their older years (Specht and others, 2014).

Consider a cross-sectional study examining the prevalence of mature (resilient) personalities at different ages in huge samples of Australian and German adults. As Figure 12.1a shows, the percentages of women classified as resilient (people ranking high on the positive Big Five traits) floated upward from a low during emerging adulthood, to a high in old age (Specht, Luhmann, & Geiser, 2014). Now scan the findings relating to self-criticism in Figure 12.1b. This chart comes from another thousand-plus person poll of Canadian adults. From a high point at age 19, notice that self-criticism scores decline for men and women at older ages (Kopala-Sibley, Mongrain, & Zuroff, 2013).

Moreover, this self-assured worldview does not signal narcissism. In creative studies conducted in Switzerland and the United States, researchers offered convincing evidence that midlife and older people have a less egocentric, more altruistic attitude toward life (Freund & Blanchard-Fields, 2014). When asked to imagine owning an apple orchard, older age groups were more prone to choose an ecology-friendly harvesting strategy over one maximizing profit. Midlife adults were more apt to donate their funds from participating in the study to a social cause than young people provided with the same choice (see Figure 12.1c). This greater generosity had nothing to do with older adults having more personal wealth, as it appeared controlling for people's income, too.

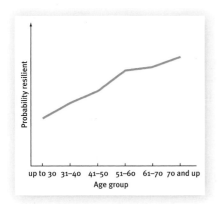

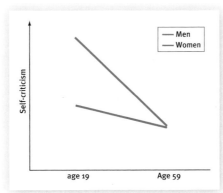

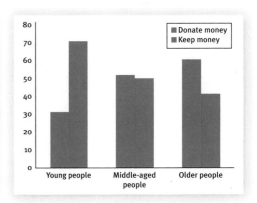

FIGURE 12.1a: **In huge cross-sectional studies conducted in Germany and Australia, the percentage of resilient personalities floated upwards in older groups:** This chart, showing the findings for women, reveals that the probability of being classified as resilient increases dramatically particularly during middle age.
Data from: Specht, Luhmann, & Geiser, 2014.

FIGURE 12.1b: **The relationship between age and self-criticism in over 300 Canadian adults ranging in age from 19 to 59, recruited from the Internet:** In this study, when people of different ages were asked to respond to items such as "There is a big difference between how I am and how I want to be," far fewer people (especially men) gave self-critical ratings at each of the older ages.
Data from: Kopala-Sibley, Mongrain, & Zuroff, 2013, p. 135.

FIGURE 12.1c: **Donation behavior at different ages in several thousand Swiss and U.S. adults:** When asked to either keep or donate the money from participating in this study to charity, notice, in particular, the dramatic rise in altruism (donating) among middle-aged people.
Data from: Freund & Blanchard-Fields, 2014.

Obviously, these findings are averages. There are clearly many, selfish "out-of-control" sixty-somethings. Perhaps you have a friend who peaked emotionally in adolescence and went on to have an unhappy life: the teenage football hero who descended into drug abuse, or your high-school prom queen who now lives homeless, on the street.

Table 12.1 showcases interesting predictors at different life stages (apart from our rankings on the Big Five) that predict either growing emotionally or having problems down the road. The last item—processing traumatic events in a thoughtful, open way—brings me to the core quality involved in adult fulfillment: generativity.

Table 12.1: Interesting Forces Promoting Maturity or Distress at Different Stages of Life

In the preteen years: *Not being in the cool kids crowd.* In following 184 adolescents, researchers found that while early adolescent "mature behaviors," such as drinking and smoking, promoted popularity in sixth or seventh grade, these cool teens were prone to have long-term difficulties with relationships and substance-abuse problems during their twenties (Allen and others, 2014; see also my popularity feature in Chapter 9).

In college: *Having prosocial values.* In exploring life goals during college and then tracking people for 20 years, researchers found that men with strong prosocial values—versus priorities revolving around making a lot of money—were most likely to be living meaningful, happy lives at the brink of middle age (Hill and others, 2011).

During adulthood: *Experiencing a medium amount of stress and coping with difficult life events in an open, productive way.* When researchers explored major life stresses and then related these reports to overall well-being, people who reported no life traumas were *more unhappy* than those who reported having a medium number of major stresses (Seery, Holman, & Silver, 2010). In following midlife women, psychologists found that if a person ranked high on openness to experience and openly processed upsetting life events, she was apt to be ranked mature at age 61 (Lilgendahl, Helson, & John, 2013).

Generativity: The Key to a Happy Life

By now you should be impressed with the power of the Big Five to predict life success. But while knowing where we stand on these core dimensions can help reveal our journey's outcome, it tells us nothing about specifics of the journey itself. Think of several friends who rank high on conscientiousness. One person might be a full-time mother; another might be a company manager; yet another might have found the outlet for his conscientiousness through being a nurse. In order to really understand what makes human beings tick, we have to move in closer and interview people about their lives. This is the strategy that Dan McAdams has used to explore personality during the adult years. Let's eavesdrop on one of McAdams's interviews:

> I was living in a rural North Dakota town and was the mother of a 4-year-old son. One summer afternoon . . . Jeff left without me and was hit by a car. When I got there, he was lying in the street unconscious . . . . I felt sure he was dying, and I didn't know of anything I could do . . . . My friend did, though, and today [Jeff] is 18 years old and very healthy. That feeling of being helpless . . . while I was sure I was watching my son die was a turning point. I decided I would never feel it again and I became an E.M.T.
>
> (quoted in McAdams, de St. Aubin, & Logan, 1993, p. 228)

In listening to these life stories, McAdams realized the power of random life events in shaping personality. Although this woman might have always ranked high in conscientiousness, the *specific* path her life took was altered by this pivotal experience. In McAdams's opinion, in order to really understand development, we need to get up close and personal and talk to people about their missions and goals.

Examining Generative Priorities

Actually, McAdam's professional mission has been to scientifically test the ideas of the pioneering theorist who *does* believe that our goals shift dramatically in different life stages: Erik Erikson. Does **generativity,** or nurturing the next generation, become our main agenda during midlife? Is Erikson (1969) correct that fulfilling our generativity is the key to feeling happy during "the afternoon" of life? When people in their forties or fifties don't feel generative, are they stagnant, demoralized, and depressed? (See Table 12.2.)

generativity In Erikson's theory, the seventh psychosocial task, in which people in midlife find meaning from nurturing the next generation, caring for others, or enriching the lives of others through their work. According to Erikson, when midlife adults have not achieved generativity, they feel stagnant, without a sense of purpose in life.

Table 12.2: Erikson's Psychosocial Stages

Life Stage	Primary Task
Infancy (birth to 1 year)	Basic trust versus mistrust
Toddlerhood (1 to 2 years)	Autonomy versus shame and doubt
Early childhood (3 to 6 years)	Initiative versus guilt
Late childhood (6 years to puberty)	Industry versus inferiority
Adolescence (teens into twenties)	Identity versus role confusion
Young adulthood (twenties to early forties)	Intimacy versus isolation
Middle adulthood (forties to sixties)	**Generativity versus stagnation**
Late adulthood (late sixties and beyond)	Integrity versus despair

To capture Erikson's concept, McAdams's research team constructed a questionnaire to generally measure generative concerns (you can take the first ten items on this scale in Table 12.3). The researchers also explored people's generative priorities by telling them to "list the top ranking agendas in your life now" (see McAdams, 2001a).

When these researchers gave their measures to young, middle-aged, and elderly people, they found few age differences in generative attitudes. People were just as likely to care about making a difference in the world at age 20 or 50 or 85.

Table 12.3: McAdams's Generative Concern Scale

True	False		
❏	❏	1.	I try to pass along the knowledge I have gained through my experiences.
❏	❏	2.	I do not feel that other people need me.
❏	❏	3.	I think I would like the work of a teacher.
❏	❏	4.	I feel as though I have made a difference to many people.
❏	❏	5.	I do not volunteer to work for a charity.
❏	❏	6.	I have made and created things that have had an impact on other people.
❏	❏	7.	I try to be creative in most things that I do.
❏	❏	8.	I think that I will be remembered for a long time after I die.
❏	❏	9.	I believe that society cannot be responsible for providing food and shelter to all homeless people.
❏	❏	10.	Others would say that I have made unique contributions to society.

Information from: McAdams & de St. Aubin, 1992, pp. 1003–1015.

How do you score on this scale measuring overall generative motivations?

Answers: 1. T, 2. F, 3. T, 4. T, 5. F, 6. T, 7. T, 8. T, 9. F, 10. T

Adults of every age derive great pleasure from engaging in generative activities. But now that he is in his sixties and has transcended identity concerns, cultivating a community garden to provide poor people with free vegetables qualifies as the generative center of this elderly man's life.

hedonic happiness Well-being defined as pure pleasure.

eudaimonic happiness Well-being defined as having a sense of meaning and life purpose.

The researchers did discover age differences in generative *priorities*—with emerging adults ranking very low on this scale (McAdams, Hart, & Maruna, 1998). Young people's goals were centered on identity issues. A 20-year-old might say, "I want to make it through college and get a good job" or "My plan is to figure out what I want to do with my life." Midlife and older adults were more likely to report: "My mission is to help my teenage son," or "My goal is to work for justice and peace in the world."

This makes sense. Remember from Chapters 3 and 6 that prosocial behaviors are in full swing by toddlerhood. There is no reason to think that our basic human drive to be nurturing changes at any life stage. But, just as Erikson would predict, we need to resolve issues related to our personal development before our primary concern shifts to giving to others in the wider world.

Is Erikson right that, as people *enter* midlife, generativity takes center stage? According to one study, "not necessarily." In following women from their forties into their sixties, researchers found that issues relating to identity ("developing as a person," "expanding myself") remained strong well into middle age. But, as these women got older, generativity gradually grew. According to this research, priorities fully focused on giving to the next generation reach a crescendo in the early sixties, once we know exactly who we are (Newton & Stewart, 2010).

Examining Adult Happiness

Is Erikson correct that generativity is the key to happiness during adult life? Here, the answer is "yes," as long as we define happiness in the right way. If we imagine happiness as simply "feeling good" (**hedonic happiness**), generativity has nothing to do with living a happy life. But, if we consider this term in its richer sense, as having purpose and meaning (**eudaimonic happiness**), then, yes, highly generative people do have exceptionally happy lives (Grossbaum & Bates, 2002; Zucker, Ostrove, & Stewart, 2002; Versey, Stewart & Duncan, 2013).

So, generativity makes sense of why sacrificing for a beloved mate makes spouses feel personally fulfilled, or why parents happily spend decades changing diapers when they could be luxuriating in hotel spas (recall the last chapter). Our main mission as adults (and starting from childhood) is *not* simply hedonic pleasure—packing in pleasurable events—but living purposeful, generative lives (Seligman, 2011). (Check out Table 12.4 for other interesting happiness facts plus another reason why just packing in pleasures *can't* permanently produce a happy life.)

When people don't have generative goals, do their lives lack meaning? As Erikson described, do these adults feel *stagnant*—purposeless and at loose ends? Read what one researcher had to say about Deborah, who, in her late forties, scored very low on generativity in his study of women's lives:

> In reference to the birth of her first child, Deborah wrote, "All actions automatic. No emotional involvement . . . ; totally self-preserving but very unpleasant." After many years of marriage, Deborah underwent a difficult divorce. She began to work in a "blur of meaningless jobs."

(adapted from Peterson, 1998, p. 12)

Table 12.4: Happiness Perceptions and Interesting Research Facts

"Youth is the happiest life stage."

Answer: *Wrong!* Emerging adulthood is the peak age for developing emotional problems. Many cross-sectional studies in Western nations agree: People are apt to be happiest in later life (more about this surprising finding in the next chapter)!

"Money can't buy happiness."

Answer: *That's true, but only once we are fairly comfortable economically.* Around the globe, poor people are significantly less happy than their more affluent counterparts. Once our basic survival needs are satisfied, the correlation between income and happiness becomes weaker—although it still exists. The main reason is probably not that getting more "things" matters, but that money can buy quality family time. And satisfying family relationships are highly related to reports of a happy life.

"I'll be happy when I get my career in order, become famous, and have the funds to eat at that five-star restaurant every night."

Answer: *Sorry, not really.* According to a phenomenon called the hedonic treadmill, when we win the lottery, graduate from college, or (in my case) get a book published, we are thrilled at first, but then revert to our normal happiness set point ("So I got an Oscar last year. What else is new?"). Therefore, piling on Kudos or engaging in pleasurable activities such as indulging in gourmet food no longer provide an emotional boost when these activities become routine. The good news is that the hedonic treadmill also applies to negative events. We adjust and then, eventually, our "natural" happiness returns.

"You can't (1) measure happiness or (2) teach people to be happy."

Answer: *Point 1 is totally false; point 2 is probably false.* Research shows that we can concretely quantify what it takes to be happy. Once people get above a ratio of 2.9 positive to negative emotions, they generally feel good about life. Therefore, happiness experts (e.g., Seligman, 2011) have developed programs to teach people to savor the moment, count their blessings, or do gratitude exercises. Still, your author (me) believes the best strategy for achieving happiness is not to spend time monitoring that feeling. When we are generative, as the text shows, a natural by-product is a happy life.

"Because happiness is an inner state, the nation we live in makes a minor impact on personal happiness."

Answer: *Wrong!* Our nation and its government greatly affects personal well-being (Ott, 2011; Pinker, 2011). As a resident of Denmark, for instance, you are probably very happy, with well-being scores topping the global charts at an average of 8 on a 10 point scale; in some African nations, the average person ranks fairly miserable (at below 4) (Wilkinson & Pickett, 2009). Check out page 367 for a surprising society-wide characteristic that predicts happiness among both affluent and poor citizens.

Information from: Jorgensen, Jamieson, & Martin, 2010; Ladis, Daniels, & Kawachi, 2009; Angelini and others, 2012; Bergsma & Ardelt, 2011; George, 2010; Helson & Soto, 2005; Windsor & Anstey, 2010.

As this case history suggests, having children does not automatically evoke generativity. You can give birth and be totally nongenerative and uninvolved. Conversely, midlife adults who never have children can be incredibly generative in the wider world (see Newton & Baltys, 2014). Classic contemporary outlets for generativity, such as environmental activism, involve caring for generations "not yet born" (Morselli, 2013). Our world-class generative role models, such as Mother Theresa or Martin Luther King, lived lives devoted (in the beautiful phrase) to "repairing the world."

The saintly life of Martin Luther King is a testament (and reminder) that the ultimate generative activity lies in devoting one's life to making a difference in the wider world.

commitment script In Dan McAdams's research, a type of autobiography produced by highly generative adults that involves childhood memories of feeling special; being unusually sensitive to others' misfortunes; having a strong, enduring generative mission from adolescence; and redemption sequences.

redemption sequence In Dan McAdams's research, a characteristic theme of highly generative adults' autobiographies, in which they describe tragic events that turned out for the best.

Examining the Childhood Memories of Generative Adults

Do the childhoods of people who embody this rich, Martin Luther King-like community-centered kind of generativity differ from those of more typical adults? To answer this question, McAdams's research team selected community leaders who scored at the upper ends of their Generative Concern Scale (see page 363) and asked them to tell their life stories. Would these autobiographies differ from those of adults such as Deborah in my previous example, who ranked low on Erikson's midlife task?

The answer was yes. The life stories of highly generative adults had themes demonstrating what the researchers called a **commitment script**. They often described early memories of feeling "blessed": "I was my grandmother's favorite"; "I was a miracle child who should not have survived." They reported feeling sensitive to the suffering of others, from a young age. They talked about having an identity revolving around generative values that never wavered from their teenage years. A 50-year-old minister in one of McAdams's studies was a teenage prostitute, and then a con artist who spent two years in a federal prison; but, throughout her life, she reported, "I was always doing ministry."

The most striking characteristic of generative adults' life stories was **redemption sequences**—examples of devastating events that turned out in a positive way (McAdams, 2006; McAdams & Bowman, 2001). For instance, in the example I just mentioned, the woman minister might view the humiliation of being sent to prison as the best thing that ever happened, the experience that turned her life around. According to McAdams (2006), early memories of feeling personally blessed, an enduring sensitivity to others' misfortunes, caring values, and, especially, being able to turn one's tragedies into growth experiences are the core ingredients of the commitment script and the main correlates of a generative adult life (see also Lilgendahl & McAdams, 2011).

What produces the kind of adult devoted to "repairing the world"? According to McAdams' interviews, one force may be the presence of caring adults in a person's past. When his research team asked people in their late fifties to pinpoint emotional turning points in their lives, adults high in generativity described critical incidents involving family members and teachers more frequently than their less generative peers. Here is an example:

> The day before my mom died, I went to the hospital . . . and I was actually on my way to pick up my senior pictures. So when I got these photographs I shared them with my mom. . . . I could just tell in her eye that she had this real proud moment . . . it was a moment I . . . treasured . . . she never saw me physically at the graduation, but in my mind I will always believe she was there in spirit. So that will always be a highlight of my life.
> (quoted in Jones & McAdams, 2013, p. 168)

If you think of your own generative role models—from a favorite teacher to, hopefully, your mom or dad—these special people are apt to be sprinkled in every ethnic group. But, interestingly, McAdams' studies consistently show that African American men and women are overrepresented in their samples of generative community-minded adults (Hart and others, 2001; McAdams, 2006; Jones & McAdams, 2013; Newton & Baltys, 2014). Does coping with discrimination—plus a strong grounding in religion—make African Americans unusually sensitive to human suffering and so prone to devote their lives to repairing the world? In support of this possibility, themes stressing progress toward overcoming adversity are central in highly generative African Americans' autobiographies (McAdams & Bowman, 2001).

In sum, this powerful generativity research explains why raindrops—meaning stressful life events—often make us more mature (recall the last item in Table 12.1 on page 362). It all depends on how we make meaning out of our personal storms. As one

61-year-old women, who grew emotionally, in a study put it: "I do not regret the past for it is the pain of my first 50 years that has brought me to where I am now" (Lilgendahl, Helson, & John, 2013, p. 413).

Wrapping Up Personality (and Well-Being)

Now, let's summarize *all* of these messages. Having read this section, here is what you might tell an emerging-adult friend who wants insights into who she will be at 40 or 59.

This group project to restore the oldest Black Baptist church in South Carolina is typical in the African American experience, where a mission to be of service—especially in a caring community that revolves around the church—is standard.

- Expect to grow in maturity and especially become much more conscientious, although, in general, your core personality will probably not change much over the years.

- Expect to become more self-assured and altruistic as you travel through middle age.

- Expect your priorities to shift toward more generative concerns and to grow in generativity, especially during late midlife.

- I predict that if you rank high on conscientiousness and the other positive Big Five traits; have prosocial, generative priorities; and deal productively with the traumas in your life, you are on track for a fulfilling middle age—but don't hold me to my word, as scientists never know for sure what the future will bring!

As a final note, I must emphasize that it's difficult to grow emotionally if you are mired in poverty or live in a society rife with conflict and corruption, where life traumas are routine. McAdams's generative community-minded African Americans were typically economically secure (Jones & McAdams, 2013). The reason why Denmark clocks in with the world's highest well-being (recall Table 12.4 on page 365) is not just that this country is comparatively affluent. People are happiest in nations where they trust their government to be fair and effective (Ott, 2011) and income inequalities are relatively small (Wilkinson & Pickett, 2009). So our own happiness depends on living in a generative society, where life isn't a zero-sum game. We are most likely to flourish as people when everyone around us is flourishing, too.

In the next section, devoted to cognition, I'll be filling in more pieces of the puzzle involved in constructing a fulfilling life.

Tying It All Together

1. Tim is going to his thirtieth college reunion, and he can't wait to find out how his classmates have changed. Statistically speaking, which two changes might Tim find in his undergraduate friends?

    a. They will be more conscientious and self-confident.

    b. They will have different priorities than they did earlier, caring more about nurturing the next generation.

    c. They will care more deeply about making money than they did before.

    d. They will be more depressed and burned out than they were earlier.

2. You are giving your best friend tips about growing emotionally and feeling fulfilled during midlife. Pick the item that should *not* be on your list:

    a. Live a calm, stress-free life.

    b. Live a generative life.

    c. Develop prosocial goals as a young person.

    d. Be conscientious and open to experience.

3. Should your professor agree with this suggestion, write about a difficult life experience, and discuss how you coped with that event.

Answers to the Tying It All Together questions can be found at the end of this chapter.

Exploring Intelligence (and Wisdom)

Remember from Chapter 7 that, when psychologists measure intelligence during childhood, they look mainly at how elementary schoolers perform on standard intelligence tests. Sometimes, they spell out different ideas about what it means to be smart, such as Gardner's multiple intelligences or Sternberg's successful intelligence. Developmentalists use standard IQ tests and nontraditional strategies to trace adult intelligence, too.

Taking the Traditional Approach: Looking at Standard IQ Tests

Think of your intellectual role model. Most likely, your mind will immediately gravitate to someone who is 50 or 80—not a person who is 20 or 25. In fact, if you are like most adults, you probably assume that, in general, people get more intelligent over the years (Sternberg & Berg, 1992).

Mid-twentieth-century psychologists had a different idea: They believed that people reach their intellectual peak in their twenties, and then intelligence steadily declines (Botwinick, 1967). They based these disturbing conclusions on studies using the (at the time) newly developed Wechsler Adult Intelligence Scale.

The **Wechsler Adult Intelligence Scale (WAIS)**, the standard test measuring adult IQ, has a similar format as the WISC, the scale for children, described in Chapter 7. It has verbal items testing different types of knowledge, such as vocabulary and adults' ability to solve math problems. It also asks test takers to perform relatively unfamiliar nonverbal activities quickly, such as putting together puzzles or arranging blocks. On this part of the test, called the performance scale, speed is essential. People must complete these tasks within a limited time.

When psychologists tested adults to derive their standards for how people should normally perform on the WAIS at different ages, they discovered that, starting in the twenties, in each older age group, average scores declined. They also found the interesting pattern in Figure 12.2 on the top of the opposite page. While scores on the verbal sections stayed stable or declined to a lesser degree, average scores on the performance scale steadily slid down, starting in people's twenties (Botwinick, 1967).

These findings would not give any fifty-something student, like Jamila in the introductory chapter vignette, confidence about venturing into a college classroom full of 20-year-olds. Luckily, however, the researchers were ignoring the huge educational differences between different cohorts at that time in U.S. history. While virtually all of the young test takers had gone to high school, many middle-aged or elderly people taking the original WAIS had probably left school in seventh or eighth grade. So the psychologists were comparing apples to oranges—adults with less education to those with much more.

How does our performance on standard intelligence tests really change as we travel through adult life? To answer this question, in the early 1960s, researchers began the **Seattle Longitudinal Study**—the definitive study of intelligence and age (Schaie, Willis, & Caskie, 2004; Schaie & Zanjani, 2006).

Imagine being a twentieth-century researcher interested in charting how people change intellectually during adulthood. If you were to carry out a cross-sectional study—comparing different age groups at the same time—your findings would be biased in a negative way. Older cohorts would be at a disadvantage, not having had as much experience taking tests, typically having gone to school for far fewer years. But if you carried out a longitudinal study, you would end up with a far-too-positive portrait of how the *average* person changes. The volunteers who enrolled in your study would probably be highly educated. Over the years, as people dropped out of your research, you would be

© william87/Kalium/age fotostock

How will this young woman's cognitive abilities change as she ages? Stay tuned for genuinely scientific answers on the next page.

Wechsler Adult Intelligence Scale (WAIS) The standard test to measure adult IQ, involving verbal and performance scales, each of which is made up of various subtests.

Seattle Longitudinal Study The definitive study of the effect of aging on intelligence, carried out by K. Warner Schaie, involving simultaneously conducting and comparing the results of cross-sectional and longitudinal studies carried out with a group of Seattle volunteers.

left with an increasingly self-selected group, the fraction of older people who were proud of proving their intellectual capacities and—as they reached their seventies—those healthy enough to take your tests (Baltes & Smith, 1997).

Faced with these contrasting biases (longitudinal research will be too positive; cross-sectional research will be biased in a negative way), the researchers devised a brilliant solution: Combine the two kinds of studies, factor out the biases of each research method, and isolate the "true" impact of age on IQ.

First, the research team selected people enrolled in a Seattle health organization who were 7 years apart in age, tested them, and compared their scores. Then, they followed each group longitudinally, testing them at 7-year intervals. At each evaluation, the psychologists selected another cross-sectional sample, some of whom they also followed over time.

Using an IQ test that, unlike the WAIS, measured five basic cognitive abilities, the researchers got a more encouraging portrait of how we change intellectually—one that fits our intuitive sense of how we should perform. Notice in looking at Figure 12.3 that, on this measure—involving, for instance, tests of vocabulary and our ability to quickly think up words—we reach our intellectual peak during our forties and early fifties (Schaie, 1996; Schaie, Willis, & Caskie, 2004). Still, the Seattle study showed the same pattern researchers first found on the WAIS. On tests measuring people's store of knowledge, such as vocabulary, scores improve till at least age 60 (Larsen, Hartmann, & Nyborg, 2007). But when a test involves doing something new very fast (such as arranging puzzles within a time limit or the word fluency measure in Figure 12.3), losses start as early as the forties (Ardila, 2007). Now, let's look at a theory that makes sense of these findings and tells us a good deal about our intellectual abilities in the real world.

Two Types of Intelligence: Crystallized and Fluid Skills

Psychologists today typically divide intelligence into two categories. **Crystallized intelligence** refers to our knowledge base, the storehouse of information that we have accumulated over the years. The verbal scale of the WAIS, with its tests of vocabulary and math, mainly measures crystallized skills. **Fluid intelligence** involves our ability to reason quickly when facing new intellectual challenges. The WAIS performance

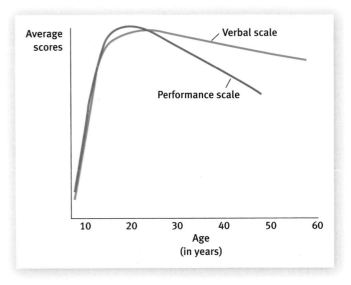

FIGURE 12.2: **Age-related changes in mean scores on the performance and verbal scales of the WAIS:** This chart showed the depressing pattern of decline from a study using the early form of the WAIS. Notice how average scores on the performance scale (items involving manipulating materials) regularly slid down starting in the twenties, while scores on the verbal scale remained more stable with age. Now compare this early age-decline with the data in Figure 12.3. Data from: Botwinick, 1967.

crystallized intelligence A basic facet of intelligence, consisting of a person's knowledge base, or storehouse of accumulated information.

fluid intelligence A basic facet of intelligence, consisting of the ability to quickly master new intellectual activities.

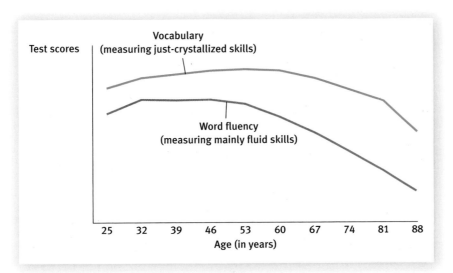

FIGURE 12.3: **Changes in two intellectual abilities over the decades in the Seattle Longitudinal Study:** Notice that scores on a test demanding a heavier component of fluid skills (word fluency, which asks people to name as many words as they can starting with a letter such as A, within a time limit) decrease after the late forties; while those on a totally crystallized test (vocabulary) stay stable into the sixties. But in general, this landmark study shows intellectual abilities peak in the fifties and decline in old age. Data from: Schaie, 1996.

scale, with its emphasis on putting together blocks or puzzles within a time limit, tends to measure fluid skills.

Fluid intelligence—because it depends on our nervous system being at its biological peak—is at its high point in our twenties and then declines. Because it measures the knowledge that we have amassed over years, crystallized intelligence tends to increase into late middle age. However, by later life, crystallized IQ declines, because our forgetting rate outpaces the new knowledge that we can absorb.

The good news is that, with regard to the most vital crystallized skill—negotiating relationships—age losses may not appear. While their slower information processing skills can impair older people's performance on standard theory of mind tasks (Henry and others, 2013), sixty-somethings seem just as good (or better) at judging people as younger adults (Hess & Smith, 2014). Plus, the losses on fluid intelligence tests are not as great for my baby boom cohort as for my parents' generation (Zelinski & Kennison, 2007), suggesting that the *Flynn effect* (mentioned in Chapters 1 and 7) also applies to the older years. The bad news is that the inevitable age-related losses on fluid IQ tests reflect a slowing of information processing that extends to many areas of life.

So, in any situation requiring multitasking, people may notice their abilities declining at a relatively young age. In your late thirties it seems harder to dribble a basketball while keeping your attention on the opposing team. You are having more trouble juggling cooking and having conversations with guests at your dinner parties than at age 25. In old age, these steady fluid losses, as you will see in Chapter 14, progress to the point where they truly interfere with daily life.

The distinction between fluid and crystallized intelligence accounts for why people in fast-paced jobs, such as air-traffic controllers, worry about being over the hill in their forties. It makes sense of why airline CEOs or professors reach their professional peak in their early sixties (but not much beyond!). Anytime an activity depends heavily on quickness, being older presents problems. Whenever an intellectual challenge involves stored knowledge, people improve into their fifties and beyond.

Suppose you are an artist or a writer. When can you expect to do your finest work? Researchers find that when a creative activity is dependent on being totally original, such as dancing or writing poetry, people tend to perform best in their thirties (see Simonton, 2007). If the form of creativity depends just on crystallized experience, such as writing nonfiction or, in my case, producing college textbooks (yes!), people perform at their best in their early sixties (Simonton, 1997, 2002). But in tracing the lives of people famous for their creative work, one researcher discovered that who we are *as people*, or our enduring abilities, outweighs the changes that occur with age. As Figure 12.4 on the next page shows, true geniuses outshine everyone else at any age (Simonton, 1997).

As his passion demands speedy mental processing, this gaming guru may feel "old" in his thirties. But this 60-year-old professor will probably see his teaching as better than ever today because his job depends almost exclusively on crystallized skills.

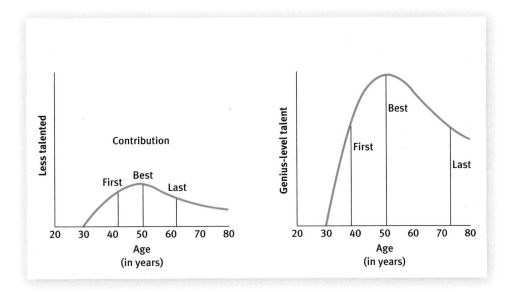

FIGURE 12.4: **Age-related changes in the career paths of geniuses and of less eminent creators:** This chart shows that people reach their peak period of creativity in midlife. However, the most gifted geniuses stand head and shoulders above their contemporaries at every age.
Data from: Simonton, 1997.

So, creatively or career-wise, expect to reach your peak in middle age (in most fields). Still, as you saw earlier with personality, expect to be the same person—to a large degree—as when you were younger. If you are exceptionally competent and creative at 30, you can stay exceptionally competent and creative at 70, or even 95. To illustrate this point, here are quotations from an interview study of creative people over age 60 (Csikszentmihalyi, 1996):

The poet Anthony Hecht, at age 70, commented:

I'm not as rigid as I was. And I can feel this in the poems . . . . They are freer metrically, . . . The earliest poems that I wrote were almost rigid in their eagerness not to make any errors. I'm less worried than that now.

(p. 215)

And the historian C. Vann Woodward, at the time in his mid-eighties, said:

Well, [today] I have . . . changed my . . . conclusions. . . . For example, that book on Jim Crow. I have done four editions of it . . . , and each time it changes . . . largely from criticisms that I have received. I think the worst mistake you could make as a historian is to be . . . contemptuous of what is new. You learn that there is nothing permanent in history. It's always changing.

(p. 216)

From Sigmund Freud, who put forth masterpieces into his eighties, to Frank Lloyd Wright, who designed world-class buildings into his ninth decade of life, history is full of examples showing that creativity can burn bright well into old age.

Is this middle-aged fashion designer at his creative peak? According to the research, the answer is yes. How proficient is he, compared to his peers ? For answers, we would want to look at this man's *enduring* creative talents from youth.

Staying IQ Smart

Returning to normally creative people, such as you and me, what qualities help *any* person stay cognitively sharp? What causes our intellectual capacities to decline at a younger-than-normal age?

HEALTH MATTERS. As our mind and our body are "all connected," the first key to staying intelligent as we age lies in staying physically fit. Hundreds of studies show that physical interventions, as varied as Taekwondo (van Dijk, Huijts, & Lodder, 2013) to resistance exercise (Chang and others, 2014), help keep intelligence fine-tuned.

The most powerful scientific evidence that our physical state affects our thinking comes from a mammoth U.S. study tracking thousands of adults. After testing physiological functions spanning heart rate to glucose metabolism, body mass index to cortisol levels, and more, scientists devised an overall physical deterioration score they labeled **allostatic load** (Karlamangla and others, 2014). As you can see in Figure 12.5, this global index of body dysregulation was strongly related to performance on executive function tests. To put these findings concretely: As an adult with an allostatic load score of 2.7 (the seventy-fifth percentile), you would rank almost three years older in your ability to quickly process information than someone of the same age with a ranking of 1 (the twenty-fifth percentile)!

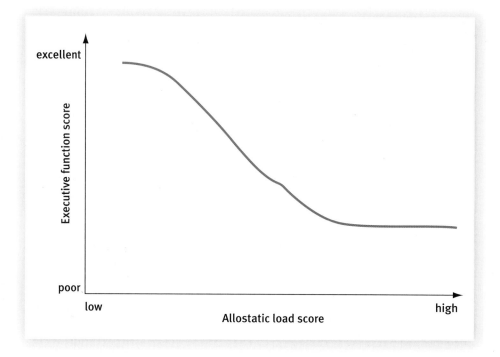

FIGURE 12.5: How allostatic load relates to scores on executive function tests in over a thousand U.S. adults with an average age in their late fifties: This chart shows concretely that body deterioration (measured by allostatic load score) is intimately tied to cognitive functioning in midlife (not just over age 65).
Data from: Karlamangla and others, 2014, p. 391.

Even more compelling (at least for me) is an eerie phenomenon gerontologists call **terminal drop.** In the first longitudinal studies of cognition, researchers were astonished to discover that they could predict which older people were more likely to die within the next few years by "larger than expected" losses in their verbal IQ (Cooney, Schaie, & Willis, 1988; Riegel & Riegel, 1972). If a person's scores on tests of vocabulary and other crystallized measures steeply declined, these changes were an ominous early warning sign of a soon-to-be-diagnosed life-threatening disease.

These studies haunted me the summer when I noticed that my father had suddenly aged mentally. My dad, who was always an intellectual whiz, had lost interest in the world. He was disoriented and depressed. A few months later, my worst fears were confirmed: My father was diagnosed with liver cancer, the illness that was to quickly end his life.

MENTAL STIMULATION (WITH PEOPLE) MAY MATTER. Because, recall from Chapter 3, environmental stimulation promotes synaptogenesis, the second key to staying intelligent should be a no-brainer: Exercise your mind!

To begin our discussion, let's return to the Big Five—this time to openness to experience. As this trait measures our tendency to reach out and seek stimulating experiences, it comes as no surprise that adults who score high on openness are apt to grow most dramatically in crystallized IQ (von Stumm, 2013).

Professional choices make a difference. People who work in complex, challenging jobs tend to become more mentally flexible with age (Schooler, 1999, 2001; Schooler, Mulatu, & Oates, 2004). Careers involving people—from hosting talk shows, to coaching teens—are especially likely to keep midlife people mentally on

allostatic load An overall score of body deterioration, gained from summing how a person functions on multiple physiological indexes. Allostatic load predicts cognitive performance during adult life.

terminal drop A research phenomenon in which a dramatic decline in an older person's scores on vocabulary tests and other measures of crystallized intelligence predicts having a terminal disease.

their toes (Finkel and others, 2009). So, one good intellectual insurance policy is to follow my advice in Chapters 10 and 11: Find a challenging, compelling, flow- inducing career!

But wait a second! Aren't adults with challenging jobs apt to be intelligent and well educated to begin with, and also younger health-wise than the average person their age? Couldn't these other forces account for why their crystallized abilities improve most with age? To *prove* that mental stimulation promotes cognitive growth, we might have to conduct an impossible (but fun) experiment: Assign young people to participate in a Jeopardy-like quiz show, or to host National Public Radio's *All Things Considered*, then compare their IQs to those of a control group in later middle age.

The good news, however, is that while we can't carry out this study with our species, it's fine to experiment on rats. And, when researchers put a group of rats in a large cage with challenging wheels and swings and then compared their cortexes with control animals, this quiz show treatment produced thicker, heavier brains (Diamond, 1988, 1993). Let's tentatively accept the widespread idea, then, that, just as physical exercise strengthens our muscles, mental exercise *may* produce a resilient mind. (I'd be careful about spending hours doing Suduko or other solitary brain-busting activities, however, on the principle that stimulation involving people works best.)

In sum, people in their forties and fifties are at the peak of their mental powers. But they will have more trouble mastering new cognitive challenges (those involving fluid skills) when under time pressure. To preserve their cognitive capacities as they age, people need to take care of their health and search out stimulating interpersonal and work experiences. And you can tell any worried 50-year-old family member who is considering going back to school that she should definitely go for it!

Obviously, this fifty-something coach needs to take care of his health in order to do his job— but the interpersonal challenges involved in dealing with these young athletes will keep him "on his toes" intellectually during his older years.

INTERVENTIONS: Keeping a Fine-Tuned Mind

Now, let's look at the lessons the research offers for any person who wants to stay mentally sharp as the years pass.

- Develop a hobby that involves physical exercise of some kind—from dancing to Taekwondo.

- Stay (or become) passionate to learn new things, and search out careers that expand your mind.

- As challenging, interpersonal activities matter most, search for careers that involve complex, people-oriented work, or try volunteer activities, like tutoring or serving on a community board.

- Understand that as you get older, new tasks involving complicated information processing will be difficult. To cope with these losses, you might adopt the following three-part strategy advocated by Paul Baltes called **selective optimization with compensation.**

selective optimization with compensation Paul Baltes's three principles for successful aging (and living): (1) selectively focusing on what is most important, (2) working harder to perform well in those top-ranking areas, and (3) relying on external aids to cope effectively.

As we move into the older years and notice we cannot function as well as we used to, Baltes believes that we need to (1) *selectively* focus on our most important activities, shedding less important priorities; (2) *optimize*, or work harder, to perform at our best in these most important areas of life; and (3) *compensate*, or rely on external aids, when we cannot cope on our own (Baltes, 2003; Baltes & Carstensen, 2003; Krampe & Baltes, 2003).

Let's take Mrs. Fernandez, whose passion is gourmet cooking. In her fifties, she might decide to give up some less important interest such as gardening, conserving her strength for the hours she spends at the stove (*selection*). She would need to work harder to prepare difficult dishes demanding split-second timing, such as her prize-winning soufflés (*optimization*). She might put a chair in the kitchen rather than

What can this white-haired college student do to ensure that he can keep up with the twenty-something classmates in this course? Try to take just this one class, rather than four or five, this term (selection); spend more time studying (optimization); and perhaps tape the lectures, so he doesn't have to just rely on his notes (compensation).

stand while preparing meals, or give up preparing dinner party feasts all by herself, and rely on her guests to bring an appetizer or dessert (*compensation*).

Although Baltes originally spelled out these guidelines to apply to successful aging, they are relevant to anyone coping with the demands of daily life—from parents struggling with *family–work conflict* (Young, Baltes, & Pratt, 2007; recall Chapter 11), to students, such as you, balancing the challenges of different courses. Because finding better life balance helps promote happiness at any age (Sheldon, Cummins, & Kamble, 2010), Table 12.5 offers a selective-optimization-with-compensation checklist to complete to help you enhance your life.

Table 12.5: Using Selective Optimization with Compensation to Construct a Fulfilling Life

Selection: List your top-ranking priorities. Estimate how much time you spend on these agendas.

1. _____   hrs _____

2. _____   hrs _____

Can you increase the time you spend on these most critical agendas and decrease the time you spend on less important concerns?

Optimization: List strategies that you could use to perform better in your top-priority areas.

1. _____

2. _____

Compensation: List external aids that might help you be more successful in managing your time and/or family and friends you can rely on to take over some jobs when you feel overwhelmed.

1. _____

2. _____

3. _____

Taking a Nontraditional Approach: Examining Postformal Thought

So far, I have been mainly discussing the insights related to intelligence derived from traditional IQ tests. But look back at the quotations from the older poet Anthony Hecht and the historian C. Vann Woodward, on page 371. The qualities these creative people were describing have nothing to do with putting together puzzles or blocks. What stands out about these men is their openness to experience and sensitivity to their inner lives. Given that standard IQ tests were devised to predict performance in school, perhaps it would make sense to come up with a test to capture the qualities that define thinking intelligently during adult life.

Jean Piaget described qualitative changes in cognition that occur in children as they age. So developmentalists drew inspiration from this landmark theory to construct an adult-relevant measure of IQ (Labouvie-Vief, 1992; Rybash, Hoyer, & Roodin, 1986; Sinnott, 2003).

Recall Piaget believed that we develop cognitively through hands-on experience with the world. Although Piaget thought that the pinnacle of mental development occurs when teens reach formal operations and reason like "real scientists," wouldn't years of living produce a more advanced kind of thinking called **postformal thought?** Let's look at what separates this adult intelligence from Piaget's formal operational stage:

POSTFORMAL THOUGHT IS RELATIVISTIC. As you saw in Chapter 9, adolescents in formal operations can argue rationally about rights and wrongs. With age and

postformal thought A uniquely adult form of intelligence that involves being sensitive to different perspectives, making decisions based on one's inner feelings, and being interested in exploring new questions.

life experience, we realize that most real-world problems do not have clear-cut "right" answers. Postformal thinkers accept the validity of different perspectives. They embrace the ambiguities of life. This awareness that the truth is relative does not mean that postformal thinkers avoid making decisions or having strong beliefs. As with C. Vann Woodward, people who reason postformally make better decisions *because* they are open to changing their ideas when faced with competing perspectives that make sense.

POSTFORMAL THOUGHT IS FEELING-ORIENTED. Teenagers in formal operations feel that by using logic, they can make sense of the world. Postformal thinkers go beyond rationality to reason in a different way. Because there is often no objectively "right" answer to life's dilemmas, thinking postformally means relying more on one's gut feelings as the basis for making decisions. As with Anthony Hecht, people who reason postformally are less rigid, more open, fully in touch with their inner lives.

POSTFORMAL THOUGHT IS QUESTION-DRIVEN. Adolescents want to get the correct answers and finish or solve tasks. Postformal thinkers are less focused on solutions. They thrive on developing new questions and reconsidering their opinions. As you saw with both Anthony Hecht and Prof. Woodward, people who think postformally enjoy coming up with new, interesting ways of looking at the world.

Clearly, we cannot measure this kind of intelligence by giving tests in which questions have a single correct answer. We need to adopt the strategy that Lawrence Kohlberg used with his moral dilemmas (recall Chapter 9): Present people with real-world situations and examine the way they think. How would you respond to this sample problem?

> John is known to be a heavy drinker, especially when he goes to parties. Mary, John's wife, warns him that if he gets drunk one more time, she will leave him and take the children. John goes to an office party and comes home drunk. Does Mary leave him? How sure are you of your answer?

If you answered this question rigidly ("Mary said she would leave, so she should; yes, I am sure I am right"), you are not thinking postformally. You must explore the consequences of leaving for Mary, for John, and for the children. You must understand that any answer you gave would be a judgment call.

Actually, astute readers may be thinking that the qualities involved in postformal thinking have uncanny parallels to the same personality attributes involved in growing emotionally with age: Be open to experience; confront and process negative life events in a thoughtful way.

Since post-formal thinking seems so linked to our enduring personality, it makes sense that simply growing older does not make people more capable of reasoning in this wiser, more "mature" way. However, one important facet of wisdom does increase in later life—our ability to take a more realistic view of societal change.

Psychologists (Grossmann and others, 2010) asked adults to talk about social/ethnic conflicts: "The Issi want to preserve that nation's traditions, and the Assari want social change. What will happen? What would you advise?" They wondered: Would older people discuss the problem from each group's vantage point and realize that the outcome was uncertain? Would they understand change comes gradually and stress the need for compromise?

As you can see by the blue dots in Figure 12.6, the answer was yes. Notice that a few middle-aged adults fit into the wise category. About half of elderly adults do not. But after the early sixties—wisdom takes off.

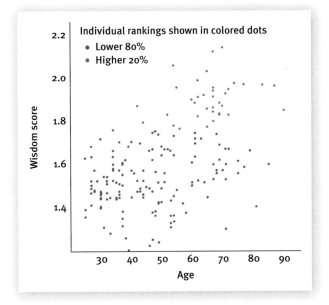

FIGURE 12.6: Age distribution of "wisdom" scores as judged by the way a random sample of Michigan adults of different ages reasons about scenarios involving ethnic and social conflicts: In this interesting study, notice that wisdom rates dramatically rise among the people in their sixties (blue dots), although about half of all elderly adults don't make it into the wise category (red dots).
Data from: Grossmann and others, 2010, p. 7248.

Now that she is 60, this woman may qualify as truly wise, particularly if she has the qualities listed here.

Rolf Bruderer/Masterfile

Now, returning to what we have learned so far, what lessons does this whole chapter have for constructing a fulfilling life? Table 12.6 summarizes *all* of these insights in a chart that offers tips for flourishing during adult life.

Until this point, I have been discussing issues that are relevant to people in their twenties, their forties and fifties, and even adults aged 95. In the next section, I'll explore transitions unique to the middle years.

Table 12.6: How to Flourish During Adulthood: A Summary Table

1. Develop a generative mission. If you feel that your life lacks purpose, try volunteering or helping others—it's addictive!

2. Try to view your failures and upsetting life experiences as learning lessons. Understand life's disappointments offer us our best opportunities to grow, provided we openly confront and process these changes.

3. To keep your mind fine-tuned, take care of your physical health and be open to experience—putting yourself in mentally stimulating situations involving people.

4. When you feel in role conflict—or that your life lacks balance—establish priorities, work hard in your most important areas, and rely on external aids to help you perform.

5. Think postformally: Be open to different perspectives; question your established ideas and ways of thinking; reflect on your feelings to help guide you in making wise life choices.

Tying It All Together

1. Andres is an air traffic controller and Mick is a historian. Pick which man is likely to reach his career peak earlier, and explain the reasons why.

2. Your author (me) is writing another textbook on lifespan development. I am also learning a new video game. Identify each type of intellectual skill involved and describe how my abilities in each of these areas are likely to change now that I am in my sixties.

3. Rick says, "I've got too much on my plate. I can't do anything well." Identify the theory discussed in this chapter that would be most helpful in addressing this problem, and explain what this theory would advise.

4. Kayla is contemplating breaking up with her boyfriend, Mark, because, she says, "He doesn't give me the attention I need." Name the advice a postformal thinker would *not* give to Kayla.
   a. "Leave the bum!"
   b. "Think of what is going on from Mark's perspective—for instance, is he overworked?"
   c. "Whatever choice you make, look at all the angles."
   d. "There may be no 'right decision.' Go with your gut."

Answers to the Tying It All Together questions can be found at the end of this chapter.

Midlife Roles and Issues

As I mentioned at the beginning of this chapter, classic midlife events can be sources of joy and issues for concern. On the uplifting side, there is that terrific life experience called grandparenthood. The downside may be the need to care for disabled aged parents, and to face sexual decline. Let's now look at these "aging phase of life" joys and concerns one by one.

Grandparenthood

The (Lakota) grandparents always took . . . the first grandchild to raise. They think that . . . they're more mature . . . and they could teach the children a lot more than the young parents. . . . I'm still trying to carry on that tradition because my grandmother raised me most of the time up until I was nine years old.

(quoted in Weibel-Orlando, 1999, p. 187)

This comment from Mrs. Big Buffalo, a Native American grandmother, reminds us that every adult role, from spouse, to parent, to worker, to grandparent, is shaped by our society. Native American and Hawaiian grandparents are apt to see raising grandchildren as "our custom" (Yancura, 2013). In Western cultures, where we put a priority on the nuclear family, grandparents are more peripheral to family life. In most societies, maternal grandparents (the daughter's parents) are more involved with the grandchildren. In China, it's the moms and dads of sons (Xu, Silverstein, & Chi, 2014).

Still, even in Western nations, where tradition dictates taking a hands-off stance, in our era of single parents and full-time working mothers, grandparents must be more involved than in the past (Dunifon, 2013). As I implied in Chapter 4, many women today help care for an infant grandchild while their sons and daughters work (Hank & Buber, 2009; McNally, Share, & Murray, 2014). Doesn't this impulse to watch over the youngest, most vulnerable family members suggest that there is a basic benefit built into grandparenthood?

Exploring the Grandparent Mission to Care

Because human beings are the only species with female bodies programmed to outlast the reproductive years, evolutionary theorists argue, the answer is yes. Menopause, they believe, evolved to offer an extra layer of mothers, without their own childrearing distractions, to care for the young (Coall & Hertwig, 2010). Put bluntly, grandmas function to help our species survive.

This lifesaving function is apparent in subsistence societies. Remember from reading the Experiencing the Lifespan box in Chapter 3 that, in Ghana, a grandma often steps in to take care of the family so her daughter can make the weekly trek to the clinic to stave off death in a young, malnourished child. Therefore, in Africa, the presence of a grandmother reduces mortality rates during the early years of life (Gibson & Mace, 2005).

In our culture, grandparents do their lifesaving selectively. As **family watchdogs**, they step in during a crisis to help the younger family members cope (Dunifon, 2013). At these times, their true value shines through. Grandparents are the family's safety net (Troll, 1983).

In more normal times, grandparents function as mediators, helping parents and children resolve their differences (Kulik, 2007). They serve as cheerleaders and reinforcers of prized family norms (Dunifon, 2013) ("Wow you got on the honor role. Nana is SO proud!"). Grandparents can be the family cement, keeping cousins close. From Christmas get-togethers to Thanksgiving dinners, "Grandma's house" is often the focal meeting point—the place where cousins regularly reconnect. As one developmentalist put it:

Grandparents serve as symbols of connectedness within and between lives; as people who can listen and have the time to do so; as reserves of time, help, and attention; as links to the unknown past; as people who are sufficiently varied, flexible, and complex to defy easy categories and clear-cut roles.

(Hagestad, 1985, p. 48)

You may notice this complexity and flexibility in your own family. One grandparent might be a shadowy figure; another may qualify as a second mother or best friend.

family watchdogs A basic role of grandparents, which involves monitoring the younger family member's well-being and intervening to provide help in a crisis.

From jumping on trampolines to taking the grandchildren to the local lake, grandparents fulfill this joyous life role in their own distinctive, personal ways.

For this grandma, spending the day with her grandson and her daughter-in-law is an absolute joy. Still, she has to be careful not to criticize this young woman's child-rearing skills or risk being cut off from future visits.

Some grandparents love to jump on trampolines; others show their love in "baking cookies" ways. An intellectual grandpa may take you to lectures; a fishing grandpa may take you on the lake.

Which Grandparents Are More or Less Involved?

What forces determine how involved a particular grandparent is likely to be? Gender matters. Study after study agrees that grandparenthood is a more joyous, emotionally central role for women than men (Findler and others, 2013). Perhaps because they have spent so many decades as "old style" distant dads, grandfathers more frequently report having trouble connecting emotionally with their grandchildren than do their wives (Ben Shlomo, 2014).

Physical proximity makes a huge difference—whether grandchildren live around the corner or many miles away (Hakoyama & MaloneBeach, 2013). As one grandfather sadly mentioned, "We get to see her maybe once or twice a year, and every time . . . I'm thrilled with the development I see but I am disappointed that I had very little to do with it" (Bangerter & Waldron, 2014, p. 92).

Age matters—being a younger grandparent (Ben Shlomo, 2014) and, especially, having young granddaughters and grandsons. Although, grandparent–grandchild involvement can be intense during the early years of life, just as they separate from their parents, older children naturally leave the grandparent orbit and prefer to be around their peers. As one grandparent lamented: "We'll come for Thanksgiving and she'll (the 19-year-old daughter) have dinner with us and then say, 'I gotta go meet my friends' . . . (and I'm thinking). Well your grandparents just drove 400 miles (to see you)" (adapted from Bangerter & Waldron, 2014).

These quotations—from a study exploring grandparent–teenager closeness—suggest that technology *can* erode these barriers of distance and age. Here is how one woman described a Skype visit with her 13-year-old granddaughter: "She just . . . put the computer on her bed and so we did a kind of virtual tour of her room and it was just like she and I were hanging . . . out. No one else in the house even knew we were talking . . . and it was really cool" (Bangerter & Waldron, 2014, p. 93).

And a side benefit of friending your grandchild on Facebook is that you can feel closely connected without having *any* conversation at all: "I keep my mouth shut" said another grandma. "They know I'm there (on Facebook) and they are comfortable with it . . . if I got on the phone with them and tried to have them tell me . . . the things they do, it wouldn't happen" (2014, p. 93).

Grandparent Problems

Grandparents take pride in the fact that they are free to "be there" to lovingly listen, and to leave the disciplining to mom and dad. But my discussion implies grandparents are really not free. For one thing, it's important to hold your tongue and not criticize your child's parenting, because your access to the grandchildren depends on having a good relationship with the generation in between (Sims & Rofail, 2013; Lou and others, 2013).

Now imagine your built-in barriers if you are a paternal grandmother, the mother of a son. Because women are closer to their own mothers (versus their mothers-in-law) and, in Western nations, control the family's social relationships, paternal grandparents are in danger of "not being there" as much as they would like.

Being in this situation created heartache for a friend of mine, when this preference for maternal moms cost her physical proximity. Her daughter-in-law decided to move across the country to be close to her own mother in Seattle, rather than stay in New York City—transforming my friend into the distant grandma she never wanted to be.

The allegiance to one's family of origin can have devastating effects after a divorce. When the wife gets custody, and especially if she remarries and has other children, she can lock her ex-husband's parents out of the family's life (Sims & Rofail, 2013).

When people get locked out of seeing their grandchildren—whether due to a divorce, being a disliked paternal grandma, or because of disputes with a biological child—you would think that courts might grant these grandparents visitation rights. You would be wrong. Some ethicists argue that simply being a grandparent doesn't give people *any* intrinsic legal rights (Draper, 2013). Yes, many states have legislation allowing grandparent visitation depending on "the best interests of the child." But consider the situation in Florida (and Canada), where these statutes have been struck down as unconstitutional, in favor of the idea that parents alone, except in cases of maltreatment, are perfectly free to decide who their child sees (Beiner and others, 2014).

Then there is the opposite situation—feeling compelled to "be there" more than you want. Let's spell out a typical scenario: Your daughter (or son) wants you to watch the baby while she is at work. You don't want to disappoint your child, but you want your own life. The *role conflict* is especially intense when grandparents assume a more demanding job—becoming full-time parents again.

Caregiving grandparents take full responsibility for raising their grandchildren. In recent decades, the ranks of these grandparents have swelled. In the 2010 census, 7.5 million U.S. children lived with a grandparent. The number of grandparents having primary care for that grandchild doubled over the past 40 years (Rubin, 2013). Although they span the socioeconomic spectrum, caregiving grandparents tend to be poor. In extreme cases, these front-line caregivers must petition the court for custody and formally adopt a granddaughter or grandson.

How does it feel to take this step? As you might expect, custodial grandparents are typically deeply distressed, mourning the fact that their own son or daughter—often because of incarceration, or drug or alcohol problems—is incapable of performing this job (Rubin, 2013). They may feel angry at being forced into this "off-time" role. But they often feel a generative, "watchdog" responsibility to protect their flesh and blood (Hayslip & Patrick, 2003). Here is what one woman had to say to the police after her drug-abusing daughter took off with a grandchild and stole her car:

> [The police in a different state] said to me, "Ma'am, if you don't get here in 72 hours, then your grandson will be put in the [state protective services system] and you will have to fight to get him." I said, "I will fight from the moment I get there if my grandson is not there for me."
>
> (quoted in Climo, Terry, & Lay, 2002, p. 25)

And another woman summed up the general feeling of the custodial grandmothers in this study when she blurted out: "Nobody is going to take [my grandson] away from me. I have done everything except give birth to him" (quoted in Climo, Terry, & Lay, 2002, p. 25).

These women, mainly in their late fifties, complained about feeling physically drained: "Some days I feel really old, like I just can't keep up with him" (quoted in Climo, Terry, & Lay, 2002, p. 23). They had mixed emotions about their situation: "Some days I feel real blessed by it, other days I want to sit and cry" (p. 25). They sometimes described redemption sequences, too: "God has given me this wonderful little boy to raise and I'm thinking, 'How many people get the opportunity to do it a second time?'" (p. 26).

Parent Care

Ask friends and family members and they will tell you that becoming a grandparent is one of the joys of being middle-aged. Words such as *joy* and *fulfillment*

caregiving grandparents
Grandparents who have taken on full responsibility for raising their grandchildren.

parent care Adult children's care for their disabled elderly parents.

do not come to mind when we imagine that second classic midlife role: caring for elderly parents. Researchers who study **parent care** speak of this family job using phrases like "burden," "hassles," and "strain" (Hunt, 2003; Son and others, 2007).

Caring for parents violates the basic principle in Western cultures that parents give to their children, not the reverse (Belsky, 1999). So, it makes sense that while older people may welcome help from siblings or a spouse, they prefer being the "givers" (or help providers) with an adult child. Moreover, as you might expect from the vow "in sickness and in health," elderly spouses find caregiving far less burdensome than daughters or sons do (Perrig-Chiello & Hutchison, 2010).

Actually, let me get personal and relate all of this to Chapter 11. When older people are happily married, sacrificing for a chronically ill spouse is *not* a burden, but a source of fulfillment. It's definitely a "labor of love."

Unfortunately, this is often not true with parent care. Because caring for an ill parent is typically a woman's job, it can produce role conflict, when a daughter or daughter-in law must cut back her work hours, or leave her career. If, as is increasingly true, a caregiving child is in her sixties or seventies, parent care may put a damper in that child's retirement plans or interfere with the need to care for her frail, disabled spouse. More rarely, a woman is pulled between two intergenerational commitments, caring for her elderly parent and watching the grandchildren full time.

At this point, I need to set the record straight: The phenomenon called the "sandwich generation"—women pulled between caring for their *young* children and disabled *elderly* parents— is fairly rare. Since parent care typically occurs in the fifties, that job usually occurs during empty nest, grandparent stage. Moreover, the classic concept that people have a predictable "midlife crisis" is another myth. The research facts show it doesn't exist for most adults.

Finally, the belief that in Asian cultures or in U.S. groups with more collectivist values, children are "happy" to care for aging parents is also untrue (Freeman and others, 2010; Hashizume, 2010). In Japan, for instance, with polls showing one in two middle-aged people want to live apart from their children when they get old, hands-on caring for elderly parents is no longer a cultural norm (Qu, 2014). In one U.S. study, if children reported that helping their aged parent was "a family obligation," they felt under *more* stress when actually providing care (Sayegh & Knight, 2011). How stressful, *generally*, is parent care?

The answer—as *developmental systems theory* predicts—is "it varies" (Merz, Schulze, & Schuengel, 2010). If the older adult's needs are minimal, a daughter is not working, and/or she is providing intense care but getting a lot of support, caring for an aged parent is no problem (DiRosa and others, 2011). But coping with other stressful commitments (such as working and caring for the grandchildren full time) and especially feeling one's brothers and sisters are

Will this middle-aged child find parent care an impossible stress? Keys lie in her parent's personality, the amount of help she needs to provide, her other commitments, and whether this daughter feels her siblings are doing their fair share.

not doing their "fair share" is a recipe for depression and poor health (Koerner, Shirai, & Kenyon, 2010; Merrill, 1996).

The older person's personality looms large. Parent care, as you will see in Chapter 14, poses particular challenges with Alzheimer's disease. According to one alarming study, if a caregiver perceived a parent as difficult and manipulative and became resentful, the situation could escalate to screaming, yelling, or threatening that person with a nursing home (Smith and others, 2011).

Still, caring for a disabled parent can have the opposite effect. It may offer its own *redemption sequence*, giving children the chance to repay a beloved mother or father for years of care (Kramer & Thompson, 2002). Moreover, as with other life stresses, productively confronting this challenge can help midlife children grow emotionally and become "wiser," especially about planning for their lives when they become old (Pope, 2013).

Balancing the need to respect a frail older parent's autonomy and knowing when to intervene (Funk, 2010); being generative with the grandchildren, but not intrusive, while balancing your own and your family's needs: These are the kinds of complex relationship challenges that explain why, in Jung's evocative words, the long "afternoon of life" *may* teach us to be wise.

Body Image, Sex, and Menopause

Jung famously believed, "We cannot live life's afternoon by the program of life's morning"—meaning that the key to growing mature with age lies in giving up the quest for physical beauty in favor of more spiritual concerns. But judged by our contemporary passion for cosmetic surgery, how many twenty-first century adults fit Jung's idea of "wise"?

The (somewhat) good news is that while fifty-something females do love to catalog each sign of physical decay, body dissatisfaction does not increase in midlife. Moreover, unless they are particularly age-phobic (Slevec & Tiggemann, 2011), many middle-aged women take a kind of middle position with regard to Jung's advice: rejecting body-altering measures, such as facelifts, but wanting to age as beautifully as possible by using creams and dyes (Muise & Desmarais, 2010). The media presence of "mature" sex symbols such as Sharon Stone suggest that today we don't have to give up our sexual selves until fairly far into life's afternoon (Weitz, 2010). What really happens sexually to *both* men and women as they age?

In her late-fifties, Sharon Stone is a glorious testament to the fact that youthful sex symbols can remain just as alluring (and natural looking!) well into the afternoon of life.

Exploring the Facts Relating to Physical Sexual Decline

The findings for middle-aged men are somewhat depressing. Older males need more time to develop an erection. They are more likely to lose an erection before ejaculation occurs. Their ejaculations become less intense. By their fifties, most men are not able to have another erection for 12 to 24 hours after having had sex (Masters & Johnson, 1966). This slower arousal to ejaculation tempo explains the popularity of the billion-dollar market for erection-stimulating drugs. Desire remains, but by late middle age, many men need extra help to implement their plans.

Because their sexual apparatus does not critically depend on blood flow, older women can be just as orgasmic at 80 as at age 20. Unfortunately, however, in middle age, women are more apt to turn off to sex than men. The reason is environmental: being without a partner (due to widowhood or divorce); having an older spouse with a chronic disease; not having anyone respond to you as a sexual human being. Menopause can indirectly affect sexuality, too.

Menopause typically occurs at about age 50, when estrogen production falls off dramatically and women stop ovulating. Specifically, the defining marker of menopause is not having menstruated for a year. As estrogen production declines and a woman approaches this milestone, her menstrual cycle becomes more irregular. During this sexual winding-down period, called *perimenopause*, as the stereotypes described in Table 12.7 on the next page suggest, many women have other physical symptoms, such as night sweats and hot flashes (sudden sensations of heat) (Lerner-Geva and others, 2010).

menopause The age-related process, occurring at about age 50, in which ovulation and menstruation stop due to the decline of estrogen.

Table 12.7: Stereotypes and Facts About Menopause

1. **The stereotype:** Women have terrible physical symptoms while going through menopause.

   The facts: Researchers find that an upsurge of minor physical complaints does occur during the few years preceding menopause: lack of energy, backaches, and joint stiffness. Many women experience hot flashes and some sleeplessness. Still, there is variability from person to person, and complaints vary from culture to culture. In one study, while fewer than half the women in a Scandinavian poll reported difficult symptoms, 2 out of 3 U.S. women did (Nappi & Kokot-Kierepa, 2010).

2. **The stereotype:** Women are very moody while going through menopause.

   The facts: Statistically speaking, women may show a minor rise in anxiety and depression as they approach menopause, when estrogen levels are waning (Avis and others, 2004). However, more recent research suggests menopause has no impact on mental health (Soares, 2013).

3. **The stereotype:** Women feel empty, "dried up," old, and asexual after menopause.

   The facts: Many women find menopause a relief. For instance, one-third of the women in Taiwan and almost half of all Australian women in a cross-cultural study said that they were happy not to have to deal with a period every month (Fu, Anderson, & Courtney, 2003). In another Danish study, at menopause, most women felt that they were entering a new, freer (and sexier) stage of life (Hvas, 2001).

This estrogen loss produces changes in the reproductive tract. After menopause, the vaginal walls thin out and become more fragile. The vagina shortens, and its opening narrows. The size of the clitoris and labia shrinks and blood flow tends to decrease. It takes longer after arousal for lubrication to begin (Masters & Johnson, 1966; Saxon, Etten, & Perkins, 2010). Women don't produce as much fluid as before. These changes can make having intercourse so painful that some women stop having sex.

wavebreakmedia/Shutterstock

The secret is that this 70-something couple may be just as passionate now as ever—because they have a more inclusive definition of lovemaking than having intercourse!

Baring the *Real* Sexual Truth

By now readers might be sadly thinking, "I'd better enjoy my current sex life, because my sexual self will probably evaporate when I get old." Not so fast!

Yes, being partnerless, or having a husband who is ill, can stop sexuality in the older years (Syme and others, 2013). However, well into later life, many couples still enjoy sex (Trudel and others, 2014). In one national Swedish study, 2 in 3 men in that nation over age 70 reported still having intercourse. The odds for 70-plus women, while 1 in 3, still show that female sexuality remains alive and well far beyond the middle years (Beckman and others, 2014).

And if you assume male performance problems signal the death of decent sex, think again. In one survey, while admitting their erectile problems were troubling, middle-aged and elderly men rejected the idea that erectile capacity defined their sexual selves (Thompson & Barnes, 2013). In an interview study, many reported becoming better lovers during life's afternoon (and evening). As Frank, age 71, explained: "As a sexual partner I am probably more considerate . . . Between 50 and 70 I . . . became more tender" (Sandberg, 2013, p. 271).

Another 84-year-old named Owe shared this delightful under-the-covers account: "It's (sex is) more carefree . . . They (people Owe's age) are lying naked together caressing each other's bodies and saying tender words . . . fondling the genitals from time to time. Back then it was the arousal and everything was over. . . . And everyday life was back. . . . This is more elongated; it can stretch over an entire evening or day" (adapted from Sandberg, 2013, p. 269).

This lovely description makes sense of why, in one survey, during their older years, men and women, lesbian, gay, and bisexual couples, described great sex in similar ways: It's all about intimacy, communication, and authenticity. Moreover, many respondents reported that their current lovemaking was better than the sex they had when young! (See Kleinplatz and others, 2013.) The only group who disagreed were sex therapists—who, perhaps by focusing mainly on what goes wrong physically, believed that sex automatically becomes more dysfunctional and dissatisfying with age.

Table 12.8 summarizes the male and female changes described in this section, and offers advice for staying passionate about sex as you age.

How do we change physically, cognitively, and personality-wise as we move into old age? Stay tuned for answers in the next part of the book, as I focus on "the evening, or twilight, of life."

Table 12.8: Staying Passionate About Sex with Age

FOR MEN

Problem	Solutions
Trouble maintaining or achieving an erection	1. Understand that some physiological slowing down is normal, and do not be alarmed by problems performing. Sexual relations need to occur more slowly; manual stimulation may be necessary to achieve erection and orgasm. Also understand that some of these very changes may make you a more creative, sensitive lover as you grow old.
	2. Stay healthy. Avoid sexually impairing conditions such as heart disease. If possible, avoid medications that have sexual side effects (such as antidepressants and blood pressure pills).
	3. If troubled by chronic problems performing, explore the medicines that are available for treating these issues, as well as devices such as the penile pump.

FOR WOMEN

Problem	Solutions
No sexual signals coming from the outside world	1. Stay sexy, be conscious of your physical appearance.
	2. Find a partner (there are many!) who appreciates you as a sexual human being.
Decline in estrogen levels makes having sexual intercourse painful	1. Consider using lubricants, such as K-Y Jelly, when having sex.
	2. Consider hormone replacement therapy (but discuss this with your doctor).

Concluding advice for both sexes: Don't accept the stereotype that sexuality declines with age. Sex has the potential to become more emotionally gratifying (meaning affection-centered) as people grow old.

Tying It All Together

1. Juanita, aged 4, has two grandmothers, Karen and Louisa. Grandma Karen is much more involved with Juanita than is Grandma Louisa. List two possible reasons why this might be. As Juanita gets older you might expect her to get *more/less* involved with Grandma Karen.

2. Poll your class. Do most people report being closest to their maternal grandmother (or grandfather)? Does your class feel that technology is increasing their sense of connection to grandparents (and, if so, perhaps they could give specific examples).

3. Kim is caring for her elderly mother, who just had a stroke. Each of the following should make Kim's job feel easier *except*:

   a. Kim views caregiving as an opportunity to repay her mom for years of love.

   b. Kim's mom has a mellow personality.

   c. Kim has several siblings.

4. For the following "age and sexuality" statements, select the right gender: *Males/ Females* decline the most physiologically *Male/female* sexuality is most affected by social issues (such as not having a partner).

5. Summarize, to a friend, how sexuality changes in middle and later life.

Answers to the Tying It All Together questions can be found at the end of this chapter.

SUMMARY

Although the boundaries of middle age span about age 40 to the early sixties, many older adults describe themselves as middle aged. Personality, specifically neuroticism, predicts whether midlife adults have an upbeat or gloomy view of the future.

Research on the **Big Five** traits shows scores on neuroticism and the other core dimensions of personality predict a variety of life outcomes. In particular, conscientiousness sets us up to age healthier and be successful in work and love. Because genetic and environmental forces converge to promote consistency, our core personality probably doesn't change much as we age. Still, people grow in conscientiousness and other positive Big Five traits as they assume adult roles. People also are more resilient, less self-critical, and seem more altruistic at older ages. Dan McAdams's research exploring Erikson's **generativity** shows that our priorities shift to "other-centered concerns" during later midlife. Generativity, while not related to **hedonic happiness**, defines **eudaimonic happiness**—living a meaningful, fulfilling adult life.

In their autobiographies, highly generative adults produce a **commitment script** and describe **redemption sequences**—negative events that turned out for the best. They also more often describe defining life events involving caring family members or teachers. The fact that African Americans may often be highly generative suggests that adversity—in moderation and handled productively—may produce emotional growth. Growing emotionally (and being highly generative) is most apt to occur when people are economically secure and live in "generative nations."

Early studies using the **Wechsler Adult Intelligence Scale (WAIS)** found that people reach their intellectual peak in their twenties—although scores on the timed performance scale tests declined more rapidly than did scores on the verbal scale. The **Seattle Longitudinal Study**—which controlled for the biases of this research—showed the same change pattern, but it also indicated that we reach our intellectual peak in midlife.

Fluid intelligence, the capacity to master unfamiliar cognitive challenges quickly, is at its height early in adulthood, and then it declines. **Crystallized intelligence,** our knowledge base, rises until well into middle age. In professions that heavily depend on crystallized knowledge—versus fast information processing—people do well into their sixties. Creativity reaches its peak in midlife, although our basic talents predict our real-world performance (at any age) best.

Staying healthy, indexed by having a low **allostatic load,** and seeking out stimulating interpersonal activities (and jobs) can prevent age-related cognitive decline. **Terminal drop,** a significant loss in IQ, can indicate that a person is near death. Using **selective optimization with compensation** helps people successfully cope with age-related losses and live more successfully at any life stage.

Postformal thinkers are sensitive to diverse perspectives, interested in exploring questions, and attuned to their inner feelings in making life decisions. The specific aspect of wise thinking, involving realistically reasoning about social conflicts in particular, may rise during later life.

Midlife Roles and Issues

Grandmotherhood may have evolved to help our species survive. In our society, grandparents act as **family watchdogs,** stepping in when the younger family members need help. Gender, physical proximity, the grandchildren's ages, and especially people's relationship with the parent generation, determine people's involvement in this joyous but constrained life role. Because women tend to be closer to their own mothers, paternal grandmothers are at risk of being less involved with the grandchildren than they want. At its extreme, people may be cut off from seeing the grandchildren after a divorce, or due to having alienated the parents. The opposite problem, being forced to be too involved, at its extreme occurs with **caregiving grandparents,** especially people needing to take full legal custody of a child.

Parent care is another family role that some middle-aged daughters may assume. While often stressful, a variety of forces affect how women feel when caring for a disabled parent, and this life role can sometimes promote emotional growth. Another midlife concern involves declining sexuality. For males, erectile capacity steadily declines. Although women show few (or no) physical sexual changes, **menopause** has the side effect of making intercourse more painful. The main reason, however, that older women may give up sex is social: being without a partner, not being viewed as sexual human beings. First-person accounts of old-age sexuality belie the standard gloom-and-doom decline message, suggesting that lovemaking can become more gratifying in later life.

KEY TERMS

Big Five, p. 358

generativity, p. 363

hedonic happiness, p. 364

eudaimonic happiness, p. 364

commitment script, p. 366

redemption sequence, p. 366

Wechsler Adult Intelligence Scale (WAIS), p. 368

Seattle Longitudinal Study, p. 368

crystallized intelligence, p. 369

fluid intelligence, p. 369

allostatic load, p. 372

terminal drop, p. 372

selective optimization with compensation, p. 373

postformal thought, p. 374

family watchdogs, p. 377

caregiving grandparents, p. 379

parent care, p. 380

menopause, p. 381

ANSWERS TO Tying It All Together QUIZZES

Exploring Personality (and Well-Being)

1. a and b

2. a

3. The answers here are up to you, but it would be best to confront and process that event in a way that might promote personal growth.

Exploring Intelligence (and Wisdom)

1. Andres will reach his career peak far earlier than Mick because his job is heavily dependent on fluid skills. A historian's job depends almost exclusively on crystallized skills.

2. Textbook writing is a crystallized skill, so I should be just as good at my life passion during my sixties—provided I don't get ill. Playing video games depends heavily on fluid skills, so I will be far worse now than when I was young.

3. The theory that applies to Rick's problem—"too much on his plate"—is Baltes's selective optimization with compensation: He needs to (1) prioritize and shed less important jobs, (2) work harder in his top-ranking areas, and (3) use external aids to help him cope.

4. a

Midlife Roles and Issues

1. Karen may live closer to Emma. Most likely she is a maternal grandma. As Juanita gets older you would expect her to be *less* involved with her grandma.

2. Answers here will vary.

3. c

4. *Males* decline the most physiologically; *female* sexuality is most affected by social issues (such as the lack of a partner).

5. Although the "physical sexual facts" show declining performance is universal, especially for men, many people remain sexually active into later life. Because sex is more centered on affection, many older adults say lovemaking is actually better at their age.

Later Life

This two-chapter book part, devoted to life's last stage, highlights how we develop and change as we move through senior citizenhood (the sixties and beyond). Chapter 13 covers issues relevant to both the young-old and old-old years. Chapter 14 emphasizes concerns that become pressing priorities in advanced old age.

Chapter 13—**Later Life: Cognitive and Socioemotional Development** begins with an overview of the historic twenty-first-century age boom, then looks at how memory changes as we age. During this discussion, you will not only learn a wealth of information about memory and aging, but also get insights into how to improve memory at any age. Then, we turn to the emotional side of life. I'll outline a creative theory and research spelling out why old age might be the best life stage, and then offer tips for living meaningfully at this pinnacle age. The second half of this chapter tackles those major later-life transitions: retirement and widowhood.

Chapter 14—**The Physical Challenges of Old Age** begins by describing the aging process and how it progresses into disease and disability. Then, I'll explore late-life sensory and motor changes and offer a detailed look at that most feared old-age illness: Alzheimer's disease. At the end of this chapter, you will learn about the living arrangements and health-care options available to people when old-age frailties strike. This chapter will open your eyes to the challenges of age-related disabilities and, hopefully, sensitize you to the need to change the wider world to promote an ideal older adult–environment fit.

PART VI

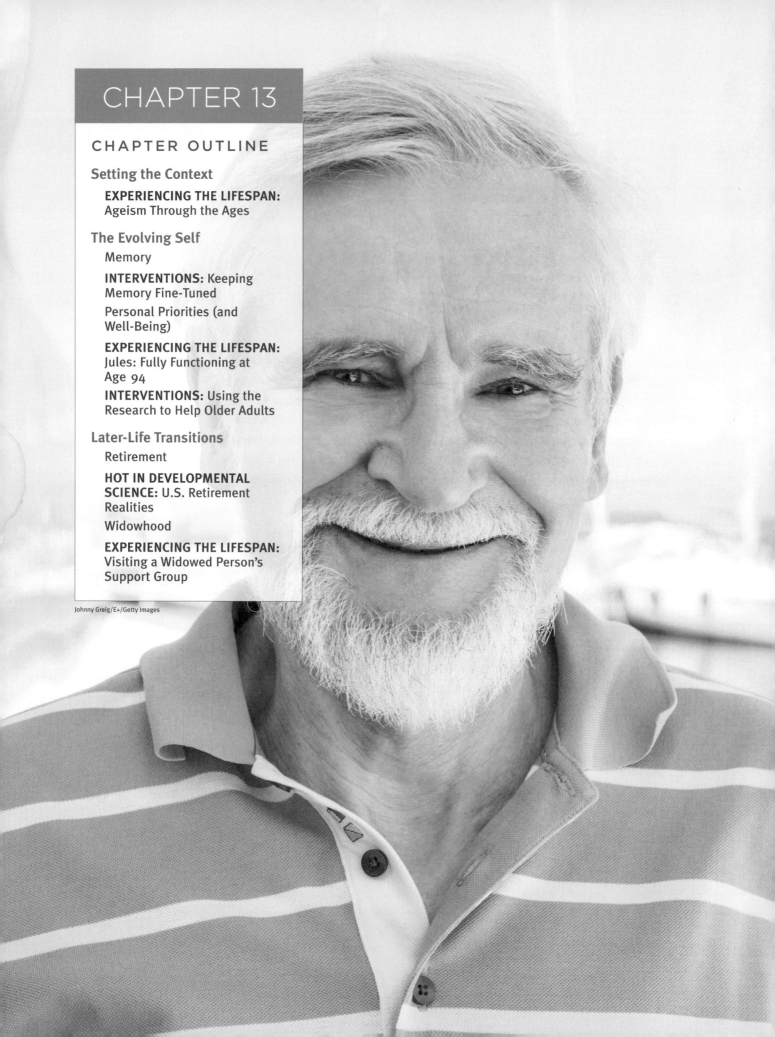

CHAPTER 13

CHAPTER OUTLINE

Later Life: Cognitive and Socioemotional Development

Ten years ago, at age 62, Susan and Carl retired. They were healthy (at the time)—and with Carl's investments and their pensions—well off. They were passionate to enjoy these final decades, to travel, to focus on the moment, to revel in this new phase of life. Carl and Susan never had children, but they had their nieces and nephews and many friends. In particular, Susan was close to her niece, Emma, who called her favorite aunt, "my adoptive mom."

For Susan and Carl, retirement meant spending time with their closest friends and family members, like Emma. It involved devoting weekdays to volunteering at church and taking those well-loved cruises to Mexico, the Mediterranean, and Marrakesh. Most of all, it meant having the joy of being together as a couple, free from the demands of work. Carl's heart disease—first diagnosed at age 66—lent poignancy to their shared life. As it turned out, their retirement years were priceless, but they were over too soon. After several bypass surgeries, and years of declining health, Carl died of a massive stroke.

After Carl's death, Susan felt numb. How can you go on without your high school sweetheart, your life love for more than 50 years? But she was astonished by her mixed emotions: the loneliness and sense of loss, even when surrounded by her friends; the incredible joy (for the priceless relationship she and Carl had); the relief that Carl never had to suffer being bedridden; pride in her ability to go on.

Actually, for the most part (bless the Lord), Susan has been amazed at her inner strength. Realizing that as an "old lady of 72" she needed to make a new life, Susan enrolled in an adult education program at the local college. With Emma's help, she mustered the courage to construct a profile on a seniors' dating website. Of course, no one will ever, ever take Carl's place. But wouldn't it be fun to try dating, liberated from the fears of being rejected or anxieties about making an adult life she had at age 21!

Susan's life changed dramatically from the time she and Carl retired until her husband got sick and died. These two chapters capture the developmental shifts people experience as they travel through the young-old (sixties and seventies) and old-old (over age 80) years. In the current chapter, I'll focus on cognition and the socioemotional side of later life. In Chapter 14, I'll be following Susan as she moves into her eighties and confronts physical frailties of advanced old age.

Susan's life differs dramatically from most elderly widows around the globe—in her lifestyle, in her open attitudes toward dating, in having the income to enjoy her older years. Still, in one way, her experience is similar to millions of other people her age. She is a foot soldier in a late-life army storming through the developed world.

median age The age at which 50 percent of a population is older and 50 percent is younger.

young-old People in their sixties and seventies.

old-old People almost age 80 and older.

Jens Lucking/MECKY/Getty Images

Long life expectancies, declining fertility, the baby boomers reaching old age—all of these forces explain why the median age of the population is increasing and why, in the decades to come, more people will look closer in age to this elderly woman than her 22-year-old granddaughter.

Setting the Context

The well-known reason for this invasion is the baby boomers marching into their young-old years. Moreover, due to our twentieth-century advances in life expectancy, when people reach that magical sixty-fifth birthday, they can now expect, on average, to live for 18 more years (Adams & Rau, 2011).

Falling fertility is also producing this unique historic demographic change (Cherlin, 2010; recall Chapter 11). When birth rates decline, the **median age** of a nation—the cutoff age at which half of the population is older and half is younger—tends to rise. With childbearing rates dipping sharply in Europe and Asia in recent decades, the median age of the population in most developed countries is now well into middle age.

The baby boomers, longevity, and low fertility are converging to produce our new, old world. You can track this demographic storm as it peaks in specific nations in Figure 13.1. In 2030 in Japan, where average life expectancy now tops age 81 and fertility rates are low, the median age of the population will be roughly age 50. In Italy, 1 out of every 2 people will be at least 52. And in that same year, roughly 1 in every 5 Americans and 1 in 4 Europeans will be over age 65 (National Center for Health Statistics, 2008).

How will you feel about living in a nation where the people with walkers may be about to outnumber the babies in strollers on your streets? For hints, you might take a trip to a U.S. city where the age storm has struck. In Sarasota, Florida, where the 65-plus population tops 30 percent, residents view age 70 as "young." You aren't defined as elderly until you make it to age 80 and above (Fishman, 2010). In Sarasota, people understand: Statistically speaking, there is a world of difference between being healthy and **young-old** and having physical frailties (or depending on those walkers) during the **old-old** years.

The health (and wealth) differences between the young-old and old-old may explain our contradictory stereotypes about later life. We have the image of the vital, energetic widow dating on-line, and the vision of the lonely, aged person languishing in a nursing home; the portrait of an affluent, retired married couple traveling the world, and picture of the depressed institutionalized elder with a dementing disease.

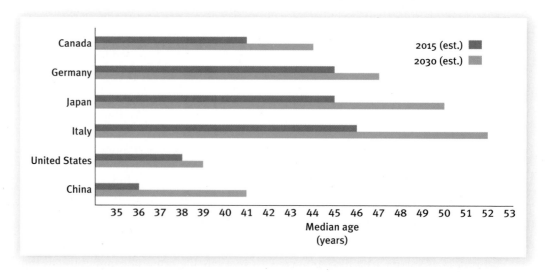

FIGURE 13.1: **Predicted median age of the population, selected countries, in 2015 and 2030:** Now, the median age of the population—the point at which half the people are younger and half are older—is 45-plus in Italy, Germany, and Japan. Also, notice how high the median ages in these nations will be in 2030. How do you think living in these "most-aged nations" will affect residents' daily lives?

Data from: Kinsella & Velkoff, 2001.

The expressions on the faces of this joyous 65-year-old and dour 90-year-old say it all. In terms of lifestyle, personality, memory, health, and everything else, there can be a world of difference between being young-old and old-old.

But amid this diversity lies consensus about the negative qualities related to being old. Worldwide, people link old age with physical and mental decline. While people in places like Sardinia, Italy, where the elderly have reputations for living healthy to the end of life, have more upbeat attitudes (Bottiroli and others, 2013), if you ask most older adults to forecast their futures, you are apt to hear gloomy comments such as, "I won't be as happy in five years as I am today" (Lang and others, 2013).

The bottom line is that everyone—young and old—is guilty of **ageism**, intensely negative attitudes about old age, although among emerging adults this aversion varies depending on personality traits such as openness to experience or whether a young person is phobic about physical decline (Allan, Johnson, & Emerson, 2014). Moreover, as the Experiencing the Lifespan box shows, in contrast to our stereotypes, throughout history, old age has also been feared as a time of unremitting loss. Luckily, we also gravitate to the elderly for classic positive traits.

ageism Stereotypic, intensely negative ideas about old age.

Experiencing the Lifespan: Ageism Through the Ages

The hair is gray. . . . The brows are gone, the eyes are blear . . . The nose is hooked and far from fair. . . . The ears are rough and pendulous. . . . The face is sallow, dead and drear. . . . The chin is purs'd . . . the lips hang loose. . . . Aye such is human beauty's lot! . . . Thus we mourn for the good old days . . . , wretched crones, huddled together by the blaze. . . .

(excerpted from an Old English poem called "Lament of the Fair Heaulmiere" [or Helmet-maker's girl], quoted in Minois, 1989, p. 230)

Many of us assume that people had better values and attitudes toward old age in "the good old days." Poems such as the one above show that we need to give that stereotype a closer look.

In ancient times, old age was seen as a miracle because it was so rare. Where there was no written language, older people were valued for their knowledge. However, this elevated status applied only to a few people—typically men—who were upper class. For slaves, servants, and women, old age was often a cruel time.

Moreover, just as today, cultures made a distinction between active, healthy older people and those who were disabled and ill. In many societies, for instance, the same person who had been revered was subjected to barbaric treatment once he outlived his usefulness—that is, became decrepit or senile. Samoans killed their elderly in elaborate ceremonies in which the victim was required to participate. Other cultures left their older people to die of neglect. Michelangelo and Sophocles, revered as old men, stand as symbols of the age-friendly attitudes of the nations in which they lived. However, the images portrayed in their creative works celebrated youth and beauty. Even in Classical Greece and Renaissance Italy—societies known for being enlightened—people believed old age was the worst time of life.

As historian Georges Minois (1989) concluded in a survey of how Western cultures treated their elders, "It is the tendency of every society to live and go on living: it extols the strength and fecundity that are so closely linked to youth and it dreads the . . . decrepitude of old age. Since the dawn of history . . . young people have regretted the onset of old age. The fountain of youth has always constituted Western man's most irrational hope" (p. 303).

(The information in this box is taken from Minois, 1989, and Fischer, 1977.)

In one U.S. poll, adults agreed that a 75-year-old would be superior to a 20-something in calmly handling conflicts (Swift, Abrams, & Marques, 2013). When undergraduates were asked to discuss the personalities of audio recordings of speakers with "elderly" and "young" voices," students did judge the old voices being less powerful. But they said they would gravitate to the elderly speakers for being gifted storytellers and being wise (Montepare, Kempler & McLaughlin-Volpe, 2014).

In these next two chapters, I'll be giving you a wealth of scientific insights into our negative old-age stereotypes—as I chart the ways thinking and physical abilities decline in the older years. But as we enter the emotional lives of the elderly, I hope to give you a more positive image of your late life future, too. Do older people really have a mellower, more balanced, wise perspective on life? Before reading the research facts relating to this topic and others, you might want to explore your personal old-age stereotypes by taking the "Is It True About the Elderly" questionnaire (Table 13.1).

Table 13.1: Is It True About the Elderly?

1. Memory stays stable through midlife, then declines in later life.

2. There is little that can be done to improve memory in old age.

3. Old people think about life more negatively than young people.

4. The typical retirement age is 65.

5. Older workers are more rigid.

6 Widowhood is always a totally devastating emotional blow.

7. Due to scientific advances, we will soon be able to live well beyond the maximum human lifespan.

8. Compared to vision difficulties, hearing losses in old age are "a piece of cake."

9. No one who has Alzheimer's disease can live a meaningful life.

10. About 50 percent of people over 65 live in nursing homes.

(I'll be discussing items 1–6 in this chapter and items 7–10 in Chapter 14.)

Answers: 1. F, 2. F, 3. F, 4. F, 5. F, 6. F, 7. F, 8. F, 9. F, 10. F

The Evolving Self

Now, let's start our research tour, by first exploring how that important component of thinking, memory, changes during our older years, and then turning to the emotional quality of later life.

Memory

When we think of specific cognitive abilities, as we get older, we can look forward to positive changes—expanding our crystallized skills, becoming wise (recall Chapter 12). If you are like people in the poll I mentioned earlier, you would believe that 75-year-olds are more talented at specific abilities such as solving crossword puzzles than the young (Swift, Abrams, & Marques, 2013). These upbeat feelings do not extend to memory. With memory, starting in midlife, we see only decline. (The classic fifty-something phrase is, "Sorry, I'm having a senior moment!") Once people reach their late sixties and seventies, the wider world is on high alert for memory problems, too.

In a classic study, psychologists demonstrated this mindset by filming actors aged 20, 50, and 70 reading an identical speech. During the talk, each person made a few references to memory problems, such as "I forgot my keys." Volunteers then watched only the young, middle-aged, or older actor and wrote about what the person was like. Many of the people who saw the 70-year-old described him as forgetful. No one who heard the identical words read by the younger adults even mentioned memory! (See Rodin & Langer, 1980.)

The reality is that, when a young person forgets something, we pass off the problem as due to external forces: "I was distracted"; "I had too much going on"; "It might be those four glasses of wine I had at dinner last night." When that person is old, we have a more ominous interpretation: "Perhaps this is the beginning of Alzheimer's disease" (Erber & Prager, 1999). When you last were with an elderly family member and she forgot a name or appointment, did the idea that "Grandma is declining mentally" cross your mind?

Scanning the Facts

Are older people's memory abilities *really* much worse than those of younger adults? Unfortunately, the answer, based on thousands of studies, is yes. In testing everything from the ability to recall unfamiliar faces to the names of new places, from remembering the content of paragraphs to recalling where objects are located in space, the elderly perform more poorly than the young (see Dixon and others, 2007, for a review).

As a memory task gets more difficult, the performance gap between young and old people expands. When psychologists ask old people to recognize an item or word they have previously seen, they do almost as well as 20-year-olds (Danckert & Craik, 2013). The elderly score comparatively worse when they need to come up with that word or name completely on their own. (The distinction here is analogous to taking a multiple-choice exam versus a short-answer test.) Older people perform even more dismally when they have to recall a face or name and link it to a specific context (Dennis and others, 2008; see also Craik, Luo, & Sakuta, 2010): "Yes, I recognize that guy . . . but was he the cable repairman or a guest at Claire's commencement party last month?"

While connecting names to places, or remembering exactly *where* we heard some bit of information, is difficult in old age, this task is not easy at any life stage. I'll never forget when a twenty-something student server blew me away with this comment: "I remember you very well, Dr. Belsky. I learned so much in your *English Literature class* three years ago."

The elderly do especially poorly on **divided-attention tasks**—situations in which they need to memorize material or perform an activity while monitoring something else. Remembering to keep checking the clock so that you don't miss your 3 p.m. class, texting or spending time on Facebook while "listening" to a lecture—these multitasking activities impair memory performance at any age (Craik, Luo, & Sakuta, 2010). Warning! This is a documented fact! But while young people can master these kinds of difficult divided-attention tasks, they are virtually impossible in old age (Gothe, Oberauer, & Kliegl, 2008).

If you can relate to this photo the next time you are tempted to text during that not-so-interesting class, keep this message in mind: *Divided-attention tasks* make memory worse!

More depressing, when researchers pile on the memory demands and add time pressures, deficits show up as early as the late twenties (Borella, Carretti, & De Beni, 2008). Returning to the previous chapter, it makes sense that when people have to remember new, random bits of information very fast, losses take place soon after youth. These requirements are prime examples of *fluid intelligence* tasks.

What is going wrong with memory as we age? Let's get insights from examining two different ways of conceptualizing "a memory": the information-processing and memory-systems approaches.

divided-attention task A difficult memory challenge involving memorizing material while simultaneously monitoring something else.

An Information-Processing Perspective on Memory Change

Remember from Chapters 3 and 5 that developmentalists who adopt an *information-processing theory* perspective on cognition see memory as progressing through stages. The gateway system, which transforms information into more permanent storage, is called *working memory.*

Working memory, as I mentioned in Chapter 5, contains a limited memory-bin space—the amount of information we can keep in our awareness. It includes an executive processor that controls our attention and transforms the contents of this temporary storage facility into material we can remember later on. Recall that, during childhood, as the frontal lobes mature, working memory-bin capacity dramatically improves. Unfortunately, as we travel through adulthood, working memory works worse and worse (McCabe and others, 2010; Reuter-Lorenz, 2013).

What explains this decline? Experts target deficits with the executive processor, that hypothetical structure responsible for manipulating material into the permanent memory store. As people age, they have more problems with focusing this master controller and so can't attend as well to what they need to learn (Müller-Oehring and others, 2013; Ofen & Shing, 2013; Rowe, Hasher, & Turcotte, 2008). One classic symptom of this *executive function* deficit, as you just saw, is that older people have exceptional trouble mastering divided-attention tasks.

When we think of executive functions such as selective attention, a particular brain structure comes to mind. Later-life memory deficits, according to current thinking, mainly reflect age-related deterioration in the frontal lobes (Reuter-Lorenz, 2013). Neuroscientists can vividly "see" this cortical thinning by taking images of the brain (Müller-Oehring, 2013; Fjell and others, 2014). Brain-imaging studies reveal an erosion of myelin in the frontal lobes is typical during the older years (Lu and others, 2013). Although they can't directly view individual neurons, based on autopsying animals, scientists now believe that synaptic loss also characterizes the elderly brain (Samson & Barnes, 2013).

How does the older brain adapt? Because brain-imaging techniques allow us to track activation patterns when adults are given memory tasks, they also offer fascinating information about this issue.

With easy memory challenges, such as remembering a few items, notice from Figure 13.2 that older adults show a broader pattern of frontal-lobe activity compared to young adults (Reuter-Lorenz, 2013; Friedman & Johnson, 2014). But, as the task

Remembering the speaker's messages at this senior citizen center lecture is going to be especially hard because older people have special trouble screening out distracting audience conversations and focusing on what they need to learn.

FIGURE 13.2: **Frontal lobe activation in young (left) and older adults (right) in a memory study:** In this fMRI study, researchers measured activation in the frontal lobes when older and younger adults were given a relatively easy laboratory memory task. Notice on the left photo that, while regions of the left hemisphere alone are activated in young adults, the older brains (right image) are working harder to master this task—as here activation occurs in both brain hemispheres.
Data from: Reuter-Lorenz & Cappell, 2008.

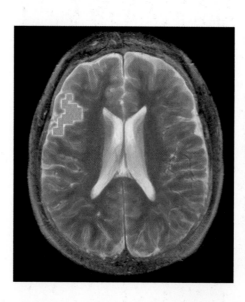

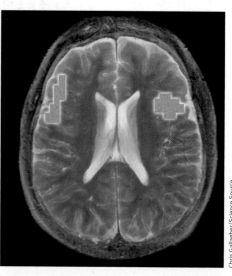

Chris Gallagher/Science Source

gets difficult, the older brain shifts to underactivation—suggesting that it totally maxed out! (See Park & McDonough, 2013; Reuter-Lorenz, 2013.)

This finding is very depressing. Does the aging brain have to work on overdrive and then ultimately "give up" (neurologically speaking) in remembering everything? Luckily, the answer is no. Some memories are more indelibly carved in our mind.

A Memory-Systems Perspective on Change

Think of the amazing resilience of some memories and the incredible vulnerability of others. Why do you automatically remember how to hold a tennis racquet even though you have not been on a court for years? Why is "George Washington," the name of our first president, locked in your mind while you are incapable of remembering what you had for dinner three days ago? These kinds of memories seem to differ in ways that go beyond how much effort went into embedding them into our minds. They seem qualitatively different in a fundamental way.

According to the **memory-systems perspective** (Craik, 2000; Tulving, 1985), there are three basic types of memory:

- **Procedural memory** refers to information that we automatically remember, without conscious reflection or thought. A real-life example involves physical skills. Once we have learned a complex motor activity, such as how to ride a bike, we automatically remember how to perform that skill once we are in that situation again.

- **Semantic memory** is our fund of basic factual knowledge. Remembering that George Washington was our first president and knowing what a bike is are examples of the kinds of information in this well-learned, crystallized database.

- **Episodic memory** refers to the ongoing events of daily life. When you remember going bike riding last Thursday or what you had for dinner last night, you are drawing on episodic memory.

As you can see in these examples and those described in Table 13.2, episodic memory is the most fragile system. A year from now you will still remember who

memory-systems perspective A framework that divides memory into three types: procedural, semantic, and episodic memory.

procedural memory In the memory-systems perspective, the most resilient (longest-lasting) type of memory; refers to material, such as well-learned physical skills, that we automatically recall without conscious awareness.

semantic memory In the memory-systems perspective, a moderately resilient (long-lasting) type of memory; refers to our ability to recall basic facts.

episodic memory In the memory-systems perspective, the most fragile type of memory, involving the recall of the ongoing events of daily life.

Table 13.2: Examples of the Differences Among Procedural, Semantic, and Episodic Memory

Procedural Memory	Semantic Memory	Episodic Memory
You get into your blue Toyota and automatically know how to drive.	You know that you have a blue Toyota.	You memorize where you left your blue Toyota in the parking lot of the amusement park.
You automatically find yourself singing the words to "Jingle Bells" when the melody comes on the radio.	You remember that "Jingle Bells" is a song.	You remember the last time you heard "Jingle Bells."
You begin to get excited as you approach your college campus for the fall semester of your senior year.	You know that you are a student at X University and that you are a psychology major.	You memorize the room number of this class during the first week of the new semester.*
I unconsciously find the letters I am typing now on my computer.	I know that I am writing a book called *Experiencing the Lifespan*.	I remember that today I must go to the library and photocopy an article on memory that I will need in preparing this chapter.

*Now that it's late in the semester, the location of this class has migrated into procedural memory; so, although you automatically walk to the door, if a friend says, "I'll meet you at class. Just tell me the room number," you are apt to draw a blank!

George Washington is (semantic memory). You will recall how to get on the bike and use the handlebars to pace your speed (procedural memory). However, even a few days later, you are likely to forget what you had for dinner on a particular night. Remembering isolated events—from what day we last went bike riding, to what we ate last Tuesday, to the paragraph you are reading now—are especially vulnerable to time.

The good news is that on tests of semantic memory older people may do as well as the young (Dixon and others, 2007). Procedural memory is amazingly long-lasting, as we know when we get on a bike after not having ridden for decades, and take off down the road. The real age loss occurs in episodic memory—remembering the details of daily life.

This decline in episodic memory is what people notice when they realize they are having more trouble remembering the name of a person at a party or where they parked the car. Our databank of semantic memories stays intact until well into later life (Ofen & Shing, 2013)—explaining why we expect older people to outperform the young at crystallized verbal challenges such as crossword puzzles. People with Alzheimer's disease can retain procedural memories after the other memory systems are largely gone. They can walk, dress themselves, and even remember (to the horror of caregivers) how to turn on the ignition and drive after losing their ability to recall basic facts, such as where they live.

The incredible resilience of procedural memory explains why your 85-year-old aunt, who was a musician, can still play the piano beautifully, even though she is now incapable of remembering family members' names. Why is this particular system the last to go? The reason, according to neuropsychologists, is that the information in procedural memory resides in a different region of the brain. When we first learn a complex motor skill, such as driving or playing an instrument, our frontal lobes are heavily involved. Then, after we have thoroughly learned that activity, this knowledge becomes automatic and migrates to a lower brain center, which frees up our frontal cortex for mastering other higher-level thinking tasks (Friedman, 2003).

Why can this elegant 85-year-old pianist still beautifully entertain you, even though she is beginning to forget basic facts about her life? Because her talents have migrated into procedural memory—the final memory system to go.

Actually, this is good. If I had to focus on remembering how to type these words on my computer, would I ever be able to simultaneously do the complicated mental work of figuring out how to describe the concepts I am explaining now?

In sum, the message with regard to age and memory is both worse and also far better than we might have thought: As we get older, we do not have to worry much about remembering basic facts. Our storehouse of crystallized knowledge is "really there." However, we will have more trouble memorizing bits of new information, and these losses in episodic memory show up at a surprisingly early age.

INTERVENTIONS: Keeping Memory Fine-Tuned

What should people do when they notice that their ability to remember life's ongoing details is worse? Let's look at three approaches:

USE SELECTIVE OPTIMIZATION WITH COMPENSATION. The first strategy is to use Baltes's three-step process, spelled out in Chapter 12: (1) Selectively focus on what you want to remember—that is, don't clog your working memory bins with irrelevant thoughts. (2) Optimize, or work hard to manipulate material in this system into permanent memory. (3) Use compensation, or external memory aids.

For example, to remember where you parked at the airport: (1) Focus on *where* you are parking when you slide your car into the spot. Don't daydream or get distracted by the need to catch the plane. (2) Work hard to encode that specific location in your brain. (3) Take a photo on your smart phone so you won't have to remember that place all on your own.

At this point, readers might be thinking: Why not just bypass those difficult executive-function challenges (selecting and optimizing) and skip to compensation, by using your phone? The problem, experts point out, is that over-relying on environmental supports can have a dark side (Lindenberger & Mayr, 2014). If an older person—or any person—depends excessively on external cues, that person is destined for problems when those supports malfunction. Put concretely, if your phone goes on the fritz, without a backup, you have lost your whole life. Moreover, no technology can eliminate our need to memorize everyday episodic facts, such as linking names to faces, remembering when we took Dr. Belsky's class, or recalling where we might have misplaced our keys two days ago. So let's turn to optimization (Baltes's step 2), by spelling out strategies for effortlessly sliding information into our memory bins.

USE MNEMONIC TECHNIQUES. Have you ever noticed that some episodic events are locked in memory (such as your wedding day or the time you and your significant other had that terrible fight), while others fade? Emotional events embed themselves solidly into memory because they activate wider regions of the brain (Dolcos & Cabeza, 2002). Therefore, the key to memorizing isolated bits of information is to make material stand out emotionally.

Mnemonic techniques are strategies to make information emotionally vivid. These approaches range from using the acronym OCEAN to help you recall the name of each Big Five trait in studying for the Chapter 12 test to, when introduced to the elderly woman in the photo below, thinking, "I'll remember her name is Mrs. Silver because of her hair."

The fact that we learn emotionally salient information without much effort may explain why our memories vary in puzzling ways in real life. A history buff soaks up every detail about the Civil War but remains clueless about where he left his socks. Because your passion is developmental science, you do well with very little studying in this course, but it takes you hours to memorize a single page in your biology text.

Actually, the principle that emotional events are locked more firmly in our brains may partly account for our impression that the elderly remember past experiences best. In fact, when researchers asked adults to remember self-defining events in their personal autobiographies ("the day I got accepted into graduate school"; "when I hit that car on Lakeshore drive in November of 1982"), the elderly did perform better than the young! (See Martinelli and others, 2013.)

WORK ON THE PERSON'S MENTAL STATE. This brings up the thought that standard laboratory memory tests are unfair to older adults. These tests require remembering random bits of episodic information. So they showcase the very memory skill that dramatically declines with age. Wouldn't the elderly do comparatively better when asked to remember emotionally salient information they need in their daily lives?

Now compound this bias with the poisonous impact of self-doubt. If you were 70 or 80, imagine how you would feel when asked to participate in a memory study. Wouldn't you be frightened, thinking, "This test might show I have Alzheimer's disease!"

Actually, just being told, "I'm giving you a memory test," makes older people feel years older (Hughes, Geraci, & De Forrest, 2013). Moreover, labeling a test as "measuring memory" impairs an older person's performance on *any* cognitive test. In one scary study, after being informed, "This is a memory test," 70 percent of older adults scored below the clinical cut-off for Alzheimer's disease on a classic diagnostic test, compared to less than one in five people not given that threat! Conversely, when researchers said a given IQ scale tapped wisdom, older people's performance improved—even though that test really measured a fluid skill (Hehman & Bugental, 2013).

mnemonic technique
A strategy for aiding memory, often by using imagery or enhancing the emotional meaning of what needs to be learned.

Ronnie Kaufman/Getty Images

Although his main goal is to greet this woman in a warm, personal way, in order to remember his new friend's name, this elderly man might want to step back and use the mnemonic strategy of forming a mental image, thinking, "I'll remember it's Mrs. Silver because of her hair."

socioemotional selectivity theory A theory of aging (and the lifespan) put forth by Laura Carstensen, describing how the time we have left to live affects our priorities and social relationships. Specifically, in later life people focus on the present and prioritize being with their closest attachment figures.

Moreover, subjective memory complaints ("I'm having terrible trouble remembering") have a tenuous relationship to an older person's actual scores on memory tests (Crumley, Stetler, & Horhota, 2014; Pearman, Hertzog, & Gerstorf, 2014). What does predict subsequent cognitive decline, one longitudinal study suggested, is depression—feeling chronically unhappy with one's current life (Goveas and others, 2014).

So, to take a family example, when my 90-year-old mother complained, "I can't remember anything," we children were wrong to *automatically* assume that she was developing Alzheimer's disease. And, in fact, after taking action to improve my mom's emotional state by moving her to a continuing care community (described in the next chapter), her memory greatly improved.

Actually, in contrast to the image of late-life memory loss as caused by an irreversible brain "condition," teaching the elderly memory improvement techniques does work (see, for instance, Borella and others, 2014). Today, these strategies have proliferated (Gajewski, 2013), with scientists training older adults on everything from video games (designed to heighten selective attention) (Toril, Reales, & Ballesteros, 2014), to mastering the demands of daily life (Burkard and others, 2014; Brom & Kliegel, 2014; McDaniel and others, 2014). Still, we do run into the problem of motivation. People tend to "get lazy" (meaning not follow through) because optimization strategies demand serious mental work! (See Burkard and others, 2014; Ennis, Hess, & Smith, 2013.)

Personal Priorities (and Well-Being)

Everyone believes that memory declines with age. But as I mentioned earlier, we have more positive ideas about our emotional lives. Does old age really bring serenity and emotional balance? Laura Carstensen believes it does.

Focusing on Time Left to Live: Socioemotional Selectivity Theory

Imagine that you are elderly and aware that you have a limited time left to live. How might your goals and priorities change? The idea that our place on the lifespan changes our life agendas is the premise of Carstensen's **socioemotional selectivity theory.**

According to Carstensen (1995), during the first half of adult life, our push is to look to the future. We are eager to make it in the wider world. We want to reach a better place at some later date. As we grow older and realize that our future is limited, we refocus our priorities. We want to make the most of our present life.

Carstensen believes that this focus on making the most of every moment explains why late life is potentially the happiest life stage. When our agenda lies in the future, we often forgo our immediate desires in the service of a later goal. Instead of telling off the boss who insults us, we hold our tongue because this authority figure holds the key to getting ahead. We are nice to that nasty person, or go to that dinner party we would rather pass up in order to advance socially or in our career. We accept the anxiety-ridden months when we first move to an unfamiliar city because we expect to feel better than ever in a year or two.

In later life, we are less interested in where we *will* be going. So we refuse to waste time with unpleasant people or enter anxiety-provoking situations because they may have a payoff at some later point. Almost unconsciously, we decide, "I don't have that long to live. I have to spend my time doing what makes me feel good emotionally *right now*."

Furthermore, when our passion lies in making the most of the present, Carstensen argues, our social priorities shift. During childhood, adolescence, and emerging adulthood our mission is to leave our attachment figures. We want to expand our social horizons, form

Socioemotional selectivity theory, with its principle that, in old age, we make the most of every moment, explains why, at celebrations, older adults are often the life of the party.

new close relationships, and connect with exciting new people who can teach us new things. Once we have achieved our life goals, we are less interested in developing new attachments. We already have our family and network of caring friends. So we center our lives on our spouse, our best friends, and our children—the people we love the most.

Actually, as we travel throughout adulthood our social networks do shrink, and we center our lives more on family than friends (Wrzus and others, 2013). Moreover, perhaps partly due to years of experience managing complex social situations (see the previous chapter), the elderly report more positive interpersonal encounters than the young (English & Carstensen, 2014).

Older people, Carstensen finds, carefully limit their social encounters, too. When her research team asked elderly and young people, "Who would you rather spend time with—a close family member, an acquaintance, or the author of a recent book?" Young people's choices were spread among the three possible partners. Older people chose overwhelmingly to be with the family member, their closest attachment figure in life (Fung, Lai, & Ng, 2001).

Socioemotional selectivity theory, with its principle that, in old age, we focus on our closest attachment figures, explains why simply spending time with each other and their grandchildren is this elderly couple's passion in life.

When Do We Prioritize the Present Regardless of Our Life Stage?

But is this change in priorities *simply* a function of being old? The answer is no. Adults with fatal illnesses also voted to spend an evening with a familiar close person. So did people who were asked to imagine that they were about to move across the country alone. According to Carstensen, whenever we see our future as limited, we pare down our social contacts, maximize our positive experiences, and spend time with the people we care about the most.

Socioemotional selectivity theory explains why—although normally you are content to live a continent away—when you are in danger of losing a loved one, you want to be physically close. So, you fly in to spend time with your beloved grandma when she is seriously ill. You insist on spending a weekend with your high school friend who is leaving for a tour of duty in the military in some dangerous part of the world.

The theory accounts for the choices my cousin Clinton made when he was diagnosed with lymphoma in his early twenties. An exceptionally gifted architect, Clinton gave up his promising career and retired to rural New Hampshire to build houses, hike, and ski for what turned out to be another quarter-century of life. Clinton's funeral, at age 50, was an unforgettable celebration—a testament to a person who, although his life was shorter than most, lived fully for longer than many people who survive to twice this age. Have you ever seen the principles of socioemotional selectivity theory in operation in your own life?

Making the Case for Old Age as the Best Time of Life

This passion to make the most of every moment may partly explain the **paradox of well-being**—the puzzling research fact that, as I mentioned in Chapter 12, happiness improves well into later life (Gana and others, 2013). Here are two additional (related) causes:

OLDER PEOPLE PRIORITIZE POSITIVE EMOTIONAL STATES. This bias to focus on positive experiences, alluded to earlier, has been so well documented by now that it has its own label: the **positivity effect.** To take one example, imagine being at a casino and sitting next to an elderly adult. Carstensen's research suggests the older person will be just as happy as you when she expects to win. But she probably won't be upset (or will get far less disturbed) when she loses (Nielsen, Knutson, & Carstensen, 2008).

People of every age, as I described in the previous section, remember emotional stimuli best. However, the elderly perform better when asked to recall happy versus sad images and faces (Simon and others, 2013).

paradox of well-being The fact that despite their physical and mental losses, the elderly report being just as happy or happier than the young.

positivity effect The tendency for older people to focus on positive experiences and screen out negative events.

Older people also view their distressing life experiences in a less gloomy way. When asked to describe an upsetting event in their past, older adults used fewer negative emotions and described far less anxiety than did younger adults (Robertson & Hopko, 2013). When Carstensen's research team had different age groups listen to stories about a 25-year-old and a 75-year-old, then asked these volunteers to retell the stories from the perspective of each person, the elderly participants used more positive statements when talking from the older person's point of view. The younger adults showed no signs of understanding that old people might think differently than the young (Sullivan, Mikels, & Carstensen, 2010). So, not only are older people adept at minimizing negativity, they have a secret knowledge you only get from reaching later life. In old age, we *can* rise above the storms of daily life.

If you need more evidence that age offers this serene bird's-eye perspective, consider a remarkable poll charting the emotional states of over 40,000 Australian adults over age 40: While younger adults were more apt to describe intense highs and lows, the elderly more often reported feeling calm and peaceful than the middle-aged group (Windsor, Burns, & Byles, 2013).

Having help from young women is likely to be a new life experience for this man. How would you feel about "the goodness of humanity," if people started treating you in this unusually caring way?

OLDER PEOPLE LIVE LESS-STRESSFUL LIVES. Actually, there are clear, external reasons why old age should be a worry-free life stage: No longer having the hassles of raising children or the gut-churning pressures to perform at work. Older people report fewer daily stresses than the young (Charles & Almeida, 2007; Charles and others, 2010; von Hippel, Henry, & Matovic, 2008). An added bonus is that the outside world treats you with special care (Luong, Charles, & Fingerman, 2010). In one study, when researchers asked adults how they would react in a difficult interpersonal situation, people said they would be prone to hold off confronting someone if that individual was old (Fingerman, Miller, & Charles, 2008). An elderly speaker alerted my class to this interesting perk when he mentioned, "The best thing about being 88 is that everyone is incredibly nice!" If strangers opened doors for you, people forgave your foibles, and everyone made a special effort to be kind, wouldn't you feel better about life and the human race?

So knowing your life will end, and many years spent living, provide surprising emotional bonuses. Moreover, in old age, people have more luxury to do just what they want, and the outside world hassles them less!

What Can Make Old Age the Unhappiest Time of Life?

But at this point, many of you may be thinking, "Something is wrong with this picture." What about the miserable elderly people who the world doesn't treat so kindly, older adults left to languish, lonely and impoverished, in their so-called golden years? When I gave talks on successful aging at local senior centers in my thirties (some gall!), I vividly recall one 89-year-old woman who put me in my place: "Wait till you are my age, young lady. Then you will *really* know how terrible it is to be old!"

The erosion of U.S. retirement as a life stage (to be described in the next section) is destined to impair the emotional quality of old age. As "social connectedness" is critical to human happiness, widowhood and outliving friends *must* take a psychological toll. Now, combine this with the physical losses of advanced old age, and it should come as no surprise that some studies show happiness takes a nosedive as people approach the old-old years (Dozeman and others, 2010; Rothermund & Brandstädter, 2003).

So, the paradox of well-being extends only so far. When people are frail or disabled and death looms on the horizon, life can lose all of its purpose and joy. As one formerly ideally-aging man wrote: "I was still driving, walking . . . and feeling pretty confident about my condition . . . at age 87; now after three more years of age-related decline, I've almost had enough. . . . Without (my wife) . . . I would be hard pressed to find reasons to get up in the morning. Even with Kathe, I've begun to feel that I've almost had enough living without the people and possessions that shaped my life" (adapted from Crum, 2014, p. 6).

Still, let's not stereotype all ninety-somethings as in a dismal holding pattern, waiting for death. As my inspiring interview with Jules in the Experiencing the Lifespan box shows, some people live exceptionally gratifying lives at the uppermost limits of life.

Experiencing the Lifespan: Jules: Fully Functioning at Age 94

It was a hot August morning at Vanderbilt University as friends, colleagues, and students gathered to celebrate the publication of his book. Their voices often cracked with emotion as they rose to testify: "You changed my life. You are an inspiration—the best therapist and supervisor I've ever had." Frail, bent over, beginning to doze—suddenly, 94-year-old Jules came to life. "My book traces the development of my ideas about ideal mental health. It's been a 60-year journey to identify the 'fully functional person' that I'm still trying to get right today." Who is this revered role model? What made Jules the person he is, and what is his philosophy about aging and life? Let's read this interview.

My parents left Europe right before the First World War. So in 1915, I was lucky enough to arrive in this world (or be born). Growing up in Baltimore, my brothers and I were incredibly close because, as the only Jewish family in our Christian immigrant neighborhood, we were living in an alien world. I vividly remember the neighborhood kids regularly taunting us as Jesus killers as we walked to school. So we learned from an early age that the world can be a dangerous place. What this experience did was to take us in the opposite direction . . . to see every person as precious, to develop attitudes that were worldwide.

When I was a teenager, and asked myself, "What is important in life?" the answer was "relationships," . . . to have a fundamental faith in people. It was clear that human beings had a long way to go to reach maturity, but you need to act ethically and lovingly. I also looked to the Bible for guidance, asking myself, "What do the ancient prophets tell us about living an ethical life?" During the Second World War my brothers and I decided we could never participate in violence, and so we were conscientious objectors. I knew I could never kill another human being.

I started out my work life as a public school teacher in Baltimore. I had no desire to get a Ph.D., but when I read a paper by Carl Rogers* in 1948, who was developing his client-centered therapy, I was electrified: Understand the person from his own framework; don't be judgmental; look beyond the diagnosis to the real human being. By listening empathically and relating unconditionally, you can guide a person toward health. Those decades I spent collaborating with Carl ended up defining my life work.

I'm still the same person as always, the same adolescent hiding in the body of a 94-year-old man—but with much more experience in living! The difference is that, physically, I am handicapped [with congestive heart failure] and so I use a shorter horizon. Instead of thinking about a year ahead, I might think about a week. . . . I am well aware that I could die any time. But it's unthinkable to me not to do therapy. I'm incomplete if I am not expressing my passion in life.

It's important never to put life in the past tense. There is no such thing as "aging" or "retirement." You are always learning and developing. When I was younger and looked to the Bible for guidance, I gravitated to the prophet Micah. Micah sums up my philosophy for living in this one sentence: "What doeth the lord require of me but to do justly, to love mercy, and to walk humbly with thy god."

*Rogers was one of the premier twentieth-century psychologists.

Decoding Some Keys to Happiness in Old Age

Do you have an old-age role model such as Jules, someone who believes he is continuing to develop as a person at age 90 or 94? What makes these people stand out? For one thing, Jules demonstrates the openness to experience, self-efficacy, and ability to reinterpret upsetting life events as growth experiences that define being wise (Etezadi & Pushkar, 2013; recall the previous chapter). What is particularly striking is this master therapist's generativity, and the fact that Jules has reached Erikson's milestone of *integrity* (see Table 13.3 on the next page). Jules knows he has lived according to the prophetic guidelines that he views at the core of having a meaningful life.

Table 13.3: Erikson's Psychosocial Stages and Tasks

Life Stage	Primary Task
Infancy (birth to 1 year)	Basic trust versus mistrust
Toddlerhood (1 to 2 years)	Autonomy versus shame and doubt
Early childhood (3 to 6 years)	Initiative versus guilt
Middle childhood (6 years to puberty)	Industry versus inferiority
Adolescence (teens into twenties)	Identity versus role confusion
Young adulthood (twenties to early forties)	Intimacy versus isolation
Middle adulthood (forties to sixties)	Generativity versus stagnation
Late adulthood (late sixties and beyond)	**Integrity versus despair**

According to Erikson, our task in later adulthood is to look back over our life to see if we accomplished what we set out to do. Older people who know they have lived fully are not afraid to die. But older adults who have serious regrets about their lives may be terrified of death and feel a sense of despair.

integrity Erik Erikson's eighth psychosocial stage, in which elderly people decide that their life missions have been fulfilled and so accept impending death.

Tim Macpherson/The Image Bank/Getty Images

Notice this man's sense of pleasure at helping his friend. Now we know that feeling generative and, especially, having a sense of life purpose, may even extend older people's lives.

Erikson believed that, to reach **integrity,** older people must review their lives and make peace with what they have previously done. But, happiness in old age does not involve dwelling on the past. As with Jules, it involves finding purpose and meaning in your present life (Burr, Santo, & Pushkar, 2011).

Moreover, younger readers might be interested to know that, apart from everything else, having a sense of life purpose also predicts living longer. In one mammoth longitudinal study, adults of every age who agreed with questionnaire items such as, "I wander aimlessly through life," died at earlier ages than their peers (Hill & Turiano, 2014).

By now you might be thinking that I am being far, far too positive. Clearly, people who remain upbeat emotionally and connected socially in advanced old age are rare. Not so fast! In four studies tracking Swedish people as they moved through their eighties, researchers did find specific groups declined dramatically cognitively or were isolated and depressed. But, the largest fraction of this oldest-old group remained stable in terms of life satisfaction and being socially engaged. They retained a reasonably good memory, too (Morack and others, 2013).

Live purposefully, be open to experience, remain lovingly attached, be generative—these are some keys to aging happily into advanced old age (and living happily during any stage of adult life!).

INTERVENTIONS: **Using the Research to Help Older Adults**

Now, let's summarize all of these messages. How can we help older people improve their memory skills? How should you think about the relationship priorities of older loved ones, and when should you worry about their emotional states? Here are some suggestions:

- As late-life memory difficulties are most likely to show up in situations where there is "a lot going on," give older people ample time to learn material and provide them with a nondistracting environment (more about this environmental engineering in Chapter 14).

- Don't stereotype older adults as having a "bad" memory. Remember that semantic memory stays stable with age, and that teaching mnemonic strategies can work. Help older people develop their memory skills by suggesting this chapter's tips. Also, however, be realistic. Tell the older person, "If you notice a decline in your ability to attend to life's details (episodic memory), that's normal. It does NOT mean you have Alzheimer's disease" (Dixon and others, 2007).

- Encourage older loved ones—even those with disabilities—to maintain a personal passion. Being "efficaciously" engaged not only helps slide information through our memory bins, but makes for a happy life.

- Using the insights that socioemotional selectivity theory offers, don't expect older people to automatically want to socialize or make new friends. When an elderly person says, "I don't want to go to the senior citizen center. All I care about is my family," she may be making an age-appropriate response.

- Don't imagine that older people are unhappy. Actually, assume the reverse is true. However, be alert to depression in someone who is physically frail and socially isolated. Again, the key to warding off depression in old age is the same as at any age: being generative, feeling closely attached, having a sense of meaning in life.

 ## Tying It All Together

1. Dwayne is planning on teaching lifespan development at the senior center. He's excited; but since, until now, he's taught only younger people, he's worried about how memory changes in his older students might affect their enjoyment of his class. Based on your understanding of which memory situations give older people the most trouble, suggest some changes Dwayne might make in his teaching.

2. Classify each of the following memory challenges as involving episodic memory, semantic memory, or procedural memory:

   a. Someone asks you for your street address.

   b. Someone asks you what you just read in this chapter.

   c. You go bike riding.

3. Which of the abilities in the previous question (1) will an older loved one retain the longest if she gets Alzheimer's disease, and (2) will start to decline relatively early in life?

4. As you study this section, come up with a vivid image to embed the major terms in your mind. (For instance, to remember *working memory*, think of a brain on a treadmill; to recall *episodic memory*, think of an episode of your favorite TV show.) Do you agree that this optimization technique, while helpful, demands mental effort?

5. You are eavesdropping on three elderly friends as they discuss their feelings about life. According to socioemotional selectivity theory, which two comments might you hear?

   a. Frances says, "Now that I'm older, I want to meet as many new people as possible."

   b. Allen reports, "I'm enjoying life more than ever today. I'm savoring every moment—and what a pleasure it is to do just what I want!"

   c. Milly mentions, "I've been spending as much time as possible with my family, the people who matter to me the most."

6. Based on this chapter, give three reasons why happiness should peak in later life.

Answers to the Tying It All Together questions can be found at the end of this chapter.

Later-Life Transitions

Now, let's look at how people find meaning as they confront the life transitions of retirement and widowhood.

Retirement

When we imagine the U.S. retirement age, we immediately think of 65. But, you might be surprised to know, the age for collecting full Social Security benefits is now 66 (and for people born after 1970, it will be 67); and for decades the "true" average U.S. retirement age was under 62 (Munnell & Rutledge, 2013). When we think of being retired, we imagine a short life stage before death. But if you leave work in your early sixties—particularly if you are female—expect to be retired for about a quarter of your total life! (See Adams & Rau, 2011.)

What caused retirement to take up such a huge chunk of the lifespan, and what is happening to this life stage in the United States today? Stay tuned as I scan the global economic retirement scene, and then offer a synopsis of current U.S. retirement trends.

Setting the Context: Differing Financial Retirement Cushions

If you are like many young people, you probably aren't sure whether retirement will continue to exist once you reach later life. Actually, there are places where retirement doesn't exist today. In Bangladesh, Jamaica, and Mexico, where more than half of all people over 65 are in the labor force, the elderly must work till they get seriously ill (Kinsella & Velkoff, 2001). The reason is that these nations lack the government-financed programs that propelled developed world retirement into a full life stage.

By the late twentieth century, government-sponsored programs, sometimes allowing retirement as young as the late fifties—were a fixture in more than 160 nations (Kinsella & Velkoff, 2001). But even in Europe, which has universal old-age government supports, retirement anxieties differ from place to place. In Scandinavia, with its shared national goal to "help everyone cradle to grave," residents feel secure that they will be helped in old age. In Central Europe, where the gaps between rich and poor are wide and economic hardship is common earlier in life, people are intensely worried about their retirement years (Hershey, Henkins, & van Dalen, 2010).

What retirement programs can affluent nations provide? For answers, let's compare Germany and the United States.

GERMANY: MERCEDES MODEL GOVERNMENT SUPPORT. Germans currently do worry more about retirement because they live in a rapidly aging nation where the government may need to cut back on the funds citizens have long enjoyed—comfortable old-age income for life. Retirement in Germany is mainly financed by employee and employer payroll taxes similar to the system we have in the United States. However, unlike in the United States, in Germany, the philosophy has traditionally been to keep people well off during their older years. When the typical German worker retires, the government has replaced roughly three-fourths of that person's working income for life. Until recently, Germans have had no worries about falling into poverty in old age. Remarkably, German retirees have had *more* spending power as they traveled further into old age (Hungerford, 2003).

THE UNITED STATES: GOING IT ALONE WITH MODEST GOVERNMENT HELP. If Germany has offered a Mercedes-like model, government-funded U.S. retirement is more like an old used car; it allows people to barely make it, but in no comfort at all. The reason is that the famous, guaranteed old-age insurance program called Social Security operates as a safety net to keep people from being destitute in old age.

Social Security, the landmark government program instituted by President Franklin D. Roosevelt in 1935 at the height of the Great Depression, gets its financing from current workers. Employees and employers pay into this program to fund today's

Social Security The U.S. government's national retirement support program.

retirees; then, when it is their turn to retire, these adults get a lifelong stipend financed by the current working population. However, with an average monthly check of $1303 in late 2014, Social Security can barely support the basics of life for older adults (Social Security Monthly Statistical Snapshot, 2014).

Private pensions (and personal savings) are supposed to take up the slack. Workers put aside a portion of each paycheck, and these funds, often matched by employer contributions, go into a tax-free account that accumulates equity. Then, at retirement, the person gets regular payouts, or a lump sum, on which to live (Johnson, 2009).

The central role of private pensions in financing retirement reflects the priority that the United States places on individual initiative. We are leery about the welfare-state implications of a federal government plan, preferring to provide tax incentives that encourage workers to plan for retirement on their own.

private pensions The major source of nongovernmental income support for U.S. retirees, in which the individual worker and employer put a portion of each paycheck into an account to help finance retirement.

 Hot in Developmental Science: U.S. Retirement Realities

The problem is that, with an average retirement nest egg of $127,000, most baby boomers haven't come close to amassing the pension cushion (at least 10 times that amount) to support a decent lifestyle for 15 or so years (Leicht & Fitzgerald, 2014; Collinson, 2014). Moreover, unfortunately, many adults have unrealistic impressions about their retirement futures, expecting help from family members or from pensions that are unlikely to exist (Whitaker & Bokemeier, 2014). What are the *real* retirement realities in the United States?

EXPECT LONGER WORKING LIVES. Hints come from asking people at the brink of retirement age. Less than one in nine baby boomers feel very confident they can retire with a comfortable lifestyle. Two out of three say they will work after age 65 (Collinson, 2014). In another poll, two in five people said they planned to work "til they drop" (reported in Leicht & Fitzgerald, 2014).

Why do people in the United States approach retirement so financially strapped? No, it's not conspicuous consumption or an inability for this "entitled cohort" to live within their means. The real problem, social critics argue, lies in rising income inequality and the eroding loss in real wages (Leicht & Fitzgerald, 2014). When your salary has not been keeping pace with the cost of living for years, you simply don't have the financial resources to save much for retirement. Now, combine this with the fact that, when the Great Recession hit in 2008, one in four people had their wages reduced or were laid off. Many baby boomers helplessly witnessed the value of their largest asset, their homes, erode.

In Chapter 10, I alluded to how the Great Recession has forced young people to postpone important events such as leaving the nest or getting married, in part because of the difficulty of finding decent jobs. But as a laid-off older job seeker during those gloomy years, you would also have considerable trouble finding work. Between 2008 and 2009, the over-55 unemployment rate soared from 3.2 to 7 percent. The median duration of joblessness for this group was 38.4 weeks at its peak (Leicht & Fitzgerald, 2014).

Moreover, even when baby boomers are fortunate to have well-paying jobs, they may be reluctant to retire for another recession-related reason: In one national poll, 7 percent of U.S. older workers said they were putting off retiring to care for struggling adult daughters and sons (Golden, 2014).

Where do women fit into this picture? As you might imagine, their less continuous work histories and lower-wage jobs (remember Chapter 11), plus longer life expectancies, make it particularly hard to amass sufficient retirement funds ("How can I save for old age when I need my income to live?") (Wang & Shi, 2014). While upper-middle-class married women entering retirement are better off, they are vulnerable to spending their nest eggs and ending their lives dependent just on Social Security. In fact, the U.S. age group most likely to live in poverty is females over 85.

AP Photo/The Star Tribune, Courtney Perry

This 70-year-old clerk would probably prefer basking at the beach to bending over a deli freezer. But given Social Security's meager allotment, millions of older Americans must work during their so-called "golden" years.

EXPECT TO CONSIDER WORKING AFTER YOU RETIRE. These economic realities partly explain why two out of three retirees in the United States do return to work (Wang & Shi, 2014). Some people are fortunate to continue working for the same employer at reduced hours. Others search for less-stressful jobs or start new, fulfilling late-life careers. Some go back to work because they miss their social attachments at a job (Wöhrmann, Deller, & Wang, 2013).

In Northern Europe, people who take post-retirement jobs are more apt to be happy, because they more often have voluntarily chosen this path (Cho & Lee, 2014; Dingemans & Henkens, 2014). But this is not true in the United States, where retirees may be forced back into the labor market to make ends meet. Perhaps, like me, you have an older friend in this situation—needing to take a low-wage job to supplement his Social Security in order to financially survive. ◐

The dismal message is that, yes, U.S. retirement is becoming a shorter, more fragile phase of life. Moreover, the income inequalities highlighted throughout this book persist into the older years. Just as being single and female predicts earlier adult poverty, the same forces spell financial trouble in later life. But even formerly upper-middle-class people caught in the net of the Great Recession are vulnerable to struggling financially in old age (Collinson, 2014). And as a woman, even if you enter retirement affluent, poverty can be the unfortunate price of surviving until advanced old age.

Now that we understand the U.S. landscape, it's time to explore other influences that go into the decision to leave work.

Exploring the Complex Push/Pull Retirement Decision

Imagine that you are in your sixties and considering leaving your job. Clearly, your primary consideration is economic: "Do I have enough money?" However, a second force that comes into play in Western nations is health: "Can I physically continue at work?" (De Preter, Van Looy, & Mortelmans, 2013; Wang & Shi, 2014). There may be another, insidious influence prompting your decision: age discrimination.

age discrimination Illegally laying off workers or failing to hire or promote them on the basis of age.

THE IMPACT OF AGE DISCRIMINATION. Age discrimination in the United States is illegal. People cannot get fired for being "too old." But because it's acceptable to get rid of more expensive workers—who tend to be older—for "business reasons," it's difficult to prove that "age" was the reason why a fifty-something worker got laid off (Rothenberg & Gardner, 2011).

Encouraging retirement via a special buyout is the preferred positive route employers use to entice Western workers to "go gently" into their retirement years (Ekerdt, 2010). In fact, in Northern Europe, lavish pension incentives often made retiring at age 60 normal, because it didn't make financial sense for people to continue to work (De Preter, Van Looy, & Mortelmans, 2013). But workers also disengage from their jobs when they identify with being " older employees," agree with the negative stereotypes attached to that category, and feel discriminated against at work (Bayl-Smith & Griffin, 2014).

Older workers are supposed to be rigid, make more mental mistakes, be fearful of technology, and be less adaptable at work (McCann & Keaton, 2013). The problem is that these images are false! In one Swedish study, age made people *more* flexible at work (Kunze, Boehm, & Bruch, 2013). Research in the United States has suggested older workers are more compliant and, amazingly, *less likely* to take time off for being sick, in addition to generally being more reliable than younger employees (Newman, 2011).

Still, these facts don't matter much when a laid-off worker of age 50 or 60 bumps up against age discrimination when looking for a new job (van Selm & Van der

Heijden, 2013). It's impossible to prove that "too old" is the reason for a given applicant being consigned to the "won't hire" pile (Neumark, 2009). However, studies suggest that given hypothetical older and younger job seekers, employers routinely go for the younger adult (Ekerdt, 2010; Rothenberg & Gardner, 2011).

THE IMPACT OF WANTING TO WORK LONGER OR RETIRE. So far, I've been focusing on the dismal forces that affect retirement: Financial problems keep people in the labor force unwillingly; health issues and age discrimination push people to retire. I've been neglecting the fact that the decision to keep working or retire is also a *positive* choice. Many baby boomers say they want to keep working after age 65 because they love their jobs (Adams & Rau, 2011; Galinsky, 2007). People may retire in order to enter an exciting, new phase of life.

Who is passionate to stay in the labor force until their seventies or up to age 85? As I implied earlier, these older adults are often healthy and highly educated workers, like Jules in the Experiencing the Lifespan box on page 401, who feel tremendous flow in their careers (Adams & Rau, 2011; Wang & Shi, 2014). What about adults who permanently retire? Are they depressed or thrilled after taking this step?

Life as a Retiree

The answer is "it depends." Retirement at age 65 typically has no effect on well-being (Wang & Shi, 2014); but leaving work early and feeling forced out of the workforce does negatively affect people's emotional and physical health (Calvo, Sarkisian, & Tamborini, 2013; Zantinge and others, 2014; Dingemans & Henkens, 2014).

Actually, the qualities that make for retirement happiness are identical to the attributes that make for a satisfying life at any age: Be open to experience, generative (Burr, Santo, & Pushkar, 2011), healthy, happily married, and have the economic resources to enjoy life (Pinquart & Schindler, 2007).

Having a serious leisure passion, such as playing the flute or volunteering at church, smooths the way to a satisfying retirement life (Heo and others, 2010). In an uncanny parallel to the research described earlier relating to life purpose, one research summary suggested that volunteering in later life significantly reduced a person's risk of death (Okun, Yeung, & Brown, 2013). In fact, you can predict whether a just-retired relative will flourish by knowing two facts: Did this person retire on time and voluntarily leave work? (Potocnik, Torera, & Peiro, 2013.) What is she like as a human being? (See Table 13.4 for a summary of these forces.)

How can you expect your relative to spend these years? Because "personality endures," one key is to look to her passions now (Atchley, 1989; Pushkar and others, 2010). So, a social activist joins the Peace Corps. A business executive volunteers at SCORE (Senior Corps of Retired Executives), advising young people about setting up small businesses. Others decide to take up new "bucket list" goals such as hiking the Himalayas or getting a history Ph.D. Many people open to experience might retire to pack in as much new learning as they possibly can.

Table 13.4: Questions to Ask to Predict If a Relative Will Be Happy as a Retiree: A Section Summary

1. Did this person want to retire or was he forced out of the workforce?

2. Is this person relying just on Social Security and/or feeling compelled to take a post-retirement job to make ends meet?

3. Is this person generative and open to experience?

4. Is this person married (happily!), and in good health?

5. Does this person have an absorbing hobby, plan to use this time giving back to the community, or have fulfilling "bucket list" goals?

These older people are enrolled in an English class in a special senior citizens college in Japan. Because many people use their retirement years to devote themselves to the human passion for learning, special educational programs for the elderly are flourishing in nations around the world.

old-age dependency ratio
The fraction of people over age 60 compared to younger, working-age adults (ages 15 to 59). This ratio is expected to rise dramatically as the baby boomers retire.

intergenerational equity
Balancing the needs of the young and old. Specifically, often referred to as the idea that U.S. government entitlements, such as Medicare and Social Security, "over-benefit" the elderly at the expense of other age groups.

A dazzling menu of options are available to older adults passionate to expand their minds, from reduced fees at colleges, to older-adult institutes, to senior citizen center classes. Readers might be interested that, in the spirit of mind expansion (not credential collection!), during the next few years, I plan to get my master's in a liberal arts program specifically for adults.

As my goal and the life agendas of millions of baby boomers reveal, in the Western world, we see the older years as a time to vigorously connect to the world (Ekerdt, 1986). However, there is a different cultural model of retirement. In the traditional Hindu perspective, later life is a time to disengage from worldly concerns. Ideally, people become wandering ascetics, renouncing their connections to loved ones and earthly pleasures in preparation for death (Savishinsky, 2004). Although this plan is rarely followed in practice (after all, our need to be closely attached is a basic human drive!), let's not assume that our "do not go gently into the sunset," keep-active retirement ideal applies around the world.

Summing Things Up: Social Policy Retirement Issues

Now, let's summarize these section messages by focusing on some critical social issues with regard to retirement.

- **Retirement is an at-risk life stage.** In the United States, the lack of pension income and other assets is the immediate threat to retiring at 65. But the other issue lies in probable future cutbacks in Social Security (perhaps an increase until age 70 for receiving full benefits, or declining support levels). In 1950, there were about 16 workers for every U.S. retiree. Soon, the **old-age dependency ratio,** or proportion of working adults to retirees, will decline to almost 2 to 1 (Johnson, 2009). Social Security was never intended to finance a stage of life. It was instituted during a time when life expectancy was far shorter, as a stopgap for when health issues made it impossible to work. Now that the age of eligibility for full Social Security benefits is rising to 67, what other changes (retrenchments) will be on the horizon when the baby boomers have all stormed into later life?

- **Older workers are (currently) an at-risk group.** From being offered incentives to retire early, to not hiring older workers—age discrimination at work is alive and well (Ekerdt, 2010; Neumark, 2009). But, the situation is changing. Anxious about their shrinking labor force, European employers are taking steps to reverse their decades-long practice of enticing older people to leave work via pension perks (van Selm & Van der Heijden, 2013). While the United States still has ample young workers to float its economy, this may not be true in another decade when the mammoth baby boom cohort all reaches 65. At that time, will U.S. employers also change their negative attitudes toward hiring older employees?

- **Older people are more at risk of being poor.** During the 1960s and 1970s, the United States took the landmark step of dramatically reducing poverty among older adults. Congress extended Social Security benefits. Our nation passed that crucial government-funded health-care program called Medicare. (You can see the dramatic effects of these programs in cutting elderly poverty-rates by turning back to Figure 4.6, on page 118.) Old-age economic hardship is currently the fate for the roughly 1 in 3 retired Americans who survive on Social Security alone (Binstock, 2010), for the many people who must keep working during their so-called golden years, and for an alarming percentage of women as they reach advanced old age. Will poverty become endemic among the over-65 population in future years?

Finally, I can't leave the topic of old-age poverty without touching on the topic of **intergenerational equity**—balancing the needs of the young and the old. Given that the U.S. elderly get Medicare and Social Security, and citizens in many other

Western nations receive even more lavish old-age aid, it's easy for social critics to argue that affluent societies are over-funding older people at the expense of the young (as reported in Moulaert & Biggs, 2013). But, abandoning these programs leaves people dependent on their families. That hurts everyone, young and old (Binstock, 2010). Suppose you had to choose between helping your children and supporting your grandmother, and destitute older people roamed the streets? Again, we are in this together. Life is not a zero-sum game.

Widowhood

Although we worry about its future, most of us associate retirement with joy. That emotion does not apply to widowhood. In a classic study of life stress, researchers ranked the death of a spouse as life's most traumatic change (Holmes & Rahe, 1967). What multiplies the pain is that today, widowhood still may strike a pre-baby boom cohort who married in their early twenties and never lived alone.

Imagine losing your life partner after 50 or 60 years. You are unmoored and adrift, cut off from your main attachment figure. Tasks that may have been foreign, such as understanding the finances or fixing the food, fall on you alone. You must remake an identity whose central focus has been "married person" for all of your adult life. Decades ago, British psychiatrist Colin Parkes (1987) beautifully described how the world tilts: "Even when words remain the same, their meaning changes. The family is no longer the same as it was. Neither is home or a marriage" (p. 93).

How do people mourn this loss? Who has special trouble with this trauma, and how can we help people cope? Let's look at these questions one by one.

Exploring Mourning

During the first months after a loved one dies, one classic study showed, people are often obsessed with the events surrounding the final event (Lindemann, 1944; Parkes, 1972). Especially if the death was sudden, husbands and wives report repeatedly going over a spouse's final days or hours. They may feel the impulse to search for their beloved, even though they know intellectually that they are being irrational. Notice that these responses have similarities to those of a toddler who frantically searches for a caregiver when she leaves the room. With widowhood—as the poignant comments of the women in the Experiencing the Lifespan box show—John Bowlby's clear-cut attachment response reemerges at full force.

Experiencing the Lifespan: Visiting a Widowed Person's Support Group

What is it like to lose your mate? What are some of the hardest things to endure in the first year after a spouse dies? Here are the responses I got when I visited a local support group for widowed people and asked the women these kinds of questions:

"I've noticed that even when I'm with other people, I feel lonely."

"I find the weekends and evenings hard, especially now that it gets dark so early."

"Sundays are my worst. You sit in church by yourself. People avoid you when you are a widow."

"I think the hardest thing is when you had a handyman and then you lose your handyman. You would be amazed at how much fixing there is that you didn't know about. My hardest jobs were George's jobs. For instance, every time I have a car problem I break down and cry."

"I was married to a handyman and a cook. He spoiled me rotten. You don't realize it until they are gone."

"For me, it's the incessant doctors' bills. I got one yesterday. It's that continual painful reminder of the death."

"And you get all this stuff from Medicare, from Social Security. This year will be the last I file with him."

"You just don't know what to do. I didn't know anything, didn't know how much money we had . . . didn't know about the insurance. . . . My family would help me out but, you know, it's funny—you don't ask."

"You have friends, but you can't really talk to them. You don't bring him up, and neither does anyone else."

"The thing that upsets me is that I'm scared that no one but me will remember that he was alive."

Experts dislike using the word "recovery" to describe bereavement, as it implies that mourning, a normal life process, is a pathological state (Sandler, Wolchik, & Ayers, 2008). Moreover, when people lose a spouse, they do not simply "get better." They emerge as different, hopefully more resilient human beings (Balk, 2008a, 2008b; Tedeschi & Calhoun, 2008). Still, as I will describe in chapter 15, after about a year, we expect widowed people to "improve" in the sense of remaking a satisfying new life. People still care deeply about their spouses. Their emotional connection remains. However, this mental image is incorporated into the survivor's evolving identity as the widowed person continues to travel through life.

Now, let's survey the research messages we get from tracking people's feelings as they move from early bereavement into what attachment theorists might label the *working model*—or constructing an independent life—phase of widowhood:

WIDOWHOOD INVOLVES FLUCTUATING EMOTIONS. Interestingly (and in contrast to the image of unremitting pain), one conclusion of these studies is that widowhood evokes contradictory emotions. In following 59 widows, psychologists charted a regular decline in depressive symptoms over time. However, life satisfaction scores showed a different pattern, dipping to a low at the first year anniversary, and then rising during the second year (Powers, Bisconti, & Bergeman, 2014). Other researchers, following a huge national sample of Australian adults, found that, after widowhood, there was a rise in well-being (Anusic, Yap, & Lucas, 2014)!

What could explain this embarrassing finding? One possibility is that, as you saw in the introductory chapter vignette, even people in the happiest long-term marriages may not realize how well they can cope on their own. When you discover that, yes, you can prepare the taxes or fix the faucet and you do not fall apart when finding yourself single after 50 or 60 years, you have a tremendous sense of self-efficacy. As the Chinese proverb puts it: Within the worst crisis lies an opportunity (or, in the last chapter's terminology, a potential redemption sequence). As I described in Chapter 12, life traumas do promote emotional growth.

This is not to minimize the health consequences of widowhood. Study after study finds that, compared to married adults, the widowed have worse mental health (Choi and Vasunilashorn, 2014; Sasson & Umberson, 2014). In one alarming Canadian finding, 2 in 5 elderly people showed chronic symptoms of depression after losing a husband or wife (Jozwiak, Preville, & Vasiliadis, 2013). The most powerful example comes from **the widowhood mortality effect**—a markedly higher risk of dying for the surviving spouse after a partner dies (Sullivan & Fenelon, 2014). Who can people most rely on for support during this difficult time?

widowhood mortality effect The elevated risk of death among surviving spouses after being widowed.

FRIENDS SEEM MORE IMPORTANT THAN CHILDREN IN DETERMINING HOW PEOPLE ADJUST. Actually the surprising answer is friends. Family members do get people over the initial bereavement hump. But, because they have their own lives, children may need to move on ("Now that it's been three months, I don't need to visit Mom every day. I have to take care of my own husband and kids"). Therefore, to cope effectively over the long term, widows need to reach out to friends (Ha & Ingersoll-Dayton, 2008). The vital role friends play in widowhood well-being was showcased in this German finding: While satisfying "family attachments" predicted happiness among married elderly women, if a female was single, her happiness depended on having good friends (Albert, Labs, & Trommsdorff, 2010).

The virtue of friends is that, not only are they companions with whom to share activities, they also

Susan Chiang/E+/Getty Images

These widows enjoying a visit to a local nature preserve illustrate just why friends seem especially important after people lose a spouse.

may allow you to more openly share your distress. For instance, in one study, Chinese widows living in Canada felt it was inappropriate to discuss their grief with family members (Martin-Matthews and others, 2013). This tendency to clam up (meaning not embarrass people by discussing your pain) may explain why widows report feeling lonely even when in a group (recall the Experiencing the Lifespan Box on page 409). And, in specifically studying loneliness among the widowed, researchers found the best cure for this common condition lay in making a new widowed friend (Utz and others, 2014).

At this point, readers may be tempted to urge everyone who has lost a spouse to join a widowed person's group. This may be a mistake. An underlying message of my discussion is that most widowed people are resilient. We are doing them a disservice by assuming they are incompetent and totally in need of help. Actually, support groups for widowed people, psychologists find, are useful mainly for people who are having unusual trouble coping with this life event (Bonanno & Lilienfeld, 2008; Onrust and others, 2010). Who has special trouble coping with widowhood?

Predicting Which Widowed Adults Are Most at Risk

Some of you might imagine that men should be most vulnerable to having serious problems after their spouse dies. Women are more emotionally embedded in relationships. They can use their close, enduring connections with friends to construct new lives. Imagine losing your only attachment figure and you will understand why, for elderly widowers living alone, suicide is a major concern (Stroebe, Schut, & Stroebe, 2007).

Lost in loneliness, spending your days staring out at sea, this classic image of the elderly widower says it all. Men—when they haven't found a new mate—can be at high risk for suicide in the older years.

Still, men have one great advantage over women in the reattachment odds—their far higher chance of finding a new mate. To give just one example, 9 out of 10 men in a study exploring dating after widowhood were actually in new relationships. But only 1 of 9 women who said they were interested in dating was able to achieve this goal (Carr & Boerner, 2013). Attend any U.S. boomer event at your local church (or older adult institute) and, like me, you might be struck by this strange thought: Have aliens swooped down and abducted all the men?

Another general risk factor, we might think, relates to whether the death was predicted or struck out of the blue (Schaan, 2013). Did your husband die unexpectedly on the golf course or pass away after years of worsening health? On-time (expected) deaths seem inherently less stressful because they give people a chance to prepare emotionally for the event. Moreover, when you have cared for a beloved partner who has suffered for years, there can be a sense of relief when the person dies.

Perhaps because males might be losing their only attachment figure, one study exploring the widowhood mortality effect showed husbands whose wives died unexpectedly were at much higher risk of dying than other widowed adults (Sullivan & Fenelon, 2014). In contrast, other researchers (Sasson & Umberson, 2014) found losing a spouse hits women harder when that event happens at an off-time (young) age—which makes sense because, as a 30- or 40-year-old widow, it's hard to find friends who share your experience and can understand your pain.

However, rather than making generalizations based on gender or age, again, in predicting reactions to widowhood we need to adopt a *developmental systems approach*—that is, consider a complex set of forces. How emotionally resilient is the widowed person? Does that individual have other attachments or a life passion to cushion the blow? (See Carr, 2004.) We also need to look at the person's married attachment style. People who are securely attached to their partner tend to have other

What should this young woman do to help her newly widowed grandma? Check out Table 13.5 below for answers.

secure attachments in the wider world. Men and women who are insecurely attached, because they generally have more trouble relating, may have trouble forming new close relationships to make up for their loss (Bonanno and others, 2002; Field, Gal-Oz, & Bonanno, 2002; Ha, 2008).

We also can't neglect the role of the wider environment. Widowhood can be a more devastating blow for working-class women because they lack the financial resources to construct a new life (Angel, Jimenez, & Angel, 2007; Sullivan & Fenelon, 2014). In one study, researchers found that, if older adults were living in an area with a high concentration of widowed people, their odds of dying after being widowed were reduced (Subramanian, Elwert, & Christakis, 2008). So moving as a couple to a senior citizen community with all those widows and widowers may have an unexpected survivor bonus in later life!

Finally, we also need to look to the way a given culture treats widowed people. To take an extreme case, let's travel to a place where being widowed (for women) can have nightmarish aspects that go well beyond losing a spouse.

Among the Igbo of West Africa, new widows must "prove" that they did not kill their spouse by sleeping with their husband's corpse. Because property rights revert to the paternal side of the family, after the man's death, his relatives feel free to take the bereaved woman's possessions and force her off her land (Cattell, 2003; Sossou, 2002). Given this totally male-dominated tilt to their society, it is no wonder that an African widow in her sixties made this comment: "I've had so much of this bossing by men. I have my house, my garden. Why should I have a man take my money and spend it on drink and other women? I am the boss now" (quoted in Cattell, 2003, p. 59).

Table 13.5 pulls together the main points of my discussion in guidelines for helping a widowed family member. As a final comment, if you are a child, please allow your widowed parent to develop a new romantic attachment! You might think that new relationships run into headwinds from children mainly after parents' divorce (see Chapter 11). But, in the dating in late life study I alluded to earlier, when father–child bonds were somewhat ambivalent, daughters in particular were apt to get very angry when their widowed dad found a replacement life love (Carr & Boerner, 2013).

In the next chapter, devoted to the physical challenges of later life, I'll be continuing this discussion by offering tips about how to sensitively treat loved ones, especially during the old-old years.

Table 13.5: Guidelines for Helping a Family Member Survive Widowhood

1. Expect your widowed relative to experience different emotions, and don't decide this person is uncaring for having positive feelings such as pride and a sense of relief.

2. Offer comfort, but don't take over everything. Let your family member connect with her new efficacious self.

3. Encourage a female relative to reach out to friends, and possibly advise joining a widowed person's group, but only if the person seems especially isolated and distressed. Also understand that your family member may have special problems if she lost her spouse at an off-time (young) age.

4. Be alert that a man, in particular, may need special help if his wife died suddenly, or if he can't find a new love relationship. Among depressed elderly widowers who don't find another mate, suicide can be a serious concern.

5. Advise seeking special help if *any* widowed family member seems genuinely depressed for over a year.

Tying It All Together

1. Joe, a baby boomer, is approaching an age when he might retire from his public school teaching job. Compared to a colleague who retired a decade ago, Joe *(pick false statement)*: (a) is apt to have lower retirement assets (due to the 2008 recession); (b) will probably retire at an older age; (c) may need to work after he does retire; (d) will be unhappy if he devotes retirement to volunteering with at risk kids.

2. Social Security provides a *lavish/meager* income that is *guaranteed by the government/ depends on personal investments.*

3. As I touched on in the text, to preserve Social Security, U.S. readers are apt to hear discussions about increasing the age of eligibility for getting full benefits to age 70. Discuss the pros and cons of this controversial idea.

4. If your favorite aunt's husband recently died, you can expect *(choose one)*: *mixed feelings of loss and self-efficacy/just sadness that gets steadily less intense.* To predict how well your relative copes, the quality of her *family/friendships* matters most.

Answers to the Tying It All Together questions can be found at the end of this chapter.

SUMMARY

Setting the Context

The **median age** of the population is rising due to declining fertility, longer life expectancies, and, of course, the baby boom. While **ageism** (negative stereotypes about the elderly) is universal, we also gravitate to the elderly for positive traits, and have contradictory old age images partly because there are such dramatic differences between being **young-old** and **old-old.**

The Evolving Self

Everyone believes that as people get older, memory declines. Elderly people do perform less well than the young on most memory tasks. Memory challenges that are more difficult—such as linking faces to specific situations, remembering bits of information quickly, and especially **divided-attention tasks**—produce the most severe deficits, and losses in these situations begin at a surprisingly young age.

Using the information-processing perspective, researchers find that as people age, working memory declines because frontal lobe executive functions are impaired. Using the **memory-systems perspective,** studies reveal few age-related losses in **semantic memory** or **procedural memory** but dramatic declines in **episodic memory.** To improve memory in old age (or at any age), use selective optimization with compensation, employ **mnemonic techniques,** and work on improving the person's mental state. Also, understand that when tests are labeled as "for memory," older people may get too anxious to perform as well as they should, and that late life memory complaints may not relate to a person's scores on objective memory tests.

Socioemotional selectivity theory suggests that in old age (or at any age), when people see their future as limited, they focus on maximizing the quality of their current life, and prefer to be with their closest attachment figures. This emphasis on enjoying the present, plus the late life **positivity effect** and lower daily stress, offer compelling reasons for the **paradox of well-being,** the fact that, in surveys, older people report high levels of happiness.

Depression does become a more serious risk when people are old-old and physically frail; but, many older adults preserve their happiness and social connections into advanced old age. Reaching **integrity,** feeling generative, and having a sense of purpose in life are keys to being happy in old age.

Later-Life Transitions

Until recently, most people retired in their early sixties and lived in that state for a large chunk of adult life. The reason was the explosion of government sponsored old-age programs offering developed-world older citizens income for life. Germany has historically been a model of the ultimate in guaranteed, comfortable government support.

In the United States, our main sources of retirement income are **Social Security, private pensions,** and savings. However, unlike in Germany, Social Security only provides a meager guaranteed income. Today, because most U.S. baby boomers don't have the funds to fully float retirement, they are planning on working until older ages. When they retire, many U.S. workers may be forced to take post-retirement jobs. The Great Recession of 2008 and the erosion of real wages have made U.S. retirement a more fragile life stage.

Older workers mainly base their retirement decisions on financial considerations, but poor health can also force people to leave work. **Age discrimination,** although illegal, also propels older people to retire. Even though most negative stereotypes about older workers are false, employers are reluctant to hire older employees. Still, the decision to retire (or not to retire) can be a positive choice. People who choose to keep working into their seventies or eighties are typically healthy and well-educated, with flow-inducing jobs.

Retirees are happy when they have retired on time, freely chosen to leave work, have few health- and money worries, are generative, open to experience, and have an enduring leisure passion. People use these years to further their generativity, to pursue other "bucket list" goals, and to learn. Baby boomers' inadequate pension and savings, looming cuts to Social Security (partly due to the rising **old-age dependency** ratio), and age discrimination in the workforce remain serious threats. Still, due to work force shortages, when the massive baby boom cohort all reaches their late sixties in the next decade, people may be more willing to hire older adults. **Intergenerational equity** issues (especially over-benefiting the elderly) are a concern in nations where retirees have traditionally had many government and pension perks.

Widowhood is a top-ranking life stress, especially when it strikes old-old people who have been married for their entire adult lives. The early symptoms of bereavement have much in common with the separation response of an infant whose caregiver leaves the room. Rather than being an unmitigated trauma, however, losing a spouse evokes many different emotions and friends loom large in how people cope. Still, widows' comparatively higher rates of depression and the **widowhood mortality effect** suggest that this major life event can take an enduring toll.

While women who lose a spouse seem more cushioned by their friend network, widowed men find it much easier to find new mates. For males being widowed suddenly (versus after a spouse's long illness) and for females losing a spouse at a too young, off-time age, widowhood seems particularly hard. Personality resilience, socioeconomic status, the person's overall life situation, and cultural forces shape the experience of widowhood, too. Children need to let widowed parents develop new romantic attachments after their mother or father has died.

KEY TERMS

median age, p. 390

young-old, p. 390

old-old, p. 390

ageism, p. 391

divided-attention task, p. 393

memory-systems perspective, p. 395

procedural memory, p. 395

semantic memory, p. 395

episodic memory, p. 395

mnemonic technique, p. 397

socioemotional selectivity theory, p. 398

paradox of well-being, p. 399

positivity effect, p. 399

integrity, p. 402

Social Security, p. 404

private pensions, p. 405

age discrimination, p. 406

old-age dependency ratio, p. 408

intergenerational equity, p. 408

widowhood mortality effect, p. 410

Amos Morgan/Photodisc/Getty Images

ANSWERS TO Tying It All Together QUIZZES

Setting the Context

1. Dwayne should present concepts more slowly (but not talk down to his audience) and refrain from presenting a good deal of information in a single session. He should tie the course content into older adults' knowledge base or crystallized skills and strive to make the material relevant personally. He might offer tips on using mnemonic techniques. He should continually work on reducing memory fears: "With your life experience, learning this stuff should be a piece of cake!"

2. a. semantic memory b. episodic memory c. procedural memory

3. 1) Bike riding, that automatic skill, is "in" procedural memory, so it can be maintained even into Alzheimer's disease. 2) Remembering the material in this chapter, since it is in the most fragile system (episodic memory), is apt to decline at a relatively young age.

4. The answers here are up to you

5. b and c

6. Older people (1) focus on enjoying the present, (2) selectively screen out negativity, and (3) live less-stressful lives.

Later-Life Transitions

1. d

2. meager/guaranteed

3. Pros: Raising the retirement age to 70 will keep Social Security solvent, encourage older people to be productive for longer, and get society used to the fact that people can function competently well into later life. Cons: Depriving people of this money will add to the pressure forcing older people to unwillingly keep working—and for the millions of workers who don't have other retirement nest eggs and health problems—have the *devastating* consequence of making people penniless in later life. Keeping older people in the labor force longer will make it more difficult for young people to get jobs or advance at work.

4. You can expect mixed feelings of intense loss and self-efficacy. The quality of your aunt's friendships will matter most.

CHAPTER 14

Antony Nagelmann/The Image Bank/Getty Images

The Physical Challenges of Old Age

At age 76, Susan was vigorous and fit. She walked a mile each day. As the community college's star pupil, she took classes three days a week. But, Susan was finding it hard to hear her professors because those young students made so much noise! Her night-vision troubles made it scary to drive home from school, especially during the dark winter months.

Susan's doctor worried about her atherosclerosis. But it was the vision and bone problems that preoccupied Susan's thoughts. What if she fell when walking to class, or had an accident on those curving highway exit ramps? When Susan almost backed into a truck on Main Street—in broad daylight!—she realized she had to quit school and consider giving up her car.

Four years later, at age 80, Susan was having trouble cooking and cleaning. She began to worry: "What will happen when I can't take care of myself?" Emma, now 50 (and single), urged Susan to move in with her: "I'm buying a condo in this terrific planned community where you don't need to drive. It has no stairs; I'll put grab bars in the bathroom. As my adoptive mom, I'd consider it a privilege to help care for you."

Susan politely said no. She was determined to plan for a future that did not involve burdening loved ones with her care. It was time to check out that beautiful assisted living facility that was advertised as being at the forefront of geriatric care. But after going on Shady Acres website, Susan almost had a heart attack. The average rates ($6,000 a month) were higher than at a four-star hotel! Thank the Lord for Carl's IRA and the long-term care insurance her husband had urged her to buy at the impossibly young age of 63. Susan put her name on the waiting list—and none too soon. Six months later, she fell, breaking her hip, and could no longer live at home.

Today, Susan uses a walker. It's hard to get dressed and use the toilet. However, when I visited her, she was surprisingly upbeat. True, life at 83 can be difficult—not simply because of a person's physical state. The problem is the ridiculous status cliques some rude old ladies have formed. Still, the facility is wonderful. She loves the activities. Old ladies can hang onto their passions, too. The monthly lectures—covering everything from great books to politics, taught by her former community college professors—are a real joy!

What enemy is Susan battling? How does physical aging turn into disease, disability, and sometimes the need for a nursing home? This chapter offers answers to these questions and many more.

In the following pages, I'll be exploring problems that some gerontologists (for example, Rowe & Kahn, 1998) have labeled as "unsuccessful aging," describing what goes physically wrong during the old-old years. By now, you should realize that equating "successful aging" with walking miles at age 90 is wrong. Successful aging means drawing on what gives your life meaning to live fully, no matter how your body behaves. It is epitomized by 94-year-old Jules, described on page 401, who—although he can barely take a step without stumbling—is sensitively doing therapy and writing books.

Aging successfully means having Jules's sense of life purpose and generative mission. But, successful aging also depends on whether the wider world offers older people the support they need to function at their best. The issue in later life is not so much being ill, but living fully in the face of chronic disease. The way people function in later life depends on their personal capacities (or nature) combined with nurture—having the right person–environment fit.

How can we engineer the right person–environment fit for older loved ones? Let's begin our search for answers by charting the aging process itself.

normal aging changes
The universal, often progressive signs of physical deterioration intrinsic to the aging process.

chronic disease Any long-term illness that requires ongoing management. Most chronic diseases are age-related and are the endpoint of normal aging changes.

ADL (activities of daily living) problems Difficulty in performing everyday tasks that are required for living independently. ADLs are classified as either basic or instrumental.

instrumental ADL problems Difficulty in performing everyday household tasks, such as cooking and cleaning.

basic ADL problems Difficulty in performing essential self-care activities, such as rising from a chair, eating, and getting to the toilet.

Tracing Physical Aging

Susan has atherosclerosis, or fatty deposits on her artery walls. Her fragile bones and vision and hearing problems are also classic signs of **normal aging**—body deterioration that advanced gradually over years. Over time, normal aging shades into disease, then disability, and, finally—by a specific barrier age—death.

PRINCIPLE #1 CHRONIC DISEASE IS OFTEN NORMAL AGING "AT THE EXTREME." Many physical losses, when they occur to a moderate degree, are called normal. When these changes become extreme, they have a different label: **chronic disease.** Susan's bone loss and atherosclerosis are perfect examples. These changes, as they progress, produce those familiar later-life illnesses—osteoporosis and heart disease.

The National Health Interview Survey (NHIS), an annual government poll of health conditions among the U.S. population, tells us other interesting illness facts. As you can see in Figure 14.1, arthritis is the top-ranking chronic illness in later life (Centers for Disease Control and Prevention [CDC], 2009). As we get older, our chance of having a variety of illnesses increases. Like arthritis, many age-related diseases are not fatal. They interfere with the ability to function in the world. So the outcome of chronic illness is not just death, but **ADL** (activities of daily living) problems—difficulties handling life.

PRINCIPLE #2 ADL IMPAIRMENTS ARE A SERIOUS RISK DURING THE OLD-OLD YEARS. ADL limitations come in two categories. **Instrumental ADL problems** refer to troubles performing tasks important for living independently, such as cooking and cleaning or driving. **Basic ADL limitations** refer to problems with basic self-care activities, such as standing or getting to the bathroom or feeding oneself. When people have these severe disabilities, they typically need full-time caregiving help.

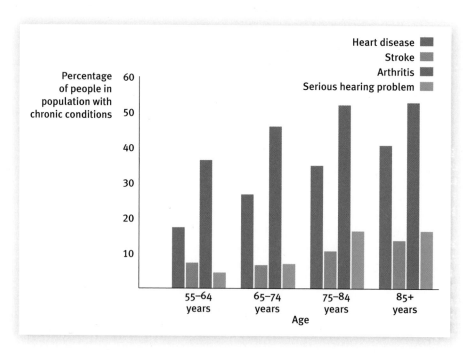

FIGURE 14.1: Prevalence of selected chronic health conditions among U.S. adults in middle and later life (percentages): As people travel into their seventies and eighties, the rates of common age-related chronic diseases rise. Although every chronic illness can impair the ability to fully enjoy life, many common chronic diseases don't actually result in death.
Data from: CDC (2009); National Center for Health Statistics (2008).

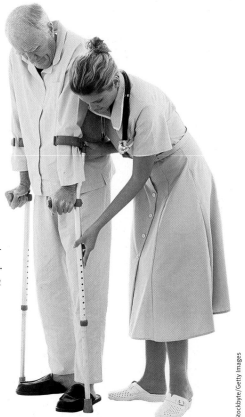

Although ADL problems can happen at any age, notice from Figure 14.2 that the old-old years are when these problems really strike. Half of all people over 85 *living in their homes*, have instrumental ADL difficulties. Basic ADL limitations, or fundamental self-care impairments, such as walking to the toilet or dressing, affect 1 in 6 of the oldest old (CDC, 2009). These statistics minimize the true rate of problems because older adults with basic ADL impairments often have to enter a nursing home.

So, yes, people can arrive at age 85 or 90 virtually disability free. But as we travel further into later life, problems physically coping become a serious risk.

PRINCIPLE #3 THE HUMAN LIFESPAN HAS A DEFINED LIMIT. A final fact about aging is that it has a fixed end. More people than ever are surviving past a century. But a miniscule fraction make it beyond that barrier age. In August 2014, worldwide, there were roughly 75 documented "super-centenarians" — people who lived until 110 and beyond (Gerontology Research Group, n.d.). Unless scientists can tamper with our built-in, species-specific *maximum lifespan*, soon after a century on this planet, we are all fated to die.

Can We Live to 1,000?

At this point, you might be thinking that many babies will soon make it to be supercentenarians. Due to scientific breakthroughs in extending the lifespan, you may have read the world is poised for the arrival of the first 1,000-year-old human being (As reported in Carnes, Olshansky, & Hayflick, 2013).

Here, you can see the real enemy in old age: It's ADL impairments. Moreover, since this 85-year-old man's difficulties standing are permanent, he was forced to enter a nursing home.

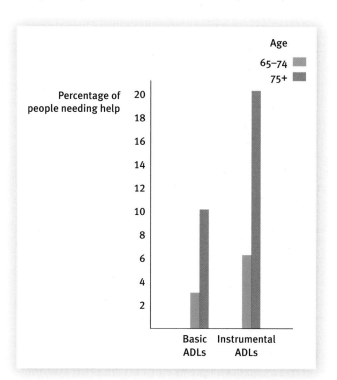

FIGURE 14.2: **Percentages of people needing assistance with instrumental ADLs and basic ADLs in the young-old years and over age 75:** Although in the sixties and early seventies the fraction of people with ADL difficulties is relatively small, the risk of having these problems escalates dramatically over age 75. (Over age 85, roughly 1 in 6 people living in the community have a basic ADL problem.)

Data from: U.S. Department of Health and Human Services, 2009.

These futuristic forecasts fall on fertile ground because one life-extension strategy has been known for 75 years. By underfeeding rats, researchers can increase the animals' maximum lifespan by up to 60 percent. The key is what one biologist calls "undernutrition without malnutrition." The animals are restricted to less food but given a nutritionally rich diet. They are allowed few empty calories (see Belsky, 1999, for review).

Calorie restriction is actually an all-purpose anti-ager, enhancing everything from glucose metabolism (Fok and others, 2013) to cardiac function (Cisiszar and others, 2013). These research findings make excellent sense because obesity, especially via its side-effect of diabetes (impaired sugar metabolism), causes every organ—from our eyes, to our heart, to our kidneys—to prematurely breakdown.

Without denying that it's important to watch your diet, however, restricting your intake *just* to live to 110 is a mistake. The calorie reduction research has typically been carried out with rats. The scientific literature is littered with miracle disease-reduction interventions—such as massive doses of vitamin A, supposed to prevent cell damage—that worked with rodents but had toxic effects on human beings!

Calorie restriction has confusing effects. Sometimes it postpones deaths in youth or allows just a small number of the most long-lived members of a species to survive longer (Gribble & Welch, 2013). There may be an unwelcome fertility trade off. Suppose you lived to 110 but put off puberty to age 25?

This species has been the target of almost all of our life-extension research carried out over the past 75 years—but it's unclear if the rat underfeeding results generalize to human beings.

Let's listen to the foremost experts in the biology of aging explain why extending the maximum lifespan in the near future is an unrealistic dream (Carnes, Olshansky, & Hayflick, 2013):

- The body breakdown involved in aging has complex causes, from multiple genetic timers to random insults that happen as cells do their metabolic work. There can't be a single magic-bullet intervention that stops aging and extends life. Even if a breakthrough technology such as stem-cell research fulfills its promise to regenerate cells lost to Parkinson's disease (Kim, Lee, & Kim, 2013), a few years later some other age-related illness, like cancer, is going to crop up. The best analogy to our aging bodies is an old car. Replacing each defective part only puts off the day when so much goes wrong that the whole system reaches its expiration date and everything stops.

- Our body's evolutionary expiration date is naturally set well below a century, because the survival of our species promotes, at best, living through the grandparent years (recall Chapter 12). Therefore, even in the most affluent nations, the probability of a twenty-first-century newborn living to 100 remains low. (It's about 4.5 percent in Japan.) So, let's celebrate our remarkable twentieth-century progress at allowing most babies born in the developed world to survive close to our expiration date. But, let's realize that extending the maximum lifespan is going to be far harder than the breakthroughs that allowed us to make it to later life.

Now let's turn to two familiar markers that affect our journey toward our expiration date (and every other aspect of our lifespan journey): socioeconomic status and gender.

Socioeconomic Status, Aging, and Disease

The most powerful evidence that poverty affects how long we live comes from scanning a few life-expectancy statistics in the developing versus the developed worlds: Babies born in South Africa can expect on average to survive to age forty years longer. Infants lucky to emerge from the womb in Monaco have a 50/50 chance of living 30 years longer—to 89 (CIA World Factbook, n.d.). This mammoth global difference is mirrored by a **socioeconomic health gap** within each country. From Canada to Cameroon and from Sweden to Somalia, affluent and well-educated people live healthier and survive for a longer time.

socioeconomic health gap The disparity, found in nations around the world, between the health of the rich and poor.

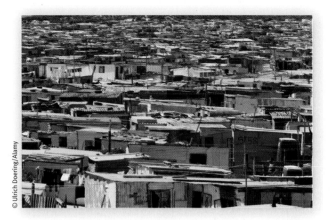 

These snapshots show visually why babies born in the affluent kingdom of Monaco statistically out-survive South African newborns by a remarkable 40 years.

When, during adulthood, is the socioeconomic health gap most pronounced? The answer, according to most (but not all) surveys, is during midlife, as normal age changes are progressing to chronic disease. For instance, in one study in Holland, only 5 percent of people in the top quarter of the income distribution reported being in poor health at age 55. For their bottom quarter counterparts, the odds were 1 in 3 (Kippersluis and others, 2010).

You may see these statistics in operation by just looking around. Notice how, by the late thirties people show clear differences in their aging rates. Although there are many exceptions, notice also that low-income adults are apt to look physically older than their chronological age. In fact, for disadvantaged Americans, "old-age" ADL impairments, not infrequently, qualify as problems of midlife (Health United States, 2009).

How far back in development can we trace this accelerated aging path? Unfortunately, based on the *fetal programming* hypothesis, its roots might emerge in the womb. Remember from Chapter 2 that *low birth weight*—which is linked to poverty—is epigenetically associated with premature heart disease and earlier death. Now recall from Chapters 4 and 5 that obesity and elevated levels of cortisol (the stress hormone) are more common among preschoolers at the low end of the socioeconomic scale. Therefore, the many health-impairing forces linked to early childhood poverty—from obesity, to chronic anxiety, to being born small—accumulate to increase our *allostatic* load, that overall marker of body breakdown signaling disease (Umberson and others, 2014; O'Donovan and others, 2013).

Now compound this with the poisonous adult lifestyle forces linked to poverty— from social-class differences in smoking (Boykin and others, 2011); to lack of exercise (who has time to work out if you are working two jobs to survive?); from poor eating habits (as high-fat foods are less expensive than fish or fresh fruit, what choices would you make if you had to save every dime?); to the stress-inducing impact of unemployment or living in crime-ridden neighborhoods.

So far, I've spelled out a dismal scenario. But, socioeconomic status involves both education and income. And, as you will see in Figure 14.3 on the next page, the educational component of SES looms large in predicting life expectancy, especially for men (OECD, 2014; Mazzonna, 2014).

Fascinating evidence that education directly affects aging involves research on telomeres, DNA sequences at the end of our chromosomes. Telomere shortening is a benchmark of cellular aging, as it shows that a particular cell has reached senescence and can no longer divide. Among a huge group of U.S. older adults, researchers found that high school graduates had shorter telomeres than people who attended college, a difference that was particularly striking among Black men (Adler and others, 2013; Mazzotti, Tufik, & Andersen, 2013). Therefore, in addition to (or due to) its other benefits, college can extend our lives!

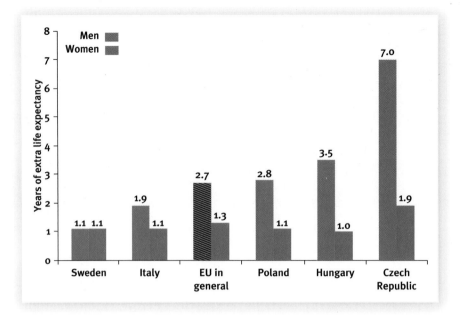

FIGURE 14.3: Life-expectancy gaps between older people with high and low levels of education in selected European countries in 2010: Notice that, while the size of the gap differs in interesting ways from nation to nation, depending partly on the given country's income inequalities, in the European Union, being well-educated gives people—mainly men—a considerable longevity boost. Data from: OECD, 2014, p. 19.

This compelling photo offers one reason for the "Hispanic paradox" (the fact that disadvantaged Latino-heritage adults tend to live a surprisingly long time): a culture immersed in intergenerational adoration and respect. The lesson: As a caring, involved grandchild of *any* cultural background, you might be "working" to help extend a beloved elderly family member's life!

Another life extender is close relationships. In one landmark study, researchers found that caring social connections were as—or more—important than good health practices in predicting how long people survived (Berkman & Breslow, 1983).

Being embedded in nurturing communities may explain "the Hispanic paradox," the fact that poverty-level U.S. Latinos outlive low-income Whites (Turra & Goldman, 2007). It accounts for why loving marriages are correlated with longevity, too (Choi & Marks, 2013). While caring attachment figures do everything from encouraging us to eat well (Friedman, 2014), to insisting we go to the doctor when we are ill, love stimulates *oxytocin* production, which, in itself, mutes the anxiety response to stress (Myers and others, 2014).

Gender, Aging, and Disease

Their wider web of social connections could be one reason why women outlive men, sometimes by an incredible decade or more (OECD, 2014). Still, the main reason for women's superior survival is biological. Having an extra X chromosome makes females physically hardier at every stage of life.

During adulthood, the main reason for this gender gap can be summed up in one phrase: fewer early heart attacks. Illnesses of the cardiovascular system (the arteries and their pump, the heart) are the top-ranking killers for both women and men. In 2014, cardiac arrests accounted for roughly 1 in 6 U.S. deaths (Go and others, 2014). However, because estrogen helps to slow the process by which fat deposits clog the arteries, men are roughly twice as likely as women to die of a heart attack in midlife (American Heart Association, 2001).

Their biological susceptibility to early heart attacks means that men tend to "die quicker and sooner." For women, the worldwide pattern is "surviving longer but being more frail" (OECD, 2014; Tareque, Begum, & Saito, 2013; Rohlfsen & Kronenfeld, 2014; Onadja and others, 2013).

It makes sense that disability is the price of traveling to the lifespan train's final stops. However, the phrase "living sicker" applies to women throughout adult life. During their twenties and thirties and forties, only women experience the physical ailments related to pregnancy and menstruation. As they age, females have higher rates of arthritis, vision impairments, and obesity—illnesses that produce ADL problems but (except in the case of obesity) don't lead to death (Whitson and others, 2010).

This male/female disability distinction brings me to a statistic called **healthy-life years**—the age at which we can expect to survive without ADL limitations. Notice from Figure 14.4, in the European Union, healthy-life years are much shorter than overall life expectancy for both sexes. But, if you look just at the length of the blue bar, notice that elderly men live healthy comparatively longer than women do. In fact, considering just healthy-life years, EU females' average six-year longevity advantage shrinks to a single year! (See OECD, 2014.)

healthy-life years The number of years people can expect to live without ADL problems.

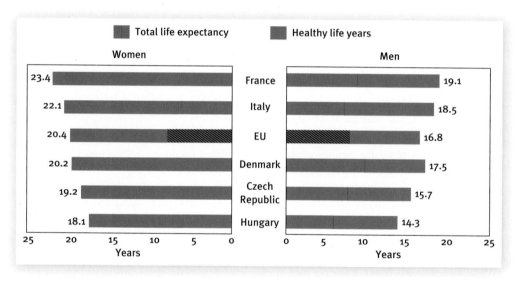

FIGURE 14.4: **Life expectancy (blue plus magenta bars) and healthy life years (blue bar) at 65, for women and men in a few European nations in 2012:** Notice that in each E.U. nation, overall life expectancy at age 65 is considerably longer than the years older people can expect to live in health. However, the gap between the two measures is wider for women than men. Bottom-line message: The statistical price of surviving into your older years is disability during the final years of your life, particularly if you are a female.

Data from: OECD, 2014, p. 19.

INTERVENTIONS: Taking a Holistic Lifespan Disease-Prevention Approach

How can we increase our healthy-life years and get closer to the biological limit of life? As I mentioned in Chapter 5, with regard to obesity, one route is to alter our epigenetic path by changing the environment from day one. Specifically:

- *Focus on childhood.* As I've been stressing throughout this book, we need to prevent premature births, make inroads in child poverty, and improve early childhood education. Now we understand that encouraging teens to enroll in and finish college can also have health benefits in middle and later life!

- *Focus on constructing caring communities.* Let's commit to making cities senior-citizen friendly (Barusch and others, 2013); and construct walkable, planned communities that allow people to exercise without going to gyms. Let's build in services that reach out to isolated neighbors and provide the nurturing social relationships that extend life.

Finally, let's appreciate the realities in Figure 14.4. Without minimizing old age's emotional benefits, even in the most health-conscious European nations, the price of living to the upper ends of the lifespan is frequently disease. Given that running for miles at age 90 is unrealistic, and we are decades from tampering with our DNA, let's use our human ingenuity to make the world user-friendly for normally aging people marching into later life. With this goal in mind, it's time to confront the conditions causing ADL problems in the flesh—sensory-motor declines and major neurocognitive disorders, or dementia.

Tying It All Together

1. When she was in her late fifties, Edna's doctor found considerable bone erosion and atherosclerosis during a checkup. At 70, Edna's been diagnosed with osteoporosis and heart disease. Did Edna:

   a. suddenly develop these diseases?

   b. have normal aging changes that slowly progressed into these chronic diseases?

   c. have both above events occur?

2. Marjorie has problems cooking and cleaning the house. Sara cannot dress herself or get out of bed without someone's help. Marjorie has _____ problems and Sara has _____ problems.

3. Laura brags that her newborn is likely to live to 120. Using the points in this section, convince Laura that she is wrong.

4. Nico and Hiromi are arguing about men's versus women's health. Nico says that women are basically "healthier"; Hiromi thinks that it's men. Explain why both Nico and Hiromi are each partly correct.

Answers to the Tying It All Together questions can be found at the end of this chapter.

Sensory-Motor Changes

What happens to vision, hearing, and motor abilities as we grow old, and how can we take action to minimize sensory-motor declines?

Our Windows on the World: Vision

One way aging affects our sight becomes evident during midlife. By their late forties and fifties, people have trouble seeing close objects. The year I turned 50, this change struck like clockwork; and I had to buy glasses to read.

presbyopia Age-related midlife difficulty with near vision, caused by the inability of the lens to bend.

Presbyopia, the term for age-related difficulties with seeing close objects, is one of those classic signs, like gray hair, showing that people are no longer young. When I squint to make out sentences, the fact of my age crosses my consciousness. I imagine students have this same thought ("Dr. Belsky is older") when they see me struggle with this challenge in class.

Other age-related changes in vision progress gradually. Older people have special trouble seeing in dim light. They are more bothered by glare, a direct beam of light hitting the eye. They cannot distinguish certain colors as clearly or see visual stimuli as distinctly as before.

What is it like to be undergoing this progression? It can be annoying to ask the server what the impossibly faint restaurant bill comes to or to fumble your way into a neighbor's seat at a darkened movie theater. For me, the most hair-raising experiences relate to driving at night. Last week, a curve of the highway exit ramp loomed out of the dark and I was inches from death. But apart from worries about night driving these problems have little effect on my life.

Unfortunately, this may not be true a decade from now. As Figure 14.5 illustrates, seeing in glare-filled environments such as a lighted medicine cabinet, or even making out the print on a white page, can be a real challenge during the old-old years.

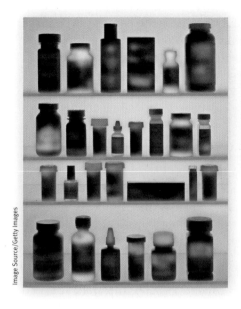

FIGURE 14.5: **How an 85-year-old might see the world:** Age-related visual losses, such as sensitivity to glare, make the world look fuzzier at age 80 or 85. So, as these images show, everything from finding a bottle of pills in the medicine cabinet to reading the print in books such as this text can be a difficult task.

These signs of normal aging—presbyopia, problems seeing in the dark, and increased sensitivity to glare—are mainly caused by changes in a structure toward the front of the eye called the **lens** (see Figure 14.6). The disk-shaped lens allows us to see close objects by curving outward. As people reach midlife, the transparent lens thickens and develops impurities, and can no longer bend. This clouding and thickening not only produces presbyopia, but also limits vision in dimly lit places where people need as much light as possible to see.

lens A transparent, disk-shaped structure in the eye, which bends to allow us to see close objects.

These changes also make older adults more sensitive to glare. Notice how, when sunlight hits a dirty window, the rays scatter and it becomes impossible for you to see out. Because they are looking at the world through a cloudier lens, older people see far less well when a beam of light shines in their eye. When this normal, age-related lens clouding becomes so pronounced that the person's vision is seriously impaired, the outcome is that familiar late-life chronic condition—a *cataract*.

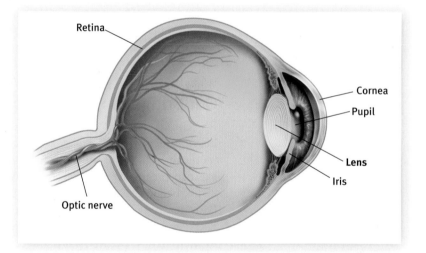

FIGURE 14.6: **The human eye:** Deterioration in many structures of the eye contributes to making older adults' vision poor. However, changes in the lens, shown here, are responsible for presbyopia and also contribute greatly to impaired dark vision and sensitivity to glare—the classic signs of "aging vision."

The good news is that cataracts are curable. The physician simply removes the defective lens and inserts a contact lens. The bad news is that the other three top-ranking old-age vision conditions—*macular degeneration* (deterioration of the receptors promoting central vision), *glaucoma* (a buildup of pressure that can damage the visual receptors), and *diabetic retinopathy* (a leakage from the blood vessels of the retina into the body of the eye)—can *sometimes* permanently impair sight.

INTERVENTIONS: Clarifying Sight

To lessen the impact of the normal vision losses basic to getting old, again, the key is to modify the wider world. People should make sure their homes are well lit, but avoid overhead light fixtures, especially fluorescent bulbs shining down directly on a bare floor, as these produce glare. They should design appliances with nonreflective materials and adjustable lighting. Putting enlarged letters and numbers on appliances will make the stove and computer keyboard easier to use.

Vision problems are a prime cause of ADL impairments because they make everything from working to walking a challenging task (Wahl and others, 2013). Poor vision is a risk factor for falling which, as you will see later, is a frightening event in later life (Ambrose, Paul, & Hausdorff, 2013; Kallstrand-Erikson and others, 2013).

This brings up the social consequences of seriously limited sight: not leaving the house because you are afraid of falling; suffering the pain of depending on loved ones for jobs you used to do: "I feel so embarrassed . . . ," said one man; ". . . I can't even change a fuse, and it's embarrassing, belittling" (quoted in Girdler, Packer, & Boldy, 2008, p. 113). People might experience the uncomfortable feeling of being "overprotected" (meaning infantilized) by well-meaning friends and family.

These fears are well founded. When researchers polled older adults attending a low-vision clinic, over time, more respondents agreed with comments such as, "People don't let me do what I could do for myself" (Cimarolli and others, 2013).

Given this danger, how can loved ones help? Encourage the person to visit a low-vision center for rehabilitation, because these programs work (Smallfield, Clem, & Myers, 2013). Consider Jim Vlock, a retired executive whose eyes were literally opened when he (reluctantly) visited a center for the visually impaired. After an evaluation, Mr. Vlock emerged laden with devices, from a talking watch, to specialized glasses for different tasks, to a computer with an enlarged screen that can "read for him." As one center director put it, "Too often we get patients who . . . have lost their jobs, their wives, their home. . . . Our philosophy is to get patients to do things for themselves so they can feel fulfilled." (See Brody, 2010.)

Actually people with vision impairments adopt different creative coping techniques on their own (Schilling and others, 2013)—from rearranging the wider world ("I make contrasts everywhere"; "I just bought new white mugs so I can see where the coffee is," said one woman), to drawing on their *positivity* skills to see life with new eyes ("Let me take pleasure in the many things I still can do"). These encouraging findings explain why even serious vision disorders are not linked to depression in old age (Kiely, Anstey, & Luszcz, 2013). This is not true of that other important sense—hearing.

Our Bridge to Others: Hearing

It's natural to worry most about losing our sight in old age. But one study showed hearing impairments are more prone to produce depression than almost any other medical problem of later life (Mener and others, 2013). The reason is that hearing loss can provoke loneliness (Kiely, Anstey, & Luszcz, 2013: Pronk, Deeg, & Kramer, 2013) because it robs us from understanding language, our bridge to other minds. Poor hearing isolates us from the human world.

Unfortunately, late-life hearing problems are common. They affect 1 in 3 people in their sixties. By the next decade, the statistics double, to almost 2 out of 3 (Bainbridge & Wallhagen, 2014). The figures are particularly alarming for men. Around the world, males are several times more likely than women to develop hearing losses in midlife (Belsky, 1999).

One reason is that age-related hearing loss has an environmental cause: exposure to noise. Men are more likely to be construction workers, ride motorcycles, and go to NASCAR races. These high-noise environments can provoke hearing handicaps at an unusually young age. Government regulations mandate hearing protection devices for workers in noisy occupations, which may partly explain why in recent decades, U.S. hearing loss rates have stabilized or declined (Bainbridge & Wallhagen, 2014). Still, from exposing ourselves to the roar of rock concerts to embedding an iPod in our ear, these statistics are apt to stay stubbornly high as today's emerging adults travel into their older years.

Presbycusis—the characteristic age-related hearing loss—is caused by the atrophy or loss of the hearing receptors, located in the inner ear (Yamasoba and others, 2013; see Figure 14.7). This irreversible change, compounded by

presbycusis Age-related difficulty in hearing, particularly high-pitched tones, caused by the atrophy of the hearing receptors located in the inner ear.

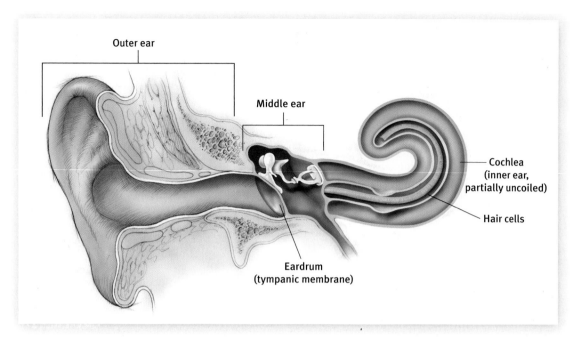

FIGURE 14.7: **The human ear:** Presbycusis is caused by the selective loss of the hearing receptors in the inner ear—called hair cells—that allow us to hear high-pitched tones—so these changes are permanent.

the neural declines discussed in the previous chapter, affect people's ability to quickly process speech as early as midlife (Clinard & Tremblay, 2013). The receptors coding high-pitched tones are most vulnerable. So, older people have special difficulties hearing consonants, for instance mistaking the word *time* for *dime*, because these sounds are delivered at a higher pitch (Bainbridge & Wallhagen, 2014).

Put yourself in the place of someone with presbycusis. Because of your speech decoding difficulties, listening to conversations feels like hearing a radio filled with static. (That's why older people complain: "I can hear you, but I can't understand you.") Because your impairment has been progressing gradually, you may not be sure you *have* a problem, thinking, "Other people talk too softly." If you are like most hearing-impaired people, you won't get a hearing aid (Laplante-Levesque, Hickson, & Worrall, 2010). Hearing aids are expensive and a hassle to manage, or so you have heard (see McCormack & Fortnum, 2013). After all, you can hear fairly well in quiet situations. It's only when it gets noisy that you can't hear at all.

Think of the pitch of the background noises surrounding you now: the hum of a computer, the sound of a car motor starting up. These sounds are lower in pitch than speech. This explains why hearing-impaired people complain about "all that noise." Background sounds overpower the higher-pitched conversations they need to understand.

Imagine having a conversation with a relative who cannot hear well—having to repeat your sentences, needing to shout to make yourself understood. Although you love your grandpa dearly, you automatically cringe when he enters the room. Now, imagine that you are a hearing-impaired person who must continually say, "Please repeat that," and you will understand why this ailment can provoke isolation. Hearing losses impair our ability to lovingly connect.

Being in a wheelchair seriously compromises anyone's quality of life. But this woman's hearing impairment, which makes having a conversation with her husband practically impossible, may be even more important in cutting her off from the outside world. Moreover, if she is like most of older people, she won't be using a hearing aid.

INTERVENTIONS: **Amplifying Hearing**

Because background noise is important in determining how well older people hear, one solution is to choose your social settings with care. Don't go to a noisy restaurant. Avoid places with low ceilings or bare floors, as they magnify sound. Install wall-to-wall carpeting in the house to help absorb background noise. Get rid of noisy appliances, such as a rattling air conditioner or fan. If a loved one is receptive, you might mention that assistive devices such as flashing phones might improve his life.

When talking to a hearing-impaired older adult, speak clearly and slowly. Face the person. Perhaps use gestures so the person can take advantage of multiple sensory cues (Diederich, Colonius, & Schomburg, 2008). But avoid *elderspeak*, the tendency to talk more in exaggerated tones ("HOW *ARE* YOU, *DARLING*? WHAT IS FOR *DINNER* TODAY?").

Elderspeak—a mode of communication we tend to naturally fall into when an older person looks physically (and so mentally) impaired—has unfortunate similarities to *infant-directed speech*. We use simpler phrases and grammar, and employ infantile "loving" words, such as *darling*, that we would never adopt when formally addressing a "real" adult (Kemper & Mitzner, 2001). I'll never forget going out to dinner with a friend in his late eighties who needed to use a walker, and cringing at how the 18-year-old server treated this intellectual man like a 2-year-old!

For your own future hearing, the message rings out loud and clear. *Avoid high-noise environments and cover your ears when you pass by noisy places.* Why do we hear so much about the need to exercise, and yet there is a deafening silence about protecting our hearing? How many of you religiously work out to prevent health problems like heart attacks but attend rock concerts without a thought? Think of the noise level at your fitness center. Could the same place where you are going to improve your health be producing this common age-related disease?

Ironically, the same noisy places that contribute to hearing losses now sometimes offer solutions for the hearing impaired. An assistive device is available in big city public venues—such as train, bus, and subway stations—that "delivers" loudspeaker announcements directly to a user's hearing aid. This microphone-attached advance, called the hearing loop, makes speech crystal clear by bypassing the cacophony of background noise. (See Hearing Loop, n.d.). The hearing loop has now migrated to some community theaters and concert halls, and speaker-to-listener microphones show promise at amplifying personal conversations, too (see Aberdeen & Fereiro, 2014).

Still no external hookup can supplant that simple device, the hearing aid. So what causes the (beautifully named) " file drawer problem," the fact that even after being fitted for a hearing aid, older people, not infrequently, give this device up?

Users complain that hearing aids (being so small) are cumbersome to adjust (McCormack & Fortnum, 2013). They are difficult to care for (Kelly and others, 2013). Worse yet, because they don't completely compensate for the selective losses I've described, they don't make your hearing perfectly normal . . . which bothers me, because I'm developing the hearing troubles discussed in this section as we speak. So if any budding mechanical genius is listening: You'll benefit humankind, make billions, and most important, *help your author*, by inventing a perfect hearing aid!

Motor Performances

Poor hearing causes heartaches when we communicate with older people one-to-one. What bothers us when we imagine the general category "old person" lies in the motor realm. The elderly are so slow!

Slowness puts older people out of sync with the physical world. It can make driving or getting across the street a challenging feat. It causes missteps in relationships, too. If you find yourself behind an elderly person at the supermarket checkout counter or an older driver going 40 in a 65-mile-per-hour zone, notice that your

elderspeak A style of communication used with an older person who seems to be physically impaired, involving speaking loudly and with slow, exaggerated pronunciation, as if talking to a baby.

Even though this aged woman may have spent her life as a Shakespeare scholar or a well-known scientist, her emerging-adult granddaughter will be tempted to talk to her frail, tiny grandma in *elderspeak*. How often have you used this patronizing type of speech with a cognitively sharp person in her eighties or nineties just because she looked as if she might be impaired?

© Ole Graf/Corbis

The huge domed ceilings are awe-inspiring, but combined with bare floors and the clatter of commuters, they make New York City's Grand Central Station an acoustic nightmare. However, thanks to the miracle of the hearing loop, people can now bypass that background noise via loudspeaker train announcements beamed directly to their hearing aids.

reaction is to get annoyed. So, age-related slowing alone may help explain why our fast-paced, time-oriented society has such negative prejudices against the old.

The slowness that is emblematic of old age is mainly caused by the loss in information-processing speed that starts decades earlier, in young adulthood (again described in Chapters 12 and 13). This slowed **reaction time**—or decline in the ability to respond quickly to sensory input—affects every action, from accelerating when the traffic light turns green, to hearing fast paced conversations, to performing well on a fluid IQ test.

Age changes in the skeletal structures propelling action compound the slowness: With *osteoarthritis*, the joint cartilage wears away, making everything from opening a jar to running for the bus an endurance test. With **osteoporosis,** the bones become porous, brittle, and fragile, and break easily. Although men can also develop osteoporosis, women, as is well known, are more susceptible to this disease. The main reason is that females—particularly slender women—have frailer, smaller bones. With this illness, the fragile bones break at the slightest pressure and cannot knit themselves back together. Hip fractures are a special danger. They are a primary reason for needing to enter a nursing home (Jette and others, 1998).

Actually, as roughly 1 in every 3 older people falls in any given year, hip fractures are not infrequent in old age. The cost of fall-related injuries in hospitalizations and nursing home placement is enough to knock society off its feet—representing at least 0.1 percent of health-care expenditures in the United States and the European Union (Ambrose, Paul, & Hausdorff, 2013).

This British road sign perfectly symbolizes our image of "the old": ADL-impaired; needing special care; most of all, impossibly slow.

INTERVENTIONS: Managing Motor Problems

As the number one risk factor for falling is dizziness (see Olsson Möller and others, 2013), physicians should be careful about over-prescribing medications to older adults. Because gait and balance difficulties make falls more likely, people need to check out exercise programs focused on improving these skills (such as Tai Chi) (Gschwind, Bridenbaugh, & Kressig, 2010). Physical exercise can even somewhat reverse balance, strength, and mobility declines that are moderately severe (Ip and others, 2013).

Older people and their loved ones might also take steps to avoid tripping by using high-quality indirect lighting (as I mentioned earlier) and low-pile, wall-to-wall carpeting in their homes. Put grab bars in places such as in the bathtub, where

reaction time The speed at which a person can respond to a stimulus. A progressive increase in reaction time is universal to aging.

osteoporosis An age-related chronic disease in which the bones become porous, fragile, and more likely to break. Osteoporosis is most common in thin women and so most common in females of European and Asian descent.

Medical scooters provide vital wheels to elderly and disabled adults—keeping this man physically connected to life.

falls are likely to occur. Install cabinet doors that open to the touch, and place shelves within easy reach. If a relative is worried about living independently, urge her to check out body sensors that signal health care providers if she trips and falls.

Actually, "lower body" impairments—because they limit mobility—are the number-one barrier to living independently in later life (Pressler & Ferraro, 2010). Suppose you needed help standing, and getting to the toilet was a scary balancing act? Still I know a man who cannot walk—and should be in a nursing home—whose life was transformed by that simple assistive device: the medical scooter. The scooter has permitted him to stay in his own home (with a lot of loving family support) and given him wheels to travel. It has also saved our government thousands of dollars in institutional care!

Table 14.1 summarizes the main points of this sensory-motor section, with special emphasis on highlighting what older adults and their loved ones can do to produce the right person–environment fit at home. How do the elderly handle that environmental challenge so important to staying independent: driving?

Table 14.1: Age-Related Sensory-Motor Changes and Interventions: A Summary

Changes	Interventions
VISION	
Problems with seeing in dimly lit places, sensitivity to glare	• Use strong, indirect light, and avoid using fluorescent bulbs.
	• Look for home appliances with large letters, nonreflective surfaces, and adjustable lighting.
	• Consider giving up driving at night and in the rain.
	• If your eyesight becomes severely impaired, go to a low-vision center for help.
HEARING	
Loss of hearing for high-pitched tones	• Reduce background noise.
	• Speak distinctly while facing the person, but avoid elderspeak.
	• Install wall-to-wall carpeting and double-paned windows in a home.
MOTOR ABILITIES	
Slower reaction time	• Be careful in speed-oriented situations.
Osteoporosis and osteoarthritis	• Search out exercise programs focused on improving balance and gait.
Gait problems	• Install low-pile carpeting to prevent tripping, grab bars, and other assistive devices at home. (The lighting interventions suggested above will also help prevent falls.)

Hot in Developmental Science: Driving in Old Age

Imagine that you are an elderly person whose vision problems or lower-body impairments are making driving dangerous. You first stop driving during rush hour. For years, you have been uncomfortable driving at night and in the rain. But even though you are aware of having problems, if you are like many older people, you cannot imagine giving up your car (Lindstrom-Forneri, Tuokko, & Rhodes, 2007). Abandoning driving means confronting the loss of independent selfhood that you first gained when you got your license as a teen. Giving up driving might even force you to abandon your home and enter a nursing home.

Actually, driving is a special concern for the elderly because it involves *many* sensory and motor skills. In addition to demanding adequate vision, driving is affected by hearing losses because we become alert to the location of other cars partly by their sound (see Munro and others, 2010). To drive well demands having the muscle strength to push down the pedals and the joint flexibility to turn the wheel. And, as anyone behind an older driver when the light turns green knows, driving is especially sensitive to slowed reaction time.

The good news is that older people—more often women than men (Sarkin and others, 2013; Tuokko and others, 2013)—limit their driving, especially when they reach the old-old years (Tuokko and others, 2013). Elderly drivers, one video study showed, pay special attention to the road when they are in heavy traffic and make left or right turns (Charlton and others, 2013). The bad news is that a small percent of drivers (roughly 1 in 10 older people in one study) rank their skills as excellent, even when on-road assessments by examiners show they are unsafe to drive (Wood, Lacherez, & Anstey, 2013). This may explain why accident rates shoot upward during *the old-old years* (Stamatiadis, 1996; see also Ross and others, 2009; see Figure 14.8).

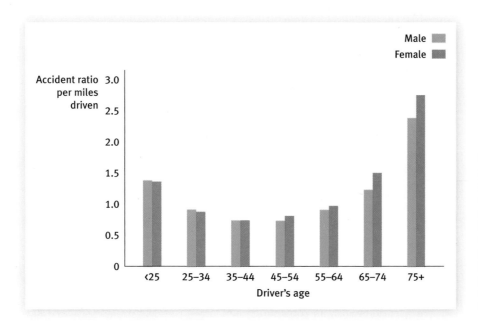

FIGURE 14.8: **Accident rates in U.S. urban areas, by age and gender:** Driving is especially dangerous for drivers age 75 and over. Notice that, if we look at per person miles driven, old-old drivers have accident rates that outpace those in the other highest-risk group—teenagers and emerging adults.

Data from: Stamatiadis, 1996.

Imagine you are a passenger and your 90-year-old uncle is behind the wheel. When should you be most concerned? Expect special trouble at complex intersections—which demand *divided attention* and complex information processing. For similar reasons, expect making difficult left turns into traffic to be unusually hair-raising (Clarke and others, 2010). Obviously, the danger accelerates in poor visibility with traffic around (Trick, Toxopeus, & Wilson, 2010).

What should society do? Our first thought would be to require yearly license renewals, accompanied by vision tests for people over 75. Still, a simple eye test will not be enough. With late-life driving difficulties, reaction-time issues loom large (Martin and others, 2010). Because the elderly have trouble processing the changing array of stimuli on the road (Roenker and others, 2003), to really weed out dangerous drivers, we might need to give each older driver neuropsychological tests (Dawson and others, 2010). Should we rely on relatives or ask physicians to report impaired

Vision problems, hearing difficulties, and especially slowed reaction time—all combine to make this 80-year-old a more dangerous driver. Moreover, he will have special trouble driving in high risk situations.

older drivers? Would you have the courage to rob your uncle of his adult status by taking away his keys?

None of these interventions speaks to the larger issue: "If I can't drive, I may have to leave my home." We need to redesign the driving environment by putting adequate lighting on road signs, streets, highways, and, especially, exit ramps. We need to construct walkable communities, invest in mass transportation, and take other steps to liberate people from cars. This mandate is mandatory to tackle our global energy problems, ballooning obesity, and the looming ADL crisis as the baby boomers move down the highway of later life.

On your way home tonight, think of how to change the driving environment to provide a better person–environment fit for older adults (and yourself!). This environmental engineering is crucial when dealing with the most feared condition of old age: major neurocognitive disorders, or dementia.

Tying It All Together

1. Roy, who is 55, is having trouble seeing in the dark and in glare-filled environments. Roy's problem is caused by the clouding of his *cornea/iris/lens*. At age 80, when Roy's condition has progressed to the point where he can't see much at all, he will have *a cataract/diabetic retinopathy/macular degeneration*, a condition that *can/cannot* be cured by surgery.

2. Dr. Jones has just given a 45-year-old a diagnosis of presbycusis. All of the following predictions about this patient are accurate except (*pick out the false statement*):
   a. The patient is likely to be a male.
   b. The patient has probably been exposed to high levels of noise.
   c. The patient is at risk for becoming isolated and depressed.
   d. The patient will hear best in noisy environments.

3. Your 75-year-old grandmother asks for advice about how to remodel her home to make it safer. Which modifications should you suggest?
   a. Install low-pile carpeting and put grab bars in the bathroom.
   b. Put fluorescent lights in the ceilings.
   c. Buy appliances with larger numerals and nonreflective surfaces.
   d. Put a skylight in the bathroom that allows direct sunlight to shine down on the medicine cabinet.
   e. Get rid of noisy air conditioners and fans.

4. Your state legislature is considering a law to require annual eye exams for drivers over the age of 75. Explain to the lawmakers why this law may not be effective, and offer some alternate strategies that could minimize the dangers of needing to drive in old age.

Answers to the Tying It All Together questions can be found at the end of this chapter.

---

major neurocognitive disorder (NCD) (also known as dementia). The general term for any illness involving serious, progressive, usually irreversible cognitive decline, that interferes with a person's ability to live independently. (A minor neurocognitive disorder is the label for a less severe impairment in memory, reasoning, and thinking which does not compromise independent living.)

Neurocognitive Disorders (NCDs)

Major neurocognitive disorder (commonly known as dementia) is the general label for any illness that produces serious, progressive, and often irreversible cognitive problems that compromise a person's ability to function. (The framers of the current U.S. diagnostic manual, *DSM-5*, distinguish between a major and minor form of NCD; with the minor form, the person has difficulties with memory and thinking that, while significant, don't prevent living independently.)

The devastating mental losses produce the total erosion of our personhood, the complete unraveling of the inner self. Younger people can also develop a neurocognitive disorder if they have a brain injury or an illness such as AIDS. However—as you will see later—these symptoms are typically produced by two specific conditions that typically strike in later life.

What is the cognitive decline really like? As you can poignantly see in the Experiencing the Lifespan box, in the earlier stages, people forget basic *semantic information*. They cannot recall core facts about their lives, such as the name of their town or how to get home. Impairments in *executive functions* are prominent. A conscientious person behaves erratically. An extrovert withdraws from the world.

Experiencing the Lifespan: An Insider Describes His Unraveling Mind

Hal is handsome and elegant, a young-looking 69. He warmly welcomes me into his apartment at the assisted-living facility. Copies of National Geographic *and* Scientific American *are laid out in stacks. Index cards list his daughters' names and phone numbers, and provide reminders about the city and the state where he lives. Hal taught university chemistry for years. When his mind began to unravel, he learned that he had the illness whose symptoms he graciously describes:*

I first noticed that I had a problem giving short speeches. You have a blank and like . . . what do I put in there. . . . I can speak. You are listening to me and you don't hear any pauses, but if you get me into something. . . . I just had one of these little pauses. I knew what I wanted to say and I couldn't get into it, so I think a little bit and wait and try to get around to it. I know it's there . . . but where do I use it? . . . It's ups and downs; and then one day you are in a deep valley. You can't get tied up in the hills and valleys because they just lead you around and it makes you more frustrated than ever. . . . If I can't get things, I just give up and then try to calm down and come back to it. Like, when I read, I get confused; but then I just stop and try again a month later. Or the people here: I know them by face, by sight, but I cannot get that focus down to memorize any names. I remember things from when I was five. It's what's happening now that doesn't make a lot of sense.

As we walk to my car after this interview, Hal's daughter fills me in:

My father seems a lot happier now that he is here. The problem is the frustration, when he tries to explain things and I can't understand and neither of us connects. Then he gets angry, and I get angry. My father has always been a very intellectual person, so feeling out of control is overwhelming for him. . . . He has days where he gets paranoid, decides that there is a conspiracy out for him. It's tiny things. A letter came to the wrong place and he went down and exploded at the people at the desk. For me the worst thing is remembering how my father was. You expect a certain response from him and you get this strange response. It's like there's a different person inside.

As the symptoms progress, every aspect of thinking is affected. Abstract reasoning becomes difficult. People can no longer think through options when making decisions. Their language abilities are compromised. People cannot name common objects, such as a shoe or a bed. Judgment is gone. Older adults may act inappropriately—undressing in public, running out in traffic. They may wander aimlessly and behave recklessly, unaware that they are endangering their lives.

When these diseases reach their later stages, people may be unable to speak or move. Ultimately, they are bedridden, unable to remember how to eat or even swallow. At this point, complications such as infections or pneumonia often lead to death.

The Dimensions of These Disorders

How long does this devastating decline path take? As you will see later, there is an in-between period between experiencing moderate memory problems and having full-blown symptoms. So it's sometimes hard to clearly define when a major neurocognitive disorder actually begins. The deterioration progresses at different rates from person to person and varies depending on the specific disease. But in general, these illnesses deserve the label chronic disease. On average, the time from diagnosis until death is approximately 4 to 10 years (Rabins, 2011; Theis & Bleiler, 2011).

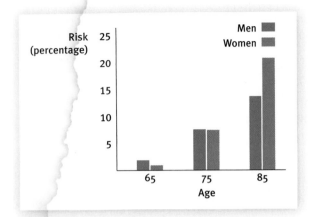

FIGURE 14.9: Estimated risks for major neurocognitive disorder in a major U.S. study, by age and sex: The good news is that our chance of getting a major neurocognitive disorder by age 65 is minuscule. The bad news is that, by age 85—especially for females—the risk accelerates.

Date from: Alzheimer's Association, 2009.

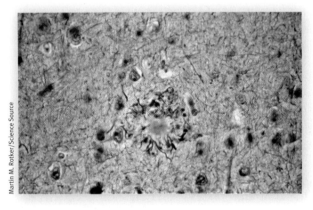

This magnified slice of the brain showing the senile plaques (dark circles) provides a disturbing window into the ravages of Alzheimer's disease.

vascular neurocognitive disorder (also known as vascular dementia). A type of age-related neurocognitive disorder caused by multiple small strokes.

neurocognitive disorder due to Alzheimer's disease (or Alzheimer's disease). A type of age-related neurocognitive disorder characterized by neural atrophy and abnormal by-products of that atrophy, such as senile plaques and neurofibrillary tangles.

neurofibrillary tangles Long, wavy filaments that replace normal neurons and are characteristic of Alzheimer's disease.

The good news is that these devastating mental impairments are typically illnesses of *advanced* old age. Among the young-old, the prevalence of these diseases is in the single digits. Over age 85, 1 in 3 people are destined to develop memory problems this severe (see Figure 14.9). While these statistics are alarming, notice the small silver lining here. Most older adults do survive sound in mind well into the old-old years.

Neurocognitive Disorders' Two Main Causes

What conditions produce these terrible symptoms? Although there is a host of rarer late life diseases, typically the older person will be diagnosed with *Alzheimer's disease* or *vascular dementia* or some combination of those two illnesses.

Vascular neurocognitive disorder (also called vascular dementia) involves impairments in the vascular (blood) system, or network of arteries feeding the brain. Here, the person's cognitive problems are caused by multiple small strokes.

Neurocognitive disorder due to Alzheimer's disease (typically called Alzheimer's disease) directly attacks the core structure of human consciousness, our neurons. With this illness, the neurons wither away and are replaced by strange wavy structures, called **neurofibrillary tangles,** and, as you can see in this photo, thick, bullet-shaped bodies of protein, called **senile plaques.**

Vascular problems—because they limit the brain's blood supply—promote this neural loss (Strand and others, 2013; Vuorinen and others, 2013). So, when an 85- or 90-year-old person develops this condition, small strokes plus Alzheimer's changes typically work together to produce the mental decline (Theis & Bleiler, 2011).

As you just saw, the number-one risk factor for developing any major neurocognitive disorder is being old-old. But there is a genetic marker that raises the chances of getting Alzheimer's disease. Roughly 15 percent of the U.S. population possesses two copies of the APOE-4 marker. Being in this unlucky group roughly doubles the chance of a person's getting ill during the young-old years (Blacker & Lovestone, 2006).

This breakthrough in the genetics of Alzheimer's poses a dilemma. Children who have witnessed a parent develop this illness are (no surprise) terrified of the disease. Knowing they don't have the genetic marker would ease their minds. But having the APOE-4 allele does not mean that a person will definitely get ill. It only shows that person is at higher risk. Would you decide to be tested? The answer, if you are like many people, might hinge on whether there are strategies to ward off the blow. Where *are* we in terms of preventing and treating Alzheimer's disease?

Targeting the Beginnings: The Quest to Nip Alzheimer's in the Bud

The main front in the war to prevent Alzheimer's centers on a protein called amyloid, a fatty substance that is the basic constituent of the senile plaques. According to much—but not all—current scientific thinking, the amyloid-laden plaques are central to producing the cortical decay (Theis & Bleiler, 2011). Efforts to dissolve the plaques in Alzheimer's patients have not worked. The challenge is to stem this amyloid cascade before the damage has occurred and people show symptoms of the disease.

This means early diagnosis is crucial. But since scientists cannot look into the brain to see the individual neurons, as of this writing there is no definitive medical test showing the person is getting ill. The current way of diagnosing Alzheimer's is to: (1) Look for a history of steady mental deterioration (rapid mental confusion signals a state called *delirium* which, in the elderly, may be due to anything from medication side effects to a heart attack); (2) rule out other physical and psychological causes; and (3) explore the person's performance on neuropsychological tests.

Older adults diagnosed with *mild cognitive impairment* are centrally important in this research goal. These people show serious learning impairments but have yet to cross the line to Alzheimer's disease. Not everyone with mild cognitive impairment makes the transition to Alzheimer's. In fact some people—those open to experience, with cognitively enriching lifestyles—can improve (Sachdev and others, 2013). How-ever, a good fraction (roughly 1 in 2 people) develops the illness within a few years (Theis & Bleiler, 2011).

The fact that the APOE-4 marker strongly predicts developing mild cognitive impairment may explain its link to full blown Alzheimer's (Brainerd and others, 2013). Other clues that a person is on the road to this illness are gait changes, walking more slowly (Verghese and others, 2013; Hausdorff & Buchman, 2013), and having difficulties with complex IADL activities, such as finding your way in unfamiliar places (see Reppermund and others, 2013). Once we have clear "biomarkers" of incipient Alzheimer's, scientists can work on developing medicines that might stop the disease in its tracks.

In the meantime, is there anything you and I can do? Adopting a heart-healthy diet is an excellent policy because, as I've been suggesting, cardiovascular problems are closely linked to cognitive loss. Although Alzheimer's is an equal-opportunity illness, affecting everyone from scholars on down, being well educated offers people a cognitive reserve to buffer the decline (Roberson, 2013; Crowe and others, 2013). (Another reason to stay in college!) Because enriching maze running challenges stimulate neurogenesis in elderly rats (Speisman and others, 2013), it's *possible* that providing mental exercise might help stave off some neural declines.

What clearly *does* improve cognitive function in middle-aged and elderly people is physical exercise (see Benedict and others, 2013). Interestingly, exercise may slow accelerated plaque formation in the very group most susceptible to Alzheimer's—adults with the APOE marker (Head and others, 2011). So, if I had to vote, my number-one candidate for an anti-Alzheimer's strategy would be *physical exercise*. Even if it doesn't help our species construct new brain cells, at a minimum, going to the gym or walking will help with the vascular component of this illness (and, of course, help prevent the lower-body problems that are such a threat to independent living in later life).

senile plaques Thick, bullet-like amyloid-laden structures that replace normal neurons and are characteristic of Alzheimer's disease.

These seventy-something dancers in the photo you first saw at the beginning of Chapter 12 are not only likely to see themselves as young, but their favorite activity may actually help prevent Alzheimer's disease!

INTERVENTIONS: Dealing with These Devastating Disorders

What about those Alzheimer's drugs we see advertised on TV? Unfortunately, their effects, put charitably, are minor at best (Rabins, 2011). With this illness, the main interventions are environmental. They involve providing the best disease–environment fit for the person and helping the second casualties of these diseases—caregivers.

FOR THE PERSON: USING EXTERNAL AIDS AND MAKING LIFE PREDICTABLE AND SAFE. Creative external aids such as using note cards can jog memory when people are in the earlier stages of Alzheimer's. It helps to put shoes right next to socks or the coffee pot by the cup, and verbally remind the person what to do. A prime concern is safety. To prevent people from wandering off (or driving off!), double-lock or put buzzers on doors. Deactivate dangerous appliances, such as the stove, and put toxic substances, such as household cleaners, out of reach. Many nursing homes feature specialized "memory units," with living environments designed to promote cognitive capacities and staff skilled in dealing with this disease. At every stage of the illness, the goals are to (1) protect people and keep them functioning as well as possible for as long as possible and (2) be caring and offer loving support.

So far, I have mainly discussed what others can do for these devastating impairments—as if the diseases had magically evaporated a human being. This assumption is wrong. The real profiles in courage are the people in the early stages of Alzheimer's who get together to problem-solve and offer each other support. What does it feel like to be losing your inner self? We already got insights from Hal in the Experiencing the Lifespan box on page 433. Now let's read what other people with early Alzheimer's have to say:

> Well, the first word that comes to my mouth is fear; becoming an infant, incontinence, not knowing who you are . . . I can go on and on, with those kinds of expressions.
>
> (quoted in MacRae, 2008, p. 400)

Outsiders can compound this terror when they develop their own memory problem—centering on the label and forgetting the human being. A woman named Bea vividly described this situation when she was first told her diagnosis:

> The last person who interviewed me was the neurologist. He was very indifferent and said it was just going to get worse. . . . Health-care professionals need to be compassionate. . . . There but for the grace of God go I.
>
> (quoted in Snyder, 1999, pp. 17–18)

Can people use their late-life *positivity* skills to act efficaciously in the face of their disease? Read what a man named Ed had to say:

> Life is a challenge . . . I am alive and I'm going to live life to the best I can. (If) people want to (say) oh what's the point in living? Well, they've stopped living. . . . you only get one chance and this is it. Make the most of it.
>
> (quoted in MacRae, 2008, p. 401)

Another man named Gorman went even further:

> This early diagnosis has given me time to enjoy the life I have now. . . .: A beautiful sunset, a tree in the spring, the rising sun. Yes, having Alzheimer's has changed my life; it has made me appreciate life more. I no longer take things for granted.
>
> (quoted in MacRae, 2008, p. 401)

Can older adults with Alzheimer's give us other insights into what it means to be wise? Judge for yourself, as you read what a loving dad named Booker said about the cycle of life:

> I'm blessed to have a wonderful daughter. I sent her to . . . school and college and now she takes care of all of my business. . . . I'm in her hands. I'm in my baby phase now, so to speak. So sometimes I call her "my mumma." . . . Yes, she's my mumma now. [Booker smiled appreciatively.] . . . She's my backbone. She's such a blessing to me.
>
> (quoted in Snyder, 1999, p. 103)

FOR THE CAREGIVER: COPING WITH LIFE TURNED UPSIDE DOWN. Imagine your beloved father or spouse has Alzheimer's or another irreversible cognitive disorder. You know that the illness is permanent. You helplessly witness your loved one deteriorate. As the disease progresses to its middle stage, you must deal with a human being who has turned alien, where the tools used in normal encounters no longer apply. The person may be physically and verbally abusive, wake and wander in the night. When the 24/7 symptoms produce total role overload (Infurna, Gerstorf, & Zarit, 2013), you face the guilt of putting your loved one in a nursing home (Graneheim, Johansson, & Lindgren, 2014). Or, you decide to put your own life on hold for years and care for the person every minute of the day.

What strategies do people use to cope? One study with African American caregivers revealed that people rely on their faith for solace: "This is my mission from God" (Dilworth-Anderson, Boswell, & Cohen, 2007). Others turn to the Alzheimer's caregiver support groups and Internet chat rooms for advice: "She seems to get worse during the night." "What works for you?" "My husband hit me the other day, and I was devastated." "Keep telling yourself it's the illness. People with these illnesses can't help how they act."

Another key lies in relishing the precious moments together you have left:

> (Tom and Jane, married for 63 years, who were being interviewed about the illness) sat close to one another on the couch . . . and shared a great deal of smiles and giggles ... and at times it felt they were the only people in the room . . . Although the stories Jane told did not always make sense, her eyes lit up whenever a question was asked about her marriage to Tom . . . What cannot be easily captured on paper were the warm interactions . . . The investigators felt privileged to be part of such a rich process in which one couple had the opportunity to share the story of their relationship together.
>
> (quoted in Daniels, Lamson, & Hodgson, 2007, p. 167)

Yes, dealing with a loved one with these disorders is embarrassing (Montoro-Rodriguez and others, 2009). It's stressful and depressing, too. But this life experience offers its own *redemption sequence*. Caregivers often report having a heightened sense of mastery after confronting this stress (Infurna, Gerstorf, & Zarit, 2013). They get a firsthand lesson in what is really important in life. One woman summed up her journey of self-awareness like this: "What it's done for me, Alzheimer's, is . . . to give me a whole new life" (quoted in Peacock and others, 2010, p. 648). (Table 14.2 summarizes these messages in a list of caregiving tips.)

Until this point, I've been exploring how older people and their loved ones can personally take action to promote the best person–environment fit when old-age frailties strike. Now, let's look at what society is doing to help.

Table 14.2: Tips for Helping People with Cognitive Disorders

1. Provide clear cues to alert the person to the surroundings, such as using note cards and labeling rooms and objects around the home (for example, use a picture of the toilet and tub at the door to the bathroom); use strong, contrasting colors to highlight the difference between different rooms in the house.

2. Protect the person from getting injured by double-locking the doors, turning off the stove, and taking away the keys to the car.

3. Offer a highly predictable, structured daily routine.

4. Don't take insulting comments personally. Try to understand that "it's the disease talking."

5. Remember that there is a real person in there. Respect the individual's personhood.

6. Try to see the silver lining; this is a time to understand what's really important in life, to grow as a person and show your love.

7. Definitely join a caregiver support group—and contact the Alzheimer's Association (http://www.alz.org).

Tying It All Together

1. Your grandmother has just been diagnosed with a major neurocognitive disorder. Describe the two disease processes that typically cause this condition.

2. Mary, age 50, is terrified of getting a neurocognitive disorder. Which statement can you make that is both accurate and comforting? *(Pick one.)* a. Don't worry. These conditions are typically illnesses of the "old-old" years. b. Don't worry. Scientists can cure these conditions when the illnesses are caught at their earliest stages.

3. You are giving a status report to a Senate Committee on biomedical efforts to prevent Alzheimer's disease. First, target the main research problem scientists face. Then, offer a tip to the worried elderly senators about a strategy that *might* help ward off the illness.

4. Mrs. Jones has just been diagnosed with early Alzheimer's disease. Her relatives might help by:

   a. taking steps to keep her safe in her home.

   b. encouraging her to attend an Alzheimer's patient support group.

   c. treating her like a human being.

   d. doing all of the above.

Answers to the Tying It All Together questions can be found at the end of this chapter.

Options and Services for the Frail Elderly

Imagine you are in your seventies, and cooking and cleaning are difficult. You have trouble walking to the mailbox or getting from your car to the store. You start out by using *selection and optimization*. You focus on your most essential activities. You spend more time on each important life task. You are determined to live independently for as long as possible. But you know that the time is coming when you will enter Baltes's full-fledged compensation mode. You will need to depend on other people for your daily needs. Where can you turn?

Setting the Context: Scanning the Global Elder-Care Scene

For most of human history, older people would never confront this challenge. Families lived in multigenerational households. When the oldest generation needed help, caregivers were right on the scene.

Today, however, this support network is fraying in some of the collectivist countries historically most committed to family care (Qu, 2014). In affluent Japan, nursing home care is becoming common. In China, young people have rapidly adopted Western individualistic lifestyles, as they move from the villages to the cities to find work. The government's one child policy in particular has left Chinese elderly fearful of what will happen when they need old-age help (Gustafson & Baofeng, 2014). So, the East is turning to the West for models of societal elderly care.

The Scandinavian countries offer some of our best examples of the elder care advanced Western societies can provide (Rodrigues & Schmidt, 2010). In Sweden, Norway, and Denmark, government-funded home health services swing into operation to help impaired older people "age in place"—meaning stay in their own homes. Innovative elderly housing alternatives dot the countryside—from multigenerational villages with a central community center providing health care to small nursing facilities with attractive private rooms (Johri, Beland, & Bergman, 2003). Because their care is free and government funded, Scandinavian older adults don't need to face that anxiety-ridden question of "can I afford to get help?"

Alternatives to Institutions in the United States

In the United States, we do have these worries. The reason is that **Medicare,** the U.S. health insurance system for the elderly, pays only for services defined as cure-oriented. It does not cover help with activities of daily living—the very services such as cooking or cleaning or bathing that might keep people out of a nursing home when they are having trouble functioning in life.

What choices do older people in the United States and other developed nations have instead of going to a nursing home? Here are the main **alternatives to institutionalization** that exist today:

- A **continuing-care retirement community** is a residential complex that provides different levels of services from independent apartments to nursing home care. Continuing care provides the ultimate person–environment fit. Residents arrive in relatively good health and then get the appropriate type of care as their physical needs change. With this type of housing, older adults are purchasing peace of mind. They know where they will be going if and when they need nursing home care.

- An **assisted-living facility** is designed for people who have ADL limitations, but not impairments that require full-time, 24-hour care. Assisted living—which has mushroomed in popularity—offers care in a less medicalized, homey setting. Residents often have private rooms with their own furniture. These settings do not have the overtones of an institutional "old-age home" (Phillips & Hawes, 2005; Yamasaki & Sharf, 2011).

- **Day-care programs** are specifically for older people who live with their families. Much like its namesake for children, adult day-care provides activities and a place for an impaired older person to go when family members are at work. Because this service allows relatives to care for a frail parent at home without having to give up their other responsibilities—day care puts off the need for a nursing home (Cho, Zarit, & Chiriboga, 2009).

- **Home health services** help people age "in place" (at home). Paid caregivers come to the house to cook, clean, and help the older adult with personal care activities such as bathing.

With their enriching activities and services and social contacts, assisted-living and continuing-care facilities can be marvelous settings in which to spend the final years of your life. ("It's like permanently living on a cruise ship," gushed a friend). However, older people must sometimes be unwillingly pushed by family members to move to these places (Koenig and others, 2014). Why?

One reason is that leaving home means shedding one's prized possessions, robbing people of the identity and memories attached to "real life" (Wiles and others, 2012). Moving can activate fears of losing privacy (Crisp and others, 2013). Yes, you won't have the scary experience of struggling to make it all alone, but you still can feel lonely, especially since you may confront the same poisonous group-status hierarchies you had to deal with during your preteen years (Ayalon & Green, 2013; Schafer, 2013). (Unfortunately, human nature doesn't change!)

Most important, in the United States, older people only have the option of moving to continuing care if they are *wealthy*—not even middle class (see Coe & Boyle, 2013). Can't we devise innovative, low-cost frail-elder-care alternatives that don't involve moving and help people who have some ADL problems but don't require that ultimate setting—the nursing home?

Medicare The U.S. government's program of health insurance for elderly people.

alternatives to institutionalization Services and settings designed to keep older people who are experiencing age-related disabilities that don't merit intense 24-hour care from having to enter nursing homes.

continuing-care retirement community A housing option characterized by a series of levels of care for elderly residents, ranging from independent apartments to assisted living to nursing home care. People enter the community in relatively good health and move to sections where they can get more care when they become disabled.

assisted-living facility A housing option providing care for elderly people who have instrumental ADL impairments and can no longer live independently but may not need a nursing home.

day-care program A service for impaired older adults who live with relatives, in which the older person spends the day at a center offering various activities.

home health services Nursing-oriented and housekeeping help provided in the home of an impaired older adult (or any other impaired person).

It's tempting menus can make continuing care delicious places for wealthy older adults to spend their last years of life—provided you can tolerate the social "risk" of not being invited to sit at this dinner table.

Nursing Home Care

Nursing homes, or **long-term-care facilities,** provide shelter and services to people with basic ADL problems—individuals who do require 24-hour caregiving help. Although adults of every age live in nursing homes, it should come as no surprise that the main risk factor for entering these institutions is being very old. The average nursing home resident is in his—or, I should say, her—late eighties and nineties. Because, as we know, females live sicker into advanced old age, women make up the vast majority of residents in long-term-care (Belsky, 2001).

What causes people to enter nursing homes? Often, a person arrives after some incapacitating event, such as breaking a hip. Given that these diseases require such daunting 24/7 care, roughly half of the nursing home population has some neurocognitive disorder such as Alzheimer's disease.

In predicting who ends up in a nursing home, both nature and nurture forces are involved. Yes, the person's biology (or physical state) does matter. But so does the environment: specifically, whether a network of attachment figures is available to provide care. Does the older adult have several family members and/or a friend willing to take the person in? The more places (and people) a frail person has "in reserve" to provide help, the lower the risk of that individual's landing in long-term care (Kasper, Pezzin, & Rice, 2010).

Just as the routes by which people arrive differ, residents take different paths once they enter nursing homes. Sometimes, a nursing home is a short stop before returning home. Or it may be a short interlude before death. Some residents live for years in long-term care.

You might be surprised to learn who is paying for these residents' care in the United States. Because people start out paying the costs out of their own pockets and "spend down" until they are impoverished, *Medicaid*, the U.S. health-care system specifically for the poor, finances our nation's nursing homes.

Evaluating Nursing Homes

Nursing homes are often viewed as dumping grounds where residents are abused or left to languish unattended until they die. How accurate are these stereotypes?

Many times, the generalizations are unfair. Nursing homes may offer perks from beauty parlors to private rooms. Residents often appreciate their newfound feelings of safety after moving (Nakrem and others, 2013). A strong movement is afoot to make nursing homes homey and "person centered," just as any other retirement home (Bishop & Stone, 2014).

We still have far to go. In one poll, more than one-half of industry experts ranked the quality of U.S. nursing homes as "fair" or "poor" (Miller, Mor, & Clark, 2010). In an alarming Michigan survey, 1 out of 5 family members reported that, yes, their impaired relative had suffered some nursing home abuse (Conner and others, 2011). (As you might imagine, "difficult" residents—that is, those with behavior problems and/or the totally physically incapacitated—are most at risk here.)

It's also difficult to erase the efficacy-eroding liabilities intrinsic to institutional life. Imagine sharing a small room with a stranger and needing to eat the food the facility serves at predetermined hours (Kane, 1995–1996). Nursing home residents can't just decide to lie in bed or refuse to take a medicine. Their every action—from sitting in a chair to being taken to the toilet—is dependent on the workers providing care. As one frustrated new resident named Luis put it: "I would say to my friends, don't go there. Go to jail instead" (quoted in Johnson & Bibbo, 2014, p. 60).

The simple act of going down steps can be an ordeal when people have ADL impairments. Imagine being this woman and knowing that, because of your osteoporosis (graphically shown in the small image at the lower left), any misstep might land you in a nursing home.

nursing home/long-term-care facility A residential institution that provides shelter and intensive caregiving, primarily to older people who need help with basic ADLs.

My discussion brings up the front-line nursing home caregivers—the **certified nurse assistant or aide.** Just as during life's early years, caregiving at the upper end of the lifespan is low-status work. Nursing home aides, like their counterparts in day-care centers, make poverty-level wages. Facilities are chronically understaffed (Teeri and others, 2008). So, even when an aide loves what she does, the job conditions can make it difficult to provide adequate care. Having worked in long-term care, I can testify that residents are sometimes left lying in urine for hours. They wait inordinately long for help getting fed. One reason is that it can take hours to feed the eight or so people in your care when dinner arrives!

Still, even some highly experienced nurses gravitate to this "low status" work. As one Swedish nurse explained: "Your relationship with the patients is completely different when you see them for years. . . . As a new nurse, your focus is on medical and technical skills. But, elderly care is so much more" (adapted from Carlson and others, 2014, pp. 764–765). Read what Jayson, a mellow, 6-foot-tall, 200-pound giant had to say about his job at a Philadelphia nursing home:

> At first I was put off by the smells. . . . Then I got moved to the Alzheimer's unit . . . and I found this to be like . . . the best task I ever had. . . . If you just come in here and say, "Okay, I got a job to do and I'm just doing my job," . . . then you're in the wrong field. . . . When somebody here dies, we all talk, we say how much we miss the person. . . . Some of them cry. . . . Some of them go to their funerals. . . . I actually spoke at some of the funerals. . . . I say how much this person meant to me.
>
> (quoted in Black & Rubinstein, 2005, pp. S-4–6)

For Jayson, who—after being shot and lingering near death—reported seeing an angel visit him in the form of a little old man, his career is a calling from God. He is flourishing in this consummately generative job. What about nursing-home residents? Can people get it together within this most unlikely setting? For uplifting answers, check out the Experiencing the Lifespan box.

certified nurse assistant or aide The main hands-on care provider in a nursing home who helps elderly residents with basic ADL problems.

Experiencing the Lifespan: Getting It Together in the Nursing Home

A few years ago, I attended an unforgettable memorial service at a Florida nursing home. Person after person rose to eulogize this woman, a passionate advocate who had worked with immense self-efficacy to make a difference in her fellow residents' lives. Then Mrs. Alonzo's son told his story. He said that he had never really known his mother. When he was young, she became schizophrenic and was shunted to an institution. Then, at age 68, Mrs. Alonzo entered the nursing home to await death. It was only in this place, where life is supposed to end, that she blossomed as a human being.

If you think that this story of emotional growth is unique, listen to this friend of mine, a psychologist who, like Jayson, finds her generativity in nursing home work:

My most amazing success entered treatment two years ago. This severely depressed resident had had an abusive marriage and suffered from enduring feelings of powerlessness and low self-esteem. I think that being sent to our institution allowed this woman to make the internal changes that she had been incapable of before. She began to look at her past and see how her experiences had shaped her poor sense of self and then to see her inner strengths. She and I formed a very close relationship.

So then she decided to work on becoming closer to her children. She had been aloof as a mother, and she told me that once her younger child had asked her to say that she loved her and she couldn't get the words out. Now, at age 89, she called this daughter, told her that she did love her and that she was sorry she couldn't say it before. Her daughters said that I had presented them with a miracle, the loving mother they always wanted. My patient made friends on the floor and became active in the residents' council. In the time we saw one another she used to tell me, "I never believed I could change at this age."

As she finished her story, my friend's eyes filled with tears: "My patient died a few months ago, and I still miss her so much."

A Few Concluding Thoughts

Dealing with ADL impairments is a vital social challenge facing our rapidly aging world. As you now know, we can't count on science to magically cure the disabilities inherent to surviving beyond our "expiration date." We need to prepare for our looming baby-boomer ADL crisis right now!

Our personal challenge, as you learned in these later-life chapters, is to live fully as long as we are alive. The Experiencing the Lifespan box you just read highlights the fact—again—that yes, it is possible to flourish even in a nursing home. It underlines the importance of close attachments in promoting a meaningful life. Plus, the story of this woman who got it together in the nursing home enriches Erikson's masterful ideas that have guided our lifespan tour: It's never too late to accomplish developmental tasks that we may have missed. People can find their real identity (or authentic self), fulfill their generativity, and so reach integrity in their final months of life!

In the next chapter, I'll continue this theme of inner development and also stress the crucial importance of making connections with loved ones as I focus directly on life's endpoint—death.

 Tying It All Together

1. You are a geriatric counselor, and an 85-year-old woman and her family come to your office for advice about the best arrangement for her care. Match the letter of each item below with the number of the suggestion that would be most appropriate if this elderly client:

   a. is affluent, worried about living alone, and has no ADL problems.

   b. has ADL impairments and is living with her family—who want to continue to care for her at home.

   c. has instrumental ADL impairments (but can perform basic self-care activities), can no longer live alone, and has a good amount of money.

   d. has basic ADL impairments.

   e. is beginning to have ADL impairments, lives alone, and has very little money (but does not qualify for Medicaid).

   (1) a continuing-care retirement facility

   (2) an assisted-living facility

   (3) a day-care program

   (4) a nursing home

   (5) There are no good alternatives you can suggest; people in this situation must struggle to cope at home.

2. Joey and Jane realize that their mother needs to go a nursing home. Which two likely comments can you make about this mother's situation—and nursing homes in general?

   a. No one in the family is available to take their mom in.

   b. Medicare will completely cover their mom's expenses.

   c. The quality of the facilities to which their mom will go may vary greatly.

   d. The staff at their mom's nursing home will almost always hate their jobs.

3. Devise some creative strategies to care for the frail elderly in their homes.

Answers to the Tying It All Together questions can be found at the end of this chapter.

SUMMARY

Tracing Physical Aging

Normal aging changes progress into **chronic disease** and finally, during the old-old years, may result in impairments in **activities of daily living (ADL) problems,** either less incapacitating **instrumental ADL problems** or **basic ADL problems**—troubles with basic self-care.

Futuristic gurus predict that we are about to extend our maximum human lifespan (about a century), especially because underfeeding can extend the maximum life span of rats. But gerontologists believe this goal is unlikely, because the cascade of faults involved in human aging ensure that our bodies must give out at about the century mark.

Socioeconomic status predicts how quickly we age and die, as shown by the wide life expectancy differences between the developed and developing worlds. The **socioeconomic health gap** refers to the fact that—within each nation—people who are affluent live healthier for a longer time. A variety of forces, starting in early childhood, make poverty a risk factor for early disability and death. Education and close attachments enhance longevity and health.

Gender also affects aging, with males dying at younger ages of heart attacks and women surviving longer but being more disabled. While females are biologically primed to live longer, considering **healthy-life years,** women only do slightly better than men. Although physical problems are the predictable price of living far into old age, improving children's lives and constructing caring communities may have dramatic health payoffs during adult life.

Sensory-Motor Changes

The classic age-related vision problems—**presbyopia** (impairments in near vision), difficulties seeing in dim light, and problems with glare—are caused by a rigid, cloudier **lens.** Modifying lighting can help compensate for these losses. Cataracts, the endpoint of a cloudy lens, can be easily treated, although the other major age-related vision impairments can cause a more permanent loss of sight. Don't overprotect visually impaired loved ones. Encourage people to visit a low vision center for help.

The common old-age hearing impairment **presbycusis** may be emotionally more troubling than vision problems because it limits a person's contact with the human world. As exposure to noise promotes this selective loss for high-pitched tones, men are at higher risk of having hearing handicaps, especially at younger ages. To help a hearing-impaired person, limit low-pitched background noise and speak distinctly—but avoid **elderspeak,** the impulse to talk to the older person like a baby. For your own future hearing, protect yourself against excessive noise. Hearing aids, unfortunately, are less user-friendly and effective than we might hope.

"Slowness" in later life is due to age-related changes in **reaction time** and skeletal conditions such as osteoarthritis and **osteoporosis** (thin, fragile bones). Osteoporosis is a special concern because falling and breaking a hip is a major reason for entering a nursing home. As mobility is crucial to late-life independence, older people must exercise and modify their homes to reduce the risk of falls.

Although the elderly drive less often, accident rates rise sharply among drivers over age 75. Solutions to the problem, such as mandatory vision tests over a certain age, may not work so well, as driving involves many sensory and motor skills. Modifying the driving environment and especially developing a car-free society are critical challenges today.

Neurocognitive Disorders (NCDs)

Major neurocognitive disorder (also known as dementia) is the label for any illness involving serious irreversible declines in cognitive functioning. The two illnesses causing these symptoms are **neurocognitive disorder due to Alzheimer's disease,** defined by neural atrophy accompanied by **senile plaques** and **neurofibrillary tangles,** and **vascular neurocognitive dementia,** caused by small strokes. These diseases typically erupt during the old-old years and progress gradually, with the person losing all functions. The APOE-4 marker predicts developing Alzheimer's disease at a relatively younger age.

To prevent the accumulation of the plaques, scientists are studying people with mild cognitive impairment and looking for risk factors that foreshadow getting ill. Today, Alzheimer's cannot be prevented or cured, although physical exercise may help ward off its onset. The key is to make environmental modifications to keep the person safe—and understand that older adults with these problems are still people. Caregivers' accounts and the testaments of people in Alzheimer's early stages offer profiles in human courage.

Options and Services for the Frail Elderly

Although, traditionally, older people lived in multigenerational households, with a built-in family support network for when they became frail, even societies historically most committed to family care (such as China and Japan) now need Western options for dealing with disabled older adults. In the United States, the major **alternatives to institutionalization—continuing-care retirement communities, assisted-living facilities, day-care programs,** and **home health services**—are typically fairly costly and not covered by **Medicare.** We need services to help people with disabilities who are not wealthy and do not need the intense care of a nursing home.

Being female, very old, and not having loved ones to take the person in are the main risk factors for entering **nursing homes,** or **long-term-care facilities.** While nursing homes vary in quality, and are improving, they still don't typically provide high-quality care. Even though the **certified nursing assistant or aide,** the main caregiver, is poorly paid, people can get tremendous gratifications from nursing home work. Society needs to prepare for an onslaught of ADL problems as the baby boomers enter their old-old years. People can develop as human beings even in a nursing home, and reach every Eriksonian milestone during their final years—or months—of life.

normal aging changes, p. 418

chronic disease, p. 418

ADL (activities of daily living) problems, p. 418

instrumental ADL problems, p. 418

basic ADL limitations, p. 418

socioeconomic health gap, p. 420

healthy-life years, p. 423

presbyopia, p. 424

lens, p. 425

presbycusis, p. 426

elderspeak, p. 428

reaction time, p. 429

osteoporosis, p. 429

major neurocognitive disorder (NCD), p. 432

vascular neurocognitive disorder, p. 434

neurocognitive disorder due to Alzheimer's disease, p. 434

neurofibrillary tangles, p. 434

senile plaques, p. 434

Medicare, p. 439

alternatives to institutionalization, p. 439

continuing-care retirement community, p. 439

assisted-living facility, p. 439

day-care program, p. 439

home health services, p. 439

nursing home/long-term-care facility, p. 440

certified nurse assistant or aide, p. 441

ANSWERS TO **Tying It All Together** QUIZZES

Tracing Physical Aging

1. b

2. Marjorie has *instrumental ADL* problems, and Sara has *basic ADL* problems.

3. Tell Laura that physical aging has such complex causes that finding any single life-extension intervention will be virtually impossible. Moreover, even if we can replace individual body parts, such as our heart, other vital organs such as our kidneys are programmed to wear out. The fact that only a tiny percentage of twenty-first-century babies is projected to live to 100 makes it unlikely that her child—or any child—can live to 120.

4. Nico and Hiromi are both correct, because although women live longer (meaning that they must be healthier), they also live "sicker" (meaning that they are more apt to be ill) throughout adulthood.

Sensory-Motor Changes

1. lens; cataract; can

2. d

3. a, c, and e. (Suggestions b and d will make grandma's eyesight worse.)

4. Tell the lawmakers that relying just on an eye exam won't be effective because driving is dependent on many sensory and motor skills. Suggest sponsoring bills to change roads by putting adequate lighting on exit ramps, more traffic signals at intersections (especially left-turn signals), and exploring other ways to make the driving environment more age-friendly. Most important, foster initiatives that don't depend on driving: Invest in public transportation. Give tax incentives to developers to embed shopping in residential neighborhoods, and encourage creative alternatives to cars.

Amos Morgan/Photodisc/Getty Images

Neurocognitive Disorders (NCDs)

1. The illnesses are neurocognitive disorder due to Alzheimer's disease, involving the deterioration of the neurons and their replacement with senile plaques and tangles, and vascular neurocognitive disorder, which involves small strokes. (Grandma—not infrequently—may have both illnesses.)

2. a

3. The main problem scientists face is diagnosing cognitive problems before they progress to the disease stage—so that we can develop treatments to ward off the illness. Tell the worried senators that they should start a fitness regimen now! While we don't have definitive evidence, there are strong hints that exercise may help stave off Alzheimer's disease.

4. d

Options and Services for the Frail Elderly

1. a, 1; b, 3; c, 2; d, 4; e, 5

2. a and c

3. Here, you can use your own creativity. My suggestions: (1) Institute a program whereby people get cash incentives to care for frail elders in their homes. (2) Build small, intergenerational living communities, with a centrally located home option specifically for the frail elderly. Residents who buy houses here would commit to taking care of the older adults in their midst. (3) Set up a Craigslist-type Web site, matching older people with a room to spare with area college students in need. Young people would live rent-free in exchange for helping the older person with cooking and shopping. (4) Establish a national scholarship program (perhaps called the "Belsky Grant"!) that would pay your tuition and living expenses if you commit to caring for frail elders in the community.

Epilogue

Now that we have reached the end of our lifespan journey, it's time to focus on life's final chapter (death) and reflect on what we've learned.

Chapter 15–**Death and Dying** is actually a perfect finale to this lifespan tour, because, not only does this milestone end our personal lives, but death is the one milestone that occurs at every life stage. How have death attitudes and practices changed throughout history, and what do people (and their grieving loved ones) feel as they deal with this final "act" of life? How has the health-care system approached the terminally ill, and what can we do to make dying more humane? These issues lead into that contemporary ethical issue: strategies for taking control of when we die.

In **Final Thoughts,** I'll take a *very* short step back to scan the high points of the journey as a whole. After you read the top four trends that stood out for me in surveying the research, take some time to think about what struck you most forcefully in reading this book.

PART VII

CHAPTER 15

Death and Dying

I was getting in the car to drive to work when Amy screamed, "Stewart! Come listen to the news!" We figured out pretty quickly that it came in right about the floor where she worked, the 96th. By the time the tower came down, we knew for sure that she died. With a normal death, you prepare for the grieving process. With a shocking death, it hits you by surprise. My wife was about to give birth to our first child, and my mother had plane tickets to come down on Friday. You get into the part of it where you mentally play back the events. Mom (typical, for her) had gone into work early so she could leave for a dentist appointment. If she'd been a less responsible person, she would not have been there at 8:46. The other weird part of it is, like, the whole country feels they own pieces of this tragedy and need to constantly remind you about it. So it doesn't go away.

My mom didn't have young children, but she was looking forward to retirement, to being a grandmother, and so she was cheated of all those things. Not only did she die in this horrible way—she died at an unacceptably early age.

. . .

In his seventies, my father seemed immortal. While he often joked about being an "old man," he had no major infirmities. At age 81, mortality hit. For a few months, Dad had been listless—not his old self, looking old. Then came the unforgettable call: "The doctor says that it's cancer of the liver. Jan, I'm going to die."

Because medicine never admits defeat, the plan was three rounds of chemotherapy, punctuated by "recovery" at home. The doctor said, "Maybe we can lick this thing," but the treatments were agonizing. Worse yet, recovery never happened. My father got weaker. After a few months, he could barely walk. Then, before going into the hospital for the third round, my mother called: "Last night we cried together and decided not to continue. We're calling in hospice. I think it's time for you to come down." My father had two more weeks to live.

A day or two before you die, you slip into a coma. It's the preceding week or two that lasts for years. Everyone has been summoned to bustle around a train that cannot be derailed. Yes, you can talk, but what do you say? My father was never a verbal man. Then, as if on cue, the disease picks up speed. From the wheelchair to becoming bedridden, the voice that mutates into a whisper, followed by waiting . . . for what? You force yourself to be at the bedside when the breathing gets slow and rattled, but you are terrified. You have never seen a dying person. You don't know how things will go. Above all, you hope that things go quickly. You can't stand to see your father suffer anymore.

M y father died in the "normal" late-twentieth-century way. Although we knew nothing about how people die, we had plenty of time to plan for the event. Dad's death came at the "right" time, at the end of a long life. The kind of death Stewart's mother faced on September 11 was horrifying, unexpected—totally outside the norm. How does death *really* happen today, compared to dying in centuries past?

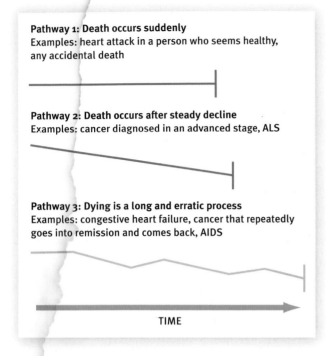

Pathway 1: Death occurs suddenly
Examples: heart attack in a person who seems healthy, any accidental death

Pathway 2: Death occurs after steady decline
Examples: cancer diagnosed in an advanced stage, ALS

Pathway 3: Dying is a long and erratic process
Examples: congestive heart failure, cancer that repeatedly goes into remission and comes back, AIDS

TIME

FIGURE 15.1: **Three pathways to death:** Although some people die suddenly, the pattern in blue and especially that in yellow are the most common pathways by which people die today.

Setting the Context

Today, as Figure 15.1 suggests, our pathways to death take different forms (Field, 2009). As happened most dramatically in the World Trade Center tragedy, roughly 1 out of every 6 or 7 people in developed nations dies without warning—as a result of an accident or, more often, of a sudden, fatal, age-related event, such as a heart attack or stroke (Enck, 2003; see the red line in Figure 15.1). My father's death fit the pattern when illnesses such as cancer are discovered at an advanced stage. Here, as the blue line shows, a person is diagnosed with a fatal disease and steadily declines.

The prolonged, erratic pattern, shown in yellow, is the most common dying pathway in our age of extended chronic disease. After developing cancer—or, like my husband, con-gestive heart failure (see the Experiencing the Lifespan Box, on page 455)—people battle that condition for years, helped by medical technology, until death occurs.

So today, deaths in affluent countries typically occur slowly. They are dominated by medical procedures. They have a protracted, uncertain course (Field, 2009; Harris and others, 2013). For most of human history, people died in a different way.

A Short History of Death

For most of human history, death was ever present—"up close and personal"—and occurred in the midst of normal life. Here is an eighteenth-century painting entitled "The Dying Request," in which a dying young woman is offering her final words to her spouse.

She contracted a summer cholera. After four days she asked to see the village priest, who came and waited to give her the last rites. "Not yet, M. le Curé, I'll let you know when the time comes." Two days later: "Go and tell M. le Curé to bring me Extreme Unction."

(reported in Walter, 2003, p. 213)

As you can see in this nineteenth-century description of the death of a French peasant woman, before modern medicine, death arrived quickly. People let nature take its course. There was nothing they could do. Dying was familiar, predictable, and normal. It was embedded in daily life (Wood & Williamson, 2003).

According to the historian Philippe Ariès (1974, 1981), while life in the Middle Ages was horrid and "wild," death was often "tame." Famine, child-birth, and infectious disease ensured that death was an expected presence throughout the lifespan. People died, as they lived, in view of the community and were buried in the churchyard in the center of town.

During the eighteenth and nineteenth centuries, death began to move off center stage when—because of fears about disease—villagers relocated burial sites to cemeteries outside of town (Kastenbaum, 2004). Then, a more dramatic change took place during the early twentieth century, when medi-cal science successfully waged war against disease. The conquest of many infectious illnesses moved dying toward the end of the lifespan, relocating it to old age (Field, 2009). Today, with 3 out of 4 deaths in the United States occurring among people over age 65 (and often happening in our eighties and nineties), the actors in the death drama are often a marginal, atypical group—nothing like you or me.

As modern medicine took over, the scene of death shifted to hospitals and nursing homes. So the act of dying was disconnected from life. Because hospitals billed themselves as places of recovery, death became a symptom of scientific failure (see Risse & Balboni, 2013). When people took their last breaths, embedded in the recesses of intensive care, health-care workers quickly erased all signs of death's presence, as they shrouded the body and shipped it to be spruced up in the funeral home (Kastenbaum, 2004). According to one social critic, by the mid-twentieth century, death had become the new "pornography"—disgusting, abnormal, never seen or talked about (Gorer, 1965).

In recent decades, society has shifted course. First, doctors did a total turnaround from the practice of concealing a devastating diagnosis—never mentioning, for instance, the "C word"—in favor of telling people, "Yes, it's cancer, and there is not much we can do." (Now that we can meticulously track each symptom on the Internet, physicians foolish enough not to be upfront about a patient's illness might be charged with malpractice or worse!) During the last 15 years, our health-care system has fully confronted the reality that "yes, people die," by developing structures to ease our passage through the terminal phase of life (Risse & Balboni, 2013). We urge everyone to do their part, by documenting in writing how they want their final act to proceed.

Cultural Variations on a Theme

While mainstream society stresses full disclosure and actively planning for our "final act," death attitudes differ from group to group even in the developed world. To demonstrate this point, let's scan the practices of a culture for whom dying remains up close and personal, but death is never openly discussed: the Hmong.

The Hmong, persecuted for centuries in China and Southeast Asia, migrated to North America after the Vietnam War and number close to a million U.S. residents today. According to Hmong tradition, mentioning dying "will unlock the gate of evil spirits," so when a person enters the terminal phase of life, no one is permitted to discuss that fact. However, when death is imminent, the family becomes intimately involved. Relatives flock around and dress the ill person in the traditional burial garment—a black robe or suit. After death arrives, they lovingly wash and groom the corpse, preparing it to be viewed.

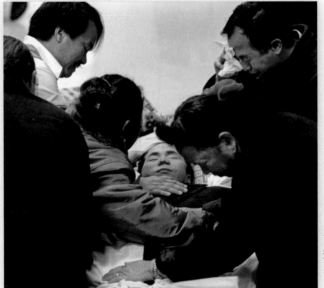

If, contrary to Hmong custom, the person dies in a hospital, it's crucial that the body *not* be immediately sent to the morgue. The family congregates at the bedside to wail and caress the corpse for hours. Then, after a lavish four-day funeral ceremony, during which the body remains in view, the deceased is lovingly dressed in warm clothing to guard against the cold, and the feet are encased in special blue shoes for the journey to the next world. At the gravesite, the coffin is reopened for a final viewing before being permanently closed (Gerdner and others, 2007). Could you participate in these activities, by giving your relative the hands-on care that the Hmong and other societies routinely provided throughout history to prepare loved ones for the grave?

Even today, small pockets of the U.S. population adopt an intensely hands-on approach to death. Here, you can see phase one in the carefully orchestrated days-long Hmong funeral ceremony—the body, dressed in its traditional garments, being caressed by distraught family members.

In this chapter, I'll explore what dying is like in the twenty-first-century West, an age of open communications, extended chronic disease, and new attention to providing quality end-of-life care. First, I'll examine the feelings of the dying person; then, turn to the health-care system; and then, return to the person to tackle those touchy issues related to controlling the timing of when we die. As you just saw with the Hmong, however, it's crucial to remember that—just as dying pathways differ—with death and dying *in general*, diversity is the main theme. We all bring unique, *equally* valid perspectives to that ultimate event of human life.

Tying It All Together

1. Imagine that you were born in the seventeenth or eighteenth century. Which statement about your dying pathway would *not* be true?

    a. You would probably have died quickly of an infectious disease.

    b. You would have died in a hospital.

    c. You would have seen death all around you from a young age.

    d. You would probably have died at a relatively young age.

2. If you follow the typical twenty-first-century pattern, as you approach death, you can expect to decline (*quickly/slowly and erratically*) due to (*an accident/an age-related chronic disease*).

3. Ella says today we live in a death-denying society. Amanda argues, "That's not true. We are paying far more attention to the experience of dying than in the past." Who is apt to be most correct, and why?

Answers to the Tying It All Together questions can be found at the end of this chapter.

The Dying Person

How do people react when they are diagnosed with a fatal illness? What are their emotions as they struggle with this devastating news? The first person to scientifically study these topics was a young psychiatrist named Elisabeth Kübler-Ross.

Kübler-Ross's Stages of Dying: Description and Critique

While working as a consultant at a Chicago hospital during the 1960s, Kübler-Ross became convinced that the health-care system was neglecting the emotional needs of the terminally ill. As part of a seminar, she got permission to interview dying patients. Many people, she found, were relieved to talk about their diagnosis and knew that their condition was terminal, even though the medical staff and family members had made valiant efforts to conceal that fact. Kübler-Ross published her discovery that open communication was important to dying people in *On Death and Dying*, a slim best-seller that ushered in a revolution in the way we treat the terminally ill.

Kübler-Ross (1969), in her **stage theory of dying**, originally proposed that we progress through five emotions in coming to terms with death: *denial, anger, bargaining, depression,* and *acceptance*. Let's now briefly look at each emotional state:

When a person first gets some terrible diagnosis, such as "You have advanced lung cancer," her immediate reaction is denial. She thinks, "There must be a mistake," and takes trips to doctor after doctor, searching for a new, more favorable set of tests. When these efforts fail, denial gives way to anger.

In the anger stage, the person lashes out, bemoaning her fate, railing at other people. One patient may get enraged at a physician: "He should have picked up my illness earlier on!" Others direct their fury at a friend or family member: "Why did I get lung cancer at 55, while my brother, who has smoked a pack of cigarettes a day since he was 20, remains in perfect health?"

Eventually, this emotion yields to a more calculating one: bargaining. Now, the person pleads for more time, promising to be good if she can put off death a bit. Kübler-Ross (1969) gives this example of a woman who begged God to let her live long enough to attend the marriage of her oldest son:

> The day preceding the wedding she left the hospital as an elegant lady. Nobody would have believed her real condition. She . . . looked radiant. I wondered what her reaction would be when the time was up for which she had bargained. . . . I will never forget the

Kübler-Ross's stage theory of dying The landmark theory, developed by psychiatrist Elisabeth Kübler-Ross, that people who are terminally ill progress through five stages in confronting their death: denial, anger, bargaining, depression, and acceptance.

moment she returned to the hospital. She looked tired and somewhat exhausted and before I could say hello, said, "Now don't forget I have another son."

(1969, p. 83)

Then, once reality sinks in, the person gets depressed and, ultimately, reaches acceptance. By this time, the individual is quite weak and no longer feels upset, angry, or depressed. She may even look forward to the end.

Kübler-Ross deserves enormous credit for alerting us to the fact that there is a living, breathing person inside the diagnosis "terminal cancer" or "end-stage heart disease." The problem is that her original ideas were embraced in a rigid, simplistic way. Here are three reasons why we *cannot* take this theory as the final word about death:

TERMINALLY ILL PEOPLE DO NOT ALWAYS WANT TO DISCUSS THEIR SITUATION. Although she never intended this message, many people read into Kübler-Ross's theory the idea that all patients want to talk about impending death. This is emphatically not true (Baile, Aaron, & Parker, 2009; Carlander and others, 2011; Shih and others, 2009). When researchers ask fatally ill patients about how they feel about discussing death, they find that people broach this subject selectively and reluctantly. As one woman said: "They're scary subjects and . . . we don't want to touch on it too much. . . ." (quoted in McGrath, 2004, p. 836). Patients avoid these discussions because they believe others won't want to hear: "I try to be open but . . . many people . . . can't manage it. They withdraw" (quoted in Saeteren, Lindström, & Nåden, 2010, p. 815). Sometimes, they shy away from these conversations to protect loved ones and themselves: "My sister is good but I couldn't load off onto her, she would just break. . . . I've got as much as I can cope with. So I can't get her upset . . . and then have . . . to calm her down" (quoted in McGrath, 2004, pp. 837, 839).

The bottom line is that people who are dying behave just as when they are living (which they are!). They are leery about bringing up painful subjects. People don't shed their sensitivity to others and feelings about what topics are appropriate to discuss when they have a terminal disease. Actually, as life is drawing to a close, preserving the quality of our attachment relationships is a *paramount* agenda — and this, as you will see, is a message I will highlight throughout this chapter.

NOT EVERY PERSON OR FAMILY FEELS IT'S BEST TO SPELL OUT "THE FULL TRUTH." As you saw earlier with the Hmong, the idea that we must inform terminally ill patients about their condition is also not universally accepted. Yes, in our individualistic society, people *say* they are interested in knowing the facts: "Information is important," said one Swedish woman with cancer. "Even if you have a short time left, you have to plan this time" (quoted in Saeteren, Lindström, & Nåden, 2010, p. 814). But they may not want doctors to get specific when the prognosis is dire (Baile, Aaron, & Parker, 2009; Innes & Payne, 2009). Families go further: "Don't tell my loved one anything at all!" Here is how one social worker described how she reacted when she received this plea from loving sons:

Hurting and sad (after learning their mom's diagnosis of inoperable cancer), . . . The older sons rushed to the clinic to make me privy to the decision. . . . "Our mother doesn't know anything and that's how we want to keep it." I could see their behavior as denial and discuss the western ethic of patient responsibility. But . . . I knew their children were protecting their mother from what they saw as worse than death: The expectation of nearing death.

(quoted in Kannai, 2008, pp. 146–147)

Having loved ones pray by a bedside can offer solace and a sense of connection during a person's final days. But to be really sensitive, this woman's family would also need to respect her privacy, taking their cues from her as to whether she *really* wanted to discuss impending death.

As this sensitive woman realized, the approach that Kübler-Ross and our culture spells out as caring can sometimes be unloving, insensitive, and rude.

PEOPLE DO NOT PASS THROUGH DISTINCTIVE STAGES IN ADJUSTING TO DEATH. Most important, Kübler-Ross's theory is wrong! People facing death do *not* progress emotionally in a stage-to-stage, cookie-cutter way. In fact, uncritically accepting Kübler-Ross's stages can be dangerous if it encourages us to distance ourselves from dying loved ones (Kastenbaum, 2004). Instead of understanding that becoming depressed is a reasonable reaction when facing a life-threatening illness, if friends and family see this feeling as "a phase," they might view this response as somehow not real. It's perfectly understandable for an ill person to get angry when others respond insensitively or don't call; but if we view this response through the lens of stage theory, we might dismiss these natural feelings of hurt as "predictable" signs of the anger stage.

Therefore, experts view Kübler-Ross's contributions with mixed emotions. Yes, she pioneered an important topic. But her theory encouraged its own insensitivity to the terminally ill (Kastenbaum, 2004).

The More Realistic View: Many Different Emotions; Wanting Life to Go On

People who are dying *do* get angry, bargain, deny their illness, and become depressed. However, as one psychiatrist argues, it's more appropriate to view these feelings as "a complicated clustering of intellectual and affective states, some fleeting, lasting for a moment, or a day" (Schneidman, 1976, p. 6). Even when people "know" their illness is terminal, the awareness of "I am dying" may not penetrate in a definitive way (Groopman, 2004; Saeteren, Lindström, & Nåden, 2010). This emotional state, called **middle knowledge,** is highlighted in this description of Rachel, a 17-year-old who knew she had end-stage cystic fibrosis.

> Rachel said . . . that when she is to die, she wanted to be here in Canuck Place (the hospice), surrounded by friends and family . . . and the nurses and doctors that can help her feel not scared. And then she said "but I have another way that I'd like to die . . . sitting on my front porch wrapped in an afghan in a rocking chair and my husband holding my hand."
>
> (Liben, Papadatou, & Wolfe, 2008, p. 858)

Moreover, as Rachel's final heart-wrenching comment suggests, when people realize that they are close to death, an emotion that often burns strong is hope (Groopman, 2004; Innes & Payne, 2009). If people are religious, their hopes may hinge on divine intervention: "God will provide a miraculous cure." Others pin their hopes on meditation, alternative therapies, or exercise. Another source of hope—as Kübler-Ross suggested—is the idea that the medical predictions can be wrong: "True, I have that diagnosis, but I know of cases where a doctor told a person with my illness she had six months left and she has been living for 10 years."

Hope, as you can see in the Experiencing the Lifespan box, doesn't mean hoping for a cure. It may mean wishing you survive through the summer, or live to see your wife's book published, and not be bedridden before you die. It can mean hoping that your love lives on in your family, or that your life work will make a difference in the world. (Remember, that's what being generative is all about.) Contrary to what Kübler-Ross implies, even reaching acceptance has nothing to do with abandoning hope. People can understand—"I'm dying"—and still have many future goals and plans.

middle knowledge The idea that terminally ill people can know that they are dying yet at the same time not completely grasp or come to terms emotionally with that fact.

Experiencing the Lifespan: Hospice Hopes

It started on a trip to Washington—David's favorite city. "Something is different with my body. I got out of breath when I took a walk around the mall." Then came the diagnosis: "You have congestive heart failure. Because your heart muscle is enlarged, fluid is accumulating around your lungs and legs. But with our medicines, you can almost certainly live—with restrictions—for some time."

During the next few years when my husband's body became badly bloated, we periodically entered the hospital, to drain off the fluid and accumulate another cocktail of pills. Then, in May 2012, due to a side effect of the medicine, my husband went into kidney failure, and we rushed to the hospital again. Just as the frantic staff was poised to transfer David to endure another heroic intervention, our cardiologist entered the room: "I'm referring your husband to hospice," he tersely stated. "There is nothing more we can do." We left the hospital that beautiful late spring afternoon to await death.

Those last few days turned into more than 9 months. With the help of just one pill to control his symptoms, David got much better. He was able to spend that summer and most of the fall walking around on his own. On the December day we finally needed to order a hospital bed, I served chili and chocolate chip cookies for dinner. Then, David just closed his eyes and died.

My husband's hope in hospice had been to live through the summer, enjoying nature and spending time sitting with me by the pool. He wanted to be alive to hold the third edition of this book, due in November, in his hands. He hated the idea of being bedridden during his final days. Hospice granted David all three of his final wishes.

Heart failure epitomizes that common twenty-first-century pathway to death. Patients have good days and bad days. They live for years in the shadow of death. Although extended, ultimately fatal, chronic illnesses can strike at any age (recall, for instance, the earlier quote relating to cystic fibrosis), most often, as with my husband, they occur *on time* in terms of our social clock, in our older years.

Drawing on Erik Erikson's theory, we might predict that facing death in our teens or early adult life is uniquely difficult. How can you reach integrity, or the sense you have fulfilled your life goals if you have not found your identity, mastered intimacy, or discovered your generative path? Because death is so appropriate at their life stage, older people don't show the classic avoidance to death-related words and phrases apparent even during middle age (De Raedt, Koster, & Ryckewaert, 2013). What do we mean by having an appropriate death?

In Search of a Good Death

Insights come from turning to religious sources. From the Old Testament (Spronk, 2004) to Hindu traditions (Gupta, 2011), religions agree that death should be celebrated after a long life. Death should be peaceful and sudden, explaining why violent deaths, like suicides or murders, are especially repellent, and why people universally reject the idea of being "tortured" by medical technology at the end of life (Enguidanos, Yonashiro-Cho, & Cote, 2013). Death is "best" when it

Deprived of life as a husband and father at an off-time age seems totally "against nature" and unfair—making this man's death in his thirties impossibly sad.

occurs in the "homeland" (not far away), accounting for why—around the globe— people prefer to die surrounded by their loved ones, and reject the sanitized, impersonal dying that takes place in intensive care (Prevost & Wallace, 2009; Shih and others, 2009).

©Mary Evans Picture Library/The Image Works

The principle that good deaths must occur "near the homeland" is embedded in many religious traditions. This nineteenth-century depiction shows a Hindu funeral ceremony, with the deceased making his final passage surrounded by loving community members while being carried ceremoniously to the grave.

A good death came to my grandmother, one beautiful summer day. Grandma, at age 98, was just beginning to get slightly frail. One afternoon, before preparing dinner for her visiting grandchildren and great-grandchildren (which she insisted on doing), she got in her car to drive to the hairdresser and—on leaving the driveway—was hit by an oncoming car. Of the eight people involved in the accident, no one was hurt but Grandma, who was killed instantly. They said she never felt any pain.

Given that our chances of being killed instantly at our doorstep, without frailties at the limit of human life, are almost nil, how can we expand on the above criteria to spell out specific dimensions of a good death? One psychologist offers the following guidelines (Corr, 1991–1992):

1. We want to minimize our physical distress, to be as free as possible from debilitating pain.

2. We want to maximize our psychological security, reduce fear and anxiety, and feel in control of how we die.

3. We want to enhance our relationships and be close emotionally to the people we care about.

4. We want to foster our spirituality and have the sense that there was integrity and purpose to our lives.

Minimize pain and fear; be close to loved ones; enhance spirituality; feel that life has meaning—these are the themes from the studies that poll caregivers about the qualities involved in a loved one's "good death" (Downey and others, 2010; Karlsson & Berggren, 2011; Leung and others, 2010; Shih and others, 2009). Yes, a strong religious faith can offer people peace in their final days (Braam, Klinkenberg, & Deeg, 2011). But it's not necessary to believe in an afterlife or any religion. Actually, in one study, the main dimension that was related to feeling comfortable about dying was having a sense of purpose in life (Ardelt & Koenig, 2006).

So again, Erikson seems right in saying that the key to accepting death is fulfilling our life tasks and, especially, our generative missions. And in Erikson's (1963) poetic words, appreciating that one's "individual life is the accidental coincidence of . . . one lifecycle within . . . history" (p. 268) can be important in embracing death, too:

Barbara turned on the lamp. . . . Her eyes were sunken and her skin was pale. It would not be long, I thought. . . . "Are you afraid?" I asked. "You know, not really,. . . . I have strange comforting thoughts. . . . When fear starts to creep up on me, I conjure up the idea that millions and millions of people have passed away before me, and millions more will pass away after I do . . . I guess if they all did it, so can I."

(Groopman, 2004, pp. 137–138)

Evan Agostini/Invision/AP

Right before going into surgery and unexpectedly dying, Joan Rivers signaled to her daughter (and broadcast to the world via youtube) that she had reached integrity—when she said, "If I die I have no regrets, because I've loved every minute of this life!"

What are your priorities for a good death? Table 15.1 offers an expanded checklist based on the principles in this section, to help you evaluate your top-ranking death goals.

Table 15.1: Evaluating Your Priorities for a Good Death: A Checklist

When you think about dying, rank how important each of these criteria might be to you as: (1) of utmost importance; (2) important, but not primary; or (3) relatively unimportant.

_____ 1. Not being a burden to my family.

_____ 2. Being at peace with death—that is, not being anxious about dying.

_____ 3. Not being in physical pain.

_____ 4. Having control over where I die—that is, being able to choose whether to die at home or in the hospital.

_____ 5. Having control over how I die—that is, being able to choose whether to be kept alive through medical interventions or to die naturally. Being able to end my life if I am terminally ill and in great pain.

_____ 6. Feeling close to my loved ones.

_____ 7. Feeling close to God.

_____ 8. Feeling that I have fulfilled my mission on earth or made a difference in the world.

Do your top-ranking priorities for dying tell you anything about your priorities for living?

Hot in Developmental Science: Evolving Ideas About Grieving

Death is just the first chapter in the survivor's ongoing life story. Although I discussed bereavement in the widowhood section in Chapter 13, let's now focus on how both psychologists and the public expect that universal experience to proceed (see Jordan & Litz, 2014; Penman and others, 2014).

In the first months after a loved one dies, people are absorbed in mourning, crying; perhaps having trouble eating and sleeping. They might be ruminating about their loved one, carrying around reminders, sharing stories, looking through photos, focusing on the person's last days. Some people literally sense their loved one's physical presence in the room (Keen, Murray, & Payne, 2013). Then, after about six months, we expect mourners to recover in the sense of reconnecting to the world (Jordan & Litz, 2014). People still care deeply about their loved one. The person's memory can be evoked on special times such as anniversaries. But this mental image becomes incorporated into the mourner's identity as that person travels through life.

Grief patterns, however, are shaped by each society's unique norms (Neimeyer, Klass, & Dennis, 2014). Some cultures expect people to pine for decades. In others, mourners are supposed to adopt a stoic stiff upper lip. There are variations in grieving in our society, too. Sometimes, people do their mourning *before a person's death*, such as when the doctor refers a loved one to hospice or after a diagnosis of Alzheimer's disease. While we are tempted to accuse these people of being callous ("She went to that party right after her mother died! She hasn't even been crying much!"), you might be surprised to know it's "normal" to not have intense symptoms even during the first few months after a significant other dies (Boerner, Mancini, and Bonanno, 2013).

But suppose it's been more than a year and your bereaved relative still cries continually, feels life is meaningless, and seems incapable of constructing a new life. Can grieving last overly long?

Very cautiously, the framers of our Western psychiatric diagnostic manuals answer yes. When the person's symptoms continue unabated or become more intense after 6 months to a year, and that individual shows no signs of reconnecting with the world, mental health workers can diagnose a condition labeled **persistent complex bereavement-related disorder,** or **prolonged grief.**

persistent complex bereavement-related disorder, or prolonged grief Controversial new diagnosis, appearing in the most recent versions of the Western psychiatric disorder manuals, in which the bereaved person shows intense symptoms of mourning with no signs of abatement, or an increase in symptoms 6 months to a year after a loved one's death.

This new diagnosis is controversial, in part because it risks reclassifying that normal life event called mourning as a pathological state. Furthermore, aren't some deaths so "bad" that prolonged grief is normal—for instance, if a loved one died violently, or due to murder or suicide, or you have the tragedy of outliving your child? 🚫

A Small, Final Note on Mourning a Child

When I worked in a nursing home, I realized that a child's death can be more upsetting than any other loss. It doesn't matter whether their "baby" dies at age 6 or in his sixties, people have special trouble coping with that unnatural event (Hayslip & Hansson, 2003). While people do eventually construct a fulfilling life, in one study, even after 4 years, many bereaved parents still showed symptoms of prolonged grief, continually yearning for their child (McCarthy and others, 2010).

A child's death may evoke powerful feelings of survivor guilt: "Why am I still alive?" If the death occurred suddenly due to an accident, there is disbelief and possibly guilt at having failed in one's mission as a parent: "I couldn't protect my baby!" (See Cole & Singg, 1998.) If the death was expected—for instance, a child died of cancer—parents have still lost their futures. They must cope with their anger that an innocent son or daughter had to suffer, unfairly robbed of life. The problem is that a child's death can never be really "good," because this off-time event shakes our worldview of the universe as predictable and fair (Neimeyer, Klass, & Dennis, 2014).

When a child has inoperable cancer *and seems to understand that he is dying*, does it help for parents to discuss death with this daughter or son? To explore this question, Swedish researchers interviewed every family who had lost a child to cancer in that country over several years (Kreicbergs and others, 2004). No parent who reported having a conversation about death with an ill daughter or son had any regrets. In contrast, more than half of the mothers and fathers who believed that their child understood what was happening but never discussed this topic felt guilty later on.

Other research has a similar message: If parents feel satisfied that they said goodbye to their child, this helps lessen the pain. Moreover, not discussing what is happening can produce enduring regrets:

> "I wish I had him back so that we could hug and kiss and say goodby" (said one anguished mother). "We never said good-bye. We faked the whole thing. . . . I just feel there was no ending, no finish . . . Yet he never took the lead . . . he never said, 'Ma, I'm dying.'"
>   (quoted in Wells-di Gregorio, 2009, p. 252).

What else helps grieving parents cope? In this situation, it helps *not to sever* the attachment bond to your child.

Design Pics RF/Leah Warkentin/Getty Images

Unless she can restore her sense of life as predictable this mother may find herself locked in prolonged grief—as the death of a child can rank as life's most devastating event.

> I talk to her . . . every night. . . . I just say . . . I'm so sorry for what you had to go through, but mommy is so proud of you.

> I'd . . . get his ashes and sit . . . and rock. I'll . . . kiss his little container thing and try to say good night to him every night when I go to bed.
>   (quoted in Foster and others, 2011, pp. 427, 428, 429, 432)

Another bereaved parent in a South American study went further:

> A month had gone by since Matais's death and I went to the hospital to give encouragement to a mother whose son was dying. . . . This is the way I honor Matais. There I meet him; there I feel him present. I immortalized him by working as a volunteer. Matais is immortalized in the things I do, in the good, in the beautiful things.
>   (Adapted from Vega, Rivera, & González, 2014, p. 171)

Actually, experts believe the key to recovering from terribly unfair deaths depends on finding new meaning in one's disrupted life story, and so restoring the idea that the universe is predictable and fair (Neimeyer, Klass, & Dennis, 2014). Grieving parents report they turned the corner when they used their tragedy as a redemption sequence to help keep their child's memory alive. Some families find solace in donating their sons' or daughters' organs to help others survive, or they may adopt a child's life passions, for instance by deciding to agitate for environmental change. As in the example above, parents may devote their lives to counseling families with an ill child (Vega, Rivera, & González, 2014). People transform bad deaths into love by working at suicide hotlines, or establishing websites to crusade against drunk driving, agitating for better fire safety laws, creating beautiful art-work, or simply marching in protest against any death they view as unfair.

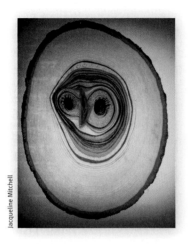

Jacqueline Mitchell

Eileen Wallach

Jac, my reference checker for this book, helped turn her boyfriend's suicide into a redemption sequence by counseling survivors of this tragedy and producing works of art in a Nashville program, "Your Heart in Art."

These examples have lessons for all of us in surviving bereavement. Give your loved one a good life. Provide the best possible death. Draw on your loss to grow as a person and enrich other people's lives.

Table 15.2 expands on the topic of bad death by exploring another off-time loss—children's grief.

Table 15.2: Bereavement at an Off-Time Age: Tips for Understanding Mourning During Childhood

Tip 1: Look to the child's developmental stage. While infants and toddlers cannot grasp the concept of death, losing a primary caregiver at this age can affect the attachment response. Preoperational preschoolers are also too young to grasp the concept that death is permanent, but their egocentric thinking may produce guilt that they caused their loved one to die through their bad thoughts. Temper tantrums, sleep disturbances, and regressing to more babyish behavior are common responses to experiencing a caregiver's death at this age. Finally, after reaching concrete operations—around age 9 or 10—children are capable of grasping the finality of death, and begin to mourn in the traditional sense. At this age, and especially adolescence, complicated bereavement responses center around acting-out behaviors and internalizing symptoms such as nonsuicidal self-injury and depression.

Tip 2: Look to the child's life situation. Most children are resilient, coping with the death of a loved one without showing *any* signs of prolonged grief. But symptoms of complicated bereavement are more likely when the death is sudden or violent, the child is already emotionally fragile, and the person's family life is unstable. The risk of long-term problems also accelerates when the young person has experienced multiple life losses. Moreover, because at this age upsetting feelings cannot be channeled into a redemption sequence, especially after losing a parent during childhood, mourning may naturally occur in extended fits and starts, with fresh waves of grief appearing during milestone events years later, such as when the person graduates from college, gets married, or becomes a parent.

Tip 3: Interventions should involve a multifaceted, community-centered approach. In helping children mourn in a healthy way, everyone—from teachers to siblings to peers—can play a vital role. The keys are to listen sensitively, offer emotional support and, rather than "ignoring" the trauma, allow the child to openly discuss and process the feelings of loss.

Information is from Barnard, Moreland, and Nagy, 1999; Christ, 2000; Baker & Sedney, 1996; Humphrey & Zimpfer, 2007, and McCarthy & Jessop, 2005.

This next section explores how the health-care system is doing in providing people for the best possible death.

 Tying It All Together

1. Sara is arguing that Kübler-Ross's conceptions about dying are "fatally flawed." Pick out the argument she should *not* use to make her case (that is, identify the false alternative):

   a. People who are dying do not necessarily want to talk about that fact.

   b. People do not go through "stages" in adjusting to impending death.

   c. People who are dying simply accept that fact.

2. If your uncle has recently been diagnosed with advanced lung cancer, he should feel (*many different emotions/only depressed/only angry*), but in general, he should have (*hope/a lot of anger*).

3. Jose says he feels comforted that his beloved uncle had a good death. Which statement is *least* likely to apply to this man:

   a. Jose's uncle died peacefully after a long life.

   b. Jose's uncle was religious.

   c. Jose's uncle died surrounded by loving attachment figures.

   d. Jose's uncle felt he had achieved his missions in life.

4. Imagine you are a psychologist, and a patient comes to your office suffering from prolonged grief. Based on this section, in a sentence, describe your main treatment goal.

Answers to the Tying It All Together questions can be found at the end of this chapter.

The Health-Care System

How does the health-care system deal with death? Let's first take a critical look at standard hospital terminal care and then explore the new health-care options designed to tame twenty-first-century death.

What's Wrong with Traditional Hospital Care for the Dying?

Most of us will die in a hospital (Prevost & Wallace, 2009). But social scientists have known for a half-century that the traditional hospital approach to dying has flaws. Consider the findings of this groundbreaking 1960s study in which sociologists entered hospitals and observed how the medical staff organized "the work" of terminal care (Glaser & Strauss, 1968).

The researchers found that, when a person was admitted to the hospital, nurses and doctors set up predictions about what pattern that individual's dying was likely to follow. This implicit **dying trajectory** then governed how the staff acted.

The problem was that dying trajectories could not be completely predicted. When someone mistakenly categorized as "having months to live" was moved to a unit in the hospital where she was not monitored, this mislabeling tended, not infrequently, to hasten death. An interesting situation happened when someone was expected to die soon and then lived on. Doctors might call loved ones to the bedside to say goodbye, only to find that the person began to improve. This "final goodbye" scenario could play out time and time again. The paradox was that if dying was "off schedule," *living* might be transformed into a negative event!

> One patient who was expected to die (quickly) had no money, but started to linger indefinitely (being paid for as a charity patient in the hospital). The money problem, however,

dying trajectory The fact that hospital personnel make projections about the particular pathway to death that a seriously ill patient will take and organize their care according to that assumption.

created much concern among both family members and the hospital administrators. . . . The doctor continually had to reassure both parties that the patient (who lived for six weeks more) would soon die; that is, to try to change their expectations back to "certain to die on time."

(Glaser & Straus, 1968, pp. 11–12)

The bottom line is that deaths don't occur according to a programmed timetable. Hospitals are structured according to the assumption that they do. This incompatibility makes for a messy dance of terminal care.

Unfortunately, since this research was conducted, the situation has not changed. According to one review of hospital records spanning 1996 to 2010, the odds of health-care workers accurately predicting the date of a patient's dying were only fifty-fifty (Phillips, Halcomb, and Davidson, 2011). So families still suffer the trauma of being caught "off guard" when faced with that event (Wells-di Gregorio, 2009). When dying proceeds according to schedule (or as expected), health-care personnel classify the death as "good." As one resident in a study reported: "I felt good that he died in a comfortable way. . . . I guess I just knew it would happen in 24 hours so it doesn't come as a shock" (quoted in Good and others, 2004, p. 944). When trajectories are mislabeled, the death is defined as "bad": "She came in for a bone marrow transplant to cure her [cancer] . . . and got pulmonary toxicity and died" (p. 945). Good deaths happen when there is smooth communication between the medical team and patients' families. Bad deaths are rife with disagreements, anger, and hurt (see Wells-di Gregorio, 2009). In fact, because of the potential for miscommunication, traditional hospital dying may be more turbulent in the twenty-first century than before.

One reason is that, today, patients do not spend weeks or months in a hospital. They often enter this setting when they are within days of death. Therefore, the health-care professionals on the death scene may not be emotionally involved with the person (Good and others, 2004). They may have little understanding of patients' and families' needs.

Disagreements between members of the health-care team add to this problem. Physicians make the final decisions about treatments; but nurses, the frontline caregivers, know the patient's and family's wishes best. Nurses may want to advocate for dying patients but be afraid of being disciplined if they speak up (Thacker, 2008; Yu & Chan, 2010). Compounding these professional conflicts are issues related to living in our multicultural society (Wells-di Gregorio, 2009). Suppose the attending doctor on the floor where your relative is dying is a recent immigrant from Beijing or Bangladesh, or your parents only speak Spanish or Swahili. How can everyone really communicate at this intensely emotional time?

How can doctors relate to immigrant women anxiously awaiting news about their ill loved ones? Issues like these loom large as hospital personnel struggle to do the right thing for families of dying patients in our contemporary multicultural society.

What underlies these conflicts is our quantum leap death-defying technologies. Physicians can offer nutrition to people through a tube into the stomach, bypassing the body's normal signal to stop eating in preparation for death. They put patients on ventilators, machines that breathe for the person, after the lungs have given out. Caring doctors may agonize about using these heroic measures (Liben, Papadatou, & Wolfe, 2008). But their mission to cure can make it difficult to resist the lure of the machines:

We were realizing that we were going to hurt him [a 40-year-old lung cancer patient who had had multiple surgeries and several strokes] if we . . . kept trying to keep a body alive that was not wanting to be alive. And everyone figured "what the heck, give it a shot."

(quoted in Good and others, 2004, p. 945)

Today, medical workers are faced with agonizing ethical choices: How long do you vigorously wage war against death, and when should you say, "enough is enough"? Shifting from the cure-at-all-costs mode can be difficult. To paraphrase one expert, it's like "deciding to play baseball while the football game is in full swing"

Rob Melnychuk/Stockbyte/Jupiter Images/Getty Images

palliative care Any intervention designed not to cure illness but to promote dignified dying.

end-of-life care instruction Courses in medical and nursing schools devoted to teaching health-care workers how to provide the best palliative care to the dying.

palliative-care service A service or unit in a hospital that is devoted to end-of-life care.

Imagine being this doctor and knowing the terminally ill patient whose chart you are reading is about to ask, "What is my prognosis?" Wouldn't it be helpful to have some end-of-life care instruction during your training to guide you about how best to respond?

(Chapple, 1999). Understanding that we can never take the mess out of dying, just as we can never take the mess out of living, let's now look at how the traditional health-care system is taking action to tame contemporary death.

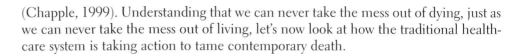

INTERVENTIONS: Providing Superior Palliative Care

Palliative care refers to any strategy designed to promote dignified dying. Palliative care includes educating health-care personnel about how to deal with dying patients; modifying the hospital structure; or providing that well-known alternative to dying in a hospital, hospice care. Let's scan these interventions one by one.

Educating Health-Care Providers

In recent decades, **end-of-life care instruction** has become a frequent component of medical and nursing training. Courses cover everything from the best drugs to control pain without "knocking the person out" to the ethics of withdrawing treatment. Instruction may involve hands-on experiences such as having medical students visit terminally ill patients in hospices (Gadoud and others, 2013) or workshops in which student nurses personally imagine what it is like to die (Liu and others, 2011).

We need to do more (Smith & Hough, 2011). In one hospital survey, although nurses reported dealing with death on a daily basis, fewer than half said they had formal training in end-of-life care within the previous three years (Thacker, 2008). Doctors want more guidance in how to discuss negative prognoses since they are naturally reluctant to convey the message, "There isn't much we can do" (Smith & Hough, 2011).

The result of this anxiety is that we sometimes get physicians who (perhaps out of their own fear) decide to take Kübler-Ross's concept of "honesty" literally, saying, "Your illness is terminal," and then bolting from the room. Or health-care providers persist in carrying out painful, futile treatments for far too long. Luckily, however, we have a hospital structure designed to ease these difficult discussions, a mainstream medical alternative devoted to promoting the best possible death.

Changing Hospitals: Palliative-Care Units

A **palliative-care service** is a special unit or service that is devoted to end-of-life care within a traditional hospital setting. Here, certain groups of inpatients—for instance, old-old people with multiple chronic illnesses and people with advanced cancer—have their care managed by a team of providers trained in when to shift from "football to baseball mode" (recall the analogy mentioned earlier). Patients enrolled in the palliative-care service are not denied cure-oriented interventions (Bonebrake and others, 2010). However, as their illness becomes terminal, the vigor of life-prolonging treatments shifts to providing the best possible "comfort care."

Families give palliative care high marks, compared to traditional end-of-life care (García-Pérez and others, 2009). These services are "cost-effective" (Meier & Beresford, 2009). Moreover—unlike what some readers may fear—having this unit at a hospital doesn't make death more likely when patients enter that institution's care (Cassel and others, 2010). So, by the first decade of the twenty-first century, many major medical centers in the developed world provided palliative-care services (Dobbins, 2007).

The global view, however, is bleak. Even in affluent nations—such as Canada—experts estimate that only 1 in 4 terminally ill people has access to hospital-based palliative care (Shariff, 2011). Of the roughly one million human

Robin Nelson/Photo Edit Inc.

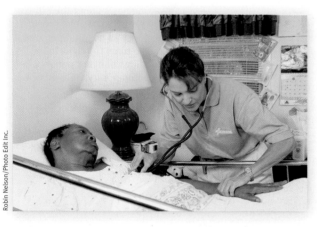

Palliative-care services, with their focus on pain control and letting patients spend their final days in a more natural setting, provide an alternative to dying in the medicalized recesses of intensive care. In this palliative-care unit, a nurse is taking the blood pressure of a patient who has had a stroke and is suffering from end-stage heart disease.

beings who die each week worldwide, a large fraction spend their final days in agony, without even over-the-counter medicines to control their pain (Clark, 2007).

State-of-the art, hospital-based palliative-care services are a welcome trend. But it still seems unfair to ask health-care professionals to embrace the enemy. Physicians in particular may shy away from dying patients because facing them means they failed in their mission to cure. Therefore, the most humane way to promote dignified dying might be to remove that act from the doctors with their cure-oriented focus and death-defying machines.

Unhooking Death from Doctors and Hospitals: Hospice Care

This is the philosophy underlying the **hospice movement**, which gained momentum in the 1970s, along with the natural childbirth movement. Like birth, hospice activists argued, death is a natural process. We need to let this process occur in the most pain-free, natural way (Corr, 2007).

Hospice workers are skilled in techniques to minimize patients' physical discomfort. They are trained in providing a humanistic, supportive psychological environment, one that assures patients and family members that they will not be abandoned in the face of approaching death (Monroe and others, 2008).

In many developed nations, hospice care is mainly delivered in a freestanding facility called a hospice. The main focus of the United States hospice movement is on providing backup care that allows people to die with dignity at home. As occurred with my husband, and as you can read in the Experiencing the Lifespan box below, multidisciplinary hospice teams go into the person's home, offering care on a part-time, scheduled, or daily basis. They provide 24-hour help in a crisis, giving family caregivers the support they need to allow their relative to spend his final days at home. Their commitment does not end after the person dies: An important component of hospice care is bereavement counseling.

hospice movement A movement, which became widespread in recent decades, focused on providing palliative care to dying patients outside of hospitals and especially on giving families the support they need to care for the terminally ill at home.

Experiencing the Lifespan: Hospice Team

What is hospice care really like? For answers, here are some excerpts from an interview I conducted with the team (nurse, social worker, and volunteer coordinator) who manages our local hospice.

Usually, we get referrals from physicians. People may have a wide community support system or be new to the area. Even when there are many people involved, there is almost always one primary caregiver, typically a spouse or adult child.

We see our role as empowering families, giving them the support to care for their loved ones at home. We go into the home as a team to make our initial assessment: What services does the family need? We provide families training in pain control, in making beds, in bathing. A critical component of our program is respite services. Volunteers come in for part of each day. They may take the children out for pizza, or give the primary caregiver time off, or just stay there to listen.

Families will say initially, "I don't think I can stand to do this." They are anxious because it's a new experience they have never been through. At the beginning, they call a lot. Then, you watch them gain confidence in themselves. We see them at the funeral and they thank us for helping them give their loved one this experience. Sometimes, the primary caregiver can't bear to keep the person at home to the end. We respect that, too.

The whole thing about hospice is choice. Some people want to talk about dying. Others just want you to visit, ask about their garden, talk about current affairs. We take people to see the autumn leaves, to see Santa Claus. Our main focus is: What are your priorities? We try to pick up on that. We had a farmer whose goal was to go to his farm one last time and say goodbye to his tractor. We got together a big tank of oxygen, and carried him down to his farm. We have one volunteer who takes a client to the mall.

We keep in close touch with the families for a year after, providing them counseling or referring them to bereavement groups in the community. Some families keep in contact with notes for years. We run a camp each summer for children who have lost a parent.

We have an unusually good support system among the staff. In addition to being with the families at 3 a.m., we call one another at all times of the night. Most of us have been working here for years. We feel we have the most meaningful job in the world.

Entering a U.S. hospice program is simple. It requires a physician to certify that the person is within six months of death. Home hospice care is less expensive than traditional end-of-life care (Bentur and others, 2014). Because Medicare fully covers this service, U.S. hospice is available to people on every rung of the economic ladder (Sengupta & others, 2014).

As you can see in Figure 15.2, in recent decades, the U.S. hospice movement has mushroomed. By 2009, roughly 2 in 5 U.S. deaths occurred in hospice care. What is the hospice experience really like?

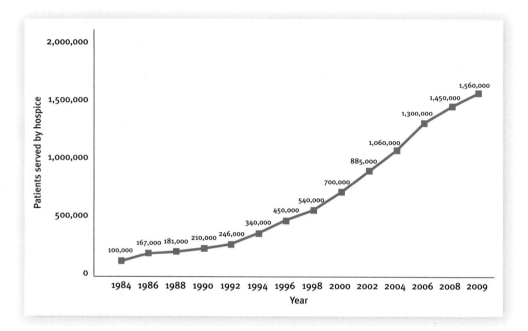

FIGURE 15.2: Patients served by hospice in the United States, 1984–2009: Notice that the number of people enrolling in hospice grew exponentially, especially during the first decade of the twenty-first century.

Data from: National Hospice and Palliative Care Organization, 2011.

Charting the U.S. Hospice Experience

Imagine that your doctor has just made the pronouncement: "I'm referring your spouse or parent to hospice. There is nothing more we can do." You must simultaneously deal with the shock of grieving and embark on a difficult, uncharted path. Passionate to offer your loved one this final demonstration of love, you are incredibly anxious about what lies ahead. What can you expect about the person's pathway to death?

The answer partly depends on the illness. If the disease is cancer, expect a more precipitous decline. With congestive heart failure or pulmonary disease, the transition to serious ADL problems is apt to be slower during the next days and weeks. Some people enter hospice bedridden and spend their final days comatose. Others, like my husband, are fully alert and able to perform basic ADL activities until their last moments of life (Harris and others, 2013). This variation partly explains why, although the average hospice stay is roughly two weeks, 1 in 10 U.S. patients spends close to a year in hospice care (Sengupta and others, 2014).

This uncertainty is scary, but your main fear is seeing your loved one suffer. The box full of medications you just got from the hospice team is frightening. Without any nursing training, will you be able to control your family member's pain?

Actually, issues relating to pain control rank among hospice caregivers primary concerns: People worry about leaving the person in agony, or they may fear that that final dose of morphine hastened death (Oliver and others, 2013; Kelley and others, 2013). As one person reported: "She (dying loved one) has chronic pain. The morphine was in an unusual bottle and I was afraid to give her too much or too little and the dropper wasn't working. It was very scary" (quoted in Kelley and others, 2013, p. 679).

These worries are not unrealistic. In one survey, 2 out of 3 U.S. hospice providers cited medication management as their most problematic issue. One in three reported frequently encountering problems in this area as they struggled to help families provide care (Joyce & Lau, 2013).

Charting the Barriers to Hospice

This discussion brings up the hurdles to hospice. As I mentioned earlier, hope is the main emotion people feel when facing a terminal disease. Entering hospice means confronting the reality, "I am going to die." Family members are naturally reluctant to bring up hospice, because they, too, may want to urge undergoing that one last curative intervention that allows a loved one to survive.

The same reluctance applies to the hospice gatekeeper—the physician. As I alluded to earlier, doctors find it difficult to "give up" on a patient they may have treated for months or years (Marmo, 2014). So, it makes sense that physicians often refrain from mentioning hospice until patients' last weeks of life, even when the ill person might have benefitted from this service for months (Snyder and others, 2013).

Another impediment relates to everyone's misconceptions about hospice care. People are not aware that patients can still receive curative interventions after entering hospice, or that it's possible to survive for months in hospice with a fairly good quality of life (see the Experiencing the Lifespan box on page 455). Particularly, minority groups may not understand that in the United States, Medicare pays for hospice (Frey and others, 2013) or realize that hospice care occurs at home (Enguidanos, Yonashiro-Cho, & Cote, 2013). African Americans may cling to aggressive cure-oriented treatments, out of a lifelong fear that traditional medicine has done them wrong (Johnson and others, 2013). Residents of rural areas may not have access to hospice teams (Lynch, 2013).

Even when patients are aware that their illness is fatal, they may be less than thrilled to have loved ones care for them during their final weeks of life. Imagine being totally taken care of by your family when you have a terminal disease. You don't have any privacy. Loved ones must bathe you and dress you; they must care for your every need. You may be embarrassed about being seen naked and incontinent; you may want time alone to vent your anguish and pain. In a hospital (or inpatient hospice), care is impersonal. At home, there is the humiliation of having to depend on the people you love most for each intimate bodily act.

Most importantly, care by strangers equals care that is free from guilt. As I described earlier in this chapter, when people are approaching death, they often want to emotionally protect their loved ones—to shield them from pain. Witnessing the toll that your disease is taking on your family may multiply the pain of dying itself.

This explains, why, in a rare interview study conducted with people receiving inpatient hospice care in Australia, patients' main worries centered around loved ones. Yes, people said, moving to hospice signaled a depressing step closer to death. But they were relieved to no longer be burdening their families: "My husband is very quiet. . . . If he feels he cannot cope, I would rather be in here if that gives him a chance to come here, spend some time and then go home and get his head together," reported one woman. A man appreciated the privacy involved in getting care from strangers. "It's going with a little bit of dignity . . . and not in a mess, . . . and not being a frightening sight to those who are sitting there" (quoted in Broom & Kirby, 2013, p. 504).

This need to preserve dignity (or face) with one's family, may explain why U.S. hospice programs are rejected among the very cultural group historically most committed to family care. When researchers polled Chinese heritage elderly living in San Francisco, people reacted with horror when they learned hospice involves care at home. One woman summed up the general feelings when she said, "If I am dying

Although this caregiving wife probably wouldn't have it any other way, deciding on home hospice care is apt to evoke scary feelings: Will I be able to control my beloved husband's pain?

I become very grumpy; it's a good idea to send me to a nursing home" (quoted in Enguidanos, Yonashiro-Cho, & Cote, 2013, p. 996).

Table 15.3 summarizes these section points in "a pros and cons of home care" chart. Now that I have surveyed the health-care options, it's time to continue our search for a "good" twenty-first-century death by returning to the dying person.

Table 15.3: Home Deaths: Pros and Cons

The case against dying at home

1. No worries about family members not being able to control your pain.

2. No fear of burdening your family with your care.

3. Privacy to vent your feelings, without family members around.

4. Avoiding the embarrassment of depending on loved ones for help with your intimate body functions.

The case in favor of dying at home

1. Avoiding having life-prolonging machines used on you.

2. Spending your final days surrounded by the people you care about most.

3. Spending your final days in the physical setting you love best.

Given these considerations, would you prefer to meet death at home?

 Tying It All Together

1. In a sentence, describe to a friend the basic message of the classic research describing the various dying trajectories discussed on pages 480–481.

2. Based on this section, which statement most accurately reflects doctors' reactions to the terminally ill? (*Pick one.*) (a) Doctors are insensitive to dying patients' needs, or (b) Doctors feel terribly upset when a patient is dying, but may feel forced to use modern technologies to "prolong" death.

3. Carol's husband has just been referred to hospice. If this couple lives in the United States, you can predict (*pick FALSE statement*):

   a. Carol will be caring for her spouse at home.

   b. If Carol's spouse has heart disease, he may decline more slowly than if he has cancer.

   c. Carol may be terribly worried about her ability to control her husband's pain.

   d. Carol will spend a good deal of money on hospice care.

4. Melanie is arguing that there's no way she will die in a hospital. She wants to end her life at home, surrounded by her husband and children. Using the information in this section, convince Melanie of the down side to spending her final days at home.

Answers to the Tying It All Together questions can be found at the end of this chapter.

The Dying Person: Taking Control of How We Die

In this section, I'll explore two strategies people can use to control their final passage and so promote a "good death." The first is an option that our society strongly encourages: People should make their wishes known in writing about their treatment preferences should they become mentally incapacitated. The second approach is controversial: People should be allowed to get help if they want to end their lives.

Giving Instructions: Advance Directives

An **advance directive** is the name for any written document spelling out instructions with regard to life-prolonging treatment when people are irretrievably ill and cannot communicate their wishes. There are four basic types of advance directives: two that the individual drafts and two that are filled out by other people, called surrogates, when the ill person is seriously mentally impaired.

- In the **living will,** mentally competent individuals leave instructions about their treatment wishes for life-prolonging strategies should they become comatose or permanently incapacitated. Although people typically fill out living wills in order to refuse aggressive medical interventions, it is important to point out that this document can also specify that every heroic measure be carried out.

- In a **durable power of attorney for health care,** individuals designate a specific person, such as a spouse or a child, to make end-of-life decisions "in their spirit" when they are incapable of making those choices known.

- A **Do Not Resuscitate (DNR) order** is filled out when the sick person is already mentally impaired, usually by the doctor in consultation with family members. This document, most often placed in a nursing home or hospital chart, stipulates that, if a cardiac arrest takes place, health-care professionals should not try to revive the patient.

- A **Do Not Hospitalize (DNH) order** is specific to nursing homes. It specifies that, during a medical crisis, a mentally impaired resident should not be transferred to a hospital for emergency care.

Advance directives have an admirable goal. Ideally, they provide a road map so that family members and doctors are not forced to guess what care the permanently incapacitated person *might* want. However, there are issues with regard to these documents too.

One difficulty is that people are naturally reluctant to think about their death (Ko & Lee, 2014). Do you or your parents have an advance directive? Even in the Netherlands, where people can choose to take their lives, less than 1 in 10 people does (as reported in van Wijmen and others, 2014).

The good news is that most older adults in the United States now have advance directives, a quantum leap from the situation a decade ago (Silveira, Wiitala, & Piette, 2014). But minorities and low-income elderly are particularly leery of filling out these documents (Ko & Lee, 2014). Imagine, for instance, that you are an African American and well aware of the sordid history of health discrimination against your group. Would you want to write a document telling medical personnel what *not* to do?

There are also serious problems with the most well-known advance directive, the living will. Because living wills are vague, these documents are subject to misinterpretations (Cicirelli, 2007): Does "no aggressive treatments" mean not putting in the feeding tube that has allowed my aunt to survive for 4 years after brain surgery? When your grandma wrote she wanted "No heroic measures," what exactly did she mean?

While we might think the solution would be to come up with specific checklists ("I don't want to be on a ventilator, but I do want a feeding tube"), can we expect people to make these detailed decisions? How many of you *really* know what being on a ventilator or having a feeding tube entails? Moreover, while you might say "no heroic measures" if you are healthy, your decisions are apt to be different when you are battling a fatal disease. Therefore, the best strategy is to have a series of evolving discussions with loved ones, and then choose a designated family member who, in consultation with the physician, makes the final choice (see, McMahan and others, 2013; van Wijmen & others, 2014).

advance directive Any written document spelling out instructions with regard to life-prolonging treatment if individuals become irretrievably ill and cannot communicate their wishes.

living will A type of advance directive in which people spell out their wishes for life-sustaining treatment in case they become permanently incapacitated and unable to communicate.

durable power of attorney for health care A type of advance directive in which people designate a specific surrogate to make health-care decisions if they become incapacitated and are unable to make their wishes known.

Do Not Resuscitate (DNR) order A type of advance directive filled out by surrogates (usually a doctor in consultation with family members) for impaired individuals, specifying that if they go into cardiac arrest, efforts should not be made to revive them.

Do Not Hospitalize (DNH) order A type of advance directive put into the charts of impaired nursing home residents, specifying that in a medical crisis they should not be transferred to a hospital for emergency care.

Experts advise this older woman to regularly have these frank conversations with her family as she prepares her durable power of attorney for health care.

This means the best advance directive is a durable power of attorney for health care. Granted, deciding on a single family member to carry out one's wishes can lead to jealousy. ("Why did Mom choose my brother and not me?") It doesn't ensure mistakes won't occur. Suppose after giving your "so called" reliable daughter power of attorney, that child elopes with a money-grubbing third husband and you realize you made the wrong choice? Still, having a defined proxy—but making sure to sit down and discuss your wishes with the family—can reduce the conflicts when you believe that Mom's suffering should not be prolonged, while your brother insists that treatment continue at all costs. These sibling disagreements are tailor-made to poison family relationships for years (or life).

By now, some readers may be getting uneasy, not about keeping people alive too long, but about the opposite problem—letting them die too soon. Let's ratchet up the anxiety as we move to the next step in the search for death with dignity: helping people take their own lives.

Deciding When to Die: Active Euthanasia and Physician-Assisted Suicide

Dr. Cox, a British rheumatologist, had a warm relationship with Mrs. Boyles, who had been his patient for 13 years. Mrs. Boyles was terminally ill, in excruciating pain and begged Dr. Cox to end her life: "Her pain was . . . grindingly severe. . . . [It] did not respond to increasingly large doses of opioids. Dr. Cox had reassured her that she would not be allowed to suffer terrible pain during her final days but was unable to honor that pledge. . . . As an act of compassion, he injected two ampoules of potassium chloride (a fatal drug). . . . The patient died a few minutes later peacefully in the presence of her (grateful) sons. . . ." Then the ward sister, out of a sense of duty . . . reported the action to the police. Told to "disregard the doctor's motives" but only rule on his "intent to kill," a jury . . . convicted Dr. Cox "amid scenes of great emotional distress in the court."

(as reported in Begley, 2008; quotes are from pp. 436 and 438)

How do you feel about this doctor's decision, the reaction of his nurse, and the jury's judgment? If you were like many people in Great Britain, you would have been outraged, believing that Dr. Cox was a hero because he acted on his mission to relieve human suffering rather than follow an unjust law (recall Kohlberg's *post-conventional stage*, in Chapter 9).

Let's first make some distinctions. **Passive euthanasia,** withdrawing potentially life-saving interventions, such as a feeding tube, is perfectly legal. (That's what advance directives specify.) But the step Dr. Cox took qualified as **active euthanasia**—taking *action* to help a person die. Active euthanasia is illegal in every nation except Belgium, Luxembourg, and the Netherlands. However, as of this writing (early 2015) a variation on active euthanasia called physician-assisted suicide is legal in Switzerland, Oregon, Montana, Vermont, and Washington State. Under strict conditions, at a terminally ill patient's request, physicians can prescribe a medication the individual can personally take to bring on death.

As the judge in the above trial spelled out, the distinction between the two types of euthanasia lies in intentions (Dickens, Boyle, & Ganzini, 2008). When we withdraw some heroic measure, we don't specifically wish for death. When doctors give a patient a lethal dose of a drug or, as in **physician-assisted suicide,** prescribe a lethal substance for a terminally ill person, they want that individual to die.

Although active euthanasia is almost universally against the law, surveys suggest practices that hasten death do routinely occur (Chambaere and others, 2011; Seale, 2009). To take a classic example, doctors may sedate a dying patient beyond the point required for pain control, and so "accelerate" that person's death (Cellarius, 2011).

passive euthanasia
Withholding potentially life-saving interventions that might keep a terminally ill or permanently comatose patient alive.

active euthanasia A deliberate health-care intervention that helps a patient die.

physician-assisted suicide A type of active euthanasia in which a physician prescribes a lethal medication to a terminally ill person who wants to die.

Polls show increasingly widespread public acceptance of active euthanasia in Western E.U. nations over the past 30 years. But this is not the case in Central and Eastern Europe, where significant fractions of citizens still believe terminating the lives of people is never justified (Cohen and others, 2013). Why?

One reason is that killing violates the principle that only God can give or take a life. So the fact that in Central and Eastern Europe people are more apt to be religious partly explains this East–West attitude split. Apart from religious considerations, there are other reasons to be leery about taking this step.

Critics fear that legalizing euthanasia may open the gates to allowing doctors and families to "pull the plug" on people who are impaired but don't want to die (Verbakel & Jaspers, 2010). Even when someone requests help to end his life, a patient might sometimes be pressured into making that decision by unscrupulous relatives who are anxious to get an inheritance and don't want to wait till the person dies. Governments might be tempted to push through euthanasia legislation to spare the expense of treating seriously disabled citizens—offering another possible reason why residents living in more authoritarian, less democratic Eastern European nations are more apt to oppose this idea (Cohen and others, 2013).

During the 1990s, Dr. Jack Kevorkian ignited a nationwide controversy when he reported having helped many terminally ill patients die and made numerous media appearances proudly showing off this "suicide machine." For reasons discussed in the text, many people reacted with horror; Dr. Kevorkian was dubbed "Dr. Death," and he was sentenced to serve time in prison for second-degree murder!

Older people, unfortunately, are apt to be against physician-assisted dying, based on personal encounters: "She (my niece) thought that I should be euthanized," reported one horrified woman. "And she actually said to me (when I was ill), 'if you were my dog I would shoot you to put you out of your misery'" (Malpas and others, 2014, p. 356).

Another issue relates to where to draw the line. Should we allow people to kill themselves when they have a painful chronic condition, but may not be fatally ill? Suppose the person is simply chronically depressed. Can permitting suicide *ever* be an ethically acceptable choice (see Berghmans, Widdershoven, & Widdershoven-Heerding, 2013; Gillett & Chamberlain, 2013; Wittwer, 2013)?

There are excellent arguments on the other side. Should patients be forced to unwillingly endure the pain and humiliation of dying when physicians have the tools to mercifully end life? Knowing the agony that terminal disease can cause, is it humane to stand by and let nature take its course? Do you believe that legalizing active euthanasia or physician-assisted suicide is a true advance in caring for the dying or its opposite, the beginning of a "slippery slope" that might end in sanctioning the killing of anyone whose quality of life is impaired?

A Looming Social Issue: Age-Based Rationing of Care

There obviously is an age component to the "slippery slope" of withholding care. As I suggested earlier, people with DNR or DNH orders in their charts are typically elderly, near the end of their natural lives. We already use passive euthanasia at the upper end of the lifespan on a case-by-case basis, holding off from giving aggressive treatments to people we deem "too frail." Should we formally adopt the principle "don't use death-defying strategies" for people after they reach a certain age?

Daniel Callahan (1988), a prominent biomedical ethicist, argues that the answer must be yes. According to Callahan, there is a time when "the never-to-be-finished fight against death" must stop. Let's now read Callahan's arguments in favor of **age-based rationing of care:**

1. *After a person has lived out a natural lifespan, medical care should no longer be oriented to resisting death.* While stressing that no precise cutoff age can be set, Callahan puts this marker at around the eighties. This does not mean that life at

age-based rationing of care The controversial idea that society should not use expensive life-sustaining technologies on people in their old-old years.

this age has no value, but rather that when people reach their old-old years, death in the near future is inevitable and this process cannot be vigorously defied.

2. *The existence of medical technologies capable of extending the lives of elderly persons who have lived out a natural lifespan creates no presumption that the technologies must be used for that purpose.* Callahan believes that the proper goal of medicine is to stave off premature death. We should not become slaves to our death-defying technology by blindly using each intervention on every person, no matter what that individual's age.

Age-based rationing of health care is poised to become an important developed world issue as the baby boomers flood into later life, and governments grapple with the astronomical health-care costs involved in keeping frail elderly people alive for years. As I mentioned in Chapter 14, we cannot count on medical miracles to cure the many physical problems that are the downside to living to our eighties and beyond.

Do you think Callahan is "telling it like it should be" from a logical, rational point of view, or do his proposals give you chills? Should we rely on markers such as life expectancy or quality of life to allocate who does or doesn't deserve to get care?

Whatever your answer to these compelling questions, you might notice that this chapter is devoted to one core lifespan concern. As we approach death, our life comes full circle, and we care only about what mattered during our first year of life—being connected to the people we most love. True, self-efficacy is important. But, when we come right down to it, attachment trumps everything else!

 Tying It All Together

1. Your mother asks you whether she should fill out an advance directive. Given what you know about these documents, what should your answer be?

   a. Go for it! But fill out a living will.

   b. Go for it! But you need to regularly discuss your preferences with each of us and complete a durable power of attorney.

   c. Avoid advance directives like the plague because your preferences will never be fulfilled.

2. Latoya and Jamal are arguing about legalizing physician-assisted suicide. Jamal is furious that this practice is not legal and feels that "people should have the right to die." Latoya is terribly worried about formally institutionalizing this practice. Using the points in this section, first make Jamal's case, and then support Latoya's argument.

3. Poll your class: How would your fellow students vote if they were on the jury deciding Dr. Cox's case? If you were the ward nurse, would you have reported this doctor's decision to the police?

Answers to the Tying It All Together questions can be found at the end of this chapter.

The Dying Person

Today, we have three major pathways to death: People die suddenly, without warning; they steadily decline after being diagnosed with a fatal disease; and, most often, they battle an ultimately fatal, chronic condition for a prolonged time. Before modern medicine people died quickly and everyone had hands-on experience with death. Then, during most of the twentieth century, medical science relocated dying to hospitals, and people avoided talking or thinking about death.

In recent decades, Western attitudes have changed. Doctors now openly discuss potentially fatal diagnoses, and society has health-care alternatives devoted to easing people's passage to death. We also urge everyone to discuss their end-of-life preferences, although talking about death is still forbidden in some cultural groups.

Elisabeth Kübler-Ross, in her **stage theory of dying**, proposed that people pass through *denial, anger, bargaining, depression,* and *acceptance* when they learn they have a fatal disease. However, we cannot take this landmark theory as the final truth. Not every person wants to talk about impending death. Sometimes it may be best not to be totally honest about a loved one's dire prognosis. Most important, terminally ill people feel many different emotions—especially hope. Rather than emotionally approaching death in "stages," patients may experience a state called **middle knowledge,** both knowing and not fully comprehending their fate. Even in the face of accepting death, dying people still have life goals.

Biblical accounts showcase the defining qualities of good deaths: It's best to die at peace after a long life, surrounded by our loved ones. Specifically, people want to die relatively free of pain and anxiety, feel in control of how they die, and end their lives feeling close to their attachment figures. Believing that we have fulfilled our purpose in living and appreciating that death is part of the universal human cycle of life is also important in accepting death.

Our culture has clear conceptions about normal mourning. After an initial period spent absorbed with their loss, we expect people to recover emotionally after about a year. When mourners still show intense symptoms after this time, they can now be diagnosed with a controversial mental health condition called **persistent complex bereavement-related disorder,** or **prolonged grief.** However, prolonged grief may be normal when parents face that off-time event, the death of a child. In this worst-case example of a bad death, it helps to openly discuss dying (if that child knows he or she is terminally ill) and say goodbye to one's son or daughter. Keeping the child alive in spirit helps mute the pain. Transforming the death into a redemption sequence allows grieving adults to restore a sense of life as predictable and fair.

The Health-Care System

A classic study of **dying trajectories** showed that because dying doesn't proceed according to a "schedule" but medical personnel assume it does, the way hospitals manage death leaves much to be desired. Communication problems among patients, families, and medical personnel, along with the fact that medical technologies can extend life beyond the time the body "wants" to die, increase the potential for undignified hospital deaths. Interventions to provide better **palliative care** include: (1) offering **end-of-life care instruction** to health-care personnel; (2) establishing hospital-based **palliative-care services;** and (3) removing the scene of dying from hospitals to the hospice.

The U.S. **hospice movement** offers backup services that allow families to let their loved ones spend their final months dying naturally, at home. Family caregivers can expect different trajectories to death depending on the person's illness. They confront scary issues relating to pain control. Difficulties relating to labeling patients as dying and simple lack of awareness are other hurdles to hospice care. Home deaths may not be the best choice if attachment-related issues such as not burdening loved ones matter most to people facing a fatal disease.

The Dying Person: Taking Control of How We Die

Advance directives—the **living will** and **durable power of attorney for health care,** filled out by the individual in health, and the **Do Not Resuscitate (DNR)** and **Do Not Hospitalize (DNH)** orders, filled out by surrogates when the person is mentally impaired—provide information about whether to use heroic measures when individuals cannot make their treatment wishes known. The best advance directive is the durable power of attorney, in which a person gives a specific family member decision-making power to decide on end-of life care.

With **active euthanasia** and **physician-assisted suicide,** physicians move beyond **passive euthanasia** (withdrawing treatments) to actively promote the deaths of seriously ill people who want to end their lives. Paramount among the objections to legalizing active euthanasia is the idea that we may open the door to killing people who don't really want to die.

A related issue is **age-based rationing of care,** whether to hold off on using expensive death-defying technologies with people who are old-old. At this moment, age-based rationing of care is poised to move center stage in Western nations, as the massive baby boom cohort enters their elderly years. The timeless message of this chapter—and the book—is that love (or, in developmental science terminology, our attachments) is at the core of human life.

KEY TERMS

ANSWERS TO Tying It All Together QUIZZES

Setting the Context

1. b

2. slowly and erratically; an age-related chronic disease

3. Amanda, because today we openly discuss death, and are making efforts to promote dignified dying.

The Dying Person

1. c

2. many different emotions; hope

3. b

4. Your goal is to restore the person's sense of meaning in life, ideally by helping that individual transform her loss into a redemption sequence.

The Health-Care System

1. Although medical personnel set up predictions about how patients are likely to die, death doesn't always go according to schedule—so these prognostications are often wrong!

2. b

3. d

4. Here's what you might say to Melanie: Would you feel comfortable about burdening your family 24/7 with the job of nursing you for months or having them manage the health crises that would occur? How would you feel having loved ones see you naked and incontinent—would you want that to be their last memory of you? Wouldn't it be better to be in a setting where trained professionals could competently manage your physical pain?

The Dying Person: Taking Control of How We Die

1. b

2. Jamal's case: We are free to make decisions about how to live our lives, so it doesn't make logical sense that we can't decide when our lives should end. Plus, it's cruel to torture fatally ill people, forcing them to suffer fruitless, unwanted pain when we can easily provide a merciful death. Latoya's argument: I'm worried that greedy relatives might pressure ill people into deciding to die "for the good of the family" (that is, to save the family money). I believe that legalizing physician-assisted suicide leaves the door open to governments deciding to kill people when they think the quality of their life is not good. Furthermore, only God can take a life!

3. Here your answers may vary in interesting ways. Enjoy the discussion!

Final Thoughts

We are done!!!!! Revising this book has been thrilling. I've gotten a birds-eye view of the research strides developmental scientists have made within just a few years. In these past three years, I've witnessed human development mature into vigorous midlife. So, bear with me as I take one last page to summarize four personal top pick new research trends.

TREND NUMBER ONE: Developmental science is a truly *global* research field.
Until recently, lifespan research was fairly uni-dimensionally focused on the United States. Now, our studies have expanded to the world. From the path-breaking European findings on day care, attachment, and, especially, emerging adulthood, to the impressive Canadian and Australian longitudinal research exploring adult life, scientists from *every* developed nation have emerged as leaders in our field. Moreover, no longer are Western research teams studying people from India or China or Iran. Now, *developing world* scientists are chiming in as full participants in our field.

TREND NUMBER TWO: Developmental scientists are tracking the roots of later development into very early life.
Another exciting advance relates to epigenetics—the elegant studies suggesting events in utero and our earliest years may help program development well into old age. Now, we know graphically that preschool poverty or stress may increase our mid-life allostatic load. We understand that our obesity pathway may be partly set in motion during the first year of life. At the same time, we realize more firmly that development occurs at *every* life stage.

TREND NUMBER THREE: Developmental scientists understand that living can be immensely fulfilling at the upper ends of life.
This brings up the studies exploring positive human development—in particular, the heartening research demonstrating that emotional growth occurs well into later life. No longer can we accept the gloom and doom idea that older people are unhappy or that the physical losses of aging extend to people's emotional lives. Not only are older people—even into their eighties—happy, scientists are homing in on the interpersonal and societal forces that make for a fulfilling old age (and happy human life!).

TREND NUMBER FOUR: Developmental scientists are making landmark strides in exploring the biology of human development.
At the same time, we know far more about the biological forces shaping behavior—from the studies tracking cortisol, or oxytocin, to the explosion of research using the fMRI and tentative findings suggesting there may be environment-sensitive genes. As I've mentioned, this biologically oriented research is in its infancy. The complexity of development can *never* be reduced to hormones, slices of DNA, or single brain parts. Still, who knows what insights we might have about genetics and the brain in the next few years!

A

A-not-B error: In Piaget's framework, a classic mistake made by infants in the sensorimotor stage, whereby babies approaching age 1 go back to the original hiding place to look for an object even though they have seen it get hidden in different place.

accommodation: In Piaget's theory, enlarging our mental capacities to fit input from the wider world.

acculturation: Among immigrants, the tendency to become similar in attitudes and practices to the mainstream culture after time spent living in a new society.

achievement tests: Measures that evaluate a child's knowledge in specific school-related areas.

active euthanasia: A deliberate health-care intervention that helps a patient die.

active forces: The nature-interacts-with-nurture principle that our genetic temperamental tendencies and predispositions cause us to actively choose to put ourselves into specific environments.

ADL (activities of daily living) problems: Difficulty in performing everyday tasks that are required for living independently. ADLs are classified as either basic or instrumental.

adolescence-limited turmoil: Antisocial behavior that, for most teens, is specific to adolescence and does not persist into adult life.

adolescent egocentrism: David Elkind's term for the tendency of young teenagers to feel that their actions are at the center of everyone else's consciousness.

adoption study: Behavioral genetic research strategy, designed to determine the genetic contribution to a given trait, that involves comparing adopted children with their biological and adoptive parents.

adrenal androgens: Hormones produced by the adrenal glands that program various aspects of puberty, such as growth of body hair, skin changes, and sexual desire.

adult attachment styles: The different ways in which adults relate to romantic partners, based on Mary Ainsworth's infant attachment styles (Adult attachment styles are classified as secure, preoccupied/ambivalent insecure, or avoidant/dismissive insecure).

adult development: The scientific study of the adult part of life.

advance directive: Any written document spelling out instructions with regard to life-prolonging treatment if individuals become irretrievably ill and cannot communicate their wishes.

age-based rationing of care: The controversial idea that society should not use expensive life-sustaining technologies on people in their old-old years.

age discrimination: Illegally laying off workers or failing to hire or promote them on the basis of age.

ageism: Stereotypic, intensely negative ideas about old age.

age norms: Cultural ideas about the appropriate ages for engaging in particular activities or life tasks.

age of viability: The earliest point at which a baby can survive outside the womb.

aggression: Any hostile or destructive act.

allostatic load: An overall score of body deterioration gained from summing how a person functions on multiple physiological indexes. Allostatic load predicts cognitive performance during adult life.

alternatives to institutionalization: Services and settings designed to keep older people, who do not merit intense 24-hour care and are experiencing age-related disabilities, from having to enter nursing homes.

amniocentesis: A second-trimester procedure that involves inserting a syringe into a woman's uterus to extract a sample of amniotic fluid, which is tested for a variety of genetic and chromosomal conditions.

amniotic sac: A bag-shaped, fluid-filled membrane that contains and insulates the fetus.

analytic intelligence: In Robert Sternberg's framework on successful intelligence, the facet of intelligence involving performing well on academic-type problems.

animism: In Piaget's theory, the preoperational child's belief that inanimate objects are alive.

anorexia nervosa: A potentially life-threatening eating disorder characterized by pathological dieting (resulting in severe weight loss and, in females, loss of menstruation) and a distorted body image.

anxious-ambivalent attachment: An insecure attachment style characterized by a child's intense distress when reunited with a primary caregiver after separation.

Apgar scale: A quick test used to assess a just-delivered baby's condition by measuring heart rate, muscle tone, respiration, reflex response, and color.

artificialism: In Piaget's theory, the pre-operational child's belief that human beings make everything in nature.

assimilation: In Jean Piaget's theory, the first step promoting mental growth, involving fitting environmental input to our existing mental capacities.

assisted-living facility: A housing option providing care for elderly people who have instrumental ADL impairments and can no longer live independently but may not need a nursing home.

assisted reproductive technology (ART): Any infertility treatment in which the egg is fertilized outside of the womb.

attachment: The powerful bond of love between a caregiver and child (or between any two individuals).

attachment in the making: Second phase of Bowlby's attachment sequence, when, from 4 to 7 months of age, babies slightly prefer the primary caregiver.

attachment theory: Theory formulated by John Bowlby centering on the crucial importance to our species' survival of being closely connected with a caregiver during early childhood and being attached to a significant other during all of life.

attention-deficit/hyperactivity disorder (ADHD): The most common childhood learning disorder in the United States, disproportionately affecting boys, characterized by inattention and hyperactivity at home and/or at school.

authoritarian parents: In the parenting-styles framework, a type of child-rearing in which parents provide plenty of rules but rank low on child-centeredness, stressing unquestioning obedience.

authoritative parents: In the parenting-styles framework, the best possible child-rearing style, in which parents rank high on both nurturance and discipline, providing both love and clear family rules.

autism spectrum disorders (ASDs): Conditions characterized by persistent, severe, widespread social and conversational deficits; lack of interest in people and their feelings; and repetitive, restricted behavior patterns, such as rocking, ritualized behavior, hypersensitivity to sensory input, and a fixation on inanimate objects. A core characteristic of these disorders is impairments in theory of mind.

autobiographical memories: Recollections of events and experiences that make up one's life history.

autonomy: Erikson's second psychosocial task, when toddlers confront the challenge of understanding that they are separate individuals.

average life expectancy: A person's fifty-fifty chance at birth of living to a given age.

avoidant/dismissive insecure attachment: A standoffish, excessively disengaged style of relating to loved ones.

avoidant attachment: An insecure attachment style characterized by a child's indifference to a primary caregiver at being reunited after separation.

axon: A long nerve fiber that usually conducts impulses away from the cell body of a neuron.

B

babbling: The alternating vowel and consonant sounds that babies repeat with variations of intonation and pitch and that precede the first words.

baby-proofing: Making the home safe for a newly mobile infant.

baby boom cohort: The huge age group born between 1946 and 1964.

basic ADL problems: Difficulty in performing essential self-care activities, such as rising from a chair, eating, and getting to the toilet.

behavioral genetics: Field devoted to scientifically determining the role that hereditary forces play in determining individual differences in behavior.

bidirectionality: The crucial principle that people affect one another, or that interpersonal influences flow in both directions.

Big Five: Five core psychological predispositions—neuroticism, extraversion, openness to

experience, conscientiousness, and agreeableness—that underlie personality.

binge eating disorder: A newly labeled eating disorder defined by recurrent, out-of-control binging accompanied by feelings of disgust.

biracial or multiracial identity: How people of mixed racial backgrounds come to terms with who they are as people in relation to their heritage.

birth defect: A physical or neurological problem that occurs prenatally or at birth.

blastocyst: The hollow sphere of cells formed during the germinal stage in preparation for implantation.

body mass index (BMI): The ratio of weight to height; the main indicator of overweight or underweight.

boundaryless career: Today's most common career path for Western workers, in which people change jobs or professions periodically during their working lives.

breadwinner role: Traditional concept that a man's job is to support a wife and children.

bulimia nervosa: An eating disorder characterized by at least biweekly cycles of binging and purging (by inducing vomiting or taking laxatives) in an obsessive attempt to lose weight.

bully-victims: Exceptionally aggressive children (with externalizing disorders) who repeatedly bully and get victimized.

bullying: A situation in which one or more children (or adults) harass or target a specific child for systematic abuse.

C

caregiving grandparents: Grandparents who have taken on full responsibility for raising their grandchildren.

centering: In Piaget's conservation tasks, the preoperational child's tendency to fix on the most visually striking feature of a substance and not take other dimensions into account.

cephalocaudal sequence: The developmental principle that growth occurs in a sequence from head to toe.

cerebral cortex: The outer, folded mantle of the brain, responsible for thinking, reasoning, perceiving, and all conscious responses.

certified nurse assistant or aide: The main hands-on care provider in a nursing home who helps elderly residents with basic ADL problems.

cervix: The neck, or narrow lower portion, of the uterus.

cesarean section (c-section): A method of delivering a baby surgically by extracting the baby through incisions in the woman's abdominal wall and the uterus.

child development: The scientific study of development from birth through adolescence.

childhood obesity: A body mass index at or above the 95th percentile compared to the U.S. norms established for children in the 1970s.

child maltreatment: Any act that seriously endangers a child's physical or emotional well-being.

chorionic villus sampling (CVS): A relatively risky first-trimester pregnancy test for fetal genetic disorders.

chromosome: A threadlike strand of DNA located in the nucleus of every cell that carries the genes, which transmit hereditary information.

chronic disease: Any long-term illness that requires ongoing management. Most chronic diseases are age-related and are the endpoint of normal aging changes.

circular reactions: In Piaget's framework, repetitive action-oriented schemas (or habits) characteristic of babies during the sensorimotor stage.

class inclusion: The understanding that a general category can encompass several subordinate elements.

clear-cut attachment: Critical human attachment phase, from 7 months through toddlerhood, defined by separation anxiety, stranger anxiety, and needing a primary caregiver close.

clique: A small peer group composed of roughly six teenagers who have similar attitudes and who share activities.

co-sleeping: The standard custom, in collectivist cultures, of having a child and parent share a bed.

cognitive behaviorism (social learning theory): A behavioral worldview that emphasizes that people learn by watching others and that our thoughts about the reinforcers determine our behavior. Cognitive behaviorists focus on charting and modifying people's thoughts.

cohabitation: Sharing a household in an unmarried romantic relationship.

cohort: The age group with whom we travel through life.

colic: A baby's frantic, continual crying during the first three months of life caused by an immature nervous system.

collaborative pretend play: Fantasy play in which children work together to develop and act out the scenes.

collectivist cultures: Societies that prize social harmony, obedience, and close family connectedness over individual achievement.

commitment script: In Dan McAdams's research, a type of autobiography produced by highly generative adults that involves childhood memories of feeling special; being unusually sensitive to others' misfortunes; having a strong, enduring generative mission from adolescence; and redemption sequences.

Common Core State Standards: Transformative U.S. public school changes, spelling out universal learning benchmarks and emphasizing teaching through scaffolding, problem solving, and communication skills.

concrete operational thinking: In Piaget's framework, the type of cognition characteristic of children aged 8 to 11, marked by the ability to reason about the world in a more logical, adult way.

conservation tasks: Piagetian tasks that involve changing the shape of a substance to determine whether children can go beyond the way that substance's visually appearance and understand that the volume is retained.

consummate love: In Robert Sternberg's triangular theory of love, the ideal form of love, in which a couple's relationship involves all three of the major facets of love: passion, intimacy, and commitment.

contexts of development: Fundamental markers, including cohort, socioeconomic status, culture, and gender, that shape how we develop throughout the lifespan.

continuing-care retirement community: A housing option characterized by a series of levels of care for elderly residents, ranging from independent apartments to assisted living to nursing home care. People enter the community in relatively good health and move to sections where they can get more care when they become disabled.

conventional level of morality: In Lawrence Kohlberg's theory, the intermediate level of moral reasoning, in which people respond to ethical issues by considering the need to uphold social norms.

corporal punishment: The use of physical force to discipline a child.

correlational study: A research strategy that involves relating two or more variables.

creative intelligence: In Robert Sternberg's framework on successful intelligence, the facet of intelligence involved in producing novel ideas or innovative work.

cross-sectional study: A developmental research strategy that involves testing different age groups at the same time.

crowd: A relatively large teenage peer group.

crystallized intelligence: A basic facet of intelligence, consisting of a person's knowledge base, or storehouse of accumulated information.

cyberbullying: Systematic harassment conducted through electronic media.

D

day-care center: A day-care arrangement in which a large number of children are cared for at a licensed facility by paid providers.

day-care program: A service for impaired older adults who live with relatives, in which the older person spends the day at a center offering various activities.

decentering: In Piaget's conservation tasks, the concrete operational child's ability to look at several dimensions of an object or substance.

deinstitutionalization of marriage: The decline in marriage and the emergence of alternate family forms that occurred during the last third of the twentieth century.

dendrite: A branching fiber that receives information and conducts impulses toward the cell body of a neuron.

depth perception: The ability to see (and fear) heights.

developed world: The most affluent countries in the world.

developing world: The more impoverished countries of the world.

developmental disorders: Learning impairments and behavioral problems during infancy and childhood.

developmentalists: Researchers and practitioners whose professional interest lies in the study of the human lifespan.

developmental systems perspective: An all-encompassing outlook on development that stresses the need to embrace a variety of theories, and the idea that all systems and processes interrelate.

deviancy training: Socialization of a young teenager into delinquency through conversations centered on performing antisocial acts.

disorganized attachment: An insecure attachment style characterized by responses such as freezing or fear when a child is reunited with the primary caregiver in the Strange Situation.

divided-attention task: A difficult memory challenge involving memorizing material while simultaneously monitoring something else.

DNA (deoxyribonucleic acid): The material that makes up genes, which bear our hereditary characteristics.

dominant disorder: An illness that a child gets by inheriting one copy of the abnormal gene that causes the disorder.

Do Not Hospitalize (DNH) order: A type of advance directive put into the charts of impaired nursing home residents, specifying that, in a medical crisis, they should not be transferred to a hospital for emergency care.

Do Not Resuscitate (DNR) order: A type of advance directive filled out by surrogates (usually a doctor in consultation with family members) for impaired individuals, specifying that if they go into cardiac arrest, efforts should not be made to revive them.

dose–response effect: Term referring to the fact that the amount (dose) of a substance, in this case the depth and length of deprivation, determines its probable effect or impact on the person (In the orphanage studies, the "response" is subsequent emotional and/or cognitive problems).

Down syndrome: The most common chromosomal abnormality, causing intellectual disability, susceptibility to heart disease, and other health problems as well as distinctive physical characteristics, such as slanted eyes and stocky build.

durable power of attorney for health care: A type of advance directive in which people designate a specific surrogate to make health-care decisions if they become incapacitated and are unable to make their wishes known.

dying trajectory: The fact that hospital personnel make projections about the particular pathway to death that a seriously ill patient will take and organize their care according to that assumption.

dyslexia: A learning disorder that is characterized by reading difficulties, lack of fluency, and poor word recognition that is often genetic in origin.

E

early childhood: The first phase of childhood, lasting from age 3 through kindergarten, or about age 5.

Early Head Start: A federal program that provides counseling and other services to low-income parents and children under age 3.

eating disorder: A pathological obsession with getting and staying thin. The two best-known eating disorders are *anorexia nervosa* and *bulimia nervosa*.

egocentrism: In Piaget's theory, the preoperational child's inability to understand that other people have different points of view from their own.

elderspeak: A style of communication used with an older person who seems to be physically impaired, involving speaking loudly and with slow, exaggerated pronunciation, as if talking to a baby.

embryonic stage: The second stage of prenatal development, lasting from week 3 through week 8.

emerging adulthood: The phase of life that begins after high school, tapers off toward the late twenties, and is devoted to constructing an adult life.

emotion regulation: The capacity to manage one's emotional state.

empathy: Feeling the exact emotion that another person is experiencing.

end-of-life care instruction: Courses in medical and nursing schools devoted to teaching health-care workers how to provide the best palliative care to the dying.

epigenetics: Research field exploring how early life events alter the outer cover of our DNA, producing lifelong changes in health and behavior.

episodic memory: In the memory-systems perspective, the most fragile type of memory, involving the recall of the ongoing events of daily life.

Erikson's psychosocial tasks: In Erik Erikson's theory, each challenge that we face as we travel through the eight stages of the lifespan.

ethnic identity: How people come to terms with who they are as people relating to their unique ethnic or racial heritage.

eudaimonic happiness: Well-being defined as having a sense of meaning and life purpose.

evocative forces: The nature-interacts-with-nurture principle that our genetic temperamental tendencies and predispositions evoke, or produce, certain responses from other people.

evolutionary psychology: Theory or worldview highlighting the role that inborn, species-specific behaviors play in human development and life.

executive functions: Any frontal-lobe ability that allows us to inhibit our responses and to plan and direct our thinking.

experience-sampling technique: A research procedure designed to capture moment-to-moment experiences by having people carry pagers and take notes describing their activities and emotions whenever the signal sounds.

externalizing tendencies: A personality style that involves acting on one's immediate impulses and behaving disruptively and aggressively.

extrinsic career rewards: Work that is performed for external reinforcers, such as pay.

extrinsic motivation: The drive to take an action because that activity offers external reinforcers such as praise, money, or a good grade.

F

face-perception studies: Research using preferential looking and habituation to explore what very young babies know about faces.

fallopian tube: One of a pair of slim, pipelike structures that connect the ovaries with the uterus.

family day care: A day-care arrangement in which a neighbor or relative cares for a small number of children in her home for a fee.

family watchdogs: A basic role of grandparents involving monitoring younger family members' well-being and intervening to provide help in cases of crisis.

family–work conflict: A situation in which people—typically parents—are torn between the demands of family and work.

fantasy play: Play that involves making up and acting out a scenario; also called *pretend play*.

fertility rate: The average number of children a woman in a given country has during her lifetime.

fertilization: The union of sperm and egg.

fetal alcohol syndrome (FAS): A cluster of birth defects caused by the mother's alcohol consumption during pregnancy.

fetal programming research: New research discipline exploring the impact of traumatic pregnancy events and intense stress on producing low birth weight, obesity, and long-term physical problems.

fetal stage: The final period of prenatal development, lasting seven months, characterized by physical refinements, massive growth, and the development of the brain.

fine motor skills: Physical abilities that involve small, coordinated movements, such as drawing and writing one's name.

flow: Mihaly Csikszentmihalyi's term for feeling total absorption in a challenging, goal-oriented activity.

fluid intelligence: A basic facet of intelligence, consisting of the ability to quickly master new intellectual activities.

Flynn Effect: Remarkable and steady rise in overall performance on IQ tests that has been occurring around the world over the past century.

food insecurity: According to U.S. Department of Agriculture surveys, the number of households that report needing to serve unbalanced meals, worrying about not having enough food at the end of the month, or having to go hungry due to lack of money (latter is *severe food insecurity*).

formal operational stage: Jean Piaget's fourth and final stage of cognitive development, reached at around age 12, and characterized by teenagers' ability to reason at an abstract, scientific level.

frontal lobes: The area at the uppermost front of the brain responsible for reasoning and planning our actions.

G

"g": Charles Spearman's term for a general intelligence factor that he claimed underlies all cognitive activities.

gang: A close-knit, delinquent peer group. Gangs form mainly under conditions of economic deprivation; they offer their members protection from harm and engage in a variety of criminal activities.

gender-segregated play: Play in which boys and girls associate only with members of their own sex—typical of childhood.

gender schema theory: Explanation for gender-stereotyped behavior that emphasizes the role of cognitions; specifically, the idea that once children know their own gender label (girl or boy), they selectively watch and model their own sex.

gene: A segment of DNA that contains a chemical blueprint for manufacturing a particular protein.

generativity: In Erikson's theory, the seventh psychosocial task, in which people in midlife find meaning from nurturing the next generation, caring for others, or enriching the lives of others through their work. According to Erikson, when midlife adults have not achieved generativity, they feel stagnant and without a sense of purpose in life.

genetic counselor: A professional who counsels parents-to-be about their own and/or their children's risk of developing genetic disorders, as well as available treatments.

genetic testing: A blood test to determine whether a person carries the gene for a given genetic disorder.

germinal stage: The first 14 days of prenatal development, from fertilization to full implantation.

gerontology: The scientific study of the aging process and older adults.

gestation: The period of pregnancy.

gifted: The label for superior intellectual functioning characterized by an IQ score of 130 or above, showing that a child ranks in the top 2 percent of his age group.

gonads: The sex organs—the ovaries in girls and the testes in boys.

goodness of fit: An ideal parenting strategy that involves arranging children's environments to suit their temperaments, minimizing their vulnerabilities and accentuating their strengths.

grammar: The rules and word-arranging systems that every human language employs to communicate meaning.

Great Recession of 2008: Dramatic loss of jobs (and consumer spending) that began with the bursting of the U.S. housing bubble in late 2007.

gross motor skills: Physical abilities that involve large muscle movements, such as running and jumping.

growth spurt: A dramatic increase in height and weight that occurs during puberty.

guilt: Feeling upset about having caused harm to a person or about having violated one's internal standard of behavior.

H

habituation: The predictable loss of interest that develops once a stimulus becomes familiar; used to explore infant sensory capacities and thinking.

Head Start: A federal program offering high-quality day care at a center and other services to help

preschoolers aged 3 to 5 from low-income families prepare for school.

healthy-life years: The number of years people can expect to live without ADL problems.

hedonic happiness: Well-being defined as pure pleasure.

holophrase: First clear evidence of language, when babies use a single word to communicate a sentence or complete thought.

home health services: Nursing-oriented and housekeeping help provided in the home of an impaired older adult (or any other impaired person).

homogamy: The principle that we select a mate who is similar to us.

homophobia: Intense fear and dislike of gays and lesbians.

hormones: Chemical substances released in the bloodstream that target and change organs and tissues.

hospice movement: A movement, which became widespread in recent decades, focused on providing palliative care to dying patients outside of hospitals and especially on giving families the support they need to care for the terminally ill at home.

hostile attributional bias: The tendency of highly aggressive children to see motives and actions as threatening when they are actually benign.

HPG axis: The main hormonal system programming puberty; it involves a triggering hypothalamic hormone that causes the pituitary gland to secrete its hormones, which in turn cause the ovaries and testes to develop and secrete the hormones that produce major body changes.

I

identity achievement: An identity status in which the person decides on a definite adult life path after searching out various options.

identity constancy: In Piaget's theory, the preoperational child's inability to grasp that a person's core "self" stays the same despite changes in external appearance.

identity diffusion: An identity status in which the person is aimless or feels totally blocked, without any adult life path.

identity foreclosure: An identity status in which the person decides on an adult life path (often one spelled out by an authority figure) without any thought or active search.

identity: In Erikson's theory, the life task of deciding who to be as a person in making the transition to adulthood.

identity statuses: James Marcia's four categories of identity formation: identity diffusion, identity foreclosure, moratorium, and identity achievement.

imaginary audience: David Elkind's term for the tendency of young teenagers to feel that everyone is watching their every action; a component of adolescent egocentrism.

immigrant paradox: The fact that despite living in poverty, going to substandard schools, and not having parents who speak the language, many immigrant children do far better than we might expect in school.

implantation: The process in which a blastocyst becomes embedded in the uterine wall.

income inequality: The gap between the rich and poor within a nation. Specifically, when income inequality is wide, a nation has a few very affluent residents and a mass of disadvantaged citizens.

individualistic cultures: Societies that prize independence, competition, and personal success.

induction: The ideal discipline style for socializing prosocial behavior, involving getting a child who has behaved hurtfully to empathize with the pain he has caused the other person.

industry versus inferiority: Erik Erikson's term for the psychosocial task of middle childhood involving managing our emotions and realizing that real-world success involves hard work.

infant-directed speech (IDS): The simplified, exaggerated, high-pitched tones that adults and children use to speak to infants that function to help teach language.

infant mortality: Death during the first year of life.

infertility: The inability to conceive after a year of unprotected sex. (Includes the inability to carry a child to term.)

information-processing approach: A perspective on understanding cognition that divides thinking into specific steps and component processes, much like a computer.

initiative versus guilt: Erik Erikson's term for the preschool psychosocial task involving actively taking on life tasks.

inner speech: In Vygotsky's theory, the way in by which human beings learn to regulate their behavior and master cognitive challenges, through silently repeating information or talking to themselves.

insecure attachment: Deviation from the normally joyful response of being united with a primary caregiver, signaling problems in the caregiver–child relationship.

instrumental ADL problems: Difficulty in performing everyday household tasks, such as cooking and cleaning.

integrity: Erik Erikson's eighth psychosocial stage, in which elderly people decide that their life missions have been fulfilled and so accept impending death.

intellectual disability: The label for significantly impaired cognitive functioning, measured by deficits in behavior accompanied by having an IQ of 70 or below.

intergenerational equity: Balancing the needs of the young and old. It is often regarded to as the idea that U.S. government entitlements, such as Medicare and Social Security, "over-benefit" the elderly at the expense of other age groups.

internalizing tendencies: A personality style that involves intense fear, social inhibition, and often depression.

intimacy: Erikson's first adult task, involving connecting with a partner in a mutually loving relationship.

intrinsic career rewards: Work that provides inner fulfillment and allows people to satisfy their needs for creativity, autonomy, and relatedness.

intrinsic motivation: The drive to act based on the pleasure of taking that action in itself, not for an external reinforcer or reward.

in vitro fertilization: An infertility treatment in which conception occurs outside of the womb; the developing cell mass is then inserted into the woman's uterus so that pregnancy can occur.

K

kangaroo care: Carrying a young baby in a sling close to the caregiver's body. This technique is most useful for soothing an infant.

Kübler-Ross's stage theory of dying: The landmark theory, developed by psychiatrist Elisabeth Kübler-Ross, that people who are terminally ill progress through five stages in confronting their death: denial, anger, bargaining, depression, and acceptance.

L

language acquisition device (LAD): Chomsky's term for a hypothetical brain structure that enables our species to learn and produce language.

learned helplessness: A state that develops when a person feels incapable of affecting the outcome of events, and gives up without trying.

lens: A transparent, disk-shaped structure in the eye, which bends to allow us to see close objects.

life-course difficulties: Antisocial behavior that, for a fraction of adolescents, persists into adult life.

lifespan development: The scientific study of development through life.

little-scientist phase: The time around age 1 when babies use tertiary circular reactions to actively explore the properties of objects, experimenting with them like "scientists."

living will: A type of advance directive in which people spell out their wishes for life-sustaining treatment in case they become permanently incapacitated and unable to communicate.

longitudinal study: A developmental research strategy that involves testing an age group repeatedly over many years.

low birth weight (LBW): A body weight at birth of less than 5 1/2 pounds.

M

major neurocognitive disorder (NCD) (also known as dementia) The general term for any illness involving serious, progressive, usually irreversible cognitive decline, that interferes with a person's ability to live independently. (A minor neurocognitive disorder is the label for a less severe impairment in memory, reasoning, and thinking which does not compromise independent living.)

marital equity: Fairness in the "work" of a couple's life together. If a relationship lacks equity, with one partner doing significantly more than the other, the outcome is typically marital dissatisfaction.

mass-to-specific sequence: The developmental principle that large structures (and movements) precede increasingly detailed refinements.

maximum lifespan: The biological limit of human life (about 105 years).

mean length of utterance (MLU): The average number of morphemes per sentence.

means–end behavior: In Piaget's framework, performing a different action to achieve a goal—an ability that emerges in the sensorimotor stage as babies approach age 1.

median age: The age at which 50 percent of a population is older and 50 percent is younger.

Medicare: The U.S. government's program of health insurance for elderly people.

memory-systems perspective: A framework that divides memory into three types: procedural, semantic, and episodic memory.

menarche: A girl's first menstruation.

menopause: The age-related process, occurring at about age 50, in which ovulation and menstruation stop due to the decline of estrogen.

micronutrient deficiency: Chronically inadequate level of a specific nutrient important to development and disease prevention, such as Vitamin A, Zinc, and/or Iron.

middle childhood: The second phase of childhood, covering the elementary school years, from about age 6 to 11.

middle knowledge: The idea that terminally ill people can know that they are dying yet, at the same time, not completely grasp or come to terms emotionally with that fact.

miscarriage: The naturally occurring loss of a pregnancy and death of the fetus.

mnemonic technique: A strategy for aiding memory, often by using imagery or enhancing the emotional meaning of what needs to be learned.

modeling: Learning by watching and imitating others.

moratorium: An identity status in which the person actively seeks out various possibilities to find a truly solid adult life path. A mature style of constructing an identity.

morpheme : The smallest unit of meaning in a particular language—for example, *boys* contains two morphemes: *boy* and the plural suffix *s*.

multiple intelligences theory: In Howard Gardner's perspective on intelligence, the principle that there are eight separate kinds of intelligence—verbal, mathematical, interpersonal, intrapersonal, spatial, musical, kinesthetic, and naturalist—plus a possible ninth form, called spiritual intelligence.

myelination: Formation of a fatty layer, encasing the axons of neurons. This process, which speeds the transmission of neural impulses, continues from birth to early adulthood.

N

natural childbirth: A general term for labor and birth without medical interventions.

naturalistic observation: A measurement strategy that involves directly watching and coding behaviors.

nature: Biological or genetic causes of development.

neonatal intensive care unit (NICU): A special hospital unit that treats at-risk newborns, such as low-birth-weight and very-low-birth-weight babies.

nest-leaving: Moving out of a childhood home and living independently.

neural tube: A cylindrical structure that forms along the back of the embryo and develops into the brain and spinal cord.

neurocognitive disorder due to Alzheimer's disease (or Alzheimer's disease): A type of age-related neurocognitive disorder characterized by neural atrophy and abnormal by-products of that atrophy, such as senile plaques and neurofibrillary tangles.

neurofibrillary tangles: Long, wavy filaments that replace normal neurons and are characteristic of Alzheimer's disease.

neuron: A nerve cell.

non-normative transitions: Unpredictable or atypical life changes that occur during development.

nonsuicidal self-injury: Cutting, burning, or purposely injuring one's body to cope with stress.

normal aging changes: The universal, often progressive signs, of physical deterioration intrinsic to the aging process.

normative transitions: Predictable life changes that occur during development.

nursing home/long-term-care facility: A residential institution that provides shelter and intensive caregiving, primarily to older people who need help with basic ADLs.

nurture: Environmental causes of development.

nurturer father: Husband who actively participates in hands-on child care.

O

object permanence: In Piaget's framework, the understanding that objects continue to exist even when we can no longer see them, which gradually emerges during the sensorimotor stage.

occupational segregation: The separation of men and women into different kinds of jobs.

off time: Being too late or too early in a culture's timetable for achieving adult life tasks.

old-age dependency ratio: The fraction of people over age 60 compared to younger, working-age adults (ages 15 to 59). This ratio is rising dramatically as the baby boomers retire.

old-old: People almost age 80 and older.

on time: Being on target in a culture's timetable for achieving adult life tasks.

operant conditioning: According to the traditional behavioral perspective, the law of learning that determines any voluntary response. Specifically, we act the way we do because we are reinforced for acting in that way.

osteoporosis: An age-related chronic disease in which the bones become porous, fragile, and more likely to break. Osteoporosis is most common in thin women and females of European and Asian descent.

ovary: One of a pair of almond-shaped organs that contain a woman's ova, or eggs.

overextension: An error in early language development in which young children apply verbal labels too broadly.

overregularization: An error in early language development, in which young children apply the rules for plurals and past tenses even to exceptions, so irregular forms sound like regular forms.

ovulation: The moment during a woman's monthly cycle when an ovum is expelled from the ovary.

ovum: An egg cell containing the genetic material contributed by the mother to the baby.

oxytocin: The hormone whose production is centrally involved in bonding, nurturing, and caregiving behaviors in our species and other mammals.

P

palliative care: Any intervention designed not to cure illness but to promote dignified dying.

palliative-care service: A service or unit in a hospital that is devoted to end-of-life care.

paradox of well-being: The fact that despite their physical and mental losses, the elderly report being just as happy or happier than the young.

parental alienation: The practice among divorced parents of badmouthing a former spouse, with the goal of turning a child against that person.

parent care: Adult children's care for their disabled elderly parents.

parenting style: In Diana Baumrind's framework, how parents align on two dimensions of child-rearing: nurturance (or child-centeredness) and discipline (or structure and rules).

passive euthanasia: Withholding potentially life-saving interventions that might keep a terminally ill or permanently comatose patient alive.

permissive parents: In the parenting-styles framework, a type of child-rearing in which parents provide few rules but rank high on child-centeredness, being extremely loving but providing little discipline.

Persistent Complex Bereavement-Related Disorder, or prolonged grief: Controversial new diagnosis, appearing in the most recent versions of the Western psychiatric disorder manuals, in which the bereaved person shows intense symptoms of mourning with no signs of abatement, or an increase in symptoms 6 months to a year after a loved one's death.

personal fable: David Elkind's term for the tendency of young teenagers to believe that their lives are special and heroic; a component of adolescent egocentrism.

person–environment fit: The extent to which the environment is tailored to our biological tendencies and talents. In developmental science, fostering this fit between our talents and the wider world is an important goal.

phoneme: The sound units that convey meaning in a given language—for example, in English, the *c* sound of *cat* and the *b* sound of *bat*.

physician-assisted suicide: A type of active euthanasia in which a physician prescribes a lethal medication to a terminally ill person who wants to die.

Piaget's cognitive developmental theory: Jean Piaget's principle that from infancy to adolescence, children progress through four qualitatively different stages of intellectual growth.

placenta: The structure projecting from the wall of the uterus during pregnancy through which the developing baby absorbs nutrients.

plastic: Malleable, or capable of being changed (used to refer to neural or cognitive development).

positivity effect: The tendency for older people to focus on positive experiences and screen out negative events.

postconventional level of morality: In Lawrence Kohlberg's theory, the highest level of moral reasoning, in which people respond to ethical issues by applying their own moral guidelines apart from society's rules.

postformal thought: A uniquely adult form of intelligence that involves being sensitive to different perspectives, making decisions based on one's inner feelings, and being interested in exploring new questions.

power assertion: An ineffective socialization strategy that involves yelling, screaming, or hitting out in frustration at a child.

practical intelligence: In Robert Sternberg's framework on successful intelligence, the facet of intelligence involved in knowing how to act competently in real-world situations.

preattachment phase: The first phase of John Bowlby's developmental attachment sequence, during the first three months of life, when infants show no visible signs of attachment.

preconventional level of morality: In Lawrence Kohlberg's theory, the lowest level of moral reasoning, in which people approach ethical issues by considering the personal punishments or rewards of taking a particular action.

preferential-looking paradigm: A research technique to explore early infant sensory capacities and cognition, drawing on the principle that we are attracted to novelty and prefer to look at new things.

preoccupied/ambivalent insecure attachment: An excessively clingy, needy style of relating to loved ones.

preoperational thinking: In Piaget's theory, the type of cognition characteristic of children aged 2 to 7, marked by an inability to step back from one's immediate perceptions and think conceptually.

presbycusis: Age-related difficulty in hearing, particularly high-pitched tones, caused by the atrophy of the hearing receptors located in the inner ear.

presbyopia: Age-related midlife difficulty with near vision, caused by the inability of the lens to bend.

preschool: A teaching-oriented group setting for children aged 3 to 5.

primary attachment figure: The closest person in a child's or adult's life.

primary circular reactions: In Piaget's framework, the first infant habits during the sensorimotor stage, centered on the body.

primary sexual characteristics: Physical changes of puberty that directly involve the organs of reproduction, such as the growth of the penis and the onset of menstruation.

private pensions: The major source of nongovernmental income support for U.S. retirees, in which the individual worker and employer put a portion of each paycheck into an account to help finance retirement.

proactive aggression: A hostile or destructive act initiated to achieve a goal.

procedural memory: In the memory-systems perspective, the most resilient (longest-lasting) type of memory; refers to material, such as well-learned physical skills, that we automatically recall without conscious awareness.

prosocial behavior: Sharing, helping, and caring actions.

proximity-seeking behavior: Acting to maintain physical contact or to be close to an attachment figure.

proximodistal sequence: The developmental principle that growth occurs from the most interior parts of the body outward.

puberty rite: A "coming of age" ritual, usually beginning at some event such as first menstruation, held in traditional cultures to celebrate children's transition to adulthood.

puberty: The hormonal and physical changes by which children become sexually mature human beings and reach their adult height.

Q

qualitative research: Occasional developmental science data-collection strategy that involves interviewing people to obtain information which cannot be quantified on a numerical scale.

quantitative research: Standard developmental science data-collection strategy that involves testing groups of people and using numerical scales and statistics.

quickening: A pregnant woman's first feeling of the fetus moving inside her body.

R

reaction time: The speed at which a person can respond to a stimulus. A progressive increase in reaction time is universal to aging.

reactive aggression: A hostile or destructive act carried out in response to being frustrated or hurt.

recessive disorder: An illness caused by inheriting two copies of the abnormal, disorder-causing gene.

redemption sequence: In Dan McAdams's research, a characteristic theme of highly generative adults' autobiographies, in which they describe tragic events that turned out for the best.

reflex: A response or action that is automatic and programmed by noncortical brain centers.

rehearsal: A learning strategy in which people repeat information to embed it in to memory.

reinforcement: Behavioral term for reward.

rejecting-neglecting parents: In the parenting-styles framework, the worst child-rearing approach, in which parents provide little discipline and little nurturing or love.

relational aggression: A hostile or destructive act designed to cause harm to a person's relationships.

reliability: In measurement terminology, a basic criterion of a test's accuracy wherein scores must be fairly similar when a person re-takes a test.

REM sleep: The phase of sleep involving rapid eye movements, when the EEG looks almost like it does during waking. REM sleep decreases as infants mature.

representative sample: A group that reflects the characteristics of the overall population.

resilient children: Children who rebound from serious early life traumas to construct successful adult lives.

reversibility: In Piaget's conservation tasks, the concrete operational child's knowledge that a specific change in the way a given substance looks can be reversed.

role: The characteristic behavior that is expected of a person in a particular social position, such as student, parent, married person, worker, or retiree.

role conflict: A situation in which a person is torn between two or more major responsibilities—for instance, parent and worker—and cannot do either job adequately.

role confusion: Erikson's term for a failure in identity formation, marked by the lack of any sense of a future adult path.

role overload: A job situation that places so many requirements or demands on workers that it becomes impossible to do a good job.

role phase: In Murstein's theory, the final mate-selection stage, in which committed partners work out their future life together.

rooting reflex: Newborns' automatic response to a touch on the cheek, involving turning toward that location and beginning to suck.

rough-and-tumble play: Play that involves shoving, wrestling, and hitting, but in which no actual harm is intended; especially characteristic of boys.

ruminative moratorium: When a young person is unable to decide between different identities, becoming emotionally paralyzed and highly anxious.

S

scaffolding: The process of teaching new skills by entering a child's zone of proximal development and tailoring one's efforts to that person's competence level.

school-to-work transition: The change from the schooling phase of life to the work world.

Seattle Longitudinal Study: The definitive study of the effect of aging on intelligence, led by K. Warner Schaie, involving simultaneously conducting and comparing the results of cross-sectional and longitudinal studies carried out with a group of Seattle volunteers.

secondary circular reactions: In Piaget's framework, habits of the sensorimotor stage lasting from about 4 months of age to the baby's first birthday, centered on exploring the external world.

secondary sexual characteristics: Physical changes of puberty that are not directly involved in reproduction.

secular trend in puberty: A century-long decline in the average age at which children reach puberty in the developed world.

secure attachment: Ideal attachment response when a child responds with joy at being united with a primary caregiver; in adulthood, the genuine intimacy that is ideal in love relationships.

secure (adult) attachment: The genuine intimacy that is ideal in love relationships.

selective attention: A learning strategy in which people manage their awareness so as to attend only to what is relevant and to filter out unneeded information.

selective optimization with compensation: Paul Baltes's three principles for successful aging (and living): (1) selectively focusing on what is most important, (2) working harder to perform well in those top-ranking areas, and (3) relying on external aids to cope effectively.

self-awareness: The ability to observe our actions from an outside frame of reference and to reflect on our inner state.

self-conscious emotions: Feelings of pride, shame, or guilt, which first emerge around age 2 and show the capacity to reflect on the self.

self-efficacy: According to cognitive behaviorism, an internal belief in our competence that predicts whether we initiate activities or persist in the face of failures, and predicts the goals that we set.

self-esteem: Evaluating oneself as either "good" or "bad" as a result of comparing the self to other people.

self-report strategy: A measurement having people report on their feelings and activities through questionnaires.

self-soothing: Children's ability, usually beginning at about 6 months of age, to put themselves back to sleep when they wake up during the night.

semantic memory: In the memory-systems perspective, a moderately resilient (long-lasting) type of memory; refers to our ability to recall basic facts.

semantics: The meaning system of a language—that is, what the words stand for.

senile plaques: Thick, bullet-like amyloid-laden structures that replace normal neurons and are characteristic of Alzheimer's disease.

sensitive period: The time when a body structure is most vulnerable to damage by a teratogen, typically when that organ or process is rapidly developing or coming "on line."

sensorimotor stage: Piaget's first stage of cognitive development, lasting from birth to age 2, when babies'

agenda is to pin down the basics of physical reality.

separation anxiety: Signal of clear-cut attachment when a baby gets upset as a primary caregiver departs.

serial cohabitation: Living sequentially with different partners outside of marriage.

sex-linked single-gene disorder: An illness, carried on the mother's X chromosome, that typically leaves the female offspring unaffected but has a fifty-fifty chance of striking each male child.

sexual double standard: A cultural code that gives men greater sexual freedom than women. Specifically, society expects males to want to have intercourse and expects females to remain virgins until they marry and be more interested in relationships than having sex.

shame: A feeling of being personally humiliated.

single-gene disorder: An illness caused by a single gene.

social-interactionist perspective: An approach to language development that emphasizes its social function, specifically that babies and adults have a mutual passion to communicate.

social clock: The concept suggesting that we regulate our passage through adulthood by an inner timetable telling us which activities are appropriate for certain ages.

social cognition: Any skill related to understanding feelings and negotiating interpersonal interactions.

socialization: The process by which children are taught to obey the norms of society and to behave in socially appropriate ways.

social networking sites: Internet sites whose goal is to forge personal connections between users.

social referencing: A baby's checking back and monitoring a caregiver for cues as to how to behave while exploring; linked to clear-cut attachment.

Social Security: The U.S. government's national retirement support program.

social smile: The first real smile, occurring at about 2 months of age.

socioeconomic health gap: The disparity, found in nations around the world, between the health of the rich and poor.

socioeconomic status (SES): A basic marker referring to status on the educational and—especially—income rungs.

Socioemotional Selectivity Theory: A theory of aging (and the lifespan) put forth by Laura Carstensen, describing how the time we have left to live affects our priorities and social relationships. Specifically in later life, people focus on the present and prioritize being with their closest attachment figures.

specific learning disorder: The label for any impairment in language or any deficit related to listening, thinking, speaking, reading, writing, spelling, or understanding mathematics.

spermarche: A boy's first ejaculation of live sperm.

stimulus phase: In Murstein's theory, the initial mate-selection stage, in which we make judgments about a potential partner based on external characteristics such as appearance.

Stimulus-Value-Role Theory: Murstein's mate-selection theory suggest that similar people pair up and that our path to commitment progresses through three phases (called the stimulus, value-comparison, and role phases).

stranger anxiety: Beginning at about 7 months of age, when a baby grows wary of people other than a primary caregiver.

Strange Situation: Mary Ainsworth's procedure to measure attachment at age 1, involving planned separations and reunions with a caregiver.

stunting: Excessively short stature in a child, caused by chronic lack of adequate nutrition.

"storm and stress": G. Stanley Hall's phrase for the intense moodiness, emotional sensitivity, and risk-taking tendencies that characterize the life stage which he labeled adolescence.

successful intelligence: In Robert Sternberg's framework, the optimal form of cognition involving having a good balance of analytic, creative, and practical intelligence.

sucking reflex: The automatic, spontaneous sucking movements newborns produce, especially when anything touches their lips.

Sudden Infant Death Syndrome (SIDS): The unexplained death of an apparently healthy infant, often while sleeping, during the first year of life.

swaddling: The standard Western infant calming technique of wrapping a baby tightly in a blanket or other garment.

sympathy: A state necessary for acting prosocially, involving feeling upset *for* a person who needs help.

synapse: The gap between the dendrites of one neuron and the axon of another, over which impulses flow.

synaptogenesis: Forming of connections between neurons at the synapses. This process, responsible for all perceptions, actions, and thoughts, is most intense during infancy and childhood but continues throughout life.

synchrony: The reciprocal aspect of the attachment relationship, with a caregiver and infant responding emotionally to each other in a sensitive, exquisitely attuned way.

syntax: The system of grammatical rules in a particular language.

T

telegraphic speech: First stage of combining words in infancy, in which a baby pares down a sentence to its essential words.

temperament: A person's characteristic, inborn style of dealing with the world.

teratogen: A substance, such as alcohol, that crosses the placenta and harms the fetus.

terminal drop: A research phenomenon in which a dramatic decline in an older person's scores on vocabulary tests and other measures of crystallized intelligence predicts having a terminal disease.

tertiary circular reactions: In Piaget's framework, "little-scientist" activities of the sensorimotor stage, beginning around age 1, involving flexibly exploring the properties of objects.

testes: Male organs that manufacture sperm.

testosterone: The hormone responsible for the maturation of reproductive organs in men as well as hair and skin changes during puberty and for sexual desire in both sexes.

theory: Any perspective explaining why people act the way they do. Theories allow us to predict behavior and also suggest how to intervene to improve behavior.

theory of mind: Children's first cognitive understanding, which appears at about age 4, that other people have different beliefs and perspectives from their own.

thin ideal: Media-driven cultural idea that females need to be abnormally thin.

toddlerhood: The important transitional stage after babyhood, from roughly 1 year to 2 1/2 years of age; defined by an intense attachment to caregivers and an urgent need to become independent.

traditional behaviorism: The original behavioral worldview that focused on charting and modifying only "objective," visible behaviors.

traditional stable career: A career path in which people settle into their permanent life's work in their twenties and often stay with the same organization until they retire.

Triangular Theory of Love: Robert Sternberg's categorization of love relationships into three facets: passion, intimacy, and commitment. When arranged at the points of a triangle, their combinations describe all of the different kinds of adult love relationships.

trimester: One of the 3-month-long segments into which pregnancy is divided.

true experiment: The only research strategy that can determine that something causes something else; involves randomly assigning people to different treatments and then looking at the outcome.

twentieth-century life expectancy revolution: The dramatic increase in average life expectancy that occurred during the first half of the twentieth century in the developed world.

twin/adoption study: Behavioral genetic research strategy that involves comparing the similarities of identical twin pairs adopted into different families, to determine the genetic contribution to a given trait.

twin study: Behavioral genetic research strategy, designed to determine the genetic contribution of a given trait, and involves comparing identical twins with fraternal twins (or with other people).

U

U-shaped curve of marital satisfaction: The most common pathway of marital happiness in the West, in which satisfaction is highest at the honeymoon, declines during the child-rearing years, then rises after the children grow up.

ultrasound: In pregnancy, an image of the fetus in the womb that helps to date the pregnancy, assess the fetus's growth, and identify abnormalities.

umbilical cord: The structure that attaches the placenta to the fetus, through which nutrients are passed and fetal wastes are removed.

underextension: An error in early language development in which young children apply verbal labels too narrowly.

undernutrition: A chronic lack of adequate food.

uterus: The pear-shaped muscular organ in a woman's abdomen that houses a developing baby.

V

validity: In measurement terminology, a basic criterion for a test's accuracy involving whether that measure reflects the real-world quality that it is supposed to measure.

value-comparison phase: In Murstein's theory, the second mate-selection stage, in which we make judgments about a partner on the basis of similar values and interests.

vascular neurocognitive disorder (also known as vascular dementia): A type of age-related neurocognitive disorder caused by multiple small strokes.

very low birth weight (VLBW): A body weight at birth of less than 3 1/4 pounds.

visual cliff: A table that appears to "end" in a drop-off at its midpoint; used to test for infant depth perception.

W

Wechsler Adult Intelligence Scale (WAIS): The standard test to measure adult IQ, involving verbal and performance scales, each of which is made up of various subtests.

widowhood mortality effect: The elevated risk of death among surviving spouses after being widowed.

Wechsler Intelligence Scale for Children (WISC): The standard intelligence test used in childhood, consisting of different scales composing a variety of subtests.

working memory: In information-processing theory, the limited-capacity gateway system containing all of the material that we can keep in awareness at a single moment. The material in this system is either processed for more permanent storage or lost.

working model: In Bowlby's theory, the mental representation of a caregiver allowing children over age 3 to be physically apart from that primary attachment figure.

Y

young-old: People in their sixties and seventies.

youth development program: Any after-school program or structured activity outside of the school day that is devoted to promoting flourishing in teenagers.

Z

zone of proximal development (ZPD): In Vygotsky's theory, the gap between a child's ability to solve a problem totally on his own and his potential knowledge if taught by a more accomplished person.

zygote: A fertilized ovum.

References

Abbasi-Shavazi, J., Mohammad J., & McDonald, P. (2008). Family change in Iran: Religion, revolution, and the state. In R. Jayakody, A. Thornton, & W. Axinn (Eds.), *International family change: Ideational perspectives* (pp. 177–198). New York, NY: Taylor & Francis Group/Erlbaum.

Abbassi, V. (1998). Growth and normal puberty. *Pediatrics, 102,* 507–511.

Abbate-Daga, G., Gramaglia, C., Amianto, F., Marzola, E., & Fassino, S. (2010). Attachment insecurity, personality, and body dissatisfaction in eating disorders. *The Journal of Nervous and Mental D\isease, 198*(7), 520–524.

Abdou, C. M., Dunkel, S. C., Campos, B., Hilmert, C. J., Dominguez, T. P., Hobel, C. J., . . . Sandman, C. A. (2010). Communalism predicts prenatal affect, stress, and physiology better than ethnicity and socioeconomic status. *Cultural Diversity & Ethnic Minority Psychology, 16*(3), 395–403.

Aberdeen, L., & Fereiro, D. (2014). Communicating with assistive listening devices and age-related hearing loss: Perceptions of older Australians. *Contemporary Nurse: A Journal for the Australian Nursing Profession, 47*(1-2), 119–131.

Abramson, L. Y., Seligman, M. E., & Teasdale, J. D. (1978). Learned helplessness in humans: Critique and reformulation. *Journal of Abnormal Psychology, 87,* 49–74.

Abu-Akel, A., & Shamay-Tsoory, S. (2011). Neuroanatomical and neurochemical bases of theory of mind. *Neuropsychologia, 49,* 2971–2984.

Abubakar, A., Holding, P., Vijver, F. J. R., Newton, C., & Baar, A. V. (2010). Children at risk for developmental delay can be recognised by stunting, being underweight, ill health, little maternal schooling or high gravity. *Journal of Child Psychology and Psychiatry, 51*(6), 652–659.

Acevedo, B. P., & Aron, A. (2009). Does a long-term relationship kill romantic love? *Review of General Psychology, 13,* 59–65.

Acevedo-Polakovich, I. D., Cousineau, J. R., Quirk, K. M., Gerhart, J. I., Bell, K. M., & Adomako, M. S. (2014). Toward an asset orientation in the study of U.S. Latina/o youth: Biculturalism, ethnic identity, and positive youth development. *The Counseling Psychologist, 42*(2), 201–229.

Adachi, P. C., & Willoughby, T. (2014). It's not how much you play, but how much you enjoy the game: The longitudinal association between adolescents' self-esteem and the frequency versus enjoyment of involvement in sports. *Journal of Youth and Adolescence, 43*(1), 137–145

Adair, L. S. (2008). Child and adolescent obesity: Epidemiology and developmental perspectives. *Physiology & Behavior, 94,* 8–16.

Adams, G. A., & Rau, B. (2011). Putting off tomorrow to do what you want today: Planning for retirement. *American Psychologist, 66*(3), 180–192.

Adi-Japha, E., Berberich-Artzi, J., & Libnawi, A. (2010). Cognitive flexibility in drawings of bilingual children. *Child Development, 81*(5), 1356–1366.

Adler, N., Pantell, M. S., O'Donovan, A., Blackburn, E., Cawthon, R., Koster, A., . . . Epel, E. (2013). Educational attainment and late life telomere length in the health, aging and body composition study. *Brain, Behavior, and Immunity, 27,* 15–21.

Adolph, K. E. (2008). Learning to move. *Current Directions in Psychological Science 17*(3), 213–218.

Adolph, K., & Berger, S. E. (2006). Motor development. In D. Kuhn, R. S. Siegler, W. Damon, & R. M. Lerner (Eds.), *Handbook of child psychology: Vol. 2, Cognition, perception, and language* (6th ed.) pp. 161–213. Hoboken, NJ: Wiley.

Aghajanian, A., & Thompson, V. (2013). Recent divorce trend in Iran. *Journal of Divorce & Remarriage, 54*(2), 112–125.

Agrawal, A., & Lynskey, M. T. (2008). Are there genetic influences on addiction: Evidence from family, adoption, and twin studies. *Addiction, 103,* 1069–1081.

Ahnert, L., Pinquart, M., & Lamb, M. (2006). Security of children's relationships with nonparental care providers: A meta-analysis. *Child Development, 74*(3), 664–679.

Ainsworth, M. D. S. (1967). *Infancy in Uganda: Infant care and the growth of love.* Baltimore, MD: Johns Hopkins Press.

Ainsworth, M. D. S. (1973). The development of infant-mother attachment. In B. M. Caldwell & H. N. Ricciuti (Eds.), *Review of child development research* (Vol. 3, pp. 1–94). Chicago, IL: University of Chicago Press.

Ainsworth, M. D. S., Blehar, M. C., Waters, E., & Wall, S. (1978). *Patterns of attachment: A psychological study of the strange situation.* Hillsdale, NJ: Erlbaum.

Aknin, L. B., Hamlin, J. K., & Dunn, E. W. (2012). Giving leads to happiness in young children. *Plos ONE, 7*(6).

Aksan, N., & Kochanska, G. (2004). Links between systems of inhibition from infancy to preschool years. *Child Development, 75*(5), 1477–1490.

Alatupa, S., Pulkki-Råback, L., Hintsanen, M., Elovainio, M., Mullola, S., & Keltikangas-Järvinen, L. (2013). Disruptive behavior in childhood and socioeconomic position in adulthood: A prospective study over 27 years. *International Journal of Public Health, 58*(2), 247–256.

Albert, I., Labs, K., & Trommsdorff, G. (2010). Are older adult German women satisfied with their lives? On the role of life domains, partnership status, and self-control. *GeroPsych, 23*(1), 39–49.

Alderson, R. M., Hudec, K. L., Patros, C. G., & Kasper, L. J. (2013). Working memory deficits in adults with attention-deficit/hyperactivity disorder (ADHD): An examination of central executive and storage/rehearsal processes. *Journal of Abnormal Psychology, 122*(2), 532–541.

Aldred, H. E. (1997). *Pregnancy and birth sourcebook: Basic information about planning for pregnancy, maternal health, fetal growth and development.* Detroit, MI: Omnigraphics.

Ali, M. M., & Dwyer, D. S. (2011). Estimating peer effects in sexual behavior among adolescents. *Journal of Adolescence, 34,* 183–190.

Allan, L. J., Johnson, J. A., & Emerson, S. D. (2014). The role of individual difference variables in ageism. *Personality and Individual Differences, 59,* 32–37.

Allemand, M., Steiger, A. E., & Hill, P. L. (2013). Stability of personality traits in adulthood: Mechanisms and implications. *Geropsych: The Journal of Gerontopsychology and Geriatric Psychiatry, 26*(1), 5–13.

Allen, J. P., Porter, M., McFarland, C., McElhaney, K. B., & Marsh, P. (2007). The relation of attachment security to adolescents' paternal and peer relationships, depression, and externalizing behavior. *Child Development, 78*(4), 1222–1239.

Allen, J. P., Schad, M. M., Oudekerk, B., & Chango, J. (2014). What ever happened to the "cool" kids? Long-term sequelae of early adolescent pseudomature behavior. *Child Development, 85*(5), 1866–1880.

Allen, T. D., & Finkelstein, L. M. (2014). Work–family conflict among members of full-time dual-earner couples: An examination of family life stage, gender, and age. *Journal of Occupational Health Psychology, 19*(3), 376–384.

Allendorf, K. (2013). Schemas of marital change: From arranged marriages to eloping for love. *Journal of Marriage and Family, 75*(2), 453–469.

Allison, C. M., & Hyde, J. S. (2013). Early menarche: Confluence of biological and contextual factors. *Sex Roles, 68*(1-2), 55–64.

Alloway, T. P., & Alloway, R. G. (2013). Working memory across the lifespan: A cross-sectional approach. *Journal of Cognitive Psychology, 25*(1), 84–93.

Alzheimer's Association. (2009). *2009 Alzheimer's disease, facts and figures,* p. 14. Retrieved from https://www.alz.org/national/documents/report_alzfactsfigures2009.pdf

Amato, P. R. (2007). Transformative processes in marriage: Some thoughts from a sociologist. *Journal of Marriage and Family, 69*(2), 305–309.

Amato, P. R. (2010). Research on divorce: Continuing trends and new developments. *Journal of Marriage and Family, 72,* 650–666.

Amato, P. R., & Hohmann-Marriott, B. (2007). A comparison of high- and low-distress marriages that end in divorce. *Journal of Marriage and Family, 69*(3), 621–638.

Ambrose, A. F., Paul, G., & Hausdorff, J. M. (2013). Risk factors for falls among older adults: A review of the literature. *Maturitas, 75*(1), 51–61.

American Academy of Pediatrics, Committee on Drugs. (2000). Use of psychoactive medication during pregnancy and possible effects on the fetus and newborn. *Pediatrics, 105,* 880–887.

American Academy of Pediatrics. (2005). Breastfeeding and the use of human milk. *Pediatrics, 115,* 496–506.

American Heart Association. (2001). *2002 heart and stroke statistical update.* Dallas, TX: American Heart Association.

American Psychiatric Association. (2013). *Diagnostic and statistical manual of mental disorders* (5th ed.). Arlington, VA: American Psychiatric Publishing.

Anakwenze, U., & Zuberi, D. (2013). Mental health and poverty in the inner city. *Health & Social Work, 38*(3), 147–157.

Andero, A. A., & Stewart, A. (2002). Issue of corporal punishment: Re-examined. *Journal of Instructional Psychology, 29,* 90–96.

Anders, T., Goodlin-Jones, B., & Zelenko, M. (1998). Infant regulation and sleep-wake state development. *Zero to Three, 19*(2), 9–14.

Anderson, J. W. (1972). Attachment behaviour out of doors. In N. Blurton Jones (Ed.), *Ethological studies of child behaviour* (pp. 199–215). London, England: Cambridge University Press.

Anderson, R., & Mitchell, E. M. (1984). Children's health and play in rural Nepal. *Social Science & Medicine, 19,* 735–740.

Andrews, T., & Knaak, S. (2013). Medicalized mothering: Experiences with breastfeeding in Canada and Norway. *The Sociological Review, 61*(1), 88–110.

Anestis, M. D., Pennings, S. M., Lavender, J. M., Tull, M. T., & Gratz, K. L. (2013). Low distress tolerance as an indirect risk factor for suicidal behavior: Considering the explanatory role of non-suicidal self-injury. *Comprehensive Psychiatry, 54*(7), 996–1002.

Angel, J. L., Jimenez, M. A., & Angel, R. J. (2007). The economic consequences of widowhood for older minority women. *The Gerontologist, 47*(2), 224–234.

Angelini, V., Cavapozzi, D., Corazzini, L., & Paccagnella, O. (2012). Age, health and life satisfaction among older Europeans. *Social Indicators Research, 105*(2), 293–308.

Annerbäck, E.-M., Svedin, C.-G., & Gustafsson, P. A. (2010). Characteristic features of severe child physical abuse—A multi-informant approach. *Journal of Family Violence, 25,* 165–172.

Anschutz, D. J., Spruijt-Metz, D., Van Strien, T., & Engels, R. C. M. E. (2011). The direct effect of thin ideal focused adult television on young girls' ideal body figure. *Body Image, 8,* 26–33.

Anusic, I., Yap, S. Y., & Lucas, R. E. (2014). Does personality moderate reaction and adaptation to major life events? Analysis of life satisfaction and affect in an Australian national sample. *Journal of Research in Personality, 51,* 69–77.

Anzman-Frasca, S., Liu, S., Gates, K. M., Paul, I. M., Rovine, M. J., & Birch, L. L. (2013). Infants' transitions out of a fussing/crying state are modifiable and are related to weight status. *Infancy, 18*(5), 662–686.

Aoyama, S., Toshima, T., Saito, Y., Konishi, N., Motoshige, K., Ishikawa, N., . . . Kobayashi M. (2010). Maternal breast milk odour induces frontal lobe activation in neonates: A NIRS study. *Early Human Development, 86,* 541–545.

Archibald, A. B., Graber, J. A., & Brooks-Gunn, J. (2003). Pubertal processes and physiological growth in adolescence. In G. R. Adams & M. D. Berzonsky (Eds.), *Blackwell handbook of adolescence* (pp. 24–47). Malden, MA: Blackwell.

Ardelt, M., & Koenig, C. S. (2006). The role of religion for hospice patients and relatively healthy older adults. *Research on Aging, 28,* 184–215.

Ardila, A. (2007). Normal aging increases cognitive heterogeneity: Analysis of dispersion in WAIS-III scores across age. *Archives of Clinical Neuropsychology, 22,* 1003–1011.

Ariès, P. (1962). *Centuries of childhood: A social history of family life.* New York, NY: Knopf.

Ariès, P. (1974). *Western attitudes toward death: From the Middle Ages to the present* (P. M. Ranum, Trans.). Baltimore, MD: Johns Hopkins University Press. Johns Hopkins University Press.

Ariès, P. (1981). *The hour of our death* (H. Weaver, Trans.). New York, NY: Knopf.

Arnett, J. J. (1999). Adolescent storm and stress, reconsidered. *American Psychologist, 54,* 317–326.

Arnett, J. J. (2004). *Emerging adulthood: The winding road from the late teens through the twenties.* New York, NY: Oxford University Press.

Arnett, J. J. (2007). The long and leisurely route: Coming of age in Europe today. *Current History: A Journal of Contemporary Affairs, 106,* 130–136.

Arnett, J. J., & Tanner, J. L. (2010). Themes and variations in emerging adulthood across social classes. In J. J. Arnett, M. Kloep, L. B. Hendry, & J. L. Tanner (Eds.), *Debating emerging adulthood: Stage or process?* (pp. 31–51). New York, NY: Oxford University Press.

Aron, A., Norman, C. C., Aron, E. N., & Lewandowski, G. (2002). Shared participation in self-expanding activities: Positive effects on experienced marital quality. In P. Noller & J. A. Feeney (Eds.),

Understanding marriage: Developments in the study of couple interaction (pp. 177–194). New York, NY: Cambridge University Press.

Asghar, S., Magnusson, A., Khan, A., Ali, K., Hussain, A. (2010). In Bangladesh, overweight individuals have fewer symptoms of depression than non-overweight individuals. *Obesity, 18*(6), 1143–1145.

Åström, J., Nakosteen, R. A., Westerlund, O., & Zimmer, M. A. (2013). Twice chosen: Spouse matching and earnings among women in first and second unions. *The Social Science Journal, 50*(3), 277–288.

Atchley, R. (1989). A continuity theory of normal aging. *The Gerontologist, 29*(2), 183–190.

AVERT. (2005, November 22). *AIDS and HIV statistics for Sub-Saharan Africa.* Retrieved from http://www.avert.org/subadults.htm

Avis, N. E., Assmann, S. F., Kravitz, H. M., Ganz, P. A., & Ory, M. (2004). Quality of life in diverse groups of midlife women: Assessing the influence of menopause, health status and psychosocial and demographic factors. *Quality of Life Research, 13*, 933–946.

Ayalon, L., & Green, V. (2013). Social ties in the context of the continuing care retirement community. *Qualitative Health Research, 23*(3), 396–406.

Baddeley, A. D. (1992). Working memory: The interface between memory and cognition. *Journal of Cognitive Neuroscience, 4*, 281–288.

Baibazarova, E., van de Beek, C., Cohen-Kettenis, P. T., Buitelaar, J., Shelton, K. H., & van Goozen, S. M. (2013). Influence of prenatal maternal stress, maternal plasma cortisol and cortisol in the amniotic fluid on birth outcomes and child temperament at 3 months. *Psychoneuroendocrinology, 38*(6), 907–915.

Baile, W. F., Aaron, J., & Parker, P. A. (2009). Practitioner-patient communication in cancer diagnosis and treatment. In S. M. Miller, D. J. Bowen, R. T. Croyle, & J. H. Rowland (Eds.), *Handbook of cancer control and behavioral science: A resource for researchers, practitioners, and policymakers* (pp. 327–346). Washington, DC: American Psychological Association.

Baillargeon, R. (1993). The object concept revisited: New direction in the investigation of infants' physical knowledge. In C. Granrud (Ed.), *Visual perception and cognition in infancy* (pp. 265–315). Hillsdale, NJ: Erlbaum.

Baillargeon, R., & DeVos, J. (1991). Object permanence in young infants: Further evidence. *Child Development, 62*, 1227–1246.

Baillargeon, R., & Graber, M. (1987). Where's the rabbit? 5.5-month-old infants' representation of the height of a hidden object. *Cognitive Development, 2*, 375–392.

Bainbridge, K. E., & Wallhagen, M. I. (2014). Hearing loss in an aging American population: Extent, impact, and management. *Annual Review of Public Health, 35*, 139–152.

Baker, J. E., & Sedney, M. A. (1996). How bereaved children cope with loss: An overview. In C. A. Corr & D. Corr (Eds.), *Handbook of childhood death and bereavement* (pp. 109–129). New York, NY: Springer.

Bal, E., Yerys, B. E., Sokoloff, J. L., Celano, M. J., Kenworthy, L., Giedd, J. N., & Wallace, G. L. (2013). Do social attribution skills improve with age in children with high functioning autism spectrum disorders? *Research in Autism Spectrum Disorders, 7*(1), 9–16.

Balk, D. E. (2008a). A modest proposal about bereavement and recovery. *Death Studies, 32*, 84–93.

Balk, D. E. (2008b). Special issue on bereavement, outcomes, and recovery: Guest editor's opening remarks. *Death Studies, 32*, 1–5.

Ball, H. (2007). Bed-sharing practices of initially breastfed infants in the first 6 months of life. *Infant and Child Development, 16*, 387–401.

Ball, H. L., & Volpe, L. E. (2013). Sudden Infant Death Syndrome (SIDS) risk reduction and infant sleep location—Moving the discussion forward. *Social Science & Medicine, 79*, 84–91.

Ballard, R. H., Holtzworth-Munroe, A., Applegate, A. G., D'Onofrio, B. M., & Bates, J. E. (2013). A randomized controlled trial of child-informed mediation. *Psychology, Public Policy, and Law, 19*(3), 271–281.

Baltes, M. M., & Carstensen, L. L. (2003). The process of successful aging: Selection, optimization, and compensation. In U. M. Staudinger & U. Lindenberger (Eds.), *Understanding human development: Dialogues with lifespan psychology* (pp. 81–104). Dordrecht, Netherlands: Kluwer Academic.

Baltes, P. B. (2003). On the incomplete architecture of human ontogeny: Selection, optimization, and compensation as foundation of developmental theory. In U. M. Staudinger & U. Lindenberger (Eds.), *Understanding human development: Dialogues with lifespan psychology* (pp. 17–43). Boston: Kluwer Academic.

Baltes, P. B., & Smith, J. (1997). A systemic-wholistic view of psychological functioning in very old age: Introduction to a collection of articles from the Berlin Aging Study. *Psychology and Aging, 12*, 395–409.

Banducci, A. N., Gomes, M., MacPherson, L., Lejuez, C. W., Potenza, M. N., Gelernter, J., & Amstadter, A. B. (2014). A preliminary examination of the relationship between the 5-HTTLPR and childhood emotional abuse on depressive symptoms in 10–12-year-old youth. *Psychological Trauma: Theory, Research, Practice, and Policy, 6*(1), 1–7.

Bandura, A. (1977). *Social learning theory.* Englewood Cliffs, NJ: Prentice Hall.

Bandura, A. (1986). *Social foundations of thought and action: A social cognitive theory.* Englewood Cliffs, NJ: Prentice-Hall.

Bandura, A. (1989). Human agency in social cognitive theory. *American Psychologist, 44*, 1175–1184.

Bandura, A. (1992). Exercise of personal agency through the self-efficacy mechanism. In R. Schwarzer (Ed.), *Self-efficacy: Thought control of action* (pp. 3–38). Washington, DC: Hemisphere.

Bandura, A. (1997). *Self-efficacy: The exercise of control.* New York, NY: Freeman.

Bane, K. (2004). *What the best college teachers do.* Cambridge, MA: President and Fellows of Harvard College.

Bangerter, L. R., & Waldron, V. R. (2014). Turning points in long distance grandparent–grandchild relationships. *Journal of Aging Studies, 29*, 88–97.

Barkin, S., Scheindlin, B., Ip, E. H., Richardson, I., & Finch, S. (2007). Determinants of parental discipline practices: A national sample from primary care practices. *Clinical Pediatrics, 46*(1), 64–69.

Barkley, R. A. (1998). *Attention-deficit hyperactivity disorder: A handbook for diagnosis and treatment* (2nd ed.). New York, NY: Guilford Press.

Barkley, R. A. (2003). Attention-deficit/hyperactivity disorder. In E. J. Mash & R. A. Barkley (Eds.), *Child psychopathology* (2nd ed. pp. 75–143). New York, NY: Guilford Press.

Barkley, R. A., & Murphy, K. R. (2006). *Attention-deficit hyperactivity disorder: A clinical workbook* (3rd ed.). New York, NY: Guilford Press.

Barnard, P., Moreland, I., & Nagy, J. (1999). *Children, bereavement and trauma: Nurturing resilience.* London, England: Jessica Kingsley.

Barnes, G. M., Hoffman, J. H., Welte, J. W., Farrell, M. P., & Dintcheff, B. A. (2007). Adolescents' time use: Effects on substance use, delinquency and sexual activity. *Journal of Youth and Adolescence, 36,* 697–710.

Barnett, M. A., Shanahan, L., Deng, M., Haskett, M. E., & Cox, M. J. (2010). Independent and interactive contributions of parenting behaviors and beliefs in the prediction of early childhood behavior problems. *Parenting: Science and Practice, 10*(1), 43–59.

Barnett, S. M., Ceci, S. J., & Williams, W. M. (2006). Is the ability to make a bacon sandwich a mark of intelligence? and other issues: Some reflections on Gardner's theory of multiple intelligences. In J. A. Schaler (Ed.) *Howard Gardner under fire: The rebel psychologist faces his critics* (pp. 95–114). Chicago, IL: Open Court.

Barnhart, C., Raval, V., Jansari, A., & Raval, P. (2013). Perceptions of Parenting Style Among College Students in India and the United States. *Journal of Child and Family Studies, 22*(5), 684–693.

Baron, I. S., & Rey-Casserly, C. (2010). Extremely preterm birth outcome: A review of four decades of cognitive research. *Neuropsychology Review, 20*(4), 430–425.

Baron-Cohen, S. (1999). The evolution of a theory of mind. In M. C. Corballis & S. E. G. Lea (Eds.), *The descent of mind: Psychological perspectives on hominid evolution* (pp. 261–277). New York, NY: Oxford University Press.

Barratt, R., Levickis, P., Naugton, G., Gerner, B., Gibbonskay, M. (2013). Why families choose not to participate in research: Feedback from non-responders. *Journal of Paediatrics and Child Health, 49*(1), 57–62.

Barrett, E. S., Tran, V., Thurston, S., Jasienska, G., Furberg, A., Ellison, P. T., & Thune, I. (2013). Marriage and motherhood are associated with lower testosterone concentrations in women. *Hormones and Behavior, 63*(1), 72–79.

Barry, R. A., & Kochanska, G. (2010). A longitudinal investigation of the affective environment in families with young children: From infancy to early school age. *Emotion, 10*(2), 237–249.

Barry, R. A., Kochanska, G., & Philibert, R. A. (2008). G × E interaction in the organization of attachment: Mother's responsiveness as a moderator of children's genotypes. *Journal of Child Psychology and Psychiatry, 49,* 1313–1320.

Barry, R. A., & Lawrence, E. (2013). "Don't stand so close to me": An attachment perspective of disengagement and avoidance in marriage. *Journal of Family Psychology, 27*(3), 484–494.

Bartlett, J. D., & Easterbrooks, M. A. (2012). Links between physical abuse in childhood and child neglect among adolescent mothers. *Children and Youth Services Review, 34*(11), 2164–2169.

Barusch, A. S. (2013). Age-friendly cities: A social work perspective. *Journal of Gerontological Social Work, 56*(6), 465–472.

Bassok, D. (2010). Do black and Hispanic children benefit more from preschool? Understanding differences in preschool effects across racial groups. *Child Development, 81*(6), 1828–1845.

Bauer, J. J., & McAdams, D. P. (2010). Eudaimonic growth: Narrative growth goals predict increases in ego development and subjective well-being 3 years later. *Developmental Psychology, 46*(4), 761–772.

Baumeister, R. F., Campbell, J. D., Krueger, J. I., & Vohs, K. D. (2003). Does high self-esteem cause better performance, interpersonal success, happiness, or healthier lifestyles? *Psychological Science in the Public Interest, 4*(1), 1–44.

Baumgartner, S. E., Sumter, S. R., Peter, J., Valkenburg, P. M., & Livingstone, S. (2014). Does country context matter? Investigating the predictors of teen sexting across Europe. *Computers in Human Behavior, 34,* 157–164.

Baumrind, D. (1971). Current patterns of parental authority. *Developmental Psychology, 4*(1, Pt. 2), 1–103.

Baumrind, D., Larzelere, R. E., & Cowan, P. A. (2002). Ordinary physical punishment: Is it harmful? Comment on Gershoff. *Psychological Bulletin, 128,* 580–589.

Bava, S., Thayer, R., Jacobus, J., Ward, M., Jernigan, T. L., & Tapert, S. F. (2010). Longitudinal characterization of white matter maturation during adolescence. *Brain Research, 1327,* 38–46.

Bayl-Smith, P. H., & Griffin, B. (2014). Age discrimination in the workplace: Identifying as a late-career worker and its relationship with engagement and intended retirement age. *Journal of Applied Social Psychology, 44*(9), 588–599.

Bayrampour, H., Heaman, M., Duncan, K. A., & Tough, S. (2013). Predictors of perception of pregnancy risk among nulliparous women. *Journal of Obstetric, Gynecologic, & Neonatal Nursing: Clinical Scholarship for the Care of Women, Childbearing Families, & Newborns, 42*(4), 416–427.

Beach, S. H., Brody, G. H., Lei, M. K., Gibbons, F. X., Gerrard, M., Simons, R. L., . . . Philibert, R. A. (2013). Impact of child sex abuse on adult psychopathology: A genetically and epigenetically informed investigation. *Journal of Family Psychology, 27*(1), 3–11.

Becker, S. P., Fite, P. J., Luebbe, A. M., Stoppelbein, L., & Greening, L. (2013). Friendship intimacy exchange buffers the relation between ADHD symptoms and later social problems among children attending an after-school care program. *Journal of Psychopathology and Behavioral Assessment, 35*(2), 142–152.

Becker, S. P., McBurnett, K., Hinshaw, S. P., & Pfiffner, L. J. (2013). Negative social preference in relation to internalizing symptoms among children with ADHD predominantly inattentive type: Girls fare worse than boys. *Journal of Clinical Child and Adolescent Psychology, 42*(6), 784–795.

Becker-Blease, K. A., Turner, H. A., & Finkelhor, D. (2010). Disasters, victimization, and children's mental health. *Child Development, 81*(4), 1040–1052.

Beckman, N., Waern, M., Östling, S., Sundh, V., & Skoog, I. (2014). Determinants of sexual activity in four birth cohorts of Swedish 70-year-olds examined 1971–2001. *Journal of Sexual Medicine, 11*(2), 401–410.

Beckmann, C. R. B., Ling, F. W., Laube, D. W., Smith, R. P., Barzansky, B. M., & Herbert, W. N. P. (2002). *Obstetrics and gynecology* (4th ed.). Baltimore, MD: Lippincott Williams & Wilkins.

Beernick, A. C. E., Swinkels, S. H. N., & Buitelaar, J. K. (2007). Problem behavior in a community sample of 14- and 19-month-old children. *European Child and Adolescent Psychiatry, 16,* 271–280.

Begley, A. M. (2008). Guilty but good: Defending voluntary active euthanasia from a virtue perspective. *Nursing Ethics, 15*(4), 434–445.

Behboodi-Moghadam, Z., Salsali, M., Eftekhar-Ardabily, H., Vaismoradi, M., & Ramezanzadeh, F. (2013). Experiences of infertility through the lens of Iranian infertile women: A qualitative study.

Japan Journal of Nursing Science, 10(1), 41–46.

Behrens, K. Y., Parker, A. C., & Haltigan, J. D. (2011). Maternal sensitivity assessed during the Strange Situation Procedure predicts child's attachment quality and reunion behaviors. *Infant Behavior and Development, 34*(2), 378–381.

Beijers, C., Burger, H., Verbeek, T., Bockting, C. H., & Ormel, J. (2014). Continued smoking and continued alcohol consumption during early pregnancy distinctively associated with personality. *Addictive Behaviors, 39*(5), 980–986.

Beijers, R., Riksen-Walraven, J. M., & de Weerth, C. (2013). Cortisol regulation in 12-month-old human infants: Associations with the infants' early history of breastfeeding and co-sleeping. *Stress: The International Journal on the Biology of Stress, 16*(3), 267–277.

Beiner, S. F., Lowenstein, L., Worenklein, A., & Sauber, S. R. (2014). Grandparents' rights: Psychological and legal perspectives. *American Journal of Family Therapy, 42*(2), 114–126.

Bell, A. S. (2011). A critical review of ADHD diagnostic criteria: What to address in the DSM-V. *Journal of Attention Disorders, 15*(1), 3–10.

Bellinger, D., Leviton, A., Waternaux, C., Needleman, H., & Rabinowitz, M. (1987). Longitudinal analyses of prenatal and postnatal lead exposure and early cognitive development. *New England Journal of Medicine, 316*, 1037–1043.

Belsky, D. W. (2013). Informing public health approaches to obesity and smoking using genome-wide association studies: Genetic epidemiology affirms the importance of early prevention. *Dissertation Abstracts International, 73*.

Belsky, D. W., Moffitt, T. E., & Caspi, A. (2013). Genetics in population health science: Strategies and opportunities. *American Journal of Public Health, 103*(S1), S73–S83.

Belsky, J. (2014). Toward an evo-devo theory of reproductive strategy, health, and longevity: Commentary on Rickard et al. (2014). *Perspectives on Psychological Science, 9*(1), 16–18.

Belsky, J. K. (1999). *The psychology of aging: Theory, research, and interventions* (3rd ed.). Pacific Grove, CA: Brooks/Cole.

Belsky, J. K. (2001). Aging. In J. Worell (Ed.), *Encyclopedia of women and gender: Sex similarities and differences and the impact of society on gender* (Vol. 1 pp. 95–108). San Diego, CA: Academic Press.

Belsky, J., & Pluess, M. (2009). Beyond diathesis stress: Differential susceptibility to environmental influences. *Psychological Bulletin, 135*(6), 885–908.

Belsky, J., & Pluess, M. (2011). Beyond adversity, vulnerability, and resilience: Individual differences in developmental plasticity. In Cicchetti, D., & Roisman, G. I. (Eds.) *The Origins and Organization of Adaptation and Maladaptation* (pp. 379–422). Hoboken, NJ: Wiley.

Belsky, J., & Pluess, M. (2013). Genetic moderation of early child-care effects on social functioning across childhood: A developmental analysis. *Child Development, 84*(4), 1209–1225.

Belsky, J., & Rovine, M. (1990). Patterns of marital change across the transition to parenthood: Pregnancy to three years postpartum. *Journal of Marriage & the Family, 52*, 5–19.

Belsky, J., & Volling, B. L. (1987). Mothering, fathering, and marital interaction in the family triad during infancy: Exploring family systems processes. In P. W. Berman & F. A. Pedersen (Eds.), *Men's transitions to parenthood: Longitudinal studies of early family experience* (pp. 37–63). Hillsdale, NJ: Erlbaum.

Belsky, J., Houts, R. M., & Pasco Fearon, R. M. (2010). Infant attachment security and the timing of puberty: Testing an evolutionary hypothesis. *Psychological Science, 21*, 1195–1201.

Belsky, J., Lang, M. E., & Rovine, M. (1985). Stability and change in marriage across the transition to parenthood: A second study. *Journal of Marriage and the Family, 47*, 855–865.

Belsky, J., Newman, D. A., Widaman, K., Rodkin, P., Pluess, M., Fraley, C., Berry, D., Helm, J., & Roisman, G. (2014). "Differential susceptibility to effects of maternal sensitivity? A study of candidate plasticity genes." *Development and Psychopathology, 1*.

Belsky, J., Steinberg, L., & Draper, P. (1991). Childhood experience, interpersonal development, and reproductive strategy: An evolutionary theory of socialization. *Child Development, 62*, 647–670.

Belsky, J., Steinberg, L. D., Houts, R. M., Friedman, S. L., DeHart, G., Cauffman, E., . . . Susman, E. (2007a). Family rearing antecedents of pubertal timing. *Child Development, 78*(4), 1302–1321.

Belsky, J., Vandell, D. L., Burchinal, M., Clarke-Stewart, K. A., McCartney, K., Owen, M. T., & The NICHD Early Child Care Research Network. (2007b). Are there long-term effects of early child care? *Child Development, 78*(2), 681–701.

Bem, S. L. (1981). Gender schema theory: A cognitive account of sex typing. *Psychological Review, 88*, 354–364.

Ben Shlomo, S. (2014). What makes new grandparents satisfied with their lives? *Stress and Health: Journal of the International Society for the Investigation of Stress, 30*(1), 23–33.

Benas, J. S., Uhrlass, D. J., & Gibb, B. E. (2010). Body dissatisfaction and weight-related teasing: A model of cognitive vulnerability to depression among women. *Journal of Behavior Therapy and Experimental Psychiatry, 41*(4), 352–356.

Benedict, C., Brooks, S. J., Kullberg, J., Nordenskjöld, R., Burgos, J., Le Grevès, M., . . . Schiöth, H. B. (2013). Association between physical activity and brain health in older adults. *Neurobiology of Aging, 34*(1), 83–90.

Beneventi, H., Tønnessen, F. E., Ersland, L., & Hugdahl, K. (2010). Working memory deficit in dyslexia: Behavioral and fMRI evidence. *International Journal of Neuroscience, 120*, 51–59.

Bengtson, V. L. (1989). The problem of generations: Age group contrasts, continuities, and social change. In V. L. Bengtson & K. W. Schaie (Eds.), *The course of later life: Research and reflections* (pp. 25–54). New York, NY: Springer.

Benjet, C., & Kazdin, A. E. (2003). Spanking children: The controversies, findings and new directions. *Clinical Psychology Review, 23*, 197–224.

Benner, A. D., Kretsch, N., Harden, P. & Crosnoe, R. (2014). Academic achievement as a moderator of genetic influences on alcohol use in adolescence. *Developmental Psychology, 50*(4), 1170–1178.

Benoit, A., Lacourse, E., & Claes, M. (2013). Pubertal timing and depressive symptoms in late adolescence: The moderating role of individual, peer, and parental factors. *Development and Psychopathology, 25*(2), 455–471.

Bentur, N., Resnizky, S., Balicer, R., & Eilat-Tsanani, T. (2014). Utilization and cost of services in the last 6 months of life of patients with cancer—with and without home hospice care. *American*

Journal of Hospice & Palliative Medicine, 31(7), 723–725.

Berger, A., Alyagon, U., Hadaya, H., Atzaba-Poria, N., & Auerbach, J. G. (2013). Response inhibition in preschoolers at familial risk for attention deficit hyperactivity disorder: A behavioral and electrophysiological stop-signal study. *Child Development, 84*(5), 1616–1632.

Berger, C., & Dijkstra, J. K. (2013). Competition, envy, or snobbism? How popularity and friendships shape antipathy networks of adolescents. *Journal of Research on Adolescence, 23*(3), 586–595.

Bergh, C., Callmar, M., Danemar, S., Hölcke, M., Isberg, S., Leon, M., . . . Södersten, P. (2013). Effective treatment of eating disorders: Results at multiple sites. *Behavioral Neuroscience, 127*(6), 878–889.

Berghmans, R., Widdershoven, G., & Widdershoven-Heerding, I. (2013). Physician-assisted suicide in psychiatry and loss of hope. *International Journal of Law and Psychiatry, 36*(5–6), 436–443.

Bergsma, A., & Ardelt, M. (2011). Self-reported wisdom and happiness: An empirical investigation. *Journal of Happiness Studies, 37*(2), 1–19.

Berk, L. E., & Winsler, A. (1999). *NAEYC research into practice series: Vol. 7. Scaffolding children's learning: Vygotsky and early childhood education.* Washington, DC: National Association for the Education of Young Children.

Berkman, L., & Breslow, L. (1983). *Health and ways of living: The Alameda County study.* New York, NY: Oxford University Press.

Berko, J. (1958). The child's learning of English morphology. *Word, 14,* 150–177.

Berkowitz, R. I., & Stunkard, A. J. (2002). Development of childhood obesity. In T. A. Wadden & A. J. Stunkard (Eds.), *Handbook of obesity treatment* (pp. 515–531). New York, NY: Guilford Press.

Berlin, L. J., Appleyard, K., & Dodge, K. (2011). Intergenerational continuity in child maltreatment: Mediating mechanisms and implications for prevention. *Child Development, 82*(1), 162–176.

Bernard, J. Y., De Agostini, M., Forhan, A., Alfaiate, T., Bonet, M., Champion, V., . . . Heude, B. (2013). Breastfeeding duration and cognitive development at 2 and 3 years of age in the EDEN Mother–Child Cohort. *Journal of Pediatrics, 163*(1), 36–42.

Berry, D., Blair, C., Ursache, A., Willoughby, M. T., & Granger, D. A. (2014). Early childcare, executive functioning, and the moderating role of early stress physiology. *Developmental Psychology, 50*(4), 1250–1261.

Bersamin, M., Bourdeau, B., Fisher, D. A., Hill, D. L., Walker, S., Grube, J. W., & Grube, E. L. (2008). *Casual partnerships: Media exposure and relationship status at last oral sex and vaginal intercourse.* Paper presented at the Biennial Meeting of the Society for Research in Adolescence, Chicago, 2008.

Berthelsen, D., & Brownlee, J. (2007). Working with toddlers in child care: Practitioners' beliefs about their role. *Early Childhood Research Quarterly, 22,* 347–362.

Berzin, S. C., & De Marco, A. C. (2010). Understanding the impact of poverty on critical events in emerging adulthood. *Youth & Society, 43*(2), 278–300.

Best, J. R., & Miller, P. H. (2010). A developmental perspective on executive function. *Child Development, 81*(6), 1641–1660.

Bianchi, S. M., & Milkie, M. A. (2010). Work and family research in the first decade of the 21st century. *Journal of Marriage and Family, 72,* 705–725.

Bianchi, S., Robinson, J. R., & Milkie, M. A. (2006). *Changing rhythms of American family life.* New York, NY: Russell Sage Foundation.

Binstock, R. H. (2010). From compassionate ageism to intergenerational conflict? *The Gerontologist, 50*(5), 574–585.

Birren, J. E., & Birren, B. A. (1990). The concepts, models, and history of the psychology of aging. In J. E. Birren & K. W. Schaie (Eds.), *Handbook of the psychology of aging* (3rd ed. pp. 3–20). San Diego, CA: Academic Press.

Bishop, C. E., & Stone, R. (2014). Implications for policy: The nursing home as a least restrictive setting. *The Gerontologist, 54*(Suppl 1), S98–S103.

Bissada, A., & Briere, J. (2001). Child abuse: Physical and sexual. In J. Worell (Ed.), *Encyclopedia of women and gender: Sex similarities and differences and the impact of society on gender* (pp. 219–232). San Diego, CA: Academic Press.

Björk, S. (2013). Doing morally intelligible fatherhood: Swedish fathers' accounts of their parental part-time work choices. *Fathering, 11*(2), 221–237.

Bjorklund, D. F. (2005). *Children's thinking: Cognitive development and individual differences* (4th ed.). Belmont, CA: Wadsworth.

Bjorklund, D. F., & Bjorklund, B. R. (1992). *Looking at children: An introduction to child development.* Monterey, CA: Brooks-Cole.

Bjorklund, D. F., & Pellegrini, A. D. (2002). *The origins of human nature: Evolutionary developmental psychology.* Washington, DC: American Psychological Association.

Bjorklund, D. F., & Rosenblum, K. E. (2001). Children's use of multiple and variable addition strategies in a game context. *Developmental Science, 4,* 184–194.

Black, H. K., & Rubinstein, R. L. (2005). Direct care workers' response to dying and death in the nursing home: A case study. *Journals of Gerontology: Psychological Sciences, 60B,* S3–S10.

Blacker, D., & Lovestone, S. (2006). Genetics and dementia nosology. *Journal of Geriatric Psychiatry and Neurology, 19,* 186–191.

Blake, W. (1794). *The schoolboy.* Retrieved from http://www.dundee.ac.uk/english/wics/blake/blake2.htm#e25

Blakemore, S., & Mills, K. L. (2014). Is adolescence a sensitive period for sociocultural processing? *Annual Review of Psychology, 65,* 187–207.

Blakemore, S.-J., Burnett, S., & Dahl, R. E. (2010). The role of puberty in the developing adolescent brain. *Human Brain Mapping, 31,* 926–933.

Blatney, M., Jelinek, M., & Osecka, T. (2007). Assertive toddler, self-efficacious adult: Child temperament predicts personality over forty years. *Personality and Individual Differences, 43,* 2127–2136.

Bleidorn, W., Kandler, C., & Caspi, A. (2014). The behavioural genetics of personality development in adulthood — Classic, contemporary, and future trends. *European Journal of Personality, 28*(3), 244–255.

Bleidorn, W., Klimstra, T. A., Denissen, J. A., Rentfrow, P. J., Potter, J., & Gosling, S. D. (2013). Personality maturation around the world: A cross-cultural examination of social-investment theory. *Psychological Science, 24*(12), 2530–2540.

Bloch, L., Haase, C. M., & Levenson, R. W. (2014). Emotion regulation predicts marital satisfaction: More than a wives' tale. *Emotion, 14*(1), 130–144.

Blomeyer, D., Friemel, C. M., Buchmann, A. F., Banaschewski, T., Laucht, M., & Schneider, M. (2013). Impact of pubertal stage at first drink on adult drinking behavior. *Alcoholism: Clinical and Experimental Research, 37*(10), 1804–1811.

Blood, R. O., & Wolfe, D. M. (1960). *Husbands and wives: The dynamics of family living.* Oxford, England: Free Press Glencoe.

Blum, D. (2002). *Love at Goon Park: Harry Harlow and the science of affection.* Cambridge, MA: Perseus.

Boden, J. M., Fergusson, D. M., & Horwood, J. (2010). Risk factors for conduct disorder and oppositional/defiant disorder: Evidence from a New Zealand birth cohort. *Journal of the American Academy of Child & Adolescent Psychiatry, 49*(11), 1125–1133.

Bodenmann, G., Charvos, L., Bradbury, T. N., Bertoni, A., Iafrate, R., Giuliani, C., . . . Behling, J. (2007). The role of stress in divorce: A three-nation retrospective study. *Journal of Social and Personal Relationships, 24*(5), 707–728.

Boerner, K., Mancini, A. D., & Bonanno, G. (2013). On the nature and prevalence of uncomplicated and complicated patterns of grief. In M. Stroebe, H. Schut, J. van den Bout (Eds.), *Complicated grief: Scientific foundations for health care professionals* (pp. 55–67). New York, NY: Routledge/Taylor & Francis Group.

Bohlin, G., Eninger, L., Brocki, K. C., & Thorell, L. B. (2012). Disorganized attachment and inhibitory capacity: Predicting externalizing problem behaviors. *Journal of Abnormal Child Psychology, 40*(3), 449–458.

Boisvert, J. A., & Harrell, W. A. (2013). The impact of spirituality on eating disorder symptomatology in ethnically diverse Canadian women. *International Journal of Social Psychiatry, 59*(8), 729–738.

Bonanno, G. A., & Lilienfeld, S. O. (2008). Let's be realistic: When grief counseling is effective and when it's not. *Professional Psychology: Research and Practice, 39*(3), 377–380.

Bonanno, G. A., Wortman, C. B., Lehman, D. R., Tweed, R. G., Haring, M., Sonnega, J., . . . Nesse, R. M. (2002). Resilience to loss and chronic grief: A prospective study from pre-loss to 18-months postloss. *Journal of Personality and Social Psychology, 83,* 1150–1164.

Bonanno, R. A., & Hymel, S. (2013). Cyber bullying and internalizing difficulties: Above and beyond the impact of traditional forms of bullying. *Journal of Youth and Adolescence, 42*(5), 685–697.

Bonebrake, D., Culver, C., Call, K., & Ward-Smith, P. (2010). Clinically differentiating palliative care and hospice.

Clinical Journal of Oncology Nursing, 14(3), 273–275.

Boonpleng, W., Park, C. G., Gallo, A. M., Corte, C., McCreary, L., & Bergren, M. D. (2013). Ecological influences of early childhood obesity: A multilevel analysis. *Western Journal of Nursing Research, 35*(6), 742–759.

Booth-LaForce, C., & Oxford, M. L. (2008). Trajectories of social withdrawal from grades 1 to 6: Prediction from early parenting, attachment, and temperament. *Developmental Psychology, 44,* 1298–1313.

Borella, E., Carretti, B., & De Beni, R. (2008). Working memory and inhibition across the adult life-span. *Acta Psychologica, 128,* 33–44.

Borella, E., Carretti, B., Cantarella, A., Riboldi, F., Zavagnin, M., & De Beni, R. (2014). Benefits of training visuo-spatial working memory in young–old and old–old. *Developmental Psychology, 50*(3), 714–727.

Borko, H., Wolf, S. A., Simone, G., & Uchiyama, K. P. (2003). Schools in transition: Reform efforts and school capacity in Washington state. *Educational Evaluation and Policy Analysis, 25,* 171–201.

Bosmans, G., Dujardin, A., Raes, F., & Braet, C. (2013). The specificity of autobiographical memories in early adolescence: The role of mother-child communication and attachment-related beliefs. *The Journal of Early Adolescence, 33*(5), 710–731.

Bottiroli, S., Cavallini, E., Fastame, M. C., & Hertzog, C. (2013). Cultural differences in rated typicality and perceived causes of memory changes in adulthood. *Archives of Gerontology and Geriatrics 57*(3), 271–281.

Botwinick, J. (1967). *Cognitive processes in maturity and old age.* New York, NY: Springer.

Bouchard, T. J., Segal, N. L., Tellegen, A., McGue, M., Keyes, M., & Kruger, R. (2004). Genetic influences on social attitudes: Another challenge to psychology from behavior genetics. In L. F. DiLalla (Ed.), *Behavior genetics principles: Perspectives in development, personality, and psychopathology.* Washington, DC: American Psychological Association Press.

Bourke, A., Boduszek, D., Kelleher, C., McBride, O., & Morgan, K. (2014). Sex education, first sex and sexual health outcomes in adulthood: Findings from a nationally representative sexual health survey. *Sex Education, 14*(3), 299–309.

Bowers, E. P., Li, Y., Kiely, M. K., Brittian, A., Lerner, J. V., & Lerner, R. M. (2010). The Five Cs model of positive youth development: A longitudinal analysis of confirmatory factor structure and measurement invariance. *Journal of Youth and Adolescence, 39,* 720–735.

Bowker, J. C., & Raja, R. (2011). Social withdrawal subtypes during early adolescence in India. *Journal of Abnormal Child Psychology, 39,* 201–212.

Bowlby, J. (1969). *Attachment and loss: Vol. 1. Attachment.* New York, NY: Basic Books.

Bowlby, J. (1973). *Attachment and loss: Vol. 2. Separation: Anxiety and anger.* New York, NY: Basic Books.

Bowlby, J. (1980). *Attachment and loss: Vol. 3. Loss: Sadness and depression.* New York, NY: Basic Books.

Boykin. S., Diez-Roux, A. V., Carnethon, M., Shrager, S., Ni, H., & Whitt-Glover, M. (2011). Racial/ethnic heterogeneity in the socioeconomic patterning of CVD risk factors in the United States: The multi-ethnic study of atherosclerosis. *Journal of Health Care for the Poor and Underserved, 22,*111–127.

Boyle, D. E., Marshall, N. L., & Robeson, W. W. (2003). Gender at play: Fourth-grade girls and boys on the playground. *American Behavioral Scientist, 46,* 1326–1345.

Braam, A. W., Klinkenberg, M., & Deeg, D. J. H. (2011). Religiousness and mood in the last week of life: An explorative approach based on after-death proxy interviews. *Journal of Palliative Medicine, 14*(1), 31–37.

Bradbury, T. N., & Karney, B. R. (2004). Understanding and altering the longitudinal course of marriage. *Journal of Marriage and Family, 66,* 862–879.

Bradley, R. H., & Coryn, R. (2013). From parent to child to parent . . . : Paths in and out of problem behavior. *Journal of Abnormal Child Psychology 41*(4), 515–529.

Brainerd, C. J., Reyna, V. F., Petersen, R. C., Smith, G. E., Kenney, A. E., Gross, C. J., . . . Fisher, G. G. (2013). The apolipoprotein E genotype predicts longitudinal transitions to mild cognitive impairment but not to Alzheimer's dementia: Findings from a nationally representative study. *Neuropsychology, 27*(1), 86–94.

Brame, R., Turner, M. C., Paternoster, R., & Bushway, S. (2012). Cumulative prevalence of arrest from ages 8 to 23 in a national sample. *Pediatrics, 129*(1), 21–27.

Bramen, J. E., Hranilovich, J. A., Dahl, R. E., Forbes, E. E., Chen, J., Toga, A. W., . . . Sowell, E. R. (2011). Puberty influences medial temporal lobe and cortical gray matter maturation differently in boys than girls matched for sexual maturity. *Cerebral Cortex, 21*(3), 636–646.

Brand, S., Gerber, M., Kalak, N., Kirov, R., Lemola, S., Clough, P. J., . . . Holsboer-Trachsler, E. (2014). Adolescents with greater mental toughness show higher sleep efficiency, more deep sleep and fewer awakenings after sleep onset. *Journal of Adolescent Health, 54*(1), 109–113.

Branje, S., Laninga-Wijnen, L., Yu, R., & Meeus, W. (2014). Associations among school and friendship identity in adolescence and romantic relationships and work in emerging adulthood. *Emerging Adulthood, 2*(1), 6–16.

Breen, A. V., Lewis, S. P., & Sutherland, O. (2013). Brief report: Non-suicidal self-injury in the context of self and identity development. *Journal of Adult Development, 20*(1), 57–62.

Bregman, H. R., Malik, N. M., Page, M. L., Makynen, E., & Lindahl, K. M. (2013). Identity profiles in lesbian, gay, and bisexual youth: The role of family influences. *Journal of Youth and Adolescence, 42*(3), 417–430.

Brendgen, M., Vitaro, F., Bukowski, W. M., Dionne, G., Tremblay, R. E., & Boivin, M. (2013). Can friends protect genetically vulnerable children from depression? *Development and Psychopathology, 25*(2), 277–289.

Bretherton, I. (2005). In pursuit of the internal working model construct and its relevance to attachment relationships. In K. E. Grossmann, K. Grossmann, & E. Waters (Eds.), *Attachment from infancy to adulthood: The major longitudinal studies* (pp. 13–47). New York, NY: Guilford Press.

Brière, F. N., Archambault, K., & Janosz, M. (2013). Reciprocal prospective associations between depressive symptoms and perceived relationship with parents in early adolescence. *Canadian Journal of Psychiatry / La Revue Canadienne de Psychiatrie, 58*(3), 169–176.

Briley, D. A., & Tucker-Drob, E. M. (2014). Genetic and environmental continuity in personality development: A meta-analysis. *Psychological Bulletin, 140*(5), 1303–1331.

Britton, M. L. (2013). Race/ethnicity, attitudes, and living with parents during young adulthood. *Journal of Marriage and Family, 75*(4), 995–1013.

Brock, R. L., & Lawrence, E. (2014). Intrapersonal, interpersonal, and contextual risk factors for overprovision of partner support in marriage. *Journal of Family Psychology, 28*(1), 54–64.

Brodhagen, A., & Wise, D. (2008). Optimism as a mediator between the experience of child abuse, other traumatic events, and distress. *Journal of Family Violence, 36*, 403–411.

Brody, G. H., Tianyi, Y., Beach, S. H., Kogan, S. M., Philibert, R. A., & Windle, M. (2014). Harsh parenting and adolescent health: A longitudinal analysis with genetic moderation. *Health Psychology, 33*(5), 401–409.

Brody, J. E. (2010, December 27). Just because one's vision is waning, hope doesn't have to. *The New York Times*, p. D2.

Brody, N. (2006). Geocentric theory: A valid alternative to Gardner's theory of intelligence. In J. A. Schaler (Ed.), *Howard Gardner under fire: The rebel psychologist faces his critics* (pp. 73–94). Chicago, IL: Open Court Publishing Co.

Brom, S. S., & Kliegel, M. (2014). Improving everyday prospective memory performance in older adults: Comparing cognitive process and strategy training. *Psychology and Aging, 29*(3), 744–755.

Bronfenbrenner, U. (1977). Toward an experimental ecology of human development. *American Psychologist, 32*, 513–531.

Bronstein, P. (1988). Father-child interaction: Implications for gender-role socialization. In P. Bronstein & C. P. Cowan (Eds.), *Fatherhood today: Men's changing role in the family* (pp. 107–124). Oxford, England: Wiley.

Brooks-Gunn, J., & Ruble, D. N. (1982). The development of menstrual-related beliefs and behaviors during early adolescence. *Child Development, 53*, 1567–1577.

Brooks-Gunn, J., & Warren, M. P. (1985). The effects of delayed menarche in different contexts: Dance and nondance students. *Journal of Youth and Adolescence, 14*, 285–300.

Brooks-Gunn, J., & Warren, M. P. (1988). The psychological significance of secondary sexual characteristics in nine- to eleven-year-old girls. *Child Development, 59*, 1061–1069.

Brooks-Gunn, J., Newman, D. L., Holderness, C. C., & Warren, M. P. (1994). The experience of breast development and girls' stories about the purchase of a bra. *Journal of Youth and Adolescence, 23*, 539–565.

Broom, A., & Kirby, E. (2013). The end of life and the family: Hospice patients' views on dying as relational. *Sociology of Health & Illness, 35*(4), 499–513.

Brotman, L. M., O'Neal, C. R., Huang, K., Gouley, K. K., Rosenfelt, A., & Shrout, P. E. (2009). An experimental test of parenting practices as a mediator of early childhood physical aggression. *Journal of Child Psychology and Psychiatry, 50*(3), 235–245.

Bryan, D. M. (2013). To parent or provide? The effect of the provider role on low-income men's decisions about fatherhood and paternal engagement. *Fathering, 11*(1), 71–89.

Buck, K. A., & Dix, T. (2012). Can developmental changes in inhibition and peer relationships explain why depressive symptoms increase in early adolescence? *Journal of Youth and Adolescence, 41*, 403–413.

Bugental, D. B., Ellerson, P. C., Lin, E. K., Rainey, B., Kokotovic, A., & O'Hara, N. (2010). A cognitive approach to child abuse prevention. *Psychology of Violence, 1*(S), 84–106.

Buhl, H. M., & Lanz, M. (2007). Emerging adulthood in Europe: Common traits and variability across five European countries. *Journal of Adolescent Research, 22*(5), 439–443.

Bukowski, W. M. (2001). Friendship and the worlds of childhood. In D. W. Nangle & C. A. Erdley (Eds.), *New directions for child and adolescent development: No. 91. The role of friendship in psychological adjustment* (pp. 93–105). San Francisco: Jossey-Bass.

Burchinal, M., Skinner, D., & Reznick, J. S. (2010). European American and African American mothers' beliefs about parenting and disciplining infants: A mixed-method analysis. *Parenting: Science and Practice, 10*, 79–96.

Bureau, J.-F., Martin, J., Freynet, N., Poirier, A. A., Lafontaine, M.-F., & Cloutier, P. (2010). Perceived dimensions of parenting and non-suicidal self-injury in young adults. *Journal of Youth and Adolescence, 39*, 484–494.

Burkard, C., Rochat, L., Blum, A., Emmenegger, J., Van der Linden, A. J., & Van der Linden, M. (2014). A daily-life-oriented intervention to improve prospective memory and goal-directed behaviour in ageing: A pilot study. *Neuropsychological Rehabilitation, 24*(2), 266–295.

Burnett, S., Thompson, S., Bird, G., & Blakemore, S. (2011). Pubertal development of the understanding of social emotions: Implications for education.

Learning and Individual Differences, 21(6), 681–689.

Burr, A., Santo, J. B., & Pushkar, D. (2011). Affective well-being in retirement: The influence of values, money, and mental health across three years. *Journal of Happiness Studies, 12,* 17–40.

Bushnell, I. W. R. (1998). The origins of face perception. In F. Simion & G. Butterworth (Eds.), *The development of sensory, motor and cognitive capacities in early infancy: From perception to cognition* (pp. 69–86). Hove, England: Psychology Press.

Bute, J. J. (2013). The discursive dynamics of disclosure and avoidance: Evidence from a study of infertility. *Western Journal of Communication, 77*(2), 164–185.

Butkovic, A., Brkovic, I., & Bratko, D. (2011). Predicting well-being from personality in adolescents and older adults. *Journal of Happiness Studies, 21,* 1–13.

Buttelmann, D., Call, J., & Tomasello, M. (2009). Do great apes use emotional expressions to infer desires? *Developmental Science, 12*(5), 688–698.

Buttenheim, A. M., & Asch, D. A. (2013). Behavioral economics: The key to closing the gap on maternal, newborn and child survival for Millennium Development Goals 4 and 5? *Maternal and Child Health Journal, 17*(4), 581–585.

Cacioppo, J. T., Cacioppo, S., Gonzaga, G. C., Ogburn, E. L., & VanderWeele, T. J. (2013). Marital satisfaction and break-ups differ across on-line and off-line meeting venues. *PNAS Proceedings of the National Academy of Sciences of the United States of America, 110*(25), 10135–10140.

Callahan, D. (1988). *Setting limits: Medical goals in an aging society.* New York, NY: Simon & Schuster.

Calvo, E., Sarkisian, N., & Tamborini, C. R. (2013). Causal effects of retirement timing on subjective physical and emotional health. *Journals of Gerontology Series B: Psychological Sciences and Social Sciences, 68B*(1), 73–84.

Campos, J. J., Anderson, D. I., Barbu-Roth, M. A., Hubbard, E. M., Hertenstein, M. J., & Witherington, D. (2000). Travel broadens the mind. *Infancy, 1,* 149–219.

Canter, A. S. (1997). The future of intelligence testing in the schools. *School Psychology Review, 26,* 255–261.

Caplan, A. L., Blank, R. H., & Merrick, J. C. (Eds.). (1992). *Compelled compassion: Government intervention in the treatment of critically ill newborns.* Totowa, NJ: Humana Press.

Cappelli, P., & Keller, J. R. (2013). Classifying work in the new economy. *The Academy of Management Review, 38*(4), 575–596.

Carlander, I., Ternestedt, B.-M., Sahlberg-Blom, E., Hellström, I., & Sandberg, J. (2011). Being me and being us in a family living close to death at home. *Qualitative Health Research, 21*(5), 683–695.

Carlson, A. G., Rowe, E., & Curby, T. W. (2013). Disentangling fine motor skills' relations to academic achievement: The relative contributions of visual-spatial integration and visual-motor coordination. *The Journal of Genetic Psychology: Research and Theory on Human Development, 174*(5), 514–533.

Carlson, E., Rämgård, M., Bolmsjö, I., & Bengtsson, M. (2014). Registered nurses' perceptions of their professional work in nursing homes and home-based care: A focus group study. *International Journal of Nursing Studies, 51*(5), 761–767.

Carlsund, Å., Eriksson, U., Löfstedt, P., & Sellström, E. (2013). Risk behaviour in Swedish adolescents: Is shared physical custody after divorce a risk or a protective factor? *European Journal of Public Health, 23*(1), 3–8.

Carnes, B., Olshansky, S., & Hayflick, L. (2013). Can human biology allow most of us to become centenarians? *Journals of Gerontology Series A: Biological Sciences and Medical Sciences, 68*(2), 136–142.

Carnevale, A., & Strohl, J. (2010). How increasing college access is increasing inequality and what to do about it. In R. D. Kahlenberg (Ed.), *Rewarding strivers: Helping low-income students succeed in college.* New York, NY: The Century Foundation Press.

Caron, S. L., & Moskey, E. G. (2002). Changes over time in teenage sexual relationships: Comparing the high school class of 1950, 1975, and 2000. *Adolescence, 37,* 515–526.

Carr, D. (2004). Gender, preloss marital dependence, and older adults' adjustment to widowhood. *Journal of Marriage and Family, 66,* 220–235.

Carr, D., & Boerner, K. (2013). Dating after late-life spousal loss: Does it compromise relationships with adult children? *Journal of Aging Studies, 27*(4), 487–498.

Carroll, J. S., Willoughby, B., Badger, S., Nelson, L. J., Barry, C. M., & Madsen, S. D. (2007). So close, yet so far away: The impact of varying marital horizons on emerging adulthood. *Journal of Adolescent Research, 22*(3), 219–247.

Carstensen, L. L. (1995). Evidence for a life-span theory of socioemotional selectivity. *Current Directions in Psychological Science, 4,* 151–156.

Carstensen, L. L., Graff, J., Levenson, R. W., & Gottman, J. M. (1996). Affect in intimate relationships: The developmental course of marriage. In C. Magai & S. H. McFadden (Eds.), *Handbook of emotion, adult development, and aging* (pp. 227–247). San Diego, CA: Academic Press.

Carter, R., Silverman, W. K., & Jaccard, J. (2013). Race and perceived pubertal transition effects on girls' depressive symptoms and delinquent behaviors. *Journal of Youth and Adolescence, 42*(8), 1155–1168.

Case, R. (1999). Conceptual development. In M. Bennett (Ed.), *Developmental psychology: Achievements and prospects* (pp. 36–54). New York, NY: Psychology Press.

Casey, B. J., & Caudle, K. (2013). The teenage brain: Self control. *Current Directions in Psychological Science, 22*(2), 82–87.

Cashmore, J., & Parkinson, P. (2008). Children's and parents' perceptions on children's participation in decision making after parental separation and divorce. *Family Court Review, 46*(1), 91–104.

Cassel, J. B., Hager, M. A., Clark, R. R., Retchin, S. M., Dimartino, J., Coyne, P. J., . . . Smith, T. J. (2010). Concentrating hospital-wide deaths in a palliative care unit: The effect of place on death and system-wide mortality. *Journal of Palliative Medicine, 13*(4), 371–374.

Castel, A. D., Lee, S. S., Humphreys, K. L., & Moore, A. N. (2010). Memory capacity, selective control, and value-directed remembering in children with and without attention-deficit/hyperactivity disorder (ADHD). *Neuropsychology, 25*(1), 15–24.

Castellanos-Ryan, N., Parent, S., Vitaro, F., Tremblay, R. E., & Séguin, J. R. (2013). Pubertal development, personality, and substance use: A 10-year longitudinal study from childhood to adolescence. *Journal of Abnormal Psychology, 122*(3), 782–796.

Cattell, M. G. (2003). African widows: Anthropological and historical perspectives. *Journal of Women & Aging, 15,* 49–66.

Caulfield, L., Richard, S. A., Rivera, J. A., Musgrove, P., & Black, R. E. (2006).

Disease control priorities in developing countries (2nd ed.). New York, NY: Oxford University Press.

Cecchini, M., Baroni, E., Di Vito, C., Piccolo, F., Aceto, P., & Lai, C. (2013). Effects of different types of contingent tactile stimulation on crying, smiling, and sleep in newborns: An observational study. *Developmental Psychobiology, 55*(5), 508–517.

Ceci, S. J., Rosenblum, T., de Bruyn, E., & Lee, D. Y. (1997). A bio-ecological model of intellectual development: Moving beyond h-sup-2. In R. J. Sternberg & E. L. Grigorenko (Eds.), *Intelligence, heredity, and environment* (pp. 303–322). New York, NY: Cambridge University Press.

Cellarius, V. (2011). 'Early terminal sedation' is a distinct entity. *Bioethics, 25*(1), 46–54.

Centers for Disease Control and Prevention. (2007). *Infant mortality statistics from the 2004 period: Linked birth/infant death data.* Retrieved from http://www.cdc.gov/nchs/data/nvsr/nvsr55/nvsr55_14.pdf

Centers for Disease Control and Prevention. (2009). *Health data interactive.* Retrieved from http://www.cdc.gov/nchs/hdi.htm

Centers for Disease Control and Prevention. (2010a). *What is assisted reproductive technology?* Retrieved from http://www.cdc.gov/art/

Centers for Disease Control and Prevention. (2010b). Increasing prevalence of parent-reported attention-deficit/hyperactivity disorder among children: United States, 2003–2007. *Morbidity and Mortality Weekly Report (MMWR), 59*(44). Retrieved from http://www.ncbi.nlm.nih.gov/pubmed/21063274

Centers for Disease Control and Prevention. (2011). *Prevalence of childhood obesity in the United States 2011–2012.* Retrieved from http://www.cdc.gov/HealthyYouth/obesity/facts.htm

Centers for Disease Control and Prevention. (n.d.). *Attention deficit hyperactivity disorder.* In *CDC FastStats.* Retrieved from http://www.cdc.gov/nchs/fastats/adhd.htm

Centers for Disease Control and Prevention. (n.d.). *Childhood obesity facts.* Retrieved from http://www.cdc.gov/HealthyYouth/obesity/facts.htm

Central Intelligence Agency. (2007). *The world factbook 2007.* Washington, DC: U.S. Government Printing Office.

Central Intelligence Agency. (2008). *The world factbook 2008.* Washington, DC: U.S. Government Printing Office.

Central Intelligence Agency. (n.d.). *World Factbook.* Retrieved from https://www.cia.gov/library/publications/the-world-factbook/

Chadwick, R., & Foster, D. (2013). Technologies of gender and childbirth choices: Home birth, elective caesarean and White femininities in South Africa. *Feminism & Psychology, 23*(3), 317–338.

Chambaere, K., Bilsen, J., Cohen, J., Onwuteaka-Philipsen, B. D., Mortier, F., & Deliens, L. (2011). Trends in medical end-of-life decision making in Flanders, Belgium 1998–2001–2007. *Medical Decision Making, 31*(3), 500–510.

Chang, H. H., Larson, J., Blencowe, H., Spong, C. Y., Howson, C. P., Cairns-Smith, S., . . . Lawn, J. E. (2013). Preventing preterm births: Analysis of trends and potential reductions with interventions in 39 countries with very high human development index. *The Lancet, 381*(9862), 223–234.

Chang, Y., Tsai, C., Huang, C., Wang, C., & Chu, I. (2014). Effects of acute resistance exercise on cognition in late middle-aged adults: General or specific cognitive improvement? *Journal of Science and Medicine in Sport, 17*(1), 51–55.

Chapple, H. S. (1999). Changing the game in the intensive care unit: Letting nature take its course. *Critical Care Nurse, 19*, 25–34.

Charles, M. (1992). Cross-national variation in occupational sex segregation. *American Sociological Review, 57*, 483–502.

Charles, S. T., & Almeida, D. M. (2007). Genetic and environmental effects on daily life stressors: More evidence for greater variation in later life. *Psychology and Aging, 22*(2), 331–340.

Charles, S. T., Luong, G., Almeida, D. M., Ryff, C., Sturm, M., & Love, G. (2010). Fewer ups and downs: Daily stressors mediate age differences in negative affect. *Journals of Gerontology: Psychological Sciences, 65B*(3), 279–286.

Charlton, J. L., Catchlove, M., Scully, M., Koppel, S., & Newstead, S. (2013). Older driver distraction: A naturalistic study of behaviour at intersections. *Accident Analysis and Prevention, 58*, 271–278.

Chen, E. S. L., & Rao, N. (2011). Gender socialization in Chinese kindergartens: Teachers' contributions. *Sex Roles, 64*, 103–116.

Chen, W., Glasser, S., Benbenishty, R., Davidson-Arad, B., Tzur, S., & Lerner-Geva, L. (2010). The contribution of a hospital child protection team in determining suspected child abuse and neglect: Analysis of referrals of children aged 0–9. *Children and Youth Services Review, 32*(12), 1664–1669.

Chen, X., & French, D. C. (2008). Children's social competence in cultural context. *Annual Review of Psychology, 59*, 591–616.

Chen, Y., McAnally, H. M., & Reese, E. (2013). Development in the organization of episodic memories in middle childhood and adolescence. *Frontiers in Behavioral Neuroscience, 7*, 84.

Cherlin, A. J. (2004). The deinstitutionalization of American marriage. *Journal of Marriage and Family, 66*, 848–861.

Cherlin, A. J. (2010). Demographic trends in the United States: A review of research in the 2000s. *Journal of Marriage and Family, 72*(3), 403–419.

Chernyak, N., & Kushnir, T. (2013). Giving preschoolers choice increases sharing behavior. *Psychological Science, 24*(10), 1971–1979.

Chertkow, H., Whitehead, V., Phillips, N., Wolfson, C., Atherton, J., & Bergman, H. (2010). Multilingualism (but not always bilingualism) delays the onset of Alzheimer disease: Evidence from a bilingual community. *Alzheimer Disease and Associated Disorders, 24*(2), 118–125.

Child Soldiers Global Report. (2008). *Coalition to stop the use of child soldiers.* Retrieved from http://www.Childsoldiersglobal-report.org

Child Trends Data Bank. (2008). Retrieved from http://www.childtrends.org/databank/

Chisolm, M. S., Cheng, D., & Terplan, M. (2014). The relationship between pregnancy intention and change in perinatal cigarette smoking: An analysis of PRAMS data. *Journal of Substance Abuse Treatment, 46*(2), 189–193.

Cho, J., & Lee, A. (2014). Life satisfaction of the aged in the retirement process: A comparative study of South Korea with Germany and Switzerland. *Applied Research in Quality of Life, 9*(2), 179–195.

Cho, S., Zarit, S. H., & Chiriboga, D. A. (2009). Wives and daughters: The differential role of day care use in the nursing home placement of cognitively impaired family members. *The Gerontologist, 49*(1), 57–67.

Cho, Y., & Haslam, N. (2010). Suicidal ideation and distress among immigrant adolescents: The role of acculturation, life stress, and social support. *Journal of Youth and Adolescence, 39*(4), 370–379.

Choi, H., & Marks, N. F. (2013). Marital quality, socioeconomic status, and physical health. *Journal of Marriage and Family, 75*(4), 903–919.

Choi, K. H., & Vasunilashorn, S. (2014). Widowhood, age heterogamy, and health: The role of selection, marital quality, and health behaviors. *Journals of Gerontology Series B: Psychological Sciences and Social Sciences, 69B*(1), 123–134.

Choi, Y., Kim, Y. S., Kim, S. Y., & Park, I. K. (2013). Is Asian American parenting controlling and harsh? Empirical testing of relationships between Korean American and Western parenting measures. *Asian American Journal of Psychology, 4*(1), 19–29.

Christ, G. H. (2000). *Healing children's grief.* New York, NY: Oxford University Press.

Christensen, J., Grønborg, T. K., Sørensen, M. J., Schendel, D., Parner, E. T., Pedersen, L. H., & Vestergaard, M. (2013). Prenatal valproate exposure and risk of autism spectrum disorders and childhood autism. *Journal of the American Medical Association, 309*(16), 1696–1703.

Christensen, K. Y., Maisonet, M., Rubin, C., Holmes, A., Flanders, W. D., Heron, J., . . . Marcus, M. (2010). Progression through puberty in girls enrolled in a contemporary British cohort. *Journal of Adolescent Health, 47*(3), 282–289.

Christian Elledge, L., Williford, A., Boulton, A. J., DePaolis, K. J., Little, T. D., & Salmivalli, C. (2013). Individual and contextual predictors of cyberbullying: The influence of children's provictim attitudes and teachers' ability to intervene. *Journal of Youth and Adolescence, 42*(5), 698–710.

Christopher, C., Saunders, R., Jacobvitz, D., Burton, R., & Hazen, N. (2013). Maternal empathy and changes in mothers' permissiveness as predictors of toddlers' early social competence with peers: A parenting intervention study. *Journal of Child and Family Studies, 22*(6), 769–778.

Chua, A. (2011). *Battle hymn of the tiger mother.* New York, NY: Penguin Press.

Chung, J. M., Robins, R. W., Trzesniewski, K. H., Noftle, E. E., Roberts, B. W., &

Widaman, K. F. (2014). Continuity and change in self-esteem during emerging adulthood. *Journal of Personality and Social Psychology, 106*(3), 469–483.

Chung-Hall, J., & Chen, X. (2010). Aggressive and prosocial peer group functioning: Effects on children's social, school, and psychological adjustment. *Social Development, 19*, 659–680.

Cicirelli, V. G. (2007). End of life decisions: Research findings and implications. In A. Tomer, P. T. Wong, & G. Eliason (Eds.), *Existential and spiritual issues in death attitudes* (pp. 115–138). Hillsdale, NJ: Erlbaum.

Cimarolli, V. R., Boerner, K., Reinhardt, J. P., & Horowitz, A. (2013). Perceived overprotection, instrumental support and rehabilitation use in elders with vision loss: A longitudinal perspective. *Psychology & Health, 28*(4), 369–383.

Clark, D. (2007). End-of-life care around the world: Achievements to date and challenges remaining. *Omega, 56*(1), 101–110.

Clarke, D. D., Ward, P., Bartle, C., & Truman, W. (2010). Older drivers' road traffic crashes in the UK. *Accident Analysis and Prevention, 42*, 1018–1024.

Class, Q. A., Khashan, A. S., Lichtenstein, P., Långström, N., & D'Onofrio, B. M. (2013). Maternal stress and infant mortality: The importance of the preconception period. *Psychological Science, 24*(7), 1309–1316.

Claxton, S. E., & van Dulmen, M. M. (2013). Casual sexual relationships and experiences in emerging adulthood. *Emerging Adulthood, 1*(2), 138–150.

Clearfield, M. W., & Jedd, K. E. (2013). The effects of socio-economic status on infant attention. *Infant and Child Development, 22*(1), 53–67.

Clerkin, S. M., Schulz, K. P., Berwid, O. G., Fan, J., Newcorn, J. H., Tang, C. Y., & Halperin, J. M. (2013). Thalamo-cortical activation and connectivity during response preparation in adults with persistent and remitted ADHD. *The American Journal of Psychiatry, 170*(9), 1011–1019.

Climo, J. J., Terry, P., & Lay, K. (2002). Using the double bind to interpret the experience of custodial grandparents. *Journal of Aging Studies, 16*, 19–35.

Clinard, C. G., & Tremblay, K. L. (2013). Aging degrades the neural encoding of simple and complex sounds in the human brainstem. *Journal of the American Academy of Audiology, 24*(7), 590–599

Coall, D. A., & Hertwig, R. (2010). Grandparental investment: Past, present, and future. *Behavioral and Brain Sciences, 33*, 1–59.

Coe, N. B., & Boyle, M. A. (2013). The asset and income profiles of residents in seniors housing and care communities: What can be learned from existing data sets. *Research on Aging, 35*(1), 50–77.

Cohen, J., Van Landeghem, P., Carpentier, N., & Deliens, L. (2013). Different trends in euthanasia acceptance across Europe. A study of 13 western and 10 central and eastern European countries, 1981–2008. *European Journal of Public Health, 23*(3), 378–380.

Cohen, O., Leichtentritt, R. D., & Volpin, N. (2014). Divorced mothers' self-perception of their divorce-related communication with their children. *Child & Family Social Work, 19*(1), 34–43.

Cohen, P. N. (2004). The gender division of labor: "Keeping house" and occupational segregation in the United States. *Gender & Society, 18*, 239–252.

Cohen, P., Kasen, S., Chen, H., Hartmark, C., & Gordon, K. (2003). Variations in patterns of developmental transmissions in the emerging adulthood period. *Developmental Psychology, 39*, 657–669.

Coie, J. D., & Dodge, K. A. (1998). Aggression and antisocial behavior. In W. Damon (Series ed.) & N. Eisenberg (Vol. Ed.), *Handbook of child psychology: Vol 3. Social, emotional, and personality development* (5th ed. pp. 779–862). Hoboken, NJ: Wiley.

Cole, B., & Singg, S. (1998). *Relationship between parental bereavement reaction factors and selected psychosocial variables.* Paper presented at the Annual Meeting of the American Psychological Society, Washington, DC.

Cole-Lewis, H. J., Kershaw, T. S., Earnshaw, V. A., Yonkers, K. A., Lin, H., & Ickovics, J. R. (2014). Pregnancy-specific stress, preterm birth, and gestational age among high-risk young women. *Health Psychology, 33*(9), 1033–1045.

Coleman-Jenson, A., Nord, M., and Singh, A. (2013). *Household food security in the United States in 2012.* U.S. Department of Agriculture, Economic Research Report No. (ERR-155).

Coley, R. L., Votruba-Drzal, E., Miller, P. L., & Koury, A. (2013). Timing, extent, and type of child care and children's behavioral functioning in kindergarten. *Developmental Psychology, 49*(10), 1859–1873.

Collignon, O., Vandewalle, G., Voss, P., Albouy, G., Charbonneau, G.,

Lassonde, M., & Lepore, F. (2011). Functional specialization for auditory-spatial processing in the occipital cortex of congenitally blind humans. *Proceedings of the National Academy of Sciences of the United States of America, 108*(11), 4435–4440.

Collins, R. L. (2011). Content analysis of gender roles in media: Where are we now and where should we go? *Sex Roles, 64,* 290–298.

Collins, R. L., Elliott, M. N., Berry, S. H., Kanouse, D. E., Kunkel, D., Hunter, S. B., & Miu, A. (2004). Watching sex on television predicts adolescent initiation of sexual behavior. *Pediatrics, 114,* e280–289.

Collinson, C. (2014, September-October). Baby boomers will trailblaze new retirement models (they have to). *Aging Today, 35*(5), 1, 7.

Colrain, I. M., & Baker, F. C. (2011). Changes in sleep as a function of adolescent development. *Neuropsychology Review, 21,* 5–21.

Compian, L., Gowen, L. K., & Hayward, C. (2004). Peripubertal girls' romantic and platonic involvement with boys: Associations with body image and depression symptoms. *Journal of Research on Adolescence, 14,* 23–47.

Conner, T., Prokhorov, A., Page, C., Fang, Y., Xiao, Y., & Post, L. A. (2011). Impairment and abuse of elderly by staff in long-term care in Michigan: Evidence from structural equation modeling. *Journal of Interpersonal Violence, 26*(1), 21–33.

Cook, C. R., Williams, K. R., Guerra, N. G., Kim, T. E., & Sadek, S. (2010). Predictors of bullying and victimization in childhood and adolescence: A meta-analytic investigation. *School Psychology Quarterly, 25*(2), 65–83.

Cook, T. D., & Furstenberg, F. F. (2002). Explaining aspects of the transition to adulthood in Italy, Sweden, Germany, and the United States: A cross-disciplinary, case synthesis approach. *Annals of the American Academy of Political and Social Science, 580,* 257–287.

Cook, T. D., Deng, Y., & Morgano, E. (2007). Friendship influences during early adolescence: The special role of friends' grade point average. *Journal of Research on Adolescence, 17*(2), 325–356.

Cooney, T. M., Schaie, K. W., & Willis, S. L. (1988). The relationship between prior functioning on cognitive and personality dimensions and subject attrition in longitudinal research. *Journals of Gerontology, 43,* 12–17.

Coontz, S. (1992). *The way we never were: American families and the nostalgia trap.* New York, NY: Basic Books.

Cornwell, T., & McAlister, A. R. (2011). Alternative thinking about starting points of obesity. Development of child taste preferences. *Appetite 56*(2), 428–439.

Corr, C. A. (1991–1992). A task-based approach to coping with dying. *Omega, 24,* 81–94.

Corr, C. A. (2007). Hospice: Achievements, legacies, and challenges. *Omega, 56*(1), 111–120.

Corsaro, W. A. (1985). *Friendship and peer culture in the early years.* Norwood, NJ: Ablex.

Corsaro, W. A. (1997). *The sociology of childhood.* Thousand Oaks, CA: Pine Forge Press/Sage.

Costos, D., Ackerman, R., & Paradis, L. (2002). Recollections of menarche: Communication between mothers and daughters regarding menstruation. *Sex Roles, 46,* 49–59.

Côté, J. E., & Levine, C. G. (2002). *Identity formation, agency, and culture: A social psychological synthesis.* Mahwah, NJ: Erlbaum.

Côté, J., & Bynner, J. M. (2008). Changes in the transition to adulthood in the UK and Canada: The role of structure and agency in emerging adulthood. *Journal of Youth Studies, 11,* 251–268.

Cotterell, J. (1996). *Social networks and social influences in adolescence.* New York, NY: Routledge.

Cowan, C. P., & Cowan, P. A. (1992). *When partners become parents: The big life change for couples.* New York, NY: Basic Books.

Cowan, P. A., Cowan, C. P., & Mehta, N. (2009). Adult attachment, couple attachment, and children's adaptation to school: An integrated attachment template and family risk model. *Attachment & Human Development, 11*(1), 29–46.

Cox, K. S., Wilt, J., Olson, B., & McAdams, D. P. (2010). Generativity, the big five, and psychosocial adaptation in midlife adults. *Journal of Personality, 78*(4), 1185–1208.

Cozzarelli, C., Karafa, J. A., Collins, N. L., & Tagler, M. J. (2003). Stability and change in adult attachment styles: Associations with personal vulnerabilities, life events, and global construals of self and others. *Journal of Social & Clinical Psychology, 22,* 315–346.

Crade, M., & Lovett, S. (1988). Fetal response to sound stimulation: Preliminary report exploring use of sound stimulation in routine obstetrical ultrasound examinations. *Journal of Ultrasound in Medicine, 7,* 499–503.

Craig, L., & Mullan, K. (2010). Parenthood, gender and work-family time in the United States, Australia, Italy, France, and Denmark. *Journal of Marriage and Family, 72*(5), 1344–1361.

Craik, F. I. M. (2000). Age-related changes in human memory. In D. C. Park & N. Schwarz (Eds.), *Cognitive aging: A primer* (pp. 75–92). New York, NY: Psychology Press.

Craik, F. I. M., Luo, L., & Sakuta, Y. (2010). Effects of aging and divided attention on memory for items and their contexts. *Psychology and Aging, 25*(4), 968–979.

Cramer, P. (2008). Identification and the development of competence: A 44-year longitudinal study from late adolescence to late middle age. *Psychology and Aging, 23,* 410–421.

Crawford, A. M., & Manassis, K. (2011) Anxiety, social skills, friendship quality, and peer victimization: An integrated model. *Journal of Anxiety Disorders, 25*(7), 924–937.

Crick, N. R., & Dodge, K. A. (1996). Social information-processing mechanisms on reactive and proactive aggression. *Child Development, 67,* 993–1002.

Crisp, D. A., Windsor, T. D., Butterworth, P., & Anstey, K. J. (2013). What are older adults seeking? Factors encouraging or discouraging retirement village living. *Australasian Journal on Ageing, 32*(3), 163–170.

Crittenden, A. (2001). *The price of motherhood: Why the most important job in the world is still the least valued.* New York, NY: Metropolitan Books.

Crosnoe, R., Wirth, R. J., Pianta, R. C., Leventhal, T., & Pierce, K. M. (2010). Family socioeconomic status and consistent environmental stimulation in early childhood. *Child Development, 81*(3), 972–987.

Crouch, J. L., Milner, J. S., Skowronski, J. J., Farc, M. M., Irwin, L. M., & Neese, A. (2010). Automatic encoding of ambiguous child behavior in high and low risk for child physical abuse parents. *Journal of Family Violence, 25,* 73–80.

Crowe, M., Clay, O., Martin, R., Howard, V., Wadley, V., Sawyer, P., & Allman, R. (2013). Indicators of childhood quality of education in relation to cognitive function in older adulthood. *Journals of*

Gerontology Series A: Biological Sciences and Medical Sciences, 68(2), 198–204.

Crum, M. (2014, September-October). On frailty and facing death. *Aging Today, 35*(5), 6.

Crumley, J. J., Stetler, C. A., & Horhota, M. (2014). Examining the relationship between subjective and objective memory performance in older adults: A meta-analysis. *Psychology and Aging, 29*(2), 250–263.

Csikszentmihalyi, M. (1990). *Flow: The psychology of optimal experience.* New York, NY: Harper & Row.

Csikszentmihalyi, M. (1996). *Creativity: Flow and the psychology of discovery and invention.* New York, NY: HarperCollins.

Csikszentmihalyi, M., & Larson, R. (1984). *Being adolescent: Conflict and growth in the teenage years.* New York, NY: Basic Books.

Csikszentmihalyi, M., & Schneider, B. L. (2000). *Becoming adult: How teenagers prepare for the world of work.* New York, NY: Basic Books.

Csiszar, A., Sosnowska, D., Tucsek, Z., Gautam, T., Toth, P., Losonczy, G., . . . Ungvari, Z. (2013). Circulating factors induced by caloric restriction in the nonhuman primate *macaca mulatta* activate angiogenic processes in endothelial cells. *Journals of Gerontology Series A: Biological Sciences and Medical Sciences, 68*(3), 235–249.

Culbert, K. M., Breedlove, S. M., Sisk, C. L., Burt, S. A., & Klump, K. L. (2013). The emergence of sex differences in risk for disordered eating attitudes during puberty: A role for prenatal testosterone exposure. *Journal of Abnormal Psychology, 122*(2), 420–432.

Cushen, P. J., & Wiley, J. (2011). Aha! Voila! Eureka! Bilingualism and insightful problem solving. *Learning and Individual Differences, 21*(4), 458–462.

CysticFibrosis.com. (n.d.). Retrieved from http://www.cysticfibrosis.com/home/

Daddis, C. (2011). Desire for increased autonomy and adolescents' perceptions of peer autonomy: "Everyone else can; why can't I?" *Child Development, 82*(4), 1310–1326.

Dahl, R. E. (2004). Adolescent brain development: A period of vulnerabilities and opportunities. In R. E. Dahl & L. P. Spear (Eds.), *Adolescent brain development: Vulnerabilities and opportunities, Volume 1021* (pp. 1–22). New York, NY: Academy of Sciences.

Damaraju, E., Caprihan, A., Lowe, J. R., Allen, E. A., Calhoun, V. D., & Phillips, J. P. (2014). Functional connectivity in the developing brain: A longitudinal study from 4 to 9 months of age. *NeuroImage, 84*, 169–180.

Danckert, S. L., & Craik, F. M. (2013). Does aging affect recall more than recognition memory? *Psychology and Aging, 28*(4), 902–909.

Daniels, K. J., Lamson, A. L., & Hodgson, J. (2007). An exploration of the marital relationship and Alzheimer's disease: One couple's story. *Families, Systems, & Health, 25*(2), 162–177.

Danziger, S., & Ratner, D. (2010). Labor market outcomes and the transition to adulthood. *The Future of Children, 20*, 1–24. Retrieved from http://www.futureofchildren.org/publications/journals/article/index.xml?journalid=72&articleid=524

Darwiche, J., Favez, N., Maillard, F., Germond, M., Guex, P., Despland, J., & de Roten, Y. (2013). Couples' resolution of an infertility diagnosis before undergoing in vitro fertilization. *Swiss Journal of Psychology, 72*(2), 91–102.

Dasen, P. R. (1977). *Piagetian psychology: Cross-cultural contributions.* New York, NY: Gardner Press.

Dasen, P. R. (1984). The cross-cultural study of intelligence: Piaget and the Baoule. *International Journal of Psychology, 19*, 407–434.

Davies, A. R., & Frink, B. D. (2014). The origins of the ideal worker: The separation of work and home in the United States from the market revolution to 1950. *Work and Occupations, 41*(1), 18–39.

Davila, J., & Kashy, D. A. (2009). Secure base processes in couples: Daily associations between support experiences and attachment security. *Journal of Family Psychology, 23*, 76–88.

Davis, A. M., Bennett, K. J., Befort, C., Nollen, N. (2011). Obesity and related health behaviors among urban and rural children in the United States: Data from the National Health and Nutrition Examination Survey 2003–2004 and 2005–2006. *Journal of Pediatric Psychology, 36*(6), 669–676.

Dawes, M., & Xie, H. (2014). The role of popularity goal in early adolescents' behaviors and popularity status. *Developmental Psychology, 50*(2), 489–497.

Dawson, J. D., Uc, E. Y., Anderson, S. W., Johnson, A. M., & Rizzo, M. (2010). Neuropsychology predictors of driving errors in older adults. *Journal of*

the American Geriatrics Society, 58(6), 1090–1096.

De Goede, I. H. D., Branje, S. J. T., & Meeus, W. H. J. (2009). Developmental changes in adolescents' perceptions of relationships with their parents. *Journal of Youth and Adolescence, 38*, 75–88.

de Mello, C. B., Rossi, A. U., Cardoso, T. G., Rivero, T. S., de Moura, L. M., Nogueira, R. G., . . . Muszkat, M. (2013). Neuroimaging and neuropsychological analyses in a sample of children with ADHD inattentive subtype. *Clinical Neuropsychiatry: Journal of Treatment Evaluation, 10*(2), 45–54.

De Preter, H., Van Looy, D., & Mortelmans, D. (2013). Individual and institutional push and pull factors as predictors of retirement timing in Europe: A multilevel analysis. *Journal of Aging Studies, 27*(4), 299–307.

De Raedt, R., Koster, E. W., & Ryckewaert, R. (2013). Aging and attentional bias for death related and general threat-related information: Less avoidance in older as compared with middle-aged adults. *Journals of Gerontology Series B: Psychological Sciences and Social Sciences, 68B*(1), 41–48.

De Ridder, S., & Van Bauwel, S. (2013). Commenting on pictures: Teens negotiating gender and sexualities on social networking sites. *Sexualities, 16*(5-6), 565–586.

De Schipper, E. J., Riksen-Walraven, J. M., & Geurts, S. A. E. (2006). Effects of child-caregiver ratio on the interactions between caregivers and children in child-care centers: An experimental study. *Child Development, 77*(4), 861–874.

De Schipper, J. C., Tavecchio, L. W. C., & van IJzendoorn, M. H. (2008). Children's attachment relationships with day care caregivers: Associations with positive caregiving and the child's temperament. *Social Development, 17*(3), 454–470.

De Wilde, K. S., Trommelmans, L. C., Laevens, H. H., Maes, L. R., Temmerman, M., & Boudrez, H. L. (2013). Smoking patterns, depression, and sociodemographic variables among Flemish women during pregnancy and the postpartum period. *Nursing Research, 62*(6), 394–404.

Dean, D. C., O'Muircheartaigh, J., Dirks, H., Waskiewicz, N., Walker, L., Doernberg, E., . . . Deoni, S. L. (2014). Characterizing longitudinal white matter development during early childhood. *Brain Structure & Function, 220*(4), 1921–1933.

Dean, R. S., & Davis, A. S. (2007). Relative risk of perinatal complications in common childhood disorders. *School Psychology Quarterly*, 22(1), 13–23.

Deardorff, J., Cham, H., Gonzales, N. A., White, R. B., Tein, J., Wong, J. J., & Roosa, M. W. (2013). Pubertal timing and Mexican-origin girls' internalizing and externalizing symptoms: The influence of harsh parenting. *Developmental Psychology*, 49(9), 1790–1804.

Deary, I. J., Whalley, L. J., Lemmon, H., Crawford, J. R., & Starr, J. M. (2000). The stability of individual differences in mental ability from childhood to old age: Follow-up of the 1932 Scottish Mental Survey. *Intelligence*, 28, 49–55.

Deater-Deckard, K., Beekman, C., Wang, Z., Kim, J., Petrill, S., Thompson, L., & DeThorne, L. (2010). Approach/positive anticipation, frustration/anger, and overt aggression in childhood. *Journal of Personality*, 78(3), 991–1010.

Deater-Deckard, K., Ivy, L., & Smith, J. (2005). Resilience in gene-environment transactions. In S. Goldstein, & R. B. Brooks (Eds.), *Handbook of resilience in children* (pp. 49–63). New York, NY: Kluwer Academic/Plenum.

DeCasper, A. J., & Fifer, W. P. (1980, June 6). Of human bonding: Newborns prefer their mothers' voices. *Science*, 208, 1174–1176.

Deci, E. L., & Ryan, R. M. (1985). The general causality orientations scale: Self-determination in personality. *Journal of Research in Personality*, 19, 109–134.

Deci, E. L., & Ryan, R. M. (2000). The "what" and "why" of goal pursuits: Human needs and the self-determination of behavior. *Psychological Inquiry*, 11, 227–268.

DeFillippi, R. J., & Arthur, M. B. (1994). The boundary-less career: A competency-based perspective. *Journal of Organizational Behavior*, 15, 307–324.

DeGarmo, D. S. (2010). Coercive and prosocial fathering, antisocial personality, and growth in children's postdivorce noncompliance. *Child Development*, 81(2), 503–516.

Degnan, K. A., Almas, A. N., & Fox, N. A. (2010). Temperament and the environment in the etiology of childhood anxiety. *Journal of Child Psychology and Psychiatry*, 51(4), 497–517.

Del Giudice, M. (2011). Alone in the dark? Modeling the conditions for visual experience in human fetuses. *Developmental Psychobiology*, 53(2), 214–219.

Delevi, R., & Weisskirch, R. S. (2013). Personality factors as predictors of sexting. *Computers in Human Behavior*, 29(6), 2589–2594.

Deligiannidis, K. M., Byatt, N., & Freeman, M. P. (2014). Pharmacotherapy for mood disorders in pregnancy: A review of pharmacokinetic changes and clinical recommendations for therapeutic drug monitoring. *Journal of Clinical Psychopharmacology*, 34(2), 244–255.

Dempster, F. N. (1981). Memory span: Sources of individual and developmental differences. *Psychological Bulletin*, 89, 63–100.

Denham, S. A. (1998). *Emotional development in young children*. New York, NY: Guilford Press.

Denham, S. A., Blair, K. A., DeMulder, E., Levitas, J., Sawyer, K., Auerbach-Major, S., & Queenan, P. (2003). Preschool emotional competence: Pathway to social competence. *Child Development*, 74, 238–256.

Deniz Can, D., Richards, T., & Kuhl, P. K. (2013). Early gray-matter and white-matter concentration in infancy predict later language skills: A whole brain voxel-based morphometry study. *Brain and Language*, 124(1), 34–44.

Dennis, C., Gagnon, A., Van Hulst, A., Dougherty, G., & Wahoush, O. (2013). Prediction of duration of breastfeeding among migrant and Canadian-born women: Results from a multi-center study. *Journal of Pediatrics*, 162(1), 72–79.

Dennis, N. A., Hayes, S. M., Prince, S. E., Madden, D. J., Huettel, S. A., & Cabeza, R. (2008). Effects of aging on the neural correlates of successful item and source memory encoding. *Journal of Experimental Psychology: Learning, Memory, and Cognition*, 34(4), 791–808.

Dennissen, J. J. A., Asendorpf, J. B., & van Aken, M. A. G. (2008). Childhood personality predicts long-term trajectories of shyness and aggressiveness in the context of demographic transitions in emerging adulthood. *Journal of Personality*, 76(1), 67–99.

Deoni, S. L., Dean, D. I., Piryatinsky, I., O'Muircheartaigh, J., Waskiewicz, N., Lehman, K., . . . Dirks, H. (2013). Breastfeeding and early white matter development: A cross-sectional study. *NeuroImage*, 82, 77–86.

Devine, R. T., & Hughes, C. (2013). Silent films and strange stories: Theory of mind, gender, and social experiences in middle childhood. *Child Development*, 84(3), 989–1003.

Dew, J., & Wilcox, W. B. (2011). If momma ain't happy: Explaining declines in marital satisfaction among new mothers. *Journal of Marriage and Family*, 73, 1–12.

DeWall, C. N., Twenge, J. M., Gitter, S. A., & Baumeister R. F. (2009). It's the thought that counts: The role of hostile cognition in shaping aggressive responses to social exclusion. *Journal of Personality and Social Psychology*, 96, 45–59.

Diamanti, A., Basso, M. S., Castro, M., Bianco, G., Ciacco, E., Calce, A., . . . Gambarara, M. (2008). Clinical efficacy and safety of parental nutrition in adolescent girls with anorexia nervosa. *Journal of Adolescent Health*, 42, 111–118.

Diamond, A. (2009). The interplay of biology and the environment broadly defined. *Developmental Psychology*, 45, 1–8.

Diamond, A., Kirkham, N., & Amso, D. (2002). Conditions under which young children can hold two rules in mind and inhibit a prepotent response. *Developmental Psychology*, 38, 352–362.

Diamond, M. C. (1988). *Enriching heredity: The impact of the environment on the anatomy of the brain*. New York, NY: Free Press.

Diamond, M. C. (1993). An optimistic view of the aging brain. *Generations*, 17(1), 31–33.

Díaz-Morales, J. F., Escribano, C., Jankowski, K. S., Vollmer, C., & Randler, C. (2014). Evening adolescents: The role of family relationships and pubertal development. *Journal of Adolescence*, 37(4), 425–432.

Dickens, B. M., Boyle, J. M., & Ganzini, L. (2008). Euthanasia and assisted suicide. In P. A. Singer, & A. M. Viens (Eds.), *The Cambridge textbook of bioethics* (pp. 72–77). New York, NY: Cambridge University Press.

Diederich, A., Colonius, H., & Schomburg, A. (2008). Assessing age-related multisensory enhancement with the time-window-of-integration model. *Neuropsychologia*, 46, 2556–2562.

Dietz, P. M., Homa, D., England, L. J., Burley, K., Tong, V. T., Dube, S. R., & Bernert, J. T. (2011). Estimates of nondisclosure of cigarette smoking among pregnant and nonpregnant women of reproductive age in the United States. *American Journal of Epidemiology*, 173(3), 355–359.

Dilworth-Anderson, P., Boswell, G., & Cohen, M. D. (2007). Spiritual and religious coping values and beliefs among African American caregivers: A qualitative study. *Journal of Applied Gerontology, 26*(4), 355–369.

Dingemans, E., & Henkens, K. (2014). Involuntary retirement, bridge employment, and satisfaction with life: A longitudinal investigation. *Journal of Organizational Behavior, 35*(4), 575–591.

DiRenzo, M. S., Greenhaus, J. H., & Weer, C. H. (2011). Job level, demands, and resources as antecedents of work-family conflict. *Journal of Vocational Behavior, 79*, 305–314.

DiRosa, M., Kofahl, C., McKee, K., Bién, B., Lamura, G., Prouskas, C., . . . Mnich, E. (2011). A typology of caregiving situations and service use in family carers of older people in six European countries. *GeroPsych, 24*(1), 5–18.

Dishion, T. J., & Tipsord, J. M. (2011). Peer contagion in child and adolescent social and emotional development. *Annual Review of Psychology, 62*, 189–214.

Dishion, T. J., McCord, J., & Poulin, F. (1999). When interventions harm: Peer groups and problem behavior. *American Psychologist, 54*, 755–764.

Dixon, R. A., Rust, T. B., Feltmate, S. E., & See, S. K. (2007). Memory and aging: Selected research directions and application issues. *Canadian Psychology, 48*(2), 67–76.

Doane, L. D., & Thurston, E. C. (2014). Associations among sleep, daily experiences, and loneliness in adolescence: Evidence of moderating and bidirectional pathways. *Journal of Adolescence, 37*(2), 145–154.

Dobbins, E. H. (2007). End-of-life decisions: Influence of advance directives on patient care. *Journal of Gerontological Nursing, 33*, 50–56.

Dodge, K. A., Coie, J. D., & Lynam, D. (2006). Aggression and antisocial behavior in youth. In N. Eisenberg, W. Damon, & R. M. Lerner (Eds.), *Handbook of child psychology: Vol. 3. Social, emotional, and personality development* (6th ed. pp. 719–788). Hoboken, NJ: Wiley.

Dolcos, F., & Cabeza, R. (2002). Event-related potentials of emotional memory: Encoding pleasant, unpleasant, and neutral pictures. *Cognitive, Affective & Behavioral Neuroscience, 2*, 252–263.

Donnellan, M. B., Conger, R. D., & Burzette, R. G. (2007). Personality development from late adolescence to young adulthood: Differential stability, normative maturity, and evidence for the maturity-stability hypothesis. *Journal of Personality, 75*(2), 237–263.

Doucet, S., Soussignan, R., Sagot, P., & Schaal, B. (2007). The "smellscape" of mother's breast: Effects of odor masking and selective unmasking on neonatal arousal, oral and visual responses. *Developmental Psychobiology, 49*, 129–138.

Douglas, P. S., & Hill, P. S. (2013). Behavioral sleep interventions in the first six months of life do not improve outcomes for mothers or infants: A systematic review. *Journal of Developmental and Behavioral Pediatrics, 34*(7), 497–507.

Douglas, S. J., & Michaels, M. W. (2004). *The mommy myth: The idealization of motherhood and how it has undermined women.* New York, NY: Free Press.

Dovis, S., Van der Oord, S., Wiers, R. W., & Prins, P. M. (2013). What part of working memory is not working in ADHD? Short-term memory, the central executive and effects of reinforcement. *Journal of Abnormal Child Psychology, 41*(6), 901–917.

Downey, L., Curtis, J. R., Lafferty, W. E., Herting, J. R., & Engelberg, R. A. (2010). The quality of dying and death questionnaire (QODD): Empirical domains and theoretical perspectives. *Journal of Pain and Symptom Management, 39*(1), 9–22.

Dozeman, E., van Marwijk, H. W., van Schaik, D. J. F., Stek, M. L., van der Horst, H. E., Beekman, A. T. F., & van Hout, H. P. (2010). High incidence of clinically relevant depressive symptoms in vulnerable persons of 75 years or older living in the community. *Aging & Mental Health, 14*, 828–833.

Drago, F. (2011). Self-esteem and earnings. *Journal of Economic Psychology, 32*, 480–488.

Draper, H. (2013). Grandparents' entitlements and obligations. *Bioethics, 27*(6), 309–316.

Driver, J., & Gottman, J. M. (2004). Daily marital interactions and positive affect during marital conflict among newlywed couples. *Family Process, 43*(3), 301–314.

Drouin, M., & Tobin, E. (2014). Unwanted but consensual sexting among young adults: Relations with attachment and sexual motivations. *Computers in Human Behavior, 31*, 412–418.

Drouin, M., Miller, D. A., & Dibble, J. L. (2014). Ignore your partners' current Facebook friends; beware the ones they add! *Computers in Human Behavior, 35*, 483–488.

Duberstein, P. R., Chapman, B. P., Sink, K. M., Tindle, H. A., Bamonti, P., Robbins, J., . . . Franks, P. (2011). Personality and risk for Alzheimer's disease in adults 72 years of age and older: A 6-year follow-up. *Psychology and Aging, 26*(2), 351–362.

Duffy, D., & Reynolds, P. (2011). Babies born at the threshold of viability: Attitudes of paediatric consultants and trainees in South East England. *Acta Paediatrica, 100*, 42–46.

Duffy, R. D., Allan, B. A., Autin, K. L., & Douglass, R. P. (2014). Living a calling and work well-being: A longitudinal study. *Journal of Counseling Psychology, 61*(4), 605–615.

Dumas, L., Lepage, M., Bystrova, K., Matthiesen, A., Welles-Nyström, B., & Widström, A. (2013). Influence of skin-to-skin contact and rooming-in on early mother–infant interaction: A randomized controlled trial. *Clinical Nursing Research, 22*(3), 310–336.

Dumontheil, I., Apperly, I. A., & Blakemore, S.-J. (2010). Online usage of theory of mind continues to develop in late adolescence. *Developmental Science, 13*(2), 331–338.

Duncan, G. J., & Brooks-Gunn, J. (2000). Family poverty, welfare reform, and child development. *Child Development, 71*, 188–196.

Duncan, G. J., Ziol-Guest, K. M., & Kalil, A. (2010). Early-childhood poverty and adult attainment, behavior, and health. *Child Development, 81*(1), 306–325.

Dunedin Multidisciplinary Health and Development Research Unit. (2014). *The Dunedin multidisciplinary health & development study.* Retrieved from http://www.duneddinstudy.otago.ac.nz/

Dunfield, K. A., Kuhlmeier, V. A. (2013). Evidence for partner choice in toddlers: Considering the breadth of other oriented behaviors. *Behavioral and Brain Sciences, 36*(1), 88–89.

Dunifon, R. (2013). The influence of grandparents on the lives of children and adolescents. *Child Development Perspectives, 7*(1), 55–60.

Dunn, J., & Hughes, C. (2001). "I got some swords and you're dead!" Violent fantasy, antisocial behavior, friendship, and moral sensibility in young children. *Child Development, 72*, 491–505.

Dunn, J., Wooding, C., & Hermann, J. (1977). Mothers' speech to young children: Variation in context. *Developmental Medicine & Child Neurology, 19*, 629–638.

Dunn, M. G., & O'Brien, K. M. (2013). Work–family enrichment among dual-earner couples: Can work improve our family life? *Journal of Counseling Psychology, 60*(4), 634–640.

Dunphy, D. C. (1963). The social structure of urban adolescent peer groups. *Sociometry, 26,* 230–246.

Duvander, A. (2014). How long should parental leave be? Attitudes to gender equality, family, and work as determinants of women's and men's parental leave in Sweden *Journal of Family Issues, 35*(7), 909–926.

Dwairy, M. (2010). Parental inconsistency: A third cross-cultural research on parenting and psychological adjustment of children. *Journal of Child and Family Studies, 19,* 23–29.

Dweck, C. S. (1986). Motivational processes affecting learning. *American Psychologist, 41,* 1040–1048.

Eccles, J. S., & Roeser, R. W. (2003). Schools as developmental contexts. In G. R. Adams & M. D. Berzonsky (Eds.), *Blackwell handbook of adolescence* (pp. 129–148). Malden, MA: Blackwell.

Economic Policy Institute. (2011). *State of Working America.* Washington, DC: EPI.

Economic Policy Institute. (n.d.). Retrieved from http://www.epi.org

Edin, K., & Kefalas, M. (2005). *Promises I can keep: Why poor women put motherhood before marriage.* Berkeley: University of California Press.

Edwards, A. C., Dodge, K. A., Latendresse, S. J., Lansford, J. E., Bates, J. E., Pettit, . . . Dick, D. M. (2010). MAOA-uVNTR and early physical discipline interact to influence delinquent behavior. *Journal of Child Psychology and Psychiatry, 51*(6), 679–687.

Eisenberg, N. (1992). *The caring child.* Cambridge, MA: Harvard University Press.

Eisenberg, N. (2003). Prosocial behavior, empathy, and sympathy. In M. H. Bornstein, L. Davidson, C. L. M. Keyes, & K. A. Moore (Eds.), *Well-being: Positive development across the life course* (pp. 253–265). Mahwah, NJ: Erlbaum.

Eisenberg, N., & Fabes, R. A. (1998). Prosocial development. In W. Damon (Series ed.) & N. Eisenberg (Vol. ed.), *Handbook of child psychology: Vol 3. Social, emotional, and personality development* (5th ed. pp. 701–778). Hoboken, NJ: Wiley.

Eisenberg, N., Guthrie, I. K., Murphy, B. C., Shepard, S. A., Cumberland, A., &

Carlo, G. (1999). Consistency and development of prosocial dispositions: A longitudinal study. *Child Development, 70,* 1360–1372.

Eisenberg, N., Hofer, C., Sulik, M. J., & Liew, J. (2014). The development of prosocial moral reasoning and a prosocial orientation in young adulthood: Concurrent and longitudinal correlates. *Developmental Psychology, 50*(1), 58–70.

Eisner, E. W. (2004). Multiple intelligences: Its tensions and possibilities. *Teachers College Record, 106,* 31–39.

Ekerdt, D. J. (1986). The busy ethic: Moral continuity between work and retirement. *The Gerontologist, 26,* 239–244.

Ekerdt, D. J. (2010). Frontiers of research on work and retirement. *Journals of Gerontology: Social Sciences, 65B*(1), 69–80.

Elder, G. H., & Caspi, A. (1988). Economic stress in lives: Developmental perspectives. *Journal of Social Issues, 44,* 25–45.

Elkind, D. (1968). Cognitive development in adolescence. In J. F. Adams (Ed.), *Understanding adolescence* (pp. 128–158). Boston: Allyn and Bacon.

Elkind, D. (1978). Understanding the young adolescent. *Adolescence, 13,* 127–134.

Elliot, S. (2012). Not my kid: What parents believe about the sex lives of their teenagers. New York, NY: University Press.

Ellis, B. J. (2004). Timing of pubertal maturation in girls: An integrated life history approach. *Psychological Bulletin, 130,* 920–958.

Ellis, B. J., Boyce, W. T., Belsky, J., Bakermans-Kranenburg, M. J., & Van Ijzendoorn, M. H. (2011a). Differential susceptibility to the environment: An evolutionary-neurodevelopmental theory. *Development and Psychopathology, 23*(1), 7–28.

Ellis, B. J., Shirtcliff, E. A., Boyce, W., Deardorff, J., & Essex, M. J. (2011b). Quality of early family relationships and the timing and tempo of puberty: Effects depend on biological sensitivity to context. *Development and Psychopathology, 23*(1), 85–99.

Elsaesser, C., Gorman-Smith, D., & Henry, D. (2013). The role of the school environment in relational aggression and victimization. *Journal of Youth and Adolescence, 42*(2), 235–249.

Enck, G. E. (2003). The dying process. In C. D. Bryant (Ed.), *Handbook of death*

& dying (pp. 457–467). Thousand Oaks, CA: Sage.

Engle, S. (n.d.). Degree attainment rates at colleges and universities: College completion declining, taking longer, UCLA study shows. *Higher Education Research Institute.* Retrieved from http://www.gseis.ucla.edu/heri/darcu_pr.html

English, T., & Carstensen, L. L. (2014). Selective narrowing of social networks across adulthood is associated with improved emotional experience in daily life. *International Journal of Behavioral Development, 38*(2), 195–202.

Englund, M. M., Egeland, B., Olivia, E. M., & Collins, W. A. (2008). Childhood and adolescent predictors of heavy drinking and alcohol use disorders in early adulthood: A longitudinal development analysis. *Addiction, 103* (Suppl. 1), 23–35.

Enguidanos, S., Yonashiro-Cho, J., & Cote, S. (2013). Knowledge and perceptions of hospice care of Chinese older adults. *Journal of the American Geriatrics Society, 61*(6), 993–998.

Ennis, G. E., Hess, T. M., & Smith, B. T. (2013). The impact of age and motivation on cognitive effort: Implications for cognitive engagement in older adulthood. *Psychology and Aging, 28*(2), 495–504.

Epstein, R. (2010). *Teen 2.0: Saving our children and families from the torment of adolescence.* New York, NY: Linton.

Epstein, R., Pandit, M., & Thakar, M. (2013). How love emerges in arranged marriages: Two cross-cultural studies. *Journal of Comparative Family Studies, 44*(3), 341–360.

Erber, J. T., & Prager, I. G. (1999). Age and memory: Perceptions of forgetful young and older adults. In T. M. Hess & F. Blanchard-Fields (Eds.), *Social cognition and aging* (pp. 197–217). San Diego, CA: Academic Press.

Erikson, E. H. (1950). *Childhood and society.* Oxford, England: Norton.

Erikson, E. H. (1963). *Childhood and society* (2nd ed.). New York, NY: Norton.

Erikson, E. H. (1968). *Identity: Youth and crisis.* New York, NY: Norton.

Erikson, E. H. (1969). *Gandhi's truth: On the origins of militant nonviolence.* New York, NY: Norton.

Erikson, E. H. (1980). *Identity and the life cycle.* New York, NY: Norton.

Erulkar, A. (2013). Adolescence lost: The realities of child marriage. *Journal of Adolescent Health, 52*(5), 513–514.

Espelage, D. L., & De La Rue, L. (2013). School bullying: Its nature and ecology. In J. C. Srabstein, J. Merrick (Eds.), *Bullying: A public health concern* (pp. 23-37). Hauppauge, NY: Nova Science.

Espeset, E. M. S., Nordbø, R. H. S., Gulliksen, K. S., Skárderud, F., Geller, J., & Holte, A. (2011). The concept of body image disturbance in anorexia nervosa: An empirical inquiry utilizing patients' subjective experiences. *Eating Disorders, 19*(2), 175–193.

Espinoza, P., Penelo, E., & Raich, R. M. (2010). Disordered eating behaviors and body image in a longitudinal pilot study of adolescent girls: What happens 2 years later? *Body Image, 7,* 70–73.

Etaugh, C. A., & Bridges, J. S. (2006). Midlife transitions. In J. Worell & C. D. Goodheart (Eds.), *Handbook of girls' and women's psychological health: Gender and well-being across the lifespan* (pp. 359–367). New York, NY: Oxford University Press.

Etezadi, S., & Pushkar, D. (2013). Why are wise people happier? An explanatory model of wisdom and emotional well-being in older adults. *Journal of Happiness Studies, 14*(3), 929–950.

Evans, A. D., Xu, F., & Lee, K. (2011). When all signs point to you: Lies told in the face of evidence. *Developmental Psychology, 47*(1), 39–49.

Evans, G. W., & Kim, P. (2013). Childhood poverty, chronic stress, self-regulation, and coping. *Child Development Perspectives, 7*(1), 43–48.

Evertsson, M. (2014). Gender ideology and the sharing of housework and child care in Sweden. *Journal of Family Issues, 35*(7), 927–949.

Fabes, R. A., Martin, C. L., & Hanish, L. D. (2003). Young children's play qualities in same-, other-, and mixed-sex peer groups. *Child Development, 74,* 921–932.

Fabian, J. (2011). Applying Roper v. Simmons in juvenile transfer and waiver proceedings: A legal and neuroscientific inquiry. *International Journal of Offender Therapy and Comparative Criminology, 55*(5), 732–755.

Facio, A., & Resett, S. (2014). Work, romantic relationships, and life satisfaction in Argentinean emerging adults. *Emerging Adulthood, 2*(1), 27–35.

Faeh, D., & Bopp, M. (2010). Increase in the prevalence of obesity in Switzerland 1982–2007: Birth cohort analysis puts recent slowdown into perspective. *Obesity, 18*(3), 644–646.

Fahs, B. (2007). Second shifts and political awakenings: Divorce and the political socialization of middle-aged women. *Journal of Divorce & Remarriage, 47*(3/4), 43-64.

Fairchild, H., & Cooper, M. (2010). A multidimensional measure of core beliefs relevant to eating disorders: Preliminary development and validation. *Eating Behaviors, 11,* 239–246.

Families and Work Institute. (2009). Times are changing: Gender and generation at work and at home. Retrieved from http://www.familiesandwork.org/site/research/reports/Times_Are_Changing.pdf

Farber, N., & Miller-Cribbs, J. E. (2014). "First train out": Marriage and cohabitation in the context of poverty, deprivation, and trauma. *Journal of Human Behavior in the Social Environment, 24*(2), 188–207.

Farmer, T. W., Hamm, J. V., Leung, M., Lambert, K., & Gravelle, M. (2011). Early adolescent peer ecologies in rural communities: Bullying in schools that do and do not have a transition during the middle grades. *Journal of Youth and Adolescence, 40*(9), 1106–1117.

Farroni, T., Massaccesi, S., & Simion, F. (2002). La direzione dello sguardo di un'altra persona puo dirigere l'attenzione del neonato? [Can the direction of the gaze of another person shift the attention of a neonate?] *Giornale Italiano di Psicologia, 29,* 857–864.

Fauth, R. C., Leventhal, T., & Brooks-Gunn, J. (2007). Welcome to the neighborhood? Long term impacts of moving to low-poverty neighborhoods on poor children's and adolescents' outcomes. *Journal of Research on Adolescence, 17*(2), 249–284.

Feeney, J. A. (1999). Adult romantic attachment and couple relationships. In J. Cassidy & P. R. Shaver (Eds.), *Handbook of attachment: Theory, research, and clinical applications* (pp. 355–377). New York, NY: Guilford Press.

Feeney, J. A., & Noller, P. (2002). Allocation and performance of household tasks: A comparison of new parents and childless couples. In P. Noller & J. A. Feeney (Eds.), *Understanding marriage: Developments in the study of couple interaction* (pp. 411–436). New York, NY: Cambridge University Press.

Feeney, J. A., Hohaus, L., Noller, P., & Alexander, R. P. (2001). *Becoming parents: Exploring the bonds between mothers, fathers, and their infants.* New York, NY: Cambridge University Press.

Feinberg, I., & Campbell, I. G. (2010). Sleep EEG changes during adolescence: An index of a fundamental brain reorganization. *Brain and Cognition, 72,* 56–65.

Feixa, C. (2011). Past and present of adolescence in society: The "teen brain" debate in perspective. *Neuroscience and Biobehavioral Reviews, 35*(8), 1634–1643.

Feldman, R., & Eidelman, A. I. (2003). Skin-to-skin contact (kangaroo care) accelerates autonomic and neurobehavioural maturation in preterm infants. *Developmental Medicine & Child Neurology, 45,* 274–281.

Ferber, R. (1985). Sleep, sleeplessness, and sleep disruptions in infants and young children. *Annals of Clinical Research, 17*(5). Special issue: Sleep research and its clinical implications, 227–234.

Ferguson, E. D., Hagaman, J. A., Maurer, S. B., Mathews, P., & Peng, K. (2013). Asian culture in transition: Is it related to reported parenting styles and transitivity of simple choices? *Journal of Applied Social Psychology, 43*(4), 730–740.

Ferland, P., & Caron, S. L. (2013). Exploring the long-term impact of female infertility: A qualitative analysis of interviews with postmenopausal women who remained childless. *The Family Journal, 21*(2), 180–188.

Fernandez, M., Blass, E. M., Hernandez-Reif, M., Field, T., Diego, M., & Sanders, C. (2003). Sucrose attenuates a negative electroencephalographic response to an aversive stimulus for newborns. *Journal of Developmental & Behavioral Pediatrics, 24,* 261–266.

Field, M. J. (2009). How people die in the United States. In J. L. Werth Jr. and D. Blevins (Eds.), *Decision making near the end of life: Issues, developments, and future directions* (pp. 63–75). New York, NY: Routledge.

Field, N. P., Gal-Oz, E., & Bonanno, G. A. (2003). Continuing bonds and adjustment at 5 years after the death of a spouse. *Journal of Consulting and Clinical Psychology, 71,* 110–117.

Field, T., Diego, M., & Hernandez-Reif, M. (2007). Massage therapy research. *Developmental Review, 27,* 75–89.

Field, T., Diego, M., & Hernandez-Reif, M. (2011). Potential underlying mechanisms for greater weight gain in massaged preterm infants. *Infant Behavior and Development, 34*(3), 383–389.

Fincham, F. D., Stanley, S. M., & Beach, S. R. (2007). Transformative processes in marriage: An analysis of emerging trends. *Journal of Marriage and Family, 69*(2), 275–292.

Findler, L., Taubman–Ben-Ari, O., Nuttman-Shwartz, O., & Lazar, R. (2013). Construction and validation of the multidimensional experience of grandparenthood set of inventories. *Social Work Research, 37*(3), 237–253.

Finegood, D. T., Merth, T. N., & Rutter, H. (2010). Implications of the Foresight Obesity System Map for solutions to childhood obesity. *Obesity, 18*(Suppl 1), S13–S16.

Finer, L. B., & Philbin, J. M. (2014). Trends in ages at key reproductive transitions in the United States, 1951–2010. *Women's Health Issues 24*(3), 1–9.

Fingerman, K. L., Miller, L., & Charles, S. (2008). Saving the best for last: How adults treat social partners of different ages. *Psychology and Aging, 23*(2), 399–409.

Finkel, D., & Pedersen, N. L. (2004). Processing speed and longitudinal trajectories of change for cognitive abilities: The Swedish Adoption/Twin Study of Aging. *Aging, Neuropsychology, and Cognition, 11*, 325–345.

Finkel, D., Andel, R., Gatz, M., & Pedersen, N. (2009). The role of occupational complexity in trajectories of cognitive aging before and after retirement. *Psychology and Aging, 24*(3), 563–573.

Fischer, D. H. (1977). *Growing old in America.* New York, NY: Oxford University Press.

Fishman, T. (2010). *Shock of gray: The aging of the world's population and how it pits young against old, child against parent, worker against boss, company against rival, and nation against nation.* New York, NY: Scribner.

Fitzpatrick, C., & Pagani, L. S. (2012). Toddler working memory skills predict kindergarten school readiness. *Intelligence, 40*(2), 205–212.

Fitzpatrick, M. J., & McPherson, B. J. (2010). Coloring within the lines: Gender stereotypes in contemporary coloring books. *Sex Roles, 62*, 127–137.

Fivush, R. (2011). The development of autobiographical memory. *Annual Review of Psychology, 62*, 559–582.

Fjell, A. M., Westlye, L. T., Grydeland, H., Amlien, I., Espeseth, T., Reinvang, I., . . . Walhovd, K. B. (2014). Accelerating cortical thinning: Unique to dementia or universal in aging? *Cerebral Cortex, 24*(4), 919–934.

Flanagan, C. A., & Stout, M. (2010). Developmental patterns of social trust between early and late adolescence: Age and school climate effects. *Journal of Research on Adolescence, 20*(3), 748–773.

Flavell, J. H. (1963). *The developmental psychology of Jean Piaget.* New York, NY: Van Nostrand.

Flavell, J. H., Beach, D. R., & Chinsky, J. M. (1966). Spontaneous verbal rehearsal in a memory task as a function of age. *Child Development, 37*, 283–299.

Flower, K. B., Willoughby, M., Cadigan, R. J., Perrin, E. M., & Randolph, G. (2008). Understanding breastfeeding initiation and continuation in rural communities: A combined qualitative/quantitative approach. *Maternal and Child Health Journal, 12*(3), 402–414.

Flynn, J. R. (2007). *What is intelligence? Beyond the Flynn effect.* New York, NY: Cambridge University Press.

Fok, W., Zhang, Y., Salmon, A., Bhattacharya, A., Gunda, R., Jones, D., . . . Pérez, V. (2013). Short-term treatment with rapamycin and dietary restriction have overlapping and distinctive effects in young mice. *Journals of Gerontology Series A: Biological Sciences and Medical Sciences, 68*(2), 108–116.

Fonseca, A., Nazaré, B., & Canavarro, M. C. (2014). Parenting an infant with a congenital anomaly: An exploratory study on patterns of adjustment from diagnosis to six months post birth. *Journal of Child Health Care, 18*(2), 111–122.

Forbush, K. T., & Hunt, T. K. (2014). Characterization of eating patterns among individuals with eating disorders: What is the state of the plate? *Physiology & Behavior, 134*, 92–109.

Ford, D. H., & Lerner, R. M. (1992). *Developmental systems theory: An integrative approach.* Newbury Park, CA: Sage.

Forster, S., Robertson, D. J., Jennings, A., Asherson, P., & Lavie, N. (2014). Plugging the attention deficit: Perceptual load counters increased distraction in ADHD. *Neuropsychology, 28*(1), 91–97.

Foss, K. A. (2010). Perpetuating "scientific motherhood": Infant feeding discourse in *Parents Magazine* 1930–2007. *Women & Health, 50*(3), 297–311.

Fossen, R. S., & Vredenburgh, D. J. (2014). Exploring differences in work's meaning: An investigation of individual attributes associated with work orientations. *Journal of Behavioral and Applied Management, 15*(2), 101–120.

Foster, R. E., Stone, F. P., Linkh, D. J., Besetsny, L. K., Collins, P. S., Saha, T., . . . Milner, J. S. (2010). Substantiation of spouse and child maltreatment reports as a function of referral source and maltreatment type. *Military Medicine, 175*(8), 560–566.

Foster, T. L., Gilmer, M. J., Davies, B., Dietrich, M. S., Barrera, M., Fairclough, . . . Gerhardt, C. A. (2011). Comparison of continuing bonds reported by parents and siblings after a child's death from cancer. *Death Studies, 35*, 420–440.

Fothergill, A. (2013). Managing childcare: The experiences of mothers and childcare workers. *Sociological Inquiry, 83*(3), 421–447.

Fowler-Brown, A. G., Ngo, L. H., Phillips, R. S., & Wee, C. C. (2010). Adolescent obesity and future college degree attainment. *Obesity, 18*(6), 1235–1241.

Fox, J., Osborn, J. L., & Warber, K. M. (2014). Relational dialectics and social networking sites: The role of Facebook in romantic relationship escalation, maintenance, conflict, and dissolution. *Computers in Human Behavior, 35*, 527–534.

Fox, S. E., Levitt, P., & Nelson, C. A. (2010). How the timing and quality of early experiences influence the development of brain architecture. *Child Development, 81*(1), 28–40.

Foynes, M. M., Platt, M., Hall, G. N., & Freyd, J. J. (2014). The impact of Asian values and victim–perpetrator closeness on the disclosure of emotional, physical, and sexual abuse. *Psychological Trauma: Theory, Research, Practice and Policy, 6*(2), 134–141.

Fraley, R. C., Roisman, G. I., Booth-LaForce, C., Owen, M. T., & Holland, A. S. (2013). Interpersonal and genetic origins of adult attachment styles: A longitudinal study from infancy to early adulthood. *Journal of Personality and Social Psychology, 104*(5), 817–838.

Francis, D. A., & DePalma, R. (2014). Teacher perspectives on abstinence and safe sex education in South Africa. *Sex Education, 14*(1), 81–94.

Frans, E. M., Sandin, S., Reichenberg, A., Långström, N., Lichtenstein, P., McGrath, J. J., & Hultman, C. M. (2013). Autism risk across generations: A population-based study of advancing grandpaternal and paternal age. *JAMA Psychiatry, 70*(5), 516–521.

Freeman, S., Kurosawa, H., Ebihara, S., & Kohzuki, M. (2010). Caregiving burden for the oldest old: A population based study of centenarian caregivers in

Northern Japan. *Archives of Gerontology and Geriatrics, 50*, 282–291.

Freund, A. M., & Blanchard-Fields, F. (2014). Age-related differences in altruism across adulthood: Making personal financial gain versus contributing to the public good. *Developmental Psychology, 50*(4), 1125–1136.

Frey, K. S., & Ruble, D. N. (1985). What children say when the teacher is not around: Conflicting goals in social comparison and performance assessment in the classroom. *Journal of Personality and Social Psychology, 48*, 550–562.

Frey, K. S., & Ruble, D. N. (1990). Strategies for comparative evaluation: Maintaining a sense of competence across the life span. In R. J. Sternberg & J. Kolligian, Jr. (Eds.), *Competence considered* (pp. 167–189). New Haven, CT: Yale University Press.

Frey, R., Gott, M., Raphael, D., Black, S., Teleo-Hope, L., Lee, H., & Wang, Z. (2013). "Where do I go from here"? A cultural perspective on challenges to the use of hospice services. *Health & Social Care in the Community, 21*(5), 519–529.

Friedman, D. (2003). Cognition and aging: A highly selective overview of event-related potential (ERP) data. *Journal of Clinical and Experimental Neuropsychology, 25*, 702–720.

Friedman, D., & Johnson, R. J. (2014). Inefficient encoding as an explanation for age-related deficits in recollection-based processing. *Journal of Psychophysiology, 28*(3), 148–161.

Friedman, E. M. (2014). Good friends, good food . . . what more could we want? Assessing the links between social relationships and dietary behaviors. A commentary on Conklin et al. *Social Science & Medicine, 100*, 176–177.

Frischen, A., Bayliss, A. P., & Tipper, S. P. (2007) Gaze cueing of attention: Visual attention, social cognition, and individual differences. *Psychological Bulletin, 133*(4), 694–724.

Frisén, A., & Holmqvist, K. (2010). What characterizes early adolescents with a positive body image? A qualitative investigation of Swedish girls and boys. *Body Image, 7*, 205–212.

Frye, A. A., & Liem, J. H. (2011). Diverse patterns in the development of depressive symptoms among emerging adults. *Journal of Adolescent Research, 26*(5), 570–590.

Fu, S.-Y., Anderson, D., & Courtney, M. (2003). Cross-cultural menopausal experience: Comparison of Australian and Taiwanese women. *Nursing & Health Sciences, 5*, 77–84.

Fuller, B., & García Coll, C. (2010). Learning from Latinos: Contexts, families, and child development in motion. *Developmental Psychology, 46*(3), 559–565.

Fung, H. H., Lai, P., & Ng, R. (2001). Age differences in social preferences among Taiwanese and mainland Chinese: The role of perceived time. *Psychology and Aging, 16*, 351–356.

Funk, L. M. (2010). Prioritizing parental autonomy: Adult children's accounts of feeling responsible and supporting aging parents. *Journal of Aging Studies, 24*(1), 57–64.

Furler, K., Gomez, V., & Grob, A. (2013). Personality similarity and life satisfaction in couples. *Journal of Research in Personality, 47*(4), 369–375.

Furler, K., Gomez, V., & Grob, A. (2014). Personality perceptions and relationship satisfaction in couples. *Journal of Research in Personality, 50*, 33–41.

Furstenberg, F. F. Jr. (2010). On a new schedule: Transitions to adulthood and family change. *The Future of Children, 20*, 67–87. Retrieved from http://www.futureofchildren/futureofchildren/publications/docs/20_01_04.pdf

Fuwa, M. (2014). Work–family conflict and attitudes toward marriage. *Journal of Family Issues, 35*(6), 731–754.

Gadoud, A., Adcock, Y., Jones, L., Koon, S., & Johnson, M. (2013). "It's not all doom and gloom": Perceptions of medical students talking to hospice patients. *Journal of Palliative Medicine, 16*(9), 1125–1129.

Gaffney, K. F., Kitsantas, P., Brito, A., & Swamidoss, C. S. (2014). Postpartum depression, infant feeding practices, and infant weight gain at six months of age. *Journal of Pediatric Health Care, 28*(1), 43–50.

Gagne, M. H., Tourigny, M., Joly, J., & Pouliot-Lapointe, J. (2007). Predictors of adult attitudes toward corporal punishment of children. *Journal of Interpersonal Violence, 22*(10), 1285–1304.

Gähler, M., & Garriga, A. (2013). Has the association between parental divorce and young adults' psychological problems changed over time? Evidence from Sweden, 1968–2000. *Journal of Family Issues, 34*(6), 784–808.

Gajewski, P. D. (2013). Abstracts of the International Conference "Aging & Cognition": Dortmund, Germany, April 25–27, 2013. *Journal of Psychophysiology, 27*(Suppl 1), 9–75.

Gajic-Veljanoski, O., & Stewart, D. E. (2007). Women trafficked into prostitution: Determinants, human rights, and health needs. *Transcultural Psychiatry, 44*(3), 338–358.

Gala, J., & Kapadia, S. (2014). Romantic love, commitment and marriage in emerging adulthood in an Indian context: Views of emerging adults and middle adults. *Psychology and Developing Societies, 26*(1), 115–141.

Galinsky, E. (2007). The changing landscape of work. *Generations, 31*(1), 16–22.

Galinsky, E., Bond, J. T., Kim, S., Backon, L., Brownfield, E., & Sakai, K. (2005). *Overwork in America: When the way we work becomes too much.* New York, NY: Families and Work Institute.

Gana, K., Bailly, N., Saada, Y., Joulain, M., & Alaphilippe, D. (2013). Does life satisfaction change in old age: Results from an 8-year longitudinal study. *The Journals of Gerontology Series B: Psychological Sciences and Social Sciences, 68B*(4), 540–552.

Gao, Y., Raine, A., Venables, P. H., Dawson, M. E., & Mednick, S. A. (2010). Reduced electrodermal fear conditioning from ages 3 to 8 years is associated with aggressive behavior at age 8 years. *Journal of Child Psychology and Psychiatry, 51*(5), 550–558.

García-Pérez, L., Linertová, R., Martín-Olivera, P., Serrano-Aguilar, P., & Benítez-Rosario, M. P. (2009). A systematic review of specialised palliative care for terminal patients: Which model is better? *Palliative Medicine, 23*(1), 17–22.

Gardner, H. (1998). A multiplicity of intelligences. *Scientific American Presents, 9*(4), 18–23.

Gardner, H. (2004). *Frames of mind: The theory of multiple intelligences.* New York, NY: Basic Books.

Gardner, H., & Moran, S. (2006). The science of multiple intelligences theory: A response to Lynn Waterhouse. *Educational Psychologist, 41*(4), 227–232.

Gardner, M., Roth, J., & Brooks-Gunn, J. (2008). Adolescents' participation in organized activities and developmental success 2 and 8 years after high school: Do sponsorship, duration, and intensity matter? *Developmental Psychology, 44*, 814–830.

Garey, A. I., & Arendell, T. (2001). Children, work, and family: Some thoughts on "mother blame." In R. Hertz & N. L. Marshall (Eds.),

Working families: The transformation of the American home (pp. 293–303). Berkeley, CA: University of California Press.

Gartstein, M. A., Bridgett, D. J., Young, B. N., Panksepp, J., & Power, T. (2013). Origins of effortful control: Infant and parent contributions. *Infancy, 18*(2), 149–183.

Gath, A. (1993). Changes that occur in families as children with intellectual disability grow up. *International Journal of Disability, Development and Education, 40*, 167–174.

Gatrell, C. J., Burnett, S. B., Cooper, C. L., & Sparrow, P. (2013). Work–life balance and parenthood: A comparative review of definitions, equity and enrichment. *International Journal of Management Reviews, 15*(3), 300–316.

Gau, S. S., & Chang, J. P. (2013). Maternal parenting styles and mother–child relationship among adolescents with and without persistent attention-deficit/hyperactivity disorder. *Research in Developmental Disabilities, 34*(5), 1581–1594.

Gavin, J., Rodham, K., & Poyer, H. (2008). The presentation of "pro-anorexia" in online group interactions. *Qualitative Health Research, 18*(3), 325–333.

Gazelle, H., & Ladd, G. W. (2003). Anxious solitude and peer exclusion: A diathesis-stress model of internalizing trajectories in childhood. *Child Development, 74*, 257–278.

Geary, D. C. (1998). *Male, female: The evolution of human sex differences.* Washington, DC: American Psychological Association.

Genevie, L. E., & Margolies, E. (1987). *The motherhood report: How women feel about being mothers.* New York, NY: Macmillan.

Gentile, K. (2014). Exploring the troubling temporalities produced by fetal personhood. *Psychoanalysis, Culture & Society, 19*(3), 279–296.

Gentzler, A. L., Oberhauser, A. M., Westerman, D., & Nardoff, D. K. (2011). College students' use of electronic communication with parents: Links to loneliness, attachment, and relationship quality. *CyberPsychology, Behavior, and Social Networking, 11*(1–2), 71–74.

George, L. K. (2010). Still happy after all these years: Research frontiers in subjective well-being in later life. *Journals of Gerontology: Social Sciences, 65B*(3), 331–339.

Geraci, A., Surian, L., Ferraro, M., & Cantagallo, A. (2010). Theory of mind in patients with ventromedial or dorsolateral prefrontal lesions following traumatic brain injury. *Brain Injury, 24*(7-8), 978–987.

Gerber, E. B., Whitebook, M., & Weinstein, R. S. (2007). At the heart of child care: Predictors of teacher sensitivity in center-based child care. *Early Childhood Research Quarterly, 22*, 327–346.

Gerdner, L. A., Cha, D., Yang, D., & Tripp-Reimer, T. (2007). The circle of life: End-of-life care and death rituals for Hmong-American elders. *Journal of Gerontological Nursing, 33*(5), 20–29.

Germo, G. R., Chang, E. S., Keller, M. A., & Goldberg, W. A. (2007). Child sleep arrangements and family life: Perspectives from mothers and fathers. *Infant and Child Development, 16*, 433–456.

Gerontology Research Group. (n.d.). Retrieved from http://www.grg.org

Gershoff, E. T. (2002). Corporal punishment by parents and associated child behaviors and experiences: A meta-analytic and theoretical review. *Psychological Bulletin, 128*, 539–579.

Gerson, M.-J., Posner, J.-A., & Morris, A. M. (1991). The wish for a child in couples eager, disinterested, and conflicted about having children. *American Journal of Family Therapy, 19*, 334–343.

Gervain, J., & Mehler, J. (2010). Speech perception and language acquisition in the first year of life. *Annual Review of Psychology, 61*, 191–218.

Gestsdottir, S., Bowers, E., von Eye, A., Napolitano, C. M., & Lerner, R. M. (2010). Intentional self regulation in middle adolescence: The emerging role of loss-based selection in positive youth development. *Journal of Youth and Adolescence, 39*, 764–782.

Gettler, L. T., McDade, T. W., Agustin, S. S., Feranil, A. B., & Kuzawa, C. W. (2013). Do testosterone declines during the transition to marriage and fatherhood relate to men's sexual behavior? Evidence from the Philippines. *Hormones and Behavior, 64*(5), 755–763.

Ghassabian, A., Herba, C. M., Roza, S. J., Govaert, P., Schenk, J. J., Jaddoe, V. W., . . . Tiemeier, H. (2013). Infant brain structures, executive function, and attention deficit/hyperactivity problems at preschool age. A prospective study. *Journal of Child Psychology and Psychiatry, 54*(1), 96–104.

Gibbins, S., & Stevens, B. (2001). Mechanisms of sucrose and nonnutritive sucking in procedural pain management in infants. *Pain Research & Management, 6*, 21–28.

Gibson, E. J., & Walk, R. D. (1960). The "visual cliff". *Scientific American, 202*(4), 64–71.

Gibson, M. A., & Mace, R. (2005). Helpful grandmothers in rural Ethiopia: A study of the effect of kin on child survival and growth. *Evolution and Human Behavior, 26*, 469–482.

Gibson-Davis, C. M. (2009). Money, marriage, and children: Testing the financial expectations and family formation theory. *Journal of Marriage and Family, 71*, 146–160.

Gibson-Davis, C., & Rackin, H. (2014). Marriage or carriage? Trends in union context and birth type by education. *Journal of Marriage and Family, 76*(3), 506–519.

Giedd, J. N., Stockman, M., Weddle, C., Liverpool, M., Alexander-Bloch, A., Wallace, G. L., & Lenroot, R. K. (2010). Anatomic magnetic resonance imaging of the developing child and adolescent brain and effects of genetic variation. *Neuropsychology Review, 20*(4), 349–361.

Gilbert-Barness, E. (2000). Maternal caffeine and its effect on the fetus. *American Journal of Medical Genetics, 93*, 253.

Gilboa, S., Shirom, A., Fried, Y., & Cooper, C. (2008). A meta-analysis of work demand stressors and job performance: Examining main and moderating effects. *Personnel Psychology, 61*(2), 227–272.

Giletta, M., Scholte, R. J., Engels, R. E., Ciairano, S., & Prinstein, M. J. (2012). Adolescent non-suicidal self-injury: A cross-national study of community samples from Italy, the Netherlands and the United States. *Psychiatry Research, 197*(1-2), 66–72.

Gillett, G., & Chamberlain, J. (2013). The clinician's dilemma: Two dimensions of ethical care. *International Journal of Law and Psychiatry, 36*(5–6), 454–460.

Gilligan, C., Attanucci, J. (1988). Two moral orientations: Gender differences and similarities. *Merrill-Palmer Quarterly: Journal of Developmental Psychology, 34*(3), 223–237.

Gilman, R., Huebner, E. S., Tian, L., Park, N., O'Byrne, J., Schiff, . . . & Langknecht, H. (2008). Cross-national adolescent multidimensional life satisfaction reports: Analysis of mean scores and response style differences. *Journal of Youth and Adolescence, 37*, 142–154.

Ginsburg, H., & Opper, S. (1969). *Piaget's theory of intellectual development: An introduction*. Englewood Cliffs, NJ: Prentice-Hall.

Giordano, P. C., Manning, W. D., & Longmore, M. A. (2010). Affairs of the heart: Qualities of adolescent romantic relationships and sexual behavior. *Journal of Research on Adolescence, 20*(4), 983–1013.

Girdler, S., Packer, T. L., & Boldy, D. (2008). The impact of age-related vision loss. *OTJR: Occupation, Participation, and Health, 28*, 110–120.

Glaser, B. G., & Strauss, A. L. (1968). *Time for dying*. Chicago, IL: Aldine.

Glenn, N. (1990). Quantitative research on marital quality in the 1980s: A critical review. *Journal of Marriage and the Family, 52*, 818–831.

Go, A. S., Mozaffarian, D., Roger, V. L., Benjamin, E. J., Berry, J. D., Blaha, M. J., . . . Turan, T. N. (2014). Executive summary: Heart disease and stroke statistics—2014 update: A report from the American Heart Association. *Circulation, 129*(3), 399–410.

Godino, L., Turchetti, D., & Skirton, H. (2013). A systematic review of factors influencing uptake of invasive fetal genetic testing by pregnant women of advanced maternal age. *Midwifery, 29*(11), 1235–1243.

Goldberg, A., Smith, J., & Kashy, D. A. (2010). Preadoptive factors predicting lesbian, gay, and heterosexual couples' relationship quality across the transition to adoptive parenthood. *Journal of Family Psychology, 24*(3), 221–232.

Goldberg, W. A., Lucas-Thompson, R. G., Germo, G. R., Keller, M. A., Davis, E. P., & Sandman, C. A. (2013). Eye of the beholder? Maternal mental health and the quality of infant sleep. *Social Science & Medicine, 79*, 101–108.

Golden, L. (2008). Limited access: Disparities in flexible work schedules and work-at-home. *Journal of Family Economic Issues, 29*, 86–109.

Golden, P. (2014, September-October). They do it for love: Many parents incur debt, delay retirement to help adult children. *Aging Today, 35*(5).

Goldman, J. G., & Coleman, S. J. (2013). Primary school puberty/sexuality education: Student-teachers' past learning, present professional education, and intention to teach these subjects. *Sex Education, 13*(3), 276–290.

Goldner, J., Peters, T. L., Richards, M. H., & Pearce, S. (2011). Exposure to community violence and protective and risky contexts among low income urban African American adolescents: A prospective study. *Journal of Youth and Adolescence, 40*, 174–186.

Goldschmidt, A. B., Wall, M. M., Loth, K. A., Bucchianeri, M. M., & Neumark-Sztainer, D. (2014). The course of binge eating from adolescence to young adulthood. *Health Psychology, 33*(5), 457–460.

Golombok, S., Mellish, L., Jennings, S., Casy, P., Tasker, F., & Lamb, M. (2014). Adoptive gay father families: Parent–child relationships and children's psychological adjustment. *Child Development, 85*(2), 456–468.

Golombok, S., Perry, B., Burston, A., Murray, C., Mooney-Somers, J., Stevens, M., & Golding, J. (2003). Children with lesbian parents: A community study. *Developmental Psychology, 39*, 20–33.

Gooch, D., Snowling, M., & Hulme, C. (2011). Time perception, phonological skills and executive function in children with dyslexia and/or ADHD symptoms. *Journal of Child Psychology and Psychiatry, 52*(2), 195–203.

Good, M.-J. D., Gadmer, N. M., Ruopp, P., Lakoma, M., Sullivan, A. M., Redinbaugh, E., Arnold, R. M., & Block, S. D. (2004). Narrative nuances on good and bad deaths: Internists' tales from high-technology work places. *Social Science & Medicine, 58*, 939–953.

Goodlin-Jones, B. L., Burnham, M. M., Gaylor, E. E., & Anders, T. F. (2001). Night waking, sleep-wake organization, and self-soothing in the first year of life. *Journal of Developmental and Behavioral Pediatrics, 22*(4), 226–233.

Gooldin, S. (2013). "Emotional rights," moral reasoning, and Jewish–Arab alliances in the regulation of in-vitro-fertilization in Israel: Theorizing the unexpected consequences of assisted reproductive technologies. *Social Science & Medicine, 83*, 90–98.

Gopnik, A. (2010). How babies think: Even the youngest children know, experience and learn far more than scientists ever thought possible. *Scientific American, 303*, 76–81.

Gordon-Larsen, P., The, N. S., & Adair, L. S. (2010). Longitudinal trends in obesity in the United States from adolescence to the third decade of life. *Obesity, 18*(9), 1801–1804.

Gordon-Messer, D., Bauermeister, J. A., Grodzinski, A., & Zimmerman, M. (2013). Sexting among young adults. *Journal of Adolescent Health, 52*(3), 301–306.

Gore, T., & Dubois, R. (1998). The "Back to Sleep" campaign. *Zero to Three, 19*(2), 22–23.

Gorer, G. (1965). *Death, grief, and mourning in contemporary Britain*. London, England: Cresset Press.

Gothe, K., Oberauer, K., & Kliegl, R. (2008). Age differences in dual-task performance after practice. *Psychology and Aging, 22*(3), 596–606.

Gottman, J. (1994). *Why marriages succeed or fail: And how you can make yours last*. New York, NY: Simon & Schuster.

Gottman, J. M. (1999). *The marriage clinic: A scientifically based marital therapy*. New York, NY: Norton.

Gould, E. (2014). Raising wages is key to improving incomes of low-income Americans. Economic Policy Institute, June 17, 2014.

Gould, L. A., & Pate, M. (2010). Discipline, docility, and disparity: A study of inequality and corporal punishment. *British Journal of Criminology, 50*, 185–205.

Gould, S. J. (1981). *The mismeasure of man*. New York, NY: Norton.

Goveas, J. S., Espeland, M. A., Hogan, P. E., Tindle, H. A., Shih, R. A., Kotchen, J. M., . . . Resnick, S. M. (2014). Depressive symptoms and longitudinal changes in cognition: Women's health initiative study of cognitive aging. *Journal of Geriatric Psychiatry and Neurology, 27*(2), 94–102.

Graber, J. A., Nichols, T. R., & Brooks-Gunn, J. (2010). Putting pubertal timing in developmental context: Implications for prevention. *Developmental Psychobiology, 52*(3), 254–262.

Graham, J., Banaschewski, T., Buitelaar, J., Coghill, D., Danckaerts, M., Dittmann, R. W., . . . Taylor, E. (2011). European guidelines on managing adverse effects of medication for ADHD. *European Child & Adolescent Psychiatry, 20*, 17–37.

Graneheim, U. H., Johansson, A., & Lindgren, B. (2014). Family caregivers' experiences of relinquishing the care of a person with dementia to a nursing home: Insights from a meta-ethnographic study. *Scandinavian Journal of Caring Sciences, 28*(2), 215–224.

Gratwick-Sarll, K., Mond, J., & Hay, P. (2013). Self-recognition of eating-disordered behavior in college women: Further evidence of poor eating disorders "mental health literacy"? *Eating Disorders: The Journal of Treatment & Prevention, 21*(4), 310–327.

Greenfield, E. A. (2010). Child abuse as a life-course social determinant of adult health. *Maturitas, 66,* 51–55.

Gribble, K. E., & Mark Welch, D. B. (2013). Life-span extension by caloric restriction is determined by type and level of food reduction and by reproductive mode in *Brachionus manjavacas* (Rotifera). *Journals of Gerontology Series A: Biological Sciences and Medical Sciences, 68*(4), 349–358.

Groen, Y., Wijers, A. A., Tucha, O., & Althaus, M. (2013). Are there sex differences in ERPs related to processing empathy-evoking pictures? *Neuropsychologia, 51*(1), 142–155.

Groeneveld, M. G., Vermeer, H. J., van IJzendoorn, M. H., & Linting, M. (2010). Children's well-being and cortisol levels in home-based and center-based childcare. *Early Childhood Research Quarterly, 25*(4), 502–514.

Groopman, J. E. (2004). *The anatomy of hope: How patients prevail in the face of illness.* New York, NY: Random House.

Grossbaum, M. F., & Bates, G. W. (2002). Correlates of psychological well-being at midlife: The role of generativity, agency and communion, and narrative themes. *International Journal of Behavioral Development, 26,* 120–127.

Grossmann, K., Grossmann, K. E., & Kindler, H. (2005). Early care and the roots of attachment and partnership representations: The Bielefeld and Regensburg longitudinal studies. In K. E. Grossmann, K. Grossmann, & E. Waters (Eds.), *Attachment from infancy to adulthood: The major longitudinal studies* (pp. 98–136). New York, NY: Guilford Press.

Grossmann, I., Na, J., Varnum, M. E. W., Park, D. C., Kitayama, S., & Nisbett, R. E. (2010). Reasoning about social conflicts improves into old age. *Psychological and Cognitive Sciences, 107*(16), 7246–7250.

Grube, J. W., Bourdeau, B., Fisher, D. A., & Bersamin, M. (2008). *Television exposure and sexuality among adolescents: A longitudinal survey study.* Paper presented at the Biennial Meeting of the Society for Research in Adolescence. Chicago, IL.

Gschwind, Y. J., Bridenbaugh, S. A., & Kressig, R. W. (2010). Gait disorders and falls. *GeroPsych, 23*(1), 21–32.

Guan, S. A., Greenfield, P. M., & Orellana, M. F. (2014). Translating into understanding: Language brokering and prosocial development in emerging adults from immigrant families. *Journal of Adolescent Research, 29*(3), 331–355.

Guardino, C. M., & Schetter, C. D. (2014). Coping during pregnancy: A systematic review and recommendations. *Health Psychology Review, 8*(1), 70–94.

Guendelman, S., Kosa, J. L., Pearl, M., Graham, S., Goodman, J., & Kharrazi, M. (2009). Juggling work and breastfeeding: Effects of maternity leave and occupational characteristics. *Pediatrics, 123,* e38–e46.

Guerra, N. G., Williams, K. R., & Sadek, S. (2011). Understanding bullying and victimization during childhood and adolescence: A mixed methods study. *Child Development, 82*(1), 295–310.

Guerri, C., & Pascual, M. (2010). Mechanisms involved in the neurotoxic, cognitive, and neurobehavioral effects of alcohol consumption during adolescence. *Alcohol, 44*(1), 15–26.

Gunderson, E. A., Gripshover, S. J., Romero, C., Dweck, C. S., Goldin-Meadow, S., & Levine, S. C. (2013). Parent praise to 1- to 3-year-olds predicts children's motivational frameworks 5 years later. *Child Development, 84*(5), 1526–1541.

Gunther Moor, B., Bos, M. N., Crone, E. A., & van der Molen, M. W. (2014). Peer rejection cues induce cardiac slowing after transition into adolescence. *Developmental Psychology, 50*(3), 947–955.

Gupta, R. (2011). Death beliefs and practices from an Asian Indian American Hindu perspective. *Death Studies, 35,* 244–266.

Gustafson, K., & Baofeng, H. (2014). Elderly care and the one-child policy: Concerns, expectations and preparations for elderly life in a rural Chinese township. *Journal of Cross-Cultural Gerontology, 29*(1), 25–36.

Guttmacher Institute. (2011a). *Facts on American Teens' Sources of Information About Sex.* New York, NY: Guttmacher Institute.

Guttmacher Institute. (2011b). *In brief: Facts on American teens' sexual and reproductive health.* New York, NY: Guttmacher Institute.

Guttmacher Institute. (2014). *Contraceptive use in the United States.* Retrieved from http://www.guttmacher.org/pubs/fb_contr_use.html

Ha, J.-H. (2008). Changes in support from confidants, children, and friends following widowhood. *Journal of Marriage and Family, 70,* 306–318.

Ha, J.-H., & Ingersoll-Dayton, B. (2008). The effect of widowhood on international ambivalence. *Journals of Gerontology: Social Sciences, 63B*(1), S49–S58.

Habermas, T., Negele, A., & Mayer, F. B. (2010). "Honey, you're jumping about"—Mothers' scaffolding of their children's and adolescents' life narration. *Cognitive Development, 25,* 339–351.

Haddad, E., Chen, C., & Greenberger, E. (2011). The role of important nonparental adults (VIPs) in the lives of older adolescents: A comparison of three ethnic groups. *Journal of Youth and Adolescence, 40,* 310–319.

Hadden, B. W., Smith, C. V., & Webster, G. D. (2014). Relationship duration moderates associations between attachment and relationship quality: Meta-analytic support for the temporal adult romantic attachment model. *Personality and Social Psychology Review, 18*(1), 42–58.

Hagestad, G. O. (1985). Continuity and connectedness. In V. L. Bengtson & J. F. Robertson (Eds.), *Grandparenthood* (pp. 31–48). Thousand Oaks, CA: Sage.

Hahn-Holbrook, J., Haselton, M. G., Schetter, C. D., & Glynn, L. M. (2013). Does breastfeeding offer protection against maternal depressive symptomatology? A prospective study from pregnancy to 2 years after birth. *Archives of Women's Mental Health, 16*(5), 411–422.

Hakoyama, M., & MaloneBeach, E. E. (2013). Predictors of grandparent–grandchild closeness: An ecological perspective. *Journal of Intergenerational Relationships, 11*(1), 32–49.

Hall, G. S. (1969). *Adolescence.* New York, NY: Arno Press. (Original work published 1904).

Hall, S. (2011). "It's going to stop in this generation": Women with a history of child abuse resolving to raise their children without abuse. *Harvard Educational Review, 81*(1), 24–49.

Halperin, J. M., & Healey, D. M. (2011). The influences of environmental enrichment, cognitive enhancement, and physical exercise on brain development: Can we alter the developmental trajectory of ADHD? *Neuroscience and Biobehavioral Reviews, 35,* 621–634.

Halpern-Meekin, S., Manning, W. D., Giordano, P. C., & Longmore, M. A. (2013). Relationship churning in emerging adulthood: On/off relationships and sex with an ex. *Journal of Adolescent Research, 28*(2), 166–188.

Hamlin, J. K. (2013a). Failed attempts to help and harm: Intention versus outcome in preverbal infants' social evaluations. *Cognition, 128*(3), 451–474.

Hamlin, J. K. (2013b). Moral judgment and action in preverbal infants and toddlers: Evidence for an innate moral core. *Current Directions in Psychological Science, 22*(3), 186–193.

Hamlin, J. K., & Wynn, K. (2011). Young infants prefer prosocial to antisocial others. *Cognitive Development, 26*, 30–39.

Hamlin, J. K., Mahajan, N., Liberman, Z., & Wynn, K. (2013). Not like me = bad: Infants prefer those who harm dissimilar others. *Psychological Science, 24*(4), 589–594.

Hampson, S. E., Edmonds, G. W., Goldberg, L. R., Dubanoski, J. P., & Hillier, T. A. (2013). Childhood conscientiousness relates to objectively measured adult physical health four decades later. *Health Psychology, 32*(8), 925–928.

Hank, K., & Buber, I. (2009). Grandparents caring for their grandchildren: Findings from the 2004 Survey of Health, Ageing, and Retirement in Europe. *Journal of Family Issues, 30*, 53–73.

Harbourne, R. T., Lobo, M. A., Karst, G. M., & Galloway, J. C. (2013). Sit happens: Does sitting development perturb reaching development, or vice versa? *Infant Behavior and Development, 36*(3), 438–450.

Harley, K., & Reese, E. (1999). Origins of autobiographical memory. *Developmental Psychology, 35*, 1338–1348.

Harlow, C. M. (Ed.). (1986). *From learning to love: The selected papers of H. F. Harlow.* New York, NY: Praeger.

Harlow, H. F. (1958). The nature of love. *American Psychologist, 13*, 673–685.

Harlow, H. F., Harlow, M. K., Dodsworth, R. O., & Arling, G. L. (1966). Maternal behavior of rhesus monkeys deprived of mothering and peer associations in infancy. *Proceedings of the American Philosophical Society, 110*, 58–66.

Harriger, J. A., Calogero, R. M., Witherington, D. C., & Smith, J. E. (2010). Body size stereotyping and internalization of the thin ideal in preschool girls. *Sex Roles, 63*, 609–620.

Harris, J. R. (1995). Where is the child's environment? A group socialization theory of development. *Psychological Review, 102*, 458–489.

Harris, J. R. (1998). *The nurture assumption: Why children turn out the way they do.* New York, NY: Free Press.

Harris, J. R. (2002). Beyond the nurture assumption: Testing hypotheses about the child's environment. In J. G. Borkowski, S. L. Ramey, & M. Bristol-Power (Eds.), *Parenting and the child's world: Influences on academic, intellectual, and social-emotional development* (pp. 3–20). Mahwah, NJ: Erlbaum.

Harris, J. R. (2006). *No two alike: Human nature and human individuality.* New York, NY: Norton.

Harris, P., Wong, E., Farrington, S., Craig, T. R., Harrold, J. K., Oldanie, B., . . . Casarett, D. J. (2013). Patterns of functional decline in hospice: What can individuals and their families expect? *Journal of the American Geriatrics Society, 61*(3), 413–417.

Harris, T. S. (2010). Bruises in children: Normal or child abuse? *Journal of Pediatric Health Care, 24*(4), 216–221.

Harrist, A. W., Thompson, S. D., & Norris, D. J. (2007). Defining quality child care: Multiple stakeholder perspectives. *Early Education and Development, 18*(2), 305–336.

Hart, H. M., McAdams, D. P., Hirsch, B. J., & Bauer, J. J. (2001). Generativity and social involvement among African Americans and White adults. *Journal of Research in Personality, 35*, 208–230.

Harter, S. (1981). A new self-report scale of intrinsic versus extrinsic orientation in the classroom: Motivational and informational components. *Developmental Psychology, 17*, 300–312.

Harter, S. (1999). *The construction of the self: A developmental perspective.* New York, NY: Guilford Press.

Harter, S. (2006). Developmental and individual difference perspectives on self-esteem. In D. K. Mroczek, & T. D. Little (Eds.), *Handbook of personality development* (pp. 311–334). Mahwah, NJ: Erlbaum.

Harter, S., & Pike, R. (1984). The pictorial scale of perceived competence and social acceptance for young children. *Child Development, 55*, 1969–1982.

Hartup, W. W., & Stevens, N. (1997). Friendships and adaptation in the life course. *Psychological Bulletin, 121*, 355–370.

Hashimoto-Torii, K., Kawasawa, Y. I., Kuhn, A., & Rakic, P. (2011). Combined transcriptome analysis of fetal human and mouse cerebral cortex exposed to alcohol. *Proceedings of the National Academy of Sciences of the United States of America, 108*(10), 4212–4217.

Hashizume, Y. (2010). Releasing from the oppression: Caregiving for the elderly parents of Japanese working women. *Qualitative Health Research, 20*(6), 830–844.

Haskett, M. E., Neupert, S. D., & Okado, Y. (2014). Factors associated with 3-year stability and change in parenting behavior of abusive parents. *Journal of Child and Family Studies, 23*(2), 263–274.

Hausdorff, J. M., & Buchman, A. S. (2013). What links gait speed and MCI with dementia? A fresh look at the association between motor and cognitive function. *Journals of Gerontology Series A: Biological Sciences and Medical Sciences, 68*(4), 409–411.

Hawkins, A., Stenzel, A., Taylor, J., Chock, V. Y. & Hugdgens, L. (2013). Variables influencing pregnancy termination following prenatal diagnosis of fetal chromosome abnormalities. *Journal of Genetic Counseling, 22*, 238–248.

Hawley, P. H., Johnson, S. E., Mize, J. A., & McNamara, K. A. (2007). Physical attractiveness in preschoolers: Relationships with power, status, aggression, and social skills. *Journal of School Psychology, 45*, 499–521.

Hayslip, B., Jr., & Hansson, R. O. (2003). Death awareness and adjustment across the life span. In C. D. Bryant (Ed.), *Handbook of death and dying* (pp. 437–447). Thousand Oaks, CA: Sage.

Hayslip, B., Jr., & Patrick, J. H. (Eds.). (2003). *Working with custodial grandparents.* New York, NY: Springer.

Hazan, C., & Shaver, P. (1987). Romantic love conceptualized as an attachment process. *Journal of Personality and Social Psychology, 52*, 511–524.

Head, D., Bugg, J. M., Goate, A. M., Fagan, A. M. Minton, M. A., Bensinger, T., . . . Morris, J. C. (2012). Exercise engagement as a moderator of the effects of APOE genotype on amyloid deposition. *Archives of Neurology, 69*(5), 636–643.

Healthychildren.org. (n.d.) Retrieved from http://www.Healthychildren.org

Healy, E., Reichenberg, A., Nam, K. W., Allin, M. G., Walshe, M., Rifkin, L., . . . Nosarti, C. (2013). Preterm birth and adolescent social functioning—Alterations in emotion-processing brain areas. *Journal of Pediatrics, 163*(6), 1596–1604.

Hearing Loop. (n.d.) Retrieved from http://www.hearingloop.com

Heatherton, T. F. (2011). Neuroscience of self and self-regulation. *Annual Review of Psychology, 62*, 363–390.

Heaven, P. C. L., Ciarrochi, J., & Vialle, W. (2008). Self-nominated peer crowds, school achievement, and psychological adjustment in adolescents: Longitudinal analysis. *Personality and Individual Differences, 44,* 977–988.

Hehman, J. A., & Bugental, D. B. (2013). "Life stage-specific" variations in performance in response to age stereotypes. *Developmental Psychology, 49*(7), 1396–1406.

Helson, R., & Soto, C. J. (2005). Up and down in middle age: Monotonic and nonmonotonic changes in roles, status, and personality. *Journal of Personality and Social Psychology, 89*(2), 194–204.

Hemar-Nicolas, V., Ezan, P., Gollety, M., Guichard, N., & Leroy, J. (2013). How do children learn eating practices? Beyond the nutritional information, the importance of social eating. *Young Consumers, 14*(1), 5–18.

Hendry, L. B., & Kloep, M. (2010). How universal is emerging adulthood? An empirical example. *Journal of Youth Studies, 13*(2), 169–179.

Hengartner, M. P., Müller, M., Rodgers, S., Rössler, W., & Ajdacic-Gross, V. (2013). Can protective factors moderate the detrimental effects of child maltreatment on personality functioning? *Journal of Psychiatric Research, 47*(9), 1180–1186.

Henry, J., Phillips, L. H., Ruffman, T., & Bailey, P. E. (2013). A meta-analytic review of age differences in theory of mind. *Psychology and Aging, 28*(3), 826–839

Henry, L. A., Messer, D. J., & Nash, G. (2012). Executive functioning in children with specific language impairment. *Journal of Child Psychology and Psychiatry, 53,* 37–45.

Hensler, B. S., Schatschneider, C., Taylor, J., & Wagner, R. K. (2010). Behavioral genetic approach to the study of dyslexia. *Journal of Developmental and Behavioral Pediatrics, 31*(7), 525–532.

Heo, J., Lee, Y., McCormick, B. P., & Pedersen, P. M. (2010). Daily experience of serious leisure, flow, and subjective well-being of older adults. *Leisure Studies, 29*(2), 207–225.

Hepach, R., Vaish, A., & Tomasello, M. (2013). A new look at children's prosocial motivation. *Infancy, 18*(1), 67–90.

Hernández–Martínez, C., Val, V. A., Subías, J. E., & Sans, J. C. (2012). A longitudinal study on the effects of maternal smoking and secondhand smoke exposure during pregnancy on neonatal neurobehavior. *Early Human Development, 88*(6), 403–408.

Herrenkohl, T. I., Hong, S., Klika, J. B., Herrenkohl, R. C., & Russo, M. J. (2013). Developmental impacts of child abuse and neglect related to adult mental health, substance use, and physical health. *Journal of Family Violence, 28*(2), 191–199.

Herrera, F. (2013). "Men always adopt": Infertility and reproduction from a male perspective. *Journal of Family Issues, 34*(8), 1059–1080.

Herrnstein, R. J., & Murray, C. A. (1994). *The bell curve: Intelligence and class structure in American life.* New York, NY: Free Press.

Hershey, D. A., Henkens, K., & van Dalen, H. P. (2010). What drives retirement income worries in Europe? A multilevel analysis. *European Journal of Ageing, 7,* 301–311.

Hertzog, C. (1996). Research design in studies of aging and cognition. In J. E. Birren, K. W. Schaie, R. P. Abeles, M. Gatz, & T. A. Salthouse (Eds.), *Handbook of the psychology of aging* (4th ed. pp. 24–37). San Diego, CA: Academic Press.

Hess, T. M., & Smith, B. T. (2014). Aging and the impact of irrelevant information on social judgments. *Psychology and Aging, 29*(3), 542–553.

Hesse-Biber, S., Livingstone, S., Ramirez, D., Barko, E. B., & Johnson, A. L. (2010). Racial identity and body image among black female college students attending predominately white colleges. *Sex Roles, 63,* 697–711.

Hetherington, E. M., & Kelly, J. (2002). *For better or for worse: Divorce reconsidered.* New York, NY: Norton.

Hewitt, B., Haynes, M., & Baxter, J. (2013). Relationship dissolution and time on housework. *Journal of Comparative Family Studies, 44*(3), 327–340.

Higher Education Research Institute. (2013). Class of 2012: Findings from the college senior survey. *HERI Research Brief.* Retrieved from http://www.heri.ucla.edu/

Hill, P. L., & Turiano, N. A. (2014). Purpose in life as a predictor of mortality across adulthood. *Psychological Science, 25*(7), 1482–1486.

Hill, P. L., Jackson, J. J., Roberts, B. W., Lapsley, D. K., & Brandenberger, J. W. (2011). Change you can believe in: Changes in goal setting during emerging and young adulthood predict later adult well-being. *Social Psychological and Personality Science, 2*(2), 123–131.

Hinde, R. A. (2005). Ethology and attachment theory. In K. E. Grossmann, K. Grossmann, & E. Waters (Eds.), *Attachment from infancy to adulthood: The major longitudinal studies* (pp. 1–12). New York, NY: Guilford Press.

Hinduja, S., & Patchin, J. W. (2013). Social influences on cyberbullying behaviors among middle and high school students. *Journal of Youth and Adolescence, 42*(5), 711–722.

Hipwell, A. E., Keenan, K., Loeber, R., & Battista, D. (2010). Early predictors of sexually intimate behaviors in an urban sample of young girls. *Developmental Psychology, 46*(2), 366–378.

Hirschfield, P. J., & Gasper, J. (2011). The relationship between school engagement and delinquency in late childhood and early adolescence. *Journal of Youth and Adolescence, 40*(1), 3–22.

Hoff-Ginsberg, E. (1997). *Language development.* Belmont, CA: Brooks/Cole.

Hoffman, M. L. (1994). Discipline and internalization. *Developmental Psychology, 30,* 26–28.

Hoffman, M. L. (2001). Toward a comprehensive empathy-based theory of pro-social moral development. In A. C. Bohart and D. J. Stipek (Eds.), *Constructive and destructive behavior: Implications for family, school, and society* (pp. 61–86). Washington, DC: American Psychological Association.

Hofstede, G. (1981). Cultures and organizations. *International Studies of Management and Organization, 10*(4), 15–41.

Hofstede, G. (2001). *Culture's consequences: Comparing values, behaviors, institutions, and organizations across nations* (2nd ed.). Thousand Oaks, CA: Sage.

Holland, J. (1997). *Making vocational choices: A theory of vocational personalities and work environments* (3rd ed.). Odessa, FL: Psychological Assessment Resources.

Holland, L. A., Brown, T. A., & Keel, P. K. (2014). Defining features of unhealthy exercise associated with disordered eating and eating disorder diagnoses. *Psychology of Sport and Exercise, 15*(1), 116–123.

Holmes, T. H., & Rahe, R. H. (1967). The social readjustment rating scale. *Journal of Psychosomatic Research, 11,* 213–218.

Hoogman, M., Onnink, M., Cools, R., Aarts, E., Kan, C., Arias Vasquez, A., . . . Franke, B. (2013). The dopamine transporter haplotype and reward-related striatal responses in adult ADHD.

European Neuropsychopharmacology, 23(6), 469–478.

Hoover, E. (2011). *The Chronicle of Higher Education: Surveys of the public and presidents*. In *College's value goes deeper than the degree, graduates say*. Retreived from http://www.chronicle.com/article/Its-More-Than_the/127534

Hopper, J. (1993). The rhetoric of motives in divorce. *Journal of Marriage & the Family*, 55, 801–813.

House, B. R., Silk, J. B., Henrich, J., Barrett, H. C., Scelza, B. A., Boyette, A. H., . . . Laurence, S. (2013). Ontogeny of prosocial behavior across diverse societies. *Proceedings of the National Academy of Sciences of the United States of America*, 110(36), 14586–14591.

Hrdy, S. B. (1999). *Mother nature: A history of mothers, infants, and natural selection*. New York, NY: Pantheon Books.

Hu, S., & Kuh, G. D. (2003). Diversity experiences and college student learning and personal development. *Journal of College Student Development*, 44, 320–334.

Huang, H., Coleman, S., Bridge, J. A., Yonkers, K., & Katon, W. (2014). A meta–analysis of the relationship between antidepressant use in pregnancy and the risk of preterm birth and low birth weight. *General Hospital Psychiatry*, 36(1), 13–18.

Huddleston, J., & Ge, X. (2003). Boys at puberty: Psychosocial implications. In C. Hayward (Ed.), *Gender differences at puberty* (pp. 113–134). New York, NY: Cambridge University Press.

Hughes, M. L., Geraci, L., & De Forrest, R. L. (2013). Aging 5 years in 5 minutes: The effect of taking a memory test on older adults' subjective age. *Psychological Science*, 24(12), 2481–2488.

Hülsheger, U. R., Lang, J. B., Depenbrock, F., Fehrmann, C., Zijlstra, F. H., & Alberts, H. M. (2014). The power of presence: The role of mindfulness at work for daily levels and change trajectories of psychological detachment and sleep quality. *Journal of Applied Psychology*, 99(6), 1113–1128.

Humphrey, G. M. & Zimpfer, D. G. (2007). *Counselling for grief and bereavement*, 2nd ed. Los Angeles, CA: Sage.

Hungerford, T. L. (2003). Is there an American way of aging? Income dynamics of the elderly in the United States and Germany. *Research on Aging*, 25, 435–455.

Hunt, C. K. (2003). Concepts in caregiver research. *Journal of Nursing Scholarship*, 35, 27–32.

Hurks, P. P. M., & Hendriksen, J. G. M. (2011). Retrospective and prospective time deficits in childhood ADHD: The effects of task modality, duration, and symptom dimensions. *Child Neuropsychology*, 17(1), 34–50.

Hurt, T. R. (2013). Toward a deeper understanding of the meaning of marriage among Black men. *Journal of Family Issues*, 34(7), 859–884.

Hutchinson, D. M., Rapee, R. M., & Taylor, A. (2010). Body dissatisfaction and eating disturbances in early adolescence: A structural modeling investigation examining negative affect and peer factors. *The Journal of Early Adolescence*, 30(4), 489–517.

Hutteman, R., Hennecke, M., Orth, U., Reitz, A. K., & Specht, J. (2014). Developmental tasks as a framework to study personality development in adulthood and old age. *European Journal of Personality*, 28(3), 267–278.

Huttenlocher, P. R. (2002). *Neural plasticity: The effects of environment on the development of the cerebral cortex*. Cambridge, MA: Harvard University Press.

Hvas, L. (2001). Positive aspects of menopause: A qualitative study. *Maturitas*, 39, 11–17.

Hwang, S.-L., Gau, S. S.-F., Hsu, W.-Y., & Wu, Y.-Y. (2010). Deficits in interval timing measured by the dual-task paradigm among children and adolescents with attention-deficit/hyperactivity disorder. *Journal of Child Psychology and Psychiatry*, 51(3), 223–232.

Hwang, W. (2013). Who are people willing to date? Ethnic and gender patterns in online dating. *Race and Social Problems*, 5(1), 28–40.

Hyde, A., Drennan, J., Butler, M., Howlett, E., Carney, M., & Lohan, M. (2013). Parents' constructions of communication with their children about safer sex. *Journal of Clinical Nursing*, 22(23-24), 3438–3446.

Hymowitz, K., Carroll, J. S., Wilcox, W. B., & Kaye, K. (2013). *Knot yet: The benefits and costs of delayed marriage in America—Report summary*. Retrieved from http://www.twentysomethingmarriage.org/

Infurna, F. J., Gerstorf, D., & Zarit, S. H. (2013). Substantial changes in mastery perceptions of dementia caregivers with the placement of a care recipient. *Journals of Gerontology Series B:*

Psychological Sciences and Social Sciences, 68(2), 202–214.

Innes, S., & Payne, S. (2009). Advanced cancer patients' prognostic information preferences: A review. *Palliative Medicine*, 23, 29–39.

Ip, E. H., Church, T., Marshall, S. A., Zhang, Q., Marsh, A. P., Guralnik, J., . . . Rejeski, W. J. (2013). Physical activity increases gains in and prevents loss of physical function: Results from the lifestyle interventions and independence for elders pilot study. *Journals of Gerontology Series A: Biological Sciences and Medical Sciences*, 68(4), 426–432.

Israel, S., Moffitt, T. E., Belsky, D. W., Hancox, R. J., Poulton, R., Roberts, B. W., Thomson, W. M., & Caspi, A. (2014). Translating personality psychology to help personalize preventive medicine for young-adult patients. *Journal of Personality and Social Psychology*, 106(3), 484–498.

Ito, M., & Sharts-Hopko, N. C. (2002). Japanese women's experience of childbirth in the United States. *Health Care for Women International*, 23, 666–677.

Ito, Y., & Izumi-Taylor, S. (2013). A comparative study of fathers' thoughts about fatherhood in the USA and Japan. *Early Child Development and Care*, 183(11), 1689–1704.

Jackson, T., & Chen, H. (2008). Predicting changes in eating disorder symptoms among Chinese adolescents: A 9-month prospective study. *Journal of Psychosomatic Research*, 64, 87–95.

Jaffe, J., & Diamond, M. O. (2011). *Reproductive trauma: Psychotherapy with infertility and pregnancy loss clients*. Washington, DC.: American Psychological Association.

Jaffee, S. R., Bowes, L., Ouellet-Morin, I., Fisher, H. L., Moffitt, T. E., Merrick, M. T., & Arseneault, L. (2013). Safe, stable, nurturing relationships break the intergenerational cycle of abuse: A prospective nationally representative cohort of children in the United Kingdom. *Journal of Adolescent Health*, 53(4, Suppl.), S4–S10.

Jang, H., Reeve, J., & Deci, E. L. (2010). Engaging students in learning activities: It is not autonomy support or structure but autonomy support and structure. *Journal of Educational Psychology*, 102(3), 588–600.

Jensen, C., Steinhausen, H., & Lauritson, M. B. (2014). Time trends over 16 years in incidence rates of autism spectrum disorders across the lifespan based on nationwide Danish register data. In *Journal of Autism Development Disorders*, 44(8), 1808–1818.

Jensen, H., Grøn, R., Lidegaard, Ø., Pedersen, L., Andersen, P., & Kessing, L. (2013). The effects of maternal depression and use of antidepressants during pregnancy on risk of a child small for gestational age. *Psychopharmacology*, 228(2), 199–205.

Jensen, T. M., Shafer, K., & Larson, J. H. (2014). (Step)parenting attitudes and expectations: Implications for stepfamily functioning and clinical intervention. *Families in Society*, 95(3), 213–220.

Jenson, W. R., Olympia, D., Farley, M., & Clark, E. (2004). Positive psychology and externalizing students in a sea of negativity. *Psychology in the Schools, 41*, 67–79.

Jette, A. M., Assmann, S. F., Rooks, D., Harris, B. A., & Crawford, S. (1998). Interrelationships among disablement concepts. *Journals of Gerontology Series A: Biological Sciences and Medical Sciences*, 53A, M395–M404.

Johns, M. M., Zimmerman, M., & Bauermeister, J. A. (2013). Sexual attraction, sexual identity, and psychosocial wellbeing in a national sample of young women during emerging adulthood. *Journal of Youth and Adolescence*, 42(1), 82–95.

Johnson, J., & Rochkind, J. (2011). *With their whole lives ahead of them: Myths and realities about why so many students fail to finish college (The Public Agenda Report).* In *The Bill and Melinda Gates Foundation.* Retrieved from http://www.publicagenda.org/files/theirwholelivesaheadofthem.pdf

Johnson, K. M. (2013). Making families: Organizational boundary work in US egg and sperm donation. *Social Science & Medicine, 99*, 64–71.

Johnson, K. S., Kuchibhatla, M., Payne, R., & Tulsky, J. A. (2013). Race and residence: Intercounty variation in black-white differences in hospice use. *Journal of Pain and Symptom Management*, 46(5), 681–690.

Johnson, M., Crosnoe, R., & Elder, G. R. (2011). Insights on adolescence from a life course perspective. *Journal of Research on Adolescence*, 21(1), 273–280.

Johnson, R. A., & Bibbo, J. (2014). Relocation decisions and constructing the meaning of home: A phenomenological study of the transition into a nursing home. *Journal of Aging Studies, 30*, 56–63.

Johnson, R. W. (2009). Employment opportunities at older ages: Introduction to the special issue. *Research on Aging, 31*, 3–16.

Johnston, L. D., O'Malley, P. M., Bachman, J. G., & Schulenberg, J. E. (2011). *Marijuana use continues to rise among U.S. teens, while alcohol use hits historic lows.* In *University of Michigan New Service: Ann Arbor, MI.* Retrieved from http://www.monitoringthefuture.org

Johnston, L. D., O'Malley, P. M., Miech, R. A., Bachman, J. G., & Schulenberg, J. E. (2014). *Monitoring the Future national survey results on drug use: 1975–2013: Overview, key findings on adolescent drug use.* Ann Arbor: Institute for Social Research, University of Michigan.

Johri, M., Beland, F., & Bergman, H. (2003). International experiments in integrated care for the elderly: A synthesis of the evidence. *International Journal of Geriatric Psychiatry, 18*, 222–235.

Joinson, C., Heron, J., Araya, R., & Lewis, G. (2013). Early menarche and depressive symptoms from adolescence to young adulthood in a UK cohort. *Journal of the American Academy of Child & Adolescent Psychiatry*, 52(6), 591–598.

Jokhi, R. P., & Whitby, E. H. (2011). Magnetic resonance imaging of the fetus. *Developmental Medicine & Child Neurology, 53*, 18–28.

Jones, B. K., & McAdams, D. P. (2013). Becoming generative: Socializing influences recalled in life stories in late midlife. *Journal of Adult Development*, 20(3), 158–172.

Jonkmann, K., Thoemmes, F., Lüdtke, O., & Trautwein, U. (2014). Personality traits and living arrangements in young adulthood: Selection and socialization. *Developmental Psychology*, 50(3), 683–698.

Jordan, A. H., & Litz, B. T. (2014). Prolonged grief disorder: Diagnostic, assessment, and treatment considerations. *Professional Psychology: Research and Practice*, 45(3), 180–187.

Jorgensen, B. S., Jamieson, R. D., & Martin, J. F. (2010). Income, sense of community and subjective well-being: Combining economic and psychological variables. *Journal of Economic Psychology*, 31(4), 612–623.

Jowett, A. (2014). "But if you legalise same-sex marriage. . .": Arguments against marriage equality in the British press. *Feminism & Psychology*, 24(1), 37–55.

Joyce, B. T., & Lau, D. T. (2013). Hospice experiences and approaches to support and assess family caregivers in managing medications for home hospice patients: A providers survey. *Palliative Medicine*, 27(4), 329–338.

Jozwiak, N., Preville, M., & Vasiliadis, H. (2013). Bereavement-related depression in the older adult population: A distinct disorder? *Journal of Affective Disorders*, 151(3), 1083–1089.

Juarascio, A. S., Shoaib, A., & Timko, C. A. (2010). Pro-eating disorder communities on social networking sites: A content analysis. *Eating Disorders, 18*, 393–407.

Judge, T. A., & Hurst, C. (2007). Capitalizing on one's advantages: Role of core self-evaluations. *Journal of Applied Psychology*, 92(5), 1212–1227.

Julian, M. M. (2013). Age at adoption from institutional care as a window into the lasting effects of early experiences. *Clinical Child and Family Psychology Review*, 16(2), 101–145.

Jung, C. G. (1933). *Modern man in search of a soul.* Oxford, England: Harcourt.

Jurkowski, J. M., Mills, L. G., Lawson, H. A., Bovenzi, M. C., Quartimon, R., & Davison, K. K. (2013). Engaging low-income parents in childhood obesity prevention from start to finish: A case study. *Journal of Community Health: The Publication for Health Promotion and Disease Prevention*, 38(1), 1–11.

Kagan, J. (1984). *The nature of the child.* New York, NY: Basic Books.

Kagan, J. (1994). *Galen's prophecy: Temperament in human nature.* New York, NY: Basic Books.

Kagan, J. (1998). *Galen's prophecy: Temperament in human nature.* Boulder, CO: Westview Press.

Källstrand-Eriksson, J., Baigi, A., Buer, N., & Hildingh, C. (2013). Perceived vision-related quality of life and risk of falling among community living elderly people. *Scandinavian Journal of Caring Sciences*, 27(2), 433–439.

Kalmijn, M. (2013). Adult children's relationships with married parents, divorced parents, and stepparents: Biology, marriage, or residence? *Journal of Marriage and Family*, 75(5), 1181–1193.

Kamp Dush, C. M., Rhoades, G. K., Sandberg-Thoma, S. E., & Schoppe-Sullivan, S. J. (2014). Commitment across the transition to parenthood among married and cohabiting couples. *Couple* and Family Psychology: Research and Practice, 3(2), 126–136.

Kane, R. A. (1995–1996). Transforming care institutions for the frail elderly: Out of one shall be many. Generations, 14(4), 62–68.

Kannai, R. (2008). Zohara. Patient Education and Counseling, 71, 145–147.

Karen, R. (1998). Becoming attached: First relationships and how they shape our capacity to love. London, England: Oxford University Press.

Karlamangla, A. S., Miller-Martinez, D., Lachman, M. E., Tun, P. A., Koretz, B. K., & Seeman, T. E. (2014). Biological correlates of adult cognition: Midlife in the United States (MIDUS). Neurobiology of Aging, 35(2), 387–394.

Karlsson, C., & Berggren, I. (2011). Dignified end-of-life care in the patients' own homes. Nursing Ethics, 18(3), 374–385.

Karni, E., Leshno, M., & Rapaport, S. (2014). Helping patients and physicians reach individualized medical decisions: Theory and application to prenatal diagnostic testing. Theory and Decision, 76(4), 451–467.

Karns, J. T. (2001). Health, nutrition, and safety. In G. Bremner & A. Fogel (Eds.), Blackwell handbook of infant development (pp. 693–725). Malden, MA: Blackwell.

Kasper, J. D., Pezzin, L. E., & Rice, J. B. (2010). Stability and changes in living arrangements: Relationship to nursing home admission and timing of placement. Journals of Gerontology: Social Sciences, 65B(6), 783–791.

Kastenbaum, R. (2004). On our way: The final passage through life and death. Berkeley, CA: University of California Press.

Kato, K., & Pedersen, N. L. (2005). Personality and coping: A study of twins reared apart and twins reared together. Behavior Genetics, 35, 147–158.

Katz, I., Kaplan, A., & Gueta, G. (2010). Students' needs, teachers' support, and motivation for doing homework: A cross-sectional study. Journal of Experimental Education, 78(2), 246–267.

Katz-Wise, S. L., Priess, A., & Hyde, J. S. (2010). Gender-role attitudes and behavior across the transition to parenthood. American Psychological Association, 46(1), 18–28.

Keefe, M. R., Karlsen, K. A., Lobo, M. L., Kotzer, A. M., & Dudley, W. N. (2006). Reducing parenting stress in families with irritable infants. Nursing Research, 55(3), 198–205.

Keel, P. K., Baxter, M. G., Heatherton, T. F., & Joiner, T. E. (2007). A 20-year longitudinal study of body weight, dieting, and eating disorder symptoms. Journal of Abnormal Psychology, 116(2), 422–432.

Keen, C., Murray, C., & Payne, S. (2013). Sensing the presence of the deceased: A narrative review. Mental Health, Religion & Culture, 16(4), 384–402.

Keijsers, L., & Poulin, F. (2013). Developmental changes in parent–child communication throughout adolescence. Developmental Psychology, 49(12), 2301–2308.

Keller, M. A., & Goldberg, W. A. (2004). Co-sleeping: Help or hindrance for young children's independence? Infant and Child Development, 13, 369–388.

Kelley, M., Demiris, G., Nguyen, H., Oliver, D. P., & Wittenberg-Lyles, E. (2013). Informal hospice caregiver pain management concerns: A qualitative study. Palliative Medicine, 27(7), 673–682.

Kellman, P. J., & Banks, M. S. (1998). Infant visual perception. In W. Damon (Series ed.) & D. Kuhn & R. S. Siegler (Vol. eds.), Handbook of child psychology: Volume 2. Cognition, perception, and language (pp. 103–146). Hoboken, NJ: Wiley.

Kelly, J. B. (2000). Children's adjustment in conflicted marriage and divorce: A decade review of research. Journal of the American Academy of Child & Adolescent Psychiatry, 39, 963–973.

Kelly, T. B., Tolson, D., Day, T., McColgan, G., Thilo, K., & Maclaren, W. (2013). Older people's views on what they need to successfully adjust to life with a hearing aid. Health and Social Care in the Community, 21 (3), 293–302.

Kelmanson, I. (2013). Swaddling: Maternal option and sleep behaviour in two-month-old infants. Child Care in Practice, 19(1), 36–48.

Kemper, S., & Mitzner, T. L. (2001). Language production and comprehension. In J. E. Birren & K. W. Schaie (Eds.), Handbook of the psychology of aging (5th ed. pp. 378–398). San Diego, CA: Academic Press.

Keyes, K. M., Smith, G., & Susser, E. E. (2014). Associations of prenatal maternal smoking with offspring hyperactivity: Causal or confounded? Psychological Medicine, 44(4), 857–867.

Keys, C. L. (2007). Promoting and protecting mental health as flourishing: A complementary strategy for improving national mental health. American Psychologist, 61, 95–108.

Kiang, L., & Fuligni, A. J. (2009). Ethnic identity and family processes among adolescents from Latin American, Asian, and European backgrounds. Journal of Youth and Adolescence, 38, 228–241.

Kiang, L., Witkow, M. R., & Champagne, M. C. (2013). Normative changes in ethnic and American identities and links with adjustment among Asian American adolescents. Developmental Psychology, 49(9), 1713–1722.

Kiely, K. M., Anstey, K. J., & Luszcz, M. A. (2013). Dual sensory loss and depressive symptoms: The importance of hearing, daily functioning, and activity engagement. Frontiers in Human Neuroscience, 7, 837.

Kiiski, J., Määttä, K., & Uusiautti, S. (2013). "For better and for worse, or until . . .": On divorce and guilt. Journal of Divorce & Remarriage, 54(7), 519–536.

Killewald, A. (2013). A reconsideration of the fatherhood premium: Marriage, coresidence, biology, and fathers' wages. American Sociological Review, 78(1), 96–116.

Kim, B., & Teti, D. M. (2014). Maternal emotional availability during infant bedtime: An ecological framework. Journal of Family Psychology, 28(1), 1–11.

Kim, J., & Cicchetti, D. (2010). Longitudinal pathways linking child maltreatment, emotion regulation, peer relations, and psychopathology. Journal of Child Psychology and Psychiatry, 51(6), 706–716.

Kim, J., & Deater-Deckard, K. (2011). Dynamic changes in anger, externalizing and internalizing problems: Attention and regulation. Journal of Child Psychology and Psychiatry, 52(2), 156–166.

Kim, M., & Park, I. J. K. (2011). Testing the moderating effect of parent-adolescent communication on the acculturation gap-distress relation in Korean American families. Journal of Youth and Adolescence, 40, 1661–1673.

Kim, S. U., Lee, H. J., & Kim, Y. B. (2013). Neural stem cell-based treatment for neurodegenerative diseases. Neuropathology, 33(5), 491–504.

Kim, S. Y., Chen, Q., Wang, Y., Shen, Y., & Orozco-Lapray, D. (2013). Longitudinal linkages among parent–child acculturation discrepancy, parenting, parent–child sense of alienation, and adolescent adjustment in Chinese immigrant families. *Developmental Psychology, 49*(5), 900–912.

Kim, S. Y., Wang, Y., Orozco-Lapray, D., Shen, Y., & Murtuza, M. (2013). Does "tiger parenting" exist? Parenting profiles of Chinese Americans and adolescent developmental outcomes. *Asian American Journal of Psychology, 4*(1), 7–18.

Kinniburgh-White, R., Cartwright, C., & Seymour, F. (2010). Young adults' narratives of relational development with stepfathers. *Journal of Social and Personal Relationships, 27*(7), 890–907.

Kins, E., & Beyers, W. (2010). Failure to launch, failure to achieve criteria for adulthood. *Journal of Adolescence Research, 25*(5), 743–777.

Kins, E., de Mol, J., & Beyers, W. (2014). "Why should I leave?" Belgian emerging adults' departure from home. *Journal of Adolescent Research, 29*(1), 89–119.

Kinsella, K., & Velkoff, V. A. (2001). *An aging world: 2001* (Series P95/01-1). Washington, DC: U.S. Census Bureau.

Kippersluis, H., O'Donnell, O., Doorslaer, E., & Ourti, T. V. (2010). Socioeconomic differences in health over the life cycle in an egalitarian country. *Social Science & Medicine, 70,* 428–438.

Kitahara, M. (1989). Childhood in Japanese culture. *Journal of Psychohistory, 17,* 43–72.

Kitzinger, S. (2000). *Rediscovering birth.* New York, NY: Pocket Books.

Kleinplatz, P. J., Ménard, A. D., Paradis, N., Campbell, M., & Dalgleish, T. L. (2013). Beyond sexual stereotypes: Revealing group similarities and differences in optimal sexuality. *Canadian Journal of Behavioural Science/Revue Canadienne des Sciences du Comportement, 45*(3), 250–258.

Kloep, M., & Hendry, L. B. (2010). Letting go or holding on? Parents' perceptions of their relationships with their children during emerging adulthood. *British Journal of Developmental Psychology, 28*(4), 817–834.

Klusmann, D. (2002). Sexual motivation and the duration of partnership. *Archives of Sexual Behavior, 31,* 275–287.

Knox, M. (2010). On hitting children: A review of corporal punishment in the United States. *Journal of Pediatric Health Care, 24*(2), 103–107.

Ko, E., & Lee, J. (2014). Completion of advance directives among low-income older adults: Does race/ethnicity matter?

American Journal of Hospice & Palliative Medicine, 31(3), 247–253.

Kochanska, G., Aksan, N., Penney, S. J., & Boldt, L. J. (2007). Parental personality as an inner resource that moderates the impact of ecological adversity on parenting. *Journal of Personality and Social Psychology, 92*(1), 136–150.

Kochanska, G., Coy, K. C., & Murray, K. T. (2001). The development of self-regulation in the first four years of life. *Child Development, 72,* 1091–1111.

Kochanska, G., & Kim, S. (2013). Early attachment organization with both parents and future behavior problems: From infancy to middle childhood. *Child Development, 84*(1), 283–296.

Kochanska, G., & Knaack, A. (2003). Effortful control as a personality characteristic of young children: Antecedents, correlates, and consequences. *Journal of Personality, 71,* 1087–1112.

Kochanska, G., Woodard, J., Kim, S., Koenig, J. L., Yoon, J. E., & Barry, R. A. (2010). Positive socialization mechanisms in secure and insecure parent-child dyads: Two longitudinal studies. *Journal of Child Psychology and Psychiatry, 51*(9), 998–1009.

Koenig, T. L., Lee, J. H., Macmillan, K. R., Fields, N. L., & Spano, R. (2014). Older adult and family member perspectives of the decision-making process involved in moving to assisted living. *Qualitative Social Work, 13*(3), 335–350.

Koerner, S. S., Shirai, Y., & Kenyon, D. B. (2010). Sociocontextual circumstances in daily stress reactivity among caregivers for elder relatives. *Journals of Gerontology: Psychological Sciences, 65B*(5), 561–572.

Kogan, A., Impett, E. A., Oveis, C., Hui, B., Gordon, A. M., & Keltner, D. (2010). When giving feels good: The intrinsic benefits of sacrifice in romantic relationships for the communally motivated. *Psychological Science, 21*(12), 1918–1924.

Kohlberg, L. (1966). Moral education in the schools: A developmental view. *School Review, 74,* 1–30.

Kohlberg, L. (1981). *The meaning and measurement of moral development.* Worcester, MA: Clark University Press.

Kohlberg, L. (1984). *The psychology of moral development: The nature and validity of moral stages.* San Francisco: Harper & Row.

Komarraju, M., Musulkin, S., & Bhattacharya, G. (2010). Role of student-faculty interactions in developing

college students' academic self-concept, motivation, and achievement. *Journal of College Student Development, 51*(1), 332–342.

Konner, M. (2010). *The evolution of childhood.* Cambridge, MA: Harvard University Press.

Kooij, D. M., Bal, P. M., & Kanfer, R. (2014). Future time perspective and promotion focus as determinants of intra-individual change in work motivation. *Psychology and Aging, 29*(2), 319–328.

Koolschijn, P. C., & Crone, E. A. (2013). Sex differences and structural brain maturation from childhood to early adulthood. *Developmental Cognitive Neuroscience, 5,* 106–118.

Kopala-Sibley, D. C., Mongrain, M., & Zuroff, D. C. (2013). A lifespan perspective on dependency and self-criticism: Age-related differences from 18 to 59. *Journal of Adult Development, 20*(3), 126–141.

Kornhaber, M., Griffith, K., & Tyler, A. (2014). It's not education by zip code anymore—but what is it? Conceptions of equity under the Common Core. *Education Policy Analysis Archives, 22,* 4.

Kornrich, S., Brines, J., & Leupp, K. (2013). Egalitarianism, housework, and sexual frequency in marriage. *American Sociological Review, 78*(1), 26–50.

Kot, F. C. (2014). The impact of centralized advising on first-year academic performance and second-year enrollment behavior. *Research in Higher Education, 55*(6), 527–563.

Kozol, J. (1988). *Rachel and her children: Homeless families in America.* New York, NY: Crown.

Kozol, J. (2005). *The shame of the nation: The restoration of apartheid schooling in America.* New York, NY: Crown.

Kramer, B. J., & Thompson, E. H. (2002). *Men as caregivers: Theory, research, and service implications.* New York, NY: Springer.

Krampe, R. T., & Baltes, P. B. (2003). Intelligence as adaptive resource development and resource allocation: A new look through the lenses of SOC and expertise. In R. J. Sternberg & E. L. Grigorenko (Eds.), *The psychology of abilities, competencies, and expertise* (pp. 31–68). New York, NY: Cambridge University Press.

Kreicbergs, U., Valdimarsdóttir, U., Onelöv, E., Henter, J.-I., & Steineck, G. (2004). Talking about death with children who have severe malignant disease.

New England Journal of Medicine, 351, 1175–1186.

Kreppner, J., Rutter, M., Marvin, R., O'Conner, T., & Sonuga-Barke, E. (2011). Assessing the concept of the "insecure-other" category in the Cassidy-Marvin scheme: Changes between 4 and 6 years in the English and Romanian adoptee study. *Social development, 20*(1), 1–16.

Kretsch, N., & Harden, K. P. (2014). Pubertal development and peer influence on risky decision making. *The Journal of Early Adolescence, 34*(3), 339–359.

Kroger, J. (2000). *Identity development: Adolescence through adulthood.* Thousand Oaks, CA: Sage.

Kronenberg, M. E., Hansel, T. C., Brennan, A. M., Osofsky, H. J., Osofsky, J. D., & Lawrason, B. (2010). Children of Katrina: Lessons learned about post-disaster symptoms and recovery patterns. *Child Development, 81*(4), 1241–1259.

Krstev, S., Marinković, J., Simić, S., Kocev, N., & Bondy, S. J. (2013). The influence of maternal smoking and exposure to residential ETS on pregnancy outcomes: A retrospective national study. *Maternal and Child Health Journal, 17*(9), 1591–1598.

Kübler-Ross, E. (1969). *On death and dying.* New York, NY: Macmillan.

Kuhn, D. (1989). Children and adults as intuitive scientists. *Psychological Review, 96,* 674–689.

Kulik, L. (2007). Contemporary midlife grandparenthood. In V. Muhlbauer, & J. C. Chrisler (Eds.), *Women over 50: Psychological perspectives* (pp. 131–146). New York, NY: Springer Science + Business Media.

Kunze, F., Boehm, S., & Bruch, H. (2013). Age, resistance to change, and job performance. *Journal of Managerial Psychology, 28*(7-8), 741–760.

Kusner, K. G., Mahoney, A., Pargament, K. I., & DeMaris, A. (2014). Sanctification of marriage and spiritual intimacy predicting observed marital interactions across the transition to parenthood. *Journal of Family Psychology, 28*(5), 604–614.

Labouvie-Vief, G. (1992). A neo-Piagetian perspective on adult cognitive development. In R. J. Sternberg & C. A. Berg (Eds.), *Intellectual development* (pp. 197–228). New York, NY: Cambridge University Press.

Labouvie-Vief, G. (2006). Emerging structures of adult thought. In J. J. Arnett & J. L. Tanner (Eds.), *Emerging adults in America: Coming of age in the 21st century* (pp. 59–84). Washington, DC: American Psychological Association.

Lachman, M. E. (2004). Development in midlife. *Annual Review of Psychology, 55,* 305–331.

Ladis, K., Daniels, N., & Kawachi, I. (2009). Exploring the relationship between absolute and relative position and late-life depression: Evidence from 10 European countries. *The Gerontologist, 50*(1), 48–59.

LaFontana, K. M., & Cillessen, A. H. N. (2010). Developmental changes in the priority of perceived status in childhood and adolescence. *Social Development, 19*(1), 130–147.

Lagattuta, K., Sayfan, L., & Blattman, A. J. (2010). Forgetting common ground: Six- to seven-year-olds have an overinterpretive theory of mind. *Developmental Psychology, 46*(6), 1417–1432.

Laible, D. J. (2004). Mother-child discourse surrounding a child's past behavior at 30 months: Links to emotional understanding and early conscience development at 36 months. *Merrill-Palmer Quarterly, 50,* 159–180.

Lamb, M. E. (1997). *The role of the father in child development* (3rd ed.). Hoboken, NJ: Wiley.

Landerl, K., & Moll, K. (2010). Comorbidity of learning disorders: Prevalence and familial transmission. *Journal of Child Psychology and Psychiatry, 51*(3), 287–294.

Landor, A., Simons, L. G., Simons, R. L., Brody, G. H., & Gibbons, F. X. (2011). The role of religiosity in the relationship between parents, peers, and adolescents in risky sexual behavior. *Journal of Youth and Adolescence, 40,* 296–309.

Lane, J. D., Wellman, H. M., Olson, S. L., Miller, A. L., Wang, L., & Tardif, T. (2013). Relations between temperament and theory of mind development in the United States and China: Biological and behavioral correlates of preschoolers' false-belief understanding. *Developmental Psychology, 49*(5), 825–836.

Lang, F. R., Weiss, D., Gerstorf, D., & Wagner, G. G. (2013). Forecasting life satisfaction across adulthood: Benefits of seeing a dark future? *Psychology and Aging, 28*(1), 249–261.

Lansford, J. E., Malone, P. S., Dodge, K. A., Pettit, G. S., & Bates, J. E. (2010). Developmental cascades of peer rejection, social information processing

biases, and aggression during middle childhood. *Development and Psychopathology, 22*(3), 593–602.

Laplante-Levesque, A., Hickson, L., & Worrall, L. (2010). Rehabilitation of older adults with hearing impairment: A critical review. *Journal of Aging and Health, 22*(2), 143–153.

Larsen, L., Hartmann, P., & Nyborg, H. (2007). The stability of general intelligence from early adulthood to middle age. *Intelligence, 36*(1), 29–34.

Larson, R. W., & Tran, S. P. (2014). Invited commentary: Positive youth development and human complexity. *Journal of Youth and Adolescence, 43*(6), 1012–1017.

Larsson, H., Andkarsater, H., Rastam, M., Chang, Z., & Lichtenstein, O. (2012). Childhood attention-deficit hyperactivity disorder as an extreme of a continuous trait: A quantitative genetic study of 8,500 twin pairs. *Journal of Child Psychology and Psychiatry, 53*(1), 73–80.

LaRusso, M. D., Romer, D., & Selman, R. L. (2008). Teachers as builders of respectful school climates: Implications for adolescent drug use norms and depressive symptoms in high school. *Journal of Youth and Adolescence, 37,* 386–398.

Larzelere, R. E., & Kuhn, B. R. (2005). Comparing child outcomes of physical punishment and alternative disciplinary tactics: A meta-analysis. *Clinical Child and Family Psychology Review, 8,* 1–37.

Latz, S., Wolf, A. W., & Lozoff, B. (1999). Cosleeping in context: Sleep practices and problems in young children in Japan and the United States. *Archives of Pediatrics & Adolescent Medicine, 153,* 339–346.

Laukkanen, J., Ojansuu, U., Tolvanen, A., Alatupa, S., & Aunola, K. (2014). Child's difficult temperament and mothers' parenting styles. *Journal of Child and Family Studies, 23*(2), 312–323.

Lavadera, A. L., Caravelli, L., & Togliatti, M. M. (2013). Child custody in Italian management of divorce. *Journal of Family Issues, 34*(11), 1536–1562.

Lavezzi, A. M., Corna, M., Mingrone, R., & Matturri, L. (2010). Study of the human hypoglossal nucleus: Normal development and morpho-functional alterations in sudden unexplained late fetal and infant death. *Brain & Development, 32,* 275–284.

Lavezzi, A. M., Matturri, L., Del Corno, G., & Johanson, C. E. (2013). Vulnerability of fourth ventricle choroid plexus in sudden unexplained fetal and infant death syndromes related to smoking mothers. *International Journal of Developmental Neuroscience, 31*(5), 319–327.

Lavner, J. A., & Bradbury, T. N. (2010). Patterns of change in marital satisfaction over the newlywed years. *Journal of Marriage and Family, 72,* 1171–1187.

Lavner, J. A., Karney, B. R., & Bradbury, T. N. (2013). Newlyweds' optimistic forecasts of their marriage: For better or for worse? *Journal of Family Psychology, 27*(4), 531–540.

Lawler, M., & Nixon, E. (2011). Body dissatisfaction among adolescent boys and girls: The effects of body mass, peer appearance culture and internalization of appearance ideals. *Journal of Youth and Adolescence, 40,* 59–71.

Lawn, J. E., Blencowe, H., Pattinson, R., Cousens, S., Kumar, R., Ibiebele, I., . . . Stanton, C. (2011). Stillbirths: Where? When? Why? How to make the data count? *The Lancet, 377*(9775), 1448–1463.

Lawson, G. W., & Keirse, M. C. (2013). Reflections on the maternal mortality Millennium Goal. *Birth: Issues in Perinatal Care, 40*(2), 96–102.

Leavitt, J. W. (1986). *Brought to bed: Childbearing in America, 1750 to 1950.* New York, NY: Oxford University Press.

Lecanuet, J. P., Graniere-Deferre, C., Jacquet, A. Y., & DeCasper, A. J. (2000). Fetal discrimination of low-pitched musical notes. *Developmental Psychobiology, 36,* 29–39.

Lee, E. A. E., & Troop-Gordon, W. (2011). Peer processes and gender role development: Changes in gender atypicality related to negative peer treatment and children's friendships. *Sex Roles, 64,* 90–102.

Lee, E. H., Zhou, Q., Ly, J., Main, A., Tao, A., & Chen, S. H. (2014). Neighborhood characteristics, parenting styles, and children's behavioral problems in Chinese American immigrant families. *Cultural Diversity & Ethnic Minority Psychology, 20*(2), 202–212.

Lee, J. (2008). "A Kotex and a smile": Mothers and daughters at menarche. *Journal of Family Issues, 29,* 1325–1347.

Lee, V. E., & Burkam, D. T. (2002). *Inequality at the starting gate: Social background differences in achievement as children begin school.* Washington, D.C. Economic Policy Institute.

Lee, Y., & Styne, D. (2013). Influences on the onset and tempo of puberty in human beings and implications for adolescent psychological development. *Hormones and Behavior, 64*(2), 250–261.

Leeming, D., Williamson, I., Lyttle, S., & Johnson, S. (2013). Socially sensitive lactation: Exploring the social context of breastfeeding. *Psychology & Health, 28*(4), 450–468.

Leicht, K. T., & Fitzgerald, S. T. (2014). The real reason 60 is the new 30: Consumer debt and income insecurity in late middle age. *The Sociological Quarterly, 55*(2), 236–260.

Lenroot, R. K., & Giedd, J. N. (2010). Sex differences in the adolescent brain. *Brain and Cognition, 72,* 46–55.

Lenz, A. S., Taylor, R., Fleming, M., & Serman, N. (2014). Effectiveness of dialectical behavior therapy for treating eating disorders. *Journal of Counseling & Development, 92*(1), 26–35.

Leppänen, P. H. T., Hämäläinen, J. A., Salminen, H. K., Eklund, K. M., Guttorm, T. K., Lohvansuu, K., . . . Lyytinen, H. (2010). Newborn brain event-related potentials revealing atypical processing of sound frequency and the subsequent association with later literacy skills in children with familial dyslexia. *Cortex, 46,* 1362–1376.

Lepper, M. R., Greene, D., & Nisbett, R. E. (1973). Undermining children's intrinsic interest with extrinsic reward: A test of the "overjustification" hypothesis. *Journal of Personality and Social Psychology, 28,* 129–137.

Lerner, R. M. (1998). Theories of human development: Contemporary perspectives. In W. Damon (Series ed.) & R. M. Lerner (Vol. ed.). *Handbook of child psychology: Vol. 1. Theoretical models of human development* (5th ed. pp. 1–24). Hoboken, NJ: Wiley.

Lerner, R. M., Dowling, E. M., & Anderson, P. M. (2003). Positive youth development: Thriving as the basis of personhood and civil society. *Applied Developmental Science, 7,* 172–180.

Lerner, R. M., Dowling, E., & Roth, S. L. (2003). Contributions of lifespan psychology to the future elaboration of developmental systems theory. In U. M. Staudinger & U. Lindenberger (Eds.), *Understanding human development: Dialogues with lifespan psychology* (pp. 413–422). Dordrecht, Netherlands: Kluwer Academic.

Lerner, R. M., von Eye, A., Lerner, J. V., Lewin-Bizan, S., & Bowers, E. P. (2010). Special issue introduction: The meaning and measurement of thriving: A view of the issues. *Journal of Youth and Adolescence, 39,* 707–719.

Lerner-Geva, L., Boyko, V., Blumstein, T., & Benyamini, Y. (2010). The impact of education, cultural background, and

lifestyle on symptoms of the menopausal transition: The Women's Health at Midlife Study. *Journal of Women's Health, 18*(5), 975–985.

Lessard, G., Flynn, C., Turcotte, P., Damant, D., Vézina, J., Godin, M., & Rondeau-Cantin, S. (2010). Child custody issues and co-occurrence of intimate partner violence and child maltreatment: Controversies and points of agreement amongst practitioners. *Child & Family Social Work, 15*(4), 492–500.

Lester, F., Benfield, N., & Fathalla, M. M. F. (2010). Global women's health in 2010: Facing the challenges. *Journal of Women's Health, 19*(11), 2081–2089.

Leung, A. K., & Chiu, C. (2011). Multicultural experience fosters creative conceptual expansion. In A. K. Leung, C. Chiu, & Y. Y. Hong (Eds.), *Cultural processes: A social psychological perspective* (pp. 263–285). New York, NY: Cambridge University Press.

Leung, K. K., Tsai, J. S., Cheng, S. Y., Liu, W. J., Chiu, T. Y., Wu, C. H., & Chen, C. Y. (2010). Can a good death and quality of life be achieved for patients with terminal cancer in a palliative care unit? *Journal of Palliative Medicine, 13*(12), 1433–1438.

Leve, L. D., Kerr, D. C. R., Shaw, D., Ge, X., Neiderhiser, J. M., Scaramella, L. V., Reid, J. B., Conger, R. & Reiss, D. (2010). Infant pathways to externalizing behavior: Evidence of Genotype X environmental interaction. *Child Development, 81*(1), 240–356.

Leventhal, T., & Newman, S. (2010). Housing and child development. *Children and Youth Services Review, 32*(9), 1165–1174.

Levine, A., & Dean, D. (2012). Generation on a tightrope: A portrait of today's college students. San Francisco: Jossey-Bass.

Lewin-Bizan, S., Lynch, A. D., Fay, K., Schmid, K., McPherran, C., Lerner, J. V., & Lerner, R. M. (2010). Trajectories of positive and negative behaviors from early- to middle-adolescence. *Journal of Youth and Adolescence, 39,* 751–763.

Lewis, A. D., Huebner, E. S., Malone, P. S., & Valois, R. F. (2011). Life satisfaction and student engagement in adolescents. *Journal of Youth and Adolescence, 40,* 249–262.

Li, F., Godinet, M. T., & Arnsberger, P. (2011). Protective factors among families with children at risk of maltreatment: Follow up to early school years. *Children and Youth Services Review, 33,* 139–148.

Li, L., Zhong, J. A., Chen, Y., Xie, Y., & Mao, S. (2014). Moderating effects of proactive personality on factors influencing work engagement based on the job demands-resources model. *Social Behavior and Personality*, 42(1), 7–16.

Li, N. P., Patel, L., Balliet, D., Tov, W., & Scollon, C. N. (2011). The incompatibility of materialism and the desire for children: Psychological insights into the fertility discrepancy among modern countries. *Social Indicators Research*, 101(3), 391–404.

Li, T., Fung, H. H., & Isaacowitz, D. M. (2011). The role of dispositional reappraisal in the age-related positivity effect. *Journals of Gerontology: Psychological Sciences*, 66B(1), 56–60.

Li, W., Farkas, G., Duncan, G. J., Burchinal, M. R., & Vandell, D. L. (2013). Timing of high-quality child care and cognitive, language, and preacademic development. *Developmental Psychology*, 49(8), 1440–1451.

Li, W., Fay, D., Frese, M., Harms, P. D., & Gao, X. Y. (2014). Reciprocal relationship between proactive personality and work characteristics: A latent change score approach. *Journal of Applied Psychology*, 99(5), 948–965.

Li, X., Ling, H., Zhang, J., Si, X., & Ma, X. (2013). Influence of timing of puberty on boys' self-concept and peer relationship. *Chinese Journal of Clinical Psychology*, 21(3), 512–514.

Li, Y., & Lerner, R. M. (2011). Trajectories of school engagement during adolescence: Implications for grades, depression, delinquency, and substance use. *Developmental Psychology*, 4(1), 233–247.

Li, Y., Johnson, B. D., & Jenkins-Guarnieri, M. A. (2013). Sexual identity development and subjective well-being among Chinese lesbians. *International Perspectives in Psychology: Research, Practice, Consultation*, 2(4), 242–254.

Liben, S., Papadatou, D., & Wolfe, J. (2008). Paediatric palliative care: Challenges and emerging ideas. *The Lancet*, 371, 852–864.

Lickenbrock, D. M., Braungart-Rieker, J. M., Ekas, N. V., Zentall, S. R., Oshio, T., & Planalp, E. M. (2013). Early temperament and attachment security with mothers and fathers as predictors of toddler compliance and noncompliance. *Infant and Child Development*, 22(6), 580–602.

Liew, J., Eisenberg, N., Spinrad, T. L., Eggum, N. D., Haugen, R. G., Kupfer, A., & Baham, M. E. (2011). Physiological regulation and fearfulness as predictors of young children's empathy-related reactions. *Social Development*, 20(1), 111–134.

Light, R. J. (2001). *Making the most of college: Students speak their minds.* Cambridge, MA: Harvard University Press.

Lightfoot, C. (1997). *The culture of adolescent risk-taking.* New York, NY: Guilford Press.

Lilgendahl, J. P., & McAdams, D. P. (2011). Constructing stories of self-growth: How individual differences in patterns of autobiographical reasonings relate to well-being in midlife. *Journal of Personality*, 79(2), 392–425.

Lilgendahl, J. P., Helson, R., & John, O. P. (2013). Does ego development increase during midlife? The effects of openness and accommodative processing of difficult events. *Journal of Personality*, 81(4), 403–416.

Lillard, A. S., Lerner, M. D., Hopkins, E. J., Dore, R. A., Smith, E. D., & Palmquist, C. M. (2013). The impact of pretend play on children's development: A review of the evidence. *Psychological Bulletin*, 139(1), 1–34.

Lim, S. L., Yeh, M., Liang, J., Lau, A. S., & McCabe, K. (2009) Acculturation gap, intergenerational conflict, parenting style, and youth distress in immigrant Chinese American families. *Marriage & Family Review*, 45, 84–106.

Lin, Y., Tsai, Y., Lai, P. (2013). The experience of Taiwanese women achieving post-infertility pregnancy through assisted reproductive treatment. *The Family Journal*, 21, 189–197.

Lindemann, E. (1944). Symptomatology and management of acute grief. *American Journal of Psychiatry*, 101, 141–148.

Lindenberger, U., & Mayr, U. (2014). Cognitive aging: Is there a dark side to environmental support? *Trends in Cognitive Sciences*, 18(1), 7–15.

Lindsey, E. W., & Colwell, M. J. (2013). Pretend and physical play: Links to preschoolers' affective social competence. *Merrill-Palmer Quarterly*, 59(3), 330–360.

Lindstrom-Forneri, W., Tuokko, H., & Rhodes, R. E. (2007). "Getting around town": A preliminary investigation of the theory of planned behavior and intent to change driving behaviors among older adults. *Journal of Applied Gerontology*, 26(4), 385–398.

Linver, M. R., Roth, J. L., & Brooks-Gunn, J. (2009). Patterns of adolescents' participation in organized activities: Are sports best when combined with other activities? *Developmental Psychology*, 45, 354–367.

Literte, P. E. (2010). Revising race: How biracial students are changing and challenging student services. *Journal of College Student Development*, 51(2), 115–135.

Liu, Y. C., Su, P. Y., Chen, C. H., Chiang, H. H., Wang, K. Y., & Tzeng, W. C. (2011). Facing death, facing self: Nursing students' emotional reactions during an experiential workshop on life-and-death issues. *Journal of Clinical Nursing*, 20(5–6), 856–863.

Loftus, J., & Andriot, A. L. (2012). "That's what makes a woman": Infertility and coping with a failed life course transition. *Sociological Spectrum*, 32(3), 226–243.

Logis, H. A., Rodkin, P. C., Gest, S. D., & Ahn, H. (2013). Popularity as an organizing factor of preadolescent friendship networks: Beyond prosocial and aggressive behavior. *Journal of Research on Adolescence*, 23(3), 413–423.

Lonardo, R. A., Giordano, P. C., Longmore, M. A., & Manning, W. D. (2009). Parents, friends, and romantic partners: Enmeshment in deviant networks and adolescent delinquency involvement. *Journal of Youth and Adolescence*, 38, 367–383.

Lopez-Caneda, E., Holguin, S., Rodrigues, C., Cadaveira, F.; Corral, M., & Doallo, S. (2014). The impact of alcohol use on inhibitory control (and vice versa) during adolescence and young adulthood: A review. *Alcohol and Alcoholism* 49(2), 173–184.

López-Guimerà, G., Levine, M. P., Sánchez-Carracedo, D., & Fauquet, J. (2010). Influence of mass media on body image and eating disordered attitudes and behaviors in females: A review of effects and processes. *Media Psychology*, 13(4), 387–416.

Lorber, M. F., O'Leary, S. G., & Smith Slep, A. M. (2011). An initial evaluation of the role of emotion and impulsivity in explaining racial/ethnic differences in the use of corporal punishment. *Developmental Psychology*, 47(6), 1744–1749.

Lorenz, K. (1935). Der Kumpan in der Umwelt des Vogels. Der Artgenosse als auslosendes Moment sozialer Verhaltungsweisen. [The companion in the bird's world. The fellow-member of the species as releasing factor of social behavior.]. *Journal für Ornithologie. Beiblatt. (Leipzig)*, 83, 137–213.

Lou, V. Q., Lu, N., Xu, L., & Chi, I. (2013). Grandparent–grandchild family capital and self-rated health of older rural Chinese adults: The role of the grandparent–parent relationship. *The Journals of Gerontology Series B: Psychological Sciences and Social Sciences,* 68B(4), 599–608.

Loukas, A., Roalson, L. A., & Herrera, D. E. (2010). School connectedness buffers the effects of negative family relations and poor effortful control on early adolescent conduct problems. *Journal of Research on Adolescence,* 20(1), 13–22.

Low income by family type. (n.d.). Retrieved from http://www.poverty.org.uk/05/index.shtml

Lowenstein, L. F. (2013). Is the concept of parental alienation a meaningful one? *Journal of Divorce & Remarriage,* 54(8), 658–667.

Lu, P. H., Lee, G. J., Tishler, T. A., Meghpara, M., Thompson, P. M., & Bartzokis, G. (2013). Myelin breakdown mediates age-related slowing in cognitive processing speed in healthy elderly men. *Brain and Cognition,* 81(1), 131–138.

Luciana, M. (2010). Adolescent brain development: Current themes and future directions. Introduction to the special issue [Editorial]. *Brain and Cognition,* 72, 1–5.

Lui, J. L., Johnston, C., Lee, C. M., & Lee-Flynn, S. C. (2013). Parental ADHD symptoms and self-reports of positive parenting. *Journal of Consulting and Clinical Psychology,* 81(6), 988–998.

Lui, P. R., & Rollock, D. (2013). Tiger mother: Popular and psychological scientific perspectives on Asian culture and parenting. *American Journal of Orthopsychiatry,* 83(4), 450–456.

Lugo-Gil, J., & Tamis-LeMonda, C. S. (2008). Family resources and parenting quality: Links to children's cognitive development across the first 3 years. *Child Development,* 79(4), 1065–1085.

Lundy, B. L. (2013). Paternal and maternal mind-mindedness and preschoolers' theory of mind: The mediating role of interactional attunement. *Social Development,* 22(1), 58–74.

Luo, S. (2014). Effects of texting on satisfaction in romantic relationships: The role of attachment. *Computers in Human Behavior,* 33, 145–152.

Luong, G., Charles, S. T., & Fingerman, K. L. (2010). Better with age: Social relationships across adulthood. *Journal of Social and Personal Relationships,* 28(1), 9–23.

Luttikhuis, H. G. M. O., Stolk, R. P., & Sauer, P. J. J. (2010). How do parents of 4- to 5-year-old children perceive the weight of their children? *Acta Paediatrica,* 99, 263–267.

Luyckx, K., Teppers, E., Klimstra, T. A., & Rassart, J. (2014). Identity processes and personality traits and types in adolescence: Directionality of effects and developmental trajectories. *Developmental Psychology,* 50(8), 2144–2153.

Lynch, S. (2013). Hospice and palliative care access issues in rural areas. *American Journal of Hospice and Palliative Medicine,* 30(2), 172–177.

Lynne-Landsman, S. D., Graber, J. A., & Andrews, J. A. (2010). Do trajectories of household risk in childhood moderate pubertal timing effects on substance initiation in middle school? *Developmental Psychology,* 46(4), 853–868.

Maccoby, E. E. (1990). Gender and relationships: A developmental account. *American Psychologist,* 45, 513–520.

Maccoby, E. E. (1998). *The two sexes: Growing up apart, coming together.* Cambridge, MA: Belknap Press of Harvard University Press.

Maccoby, E. E. (2002). Gender and group process: A developmental perspective. *Current Directions in Psychological Science,* 11, 54–58.

Maccoby, E. E., & Martin, J. A. (1983). Socialization in the context of the family: Parent-child interaction. In P. H. Mussen (Series ed.) & E. M. Hethenington (Vol. ed.), *Handbook of child psychology: Vol. 4. Socialization, personality, and social development* (4th ed. pp. 1–101). New York, NY: Wiley.

Macek, P., Bejcek, J., & Vanickova, J. (2007). Contemporary Czech emerging adults: Generation growing up in the period of social changes. *Journal of Adolescent Research,* 22(5), 444–474.

Mackinnon, S. P., Nosko, A., Pratt, M. W., & Norris, J. E. (2011). Intimacy in young adults' narratives of romance and friendship predicts Eriksonian generativity: A mixed method analysis. *Journal of Personality,* 79(3), 587–617.

MacMillan, H. L., Tanaka, M., Duku, E., Vaillancourt, T., & Boyle, M. H. (2013). Child physical and sexual abuse in a community sample of young adults: Results from the Ontario Child Health Study. *Child Abuse & Neglect: The International Journal,* 37(1), 14–21.

MacRae, H. (2008). Making the best you can of it: Living with early-state Alzheimer's disease. *Sociology of Health & Wellness,* 30(3), 396–412.

Madigan, S., Atkinson, L., Laurin, K., & Benoit, D. (2013). Attachment and internalizing behavior in early childhood: A meta-analysis. *Developmental Psychology,* 49(4), 672–689.

Maggs, J. L., Patrick, M. E., & Feinstein, L. (2008). Childhood and adolescent predictors of alcohol use and problems in adolescence and adulthood in the National Child Development Study. *Addiction,* 103 (Suppl. 1), 7–22.

Magnuson, K., & Shager, H. (2010). Early education: Progress and promise for children from low-income families. *Children and Youth Services Review,* 32, 1186–1198.

Malacrida, C., & Boulton, T. (2014). The best laid plans? Women's choices, expectations and experiences in childbirth. *Health: An Interdisciplinary Journal for the Social Study of Health, Illness and Medicine,* 18(1), 41–59.

Males, M. (2009). Does the adolescent brain make risk taking inevitable? *Journal of Adolescent Research* 24, 3–20.

Malin, H., Reilly, T. S., Quinn, B., & Moran, S. (2014). Adolescent purpose development: Exploring empathy, discovering roles, shifting priorities, and creating pathways. *Journal of Research on Adolescence,* 24(1), 186–199.

Mallard, S. R., Connor, J. L., & Houghton, L. A. (2013). Maternal factors associated with heavy periconceptional alcohol intake and drinking following pregnancy recognition: A post-partum survey of New Zealand women. *Drug and Alcohol Review,* 32(4), 389–397.

Malpas, P. J., Wilson, M. R., Rae, N., & Johnson, M. (2014). Why do older people oppose physician-assisted dying? A qualitative study. *Palliative Medicine,* 28(4), 353–359.

Mandler, J. M. (2007). On the origins of the conceptual system. *American Psychologist,* 62(8), 741–751.

Manfra, L., & Winsler, A. (2006). Preschool children's awareness of private speech. *International Journal of Behavioral Development,* 30(6), 537–549.

Manning, W. D., Brown, S. L., & Payne, K. K. (2014). Two decades of stability and change in age at first union formation. *Journal of Marriage and Family,* 76(2), 247–260.

Manning, W. D., Giordano, P. C., & Longmore, M. A. (2006). Hooking up: The relationship contexts of "nonrelationship" sex. *Journal of Adolescent Research,* 21(5), 459–483.

Manning, W. D., Longmore, M. A., & Giordano, P. C. (2007). The changing institution of marriage: Adolescents' expectation to cohabit and to marry. *Journal of Marriage and Family, 69*(3), 559–575.

Mao, A., Burnham, M. M., Goodlin-Jones, B. L., Gaylor, E. E., & Anders, T. F. (2004). A comparison of the sleep-wake patterns of cosleeping and solitary-sleeping infants. *Child Psychiatry & Human Development, 35,* 95–105.

Marcia, J. E. (1966). Development and validation of ego-identity status. *Journal of Personality and Social Psychology, 3,* 551–558.

Marcia, J. E. (1987). The identity status approach to the study of ego identity development. In T. Honess & K. Yardley (Eds.), *Self and identity: Perspectives across the lifespan* (pp. 161–171). New York, NY: Routledge.

Marieb, E. N. (2004). *Human anatomy & physiology* (6th ed.). New York, NY: Pearson Education.

Markey, P. M., & Markey, C. N. (2007). Romantic ideals, romantic obtainment, and relationship experiences: The complementarity of interpersonal traits among romantic partners. *Journal of Social and Personal Relationships, 24*(4), 517–533.

Markey, P., Markey, C., Nave, C., & August, K. (2014). Interpersonal problems and relationship quality: An examination of gay and lesbian romantic couples. *Journal of Research in Personality, 51,* 1–8.

Marlier, L., Schaal, B., & Soussignan, R. (1998). Neonatal responsiveness to the odor of amniotic and lacteal fluids: A test of perinatal chemosensory continuity. *Child Development, 69,* 611–623.

Marmo, S. (2014). Recommendations for hospice care to terminally ill cancer patients: A phenomenological study of oncologists' experiences. *Journal of Social Work in End-of-Life & Palliative Care, 10*(2), 149–169.

Marsiglio, W. (2004). When stepfathers claim stepchildren: A conceptual analysis. *Journal of Marriage and Family, 66,* 22–39.

Martin, A. J., Mansour, M., Anderson, M., Gibson, R., Liem, G. D., & Sudmalis, D. (2013). The role of arts participation in students' academic and nonacademic outcomes: A longitudinal study of school, home, and community factors. *Journal of Educational Psychology, 105*(3), 709–727.

Martin, C. L., & Dinella, L. M. (2002). Children's gender cognitions, the social environment, and sex differences in cognitive domains. In A. McGillicuddy-De Lisi & R. De Lisi (Eds.), *Biology, society, and behavior: The development of sex differences in cognition* (pp. 207–239). Westport, CT: Ablex.

Martin, C. L., & Fabes, R. A. (2001). The stability and consequences of young children's same-sex peer interactions. *Developmental Psychology, 37,* 431–446.

Martin, C. L., & Ruble, D. N. (2010). Patterns of gender development. *Annual Review of Psychology, 61.* 353–381.

Martin, J. A., Hamilton, B. E., Menacker, F., Sutton, P. D., & Mathews, T. J. (2005, November 15). *Preliminary births for 2004: Infant and maternal health.* Hyattsville, MD: National Center for Health Statistics.

Martin, K. A. (1996). *Puberty, sexuality, and the self: Boys and girls at adolescence.* New York, NY: Routledge.

Martin, P., Audet, T., Corriveau, H., Hamel, M., D'Amours, M., & Smeesters, C. (2010). Comparison between younger and older drivers of the effect of obstacle direction on the minimum obstacle distance to brake and avoid a motor vehicle accident. *Accident Analysis and Prevention, 42*(4), 1144–1150.

Martinelli, P., Anssens, A., Sperduti, M., & Piolino, P. (2013). The influence of normal aging and Alzheimer's disease in autobiographical memory highly related to the self. *Neuropsychology, 27*(1), 69–78.

Martin-Matthews, A., Tong, C. E., Rosenthal, C. J., & McDonald, L. (2013). Ethno-cultural diversity in the experience of widowhood in later life: Chinese widows in Canada. *Journal of Aging Studies, 27*(4), 507–518.

Martins, M. V., Peterson, B. D., Costa, P., Costa, M. E., Lund, R., & Schmidt, L. (2013). Interactive effects of social support and disclosure on fertility-related stress. *Journal of Social and Personal Relationships, 30*(4), 371–388.

Marysko, M., Finke, P., Wiebel, A., Resch, F., & Moehler, E. (2010). Can mothers predict childhood behavioral inhibition in early infancy? *Child and Adolescent Mental Health, 15*(2), 91–96.

Masoro, E. (1999). *Challenges of biological aging.* New York, NY: Springer.

Masten, A. S. (2004). Regulatory processes, risk, and resilience in adolescent development. In R. E. Dahl & L. P. Spear (Eds.), *Adolescent brain development: Vulnerabilities and opportunities* (Vol. 1021 pp. 310–319). New York, NY: New York Academy of Sciences.

Masters, W. H., & Johnson, V. E. (1966). *Human sexual response.* Boston, MA: Little, Brown.

Masuda, A., Boone, M. S., & Timko, C. A. (2011). The role of psychological flexibility in the relationship between self-concealment and disordered eating symptoms. *Eating Behaviors, 12,* 131–135.

Matton, A., Goossens, L., Braet, C., & Van Durme, K. (2013). Continuity in primary school children's eating problems and the influence of parental feeding strategies. *Journal of Youth and Adolescence, 42*(1), 52–66.

May, J. S., & Beaver, K. M. (2014). The neuropsychological contributors to psychopathic personality traits in adolescence. *International Journal of Offender Therapy and Comparative Criminology, 58*(3), 265–285.

Mayberry, M. L., & Espelage, D. L. (2007). Associations among empathy, social competence, & reactive/proactive aggression subtypes. *Journal of Youth and Adolescence, 36,* 787–798.

Mayeux, L., & Cillessen, A. H. N. (2008). It's not just being popular, it's knowing it, too: The role of self-perceptions of status in the associations between peer status and aggression. *Social Development, 17,* 871–888.

Maynard, A. E., & Greenfield, P. M. (2003). Implicit cognitive development in cultural tools and children: Lessons from Maya Mexico. *Cognitive Development, 18,* 489–510.

Mayseless, O., & Keren, E. (2014). Finding a meaningful life as a developmental task in emerging adulthood: The domains of love and work across cultures. *Emerging Adulthood, 2*(1), 63–73.

Mazzonna, F. (2014). The long lasting effects of education on old age health: Evidence of gender differences. *Social Science & Medicine, 101,* 129–138.

Mazzotti, D. R., Tufik, S., & Andersen, M. L. (2013). A step forward in understanding the association between social attainment and health disparities: Evidence from late life telomere length and educational level. *Brain, Behavior, and Immunity, 27,* 13–14.

McAdams, D. P. (2001a). Generativity in midlife. In M. E. Lachman (Ed.), *Handbook of midlife development* (pp. 395–443). Hoboken, NJ: Wiley.

McAdams, D. P. (2001b). The psychology of life stories. *Review of General Psychology, 5,* 100–122.

McAdams, D. P. (2006). *The redemptive self: Stories Americans live by.* New York, NY: Oxford University Press.

McAdams, D. P. (2013). The psychological self as actor, agent, and author. *Perspectives on Psychological Science, 8*(3), 272–295.

McAdams, D. P., & Bowman, P. J. (2001). Narrating life's turning points: Redemption and contamination. In D. P. McAdams, R. Josselson, & A. Lieblich (Eds.), *Turns in the road: Narrative studies of lives in transition* (pp. 3–34). Washington, DC: American Psychological Association.

McAdams, D. P., & de St. Aubin, E. (1992). A theory of generativity and its assessment through self-report, behavioral acts, and narrative themes in autobiography. *Journal of Personality and Social Psychology, 62,* 1003–1015.

McAdams, D. P., de St. Aubin, E., & Logan, R. L. (1993). Generativity among young, midlife, and older adults. *Psychology and Aging, 8,* 221–230.

McAdams, D. P., Hart, H. M., & Maruna, S. (1998). The anatomy of generativity. In D. P. McAdams & E. de St. Aubin (Eds.), *Generativity and adult development: How and why we care for the next generation* (pp. 7–43). Washington, D.C.: American Psychological Association.

McAlister, A. R., & Peterson, C. C. (2013). Siblings, theory of mind, and executive functioning in children aged 3–6 years: New longitudinal evidence. *Child Development, 84*(4), 1442–1458.

McCabe, D. P., Roediger, H. L., McDaniel, M. A., Balots, D. A., & Hambrick, D. Z. (2010). The relationship between working memory capacity and executive functioning: Evidence for a common executive attention construct. *Neuropsychology, 24*(2), 223–243.

McCann, R. M., & Keaton, S. A. (2013). A cross cultural investigation of age stereotypes and communication perceptions of older and younger workers in the USA and Thailand. *Educational Gerontology, 39*(5), 326–341.

McCarthy, J. R., & Jessop, J. (2005). *Young people, bereavement and loss: Disruptive transitions?* London, England: National Children's Bureau.

McCarthy, M. C., Clarke, N. E., Ting, C. L., Conroy, R., Anderson, V. A., & Heath, J. A. (2010). Prevalence and predictors of parental grief and depression after the death of a child from cancer. *Journal of Palliative Medicine, 13*(11), 1321–1326.

McCarthy, M. M. (2013). A piece in the puzzle of puberty. *Nature Neuroscience, 16*(3), 251–253.

McClintock, M. K., & Herdt, G. (1996). Rethinking puberty: The development of sexual attraction. *Current Directions in Psychological Science, 5,* 178–183.

McCloskey, L. A. (2013). The intergenerational transfer of mother–daughter risk for gender-based abuse. *Psychodynamic Psychiatry, 41*(2), 303–328.

McCormack, A., & Fortnum, H. (2013). Why do people fitted with hearing aids not wear them? *International Journal of Audiology, 52*(5), 360-368.

McCreight, B. S. (2004). A grief ignored: Narratives of pregnancy loss from a male perspective. *Sociology of Health and Illness, 26,* 326–350.

McDaniel, M. A., Binder, E. F., Bugg, J. M., Waldum, E. R., Dufault, C., Meyer, A., . . . Kudelka, C. (2014). Effects of cognitive training with and without aerobic exercise on cognitively demanding everyday activities. *Psychology and Aging, 29*(3), 717–730.

McDonald, K. L., Malti, T., Killen, M., & Rubin, K. H. (2014). Best friends' discussions of social dilemmas. *Journal of Youth and Adolescence, 43*(2), 233–244.

McElwain, N. L., Booth-LaForce, C., & Wu, X. (2011). Infant–mother attachment and children's friendship quality: Maternal mental-state talk as an intervening mechanism. *Developmental Psychology, 47*(5), 1295–1311.

McFarlane, T., Urbszat, D., & Olmsted, M. P. (2011). "I feel fat": An experimental induction of body displacement in disordered eating. *Behaviour Research and Therapy, 49,* 289–293.

McGeown, K. (2005). *Life in Ceasuseascu's institutions.* Retrieved from http://news.bbc.co.uk/2/hi/europe/4630855.stm

McGill, B. S. (2014). Navigating new norms of involved fatherhood: Employment, fathering attitudes, and father involvement. *Journal of Family Issues, 35*(8), 1089–1106.

McGrath, A., Sharpe, L., Lah, S., & Parratt, K. (2014). Pregnancy-related knowledge and information needs of women with epilepsy: A systematic review. *Epilepsy & Behavior, 312,* 46–255.

McGrath, P. (2004). Affirming the connection: Comparative findings on communication issues from hospice patients and hematology survivors. *Death Studies, 28,* 829–848.

McIntosh, H., Metz, E., & Youniss, J. (2005). Community service and identity formation in adolescents. In J. L. Mahoney, R. W. Larson, & J. S. Eccles (Eds.), *Organized activities as contexts of development: Extracurricular activities, after-school and community programs* (pp. 331–351). Mahwah, NJ: Erlbaum.

McKay, A., & Barrett, M. (2010). Trends in teen pregnancy rates from 1996–2006: A comparison of Canada, Sweden, U.S.A., and England/Wales. *Canadian Journal of Human Sexuality, 19*(1–2), 43–52.

McLaughlin, K. A., Fox, N. A., Zeanah, C. H., Sheridan, M. A., Marshall, P., & Nelson, C. A. (2010). Delayed maturation in brain electrical activity partially explains the association between early environmental deprivation and symptoms of attention-deficit/hyperactivity disorder. *Biological Psychiatry, 68*(4), 329–336.

McLaughlin, K. A., Zeanah, C. H., Fox, N. A., & Nelson, C. A. (2012). Attachment security as a mechanism linking foster care placement to improved mental health outcomes in previously institutionalized children. *Journal of Child Psychology and Psychiatry, 53*(1), 46–55.

McLeskey, J., Waldron, N. L., & Redd, L. (2014). A case study of a highly effective, inclusive elementary school. *Journal of Special Education, 48*(1), 59–70.

McMahan, R. D., Knight, S. J., Fried, T. R., & Sudore, R. L. (2013). Advance care planning beyond advance directives: Perspectives from patients and surrogates. *Journal of Pain and Symptom Management, 46*(3), 355.

McMener, D. J., Betz, J., Genther, D. J., Chen, D., & Lin, F. R. (2013). Hearing loss and depression in older adults. *Journal of the American Geriatrics Society, 61*(9), 1627–1629.

McNally, S., Share, M., & Murray, A. (2014). Prevalence and predictors of grandparent childcare in Ireland: Findings from a nationally representative sample of infants and their families. *Child Care in Practice, 20*(2), 182–193.

McNeely, C. A., & Barber, B. K. (2010). How do parents make adolescents feel loved? Perspectives on supportive parenting from adolescents in 12 cultures. *Journal of Adolescent Research, 25*(4), 601–631.

McNiel, M. E., Labbok, M. H., & Abrahams, S. W. (2010). What are the risks associated with formula feeding? A re-analysis and review. *Birth: Issues in Prenatal Care, 37*(1), 50–58.

Meeus, W. (2011). The study of adolescent identity formation 2000–2010: A review of longitudinal research. *Journal of Research on Adolescence, 21*(1), 75–94.

Meier, D. E., & Beresford, L. (2009). Palliative care cost research can help other palliative care programs make their case. *Journal of Palliative Medicine, 23,* 15–20.

Melby-Lervåg, M., & Hulme, C. (2013). Is working memory training effective? A meta-analytic review. *Developmental Psychology, 49*(2), 270–291.

Melendez, M. C., & Melendez, N. B. (2010). The influence of parental attachment on the college adjustment of White, Black, and Latina/Hispanic women: A cross-cultural investigation. *Journal of College Student Development, 51*(4), 419–435.

Melinder, A., Baugerud, G. A., Ovenstad, K. S., & Goodman, G. S. (2013). Children's memories of removal: A test of attachment theory. *Journal of Traumatic Stress, 26*(1), 125–133.

Mellor, D., Fuller-Tyszkiewicz, M., McCabe, M. P., & Ricciardelli, L. A. (2010). Body image and self-esteem across age and gender: A short-term longitudinal study. *Sex Roles, 63*(9–10), 672–681.

Meltzoff, A. N., & Moore, M. K. (1977, October 7). Imitation of facial and manual gestures by human neonates. *Science, 198,* 75–78.

Menard, J. L., & Hakvoort, R. M. (2007). Variations of maternal care alter offspring levels of behavioral defensiveness in adulthood: Evidence for a threshold model. *Behavioral Brain Research, 176,* 302–313.

Mence, M., Hawes, D. J., Wedgwood, L., Morgan, S., Barnett, B., Kohlhoff, J., & Hunt, C. (2014). Emotional flooding and hostile discipline in the families of toddlers with disruptive behavior problems. *Journal of Family Psychology, 28*(1), 12–21.

Mendle, J., Harden, K. P., Brooks-Gunn, J., & Graber, J. A. (2010). Development's tortoise and hare: Pubertal timing, pubertal tempo, and depressive symptoms in boys and girls. *Developmental Psychology, 46*(5), 1341–1353.

Mendonça, M., & Fontaine, A. M. (2013). Late nest leaving in Portugal: Its effects on individuation and parent–child relationships. *Emerging Adulthood, 1*(3), 233–244.

Merrill, D. M. (1996). Conflict and cooperation among adult siblings during the transition to the role of filial caregiver. *Journal of Social and Personal Relationships, 13*(3), 399–413.

Merz, E. M., Schulze, H. J., & Schuengel, C. (2010). Consequences of filial support for two generations: A narrative and quantitative review. *Journal of Family Issues, 31*(11), 1530–1554.

Meuwly, N., Feinstein, B. A., Davila, J., Nuñez, D. G., & Bodenmann, G. (2013). Relationship quality among Swiss women in opposite-sex versus same-sex romantic relationships. *Swiss Journal of Psychology, 72*(4), 229–233.

Michalczyk, K., Malstädt, N., Worgt, M., Könen, T., & Hasselhorn, M. (2013). Age differences and measurement invariance of working memory in 5- to 12-year-old children. *European Journal of Psychological Assessment, 29*(3), 220–229.

Miche, M., Elsässer, V. C., Schilling, O. K., & Wahl, H. (2014). Attitude toward own aging in midlife and early old age over a 12-year period: Examination of measurement equivalence and developmental trajectories. *Psychology and Aging, 29*(3), 588–600.

Midei, A. J., Matthews, K. A., Chang, Y., & Bromberger, J. T. (2013). Childhood physical abuse is associated with incident metabolic syndrome in midlife women. *Health Psychology, 32*(2), 121–127.

Mikaeili, N., Barahmand, U., & Abdi, R. (2013). The prevalence of different kinds of child abuse and the characteristics that differentiate abused from non-abused male adolescents. *Journal of Interpersonal Violence, 28*(5), 975–996.

Mikkelsen, A. T., Madsen, S. A., & Humaidan, P. (2013). Psychological aspects of male fertility treatment. *Journal of Advanced Nursing, 69*(9), 1977–1986.

Mikulincer, M., Florian, V., Cowan, P. A., & Cowan, C. P. (2002). Attachment security in couple relationships: A systemic model and its implications for family dynamics. *Family Process, 41,* 405–434.

Miller, B. J., & Lundgren, J. D. (2010). An experimental study of the role of weight bias in candidate evaluation. *Obesity, 18*(4), 712–718.

Miller, D., & Daniel, B. (2007). Competent to cope, worthy of happiness? How the duality of self-esteem can inform a resilience-based classroom environment. *School Psychology International, 28*(5), 605–622.

Miller, E. A., Mor, V., & Clark, M. (2010). Reforming long-term care in the United States: Findings from a national survey of specialists. *The Gerontologist, 50*(2), 238–252.

Miller, G. E., Chen, E., & Parker, K. J. (2011). Psychological stress in childhood and susceptibility to the chronic diseases of aging: Moving toward a model of behavioral and biological mechanisms. *Psychological Bulletin, 137*(6), 959–997.

Miller, P., Votruba-Drzal, E., & Setodji, C. (2013). Family income and early achievement across the urban rural continuum. *Developmental Psychology, 49*(8), 1452–1465.

Miller, W. D., Sadegh-Nobari, T., & Lillie-Blanton, M. (2011). Healthy starts for all: Policy prescriptions. *American Journal of Preventive Medicine, 40*(1), S19–S37.

Mills, R., Scott, J., Alati, R., O'Callaghan, M., Najman, J. M., & Strathearn, L. (2013). Child maltreatment and adolescent mental health problems in a large birth cohort. *Child Abuse & Neglect: The International Journal, 37*(5), 292–302.

Miniño, A. M., Arias, E., Kochanek, K. D., Murphy, S. L., & Smith, B. L. (2002, September 16). *Deaths: Final data for 2000.* National Vital Statistics Reports, 50(16).

Minois, G. (1989). *History of old age: From antiquity to the Renaissance* (S. H. Tenison, Trans.). Chicago, IL: University of Chicago Press.

Mintz, S. (2004). *Huck's raft: A history of American childhood.* Cambridge, MA: Belknap Press of Harvard University Press.

Mirecki, R. M., Brimhall, A. S., & Bramesfeld, K. D. (2013). Communication during conflict: Differences between individuals in first and second marriages. *Journal of Divorce & Remarriage, 54*(3), 197–213.

Mirecki, R. M., Chou, J. L., Elliott, M., & Schneider, C. M. (2013). What factors influence marital satisfaction? Differences between first and second marriages. *Journal of Divorce & Remarriage, 54*(1), 78–93.

Mistry, J., Chaudhuri, J., & Diez, V. (2003). Ethnotheories of parenting: Integrating culture and child development. In R. M. Lerner, F. H. Jacobs, & D. Wertlieb (Eds.), *Handbook of applied developmental science: Promoting positive child, adolescent, and family development through research, policies, and programs* (pp. 233–256). Thousand Oaks, CA: Sage.

Modell, J. (1989). *Into one's own: From youth to adulthood in the United States, 1920–1975*. Berkeley, CA: University of California Press.

Modin, B., Östberg, V., & Almquist, Y. (2011). Childhood peer status and adult susceptibility to anxiety and depression. A 30-year hospital follow-up. *Journal of Abnormal Child Psychology, 39*, 187–199.

Moehler, E., Kagan, J., Oelkers-Ax, R., Brunner, R., Poustka, L., Haffner, J., & Resch, F. (2008). Infant predictors of behavioural inhibition. *British Journal of Developmental Psychology, 26*(1), 145–150.

Moffitt, T. E. (1993). Adolescence-limited and life-course-persistent antisocial behavior: A developmental taxonomy. *Psychological Review, 100*, 674–701.

Moilanen, K. L., Crockett, L. J., Raffaelli, M., & Jones, B. L. (2010). Trajectories of sexual risk from middle adolescence to early adulthood. *Journal of Research on Adolescence, 20*(1), 114–139.

Molden, D. C., & Dweck, C. S. (2006). Finding "meaning" in psychology: A lay theories approach to self-regulation, social perception, and social development. *American Psychologist, 61*, 192–203.

Molloy, L. E., Gest, S. D., & Rulison, K. L. (2011). Peer influences on academic motivation: Exploring multiple methods of assessing youths' most "influential" peer relationships. *The Journal of Early Adolescence, 31*(1), 13–40.

Monahan, K. C., Dmitrieva, J., & Cauffman, E. (2014). Bad romance: Sex differences in the longitudinal association between romantic relationships and deviant behavior. *Journal of Research on Adolescence, 24*(1), 12–26.

Monroe, B., Hansford, P., Payne, M., & Sykes, N. (2008). St. Christopher's and the future. *Omega: Journal of Death and Dying. Special Issue: "Hospice heritage," in memory of Dame Cicely Saunders, 56*, 63–75.

Montemurro, B. (2014). Getting married, breaking up, and making up for lost time: Relationship transitions as turning points in women's sexuality. *Journal of Contemporary Ethnography, 43*(1), 64–93.

Montepare, J. M., Kempler, D., & McLaughlin-Volpe, T. (2014). The voice of wisdom: New insights on social impressions of aging voices. *Journal of Language and Social Psychology, 33*(3), 241–259.

Montoro-Rodriguez, J., Kosloski, K., Kercher, K., & Montgomery, R. J. V. (2009). The impact of social embarrassment on caregiving distress in a multicultural sample of caregivers. *Journal of Applied Gerontology, 28*, 195–217.

Mooney, A., Brannen, J., Wigfall, V., & Parutis, V. (2013). The impact of employment on fatherhood across family generations in White British, Polish and Irish origin families. *Community, Work & Family, 16*(4), 372–389.

Morack, J., Ram, N., Fauth, E. B., & Gerstorf, D. (2013). Multidomain trajectories of psychological functioning in old age: A longitudinal perspective on (uneven) successful aging. *Developmental Psychology, 49*(12), 2309–2324.

Moreno, M., & Trainor, M. E. (2013). Adolescence extended: Implications of new brain research on medicine and policy. *Acta Paediatrica, 102*(3), 226–232.

Morgan, E. M. (2013). Contemporary issues in sexual orientation and identity development in emerging adulthood. *Emerging Adulthood, 1*(1), 52–66.

Morgan, E. M., Thorne, A., & Zubriggen, E. L. (2010). A longitudinal study of conversations with parents about sex and dating during college. *Developmental Psychology, 46*(1), 139–150.

Morgan, H. J., & Shaver, P. R. (1999). Attachment processes and commitment to romantic relationships. In J. M. Adams & W. H. Jones (Eds.), *Handbook of interpersonal commitment and relationship stability* (pp. 109–124). Dordrecht, Netherlands: Kluwer Academic.

Morgan, J. K., Shaw, D. S., & Forbes, E. E. (2014). Maternal depression and warmth during childhood predict age 20 neural response to reward. *Journal of the American Academy of Child & Adolescent Psychiatry, 53*(1), 108–117.

Morrissey, T. W., Dunifon, R. E., & Kalil, A. (2011). Maternal employment, work schedules, and children's body mass index. *Child Development, 82*(1), 66–81.

Morselli, D. (2013). The olive tree effect: Future time perspective when the future is uncertain. *Culture & Psychology, 19*(3), 305–322.

Mortensen, E. L., Michaelsen, K. F., Sanders, S. A., & Reinisch, J. M. (2002). The association between duration of breastfeeding and adult intelligence. *Journal of the American Medical Association, 287*, 2365–2371.

Mosko, S., Richard, C., & McKenna, J. (1997). Maternal sleep and arousals during bedsharing with infants. *Sleep: Journal of Sleep Research & Sleep Medicine, 20*, 142–150.

Moss, E., Cyr, C., Bureau, J.-F., Tarabulsy, G. M., & Dubois-Comtois, K. (2005). Stability of attachment during the preschool period. *Developmental Psychology, 41*, 773–783.

Moulaert, T., & Biggs, S. (2013). International and European policy on work and retirement: Reinventing critical perspectives on active ageing and mature subjectivity. *Human Relations, 66*(1), 23–43.

Muehlenkamp, J. J., Claes, L., Havertape, L., & Plener, P. L. (2012). International prevalence of adolescent non-suicidal self-injury and deliberate self-harm. *Child and Adolescent Psychiatry and Mental Health, 6*, 1–9.

Mueller, C. M., & Dweck, C. S. (1998). Praise for intelligence can undermine children's motivation and performance. *Journal of Personality and Social Psychology, 75*(1), 33–52.

Muise, A., & Desmarais, S. (2010). Women's perceptions and use of "anti-aging" products. *Sex Roles, 63*, 126–137.

Müller-Oehring, E. M., Schulte, T., Rohlfing, T., Pfefferbaum, A., & Sullivan, E. V. (2013). Visual search and the aging brain: Discerning the effects of age-related brain volume shrinkage on alertness, feature binding, and attentional control. *Neuropsychology, 27*(1), 48–59.

Mulvaney, M. K., & Mebert, C. J. (2007). Parental corporal punishment predicts behavior problems in early childhood. *Journal of Family Psychology, 21*(3), 389–397.

Munnell, A. H., & Rutledge, M. S. (2013). The effects of the great recession on the retirement security of older workers. *Annals of the American Academy of Political and Social Science, 650*(1), 124–142.

Munro, C. A., Jefferys, J., Gower, E. W., Muñoz, B. E., Lyketsos, C. G., Keay, L., . . . West, S. K. (2010). Predictors of lane- change errors in older drivers. *Journal of the American Geriatrics Society, 58*, 457–464.

Munroe, R. L. (2010). Following the Whitings: The study of male pregnancy symptoms. *Journal of Cross-Cultural Psychology, 41*(4), 592–604.

Murray, A. L., Scratch, S. E., Thompson, D. K., Inder, T. E., Doyle, L. W., Anderson, J. I., & Anderson, P. J. (2014). Neonatal brain pathology predicts adverse attention and processing speed outcomes in very preterm and/or very low birth weight children. *Neuropsychology*, 28(4), 552–562.

Murray, C. (2012). *Coming apart: The state of White America, 1960–2010*. New York, NY: Crown Forum.

Murray, S. L., & Holmes, J. G. (1997). A leap of faith? Positive illusions in romantic relationships. *Personality and Social Psychology Bulletin*, 23, 586–604.

Murray, S. L., Bellavia, G. M., Rose, P., & Griffin, D. W. (2003). Once hurt, twice hurtful: How perceived regard regulates daily marital interactions. *Journal of Personality and Social Psychology*, 84, 126–147.

Murray, S. L., Holmes, J. G., Bellavia, G., Griffin, D. W., & Dolderman, D. (2002). Kindred spirits? The benefits of egocentrism in close relationships. *Journal of Personality and Social Psychology*, 82, 563–581.

Murray, S. L., Holmes, J. G., Dolderman, D., & Griffin, D. W. (2000). What the motivated mind sees: Comparing friends' perspectives to married partners' views of each other. *Journal of Experimental Social Psychology*, 36, 600–620.

Murstein, B. I. (1999). The relationship of exchange and commitment. In J. M. Adams & W. H. Jones (Eds.), *Handbook of interpersonal commitment and relationship stability* (pp. 205–219). Dordrecht, Netherlands: Kluwer Academic.

Murstein, B. I., Reif, J. A., & Syracuse-Siewert, G. (2002). Comparison of the function of exchange in couples of similar and differing physical attractiveness. *Psychological Reports*, 91, 299–314.

Must, A., Naumova, E. N., Phillips, S. M., Blum, M., Dawson-Hughes, B., & Rand, W. M. (2005). Childhood overweight and maturational timing in the development of adult overweight and fatness: The Newton Girls Study and its follow-up. *Pediatrics*, 116, 620–627.

Muzik, M., Bocknek, E. L., Broderick, A., Richardson, P., Rosenblum, K. L., Thelen, K., & Seng, J. S. (2013). Mother–infant bonding impairment across the first 6 months postpartum: The primacy of psychopathology in women with childhood abuse and neglect histories. *Archives of Women's Mental Health*, 16(1), 29–38.

Myers, A. J., Williams, L., Gatt, J. M., McAuley-Clark, E., Dobson-Stone, C., Schofield, P. R., & Nemeroff, C. B. (2014). Variation in the oxytocin receptor gene is associated with increased risk for anxiety, stress and depression in individuals with a history of exposure to early life stress. *Journal of Psychiatric Research*, 59, 93–100.

Myers, L. L., & Wiman, A. M. (2014). Binge eating disorder: A review of a new DSM diagnosis. *Research on Social Work Practice*, 24(1), 86–95.

Nakrem, S., Vinsnes, A. G., Harkless, G. E., Paulsen, B., & Seim, A. (2013). Ambiguities: Residents' experience of "nursing home as my home." *International Journal of Older People Nursing*, 8(3), 216–225.

Nappi, R. E., & Kokot-Kierepa, M. (2010). Women's voices in the menopause: Results from an international survey on vaginal atrophy. *Maturitas*, 67, 233–238.

National Center for Children in Poverty (NCCP). (2014). Retrieved from http://www.nccp.org

National Center for Health Statistics. (2008). *Health, United States, 2007: With chartbook on trends in the health of Americans*. Hyattsville, MD: U.S. Government Printing Office.

National Center on Education Statistics, Fast Facts. (n.d.). *Employment rates of college graduates*. Retrieved from http://www.nces.ed.gov/fastfacts

National Down Syndrome Society. (n.d.). *What is Down Syndrome?* Retrieved from http://www.ndss.org/Down-Syndrome/What-Is-Down-Syndrome

National Health and Nutrition Examination Survey. (2004). *Clinical growth charts*. In *National Center for Health Statistics (U.S. Department of Health & Human Services [USDHHS])*. Retrieved from: http://www.cdc.gov/nchs/about/major/nhanes/growthcharts/clinical_charts.htm

National Hospice and Palliative Care organization (2011). *Patients served by hospice in the United States, 1984–2009*. In *NHPCO*. Retrieved from http://www.nhpco.org/files/public/Statistics_Research/Graph-of-hospice_1982_2009.pdf

Natsuaki, M. N., Leve, L. D., Harold, G. T., Neiderhiser, J. M., Shaw, D. S., Ganiban, J., . . . Reiss, D. (2013). Transactions between child social wariness and observed structured parenting: Evidence from a prospective adoption study. *Child Development*, 84(5), 1750–1765.

Natsuaki, M., Ge, X., & Wenk, E. (2008). Continuity and changes in the developmental trajectories of criminal career: Examining the roles of timing of first arrest and high school graduation. *Journal of Youth and Adolescence*, 37, 431–444.

Naughton, F., Eborall, H., & Sutton, S. (2013). Dissonance and disengagement in pregnant smokers: A qualitative study. *Journal of Smoking Cessation*, 8(1), 24–32.

Neberich, W., Penke, L., Lehnart, J., & Asendorpf, J. B. (2010). Family of origin, age at menarche, and reproductive strategies: A test of four evolutionary-developmental models. *European Journal of Developmental Psychology*, 7(2), 153–177.

Neff, L. A., & Geers, A. L. (2013). Optimistic expectations in early marriage: A resource or vulnerability for adaptive relationship functioning? *Journal of Personality and Social Psychology*, 105(1), 38–60.

Negriff, S., Dorn, L. D., Pabst, S. R., & Susman, E. J. (2011). Morningness/eveningness, pubertal timing, and substance use in adolescent girls. *Psychiatry Research*, 185, 408–413.

Neimeyer, R. A., Klass, D., & Dennis, M. R. (2014). A social constructionist account of grief: Loss and the narration of meaning. *Death Studies*, 38(8), 485–498.

Nelson, K. (1974). Concept, word, and sentence: Interrelations in acquisition and development. *Psychological Review*, 81, 267–285.

Nelson, K., & Fivush, R. (2004). The emergence of autobiographical memory: A social cultural developmental theory. *Psychological Review*, 111, 486–511.

Nelson, L. J., Duan, X. X., Padilla-Walker, L. M., & Luster, S. S. (2013). Facing adulthood: Comparing the criteria that Chinese emerging adults and their parents have for adulthood. *Journal of Adolescent Research*, 28(2), 189–208.

Nelson, S. K., Kushlev, K., & Lyubomirsky, S. (2014). The pains and pleasures of parenting: When, why, and how is parenthood associated with more or less well-being? *Psychological Bulletin*, 140(3), 846–895.

Nepomnyaschy, L., & Teitler, J. (2013). Cyclical cohabitation among unmarried parents in fragile families. *Journal of Marriage and Family*, 75(5), 1248–1265.

Neugarten, B. (1972). Personality and the aging process. *The Gerontologist*, 12(1, Pt. 1), 9–15.

Neugarten, B. L. (1979). Time, age, and the life cycle. *American Journal of Psychiatry*, 136, 887–894.

Neumark, D. (2009). The Age Discrimination in Employment Act and the challenge of population aging. *Research on Aging*, 31, 41–68.

Newcomb, A. F., & Bagwell, C. L. (1995). Children's friendship relations: A meta-analytic review. *Psychological Bulletin, 117,* 306–347.

Newman, K. L. (2011). Sustainable careers: Lifecycle engagement in work. *Organizational Dynamics, 40,* 136–143.

Newton, N. J., & Baltys, I. H. (2014). Parent status and generativity within the context of race. *International Journal of Aging & Human Development, 78*(2), 171–195.

Newton, N., & Stewart, A. J. (2010). The midlife ages: Change in women's personalities and social roles. *Psychology of Women's Quarterly, 31,* 75–84.

NICHD Early Child Care Research Network. (2003). Does amount of time spent in child care predict socioemotional adjustment during the transition to kindergarten? *Child Development, 74,* 976–1005.

NICHD Early Child Care Research Network. (2004). Type of child care and children's development at 54 months. *Early Childhood Research Quarterly, 19,* 203–230.

NICHD Early Child Care Research Network. (2006). Child-care effect sizes for the NICHD Study of Early Child Care and Youth Development. *American Psychologist, 61,* 99–116.

Nicolopoulou, A., Barbosa de Sá, A., Ilgaz, H., & Brockmeyer, C. (2010). Using the transformative power of play to educate hearts and minds: From Vygotsky to Vivian Paley and beyond. *Mind, Culture, and Activity, 17,* 42–58.

Nicolson, R. I., & Fawcett, A. J. (2011). Dyslexia, dysgraphia, procedural learning and the cerebellum. *Cortex, 47,* 117–127.

Nielsen, L., Knutson, B., & Carstensen, L. L. (2008). Affect dynamics, affective forecasting, and aging. *Emotion, 8*(3), 318–330.

Nikulina, V., & Widom, C. S. (2013). Child maltreatment and executive functioning in middle adulthood: A prospective examination. *Neuropsychology, 27*(4), 417–427.

Nomaguchi, K. M., & DeMaris, A. (2013). Nonmaternal care's association with mother's parenting sensitivity: A case of self-selection bias? *Journal of Marriage and Family, 75*(3), 760–777.

Nomaguchi, K., & House, A. N. (2013). Racial-ethnic disparities in maternal parenting stress: The role of structural disadvantages and parenting values. *Journal of Health and Social Behavior, 54*(3), 386–404.

Normand, S., Schneider, B., Lee, M., Maisonneuve, M., Chupetlovska-Anastasova, A., Kuehn, S., & Robaey, P. (2013). Continuities and changes in the friendships of children with and without ADHD: A longitudinal, observational study. *Journal of Abnormal Child Psychology, 41*(7), 1161–1175.

Norwood, S. J., Bowker, A., Buchholz, A., Henderson, K. A., Goldfield, G., & Flament, M. F. (2011). Self-silencing and anger regulation as predictors of disordered eating among adolescent females. *Eating Behaviors, 12,* 112–118.

O'Donovan, A., Slavich, G. M., Epel, E. S., & Neylan, T. C. (2013). Exaggerated neurobiological sensitivity to threat as a mechanism linking anxiety with increased risk for diseases of aging. *Neuroscience and Biobehavioral Reviews, 37*(1), 96–108.

O'Rourke, N., Neufeld, E., Claxton, A., & Smith, J. A. Z. (2010). Knowing me—knowing you: Reported personality and trait discrepancies as predictors of marital idealization between long-wed spouses. *Psychology and Aging, 25*(2), 412–421.

Oas, P. T. (2010). Current status on corporal punishment with children: What the literature says. *American Journal of Family Therapy, 38*(5), 413–420.

Obradović, J., Burt, K. B., & Masten, A. S. (2010). Testing a dual cascade model linking competence and symptoms over 20 years from childhood to adulthood. *Journal of Clinical Child and Adolescent Psychology, 39*(1), 90–102.

Oddo, S., Lux, S., Weiss, P. H., Schwab, A., Welzer, H., Markowitsch, H. J., & Fink, G. R. (2010). Specific role of medial prefrontal cortex in retrieving recent autobiographical memories: An fMRI study of young female subjects. *Cortex, 46,* 29–39.

OECD. (2014). *Health at a Glance: Europe 2014,* In *OECD Publishing.* Retrieved from http://www.oecd.org/health/health-at-a-glance-europe-23056088.htm

Ofen, N., & Shing, Y. L. (2013). From perception to memory: Changes in memory systems across the lifespan. *Neuroscience and Biobehavioral Reviews, 37*(9, Part B), 2258–2267.

Okun, M. A., Yeung, E. W., & Brown, S. (2013). Volunteering by older adults and risk of mortality: A meta-analysis. *Psychology and Aging, 28*(2), 564–577.

Oldehinkel, A. J., & Bouma, E. C. (2011). Sensitivity to the depressogenic effect of stress and HPA-axis reactivity in adolescence: A review of gender differences. *Neuroscience and Biobehavioral Reviews, 35*(8), 1757–1770.

Oliver, D. P., Wittenberg-Lyles, E., Washington, K., Kruse, R. L., Albright, D. L., Baldwin, P. K., . . . Demiris, G. (2013). Hospice caregivers' experiences with pain management: "I'm not a doctor, and I don't know if I helped her go faster or slower." *Journal of Pain and Symptom Management, 46*(6), 846–858.

Olsson Möller, U., Midlöv, P., Kristensson, J., Ekdahl, C., Berglund, J., & Jakobsson, U. (2013). Prevalence and predictors of falls and dizziness in people younger and older than 80 years of age—A longitudinal cohort study. *Archives of Gerontology and Geriatrics, 56*(1), 160–168.

Olthof, T. (2012). Anticipated feelings of guilt and shame as predictors of early adolescents' antisocial and prosocial interpersonal behaviour. *European Journal of Developmental Psychology, 9*(3), 371–388.

Olweus, D., Limber, S., & Mihalic, S. F. (1999). *Blueprints for violence prevention, Book 9: Bullying prevention program.* Boulder, CO: Center for the Study and Prevention of Violence, Institute of Behavioral Science, University of Colorado at Boulder.

Omar, H., McElderry, D., & Zakharia, R. (2003). Educating adolescents about puberty: What are we missing? *International Journal of Adolescent Medicine and Health, 15,* 79–83.

Onadja, Y., Atchessi, N., Soura, B. A., Rossier, C., & Zunzunegui, M. (2013). Gender differences in cognitive impairment and mobility disability in old age: A cross-sectional study in Ouagadougou, Burkina Faso. *Archives of Gerontology and Geriatrics, 57*(3), 311–318.

Onrust, S., Willemse, G., VanDenBout, J., & Cuijpers, P. (2010). Effects of a visiting service for older widowed individuals: A randomized clinical trial. *Death Studies, 34*(9), 777–803.

Osofsky, J. D., & Lieberman, A. F. (2010). A call for integrating a mental health perspective into systems of care for abused and neglected infants and young children. *American Psychologist, 66*(2), 120–128.

Ostrov, J. M., & Godleski, S. A. (2010). Toward an integrated gender-linked model of aggression subtypes in early and middle childhood. *Psychological Review, 117*(1), 233–242.

Ostrov, J. M., Murray-Close, D., Godleski, S. A., & Hart, E. J. (2013). Prospective associations between forms and functions of aggression and social and affective processes during early childhood. *Journal of Experimental Child Psychology*, 116(1), 19–36.

Ott, J. C. (2011). Government and happiness in 130 nations: Good governance fosters higher level and more equality of happiness. *Social Indicators Research*, 102(1), 3–22.

Ott, M. A., Millstein, S. G., Ofner, S., & Halpern-Felsher, B. L. (2006). Greater expectations: Adolescents' positive motivations for sex. *Perspectives on Sexual and Reproductive Health*, 38, 84–89.

Otterman, G., Lainpelto, K., & Lindblad, F. (2013). Factors influencing the prosecution of child physical abuse cases in a Swedish metropolitan area. *Acta Paediatrica*, 102(12), 1199–1203.

Overall, N. C., Fletcher, G. O., & Simpson, J. A. (2010). Helping each other grow: Romantic partner support, self-improvement, and relationship quality. *Personality and Social Psychology Bulletin*, 36(11), 1496–1513.

Owens, E. B., & Hinshaw, S. P. (2013). Perinatal problems and psychiatric comorbidity among children with ADHD. *Journal of Clinical Child and Adolescent Psychology*, 42(6), 762–768.

Pace, C. S., & Zavattini, G. C. (2011). "Adoption and attachment theory": The attachment models of adoptive mothers and the revision of attachment patterns of their late-adopted children. *Child Care, Health and Development*, 37(1), 82–88.

Paechter, C. (2013). Concepts of fairness in marriage and divorce. *Journal of Divorce & Remarriage*, 54(6), 458–475.

Paek, H.-J., Nelson, M. R., & Vilela, A. M. (2011). Examination of gender-role portrayals in television advertising across seven countries. *Sex Roles*, 64, 192–207.

Paikoff, R. L., & Brooks-Gunn, J. (1991). Do parent-child relationships change during puberty? *Psychological Bulletin*, 110, 47–66.

Palkovitz, R. J. (2002). *Involved fathering and men's adult development: Provisional Balances.* Mahwah, NJ: Erlbaum.

Palladino, G. (1996). *Teenagers: An American history.* New York, NY: Basic Books.

Palley, E., & Shdaimah, C. (2011). Child care policy: A need for greater advocacy. *Children and Youth Services Review*, 33, 1159–1165.

Parackal, S. M., Parackal, M. K., & Harraway, J. A. (2013). Prevalence and

correlates of drinking in early pregnancy among women who stopped drinking on pregnancy recognition. *Maternal and Child Health Journal*, 17(3), 520–529.

Parent, A.-S., Teilmann, G., Juul, A., Skakkebaek, N. E., Toppari, J., & Bourguignon, J.-P. (2003). The timing of normal puberty and the age limits of sexual precocity: Variations around the world, secular trends, and changes after migration. *Endocrine Reviews*, 24, 668–693.

Parent, M. C., & Moradi, B. (2011). His biceps become him: A test of objectification theory's application to drive for muscularity and propensity for steroid use in college men. *Journal of Counseling Psychology*, 58, 246–256.

Parham-Payne, W., Dickerson, B. J., & Everette, T. D. (2013). Trading the picket fence: Perceptions of childbirth, marriage, and career. *Journal of Sociology and Social Welfare*, 40(3), 85–104.

Park, D. C., & McDonough, I. M. (2013). The dynamic aging mind: Revelations from functional neuroimaging research. *Perspectives on Psychological Science*, 8(1), 62–67.

Park, Y. S., Kim, B. S. K., Chiang, J., & Ju, C. M. (2010). Acculturation, enculturation, parental adherence to Asian cultural values, parenting styles, and family conflict among Asian American college students. *Asian American Journal of Psychology*, 1(1), 67–79.

Parkes, A., Wight, D., Hunt, K., Henderson, M., & Sargent, J. (2013). Are sexual media exposure, parental restrictions on media use and co-viewing TV and DVDs with parents and friends associated with teenagers' early sexual behaviour? *Journal of Adolescence*, 36(6), 1121–1133.

Parkes, C. M. (1987). *Bereavement: Studies of grief in adult life* (2nd ed.). Madison, CT: International Universities Press.

Pasco Fearon, R. M., & Belsky, J. (2011). Infant–mother attachment and the growth of externalizing problems across the primary-school years. *Journal of Child Psychology and Psychiatry*, 52(7), 782–791.

Pasco Fearon, R., Bakermans-Kranenburg, M. J., van IJzendoorn, M. H., Lapsley, A., & Roisman, G. I. (2010). The significance of insecure attachment and disorganization in the development of children's externalizing behavior: A meta-analytic study. *Child Development*, 81(2), 435–456.

Pascuzzo, K., Cyr, C., & Moss, E. (2013). Longitudinal association between adolescent attachment, adult romantic attachment, and emotion regulation

strategies. *Attachment & Human Development*, 15(1), 83–103.

Patall, E. A., Cooper, H., & Robinson, J. C. (2008). The effects of choice on intrinsic motivation and related outcomes: A meta-analysis of research findings. *Psychological Bulletin*, 134(2), 270–300.

Paul, A. M. (2010). *Origins: How the nine months before birth shape our lives.* New York, NY: Free Press.

Paul, I. M., Savage, J. S., Anzman, S. L., Beiler, J. S., Marini, M. E., Stokes, J. L., & Birch, L. L. (2011). Preventing obesity during infancy: A pilot study. *Obesity*, 19(2), 353–361.

Paulus, M., & Moore, C. (2014). The development of recipient-dependent sharing behavior and sharing expectations in preschool children. *Developmental Psychology*, 50(3), 914–921.

Paulussen-Hoogeboom, M. C., Stams, G. J. J. M., Hermanns, J. M. A., & Peetsma, T. T. D. (2007). Child negative emotionality and parenting from infancy to preschool: A meta-analytic review. *Developmental Psychology*, 43(2), 438–453.

Pavarini, G., de Hollanda Souza, D., & Hawk, C. K. (2013). Parental practices and theory of mind development. *Journal of Child and Family Studies*, 22(6), 844–853.

Peach, H. D., & Gaultney, J. F. (2013). Sleep, impulse control, and sensation-seeking predict delinquent behavior in adolescents, emerging adults, and adults. *Journal of Adolescent Health*, 53(2), 293–299.

Peacock, S., Forbes, D., Markle-Reid, M., Hawranik, P., Morgan, D., Jansen, L., & Henderson, S. R. (2010). The positive aspects of the caregiving journey with dementia: Using a strengths-based perspective to reveal opportunities. *Journal of Applied Gerontology*, 29(5), 640–659.

Peake, S. J., Dishion, T. J., Stormshak, E. A., Moore, W. E., & Pfeifer, J. H. (2013). Risk-taking and social exclusion in adolescence: Neural mechanisms underlying peer influences on decision-making. *Neuroimage*, 82, 23–34.

Pearman, A., Hertzog, C., & Gerstorf, D. (2014). Little evidence for links between memory complaints and memory performance in very old age: Longitudinal analyses from the Berlin Aging Study. *Psychology and Aging*, 29(4), 828–842.

Pearson, D. A., Santos, C. W., Aman, M. G., Arnold, L. E., Casat, C. D., Mansour, R., . . . Cleveland, L. A. (2013). Effects of extended release methylphenidate treatment on ratings of attention-deficit/hyperactivity disorder (ADHD) and associated behavior in children with autism spectrum disorders and ADHD symptoms. *Journal of Child and Adolescent Psychopharmacology, 23*(5), 337–351.

Peck, S. C., Vida, M., & Eccles, J. S. (2008). Adolescent pathways to adulthood drinking: Sport activity involvement is not necessarily risky or protective. *Addiction, 103* (Suppl. 1), 69–83.

Pedersen, N. L. (1996). Gerontological behavior genetics. In J. E. Birren, K. W. Schaie, R. P. Abeles, M. Gatz, & T. A. Salthouse (Eds.), *Handbook of the psychology of aging* (4th ed. pp. 59–77). San Diego, CA: Academic Press.

Pellegrini, A. D. (2006). The development and function of rough-and-tumble play in childhood and adolescence: A sexual selection theory perspective. In A. Göncü & S. Gaskins (Eds.), *Play and development: Evolutionary, sociocultural, and functional perspectives. The Jean Piaget Symposium Series* (pp. 77–98). Mahwah, NJ: Erlbaum.

Pellegrini, A. D., & Smith, P. K. (Eds.). (2005). The nature of play: Great apes and humans. New York, NY: Guilford Press.

Pellegrini, A. D., Long, J. D., Roseth, C. J., Bohn, C. M., & Van Ryzin, M. (2007). A short-term longitudinal study of preschoolers' (*Homo sapiens*) sex segregation: The role of physical activity, sex, and time. *Journal of Comparative Psychology, 121*(3), 282–289.

Pelts, M D. (2014). Look back at the defense of marriage act: Why same-sex marriage is still relevant for social work. *Journal of Woman and Social work, 29*(2). 237–247

Penman, E. L., Breen, L. J., Hewitt, L. Y., & Prigerson, H. G. (2014). Public attitudes about normal and pathological grief. *Death Studies, 38*(8), 510–516.

Peper, J. S., & Dahl, R. E. (2013). The teenage brain: Surging hormones—Brain-behavior interactions during puberty. *Current Directions in Psychological Science, 22*(2), 134–139.

Pérez-Edgar, K., Bar-Haim, Y., McDermott, J. M., Chronis-Tuscano, A., Pine, D. S., & Fox, N. A. (2010a). Attention biases to threat and behavioral inhibition in early childhood shape adolescent social withdrawal. *Emotion, 10,* 349–357.

Pérez-Edgar, K., McDermott, J. N., Korelitz, K., Degnan, K. A., Curby, T. W., Pine, D. S., & Fox, N. A. (2010b).

Patterns of sustained attention in infancy shape the developmental trajectory of social behavior from toddlerhood through adolescence. *Developmental Psychology, 46*(6), 1723–1730.

Perrig-Chiello, P., & Hutchison, S. (2010). Family caregivers of elderly persons: A differential perspective on stressors, resources, and well-being. *GeroPsych, 23*(4), 195–206.

Perrone-McGovern, K. M., Wright, S. L., Howell, D. S., & Barnum, E. L. (2014). Contextual influences on work and family roles: Gender, culture, and socioeconomic factors. *The Career Development Quarterly, 62*(1), 21–28.

Perry, A. R., & Langley, C. (2013). Even with the best of intentions: Paternal involvement and the theory of planned behavior. *Family Process, 52*(2), 179–192.

Perry, S. L. (2013). Religion and Whites' attitudes toward interracial marriage with African Americans, Asians, and Latinos. *Journal for the Scientific Study of Religion, 52*(2), 425–442.

Perry, W. (1999). *Forms of ethical and intellectual development in the college years: A scheme.* San Francisco: Jossey-Bass.

Persike, M., & Seiffge-Krenke, I. (2014). Is stress perceived differently in relationships with parents and peers? Inter- and intra-regional comparisons on adolescents from 21 nations. *Journal of Adolescence, 37*(4), 493–504.

Peskin, J. (1992). Ruse and representations: On children's ability to conceal information. *Developmental Psychology, 28,* 84–89.

Peterson, B. E. (1998). Case studies of midlife generativity: Analyzing motivation and realization. In D. P. McAdams & E. de St. Aubin (Eds.), *Generativity and adult development: How and why we care for the next generation* (pp. 101–131). Washington, DC: American Psychological Association.

Petraglia, F., Serour, G. I., & Chapron C. (2013). The changing prevalence of infertility. *International Journal of Gynecology Obstetrics, 123* (Suppl. 2), S4–8.

Petts, R. J. (2014). Family, religious attendance, and trajectories of psychological well-being among youth. *Journal of Family Psychology, 28*(6), 759–768.

Pfinder, M., Kunst, A. E., Feldmann, R., van Eijsden, M., & Vrijkotte, T. M. (2014). Educational differences in continuing or restarting drinking in early and late pregnancy: Role of psychological and physical problems. *Journal of*

Studies on Alcohol and Drugs, 75(1), 47–55.

Pharo, H., Sim, C., Graham, M., Gross, J., & Hayne, H. (2011). Risky business: Executive function, personality, and reckless behavior during adolescence and emerging adulthood. *Behavioral Neuroscience, 125*(6), 970–978.

Phelan, P., Davidson, A. L., & Yu, H. C. (1998). *Adolescents' worlds: Negotiating family, peers, and school.* New York, NY: Teachers College Press.

Phillips, C. D., & Hawes, C. (2005). Care provision in housing with supportive services: The importance of care type, individual characteristics, and care site. *Journal of Applied Gerontology, 24,* 55–67.

Phillips, D. A., & Lowenstein, A. E. (2011). Early care, education and child development. *American Review of Psychology, 62,* 483–500.

Phillips, D. P., Brewer, K. M., & Wadensweiler, P. (2011). Alcohol as a risk factor for sudden infant death syndrome (SIDS). *Addiction, 106*(3), 516–525.

Phillips, J. L., Halcomb, E, J., & Davidson, P. M. (2011). End-of-life care pathways in acute and hospice care: An integrative review. *Journal of Pain and Symptom Management, 41*(5), 940–955.

Phinney, J. S. (2006). Acculturation is not an independent variable: Approaches to studying acculturation as a complex process. In M. H. Bornstein & L. R. Cote (Eds.), *Acculturation and parent-child relationships: Measurement and development* (pp. 79–95). Mahwah, NJ: Erlbaum.

Piaget, J. (1950). *The psychology of intelligence.* Oxford, England: Harcourt.

Piaget, J. (1962). *Play, dreams and imitation in childhood.* New York, NY: Norton. (Original work published 1951).

Piaget, J. (1965). *The moral judgment of the child* (Paperback ed.). New York, NY: Free Press.

Piaget, J. (1971). *The psychology of intelligence.* London, England: Routledge & Kegan Paul. (Original work published 1950).

Pierce, L., Dahl, M. S., & Nielsen, J. (2013). In sickness and in wealth: Psychological and sexual costs of income comparison in marriage. *Personality and Social Psychology Bulletin, 39*(3), 359–374.

Pinker, S. (2011). *The better angels of our nature: Why violence has declined.* New York, NY: Viking.

Pinquart, M. (2013). Do the parent–child relationship and parenting behaviors differ between families with a child with and without chronic illness? A meta-analysis. *Journal of Pediatric Psychology*, 38(7), 708–721.

Pinquart, M., & Schindler, I. (2007). Changes of life satisfaction in the transition to retirement: A latent-class approach. *Psychology and Aging*, 22(3), 442–455.

Pinquart, M., Feußner, C., & Ahnert, L. (2013). Meta-analytic evidence for stability in attachments from infancy to early adulthood. *Attachment & Human Development*, 15(2), 189–218.

Pitkanen, T., Kokko, K., Lyyra, A., & Pulkkinen, L. (2008). A developmental approach to alcohol drinking behaviour in adulthood: A follow-up study from age 8 to 42. *Addiction*, 103 (Suppl. 1), 48–68.

Pitrou, I., Shojaei, T., Wazana, A., Gilbert, F., & Kovess-Masféty, V. (2010). Child overweight, associated psychopathology, and social functioning: A French school-based survey in 6- to 11-year-old children. *Obesity*, 18(4), 809–817.

Pitzer, L. M., & Fingerman, K. L. (2010). Psychosocial resources and associations between childhood physical abuse and adult well-being. *Journals of Gerontology: Psychological Sciences*, 65B(4), 425–433.

Plomin, R., & Bergeman, C. S. (1991). The nature of nurture: Genetic influence on "environmental" measures. *Behavioral and Brain Sciences*, 14, 373–427.

Plomin, R., & Spinath, F. M. (2004). Intelligence: Genetics, genes, and genomics. *Journal of Personality and Social Psychology*, 86, 112–129.

Plomin, R., DeFries, J. C., Craig, I. W., & McGuffin, P. (2003). Behavioral genomics. In R. Plomin, J. C. DeFries, I. W. Craig, & P. McGuffin (Eds.), *Behavioral genetics in the postgenomic era* (pp. 531–540). Washington, DC: American Psychological Association.

Pluess, M., & Belsky, J. (2010). Differential susceptibility to parenting and quality child care. *Developmental Psychology*, 46(2), 379–390.

Pnevmatikos, D., & Trikkaliotis, I. (2013). Intraindividual differences in executive functions during childhood: The role of emotions. *Journal of Experimental Child Psychology*, 115(2), 245–261.

Poirier, F. E., & Smith, E. O. (1974). Socializing functions of primate play. *American Zoologist*, 14, 275–287.

Polanco-Roman, L., & Miranda, R. (2013). Culturally related stress, hopelessness, and vulnerability to depressive symptoms and suicidal ideation in emerging adulthood. *Behavior Therapy*, 44(1), 75–87.

Poortman, A. R., & Seltzer, J. A. (2007). Parents' expectations about childrearing after divorce: Does anticipating difficulty deter divorce? *Journal of Marriage and Family*, 69(1), 254–269.

Pope, N. D. (2013). Views on aging: How caring for an aging parent influences adult daughters' perspectives on later life. *Journal of Adult Development*, 20(1), 46–56.

Porfeli, E. J., & Mortimer, J. T. (2010). Intrinsic work value-reward dissonance and work satisfaction during young adulthood. *Journal of Vocational Behavior*, 76, 507–519.

Potocnik, K., Tordera, N., & Peiro, J. (2013). Truly satisfied with your retirement or just resigned? Pathways toward different patterns of retirement satisfaction. *Journal of Applied Gerontology*, 32(2), 164–187.

Potter, D. (2010). Psychosocial well-being and the relationship between divorce and children's academic achievement. *Journal of Marriage and Family*, 72, 933–946.

Potts, M., Prata, N., & Sahin-Hodoglugil, N. N. (2010). Maternal mortality: One death every 7 min. *The Lancet*, 375(9728), 1762–1763.

Poulin, F., & Chan, A. (2010). Friendship stability and change in childhood and adolescence. *Developmental Review*, 30(3), 257–272.

Poulin, M., & Silver, R. (2008). World benevolence beliefs and well-being across the lifespan. *Psychology and Aging*, 23, 19.

Powers, S. M., Bisconti, T. L., & Bergeman, C. S. (2014). Trajectories of social support and well-being across the first two years of widowhood. *Death Studies*, 38(8), 499–509.

Prakash, K., & Coplan, R. J. (2007). Socioemotional characteristics and school adjustment of socially withdrawn children in India. *International Journal of Behavioral Development*, 31(2), 123–132.

Preßler, A., Krajewski, K., & Hasselhorn, M. (2013). Working memory capacity in preschool children contributes to the acquisition of school relevant precursor skills. *Learning and Individual Differences*, 23, 138–144.

Pressler, K. A., & Ferraro, K. F. (2010). Assistive device use as a dynamic acquisition process in later life. *The Gerontologist*, 50(3), 371–381.

Preston, S. H. (1991). *Fatal years: Child mortality in late nineteenth-century America*. Princeton, NJ: Princeton University Press.

Prevost, S. S., & Wallace, J. B. (2009). Dying in institutions. In J. L. Werth, & D. Blevins (Eds.), *Decision making near the end-of-life: Issues, developments, and future directions. Series in death, dying and bereavement* (pp. 189–208). New York, NY: Routledge/Taylor & Francis Group.

Prinstein, M. J., & La Greca, A. M. (2002). Peer crowd affiliation and internalizing distress in childhood and adolescence: A longitudinal follow-back study. *Journal of Research on Adolescence*, 12, 325–351.

Pronk, M., Deeg, D. H., & Kramer, S. E. (2013). Hearing status in older persons: A significant determinant of depression and loneliness? Results from the Longitudinal Aging Study Amsterdam. *American Journal of Audiology*, 22(2), 316–320.

Pryor, J. H., Hurtado, S., SeAngelo, L., Blake, L. P., & Tran, S. (2011). The American freshman: National norms Fall 2010. Los Angeles, Higher Education Research Institute, UCLA.

Puhl, R. M., & Heuer, C. A. (2010). Obesity stigma: Important considerations for public health. *American Journal of Public Health*, 100(6), 1019–1028.

Puhl, R. M., & Latner, J. D. (2007). Stigma, obesity, and the health of the nation's children. *Psychological Bulletin*, 133(4), 557–580.

Pungello, E. P., Kainz, K., Burchinal, M., Wasik, B. H., Sparling, J. J., Ramey, C. T., & Campbell, F. A. (2010). Early educational intervention, early cumulative risk, and the early home environment as predictors of young adult outcomes within a high-risk sample. *Child Development*, 81(1), 410–426.

Pushkar, D., Chaikelson, J., Conway, M., Etezadi, J., Giannopolous, C., Li, K., & Wrosch, C. (2010). Testing continuity and activity variables as predictors of positive and negative affect in retirement. *Journals of Gerontology: Psychological Sciences*, 65B(1), 42–49.

Qu, Y. (2014). The comparative study of household elderly care in China, the Philippines and Japan. *Home Health*

Care Management and Practice, 26(3),175–181.

Rabin, J. S., Gilboa, A., Stuss, D. T., Mar, R. A., & Rosenbaum, R. S. (2010). Common and unique neural correlates of autobiographical memory and theory of mind. *Journal of Cognitive Neuroscience,* 22(6), 1095–1111.

Rabins, P. V. (2011, April). Memory. *The John Hopkins White Papers,* 48.

Rahman, A., Iqbal, Z., & Harrington, R. (2003). Life events, social support and depression in childbirth: Perspectives from a rural community in the developing world. *Psychological Medicine,* 33, 1161–1167.

Raj, A., & Boehmer, U. (2013). Girl child marriage and its association with national rates of HIV, maternal health, and infant mortality across 97 countries. *Violence Against Women,* 19(4), 536–551.

Rambaran, A. J., Dijkstra, J. K., & Stark, T. H. (2013). Status-based influence processes: The role of norm salience in contagion of adolescent risk attitudes. *Journal of Research on Adolescence,* 23(3), 574–585.

Ramsay, S. M., & Santella, R. M. (2011). The definition of life: A survey of obstetricians and neonatologists in New York City hospitals regarding extremely premature births. *Maternal and Child Health Journal,* 15, 446–452.

Ranta, M., Dietrich, J., & Salmela-Aro, K. (2014). Career and romantic relationship goals and concerns during emerging adulthood. *Emerging Adulthood,* 2(1), 17–26.

Rapport, M. D., Orban, S. A., Kofler, M. J., & Friedman, L. M. (2013). Do programs designed to train working memory, other executive functions, and attention benefit children with ADHD? A meta-analytic review of cognitive, academic, and behavioral outcomes. *Clinical Psychology Review,* 33(8), 1237–1252.

Ratner, N. B. (2013). Why talk with children matters: Clinical implications of infant- and child-directed speech research. *Seminars in Speech and Language,* 34(4), 203–214.

Rauer, A. J., Pettit, G. S., Lansford, J. E., Bates, J. E., & Dodge, K. A. (2013). Romantic relationship patterns in young adulthood and their developmental antecedents. *Developmental Psychology,* 49(11), 2159–2171.

Raver, C. C., Blair, C., & Willoughby, M. (2013). Poverty as a predictor of 4-year-olds' executive function: New perspectives on models of differential susceptibility. *Developmental Psychology,* 49(2), 292–304.

Raz, S., Newman, J., DeBastos, A. K., Peters, B. N., & Batton, D. G. (2014). Postnatal growth and neuropsychological performance in preterm-birth preschoolers. *Neuropsychology,* 28(2), 188–201.

Reddy, V., Liebal, K., Hicks, K., Jonnalagadda, S., & Chintalapuri, B. (2013). The emergent practice of infant compliance: An exploration in two cultures. *Developmental Psychology,* 49(9), 1754–1762.

Regan, P., & Ball, E. (2013). Breastfeeding mothers' experiences: The ghost in the machine. *Qualitative Health Research,* 23(5), 679–688.

Reijneveld, S. A., van der Wal, M. F., Brugman, E., Sing, R. A. H., & Verloove-Vanhorick, S. P. (2004). Infant crying and abuse. *Lancet,* 364, 1340–1342.

Reimer, J., Paolitto, D. P., & Hersh, R. H. (1983). *Promoting moral growth: From Piaget to Kohlberg* (2nd ed.). New York, NY: Longman.

Reimer, K. (2003). Committed to caring: Transformation in adolescent moral identity. *Applied Developmental Science,* 7, 129–137.

Reiss, D., Eccles, J. S., & Nielsen, L. (2014). Conscientiousness and public health: Synthesizing current research to promote healthy aging. *Developmental Psychology,* 50(5), 1303–1314.

Reissman, C., Aron, A., & Bergen, M. R. (1993). Shared activities and marital satisfaction: Causal direction and self-expansion versus boredom. *Journal of Social and Personal Relationships,* 10, 243–254.

Reppermund, S., Brodaty, H., Crawford, J. D., Kochan, N. A., Draper, B., Slavin, M. J., . . . Sachdev, P. S. (2013). Impairment in instrumental activities of daily living with high cognitive demand is an early marker of mild cognitive impairment: the Sydney Memory and Ageing Study. *Psychological Medicine,* 43(11), 2437–2445.

Reskin, B. (1993). Sex segregation in the workplace. *Annual Review of Sociology,* 19, 241–270.

Reuter-Lorenz, P. A. (2013). Aging and cognitive neuroimaging: A fertile union. *Perspectives on Psychological Science,* 8(1), 68–71.

Reuter-Lorenz, P. A., & Cappell, K. A. (2008). Neurocognitive aging and the compensation hypothesis. *Current Directions in Psychological Science,* 17(3), 177–182.

Ridgway, A., Northup, J., Pellegrin, A., LaRue, R., & Hightsoe, A. (2003). Effects of recess on the classroom behavior of children with and without attention-deficit hyperactivity disorder. *School Psychology Quarterly,* 18, 253–268.

Riegel, K. F., & Riegel, R. M. (1972). Development, drop, and death. *Developmental Psychology,* 6, 306–319.

Rilling, J. K. (2013). The neural and hormonal bases of human parental care. *Neuropsychologia,* 51(4), 731–747.

Rinehart, M. S., & Kiselica, M. S. (2010). Helping men with the trauma of miscarriage. *Psychotherapy: Theory, Research, Practice, Training,* 47(3), 288–295.

Rispoli, K. M., McGoey, K. E., Koziol, N. A., & Schreiber, J. B. (2013). The relation of parenting, child temperament, and attachment security in early childhood to social competence at school entry. *Journal of School Psychology,* 51(5), 643–658.

Risse, G. B., & Balboni, M. J. (2013). Shifting hospital–hospice boundaries: Historical perspectives on the institutional care of the dying. *American Journal of Hospice & Palliative Medicine,* 30(4), 325–330.

Ritchie, R. A., Meca, A., Madrazo, V. L., Schwartz, S. J., Hardy, S. A., Zamboanga, B. L., . . . Lee, R. M. (2013). Identity dimensions and related processes in emerging adulthood: Helpful or harmful? *Journal of Clinical Psychology,* 69(4), 415–432.

Roberts, A. L., Lyall, K., Rich-Edwards, J. W., Ascherio, A., & Weisskopf, M. G. (2013). Association of maternal exposure to childhood abuse with elevated risk for autism in offspring. *JAMA Psychiatry,* 70(5), 508–515.

Roberts, A., & Good, E. (2010). Media images and female body dissatisfaction: The moderating effects of the Five-Factor traits. *Eating Behaviors,* 11(4), 211–216.

Robertson, I. H. (2013). A noradrenergic theory of cognitive reserve: Implications for Alzheimer's disease. *Neurobiology of Aging,* 34(1), 298–308.

Robertson, S. C., & Hopko, D. R. (2013). Emotional expression during autobiographical narratives as a function of aging: Support for the socioemotional selectivity theory. *Journal of Adult Development,* 20(2), 76–86.

Robles, T. F., Slatcher, R. B., Trombello, J. M., & McGinn, M. M. (2014). Marital quality and health: A meta-analytic review. *Psychological Bulletin, 140*(1), 140–187.

Rodin, J., & Langer, E. J. (1980). Aging labels: The decline of control and the fall of self-esteem. *Journal of Social Issues, 36*, 12–29.

Rodkin, P. C., & Roisman, G. I. (2010). Antecedents and correlates of the popular-aggressive phenomenon in elementary school. *Child Development, 81*(3), 837–850.

Rodkin, P. C., Ryan, A. M., Jamison, R., & Wilson, T. (2013). Social goals, social behavior, and social status in middle childhood. *Developmental Psychology, 49*(6), 1139–1150.

Rodrigues, R., & Schmidt, A. E. (2010). Expenditures for long-term care: At the crossroads between family and state. *GeroPsych, 23*(4), 183–193.

Rodriguez, C. M., & Henderson, R. C. (2010). Who spares the rod? Religious orientation, social conformity, and child abuse potential. *Child Abuse & Neglect, 34*, 84–94.

Roenker, D. L., Cissell, G. M., Ball, K. K., Wadley, V. G., & Edwards, J. D. (2003). Speed-of-processing and driving simulator training result in improved driving performance. *Human Factors, 45*, 218–233.

Roffwarg, H. P., Muzio, J. N., & Dement, W. C. (1966, April 29). Ontogenetic development of the human sleep-dream cycle. *Science, 152*, 604–619.

Rogoff, B., Paradise, R., Arauz, R. M., Correa-Chavez, M., & Angelillo, C. (2003). Firsthand learning through intent participation. *Annual Review of Psychology, 54*, 175–203.

Rohlfsen, L. S., & Kronenfeld, J. J. (2014). Gender differences in functional health: Latent curve analysis assessing differential exposure. *Journals of Gerontology Series B: Psychological Sciences and Social Sciences, 69*(4), 1.

Rojas-Flores, L., Herrera, S., Currier, J. M., Lin, E. Y., Kulzer, R., & Foy, D. W. (2013). "We are raising our children in fear": War, community violence, and parenting practices in El Salvador. *International Perspectives in Psychology: Research, Practice, Consultation, 2*(4), 269–285.

Romano, E., Babchishin, L., Pagani, L. S., & Kohen, D. (2010). School readiness and later achievement: Replication and extension using a nationwide Canadian survey. *Developmental Psychology, 46*(5), 995–1007.

Romeo, R. D. (2013). The teenage brain: The stress response and the adolescent brain. *Current Directions in Psychological Science, 22*(2), 140–145.

Rorie, M., Gottfredson, D. C., Cross, A., Wilson, D., & Connell, N. M. (2011). Structure and deviancy training in after-school programs. *Journal of Adolescence, 34*, 105–117.

Rose, A. J., & Asher, S. R. (2000). Children's friendships. In C. Hendrick & S. S. Hendrick (Eds.), *Close relationships: A sourcebook* (pp. 47–57). Thousand Oaks, CA: Sage.

Rose, J., Vassar, R., Cahill-Rowley, K., Guzman, X., Stevenson, D. K., & Barnea-Goraly, N. (2014). Brain microstructural development at near-term age in very-low-birth-weight preterm infants: An atlas-based diffusion imaging study. *Neuroimage, 86*, 244–256.

Rosenfield, R. L., Lipton, R. B., & Drum, M. L. (2009). Thelarche, pubarche, and menarche attainment in children with normal and elevated body mass index. *Pediatrics, 123*, 84–88.

Rosenthal, M., Wallace, G. L., Lawson, R., Wills, M. C., Dixon, E., Yerys, B. E., & Kenworthy, L. (2013). Impairments in real-world executive function increase from childhood to adolescence in autism spectrum disorders. *Neuropsychology, 27*(1), 13–18.

Roseth, C. J., Pellegrini, A. D., Dupuis, D. N., Bohn, C. M., Hickey, M. C., Hilk, C. L., & Peshkam, A. (2011). Preschoolers' bistrategic resource control, reconciliation, and peer regard. *Social Development, 20*(1), 185–211.

Ross, L. A., Clay, O. J., Edwards, J. D., Ball, K. K., Wadley, V. G., Vance, D. E., . . . Joyce, J. J. (2009). Do older drivers at-risk for crashes modify their driving over time? *Journals of Gerontology: Psychological Sciences, 64B*, 163–170.

Rosti, R. O., Sadek, A. A., Vaux, K. K., & Gleeson, J. G. (2014). The genetic landscape of autism spectrum disorders. *Developmental Medicine & Child Neurology, 56*(1), 12–18.

Rothenberg, J. Z., & Gardner, D. S. (2011). Protecting older workers: The failure of the Age Discrimination in Employment Act of 1967. *Journal of Sociology & Social Welfare, 38*(1), 9–30.

Rothermund, K., & Brandtstädter, J. (2003). Depression in later life: Cross-sequential patterns and possible determinants. *Psychology and Aging, 18*, 80–90.

Rothman, R. (2014). The Common Core takes hold: Implementation moves steadily forward. *Education Next, 14*(3), 16–22.

Roussotte, F., Soderberg, L., & Sowell, E. (2010). Structural, metabolic and functional brain abnormalities as a result of prenatal exposure to drugs of abuse: Evidence from neuroimaging. *Neuropsychology Review, 20*(4), 376–397.

Rowe, D. C. (2003). Assessing genotype-environment interactions and correlations in the postgenomic era. In R. Plomin, J. C. DeFries, I. W. Craig, & P. McGuffin (Eds.), *Behavioral genetics in the postgenomic era* (pp. 71–86). Washington, DC: American Psychological Association.

Rowe, G., Hasher, L., & Turcotte, J. (2008). Age differences in visuospatial working memory. *Psychology and Aging, 23*(1), 79–84.

Rowe, J. W., & Kahn, R. L. (1998). *Successful aging.* New York, NY: Pantheon Books.

Rowe, M. L., Levine, S. C., Fisher, J. A., & Goldin-Meadow, S. (2009). Does linguistic input play the same role in language learning for children with and without early brain injury? *Developmental Psychology, 45*, 90–102.

Royal College of Obstetricians and Gynaecologists [RCOG]. (1999). *Alcohol consumption in pregnancy.* Retrieved from http://www.rcog.org/uk/index.asp?PageID=509

Rubin, K. H., Bukowski, W. M., & Parker, J. G. (2006). Peer interactions, relationships, and groups. In N. Eisenberg, W. Damon, & R. M. Lerner (Eds.), *Handbook of child psychology: Vol. 3. Social, emotional, and personality development* (6th ed. pp. 571–645). Hoboken, NJ: Wiley.

Rubin, M. (2013). Grandparents as caregivers: Emerging issues for the profession. *Journal of Human Behavior in the Social Environment, 23*(3), 330–344.

Ruble, D. N., Martin, C., & Berenbaum, S. A. (2006). Gender development. In N. Eisenberg, W. Damon, & R. M. Lerner (Eds.), *Handbook of child psychology: Vol. 3. Social, emotional, and personality development* (6th ed. pp. 858–932). Hoboken, NJ: Wiley.

Runions, K. C. (2013). Toward a conceptual model of motive and self-control in cyber-aggression: Rage, revenge, reward, and recreation. *Journal of Youth and Adolescence, 42*(5), 751–771.

Runions, K. C., & Keating, D. P. (2010). Anger and inhibitory control as moderators of children's hostile attributions and aggression. *Journal of Applied Developmental Psychology, 31,* 370–378.

Rusbult, C. E., Kumashiro, M., Kubacka, K. E., & Finkel, E. J. (2009). "The part of me that you bring out": Ideal similarity and the Michelangelo phenomenon. *Journal of Personality and Social Psychology, 96,* 61–82.

Rushton, J. P., & Jensen, A. R. (2005). Thirty years of research on race differences in cognitive ability. *Psychology, Public Policy, and Law, 11,* 235–294.

Russell, V. M., Baker, L. R., & McNulty, J. K. (2013). Attachment insecurity and infidelity in marriage: Do studies of dating relationships really inform us about marriage? *Journal of Family Psychology, 27*(2), 242–251.

Ryan, J. J., Glass, L. A., & Bartels, J. M. (2010). Stability of the WISC-IV in a sample of elementary and middle school children. *Applied Neuropsychology, 17*(1), 68–72.

Ryan, R. M., Deci, E. L., Grolnick, W. S., & La Guardia, J. G. (2006). The significance of autonomy and autonomy support in psychological development and psychopathology. In D. Cicchetti & D. J. Cohen (Eds.), *Developmental psychopathology: Vol. 1. Theory and method* (2nd ed. pp. 795–849). Hoboken, NJ: John Wiley & Sons Inc.

Ryan-Krause, P. (2011). Attention deficit hyperactivity disorder: Part III. *Journal of Pediatric Health Care, 25*(1), 50–53.

Rybash, J. M., Hoyer, W. J., & Roodin, P. (1986). *Adult cognition and aging: Developmental changes in processing, knowing, and thinking.* New York, NY: Pergamon Press.

Ryeng, M. S., Kroger, J., & Martinussen, M. (2013). Identity status and self-esteem: A meta-analysis. *Identity: An International Journal of Theory and Research, 13*(3), 201–213.

Saarni, C. (1999). *The development of emotional competence.* New York, NY: Guilford Press.

Sabey, A. K., Rauer, A. J., & Jensen, J. F. (2014). Compassionate love as a mechanism linking sacred qualities of marriage to older couples' marital satisfaction. *Journal of Family Psychology, 28*(5), 594–603.

Sabik, N. J., Cole, E. R., & Ward, L. M. (2010). Are all minority women equally buffered from negative body image? Intra-ethnic moderators of the buffering hypothesis. *Psychology of Women Quarterly, 34*(2), 139–151.

Sachdev, P. S., Lipnicki, D. M., Crawford, J., Reppermund, S., Kochan, N. A., Trollor, J. N., . . . Team, A. S. (2013). Factors predicting reversion from mild cognitive impairment to normal cognitive functioning: A population-based study. *Plos ONE, 8*(3).

Saenz, J., & Alexander, G. M. (2013). Postnatal testosterone levels and disorder relevant behavior in the second year of life. *Biological Psychology, 94*(1), 152–159.

Saeteren, B., Lindström, U. Å., & Nåden, D. (2010). Latching onto life: Living in the area of tension between the possibility of life and the necessity of death. *Journal of Clinical Nursing, 20,* 811–818.

Saewyc, E. M. (2011). Research on adolescent sexual orientation: Development, health disparities, stigma, and resilience. *Journal of Research on Adolescence, 21*(1), 256–272.

Samimi, P., & Alderson, K. G. (2014). Sexting among undergraduate students. *Computers in Human Behavior, 31,* 230-241.

Samson, D., & Apperly, I. A. (2010). There is more to mind reading than having theory of mind concepts: New directions in theory of mind research. *Infant and Child Development, 19,* 443–454.

Samson, R. D., & Barnes, C. A. (2013). Impact of aging brain circuits on cognition. *European Journal of Neuroscience, 37*(12), 1903–1915.

Sánchez, B., Esparza, P., Cölon, Y., & Davis, K. E. (2010). Tryin' to make it during the transition from high school: The role of family obligation attitudes and economic context for Latino emerging adults. *Journal of Adolescent Research, 25*(6), 858–884.

Sánchez-Mora, C., Cormand, B., Ramos-Quiroga, J. A., Hervás, A., Bosch, R., Palomar, G., . . . Ribasés, M. (2013). Evaluation of common variants in 16 genes involved in the regulation of neurotransmitter release in ADHD. *European Neuropsychopharmacology, 23*(6), 426–435.

Sánchez-Villegas, A., Pimenta, A. M., Beunza, J. J., Guillen-Grima, F., Toledo, E., & Martinez-Gonzalez, M. A. (2010). Childhood and young adult overweight/obesity and incidence of depression in the SUN Project. *Obesity, 18*(7), 1443–1448.

Sandberg, L. (2013). Just feeling a naked body close to you: Men, sexuality and intimacy in later life. *Sexualities, 16*(3-4), 261–282.

Sandberg-Thoma, S. E., & Kamp Dush, C. M. (2014). Casual sexual relationships and mental health in adolescence and emerging adulthood. *Journal of Sex Research, 51*(2), 121–130.

Sandler, I. N., Wheeler, L. A., & Braver, S. L. (2013). Relations of parenting quality, interparental conflict, and overnights with mental health problems of children in divorcing families with high legal conflict. *Journal of Family Psychology, 27*(6), 915–924.

Sandler, I. N., Wolchik, S. A., & Ayers, T. S. (2008). Resilience rather than recovery: A contextual framework on adaptation following bereavement. *Death Studies, 32,* 59–73.

Santesso, D. L., Schmidt, L. A., Trainor, L. J. (2007). Frontal brain electrical activity (EEG) and heart rate in response to affective infant-directed (ID) speech in 9-month-old infants. *Brain and Cognition, 65,* 14–21.

Sarkin, A., Tally, S., Wooldridge, J., Choi, K., Shieh, M., & Kaplan, R. (2013). Gender differences in adapting driving behavior to accommodate visual health limitations. *Journal of Community Health, 38*(6), 1175–1181.

Sasson, I., & Umberson, D. J. (2014). Widowhood and depression: New light on gender differences, selection, and psychological adjustment. *Journals of Gerontology Series B: Psychological Sciences and Social Sciences, 69B*(1), 135–145.

Sattler, J. M. (2001). *Assessment of children: Cognitive applications* (4th ed.). La Mesa, CA: Sattler.

Savage, C. L., Anthony, J., Lee, R., Kappesser, M. L., & Rose, B. (2007). The culture of pregnancy and infant care in African American women: An ethnographic study. *Journal of Transcultural Nursing, 18*(3), 215–223.

Savin-Williams, R. C. (2001). *Mom, Dad, I'm gay. How families negotiate coming out.* Washington, DC: American Psychological Association.

Savin-Williams, R. C. (2008). Then and now: Recruitment, definition, diversity, and positive attributes of same-sex populations. *Developmental Psychology, 44*(1), 135–138.

Savishinsky, J. (2004). The volunteer and the Sannyasin: Archetypes of retirement in America and India. *International Journal of Aging & Human Development, 59,* 25–41.

Saxon, S. V., Etten, M., & Perkins, E. A. (2010). *Physical change and aging: A guide for the helping professions* (5th ed.). New York, NY: Springer.

Sayegh, P., & Knight, B. G. (2011). The effects of familism and cultural justification on the mental and physical health of family caregivers. *Journals of Gerontology: Psychological Sciences, 66B*(1), 3–14.

Sayer, L. C., Bianchi, S. M., & Robinson, J. P. (2004). Are parents investing less in children? Trends in mothers' and fathers' time with children. *American Journal of Sociology, 110,* 1–43.

Scales, P. C., Benson, P. L., & Roehlkepartain, E. C. (2011). Adolescent thriving: The role of sparks, relationships, and empowerment. *Journal of Youth and Adolescence, 40*(3), 263–277.

Scarr, S. (1997). Behavior-genetic and socialization theories of intelligence: Truce and reconciliation. In R. J. Sternberg & E. L. Grigorenko (Eds.), *Intelligence, heredity, and environment* (pp. 3–41). New York, NY: Cambridge University Press.

Scarr, S., & Deater-Deckard, K. (1997). Family effects on individual differences in development. In S. S. Luthar, J. A. Burack, D. Cicchetti, J. R. Weisz (Eds.), *Developmental psychopathology: Perspectives on adjustment, risk, and disorder* (pp. 115–136). New York, NY: Cambridge University Press.

Schaan, B. (2013). Widowhood and depression among older Europeans—The role of gender, caregiving, marital quality, and regional context. *Journals of Gerontology Series B: Psychological Sciences and Social Sciences, 68B*(3), 431–442.

Schafer, M. H. (2013). Structural advantages of good health in old age: Investigating the health-begets-position hypothesis with a full social network. *Research on Aging, 35*(3), 348–370.

Schaie, K. W. (1996). Intellectual development in adulthood. In J. E. Birren, K. W. Schaie, R. P. Abeles, M. Gatz, & T. A. Salthouse (Eds.), *Handbook of the psychology of aging* (4th ed. pp. 266–286). San Diego, CA: Academic Press.

Schaie, K. W., & Zanjani, F. A. K. (2006). Intellectual development across adulthood. In C. Hoare (Ed.), *Handbook of adult development and learning* (pp. 99–122). New York, NY: Oxford University Press.

Schaie, K. W., Willis, S. L., & Caskie, G. I. L. (2004). The Seattle Longitudinal Study: Relationship between personality and cognition. *Aging, Neuropsychology, and Cognition, 11,* 304–324.

Schellinger, K., & Talmi, A. (2013). Off the charts? Considerations for interpreting parent reports of toddler hyperactivity. *Infant Mental Health Journal, 34*(5), 417–419.

Scheres, A., Tontsch, C., & Lee Thoeny, A. (2013). Steep temporal reward discounting in ADHD-Combined type: Acting upon feelings. *Psychiatry Research, 209*(2), 207–213.

Schilling, O. K., Wahl, H., Boerner, K., Reinhardt, J. P., Brennan-Ing, M., & Horowitz, A. (2013). Change in psychological control in visually impaired older adults over 2 years: Role of functional ability and depressed mood. *Journals of Gerontology Series B: Psychological Sciences and Social Sciences, 68*(5), 750–761.

Schirduan, V., & Case, K. (2004). Mindful curriculum leadership for students with attention deficit hyperactivity disorder: Leading in elementary schools by using multiple intelligences theory (SUMIT). *Teachers College Record, 106,* 87–95.

Schlegel, A. (1995). The cultural management of adolescent sexuality. In P. R. Abramson & S. D. Pinkerton (Eds.), *Sexual nature, sexual culture* (pp. 177–194). Chicago, IL: University of Chicago Press.

Schlegel, A., & Barry, H., III. (1991). *Adolescence: An anthropological inquiry.* New York, NY: Free Press.

Schlinger, H. D. (2003). The myth of intelligence. *Psychological Record, 53,* 15–32.

Schmid, G., Schreier, A., Meyer, R., & Wolke, D. (2010). A prospective study in the persistence of infant crying, sleeping and feeding problems and preschool behavior. *Acta Pædiatrica, 99,* 286–290.

Schneidman, E. (Ed.). (1976). *Death: Current perspectives.* Palo Alto, CA: Mayfield.

Scholte, R., Sentse, M., & Granic, I. (2010). Do actions speak louder than words? Classroom attitudes and behavior in relation to bullying in early adolescence. *Journal of Clinical Child & Adolescent Psychology, 39*(6), 789–799.

Schooler, C. (1999). The workplace environment: Measurement, psychological effects, and basic issues. In S. L. Friedman & T. D. Wachs (Eds.), *Measuring environment across the life span: Emerging methods and concepts* (pp. 229–246). Washington, D.C.: American Psychological Association.

Schooler, C. (2001). The intellectual effects of the demands of the work environment. In R. J. Sternberg & E. L. Grigorenko (Eds.), *Environmental effects on cognitive abilities* (pp. 363–380). Mahwah, NJ: Erlbaum.

Schooler, C., Mulatu, M. S., & Oates, G. (2004). Occupational self-direction, intellectual functioning, and self-directed orientation in older workers: Findings and implications for individuals and societies. *American Journal of Sociology, 110,* 161–197.

Schoon, I., & Duckworth, K. (2010). Leaving school early—and making it: Evidence from two British cohorts. *European Psychologist, 15*(4), 283–292.

Schramm, D. G., Harris, S. M., Whiting, J. B., Hawkins, A. J., Brown, M., & Porter, R. (2013). Economic costs and policy implications associated with divorce: Texas as a case study. *Journal of Divorce & Remarriage, 54*(1), 1–24.

Schreiner, L. A., Noel, P., Anderson, E., & Cantwell, L. (2011). The impact of faculty and staff on high-risk college student persistence. *Journal of College Student Development, 52*(3), 321–338.

Schroeder, R. D., & Mowen, T. J. (2014). Parenting style transitions and delinquency. *Youth & Society, 46*(2), 228–254.

Schueler, C. M., & Prinz, R. J. (2013). The role of caregiver contingent responsiveness in promoting compliance in young children. *Child Psychiatry and Human Development, 44*(3), 370–381.

Schwartz, C. E., Wright, C. I., Shin, L. M., Kagan, J., & Rauch, S. L. (2003, June 20). Inhibited and uninhibited infants "grown up": Adult amygdalar response to novelty. *Science, 300,* 1952–1953.

Schwartz, S. J., Zamboanga, B. L., Luyckx, K., Meca, A., & Ritchie, R. A. (2013). Identity in emerging adulthood: Reviewing the field and looking forward. *Emerging Adulthood, 1*(2), 96–113.

Scrimgeour, M. B., Blandon, A. Y., Stifter, C. A., & Buss, K. A. (2013). Cooperative coparenting moderates the association between parenting practices and children's prosocial behavior. *Journal of Family Psychology, 27*(3), 506–511.

Scrimsher, S., & Tudge, J. (2003). The teaching/learning relationship in the first years of school: Some revolutionary implications of Vygotsky's theory. *Early Education and Development, 14,* 293–312.

Seale, C. (2009). Legalisation of euthanasia or physician-assisted suicide: Survey of doctors' attitudes. *Palliative Medicine, 23,* 205–212.

Sebastian, C., Viding, E., Williams, K. D., & Blakemore, S.-J. (2010). Social brain development and the affective consequences of ostracism in adolescence. *Brain and Cognition, 72,* 134–145.

Sebastián-Enesco, C., Hernández-Lloreda, M. V., & Colmenares, F. (2013). Two and a half-year-old children are prosocial even when their partners are not. *Journal of Experimental Child Psychology, 116*(2), 186–198.

Seery, M. D., Holman, E. A., & Silver, R. C. (2010). Whatever does not kill us: Cumulative lifetime adversity, vulnerability, and resilience. *Journal of Personality and Social Psychology, 99*(6) 1025–1041.

Seiffge-Krenke, I. (2010). Predicting the timing of leaving home and related developmental tasks: Parents' and children's perspectives. *Journal of Social and Personal Relationships, 27*(4), 495–518.

Seiffge-Krenke, I. (2013). "She's leaving home . . ." Antecedents, consequences, and cultural patterns in the leaving home process. *Emerging Adulthood, 1*(2), 114–124.

Seiffge-Krenke, I., Persike, M., & Luyckx, K. (2013). Factors contributing to different agency in work and study: A view on the "forgotten half." *Emerging Adulthood, 1*(4), 283–292.

Self-Brown, S. R., & Mathews, S. (2003). Effects of classroom structure on student achievement goal orientation. *Journal of Educational Research, 97,* 106–111.

Seligman, M. P. (2011). *Flourish: A visionary new understanding of happiness and well-being.* New York, NY: Free Press.

Sengupta, M., Park-Lee, E., Valverde, R., Caffrey, C., & Jones, A. (2014). Trends in length of hospice care from 1996 to 2007 and the factors associated with length of hospice care in 2007: Findings from the National Home and Hospice Care Surveys. *American Journal of Hospice and Palliative Medicine, 31*(4), 356–364.

Sercombe, H. (2010). The gift and the trap: Working the "teen brain" into our concept of youth. *Journal of Adolescent Health, 25*(1), 31–47.

Settersten, R. A., & Ray, B. (2010). *What's going on with young people today? The long and twisting path to adulthood.* In *The Future of Children, 20*(1), 1–21. Retrieved from www.princeton.edu/futureofchildren/publications/docs/20_01_02.pdf

Shafer, E. F. (2011). Wives' relative wages, husbands' paid work hours, and wives' labor-force exit. *Journal of Marriage and Family, 73,* 250–263.

Shafer, K., & James, S. L. (2013). Gender and socioeconomic status differences in first and second marriage formation. *Journal of Marriage and Family, 75*(3), 544–564.

Shahaeian, A., Peterson, C. C., Slaughter, V., & Wellman, H. M. (2011). Culture and the sequence of steps in theory of mind development. *Developmental Psychology, 47*(5), 1239–1247.

Shalev, I., Moffitt, T. E., Braithwaite, A. W. , Danese, A., Fleming, N. I., Goldman-Mellor, S., . . . Caspi, A. (2014). Internalizing disorders and leukocyte telomere erosion: a prospective study of depression, generalized anxiety disorder and post-traumatic stress disorder. *Molecular Psychiatry, 19*(11), 1163–1170.

Shanahan, M. J., Hill, P. L., Roberts, B. W., Eccles, J., & Friedman, H. S. (2014). Conscientiousness, health, and aging: The Life Course of Personality Model. *Developmental Psychology, 50*(5), 1407–1425.

Shapero, B. G., Black, S. K., Liu, R. T., Klugman, J., Bender, R. E., Abramson, L. Y., & Alloy, L. B. (2014). Stressful life events and depression symptoms: The effect of childhood emotional abuse on stress reactivity. *Journal of Clinical Psychology, 70*(3), 209–223.

Shariff, M. J. (2011). Navigating assisted death and end-of-life care. *Canadian Medical Association Journal, 183*(6), 643–644.

Shaywitz, S. E., Morris, R., & Shaywitz, B. A. (2008). The education of dyslexic children from childhood to young adulthood. *Annual Review of Psychology, 59,* 451–475.

Shearer, C. L., Crouter, A. C., & McHale, S. M. (2005). Parents' perceptions of changes in mother-child and father-child relationships during adolescence. *Journal of Adolescent Research, 20,* 662–684.

Sheehan, A., Schmied, V., & Barclay, L. (2013). Exploring the process of women's infant feeding decisions in the early postbirth period. *Qualitative Health Research, 23*(7), 989–998.

Shelden, R. G., Tracy, S. K., & Brown, W. B. (1997). *Youth gangs in American society.* Belmont, CA: Wadsworth.

Sheldon, K. M., Cummins, R., & Kamble, S. (2010). Life balance and well-being: Testing a novel conceptual and measurement approach. *Journal of Personality, 78*(4), 1093–1133.

Sheridan, A., Murray, L., Cooper, P. J., Evangeli, M., Byram, V., & Halligan, S. L. (2013). A longitudinal study of child sleep in high and low risk families: Relationship to early maternal settling strategies and child psychological functioning. *Sleep Medicine, 14*(3), 266–273.

Shih, F., Lin, H., Gau, M., Chen, C., Hsiao, S., Shih, S., Sheu, S. J. (2009). Spiritual needs of Taiwan's older patients with terminal cancer. *Oncology Nursing Forum, 36,* e31–e38.

Shochat, T., Cohen-Zion, M., & Tzischinsky, O. (2014). Functional consequences of inadequate sleep in adolescents: A systematic review. *Sleep Medicine Reviews, 18*(1), 75–87.

Shonkoff, J. P., & Phillips, D. A. (2000). Growing up in child care. In J. P. Shonkoff & D. A. Phillips (Eds.), *From neurons to neighborhoods: The science of early childhood development* (pp. 297–327). Washington, DC: National Academy Press.

Short, M. A., Gradisar, M., Lack, L. C., & Wright, H. R. (2013). The impact of sleep on adolescent depressed mood, alertness and academic performance. *Journal of Adolescence, 36*(6), 1025–1033.

Shulman, E. P., & Cauffman, E. (2013). Reward-biased risk appraisal and its relation to juvenile versus adult crime. *Law and Human Behavior, 37*(6), 412–423.

Shulman, S., & Connolly, J. (2013). The challenge of romantic relationships in emerging adulthood: Reconceptualization of the field. *Emerging Adulthood, 1*(1), 27–39.

Sibley, M. H., Pelham, W. E., Molina, B. G., Gnagy, E. M., Waschbusch, D. A., Biswas, A., . . . Karch, K. M. (2011). The delinquency outcomes of boys with ADHD with and without comorbidity. *Journal of Abnormal Child Psychology. 39*(1), 21–32.

Sieswerda-Hoogendoorn, T., Bilo, R. A., van Duurling, L. L., Karst, W. A., Maaskant, J. M., van Aalderen, W. M., & van Rijn, R. R. (2013). Abusive head trauma in young children in the Netherlands: Evidence for multiple incidents of abuse. *Acta Paediatrica, 102*(11), e497–501.

Silveira, M. J., Wiitala, W., & Piette, J. (2014). Advance directive completion by elderly Americans: A decade of change. *Journal of the American Geriatrics Society, 62*(4), 706–710.

Silventoinen, K., Haukka, J., Dunkel, L., Tynelius, P., & Rasmussen, F. (2008). Genetics of pubertal timing and its associations with relative weight in childhood and adult height: The Swedish young male twins study. *Pediatrics, 121*(4), 885–891.

Silvetti, M., Castellar, E. N., Roger, C., & Verguts, T. (2014). Reward expectation and prediction error in human medial frontal cortex: An EEG study. *Neuroimage, 84*, 376–382.

Simmons, R. G., & Blyth, D. A. (1987). *Moving into adolescence: The impact of pubertal change and school context.* Hawthorne, NY: Aldine.

Simon, T., Suengas, A. G., Ruiz, G. L., & Bandres, J. (2013). Positive bias is a defining characteristic of aging to the same extent as declining performance. *International Journal of Psychology, 48*(4), 704–714.

Simons, D. A., & Wurtele, S. K. (2010). Relationships between parents' use of corporal punishment and their children's endorsement of spanking and hitting other children. *Child Abuse & Neglect, 34*, 639–646.

Simonton, D. K. (1997). Creative productivity: A predictive and explanatory model of career trajectories and landmarks. *Psychological Review, 104*, 66–89.

Simonton, D. K. (2002). Longitudinal changes in creativity. In D. K. Simonton (Ed.), *Great psychologists and their times: Scientific insights into psychology's history* (pp. 67–101). Washington, DC: American Psychological Association.

Simonton, D. K. (2007). Creative life cycles in literature: Poets versus novelists or conceptualists versus experimentalists? *Psychology of Aesthetics, Creativity, and the Arts, 1*(3), 133–139.

Simpson, J. A., Collins, W. A., Tran, S., & Hayden, K. C. (2007). Attachment and the experience and expression of emotions in romantic relationships: A developmental perspective. *Journal of Personality and Social Psychology, 92*(2), 355–367.

Sims, M., & Rofail, M. (2013). The experiences of grandparents who have limited or no contact with their grandchildren. *Journal of Aging Studies, 27*(4), 377–386.

Sinnott, J. D. (2003). Postformal thought and adult development: Living in balance. In J. Demick & C. Andreoletti (Eds.), *Handbook of adult development* (pp. 221–238). New York, NY: Kluwer Academic/Plenum.

Sjörs, G. (2010). Treatment decisions for extremely preterm newborns: Beyond gestational age. *Acta Paediatrica, 99*(12), 1761–1762.

Skinner, B. F. (1960). *The behavior of organisms: An experimental analysis.* New York, NY: Appleton-Century-Crofts.

Skinner, B. F. (1974). *About behaviorism.* New York, NY: Knopf.

Skogli, E. W., Teicher, M. H., Andersen, P. N., Hovik, K. T., & Øie, M. (2013). ADHD in girls and boys—Gender differences in co-existing symptoms and executive function measures. *BMC Psychiatry, 13*, 298.

Skoog, T., Stattin, H., Ruiselova, Z., & Özdemir, M. (2013). Female pubertal timing and problem behaviour: The role of culture. *International Journal of Behavioral Development, 37*(4), 357–365.

Skoranski, A. M., Most, S. B., Lutz-Stehl, M., Hoffman, J. E., Hassink, S. G., & Simons, R. F. (2013). Response monitoring and cognitive control in childhood obesity. *Biological Psychology, 92*(2), 199–204.

Slater, A. (2001). Visual perception. In G. Bremner & A. Fogel (Eds.), *Blackwell handbook of infant development* (pp. 5–34). Malden, MA: Blackwell.

Slater, A., Quinn, P.C., Kelly, D. J., Lee, K., Longmore, C.A., McDonald, P.R., & Pascalis, O. (2010). The shaping of the face space in early infancy: Becoming a native face processor. *Child Development Perspectives, 4*(5), 201–211.

Slaughter, V., Peterson, C. C., & Moore, C. (2013). I can talk you into it: Theory of mind and persuasion behavior in young children. *Developmental Psychology, 49*(2), 227–231.

Slavin, R. E., Cheung, A., Holmes, G., Madden, N. A., & Chamberlain, A. (2013). Effects of a data-driven district reform model on state assessment outcomes. *American Educational Research Journal, 50*(2), 371–396.

Slevec, J., & Tiggemann, M. (2011). Attitudes toward cosmetic surgery in middle-aged women: Body image, aging anxiety, and the media. *Psychology of Women Quarterly, 35*(4), 617–629.

Slobin, D. I. (1972). Children and language: They learn the same way all around the world. *Psychology Today, 6*(2), 71–74, 82.

Smallfield, S., Clem, K., & Myers, A. (2013). Occupational therapy interventions to improve the reading ability of older adults with low vision: A systematic review. *American Journal of Occupational Therapy, 67*(3), 288–295.

Smetana, J. G., Campione-Barr, N., & Metzger, A. (2006). Adolescent development in interpersonal and societal contexts. *Annual Review of Psychology, 57*, 255–284.

Smetana, J. G., Kochanska, G., & Chuang, S. (2000). Mothers' conceptions of everyday rules for young toddlers: A longitudinal investigation. *Merrill-Palmer Quarterly, 46*, 391–416.

Smith, A. K., Rhee, S. H., Corley, R. P., Friedman, N. P., Hewitt, J. K., & Robinson, J. L. (2012). The magnitude of genetic and environmental influences on parental and observational measures of behavioral inhibition and shyness in toddlerhood. *Behavior Genetics, 42*(5), 764–777.

Smith, A. R., Chein, J., & Steinberg, L. (2013). Impact of socio-emotional context, brain development, and pubertal maturation on adolescent risk-taking. *Hormones and Behavior, 64*(2), 323–332.

Smith, G. R., Williamson, G. M., Miller, L. S., & Schultz, R. (2011). Depression and quality of informal care: A longitudinal investigation of caregiving stressors. *Psychology and Aging, 15*(3), 385–396.

Smith, J. P., & Ellwood, M. (2011). Feeding patterns and emotional care in breastfed infants. *Social Indicators Research, 101*, 227–231.

Smith, L., & Hough, C. L. (2011). Using death rounds to improve end-of-life education for internal medicine residents. *Journal of Palliative Medicine, 14*(1), 55–58.

Smith, M. E. (1926). An investigation of the development of the sentence and the extent of vocabulary in young children. *University of Iowa Studies: Child Welfare, 3*, 92.

Smith, R. L., Rose, A. J., & Schwartz-Mette, R. A. (2010). Relational and overt aggression in childhood and adolescence: Clarifying mean-level gender differences and associations with peer acceptance. *Social Development, 19*(2), 243–269.

Smock, P. J., Manning, W. D., & Porter, M. (2005). "Everything's there except money": How money shapes decisions to marry among cohabitors. *Journal of Marriage and Family, 67*, 680–696.

Smolak, L., & Stein, J. A. (2010). A longitudinal investigation of gender role and muscle building in adolescent boys. *Sex Roles, 63*, 738–746.

Smolucha, L., & Smolucha, F. (1998). The social origins of mind: Post-Piagetian perspectives on pretend play. In O. N. Saracho & B. Spodek (Eds.),

Multiple perspectives on play in early childhood education (pp. 34–58). Albany, NY: State University of New York Press.

Snarey, J. R. (1985). Cross-cultural universality of social-moral development: A critical review of Kohlbergian research. *Psychological Bulletin, 97,* 202–232.

Snyder, L. (1999). *Speaking our minds: Personal reflections from individuals with Alzheimer's.* New York, NY: Freeman.

Snyder, S., Hazelett, S., Allen, K., & Radwany, S. (2013). Physician knowledge, attitude, and experience with advance care planning, palliative care, and hospice: Results of a primary care survey. *American Journal of Hospice and Palliative Medicine, 30*(5), 419–424.

Soares, C. (2013). Depression in peri- and post-menopausal women: Prevalence, pathophysiology and pharmacological management. *Drugs and Aging, 30*(9), 677–685.

Social Security Monthly Statistical Snapshot, October, 2014. (2014). Retrieved from: http://www.ssa.gov/

Society for Assisted Reproductive Technologies. (n.d.). Retrieved from http://www.sart.org/

Soderlund, G., Sikstrom, S., & Smart, A. (2007). Listen to the noise: Noise is beneficial for cognitive performance in ADHD. *Journal of Child Psychology and Psychiatry, 48*(8), 840–847.

Soenens, B., & Vansteenkiste, M. (2010). A theoretical upgrade of the concept of parental psychological control: Proposing new insights on the basis of self-determination theory. *Developmental Review, 30*(1), 74–99.

Solmeyer, A. R., McHale, S. M., & Crouter, A. C. (2014). Longitudinal associations between sibling relationship qualities and risky behavior across adolescence. *Developmental Psychology, 50*(2), 600–610.

Son, J., Erno, A., Shea, G., Femia, E. E., Zarit, S. H., & Stephens, M. P. (2007). The caregiver stress process and health outcomes. *Journal of Aging and Health, 19,* 871–887.

Sonuga-Barke, E. J. S., & Halperin, J. M. (2010). Developmental phenotypes and causal pathways in attention deficit/hyperactivity disorder: Potential targets for early intervention? *Journal of Child Psychology & Psychiatry, 51*(4), 368–389.

Sonuga-Barke, E. S., Brandeis, D., Cortese, S., Daley, D., Ferrin, M., Holtmann, M., . . . Sergeant, J. (2013). Nonpharmalogical interventions for ADHD:

Systematic review and meta analyses of randomized controlled trials of dietary and psychological treatments. *American Journal of Psychiatry, 170*(3), 275–289.

Soric, M., & Misigoj-Durakovic, M. (2010). Physical activity levels and estimated energy expenditure in overweight and normal-weight 11-year-old children. *Acta Paediatrica, 99,* 244–250.

Sossou, M.-A. (2002). Widowhood practices in West Africa: The silent victims. *International Journal of Social Welfare, 11,* 201–209.

Souza, J., Gülmezoglu, A., Vogel, J., Carroli, G., Lumbiganon, P., Qureshi, Z., Costa, M. J., et al. (2013). Moving beyond essential interventions for reduction of maternal mortality (the WHO Multicountry Survey on Maternal and Newborn Health): A cross-sectional study. *The Lancet, 381*(9879), 1747–1755.

Spangler, G., & Zimmermann, P. (2014). Emotional and adrenocortical regulation in early adolescence: Prediction by attachment security and disorganization in infancy. *International Journal of Behavioral Development, 38*(2), 142–154.

Spear, L. P. (2008). The psychology of adolescence. In K. K. Kline (Ed.), *Authoritative Communities: The Scientific Cases for Nurturing the Whole Child* (pp. 263–280). New York, NY: Springer-Verlag.

Specht, J., Bleidorn, W., Denissen, J. A., Hennecke, M., Hutteman, R., Kandler, C., . . . Zimmermann, J. (2014). What drives adult personality development? A comparison of theoretical perspectives and empirical evidence. *European Journal of Personality, 28*(3), 216–230.

Specht, J., Luhmann, M., & Geiser, C. (2014). On the consistency of personality types across adulthood: Latent profile analyses in two large-scale panel studies. *Journal of Personality and Social Psychology, 107*(3), 540–556.

Speisman, R. B., Kumar, A., Rani, A., Pastoriza, J. M., Severance, J. E., Foster, T. C., & Ormerod, B. K. (2013). Environmental enrichment restores neurogenesis and rapid acquisition in aged rats. *Neurobiology of Aging, 34*(1), 263–274.

Spencer, S. V., Bowker, J. C., Rubin, K. H., Booth-LaForce, C., & Laursen, B. (2013). Similarity between friends in social information processing and associations with positive friendship quality and conflict. *Merrill-Palmer Quarterly, 59*(1), 106–131.

Spense, A. (1989). *The biology of human aging.* Englewood Cliffs, NJ: Prentice Hall.

Spinath, B., & Steinmayr, R. (2008). Longitudinal analysis of intrinsic motivation and competence beliefs: Is there a relation over time? *Child Development, 49,* 1555–1569.

Spronk, K. (2004). Good death and bad death in ancient Israel according to biblical lore. *Social Science & Medicine, 58,* 985–995.

Sroufe, L. A. (2000). Early relationships and the development of children. *Infant Mental Health Journal, 21,* 67–74.

St. James-Roberts, I. (2007). Helping parents to manage infant crying and sleeping: A review of the evidence and its implications for services. *Child Abuse Review, 16,* 47–69.

Stafford, L., David, P., & McPherson, S. (2014). Sanctity of marriage and marital quality. *Journal of Social and Personal Relationships, 31*(1), 54–70.

Staikova, E., Gomes, H., Tartter, V., McCabe, A., & Halperin, J. M. (2013). Pragmatic deficits and social impairment in children with ADHD. *Journal of Child Psychology and Psychiatry, 54*(12), 1275–1283.

Stamatakis, E. E., Zaninotto, P. P., Falaschetti, E. E., Mindell, J. J., & Head, J. J. (2010). Time trends in childhood and adolescent obesity in England from 1995 to 2007 and projections of prevalence to 2015. *Journal of Epidemiology and Community Health, 64*(2), 167–174.

Stamatiadis, N. (1996). Gender effect on the accident patterns of elderly drivers. *Journal of Applied Gerontology, 15,* 8–22.

Stange, J. P., Hamlat, E. J., Hamilton, J. L., Abramson, L. Y., & Alloy, L. B. (2013). Overgeneral autobiographical memory, emotional maltreatment, and depressive symptoms in adolescence: Evidence of a cognitive vulnerability–stress interaction. *Journal of Adolescence, 36*(1), 201–208.

Stark, R., Bauer, E., Merz, C. J., Zimmermann, M., Reuter, M., Plichta, M. M., . . . Herrmann, M. J. (2011). ADHD related behaviors are associated with brain activation in the reward system. *Neuropsychologia, 49,* 426–434.

Stattin, H., & Magnusson, D. (1990). *Pubertal maturation in female development.* Hillsdale, NJ: Erlbaum.

Stebbins, H., & Knitzer, J. (2007). *State early childhood policies.* New York, NY:

Columbia University, National Center for Children in Poverty.

Steele, S., Joseph, R. M., & Tager-Flusberg, H. (2003). Brief report: Developmental change in theory of mind abilities in children with autism. *Journal of Autism and Developmental Disorders, 33,* 461–467.

Steger, M. F., Littman-Ovadia, H., Miller, M., Menger, L., & Rothmann, S. (2013). Engaging in work even when it is meaningless: Positive affective disposition and meaningful work interact in relation to work engagement. *Journal of Career Assessment, 21*(2), 348–361.

Stein, A., Malmberg, L., Leach, P., Barnes, J., & Sylva, K. (2013). The influence of different forms of early childcare on children's emotional and behavioural development at school entry. *Child: Care, Health and Development, 39*(5), 676–687.

Stein, J. H., & Reiser, L. W. (1994). A study of White middle-class adolescent boys' responses to "semenarche" (the first ejaculation). *Journal of Youth and Adolescence, 23,* 373–384.

Steinberg, L. (2001). We know some things: Parent-adolescent relationships in retrospect and prospect. *Journal of Research on Adolescence, 11,* 1–19.

Steinberg, L. (2005). Cognitive and affective development in adolescence. *Trends in Cognitive Sciences, 9,* 69–74.

Steinberg, L. (2008). A social neuroscience perspective on adolescent risk-taking. *Developmental Review, 28,* 78–106.

Steinberg, L. (2010). A behavioral scientist looks at the science of adolescent brain development. *Brain and Cognition, 72,* 160–164.

Steinberg, L., & Hill, J. P. (1978). Patterns of family interaction as a function of age, the onset of puberty, and formal thinking. *Developmental Psychology, 14,* 683–684.

Sternberg, R. J. (1984). Toward a triarchic theory of human intelligence. *Behavioral and Brain Sciences, 7,* 269–315.

Sternberg, R. J. (1986). A triangular theory of love. *Psychological Review, 93,* 119–135.

Sternberg, R. J. (1988). Triangulating love. In R. J. Sternberg & M. L. Barnes (Eds.), *The psychology of love* (pp. 119–138). New Haven, CT: Yale University Press.

Sternberg, R. J. (1996). *Successful intelligence: How practical and creative intelligence determine success in life.* New York, NY: Simon & Schuster.

Sternberg, R. J. (1997). The triarchic theory of intelligence. In D. P. Flanagan, J. L. Genshaft, & P. L. Harrison (Eds.), *Contemporary intellectual assessment: Theories, tests, and issues* (pp. 92–104). New York, NY: Guilford Press.

Sternberg, R. J. (2004). A triangular theory of love. In H. T. Reis & C. E. Rusbult (Eds.), *Close relationships: Key readings* (pp. 213–227). Phildelphia, PA: Taylor & Francis.

Sternberg, R. J. (2007). Who are the bright children? The cultural context of being and acting intelligent. *Educational Researcher, 36*(3), 148–155.

Sternberg, R. J. (2010). WICS: A new model for school psychology. *School Psychology International, 31*(6), 599–616.

Sternberg, R. J., & Berg, C. A. (1992). *Intellectual development.* New York, NY: Cambridge University Press.

Sternberg, R. J., Grigorenko, E. L., & Bundy, D. A. (2001). The predictive value of IQ. *Merrill-Palmer Quarterly, 47,* 1–41.

Sternberg, R. J., Grigorenko, E. L., & Kidd, K. K. (2005). Intelligence, race, and genetics. *American Psychologist, 60,* 46–59.

Sternberg, R. J., Jarvin, L., Birney, D. P., Naples, A., Stemler, S. E., Newman, T., . . . Grigorenko, E. L. (2014). Testing the theory of successful intelligence in teaching grade 4 language arts, mathematics, and science. *Journal of Educational Psychology, 106*(3), 881–899.

Sternberg, R. J., Torff, B., & Grigorenko, E. L. (1998). Teaching for successful intelligence raises school achievement. *Phi Delta Kappa, 79,* 667–669.

Sticca, F., & Perren, S. (2013). Is cyberbullying worse than traditional bullying? Examining the differential roles of medium, publicity, and anonymity for the perceived severity of bullying. *Journal of Youth and Adolescence, 42*(5), 739–750.

Stice, E., Ng, J., & Shaw, H. (2010). Risk factors and prodromal eating pathology. *Journal of Child Psychology and Psychiatry, 51*(4), 518–525.

Stiles, J., & Jernigan, T. L. (2010). The basics of brain development. *Neuropsychology Review, 20*(4), 327–348.

Stipek, D. J. (1996). Motivation and instruction. In D. C. Berliner & R. C. Calfee (Eds.), *Handbook of educational psychology* (pp. 85–113). New York, NY: Macmillan.

Stipek, D. J. (1997). Success in school—For a head start in life. In S. S. Luthar, J. A. Burack, D. Cicchetti, & J. R. Weisz (Eds.), *Developmental psychopathology: Perspectives on adjustment, risk, and disorder* (pp. 75–92). New York, NY: University Press.

Stoltenborgh, M., Bakermans-Kranenburg, M. J., van IJzendoorn, M. H., & Alink, L. A. (2013). Cultural–geographical differences in the occurrence of child physical abuse. A meta-analysis of global prevalence. *International Journal of Psychology, 48*(2), 81–94.

Strand, B. H., Langballe, E. M., Hjellvik, V., Handal, M., Næss, Ø., Knudsen, G. P., . . . Bjertness, E. (2013). Midlife vascular risk factors and their association with dementia deaths: Results from a Norwegian prospective study followed up for 35 years. *Journal of the Neurological Sciences, 324*(1–2), 124–130.

Stremler, R., Hodnett, E., Kenton, L., Lee, K., Weiss, S., Weston, J., & Willan, A. (2013). Effect of behavioural-educational intervention on sleep for primiparous women and their infants in early postpartum: Multisite randomised controlled trial. *BMJ (British Medical Journal), 346.*

Striegel-Moore, R. H., & Bulik, C. M. (2007). Risk factors for eating disorders. *American Psychologist, 62*(3), 181–198.

Strier, R. (2014). Unemployment and fatherhood: Gender, culture and national context. *Gender, Work and Organization, 21*(5), 395–410.

Stringer, K. J., & Kerpelman, J. L. (2010). Career identity development in college students: Decision making, parental support, and work experience. *Identity: An International Journal of Theory, 10,* 181–200.

Stroebe, M., Schut, H., & Stroebe, W. (2007). Health outcomes of bereavement. *The Lancet, 370,* 1960–1973.

Strohmeier, D., Kärnä, A., & Salmivalli, C. (2010). Intrapersonal and interpersonal risk factors for peer victimization in immigrant youth in Finland. *Developmental Psychology, 47,* 248–258.

Stronach, E. P., Toth, S. L., Rogosch, F., Oshri, A., Manly, J. T., & Cicchetti, D. (2011). Child maltreatment, attachment security, and internal representations of mother and mother–child relationships. *Child Maltreatment, 16,* 137–145.

Sturaro, C., van Lier, P. A. C., Cuijpers, P., & Koot, H. M. (2011). The role of peer relationships in the development of early school age externalizing problems. *Child Development, 82*(3), 758–765.

Suanet, B., van der Pas, S., & van Tilburg, T. G. (2013). Who is in the stepfamily? Change in stepparents' family boundaries between 1992 and 2009. *Journal of Marriage and Family*, 75(5), 1070–1083.

Suárez-Orozco, C., Gaytán, F. X., Bang, H. J., Pakes, J., O'Connor, E., & Rhodes, J. (2010). Academic trajectories of newcomer immigrant youth. *Developmental Psychology*, 46(3), 602–618.

Subrahmanyam, K., Greenfield, P. M., & Tynes, B. (2004). Constructing sexuality and identity in an online teen chat room. *Journal of Applied Developmental Psychology. Special Issue: Developing Children, Developing Media: Research from Television to the Internet from the Children's Digital Media Center*, 25, 651–666.

Subramanian, S. V., Elwert, G., & Christakis, N. (2008). Widowhood and mortality among the elderly: The modifying role of neighborhood concentration of widowed individuals. *Social Science & Medicine*, 66(4), 873–884.

Sullivan, A. R., & Fenelon, A. (2014). Patterns of widowhood mortality. *The Journals of Gerontology Series B: Psychological Sciences and Social Sciences*, 69B(1), 53–62.

Sullivan, H. S. (1953). *The interpersonal theory of psychiatry*. New York, NY: Norton.

Sullivan, S. J., Mikels, J. A., & Carstensen, L. L. (2010). You never lose the ages you've been: Affective perspective taking in older adults. *Psychology and Aging*, 25(1), 229–234.

Sun, S. S., Schubert, C. M., Chumlea, W. C., Roche, A. F., Kulin, H. E., Lee, P. A., . . . Ryan, A. S. (2002). National estimates of the timing of sexual maturation and racial differences among U.S. children. *Pediatrics*, 110, 911–919.

Sung-Chan, P., Sung, Y. W., Zhao, X., & Brownson, R. C. (2013). Family-based models for childhood-obesity intervention: A systematic review of randomized controlled trials. *International Association for the Study of Obesity*, 14, 265–278.

Suomi, S. J. (2004). How gene-environment interactions shape biobehavioral development: Lessons from studies with rhesus monkeys. *Research in Human Development*, 1, 205–222.

Super, C. M., & Harkness, S. (2003). The metaphors of development. *Human Development*, 46, 3–23.

Super, D. E. (1957). *The psychology of careers: An introduction to vocational development*. New York, NY: Harper.

Surra, C. A., & Hughes, D. K. (1997). Commitment processes in accounts of the development of premarital relationships. *Journal of Marriage and Family*, 59, 5–21.

Surra, C. A., Hughes, D. K., & Jacquet, S. E. (1999). The development of commitment to marriage: A phenomenological approach. In J. M. Adams & W. H. Jones (Eds.), *Handbook of interpersonal commitment and relationship stability* (pp. 125–148). Dordrecht, Netherlands: Kluwer Academic.

Sussman, S., & Arnett, J. J. (2014). Emerging adulthood: Developmental period facilitative of the addictions. *Evaluation & the Health Professions*, 37(2), 147–155.

Sussman, S., Pokhrel, P., Ashmore, R. D., & Brown, B. B. (2007). Adolescent peer group identification and characteristics: A review of the literature. *Addictive Behaviors*, 32, 1602–1627.

Sutin, A. R., Zonderman, A. B., Ferrucci, L., & Terracciano, A. (2013). Personality traits and chronic disease: Implications for adult personality development. *The Journals of Gerontology Series B: Psychological Sciences and Social Sciences*, 68B(6), 912–920.

Švab, A., & Humer, Ž. (2013). "I only have to ask him and he does it . . ." Active fatherhood and (perceptions of) division of family labour in Slovenia. *Journal of Comparative Family Studies*, 44(1), 57–78.

Svensson, B., Bornehag, C.-G., & Janson, S. (2011). Chronic conditions in children increase the risk for physical abuse—but vary with socio-economic circumstances. *Acta Paediatrica*, 100, 407–412.

Swann, W. B., Chang-Schneider, C., & McClarty, K. L. (2007). Do people's self-views matter? *American Psychologist*, 62(2), 84–94.

Swift, H. J., Abrams, D., & Marques, S. (2013). Threat or boost? Social comparison affects older people's performance differently depending on task domain. *Journals of Gerontology Series B: Psychological Sciences and Social Sciences*, 68B(1), 23–30.

Swinburn, B. A., & de Silva-Sanigorski, A. M. (2010). Where to from here for preventing childhood obesity: An international perspective. *Obesity*, 18(Suppl. 1), S4–S7.

Syed, A., & Azmitia, M. (2009). Longitudinal trajectories of ethnic identity during the college years. *Journal of Research on Adolescence*, 19(4), 601–624.

Syme, M. L., Klonoff, E. A., Macera, C. A., & Brodine, S. K. (2013). Predicting sexual decline and dissatisfaction among older adults: The role of partnered and individual physical and mental health factors. *Journals of Gerontology Series B: Psychological Sciences and Social Sciences*, 68B(3), 323–332.

Tadmor, C. T., Tetlock, P. E., & Peng, K. (2009). Acculturation strategies and integrative complexity: The cognitive implications of biculturalism. *Journal of Cross-Cultural Psychology*, 40, 105–139.

Tambalis, K. D., Panagiotakos, D. B., Kavouras, S. A., Kallistratos, A. A., Moraiti, I. P., Douvis, S. J., . . . Sidossis, L. S. (2010). Eleven-year prevalence trends of obesity in Greek children: First evidence that prevalence of obesity is leveling off. *Obesity*, 18(1), 161–166.

Tanner, J. L. (2006). Recentering during emerging adulthood: A critical turning point in life span human development. In J. J. Arnett & J. L. Tanner (Eds.), *Emerging adults in America: Coming of age in the 21st century* (pp. 21–55). Washington, DC: American Psychological Association.

Tanner, J. L., & Arnett, J. J. (2010). Presenting "emerging adulthood": What makes it developmentally distinctive. In J. J. Arnett, M. Kloep, L. B. Hendry, & J. L. Tanner (Eds.), *Debating emerging adulthood: Stage or process?* (pp. 13–30). New York, NY: Oxford University Press.

Tanner, J. M. (1955). *Growth at adolescence*. Oxford, England: Blackwell.

Tanner, J. M. (1978). *Foetus into man: Physical growth from conception to maturity*. Cambridge, MA: Harvard University Press.

Tareque, M. I., Begum, S., & Saito, Y. (2013). Gender differences in disability-free life expectancy at old ages in Bangladesh. *Journal of Aging and Health*, 25(8), 1299–1312.

Tarrant, R. C., Sheridan-Pereira, M., McCarthy, R. A., Younger, K. M., & Kearney, J. M. (2013). Mothers who formula feed: Their practices, support needs and factors influencing their infant feeding decision. *Child Care in Practice*, 19(1), 78–94.

Taumoepeau, M., & Reese, E. (2013). Maternal reminiscing, elaborative talk, and children's theory of mind: An intervention study. *First Language*, 33(4), 388–410.

Taveras, E. M., Hohman, K. H., Price, S. N., Rifas-Shiman, S. L., Mitchell, K., Gortmaker, S. L., & Gillman, M. W.

(2011). Correlates of participation in a pediatric primary care-based obesity prevention intervention. *Obesity, 19*(2), 449–452.

Taylor, C. A., Hamvas, L., & Paris, R. (2011). Perceived instrumentality and normativeness of corporal punishment use among black mothers. *Family Relations, 60*, 60–72.

Taylor, J. L., & Mailick, M. R. (2014). A longitudinal examination of 10-year change in vocational and educational activities for adults with autism spectrum disorders. *Developmental Psychology, 50*(3), 699–708.

Taylor, Z. E., Eisenberg, N., Spinrad, T. L., Eggum, N. D., & Sulik, M. J. (2013). The relations of ego-resiliency and emotion socialization to the development of empathy and prosocial behavior across early childhood. *Emotion, 13*(5), 822–831.

Tedeschi, R. G., & Calhoun, L. G. (2008). Beyond the concept of recovery: Growth and the experience of loss. *Death Studies, 32*(1), 27–39.

Teeri, S., Valimaki, M., Katajisto, J., & Leino-Kilpi, H. (2008). Maintenance of parents' integrity in long-term institutional care. *Nursing Ethics, 15*(4), 523–535.

Telzer, E. H., Flannery, J., Shapiro, M., Humphreys, K. L., Goff, B., Gabard-Durman, L., . . . Tottenham, N. (2013). Early experience shapes amygdala sensitivity to race: An international adoption design. *Journal of Neuroscience, 33*(33), 13484–13488.

Telzer, E. H., Fuligni, A. J., Lieberman, M. D., & Galván, A. (2013). The effects of poor quality sleep on brain function and risk taking in adolescence. *Neuroimage, 71*, 275–283.

Terplan, M., Cheng, D., & Chisolm, M. S. (2014). The relationship between pregnancy intention and alcohol use behavior: An analysis of PRAMS data. *Journal of Substance Abuse Treatment, 46*(4), 506–510.

Teskereci, G., & Oncel, S. (2013). Effect of lifestyle on quality of life of couples receiving infertility treatment. *Journal of Sex & Marital Therapy, 39*(6), 476–492.

Teti, D. M., Kim, B., Mayer, G., & Countermine, M. (2010). Maternal emotional availability at bedtime predicts infant sleep quality. *Journal of Family Psychology, 24*, 307–315.

Thacker, K. S. (2008). Nurses' advocacy behaviors in end-of-life nursing care. *Nursing Ethics, 15*(2), 174–185.

Thai, N. D., Connell, C. M., & Tebes, J. (2010). Substance use among Asian American adolescents: Influence of race, ethnicity, and acculturation in the context of key risk and protective factors. *Asian American Journal of Psychology, 1*(4), 261–274.

Thaler, N. S., Goldstein, G., Pettegrew, J. W., Luther, J. F., Reynolds, C. R., & Allen, D. N. (2013). Developmental aspects of working and associative memory. *Archives of Clinical Neuropsychology, 28*(4), 348–355.

Thapar, A., Cooper, M., Eyre, O., & Langley, K. (2013). Practitioner review: What have we learnt about the causes of ADHD? *Journal of Child Psychology and Psychiatry, 54*(1), 3–16.

Theis, W., & Bleiler, L. (2011). Alzheimer's Association report: 2011 Alzheimer's disease facts and figures. *Alzheimer's & Dementia, 7*, 208–244.

Thiessen, E. D., Hill, E. A., & Saffran, J. R. (2005). Infant-directed speech facilitates word segmentation. *Infancy, 7*, 53–71.

Thomaes, S., Stegge, H., & Olthof, T. (2007). Externalizing shame responses in children: The role of fragile-positive self-esteem. *British Journal of Developmental Psychology, 25*(4), 559–577.

Thoman, E. B., & Whitney, M. P. (1990). Behavioral states in infants: Individual differences and individual analyses. In J. Colombo & J. W. Fagen (Eds.), *Individual differences in infancy: Reliability, stability, prediction* (pp. 113–135). Hillsdale, NJ: Erlbaum.

Thomas, A., & Chess, S. (1977). *Temperament and development*. Oxford, England: Brunner/Mazel.

Thomas, A., Chess, S., & Birch, H. G. (1968). *Temperament and behavior disorders in children*. New York, NY: New York University Press.

Thomas, J. R., & French, K. E. (1985). Gender differences across age in motor performance: A meta-analysis. *Psychological Bulletin, 98*, 260–282.

Thompson, E. J., & Barnes, K. (2013). Meaning of sexual performance among men with and without erectile dysfunction. *Psychology of Men & Masculinity, 14*(3), 271–280.

Thompson, R. A., & Newton, E. K. (2013). Baby altruists? Examining the complexity of prosocial motivation in young children. *Infancy, 18*(1), 120–133.

Thompson, R., Lee, C., & Adams, J. (2013). Imagining fatherhood: Young Australian men's perspectives on fathering. *International Journal of Men's Health, 12*(2), 150–165.

Thompson-Brenner, H. (2013). The good news about psychotherapy for eating disorders: Comment on Warren, Schafer, Crowley, and Olivardia. *Psychotherapy, 50*(4), 565–567.

Tomlinson, M., Cooper, P., & Murray, L. (2005). The mother-infant relationship and infant attachment in a South African peri-urban settlement. *Child Development, 76*, 1044–1054.

Toomey, R. B., Umaña-Taylor, A. J., Updegraff, K. A., & Jahromi, L. B. (2013). Ethnic identity development and ethnic discrimination: Examining longitudinal associations with adjustment for Mexican-origin adolescent mothers. *Journal of Adolescence, 36*(5), 825–833.

Top 10 Best Dating Sites. (2014). *10 best dating sites, dating site reviews of Match.com.* Retrieved from http://www.top10bestdtingsites.com/index

Toril, P., Reales, J. M., & Ballesteros, S. (2014). Video game training enhances cognition of older adults: A meta-analytic study. *Psychology and Aging, 29*(3), 706–716.

Tornello, S., & Patterson, C. J. (2012). Gay fathers in mixed-orientation relationships: Experiences of those who stay in their marriages and of those who leave. *Journal of GLBT Family Studies, 81*(1), 85–98.

Touchette, E., Henegar, A., Godart, N. T., Pryor, L., Falissard, B., Tremblay, R. E., & Côté, S. M. (2011). Subclinical eating disorders and their comorbidity with mood and anxiety disorders in adolescent girls. *Psychiatry Research, 185*, 185–192.

Trentowska, M., Svaldi, J., & Tuschen-Caffier, B. (2014). Efficacy of body exposure as treatment component for patients with eating disorders. *Journal of Behavior Therapy and Experimental Psychiatry, 45*(1), 178–185.

Triana, M. (2011). A woman's place and a man's duty: How gender role incongruence in one's family can result in home-related spillover discrimination at work. *Journal of Business Psychology, 26*, 71–86.

Triandis, H. C. (1995). *Individualism & collectivism*. Boulder, CO: Westview Press.

Trick, L. M., Toxopeus, R., & Wilson, D. (2010). The effects of visibility conditions, traffic density, and navigational challenge in speed compensation and driving performance in older adults.

Accident Analysis and Prevention, 42, 1661–1671.

Troll, L. E. (1983). Grandparents: The family watchdog. In T. H. Brubaker (Ed.), *Family relationships in later life* (pp. 63–74). Beverly Hills, CA: Sage.

Trommsdorff, G., Friedlmeier, W., & Mayer, B. (2007). Sympathy, distress, and prosocial behavior of preschool children in four cultures. *International Journal of Behavioral Development,* 31(3), 284–293.

Troop-Gordon, W., Visconti, K. J., & Kuntz, K. J. (2011). Perceived popularity during early adolescence: Links to declining school adjustment among aggressive youth. *The Journal of Early Adolescence,* 31(1), 125–151.

Trudel, G., Dargis, L., Villeneuve, L., Cadieux, J., Boyer, R., & Préville, M. (2014). Marital, sexual and psychological functioning of older couples living at home: The results of a national survey using longitudinal methodology (Part II). *Sexologies: European Journal of Sexology and Sexual Health / Revue Européenne de Sexologie et de Santé Sexuelle,* 23(2), e35–e48.

Tulving, E. (1985). How many memory systems are there? *American Psychologist,* 40, 385–398.

Tummers, L. G., & Den Dulk, L. (2013). The effects of work alienation on organizational commitment, work effort and work-to-family enrichment. *Journal of Nursing Management,* 21(6), 850–859.

Tuokko, H., Myers, A., Jouk, A., Marshall, S., Man-Son-Hing, M., Porter, M. M., . . . Vrkljan, B. (2013). Associations between age, gender, psychosocial and health characteristics in the Candrive II study cohort. *Accident Analysis and Prevention,* 61, 267–271.

Turkheimer, E. (2004). Spinach and ice cream: Why social science is so difficult. In L. F. DiLalla (Ed.) *Behavior genetic principles: Perspectives in development, personality, and psychopathology.* Washington, DC: American Psychological Association Press.

Turkheimer, E., Haley, A., Waldron, M., D'Onofrio, B., & Gottesman, I. I. (2003). Socioeconomic status modifies heritability of IQ in young children. *Psychological Science,* 14, 623–628.

Turkington, C., & Alper, M. M. (2001). *The encyclopedia of fertility and infertility.* New York, NY: Facts on File.

Turkle, S. (2011). *Alone together: Why we expect more from technology and less from each other.* New York, NY: Basic Books.

Turra, C. M., & Goldman, N. (2007). Socioeconomic differences in mortality among U.S. adults: Insights into the Hispanic paradox. *Journals of Gerontology,* 62B(3), S184–S192.

Twenge, J. M. (2006). *Generation me: Why today's young Americans are more confident, assertive, entitled — and more miserable than ever before.* New York, NY: Free Press.

U.S. Bureau of Labor Statistics. (2014). *Women in the labor force: A databook.* Retrieved from http://www.bls.gov/opub/reports/cps/women-in-the-labor-force-a-databook-2014.pdf

U.S. Census Bureau. (2012). Retrieved from http://www.census.gov

U.S. Census Bureau. (2014). *U.S. white population a minority by 2042.* In *State and County QuickFacts.* Retrieved from http://www.quickfacts.census.gov/qfd/states/00000.html

U.S. Department of Health and Human Services. (2003). *State-funded pre-kindergarten: What the evidence shows.* Retrieved from http://aspe.hhs.gov/hsp/state-funded-pre-k/index.htm

U.S. Department of Health and Human Serices. (2009). *Summary health statistics for U.S. adults: National health interview survey,* 10(249). Retrieved from http://www.cdc.gov/nchs/data/series/sr_10/sr10_249.pdf

U.S. Department of Labor. (2011). *Usual weekly earnings of wage and salary workers first quarter 2011.* Retrieved from http://www.bls.gov/news.release/archives/wkyeng_04192011.pdf

Udry, J. R. (1990). Biosocial models of adolescent problem behaviors. *Social Biology,* 37, 1–10.

Udry, J. R. (2000). Biological limits of gender construction. *American Sociological Review,* 65, 443–457.

Udry, J. R., & Campbell, B. C. (1994). Getting started on sexual behavior. In A. S. Rossi (Ed.), *Sexuality across the life course* (pp. 187–207). Chicago, IL: University of Chicago Press.

Ueno, K. (2010). Same-sex experience and mental health during the transition between adolescence and young adulthood. *The Sociological Quarterly,* 51, 484–510.

Uji, M., Sakamoto, A., Adachi, K., & Kitamura, T. (2014). The impact of authoritative, authoritarian, and permissive parenting styles on children's later mental health in Japan: Focusing on parent

and child gender. *Journal of Child and Family Studies,* 23(2), 293–302.

Umberson, D., Pudrovska, T., & Reczek, C. (2010). Parenthood, childlessness, and well-being: A life course perspective. *Journal of Marriage and Family,* 72, 612–629.

Umberson, D., Williams, K., Thomas, P. A., Liu, H., & Thomeer, M. B. (2014). Race, gender, and chains of disadvantage: Childhood adversity, social relationships, and health. *Journal of Health & Social Behavior,* 55(1), 20–38.

Umemura, T., Jacobvitz, D., Messina, S., & Hazen, N. (2013). Do toddlers prefer the primary caregiver or the parent with whom they feel more secure? The role of toddler emotion. *Infant Behavior and Development,* 36(1), 102–114.

UNICEF (United Nations Children's Fund). (2000). *The time to sow.* Retrieved from http://www.unicef.org/pon00/pon00_3.pdf

UNICEF (United Nations Children's Fund). (2002). *The state of the world's children 2003.* New York, NY: UNICEF.

UNICEF (United Nations Children's Fund). (2009). *The state of the world's children: Maternal and newborn health, 2009.* Retrieved from http://www.unicef.org/publications/index_47127.html

Urban, J. B., Lewin-Bizan, S., & Lerner, R. M. (2010). The role of intentional self regulation, lower neighborhood ecological assets, and activity involvement in youth developmental outcomes. *Journal of Youth and Adolescence,* 39, 783–800.

Utz, R. L., Swenson, K. L., Caserta, M., Lund, D., & deVries, B. (2014). Feeling lonely versus being alone: Loneliness and social support among recently bereaved persons. *Journals of Gerontology Series B: Psychological Sciences and Social Sciences,* 69B(1), 85–94.

Vaaler, M. L., Stagg, J., Parks, S. E., Erickson, T., & Castrucci, B. C. (2010). Breast-feeding attitudes and behavior among WIC mothers in Texas. *Journal of Nutrition Education and Behavior,* 42(35), S30–S38.

Valentino, K., Nuttall, A. K., Comas, M., McDonnell, C. G., Piper, B., Thomas, T. E., & Fanuele, S. (2014). Mother–child reminiscing and autobiographical memory specificity among preschool-age children. *Developmental Psychology,* 50(4), 1197–1207.

van Aken, C., Junger, M., Verhoeven, M., van Aken, M. A. G., & Deković, M. (2008). The longitudinal relations between parenting and toddlers' attention problems and aggressive behaviors. *Infant Behavior and Development, 31,* 432–446.

van der Pas, S., van Tilburg, T. G., & Silverstein, M. (2013). Stepfamilies in later life. *Journal of Marriage and Family, 75*(5), 1065–1069.

Van Dijck, J. (2013). *The culture of connectivity: A critical history of social media.* Oxford, England: Oxford University Press.

van Dijk, G. P., Huijts, M., & Lodder, J. (2013). Cognition improvement in Taekwondo novices over 40. Results from the SEKWONDO Study. *Frontiers in Aging Neuroscience, 5,* 74.

van Geel, M., & Vedder, P. (2011). The role of family obligations and school adjustment in explaining the immigrant paradox. *Journal of Youth and Adolescence, 40,* 187–196.

van Harmelen, A. L., van Tol, M. J., van der Wee, N. J. A., Veltman, D. J., Aleman, A., Spinhoven, P., . . . Elzinga, B. M. (2010). Reduced medial prefrontal cortex volume in adults reporting childhood emotional maltreatment. *Biological Psychiatry, 68,* 832–838.

van IJzendoorn, M. H., & Sagi, A. (1999). Cross-cultural patterns of attachment: Universal and contextual dimensions. In J. Cassidy & P. R. Shaver (Eds.), *Handbook of attachment: Theory, research, and clinical applications* (pp. 713–734). New York, NY: Guilford Press.

van Selm, M., & Van der Heijden, B. M. (2013). Communicating employability enhancement throughout the life-span: A national intervention program aimed at combating age-related stereotypes at the workplace. *Educational Gerontology, 39*(4), 259–272.

van Steenbergen, E. F., Kluwer, E. S., & Karney, B. R. (2014). Work–family enrichment, work–family conflict, and marital satisfaction: A dyadic analysis. *Journal of Occupational Health Psychology, 19*(2), 182–194.

van Wijmen, M. S., Pasman, H. W., Widdershoven, G. M., & Onwuteaka-Philipsen, B. D. (2014). Motivations, aims and communication around advance directives: A mixed-methods study into the perspective of their owners and the influence of a current illness. *Patient Education and Counseling, 95*(3), 393–399.

Vanassche, S., Swicegood, G., & Matthijs, K. (2013). Marriage and children as a key to happiness? Cross-national differences in the effects of marital status and

children on well-being. *Journal of Happiness Studies, 14*(2), 501–524.

Vandell, D. L., Burchinal, M., Vandergrift, N., Belsky, J., & Steinberg, L. (2010). Do effects of early child care extend to age 15 years? Results from the NICHD Study of Early Child Care and Youth Development. *Child Development, 81*(3), 737–756.

Vaughn, L. M., Ireton, C., Geraghty, S. R., Diers, T., Niño, V., Falciglia, G. A., . . . Mosbaugh, C. (2010). Sociocultural influences on the determinants of breast-feeding by Latina mothers in the Cincinnati area. *Family & Community Health, 33*(4), 318–328.

Vazsonyi, A. T., & Chen, P. (2010). Entry risk into the juvenile justice system: African American, American Indian, Asian American, European American, and Hispanic children and adolescents. *Journal of Child Psychology and Psychiatry, 51*(6), 668–678.

Veenstra, R., Huitsing, G., Dijkstra, J., & Lindenberg, S. (2010). Friday on my mind: The relation of partying with antisocial behavior of early adolescents. The TRAILS Study. *Journal of Research on Adolescence, 20*(2), 420–431.

Vega, P., Rivera, M. S., & González, R. (2014). When grief turns into love: Understanding the experience of parents who have revived after losing a child due to cancer. *Journal of Pediatric Oncology Nursing, 31*(3), 166–176.

Verbakel, E., & Jaspers, E. (2010). A comparative study on permissiveness toward euthanasia: Religiosity, slippery slope, autonomy, and death with dignity. *Public Opinion Quarterly, 74*(1), 109–139.

Verghese, J., Wang, C., Lipton, R. B., & Holtzer, R. (2013). Motoric cognitive risk syndrome and the risk of dementia. *Journals of Gerontology Series A: Biological Sciences and Medical Sciences, 68*(4), 412–418.

Verhoeven, M., Junger, M., Aken, C., Dekovic, A., & Sken, M. A. G. (2010). Parenting and children's externalizing behavior: Bidirectionality during toddlerhood. *Journal of Applied Developmental Psychology, 31,* 93–105.

Versey, H. S., Stewart, A. J., & Duncan, L. E. (2013). Successful aging in late midlife: The role of personality among college-educated women. *Journal of Adult Development, 20*(2), 63–75.

Verweij, E., Oepkes, D., de Vries, M., van den Akker, M., van den Akker, E. S., & de Boer, M. A. (2013). Non-invasive prenatal screening for trisomy 21: What women want and are willing to pay.

Patient Education and Counseling, 93(3), 641–645.

Vespa, J., Lewis, J. M., & Kreider, R. M. (2013). *America's families and living arrangements: 2012.* Washington, D.C.: U.S. Census Bureau.

Vespa. J (2014). Historical trends in the marital intentions of one time and serial cohabitors. *Journal of Marriage and Family, 76,* 207–217.

Vianna, E., & Stetsenko, A. (2006). Embracing history through transforming it: Contrasting Piagetian versus Vygotskian (activity) theories of learning and development to expand constructivism within a dialectical view of history. *Theory & Psychology, 16*(1), 81–108.

Victor, S. E., Glenn, C. R., & Klonsky, E. D. (2012). Is non-suicidal self-injury an "addiction"? A comparison of craving in substance use and non-suicidal self-injury. *Psychiatry Research, 197*(1–2), 73–77.

Virmani, E.A., & Ontai, L.L. (2010). Supervision and training in child care: Does reflective supervision foster caregiver insightfulness? *Infant Mental Health Journal, 31*(1), 16–32.

Volk, H. E., Lurmann, F., Penfold, B., Hertz-Picciotto, I., & McConnell, R. (2013). Traffic-related air pollution, particulate matter, and autism. *JAMA Psychiatry, 70*(1), 71–77.

Volkmar, F. Siegel, M., Woodbury-Smith, M., King, B., McCracken, J., & State, M. (2014). Practice parameter for the assessment and treatment of children and adolescents with autism spectrum disorder. *Journal of the American Academy of Child & Adolescent Psychiatry, 53*(2), 237–257.

von der Lippe, A., Eilertsen, D. E., Hartmann, E., & Killèn, K. (2010). The role of maternal attachment in children's attachment and cognitive executive functioning: A preliminary study. *Attachment & Human Development, 12*(5), 429–444.

von Hippel, W., Henry, J. D., & Matovic, D. (2008). Aging and social satisfaction: Offsetting positive and negative effects. *Psychology and Aging, 23,* 435–439.

Von Raffler-Engel, W. (1994). *The perception of the unborn across the cultures of the world.* Seattle, WA: Hogrefe & Huber.

von Stumm, S. (2013). Investment traits and intelligence in adulthood: Assessment and associations. *Journal of Individual Differences, 34*(2), 82–89.

Votruba-Drzal, E., Coley, R. L., Koury, A. S., & Miller, P. (2013). Center-based child care and cognitive skills development: Importance of timing and household resources. *Journal of Educational Psychology, 105*(3), 821–838.

Vouloumanos, A., Werker, J. F., Hauser, M. D., & Martin, A. (2010). The tuning of human neonates' preference for speech. *Child Development, 81*(2), 517–527.

Vreeswijk, C. M., Maas, A. M., Rijk, C. M., & van Bakel, H. A. (2014). Fathers' experiences during pregnancy: Paternal prenatal attachment and representations of the fetus. *Psychology of Men & Masculinity, 15*(2), 129–137.

Vuorinen, M., Kåreholt, I., Julkunen, V., Spulber, G., Niskanen, E., Paajanen, T., . . . Solomon, A. (2013). Changes in vascular factors 28 years from midlife and late-life cortical thickness. *Neurobiology of Aging, 34*(1), 100–109.

Vygotsky, L. S. (1962). *Thought and language* (E. Hanfmann & G. Vakar, Eds. & Trans.). New York, NY: MIT Press and Wiley. (Original work published 1934).

Vygotsky, L. S. (1978). *Mind in society: The development of higher psychological processes* (M. Cole, V. John-Steiner, S. Scribner, & E. Souberman, Eds.). Cambridge, MA: Harvard University Press. (Original work published 1935).

Waasdorp, T. E., Baker, C. N., Paskewich, B. S., & Leff, S. S. (2013). The association between forms of aggression, leadership, and social status among urban youth. *Journal of Youth and Adolescence, 42*(2), 263–274.

Waasdorp, T. E., Bradshaw, C. P., Duong, J. (2011). The link between parents' perceptions of the school and their responses to school bullying: Variation by child characteristics and the forms of victimization. *Journal of Educational Psychology, 103*(2), 324–335.

Wadsworth, B. J. (1996). *Piaget's theory of cognitive and affective development: Foundations of constructivism* (5th ed.). White Plains, NY: Longman.

Wagner, J., Lüdtke, O., Jonkmann, K., & Trautwein, U. (2013). Cherish yourself: Longitudinal patterns and conditions of self-esteem change in the transition to young adulthood. *Journal of Personality and Social Psychology, 104*(1), 148–163.

Wagner, T. (2000). *How schools change: Lessons from three communities revisited* (2nd ed.). New York, NY: RoutledgeFalmer.

Wahl, H., Heyl, V., Drapaniotis, P. M., Hörmann, K., Jonas, J. B., Plinkert, P. K., & Rohrschneider, K. (2013). Severe vision and hearing impairment and successful aging: A multidimensional view. *The Gerontologist, 53*(6), 950–962.

Waldinger, R. J., & Schulz, M. S. (2010). What's love got to do with it? Social functioning, perceived health and daily happiness in married octogenarians. *Psychology and Aging, 25*(2), 422–431.

Wallerstein, J., Lewis, J., & Packer Rosenthal, S. (2013). Mothers and their children after divorce: Report from a 25-year longitudinal study. *Psychoanalytic Psychology, 30*(2), 167–184.

Walsh, J. L. (2008, March). *Magazine reading as a longitudinal predictor of women's sexual norms and behaviors.* Paper presented at 12th Biennial Meeting of Society for Research on Adolescence, Chicago, IL.

Walter, T. (2003, July 24). Historical and cultural variants on the good death. *BMJ (British Medical Journal), 327,* 218–220.

Walton, K. E., Huyen, B. T., Thorpe, K., Doherty, E. R., Juarez, B., D'Accordo, C., & Reina, M. T. (2013). Cross-sectional personality differences from age 16–90 in a Vietnamese sample. *Journal of Research in Personality, 47*(1), 36–40.

Walvoord, E. C. (2010). The timing of puberty: Is it changing? Does it matter? *Journal of Adolescent Health, 47,* 433–439.

Wang, H., & Abbott, D. A. (2013). Waiting for Mr. Right: The meaning of being a single educated Chinese female over 30 in Beijing and Guangzhou. *Women's Studies International Forum, 40,* 222–229.

Wang, M., & Saudino, K. J. (2013). Genetic and environmental influences on individual differences in emotion regulation and its relation to working memory in toddlerhood. *Emotion, 13*(6), 1055–1067.

Wang, M., & Shi, J. (2014). Psychological research on retirement. *Annual Review of Psychology, 65,* 209–233.

Wang, S., Yang, Y., Xing, W., Chen, J., Liu, C., & Luo, X. (2013). Altered neural circuits related to sustained attention and executive control in children with ADHD: An event-related fMRI study. *Clinical Neurophysiology, 124*(11), 2181–2190.

Warr, M. (2007). The tangled web: Delinquency, deception, and parental attachment. *Journal of Youth and Adolescence, 36,* 607–622.

Warren, C. S., Schafer, K. J., Crowley, M. J., & Olivardia, R. (2013). Demographic and work-related correlates of job burnout in professional eating disorder treatment providers. *Psychotherapy, 50*(4), 553–564.

Warren, C. S., Schoen, A., & Schafer, K. J. (2010). Media internalization and social comparison as predictors of eating pathology among Latino adolescents: The moderating effect of gender and generational status. *Sex Roles, 63,* 712–724.

Waterman, A. S. (1999). Identity, the identity statuses, and identity status development: A contemporary statement. *Developmental Review, 19,* 591–621.

Watson, J. B. (1930). *Behaviorism* (Revised ed.). New York, NY: Norton.

Watson, L. B., & Ancis, J. R. (2013). Power and control in the legal system: From marriage/relationship to divorce and custody. *Violence Against Women, 19*(2), 166–186.

Watson, J. B. (with the assistance of Watson, R. R.). (1972). *Psychological care of infant and child.* New York, NY: Arno Press. (Original work published 1928).

Wattis, L., Standing, K., & Yerkes, M. A. (2013). Mothers and work–life balance: Exploring the contradictions and complexities involved in work–family negotiation. *Community, Work & Family, 16*(1), 1–19.

Wedding, D., Kohout, J., Mengel, M. B., Ohlemiller, M., Ulione, M., Cook, K., . . . Braddock, S. (2007). Psychologists' knowledge and attitudes about fetal alcohol syndrome, fetal alcohol spectrum disorders, and alcohol use during pregnancy. *Professional Psychology: Research and Practice, 38*(2), 208–213.

Weibel-Orlando, J. (1999). Powwow princesses and gospelettes: Growing up in grandmother's world. In M. Schweitzer (Ed.), *Indian grandparenthood* (pp. 181–202). Albuquerque, NM: University of New Mexico Press.

Weisfeld, G. (1997). Puberty rites as clues to the nature of human adolescence. *Cross-Cultural Research: The Journal of Comparative Social Science, 31,* 27–54.

Weitz, R. (2010). Changing the scripts: Midlife women's sexuality in contemporary U.S. film. *Sexuality & Culture, 14,* 17–32.

Wells-di Gregorio, S. W. (2009). Family end-of-life decision making. In J. Werth & D. Blevins (Eds.), *Decision making near the end of life: Recent developments and future directions* (pp. 247–280). New York, NY: Routledge.

Wender, P. H., Reimherr, F. W., Marchant, B. K., Sanford, M. E., Czajkowski, L. A., & Tomb, D. A. (2011). A one year trial of methylphenidate in the treatment of ADHD. *Journal of Attention Disorders, 15*(1), 36–45.

Werner, N. E., & Hill, L. G. (2010). Individual and peer group normative beliefs about relational aggression. *Child Development, 81*(3), 826–836.

Werth, B., & Tsiaras, A. (2002). *From conception to birth: A life unfolds.* New York, NY: Doubleday.

Wertz, R. W., & Wertz, D. C. (1989). *Lying-in: A history of childbirth in America* (expanded ed.). New Haven, CT: Yale University Press.

Whitaker, E. A., & Bokemeier, J. (2014). Patterns in income source expectations for retirement among preretirees. *Research on Aging, 36*(4), 467–496.

White, B. A., Jarrett, M. A., & Ollendick, T. H. (2013). Self-regulation deficits explain the link between reactive aggression and internalizing and externalizing behavior problems in children. *Journal of Psychopathology and Behavioral Assessment, 35*(1), 1–9.

White, J. (2006). Multiple invalidities. In J. A. Schaler (Ed.), *Howard Gardner under fire: The rebel psychologist faces his critics* (pp. 45–71). Chicago, IL: Open Court.

White, L., & Edwards, J. N. (1990). Emptying the nest and parental well-being: An analysis of national panel data. *American Sociological Review, 55*, 235–242.

Whiteman, S. D., McHale, S. M., & Crouter, A. C. (2007). Longitudinal changes in marital relationships: The role of offspring's pubertal development. *Journal of Marriage and Family, 69*(4), 1005–1020.

Whiteman, S. D., McHale, S. M., & Crouter, A. C. (2010). Family relationships from adolescence to early adulthood: Changes in the family system following firstborns' leaving home. *Journal of Research on Adolescence, 21*(2), 461–474.

Whiting, J. B., Smith, D. R., Barnett, T., & Grafsky, E. L. (2007). Overcoming the Cinderella myth: A mixed methods study of successful stepmothers. *Journal of Divorce & Remarriage, 47*(1-2), 95–109.

Whitson, H. E., Landerman, L. R., Newman, A. B., Fried, L. P., Pieper, C. F., & Cohen, H. J. (2010). Chronic medical conditions and the sex-based disparity

in disability: The cardiovascular health study. *Journals of Gerontology: Medical Sciences, 65A*(12), 1325–1331.

Whitton, S. W., Stanley, S. M., Markman, H. J., & Johnson, C. A. (2013). Attitudes toward divorce, commitment, and divorce proneness in first marriages and remarriages. *Journal of Marriage and Family, 75*(2), 276–287.

Wiik, K. L., Loman, M. M., Van Ryzin, M. J., Armstrong, J. M., Essex, M. J., Pollak, S. D., & Gunnar, M. R. (2011). Behavioral and emotional symptoms of post-institutionalized children in middle childhood. *Journal of Child Psychology and Psychiatry, 52*(1), 56–63.

Wiles, J. L., Leibing, A., Guberman, N., Reeve, J., & Allen, R. S. (2012). The meaning of "aging in place" to older people. *The Gerontologist, 52*(3), 357–366.

Wilkinson, R., & Pickett, K. (2009). *The spirit level: Why greater equality makes societies stronger.* New York, NY: Bloomsbury Press.

Williams, D. M., & Bowler, D. M. (2014). Autism spectrum disorder: Fractionable or coherent? *Autism, 18*(1), 2–5.

Williams, K., Donaghue, N., & Kurz, T. (2013). "Giving guilt the flick"? An investigation of mothers' talk about guilt in relation to infant feeding. *Psychology of Women Quarterly, 37*(1), 97–112.

Williamson, R. A., Donohue, M. R., & Tully, E. C. (2013). Learning how to help others: Two-year-olds' social learning of a prosocial act. *Journal of Experimental Child Psychology, 114*(4), 543–550.

Willoughby, T., Good, M., Adachi, P. C., Hamza, C., & Tavernier, R. (2013). Examining the link between adolescent brain development and risk taking from a social–developmental perspective. *Brain and Cognition, 83*(3), 315–323.

Wilson, A. C., & Huston, T. L. (2013). Shared reality and grounded feelings during courtship: Do they matter for marital success? *Journal of Marriage and Family, 75*(3), 681–696.

Wilson, S. M., Ngige, L. W., & Trollinger, L. J. (2003). Connecting generations: Paths to Maasai and Kamba marriage in Kenya. In R. R. Hamon & B. B. Ingoldsby (Eds.), *Mate selection across cultures* (pp. 95–118). Thousand Oaks, CA: Sage.

Wilson, T. W., Franzen, J. D., Heinrichs-Graham, E., White, M. L., Knott, N. L., & Wetzel, M. W. (2013). Broadband neurophysiological abnormalities in the medial prefrontal region of the

default-mode network in adults with ADHD. *Human Brain Mapping, 34*(3), 566–574.

Wilson, T., Karimpour, R., & Rodkin, P. C. (2011). African American and European American students' peer groups during early adolescence: Structure, status, and academic achievement. *The Journal of Early Adolescence, 31*(1), 74–98.

Wimmer, H., & Perner, J. (1983). Beliefs about beliefs: Representation and constraining function of wrong beliefs in young children's understanding of deception. *Cognition, 13*, 103–128.

Windsor, T. D., & Anstey, K. J. (2010). Age differences in psychosocial predictors of positive and negative affect: A longitudinal investigation of young, midlife, and older adults. *Psychology and Aging, 25*(3), 641–652.

Windsor, T. D., & Butterworth, P. (2010). Supportive, aversive, ambivalent, and indifferent partner evaluations in midlife and young-old adulthood. *Journals of Gerontology: Psychological Sciences, 65B*(3), 287–295.

Windsor, T. D., Burns, R. A., & Byles, J. E. (2013). Age, physical functioning, and affect in midlife and older adulthood. *Journals of Gerontology Series B: Psychological Sciences and Social Sciences, 68B*(3), 395–399.

Wittwer, H. (2013). The problem of the possible rationality of suicide and the ethics of physician-assisted suicide. *International Journal of Law and Psychiatry, 36*(5–6), 419–426.

Witvliet, M., Olthof, T., Hoeksma, J. B., Goossens, F. A., Smits, M. S. I., & Koot, H. M. (2010). Peer group affiliation of children: The role of perceived popularity, likeability, and behavioral similarity in bullying. *Social Development, 19*(2), 285–303.

Wöhrmann, A. M., Deller, J., & Wang, M. (2013). Outcome expectations and work design characteristics in post-retirement work planning. *Journal of Vocational Behavior, 83*(3), 219–228.

Wolfe, D. A. (2011). Risk factors for child abuse perpetration. In J. W. White, M. P. Koss, & A. E. Kazdin (Eds.), *Violence against women and children: Vol. 1. Mapping the terrain* (pp. 31–53). Washington, D.C.: American Psychological Association.

Wood, D., Bruner, J. S., & Ross, G. (1976). The role of tutoring in problem solving. *Journal of Child Psychology and Psychiatry, 17*, 89–100.

Wood, J. M., Lacherez, P. F., & Anstey, K. J. (2013). Not all older adults have insight into their driving abilities: Evidence from an on-road assessment and implications for policy. *Journals of Gerontology Series A: Biological Sciences and Medical Sciences, 68*(5), 559–566.

Wood, W. R., & Williamson, J. B. (2003). Historical changes in the meaning of death in the western tradition. In C. D. Bryant (Ed.), *Handbook of death & dying* (pp. 14–23). Thousand Oaks, CA: Sage.

Wood-Barcalow, N. L., Tylka, T. L., & Augustus-Horvath, C. L. (2010). "But I like my body": Positive body image characteristics and a holistic model for young-adult women. *Body Image, 7,* 106–116.

Woodruff, K., & Lee, B. (2011). Identifying and predicting problem behavior trajectories among pre-school children investigated for child abuse and neglect. *Child Abuse & Neglect, 35*(7), 491–503.

World Health Organization. (2003b). *Kangaroo mother care: A practical guide.* Geneva, Switzerland: Department of Reproductive Health and Research, World Health Organization.

World Life Expectancy. (2011). *World health rankings.* Retrieved from http://www.worldlifeexpectancy.com/world-health-rankings

Wray-Lake, L., Crouter, A. C., & McHale, S. M. (2010). Developmental patterns in decision-making autonomy across middle childhood and adolescence: European American parents' perspectives. *Child Development, 81*(2), 636–651.

Wright, M. O., & Masten, A. S. (2005). Resilience processes in development: Fostering positive adaptation in the context of adversity. In S. Goldstein & R. B. Brooks (Eds.), *Handbook of resilience in children* (pp. 17–37). New York, NY: Kluwer Academic/Plenum.

Wrzus, C., Hänel, M., Wagner, J., & Neyer, F. J. (2013). Social network changes and life events across the life span: A meta-analysis. *Psychological Bulletin, 139*(1), 53–80.

Wu, C., & Chao, R. K. (2011). Intergenerational cultural dissonance in parent-adolescent relationships among Chinese and European Americans. *Developmental Psychology, 47*(2), 493–508.

Wymbs, B. T., & Pelham, Jr., W. E. (2010). Child effects on communication between parents of youth with and without attention-deficit/hyperactivity disorder. *Journal of Abnormal Psychology, 119*(2), 366–375.

Xia, Y. R., & Zhou, Z. G. (2003). The transition of courtship, mate selection, and marriage in China. In R. R. Hamon & B. B. Ingoldsby (Eds.), *Mate selection across cultures* (pp. 231–246). Thousand Oaks, CA: Sage.

Xu, H., Wen, L. M., Rissel, C., & Baur, L. A. (2013). Smoking status and factors associated with smoking of first-time mothers during pregnancy and postpartum: Findings from the Healthy Beginnings Trial. *Maternal and Child Health Journal, 17*(6), 1151–1157.

Xu, L., Silverstein, M., & Chi, I. (2014). Emotional closeness between grandparents and grandchildren in rural China: The mediating role of the middle generation. *Journal of Intergenerational Relationships, 12*(3), 226–240.

Yamasaki, J., & Sharf, B. F. (2011). Opting out while fitting in: How residents make sense of assisted living and cope with community life. *Journal of Aging Studies, 25*(1), 13–21.

Yamasoba, T., Lin, F. R., Someya, S., Kashio, A., Sakamoto, T., & Kondo, K. (2013). Current concepts in age-related hearing loss: Epidemiology and mechanistic pathways. *Hearing Research, 303,* 30–38.

Yancey, G. A., & Yancey, S. W. (2002). *Just don't marry one: Interracial dating, marriage, and parenting.* Valley Forge, PA: Judson Press.

Yancura, L. A. (2013). Justifications for caregiving in White, Asian American, and Native Hawaiian grandparents raising grandchildren. *Journals of Gerontology Series B: Psychological Sciences and Social Sciences, 68B*(1), 139–144.

Yang, C. K., & Hahn, H. M. (2002). Cosleeping in young Korean children. *Journal of Developmental & Behavioral Pediatrics, 23,* 151–157.

Yang, P., Chen, Y., Yen, C., & Chen, H. (2014). Psychiatric diagnoses, emotional-behavioral symptoms and functional outcomes in adolescents born preterm with very low birth weights. *Child Psychiatry and Human Development, 46,* 358–366.

Yates, M., & Youniss, J. (1998). Community service and political identity development in adolescence. *Journal of Social Issues, 54,* 495–512.

Yeung, W. J., & Hu, S. (2013). Coming of age in times of change: The transition to adulthood in China. *Annals of the American Academy of Political and Social Science, 646*(1), 149–171.

You, J., Lin, M., & Leung, F. (2013). Functions of non-suicidal self-injury among Chinese community adolescents. *Journal of Adolescence, 36*(4), 737–745.

Young, L. M., Baltes, B. B., & Pratt, A. K. (2007). Using selection, optimization, and compensation to reduce job/family stressors: Effective when it matters. *Journal of Business and Psychology, 21*(4), 511–539.

Young, S., & Amarasinghe, J. M. (2010). Practitioner review: Non-pharmacological treatments for ADHD: A lifespan approach. *Journal of Child Psychology and Psychiatry, 51*(2), 116–133.

Yu, H. U., & Chan, S. (2010). Nurses' response to death and dying in an intensive care unit—A qualitative study. *Journal of Clinical Nursing, 19,* 1167–1169.

Yudell, M., Tabor, H. K., Dawson, G., Rossi, J., & Newschaffer, C. (2013). Priorities for autism spectrum disorder risk communication and ethics. *Autism, 17*(6), 701–722.

Zaichkowsky, L. D., & Larson, G. A. (1995). Physical, motor, and fitness development in children and adolescents. *Journal of Education, 177,* 55–79.

Zantinge, E. M., van den Berg, M., Smit, H. A., & Picavet, H. J. (2014). Retirement and a healthy lifestyle: Opportunity or pitfall? A narrative review of the literature. *European Journal of Public Health, 24*(3), 433–439.

Zayas, V., Mischel, W., Shoda, Y., & Aber, J. L. (2011). Roots of adult attachment: Maternal caregiving at 18 months predicts adult peer and partner attachment. *Social Psychological and Personality Science, 2*(3), 289–297.

Zeanah, C. H., Berlin, L. J., & Boris, N. W. (2011). Practitioner review: Clinical applications of attachment theory and research for infants and young children. *Journal of Child Psychology and Psychiatry, 52*(8), 819–833.

Zelinski, E. M., & Kennison, R. F. (2007). Not your parents' test scores: Cohort reduces psychometric aging effects. *Psychology and Aging, 22*(3), 546–557.

Zerbe, K. (2013). Personal meaning and eating disorder treatment: Comment on Warren et al. *Psychotherapy, 50*(4), 573–575.

Zeskind, P. S., & Lester, B. M. (2001). Analysis of infant crying. In L. T. Singer & P. S. Zeskind (Eds.), *Biobehavioral assessment of the infant* (pp. 149–166). New York, NY: Guilford Press.

Zettergren, P. (2007). Cluster analysis in sociometric research: A pattern-oriented approach to identifying temporally stable peer status groups of girls. *The Journal of Early Adolescence, 27*, 90–114.

Zhan, J.-Y., Wilding, J., Cornish, K., Shao, J., Xie, C.-H., Wang, Y.-H., . . . Zhao, Z.-Y. (2011). Charting the developmental trajectories of attention and executive function in Chinese school-aged children. *Child Neuropsychology, 17*, 82–95.

Zimmer-Gembeck, M. J., & Helfand, M. (2008). Ten years of longitudinal research on U.S. adolescent sexual behavior: Developmental correlates of sexual intercourse, and the importance of age, gender and ethnic background. *Developmental Review, 28*, 153–224.

Zimmermann, P., & Iwanski, A. (2014). Emotion regulation from early adolescence to emerging adulthood and middle adulthood: Age differences, gender differences, and emotion-specific developmental variations. *International Journal of Behavioral Development, 38*(2), 182–194.

Zoccolotti, P., & Friedmann, N. (2010). From dyslexia to dyslexias, from dysgraphia to dysgraphias, from a cause to causes: A look at current research on developmental dyslexia and dysgraphia. *Cortex: A Journal Devoted to the Study of the Nervous System and Behavior, 46*(10), 1211–1215.

Zucker, A. N., Ostrove, J. M., & Stewart, A. J. (2002). College-educated women's personality development in adulthood: Perceptions and age differences. *Psychology and Aging, 17*, 236–244.

Note: Page numbers followed by f indicate figures; those followed by t indicate tables.

Groopman, J. E., 454, 456
Grossbaum, M. F., 364
Grossmann, I., 375, 375f
Grube, J. W., 251
Gschwind, Y. J., 429
Guan, S. A., 282
Guardino, C. M., 44, 50
Guendelman, S., 78
Guerra, N. G., 180, 192, 193
Guerri, C., 275
Gueta, G., 221
Gunderson, E. A., 175
Gunther Moor, B., 266
Gupta, R., 455
Gustafsson, P. A., 208
Guttmacher Institute, 243, 250, 250f, 251, 253, 253f

H
Ha, J.-H., 410, 412
Haase, C. M., 335
Habermas, T., 159
Haddad, E., 273
Hadden, B. W., 320
Hagestad, G. O., 377
Hahn, H. M., 85
Hahn-Holbrook, J., 78
Hakoyama, M., 378
Hakvoort, R. M., 82
Halcomb, E., J., 461
Hall, G. S., 4, 6, 260, 266
Hall, S., 208
Halperin, J. M., 154, 156
Halpern-Meekin, S., 314
Haltigan, J. D. ., 112
Hamlin, J. K., 98, 99
Hampson, S. E., 360
Hamvas, L., 206
Hank, K., 377
Hansson, R. O., 458
Harbourne, R. T., 92
Harden, K. P., 241
Harkness, S., 171
Harley, K., 159
Harlow, C. M., 109
Harlow, H., 108
Harraway, J. A., 49
Harrell, W. A., 248
Harriger, J. A., 245
Harrington, R., 44
Harris, J. R., 204, 282
Harris, P., 450, 464
Harris, T. S., 209
Harrist, A. W., 122
Hart, H. M., 364, 366
Harter, S., 170, 171, 172, 173f, 175, 221, 244
Hartup, W. W., 188
Hasher, L., 394
Hashimoto-Torii, K., 49
Haskett, M. E., 209
Haslam, N., 282

Hasselhorn, M., 151
Hausdorff, J. M., 426, 429, 435
Hawes, C., 439
Hawk, C. K., 162
Hawkins, A., 56
Hawley, P. H., 191
Hay, P., 246
Hayflick, L., 419, 420
Haynes, M., 337
Hayslip, B., Jr., 379, 458
Hayward, C., 245
Hazan, C., 318
Healey, D. M., 154, 156
Healthychildren.org, 200
Healy, E., 64
Hearing Loop, 428
Heatherton, T. F., 162t
Heaven, P. C. L., 284
Hecht, A., 371, 374, 375
Hehman, J. A., 397
Helfand, M., 250
Helson, R., 359, 362, 365t, 367
Hemar-Nicolas, V., 141
Henderson, R. C., 206
Hendriksen, J. G. M., 154
Hendry, L. B., 295, 297
Hengartner, M. P., 209
Henkens, K., 404, 406, 407
Henry, J., 370
Henry, J. D., 400
Henry, L. A., 215t
Hensler, B. S., 215t
Heo, J., 407
Hepach, R., 175, 176
Herdt, G., 234, 249
Hernandez-Reif, M., 82
Hernández–Martínez, C., 49
Herrenkohl, T. I., 208
Herrera, D. E., 277
Herrera, F., 57
Herrnstein, R. J., 217
Hersh, R. H., 264, 264t
Hershey, D. A., 404
Hertwig, R., 377
Hertzog, C., 27, 398
Hess, T. M., 370, 398
Hesse-Biber, S., 246
Hetherington, E. M., 337
Heuer, C. A., 140
Hewitt, B., 337
Hickson, L., 427
Higher Education Research Institute, 304
Hill, E. A., 101
Hill, J. P., 281
Hill, L. G., 190, 193
Hill, P. L., 360, 362, 402
Hill, P. S., 84
Hinde, R. A. ., 109
Hinduja, S., 193
Hinshaw, S. P., 154
Hipwell, A. E., 250

Hirschfield, P. J., 272, 277
Hodgson, J., 437
Hoff-Ginsberg, E., 100, 101
Hoffman, M. L., 177
Hofstede, G., 10
Hohmann-Marriott, B., 338
Holland, L. A., 246
Holman, E. A., 362
Holmes, J. G., 316
Holmes, T. H., 409
Holmqvist, K., 248
Holt, A., 215
Hoogman, M., 154
Hoover, E., 309
Hopko, D. R., 400
Hopper, J., 337
Horhota, M., 398
Hough, C. L., 462
Houghton, L. A., 50
House, A. N., 202
House, B. R., 175
Houts, R. M., 239
Hoyer, W. J., 374
Hrdy, S. B., 5, 6
Hu, S., 295, 299, 310
Huang, H., 48
Huddleston, J., 237
Hughes, C., 160, 184
Hughes, D. K., 316, 317t
Hughes, M. L., 397
Huijts, M., 371
Hulme, C., 154, 155
Hülsheger, U. R., 348
Humaidan, P., 57
Humer, Ž., 344
Humphrey, G. M., 459t
Hungerford, T. L., 404
Hunt, C. K., 380
Hunt, T. K., 247
Hurks, P. P. M., 154
Hurst, C., 348
Hurt, T. R., 335
Huston, T. L., 316
Hutchinson, D. M., 245
Hutchison, S., 380
Hutteman, R., 360
Huttenlocher, P. R., 41f, 47t
Hvas, L., 382t
Hwang, S.-L., 154
Hwang, W., 312
Hyde, A., 243, 249
Hyde, J. S., 242, 341
Hymel, S., 193
Hymowitz, K., 7

I
Infurna, F. J., 437
Ingersoll-Dayton, B., 410
Innes, S., 453, 454
Ip, E. H., 429
Iqbal, Z., 44
Israel, S., 28

Ito, M., 36
Ito, Y., 344
Ivy, L., 204
Iwanski, A., 305
Izumi-Taylor, S., 344

J
Jaccard, J., 241
Jackson, T., 245
Jacquet, S. E., 316, 317t
Jaffe, J., 45, 59
Jaffee, S. R., 209
James, S. L., 338
James, W., 88, 90
Jamieson, R. D., 365t
Jang, H., 222
Janosz, M., 273
Janson, S., 208
Jaspers, E., 469
Jedd, K. E., 119
Jelinek, M., 194
Jenkins-Guarnieri, M. A., 313
Jensen, A. R., 217
Jensen, C., 163f
Jensen, H., 48
Jensen, J. F., 335
Jenson, W. R., 181, 339
Jernigan, T. L., 41, 74, 75, 76t
Jessop, J., 459t
Jette, A. M., 429
Jimenez, M. A., 412
Johansson, A., 437
John, O. P., 359, 362, 367
Johns, M. M., 314
Johnson, B. D., 313
Johnson, J., 307
Johnson, J. A., 391
Johnson, K. M., 59
Johnson, K. S., 465
Johnson, M., 295
Johnson, R. A., 440
Johnson, R. J., 394
Johnson, R. W., 408
Johnson, V. E., 381, 382
Johnston, L. D., 268, 269f
Johri, M., 438
Joinson, C., 242
Jokhi, R. P., 55
Jones, B. K., 366, 367
Jonkmann, K., 361
Jordan, A. H., 457
Jorgensen, B. S., 365t
Joseph, R. M., 162
Jowett, A., 313
Joyce, B. T., 465
Jozwiak, N., 410
Juarascio, A. S., 246
Judge, T. A., 348
Julian, M. M., 116
Jung, C. G., 356, 381
Jurkowski, J. M., 141

Poulin, F., 188, 281, 285
Poulin, M., 27, 27f
Powers, S. M., 410
Poyer, H., 246
Prager, I. G., 393
Prakash, K., 170
Prata, N., 63
Pratt, A. K., 374
Preßler, A., 151
Pressler, K. A., 430
Preston, S. H., 78
Preville, M., 410
Prevost, S. S., 455, 460
Priess, A., 341
Prinstein, M. J., 284, 285f
Prinz, R. J., 126
Pronk, M., 426
Pryor, J. H., 299, 304
Pudrovska, T., 331
Puhl, R. M., 140, 141
Pungello, E. P., 120
Pushkar, D., 401, 402, 407

Q
Qu, Y., 380, 438

R
Rabin, J. S., 162t
Rabins, P. V., 433, 435
Rackin, H., 330, 332
Rahe, R. H., 409
Rahman, A., 44
Raich, R. M., 247
Raj, A., 63
Raja, R., 170
Rambaran, A. J., 273
Ramsay, S. M., 64
Ranta, M., 314
Rao, N., 187
Rapaport, S., 55, 56
Rapee, R. M., 245
Rapport, M. D., 155
Ratner, D., 295
Ratner, N. B., 101
Rau, B., 390, 404, 407
Rauer, A. J., 314, 335
Raver, C. C., 119
Ray, B., 296
Raz, S., 64
Reales, J. M., 398
Reczek, C., 331
Redd, L., 220
Reddy, V., 125
Reese, E., 159, 160
Reeve, J., 222
Regan, P., 78–79
Reif, J. A., 315
Reijneveld, S. A., 208
Reimer, J., 264, 264t
Reimer, K., 265
Reiser, L. W., 237, 241
Reiss, D., 359

Reissman, C., 334
Reppermund, S., 435
Resett, S., 314
Reskin, B., 351
Reuter-Lorenz, P. A., 394, 394f, 395
Rey-Casserly, C., 65
Reynolds, P., 64
Reznick, J. S., 206, 207
Rhodes, R. E., 430
Rice, J. B., 440
Richard, C., 86t
Richards, T., 101, 101f
Ridgway, A., 155
Riegel, K. F., 372
Riegel, R. M., 372
Riksen-Walraven, J. M., 78, 86t, 122
Rilling, J. K., 115
Rinehart, M. S., 45
Rispoli, K. M., 115
Risse, G. B., 451
Rivera, M. S., 458, 459
Rivers, J., 456
Roalson, L. A., 277
Roberts, A., 245
Roberts, A. L., 163
Robertson, S. C., 400
Robinson, J. C., 221, 222
Robinson, J. P., 344f
Robinson, J. R., 343, 345
Robles, T. F., 333
Rochkind, J., 307
Rodham, K., 246
Rodin, J., 393
Rodkin, P. C., 180, 189, 190t, 191, 272
Rodrigues, R., 438
Rodriguez, C. M., 206
Roehlkepartain, E. C., 274
Roenker, D. L., 431
Roeser, R. W., 242
Rofail, M., 378, 379
Roffwarg, H. P., 83f
Rogers, C., 401
Rogoff, B., 149
Rohlfsen, L. S., 422
Roisman, G. I., 189
Rojas-Flores, L., 202
Rollock, D., 202
Romano, E., 181
Romeo, R. D., 271
Romer, D., 277
Roodin, P., 374
Roosevelt, E., 191
Roosevelt, F. D., 6, 404
Rorie, M., 277, 285
Rose, A. J., 179, 187, 188
Rose, J., 64
Rosenblum, K. E., 149
Rosenfield, R. L., 238
Rosenthal, M., 162

Roseth, C. J., 180
Ross, G., 149
Ross, L. A., 431
Rosti, R. O., 163
Roth, J. L., 277
Roth, S. L., 23
Rothenberg, J. Z., 406, 407
Rothermund, K., 400
Rothman, R., 223
Rousseau, J. J., 6
Roussotte, F., 49
Rovine, M., 340, 341
Rowe, D. C., 17
Rowe, E., 138
Rowe, G., 394
Rowe, J. W., 417
Rowe, M. L., 75
Royal College of Obstetricians and Gynaecologists [RCOG]., 49
Rubin, K. H., 188
Rubin, M., 379
Rubinstein, R. L., 441
Ruble, D. N., 171, 185, 187
Rulison, K. L., 272, 284
Runions, K. C., 181, 193
Rusbult, C. E., 316
Rushton, J. P., 217
Russell, V. M., 320
Rutledge, M. S., 404
Rutter, H., 140
Ryan, J. J., 216
Ryan, R. M., 222
Ryan-Krause, P., 155
Rybash, J. M., 374
Ryckewaert, R., 455
Ryeng, M. S., 302

S
Saarni, C., 177
Sabey, A. K., 335
Sabik, N. J., 246
Sachdev, P. S., 435
Sadegh-Nobari, T., 119, 120
Saenz, J., 186
Saeteren, B., 453, 454
Saffran, J. R., 101
Sagi, A., 113, 114, 114f
Sahin-Hodoglugil, N. N., 63
Saito, Y., 422
Sakuta, Y., 393
Salmela-Aro, K., 314
Samimi, P., 318t
Samson, D., 160
Samson, R. D., 394
Sánchez, B., 298
Sánchez-Mora, C., 154
Sánchez-Villegas, A., 141
Sandberg, L., 382, 383
Sandberg-Thoma, S. E., 314
Sandler, I. N., 210f, 211, 410
Santella, R. M., 64

Santesso, D. L., 101
Santo, J. B., 402, 407
Sarkin, A., 431
Sarkisian, N., 407
Sasson, I., 410, 411
Sattler, J. M., 214
Saudino, K. J., 125
Sauer, P. J. J., 141
Savage, C. L., 44
Savin-Williams, R. C., 312
Savishinsky, J., 408
Saxon, S. V., 382
Sayegh, P., 380
Sayer, L. C., 344f
Sayfan, L., 160
Scales, P. C., 274
Scarr, S., 19, 204
Schaal, B., 88
Schaan, B., 411
Schafer, K. J., 244
Schafer, M. H., 439
Schaie, K. W., 368, 369, 369f, 372
Schellinger, K., 124
Scheres, A., 155
Schetter, C. D., 44, 50
Schilling, O. K., 426
Schindler, I., 407
Schirduan, V., 219
Schlegel, A., 232
Schlinger, H. D., 217
Schmid, G., 81
Schmidt, A. E., 438
Schmidt, L. A., 101
Schmied, V., 78
Schneider, B. L., 304–305
Schneidman, E., 454
Schoen, A., 244
Scholte, R., 188, 193
Schomburg, A., 428
Schoon, I., 308
Schramm, D. G., 209
Schreiner, L. A., 309, 310
Schroeder, R. D., 202
Schueler, C. M., 126
Schuengel, C., 380
Schulz, M. S., 333
Schulze, H. J., 380
Schut, H., 411
Schwartz, C. E., 127
Schwartz, S. J., 302
Schwartz-Mette, R. A., 179, 187
Scrimgeour, M. B., 177
Scrimsher, S., 149
Seale, C., 468
Sebastian, C., 266
Sebastián-Enesco, C., 175
Seery, M. D., 362
Seiffge-Krenke, I., 290, 290f, 297, 298, 308
Self-Brown, S. R., 221
Seligman, M. P., 364

Note: Page numbers followed by f indicate figures; those followed by t indicate tables.